Encyclopedia of
Learning and Memory

Editorial Board

Encyclopedia of Learning and Memory

Larry R. Squire
Editor in Chief

Macmillan Publishing Company
NEW YORK

Maxwell Macmillan Canada
TORONTO

Maxwell Macmillan International
NEW YORK · OXFORD · SINGAPORE · SYDNEY

Macmillan Publishing Company
866 Third Avenue, New York, NY 10022

Maxwell Macmillan Canada, Inc.
1200 Eglinton Avenue East, Suite 200, Don Mills, Ontario M3C 3N1

Macmillan, Inc. is part of the Maxwell Communication Group of Companies.

Library of Congress Catalog Card Number: 92–15964

Printed in the United States of America

Printing Number
1 2 3 4 5 6 7 8 9 10

Library of Congress Cataloging-in-Publication Data

Encyclopedia of learning and memory / Larry R. Squire, editor in
   chief
      p.   cm.
   Includes bibliographical references and index.
   ISBN 0-02-897408-5 (alk. paper)
   1. Learning, Psychology of—Encyclopedias.   2. Memory—
—Encyclopedias.   3. Learning in animals—Encyclopedias.   4. Animal
memory—Encyclopedias.   5. Neuropsychology—Encyclopedias.
I. Squire, Larry R.
BF318.E53   1992
153.1′03—dc20   92–15964
                                                                CIP

Our thanks to Professor Eliot Hearst for his help with historical photographs.

The paper used in this publication meets the minimum requirements of American National Standard for Information Sciences—Permanence of Paper for Printed Library Materials. ANSI Z39.48–1984.

Contents

v

Editorial and Production Staff

Philip Friedman
Publisher

Elly Dickason
Editor in Chief, Macmillan Reference

David Eckroth
Executive Editor

Jonathan Wiener
Project Editor

Karin K. Vanderveer
Assistant Editor

Elizabeth Wilson
Copy-editor

Donald Spanel   Joseph Ruddick
Proofreaders

Cynthia Crippen
Indexer

Lynn Constantinou
Production Manager

PREFACE

Most animals, including humans, have the ability to change in response to the individual events that occur during their lifetimes. This capacity results from the simple fact that the experiences that an animal has will modify its nervous system so that it can later behave differently as a result of its experience. These changes make it possible for organisms to learn and then to retain what has been learned in a form that can be expressed at a later time. *Learning* refers to the process of acquiring new information, and *memory* refers to the persistence of learning as stored information.

Many different questions can be asked about learning and memory. What determines what is retained and what is lost? Can memory be improved? What is forgetting? Is memory one thing or many different things? How does the brain accomplish learning and memory? Where is memory stored? What are the molecular and cellular events that occur in the brain when memory is stored? During the past few decades, an enormous amount has been learned about these matters, and currently memory is an active topic for psychological and biological research. Questions about memory can be usefully addressed at any of several different levels of analysis. There are questions about single neurons and their connections (synapses), questions about neural networks and brain systems, and questions about the organization of behavior—for example, the laws and observations that describe the rich phenomenology of human learning.

The *Encyclopedia of Learning and Memory* is a compendium of 189 articles that encompass the full range of current knowledge about learning and memory. The articles have been prepared by leading scholars in neuroscience and psychology who are active researchers in this rapidly growing discipline. The articles also include twenty-six biographies of individuals who have contributed importantly to current knowledge, as well as information about the molecular and cellular biology of memory, plasticity in neurons and neural networks, brain systems involved in memory, and phenomena of behavioral memory. The articles are directed especially toward understanding human memory, but the *Encyclopedia* also provides thorough coverage of important and essential work with experimental animals, including both invertebrates and vertebrates, which has provided much of what is currently understood about learning and memory.

All of the entries are original contributions from active scholars and researchers, written for a readership of students, teachers, journalists, and members of the educated public. The articles range in length from 500 to 2,000 words. Entries are arranged alphabetically. Most entries are accompanied by a bibliography listing suggestions for further reading. The entries are also linked by a comprehensive set of cross references. Thus, when a reader encounters a term printed in small capital letters, that term is the subject of a separate entry. For example, in the article entitled "Infantile Amnesia" one finds cross-references to articles on PROSE RETENTION, EXPERTS' MEMORIES, and CODING PROCESSES: ORGANIZATION OF MEMORY. The reader will also encounter cross references at the ends of entries, such as "(See also IMPLICIT MEMORY.)."

In addition, the *Encyclopedia* includes so-called blind entries to facilitate access to main articles. These are arranged alphabetically through the *Encyclopedia* and are intended to direct the reader to appropriate articles (for example, "Drugs. *See* Drugs and Memory; Electroconvulsive Therapy and Memory Loss; Pharmacological Treatment of Memory Deficits"). An additional feature is the use of guideposts. When there is a group of related articles on a single topic, a short guidepost is available to orient the reader to the topic. For example, for the area of invertebrate learning, a short article appears to orient the reader to the six articles about learning in invertebrates.

Although the quality of the *Encyclopedia* depends ultimately on the individual contributions, much of its success is owed to the five associate editors who worked tirelessly to identify topics, work out the organization of the project, and suggest contributors. At Macmillan, David Eckroth, Elly Dickason, and Jonathan Wiener provided support and expert editorial guidance throughout the project. The finished project provides the broadest and the richest introduction to the topic of learning and memory that is available anywhere.

LARRY R. SQUIRE

LIST OF ARTICLES

LIST OF CONTRIBUTORS

Abramson, Charles I.
*State University of New York Health Science
Center, Brooklyn*
Insect Learning

Ahn, Woo-Kyoung
University of Michigan
Concepts and Categories, Learning of

Albert, Marilyn S.
Massachusetts General Hospital
Alzheimer's Disease: Behavioral Aspects

Alsop, Brent
Dalhousie University, Halifax, Canada
Operant Behavior

Amsel, Abram
University of Texas
Hull, Clark

Anagnostopoulos, Georgios
University of California, San Diego
Aristotle

Bachevalier, Jocelyne
National Institute of Mental Health
Sex Differences in Learning in Animals

Baddeley, Alan D.
*MRC Applied Psychology Unit, Cambridge,
England*
Working Memory: Humans

Bailey, Craig H.
*Columbia University College of Physicians and
Surgeons*
Morphological Basis of Learning and Memory:
Invertebrates

Bandura, Albert
Stanford University
Observational Learning

Barr, William B.
Medical College of Pennsylvania
Knowledge Systems

Bartelt, Michael J.
Ohio University
Spinal Plasticity

Barto, Andrew G.
University of Massachusetts
Algorithms, Learning

Baudry, Michel
University of Southern California
Long-Term Potentiation: Maintenance; Neuro-
transmitter Systems and Memory

Bellezza, Francis S.
Ohio University
Mnemonic Devices

Benedict, Ralph H. B.
Johns Hopkins Medical Institutions
Dementia

Bingman, Verner P.
Bowling Green State University
Migration, Navigation, and Homing

Bjork, Robert A.
University of California, Los Angeles
Interference and Forgetting

Bolhuis, Johan J.
Cambridge University, Cambridge, England
Imprinting: Behavioral Aspects

Bolles, Robert C.
University of Washington
Learning Theory

Brandt, Jason
Johns Hopkins Medical Institutions
Dementia

Brush, F. Robert
Purdue University
Behavioral Phenomena; Avoidance Learning, Active and Passive

Byrne, John H.
University of Texas Medical School
Aplysia; Classical Conditioning and Operant Conditioning; Conditioning, Cellular and Network Schemes for Higher-Order Features of Classical

Carew, Thomas J.
Yale University
Aplysia: Development of Processes Underlying Learning

Castellucci, Vincent
IRCM Clinical Research Institute, Montreal, Canada
Aplysia: Molecular Basis of Long-Term Sensitization

Catania, A. Charles
University of Maryland—Baltimore County
Reinforcement

Chase, Chris
Rutgers University
Learning Disabilities: Cognitive Aspects

Churchland, Patricia Smith
University of California, San Diego
Aristotle

Corey-Bloom, Jody
San Diego VA Medical Center
Pharmacologic Treatment of Memory Deficits

Cotman, C. W.
University of California, Irvine
Glutamate Receptors and Their Characterization

Craik, Fergus I. M.
University of Toronto, Toronto, Canada
Aging and Memory in Humans

Crow, Terry J.
University of Texas Medical School
Invertebrate Learning: Associative Learning in *Hermissenda*

Crowder, Robert G.
Yale University
Eidetic Imagery; McGeoch, John; Sensory Memory

Culicover, Peter
Ohio State University
Language Learning: Humans

Davis, Joel L.
University of Southern California
Neurotransmitter Systems and Memory

Davis, Michael
Yale University School of Medicine
Habituation and Sensitization in Vertebrates; Neural Substrates of Classical Conditioning: Fear-Potentiated Startle

Day, Jonathan R.
University of Southern California
Guide to the Anatomy of the Brain: Synapse

Desimone, Robert
National Institute of Mental Health
Primates, Visual Attention in

Dickinson, Anthony
Cambridge University, Cambridge, England
Konorski, Jerzy

Disterhoft, John F.
Northwestern University Medical School
Olds, James

Donegan, Nelson
Yale University
Neural Computation: Cerebellum

Dosher, Barbara Anne
Columbia University
Memory Search

Doupe, Allison J.
Caifornia Institute of Technology
Bird Song Learning: Neurobiology

Dudai, Yadin
Weizmann Institute of Science, Rehovot, Israel
Invertebrate Learning: Neurogenetic Analysis of Learning in *Drosophila*

Egger, M. David
University of Medicine and Dentistry of New Jersey
Habituation and Sensitization in Vertebrates

Erdelyi, Matthew Hugh
Brooklyn College
Freud, Sigmund

Ericsson, K. Anders
University of Colorado
Experts' Memories

Estes, W. K.
Harvard University
Mathematical Learning Theory

Farah, Martha
Carnegie-Mellon University
Visual Object Agnosia

Finkel, Leif H.
University of Pennsylvania
Neural Computation: Neocortex

Fowler, Anne
Bryn Mawr College
Mental Retardation

Frost, William
University of Texas Medical School
Invertebrate Learning: Habituation and Sensitization in *Tritonia*

Furedy, John J.
University of Toronto, Toronto, Canada
Pavlov, Ivan

Fuster, Joaquin M.
University of California, Los Angeles
Prefrontal Cortex and Memory in Primates

Gabriel, Michael
University of Illinois
Avoidance Learning, Neural Substrates of

Garcia, John
University of California, Los Angeles
Taste Aversion and Preference Learning in Animals

Gardiner, John M.
City University, London, England
Modality Effects

Geiselman, R. Edward
University of California, Los Angeles
Hypnosis and Memory

Gelperin, A.
AT&T Bell Labs
Invertebrate Learning: Associative Learning in *Limax*

Gillette, Rhanor
University of Illinois
Invertebrate Learning: Associative Learning in *Pleurobranchaea*

Glenberg, Arthur
University of Wisconsin
Distributed Practice Effects

Glisky, Elizabeth L.
University of Arizona
Rehabilitation of Memory Disorders

Gold, Paul E.
University of Virginia
Memory Consolidation

Goldberg, Elkhonon
Medical College of Pennsylvania
Knowledge Systems; Luria, A. R.

Gormezano, I.
University of Iowa
Conditioning, Classical and Instrumental

Gottlieb, Gilbert
University of North Carolina at Greensboro
Thorndike, Edward

Granger, Richard
University of California, Irvine
Neural Computation: Olfactory Cortex

Graybiel, Ann M.
Massachusetts Institute of Technology
Guide to the Anatomy of the Brain: Basal Ganglia

Greene, Robert L.
Case Western Reserve University
Repetition and Learning

Greenough, William T.
University of Illinois
Morphological Basis of Learning and Memory: Vertebrates

Gruber, Howard E.
Columbia University
Piaget, Jean

Gustafsson, Bengt
Göteborgs Universitet, Göteborg, Sweden
Long-Term Potentiation: Overview; Cooperativity and Associativity

Hagger, Corinne
National Institute of Mental Health
Sex Differences in Learning in Animals

Healy, Alice F.
University of Colorado
Serial Organization

Hearst, Eliot
Indiana University
Watson, John B.

Hendry, Stewart
University of California, Irvine
Guide to the Anatomy of the Brain: Cerebral Neocortex

Hertel, Paula
Trinity University
Emotion, Mood, and Memory

Hilgard, Ernest R.
Stanford University
Guthrie, Edwin R.

Hineline, Philip N.
Temple University
Behaviorism

Honig, W. K.
Dalhousie University, Halifax, Canada
Operant Behavior

Horn, Gabriel
Cambridge University, Cambridge, England
Imprinting: Behavioral Aspects; Imprinting: Neural Substrates

Ito, Masao
RIKEN, Wako, Saitama, Japan
Long-Term Depression in the Cerebellum, Neocortex, and Hippocampus

Jones, Gregory V.
University of Warwick, Coventry, England
Tip-of-the-Tongue Phenomenon

Kaas, Jon H.
Vanderbilt University
Neocortical Plasticity: Adult Visual Cortex—Neural Conditioning and Map Rearrangement; Neocortical Plasticity: Somatosensory Cortex

Kail, Robert
Purdue University
Children, Development of Memory in

Kapp, Bruce S.
University of Vermont
Neural Substrates of Classical Conditioning: Cardiovascular Responses

Kendler, Howard H.
University of California
Spence, Kenneth

Kihlstrom, John F.
University of Arizona
Amnesia, Functional

King, Frederick A.
Emory University
Animal Use in Research

Kolb, Bryan
University of Lethbridge, Lethbridge, Canada
Harlow, Harry F.

Kotovsky, Kenneth
Carnegie-Mellon University
Problem Solving

Krasne, Franklin B.
University of California, Los Angeles
Invertebrate Learning: Nonassociative Learning in Crayfish

Kritchevsky, Mark
University of California, San Diego
Amnesia, Transient Global

Lavond, David
University of Southern California
Visual Memory, Brightness and Flux in

LeDoux, Joseph E.
New York University
Neural Substrates of Emotional Memory

Leitner, Rick L.
University of Washington
Reconstructive Memory

Levin, Harvey S.
University of Texas Medical Branch at Galveston
Head Injury

Levine, Seymour
Stanford University School of Medicine
Early Experience and Learning

*Lister, Richard G.
National Institute on Aging
Drugs and Memory

Lockhart, Robert S.
University of Toronto, Toronto, Canada
Coding Processes: Levels of Processing; Measurement of Memory

Loftus, Elizabeth F.
University of Washington
Reconstructive Memory

---

* Deceased.

Logan, Gordon D.
University of Illinois
Attention and Memory

Lynch, Gary
University of California, Irvine
Long-Term Potentiation: Maintenance; Neural Computation: Olfactory Cortex

MacLeod, Colin M.
University of Toronto, Toronto, Canada
Individual Differences in Learning and Memory

Maier, Steven
University of Colorado
Learned Helplessness

Markowska, Alicja L.
Johns Hopkins University
Working Memory: Animals

Marler, Peter R.
University of California, Davis
Bird Song Learning: Behavioral Aspects

Marschark, Marc
University of North Carolina at Greensboro
Coding Processes: Imagery

McClelland, James L.
Carnegie-Mellon University
Parallel Distributed Processing Models of Memory

McDaniel, Mark A.
Purdue University
Prose Retention

McElree, Brian
Columbia University
Memory Search

McGaugh, James L.
University of California, Irvine
Hormones and Memory; Memory Consolidation

McNaughton, Bruce L.
University of Arizona
Neural Computation: Hippocampus

McNeill, Thomas H.
University of Southern California
Guide to the Anatomy of the Brain: Synapse

Medin, Douglas L.
University of Michigan
Concepts and Categories, Learning of

Meltzoff, Andrew N.
University of Washington
Infancy, Memory in

Menzel, Randolf
Freie Universität, Berlin, Germany
Invertebrate Learning: Associative Learning in
Bees

Mesulam, M-Marsel
Harvard Medical School
Guide to the Anatomy of the Brain: Basal Fore-
brain

Milner, Peter M.
McGill University, Montreal, Canada
Hebb, Donald

Morrell, Frank
Rush–Presbyterian–St. Luke's Medical Center
Kindling

Morris, R. G. M.
*University of Edinburgh Medical School, Edin-
burgh, Scotland*
Long-Term Potentiation: Behavioral Role

Moscovitch, Morris
University of Toronto, Toronto, Canada
Frontal Lobes and Memory

Murray, Elisabeth A.
National Institute of Mental Health
Primates, Visual Perception and Memory in Non-
human

Murray, David J.
Queens University, Kingston, Canada
Bartlett, Frederic

Nadel, Lynn
University of Arizona
Spatial Learning

Neisser, Ulric
Emory University
Amnesia, Infantile; Natural Settings, Memory in

Nelson, Thomas O.
University of Washington
Metamemory

Newell, Karl M.
University of Illinois
Motor Skills

Olton, David S.
Johns Hopkins University
Working Memory: Animals

Patterson, Michael M.
Ohio University
Spinal Plasticity

Pearce, John M.
University of Wales—College of Cardiff
Behavioral Phenomena: Conditioning, Classical

Petersen, Steven
Washington University School of Medicine
Positron Emission Tomography

Plante, Elena
University of Arizona
Learning Disabilities: Neurological Aspects

Price, Donald L.
Johns Hopkins University
Alzheimer's Disease: Neural and Molecular Basis

Price, Joseph L.
Washington University School of Medicine
Guide to the Anatomy of the Brain: Amygdala

Rachman, Stanley J.
*University of British Columbia, Vancouver,
Canada*
Behavior Therapy; Phobias

Ratcliff, Roger
Northwestern University
Models of Memory

Renner, Michael J.
Memphis State University
Curiosity and Exploration

Riley, Donald A.
University of California, Berkeley
Tolman, Edward C.

Roediger, Henry L., III
Rice University
Retrieval Processes in Memory

Roitblat, Herbert L.
University of Hawaii
Comparative Cognition

Rose, Steven P. R.
Open University, Milton Keynes, England
Protein Synthesis in Long-Term Memory in Vertebrates

Rosenzweig, Mark
University of California, Berkeley
Tolman, Edward C.

Rozin, John
University of Pennsylvania
Food Aversion and Preference Learning in Humans

Rubin, David C.
Duke University
Oral Traditions

Rumbaugh, Duane M.
Georgia State University
Language Learning: Nonhuman Primates

Salzinger, Kurt
Polytechnic University
Skinner, B. F.

Savage-Rumbaugh, E. Sue
Georgia State University
Language Learning: Nonhuman Primates

Schacter, Daniel L.
Harvard University
Amnesia, Functional; Implicit Memory; Semon, Richard

Schvaneveldt, Roger
New Mexico State University
Coding Processes: Organization of Memory

Schwartz, James H.
Columbia University College of Physicians and Surgeons
Second Messenger Systems

Sejnowski, Terrence J.
Salk Institute
Neural Computation: Approaches to Learning

Shepherd, Gordon M
Yale University School of Medicine
Guide to the Anatomy of the Brain: Olfactory Cortex

Sherry, David F.
University of Western Ontario, London, Canada
Evolution and Learning; Lorenz, Konrad

Shettleworth, Sara J.
University of Toronto, Toronto, Canda
Foraging

Shimamura, Arthur P.
University of California, Berkeley
Amnesia, Organic

Shinkman, Paul G.
University of North Carolina
Neocortical Plasticity: Development of the Visual System; Neocortical Plasticity: Adult Visual Cortex—Neural Conditioning and Map Rearrangement

Shoben, Edward J.
University of Illinois
Semantic Memory

Shors, Tracey J.
Princeton University
Stress and Memory

Siegelbaum, Steven A.
Columbia University College of Physicians and Surgeons
Membrane Channels and Their Modulation in Learning and Memory

*Signoret, Jean-Louis
Hôpital de la Salpêtrière, Paris, France
Ribot, Théodule

Singer, Wolf
Max-Planck-Institut für Hirnforschung, Frankfurt, Germany
Neocortical Plasticity: Adult Visual Cortex—Adaptation and Reorganization

Sisodia, Sangram S.
Johns Hopkins University
Alzheimer's Disease: Neural and Molecular Basis

Slamecka, Norman J.
University of Toronto, Toronto, Canada
Forgetting

Smith, Brian H.
Ohio State University
Insect Learning

Smith, Mary Lou
University of Toronto, Toronto, Canada
Material-Specific Memory Deficits

Sokolov, E. N.
Moscow State University, Moscow, Russia
Orienting Reflex Habituation

Somogyi, Peter
MRC Anatomical Neuropharmacology Unit, Oxford, England
Guide to the Anatomy of the Brain: Neuron

Spear, Norman E.
State University of New York at Binghamton
Hunter, Walter S.

Squire, Larry R.
University of California, San Diego
Electroconvulsive Therapy and Memory Loss; Positron Emission Tomography

---

* Deceased.

Steinmetz, Joseph E.
Indiana University
Neural Substrates of Classical Conditioning: Discrete Behavioral Responses

Suchecki, Deborah
Stanford University (Fellowship from Conselho Nacional de Pesquisa Científica e Tecnologica of Brazil)
Early Experience and Learning

Supple, William F.
University of Vermont
Neural Substrates of Classical Conditioning: Cardiovascular Responses

Swanson, Larry W.
University of Southern California
Cajal, Santiago Ramón y; Guide to the Anatomy of the Brain: Hippocampus

Tallal, Paula A.
Rutgers University
Learning Disabilities: Cognitive Aspects

Thal, Leon J.
San Diego VA Medical Center
Pharmacologic Treatment of Memory Deficits

Thomas, David R.
University of Colorado
Discrimination and Generalization

Thompson, Charles P.
Kansas State University
Mnemonists

Thompson, Richard F.
University of Southern California
Lashley, Karl; Localization of Memory Traces

Treffert, Darold A.
Brookside Medical Center
Savant Syndrome

Tsien, Richard W.
Stanford University School of Medicine
Long-Term Potentiation: Signal Transduction Mechanisms and Early Events

Tulving, Endel
University of Toronto, Toronto, Canda
Ebbinghaus, Hermann; Episodic Memory

Ungerleider, Leslie G.
National Institute of Mental Health
Primates, Visual Perception and Memory in Non-
human

Voytko, Mary Lou
Johns Hopkins Medical School
Working Memory: Animals

Watkins, Michael J.
Rice University
Memory Span

Watts, Alan G.
University of Southern California
Guide to the Anatomy of the Brain: Overview

Waymire, Jack C.
University of Texas Medical School
Activity-Dependent Regulation of Neuro
transmitter Synthesis

Weinberger, Norman M.
University of California, Irvine
Neocortical Plasticity: Auditory Cortex

Weingartner, Herbert J.
National Institute on Aging
Drugs and Memory

Welker, W. I.
University of Wisconsin
Guide to the Anatomy of the Brain: Cerebellum

Wenk, Gary L.
University of Arizona
Aging Animals, Pharmacological Manipulations
of Memory in

White, Sheldon H.
Harvard University
James, William

Whitlow, J. W., Jr.
Rutgers University
Associationism

Whittemore, E. R.
University of California, Irvine
Glutamate Receptors and Their Characterization

Wigström, Holger
Göteborgs Universitet, Göteborg, Sweden
Long-Term Potentiation: Overview; Cooperativ-
ity and Associativity

Winocur, Gordon
Trent University, Peterborough, Canada
Frontal Lobes and Memory

Wishart, Jennifer G.
University of Edinburgh, Edinburgh, Scotland
Object Concept, Acquisition of

Wittrock, M. C.
University of California, Los Angeles
School Learning

Wood, David C.
University of Pittsburgh
Unicellular Organisms, Learning and Adaptive
Plasticity in

Woodruff-Pak, Diana S.
Temple University
Aging and Memory in Animals

Yarbrough, Cathy J.
Emory University
Animal Use in Research

Zucker, Robert S.
University of California, Berkeley
Posttetanic Potentiation

Zurif, Edgar
Brandeis University
Aphasia

ACTIVITY-DEPENDENT REGULATION OF NEUROTRANSMITTER SYNTHESIS

Activity-dependent regulation of neurotransmitter synthesis refers to the ability of certain types of nerve cells to change the amount of neurotransmitter they synthesize in response to the amount of activity they experience. The study of the mechanisms underlying this regulation is prompted by the belief that these mechanisms are important not only for maintaining a source of neurotransmitter but also for adaptive changes that take place in certain nerve cells during learning and memory. It is important to note, however, that a basic postulate necessary for neurotransmitter synthesis regulation to be a mechanism for learning and memory is that increased neurotransmitter synthesis acts to increase neurotransmitter secretion and, as a consequence, synaptic strength. As yet, it has not been technically possible to demonstrate a causal relationship between activity-dependent regulation of neurotransmitter synthesis and an increase in neurotransmitter secretion. Still, activity-dependent regulation of neurotransmitter synthesis remains an important candidate for the cause of neuroplastic changes that underlie learning and memory. Three of the neurotransmitters that have shown activity-dependent regulation of synthesis are acetylcholine, the catecholamines, and serotonin. The mechanisms of the synthesis of these three neurotransmitters will be reviewed and possible roles of their regulatory mechanisms in learning and memory considered.

Depending upon both the type of nerve cell and the time scale over which adaptation occurs, the cellular and biochemical mechanisms responsible for activity-dependent regulation of neurotransmitter synthesis vary. The time scale of changes ranges from very rapid, short-term changes (scale of minutes) in which covalent modification of protein structure is involved, to more delayed, longer-term changes (scale of days). These latter are due to alterations in genetic expression of enzymes involved in neurotransmitter synthesis. Some neurotransmitters, such as the catecholamines, are regulated at both short- and long-term levels, while others, such as acetylcholine and serotonin, are regulated only at a short-term level. The mechanisms of these regulatory processes are often similar to cellular and biochemical mechanisms used in nonneural cells to regulate the synthesis of other messenger molecules, such as hormones, or to regulate the biochemical pathways of intermediary metabolism.

Acetylcholine is a neurotransmitter in the autonomic nervous system and the central nervous system (CNS), and at the neuromuscular junction. Although its turnover is among the most rapid of neurotransmitters, its concentration within nerve tissue fluctuates very little. This remarkable stability occurs because precursors for acetylcholine synthesis, acetylcoenzyme A and choline, exist in a steady-state equilibrium with choline acetyltransferase (CAT), the enzyme that catalyzes acetylcholine synthesis (Jope, 1979). For this reason, acetylcholine synthesis is usually well below its maximal rate. This means that any change in the concentration of acetylcholine or its precursors will change acetylcholine synthesis. Experiments in several different types of cholinergic cells have verified this and have shown that, physiologically, transport of choline into the cholinergic neuron is the controlling step in the synthesis of acetylcholine. For example, choline addition to perfused slices of brain tissue markedly increases the rate of acetylcholine synthesis. Increased neuronal activity also causes an increase in choline uptake (Simon and Kuhar, 1975). Most important, enhanced choline uptake in neurally stimulated cholinergic tissue persists far beyond the period of increased stimulation. Thus, it is speculated that increased choline uptake is not due merely to a shift in the equilibrium of the CAT-catalyzed reaction; instead, choline uptake is regulated by neural activity, which entails a modification of the choline transport mechanism itself. Thus, the regulation of choline uptake by nerve activity may serve as a mechanism for maintaining or increasing the strength of cholinergic synapses. As such, this mechanism may be important in modulating cholinergic neurotransmission and is a good candidate for the site of the neuroplastic changes occurring during learning. Despite the evidence of activity-dependent regulation of choline uptake, little information concerning the mechanism of this regulation has emerged. For example, evidence has been sought, with little success, for the existence of a physiological mechanism that regulates choline uptake at the cholinergic nerve ending. Thus, although it appears that nerve activity modifies acetylcholine synthesis through changes in choline uptake, the mechanism of the link between nerve activity and choline transport remains unknown.

Catecholamines—dopamine, norepinephrine, and epinephrine—are neurotransmitters in the sympathetic limb of the autonomic nervous system and in several groups of neurons in the CNS. These compounds have broad functional roles that extend from the regulation of autonomic function to the control of emotion, mood, and memory. In contrast with the lack of an apparent mechanism linking nerve activity and the regulation of choline uptake, catecholamine-synthesizing cells appear to have numerous mechanisms in place to regulate catecholamine levels in response to nerve activity. Nerve activity–related regulation of catecholamine synthesis exists in both the peripheral and the central nervous systems and at short- and long-term levels (Masserano et al., 1989). Both short- and long-term levels of regulation occur at the same step in synthesis of catecholamines, the hydroxylation of tyrosine to form dopa. The enzyme catalyzing this reaction, tyrosine hydroxylase, is the first of four enzymatic steps in the catecholamine synthesis pathway. Because tyrosine hydroxylase is present in lower concentration than the other enzymes of the synthesis pathway, it restricts the total amount of neurotransmitter synthesized.

Tyrosine hydroxylase is a tetramer, made up of four identical subunits. It uses oxygen and a pteridine cofactor, tetrahydrobiopterin, to convert tyrosine to dopa. Because tetrahydrobiopterin is also at a low concentration, its availability may be an additional factor in the regulation of catecholamine synthesis. Two separate but interacting mechanisms appear to be important in short-term nervous activity stimulation of catecholamine synthesis. One is end-product feedback inhibition of tyrosine hydroxylase activity by the catecholamine products of the pathway (Masserano et al., 1989). The second is modification of tyrosine hydroxylase's structure by the placement of phosphate groups on the tyrosine hydroxylase molecule. The latter process, termed phosphorylation, is catalyzed by protein kinases (Zigmond, Schwarzschild, and Rittenhouse, 1989). Phosphorylation is commonly used to modify proteins involved in regulation. The hypothesis that tyrosine hydroxylase is regulated by end-product feedback inhibition proposes that a pool of intracellular catecholamines, present in the region of the cell containing tyrosine hydroxylase, chronically inhibits the enzyme's activity. When catecholamines are secreted, as is the case during increased nervous activity, the inhibition is decreased and catecholamines are synthesized to replace those secreted.

Feedback inhibition is not very appealing as a candidate for synaptic plasticity at the catecholaminergic synapse because it would appear only to maintain catecholamine stores rather than to increase them. At any rate, feedback inhibition became less attractive as an explanation for short-term catecholamine synthesis regulation in general when it was discovered that tyrosine hydroxylase in stimulated tissue retains its activation even after it is separated from catecholamines (Masserano et al., 1989). This activation of tyrosine hydroxylase was subsequently shown to be due to a reversible alteration in the tyrosine hydroxylase structure in response to nerve activation. This alteration is due to activity-dependent phosphorylation of tyrosine hydroxylase (Zigmond, Schwarzschild, and Rittenhouse, 1989). Phosphorylation of tyrosine hydroxylase is an ideal candidate to underlie neuroplasticity because it provides a number of potential mechanisms for increasing the neurotransmitter synthesis capacity of the catecholaminergic cells.

It is now known that at least three independent protein kinases phosphorylate tyrosine hydroxylase on four different sites within each of the four tyrosine hydroxylase subunits. Each of these protein kinases is activated by intracellular messengers that act as mediators of extracellular signals. These protein kinases are cyclic adenosine monophosphate-dependent protein kinase (A kinase), calcium-calmodulin-dependent protein kinase II (Ca/CAM kinase II), and calcium-phospholipid-dependent protein kinase (C kinase) (Zigmond, Schwarzschild, and Rittenhouse, 1989). Both A kinase and C kinase phosphorylate tyrosine hydroxylase at one site on each enzyme subunit (Campbell, Hardie, and Vulliet, 1986). This phosphorylation has three major effects on the enzyme's function: It increases the affinity of the enzyme for tetrahydrobiopterin cofactor (the cofactor is normally present below optimal concentrations), it reduces the efficacy of catecholamine inhibition of tyrosine hydroxylase, and it causes the enzyme to be more active at pH's found inside nerve cells (Masserano et al., 1989). All three changes enhance the activity of tyrosine hydroxylase and increase catecholamine synthesis. Phosphorylation of tyrosine hydroxylase by Ca/CAM kinase II, in comparison, occurs on another site on the tyrosine hydroxylase molecule (Campbell, Hardie, and Vulliet, 1986). This phosphorylation increases the maximal catalytic activity of the tyrosine hydroxylase. Besides the phosphorylation of tyrosine hydroxylase by these three protein kinases, phosphorylation occurs on two other sites within each subunit (Haycock, 1990). The protein kinases responsible for these phosphorylations and their influence on tyrosine hydroxylase enzyme activity is not known.

Which of these mechanisms act to regulate the synthesis of catecholamines in response to neural activity, and how may they related to learning and memory? Although these questions have been difficult to answer, some conclusions are possible. Under circumstances of cell depolarization, such as when a nerve impulse invades the nerve terminal or during cholinergic neurotransmission at the adrenal medulla, the phosphorylation and activation of tyrosine hydroxylase by Ca/CAM kinase II appear to be responsible for activation of tyrosine hydroxylase (Waymire et al., 1988). The proposed model of the regulation of tyrosine hydroxylase by Ca/CAM kinase II entails a cascade with calcium influx occurring in response to cell depolarization. This rise in intracellular calcium causes calcium-dependent phosphorylation and activation of tyrosine hydroxylase and increases catecholamine synthesis. Any condition that increases the size of this phosphorylation is predicted to enhance the synthesis of catecholamines. And this may translate into increased neurotransmitter release and synaptic strength. The second mechanism known to regulate catecholamine synthesis is the phosphorylation of tyrosine hydroxylase in response to neurotransmitters that do not act by depolarizing cells. These agonists include neuropeptides, such as those of the secretin family, and appear to increase the level of the second messenger, cyclic adenosine monophosphate (cAMP) (Waymire et al., 1991). In this case A kinase–mediated phosphorylation of tyrosine hydroxylase occurs and increased catecholamine synthesis ensues. Activation of tyrosine hydroxylase is achieved through increased affinity for cofactor and decreased sensitivity to catecholamine feedback inhibition. This A kinase–mediated regulation of tyrosine hydroxylase provides a mechanism for synaptic inputs to modulate catecholamine synthesis capacity at the catecholaminergic nerve terminal by activating presynaptic receptors linked to adenylate cyclase. This mechanism is relevant to synaptic plasticity because it provides a means for other neurotransmitters to modulate the catecholaminergic synapse by increasing catecholamine synthesis. It will be important to understand the significance of this type of regulation.

Catecholamine synthesis is also regulated at a chronic, long-term level in response to persistent or extreme neural activation. In this case the amount of the enzymes in the catecholamine synthetic pathway, and especially tyrosine hydroxylase, is elevated in response to increased synaptic activity. For example, drugs or conditions, such as stress, that increase the autonomic nerve activity increase the level of tyrosine hydroxylase in peripheral autonomic cells (Thoenen, Mueller, and Axelrod, 1969). Because cutting the innervation to these cells blocks the increase, the influence is thought to be transsynaptic. Because a rise in tyrosine hydroxylase messenger RNA precedes the increase in protein, the mechanism of the synaptically induced changes in tyrosine hydroxylase is believed to be increased transcription of the gene encoding tyrosine hydroxylase. The observation that drugs that increase CNS neuronal activity also induce increased levels of CNS tyrosine hydroxylase shows that central tyrosine hydroxylase levels are also regulated by neuronal activity. This nerve activity–dependent regulation of tyrosine hydroxylase synthesis is an attractive candidate for learning and memory because the increase in tyrosine hydroxylase level is expected to increase the strength of the activated synapses. Whether this is the case is not yet known. Even so, a considerable effort is being carried out to understand as much as possible about transsynaptic regulation of tyrosine hydroxylase level because it is likely the best example known of synaptically mediated regulation of protein synthesis.

Principal issues that remain unresolved concerning the mechanism of the long-term regulation of tyrosine hydroxylase are the identity of the neurotransmitters responsible for the synaptic activation and the nature of the intracellular mechanisms responsible for increased transcription. In a model tissue, the adrenal medulla, acetylcholine is thought to be the signal that modulates tyrosine hydroxylase level. In this tissue acetylcholine stimulates cAMP level and activates A kinase. The protein kinase migrates to the cell nucleus to regulate the rate of tyrosine hydroxylase transcription by phosphorylating regulatory proteins associated with the tyrosine hydroxylase gene (Kurosawa, Guidotti, and Costa, 1976). An unresolved issue in this simple model is whether acetylcholine stimulates a rise in cAMP or whether other transmitters act at the cholinergic synapse. Because neuropeptides are secreted along with acetylcholine at some cholinergic synapses, it has been suggested that these agonists are responsible for long-term regulation of tyrosine hydroxylase level (Wessels-Reiker et al., 1991). Also, it is not clear whether transcription is regulated solely through A kinase. Because several regulatory domains exist in the tyrosine hydroxylase gene, it appears that protein kinases other than the A kinase are likely to be involved. In addition it is possible that a recently discovered, rapidly synthesized protein, c-Fos, may serve as a protein factor regulating tyrosine hydroxylase transcription.

Serotonin is also regulated by neural activity. In many ways the synthesis and regulation of this neurotransmitter are similar to those of catecholamines. Tryptophan hydroxylase catalyzes the first step in the biosynthetic pathway in a manner analogous to the action of tyrosine hydroxylase, and tetrahydrobiopterin is the cofactor (Kaufman, 1985). Unlike tyrosine hydroxylase, end products of the serotoninergic pathway do not inhibit tryptophan hydroxylase. In addition, under normal conditions, the concentration of tryptophan in blood and cells is well below the level necessary to saturate the hydroxylase. This means that factors that influence the transport of tryptophan into sero-

toninergic neurons are predicted to influence serotonin synthesis. Thus far, however, no evidence exists to show that neuronal activity influences either CNS tryptophan levels or tryptophan uptake into serotoninergic neurons (Hamon et al., 1981). For example, in the studies of neurally mediated increase in serotonin synthesis, tryptophan concentration or uptake in terminal fields does not change. The more likely explanation for neural activity regulation of serotonin synthesis is that, as with tyrosine hydroxylase, tryptophan hydroxylase's intrinsic activity is increased by phosphorylation (Hamon et al., 1981). Tryptophan hydroxylase is a substrate for Ca/CAM kinase II, and phosphorylation causes an increase in the activity of the enzyme. As yet, however, no evidence exists of a direct relationship between tryptophan hydroxylase phosphorylation and increased serotonin synthesis. It is also not known whether tryptophan hydroxylase can be phosphorylated on multiple sites by different protein kinases similar to tyrosine hydroxylase.

In conclusion, it is apparent that the understanding of the activity-dependent regulation of catecholamines is much more complete than for other neurotransmitters, such as acetylcholine and serotonin. For some neurotransmitter systems—the amino acids and purines, for example—we know virtually nothing about their synthesis regulation, so it is not clear whether it is activity-dependent. This is primarily because these compounds are so intimately associated with intermediary metabolism that it is difficult to separate their neurotransmitter-related metabolism from that associated with general cell function. One generalization emerging from the studies of the mechanisms of activity-dependent regulation of catecholamine and serotonin synthesis is the prominent position protein phosphorylation appears to play as a mechanism in both short- and long-term regulation. In the future, studies will very likely be directed to applying the understanding being gained of the mechanisms regulating catecholamine synthesis to other neurotransmitters. And although it is important to continue to investigate the mechanisms involved in activity-dependent regulation of neurotransmitter synthesis, it is also important to recognize that the role of neurotransmitter synthesis regulation in higher functions, such as learning and memory, is at present still hypothetical.

(See also PROTEIN SYNTHESIS IN LONG-TERM MEMORY IN VERTEBRATES.)

REFERENCES

Campbell, D. G., Hardie, D. G., and Vulliet, P. R. (1986). Identification of four phosphorylation sites in the N-terminal region of tyrosine hydroxylase. *Journal of Biological Chemistry 261,* 10489–10492.

Hamon, M., Bourgoin, S. Artaud, F., and El Mestikawy, S. (1981). The respective roles of tryptophan uptake and tryptophan hydroxylase in the regulation of serotonin synthesis in the central nervous system. *Journal de Physiologie* (Paris) *77,* 269–279.

Haycock, J. W. (1990). Phosphorylation of tyrosine hydroxylase in situ at serine 8, 19, 31 and 40. *Journal of Biological Chemistry 265,* 11682–11691.

Jope, R. S. (1979). High affinity choline transport and acetylCoA production in brain and their roles in the regulation of acetylcholine synthesis. *Brain Research Review 1,* 313–344.

Kaufman, S. (1985). Regulatory properties of phenylalanine, tyrosine and tryptophan hydroxylases. *Transactions of the Biochemical Society 13,* 433–436.

Kurosawa, A., Guidotti, A., and Costa, E. (1976). Induction of tyrosine 3-monooxygenase in adrenal medulla: Role of protein kinase activation and translocation. *Science 193,* 691–693.

Masserano, J. M., Vulliet, P. R., Tank, A. W., and Weiner, N. (1989). The role of tyrosine hydroxylase in the regulation of catecholamine synthesis. In U. Trendelenburg and N. Weiner, eds., *Catecholamines,* vol. 2, pp. 427–469. New York: Springer-Verlag.

Simon, J. R., and Kuhar, M. J. (1975). Impulse-flow regulation of high affinity choline uptake in brain cholinergic nerve terminals. *Nature 255,* 162–163.

Thoenen, H., Mueller, R. A., and Axelrod, J. (1969). Transsynaptic induction of adrenal tyrosine hydroxylase. *Journal of Pharmacology and Experimental Therapeutics 169,* 249–254.

Waymire, J. C., Craviso, G. L., Lichteig, K., Johnston, J. P., Baldwin, C., and Zigmond, R. E. (1991). Vasoactive intestinal peptide stimulates catecholamine biosynthesis in isolated adrenal chromaffin cells: Evidence for a 3′,5′-cyclic adenosine monophosphate dependent phosphorylation and activation of tyrosine hydroxylase. *Journal of Neurochemistry 57,* 1313–1324.

Waymire, J. C., Johnston, J. P., Hummer-Lickteig, K., Lloyd, A., Vigny, A., and Craviso, G. L. (1988). Phosphorylation of bovine adrenal chromaffin cell tyrosine hydroxylase. Temporal correlation of acetylcholine's effect on site phosphorylation, enzyme activation, and catecholamine synthesis. *Journal of Biological Chemistry 263,* 12439–12447.

Wessels-Reiker, M., Haycock, J. W., Howlett, A. C., and Strong, R. (1991). Vasoactive intestinal polypeptide induces tyrosine hydroxylase in PC12 cells. *Journal of Biological Chemistry 266,* 9347–9350.

Zigmond, R. E., Schwarzschild, M. A., and Rittenhouse, A. R. (1989). Acute regulation of tyrosine hydroxylase by nerve activity and by neurotransmitters via phosphorylation. *Annual Review of Neuroscience 12,* 415–461.

Jack C. Waymire

AGING

See Alzheimer's Disease; Pharmacological Treatment of Memory Deficits

AGING ANIMALS, PHARMACOLOGICAL MANIPULATIONS OF MEMORY IN

Psychopharmacology is the study of the effects of drugs on brain function. The specific brain functions of interest here are learning and memory. This entry presents recent studies using specific drugs that may reverse memory impairments associated with aging. Scientific investigations involving both humans and laboratory animals will be discussed. Many research studies must use laboratory animals, frequently rats and mice, because the experimental drugs might have unpleasant or harmful effects on humans. By testing these drugs on laboratory animals, we may one day be able to prevent serious age-related disorders of the human brain, such as Parkinson's disease and ALZHEIMER'S DISEASE, and we may all ultimately benefit.

Our ability to learn may be less than desired any time the demands of the task are greater than our psychological resources, particularly during aging. Although aged individuals differ in the extent to which each cognitive function is impaired, a substantial percentage of the population experience a decline in learning abilities as they grow older. *Cognitive enhancers* are drugs that can augment the brain's resources and improve learning and memory. Impaired aged individuals are obviously candidates for taking these cognitive enhancers.

Laboratory experiments typically give healthy young and aged subjects (usually animals but sometimes humans) memory tasks in which the experimental conditions are arranged so that performance is less than perfect. Selected drugs are then given, either once or over a prolonged period of time, and each subject's memory abilities are determined. Obviously, the ultimate goal of these studies with cognitive enhancers is to improve memory. To do this, scientists presume that the drug must somehow improve the function of a specific brain region or regions. There are two critical concerns that scientists have in relation to these investigations. First, the brain may already be functioning at a maximal level of performance. It may be that we cannot enhance the brain any further regardless of the drug therapy. In addition, there are important moral and legal questions that have been raised; for example, is it appropriate to attempt to enhance normal brain function? Second, scientists often assume that normal memory function can be restored by affecting only a single brain region or system. We may ultimately realize that the most important factor is the relative balance of activity between the different brain regions rather than the function of a single system. Most treatments include the use of a single drug to enhance normal function or to compensate for the loss of a particular brain system. It may ultimately become necessary to alter the function of many brain regions rather than just one.

Research on cognitive enhancers for the aged patient is based upon the assumption that the aged brain remains somewhat plastic in a percentage of the population, even if the amount of that plasticity is decreased. *Plasticity* here is intended to mean the ability of the brain to compensate for changes associated with aging. Ideally, cognitive enhancers should influence these plastic brain systems and somehow compensate for other aging-impaired brain systems. One important brain system that degenerates with aging is the *cholinergic* system. It has been given this name because of the characteristic chemical substance that brain cells within this system produce. The cholinergic system has been shown to have a very important role in learning and memory. Unfortunately, the normal function of cholinergic cells in many brain regions declines with aging in both humans and animals. Recent attempts have been made to enhance the function of the cholinergic system by adding specific nutrients to the diet, such as lecithin or choline. These nutrients may improve the ability of the cholinergic cells to function by providing the chemical building blocks for *acetylcholine*. Acetylcholine is a neurotransmitter that is excreted by cholinergic cells. Neurotransmitters allow brain cells (neurons) to communicate with each other.

This communication between neurons may underlie the processes of learning and memory. When specific nutrients are provided in the diet, more acetylcholine can be produced, communication between neurons can be improved, and learning abilities should be enhanced in aged humans and laboratory animals. However, it is important to recognize that the precise mechanism underlying the benefit of nutrient therapy is unknown.

An alternative way to enhance cholinergic function is to prolong the lifespan of the neurotransmitter acetylcholine. Once acetylcholine is released by a neuron, it is quickly destroyed. The longer acetylcholine remains active, the more cell-to-cell communication can be achieved. The drug *physostigmine* can prolong the activity of acetylcholine. This drug has been tested in aged humans and laboratory animals with slight memory loss as well as in humans with severe dementia. It can produce a noticeable improvement in some patients but not in others. Unfortunately, it produces some unpleasant side effects and patients do not enjoy taking it every day. Other drugs that act in a similar fashion, but have fewer side effects, have been investigated; they include tetrahydroacridine and galanthamine.

Aging is accompanied by impaired blood flow to the brain. Many *vasodilators* (i.e., drugs that permit increased blood flow) have been investigated. It is assumed that improved circulation to the brain will improve learning and memory. It is worth noting that some of the most promising vasodilators such as Hydergine, the nootropics, and pentoxifylline (each is discussed below), may also influence the cholinergic system. Cholinergic cells may in turn influence the blood flow into the brain. Cognitive enhancers that improve cholinergic function may therefore indirectly improve blood flow into the brain.

One of the most studied drugs in this class of drugs is Hydergine. Though the actual mechanism of Hydergine is unknown, its chemical structure suggests that it may interact with four different brain systems that have been shown to degenerate with aging, both enhancing their function directly and restoring the normal balance among them.

The next important class of drugs is the nootropics. This class includes the drugs piracetam, oxiracetam, and aniracetam. The mechanism that underlies the effects of nootropic drugs is unknown, but they may interact with specific chemical neurotransmitters in the brain. Nootropics have been investigated for their ability to improve the efficiency of higher brain functions, such as learning and memory. These drugs, given immediately prior to behavioral testing, enhance performance of aged and young rats, monkeys, and humans in a variety of experimental situations. Piracetam, in particular, has been suggested for the treatment of many common symptoms of the elderly, including senile dementia, memory disturbances, mild or severe head injuries, and language disturbances.

Pentoxifylline is a cognitive enhancer whose chemical structure closely resembles that of the active ingredient of coffee. Its use in treatment of humans enhances brain blood flow and improves many of the clinical symptoms associated with aging, including memory loss, dizziness, and insomnia. It is interesting that when caffeine is given to normal individuals, it enhances both mood and memory. These subjects also report an improved feeling of well-being and are more alert, calmer, and more interested in the experiment.

Vasopressin is a protein found naturally in the brain. Although it may not alter brain blood flow, it may facilitate brain processes that underlie learning and memory in normal and aged animals and humans.

The ability of elderly humans and laboratory animals to regulate blood levels of glucose is impaired. Glucose is a very important source of energy for the brain. This impaired regulation of blood glucose, and its altered uptake into the brain, may contribute to the dysfunction of the cholinergic system and underlie the memory impairment associated with aging. It has been demonstrated that this deficit in the regulation of blood glucose is closely related to the ability of elderly human and animal subjects to perform a difficult memory task. This may explain why injections of glucose can improve memory in aged humans and laboratory animals. Many drugs and life events (such as stress) may increase blood glucose levels and therefore indirectly modulate memory. The effects of glucose on learning and memory probably depend on the brain's cholinergic system. Cholinergic cells require glucose to make acetylcholine. Too little glucose may lead to too little acetylcholine and thereby an impaired memory.

Many of the brain processes that are influenced by cognitive enhancers are very complex. This feature of the brain contributes to the difficulty in designing an effective cognitive enhancer. However, this complexity suggests that one individual will respond favorably to a particular therapy because of the peculiar nature of his or her condition, while another individual, with a different underlying brain disorder, may not respond. Scientists must be prepared for the possibility that future cognitive enhancers may find only limited use in certain populations. The cognitive enhancers of the future may be tailored to different populations (e.g., the young or the aged) according to the nature of the enhancement required or to the type of degeneration or injury that is thought to exist within the brain. The risk is that this approach could lead to extensive polypharmacy (i.e., the use of many different drugs simultaneously) in an aged patient. This is unfortunate because the elderly are least able to tolerate the side effects of so many drugs. Scientists must therefore be very careful to design drug therapies that will avoid unwanted complications, which might undermine the benefits of the treatment.

(See also DRUGS AND MEMORY.)

REFERENCES

Bartus, R. T., Dean, R. L., Beer, B., and Lippa, A. S. (1982). The cholinergic hypothesis of geriatric memory dysfunction. *Science 217,* 408–417.

Dimond, S. G., and Brouwers, Y. M. (1976). Increase in the power of human memory in normal man through the use of drugs. *Psychopharmacology 49,* 307–309.

Drachman, D. A., and Leavitt, J. (1974). Human memory and the cholinergic system. *Archives of Neurology 30,* 13–121.

Olton, D. S., and Wenk, G. L. (1990). The development of behavioral tests to assess the effects of cognitive enhancers. *Pharmacopsychiatry 23,* 65–69.

Thal, L. J., Fuld, P. A., Masur, D. M., and Sharpless, N. S. (1983). Oral physostigmine and lecithin improve memory in Alzheimer's disease. *Annals of Neurology 13,* 491–496.

Wenk, G. L. (1989a). An hypothesis on the role of glucose in the mechanism of action of cognitive enhancers. *Psychopharmacology 99,* 431–438.

————— (1989b). Nutrition—cognition and memory. In R. B. Weg, ed., *Topics in geriatric rehabilitation,* vol. 6, *Nutrition and rehabilitation.* Rockville, Md.: Aspen Publishers.

Wenk, G. L., and Olton, D. S. (1989). Cognitive enhancers: Potential strategies and experimental results. *Progress in Neuro-Psychopharmacology and Biological Psychiatry 13,* S117–S139. Good reference source with extensive bibliography.

Gary L. Wenk

AGING AND MEMORY IN ANIMALS

There are a number of useful animal models of learning and memory in normal aging, which have expanded our knowledge and extended the prospects for ameliorating learning and memory deficits. While ALZHEIMER'S DISEASE (AD) has not been observed in animals, there are some important animal models of learning and memory in AD. Two features of animal models make them invaluable: (1) The life spans of most animals are considerably shorter than the human life span, compressing the time required to observe processes of aging; (2) Invasive or high-risk observations and experimental manipulations are feasible with animals but not with humans.

Bartus, Flicker, and Dean (1983) created logical criteria for developing animal behavioral models of aging. These criteria are presented in Table 1 and will be used to assess the animal models of learning and memory tasks such as conditioning (see CONDITIONING, CLASSICAL AND INSTRUMENTAL; OPERANT BEHAVIOR), SPATIAL LEARNING and memory, and PROBLEM SOLVING.

Classical Conditioning

Research using eyeblink classical conditioning shows promise in elucidating neurobiological mechanisms in learning, memory, and aging and has met all requirements of the criteria in Table 1 (Woodruff-Pak, Logan, and Thompson, 1990). First, eyeblink classical conditioning displays natural age-related deficits in rabbits, cats, and rats. Second, the similarities between age differences in classical conditioning in rabbits and humans are striking. Third, neurobiological age-related changes that are likely to be involved with the behavioral changes occur in humans as well as rabbits (i.e., Purkinje cell loss). With regard to the fourth criterion, involving artificial inducement of behavioral and neurobiological aging changes in young animals, aspiration of cerebellar cortex delayed but did not prevent acquisition in young rabbits (Lavond and Steinmetz, 1989). Young rabbits subjected to this treatment required almost six times as many trials to attain the learning criterion—a rate of learning comparable to that of older rabbits. The aspiration removes Purkinje cells and simulates behavioral aging quite well. Criterion

Table 1.   Logical Criteria for Developing Animal Models of Learning, Memory, and Aging

1. Behavior measured should display natural age-related deficits in the species used.
2. Conceptual or operational similarities should exist between that behavior and relevant behavioral changes in aged humans.
3. Species selected should share some of the age-related neurobiological changes observed in humans, especially those that correlate with the behavioral deficit measured.
4. If a behavioral deficit is artificially induced in younger subjects, concomitant changes in the central nervous system function should mimic some of those known to exist in aged subjects.
5. Some of the drugs known to improve behavior in the aged in clinical trials should also produce positive neurobiological and behavioral effects in the animal model.

Adapted from Bartus, Flicker, and Dean (1983).

5, involving pharmacological manipulation to ameliorate age-related deficits in classical conditioning, was satisfied by the demonstration that nimodipine accelerates rate of acquisition in old rabbits (Deyo, Straube, and Disterhoft, 1989), as does BMY 21502 (Woodruff-Pak et al., 1991).

Operant Conditioning

The type of operant conditioning for which there appear to be the largest age differences is avoidance conditioning. In this paradigm a response is emitted that enables the organism to avoid receipt of a noxious stimulus event. The passive avoidance task reinforces rodents for remaining on one side of a chamber. As soon as they cross to the opposite side of the chamber, they receive a paw shock. Retention of this passive response over a 4-hour period shows moderate age differences, and retention over a 24-hour period shows robust age differences.

Certain operational similarities exist between the passive avoidance retention deficit in rats and impairment of recent memory observed in aged human and nonhuman primates. The event to be remembered is brief and discrete, there is little or no practice or rehearsal, and retention decays

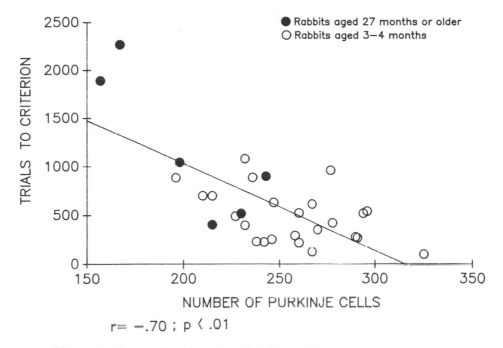

Figure 1. Scatter plot of number of Purkinje cells in selected portions of cerebellar cortex (vermis and right and left Larsell's area HVI) and trials to learning criterion in the trace classical conditioning paradigm with a 250-millisecond tone conditioned stimulus (CS) and 500-millisecond trace or silent period before the 100-millisecond corneal airpuff unconditioned stimulus (US). Thus, the CS-US interval was 750 milliseconds. Rabbits ranged in age from 3 to 50 months, but 24 of the 30 rabbits shown here were aged 3 to 4 months. *Data from Woodruff-Pak, Cronholm, and Sheffield, 1990.*

rapidly, usually within hours after the event. Bartus et al. (1981) used pharmacological agents to determine if the passive avoidance memory deficit could be ameliorated. Striking improvement on the task was caused by combining choline and piracetam. The synergistic action of the two agents supports the hypothesis that multiple, interactive neurochemical dysfunctions or deficient metabolic pathways may be involved in age-related memory impairment.

Instrumental Learning

A multiple choice-point maze is the typical apparatus for studying instrumental learning. The task of the animal is to learn the shortest path to the end of the maze, where it is rewarded. Ingram (1988) used rats (Wistar, C57BL/6, F-344) and mice (A/J, C3B10RF$_1$) at a number of points in the life span to generalize the age-related changes over ages, strains, and species.

From the perspective of the logical criteria for the development of animal models, the rodent maze model shows a robust effect of aging (criterion 1), it uses species demonstrating neurobiological age changes shared with humans (criterion 3), and age simulation in young rodents mimics aging effects (criterion 4). Criterion 3, involving the parallels between the behavioral changes in humans and in rodents performing a similar task, is not met by this animal model because very few human aging studies of maze learning have been conducted. Although criterion 5, involving pharmacological agents producing ameliorative effects, has not been met, drug studies to ameliorate learning in this animal model were attempted.

Maze learning provides an example of an animal model with robust aging effects replicated across several species that has thus far provided little insight about neurobiological mechanisms of aging. This is so because the neurobiology of the behavior is not defined in young rodents. Animal models for which the underlying neurobiological mechanisms are known or at least partially established may result in more rapid progress in research on learning, memory, and aging.

Learning and Memory for Spatial Relations

Spatial memory has been operationally defined as the ability of an organism to know or to have a representation of where it is and thus to navigate effectively in its environment (Barnes, 1988). In old age, spatial memory is less efficient in humans and animals. The intact functioning of the hippocampus is necessary for learning and remembering spatial tasks in rats and humans. Thus, spatial memory in rats is a useful animal model of learning, memory, and aging because it parallels human behavioral and neurobiological aging, and its brain substrates have been identified.

From the perspective of the criteria listed in Table 1 for successful animal models of learning, memory, and aging, the rodent model for spatial memory is most useful. Normal older rats have deficits in spatial information processing, and these deficits are similar to poorer performance of older humans on spatial tasks. Age-related neurobiological changes in the hippocampus occur in rats and humans, and in both species the neurobiological changes appear to be responsible for the behavioral deficits. Hippocampal damage in young humans and rats mimics the behavioral results in older humans and rats. Drugs affecting hippocampal efficiency in older rats improve their spatial behavior. This animal model has been useful in the description, explanation, and amelioration of spatial memory deficits in old age.

Tasks Assessing Short-Term Memory in Nonhuman Primates

The animal models that are the most similar genetically, anatomically, physiologically, and behaviorally to humans are nonhuman primates. It is with monkeys and apes that we can most easily make generalizations from animal models to humans. Particularly in the realm of behavior, nonhuman primates have capacities that provide the closest parallel to humans. With regard to neurobiological processes of aging, nonhuman primates are among the few species that develop senile plaques similar to those observed in the brains of aged humans

and, in greater numbers, in patients with AD (see, e.g., Walker et al., 1988).

The short-term memory dysfunction in aged monkeys bears a strong resemblance to short-term memory loss observed in aged humans. Because of the parallels between the performance of aged monkeys and aged normal and demented humans, the aged monkeys are useful animal models. They can be used to study memory dysfunction in aging, and they are useful in evaluating experimental drugs intended to treat memory impairment.

The animal model of nonhuman primates for short-term memory loss in aging meets all of the criteria for developing animal behavioral models listed in Table 1. The memory deficit occurs naturally, and it parallels extremely well the short-term memory deficit observed in normal aging and exacerbated in AD. Neurobiological changes occurring in aging nonhuman primates resemble human neurobiological aging phenomena more closely than do any nonprimate animal models. Inducing the aging effects in young nonhuman primates with anatomical and/or neurochemical lesions mimics aging processes, and drug facilitation is parallel in the animal model and humans. This is an excellent animal model for human aging; it is limited only by expense, by the long life spans of nonhuman primates, and by the scarcity of aged nonhuman primates.

Animal Models of Learning and Memory in Alzheimer's Disease

There is evidence in humans of severe deterioration in the nucleus basalis of Meynert in AD (see, e.g., Whitehouse et al., 1981). These results gave new momentum to the development of potential animal models of the disease. Although AD appears to be unique to humans, certain aspects of it, such as the loss of cells in the nucleus basalis, can be modeled in animals.

Cholinergic System Lesions

In rodents the homologue for the nucleus basalis of Meynert is the magnocellular nuclei of the basal forebrain (MNBF). Lesions of this region produce cholinergic hypofunction in the cortex and behavioral impairment such as poor retention in a passive avoidance task, serial spatial discrimination reversal, and poor radial maze performance, making it a most useful model.

Given that the cholinergic system plays a critical role in memory and that impairment of this system mimics some of the behavioral loss in AD, it is desirable to produce lesions of the entire cholinergic system and only the cholinergic system. With surgical techniques, this task is impossible. Chemical, electrolytic, or radio-frequency lesions result in abrupt structural traumatization of a specific brain area, which is quite unlike the comparatively slow loss of cholinergic neurons. Furthermore, local circuits and noncholinergic neurons are unavoidably involved. With pharmacological techniques, the disruption is a closer simulation of degenerative processes in AD.

A cholinergic neurotoxin called AF64A was developed that selectively impairs the cholinergic neurotransmitter system. Comparisons among neurotoxins for the cholinergic system led Hanin et al. (1987) to conclude that AF64A induces a persistent cholinergic deficiency of presynaptic origin. It is potentially a useful model for AD, and trials with it indicate that neurochemical and behavioral changes induced by AF64A parallel changes observed in AD. Experiments with AF64A and the cholinergic facilitator physostigmine have demonstrated that memory deficits induced by administration of AF64A can at least be partially reversed.

Aluminum-Induced Neurofibrillary Tangles

The injection of aluminum into the nervous systems of cats and rabbits results in the development of neurofibrillary tangles. Rabbits injected in this manner cannot acquire the conditioned eyeblink response. The approach appeared particularly relevant for AD when the presence of aluminum in the nuclear region of neurofibrillary tangles containing neuronal cells from AD patients was reported. While this procedure was initially received with enthusiasm as a means to simulate human aging phenomena that normally do not occur in animals, the technique has proved disappointing. Fisher and Hanin (1986) pointed out that central cholinergic activity, which is markedly reduced in AD, is normal in aluminum-treated rabbits. Wisniewski, Iqbal, and McDermott (1980) observed that the effect of aluminum on cholinergic markers such as choline acetyltransferase is minimal. The ultrastructure and biochemical content of aluminum-induced neurofibrillary tangles in animals are different from those of human neurofibrillary tan-

gles, and the distribution of aluminum-induced neurofibrillary tangles in animal brains differs from the distribution in human brains.

While each animal model has limitations, the value of animal models for research on learning, memory, and aging is immeasurable. For example, drug intervention is one of the strongest prospects available for memory loss in aging and dementia, and it could not be contemplated, let alone initiated, without animal models. It is only with animal models that we will develop a complete body of knowledge about learning, memory, and aging and devise the means to ameliorate memory dysfunction such as that accompanying AD.

REFERENCES

Barnes, C. A. (1988). Aging and the physiology of spatial memory. *Neurobiology of Aging 9*, 563–568.

Bartus, R. T., Dean, R. L., Sherman, K. A., Friedman, E., and Beer, B. (1981). Profound effects of combining choline and piracetam on memory enhancement and cholinergic function in aged rats. *Neurobiology of Aging 2*, 105–111.

Bartus, R. T., Flicker, C., and Dean, R. L. (1983). Logical principles for the development of animal models of age-related memory impairments. In T. Crook, S. Ferris, and R. T. Bartus, eds., *Assessment in geriatric psychopharmacology*. Madison, Conn.: Mark Powley Associates.

Deyo, R. A., Straube, K. T., and Disterhoft, J. F. (1989). Nimodipine facilitates associative learning in aging rabbits. *Science 243*, 809–811.

Fisher, A., and Hanin, I. (1986). Potential animal models for senile dementia of Alzheimer's type, with emphasis of AF64A-induced cholinotoxicity. *Annual Review of Pharmacology and Toxicology 26*, 161–181.

Hanin, I., Fisher, A., Hortnagl, H., Leventer, S. M., Potter, P. E., and Walsh, T. J. (1987). Ethylcholine aziridinium (AF64A; ECMA) and other potential cholinergic neuron–specific neurotoxins. In H. Y. Meltzer, ed., *Psychopharmacology: The third generation of progress*. New York: Raven Press.

Ingram, D. (1988). Complex maze learning in rodents as a model of age related memory impairment. *Neurobiology of Aging 9*, 475–485.

Lavond, D. G., and Steinmetz, J. E. (1989). Acquisition of classical conditioning without cerebellar cortex. *Behavioural Brain Research 33*, 113–164.

Walker, L. C., Kitt, C. A., Cork, L. C., Struble, R. G., Dellovade, T. L., and Price, D. L. (1988). Multiple transmitter systems contribute neurites to individual senile plaques. *Journal of Neuropathology and Experimental Neurology 47*, 370–381.

Whitehouse, P. J., Price, D. L., Clark, A. W., Coyle, J. T., and DeLong, M. R. (1981). Alzheimer's disease: Evidence for selective loss of cholinergic neurons in the nucleus basalis. *Annals of Neurology 10*, 122–126.

Wisniewski, H. M., Iqbal, K., and McDermott, J. R. (1980). Aluminum-induced neurofibrillary changes: Its relationship to senile dementia of Alzheimer's type. *Neurotoxicology 1*, 121–124.

Woodruff-Pak, D. S., Cronholm, J. F., and Sheffield, J. B. (1990). Purkinje cell number related to rate of classical conditioning. *NeuroReport 1*, 165–168.

Woodruff-Pak, D. S., Logan, C. G., and Thompson, R. F. (1990). Neurobiological substrates of classical conditioning across the life span. In A. Diamond, ed., *The development and neural bases of higher cognitive functions*. New York: New York Academy of Sciences Press.

Woodruff-Pak, D. S., Sasse, D. K., Coffin, J. M., Haunton-Kreps, M., and Moon, S. L. (1991). The effect of BMY 21502 on classical conditioning of the eyeblink response in young and older rabbits. In *Proceedings of the Sixth Meeting of the International Study Group on the Pharmacology of Memory Disorders Associated wtih Aging*, pp. 563–567. Boston: Center for Brain Sciences and Metabolism Charitable Trust.

Diana S. Woodruff-Pak

AGING AND MEMORY IN HUMANS

One of the commonest complaints of older people is that their memory is not what it used to be. The validity of such subjective reports is borne out, in general, by the scientific literature: Memory performance does decline as a function of the normal aging process in healthy adults, although the decline is much more evident with some materials and tasks than it is with others. This variability has given researchers useful clues to the specific memory components or processes that are particularly vulnerable to the effects of aging. Some of this work is described below.

It should be noted that virtually all the studies described use the cross-sectional method of age comparison; that is, a group of young adults (often college students in their early twenties) is compared with a group of older adults (usually community-dwelling volunteers in their sixties and seventies). Additionally, some studies incorporate middle-aged groups of people in their forties and fifties. The cross-sectional method is much more practicable than within-subject longitudinal studies, but it does leave open the possibility that the differences observed between the groups may be attributable to causes other than aging—to differences in education or motivation, for example. Obviously researchers take pains to minimize the possibility of such artifacts, and they do this by matching the groups on educational level, on vocabulary (a rough measure of verbal intelligence), and on other indicators of intelligence and socioeconomic status. A further point is that many crucial experimental results take the form of interactions between age and some experimental variable; that is, one condition of the experiment is associated with large age-related differences, whereas another condition is associated with much smaller differences, even though the same subjects are used. The finding of such differential effects makes it harder to argue that group differences are a function, say, of reduced motivation in the older sample.

Like other experimental explorations of individual differences in memory ability (see INDIVIDUAL DIFFERENCES IN LEARNING AND MEMORY), the work on aging has been carried out within various theoretical frameworks and with a view to establishing some theoretical point. In this brief article it is not possible to go into details of theoretical motivation in most cases; instead, some major findings will be described under the very general headings of short-term and long-term memory functions, and implications for current theories will be pointed out wherever appropriate.

Age Differences in Short-Term Retention

The phrase *short-term retention* is used here to refer to situations in which subjects retain a small amount of material over several seconds. Within such situations, two rather different types of tasks may be distinguished: primary memory and working memory tasks. In primary memory tasks the subject reproduces the material in much the same form as it was presented; in working memory tasks, the subject must both retain the material and simultaneously carry out further processing operations on that material or on other incoming stimuli (see also WORKING MEMORY: HUMANS). The distinction is an important one in the context of studies of aging because age differences are slight or nonexistent in primary memory tasks, but age-related decrements are substantial in working memory tasks. Some theorists have suggested that primary memory and working memory represent separate underlying memory systems, whereas others, such as Craik and Rabinowitz (1984), have taken the view that the two types of short-term retention represent the end points of a continuum of different tasks, and that tasks demanding greater amounts of concurrent processing are closer to the working memory end.

Experimental situations requiring little processing of the retained material include memory span, the Brown-Peterson task, and recall of the last few words in a free recall list (the recency effect). In a memory span task, the subject reproduces a short string of numbers, letters, or words, *span* being the longest string possible; in the Brown-Peterson task, the subject holds a small amount of material (e.g., three unrelated letters) and reproduces them after 5, 10, or 20 seconds of intervening activity. All three situations may be described loosely as primary memory tasks, and the results of many experiments agree that adult age differences are very small on these paradigms. In contrast, when subjects must continually switch attention between the material retained and some other ongoing activity, older people perform less well than their younger counterparts. One such task involves presenting subjects with a series of sentences to be understood and acted on (for example, deciding whether the statement is true or false), with the further requirement that the subject remember the last word of each successive sentence and reproduce the string of last words after the series of sentences has been presented. This is a classic working memory task, and one in which older people do less well.

Hasher and Zacks (1988) have made the interesting suggestion that older people may be less able to inhibit task-irrelevant processing, like daydreaming or thinking of personal concerns. This off-task information therefore intrudes into their ongoing processing activities and reduces the effective storage space in working memory. This suggestion is in line with the complaint of many older people that they are less able to concentrate than they were formerly, and are more vulnerable to distraction.

In summary, when older people can concentrate on a small amount of information (like a telephone number) and are allowed to reproduce it without interference from a second task or from some distracting source of information, they can perform at the level of younger adults. When distraction is present, however, or the material held in mind must be transformed or manipulated, the older adults are at a disadvantage.

Age Differences in Long-Term Retention

In the case of memory for past events, age-related differences in performance are much greater in some situations than in others. Researchers have therefore focused on two major questions: (1) What is the locus of the age difference when age-related losses are observed? (2) What factors act to reduce or enhance the differences? With respect to the first question, the obvious candidates are age differences in the encoding or acquisition phase (see CODING PROCESSES), or differences in the ability to retrieve information (see RETRIEVAL PROCESSES). In an influential article, Hasher and Zacks (1979) proposed that age-associated differences are associated with *effortful* processes such as elaborative rehearsal and organization of incoming material. Their notion was that the execution of such processes depends on the operations of a limited-capacity attentional mechanism, and that the capacity of this mechanism decreases with age in adulthood. Other theorists have suggested the similar notion that mental processes require appropriate energy resources, and that the pool of available processing resources declines with age.

Hasher and Zacks (1979) concentrated on encoding operations, but they might well have included effortful retrieval operations in their list of processes vulnerable to aging. Burke and Light (1981) explicitly suggested that older people have particular difficulty with memory retrieval, an idea endorsed by Craik (1983), who added the idea that retrieval tasks vary in difficulty, depending on how much environmental support the appropriate retrieval operations receive from the task or from the materials. For example, the delayed recall of a long list of words provides little support; it is an effortful task, and thus large age-related decrements would be expected. On the other hand, if the words are re-presented in a recognition test, the support is greater and age-related losses should be smaller. Much of the empirical evidence is in line with these ideas.

Encoding Differences

From the preceding argument it might be expected that older people would benefit disproportionately from manipulations that enrich encoding and thereby make acquisition easier and less effortful. Some experiments have shown this pattern of age-related compensation, but other paradigms show equal benefits to young and old participants, and still others have found disproportionate benefits to *younger* subjects. For example, Lars Bäckman (1986) found that age differences in the recall of lists of short sentences were least when the sentences were presented at a slow rate, and simultaneously in both auditory and visual form; this result thus illustrates the compensation pattern. Other experiments have boosted encoding by requiring subjects to fill in missing letters in synonym pairs (e.g., quick-F—ST), or to perform brief motor actions (e.g., "scratch your ear," "point to the window"); these manipulations enhance later recall of the words or verbal commands, and most studies have found an equivalent enhancement in young and old subjects. Finally, the result of a greater benefit to younger participants was found by Jan Rabinowitz (1989) in a recall study in which standard conditions were compared with optimal study conditions in which subjects chose their own pace and made notes about the words on the list. In general, then, there is evidence that aging is associated with less effective encoding for later memory; in some cases this inefficiency can be compensated for, but the parameters of this compensation are not well understood at present.

Retrieval Differences

One line of evidence that has been taken to implicate retrieval difficulties in older people is that age-related decrements are typically much smaller in recognition memory tests than in recall tests. The assumption here is that unaided recall is more effortful, and that these more effortful retrieval operations are particularly difficult for older subjects. Studies by Macht and Buschke (1983) and by Craik and McDowd (1987) have shown directly that performance of a reaction-time (RT) task is detrimentally affected when it is performed while recalling a list of words, and that this decrement is greater for older subjects. This is the expected result if recall and performance of the RT task both draw on the same limited pool of processing resources, which is smaller in the case of older participants.

A related study by Ceci and Tabor (1981) explored the dimension of flexibility in recall by presenting drawings that either were related to common themes (e.g., "associated with the North Pole") or were members of semantic categories (e.g., dwellings). During recall, subjects moved from one type of organizer to another to aid their performance, and greater flexibility in this sense related to higher levels of recall; importantly, younger subjects showed greater flexibility in using the different types of organizer.

Older subjects also experience difficulty in retrieving facts and knowledge from SEMANTIC MEMORY. One well-known example is the problem that many older people report in retrieving names; such anecdotal reports have been verified in a study conducted by Cohen and Faulkner (1986). Although proper names seem to give particular trouble, the retrieval of words can also be a problem. A nice example of this situation is provided in an experiment by Bowles and Poon; although older subjects typically do *better* than their younger counterparts on standard vocabulary tests, Bowles and Poon (1985) found substantial age-related decrements in a task in which definitions were provided and subjects had to retrieve the specified word. It thus seems that retrieval processes are particularly difficult for older people—from both episodic and semantic memory. In some cases (e.g., recognition) the provision of more complete retrieval information appears to be of greater benefit to the older group.

Nonverbal Memory

Most experiments on memory and aging have focused on the retention of verbal materials, but several studies have explored age differences in memory for pictures, faces, and other nonverbal stimuli. For example, several experiments have shown that age differences in *recognition* of scenes or drawings are typically slight, although younger subjects show superior *recall* of the same stimuli. Studies on memory for faces generally show the same pattern; age differences in later recognition of novel faces are usually small, unless the faces were shown only briefly during the learning phase or the recognition test is made very difficult by including similar faces as distractor items. Several investigators have studied age differences in memory for spatial information (see SPATIAL LEARNING), either by asking subjects to remember the position of objects in a spatial matrix or by using more realistic model towns or streetscapes. The general finding has been that older people do perform less well in these situations, although it should be borne in mind that the experiments use rather artificial situations; older people may do better when using real-life spatial information.

Memory for Remote Events

Older people often report that whereas their memory for recent events is poor, they can remember events from their youth perfectly well. However, there are a number of problems in accepting these anecdotal statements as scientific evidence. First, the events recollected from 50 or 60 years ago are typically not everyday details, but are more likely to be salient or emotional occurrences. Second, the events in question have usually been recalled many times, so they are not really being retrieved from the distant past; to some extent they are being retrieved from the last recollection, and are probably quite prone to unconscious embellishment and change. Scientific studies have tested memory for public events, faces in the news, or television programs; typically, such studies have shown a progressive decline in accurate recollection as the events become more remote. One technique that does suggest better recollection of events in youth is one in which subjects give a personal memory in response to a stimulus word (e.g., policeman, airport); elderly participants tend to respond with many experiences from the age range 10 to 30, although researchers have suggested that this finding may not reflect better encoding of events in these years so much as differential sampling from that period, which is typically rich in salient life events.

Memory for Source and for the Future

Two topics that have attracted researchers recently are (1) age differences in memory for the source or initial context in which a person was encountered or a fact was learned, and (2) age differences in remembering to carry out future actions, prospective memory. Several studies have shown that older people are more likely than their younger counterparts to forget initial context; they are therefore more likely to remember facts but not where or when they were learned, or to find a face familiar but be unable to recollect where they

met the person. The evidence on prospective memory is mixed at present; a few studies have shown that older people are less able to remember to carry out some future action, a finding in line with anecdotal reports of increased forgetfulness as people age. Other well conducted studies have found no age-related losses in this ability, however, so further research is required to elucidate the relevant factors.

Explicit and Implicit Memory

Most memory tasks involve the conscious recollection of the original event, and researchers have referred to these tasks (e.g., recall, recognition) as explicit tests of memory. However, memory can also be demonstrated implicitly, without asking the subject to recollect the initial episode—for example, by presenting a word (e.g., ASSASSIN) and later asking the subject to complete a word fragment (A - - A - - IN). Performance on the word completion task is substantially better if the target word was in the previously presented list than if it was not. Researchers have found that amnesic patients perform at normal levels on implicit memory tasks, and the same result has been found with respect to normal aging.

An illustrative experiment is one by Light and Singh (1987), who presented a list of words, then tested memory either explicitly, by providing the first three letters of target words as cues, or implicitly, by providing the first three letters of target words, with the instruction to complete the word stem with the first word that came to mind. Young subjects outperformed their elders in the explicit cued recall test, but the age groups were equally likely to complete the word stems with target words in the implicit test. It appears that older people encode events sufficiently well to carry out implicit memory tasks at the level of younger subjects; their memory problems arise in connection with the ability to reinstate some aspect of the original event in conscious awareness. (See also IMPLICIT MEMORY.)

Remediation

If older people exhibit poorer memory abilities under many conditions, can anything be done to restore performance levels? One answer may be biological; many pharmaceutical companies are attempting to develop products to alleviate memory problems, but none is available at present (see also DRUGS AND MEMORY). At the psychological level, several studies have shown that it is perfectly possible to teach older people mnemonic skills that lead to dramatic improvements in their ability to recall words or names. One example is provided by the work of Kliegl et al. (1989), who taught younger and older subjects a series of local landmarks; once the landmarks were thoroughly memorized, they acted as mnemonic pegs on which to hang a series of words through the processes of association and imagery. Using this method of loci, elderly subjects could increase their serial recall from less than ten words up to almost forty words after a single presentation, provided that ample time was allowed for encoding and retrieval. This result is basically a hopeful one, although two caveats are in order. The first is that the technique did not reduce age differences—younger subjects profited even more from learning the skill; the second point is that in similar investigations, researchers have found that older people typically do not use their laboratory-learned skills in real life. Further work is needed to devise more congenial techniques that can be incorporated without too much effort into the normal activities of daily living.

REFERENCES

Bäckman, L. (1986). Adult age differences in cross-modal recoding and mental tempo, and older adults' utilization of compensatory task conditions. *Experimental Aging Research 12,* 135–140.

Bowles, N. L., and Poon, L. W. (1985). Aging and retrieval of words in semantic memory. *Journal of Gerontology 40,* 71–77.

Burke, D. M., and Light, L. L. (1981). Memory and aging: The role of retrieval processes. *Psychological Bulletin 90,* 513–540.

Ceci, S. J., and Tabor, L. (1981). Flexibility and memory: Are the elderly really less flexible? *Experimental Aging Research 7,* 147–158.

Cohen, G., and Faulkner, D. (1986). Memory for proper names: Age differences in retrieval. *British Journal of Developmental Psychology 4,* 187–197.

Craik, F. I. M. (1983). On the transfer of information from temporary to permanent memory. *Philosophical Transactions of the Royal Society of London B302,* 341–359.

Craik, F. I. M., and Jennings, J. M. (1992). Human memory. In F. I. M. Craik and T. A. Salthouse, eds., *Handbook of aging and cognition.* Hillsdale, N.J.: Erlbaum.

Craik, F. I. M., and McDowd, J. M. (1987). Age differences in recall and recognition. *Journal of Experimental Psychology: Learning, Memory, and Cognition 12,* 474–479.

Craik, F. I. M., and Rabinowitz, J. C. (1984). Age differences in the acquisition and use of verbal information. In H. Bouma and D. G. Bouwhuis, eds., *Attention and performance X.* Hillsdale, N.J.: Erlbaum.

Hasher, L., and Zacks, R. T. (1979). Automatic and effortful processes in memory. *Journal of Experimental Psychology: General 108,* 356–388.

—— (1988). Working memory, comprehension, and aging: A review and a new view. In G. H. Bower, ed., *The psychology of learning and motivation,* vol. 22, pp. 193–225. New York: Academic Press.

Kliegl, R., Smith, J., and Baltes, P. B. (1989). Testing-the-limits and the study of adult age differences in cognitive plasticity of a mnemonic skill. *Developmental Psychology 25,* 247–256.

Light, L. L. (1991). Memory and aging: Four hypotheses in search of data. *Annual Review of Psychology 42,* 333–376.

Light, L. L., and Singh, A. (1987). Implicit and explicit memory in young and older adults. *Journal of Experimental Psychology: Learning, Memory, and Cognition 13,* 531–541.

Macht, M. L., and Buschke, H. (1983). Age differences in cognitive effort in recall. *Journal of Gerontology 38,* 695–700.

Rabinowitz, J. C. (1989). Age deficits in recall under optimal study conditions. *Psychology and Aging 4,* 378–386.

Salthouse, T. A. (1982). *Adult cognition: An experimental psychology of human aging.* New York: Springer-Verlag.

Fergus I. M. Craik

ALGORITHMS, LEARNING

Learning algorithms are sets of rules, usually expressed as mathematical equations or computer instructions, that can be followed to generate behavior exhibiting aspects of learning. Also called learning *procedures, methods,* or *rules,* learning algorithms are essential components of mathematical models of biological learning, and of technological devices engineered to improve their own performance with experience. Learning algorithms have been studied extensively in artificial intelligence as algorithms for machine learning and in engineering disciplines such as adaptive control, adaptive filtering, and adaptive pattern classification, where they appear as parameter estimation algorithms. They also play a major role in connectionist, or artificial neural network, systems, where they usually appear as rules for adjusting the strengths of connections between network elements representing neurons. These connections correspond to synapses by which neurons communicate with other neurons, and with sensory and motor mechanisms. In some connectionist systems, learning algorithms are models of the neurobiological mechanisms believed to produce learning through experience-dependent changes in neurons and synapses. Often based on extreme simplifications of neurobiological mechanisms, these learning algorithms nevertheless reveal the logical strengths and weaknesses of the hypotheses on which they rest. Other connectionist learning algorithms are motivated by the objective of modeling animal behavior or of solving practical problems through learning.

Donald HEBB's 1949 hypothesis about how neural circuits might learn associations between events is one of the earliest and most influential hypotheses suggesting learning algorithms for neural networks. Hebb hypothesized that when a neuron, A, repeatedly and persistently takes part in firing another neuron, B, the synapses by which A stimulates B are strengthened. As a result, it becomes easier for neuron A to fire neuron B in the future. Consequently, any event that stimulates neuron A may also come to stimulate neuron B, and thus become associated with the consequences of B's firing as well as with other events that stimulate B.

Turning this hypothesis into a learning algorithm requires precise definitions of the variables involved and how they interact. One of the simplest

ways to do this is to consider the situation in which neuron B receives input from other neurons, labeled 1, 2, $\cdots$, n, any of which can play the role of neuron A in Hebb's hypothesis. Let $X_B(t)$ be a positive number representing the activity level (the instantaneous rate of firing) of neuron B at time t. Similarly, for i = 1, 2, $\cdots$, n, let $X_i(t)$ represent the activity levels at time t of neurons 1, 2, $\cdots$, n (see Figure 1). To represent how the activity of neuron B depends on the activities of the other neurons, the simplest assumption is that $X_B(t)$ is a weighted sum of the activities of the other neurons, where each weight represents the current strength of a synapse. If $W_i(t)$ is the strength at time t of the synapse by which neuron i influences neuron B, this means that

$$X_B(t) = W_1(t) X_1(t) + \cdots + W_n(t) X_n(t). \quad (1)$$

Hebb's hypothesis suggests how the synaptic strengths change over time, depending on the other variables. The extent to which neuron i is taking part in firing neuron B is often represented by the *product* of the activity levels of neuron B and neuron i: $X_B(t) X_i(t)$. This product is large when the activity levels of both neurons are high, and it is small when the activity level of one or both neurons is close to zero. Thus, if neuron i persistently takes part in firing neuron B, this product will be large for many times t. This leads to a rule for changing synaptic strengths that can be written as

$$W_i(t + \Delta t) = W_i(t) + c W_B(t) X_i(t), \quad (2)$$

for each i, where Δt is a small time increment and c is a small positive number. Selecting values for Δt and c determines how rapidly the synaptic strengths change. According to Equation 2, at any time t when the activity levels of neurons i and B are both greater than zero, $X_B(t)X_i(t)$ is greater than zero and the synaptic strength $W_i(t)$ increases from time t to time t + Δt. According to Equation 1, this larger synaptic weight means that neuron i's activity will contribute more to the activity of neuron B in the future. Equations 1 and 2 comprise a learning algorithm; both are needed to compute the values of the synaptic strengths when the values $X_i(t)$, i = 1, 2, $\cdots$, n, are given for each time t. This is the simplest of many learning algorithms based on Hebb's hypothesis, and despite many shortcomings, it has played an important role in connectionist theories of learning. Brown et al.

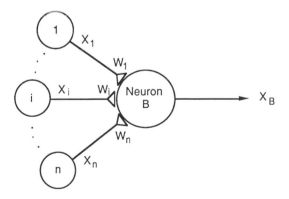

Figure 1.   Neurons 1, 2, $\cdots$, n provide input to neuron B.

(1990) discuss this and many other Hebbian learning algorithms, and how well they model synaptic properties actually observed in physiological experiments.

Other learning algorithms have been designed to have specific theoretical properties. Prominent among these is the *least mean square* (LMS) algorithm proposed by Widrow and Hoff in 1960. Like the Hebbian algorithm described above, it can be described as a way of changing the synaptic weights of a neuronlike element, but it requires another variable to provide a *training signal* to the learning process. This signal tells the element what its activity should be for a collection of input signals; it is said to provide the *desired outputs* or *target outputs*. If $Z(t)$ denotes the target output at time t for an element whose output is $X(t)$, then $Z(t) - X(t)$ gives the *error* in the element's output: the discrepancy between what the element's activity should be and what it actually is. The LMS algorithm is an *error-correction* algorithm because it changes synaptic weights so as to reduce the sizes of the errors gradually over time.

If $X(t)$ is a weighted sum of inputs as given by Equation 1, then the LMS algorithm specifies that the synaptic weights change as follows:

$$W_i(t + \Delta t) = W_i(t) + c\,[Z(t) - X(t)\,]\,X_i(t). \quad (3)$$

This means that when the element's output, $X(t)$, is too low, the error is positive and the synaptic weight, $W_i(t)$, increases (assuming both c and $X_i(t)$ are positive). On the other hand, when the element's output is too high, the error is negative and the weight decreases. In either case, this change in synaptic weight tends to make the element's output more nearly equal to the target output when input element i is active in the future. A similar error-correction algorithm, known as the Perceptron learning algorithm, differs from the LMS algorithm in that the error is sensitive only to the difference in the signs of the desired and actual outputs, and not to the difference in their sizes.

The LMS algorithm is closely related to an influential model of Pavlovian CONDITIONING proposed by Rescorla and Wagner (1972). Instead of changes in synaptic strengths, this model defines changes in the *associative strengths* between conditioned stimuli (CSs) and an unconditioned response (UR). When the animal's expectations about the events following a CS disagree with what actually occurs, the CS's associative strength changes so as to reduce the amount of disagreement in the future.

Suppose an animal is presented with a cue A, such as a tone, followed by an unconditioned stimulus (US), such as an air puff in the vicinity of the eye that triggers a reflexive eyeblink, the UR. According to the Rescorla-Wagner model, as a result of this trial, the change in the strength of the association between A and the UR, which they denoted as ΔV_A, is represented as

$$\Delta V_A = \alpha_A \beta [\lambda - V_{AX}], \quad (4)$$

where α_A is a positive constant depending on the nature of cue A, β and λ are positive constants depending on the nature of the US, and V_{AX} is the associative strength of the compound stimulus consisting of cue A together with all the other stimuli, X, present on the trial. One can think of V_{AX} as the total expectation generated by the stimulus compound AX; it is usually assumed to be the sum of the associative strengths of all of the stimuli present on the trial. An equation like Equation 4 applies to the associative strengths of all the stimuli present on the trial, including those present in the compound X; the associative strengths of stimuli not present on a trial are unchanged.

Although the Rescorla-Wagner model and the LMS algorithm were developed independently and for different purposes, they are almost identical in mathematical form. The role of the target output of the LMS algorithm is played by λ, which is different for different USs; the total expectation, V_{AX}, corresponds to the output of the LMS element, $X(t)$; and the provision of the Rescorla-Wagner model that only the associative strengths of stimuli present on a trial are changed is enforced in the LMS algorithm by the presence of the factor $X_i(t)$ on the right-hand side of the LMS equation (Equation 3). The positive constant c of the LMS algorithm corresponds to $\alpha_A \beta$ of the Rescorla-Wagner algorithm. That the latter depends on the stimulus A, whereas the former does not, is the only mathematical difference between the LMS algorithm and the Rescorla-Wagner model.

Theories of the LMS algorithm and many other learning algorithms depend on viewing the learning process as a search for the set of synaptic weights that are best according to some measure of the algorithm's performance. For example, the LMS algorithm can be understood in terms of an error surface that assigns to each possible set of weights the average, or mean, of the squared error that would be obtained using that set of weights for all relevant inputs. The current weights correspond to a point on this surface, and the LMS algorithm changes the weights by moving this point down the slope of the surface toward a point corresponding to a set of weights minimizing the error. It is called a *gradient-descent* algorithm because the direction of steepest slope is given mathematically by the gradient of the error measure. A gradient-descent algorithm finds a local minimum, meaning a point that is better than neighboring points, although a better set of weights may exist. However, when the element's output is a linear function of its inputs, as given by Equation 1, the error surface has a single minimum. In this case, the LMS algorithm finds the best set of weights—that is, the weights producing the least-mean-square error over the relevant inputs, thus justifying the algorithm's name.

A generalization of the LMS algorithm known as the *error back-propagation* algorithm has been influential in connectionist research. (Hinton [1989] provides details about this and other connectionist learning algorithms.) In its simplest form, this is a gradient-descent algorithm that applies to networks of neuronlike elements connected in multiple layers and capable of computing nonlinear functions of the network's input. An error for each element is computed, based on the output error of the network, by propagating this output error back through the network in the direction opposite to the flow of element activity. Mathematically, this process computes the gradient of the error surface at the point corresponding to all the current weights in the network. Unlike the linear LMS algorithm, however, the error back-propagation algorithm is not guaranteed to find the best weights because the error surface generally has a complex topography with many local minima.

Learning algorithms are often categorized according to properties of the learning problems for which they are best suited. Although this can be misleading because a learning algorithm can be used in different ways to solve different kinds of problems, it is nevertheless useful to describe these categories. A learning algorithm is *unsupervised* if it does not rely on training signals to provide target outputs. Unsupervised learning algorithms are useful for recoding sensory signals, often to reduce their complexity while preserving information content. The Hebbian learning algorithm described above is most often used for unsupervised learning. When a learning algorithm requires target outputs, it is said to be *supervised,* or to

perform "learning with a teacher." The LMS and error back-propagation algorithms are supervised learning algorithms. The utility of supervised learning algorithms arises from their ability to provide outputs for novel inputs on which they have never been trained, producing a kind of extrapolation from the training data, often called *generalization.* Whereas target outputs explicitly tell the learning system what its output should be, it is possible to learn with less informative training information. *Reinforcement learning* algorithms rely on receiving signals evaluating the quality of the learning system's output, but unlike the errors determined from target outputs, these signals do not directly specify what changes would improve the output. Reinforcement learning algorithms have to discover how to improve their behavior by trying various outputs and comparing the resulting evaluations. A key issue discussed in the review article by Barto (1990) is the source of training information in applications of supervised and reinforcement learning algorithms. Often great ingenuity is required to obtain training information of the quality required by a learning algorithm.

(See also NEURAL COMPUTATION.)

REFERENCES

Barto, A. G. (1990). Connectionist learning for control: An overview. In T. Miller, R. S. Sutton, and P. J. Werbos, eds., *Neural networks for control,* pp. 5–58. Cambridge, Mass.: MIT Press.

Brown, T. H., Kairiss, E. W., and Keenan, C. L. (1990). Hebbian synapses: Biophysical mechanisms and algorithms. *Annual Review of Neuroscience 13,* 475–511.

Hebb, D. O. (1949). *The organization of behavior.* New York: Wiley.

Hinton, G. E. (1989). Connectionist learning procedures. *Artificial Intelligence 40,* 185–234.

Rescorla, R. A., and Wagner, A. R. (1972). A theory of Pavlovian conditioning: Variations in the effectiveness of reinforcement and non-reinforcement. In A. H. Black and W. F. Prokasy, eds., *Classical conditioning,* vol. 2, Current research and theory, pp. 64–99. New York: Appleton.

Widrow, B., and Hoff, M. E. (1960). Adaptive switching circuits. In *1960 IRE WESCON convention record,* pp. 96–104. New York: IRE. Reprinted in J. A. Anderson and E. Rosenfeld, eds., *Neurocomputing: Foundations of research,* pp. 123–134. Cambridge, Mass.: MIT Press, 1988.

Andrew G. Barto

ALZHEIMER'S DISEASE

[*This entry consists of two articles examining Alzheimer's disease from different points of view:* Cognitive Aspects *and* Neural and Molecular Basis.]

Cognitive Aspects

Alzheimer's disease (AD) is the most common cause of DEMENTIA in the elderly, affecting 50 percent to 70 percent of patients with symptoms of dementia. To be called demented, an individual must show a progressive decline in many areas of mental ability. In the case of AD, these declines are occurring because of cell loss and other specific pathological changes that are impairing the ability of the brain to function normally. In the beginning of the disease, only some parts of the brain are affected, but as it progresses, more and more of the brain succumbs to the disease. Eventually, so many parts of the brain are involved that patients cannot move around normally and feed themselves. They then become susceptible to other diseases, such as pneumonia, that ultimately lead to death. The duration of the disease can differ widely among individuals, lasting from 5 to 15 years. Many drugs are being developed to treat it, but at the present time there is no way of preventing the progression of the disease.

When the disease was first described by Alois Alzheimer in 1907, it was thought to affect only persons under the age of 65. In the 1960s, researchers discovered that patients who were previously thought to have severe cognitive decline because of diseases in the blood vessels of the brain (cerebrovascular disease or "hardening of the arteries") in fact exhibited the pathological hallmarks of AD on autopsy (neurofibrillary tangles and neuritic plaques). The realization that AD affects persons of all ages is, therefore, a relatively new one. Since the number of people under the age of 65 who are affected by the disease is small (less than 2 percent), it used to be considered a rare disorder. Now it is understood that AD increases in prevalence as people get older. Among people 65 to 85 its prevalence is 5 percent to 15 percent, and over the age of 85, approximately 30 percent to 47 percent of people have AD. Therefore, it is now considered a common disorder. Among people over the age of 65 it is the fourth leading cause of death.

Despite a large amount of research in recent years, AD is still difficult to diagnose during life. There is no single test that one can give to be certain that someone has the disease, short of examining brain tissue through a brain biopsy. Researchers have therefore developed a number of conventions to communicate the degree to which patients have been examined and the diagnostic criteria that the patients meet. Patients who have been carefully examined during life and who meet clinical research criteria, but have not had a brain biopsy, are said to have *probable* AD, or probable dementia of the Alzheimer type. Patients who have had dementia during life, and in whom results of an examination of brain tissue meet pathological research criteria for the disease, are said to have *definite* AD.

The earliest symptom of AD in the majority of patients is severe difficulty in learning new information (i.e., anterograde memory impairment). This is revealed in everyday life by increasing forgetfulness for day-to-day events; first, patients may entirely forget a recent event from one week to the next, then from one day to the next, and finally from one minute to the next. Nearly all aspects of new learning are impaired by AD. It is not, for example, limited to information that the patient is consciously trying to learn (i.e., explicit or EPISODIC MEMORY), as is true in some amnesic disorders. Patients also have difficulty learning some types of information to which they are exposed but which they have not been specifically asked to remember (i.e., IMPLICIT MEMORY). This difficulty with implicit knowledge is variable, since patients with AD are not uniformly impaired on all implicit memory tasks. The same is true for their ability to learn new general skills (i.e., procedural knowledge). Patients have difficulty on some kinds of skill learning tasks but not others; for example, learning of motor skills is frequently spared. Early in the course of the disease the patients' memory for remote events is generally intact. As the disease progresses, remote events also become lost, but in a graded order; the most recent periods of history are lost first. It is only when patients are severely impaired that the most remote memories from their childhood are lost.

The anterograde memory impairment in AD is extremely dramatic because of the rapidity with which information is lost over a delay. Recent studies suggest that the most rapid loss of information is in the first 10 minutes after the patient has been exposed to something new. The best way to reveal this rapid loss of information is to give a patient something new to learn—for example, a story—and to ask him/her to state how much is remembered immediately, and then after a delay. The delay should be less than 10 minutes, because after 10 minutes most types of patients, and even normal older persons, forget a substantial amount of information. For example, patients with other forms of dementia, such as Pick's disease or Huntington's disease, also have difficulty learning and retaining new information, but if delays are less than 10 minutes, their retention is significantly better than that of AD patients. If delays are longer than 10 minutes, then normals and patients with other dementing diseases do not differ significantly from one another.

Two types of changes in the brain are primarily responsible for the severe anterograde memory impairment in AD. The first is damage to the hippocampus, a region in the temporal lobe that is most essential for normal human memory (see GUIDE TO THE ANATOMY OF THE BRAIN) Large numbers of neurofibrillary tangles and neuritic plaques (the pathological hallmarks of AD) are deposited in the hippocampus, particularly in the pathways leading to and from the hippocampus (the entorhinal cortex and the subiculum; respectively). There are also declines in the concentration of a number of neurotransmitters, the chemicals that are responsible for the transmission of nerve signals, in the brain. One neurotransmitter in particular, acetylcholine, which is important for normal human memory, declines by up to 70 percent in AD. The combination of these structural and chemical changes is probably responsible for the fact that the anterograde memory impairment in AD is more severe than in other patient groups.

Since patients with AD have impairments in other areas of cognitive function besides memory, it is likely that these difficulties interact with the memory impairment to increase its severity. One of the other changes that occur in the majority of patients is difficulty with a group of abilities that are collectively called *executive functions*. These abilities include concept formation, directed attention, and the concurrent manipulation of information. Recent studies suggest that early in the course of disease, most patients with AD have problems with the concurrent manipulation of information. This gives them difficulty with tasks that require the manipulation of several different components simultaneously, even when the individual components of the tasks are very well learned (e.g., preparing meals, paying bills, balancing a checkbook). That is why it sometimes seems

as if the patients have difficulty with remote memory early in the course of disease. However, when the tasks are broken down into their constituent parts, patients can perform them.

The underlying cause of this problem is unclear. It may be the result of pathological changes in subcortical structures, such as the basal forebrain, which modulates cortical function. Another possible cause may be the loss of fibers that connect different parts of the cortex to one another, the corticocortical fibers. The partial degeneration of this intracortical projection system early in the course of the disease could produce difficulties in performing tasks that require the rapid and simultaneous integration of multiple types of information.

As the disease progresses, there begins to be a loss of the basic linguistic knowledge that forms our sense of the associations among words, semantic knowledge or SEMANTIC MEMORY. Patients with AD begin to have difficulty with a number of linguistic tasks when they are mildly-to-moderately impaired. These difficulties affect the ability to produce the name of an object when shown the object itself or a picture of the object (confrontation naming). They also affect the ability to produce rapidly a series of words that belong to a particular category, such as vegetables or words starting with the letter *s* (verbal fluency). There is currently a debate among researchers concerning the underlying nature of the semantic knowledge difficulty in Alzheimer patients. Some argue that there is a breakdown in the structure of semantic knowledge, and that patients have actually lost knowledge they once possessed. Others argue that semantic knowledge is relatively intact in mildly and moderately impaired patients but more difficult to access; thus, when one asks them to intentionally search their semantic memory for information, they have difficulty, but if their semantic knowledge is evaluated indirectly, it appears to be preserved. It has been difficult to resolve this debate because the results of existing studies are contradictory.

The relationship between the cognitive changes that occur in AD and the changes that occur in normal, healthy people as they age is also unclear. Researchers wonder whether AD and normal aging are on a continuum, suggesting that if everyone lived long enough, they would develop AD. The alternative point of view is that AD is a disease distinct from normal aging.

It is generally agreed that as normal, healthy people get older, many of them demonstrate declines in some aspects of memory ability, particularly delayed recall. This was once referred to as *benign senescent forgetfulness*; more recently the term *age-associated memory impairment* has been applied to such individuals. However, many healthy older individuals, even those in their eighties and nineties, do not demonstrate these declines.

Moreover, if one follows older persons with evidence of every mild memory problems over the course of 10–12 years, some will develop AD and some will not. Recent studies indicate that approximately two-thirds of such patients will ultimately be diagnosed with AD, while one-third will continue to have evidence of memory difficulty, in day-to-day life and on formal testing, that does not get worse. It is, however, unclear what the 20- or 30-year outcome of these individuals will be; thus the issue remains unresolved.

In summary, AD is a common and serious disorder that is caused by damage to the structure and function of the brain. The cause of the disease is currently unknown, and there are no effective treatments at the present time. It produces a gradual and progressive decline in cognitive function. The most common early symptom is a dramatic loss of new information over a brief delay, but ultimately all aspects of mental ability are affected.

REFERENCES

Bayles, K. A., and Kaszniak, A. W. (1987). *Communication and cognition in normal aging and dementia.* Boston: Little, Brown.

Katzman, R. (1986). Alzheimer's disease. *New England Journal of Medicine 314,* 964–973.

Moss, M. B., and Albert, M. (1988). Alzheimer's disease and other dementing disorders. In M. S. Albert and M. B. Moss, eds., *Geriatric Neuropsychology,* pp. 145–178. New York: Guilford.

Nebes, R. D. (1992). Cognitive dysfunction in Alzheimer's disease. In F. I. M. Craik and T. Salthouse, eds., *Handbook of cognitive aging.* Hillsdale, N.J.: Erlbaum.

Wurtman, R. J. (1984). Alzheimer's disease. *Scientific American* (January), 62–74.

Marilyn S. Albert

Neural and Molecular Basis

Alzheimer's disease (AD), the most prevalent type of DEMENTIA occurring in the elderly (Evans et al.,

1989), is manifested by progressive impairments in memory, learning, language, visual-spatial skills, judgment, and behavior (McKhann et al., 1984). Eventually patients become mute, incontinent, bedridden, and unable to care for themselves. The cause of death is usually an intercurrent medical illness. History, expert examination, and a variety of laboratory tests, including brain imaging, allow a diagnosis of probable AD with a high degree of accuracy. Because there is no definitive clinical test, a diagnosis is established by the assessment of the number of neuritic or senile plaques and neurofibrillary tangles (NFTs) in brain tissue obtained at biopsy or at postmortem examination.

Involvement of Specific Brain Regions/ Neuronal Populations

Brain weight is reduced, and atrophy is most prominent in the frontal and temporal lobes and in the anterior portion of the parietal lobe. AD selectively affects specific regions of the brain and certain populations of neurons (Price, 1986). Cortical neurons, particularly glutaminergic pyramidal neurons in layers III and V, develop neuritic pathology and NFTs; eventually these cells degenerate. The involvement of subsets of cortical interneurons is reflected in reduced levels of somatostatin and corticotropin-releasing hormone immunoreactivities. In entorhinal cortex and hippocampus, pyramidal neurons degenerate, interrupting circuits critical for memory (Van Hoesen and Damasio, 1987). Cholinergic neurons of the basal forebrain magnocellular complex develop NFTs, and their distal axons/nerve terminals form neurites in some plaques. Cholinergic markers, such as choline acetyltransferase (ChAT), are reduced in amygdala, hippocampus, and neocortex. Levels of M2 muscarinic receptor subtypes and densities of nicotinic receptors may be decreased in these areas. Monoaminergic neurons of the locus coeruleus and raphe complex also show degenerative changes.

Abnormalities of the Neuronal Cytoskeleton

Neurofibrillary tangles are argentophilic fibrillary structures within perikarya and dendrites of neurons. Ultrastructurally, NFTs are composed primarily of insoluble 10-nanometer paired helical filaments (PHFs). In immunocytochemical studies, several cellular constituents appear to be associated within NFTs, including microtubule-associated proteins (MAP2 and tau), phosphorylated epitopes of the 200-kilodalton neurofilament protein, and ubiquitin, but tau appears to be the major component of PHFs (Lee et al., 1991). This soluble protein, whose six isoforms are generated by alternative messenger RNA (mRNA) splicing from a single gene, can be phosphorylated, is enriched in axons, promotes microtubule assembly and stabilization, and is critical in the cross bridging and bundling of microtubules (Goedert, Crowther, and Garner, 1991). Vigorous solubilization of dispersed PHF preparations shows three modified tau bands (60, 64, and 68 kilodaltons) that are absent from control brains, an observation consistent with the idea that PHFs contain modified holo-tau (Lee et al., 1991). Abnormal tau phosphorylation appears to be critical for the genesis of PHFs and NFTs. Because tau is important in establishing and manufacturing cell geometry, intracellular motility, and axonal transport, perturbations of tau can result in severe dysfunction of neurons. Increased amounts of abnormally phosphorylated tau may lead to the formation of poorly soluble filamentous structures that eventually form cross-linked insoluble PHFs. When these neurons degenerate, extracellular tombstone NFTs mark the locations of affected cells.

Senile Plaques/Amyloidogenesis

Senile plaques, which occur in amygdala, hippocampus, and neocortex, have two principal components: enlarged neuronal processes (neurites) visualized with silver stains, and extracellular deposits of amyloid stained by thioflavine S or Congo red (Price, 1986). Neurites are abnormal axons, nerve terminals, and dendrites enriched in PHFs, straight filaments, neurofilaments, and various membraneous organelles. Amyloid appears as 8-nanometer extracellular filaments composed principally of a roughly 4-kilodalton amyloidogenic peptide, termed β/A4 or amyloid-β protein (β/A4 or AβP) (Glenner and Wong, 1984) containing fourteen to fifteen amino acids of the transmembrane domain and twenty-eight amino acids of the extracel-

lular domain of a larger precursor protein (amyloid precursor protein [APP]) (Kang et al., 1987). The APP gene, located on the long arm of chromosome 21 (21q21), is transcribed to at least four β/A4-encoding APP mRNA that are translated to APP-695, 714, 751, and 770. With the exception of APP-695, all of these APPs have a domain that shares homology with the Kunitz class of serine protease inhibitors (Kitaguchi et al., 1988). In cell culture, APP isoforms are cleaved within the β/A4 domain, releasing a large ectodomain (Sisodia et al., 1990). The cleavage site is C-terminal to lysine residue 687, which lies adjacent to the hydrophobic membrane-spanning domain (Esch et al., 1990). Similar processes occur in vivo, and C-terminal truncated forms are present in human cerebrospinal fluid. In the central nervous system, APP mRNA and proteins are present in many neurons; for example, in pyramidal neurons of primate cortex, APP immunoreactivity is present in cell bodies, dendrites, and axons (Martin et al., 1991). Axonal transport studies have shown that full-length APP is rapidly transported (Koo et al., 1990) and is presumably delivered to nerve terminals. However, little is known about the fates and functions of neuronal APP.

Mechanisms that lead to the formation of β/A4 are not well understood. Because cleavage of APP occurs within the β/A4, the products of constitutive processing cannot contribute to the formation of β/A4, and it is believed that aberrant cleavage of APP generates the amyloidogenic 4-kilodalton β/A4. This idea is supported by the finding that in aged nonhuman primates, swollen APP-laden neurites are often decorated by β/A4 deposits (Martin et al., 1991). It is uncertain whether β/A4 has significant biological activities; intracerebral administration of residues 25–35 of β/A4 may have trophic (nutritive) or toxic effects, depending on dose (Yankner, Caceres, and Duffy, 1990).

Because the deposition of β/A4 occurs in several settings, it is thought that a variety of convergent mechanisms can lead to amyloidogenesis. Individuals with Down's syndrome (trisomy 21) develop AD-like pathology. Autosomal inheritance of the disease has been described in some families with early-onset illness. In these families, the disease is linked to markers on chromosome 21 (St. George-Hyslop et al., 1987), but, as shown by the presence of recombination events in some of these families, millions of bases separate the familial AD markers from the APP gene. However, recent studies indicate that several families with the early-onset autosomal dominant disease show a point mutation at position 717 of APP-770 within the transmembrane helix of APP, two amino acids downstream of the C-terminus of AβP (Goate et al., 1991). It is now believed that nonallelous heterogeneity exists among cases of familial AD (St. George-Hyslop et al., 1990). The contributions of this mutation and, potentially, other mutations to β/A4 deposition are not yet clear, but their roles in amyloidogenesis can be tested in transgenic mice. If these animals develop β/A4 deposits in the brain, the model will allow direct examination of mechanisms that lead to this type of amyloidogenesis and will provide an opportunity to test strategies to prevent its occurrence.

Therapy

At present, there is no satisfactory treatment for AD. During the 1980s, therapeutic approaches focused on restoring functions of perturbed transmitter circuits, particularly the basal forebrain cholinergic system. Cholinometric strategies have included precursor loading (choline and lecithin), agonists (arecoline), and anticholinesterase (physostygmine and tetrahydroaminocridine). Although these treatment protocols have produced improvement in some patients, consistent, sustained effects have not been demonstrable. Moreover, these strategies will not slow the pace of the disease. More recent experimental research has focused on approaches to promote the functional survival of vulnerable neurons. Because basal forebrain cholinergic neurons express receptors for nerve growth factor (NGF) and respond to NGF, it has been suggested that treatment with NGF may cause improvement in brain functions dependent on this cholinergic system and may ameliorate some of the degenerative abnormalities that occur in these cells. If ongoing experimental studies with recombinant NGF (Koliatsos et al., 1990) prove to be promising and nontoxic, it is likely that there will be an NGF trial in individuals with AD by the mid 1990s. As more is learned about the causes and mechanisms of cytoskeletal pathology and amyloidogenesis, new therapeutic strategies directed at these processes will be developed. (See also PHARMACOLOGICAL TREATMENT OF MEMORY DEFICITS.)

REFERENCES

Esch, F. S., Keim, P. S., Beattie, E. C., Blacher, R. W., Culwell, A. R., Oltersdorf, T., McClure, D., and Ward, P. J. (1990). Cleavage of amyloid β peptide during constitutive processing of its precursor. *Science 248,* 1122–1124.

Evans, D. A., Funkenstein, H. H., Albert, M. S., Scherr, P. A., Cook, N. R., Chown, M. J., Hebert, L. E., Hennekens, C. H., and Taylor, J. O. (1989). Prevalence of Alzheimer's disease in a community population of older persons: Higher than previously reported. *Journal of the American Medical Association 262,* 2551–2556.

Glenner, G. G., and Wong, C. W. (1984). Alzheimer's disease: Initial report of the purification and characterization of a novel cerebrovascular amyloid protein. *Biochemical and Biophysical Research Communications 120,* 885–890.

Goate, A., Chartier-Harlin, M.-C., Mullan, M., Brown, J., Crawford, F., Fidani, L., Giuffra, L., Haynes, A., Irving, N., James, L., Mant, R., Newton, P., Rooke, K., Roques, P., Talbot, C., Pericak-Vance, M., Roses, A., Williamson, R., Rossor, M., Owen, M., and Hardy, J. (1991). Segregation of a missense mutation in the amyloid precursor protein gene with familial Alzheimer's disease. *Nature 349,* 704–706.

Goedert, M., Crowther, R. A., and Garner, C. C. (1991). Molecular characterization of microtubule-associated proteins tau and MAP2. *Trends in Neuroscience 14,* 193–199.

Kang, J., Lemaire, H.-G., Unterbeck, A., Salbaum, J. M., Masters, C. L., Grzeschik, K.-H., Multhaup, G., Beyreuther, K., and Müller-Hill, B. (1987). The precursor of Alzheimer's disease amyloid A4 protein resembles a cell-surface receptor. *Nature 325,* 733–736.

Kitaguchi, N., Takahashi, Y., Tokushima, Y., Shiojiri, S., and Ito, H. (1988). Novel precursor of Alzheimer's disease amyloid protein shows protease inhibitory activity. *Nature 331,* 530–532.

Koliatsos, V. E., Nauta, H. J. W., Clatterbuck, R. E., Holtzman, D. M., Mobley, W. C., and Price, D. L. (1990). Mouse nerve growth factor prevents degeneration of axotomized basal forebrain cholinergic neurons in the monkey. *Journal of Neuroscience 10,* 3801–3813.

Koo, E. H., Sisodia, S. S., Archer, D. R., Martin, L. J., Weidemann, A., Beyreuther, K., Fischer, P., Masters, C. L., and Price, D. L. (1990). Precursor of amyloid protein in Alzheimer disease undergoes fast anterograde axonal transport. *Proceedings of the National Academy of Sciences 87,* 1561–1565.

Lee, V. M.-Y., Balin, B. J., Otvos, L., Jr., and Trojanowski, J. Q. (1991). A68: A major subunit of paired helical filaments and derivatized forms of normal tau. *Science 251,* 675–678.

Martin, L. J., Sisodia, S. S., Koo, E. H., Cork, L. C., Dellovade, T. L., Weidemann, A., Beyreuther, K., Masters, C., and Price, D. L. (1991). Amyloid precursor protein in aged nonhuman primates. *Proceedings of the National Academy of Sciences 88,* 1461–1465.

McKhann, G., Drachman, D., Folstein, M., Katzman, R., Price, D., and Stadlan, E. M. (1984). Clinical diagnosis of Alzheimer's disease: Report of the NINCDS-ADRDA Work Group under the auspices of Department of Health and Human Services Task Force on Alzheimer's Disease. *Neurology 34,* 939–944.

Price, D. L. (1986). New perspectives on Alzheimer's disease. *Annual Review of Neuroscience 9,* 489–512.

Sisodia, S. S., Koo, E. H., Beyreuther, K., Unterbeck, A., and Price, D. L. (1990). Evidence that β-amyloid protein in Alzheimer's disease is not derived by normal processing. *Science 248,* 492–495.

St. George-Hyslop, P. H., Haines, J. L., Farrer, L. A., Polinsky, R., Van Broeckhoven, C., Goate, A., McLachlan, D. R. C., Orr, H., Bruni, A. C., Sorbi, S., Rainero, I., Foncin, J.-F., Pollen, D., Cantu, J.-M., Tupler, R., Voskresenskaya, N., Mayeux, R., Growdon, J., Fried, V. A., Myers, R. H., Nee, L., Backhovens, H., Martin, J.-J., Rossor, M., Owen, M. J., Mullan, M., Percy, M. E., Karlinsky, H., Rich, S., Heston, L., Montesi, M., Mortilla, M., Nacmias, N., Gusella, J. F., Hardy, J. A., et al. (1990). Genetic linkage studies suggest that Alzheimer's disease is not a single homogeneous disorder. *Nature 347,* 194–197.

St. George-Hyslop, P. H., Tanzi, R. E., Polinsky, R. J., Haines, J. L., Nee, L., Watkins, P. C., Myers, R. H., Feldman, R. G., Pollen, D., Drachman, D., Growdon, J., Bruni, A., Foncin, J.-F., Salmon, D., Frommelt, P., Amaducci, L., Sorbi, S., Piacentini, S., Stewart, G. D., Hobbs, W. J., Conneally, P. M., and Gusella, J. F. (1987). The genetic defect causing familial Alzheimer's disease maps on chromosome 21. *Science 235,* 885–890.

Van Hoesen, G. W., and Damasio, A. R. (1987). Neural correlates of cognitive impairment in Alzheimer's disease. In *Handbook of physiology,* sec. 1: *The nervous system, vol. 5, Higher functions of the brain,* pt. 2, pp. 871–898. Bethesda, Md.: American Physiological Society.

Yankner, B. A., Caceres, A., and Duffy, L. K. (1990). Nerve growth factor potentiates the neurotoxicity of β amyloid. *Proceedings of the National Academy of Sciences 87,* 9020–9023.

Donald L. Price
Sangram S. Sisodia

AMNESIA

See Alzheimer's Disease; Amnesia, Functional; Amnesia, Infantile; Amnesia, Organic; Amnesia, Transient Global; Head Injury; Material-Specific Memory Deficits; Rehabilitation of Memory Disorders

AMNESIA, FUNCTIONAL

Analyses of learning and memory increasingly attempt to take account of clinical and experimental research on individuals with amnesia. Most of this literature has focused on pathologies of memory associated with demonstrable brain lesions (e.g., the amnesic syndrome; see AMNESIA, ORGANIC) or the administration of centrally acting drugs (e.g., barbiturates, benzodiazepines, and anesthetics), a research strategy that affords information about the biological substrates of certain cognitive functions. However, other sorts of disorders have also been of interest. The term *functional amnesia* refers to a collection of memory disorders attributable to instigating processes that do not result in damage or injury to the brain but produce more FORGETTING than would normally occur in the absence of those instigating processes.

The Pathological Amnesias

One major category of functional amnesia occurs within the context of diagnosable psychopathology, especially the dramatic "dissociative disorders" listed in the *Diagnostic Statistical Manual,* third edition, revised (DSM-III-R) of the American Psychiatric Association (1987). In current diagnostic nosology, this category includes a wide variety of syndromes whose common core is an alteration in consciousness affecting memory and identity. The classic forms are psychogenic amnesia and fugue, multiple personality disorder, and depersonalization and derealization.

In *psychogenic amnesia* (also known as limited amnesia), the patient suffers a loss of autobiographical memory for certain past experiences. It is frequently observed in cases of violent crime (interestingly, it can affect either victims or perpetrators), war neurosis, and other types of posttraumatic stress disorder.

In *psychogenic fugue* (also known as functional retrograde amnesia), the amnesia is much more extensive, covering the whole of the individual's past life, and is commonly coupled with a loss of personal identity—and, often, physical relocation. The classic instance is Ansel Bourne, studied by William JAMES in the nineteenth century. The onset of the fugue is typically associated with a physical or mental trauma; if the loss of memory and identity is accompanied by relocation, the condition may go unnoticed until the patient is asked a question about himself or herself that cannot be answered satisfactorily. In contrast with the retrograde amnesias associated with organic factors (e.g., electroconvulsive therapy or closed head wound), most fugues cover the patient's entire life history. Recovery typically begins with the patient's recognition of loss of identity. This is followed by the recovery of identity and memory per se, either spontaneously or in response to the appearance of a relative or other salient cue (sometimes abetted by hypnosis or sodium amytal). When the fugue is resolved, the patient is typically left with a limited amnesia covering the period of the fugue.

In *multiple personality,* a single individual appears to manifest two or more distinct identities that alternate in control over conscious experience, thought, and action. Before World War II, the typical case presented with only two or three such "ego states"; interestingly, more recent cases have tended to present more than this number. The classic case is "Eve," whose three personalities were studied by Corbett Thigpen and Hervey Cleckley in the 1950s. Although DSM-III-R does not require amnesia for this diagnosis, the personalities are commonly separated by some degree of amnesia. This amnesic barrier may be symmetrical, in which case each ego state is ignorant of the other(s); or, more commonly, asymmetrical, in which case an ego state may be aware of some of its counterparts but ignorant of others.

In *depersonalization* the person believes that he or she has changed in some way, or is somehow unreal; in *derealization* the same beliefs are held about one's surroundings. Because these beliefs are objectively inappropriate, these experiences can be construed as disorders of memory: The person fails to recognize some object, self, or situation with which he or she is objectively quite familiar. Episodes of depersonalization and derealization commonly occur in response to stress; they may also be induced by psychedelic drugs, and occur spontaneously in a substantial proportion of the normal population.

The dissociative disorders have been of interest at least since the time of Sigmund FREUD and Pierre Janet. Unfortunately, despite the publication of a number of dramatic clinical case narratives, these disorders rarely have been studied with controlled experimental procedures. For example, little is known about psychogenic amnesia beyond anecdotes. A few cases of fugue and multiple personality have been studied in the laboratory, but we have no idea how representative they are. Nevertheless, the available evidence suggests a pattern of selective memory deficit that is in some respects similar to that observed in organic amnesia. Thus, psychogenic fugue impairs memory for past experiences and other aspects of self-knowledge, but leaves the patient's repertoire of procedural and semantic knowledge largely intact. Moreover, the deficits in EPISODIC MEMORY most commonly impair explicit memory (conscious recollection of the past) but leave IMPLICIT MEMORY (unintentional use of knowledge gained through past experiences) relatively spared. However, it should be noted that most case studies of fugue and multiple personality have not been done with a formal taxonomy of memory structures and processes in mind, and thus have not provided a thorough survey of learning and memory functions.

The Nonpathological Amnesias

In other forms of functional amnesia, dramatic forgetting occurs in the ordinary course of everyday living. For example, people commonly fail to remember their dreams and other events of the night's sleep (e.g., episodes of brief awakening, sleepwalking, or sleeptalking, or noises in the ambient environment). In addition, attempts to demonstrate sleep learning have been almost uniformly unsuccessful. Theoretical accounts of this memory deficit usually revolve around encoding factors. For example, it has been hypothesized that sleep inhibits the higher cortical centers that support perceptual processing. However, a strong view of cortical inactivity during sleep is not supported by psychophysiological evidence such as evoked potentials. More likely, the answer lies in the sleeper's failure to engage in strategic, attention-consuming activities that support the encoding of retrievable memories. On the retrieval side, the possibility has been raised that memory for sleep events is state-dependent, a hypothesis that will prove difficult to test.

Another example of nonpathological functional amnesia concerns memory for infancy and childhood. People rarely remember much of their lives before age 5 or so; the earliest memory is typically dated between the third and fourth birthdays, and memory does not become continuous until after about age 7. As with sleep, most theoretical accounts of this developmental amnesia focus on encoding factors. For example, infantile amnesia (covering the first 2 years of life) may reflect the child's relative inability to encode symbolic, and especially linguistic, representations of events; even older children lack the information-processing capacity to encode retrievable memories. Other investigators, influenced by Piagetian theory, have suggested that memories encoded by "pre-operational" schemata may be inaccessible to retrieval by the more elaborate schemata characteristic of adult thought. A third, "ecological" viewpoint suggests that the environment does not offer the young child support in encoding distinctive episodic memory traces. However, aside from studies of infantile amnesia in rats, whose results implicate encoding processes, perhaps the most interesting aspect of infantile and childhood amnesia is how seldom any of these hypotheses have been subject to empirical test. (See also AMNESIA, INFANTILE.)

In addition to these universal instances of functional amnesia, a dramatic form of forgetting may be induced in a minority of the population by means of hypnosis. Posthypnotic amnesia rarely occurs in the absence of specific suggestions, a fact that distinguishes posthypnotic amnesia from state-dependent memory. And the amnesia can be reversed by administration of a prearranged reversibility cue, indicating that the amnesia affects retrieval, not encoding, processes. In some ways, posthypnotic amnesia resembles the memory disorders observed in psychogenic amnesia, fugue, and multiple personality. Thus, it affects memory for events the subject experienced while hypnotized, but not procedural or context-free declarative knowledge acquired during hypnosis. More important, posthypnotic amnesia impairs explicit, but spares implicit, expressions of episodic memory: Priming, interference, and savings in relearning are all unaffected by amnesia suggestions. Finally, as with the pathological syndromes, theoretical interpretation of posthypnotic amnesia is made difficult by the fact that the impairment of memory is suggested, not spontaneous, and is affected by such interpersonal factors as the subject's beliefs and expectations, relationship with the hypnotist, and general sociocultural background. (See also HYPNOSIS AND MEMORY.)

Repression and Dissociation

Historically, the absence of demonstrable brain damage has led to theoretical accounts of the functional amnesias that remain on a purely psychological level of explanation. Since the nineteenth century, two competing mechanisms have been offered: repression and dissociation. Repression, as defined by Freud, is the motivated forgetting of material (typically relating to sexual or aggressive ideas and impulses) that conflicts with physical reality or social sanctions. Dissociation, as discussed by Janet and by Morton Prince, is a "splitting off" from awareness of a set of percepts, memories, thoughts, or feelings, so that they are inaccessible to conscious perception and recollection. Although dissociation may occur in response to stress, and affect anxiety-laden percepts and memories, neither condition is a necessary precondition. Moreover, while Freud argued that repressed contents could be known only by inference (because they were expressed only symbolically), Janet argued that dissociated contents could be recovered directly.

For a long time, repression was favored over dissociation, as part of the general dominance of Freudian psychoanalysis within psychopathology and psychotherapy. More recently, however, the concept of dissociation as a psychological mechanism has been revived by Ernest Hilgard and others, as indicated by the label "dissociative disorders" given to the pathological forms of functional amnesia listed in DSM-III-R.

It should be recognized that the term *functional* has a certain ambiguity about it. Obviously, the functional amnesias, as mental states, are accompanied by correlated changes in brain state—although these physiological changes cannot be said to "cause" the amnesia in the same sense that hippocampal damage does. With respect to some of the syndromes described here, it seems likely that advances in psychobiology will pinpoint such causal relationships. For example, infantile amnesia (in rats, at least) has been attributed to incomplete myelinization of neural tissue, hippocampal development, and cortical maturation. And, arguably, the amnesia observed upon awakening is attributable to the profound brain changes that occur during sleep. For other functional disorders of memory, such as those associated with psychogenic amnesia, fugue, multiple personality, and hypnosis, it may be that future research will pinpoint similar brain changes that underlie these phenomena. Thus, just as general paresis was classified as a functional disorder for more than 400 years until the discovery of the syphilis spirochete, so it may be that future editions of this encyclopedia will find "functional amnesia" to be an empty category.

REFERENCES

American Psychiatric Association Staff (1987). *Diagnostic and statistical manual of mental disorders DSM-III-R.* Washington, D.C.: American Psychiatric Press.

Eich, E. (1990). Learning during sleep. In R. R. Bootzin, J. F. Kihlstrom, and D. L. Schacter, eds., *Sleep and cognition,* pp. 88–108. Washington, D.C.: American Psychological Association.

Kihlstrom, J. F. (1985). Posthypnotic amnesia and the dissociation of memory. In G. H. Bowers, ed., *The psychology of learning and motivation,* vol. 19, pp. 131–178. New York: Academic Press.

Kihlstrom, J. F., Tataryn, D. J., and Hoyt, I. P. (1991). Dissociative disorders. In P. B. Sutker and H. E. Adams, eds., *Comprehensive handbook of psychopathology,* 2nd ed. New York: Plenum.

Schacter, D. L. (1987). Implicit memory: History and current status. *Journal of Experimental Psychology: Learning, Memory, and Cognition 13,* 501–518.

Schacter, D. L., and Kihlstrom, J. F. (1989). Functional amnesia. In F. Boller and J. Grafman, eds., *Handbook of neuropsychology,* vol. 3, pp. 209–231. Amsterdam: Elsevier.

White, S. H., and Pillemer, D. B. (1979). Childhood amnesia and the development of a socially accessible memory system. In J. F. Kihlstrom and F. J. Evans, eds., *Functional disorders of memory,* pp. 29–73. Hillsdale, N.J.: Erlbaum.

John F. Kihlstrom
Daniel L. Schacter

AMNESIA, INFANTILE

It was Sigmund FREUD who defined infantile amnesia as a theoretical problem. Why do we remember so little from the first few years of our lives? It is not simply because they were long ago. While it is true that memory dims with the passage of time—studies of memory in natural settings show a fairly regular forgetting curve for life events— recall of early childhood is far below what that curve would predict. This does not mean that the phenomenon is inexplicable: A number of factors, both physiological and cognitive, probably contribute to the difficulty of remembering one's early childhood. Before reviewing those factors, however, it is appropriate to begin with Freud's original hypothesis.

Psychoanalytic Theories

Freud attributed infantile amnesia to *repression.* In his view, early childhood is characterized by strong sexual feelings and fantasies that become unacceptable in later life. All memories of those feelings are therefore kept from awareness, along with any recollections that might bring them to mind by association. The few images that do survive from this period are only indirectly related to real events; as "screen memories," they may function to deflect awareness from the repressed material.

This view of the causes of forgetting in infantile amnesia no longer seems plausible, and has been largely replaced by the physiological and cognitive theories discussed below. However, it may be true that the few recollections that do survive have some special meaning. These recollections can be interpreted in various ways: Alfred Adler, once Freud's disciple, believed that people's earliest memories are clues to their basic characters and motives. There is no decisive evidence for or against this claim.

Basic Findings

One way of assessing the scope of infantile amnesia is to ask adults to describe their earliest recollections and to estimate their age at the time of the event in question. Studies using this method show wide individual differences in the age for "my earliest memory," with an average around 3½ years. Memories from the first year or two of life, when they exist at all, usually represent repeated scenes or experiences rather than specific events. (Despite occasional claims made for hypnosis and other alleged techniques of memory enhancement, there are probably no genuine episodic memories from the first year.) When such recollections are cross-checked with the subject's parents, most seem to be substantially accurate. They do not necessarily depend on family narratives or photographs, though these can aid memory.

As a rule, early memories are fragmentary: There is no sense of a coherent remembered life narrative. It is difficult to define the onset of that narrative precisely, and hence to say when infantile amnesia finally ends. Freud put its close at the "sixth or eighth year," but that estimate may have been too late in life. In any event, it is useful to divide the "amnesic" period into two parts. The first phase (up to age 2 or 3) produces very few episodic memories. More can be recalled from the second phase, but even those memories are not retrieved in any systematic manner and do not form a continuous narrative.

Maturation of the Nervous System

In many mammals, the brain is not fully mature at birth. This can result in a deficit roughly analogous to infantile amnesia: Responses learned by 12-day-old rats, for example, are not retained as well as those learned by adult rats. Immaturity of the nervous system probably plays a role in human infantile amnesia as well, especially in the first 2 years.

This hypothesis becomes even more attractive in light of the modern distinction between different memory systems. Normal recall of life experiences, or EPISODIC MEMORY, depends on a critical midbrain structure called the hippocampus (see GUIDE TO THE ANATOMY OF THE BRAIN); other forms of memory apparently do not. Hippocampal lesions in adults produce deficits in episodic memory (the amnesiac syndrome) but have little effect on skill learning. Nadel and Zola-Morgan (1984) have pointed out that a similar dissociation appears in the first years of life. Although this is the period most subject to infantile amnesia (i.e., no events are later remembered), it is also a time of very rapid learning: Children acquire language, learn complex motor skills and social routines, and master the local environment. These forms of learning do not undergo any obvious subsequent loss. It seems that early infantile amnesia is limited to just those memory functions that depend on the hippocampus in adults. This is what a maturational hypothesis would suggest: The hippocampus and related structures develop more slowly than other parts of the brain and may not be fully functional until about 18 to 36 months.

Episodic Memory in Young Children

While the early phase of infantile amnesia may result from the slow maturation of underlying mechanisms, this is probably not crucial after the second year. Recent studies of the development of memory (see CHILDREN, DEVELOPMENT OF MEMORY IN) show that 2½-year-olds can readily recall individual events, such as trips or holidays, that took place 6 months earlier. Nor is 6 months an upper limit: in a study by Fivush and Hamond (1990), children who had been asked to recall a number of past events at the age of 2½ were reinterviewed 18 months later. Despite the long delay most of these (now) 4-year-olds still remembered the experiences they had reported before, often adding details that had gone unmentioned at the first interview. Thus the adult "amnesia" for the years from 2 to 5 is not due to the absence of basic episodic memory mechanisms at that age.

Cognitive Structures and the Life Narrative

Many lines of research have shown that successful recall depends on the existence of appropriate cognitive structures, or schemata. Whether the material to be remembered consists of stories (see PROSE RETENTION), chess positions (see EXPERTS' MEMORIES), or laboratory lists (see CODING PROCESSES: ORGANIZATION OF MEMORY), it is learned and retrieved most effectively by people who can relate it to a systematic framework. Without some such schema, recall is only partial and fragmentary.

This principle also applies to the recall of life events. As adults, we think of our lives as having a definite course marked by certain milestones and periods: progression through school, a succession of friends, a number of developmental phases, special events that occurred at certain dates and times, perhaps marriage, employment, and the like. We have a schema for each of these events individually, and our life narrative as a whole helps us retrieve the ones we want to remember. Lacking these schemata, young children often do not interpret events as an adult would. Even more important, they do not think of their experiences as linked to a sequence of dates and stages, that is, as parts of a life narrative. This often makes their reactions more spontaneous and natural than those of adults (as Ernst Schachtel noted in a famous discussion of infantile amnesia; see Neisser, 1982), but it also makes those reactions—and the events that produced them—harder to remember. It is probably because the events of these years are not linked to any systematic cognitive structures, either within or across events, that they are so difficult to recall in later life.

REFERENCES

Fivush, R., and Hamond, N. R. (1990). Autobiographical memory across the preschool years: Toward reconceptualizing childhood amnesia. In R. Fivush and J. A. Hudson, eds., *Knowing and remembering in young children,* pp. 223–248. New York: Cambridge University Press.

Freud, S. (1960). Three essays on the theory of sexuality: II. Infantile sexuality. In *The complete psychological writings of Sigmund Freud,* vol. 7, pp. 173–206. London: Hogarth. The original definition of infantile amnesia. First published in 1905.

Nadel, L., and Zola-Morgan, S. (1984). Infantile amnesia: A neurobiological perspective. In M. Moscovitch, ed., *Infant memory,* pp. 145–172. New York: Plenum. Reviews the evidence for the hippocampal hypothesis.

Neisser, U., ed. (1982). *Memory observed: Remembering in natural contexts.* New York: Freeman. Includes papers on infantile amnesia and early memories by Freud, Schachtel, and others.

Spear, N. E., and Campbell, B. A., eds. (1979). *Ontogeny of learning and memory.* Hillsdale, N.J.: Erlbaum. A review of the development of memory in animals.

White, S. H., and Pillemer, D. B. (1979). Childhood amnesia and the development of a socially accessible memory system. In J. F. Kihlstrom and F. J. Evans, eds., *Functional disorders of memory,* pp. 29–73. Hillsdale, N.J.: Erlbaum. A good overview of theories of infantile amnesia.

Ulric Neisser

AMNESIA, ORGANIC

Organic amnesia is a neurological disorder that affects learning and memory but leaves other mental abilities relatively preserved. One important aim of research on this disorder is to understand how learning and memory are disrupted by brain dysfunction in order to obtain clues to brain organization and normal memory processes.

Much of the current interest in memory and brain function was initiated by Milner and colleagues (Milner, Corkin, and Teuber, 1968). They studied a now-famous patient with organic amnesia, H. M., who in 1953 underwent surgery for relief of severe epileptic seizures. The surgery involved bilateral excision of the *medial temporal region,* which reportedly included removal of the amygdala, anterior two thirds of the hippocampus, and hippocampal gyrus (see Figure 1). Following surgery, H. M.'s seizure activity was attenuated, but he exhibited a profound *anterograde amnesia*—that is, he was unable to remember events and information encountered since his operation. Despite this severe impairment in new learning ability, there was no detectable impairment in intellectual or language abilities. There was some *retrograde amnesia,* that is, impairment of memory for events that occurred before the onset of amnesia. For example, H. M. could not remember the layout of the hospital ward or recognize members of the medical staff. Moreover, he could not recall the death of a favorite uncle who had died 3 years previously. Yet, following surgery, H. M.'s retrograde amnesia was not severe, as indicated by the fact that he performed as well as control subjects on a test of memory for faces of celebrities who became famous prior to 1950. He was also capable of recalling well-formed autobiographical episodes from his adolescence.

H. M. is still alive, and clinical observations indicate that memory for ongoing events is severely impaired. For example, 30 minutes after eating lunch, H. M. could not recall what he had eaten and could not even recall if he had had lunch at all. H. M. is aware of his disorder and has reflected upon his impairment as always "waking from a dream." In other words, he seems to lack continuity in the memory of events across time, even when the events are separated by only a few minutes. Thus, the central feature of H. M.'s memory disorder is anterograde amnesia or new-learning impairment. This impairment affects information received from all sensory modalities and includes impairment of both verbal and nonverbal (e.g., spatial) memory. For example, H. M. has failed to acquire new vocabulary words that have been added to the dictionary since his surgery. He also exhibits severe impairment on laboratory tests of word and picture recall, cued-word learning (e.g., learning word pairs), and recognition memory.

Despite the severity of his amnesia, H. M. can think and act normally, as indicated by his preserved I.Q. Indeed, even some memory functions are spared, such as short-term memory, which can be measured by intact performance on tests of immediate digit span (see MEMORY SPAN). Nevertheless, as soon as information is out of conscious experience, it is forgotten. The analysis of H. M.'s amnesia stands as a milestone in our progress to understand memory in the brain. He has provided the crucial evidence for the specific role of the medial temporal region in the process of memory

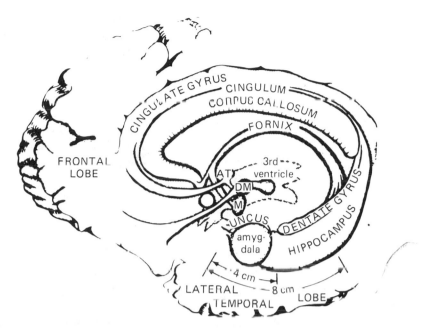

Figure 1. Schematic drawing of the medial surface of the human brain showing structures in the medial temporal lobe (e.g., hippocampus, amygdala) and in the diencephalic midline (e.g., dorsomedial [DM] and anterior [AT] thalamic nuclei, mammillary nucleus [M]). *Reprinted with permission from Squire, 1984.*

formation and storage. Indeed, the analysis of H. M. by Milner and colleagues has provided the impetus for many important animal and human studies on the role of the medial temporal region in learning and memory.

The Anatomy of Memory

There are other neurological disorders that damage the medial temporal region and thus produce an amnesic syndrome similar to that seen in H. M. For example, tumors, head injuries, or vascular disorders (e.g., strokes) in this region can cause organic amnesia. Also, some neurological disorders—such as viral infection, ischemia (i.e., loss of blood flow to the brain), or hypoxia (i.e., loss of oxygen to the brain)—particularly damage the medial temporal region. In these disorders, anterograde amnesia is often the outstanding cognitive impairment, though retrograde amnesia can also occur. General intellectual abilities and short-term memory are generally intact.

An amnesic patient studied by Zola-Morgan, Squire, and Amaral (1986) has provided additional clues concerning the prominent role of the hippocampus in memory. Patient R. B. became amnesic in 1978, when he experienced an ischemic episode that occurred during open-heart surgery. R. B. was given extensive neuropsychological assessment and was found to exhibit anterograde amnesia but little if any retrograde amnesia. In 1983, R. B. suffered a fatal cardiac arrest, and, with the encouragement of his family, a comprehensive examination of his brain was performed. This examination revealed a discrete bilateral lesion restricted to a portion of the hippocampus called the CA1 subfield. R. B. represents the first extensively studied case of amnesia that occurred as a result of damage restricted to the hippocampus.

Another area of the brain, the *diencephalic midline,* can also produce organic amnesia (see Figure 1). This area includes various midline thalamic nuclei (nuclei are bundles of neurons) as well as subthalamic nuclei. These nuclei receive and send projections to various areas in the brain, including the medial temporal region. Patients with neurological damage due to cerebrovascular stroke or head injury in this area often exhibit organic amnesia.

The best-studied cases of amnesia resulting from

damage to the diencephalic midline are patients with *Korsakoff's syndrome.* As reviewed by Butters and Cermak (1980), Korsakoff's syndrome is an amnesic disorder that develops after many years of chronic alcohol abuse and nutritional deficiency. Studies by Victor, Adams, and Collins (1971) of postmortem brain tissue show bilateral damage along the diencephalic midline, typically involving the dorsomedial thalamic nuclei and a subthalamic nucleus called the mammillary bodies. In addition, cortical atrophy and cerebellar damage are often observed.

Patients with Korsakoff's syndrome exhibit severe anterograde amnesia and often extensive retrograde amnesia. The severity of retrograde amnesia, however, is variable among these patients, with some showing extensive retrograde amnesia and others showing little. One factor that complicates the characterization of the memory impairment in Korsakoff's syndrome is widespread cortical atrophy, which is presumed to be a consequence of chronic alcohol abuse. Indeed, some mental functions, such as stimulus encoding, attention, and problem solving, are impaired in patients with Korsakoff's syndrome but not in other amnesic patients. Moreover, patients with Korsakoff's syndrome are often emotionally flat, apathetic, and without insight about their deficit. These additional cognitive and personality disorders may occur as a result of extensive cortical damage, in particular damage to the prefrontal cortex.

Not all amnesic syndromes are permanent. For example, head injury can cause a transient and selective memory impairment. Following initial stages of unconsciousness or confusion, anterograde and retrograde amnesia occurs, and the severity of anterograde amnesia is often correlated with the temporal extent of retrograde amnesia. Retrograde amnesia tends to follow *Ribot's law,* which states that memory for the recent past is affected more severely than memory for the distant past (see also RIBOT, THÉODULE). Amnesia following head trauma can last for minutes, days, or even weeks. In mild trauma cases, new learning ability recovers to premorbid levels. In more severe cases, both amnesia and other cognitive impairment can be long-lasting and sometimes permanent.

Amnesia can also occur after *electroconvulsive therapy* (ECT), which is sometimes prescribed for severe depressive illness. Anterograde amnesia can be quite severe, particularly in patients who receive bilateral ECT. Retrograde amnesia is often temporally graded, following Ribot's law. By sev-

eral months after ECT treatment, there is extensive recovery of new learning capacity. Retrograde amnesia also resolves considerably when testing occurs 6–9 months after ECT. Although the biological factors that cause the transient amnesic disorder following ECT are not well understood, it is known that the hippocampus has one of the lowest seizure thresholds of all brain structures. Thus, hippocampal functioning may be particularly compromised following ECT. (See also ELECTROCONVULSIVE THERAPY AND MEMORY LOSS.)

Advances in neuroimaging techniques, such as computed tomography (CT), magnetic resonance (MR) imaging, and POSITRON EMISSION TOMOGRAPHY (PET), have allowed more detailed analysis of the brain areas that are damaged in neurological patients. For example, analyses of CT brain scans of patients with Korsakoff's syndrome corroborated postmortem findings by identifying signs of increased fluid and low neural density in the midline diencephalic region. A new technique has been developed for MR imaging of the hippocampus (Press, Amaral, and Squire, 1989). This technique produces a clear cross-sectional image of the hippocampal formation and has already provided remarkable images of the extent of hippocampal damage in amnesic patients. For example, it was shown that, compared with control subjects, amnesic patients exhibited an average loss of 49 percent of tissue in the area of the hippocampal formation. Despite this tissue loss in the hippocampal area, the average area of the temporal lobe in these patients was nearly identical to that of control subjects. Although PET analyses of amnesic patients have not been thoroughly studied, they offer another approach to the physiological dysfunction associated with organic amnesia.

Preserved Memory Functions in Amnesia

One of the most striking findings is that amnesic patients can perform in an entirely normal fashion on certain *implicit* or *nondeclarative* memory tests (see IMPLICIT MEMORY). These tests involve habit or automatic learning, such as the kind of memory expressed on tests of skill learning, classical conditioning, and "priming." For example, H. M. showed considerable retention of perceptual-motor skill on a mirror drawing task in which he was required to trace the outline of a star while viewing the star in a mirror. The task is difficult at first but then becomes easier and easier with practice. H. M. also exhibited skill learning on a pursuit-rotor task in which a stylus must be kept on a rotating target. In these tests, H. M. performed as a skilled individual but did not have conscious knowledge of having performed the task before. Preserved skill learning has been observed in other cases of amnesia as well, for example, normal pursuit-rotor skill learning and 1-week retention in three patients with Korsakoff's syndrome and two patients with amnesia due to viral encephalitis. Also, in a jigsaw puzzle assembly task, these amnesic patients exhibited faster completion times across six trials and good retention when the same puzzle was given 1 week later.

Cohen and Squire (1980) observed preserved skill learning by amnesic patients on a mirror reading task. In this task, subjects were asked to read mirror-reversed words. Patients with Korsakoff's syndrome, patients prescribed ECT, and patient N. A. improved their reading speed of mirror-reversed words across training sessions to the same extent as control subjects. Moreover, amnesic patients exhibited normal retention of the mirror-reading skill even when they were tested 1 month after learning. Despite this intact skill learning performance, patients failed to recognize the words used in the task. Moreover, the patients often did not even recognize the testing apparatus, nor did they have conscious recollection of having engaged in the task before. Performance by amnesic patients in these tasks indicates that skill learning can be preserved even when the patient has little or no recollection of having acquired the skill. These findings suggest that amnesic patients can exhibit a certain "unconscious" form of knowledge ("knowing how") in the absence of explicit or declarative knowledge ("knowing that").

There are several other forms of preserved memory function in amnesia. One form is illustrated by an early anecdote of "unconscious" memory that was reported by Claparede. During an interview with an amnesic patient, Claparede hid a pin between his fingers and surreptitiously pricked the patient on the hand. At a later time during the interview, he once again reached for the patient's hand, but the patient quickly withdrew her hand. The patient did not acknowledge the previous incident, and, when asked why she withdrew her hand, she simply stated, "Sometimes pins are hidden in people's hands." This anecdote is an example of stimulus-response learning without awareness. Another form of such learning was demonstrated by

Weiskrantz and Warrington (1979), who assessed Pavlovian classical conditioning of the eyeblink response in two amnesic patients (see CONDITIONING, CLASSICAL AND INSTRUMENTAL). These patients retained the eyeblink response for as long as 24 hours, even though they did not recognize the test apparatus.

A memory phenomenon known as *priming* is also preserved in amnesia. Priming is an automatic facilitation or bias in performance as a result of recently encountered information. The seminal evidence for preservation of priming in amnesia came from Warrington and Weiskrantz (1968). Amnesic patients were asked to identify words or pictures that were presented in a degraded form. If the subject could not identify the stimulus, a succession of less degraded versions of the stimulus were shown until identification was successful. When amnesic patients were asked to identify the same degraded words or pictures at a later time, their performance was facilitated by the previous experience; that is, they were able to identify the stimuli more quickly. This priming effect occurred despite failure to discriminate previously presented stimuli from new ones in a recognition memory test.

Graf, Squire, and Mandler (1984) used a word completion task to study priming effects. In this task, words (e.g., *motel*) are presented to the subject and later cued by three-letter word stems (e.g., *mot*). Subjects are asked to say the first word that comes to mind for each word stem. In both amnesic patients and control subjects, the tendency to use previously presented words in the word completion test was increased by 100 percent to 200 percent over baseline levels. In this test, words appear to "pop" into mind, and amnesic patients exhibited this effect to the same level as control subjects. However, when subjects were asked to use the same word stems as aids to recollect words from the study session, the control subjects exhibited better performance than amnesic patients.

A variety of priming paradigms have since been used to demonstrate preserved priming in amnesia. For example, in one task subjects were presented words (e.g., *baby*) and later asked to "free associate" to related words (e.g., *child*). Amnesic patients exhibited a normal bias to use recently presented words in this word association task. This finding suggests that semantic associations can also be used to prime information in memory. This priming effect and others are short-lasting and decline to baseline levels after a 2-hour delay. Although patients with circumscribed diencephalic or medial temporal lesions exhibit normal priming effects, patients with the clinical diagnosis of Alzheimer's disease do not. For example, impaired word completion and word association priming have been observed in patients with senile dementia of the Alzheimer type (see ALZHEIMER'S DISEASE). These findings suggest that priming effects may depend critically on neocortical areas that are damaged in Alzheimer's disease.

Demonstrations of preserved memory functions in amnesic patients suggest that some memory processes can be dissociated from the brain regions that are damaged in organic amnesia. As reviewed by Squire (1984, 1987), various taxonomies have been used to distinguish the memory forms that are impaired in amnesia from those that are preserved. For example, many distinguish between conscious recollection and unconscious or automatic memory. Squire and colleagues suggested that amnesia impairs *declarative* memory and spares *procedural* or *nondeclarative* memory. Others have used related terms such as *explicit* and *implicit* memory or *memory* and *habit*. Such descriptions provide a framework for theoretical views about the organization of memory in the brain.

Memory Systems in the Brain

Findings from amnesic patients have led to the conclusion that there are multiple memory systems in the brain, such that some forms exist entirely outside the brain regions that are damaged in organic amnesia. Amnesic patients apparently cannot explicitly or consciously recollect information learned since the onset of amnesia. The impairment is often thought to affect the ability to store and also to retrieve newly learned information. Amnesic patients, however, can often perform in a normal fashion on certain "indirect" tests of memory—tests that do not require conscious recollection of past learning sessions. Tests of skill learning, classical conditioning, and priming can be characterized as indirect or implicit tests.

Various theories have been proposed to describe the amnesic disorder. Squire and colleagues have specified a neurological basis for declarative memory—the form of memory that is impaired in amnesia. It is hypothesized that declarative memory involves a storage or consolidation process that depends critically on the interaction of the hippocampus with areas in neocortex. The hippocampal "system" receives projections from many neocortical areas. Thus this region may be involved in relating or connecting information between various neocortical areas so that memory storage and retrieval can be accomplished quickly and efficiently. Warrington and Weiskrantz (1982) have suggested that amnesia is due to a disruption of diencephalic midline projections that connect the medial temporal region to the prefrontal cortex. Similarly, Mishkin (1982) has suggested that amnesia is caused by disruption of the interaction of the hippocampus and amygdala with structures in neocortex and in the diencephalic midline (mediodorsal and anterior nuclei of the thalamus).

In summary, neuropsychological studies of memory functions in amnesic patients have provided useful information about the organization of memory systems in the brain. Damage to the medial temporal region or diencephalic midline causes an amnesic syndrome in which conscious or declarative memory is severely impaired. Interestingly, other implicit or procedural functions (e.g., skills, habits) are entirely preserved. These findings suggest that there are multiple memory systems in the brain and that one system can be dissociated from other memory and cognitive systems. These findings may offer important avenues for both rehabilitative and pharmacological interventions. That is, it may be possible to develop more efficient and more specific diagnoses and therapies for neurological patients as well as for individuals with more subtle forms of memory dysfunction, such as that observed in aging.

REFERENCES

Andreason, N. C. (1988). Brain imaging: Applications in psychiatry. *Science 239,* 1381–1388.

Butters, N., and Cermak, L. S. (1980). Alcoholic Korsakoff's syndrome: An information processing approach. New York: Academic Press.

Cohen, N. J., and Squire, L. R. (1980). Preserved learning and retention of pattern analyzing skill in amnesia: Association of knowing how and knowing that. *Science 210,* 207–209.

Corkin, S. (1984). Lasting consequences of bilateral medial temporal lobectomy: Clinical course and experimental findings in H. M. *Seminars in Neurology 4,* 249–259.

Graf, P., Squire, L. R., and Mandler, G. (1984). The information that amnesic patients do not forget. *Journal of Experimental Psychology: Learning, Memory, Cognition 10,* 164–178.

Graff-Radford, N. R., Tranel, D., VanHoesen, G. W., and Brandt, J. P. (1990). Diencephalic amnesia. *Brain 113,* 1–25.

Milner, B., Corkin, S., and Teuber, H. (1968). Further analysis of the hippocampal amnesic syndrome: 14-year follow-up study of H. M. *Neuropsychologia 6,* 215–234.

Mishkin, M. (1982). A memory system in the monkey. In D. E. Broadbent and L. Weiskrantz, eds., *The neuropsychology of cognitive function,* pp. 85–95. London: The Royal Society.

Press, G. A., Amaral, D. G., and Squire, L. R. (1989). Hippocampal abnormalities in amnesic patients revealed by high-resolution magnetic resonance imaging. *Nature 341,* 54–57.

Schacter, D. L. (1987). Implicit memory: History and current status. *Journal of Experimental Psychology: Learning, Memory, Cognition 13,* 501–518.

Shimamura, A. P. (1989). Disorders of memory: The cognitive science perspective. In F. Boller and J. Grafman, eds., *Handbook of neuropsychology,* pp. 35–73. Amsterdam: Elsevier.

——— (1986). Priming in amnesia: Evidence for a dissociable memory function. *Quarterly Journal of Experimental Psychology 38A,* 619–644.

Squire, L. R. (1987). *Memory and brain.* New York: Oxford University Press.

——— (1984). The neuropsychology of memory. In P. Marler and H. Terrace, eds., *The biology of learning.* Berlin: Springer-Verlag.

Victor, M., Adams, R. D., and Collins, G. H. (1971). *The Wernicke-Korsakoff syndrome.* Philadelphia: Davis.

Warrington, E. K., and Weiskrantz, L. (1982). Amnesia: A disconnection syndrome? *Neuropsychologia 20,* 233–248.

——— (1968). New method of testing long-term retention with special reference to amnesic patients. *Nature 217,* 972–974.

Weiskrantz, L., and Warrington, E. K. (1978). Conditioning in amnesic patients. *Neuropsychologia 17,* 187–194.

Zola-Morgan, S., Squire, L. R., and Amaral, D. G. (1986). Human amnesia and the medial temporal region: Enduring memory impairment following a bilateral lesion limited to field CA1 of the hippocampus. *Journal of Neuroscience 6,* 2950–2967.

Arthur P. Shimamura

AMNESIA, TRANSIENT GLOBAL

Transient global amnesia (TGA) is a benign neurological condition in which the prominent deficit is a temporary organic amnesic syndrome. The episode of TGA is stereotyped. It usually begins suddenly, lasts for at least several hours, and resolves gradually over several hours to a day. Careful examination during TGA shows that the patient has a relatively isolated amnesic syndrome. Vision, hearing, sensation, strength, and coordination are normal. Language, spatial abilities, and general intellectual function also are normal, and the TGA patient can repeat a list of numbers or words. In contrast, the patient can recall little of any verbal or nonverbal material presented minutes before. The TGA patient often repeats the same question many times because of inability to remember the answer that was just given. Frequently repeated questions include "Is there something the matter with me?" and "What's wrong, have I had a stroke?" During TGA the patient has a patchy loss of recall for events dating from several hours to many years before the attack. Older memories are spared, and the patient does not lose personal identity. TGA patients examined carefully after the episode are normal except for an inability to recall the episode.

TGA generally occurs in persons over age 50, and 75 percent of patients are 50 to 69 years old. Men and women are affected with nearly equal frequency. The estimated incidence is 5.2 per 100,000 per year for persons of all ages and 23.5 per 100,000 per year for persons older than 50 years. A third of TGA attacks are precipitated by physical or psychological stress, including strenuous exertion, sexual intercourse, intense emotion, pain, exposure to intense heat or cold, and minor or major medical procedures. TGA has a recurrence rate of 3–5 percent per year for at least 5 years after the initial episode. However, the patient with TGA does not appear to have an increased risk of developing permanent memory deficit or other cognitive dysfunction, and TGA patients have an incidence of subsequent stroke equal to the incidence of a comparable population.

There are no laboratory abnormalities associated with TGA. Blood, urine, and spinal fluid examination, electrocardiogram, electroencephalogram, brain computerized tomography, and magnetic resonance imaging are normal.

Only twenty-two patients have been examined with formal neuropsychological tests during TGA. Of these, eleven were studied with a single battery of memory tests that also had been given to patients with chronic organic amnesia. All of the eleven patients had severe anterograde amnesia (i.e., inability to learn new material) for verbal and nonverbal material, and their test scores were similar to scores obtained by well-studied patients with chronic organic amnesia. The severity of the anterograde amnesia appeared to correlate with the time since onset of TGA. There was no evidence for material-specific, or partial, amnesia—no TGA patient had a significant disparity between the degree of anterograde amnesia for verbal and nonverbal material. The patients also had a temporally graded retrograde amnesia (i.e., inability to recall events that occurred before the onset of amnesia) covering at least 20 years prior to TGA onset. Again, their test scores were similar to the scores of many well-studied patients with chronic organic amnesia. The retrograde amnesia was patchy—all patients were able to recall some events that occurred within the time interval affected by retrograde amnesia. Indeed, during TGA some memories were recalled, albeit incompletely, that were less than 1 to 2 months old. The temporally graded retrograde amnesia was similar for both public and personal events. During the episode, TGA patients performed normally on almost all other formal neuropsychological tests.

It is likely that TGA is caused by temporary dysfunction of either (1) bilateral medial temporal lobe structures including field CA1 of the hippocampus and adjacent, anatomically related structures, or (2) bilateral medial diencephalic structures including the dorsomedial nucleus of the thalamus, the mammillothalamic tract, and the mammillary bodies. The exact cause of TGA is not known, although it appears to be a benign condition that requires no medical treatment.

REFERENCES

Kritchevsky, M. (1987). Transient global amnesia: When memory temporarily disappears. *Postgraduate Medicine 82,* 95–100.

——— (1989). Transient global amnesia. In F. Boller and J. Graffman, eds., *Handbook of neuropsychology,* vol. 3, ch. 7, pp. 167–182. Amsterdam: Elsevier.

Mark Kritchevsky

AMYGDALA

See Guide to the Anatomy of the Brain

ANIMAL COGNITION

See Comparative Cognition

ANIMALS

[*There are articles on animals throughout the* Encyclopedia. *For entries on animals in general, see*

Aging and Memory in Animals
Animal Use in Research
Evolution and Learning
Foraging
Imprinting
Migration, Navigation, and Homing
Sex Differences in Learning in Animals
Taste Aversion and Preference Learning in Animals
Working Memory: Animals

For entries on certain groups of animals, see

Bird Song Learning
Habituation and Sensitization in Vertebrates
Insect Learning
Invertebrate Learning
Language Learning: Nonhuman Primates
Morphological Basis of Learning and Memory: Invertebrates; Vertebrates
Prefrontal Cortex and Memory in Primates
Primates, Visual Attention in
Protein Synthesis in Long-Term Memory in Vertebrates
Unicellular Organisms, Learning and Adaptive Plasticity in

See also the Index for specific animals.]

ANIMAL USE IN RESEARCH

For well over a century, animal research has played an important role in practically every major achievement in the prevention and treatment of human and animal health problems. Research with laboratory animals underlies much of our understanding of human and animal behavior, anatomy, physiology, immunology, virology, brain and nervous system, endocrinology, reproductive biology, and other areas related to biomedical and behavioral research.

Animals ranging from the primitive *Aplysia,* a marine snail, to the highly complex primate have been crucial to research on the principles and the physical bases of learning and memory. Animals with a comparatively simple nervous system, such as the *Aplysia,* with its mere 15,000 nerve cells, provide a relatively simple arrangement for reflexes that serve as a model for organisms that are far more complex neurologically, such as primates with nervous systems containing 75 billion interconnected neurons.

Other complex organisms that have advanced learning and memory research include rodents, dogs, and cats. In studies with dogs, Pavlov defined the conditioned stimulus. This discovery, showing that a previously ineffectual stimulus could elicit a particular response when paired with an effective or unconditioned stimulus, had an immense influence on subsequent research on learning and theories of human behavior.

Animal studies have revealed that learning does not occur in a single locus or a few higher structures of the brain. For example, Thompson's habituation studies with cats showed that learning, at least of the simplest sort, can occur within the spinal cord. In studies of monkeys, Zola-Morgan and Squire have shown that the hippocampus serves recent rather than remote memory, and Goldman-Rakic has shown that the frontal lobe is important for working memory.

Many animal studies of learning and memory have been basic research, not intended to produce an immediate human application but to improve our scientific knowledge about fundamental biological and behavioral activities. Clinicians and scientists have drawn upon this knowledge to develop behavioral modification therapies, which today are used in the treatment of enuresis, addictive behaviors, and compulsive behaviors such as overeating and anorexia nervosa.

The use of biofeedback techniques with humans originated in basic studies on the behavioral conditioning of so-called involuntary neuromuscular activities in rats and other animal species. Today behavioral biofeedback control of blood pressure in hypertension aids in reducing heart attacks; and in the case of paralyzed patients it can help to elevate blood pressure in hypotensive conditions, making it possible for those who would otherwise have to remain recumbent to sit upright. Biofeedback techniques also are used in the reduction and control of pain, the correction of spinal curvature, and the relief of insomnia.

Language formation studies in the great apes have led to new concepts and practical methods that have given language skills to severely retarded children and young people who, prior to this work, had no expressive language ability. Today many of these individuals can for the first time express linguistically their needs and feelings, and understand what others are saying to them.

Animal research on conditioned taste aversion has led to new and practical behavioral methods for helping those who have undergone radiation therapy for cancer to take an interest in foods that are essential for proper nutrition and recovery, and to avoid food preferences that interfere with good nutrition.

Behavioral studies of the early development of vision in cats and primates—studies that could not be carried out in children—have led to new practices in pediatric ophthalmology that can prevent loss of vision in children with cataracts and strabismus.

Behavioral modification and behavioral therapy, widely accepted techniques for modifying alcohol, drug, and tobacco addiction, obesity, and other problems stemming in part from faulty behavior, have at their roots a long history of animal studies in learning theory and reward systems.

Programmed instruction, so valuable in educational and training programs, can trace its origins and scientific basis to a vast array of operant and instrumental learning studies in animals.

Results of primate studies in mother-infant bonding, depression, aggression, sexual development, infant abuse, and intellectual development have in some instances been incorporated into human child-rearing practices.

Since 1901, seventy-six Nobel Prizes have been awarded in medicine or physiology. Fifty-four of these recognized achievements based on research with animals. Despite such solid indicators of the value of animal research to medicine and science, numerous radical organizations believe that all biomedical and behavioral studies with animals should be ended.

The animal rights movement is generally considered by the scientific community to be fundamentally antiscientific, anti-intellectual, and antihumanistic. The public, however, often is vulnerable to the arguments of the movement, in large measure because of our nation's distressingly low level of scientific literacy. Two of the fundamental reasons that the public does not know the language of science are inadequate science education and the priorities held by society. For example, our society measures an individual's intellectual achievement and sophistication by knowledge of the arts, history, philosophy, economics, politics, and language but tends to disregard and excuse ignorance of science and the central role it has played in bringing about vast improvements in the quality of life and knowledge that produces freedom and objectivity of thought.

Currently, unless they pursue advanced degrees in the biological or behavioral sciences, many graduates of outstanding colleges and universities frequently are inadequately instructed about the nature and processes of the life sciences and the value of animal research. After completing their formal educations, most people have fewer opportunities to learn about scientific process and the value of animal research. The news media, the primary source of medical and science news for the public, rarely describe how a breakthrough in human medicine occurred.

The following briefly explains the agenda of the animal rights movement, its tactics, the facts about so-called alternatives to animal research, and some of the reasons that the public pays attention to the animal rightists.

Animal Rights Versus Animal Welfare

Animal welfare differs significantly from animal rights. Kenneth N. Gray defined animal welfare as "the human responsibility for all aspects of animal wellbeing, including proper housing, nutrition, disease prevention and treatment, careful handling and more" (1990, p. 24A). Supporters of animal welfare are not necessarily opposed to animal research; they are concerned that animals be treated as humanely as possible and used when necessary for advancement of scientific, medical, and behavioral knowledge.

Supporters of animal rights, however, believe that any use of animals, whether it be for food, clothing, education, or research, is unethical and therefore wrong. The animal rightists' philosophical premise is that animals have moral rights equal to those of humans. "Animals are not ours to eat, wear or experiment on" is the banner of one animal rights group—indeed, of the movement itself.

It is not known how many people who say that they believe in "animal rights" actually support and follow the extreme philosophical viewpoint exhibited by animal rights movement leader Ingrid Newkirk, who compares the killing of broiler chickens to the slaughter of people in the Nazi concentration camps during World War II. Indeed, the animal rightists frequently compare animal research laboratories to Nazi concentration camps, an inverted and uninformed historical perspective.

Tactics of Animal Rightists

Using their multimillion-dollar treasuries, animal rights groups bombard the public with costly full-page advertisements in major newspapers and magazines, frequent and constant mailings of newsletters and brochures, television and radio announcements, videotapes, movies, protest rallies, rock concerts, and other means of publicity. The animal rightists' actions include breaking into laboratories, stealing animals and research documents, making threatening telephone calls and writing threatening letters to scientists and their families, and producing fake and actual bombs.

Animal rightists argue that animal research is unnecessary and cruel, that laboratory animals can be replaced by computer simulations and cell cultures, and that the major health problems of humans can be prevented. Frederick K. Goodwin (1990), administrator of the Alcohol, Drug Abuse and Mental Health Administration, has described these claims as secondary arguments used by the animal rightists because the ethical premise that rats and other animals have the same right to life as humans would not be universally popular.

Minimal use of facts and maximal use of distortion and emotional appeal characterize the animal rightists' information campaign. Richard Traystman stated, "Animal activists have . . . mastered the techniques of being deliberately dishonest and of misinforming the public" (1990, p. 3). Many examples of distortion can be provided. One occurred in an Atlanta radio interview in 1990 when an animal rights leader claimed that behavioral research with animals had not benefited humans. As demonstrated earlier in this article, behavioral research has contributed significantly to human welfare.

The animal rightists' use of emotion is illustrated by their almost exclusive concentration on research with dogs, cats, and primates even though 90 percent of laboratory animals are rodents. In addition to featuring animals that are emotionally appealing, the animal rightists selectively target certain types of research for their attack. Addiction studies today are among the most common, presumably to appeal to members of the public who regard people with addiction as less worthy of our concern than are individuals with disorders that are not "self-inflicted."

The value of animal research to studies of addiction has been stressed by many scientific authorities. Animal rightists often contend that funds spent on addiction research with animals depletes the funding needed for treatment facilities. However, for every $100 spent by the federal government in 1990 on health care for mental and addictive disorders, less than 20 cents went to animal research.

In addition to taking advantage of the public's lack of understanding of the role of research in medicine and science, the animal rights movement exploits people's concern for animals by, for example, claiming that animals in research are tortured or suffer pain. Most studies do not expose animals to pain. In 1984, the U.S. Department of Agriculture reported that 61 percent of laboratory animals were in studies that did not expose them to painful procedures. Another 31 percent were involved in studies that were potentially painful, but this potential was eliminated or maximally reduced by the administration of anesthesia or analgesia. The remaining 8 percent were involved in studies often directly related to pain. These studies were designed to understand the basis of pain and develop ways to prevent or control it. Chronic pain is one of the most distressful and costly health problems, consuming an estimated $50 billion a year in medical expenses and lost productivity and income.

Research on pain with laboratory animals has been productive. Based on studies that found stimulating electrodes could reduce or inhibit pain in animals, physicians may implant electrodes in specific parts of the brain and spinal nerves of persons suffering from chronic pain. Activating the electrodes with radio transmitters has led a number of patients to experience long periods of relief.

An interesting and important question is why people are willing to deny themselves and others the benefits from animal research. Richard Conniff may have some answers:

> How thoroughly the modern world has accepted the worthlessness of human beings, and in equal and opposite measure, the sentimental importance of in-

dividual animal lives. . . . Like a bad marriage, society is degenerating into a foul entanglement characterized by mutual loathing and moral one-upmanship, where the milk of human kindness [flows] only for Muffin the cat (1990, pp. 120, 121).

Alternatives

The animal rightists particularly take advantage of the public's scientific illiteracy by claiming that so-called alternative techniques, such as cell and tissue cultures, computers, and simulations of biological systems and mathematical models can fully replace research on living animals.

Nonanimal research systems, such as those promoted by the animal rightists as substitutes for laboratory animals, *were developed by scientists* to make research more efficient, more humane, and less costly. Laboratory cultures and computer simulations do play important roles in research and have enabled the performance of studies not possible with animals. Both cultures and computers have, in some instances, allowed scientists to avoid the use of animals at certain stages of research. But alternative methods, as they are called, are in reality *adjunct* and *complementary* to the need for the use of whole, intact animals. This is because the intact biological system provided by live animals cannot be fully reproduced by computers and cultures. In addition, cells in isolation do not act or react the same as cells in an intact system. The interaction of, for example, cardiovascular, hepatic, and nervous systems cannot be studied in cell cultures. Whole, intact living organisms are required for the study of the interrelations of biological systems.

While the ingenious manipulation of a computer can rearrange data and perform operations that may hypothesize a new phenomenon, physiological process, or chemical substance, scientists will not know whether it truly exists in the living organism until it is actually found in animals or humans. While beneficial in developing or suggesting new lines of scientific inquiry and in developing new mechanisms or techniques, computer simulations have inherent limitations, such as the nature of the simulation. The validity of any model is based on its similarity to the original. Since much about the human and animal biological systems is unknown, a computer cannot fully simulate human functions. The Office of Technology Assessment noted, "To construct a computer simulation that would fully replace the use of a live organism in behavior research should require knowing everything about the behavior in question, which in turn would eliminate the need for computer simulation for the research proposed" (1986, p. 26).

Cell and tissue cultures serve a number of important uses as alternatives to whole animals in toxicity testing, for instance. But a total disease process or a whole, functioning organ is not found in a petri dish or test tube of cells. Scientists will indeed discover clues through cell cultures that, together with research on intact animals, may be vital to solving the problem at hand, but cells alone do not suffice. For many problems, culture methods are wholly inadequate by themselves. As noted by the Office of Technology Assessment in its congressional report, *Alternatives of Animal Use in Research, Testing and Education,* "isolated systems give isolated results that may bear little relation to results obtained from the integrated systems of whole animals" (1986, p. 20).

The Response of Science

Scientists and their institutions must become more involved in education at all levels from kindergarten through secondary school, as well as in informational programs for the public, administrators, and legislators. The goal is to explain clearly and practically how discoveries through basic research with animals have laid the groundwork for remarkable advances in both human and animal health; how and why invertebrates, rodents, carnivores, and other laboratory animals are used to test the safety and effectiveness of drugs, to develop vaccines and new treatments, and to establish a foundation of basic scientific knowledge about behavior and biology. The people of our nation, who as taxpayers ultimately pay for most research, must be informed of what goes on in science, how the animals are treated, and the rich rewards to society that research brings. The continued existence of biomedical and behavioral research will depend upon a major, sustained public information campaign conducted with the full participation and cooperation of all the life sciences.

REFERENCES

Brown, C. (1983). She's a portrait of zealotry in plastic shoes. *Washington Post,* November 13, p. B1.

Coalition for Animals and Animal Research Newsletter. P.O. Box 8060. Berkeley, Calif. 94707-8060.

Cohen, C. (1986). The case for the use of animals in biomedical research. *New England Journal of Medicine 315,* 865–870.

Conniff, R. (1990). Fuzzy-wuzzy thinking about animal rights. *Audubon 92* (November), 120–133.

Foundation for Biomedical Research (1990). *Portraits of a partnership in life, the remarkable story of research, animals and man.* Washington, D.C.: Foundation for Biomedical Research.

Friedman, H. R., and Goldman-Rakic, P. (1988). Activation of the hippocampus and dentate gyrus by working memory: A 2-deoxyglucose study of behaving rhesus monkeys. *Journal of Neuroscience 8,* 4693–4706.

Goldstein, A., and Kalant, H. (1990). Drug policy: Striking the right balance. *Science 249* (September 28), 1513–1521.

Goodwin, F. K. (1990). Animal rights advocates taking anti-science stance. *Atlanta Journal and Constitution,* April 22, p. G-3.

Graham, R. B. (1990). *Physiological psychology.* Belmont, Calif.: Wadsworth.

Gray, K. N. (1990). Beware animal rights propaganda in classroom. *Houston Chronicle,* November 9, p. 18B.

Hendee, W. R., and Loeb, J. M. (1988). Science literacy and the role of the physician. *Journal of the American Medical Association 260* (October 7), 1941–1942.

Hendee, W. R., Loeb, J. M., Schwartz, M. R., and Smith, S. J. (1989). *Use of animals in biomedical research.* Washington, D.C.: American Medical Association.

Henshaw, D. (1989). *Animal welfare: The story of the Animal Liberation Front.* London: Fontana Books.

Hubbell, J. G. (1990). The "animal rights" war on medicine. *Reader's Digest* (June), 70–76.

Kennedy, D. (1987). The anti-scientific method. *Wall Street Journal,* October 29, p. 26.

King, F. A. (1986). Philosophical and practical issues in animal research involving pain and stress. *Annals of the New York Academy of Sciences 467,* 405–409.

——— (1990a). Animal research: Rationale, conduct, benefits and education. Paper presented at the National Association of Biology Teachers Convention, Dallas, November 8.

——— (1990b). Animal rights: The problem and the response. Paper presented at the NIH Conference on Animal Care and Use and Policy Issues in the 1990s. Bethesda, Md., November 16–17.

——— (1991). Animal research: Our obligation to educate. In M. A. Novak and A. J. Petto, eds., *Through the looking glass, issues of psychological well-being in captive nonhuman primates.* Washington, D.C.: American Psychological Association.

King, F. A., and Yarbrough, C. (1985). Medical and behavioral benefits from primate research. *The Physiologist 28,* 75–85.

King, F. A., Yarbrough, C. J., Anderson, D. C., Gordon, T. P., and Gould, K. G. (1988). Primates. *Science 240* (June 10), 1475–1482.

McCabe, K. (1986). Who will live, who will die? *The Washingtonian 21,* 112–156.

McDonald, K. A. (1989). 1 in 18 Americans is found "scientifically literate." *The Chronicle of Higher Education,* January 25, p. A7.

Miller, N. E. (1985). The value of behavioral research on animals. *American Psychologist 40,* 425.

Office of Technology Assessment. (1986). *Alternatives of animal use in research, testing and education,* OTA-BA-273. Washington, D.C.: U.S. Government Printing Office.

Thompson, R. F., and Glanzman, D. L. (1976). Neural and behavioral mechanisms of habituation and sensitization. In T. J. Tighe and R. N. Leaton, eds., *Habituation: Perspectives from child development, animal behavior, and neurophysiology.* Hillsdale, N.J.: Erlbaum.

Traystman, R. J. (1990). The goal of animal welfare, animal "rights" and antivivisectionist groups in the United States *Journal of Neurological Anesthesiology 2* (3), 1–6.

U.S. Department of Education. (1983). *A nation at risk: The imperative for educational reform. A report to the nation and the secretary of education.* Washington, D.C.: National Commission on Excellence in Education.

Westheimer, F. H. (1987). Are our universities rotten to the "core"? *Science 236,* 1165–1166.

Frederick A. King
Cathy J. Yarbrough

APHASIA

Aphasia is the term applied to language disorders resulting from brain damage due to stroke, tumor, or trauma. Clinical observations of these language disorders have yielded two descriptive generalizations: (1) left-hemisphere damage, but not right-hemisphere damage, disrupts language use; (2) within the left hemisphere, damage in different locations undermines language in different ways.

These broad descriptions are currently being detailed in interesting ways, but primarily in terms of linguistically based representations and processes. Considerations of memory capacity—clearly an important part of any fully elaborated theory of language processing—have been entered, if at all, in rather ad hoc fashion. As will be apparent in what follows, researchers are only now starting to explore the possibility that aphasic phenomena will permit some understanding of how memory capacity constrains language processing.

Nineteenth-Century Aphasiology: Sensory and Motor Engrams

The beginning of modern aphasia research turns on the descriptions offered by two nineteenth-century neurologists, Paul Broca and Carl Wernicke. These descriptions still have merit (Geschwind, 1970).

Broca's aphasia (the name now given to Broca's observations) typically results from damage to the cortical territory supplied by the upper portion of the left middle-cerebral artery. It involves at least the lower part of the left frontal lobe, just in front of the primary motor zone that enervates the muscles involved in speech (Broca's area). Although patients with this form of aphasia show relatively good comprehension at the conversational level, they produce little speech and do so slowly, with effort and poor articulation. Also, their speech is telegraphic or agrammatic: They tend to omit articles, connective words, and grammatical inflections, and they produce, at best, only simple syntactic forms.

Wernicke's aphasia (attributed to Wernicke's original observations) usually results from a lesion in the posterior region of the left hemisphere, specifically, to the area adjacent to that involved in hearing. Patients with damage to this area (Wernicke's area) produce a form of speech strikingly different from that of patients with Broca's aphasia; it is rapid and effortless, with a superficially normal syntactic appearance. Yet their speech is remarkably empty of content and often contains errors of word choice (e.g., *boy* for *girl*). Moreover, patients with Wernicke's aphasia show a profound comprehension deficit.

Given the relation of these two distinct kinds of language disruptions to specific areas of brain damage, Wernicke theorized that the brain organizes language in the form of anatomically discrete interconnected centers. Wernicke's area was claimed to be the center for the sensory engrams or memories of words, and Broca's area, the center for motor engrams of words, that is, for the memory representations implicated in producing them. Comprehension, in this view, resulted from a hearing sensation triggering a sensory word image; the word image, in turn, evoked a memory representation of the entity or action designated by the word. Production was likewise seen as the activation of a chain of memory representations or engrams, the evocation of the memory representation of the object to be named serving to trigger the motor images expressed in articulation. What was not resolved in this formulation was whether aphasic disturbances are the consequence of a loss of the relevant memory representations of words or the result of a disruption to their arousability—that is, whether a failure of long-term storage or a disorder of the mechanisms that access stored information.

The fundamental problem with Wernicke's theory lay elsewhere, however. It had to do with the fact that its basic unit of analysis was the isolated word; sentences were viewed merely as chains of words, and their meanings, as chains of stored word concepts. But our capacity to create and understand sentences requires a much more complex characterization than that offered by Wernicke. The principles that govern the formation and order of words and phrases in utterances cannot be elaborated on the basis of a linear sequence of autonomous words, nor can they be explained by appeal to the nature of the concepts expressed by words (Chomsky, 1980).

This limitation of Wernicke's theory was recognized early on. Almost from its inception, Wernicke's "word aphasiology" was criticized for its failure to do justice to the complexity of aphasic phenomena. But given the comparatively restricted linguistic theorizing of that period, attempts to shift analyses of aphasia from the word to the sentence level—to focus on such features as agrammatism—remained undeveloped (De-Bleser, 1987). Only relatively recently has there been a concerted effort to study aphasic phenomena in terms of grammatical (sentence-processing) capacity.

Sentence-Processing Problems in Aphasia

The modern focus on sentence-level aphasic phenomena can be traced to a number of studies of comprehension in Broca's aphasia that appeared in close succession in the 1970s—studies that sought to determine the basis for what clinically appeared to be relatively intact comprehension. Typically assessing comprehension by having pa-

tients point to the correct depictions of orally delivered sentences, these studies documented the patients' abnormal reliance on semantic and pragmatic cues and their corresponding inability to carry out normal syntactic analysis. Thus, on the basis of semantic constraints, the patients could understand sentences of the type "The apple that the boy is eating is red." But they failed to interpret sentences like "The girl that the boy is chasing is tall," that is, sentences in which either entity (*boy* or *girl*) is equally capable of performing the action (*chase*) and for which, therefore, comprehension depends on syntactic analysis. Their syntactic problem was also revealed by their inability to comprehend sentences that depended on the processing of grammatical morphemes—by their inability, for example, to distinguish the meaning of "He showed her the baby pictures" from the meaning of "He showed her baby the pictures." (See Zurif [1980] for a review.)

Taken together, these studies indicated that the Broca's patients' relatively intact comprehension skills were somewhat illusory. They could carry out semantic inference but seemed unable to use features of sentence *form* to guide interpretation. In the sweeping terms used at the time, Broca's aphasic patients were said to be as agrammatic in comprehension as in production; left anterior brain damage—the area implicated in Broca's aphasia—was claimed to produce an overarching syntactic limitation. The message for memory theorists was clear: left anterior brain damage causes the *loss* of the long-term memory storage of the rules and representations that define syntactic competence.

Recent experimental findings have contradicted this message, however. First, not all patients show an overarching syntactic limitation. A number of single cases of Broca's aphasia have been reported in which agrammatic output has been observed to coexist with intact syntactic comprehension skills (Goodglass and Menn, 1985). Are these patients anomalous outliers, possibly reflecting neurological damage that contrasts with the lesion sites implicated in patients with overarching agrammatism? (After all, little is known about the precise neuroanatomical underpinnings of Broca's aphasia.) Or must these exceptions be considered as important contraindications of the generalization that somewhere within the left anterior cortex, lesions disrupt syntactic capacity for both speaking and listening? The significance of these case reports is yet to be determined.

Second, even the many Broca's patients who

do show syntactic comprehension problems do not seem entirely without syntactic capacity. They are not totally reliant on semantic and pragmatic cues to meaning. In this respect, Broca's patients lately have been found to understand not only simple active-voice sentences but also some constructions—for example, certain kinds of relative-clause constructions ("subject relatives")—that require a tacit appreciation of *hierarchically* arranged grammatical configurations. Indeed, one linguistically based account specifies only a *minimal* change in the normal (hierarchical) representational capacity in order to account for those comprehension problems that Broca's patients do show—for their inability, for example, to understand passive-voice constructions (Grodzinsky [1990] and references therein). The central claim in this account is that the only kinds of syntactic features which Broca's patients have trouble representing for the purpose of comprehension are those involved in constituent movement (in the mapping from deep to surface linguistic structures). The details of this account and of the criticisms that have been leveled against it are beyond the scope of this entry. The point it makes, however, must now be given serious consideration: that left anterior brain damage, even when it causes comprehension problems, does not totally eradicate syntactic capabilities.

Moreover, such syntactic limitations as are shown in comprehension do not seem attributable to a failure of linguistic *knowledge*. That is, the problem does not seem to implicate the long-term storage of linguistic rules and representations. Rather, the problem seems to involve processes that *implement* the long-term representations—processes that operate upon linguistic representations in real time for the purposes of speaking and listening. For example, Broca's patients recognize grammatical morphemes (function words such as *the* and *but*) as words that belong to their language, thereby pointing to the ultimate availability of these vocabulary elements. Yet they fail to use such words normally for the purpose of phrasal analysis while listening to a sentence (Zurif, Swinney, and Garrett, 1990).

Working Memory Problems in Aphasia

One focus of the current examination of real-time sentence processing in aphasia is on memory capacity—not on long-term storage systems but on working memory systems. Thus, it has been proposed that agrammatic comprehension is the consequence of memory limitations statable in terms of either reduced short-term storage capacity or greater decay rate (Kolk and van Grunsven, 1985). However, this proposal and its variants are blunted by the fact that comprehension deficits in agrammatic Broca's patients emerge only in certain syntactic environments, and not as the uniform consequence of an overriding memory limitation, one that might be expected to limit comprehension no matter what the syntactic form of the sentence.

Clearly, there remains much to discover both about how memory capacity constrains sentence processing and about the neurological (neuroanatomical) underpinnings of such constraints. Still, the search space has been narrowed: As already stated, it no longer seems likely that agrammatic comprehension is the reflection of a loss of grammatical knowledge. Thus, although the characterization of this disorder requires the invocation of linguistically specific rules and representations, it no longer seems likely that the disorder results from a failure of the long-term storage of these rules and representations. Rather, it seems to implicate the processes—including, in some complicated fashion, working memory systems—that act upon such knowledge representations in real time.

(See also LANGUAGE LEARNING: HUMANS.)

REFERENCES

Chomsky, N. (1980). Rules and representations. *The Behavioral and Brain Sciences 3,* 1–62.

DeBleser, R. (1987). From agrammatism to paragrammatism. *Cognitive Neuropsychology 4,* 187–256.

Geschwind, N. (1970). Organization of language and the brain. *Science 170,* 940–944.

Goodglass, H., and Menn, L. (1985). Is agrammatism a unitary phenomenon? In M.-L. Kean, ed., *Agrammatism.* San Diego, Calif.: Academic Press.

Grodzinsky, Y. (1990). *Theoretical perspectives on language deficits.* Cambridge, Mass.: MIT Press.

Kolk, H., and van Grunsven, M. (1985). Agrammatism as a variable phenomenon. *Cognitive Neuropsychology 2,* 347–384.

Zurif, E. B. (1980). Language mechanisms: A neuropsychological approach. *American Scientist 68,* 305–311.

Zurif, E. B., Swinney, D., and Garrett, M. (1990). Lexical processing and sentence comprehension in aphasia. In A. Caramazza, Ed., *Cognitive neuropsychology and neurolinguistics.* Hillsdale, N.J.: Erlbaum.

Edgar Zurif

APLYSIA

[The sea snail Aplysia *has been one of the invertebrates most studied from the point of view of learning and memory. This article on* Aplysia *consists of three sections:*

Classical Conditioning and Operant
 Conditioning
Molecular Basis of Long-Term Sensitization
Development of Processes Underlying Learning]

Classical Conditioning and Operant Conditioning

The simple nervous system and the relatively large identified neurons of the marine mollusk *Aplysia* provide a model system in which to examine the cellular mechanisms of two forms of associative learning: classical conditioning and operant (instrumental) conditioning. (See also CONDITIONING, CLASSICAL AND INSTRUMENTAL.)

Classical Conditioning of the Siphon-Gill Withdrawal Reflex

Behavioral Studies

A tactile or electrical stimulus delivered to the siphon results in a reflex withdrawal of the gill and siphon, which presumably serves the defensive role of protecting these sensitive structures from potentially harmful stimuli. The reflex exhibits several simple forms of learning including habituation, sensitization (see "Molecular Basis of Long-Term Sensitization" below), and classical conditioning. In the studies of classical conditioning the conditioned stimulus (CS) was a brief, weak tactile stimulus to the siphon, which by itself produced a small siphon withdrawal. The unconditioned stimulus (US) was a short-duration strong (noxious) electric shock to the tail, which by itself produced a large withdrawal of the siphon. After fifteen pairings at an interval of 5 minutes, the ability of the CS to produce siphon withdrawal (the conditioned response, CR) was enhanced beyond that produced by presentations of the US alone (sensitization control) or explicitly unpaired or random presentations of the CS and the US (Carew, Walters, and

Kandel, 1981). The conditioning persisted for as long as 4 days. Carew and colleagues (1983) also found that this reflex exhibited differential classical conditioning. Differential associative learning could be produced by delivering one CS to the siphon and another to the mantle region, or by delivering the CS+ and CS− to different parts of the siphon. As in the previous studies, the US was an electric shock delivered to the tail.

Neural Mechanisms of Classical Conditioning in Aplysia

A cellular mechanism called activity-dependent neuromodulation may contribute to associative learning in *Aplysia* (Hawkins et al., 1983; Walters and Byrne, 1983). A general cellular scheme of activity-dependent neuromodulation is illustrated in Figure 1. Two sensory neurons (SN1 and SN2), which constitute the pathways for the conditioned stimuli (CS), make weak subthreshold connections to a motor neuron. Delivering a reinforcing or unconditioned stimulus (US) alone has two effects. First, the US activates the motor neuron and produces the unconditioned response (UR). Second, the US activates a diffuse modulatory system that nonspecifically enhances transmitter release from all the sensory neurons. This nonspecific enhancement contributes to sensitization. Temporal specificity, characteristic of associative learning, occurs when there is pairing of the CS (spike activity in SN1) with the US, causing a selective amplification of the modulatory effects in that specific sensory neuron. Unpaired activity does not amplify the effects of the US in SN2. The amplification of the modulatory effects in the paired sensory neuron leads to an enhancement of the ability of SN1 to activate the motor neuron and produce the CR.

As discussed below under "Molecular Basis of Long-Term Sensitization," experimental analyses of sensitization of defensive reflexes in *Aplysia* have shown that the neuromodulator released by the reinforcing stimulus acts, at least in part, by activating the enzyme adenylate cyclase and thereby increases the synthesis of the second messenger cAMP (cyclic AMP), which activates the cAMP-dependent protein kinase; the subsequent protein phosphorylation leads to a reduction of potassium currents in the sensory neurons. Consequently, action potentials elicited after the reinforcing stimulus are broader (because there is less repolarizing K^+ current), causing an enhanced influx of Ca^{2+}. The enhanced influx of Ca^{2+} triggers

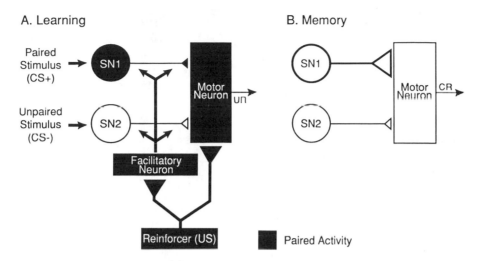

Figure 1.   General model of activity-dependent neuromodulation. (A) Learning: Shading indicates paired activity. A motivationally potent reinforcing stimulus activates a motor neuron to produce the unconditioned response (UR) and a facilitatory or modulatory system that regulates the strength of the connection between sensory neurons (SN1 and SN2) and the motor neuron. Increased spike activity in one sensory neuron (SN1) immediately before the modulatory signal amplifies the degree and duration of the modulatory effects, perhaps through the Ca^{2+} sensitivity of the modulatory evoked second messenger. The unpaired sensory neuron (SN2) does not show an amplification of the modulatory effects. (B) Memory: The amplified modulatory effects cause long-term increases in transmitter release and/or excitability of the paired neuron, which in turn strengthens the functional connection between the paired sensory neuron (SN1) and the motor neuron. The associative enhancement of synaptic strength represents the conditioned response (CR).

greater release of transmitter from the sensory neurons, which causes increased activation of motor neurons and, thus, sensitization of the reflex. The pairing specificity of the associative conditioning is due, at least in part, to an increase in the level of cAMP beyond that produced by the modulator alone (Abrams and Kandel, 1988; Ocorr, Walters, and Byrne, 1985). It appears that the influx of Ca^{2+} associated with the CS (spike activity) amplifies the US-mediated modulatory effect by interacting with a Ca^{2+}-sensitive component of the adenylate cyclase (Abrams and Kandel, 1988; Schwartz et al., 1983). A critical role for Ca^{2+}-stimulated cyclase is also suggested by studies of *Drosophila* showing that the particulate adenylate cyclase of a mutant deficient in associative learning exhibits a loss of Ca^{2+}/calmodulin sensitivity (see INVERTE-BRATE LEARNING: NEUROGENETIC ANALYSIS OF LEARNING IN DROSOPHILA).

An important conclusion is that this mechanism for associative learning is simply an elaboration of mechanisms already in place that mediate sensitization, a simpler form of learning. This finding raises the interesting possibility that even more complex forms of learning may use simpler forms as building blocks, an idea that has been suggested by some psychologists for many years but one that until now has not been testable at the cellular level (see CONDITIONING, CELLULAR AND NETWORK SCHEMES FOR HIGHER-ORDER FEATURES OF CLASSICAL).

Operant Conditioning

The mechanistic analysis of operant conditioning has not proceeded as rapidly as that for classical conditioning. Nevertheless, several behaviors in *Aplysia* can be conditioned using operant procedures. The behavioral analyses described below provide a starting point for subsequent cellular analyses.

Conditioned Modification of Feeding Behavior in Aplysia

Feeding behavior in *Aplysia* can be modified by pairing feeding with negative reinforcement. In the presence of food wrapped in a tough plastic net, *Aplysia* bite and attempt to swallow the food. However, netted food cannot be swallowed, and it is rejected. The inability to consume food appears to be an aversive stimulus that modifies feeding behavior, since trained animals do not attempt to bite netted food. Pairing successful food consumption with feeding behavior produces changes opposite to those produced by failed attempts to consume food (Susswein, Schwarz, and Feldman, 1986). Putative command neurons controlling feeding behavior have been identified. Thus, it may be possible to identify elements in the circuit that are modified by the conditioning procedure and examine the underlying mechanisms.

Operant Conditioning of Head Waving in Aplysia

Head waving is a natural behavior exhibited by *Aplysia*. Cook and Carew (1986) punished head waving toward one side or the other by the presentation of aversive bright lights. After training, *Aplysia* that received contingent reinforcement spent significantly more test time on the nonpunished ("safe") side compared with their own behavior during the baseline phase and compared with yoked controls in which illumination was unrelated to the behavioral response of the animal. When contingencies of reinforcement were subsequently reversed (safe side punished and vice versa), the contingent group showed a marked decrease in turning toward the now-punished side. When trained *Aplysia* were given 10 minutes of training in which turning was not correlated with the light, they exhibited significant retention. Because neurons controlling neck muscles have been identified (Cook and Carew, 1989), the cellular mechanisms of this example of operant conditioning in *Aplysia* can begin to be analyzed.

Operant Conditioning of Gill Withdrawal in Aplysia

Operant conditioning of gill withdrawal has been reported (Hawkins, Clark, and Kandel, 1985). In a paradigm similar to that described for head waving, an aversive stimulus (electric shock to the siphon) was paired with relaxation of the gill be-

yond a criterion level (20 percent of full contraction). Animals that received contingent training spent a significantly greater percentage of time with their gills contracted beyond the criterion level than did yoked controls. Moreover, the performance of trained animals was better than that of yoked controls in subsequent training sessions.

Conclusions

One of the important findings to emerge from recent studies on invertebrates is their capacity to exhibit various forms of associative learning (see entries under INVERTEBRATE LEARNING). Of particular significance is the finding that at least some mollusks, such as *Limax*, exhibit higher-order features of classical conditioning, such as second-order conditioning and blocking. Contextual conditioning, conditioned discrimination learning, and contingency effects have been described in *Aplysia* (Colwill, Absher, and Roberts, 1988; Hawkins, Carew, and Kandel, 1986). Such higher-order features can be viewed in a cognitive context, and raise the interesting possibility that other quasi-cognitive phenomena will be identified as the behavioral capabilities of these animals are investigated further. Since many of the invertebrates reviewed in the *Encyclopedia* are amenable to cellular analysis, an examination of cognitive properties at the cellular level may be possible.

The possibility of relating cellular changes to complex behavior in invertebrates is encouraged by the progress that has already been made in examining the neural mechanisms of simple forms of nonassociative and associative learning. The results of these analyses of *Aplysia* have shown that (1) learning involves changes in existing neural circuitry (one does not need the growth of new synapses and the formation of new circuits for learning and short-term memory to occur); (2) learning involves the activation of SECOND MESSENGER SYSTEMS; (3) the second messengers affect multiple subcellular processes to alter the responsiveness of the neuron (at least one locus for the storage and readout of memory is the alteration of specific membrane currents); and (4) long-term memory requires new protein synthesis, whereas short-term memory does not.

While considerable progress has been made in the analysis of simple forms of learning in *Aplysia*, other invertebrates, and vertebrate model systems, there is still no complete mechanistic analysis available for any single example of simple learning. Many of the technical obstacles are being overcome, however, and within the next few years it is likely that the analyses of several examples of learning will be fairly complete.

For the near future, major questions to be answered include the following: (1) To what extent are mechanisms for classical conditioning common both within any one species and between different species? (2) What is the relationship between the initial induction of neuronal change (acquisition of learning) and the maintenance of the associative change (retention of learning)? (3) What are the relationships among different forms of learning, such as sensitization, classical conditioning, and operant conditioning?

More ambitious questions include the analysis of cognitive phenomena and whether such learning involves processes and mechanisms fundamentally different from those underlying classical conditioning. Interestingly, much theoretical work has shown that artificial neural networks based on relatively simple learning rules have interesting computational capabilities and quasi-cognitive properties (see NEURAL COMPUTATION: APPROACHES TO LEARNING). Thus, it is interesting to speculate that the critical distinction between simple and complex cognitive examples of learning will be found not at the level of basic cellular mechanisms but, rather, at the level of the neural network and the specificity of neuronal connections.

REFERENCES

Abrams, T. W., and Kandel, E. R. (1988). Is contiguity detection in classical conditioning a system or cellular property? Learning in *Aplysia* suggests a possible site. *Trends in Neurosciences 11*, 128–135.

Carew, T. J., Hawkins, R. D., and Kandel, E. R. (1983). Differential classical conditioning of a defensive withdrawal reflex in *Aplysia californica. Science 219*, 397–400.

Carew, T. J., Walters, E. T., and Kandel, E. R. (1981). Classical conditioning in a simple withdrawal reflex in *Aplysia californica. Journal of Neuroscience 1*, 1426–1437.

Colwill, R. M., Absher, R. A., and Roberts, M. L. (1988). Context-US learning in *Aplysia californica. Journal of Neuroscience 8*, 4434–4439.

Cook, D. G., and Carew, T. J. (1986). Operant conditioning of head waving in *Aplysia. Proceedings of the National Academy of Sciences of the United States of America 83*, 1120–1124.

———— (1989). Operant conditioning of head-waving in *Aplysia.* I. Identified muscles involved in the operant response. *Journal of Neuroscience 9*, 3097–3106.

Hawkins, R. D., Abrams, T. W., Carew, T. J., and Kandel, E. R. (1983). A cellular mechanism of classical conditioning in *Aplysia:* Activity-dependent amplification of presynaptic facilitation. *Science 219*, 400–405.

Hawkins, R. D., Carew, T. J., and Kandel, E. R. (1986). Effects of interstimulus interval and contingency on classical conditioning of the *Aplysia* siphon withdrawal reflex. *Journal of Neuroscience 6*, 1695–1701.

Hawkins, R. D., Clark, G. A., and Kandel, E. R. (1985). Operant conditioning and differential classical conditioning of gill withdrawal in *Aplysia. Society for Neuroscience Abstracts 11*, 796.

Ocorr, K. A., Walters, E. T., and Byrne, J. H. (1985). Associative conditioning analog selectively increases cAMP levels of tail sensory neurons in *Aplysia. Proceedings of the National Academy of Sciences of the United States of America 82*, 2548–2552.

Schwartz, J. H., Bernier, L., Castellucci, V. F., Polazzolo, M., Saitoh, T., Stapleton, A., and Kandel, E. R. (1983). What molecular steps determine the time course of the memory for short-term sensitization in *Aplysia? Cold Spring Harbor Symposium on Quantitative Biology 48*, 811–819.

Susswein, A. J., Schwarz, M., and Feldman, E. (1986). Learned changes of feeding behavior in *Aplysia* in response to edible and inedible foods. *Journal of Neuroscience 6*, 1513–1527.

Walters, E. T., and Byrne, J. H. (1983). Associative conditioning of single sensory neurons suggests a cellular mechanism for learning. *Science 219*, 405–408.

John H. Byrne

Molecular Basis of Long-Term Sensitization

When a test stimulus triggers a reflex, the amplitude of the response can be modified by applying another, stronger or noxious stimulus to the subject. If the two stimuli are not specifically paired in time, this procedure is called *sensitization.* The amplitude of the response can be increased (positive sensitization) or decreased (negative sensitization). This phenomenon is found in all types of animals and is considered by many to be a simple form of learning. As the stimulation protocol is varied, the changes of the response amplitude can last from a few minutes (short-term) to several days or weeks (long-term).

The cellular and molecular basis of this form

of learning was studied in the marine mollusk *Aplysia*. This snail, like many other invertebrates, has been used to study basic questions in neurobiology (Kandel, 1979). The relative simplicity of the nervous system of *Aplysia* permits the neuroscientists to relate cellular changes at specific synapses to specific changes in behavior of the animal. It is possible in this system to study the biochemical mechanisms underlying short-term and long-term sensitization and the relationship between them.

Sensitization of the Gill and Siphon Withdrawal Reflex and of the Tail Withdrawal Reflex

Two reflexes in *Aplysia* have been used to study the cellular mechanisms of sensitization: the gill and siphon withdrawal reflex and the tail withdrawal reflex. Both reflexes can be facilitated for several minutes in the intact animal. For example, when an *Aplysia* is rested or unstimulated, a light touch (test stimulation) to its siphon skin evokes a contraction of its gill and its siphon. The amplitude and the duration of this response can be enhanced if a stronger stimulation (facilitating stimulus) is applied to the same spot or to any other part of the animal. The facilitation of the reflex is called sensitization. It is possible to depress the amplitude of the response by repeating the test stimulation at regular intervals; this simple form of learning is called habituation. The facilitation of a habituated response is called a dishabituation. The facilitation of the gill and siphon withdrawal reflex or the tail withdrawal reflex can last several minutes to several days; it is dependent on the number and the strength of the facilitating stimuli.

The first step in the study of sensitization was to identify the neurons that are causally related to the reflex under investigation. Several key components of the neural circuit mediating the gill and siphon withdrawal and tail withdrawal reflexes are now known. We will discuss mainly the gill and siphon withdrawal, but the general findings and conclusions are similar for both reflexes. The neural network has two main pathways. There is a direct route or monosynaptic pathway that is the junction between the mechanoreceptor neurons of the skin and the motor neurons that make the gill and the siphon contract. There is also an indirect (polysynaptic) route via the interneurons between the sensory neurons and the motor neurons of the reflex. Some interneurons are excitatory, and others are inhibitory. It is possible to record from all these neurons when the reflex is evoked (Hawkins and Schacher, 1989). It was found that during facilitation of the reflex, the efficacy of the connection between the sensory neurons and the motor neurons is increased. This is not the only site where physiological changes can be observed, but it is an important one at which most of the studies have been done.

The increase in transmitter release is due to the action of some facilitating neurons that are activated by the facilitating stimulation. Some of these neurons that have been identified use 5-hydroxytryptamine (serotonin), others a small peptide called SCP; the transmitter of others is still unknown (Abrams et al., 1984).

During short-term facilitation, there is increased probability of transmitter release. Every time an action potential sweeps down the terminals of the sensory neuron, more packets of the excitatory transmitter are released; the excitatory postsynaptic potential (EPSP) that is recorded in the motor neurons is larger. It is believed that at least two mechanisms are involved in the increase of transmitter release (Braha et al., 1990). One mechanism is dependent on the activity of an enzyme (A kinase) that in turn depends on the formation of a second messenger called cyclic adenosine monophosphate (cAMP), and a second mechanism is dependent on another kinase (C kinase). (For review see SECOND MESSENGER SYSTEMS.)

The following sequence of events is thought to occur when the synaptic transmission is increased. First the facilitating stimulation activates some interneurons. These neurons release a transmitter such as serotonin or SCP. The transmitter molecules are recognized by receptor molecules on the membrane of the sensory neurons. These receptors are coupled to the enzyme adenylate cyclase, which changes adenosine triphosphate (ATP) molecules into cAMP molecules. The cAMP activates a cAMP-dependent protein kinase, A kinase, which will phosphorylate (add a phosphate group to) some substrate proteins. Some of these proteins, when phosphorylated, will change the properties of a special potassium channel (S channel). This potassium channel normally contributes to the repolarization of the sensory neuron action potential. When the channel properties are changed, the action potential of the sensory neuron lasts longer. The increase in duration of the action potential allows the voltage-dependent calcium channel to stay open for a longer time, and the net result is that more calcium enters the sensory neuron during each action potential. This increase in calcium flux leads to a greater amount of calcium-dependent transmitter release. At the same time, C. kinase is activated. It may be important in mobilizing the transmitter for greater release.

To summarize at this point, during short-term facilitation of the reflex, at least one physiological change is observed: There is an increase in transmitter release at the synapse between the sensory neurons and the motor neurons. There are at least two mechanisms involved: The first is cAMP-dependent and leads to an increased duration of the sensory neuron action potential, an increase in neuronal excitability; the second is not dependent on cAMP and change of neuronal excitability. The relative importance of these two mechanisms and the relationship between them is still under investigation. Most probably, several biochemical reactions are important during synaptic facilitation, and it is necessary to identify the essential molecules for it. There are already candidate proteins that are phosphorylated during facilitation, but their role in the modulation of the potassium channel or transmitter mobilization is not yet established.

Even if all the mechanisms for short-term sensitization are not fully understood, there are many questions that scientists want to ask about their relationship to those for long-term sensitization. Can the EPSP facilitation be prolonged to last several hours or days, as is the case for the reflex? What are the distinctions between short-term and long-term effects? Are the same synaptic sites in the neural network involved? Are there entirely new mechanisms involved? What are the signals used by the central nervous system to induce more permanent alterations?

In the case of the withdrawal reflex, an arbitrary time was first chosen to distinguish between short-term and long-term changes; a period of 24 hours or more was considered to be long-term and a period of less than 24 hours short-term. The final word is not in yet, since it is possible that families of mechanisms having different time scales exist. The fact that in some conditions the reflex in the intact animal was enhanced for several minutes and in other conditions it was enhanced for days suggested the 24-hour period as a first time point to consider.

The first question was whether the connection that changed during short-term sensitization was altered during a protocol that facilitated the reflex

for several days. It was found that the amplitudes of the EPSPs evoked by sensory neurons in the nervous system of long-term sensitized animals were twice as large as those in unsensitized or control animals (Frost et al., 1985). This indicated that, as in short-term facilitation of the reflex, a monosynaptic connection could change for a longer period. Again, this did not suggest that it was the only locus of alteration, but it did show that short-term and long-term modifications could be observed at a single synapse.

A second question was whether a single facilitating transmitter was sufficient to trigger a long-term physiological change. This was examined by taking advantage of the fact that the monosynaptic connection can be studied in isolation. One can put one sensory neuron and one motor neuron in the same experimental dish. After a few days, the chemical synapse between the two cells is formed. Its properties are similar to the synapse observed in the intact nervous system. The synaptic release can be increased by a brief exposure to serotonin. If the exposures are repeated to simulate an intact animal training procedure, the facilitation can last a few days. For example, one can test the amplitude of the EPSP on day 1 and retest it on day 2. When this was done, it was found that the EPSP could double its amplitude (Glanzman, Kandel, and Schacher, 1990). When the small facilitating peptide SCP or an analog of cAMP was used instead of serotonin, a similar effect was observed. It was also observed that the excitability of the sensory neuron and the probability of release were increased, and that many proteins that were phosphorylated by short exposure to serotonin (which produces short-term facilitation) were phosphorylated for more than 24 hours when the protocol to induce long-term facilitation was used (Sweatt and Kandel, 1989). This indicated that one site of change, the sensory neuron, is shared by short-term and long-term sensitization. Actually, the same facilitating substances, a common potassium current and one second messenger, are common in both instances.

Since those properties are shared, one critical issue is to attempt to dissociate long-term changes from short-term changes in the hope of studying the transition (if any) between short-lasting and longer-lasting modifications. One widely held idea is that to consolidate a change in the nervous system, new proteins are needed. In other words, to modify the physiology of a neuron or a synapse in a more permanent way, ionic channels, neuronal components related to the releasing zones, receptors, or enzymes could be modified, added, or removed.

A first set of studies suggested that such changes were indeed occurring. Intact animals were trained for a few days, then their nervous systems were taken and individual sensory neurons were injected intracellularly with an opaque substance (HRP) that allowed their serial reconstructions through light and electron microscopy. The branches of the sensory neurons from the sensitized animals were more numerous, and they had more synaptic boutons than those of unsensitized animals. On average the cellular specializations (active zones) at which transmitter release takes place were more numerous in the boutons of the sensitized animals (Bailey and Chen, 1989). (See MORPHOLOGICAL BASIS OF LEARNING AND MEMORY: INVERTEBRATES.)

A second set of studies used reversible protein synthesis inhibitors or inhibitors of messenger RNA. When these drugs were used on the reflex or on isolated neurons, long-term facilitation was not observed (Castellucci et al., 1989). On the other hand, these drugs did not interfere with short-term facilitation of the reflex, short-term excitability change of the sensory neuron, or short-term facilitation of the EPSP. An important observation was that the drugs had to be present only when the facilitating protocol or transmitter was presented. There was a time window (a few hours) during which critical signals and macromolecule synthesis were needed for the reflex to transform from a short-lasting into a longer-lasting state.

A third set of experiments attempted to identify the candidate proteins that could play an essential role in triggering the changes of long-term sensitization or in its maintenance. One approach was to mark proteins with radioactive amino acids in the nervous systems of trained and control animals at different times during or after training. The labeled proteins were then extracted and separated on two-dimensional gels. The gels were analyzed and the relative proportion of all detected proteins was measured. Several protein candidates were found (Barzilai et al., 1989; Castellucci et al., 1988; Eskin, Garcia, and Byrne, 1989). What remains to be done is to characterize their cellular and intracellular distribution, to identify their amino acid composition, and to establish how they are regulated and how essential they are for the onset and the maintenance of long-term changes.

There are two additional observations of interest for understanding some of the mechanisms involved in triggering long-term changes. The first is that the proportion of the subunits of the cAMP-dependent protein kinase (A kinase) is changed in ganglions of long-term sensitized animals, which suggests that the A kinase may be more sensitive to cAMP changes (Bergold et al., 1990). The second observation is that the C kinase enzymes are more associated with the neuronal membrane in sensitized animals than in control ones (Sacktor and Schwartz, 1990). The significance of these two findings is not yet fully understood, but they imply that various metabolic reactions can be modified in a permanent way and that this modification results in a totally new neuronal function.

Conclusions

It appears that one can dissociate short-term effects from the long-term ones by their dependence on new protein synthesis. One can conceive that some regulatory signals are sent to the neurons involved in long-term changes, and these signals induce a family of events that lead to changes such as modified ionic channels, altered metabolism, or new neuronal structures. The key questions are What are the early and necessary signals that trigger the first wave of changes, and what are the gene products that are generated? Which ones are essential, necessary, and sufficient? Are there several mechanisms with different time courses for different learning or training protocols? How many common proteins are changed in various types of learning? Are the rules similar for invertebrate and vertebrate nervous systems? How early can one detect the more permanent changes? Is there a way to delete a modification once it is established? These questions need to be examined. The answers will be important for understanding both long-term sensitization and other forms of long-term learning.

(See also PROTEIN SYNTHESIS IN LONG-TERM MEMORY IN VERTEBRATES.)

REFERENCES

Abrams, T. W., Castellucci, V. F., Camardo, J. S., Kandel, E. R., and Lloyd, P. E. (1984). Two endogenous neuropeptides modulate the gill and siphon withdrawal reflex in *Aplysia* by presynaptic facilitation involving cAMP-dependent closure of a serotonin-sensitive potassium channel. *Proceedings of the National Academy of Sciences 81,* 7956–7960.

Bailey, C. H., and Chen, M. (1989). Structural plasticity at identified synapses during long-term memory in *aplysia. Journal of Neurobiology 20,* 356–372.

Barzilai, A., Kennedy, T. E., Sweatt, J. D., and Kandel, E. R. (1989). K-H1 modulates protein synthesis and the expression of specific proteins during long-term facilitation in *Aplysia* sensory neurons. *Neuron 2,* 1577–1586.

Bergold, P. J., Sweatt, D., Winicov, I., Weiss, K. R., Kandel, E. R., and Schwartz, J. H. (1990). Protein synthesis during acquisition of long-term facilitation is needed for the persistent loss of regulatory subunits of the *Aplysia* cAMP-dependent protein kinase. *Proceedings of the National Academy of Sciences 87,* 3788–3791.

Braha, O., Dale, N., Hochner, B., Klein, M., Abrams, T. W., and Kandel, E. R. (1990). Second messengers involved in the two processes of presynaptic facilitation that contribute to sensitization and dishabituation in *Aplysia* sensory neurons. *Proceedings of the National Academy of Sciences 87,* 2040–2044.

Castellucci, V. F., Blumenfeld, H., Goelet, P., and Kandel, E. R. (1989). Inhibitor of protein synthesis blocks long-term behavioral sensitization in the isolated gill-withdrawal reflex of *Aplysia. Journal of Neurobiology 20,* 1–9.

Castellucci, V. F., Kennedy, T. E., Kandel, E. R., and Goelet, P. (1988). A quantitative analysis of 2-D gels identifies proteins whose labeling is increased following long-term sensitization in *Aplysia. Neuron 1,* 321–328.

Eskin, A., Garcia, K. S., and Byrne, J. H. (1989). Information storage in the nervous system of *Aplysia:* Specific proteins affected by serotonin and cAMP. *Proceedings of the National Academy of Sciences 86,* 2458–2462.

Frost, W. N., Castellucci, V. F., Hawkins, R. D., and Kandel, E. R. (1985). Monosynaptic connections made by the sensory neurons of the gill- and siphon-withdrawal reflex in *Aplysia* participate in the storage of long-term memory for sensitization. *Proceedings of the National Academy of Sciences 82,* 8266–8269.

Glanzman, D. L., Kandel, E. R., and Schacher, S. (1990). Target-dependent structural changes accompanying long-term synaptic facilitation in *Aplysia* neurons. *Science 249,* 799–802.

Hawkins, R. D., and Schacher, S. (1989). Identified facilitator neurons L29 and L28 are excited by cutaneous stimuli used in dishabituation, sensitization, and classical conditioning of *Aplysia. Journal of Neuroscience 9,* 4236–4245.

Kandel, E. R. (1979). *Behavioral biology of* Aplysia: *A contribution to the comparative study of opisthobranch molluscs.* San Francisco: Freeman.

Sacktor, T. C., and Schwartz, J. H. (1990). Sensitizing stimuli cause translocation of protein kinase C in *Aplysia* sensory neurons. *Proceedings of the National Academy of Sciences 87,* 2036–2039.

Sweatt, J. D., and Kandel, E. R. (1989). Persistent and transcriptionally-dependent increase in protein phosphorylation in long-term facilitation of *Aplysia* sensory neurons. *Nature 339,* 51–54.

Vincent Castellucci

Development of Processes Underlying Learning

In the 1980s exciting progress was made in understanding a variety of developmental processes, ranging from principles governing the birth, differentiation, and migration of nerve cells to the mechanisms underlying the functional assembly of complex neural circuits. In addition to the intrinsic interest in development as a fundamental field of inquiry, the analysis of development has a secondary gain: By affording the experimental opportunity of examining early-emerging processes in functional isolation from later-emerging ones, development can serve as a powerful analytic tool with which to dissect and examine specific behavioral, cellular, and molecular processes as they are expressed and integrated during ontogeny.

In recent years a developmental strategy such as that described above has been very useful in furthering the analysis of learning and memory in the marine mollusk *Aplysia,* a preparation that has proved to be quite powerful for cellular and molecular studies of several forms of learning (see "Molecular Basis of Long-Term Sensitization" above). Specifically, using this strategy, it has been possible to identify and dissociate multiple components of nonassociative learning on both behavioral and cellular levels. This type of analysis has also revealed previously unappreciated behavioral and cellular processes in *Aplysia.* Moreover, the developmental dissociation of different components of learning in juvenile *Aplysia* prompted a similar analysis in adult animals, where the same clearly dissociable components of learning were identified. Thus an analysis of the developmental assembly of learning has provided important insights into the final phenotypic expression of learning in the adult.

The Development of *Aplysia*

The life cycle of *Aplysia* can be divided into five phases: (1) an *embryonic* phase (lasting about 10 days, from fertilization to hatching); (2) a *plank-tonic* larval phase (lasting about 35 days); (3) a *metamorphic* phase (lasting only 2–3 days); (4) a *juvenile* phase (lasting at least 90 days), and (5) the *adult* phase, defined as the onset of reproductive maturity. These five phases can be further divided into thirteen discrete stages, each defined by a specific set of morphological criteria (Kriegstein, 1977). In the analysis of learning that will be described here, most work has focused on the juvenile phase of development (stages 9 through 12), since it is during this time that many of the behavioral systems of interest emerge.

Forms of Learning and Developmental Timetables

In adult *Aplysia* the siphon withdrawal reflex exhibits both nonassociative and associative forms of learning. The developmental analysis thus far carried out in *Aplysia* has focused primarily on nonassociative learning in that reflex. The three most common forms of nonassociative learning are habituation, dishabituation, and sensitization. *Habituation* refers to a decrease in response magnitude occurring as a function of repeated stimulation to a single site; *dishabituation* describes the facilitation of a habituated response by the presentation of a strong or novel stimulus, usually to another site; *sensitization* refers to the facilitation of nondecremented responses by a similar strong or novel stimulus. Using a behavioral preparation that permitted quantification of siphon withdrawal throughout juvenile development, Rankin and Carew (1987, 1988) found that these three forms of nonassociative learning emerged according to different developmental timetables. Habituation of siphon withdrawal was present very early (in stage 9) and progressively matured across all juvenile stages in terms of its interstimulus interval (ISI) function: In young animals, extremely short ISIs were necessary to produce habituation, whereas in older animals, progressively longer ISIs could be used to produce habituation. Dishabituation (produced by tail shock) emerged soon after habituation, in a distinct and later stage (stage 10). However, sensitization (also produced by tail shock) did not emerge until surprisingly late in juvenile development (stage 12), at least 60 days after the emergence of dishabituation (Figure 1).

The observation that dishabituation and sensiti-

zation can be developmentally dissociated raises important theoretical questions for a complete explanation of nonassociative learning. For example, until recently a commonly held view was that nonassociative learning could be accounted for by a *dual process* theory involving two opposing processes: a single decrementing process that gives rise to habituation, and a single facilitatory process that underlies both dishabituation and sensitization (Groves and Thompson, 1970; Carew, Castellucci, and Kandel, 1971). A key prediction of this view is that dishabituation and sensitization should always occur together. However, the developmental dissociation of these processes, together with recent behavioral and cellular evidence in adult *Aplysia* (see below), suggests that a dual-process view is inadequate to account for nonassociative learning in *Aplysia.*

The emergence of sensitization in stage 12 is not confined to the siphon withdrawal reflex in *Aplysia.* Stopfer and Carew (1988) examined another response system, escape locomotion, and found that sensitization in that system also emerges in stage 12. Thus sensitization is expressed in two different systems, one a graded reflex and the other a centrally programmed cyclical behavior, at the same time in development. This raises the interesting hypothesis that one or more developmental signals may switch on the general process of sensitization in stage 12, not only in individual response systems but in the whole animal.

Cellular Analogues of Learning and Behavioral Learning

The developmental separation of different learning processes described above provides the opportunity to examine the unique contribution of specific cellular mechanisms to each form of learning. An important step in such a cellular analysis is to show that the cellular analogue of each form of learning can be identified in the central nervous system of juvenile *Aplysia* and that these analogues exhibit a developmental time course parallel to the behavioral expression of the learning. The identified motor neuron can serve as a reliable cellular monitor of plasticity in the afferent input to the siphon withdrawal reflex.

The developmental emergence of the cellular analogue of habituation (synaptic decrement) and of dishabituation (facilitation of decremented syn-

BEHAVIORAL ANALYSIS

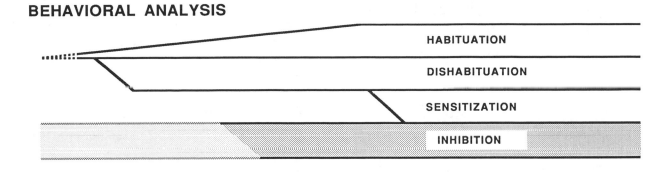

CELLULAR ANALYSIS

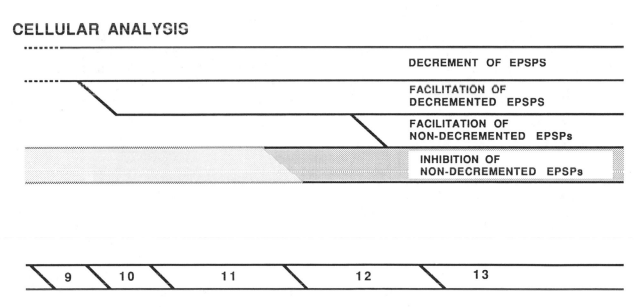

DEVELOPMENTAL STAGES

Figure 1. Summary of developmental timetables for different forms of learning and their respective cellular analogues. *Behavioral analysis:* Habituation is present as early as has been examined, in stage 9; dishabituation emerges soon after habituation, in stage 10; sensitization does not emerge until 60 days after dishabituation, in mid to late stage 12. Behavioral inhibition has been measured as early as stage 11 (indicated by shading) but may emerge even earlier. *Cellular analysis:* The cellular analogue of habituation (homosynaptic decrement of EPSPs in neuron R2) is present in stage 9; the analogue of dishabituation (facilitation of *decremented* EPSPs in R2) emerges in stage 10; the analogue of sensitization (facilitation of *nondecremented* EPSPs in R2) emerges between early and mid stage 12. Inhibition of nondecremented EPSPs in R2 has been detected as early as early stage 12 (indicated by shading) but, as with behavioral inhibition, may emerge even earlier. Thus there is a close developmental parallel between the emergence of each behavioral form of learning (as well as behavioral inhibition) and its respective cellular analogue.

aptic potentials) was first examined by Rayport and Camardo (1984). They found that synaptic decrement could be observed in neuron R2 as early as stage 9, and that facilitation of depressed synaptic potentials emerged in stage 10. Nolen and Carew (1988) then examined the emergence of the cellular analogue of sensitization (facilitation of nondecremented synaptic potentials) in R2. They found that the analogue of sensitization emerged between early and middle stage 12, many weeks after the emergence of the analogue of dishabituation. Taken collectively, these results illustrate two important points. First, the cellular analogue of each form of learning emerges in close temporal register with its respective behavioral form (Figure 1). Second, just as dishabituation and sensitization can be developmentally dissociated on a behavioral level, so their cellular analogues can be developmentally dissociated as well.

A Novel Inhibitory Process

When the effects of sensitization training (i.e., the effects of tail shock on nondecremented reflex responses) in different developmental stages were examined, an unexpected effect of tail shock was discovered: Prior to the emergence of sensitization in stage 12, tail shock had an *inhibitory* effect on reflex responsiveness (Rankin and Carew, 1988). The properties of this inhibitory process in juvenile *Aplysia* have been studied by Rankin and Carew (1989), who found that tail shock–induced inhibition of siphon withdrawal can be detected in two ways: (1) by reduction of reflex responsiveness and (2) by the apparent competition of the inhibitory process with the facilitatory process of dishabituation. Specifically, they found that as levels of tail shock were increased, progressively *more* inhibition resulted and, concomitantly, progressively *less* dishabituation was produced, suggesting the hypothesis that the tail shock–induced inhibition could significantly retard the expression of dishabituation in early developmental stages. Finally, as the process of sensitization matured, there was a clear transition from the inhibitory effect of tail shock to reflex *facilitation* between early and late stage 12.

In parallel with the behavioral reflection of inhibition described above, Nolen and Carew (1988) identified a clear cellular analogue of this inhibitory process. Specifically, they found that prior to the

emergence of the cellular analogue of sensitization in mid to late stage 12, activation of the pathway from the tail produced significant *inhibition* of nondecremented synaptic responses in neuron R2 (Figure 1). As with the behavior, there was a clear transition from inhibition to facilitation in mid to late stage 12.

The inhibitory process first identified in juvenile *Aplysia* has received considerable attention in the adult. Several laboratories have observed behavioral tail shock–induced inhibition of the siphon withdrawal reflex (Marcus et al., 1988; Mackey et al., 1987; Krontiris-Litowitz, Erikson, and Walters, 1987), and important progress has been made in studying the cellular mechanisms underlying the inhibitory process. For example, Mackey et al. (1987) found that tail shock produced presynaptic inhibition of the transmission from siphon sensory neurons. More recently, Wright, Marcus, and Carew (1991) found that polysynaptic input to the siphon motor neurons plays an important role in mediating tail shock–induced inhibition, and Wright and Carew (1990) found that a single identified inhibitory interneuron in the abdominal ganglion, cell L16, can account for most, if not all, of the inhibition of siphon withdrawal following tail shock. Finally, Fitzgerald and Carew (1991) found that serotonin, a known facilitatory neuromodulator in *Aplysia*, can also mimic the inhibitory effects of tail shock. It will be of considerable interest to study the development of these inhibitory mechanisms and examine the way in which they are integrated with facilitatory forms of behavioral plasticity.

Behavioral Dissociation of Dishabituation, Sensitization, and Inhibition in Adults

The developmental studies described above show that dishabituation, sensitization, and a novel inhibitory process, as well as their respective cellular analogues, can each be dissociated in juvenile animals. It is possible, however, that these processes, although separable during ontogeny, are not distinct in the final adult phenotype. Thus an important question arose as to whether the same forms of behavioral plasticity could be identified and separated in adult animals. Marcus et al. (1988) addressed this issue by examining, in adult *Aplysia*, the effects of a wide range of tail-shock intensities, at several times after tail shock, on both habituated and nonhabituated siphon withdrawal responses. They found that dishabituation and sensitization could be clearly dissociated in adult animals in two ways.

First was time of onset. When tested soon (90 seconds) after tail shock, dishabituation was evident at a variety of stimulus intensities, whereas, in this early test, sensitization was not exhibited at *any* stimulus intensity. In fact, examining non-decremented responses revealed that tail shock produced *inhibition* of reflex amplitude. Although no sensitization was evident in the 90-second test, in subsequent tests (20–30 minutes after tail shock) significant sensitization was observed. Thus, dishabituation has an early onset (within 90 seconds), whereas sensitization has a very delayed onset (20–30 minutes) after tail shock. Juvenile *Aplysia* also exhibit delayed-onset sensitization that emerges in early stage 12, at least 30 days after the emergence of dishabituation.

Second was stimulus intensity. When a range of stimulus intensities to the tail was examined, maximal dishabituation was produced by relatively weak stimuli, whereas maximal sensitization was produced by stronger stimuli. Moreover, the stimulus intensity that was most effective in producing dishabituation produced *no* sensitization, and the intensity that was most effective in producing sensitization produced *no* significant dishabituation. Thus, as in juvenile *Aplysia* (Rankin and Carew, 1989), the processes of dishabituation, sensitization, and inhibition can be behaviorally dissociated in adult animals.

The behavioral observations described above raise important questions about the cellular processes underlying the dissociation of dishabituation and sensitization. One possibility is that these two forms of learning reflect different underlying cellular mechanisms. Alternatively, the same or related mechanisms may be involved in both forms of learning, and the dissociation we observe could be due to differential interaction of the inhibitory process with dishabituation and sensitization. Behavioral results alone cannot distinguish between these possibilities. However, progress has been made in elucidating the cellular mechanisms underlying dishabituation and sensitization (Hochner et al., 1986) as well as inhibition (Mackey et al., 1987; Bellardetti, Kandel, and Siegelbaum, 1987; Wright, Marcus, and Carew, 1991; Wright and Carew, 1990). Thus it will be important to determine the degree to which these different cellular processes can account for the behavioral dissociations that are observed in both developing and adult *Aplysia.*

Summary and Conclusions

A developmental analysis in *Aplysia* has shown that different forms of learning, as well as their cellular analogues at central synapses, emerge according to very different developmental timetables. These studies have allowed the dissociation of four behavioral processes (Figure 1): two decrementing (habituation and inhibition) and two facilitatory (dishabituation and sensitization). Whether these dissociations are produced by different facilitatory mechanisms, by differential interactions of inhibition with decremented and nondecremented responses, or by some combination of these alternatives, our results suggest that a dual-process view of nonassociative learning, which postulates a single decremental and a single incremental process, requires revision, and that a multiple-process view, which includes the possibility of inhibitory as well as facilitatory interactions, is necessary to account adequately for the mechanisms underlying nonassociative learning.

The developmental studies discussed in this brief review have focused only on nonassociative learning in *Aplysia,* and only on short-term learning, which is retained for a relatively brief time (minutes to hours). However, *Aplysia* is also capable of exhibiting a variety of forms of associative learning. Moreover, in addition to short-term forms, both nonassociative and associative learning in *Aplysia* can exist in long-term forms lasting days to weeks (see the other sections of this composite article). It will be of interest to examine the development of these additional processes in order to gain insights into theoretically important questions such as the relationships between nonassociative and associative learning and between short-term and long-term memory. As a step in this direction, Carew, Wright, and McCance (1989) have established that long-term memory for sensitization emerges in exactly the same stage as short-term memory, stage 12. This observation lends support to the notion that short- and long-term memory may be mechanistically interrelated in *Aplysia* (Golet et al., 1986). By analyzing the development of these diverse processes at synaptic, biophysical, and molecular levels, it may be possible to gain unique insights into the substrates underlying learning and memory by examining their developmental assembly.

REFERENCES

Bellardetti, F., Kandel, E. R., and Siegelbaum, S. (1987). Neuronal inhibition by the peptide FMRFamide involves opening of S K$^+$ channels. *Nature 325,* 153–156.

Carew, T. J., Castellucci, V. F., and Kandel, E. R. (1971). Analysis of dishabituation and sensitization of the gill withdrawal reflex in *Aplysia. International Journal of Neuroscience 2,* 79–98.

Carew, T. J., Wright, W. G., and McCance, E. F. (1989). Development of long-term memory in *Aplysia:* Long-term sensitization is present when short-term sensitization first emerges. *Society for Neuroscience Abstracts 15,* 1285.

Fitzgerald, K., and Carew, T. J. (1991). Serotonin mimics tail shock in producing transient inhibition in the siphon withdrawal reflex of *Aplysia. Journal of Neuroscience 11,* 2510–2518.

Golet, P., Castellucci, V. F., Schacher, S., and Kandel, E. R. (1986). The long and short of long-term memory—a molecular framework. *Nature 322,* 419–422.

Groves, P. M., and Thompson, R. F. (1970). Habituation: A dual process theory. *Psychological Review 77,* 419–450.

Hochner, B., Klein, M., Schacher, S., and Kandel, E. R. (1986). Additional component in the cellular mechanism of presynaptic facilitation contributes to behavioral dishabituation in *Aplysia. Proceedings of the National Academy of Sciences 83,* 8794–8798.

Kriegstein, A. R. (1977). Stages in post-hatching development of *Aplysia californica. Journal of Experimental Zoology 199,* 275–288.

Krontiris-Litowitz, J. K., Erikson, M. T., and Walters, E. T. (1987). Central suppression of defensive reflexes in *Aplysia* by noxious stimulation and by factors released from body wall. *Society for Neuroscience Abstracts 13,* 815.

Mackey, S. L., Glanzman, D. L., Small, S. A., Dyke, A. M., Kandel, E. R., and Hawkins, R. D. (1987). Tail shock produces inhibition as well as sensitization of the siphon-withdrawal reflex of *Aplysia:* Possible behavioral role for presynaptic inhibition mediated by the peptide Phe-Met-Arg-Phe-NH$_2$. *Proceedings of the National Academy of Sciences 84,* 8730–8734.

Marcus, E. A., Nolen, T. G., Rankin, C. H., and Carew, T. J. (1988). Behavioral dissociation of dishabituation, sensitization, and inhibition in *Aplysia. Science 241,* 210–213.

Nolen, T. G., and Carew, T. J. (1988). A cellular analog of sensitization emerges at the same time in development as behavioral sensitization in *Aplysia. Journal of Neuroscience 8,* 212–222.

Rankin, C. H., and Carew, T. J. (1987). Development of learning and memory in *Aplysia:* II. Habituation and dishabituation. *Journal of Neuroscience 7,* 133–144.

——— (1988). Dishabituation and sensitization emerge as separate processes during development in *Aplysia. Journal of Neuroscience 8,* 197–211.

——— (1989). Developmental analysis in *Aplysia* reveals inhibitory as well as facilitatory effects of tail shock. *Behavior and Neuroscience 103,* 334–344.

Rayport, S. G., and Camardo, J. S. (1984). Differential emergence of cellular mechanisms mediating habituation and sensitization in the developing *Aplysia* nervous system. *Journal of Neuroscience 4,* 2528–2532.

Stopfer, M., and Carew, T. J. (1988). Development of sensitization of escape locomotion in *Aplysia. Journal of Neuroscience 8,* 223–230.

Wright, W. G., and Carew, T. J. (1990). Contributions of interneurons to tail-shock induced inhibition of the siphon withdrawal reflex in *Aplysia. Society for Neuroscience Abstracts 16,* 20.

Wright, W. G., Marcus, E. A., and Carew, T. J. (1991). A cellular analysis of inhibition in the siphon withdrawal reflex of *Aplysia. Journal of Neuroscience 11,* 2498–2509.

Thomas J. Carew

ARISTOTLE

Aristotle was born in northern Greece, in the town of Stagira, in 384 B.C. At 17, he went to Athens and became a student in Plato's Academy, where he remained for 20 years. Although greatly influenced by Plato and by the pre-Socratic philosophers, especially Empedocles, Aristotle was a highly original thinker and a disciple of no one. In 347 B.C. he left Athens and traveled extensively in Asia Minor, becoming tutor to Alexander the Great in 342 B.C. Seven years later he returned to Athens and began his own school, the Lyceum. After the death of Alexander the Great in 323 B.C., he left Athens, and died the following year in Chalcis, a few miles north of Athens.

In his main work on memory, *De memoria et reminiscentia,* Aristotle tries to dissect out the central phenomena to be explained, and suggests mechanical explanations of a very general sort to account for them. In his scientific works, Aristotle typically seeks the reality behind the appearances,

Figure 1. Aristotle. *Courtesy National Library of Medicine.*

and expects that the reality may be different from what it seems. This is especially forward-looking in the case of mental phenomena, where subsequent thinkers, such as Descartes (1649) and Vendler (1984), standardly insist that mental reality must be exactly as it seems. Aristotle's collection of memory phenomena displays some systematicity, and with characteristic insight, he lights on several basically correct classifications. Nevertheless, to modern eyes some of his collection is a bit of a jumble, and the mechanical explanations tendered are so implausible that they must have been no more than helpful metaphors to him.

It is Aristotle's relentlessly naturalistic perspective, however, that gives him a decidedly modern stamp. That is, he sought physical rather than supernatural or spiritual explanations for memory phenomena, and he knew very well the importance of observations even though his own were occasionally more assumptions than well-sampled observations. For example, he thought women had fewer teeth than men. In the absence of a developed biology, experimental psychology, or neuroscience, he could hardly be expected either to envisage explanations in terms of neuronal connec-

tivity or to know how to penetrate learning phenomena at the behavioral level.

Observations and Explanations

In memory and learning phenomena, Aristotle's fundamental distinction is between (1) recalling to mind at a time and (2) information storage, or as he puts it, between remembering, which is "the reinstatement in consciousness of something that was there before" (451b6), and memory, "the existence, potentially, in the mind" (452a10), of an earlier perception or conception. In modern parlance, this is the distinction between remembering in the occurrent sense and remembering in the "stored" or dispositional sense. The central problems, in Aristotle's view, are to explain three things: (1) how a perception of a state of affairs can be stored, (2) how it can be brought to mind later, and (3) when it is brought to mind, the relation between the representation and the original state of affairs, now absent, such that the first is a memory of the second and is known to be such. In contemporary dress, these are the problems of information storage, information retrieval, and the general problem of how representations represent.

Aristotle tries to explain information storage by appeal to the analogy of imprinting soft wax with a seal. He reasons that sense perception is somehow like a picture, and that it is the perception picture that stamps its likeness to create a memory. Apparently it is stamped on the soul, though Aristotle has a physicalistic, not a supernatural, conception of the soul. At any rate, the perception is stamped on some sort of physical stuff that can be in causal interaction with it and can take on some of its properties. This helps address the representation problem. The imprint (memory representation) resembles, physically, the perception (perceptual representation), which in turn resembles, physically, that of which it is a perception. So by transitivity of resemblance, there is a correlation between stored representation and original state of affairs. Aristotle's conclusion that there must be a resemblance was taken as axiomatic by most subsequent thinkers, and they searched for the parameters of physical resemblance. Recent research, especially in computer science and neuroscience, has revealed that representation does not require resemblance in any straightforward sense, a radical departure from earlier theories.

In asking how representations represent, Aristotle identified a truly fundamental problem. Still only partially solved, it remains a central problem, though it is now addressed within the framework of modern psychology, philosophy, neuroscience, and computer science.

Understanding the importance of broad systematicity in a theory, Aristotle tests a theory's strength by seeing how much can be encompassed within its ambit. Thus he claims that the stuff which receives the imprint may have varying degrees of imprintability. Explanations are then forthcoming for one's poor recollection of early childhood and for declining memory in the elderly: In very young children the stuff is too much like running water to take the imprint; in older humans, the stuff hardens and no longer is very impressible. Extending further, Aristotle thinks a related explanation will apply to his observation that those who are "too quick" and those who are "too slow" also have poor memories. Exactly what phenomenon he is addressing here is unclear, and this may be one of those inexplicable Aristotelian "observations" that need a much broadened data base.

The representation problem, Aristotle notices, has a further dimension. When an image from memory comes to mind, how do we know that it is a memory, rather than a thought or image without relation to bygone events? That is, how does the occurrent presentation carry the information that it is a memory? His answer has two parts. First, sometimes we do get confused, and we think a presentation is a memory when it is not (false memory); and sometimes we have a memory presentation but are unaware that it is a memory. So the system is imperfect. Second, when the system does work, it is because for animals with memory, "the organ whereby they perceive time is also that whereby they remember" (449b30). The idea here is that when perceptions are stored as memories, they are also somehow indexed as to time, so that the imprint bears not only the perception's shape but also its "whenness."

Retrieval appears to require something like an image or an iconic presentation that resembles the original perception. The mechanism of retrieval should, one surmises, have to do with something taking up the stored imprint and re-presenting it, but in fact Aristotle says nothing of this. Instead he discusses the phenomenon of association, noting that events experienced together are often remembered together. He explains associated recollections by saying that the "movement" of a perception causes the "movement" of the memory. He sees, therefore, that part of the theory of storage will include the relations between associated memories, but he neither provides an account of those storage relations nor elaborates on how information is retrieved by the "movements" (451b15–30). (See also ASSOCIATIONISM.)

In *Historia animalium* Aristotle suggests that humans and animals differ in that humans alone can remember something at will (488b25), though he also notes in *De memoria et reminiscentia* that recollections can occur without effort. Indeed, he observes that melancholics often have obsessive memories, try though they might to repress them. Again, in the physicalist spirit, he conjectures that melancholics have more moisture around their sense perception center, which is easily set in motion, thus explaining the memory's being presented again and again despite one's will.

Aristotle believed that animals differ in whether they have the capacity to store their perceptions; animals with the capacity to do so have genuine knowledge of their world, whereas animals lacking the capacity merely respond to their current perceptions on the basis of their innate dispositions. The advantage of storing perceptions is that the stored items may come to have systematic relations among themselves, with the result that the animal can recognize different individuals as belonging to the same category. In humans this means, for example, that a pine tree, a yew, and an olive tree may all be recognized as similar despite differences in shape, size, and color. He says that the soul is so constituted that the universal "tree" can be developed from the stored perceptions of individually distinct items. A slug, on the other hand, lacks the capacity to generalize across individuals because it lacks the capacity to store information.

In Aristotle's view, storing information provides the similarity substructure underpinning both scientific categorization and the skilled knowledge displayed by craftsmen who can make many different clay pots or can sail under many different conditions. In modern guise, his idea is that generalization to items that are relevantly similar but incidentally different, both perceptually and behaviorally, requires information storage. Additionally, he regards this capacity as enabling experience, the reason being that experience requires understanding, which in turn requires categorization of perceptions. Consequently, animals such as humans have genuine experience; animals such as slugs do not (*Posterior Analytics,* 99b36;100a5).

In the event of an inclination to feel smug about Aristotle's shortcomings, it is well to note that even current classifications of learning phenomena are controversial and tentative, and experimental psychologists are sometimes chided for doing little more than codifying common sense. Nor, of course, should Aristotle himself be blamed for the slavish adoption of his every word by uncritical monks in the Middle Ages. Aristotle the scientist-philosopher was anything but dogmatic. Recent physical explanations—while not mechanical, but electrical and biochemical—sit well with his abiding naturalism.

For a very long period in the history of thought, Aristotle's views on virtually everything were taken as authoritative. While his *Metaphysics* probably had the greatest impact, the work on memory was not especially influential.

REFERENCES

Aristotle. (1941). *De anima,* trans. by J. A. Smith. In *The basic works of Aristotle,* Richard McKeon, ed. New York: Random House.

_____. (1941). *De memoria et reminiscentia,* trans. by J. I. Beare. In *The basic works of Aristotle,* Richard McKeon, ed. New York: Random House.

_____. (1975). *Aristotle's Posterior analytics,* trans. by J. Barnes. Oxford: Clarendon Press.

Beare, J. I. (1906). *Greek theories of elementary cognition.* Oxford: Clarendon Press.

Descartes, R. (1649). *Les passions de l'âme.* English translation in E. S. Haldane and G. R. T. Ross, trans. ([1911] 1968), *The philosophical works of Descartes.* 2 vols. Cambridge: Cambridge University Press.

Edel, A. (1982). *Aristotle and his philosophy.* Chapel Hill: University of North Carolina Press.

Kahn, C. H. (1966). Sensation and consciousness in Aristotle's psychology. *Archiv für Geschichte der Philosophie 48,* 43–81.

Ross, W. D. (1923). *Aristotle.* London: Trinity Press. Reprinted, Cleveland: Meridian Books, 1959.

_____. (1955). *Aristotle's "Parva naturalia."* Oxford: Oxford University Press.

Sorabji, R. (1972). *Aristotle on Memory.* London: Trinity Press.

Vendler, Z. (1984). *The matter of minds.* Oxford: Oxford University Press.

Patricia Smith Churchland
Georgios Anagnostopoulos

ASSOCIATIONISM

Associationism is the doctrine that mental processes can be explained in terms of hypothetical relations, termed *associations,* between certain basic mental units, such as sensations, images, or ideas. (What constitutes a "basic mental unit" remains an issue, as discussed below.) *Philosophical associationism* is concerned with developing theories of epistemology and ontology, that is, with issues regarding the logical status of what we know and how we know it. *Psychological associationism* is concerned with developing theories of cognitive processes, including learning, memory, and thought. The doctrine applies to mental processes both in nonhuman animals and in humans.

Associationism has been cast in a weak and a strong form. The weak form maintains that some, but not necessarily all, aspects of cognition can be explained in the language of associations. This form of associationism can be traced to Aristotle, who proposed that the recollection of past information involves what today are called "associative retrieval mechanisms." The associative character of some acts of remembering is readily apparent to everyone, and modern theories of memory almost universally accord a prominent place to associative mechanisms. The strong form of associationism maintains that all aspects of cognition can be explained with associative principles and that nothing more is needed. This form emerged from the writings of seventeenth- and eighteenth-century British philosophers seeking a psychological equivalent of Isaac Newton's universal law of gravitation. The radical simplicity of explaining all cognition in terms of a single mechanism has remained an alluring challenge to many theorists, and associationism in its strong form can still be seen in recent connectionistic modeling of cognition.

History of Associationism

The first statement of an associative principle is conventionally attributed to the ancient Greek philosopher ARISTOTLE (384–322 B.C.), who proposed that "acts of recollection, as they occur in experience, are due to the fact that one movement [that is, thought] has by nature another that succeeds it in regular order" (1966, p. 328). In other words, one thought leads to another, an observation illustrated by many authors through the ages. The French philosopher and mathematician René Descartes (1596–1650), for example, described how he had come to feel more loving toward cross-eyed people because they reminded him of a girl he loved. In addition, at least since classical antiquity, practitioners of the "art of memory" have advocated the deliberate use of associations between different ideas as an aid to remembering. The best-known example of this is the "method of loci," said to have been used by the orator Simonides to identify victims buried under the rubble of a collapsed building. Simonides had associated people with the locations in which they sat.

Associationism as a doctrine did not really emerge until the seventeenth century, with the rise of the British empiricist philosophers, beginning with Thomas Hobbes (1588–1679). In his treatise *Leviathan,* Hobbes claimed that "besides Sense, and Thoughts, and the Trayne of thoughts [i.e., associations], the mind of man has no other motion." However, credit for the doctrine of associationism has traditionally been given to John Locke (1632–1704), who introduced the phrase "association of ideas" in his *Essay Concerning Human Understanding.* Despite their philosophical empiricism, the British associationists did not do empirical research and did not distinguish between philosophical and psychological issues. Nonetheless, the first systematic application of psychological associationism can be discerned in George Berkeley's analysis of the perception of space (1733). This was followed by David Hartley's attempt (1749) to supply a plausible physiological basis for associations; Hartley also applied principles of associationism to explain all aspects of human knowledge. This tradition culminated in the James Mill's associative analysis of thought and language in 1829.

The appearance of psychology as a separate discipline in the latter part of the nineteenth century coincided with the development of psychological theories based on associative principles, which tested those principles against empirical data. Hermann EBBINGHAUS (1850–1909) demonstrated how to conduct a rigorous experimental analysis of memory and reported the first controlled tests of associationism as an account of human memory. Wilhelm Wundt (1832–1920) and his students tried to account for the character of thoughts and ideas in terms of assocations among simpler elements. Edward THORNDIKE (1874–1949) applied associationism to the analysis of animal as well as

human behavior, and Ivan PAVLOV (1849–1936) developed a physiologically oriented associationism to explain the phenomena of conditioned reflexes. The ascendance of behaviorism, especially in American psychology, was accompanied by a rise in the status of associative accounts of many psychological phenomena. The decline of behaviorism during the 1950s and 1960s, and the emergence of the information-processing framework, led to waning interest in associationism. Beginning in the 1970s, however, computer-based models of cognition such as John Anderson and Gordon Bower's Human Associative Memory (HAM) model have nourished the growth of *neoassociationism.* Most recently, the associationist tradition has been expressed in parallel distributed processing (PDP) models of cognitive processes, described by Rumelhart and McClelland (1986), for example (see PARALLEL DISTRIBUTED PROCESSING MODELS OF MEMORY).

Three Issues of Associationism

Associationism identifies three major problems to solve for understanding cognition: (1) What are the basic elements that become associated, and what kinds of associations relate them? (2) Under what conditions are associations created? (3) How can complex phenomena be explained in terms of the associations of the basic elements?

Identifying the Basic Elements and Types of Associations

For Aristotle, the elements of association were thoughts, and the nature of a thought was left open. Much of the later tradition of associationism tried to define the elements that enter into associations more precisely. The attempt to restrict the basic elements of association led James Mill to his famous proposal that his idea of a house was literally composed of his ideas of all its constituents: "brick is one complex idea, mortar is another complex idea; these ideas, with ideas of position and quantity, compose my idea of a wall" (1869, p. 115), and so on. From a modern perspective, efforts such as Mill's were largely fruitless, and current views are similar to Aristotle's. Thus, depending on their level of analysis, different associative theories of human cognition may treat phonemes, letters, words, images, propositions, or episodes as the elements of association.

Attempts to restrict the elements of association in behavioristic theories have been largely abandoned. Thus, Edwin GUTHRIE's proposal that associations develop between movement-produced stimuli and muscle twitches, for example, has been supplanted by Edward TOLMAN's proposal that associations develop between perceptions and "molar" aspects of behavior. ("Molar" analyses describe actions in relation to their outcomes and are contrasted with "molecular" analyses. To say that someone stops a car at a red light is to provide a molar description; a molecular analysis of the same action would try to describe the actual movements involved. These would differ, depending on whether a hand brake or a foot brake was used and, for the latter, on whether the left or right foot was applied to the brake, for instance.)

Allowing different kinds of elements to enter into associations gives modern associative theories considerable flexibility. Additional flexibility is provided by recognizing the existence of different kinds of associations. Early associationists, such as David Hartley, only distinguished between *simultaneous associations,* in which elements are present at the same time, as in the red color and round shape of an apple, and *successive associations,* in which elements are present in succession, as in the red color of a whole apple and the taste of the first bite. These are nondirectional associations, however; thinking of either associated element leads to thought of the other.

Nondirectional association is illustrated at the top of Figure 1 with the pair Black-White. Modern associationism also allows a wide variety of different kinds of associations, illustrated in the remainder of Figure 1. Directional associations, in which one element calls forth the other, but not vice versa, as in Black-Board; chain associations, in which one element of a series calls forth not only its immediate successor but later elements as well, as in the alphabetic sequence ABC; labeled associations, in which one element is associated in different ways with other elements, as Robin is associated with Bird by the Is A relation and is associated with Can Sing by the Has As Property relation; and hierarchical associations, in which one element controls the associations over a subset of elements.

Identifying the Conditions of Association

Perhaps the most persistent thread of the associative tradition has been to identify the necessary

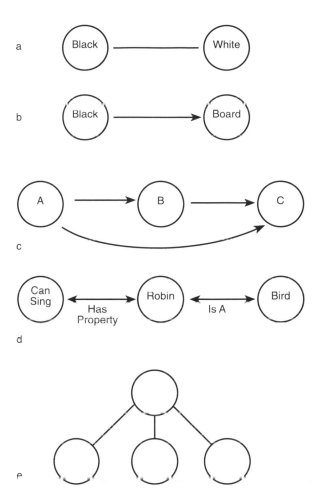

Figure 1. Illustration of various types of associations: (a) nondirected association; (b) directed association; (c) chain association; (d) labeled associations; and (e) hierarchical associations.

and sufficient conditions that establish associations between the elements of cognition. Aristotle proposed three principles by which associations are formed: *contiguity*—two thoughts that have been held in mind at the same time will become associated (e.g., lion and circus; witch and Halloween); *similarity*—one thought may be associated with a similar thought (e.g., lion and tiger; witch and wizard); and *contrast*—one thought may be associated with a contrasting thought (e.g., lion and lamb; Woody Allen and Arnold Schwarzenegger). After Aristotle many authors, including Locke, Hartley, and James Mill, tried to reduce the principles to the single principle that associations are established solely by contiguity. However, all of these authors were concerned with the *necessary* conditions for producing associations.

The first attempt to identify the *sufficient* conditions for producing associations was Thomas Brown's (1778–1820) description of the *secondary laws of association*. These nine laws stated that associations would be more or less likely, depending on (1) the duration of rehearsal, (2) the "liveliness" of the ideas, (3) the frequency of repetition, (4) the recency of exposure, (5) the degree of freedom from competing associations, (6) constitutional differences, (7) emotional tone, (8) bodily state, and (9) meaningfulness to the individual. Brown's list remains sound today.

A major discovery of modern research concerns the degree to which a particular experience will produce new associations or strengthen existing ones. Little or no change in associations will occur if a given experience is well predicted by prior associations. For example, someone who first associates high fever with flu will not readily form an association between achiness and flu, if later both high fever and achiness occur with flu. This regularity is referred to as the *Rescorla-Wagner rule* in animal learning and as the *delta rule* in connectionist modeling.

Explaining Complex Behavior in Terms of Simple Associations

The challenge of associationism is to explain complex phenomena in terms of simple associative principles. Its glory lies in successful attempts to do so.

Early associationists, such as Locke, emphasized the ability of associative principles to explain bizarre behavior. Locke, for example, related the story of a young man who had learned to dance in a room that contained a particular chest, and was afterward able to dance only in the presence of the chest. Sigmund FREUD (1856–1939), who relied on the *method of free association* in his clinical work, used associationism to explain bizarre dream content. In a famous study, the founder of behaviorism, John WATSON (1878–1958), apparently created an association between white furry animals and fear in the young boy known as little Albert by producing a loud sound when the boy was in the presence of a white rat.

More recent associationists have been equally interested in using associative principles to explain normal behavior. Beginning with Pavlov's demonstration that puppies must learn to associate the sight of food with its taste, many examples of associative learning during normal development have been found. As noted above, the assumption that associations play some role in memory is ancient. However, the importance of such a role has been greatly amplified in modern theories of learning and memory, which provide many examples of quantitative descriptions of recall and recognition. A tour de force of associationism is the simulation of language acquisition with the NETTalk model (Sejnowski and Rosenberg, 1987). Cultural processes have also been examined in terms of associative principles.

Criticisms of Associationism

Associationism has been criticized for being (a) empty of real content, (b) logically inadequate, and (c) scientifically inadequate. The first criticism is justified when "association" is used as a synonym for "relation." In modern associative theories, however, associations are just one type of relation. The second criticism is justified for a particular set of assumptions that characterize the *terminal metapostulate,* or TMP (Bever et al., 1968), but many associationists reject the TMP. The third criticism can be resolved only in the marketplace of ideas that makes science a dynamic enterprise. Historically, associationism has resisted including any structural or organizational constructs other than associations. However, modern associative theories have conceded, to a greater or lesser extent, the need for some organizational constructs. Associationism therefore remains a vital perspective on psychological processes.

REFERENCES

Anderson, John R., and Bower, Gordon, H. (1973). *Human associative memory.* Washington, D.C.: Winston. Chapter 2 presents a capsule history of associationism from a neoassociationist view.

Aristotle. *De memoria et reminiscentia.* Translated by J. I. Beare. Selection 65 in R. J. Herrnstein and E. G. Boring, eds., *Source book in the history of psychology,* pp. 328–329. Cambridge, Mass.: Harvard University Press, 1966.

Bever, T. G., Fodor, J., and Garrett, M. A. (1968). A formal limitation of associationism. In T. R. Dixon and D. L. Horton, eds., *Verbal behavior and general behavior theory.* Englewood Cliffs, N.J.: Prentice-Hall. A statement of the terminal metapostulate.

Dickinson, A. (1980). *Contemporary animal learning theory.* New York: Cambridge University Press.

Ebbinghaus, H. (1964). *Memory: A contribution to experimental psychology.* Translated by H. A. Ruger and C. E. Bussenius. New York: Dover. (Originally published in 1885).

Freud, Sigmund. (1960). *The psychopathology of everyday life,* trans. by James Strachey. London: Hogarth Press. First published 1901. This book gives many examples of associationist reasoning without demanding mastery of psychoanalytic theory; Chapter 1 provides an excellent illustration of Freud's associative theorizing.

Guthrie, E.R. (1935). *The psychology of learning.* New York: Harper & Row.

Hartley, David. (1749). *Observations on man, his frame, his duty, and his expectations.* London and Bath: Richardson.

Mill, James. (1869). *Analysis of the phenomena of the human mind,* 2nd ed. London: Longman, Green, Reader & Dyer.

Rumelhart, David, and McClelland, James. (1986). *Parallel distributed processing.* Cambridge, Mass.: MIT Press.

Sejnowski, T., and Rosenberg, C. (1987). Parallel networks that learn to pronounce English text. *Complex Systems 1,* 145–168.

Thorndike, E.L. (1903). *Educational psychology.* New York: Lemcke and Buechner.

J. W. Whitlow, Jr.

ATTENTION DEFICIT DISORDER

See Learning Disabilities

ATTENTION AND MEMORY

Attention and memory are intricately related in fact and intimately related in theory. The facts suggest that attention determines what goes into memory and what comes out of it, and that memory provides attention with the choices among which it selects. William JAMES (1890) saw a fundamental similarity between attention and primary or short-term memory; primary memory contained the current contents of attention. Miller (1956) pointed out similar capacity limitations in attention and short-term memory paradigms. Broadbent's (1958) single-channel theory was a theory of mem-

ory as much as one of attention. Like James, Broadbent identified short-term memory with the contents of the attention. But unlike James, he proposed an information-processing model to account for attentional and memorial phenomena. Later, Atkinson and Shiffrin (1968) proposed complex models in which attention and memory worked together. They distinguished among sensory, short-term, and long-term memories and proposed that attention governs the interactions between them, determining what information goes where in the system. Recent memory theories address the computations underlying encoding and retrieval, and focus on cuing and context effects as the major phenomena to be explained. Cuing and context effects are brought about by manipulating attention, so they can be thought of as attention effects as much as memory effects. Recent attention theories address skill acquisition and automaticity, focusing on the learning mechanism and the conditions under which skills can be acquired. Skills and automatisms necessarily depend on memory, and so can be thought of as memory effects as much as attention effects.

What Is Attention?

Attention is a central selective process involved in perception, cognition, and action. It is defined operationally by requiring subjects to choose between equally potent sources of stimulation or equally valid ways of interpreting a stimulus situation. Researchers commonly distinguish between *input selection,* in which subjects must choose to process one of several potential stimuli and ignore the others (e.g., listening to one conversation at a cocktail party), and *analyzer selection,* in which subjects must choose one of several ways of processing a stimulus (e.g., deciding whether a word rhymes with *play* versus whether it represents a living thing). There is a great deal of research on the selective nature of attention, addressing both input and analyzer selection.

Until recently, it was generally believed that the capacity for attentional selection was limited. This idea was central in *capacity* or *resource* theories, such as Kahneman's (1973). According to such theories, the quality of performance depends on the amount of attention deployed, and a great deal of evidence can be interpreted in that way. Recently, however, several researchers, arguing on logical and empirical grounds, have challenged the idea that there are resource limitations on attention. They claim that the requirement for coherent action, not the scarcity of resources, forces people to perceive, think, and act selectively; and they provide alternative interpretations for the effects previously attributed to capacity limitations.

Research on memory and attention has addressed the selective nature of attention as well as the effects of attentional capacity limitations. Memory has been one of several dependent variables used in debates about selective attention, addressing what happens to items that are not attended (some theories claim unattended items receive no processing; others claim they receive attenuated processing) and the locus of selection (where attentional selection occurs in the cognitive system, at early or late stages of processing). The effects of capacity limitations have been addressed in research investigating the *effort hypothesis,* which claims that memory performance is better the greater the effort (capacity) expended at encoding.

Attention and Sensory Memory

The traditional three-store model distinguishes SENSORY MEMORY, *short-term memory* (STM), and *long-term memory* (LTM) (see, e.g., Atkinson and Shiffrin, 1968). There are several sensory memories, one for each modality. Sensory memory represents the interface between perception and cognition. Sensory memory is unlimited in capacity and brief in duration. It represents the perceptual aftereffects of stimulation, maintaining a "literal" copy of the stimulus for 250 milliseconds to 3 seconds, depending on the modality and the method of measurement.

Attention is commonly viewed as the mechanism that transfers information from sensory memory to STM. Sensory memory is *preattentive,* containing relatively unprocessed information that has not yet been categorized. Attending to items in sensory memory transfers them to STM, assigning them a categorical representation. The transfer process is thought to be serial, one item at a time.

The idea that sensory memory is preattentive relates it to the controversy surrounding *early versus late selection,* which is concerned with the level of processing that can be attained without attention (i.e., before attention enters the chain of processing). Advocates of early selection claim that only physical features can be processed without attention (hence, only physical features are held in sensory memory); advocates of late selection claim that semantic features can be processed without attention (hence, semantic features are held in sensory memory). The debate has continued since the 1950s with no sign of resolution in sight.

Attention and STM

Attention and STM are closely related: Attention is the process that keeps information active in the mind, and STM is the place where it is kept active. Short-term memory is severely limited in capacity—memory span rarely exceeds nine items—and is relatively brief in duration, lasting about 20 seconds if it is not refreshed. Attention has been invoked to explain both of these characteristics.

The capacity of STM has been related theoretically to the capacity of attention. In resource theories, STM is the portion of LTM that is currently active. The activation derives from external stimulation and from the allocation of attentional capacity. The amount of LTM that can be activated is limited by the amount of capacity that can be allocated. Consequently, STM will be limited. Other theories, such as Broadbent's, emphasize temporal properties of memory processes; STM is the amount of information that can be held in a rehearsal buffer without being refreshed (i.e., the number of things that can be held in mind and repeated covertly). Information is cycled through the rehearsal buffer at a rate determined by the kind of processing required. In verbal rehearsal, the rate depends on the rate of articulation. Roughly, STM contains the amount that can be articulated in 1.5 seconds.

The duration of STM depends on the availability of attention to maintain information. If attention is paid continuously, the information can be retained indefinitely; if attention is distracted, information is lost rapidly. This is amply demonstrated in the well-replicated Brown-Peterson distractor task, in which people are given short lists (e.g., three consonants) and are engaged in a distractor task (e.g., counting backwards by threes) for a brief time. Information may be forgotten completely if attention is distracted for 20 seconds. Muter (1980) found complete decay within 3 seconds if people did not expect to have to recall the memory list.

Attention and Long-Term Memory

In three-store models, attention (in the form of control processes, such as rehearsal) was the process that transferred information from STM to LTM. A number of experiments, such as Rundus's (1971), demonstrated that long-term retention depended on the amount of rehearsal an item received. The more rehearsal, the better the retention. Research conducted in traditions other than the three-store model confirms the importance of attention as a determinant of long-term storage. Attention is sufficient for long-term storage, and it appears to be necessary as well.

The sufficiency of attention for long-term storage is demonstrated by the well-replicated equivalence of incidental and intentional learning when attention is controlled (e.g., Craik and Tulving, 1975). There appears to be no "store" instruction in the cognitive repertoire. People do not need to intend to remember something; they need only attend to it. When people intend to commit something to memory, they attend to the item. Intending to store information amounts to deliberately attending to it.

The necessity of attention for long-term storage is evidenced by the poor retention of unattended items. If information is not attended, it is generally lost within seconds (i.e., as soon as sensory memory decays). Moreover, retention of attended items depends on the amount or the quality of attention available at input: Items presented when attention is taxed by a concurrent task are poorly remembered, relative to single-task control conditions.

Claims by Hasher and Zacks (1979) and others that some attributes, such as frequency and location, are processed automatically would seem to challenge the conclusion that attention is necessary for long-term storage. However, the challenge depends on what one means by automaticity. Automatic processing is often defined as processing without attention (e.g., Posner and Snyder, 1975). Another approach is to define it as processing that follows as an obligatory consequence of attention to a stimulus (e.g., Logan, 1988). There is abundant evidence that location and frequency information is not processed independently of attention. Concurrent tasks that load attention, for example, im-

pair memory for location and frequency. Thus, location and frequency are not processed automatically in the sense that they are processed independently of attention. Rather, the data are consistent with the idea that automatic processing is an obligatory consequence of attention. Location and frequency information is encoded whenever a person attends to an item. How well it is encoded depends on the prevailing conditions of attention; the better the quality of attention, the better the encoding. This view of automaticity suggests that attention is both necessary and sufficient for long-term storage.

Conclusions about attention and long-term storage apply primarily to studies of explicit memory. Very few studies have examined the role of attention in IMPLICIT MEMORY. The results with implicit memory are not clear. On the one hand, there is some evidence of long-term retention of unattended information (Eich, 1984). On the other hand, there is evidence that dual-task conditions impair some kinds of implicit learning (Nissen and Bullemer, 1987). Further research will be required before firm conclusions can be reached.

Attention, Encoding, and Retrieval

A great deal of memory research has addressed the effects of variation in conditions of encoding (levels-of-processing effects) and variation in the match between conditions of encoding and conditions of retrieval (encoding specificity effects). These effects can be interpreted as attentional effects produced by variation in analyzer selection. Levels-of-processing effects reflect the memorial consequences of attending to different aspects of a stimulus. Attention to semantic properties generally leads to better memory than does attention to physical properties. Attention theories do not explain why "deeper" processing leads to better retention than "shallower" processing, but they do explain why different things should be remembered after different orienting tasks: Memory depends on the stimulus as it is attended to and interpreted by the subject, not on the stimulus as presented by the experimenter. The same physical stimulus presented under different orienting tasks lead to different memory representations.

Encoding specificity effects can also be interpreted as attentional effects. In general, memory is better when the conditions of retrieval match the conditions of encoding than when they differ. Conditions of encoding and retrieval may be external stimulus events, such as the context in which the memory task occurs (e.g., testing memory on the surface of the ocean or on the bottom), or they may be internal states induced by orienting tasks. In either case, memory is better when subjects are likely to attend to the same things at study and at test, either because the environment contains the same things to attend to or because the orienting task directs attention to the same stimulus properties. Studies in this tradition have shown that changes in context have more powerful effects when they are noticed (i.e., attended) by the subject than when they are not.

(See also CODING PROCESSES.)

Attention, Automaticity, and Memory

Recent research on automaticity has special relevance to memory. Empirically, automaticity refers to processing that is fast, effortless, and obligatory, such as reading familiar words or recognizing close friends and members of one's immediate family. Theoretically, automaticity is defined in terms of some underlying mechanism. In the context of capacity theories, it used to be defined as processing without attention (without attentional resources). A more modern approach is to define automaticity as processing that depends on memory retrieval. From this perspective, novice performance is thought to depend on some general algorithm for performing the task, whereas skilled or automatized performance depends on retrieval of past solutions from memory without executing the algorithm. Attention is not withdrawn from processing as performance becomes automatic. Instead, attention is directed to different aspects of processing, to what the stimulus retrieves from memory rather than to the algorithm that would apply to the stimulus (see Logan, 1988). From this perspective, automaticity is a memory phenomenon, governed by the theoretical and empirical principles that govern memory. This opens up new areas of research, relating automaticity to the memory literature.

An older issue concerns memory for stimuli that are processed automatically. Common lore and some data suggest that stimuli processed automatically are not well remembered. The resource perspective would interpret poor memory as evidence

that stimuli processed automatically did not receive attention. The memory perspective would interpret poor memory as an interference effect: Stimuli that can be processed automatically are very familiar, very similar to many stimuli that have been processed in the past. Discriminating one such stimulus from a host of similar ones would be difficult. By contrast, unfamiliar stimuli would be easy to remember because very few like them have been processed before.

Future Directions

Attention and memory are intricately related in fact and intimately related in theory, but the relations have only begun to be explored. The evidence suggests that attention is important to virtually every aspect of memory and that memory is important to virtually every aspect of attention. It suggests that the relations between attention and memory will be fertile grounds for future research. However, the surface has only been scratched. Concerted effort, both theoretical and empirical, will be necessary before the field will bear the fruit it is capable of producing.

REFERENCES

Atkinson, R. C., and Shiffrin, R. M. (1968). Human memory: A proposed system and its control processes. In K. W. Spence and J. T. Spence, eds., *The psychology of learning and motivation: Advances in theory and research,* vol. 2. New York: Academic Press.

Broadbent, D. E. (1958). *Perception and communication.* London: Pergamon.

Craik, F. I. M., and Tulving, E. (1975). Depth of processing and the retention of words in episodic memory. *Journal of Experimental Psychology: General 104,* 268–294.

Eich, E. (1984). Memory for unattended events: Remembering with and without awareness. *Memory and Cognition 12,* 105–111.

Hasher, L., and Zacks, R. T. (1979). Automatic and effortful processes in memory. *Journal of Experimental Psychology: General 108,* 356–388.

James, W. (1890). *Principles of psychology.* Boston: Holt.

Kahneman, D. (1973). *Attention and effort.* Englewood Cliffs, N.J.: Prentice-Hall.

Logan, G. D. (1988). Toward an instance theory of automatization. *Psychological Review 95,* 492–527.

Miller, G. A. (1956). The magical number seven, plus or minus two: Some limits on our capacity for processing information. *Psychological Review 63*, 81–97.

Muter, P. (1980). Very rapid forgetting. *Memory and Cognition 8*, 174–179.

Nissen, M. J., and Bullemer, P. (1987). Attentional requirements of learning: Evidence from performance measures. *Cognitive Psychology 19*, 1–32.

Posner, M. I., and Snyder, C. R. R. (1975). Attention and cognitive control. In R. L. Solso, ed., *Information processing and cognition: The Loyola symposium*, pp. 55–85. Hillsdale, N.J.: Erlbaum.

Rundus, D. (1971). Analysis of rehearsal processes in free recall. *Journal of Experimental Psychology 89*, 63–77.

Gordon D. Logan

AUDITORY MEMORY

See Modality Effects

AVOIDANCE LEARNING, NEURAL SUBSTRATES OF

Animals learn to avoid pain provided that warning stimuli are available to signal pain-inducing events. Such learning is generally of two types, active and inhibitory. *Active avoidance* refers to movements learned in response to warning stimuli for the purpose of avoiding pain. *Inhibitory avoidance* refers to immobility, learned because movement in the presence of warning stimuli has previously led to pain.

Limbic and Motor Systems

Research implicates the brain's limbic and motor systems in the mediation of avoidance learning. The limbic system is a vast network of interconnected regions including the hippocampus, amygdala, limbic thalamus, and cingulate area of the cerebral cortex. Relevant parts of the motor system include subcortical structures of the basal ganglia: the caudate nucleus and the nucleus accumbens. Since virtually all laboratory studies of avoidance learning involve locomotion (or its inhibition),

areas of the brain stem concerned with the initiation and maintenance of locomotion are also involved. (SEE GUIDE TO THE ANATOMY OF THE BRAIN.)

Theoretical Overview: WHAT and WHEN

Available data indicate that in avoidance learning the motor system acts as a WHAT system, and the limbic system acts as a WHEN system. The WHAT system determines what is to be done, that is, the particular behavior to be performed. Its functions include learning and remembering the response to be performed; making ready or "priming" the response when the avoidance situation is encountered; and executing the response. The WHAT system is relatively poor when it comes to remembering important signals in the environment, including the warning stimuli that call for avoidance behavior. These are the functions for which the WHEN system is specialized. This system learns about and remembers the warning stimuli, and it issues *command volleys* of neuronal activity that tell the WHAT system precisely when to execute the avoidance response (see Figure 1).

Data supporting these ideas come from studies of the effects of experimentally induced brain damage (lesions) and from studies of the activity of brain neurons during avoidance learning. The relevant research, summarized below, is reviewed by Gabriel (1990). Citations of studies not included in the review are given in the text below.

Active Avoidance Learning

Experimental lesions in the *medial dorsal* (MD) and *anterior* (AN) nuclei of the limbic thalamus, or lesions of the cingulate cortical areas that receive input from these thalamic nuclei, render rats, cats, and rabbits incapable of active avoidance learning. Lesions in only one of the nuclei, or in the cingulate cortical projection field of a single nucleus, yield partial learning deficits as described below. The laboratory tasks used in these studies involve learning to jump over a barrier or learning to step in an activity wheel, in order to avoid mild electric shock signaled by tone or light warning stimuli. The inability to learn in animals with these lesions is a true learning deficit, not an inability to move or to perceive the warning stimuli.

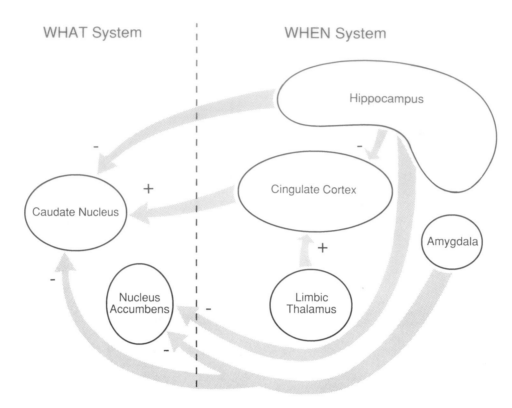

Figure 1.   Schematic diagram of the information flows among brain structures involved in avoidance learning. The plus and minus signs represent, respectively, transmissions relevant to active and inhibitory avoidance behavior.

The specific involvement of the limbic structures in avoidance learning is further supported by data indicating that cerebellar lesions, which block *classical conditioning* of eyeblink responses, do not affect avoidance learning in rabbits.

Studies of *neuronal activity* during active avoidance learning by rabbits in the activity wheel task have shown that limbic thalamic and cingulate cortical neurons "learn" to produce impulses in response to the warning tone that signals shock. Impulse rate in trained rabbits increased just after the warning stimulus and reached maximum just before the rabbits stepped, suggesting that stepping was triggered by the neuronal activity.

Cingulate cortical neurons send axons to motor areas such as the caudate nucleus. Active avoidance learning is impaired in animals with lesions in the caudate nucleus. Therefore, the flow of nerve impulses from the cingulate cortex to the caudate nucleus and possibly to other motor areas is likely responsible for initiating active avoidance responses. At the theoretical level, the role of the caudate nucleus represents the function of the WHAT system, and the information flow from the limbic thalamus and the cingulate cortex to the caudate nucleus represents the command volley issued by the WHEN system.

Two forms of neuronal "learning" have been noted in the limbic thalamus and in the cingulate cortex during the acquisition of the stepping avoidance response by rabbits. One is *discriminative* or *selective neuronal activity,* a higher rate of nerve impulses in trained animals to the warning tone than to differently pitched nonwarning tones. The second form of neuronal learning is *excitatory modulation* (EM), a dramatic increase of impulse firing rate, in trained rabbits, in response to both warning and nonwarning tones. Two facts indicate that EM is truly a learning-related change and not merely a reflection of general excitement or arousal: (1) EM does not occur when rabbits experience repeated sessions with shock and nonwarning tones, that is, tones that do not predict the occurrence of shock; (2) EM occurs at different rates in different nuclei of the limbic thalamus. (General *arousal* or excitement would be expected to increase neuronal activity simultaneously in many brain areas.) Although they are combined in the limbic thalamus, EM and the selective activity have different brain origins.

Origins of EM

Experimental lesions in a large fiber tract (the *mammillothalamic tract*) that runs from the hypothalamus to the AN block the development of EM in the AN, and such lesions diminish performance efficiency of the avoidance response. Binding of the high-affinity ligand *oxotremorine* to *muscarinic acetylcholine receptors* increases in the AN during learning (Vogt et al., 1991), and *scopolamine hydrobromide*, which blocks these receptors, abolishes the EM in the AN, as well as performance of the avoidance behavior. These results suggest that EM is due to stimulation by acetylcholine of the increased numbers of receptors in the AN. Acetylcholine is available from axons of *brain-stem tegmental neurons* that terminate in the AN. Cholinergic stimulation may increase the excitation of AN neurons by enhancing the release of the mammillothalamic tract neurotransmitter or by increasing the excitability of AN neurons in response to that neurotransmitter. Thus, to summarize, EM originates in the limbic thalamus and has the function of amplifying the selective discharges as they are relayed to the cingulate cortex.

Origins of Selective Activity

Available data indicate that selective firing in the limbic thalamus may originate in the *medial geniculate nucleus* (MGN), the thalamic portion of the ascending sensory (auditory) pathway for hearing. Several studies have shown that MGN neurons develop selective discharges during learning. Pathways whereby selective activity accesses the limbic thalamus are as yet unknown.

Inhibitory Avoidance Learning

Many experimental procedures have been used to study inhibitory avoidance learning, such as the delivery of shock after performance of an unlearned response by rats (moving from a lighted area to an innately preferred dark area), the delivery of shock after performance of a previously learned response (running in a maze alley for food or water reinforcement), or assessing choice behavior such as the relative amount of time spent in neutral areas compared with time spent in areas previously established as dangerous. The timing of avoidance responses is not greatly critical for mastery of commonly employed inhibitory avoidance tasks because subjects' are not required, as in active avoidance tasks, to produce discrete behaviors at particular moments. Instead, behavior must be suppressed in response to configurations of static, continuously present environmental stimuli.

Damage to the *hippocampal formation,* a limbic area of the cerebral cortex importantly involved in complex memory functions, is detrimental to inhibitory avoidance learning. Hippocampal involvement may reflect the fact that the warning stimuli in many inhibitory avoidance tasks have typically been experimental environments or places, rather than discrete stimuli such as tones. Successful performance in such tasks depends on the *cognitive mapping* functions of the hippocampus, including remembering whether particular environments are dangerous or safe (see Nadel, O'Keefe, and Black, 1975). This raises the question of how hippocampal cognitive mapping operations give rise to the suppression of movement toward dangerous environments. It has been suggested that this suppression is the result of flow of information over a massive WHEN system pathway from the *subicular complex* of the hippocampal formation to the nucleus accumbens, a WHAT system component implicated in the suppression of locomotion. However, other studies suggest that the caudate nucleus is involved in the suppression of behavior in inhibitory avoidance learning.

Lesions of the *amygdala* selectively impair inhibitory avoidance learning in highly aversive learning situations, but not when mild aversive stimulation is employed, and not in simple appetitive learning situations (McGaugh and Cahill, 1990). Amygdaloid projections to the nucleus accumbens may thus represent a critical pathway for the flow of command volleys from the WHEN system to the WHAT system in the highly aversive learning situations. In short, hippocampus, amygdala, and possibly other limbic WHEN system areas are likely sources of training-induced command volleys to the WHAT system that inhibit movement. Particular WHEN system areas may subserve specific functions such as cognitive mapping or emergency signaling in highly aversive tasks.

REFERENCES

Gabriel, M. (1990). Functions of the anterior and posterior cingulate cortex during avoidance learning in rabbits. In H. B. M. Ulyings, C. G. Van Eden, J. P. C. DeBruin, M. A. Corner, and M. G. P. Feenstra, eds., The prefrontal cortex: Its structure, function and pathology. *Progress in Brain Research 85,* 457–473.

McGaugh, J. L., and Cahill, L. (1990). Amygdaloid complex lesions differentially affect retention of tasks using appetitive and aversive reinforcement. *Behavioral Neuroscience 104,* 532–543.

Nadel, L., O'Keefe, J., and Black, A. (1975). Slam on the brakes: A critique of Altman, Brunner and Bayer's response-inhibition model of hippocampal function. *Behavioral Biology 14,* 151–162.

Vogt, B. A., Gabriel, M., Vogt, L. J., Poremba, A., Jensen, E. L., Kubota, Y., and Kang, E. (1991). Muscarinic receptor binding increases in anterior thalamus and cingulate cortex during discriminative avoidance learning. *Journal of Neuroscience 11,* 1508–1514.

Michael Gabriel

B

BARTLETT, FREDERIC

Frederic Charles Bartlett (1886–1969) was born on October 20, 1886, in Stow on the Wold, Gloucestershire. He studied literature, logic, and philosophy before becoming a tutor at Cambridge in 1909. At Cambridge his interests turned to psychology; he was awarded a fellowship at St. John's College in 1913 and obtained a first-class degree in moral sciences in 1914. At that time Cambridge was in the forefront of the movement to make experimental psychology a recognized branch of science in the British university system; C. S. Myers had not only campaigned for Cambridge to build a laboratory, a wish fulfilled in 1912, but also had helped to found the *British Journal of Psychology* in 1904. When World War I broke out in 1914, Myers appointed Bartlett as "relief director" of the laboratory. Bartlett instigated research into a variety of topics, including studies of the detection of faint sounds, a project in which he collaborated with E. M. Smith, whom he married in 1920, and studies of individual differences in the way subjects described pictures. These individual differences, Bartlett believed, reflected above all subjective interests and socially determined interpretations; he ascribed the latter to "conventionalization," and over the next few years he focused his attention on the role of conventionalization not only in perception but also in the retrieval of memories.

In 1922 Myers left Cambridge to head the National Institute for Industrial Psychology, and Bartlett was appointed reader and director of the Cambridge laboratory; two years later he also became editor of the *British Journal of Psychology,* a position he occupied for twenty-four years. In 1931 he was elected to a chair in experimental psychology at Cambridge. During his term as director of the laboratory, the number of faculty members grew and an increasing number of students graduated in experimental psychology. An indication of the success of the program was that of the sixteen professorships of psychology in Great Britain in 1957, ten were held by students of Myers and Bartlett. During the years between 1922 and the outbreak of World War II, Bartlett continued his

Figure 1. F. C. Bartlett. *Courtesy University of Cambridge.*

71

studies on conventionalization and memorizing and wrote three books that attest to his interest in applied psychology: *Psychology and the Soldier* (1927), which dealt with personnel selection and war neuroses, among other topics; *Psychology and Primitive Culture* (1923), in which he stressed the similarities rather than the differences between people in different societies; and *The Problem of Noise* (1934).

The work for which Bartlett is best known is *Remembering* (1932), an elaboration of his research on conventionalization. In it he describes how he used two experimental paradigms to study memory, the method of repeated reproduction, in which a subject studied a story or a picture and then reproduced it several times over a period of weeks or months; and the method of serial reproduction, in which a subject recalled a story or a picture, then passed this production on to a second subject, who studied and reproduced it, and so on down a chain of subjects. Bartlett observed that the two methods yielded similar results: recall was not duplicative but represented a reconstruction of the original story or picture based on memories of key details; the reconstruction could be biased by conventionalization and importation.

Since recall was not simply a duplication of the same pattern over and over again, Bartlett, following the suggestion of his neurologist friend Sir Henry Head, argued that memories were not stored as static traces waiting to be revived; instead they formed parts of large complexes, called *schemata*, in which individual components could be changed any time there was a retrieval act. He argued that if traces were lifeless entities waiting to be revived, we should always be at the mercy of old habits; but with a schema one could revive individual memories that had been laid down at widely varying periods of time and from them form new combinations. He believed that consciousness had evolved for this purpose, the "looking at" or "turning round on" one's own schemata; the ability to do this was greatly aided by the use of visual images in addition to speech memory.

This kind of insight could not be gained, argued Bartlett, from studies of rote memory along the lines of Ebbinghaus's experiments; furthermore, the schema theory allowed closer ties to be formed between experimental psychology and social psychology. Schemata, he believed, were held together by "appetites, instincts, interests, and ideals," the first laid down particularly in childhood; the latter two, in later life.

Bartlett's career following the publication of *Remembering* was mainly devoted to applied psychology; he was the director of the Applied Psychology Unit at Cambridge from 1944 to 1953 and was knighted in 1948. In a book entitled *Thinking* (1958) he discussed the development of the schema theory as an example of scientific thinking. He died on September 30, 1969. An obituary and bibliography is supplied by Broadbent (1970); a biography is given by Crampton (1978); and Bartlett himself wrote a short autobiography in 1936.

REFERENCES

Bartlett, F. C. (1923). *Psychology and primitive culture.* London: Cambridge University Press.

———— (1927). *Psychology and the soldier.* London: Cambridge University Press.

———— (1934). *The problem of noise.* London: Cambridge University Press.

———— (1932). *Remembering: A study in experimental and social psychology.* London: Cambridge University Press. (Paperback ed., 1964.)

———— (1936). "Autobiography." In C. Murchison, ed., *History of psychology in autobiography,* vol. 3. Worcester, Mass.: Clark University Press.

———— (1958). *Thinking: An experimental and social study.* London: George Allen and Unwin.

Broadbent, D. E. (1970). "Obituary of Sir F. C. Bartlett." *Biographical Memoirs of Fellows of the Royal Society* 16, 1–16.

Crampton, C. (1978). The Cambridge school. The life, works, and influence of James Ward, W. H. R. Rivers, C. S. Myers and Sir Frederic Bartlett. Ph.D. thesis, University of Edinburgh.

David J. Murray

BASAL FOREBRAIN

See Amnesia, Organic; Guide to the Anatomy of the Brain

BASAL GANGLIA

See Guide to the Anatomy of the Brain

BEHAVIORAL PHENOMENA: ACTIVE AND PASSIVE AVOIDANCE LEARNING

Avoidance learning is the behavioral product of an instrumental (operant) training procedure in which a more or less predictable aversive event, typically electric shock, does *not* occur contingent upon the occurrence or nonoccurrence of a specified response by the learning organism. Avoidance training occurs in two forms: active and passive. In the active form, the avoidance contingency depends on the *occurrence* of a specified response on the part of the organism; in the passive form, the avoidance contingency depends on the *nonoccurrence* (i.e., the suppression) of some specified response. The response to be suppressed may be either spontaneous or learned by virtue of prior reward training. In both forms, however, the avoidance contingency consists of the prevention or omission of a somewhat predictable noxious event. Noxious events are defined in terms of the preference relation in which the absence of the event is preferred (measured by choice) to the presence of the event. Usually the noxious event is electric shock, but loud noise, blasts of air, and high and low temperatures have been used.

Avoidance training also utilizes one of two procedures: discrete-trial or free-operant. In the discrete-trial procedure a distinctive stimulus, called a *warning signal* (WS), signals the organism that the occurrence of the aversive event (e.g., electric shock) is imminent. In most experiments the WS-shock interval is 5 to 60 seconds in duration. In the active form, making the specified response during the WS-shock interval terminates the WS and prevents the occurrence of the shock. In the passive form, suppression of the specified response during the WS-shock interval prevents the occurrence of the shock. In both forms an *intertrial interval* (ITI) intervenes between successive presentations of the WS, usually in the range of 0.5 to 5.0 minutes.

In the active free-operant procedure there are no discrete trials signaled by WSs. Instead, the avoidance contingency is dependent on time. Specifically, two timers control events: a response-shock (R-S) timer (e.g., set for 30 seconds) and a shock-shock (S-S) timer (e.g., set for 5 seconds). Training starts with the S-S timer operating. Every time it runs out, it restarts and delivers an inescapable shock of some duration (e.g., 0.5 second). The specified response turns off the S-S timer and starts the R-S timer. Every additional response resets the R-S timer to its full value. If the R-S timer runs out, it presents a shock and starts the S-S timer (Sidman, 1953). This procedure has been used only in the active form. A variation of this procedure eliminates the S-S timer and makes shock termination contingent upon the specified response rather than upon a fixed duration of shock.

In addition, a free-operant passive procedure, known as *punishment,* simply takes a response, which occurs spontaneously or by virtue of prior reward training, and makes shock or some other aversive event contingent on the occurrence of that response. The response is usually suppressed. This is also called *passive avoidance training.* It has been used in a procedure in which an animal such as a mouse or rat runs from a brightly lighted elevated platform into a dark compartment where it receives a single electric shock. The tendency to enter the dark compartment is innate, and the single punishment results in subsequent long latencies to reenter the dark compartment. This is called one-trial passive avoidance training, and it has been used extensively in the study of memory because the learning event is fixed in time, which allows analysis and manipulation of temporarily constrained neuropharmacological and endocrine processes associated with learning. Alternatively, a hungry animal may initially be rewarded with food for pressing a lever and subsequently shocked for making that same response. Usually several shocks are required to suppress the lever pressing.

Warner (1932) was the first to use a discrete-trial active avoidance procedure to study the association span of the white rat (using WS-shock intervals of 1 to 30 seconds); he used what has become known as a shuttle box, a two-compartment box in which the animal is required to run or jump back and forth between the two compartments to avoid the shock.

The reason these procedures and the behaviors they produce have been of interest to psychologists stems from early behaviorism in this country. Watson and, especially, Thorndike postulated that learned responses were a product of their consequences. That is, a response occurs, a pleasurable or aversive event ensues, and the response is reinforced (increases) if the event is pleasurable or punished (decreases) if the event is aversive.

Hilgard and Marquis (1940), two early behavioral theorists, had trouble accounting for avoidance learning because it was a product of a procedure where the reinforcing event was the response-contingent *absence* of an event, not the response-contingent *presence* of an event:

> Learning in this [avoidance] situation appears to be based in a real sense on the avoidance of the shock. It differs clearly from other types of instrumental training in which the conditioned response is followed by a definite stimulus change—food or the cessation of shock [reward training (positive reinforcement) or escape training (negative reinforcement)]. In instrumental avoidance training the new response is strengthened in the absence of any such stimulus; indeed, it is strengthened because of the absence of such a stimulus. Absence of stimulation can obviously have an influence on behavior only if there exists some sort of preparation for or expectation of the stimulation. (pp. 58–59)

This theoretical problem was ostensibly solved by Mowrer (1950), supported by Solomon and Wynne (1954) and Rescorla and Solomon (1967), by postulating that *Pavlovian conditioning* of fear on early escape trials, in which the WS is paired with shock, provided the acquired motivation to terminate the WS (now a conditioned aversive stimulus), thus providing secondary (acquired) negative reinforcement for the escape-from-fear response (i.e., the avoidance response). Others thought that the fear response was *instrumentally* reinforced by the termination of shock (Miller, 1951), but the upshot was the same: Reduction of fear by termination of the WS, whether acquired by Pavlovian or instrumental means, was the source of the acquired negative reinforcement for the avoidance response. Thus, two processes were postulated, acquisition of fear during escape trials (by Pavlovian or operant conditioning) and acquisition of the instrumental avoidance response, reinforced by fear reduction. This theoretical interpretation was supported by the results of an elegant experiment by Kamin (1956). Additional research in support of two-process theory used a transfer paradigm in which animals were given Pavlovian conditioning in one situation, and the effects of those conditioned stimuli were observed when they were subsequently superimposed on an operant baseline of responding in another situation (e.g., Solomon and Turner, 1960). Today, this two-process theory provides the best account of avoidance learning in its various forms.

In general, some animals of most species learn the avoidance contingency, whether it be in the active or the passive form, using discrete-trial or free-operant procedures. Dogs are particularly ad-

ept at avoidance learning in an active, discrete-trial shuttle-box procedure and typically show strong resistance to extinction (Solomon and Wynne, 1954). In contrast, rats are particularly difficult to train in an active, lever-press, discrete-trial procedure and require special training procedures (Berger and Brush, 1975). Thus, there are important differences among species and response requirements. Additionally, in all forms of avoidance learning—active and passive, discrete-trial and free-operant—there are enormous individual differences. Some individuals of whatever species learn rapidly and well, whereas others do not (Brush, 1966).

In view of these findings it is not surprising that several investigators have genetically selected for differences in avoidance learning. Bignami (1965) reported the first experiment with Wistar albino rats in which the selectively bred phenotypes were good or poor at avoidance learning in a shuttle box. The resulting strains are known as the Roman High Avoidance and Roman Low Avoidance strains (RHA and RLA, respectively). Training consisted of five daily sessions of fifty trials each. Selection was based on the number of avoidance responses during the first two sessions (many or few) and on good or poor retention from each session to the next. Selection was highly effective, because by the fifth generation the RHA and RLA animals avoided, respectively, on 68 percent and 20 percent of the trials.

In 1977 Brush reported on the development of the Syracuse High Avoidance and Syracuse Low Avoidance strains (SHA and SLA, respectively). Long-Evans hooded rats were trained for sixty trials in automated shuttle boxes. The data from over twenty generations of selection indicated that shuttle-box avoidance learning is heritable: SHA and SLA animals avoided on 67 percent and 0 percent of the sixty trials of training. Realized heritability (h^2, which can range between 0.0 and 1.0; Falconer, 1960) was estimated to be 0.16 in each strain, a value comparable with that found in other selection studies (Brush, Froehlich, and Sakellaris, 1979).

In 1978 Bammer reported on the first six generations of selective breeding of Sprague-Dawley albino rats for high and low levels of avoidance responding in a shuttle box. The resulting strains are known as the Australian High Avoidance and Australian Low Avoidance strains (AHA and ALA, respectively). Training consisted of fifty trials in one or more daily sessions. Realized heritability over the first five generations of selection was 0.18 and 0.27 for the AHA and ALA strains, respectively.

A unidirectionally selected strain, known as the Tokai High Avoider (THA), was bred in Japan from Wistar stock using a lever-press response and a free-operant procedure (S-S = 5 seconds, R-S = 30 seconds, shock duration = 0.5 second). The selection criterion was an avoidance rate of more than 95 percent in the last five of ten daily one-hour training sessions. Selection was successful: THA males and females learn faster and to a higher level of performance than unselected control animals from the original stock.

The fact that so many selective breeding experiments for avoidance behavior have been successful is a clear indicator of the extent to which this kind of behavior is under genetic control. In each experiment the individual variability within each strain becomes less as selection progresses, and it appears not to matter what the details of the training procedures are. For example, SHA animals do better than controls in a free-operant procedure, and THA animals do better than controls in discrete-trial shuttle-box training. Similarly, AHA animals outperform ALA animals in a discrete-trial avoidance task quite different from the one in which they were selected. Thus, it is clear that avoidance learning is strongly influenced by genetic factors, and many behavioral, physiological, and anatomical correlates of avoidance learning have been identified. Several of those correlates appear to be closely linked, genetically, to the avoidance phenotypes. Current research is devoted to identifying the mechanisms by which genes determine avoidance learning. Using modern molecular-genetic technology, researchers will soon be able to identify those genes.

REFERENCES

Bammer, G. (1978). Studies on two new strains of rats selectively bred for high or low conditioned avoidance responding. Paper presented at the Annual Meeting of the Australian Society for the Study of Animal Behavior, Brisbane.

Berger, D. F., and Brush, F. R. (1975). Rapid acquisition of discrete-trial lever-press avoidance: Effects of signal-shock interval. *Journal of the Experimental Analysis of Behavior 24,* 227–239.

Bignami, G. (1965). Selection for high rates and low rates of avoidance conditioning in the rat. *Animal Behavior 13,* 221–227.

Brush, F. R. (1966). On the differences between animals that learn and do not learn to avoid electric shock. *Psychonomic Science 5,* 123–124.

——— (1977). Behavioral and endocrine characteristics of rats selectively bred for good and poor avoidance behavior. *Activitas Nervosa Superioris 19,* 254–255.

Brush, F. R., Froehlich, J. C., and Sakellaris, P. C. (1979). Genetic selection for avoidance behavior in the rat. *Behavior Genetics 9,* 309–316.

Falconer, D. S. (1960). *Introduction to quantitative genetics.* London: Oliver & Boyd.

Hilgard, E. R., and Marquis, D. G. (1940). *Conditioning and learning.* New York: Appleton-Century-Crofts.

Kamin, L. J. (1956). The effect of termination of the CS and avoidance of the US on avoidance learning. *Journal of Comparative and Physiological Psychology 49,* 420–424.

Miller, N. E. (1951). Learnable drives and rewards. In S. S. Stevens, ed., *Handbook of experimental psychology.* New York: Wiley.

Mowrer, O. H. (1950). On the dual nature of learning—a reinterpretation of "conditioning" and "problem solving." In Mowrer's *Learning theory and personality dynamics.* New York: Ronald Press.

Rescorla, R. A., and Solomon, R. L. (1967). Two-process learning theory: Relationships between Pavlovian conditioning and instrumental learning. *Psychological Review 74,* 151–182.

Sidman, M. (1953). Two temporal parameters of the maintenance of avoidance behavior by the white rat. *Journal of Comparative and Physiological Psychology 46,* 253–261.

Solomon, R. L., and Turner, L. H. (1960). Discriminative classical conditioning under curare can later control discriminative avoidance responses in the normal state. *Science 132,* 1499–1500.

Solomon, R. L., and Wynne, L. C. (1954). Traumatic avoidance learning: The principles of anxiety conservation and partial irreversibility. *Psychological Review 61,* 353–385.

Warner, L. H. (1932). The association span of the white rat. *Journal of Genetic Psychology 39,* 57–89.

F. Robert Brush

BEHAVIORAL PHENOMENA: CLASSICAL CONDITIONING

An important aim of research into classical conditioning has been to examine the way in which it is affected by a variety of procedural manipulations. The reason for this research stems not so much from a desire to find new ways of changing an animal's behavior as from the desire to understand the fundamental mechanisms of associative learning. Most theorists now accept that the repeated pairing of a conditioned and unconditioned stimulus (CS and US) can promote the growth of an association between internal representations of these events. Once formed, the association then permits a presentation of the CS to activate the representation of the US, and this, in turn, leads to the performance of a conditioned response (CR). Various conditioning phenomena indicate, however, that such learning does not occur automatically whenever the CS and US are paired. Further, they show that associations other than those between representations of the CS and US can be formed during conditioning.

Latent Inhibition

If animals are repeatedly exposed to the CS by itself, then subsequent conditioning may progress more slowly than when the CS is novel. Such a retardation of conditioning by pre-exposure to the CS is referred to as *latent inhibition* (Lubow, 1973).

Theories differ in the way this loss of effectiveness of the CS is assumed to occur. According to Wagner (1976), the effectiveness of a stimulus is related to the amount of rehearsal it initiates in short-term memory, and this, in turn, is assumed to depend upon whether or not the stimulus is unexpected. Wagner has suggested that a stimulus will be unexpected whenever it occurs for the first few times in a different environment.

Other theorists have argued that the effectiveness of a stimulus is determined by the amount of attention it receives. According to Pearce and Hall (1980), attention to a stimulus will decline whenever it is consistently followed by the same outcome. Support for their theory comes from studies showing that latent inhibition may occur during conditioning. In one experiment, for example, rats repeatedly received a tone followed by a weak footshock. Then, in a test stage, the tone was paired with a different US. Conditioning with the tone in the test stage progressed more slowly than for subjects receiving the same CS–US pairings but with a novel CS. On the other hand, Mackintosh (1975) has proposed that attention to stimuli that are the best available predictors of reinforcement will increase, but attention to stimuli that are unin-

formative about the occurrence of a US will decline. Support for this proposal comes from studies of learned irrelevance, in which a CS and US are presented randomly with respect to each other. This treatment, which ensures that the CS is uninformative about the occurrence of the US, severely disrupts conditioning when the CS and US are eventually paired.

The available evidence does not allow a choice to be made between these different theories. Instead, it is likely that the processes governing the effectiveness of a CS are more sophisticated than is acknowledged by any one theory.

Compound Conditioning

Very often the outcome of conditioning with a CS is influenced by the stimuli that accompany it. Pavlov (1927) describes a study in which the US was signaled by a light presented simultaneously with a loud tone. Test trials with the light alone after compound conditioning failed to reveal a CR during this stimulus, even though conditioning had been shown to be effective when the light by itself was paired with the US. The presence of the tone can thus be said to *overshadow* conditioning with the light on compound trials.

Overshadowing is not always this effective. Depending on their relative intensities, the presence of one stimulus may only partially overshadow, or have no effect at all on, conditioning with another. A second factor that can influence overshadowing is whether one of the elements of the compound has been paired with the US prior to compound conditioning. Table 1 summarizes the design of a typical *blocking* experiment that was conducted by Kamin (1969). The experiment contained an experimental (E) and a control (C) group and was conducted in three stages. In the first stage, only experimental subjects received conditioning in which a 3-minute white noise was followed immediately by a mild shock to the feet. Eventually an aversive CR was observed whenever the noise was presented. The second stage of conditioning was similar to the first, except that a light accompanied the noise on every trial, and both groups received this training. In a final test stage, in which the light was presented alone, it was found that although this stimulus elicited a relatively strong CR in group C, it had very little influence on the behavior of group E. The initial condi-

Table 1.   Design of a Blocking Experiment by Kamin (1969)

Group	Stage 1	Stage 2	Test
E	Noise $\rightarrow$ shock	Light + noise $\rightarrow$ shock	Light
C		Light + noise $\rightarrow$ shock	Light

tioning with the noise thus appears to have prevented, or blocked, conditioning with the light in group E.

Blocking is said to demonstrate that during conditioning the US must be surprising if it is to enter into an association. Thus, during stage 2, the occurrence of shock for group E should not be surprising, because it is accurately predicted by the noise, and learning about the light does not take place. In contrast, the occurrence of shock should be surprising for group C, at least at the outset of stage 2, and some aversive conditioning with the light is possible.

Support for this interpretation comes from studies that have examined the influence of surprise on blocking. In one of his experiments Kamin (1969) employed a weak shock for the conditioning trials in stage 1, and a stronger shock for stage 2. Subsequent test trials revealed a substantial CR during the CS that had been introduced in the second stage of the experiment. In other words, the surprising increase in the magnitude of shock for compound conditioning was found to be sufficient to attenuate blocking. There are conflicting views as to why surprise is so influential in blocking. Wagner (1976) and Wagner and Rescorla (1972) have argued that surprise enhances the effectiveness of the US for conditioning, whereas Mackintosh (1975) and Pearce and Hall (1980) maintain that surprise enhances the effectiveness of the CS for conditioning.

Conditioned Inhibition

The studies considered above have all employed *excitatory conditioning,* in which the CS is followed by a US. In contrast, studies of *inhibitory conditioning* employ a design in which the CS signals the absence of a US. Hearst and Franklin (1977) placed hungry pigeons in a chamber in which a keylight was occasionally illuminated and food was presented for brief periods when the light was absent. As this training progressed the birds began to move away from the key whenever

it was illuminated. Because the light signaled the absence of a US, it became a *conditioned inhibitor* and elicited the CR of withdrawal.

Very often, conditioned inhibitors do not acquire the capacity to elicit CRs and special techniques are required to reveal the effectiveness of inhibitory conditioning. One technique, known as the *retardation test,* consists of pairing the conditioned inhibitor with the US that it previously signaled would not occur. Conditioning generally progresses very slowly in these circumstances, which can be seen as an indication that the original training endowed the CS with properties that are antagonistic with those acquired during excitatory conditioning. In another technique, known as the *summation test,* the conditioned inhibitor is presented in compound with a CS that has been paired previously with the US in question. Evidence of successful inhibitory conditioning is then revealed by a lower level of responding on compound trials than when the excitor is presented alone.

Second-Order Conditioning

In studies of *second-order,* or higher-order, *conditioning,* one stimulus, CS1, is first paired with a US until it reliably elicits a CR, then a second stimulus, CS2, is paired with CS1, but on these trials the US is omitted. This training often results in a CR being performed during CS2. This response may at first be quite vigorous, but because the US is withheld whenever CS2 is presented, the responses elicited by CS2 eventually weaken.

Despite its transitory nature, second-order conditioning has proved to be a valuable tool for understanding the type of associations that can be formed during conditioning. Consider the design of an experiment by Rashotte, Griffin, and Sisk (1977) using pigeons, with food as the US (Table 2). After receiving first- and second-order conditioning, subjects in group E but not group C were given trials in which CS1 was presented without the US. Subsequent test trials with CS2 revealed a significantly higher level of responding in Group C than in

Table 2. Summary of the Design of a Second-Order Conditioning Study by Rashotte, Griffin, and Sisk (1977)

Group	First-Order Conditioning	Second-Order Conditioning	Extinction	Test
E	CS1 → food	CS2 → CS1	CS1	CS2
C	CS1 → food	CS2 → CS1	—	CS2

Group E. In other words, presenting CS1 alone seriously weakened the effectiveness of second-order conditioning with CS2. One explanation for this outcome is that first-order conditioning resulted in growth of an association between internal representations of CS1 and the US, and second-order conditioning resulted in the growth of an association between CS2 and CS1. Presentations of CS2 then excite the CS1 representation, which excites the representation of the US and leads to the occurrence of the second-order CR. The trials with CS1 alone should break the second link in this chain and make it impossible for CS2 to elicit a response by activating the US representation.

Experiments based on this design do not always yield the same outcome. Rizley and Rescorla (1972) conducted a study that followed the design summarized in Table 2, but this time the US was shock and the subjects were rats. When the test trials with CS2 were conducted, both groups responded at a similar high level, which indicates that second-order conditioning was unaffected by the extinction trials with CS1. The implication of this outcome is that second-order conditioning resulted in the growth of an association between CS2 and the response of anxiety aroused by CS1. Once such an association is formed, manipulations of the CS1–shock association would then be unable to influence responding during CS2.

There is evidence, therefore, that two different types of association can develop during second-order conditioning. At present the factors that determine whether one sort of association or the other is formed are not fully understood.

Conditional Discriminations

In a conditional discrimination, the presence or absence of one stimulus indicates whether or not a US will follow another stimulus. Animals may receive training in which one stimulus (A) alone is followed by a US, whereas a compound of A with another stimulus (X) is followed by nothing. Animals can often make discriminations of this kind with relative ease, and the main focus of interest is on understanding how they do so. In the example just cited it is generally accepted that the discrimination depends upon A becoming associated with the US, and X acquiring inhibitory properties that counteract the effects of A whenever the stimuli are presented together. Other experimental designs require more complex explanations.

Rescorla (1985) describes an experiment in which a 5-second CS (X) was followed by food when it was presented during the final part of a 15-second stimulus (A); but when X was presented in the absence of A, then food was never presented. The result of this training was that a vigorous CR was recorded only during X when accompanied by A. The absence of a response during either A alone or X alone makes it difficult to attribute responding during the compound to the growth of an association between A and food, or between X and food. Instead, it has been argued that the principles of associative learning must be elaborated upon to accommodate this type of result.

One suggestion is that the above discrimination depends upon the development of a new type of association. This association permits one stimulus, A in the above example, to modulate the extent to which another stimulus, X, can activate the representation of food (see Holland, 1985; Rescorla, 1985). A rather different suggestion is that Rescorla's (1985) results were due to the growth of a configural association between a representation of the AX compound and food (Wagner and Rescorla, 1972; Pearce, 1987b). The relative merits of these theories remain to be established.

Conclusions

Two principal conclusions can be drawn from the studies described above. First, conditioning is not the result of some automatic process that is effective whenever a CS and US are paired. Instead, the operation of certain information-processing mechanisms appears to be essential if conditioning is to be successful. At the very least, for conditioning to be fully effective the representation of the CS must be maximally active, perhaps by virtue of being attended to, and the representation of the US must be fully active, perhaps by virtue of being surprising.

The second conclusion is that different methods of conditioning may result in the development of different types of associations. A goal for future research is to understand the nature of these different associations, and to identify the circumstances responsible for their development.

Further Reading

A relatively simple discussion of the issues raised above is presented in Pearce (1987a). More detailed coverage is provided by Mackintosh (1983).

REFERENCES

Hearst, E., and Franklin, S. R. (1977). Positive and negative relations between a signal and food: Approach-withdrawal behavior. *Journal of Experimental Psychology: Animal Behavior Processes 3*, 37–52.

Holland, P. C. (1985). The nature of conditioned inhibition in serial and simultaneous feature negative discriminations. In R. R. Miller and N. E. Spear, eds., *Information processing in animals: Conditioned inhibition.* Hillsdale, N.J.: Erlbaum.

Kamin, L. J. (1969). Predictability, surprise attention, and conditioning. In B. A. Campbell and R. M. Church, eds., *Punishment and aversive behavior.* New York. Appleton-Century-Crofts.

Lubow, R. E. (1973). Latent inhibition. *Psychological Bulletin 79,* 398–407.

Mackintosh, N. J. (1975). A theory of attention: Variations in the associability of stimuli with reinforcement. *Psychological Review 82,* 276–298.

———— (1983). *Conditioning and associative learning.* Oxford: Oxford Univ. Press.

Pavlov, I. P. (1927). *Conditioned reflexes.* Oxford: Oxford Univ. Press.

Pearce, J. M. (1987a). *Introduction to animal cognition.* London: Erlbaum.

———— (1987b). A model of stimulus generalization for Pavlovian conditioning. *Psychological Review 94,* 61–73.

Pearce, J. M., and Hall, G. (1980). A model for Pavlovian learning: Variations in the effectiveness of conditioned but not unconditioned stimuli. *Psychological Review 82,* 532–552.

Rashotte, M. E., Griffin, R. W., and Sisk, C. L. (1977). Second-order conditioning of the pigeon's key peck. *Animal Learning and Behavior 5,* 25–38.

Rescorla, R. A. (1985). Conditioned inhibition and facilitation. In R. R. Miller and N. E. Spear, eds., *Information processing in animals: Conditioned inhibition.* Hillsdale, N.J.: Erlbaum.

Rizley, R. C., and Rescorla, R. A. (1972). Associations in second-order conditioning and sensory preconditioning. *Journal of Comparative and Physiological Psychology 81,* 1–11.

Wagner, A. R. (1976). Priming in STM: An information-processing mechanism for self-generated or retrieval-generated depression in performance. In T. J. Tighe and R. N. Leaton, eds., *Habituation: Perspectives from child development, animal behavior, and neuropsychology.* Hillsdale, N.J.: Erlbaum.

Wagner, A. R., and Rescorla, R. A. (1972). Inhibition in Pavlovian conditioning: Application of a theory. In M. S. Halliday and R. A. Boakes, eds. *Inhibition and learning.* London: Academic Press.

John M. Pearce

BEHAVIORISM

Most generally, behaviorism is a viewpoint that takes psychological phenomena as physical activity rather than as belonging to a special domain of mental events. For a behaviorist, then, psychology is the study of behavior and its physical, mainly environmental, determinants rather than of the nature of experience or of mental process. Behaviorism originated in natural-science traditions of the late nineteenth century, and precursors of its methods and concepts developed at the turn of the century in the work of E. L. THORNDIKE and I. P. PAVLOV, as well as of several other psychologists and physiologists (Day, 1980; Herrnstein, 1969). But behaviorism as a distinct viewpoint came to be recognized with the publication of John B. WATSON's "Psychology as the Behaviorist Views It" (1913). Identification of behaviorism with the controversial Watson has persisted despite the fact that it subsequently developed into several distinct traditions that bear only a family resemblance to Watson's views and to each other (Malone, 1990; Zuriff, 1985). The predominant contemporary behaviorist position derives from the work of B. F. SKINNER, which differs from other behaviorisms in its detailed account of verbal functioning and in its inclusion of activities such as thinking and feeling as behavior to be accounted for, while maintaining a primary focus on behavior-environment relations rather than upon processes inferred as underlying those relations.

Behaviorism originated in opposition to an orthodox psychology that attempted to analyze conscious experience by focusing upon reports by observers who were trained to examine their own mental functions through techniques of introspection. Watson boldly rejected this, asserting that behavior, per se, is the proper domain of psychology. For Watson, prediction and control of overt behavior, rather than introspection of mental processes, formed the basis for an objective, scientific psychology. Behavior was to be analyzed into stimulus-response (S-R) units without appeal to hypothetical activities of brain or mind. The units could be of widely varying size, from the relatively molecular eyeblink elicited by a flash of light to the more "molar" shopping trip as response to an empty cupboard. Watson emphasized the continuity between human and nonhuman species, and he stressed the importance of learning, in animals as well as in humans, as the fundamental basis for understanding psychological process.

A neobehaviorism that came to the fore in the 1930s, that of Clark L. HULL and his student Kenneth SPENCE, dominated until midcentury. Like Watson, Hull described behavior as comprised of S-R units, but whereas Watson had presented S-R analyses as adjustable in scale, the Hull-Spence approach focused on molecular building blocks that were described as forming chains of connecting events between environmental stimuli and observed behavior. These mediating events included hypothetical (but presumably physical) stimulus traces, covert responses, and response-produced stimuli. Learned S-R units were called habits. Hull contrived an elaborate theory whose theorems and postulates, presented in geometer's style, were concerned with the formation of habit strength and with the mechanistic conversion of habit strength into overt action. The theory was published as essentially complete in 1943. Although highly touted, it proved ponderous, with numerous terms that were difficult to evaluate; it fell of its own weight within a decade. Nevertheless, Hullian students gained dominant positions within academic psychology, and elements of that approach can

be discerned to this day in theorizing that rests on the metaphor of mechanical associative connections. Hull's emphasis on formal hypothesis testing, directed at hypothetical constructs that are anchored to observable events as specified by operational definitions, also survives as a "methodological behaviorism" (Skinner, 1945) that has permeated much of psychology.

A counterpoint to Hull's views in the 1930s and 1940s was provided by Edward C. TOLMAN, who attempted to include purposive, intentional language within a behavioristic system. He invoked terms like *purpose, expectation,* and *cognition* to capture the larger-scale, goal-oriented "molar" organization of behavior. Tolman asserted that these terms need not imply anything nonphysical or mentalistic; indeed, he employed them in accounting for behavior of laboratory rats as well as of humans. But Tolman undermined such disclaimers by characterizing his view as S-O-R theory, with the "O" denoting a special role for processes within the behaving organism. The learning of complex relationships, often characterized as "cognitive maps," was said to mediate between environment and behavior. Critics of Tolman's account suggested that it left the organism "buried in thought." To the extent that he addressed the sources of action, Tolman placed them within the organism, which tended to link his account with traditional mentalistic explanations of action. Thus it is not surprising that Tolman's inclusion of intentional language never was accepted by the broader behavioristic community.

B. F. Skinner also departed from the S-R behavioral mainstream of the 1930s and 1940s, but in very different ways. He rejected mentalistic terms as "misleading fictions" while including the relationships that were Tolman's primary concern. Skinner's first conceptual innovation was to reformulate the reflex; he described this simplest unit of behavior not as stimulus-response connection but rather as directly observable abstraction, a correlation between classes of stimuli and classes of responses. Then Skinner distanced his theory still further from mediational notions of mechanism and associative connection by delineating nonreflexive behavioral units that he called operants (see OPERANT BEHAVIOR). Operants act upon the environment; they are selected by their consequences through processes denoted as *reinforcement, punishment,* and *extinction.* Operants can range from small to large in scale, and they are defined not only by the consequences that shape or maintain them but also by the contexts within which the selecting consequences have occurred. The result is a three-term relationship comprised of classes of responses, consequences, and discriminative stimuli.

Operant behavior often is characterized in ordinary language as intentional and purposive, thus having the "molar" characteristics that were Tolman's primary concern. But the traditional appeal to mentalistic intention is replaced by environment-based selection in this account of action, just as in Darwinian biology natural selection replaces divine intention in the account of new species. Learning of new behavior is readily demonstrated by rapidly shaping new patterns through differential reinforcement and through gradual fading of discriminative stimuli. In later work, Skinner (1984) described selectionist principles as applying to behavior patterns at the evolutionary level as well as at the level of cultural practice, giving accounts with close affinity to contemporary work in anthropology (e.g. Lloyd, 1985) and biology (Dawkins, 1982; Smith, 1986).

While his theory also included other principles, Skinner emphasized reinforcement as a basic relation, examining its properties and its broad implications. Empirically, he asked what would happen if only some occurrences of a response are reinforced; he devised schedules of reinforcement to explore the many ways in which this can happen, and their effects on rates, patterning, and persistence of behavior. Contemporary research has extended this to examine issues such as the conditions of self-control and preferences among schedules that are relevant to microeconomics (e.g., Rachlin, 1989) and to biological theories of foraging (e.g., Fantino and Abarca, 1985). Interpretatively, Skinner addressed the functional characteristics of verbal behavior, describing how an individual affects the behavior of others and how others teach the individual's verbal discriminations (Skinner, 1957). His approach initially was not welcomed by linguists, but some recent developments in linguistics appear more congenial to it (Andresen, 1990). The analysis includes activities like thinking, feeling, and even introspecting as behavior to be accounted for rather than as special bases for explaining overt action. It asserts that we know our private thoughts and feelings less well than we know external events, because the world cannot as accurately teach us to discriminate the former (Skinner, 1963). This provocative position gains independent support from the philosophies of Ryle (Schnaitter, 1985) and Wittgenstein (Day, 1969).

Skinner also addressed ethical and social issues in light of reinforcement-based principles—speculatively in *Walden Two,* a utopian novel that sketches an experimental approach to communal living, and analytically in essays such as "The Ethics of Helping People" (Skinner, 1978), which asserts that human rights properly concern the empowerment of effective action rather than access to things or services. Extensive discussions of these and other implications of reinforcement theory are provided by Skinner (1971, 1974), and by Catania and Harnad (1988). Contemporary behavioral research related to language emphasizes relationships between verbal and nonverbal behavior (e.g., Hayes, 1989; Cerutti, 1989) and issues such as the nature and origins of symbolic functioning (Sidman, 1986).

Of contemporary approaches, the most distinctly behavioral one is behavior analysis. Extending from Skinner's work, it differs philosophically and conceptually from other behaviorisms as well as from mainstream psychology (Lee, 1988). Its pragmatic contributions have proved effective in such diverse settings as health maintenance programs concerned with weight control, smoking, and wearing of automobile seat belts; airlines' "frequent flier" marketing techniques; techniques for basic research on drug addiction as well as for its treatment; educational techniques of documented effectiveness for handicapped and disadvantaged, as well as for mainstream, children (Becker, 1978; Wolf et al., 1987); and innovative formats for personalized instruction at the college level (Keller, 1977). Contemporary behaviorists are represented by professional organizations that include several thousand researchers, scholars, and practitioners (Thompson, 1988), and whose work is represented by more than a score of primarily behavioral journals (Wyatt et al., 1986). Thus, behaviorism has extended well beyond, while continuing an appositional role within, the specialized field where it began.

REFERENCES

Andresen, J. T. (1990). Skinner and Chomsky thirty years later. *Historiographia Linguistica 17,* 145–165.

Becker, W. C. (1978). The national evaluation of Follow-Through: Behavior theory-based programs come out on top. *Education and Urban Society 10,* 431–458.

Catania, A. C., and Harnad, S. (1988). *The selection of behavior; the operant behaviorism of B. F. Skinner: Comments and consequences.* New York: Cambridge University Press.

Cerutti, D. T. (1989). Discrimination theory of rule-governed behavior. *Journal of the Experimental Analysis of Behavior 51,* 257–276.

Dawkins, R. (1982). *The extended phenotype.* San Francisco: Freeman.

Day, W. F. (1969). On certain similarities between the *Philosophical Investigations* of Ludwig Wittgenstein and the operationism of B. F. Skinner. *Journal of the Experimental Analysis of Behavior 12,* 489–506.

——— (1980). The historical antecedents of contemporary behaviorism. In R. W. Rieber and K. Salzinger, eds., *Psychology: Theoretical-historical perspectives,* pp. 203–262. New York: Academic Press.

Fantino, E., and Abarca, N. (1985). Choice, optimal foraging, and the delay-reduction hypothesis. *Behavioral and Brain Sciences 8,* 315–362.

Hayes, S. C., ed. (1989). *Rule-governed behavior: Cognition, contingencies, and instructional control.* New York: Plenum.

Herrnstein, R. J. (1969). Behaviorism. In D. L. Krantz, ed., *Schools of psychology: A symposium,* pp. 51–68. New York: Appleton-Century-Crofts.

Hull, C. L. (1943). *Principles of behavior.* New York: Appleton-Century-Crofts.

Keller, F. S. (1977). *Summers and sabbaticals: Selected papers on psychology and education.* Champaign, Ill.: Research Press.

Lee, V. (1988). *Beyond behaviorism.* Hillsdale, N.J.: Erlbaum.

Lloyd, K. E. (1985). Behavioral anthropology: A review of Marvin Harris's *Cultural Materialism. Journal of the Experimental Analysis of Behavior 43,* 279–287.

Malone, J. C. (1990). *Theories of learning: A historical approach.* Belmont, Calif.: Wadsworth.

Rachlin, H. (1989). *Judgment, decision, and choice: A cognitive/behavioral synthesis.* New York: W. H. Freeman.

Schnaitter, R. (1985). The haunted clockwork: Reflections on Gilbert Ryle's *The concept of mind. Journal of the Experimental Analysis of Behavior 43,* 145–153.

Sidman, M. (1986). Functional analysis of emergent verbal classes. In T. Thompson and M. D. Zeiler, eds., *Analysis and integration of behavioral units,* pp. 213–245. Hillsdale, N.J.: Erlbaum.

Skinner, B. F. (1938). *The behavior of organisms: An experimental analysis.* New York: Appleton-Century-Crofts.

——— (1945). The operational analysis of psychological terms. *Psychological Review, 52,* 270–277, 291–294.

——— (1948). *Walden two.* New York: Macmillan.

——— (1957). *Verbal behavior.* New York: Appleton-Century-Crofts.

——— (1963). Behaviorism at fifty. *Science 134,* 566–602.

——— (1971). *Beyond freedom and dignity.* New York: Knopf.

——— (1974). *About behaviorism.* New York: Knopf.

——— (1978). *Reflections on behaviorism and society.* Englewood Cliffs, N.J.: Prentice-Hall.

——— (1984). Selection by consequences. *Science 213,* 501–504.

Smith, T. L. (1986). Biology as allegory: A review of Elliott Sober's *The nature of selection. Journal of the Experimental Analysis of Behavior 46,* 105–112.

Thompson, T. (1988). Benedictus behavior analysis: B. F. Skinner's magnum opus at fifty. *Contemporary Psychology 33,* 397–402.

Tolman, E. C. (1932). *Purposive behavior in animals and men.* New York: Appleton-Century-Crofts.

Watson, J. B. (1913). Psychology as the behaviorist views it. *Psychological Review 20,* 158–177.

——— (1919). *Psychology from the standpoint of a behaviorist.* Philadelphia: J. B. Lippincott.

Wolf, M. M., Braukmann, C. J., and Ramp, K. A. (1987). Serious delinquent behavior as part of a significantly handicapping condition: Cures and supporting environments. *Journal of Applied Behavior Analysis 20,* 347–359.

Wyatt, W. J., Hawkins, R. P., and Davis, P. (1986). Behaviorism: Are reports of its death exaggerated? *The Behavior Analyst 9,* 101–105.

Zuriff, G. E. (1985). *Behaviorism: A conceptual reconstruction.* New York: Columbia University Press.

Philip N. Hineline

BEHAVIOR THERAPY

Behavior therapy is a term used to describe a number of therapeutic procedures that share certain assumptions about the nature of behavioral and psychological problems and how they can best be overcome. The procedures can be classified into three main groups: fear-reduction procedures, operant conditioning procedures, and aversive techniques.

The major fear-reduction procedures consist of *systematic desensitization,* in which the person is trained to imagine a series of increasingly fearful images while in a state of relaxation; *therapeutic modeling,* in which the person observes and then imitates a therapist model engaging in increasingly close contact with the frightening object or situation; and *flooding,* in which the phobic person is exposed to intensely fearful stimulus situations for prolonged periods. In all of these methods, the phobic person is exposed to the real or imaginal fear stimulus repeatedly and/or for prolonged periods, and in all of them attempts to escape from or avoid the fear stimulus are discouraged (*response prevention*). The combination of exposure and response prevention has proved to be a robust and dependable means for reducing fear, and the clinical efficacy of this combination, in each of the three forms of fear-reduction procedures, has been confirmed in numerous controlled clinical trials (Marks, 1987; O'Leary and Wilson, 1987).

All three methods can be traced back to Pavlov's work on conditioning, and especially to his research on experimental neurosis. In developing the first of the modern methods, systematic desensitization, Wolpe (1958) was influenced by the writings of PAVLOV and the modern learning theorists, especially Clark HULL. Having rejected the psychodynamic approach, Wolpe attempted to apply modern learning techniques to psychological problems, particularly those in which anxiety is prominent. After completing a series of animal experiments, he concluded that graded, gradual reexposures to a fearful stimulus is the best way to weaken or eliminate the fear. He also concluded that the fear-reduction process can be facilitated by the deliberate superimposition on the evoked fear response of a competing incompatible response (such as relaxation imposed on a fear response). Each occasion on which an incompatible response is imposed over the fear response is an instance of reciprocal inhibition. Wolpe argued that repeated instances of such reciprocal inhibition give rise to a relatively permanent form of conditioned inhibition (of fear), and that the therapeutic effects are a direct consequence of the reciprocal inhibition.

Desensitization is the earliest and best-established of the methods, but Wolpe also introduced a number of other therapeutic procedures. Most attention, however, has been devoted to desensitization, which has been the subject of considerable experimental work and testing. This research, in addition to advancing the therapeutic efficacy of these results, eventually gave rise to a fresh view of fear itself.

Additions to and improvements of the clinical techniques were introduced in the early 1970s, and for certain types of anxiety disorder (such as panic disorder, agoraphobia, obsessional disorders, simple phobias), therapeutic modeling replaced desensitization as the method of choice.

In most cases, therapeutic modeling and flooding are carried out "in vivo," an unfortunately chosen term that here means exposure to the fear stimulus rather than to an imaginal representation of the stimulus (as in the desensitization procedure). The development of therapeutic modeling, largely the result of Bandura's work (1969), consists of repeated exposures to the fear stimulus. The phobic person first watches and then imitates the approach behavior of a therapeutic model. The method is effective and well accepted by most subjects, clients, and patients. Flooding is seldom the first choice of treatment but can be used in certain cases such as extensive obsessional/compulsive problems. Systematic desensitization remains useful for numerous problems, especially those in which direct exposure is impractical or unacceptable, as in the treatment of certain sexual disorders and social phobias.

All of the fear-reduction techniques are applications of learning procedures to clinical problems, and in common with the other forms of behavior therapy are based on the assumption that most psychological problems can be overcome by the use of conditioning or other learning processes. In the early stages of behavior therapy, it was assumed that most psychological problems are the result of faulty learning (for instance, "Symptoms are unadaptive responses" and "Symptoms are evidence of faulty learning"; Eysenck and Rachman, 1965, p. 12). Furthermore, it was argued that problems that are the result of faulty learning can be unlearned. In due course, more complex explanations were substituted.

The second form of behavior therapy, consisting of the application of *operant conditioning* ideas and procedures to clinical problems, was engineered in the United States and applied mainly to the psychological problems of children and adults with severe handicaps (e.g., mentally retarded people in or out of institutions, and people with chronic and serious psychiatric disturbances, especially chronic schizophrenia). The fear-reduction techniques were developed mainly in Britain and were and are used predominantly in dealing with adult neurotic problems, especially anxiety disorders such as obsessional disorders, panic disorders, social phobias, and circumscribed phobias.

The clinical application of operant conditioning later referred to as *reinforcement therapy* was a direct application of Skinnerian ideas, with emphasis on the consequences of behavior. Behavior that is followed by a reward will be strengthened and behavior that is followed by nonreward will be weakened.

The first application consisted of a series of attempts to treat schizophrenic problems in laboratory settings, but only limited success was achieved until the methods were applied, often with considerable ingenuity, to the maladaptive behavior of institutionalized patients with chronic psychiatric disorders (e.g., Ayllon and Azrin, 1968). Notable advances were made by the selective reinforcement of desirable behavior (e.g., self-care, eating) and the withholding of (social) reinforcement after undesirable behavior. Many of these useful advances were later incorporated into an institutional program that Ayllon and Azrin, two pioneers of this work, called the *token economy* (exchangeable tokens having replaced tangible rewards). The fact that the large ambitions of the earlier workers who expected reinforcement therapy to eliminate these psychiatric problems were never achieved does not detract from the contribution that this form of therapy continues to make. It is widely used to modify the maladaptive behavior of retarded children and adults, patients with chronic psychiatric disorders, children with speech or other behavioral deficits, and in educational settings.

Aversion therapy is a direct application of Pavlovian conditioning to appetitive but maladaptive behavior such as the excessive use of alcohol, and was originally prompted by the discovery that laboratory animals can develop conditioned nausea reactions to the stimuli that are associated with the administration of drugs that induce nausea. In order to convert the aberrant stimuli (such as inappropriate sexual stimuli, alcohol) into conditioned stimuli for nausea or other unpleasant responses, the alcohol or sexual stimuli are contingently followed by aversive stimulation. The earlier and still most common form of aversion therapy consists of pairing an alcohol conditioned stimulus with aversive nausea induced by drugs. This form of chemical aversion therapy is used mainly in the treatment of alcoholism; the other technique, *electrical aversion therapy,* in which the aversive stimulus is an electric shock, is used mainly in the treatment of aberrant sexual behavior such as pedophilia. Although aversion therapy appears to make a useful contribution to dealing with alcohol and sexual problems, it is rarely sufficient and nowadays is used as part of a wider therapeutic program that typically includes counseling, group therapy,

and family therapy. This insufficiency, the ethical problems involved in the deliberate application of aversive stimuli, and the fact that the precise nature of the conditioning processes involved in aversion therapy is not fully understood have combined to limit the use of aversion therapy.

The other two forms of behavior therapy also have their limitations, and therefore clinicians have been receptive to the growing influence of cognitive analyses of psychological and clinical phenomena. Behavior therapy has been expanded to include the influence of cognitive factors, and most practitioners now favor *cognitive behavior therapy,* which combines the original forms of behavior therapy with cognitive analyses of the problem and cognitive procedures for helping to deal with them. Thus far, cognitive behavior therapy appears to have achieved most success in the treatment of depression (e.g., Beck, 1976; O'Leary and Wilson, 1987).

REFERENCES

Ayllon, T., and Azrin, N. (1968). *The token economy.* New York: Appleton.

Bandura, A. (1969). *Principles of behavior modification.* New York: Holt.

Beck, A. (1976). *Cognitive therapy and the emotional disorders.* New York: International University Press.

Eysenck, H., and Rachman, S. (1965). *The causes and cures of narcosis.* London: Routledge and Kegan Paul.

Marks, I. (1987). *Fears, phobias, and rituals.* Oxford: Oxford University Press.

O'Leary, K., and Wilson, G. T. (1987). *Behavior therapy,* 2nd ed. Englewood Cliffs, N.J.: Prentice-Hall.

Rachman, S. (1990). *Fear and courage,* 2nd ed. New York: W. H. Freeman.

Wolpe, J. (1958). *Psychotherapy by reciprocal inhibition.* Stanford, Calif.: Stanford University Press.

Stanley J. Rachman

BIRD SONG LEARNING

[*This article consists of two sections,* Behavioral Aspects *by Peter Marler and* Neurobiology *by Allison Doupe.*]

Behavioral Aspects

Learned Dialects in Bird Song

All birds have a repertoire of up to twenty or so distinct vocal sounds that they use for communication about danger, food, sex, or group movements, and for many other purposes. Often a distinction can be made between a bird's calls, which are usually brief and monosyllabic, and its songs, which are more extended patterns of sound, often tonal and melodic and a source of pleasure for many human listeners. Songs of songbirds are usually, though not always, a male prerogative. Unlike most calls, songs are learned: They develop abnormally if a young male is reared out of hearing of the sounds of adults (Figure 1). A common consequence of this dependence on learning is the emergence of local song dialects, varying on much the same geographic scale as dialects in human speech. Songs from a bird's own dialect are especially potent as vocal signals, both to territorial males and to females ready to mate (Balaban, 1988).

Birds are unique among animals in the many analogies that can be struck between song learning and the acquisition of human speech. Avian vocal development provides one of the few tractable animal models for studying the behavioral, hormonal, and neural bases of vocal plasticity (Konishi, 1985; Marler, 1991b). No nonhuman primate is known that depends upon learning for the development of its natural vocal repertoire. Other than humans, cetaceans are the only mammals that appear to rely on learning for vocal development. The avian groups known to have learned songs include hummingbirds, parrots, and all oscine songbirds. Probably about half of the 7,000 or so bird species engage in some form of vocal learning.

Sensitive Periods for Learning

There is an underlying pattern in the steps typically required in learning to sing. First is the acquisition phase, when a bird hears songs and commits some of them to memory. These are stored for a period that varies in duration from species to species—

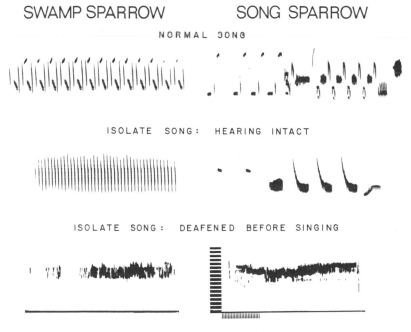

Figure 1.   Sound spectrograms of six songs, each about 2 seconds in duration, of male swamp sparrows and song sparrows. Two are typical songs heard in nature, two were developed by males reared in isolation from adult song, and two are songs of males deafened at 20 days of age. Frequencies are marked at 500 hertz intervals. The time marker is 0.5 second.

from days to months—until the bird begins to re-call songs from memory and starts to produce imitations, sometimes faithful to the original model, sometimes departing from it radically. There is thus a separation in time of the acquisition or sensory phase and the production or sensorimotor phase, ending with the production of crystallized, adult song (Marler, 1991a).

There are often sensitive periods for song acquisition, sometimes restricted to a short period early in life, and sometimes extending into adulthood. Even close relatives, such as sparrows and canaries, may differ in this respect. Several species of sparrows have a sensitive period for acquiring songs beginning at about 20 days of age, soon after young males become independent from their parents, and ending 4 to 6 weeks later (Marler, 1987; Clayton, 1989). Such sensitive periods for learning are variable within limits, depending on the strength of song stimulation and the influence of physiological factors, such as hormonal states, that vary with the season. If young are hatched late in the season and singing has already ceased for that year, closure of the sensitive period may be delayed until the following spring. The experimental withholding of stimulation by songs of the birds' own species can also delay closure of the learning period (Kroodsma and Pickert, 1980).

"Overproduction" in Song Development

The young male songbird typically begins singing sometime after learned songs have been memorized, but the imitations are not fully formed. Instead, the young male starts with *subsong,* an amorphous, noisy twittering that changes gradually, first into *plastic song,* which also is highly variable but contains the first obvious signs of mature song structure, finally crystallizing into the stable patterns of mature, adult song (Figure 2). Subsong resembles the babbling of human infants, and may be important for developing the motor skills of singing and other prerequisites for song learning, such as the ability to guide the voice by the ear. Rehearsal of previously memorized song patterns begins in plastic song. Often more plastic song themes are produced than are needed for mature singing (Figure 3), and many are discarded when song crystallization occurs. These memorized but rejected songs may provide a potential memory

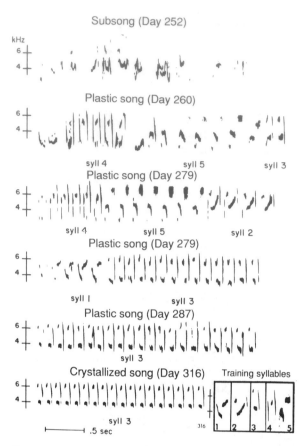

Figure 2. Samples from the process of song development in a single male swamp sparrow, ranging from subsong to crystallized song. The age of the bird ranges from 252 to 316 days. This bird was trained with tape-recorded songs, syllables of some of which are indicated in the box insert. As indicated by the labels, early efforts to reproduce imitations of these songs months later are imperfect in early plastic song, but they improve as progress toward crystallized song is made. The overproduction of song types during plastic song can also be seen. The two song types in the crystallized repertoire of this male consisted of syllable types 2 and 3.

bank of songs heard in youth, perhaps consulted later in life in assessing the songs of others (Marler and Peters, 1982).

Effects of Isolation and Deafness

Regardless of whether they have had the chance to learn, songbirds can always produce some aspects of the normal song of their species. When sparrows are raised in isolation, for example, the

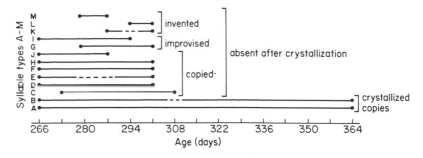

Figure 3. A diagram of song development in the male swamp sparrow shown in Figure 2, illustrating overproduction in plastic song, and the discarding of many themes at the time of song crystallization, around 300 days of age. *Reproduced with permission from Marler and Peters, 1982.*

note structure and tonal quality of their songs is abnormal, but each species still produces some basic features of normal song "syntax" (Figure 1). These features are produced irrespective of whether they were represented in any songs a male may have learned.

We gain some insight into the basis of this ability to produce certain normal song features by studying the songs of deaf birds, which are highly abnormal and variable in structure (Figure 1). This degraded form of singing results both if a male becomes deaf before song stimulation and if he is deafened after song stimulation but before the development of singing. There seems to be no internal brain circuitry that makes memorized songs directly available to guide motor development. To transform a memorized song into a produced song, the bird must be able to hear its own voice. We infer that there must be auditory templates for song, involved in guiding song production, conceived of as neural mechanisms in the auditory circuitry of the songbird brain that must vary in their specifications from species to species (Konishi, 1965; Marler and Sherman, 1983).

Natural bird songs are highly species-specific, and ornithologists often rely on song identification for species diagnosis, especially in densely wooded habitats. Songs of early-deafened songbirds are almost lacking in species specificity and are often indistinguishable between species (Figure 1). Songs of males raised in isolation but with hearing intact fall somewhere between, always retaining some species-typical features but lacking others. By playback of tape-recorded songs to wild territorial males and to females in hormonally induced estrus, it can be shown that experienced birds of both sexes completely disregard deaf songs as so-

cial signals. Normal songs evoke aggressive responses in same-species males and elicit courtship in females. Songs of other species have no effect, and deaf songs are just as ineffective. Songs of social isolates are intermediate in effectiveness. Thus the efficacy of bird song as a social signal is augmented both by the effects of learning and by developmental involvement of innate auditory templates for song.

Learning Preferences

There are other indications of involvement of innate processes in the learning process. If males of two species, such as swamp and song sparrows, are brought into the laboratory and exposed to tape recordings of songs of both species, each displays a clear preference for its own kind, even if he has never heard his own species's song before (Marler and Peters, 1989). This preference is not binding, however. A song of another species that a male will reject, if given a choice, may become acceptable if it is the only option (Figure 4), especially when it is presented in a highly interactive situation by a live tutor (Baptista and Petrinovich, 1986).

Song learning displays many unusual features, some of which recur in other circumstances, as in IMPRINTING. The frequent occurrence of relatively short sensitive periods for learning has already been noted. Unlike many other forms of learning, the process of song acquisition does not require any external reinforcement, even though social stimulation may augment the acquisition process. It suffices that the bird simply be exposed to the

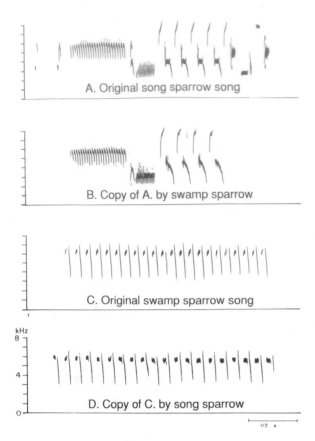

A. Original song sparrow song

B. Copy of A. by swamp sparrow

C. Original swamp sparrow song

D. Copy of C. by song sparrow

Figure 4.   Examples of birds copying songs of another species from tape recordings in the laboratory when songs of their own species are withheld. *From unpublished data of Marler and Peters.*

appropriate stimulus inputs at the appropriate stage of its development. Learning can occur with remarkably few exposures to a bird's own species song, especially at the height of the sensitive period. Sparrows will learn from 100 to 400 tape-recorded songs, both conspecific and heterospecific, and some acquisition occurs from thirty repetitions of a conspecific song. European blackbirds have learned after as few as fifteen to twenty song presentations on a single day. The virtuoso in this regard is the nightingale, which can learn a sequence of song types accurately after twenty presentations during the sensitive period. Some exceptional individuals succeed after as few as five presentations. Especially interesting is the way in which nightingales handle long strings of songs. Individual males have a repertoire of up to 200 song types, delivered one by one in a regular sequence. Experiments have shown that males can learn strings of up to sixty different songs and reproduce them in the original order, but sequenc-

ing was retained only in subsequences of three to seven songs. After producing such a matched sequence, a bird then switched to another subset, beginning at a different point. The nightingales behaved as though they divided the string of sixty songs into manageable subsets of up to seven songs, perhaps as a strategy for memorizing long sequences (Hultsch and Todt, 1988).

Song Development as a Creative Process

Perhaps the most mysterious and intriguing aspect of all is the ability of songbirds to invent new sounds (Marler, 1991a). This can be achieved in several different ways. Sometimes phrases are simply invented. At other times, a memorized theme is subjected to progressive improvisation, especially during the progression through plastic song. In some species inventiveness is more constrained, and memorized songs retain much of their original structure; but they may be broken down into component phrases and recombined to re-create new sequences. In this way, parts can be exchanged within a song, between songs learned at the same time, and even between songs that have been acquired many months apart (Figure 5). Bird species differ strikingly in the style of inventiveness that they favor, in the degree to which they indulge in invention, and in the aspect of song to which it is applied. The very large individual repertoires that males of some bird species possess, sometimes with hundreds of song types, are often built up by repeating this process of segmentation and recombination.

Conclusions

As more bird species are studied, it becomes increasingly clear that each has its own special way of approaching the song learning process. Some species learn readily from song stimulation alone, and often remarkably few song stimuli are necessary. Others take longer or require social stimulation for learning to occur. Often birds can be persuaded to learn songs of other species while having some foreknowledge of what their own species songs sound like and favoring them if given a choice. Some birds are faithful to the songs they imitate, and others use them as a basis for improvisation, retaining certain features of the model and

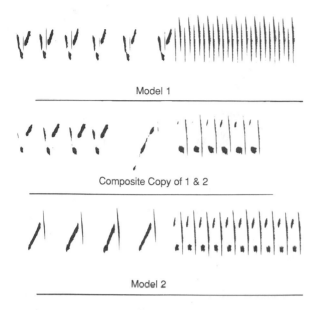

Figure 5. Song sparrows often create new themes by breaking learned songs into their component syllables and recombining them in various ways. Illustrated here is the song of a laboratory-reared song sparrow exposed to an array of synthetic songs. It learned two of these and recombined parts of them, as illustrated, to create a crude approximation of normal song sparrow song syntax.

changing others. We can draw the inference from behavioral studies that the brain of each bird species brings a distinctive set of properties and predispositions to the task of learning to sing. The challenge for the neurobiologist is to understand both the basic brain mechanisms that underlie the general learning abilities of all songbirds and the more subtle means by which each species adds its own unique flavor to the process of developing a song that is adapted to its particular social and ecological circumstances.

REFERENCES

Balaban, E. (1988). Bird song syntax: Learned intraspecific variation is meaningful. *Proceedings of the National Academy of Sciences 85,* 3657–3660.

Baptista, L. F., and Petrinovich, L. (1986). Song development in the white-crowned sparrow: Social factors and sex differences. *Animal Behavior 34,* 1359–1371.

Clayton, N. S. (1989). Song, sex and sensitive phases in the behavioral development of birds. *Trends in Evolution and Ecology 4,* 82–84.

Hultsch, H., and Todt, D. (1988). Song acquisition and acquisition constraints in the nightingale, *Luscinia megarhynchos. Naturwissenschaften 76,* 83–85.

Konishi, M. (1965). The role of auditory feedback in the control of vocalization in the white-crowned sparrow. *Zeitschrift für Tierpsychologie 22,* 770–783.

——— (1985). Birdsong: From behavior to neuron. *Annual Review of Neuroscience 8,* 125–170.

Kroodsma, D. E., and Pickert, R. (1980). Environmentally dependent sensitive periods for avian vocal learning. *Nature 288,* 477–479.

Marler, P. (1987). Sensitive periods and the role of specific and general sensory stimulation in birdsong learning. In J. P. Rauschecker and P. Marler, eds., *Imprinting and cortical plasticity,* pp. 99–135. New York: Wiley.

——— (1991a). Differences in behavioural development in closely related species: Birdsong. In P. Bateson, ed., *The development and integration of behaviour,* pp. 41–68. Cambridge: Cambridge University Press.

——— (1991b). Song-learning behavior: The interface with neuroethology. *Trends in Neuroscience 14,* 199–206.

Marler, P., and Peters, S. (1982). Developmental overproduction and selective attrition: New processes in the epigenesis of birdsong. *Developmental Psychobiology 15,* 369–378.

——— (1989). Species differences in auditory responsiveness in early vocal learning. In R. Dooling and S. Hulse, eds., *The comparative psychology of audition: Perceiving complex sounds,* pp. 243–273. Hillsdale, N.J.: Erlbaum.

Marler, P., and Sherman, V. (1983). Song structure without auditory feedback: Emendations of the auditory template hypothesis. *Journal of Neuroscience 3,* 517–531.

Peter R. Marler

Neurobiology

Bird song has many features that make it useful for studying the neural basis of learning. The behavior has been well studied (see "Behavioral Aspects," above) and shares numerous properties with other complex forms of learning. Song is an intricate motor act that is learned in distinct phases during the course of a young bird's life and depends on the animal's auditory experience. There are sensitive or critical periods for song learning, just as there are for some types of human learning, especially that of language (see LANGUAGE LEARNING). Moreover, bird song is sexually dimorphic: the

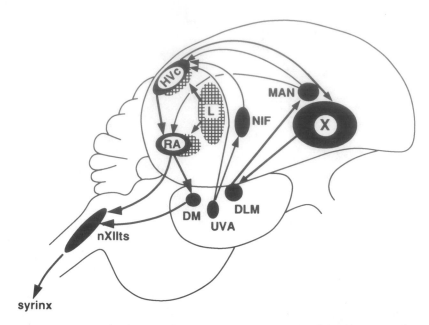

Figure 1.   The song system. This diagram shows most of the known nuclei and connections in the song system. The pathway from NIF (nucleus interface) to the syrinx via HVc (ventral nucleus of the hyperstriatum, caudal part), RA (robust nucleus of the archistriatum), DM (dorsomedial nucleus of nucleus intercollicularis), and nXIIts (tracheosyringeal portion of the hypoglossal nucleus) comprises the motor pathway for song. Area X, DLM (medial portion of the dorsolateral thalamus), and MAN (magnocellular nucleus of the anterior neostriatum) form a circuit joining HVc to RA. UVA (uvaeform nucleus of the thalamus) connects to its counterpart on the other side of the brain and is the only song nucleus known to have contralateral connections. Hatched areas indicate the primary auditory area of the avian forebrain, Field L, and its projections to the vicinity of the song nuclei.

male sings, whereas in many species the female sings little if at all, and sex steroids influence both the adult song behavior and its development. Finally, a discrete set of brain areas (Nottebohm, 1980), often called the *song system,* controls song learning and production. This suggests a possible location for the neural changes associated with song learning.

The Song System

The song system consists of numerous interconnected nuclei and occupies a relatively large volume of brain (Figure 1). The brain area nXIIts (the tracheosyringeal portion of the hypoglossal nucleus) contains the motor neurons that control the musculature of the bird's vocal organ, the syrinx. The pathway from NIF (the nucleus interface)

though HVc (the caudal portion of the ventral nucleus of the hyperstriatum) to RA (the robust nucleus of the archistriatum) and thence to nXIIts constitutes a motor pathway specialized for song production. The anterior forebrain song nuclei MAN (the magnocellular nucleus of the anterior neostriatum) and area X, as well as the thalamic nucleus that interconnects them, DLM (the medial portion of the dorsolateral nucleus of the thalamus), form a second pathway connecting HVc to RA. All of the song nuclei are present bilaterally, and the thalamic song nucleus Uva (the uvaeform nucleus) forms a connection between the two sides.

The presence of a song system is particularly associated with the learning of song, not just with song production. These brain areas are found only in birds that sing and that learn their song by reference to auditory information. The vast majority of vocal learners are passerine songbirds, but evolutionarily unrelated species that are vocal mimics, such as parrots, are also found to have structures resembling HVc and RA.

A Motor Pathway for Song

The evidence for a specialized motor pathway for song comes from two sources. Behavioral studies show that lesions of HVc, RA, or the hypoglossal nerve cause severe disruption of adult song (Nottebohm, 1980). Furthermore, electrophysiological recordings in NIF, HVc, and RA of awake birds reveal neurons whose activity is highly correlated with singing. NIF may be the birdsong pattern generator, because section of the tract from NIF to HVc destroys the patterning of song, while lesions of Uva do not (McCasland, 1987).

The song motor commands must ultimately be translated into a pattern of syringeal muscle activation and respiratory control. Intrabronchial measurements of both airflow and sound from each syringeal half have begun to shed light on how the syrinx functions to produce sound (Suthers, 1990). Similarly, electromyographic recordings from syringeal muscles in awake birds reveal the activity of the intrinsic vocal musculature during vocalization and respiration (Vicario, 1991). The output nucleus of the song system, nXIIts, has a map of the muscles of the syrinx: All motor neurons projecting to a particular syringeal muscle are clustered together in discrete zones within the motor nucleus. RA also has zones of premotor neurons that project to the corresponding muscle control area in nXIIts. The dorsal portion of RA does not project to nXIIts but to the dorsomedial nucleus (DM) of the midbrain, an area thought to be involved in vocalization and respiration in all birds, including nonsongbirds (Figure 1; Vicario, 1991). Neurons in DM then project to nXIIts, suggesting that RA has two parallel and perhaps functionally different inputs to the syringeal motor neurons. Unlike lesions of HVc or RA, which completely disrupt song, bilateral section of the nerve from nXIIts to the syringeal muscles disrupts the acoustic structure of song but leaves its gross temporal structure essentially intact. Thus, the timing information for song, although present in HVc and RA, does not strictly depend on the connection from nXIIts to the syringeal muscles. Perhaps timing cues are also relayed by connections (yet to be described) from RA to respiratory muscles and control centers.

The presence of specialized brain areas for vocal production is one of many attributes bird song shares with human speech. Another feature of the human brain is lateralization, with the left hemisphere specialized for language. Experiments in the canary raised the possibility that the songbird brain hemispheres might be lateralized as well. Lesions of the left hypoglossal nerve of the left HVc of canaries cause more disruption of song than similar lesions of the right side (Nottebohm, 1980). Subsequent investigation suggests that the interpretation of these results is not simple. In canaries, the musculature of the left side of the syrinx is much larger than that of the right. Because each hemisphere controls only the vocal musculature of the same side, a central lesion on the left would disable the more massive left musculature, and thus would have more effect than a right-sided lesion. This result would not necessarily imply a hemispheric specialization, but simply reflect the peripheral asymmetry. Further studies of song-related neural activity in canary HVc suggest that both hemispheres make equal contributions to song (McCasland, 1987).

Song-Selective Auditory Pathways

Both auditory experience and feedback are crucial to song learning. As described under "Behavioral Aspects," above, a young male songbird must first hear and memorize a tutor song during a critical period in early life. This has been called the *sensory* phase of learning. During a second, *sensorimotor* phase of learning, the young bird begins to sing. He gradually refines his initially crude and rambling vocal output, until it closely matches the memorized song or *template*. This becomes his "crystallized" adult song. In order to accomplish this matching, the bird must be able to hear his own vocalizations, although he no longer needs to hear the tutor song. After crystallization, songbirds are much less dependent on auditory feedback for normal song production (Konishi, 1989).

Because auditory feedback is used to correct vocal motor output during song learning, there must be a link between the auditory system and the vocal motor pathway. In addition, there must be brain mechanisms for very specific recognition of song and songlike vocalizations. Auditory information is relayed to the songbird forebrain as in all other birds, travelling from the cochlear nuclei through the thalamus to the forebrain primary auditory area, Field L. Anatomical experiments show that Field L projects to the vicinity of HVc and RA (Nottebohm, 1980; see Figure 1). In addition to song-related motor neurons, HVc also contains neurons that respond to auditory stimuli. Some of these HVc auditory neurons are song-selective: They respond best of all to the bird's own song, even in comparison with very similar songs of conspecifics (Margoliash, 1983). HVc song-selective neurons are also sensitive to temporal order: They are activated much more strongly by the bird's own song when the syllables are in the normal sequence than when the identical song components are played out of order or in reverse (Figure 2). This high degree of selectivity in individual neurons provides a possible mechanism for extremely specific recognition of song. Furthermore, because the bird's own song is learned during development, this song selectivity must also be learned. In fact, studies in young birds have shown that these neurons acquire their specificity during sensorimotor learning.

Recent lesion studies have shown that the anterior forebrain pathway containing MAN and X (Figure 1) plays an important role in song learning but is not an essential part of the motor pathway for song in the adult. Lesions of MAN or X have no apparent effect on adult song production, but destruction of either of these areas in young birds results in markedly abnormal song (Bottjer, Miesner, and Arnold, 1984; Sohrabji, Nordeen, and Nordeen, 1990; Scharff and Nottebohm, 1991). There are song-selective auditory neurons, similar to those in HVc, in every nucleus in this loop—X, DLM, and MAN (Doupe and Konishi, 1991). Like the neurons in HVc, these auditory neurons appear to acquire their song selectivity in parallel with song acquisition. Thus one essential role of this circuit in learning may be the auditory recognition and feedback so crucial to normal song development.

The song-selective auditory loop from HVc to the anterior forebrain eventually projects back into the motor pathway through its connection to RA (Figure 1). The neurons from MAN synapse onto premotor RA neurons that also receive input from HVc. Many RA neurons respond to song: Investigation of their auditory properties reveals that these

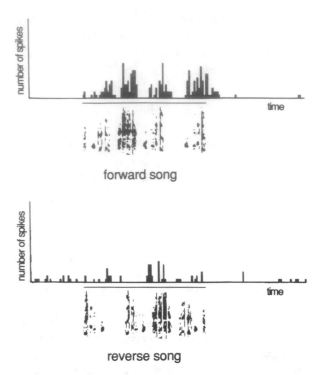

Figure 2. A song-selective HVc neuron. HVc auditory neurons respond very strongly to the presentation of the experimental animal's own song (*upper panel*), but show little response to the same song played in reverse (*lower panel*). The neuronal response is measured as number of action potentials versus time, and the song is shown below each trace in the form of a sonogram, a plot of sound frequency versus time.

cells receive a direct song-selective input from HVc neurons, in addition to their indirect auditory projection from HVc through the loop via X and MAN (Doupe and Konishi, 1991). Thus, along with the motor pathway for song, there are two highly specialized auditory circuits for song, which converge onto a song motor nucleus. This convergence of auditory and motor inputs makes RA a possible site for the auditory guidance of vocal motor development during learning.

Both MAN and HVc terminals activate glutamate receptors on RA neurons, but MAN neurons activate *n*-methyl-*d*-aspartate (NMDA) receptors, while HVc neurons activate primarily non-NMDA receptors (Mooney and Konishi, 1991). The NMDA subclass of glutamate receptors is thought to play a role in some forms of synaptic plasticity. Thus potential cellular mechanisms for learning are also present at this locus of auditory-motor convergence. This system has the potential to provide general insights into the neural basis of complex motor learning and its guidance by sensory input. (See also GLUTAMATE RECEPTORS AND THEIR CHARACTERIZATION.)

Development and Sexual Dimorphism of the Song System

It is a striking feature of the song system that it continues to develop after hatching, during song learning. Administration of ^{3}H-thymidine can be used to label neurons undergoing their last cell division, or "birthday." Such birthdating of song nuclei shows that MAN and RA are "born" before hatching, but that there is significant neurogenesis in HVc and X in the first several months after hatching (Nordeen and Nordeen, 1988). There is also naturally occurring cell death during postnatal development. In male zebra finches, many MAN neurons die around 5 weeks after hatching. Synaptic connectivity continues to develop at these late stages as well. The motor projection from HVc reaches its target nucleus RA by postnatal day 15, but then "waits" outside RA for approximately 10 days before growing in and completing the circuit (Konishi and Akutagawa, 1985). Interestingly, male zebra finches first begin to sing at the time of in growth of HVc axons into RA. In contrast to the HVc-to-RA synapses, the connections from MAN to RA (and in fact from HVc to MAN via X and DLM) are present and functional by day 15.

Bird song is sexually dimorphic: Male birds sing for courtship and territorial defense, while female birds sing much less or not at all. The behavioral dimorphism between males and females has a striking correlate in the sexual dimorphism of the song system itself. The song nuclei are much larger in males than in females (Nottebohm, 1980; see Figure 3). This size difference is due to a larger number of neurons in male nuclei as well as to increased size of both the soma and the dendritic arbor of male neurons (Gurney, 1981). Neurons in a number of the song nuclei directly bind androgens, and in the male, there is a larger number of such androgen target cells than in the female. Finally, even some of the synaptic connections are sexually dimorphic. In young female zebra finches, HVc neurons grow towards RA and "wait" outside the target just as in the male, but unlike in the male they never enter the nucleus, and RA eventually atrophies (Konishi and Akutagawa, 1985). Perhaps the lack of an important connection in the motor pathway explains the fact that the female zebra finch never sings.

Both singing and the song system are influenced by steroid hormones. Singing is much increased when androgen levels are high, for instance during the breeding season in the spring. In male canaries, there is also a seasonal variation in the size of the song nuclei, with HVc and RA enlarging by approximately 50 percent in the spring (Nottebohm, 1981). This volume increase is primarily due to marked dendritic growth, which results in increased synapses. In some species such as canaries and white-crowned sparrows, adult females will respond to injections of testosterone by beginning to sing and rapidly going through the sensorimotor phase of learning. These injections also induce marked growth of the song nuclei (Nottebohm, 1980).

The influence of sex steroids on the development of the song system has been extensively studied in zebra finches, where the differences between the male and female song systems are especially pronounced (Figure 3). Female zebra finches have very small and shrunken song nuclei and, unlike canaries, do not respond to testosterone administration in adulthood with song. If given estrogen early in life, however, female zebra finch chicks develop masculinized song nuclei (Gurney, 1981). Their nuclei do not shrink and even increase in size, and they retain a larger number of androgen target cells. Moreover, HVc axons enter RA and form synapses. Unlike normal female zebra finches, such estrogen-treated females do respond to testosterone treatment in adulthood by singing, as well as with further increases in the size of their song nuclei. This two-step action of hormones in the song system is similar to the actions of steroid hormones in other neural systems. Early effects, when brain structure is permanently affected, have been called *organizational*; later effects, when hormones act on the neural organization and elicit a response, are *activational*. Although it may seem surprising that estrogen is the masculinizing hormone, this is true in many mammalian sexually dimorphic systems as well, where testosterone is aromatized to estrogen, which then acts as the masculinizing hormone.

What is the cellular basis of the sex steroid effects on the songbird brain? RA neurons can be labelled with ^{3}H-thymidine in the egg and counted at vari-

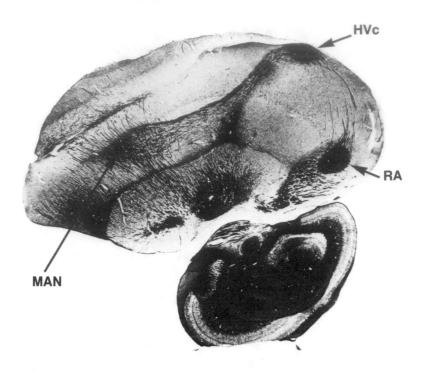

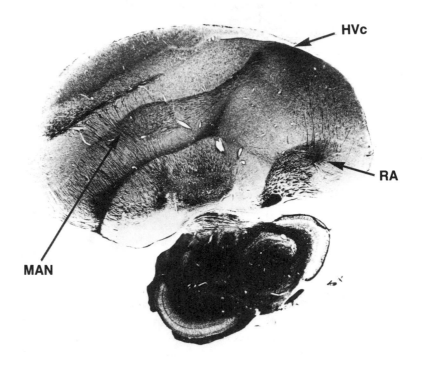

Figure 3. Sexual dimorphism of the songbird brain. These sections from corresponding areas of a male (*upper panel*) and a female (*lower panel*) zebra finch brain reveal the marked difference in size between the male and female song nuclei. HVc, ventral nucleus of the hyperstriation (caudal part); MAN, magnocellular nucleus of the anterior neostriatum; RA, robust nucleus of the archistriatum.

ous ages in normal and estrogen-treated female zebra finches. This experiment demonstrates that steroids prevent neuronal cell death that normally occurs in female RA in the first few weeks after hatching (Konishi, 1989). Thus both sexes possess the "instructions," presumably genetic, that initiate development of the song system. In females, however, the song system atrophies in the absence of the masculinizing hormone. In theory, differential neurogenesis might also play a role in generating the sexual dimorphism. The HVc and X nuclei of males and estrogen-treated females contain larger numbers of postnatally generated neurons than do those of normal females (Nordeen and Nordeen, 1988). Such increases could reflect increased neurogenesis in response to steroids. This has been difficult to determine experimentally, however, and the increase in cell numbers in the male is certainly due in part to steroid-enhanced survival of newly generated neurons (Kirn and DeVoogd, 1989).

There is a critical period for the masculinizing action of estrogen. Twelve days of treatment are adequate for masculinizing a female zebra finch, but this steroid treatment must occur before day 45 in order to be effective, which is about the time when RA appears shrunken (Konishi, 1989). This raises the possibility that the critical period closes in part because all the cells that might be masculinized have died. The site of estrogen action on the song system remains somewhat puzzling. HVc is the only song nucleus containing cells with estrogen receptors (Gahr, Fluegge, and Guettinger, 1987). One possibility is that estrogen acts only on HVc, and the effects on other parts of the song system are mediated by cascadelike transsynaptic events. Such indirect hormone effects have been seen in other sexually dimorphic systems, for instance in the motor neurons innervating the penile musculature (Rand and Breedlove, 1988). (See also HORMONES AND MEMORY; SEX DIFFERENCES IN LEARNING IN ANIMALS.)

Another unusual feature of the songbird brain and, in fact, of avian brains in general is that neurogenesis does not end after postnatal development, as it does in mammals. Neurogenesis continues to occur in portions of the germinal zone in adult birds, and these newly generated neurons migrate out into the forebrain and are incorporated into the neural circuitry. Some of these neurons in HVc project to RA (Alvarez-Buylla, Theelen, and Nottebohm, 1988). It is not yet clear, however, what

significance this phenomenon has for song learning. The new neurons occur throughout the forebrain, in females as well as males. They are found in one-time learners such as zebra finches as well as in open learners like canaries, and even in nonsongbirds. Nonetheless, this phenomenon suggests that adult birds retain a remarkable ability to generate new neurons as well as a preservation of the cues for axon guidance and neuronal specification in their brains.

An intriguing feature of the song system is that numerous dramatic developmental changes such as birth and death of neurons, axonal outgrowth, and synaptogenesis take place in the first few months of life, coincident with song learning. Do these changes cause the song learning; are they a consequence of the learning? One of the advantages of the song system is that learning can be behaviorally manipulated. For instance, the critical period for learning of the tutor song can be extended by visual or acoustic isolation, or the animal can be completely deprived of auditory input by deafening. In such birds, even though the timetable for learning has been altered, the postnatal neurogenesis in HVc and X and the volume changes of the song nuclei occur just as in normal animals. Similarly, it is now clear that seasonal increases and decreases in HVc volume occur both in some species that learn again every season and in some that do not (Brenowitz et al., 1991). Therefore, the morphological changes do not necessarily reflect learning. Rather, neural development occurs simultaneously with song learning, presumably under the control of sex steroids and other innate factors, and provides a substrate that can be used in learning. The effects of learning are likely to be represented by finer-scale changes in synaptic morphology and functional neuronal properties.

Summary

The song system of passerine songbirds is a series of discrete and interconnected brain areas that has evolved in birds that learn to sing by copying external models. It contains a pathway specialized for the motor production of song, and several auditory pathways that contain complex auditory neurons selective for the bird's own song. The properties of neurons in these pathways reflect the learning of song during early development. The interaction between these auditory and motor neurons must mediate the auditory-motor matching so crucial to song learning. The study of this system will ultimately allow a description of the learning of a complex behavior in terms of neural properties and interconnections.

Like the singing behavior, the song system is sexually dimorphic. There are differences between males and females in terms of neuronal size, number, dendritic branching, steroid hormone uptake, and synaptic connectivity. Both the development and adult function of this system are influenced by sex steroids. During a critical period in early development, estrogen acts both directly and indirectly to masculinize song nuclei by preventing neuronal death and stimulating neuronal growth. In adulthood, testosterone activates singing and causes further cellular changes that promote song. The song system offers rich material for the cellular and molecular analysis of the development of a complex neural system.

REFERENCES

Alvarez-Buylla, A., Theelen, M., and Nottebohm, F. (1988). Birth of projection neurons in the higher vocal center of the canary forebrain before, during, and after song learning. *Proceedings of the National Academy of Sciences (USA) 85,* 8722–8726.

Bottjer, S. W., Miesner, E. A., and Arnold, A. P. (1984). Forebrain lesions disrupt development but not maintenance of song in passerine birds. *Science 224,* 901–903.

Brenowitz, E. A., Nalls, B., Wingfield, J. C., and Kroodsma, D. E. (1991). Seasonal changes in avian song nuclei without seasonal changes in song repertoire. *Journal of Neuroscience 11* (5):1367–1374.

Doupe, A. J., and Konishi, M. (1991). Song-selective auditory circuits in the vocal control system of the zebra finch. *Proceedings of the National Academy of Sciences (USA) 88,* 11339–11343.

Gahr, M., Fluegge, G., and Guettinger, H.-R. (1987). Immunocytochemical localization of estrogen-binding neurons in the forebrain of the zebra finch. *Brain Research 402,* 173–177.

Gurney, M. E. (1981). Hormonal control of cell form and number in the zebra finch song system. *Journal of Neuroscience 1* (6):658–673.

Kirn, J. R., and DeVoogd, T. J. (1989). Genesis and death of vocal control neurons during sexual differentiation in the zebra finch. *Journal of Neuroscience 9,* (9):3179–3187.

Konishi, M. (1989). Birdsong for neurobiologists. *Neuron 3,* 541–549.

Konishi, M., and Akutagawa, E. (1985). Neuronal growth, atrophy and death in a sexually dimorphic song nucleus in the zebra finch. *Nature 315,* 145–147.

Margoliash, D. (1983). Acoustic parameters underlying the responses of song-specific neurons in the white-crowned sparrow. *Journal of Neuroscience 3,* (5): 1039–1057.

McCasland, J. S. (1987). Neuronal control of bird song production. *Journal of Neuroscience 7,* 23–39.

Mooney, R., and Konishi, M. (1991). Two distinct inputs to an avian song nucleus activate different glutamate receptor subtypes on individual neurons. *Proceedings of the National Academy of Sciences (USA)* 88, 4075–4079.

Nordeen, E. J., and Nordeen, K. W. (1988). Sex and regional differences in the incorporation of neurons born during song learning in zebra finches. *Journal of Neuroscience 8,* 2869–2874.

Nottebohm, F. (1980). Brain pathways for vocal learning in birds: A review of the first ten years. *Progress in Psychobiology and Physiological Psychology 9,* 85–124.

Nottebohm, F. (1981). A brain for all seasons: Cyclical anatomical changes in song control nuclei of the canary brain. *Science 214,* 1368–1370.

Rand, M. N., and Breedlove, S. M. (1988). Progress report on a hormonally sensitive neuromuscular system. *Psychobiology 16,* 398–405.

Scharff, C., and Nottebohm, F. (1991). A comparative study of the behavioral deficits following lesions of various parts of the zebra finch song system: Implications for vocal learning. *Journal of Neuroscience 11,* 2896–2913.

Sohrabji, F., Nordeen, E. J., and Nordeen, K. W. (1990). Selective impairment of song learning following lesions of a forebrain nucleus in the juvenile zebra finch. *Behavioral Neurology and Biology 53,* 51–63.

Suthers, R. A. (1990). Contributions to birdsong from the left and right sides of the intact syrinx. *Nature 347* (6292):473–477.

Vicario, D. S. (1991). Neural mechanisms of vocal production in songbirds. *Current Opinion in Neurobiology 1* (4:):595–600.

Allison J. Doupe

CAJAL, SANTIAGO RAMÓN Y

Santiago Ramón y Cajal (1852–1934), born in the small Spanish town of Petilla de Aragón on May 1, 1852, was a major figure in the history of neuroanatomy. As related in his delightful autobiography, he was somewhat mischievous as a child and determined to become an artist, much to the consternation of his father, a respected local physician. Eventually, however, he entered the University of Zaragoza, and received a degree in medicine in 1873. As a professor of anatomy at Zaragoza, his interests were mostly in bacteriology until 1887, when he visited Madrid and first saw through the microscope histological sections of brain tissue treated with the Golgi method, which had been introduced in 1873.

Although very few workers had employed this technique, Cajal immediately saw that it offered great hope in solving one of the most vexing and fundamental problems in morphology: How do nerve cells interact with each other? This realization galvanized and directed the rest of his scientific life, which was extremely productive in originality, scope, and accuracy.

To place Cajal's work in historical perspective, one must recall that while studies of the gross anatomy of the brain can be traced back as far as Aristotle, the first real insight into the disposition of its major fiber tracts was not gained until the middle of the nineteenth century, and even then the interpretation of this information was subject to great controversy. Shortly after Jacob Schleiden, Theodor Schwann, and Rudolf Virchow proposed the cell theory in the 1830s, Joseph von Gerlach, Sr., and Otto Friedrich Karl Dieters suggested that nerve tissue was special in the sense that nerve cells are not independent units but instead form a continuous syncytium or reticular net. This concept was later refined by Camillo Golgi, who concluded that the axons of nerve cells form a continuous reticular net, whereas their dendrites serve a nutritive role, much like the roots of a tree.

Using Golgi's technique, Cajal almost immediately arrived at the opposite conclusion, from his examination first of the cerebellum, and then of

Figure 1. Santiago Ramón y Cajal.

a wide variety of other sensory and motor systems. In short, he proposed that neurons interact by way of contact rather than continuity. His work on both the mature and the developing nervous system (he discovered the growth cone in 1890) provided the best evidence for the neuron doctrine (that neurons are independent units or cells, as in other tissues) until the introduction of the electron microscope in the 1950s.

Important as this evidence was, Cajal's greatest conceptual achievement was the law of dynamic polarity. Based on his analysis of Golgi-impregnated neurons in the retina and other sensory systems, where the direction of information flow from the periphery to the central nervous system seems obvious, Cajal concluded that, in general, the dendrites and perikaryon of a neuron receive information, whereas its axon transmits information. This brilliant generalization allowed him to lay out the basic organization of circuitry throughout the nervous system. This research was summarized in the monumental three-volume work *Textura del sistema nervioso del hombre y de los vertebrados,* published between 1899 and 1904, then expanded and translated into the definitive French edition, *Histologie du système nerveux de l'homme et des vertébrés* (1909–1911). This account deals systematically with all parts of the mammalian nervous system and many aspects of its development, and provides a great deal of information on the organization of the nervous system in fish, amphibians, reptiles, and birds.

Cajal next examined in great detail the histological changes that can be observed during the degeneration and regeneration of neural tissue following damage. The results of this work were summarized in another monumental work that is still well worth reading, the two-volume *Degeneration and Regeneration of the Nervous System,* first published in Spanish in 1913–1914.

Cajal received many honors, including the Nobel Prize, which he shared with a contentious Golgi in 1906. By the time he died, at the age of 82 in 1934, he had become one of the most famous and revered Spaniards of the twentieth century. In addition to the neurohistological work outlined above, he wrote widely appreciated books on color photography, advice to young investigators, and well-known Spanish aphorisms.

Cajal's description of the organization of cerebral cortical circuitry is unparalleled in depth and breadth. As early as 1894 he advanced the hypothesis that the remarkable intellectual growth seen in people who engage in continuous mental exercise is due to an enhanced elaboration of axon collaterals and dendritic processes within cortical circuitry (see also GUIDE TO THE ANATOMY OF THE BRAIN: sections on NEURON and SYNAPSE.)

REFERENCES

Cajal, S. Ramón y (1899–1904). *Textura del sistema nervioso del hombre y de los vertebrados,* 3 vols. Madrid: N. Moya.

—— (1909–1911). *Histologie du système nerveux de l'homme et des vertébrés,* L. Azoulay, trans., 2 vols. Paris: Norbert Maloine.

—— (1928). *Degeneration and regeneration of the nervous system,* R. M. May, trans. and ed., 2 vols. London: Oxford University Press.

—— (1989). *Recollections of my life,* E. H. Craigie with J. Cano, trans. Cambridge, Mass.: MIT Press.

—— (1990). *New ideas on the structure of the nervous system in man and vertebrates,* N. Swanson and L. W. Swanson, trans. Cambridge, Mass.: MIT Press.

De Filipe, J., and E. G. Jones. (1988). *Cajal on the cerebral cortex.* New York: Oxford University Press.

Larry W. Swanson

CATEGORIES

See Concepts and Categories, Learning of

CEREBELLUM

See Guide to the Anatomy of the Brain; Neural Computation

CEREBRAL NEOCORTEX

See Guide to the Anatomy of the Brain

CHILDREN, DEVELOPMENT OF MEMORY IN

On most measures, memory improves through childhood and adolescence. One measure that illustrates typical change is *digit span,* which is commonly included on tests of intelligence. Here, the examiner presents a set of digits aloud, at a rate of approximately one digit per second. The child's task is to recall the digits aloud in the order in which they were presented. The examiner begins with a set of two digits. If the child recalls these digits accurately, one digit is added to the set. Additional digits are added in this manner until children can no longer recall the entire set accurately. The largest set recalled accurately defines the child's digit span. (See also MEMORY SPAN.)

At any age, individual children will differ in digit span. However, the average digit span is approximately two digits at age 2 years, four digits at age 5, five digits at age 7, six digits at age 9, and seven digits by adolescence. These results are typical for most measures of memory, which show rapid change during early childhood, smaller change in late childhood, and adult levels of performance during early to middle adolescence. Another way to view these results is to say that digit span increases by a factor of three over the course of childhood and adolescence.

These dramatic changes in memory during childhood and adolescence have been investigated extensively by developmental psychologists. In addition, developmental psychologists have investigated the origins of memory in infancy. These topics are discussed in detail next.

Origins of Memory in Infancy

Psychologists have long been interested in infants' ability to remember experiences from very early in life. However, most of the methods used to study memory in children and adolescents cannot be used with infants because they require people to speak or write. Consequently, the study of infants' memory became possible only after psychologists devised techniques that took advantage of infants' abilities to respond in other ways.

Rovee-Collier and her colleagues have demonstrated that kicking could be used to study infant memory (Rovee-Collier, 1989). A mobile is placed over an infant's crib, and a ribbon connects the infant's leg to the mobile. Infants kick vigorously just a few minutes after their leg is connected to the mobile, demonstrating that they have learned the relation between their kicking and the mobile's movement. To study infant memory, time is allowed to pass, then the infant's leg is reconnected to the mobile. If the infant begins, almost immediately, to kick vigorously, then the infant apparently has remembered the relation between its kicking and the mobile's movement. If, instead, kicking gradually becomes more vigorous—as if the infant is relearning the relation—then the infant has forgotten the relation.

Research based on techniques like these has demonstrated that by the age of 3 months, infants will remember that link between kicking and the moving mobile for up to 14 days. That is, when an infant's leg is reconnected to the mobile within 14 days of the original learning, the infant will kick vigorously, without the need to relearn the relation.

Even newborns are able to remember. This is documented by research in which infants are first shown a picture such as a checkerboard. Then they are shown a pair of pictures: the checkerboard seen previously and a new picture. Infants typically look longer at the new picture, presumably because they recall having seen the checkerboard already.

(See also AMNESIA, INFANTILE; INFANCY, MEMORY IN.)

How Memory Develops during Childhood and Adolescence

Two factors play a critical role in the development of memory during childhood and adolescence: greater use of strategies and greater task-relevant knowledge.

Developmental Change in Use of Memory Strategies

A strategy is any deliberate act that is designed to improve retention. For example, if asked to remember a telephone number, many people spontaneously repeat the numbers mentally, a strategy known as rehearsal. As another example, when it is important to remember to take something from home to school or to the office, people may place the object near a door or near car keys; the object thus serves as its own reminder.

As children grow, they are more likely to use strategies to help them remember. In addition, as they develop, children and adolescents tend to use more effective strategies. To illustrate this sequence of change, consider age-related change in two strategies:

Looking. When the memory task is to remember a person's actions or to remember the location of an object, looking carefully at the person or the object is a good first step towards memorization. By age 3, children will use this memory strategy. That is, if they are told that they must remember another person's actions, they will watch that person much more carefully than if they have not been told to remember the person's actions.

Rehearsal. As described above, rehearsal refers to repetitive naming of information to be remembered. Typically, children start to rehearse at about age 6 or 7 years; after age 7, they become more adept at rehearsal, rehearsing more information simultaneously and organizing the information during rehearsal. For example, if children are told to remember words such as *apple, car, grape, bus, banana, bike,* preschool children will not rehearse, and, consequently, they will recall few of the words. Typically, 6- to 8-year-olds rehearse the words in the order in which they were presented. After hearing the last word in this sequence (*bike*), a typical rehearsal set for a child at this age might be *bus, banana, banana, bike.* By the age of 10 to 12 years, children do not simply parrot the sequence of words as presented. Instead, they take advantage of the relations that exist between words and might rehearse *banana, apple, banana, car, bus, bike. . . .* Thus, children's rehearsal often is limited to rote repetition of the material to be remembered. In contrast, adolescents rehearse more flexibly; they modify the strategy as necessary to fit the nature of the material.

The general trend for children to use strategies more often and more effectively as they grow apparently reflects parallel developmental changes in children's ability to *diagnose* memory tasks and to *monitor* the effectiveness of their chosen strategy. That is, young children often underestimate the difficulty of memory problems, and, consequently, may underestimate the need for a strategy to remember effectively. For example, after the

requirements of a digit-span task are explained to 5- and 6-year-olds, many children at this age estimate that they will recall nine to ten digits accurately, a value that far exceeds their actual performance. Because they believe, incorrectly, that the span task is easy, children may see little need to use a strategy to improve performance. In contrast, older children and adolescents are better able to judge the difficulty of memory tasks. Consequently, they are more likely to select an effective memory strategy.

As children develop they are also more likely to pay attention to the impact of their strategy on performance. By analyzing the effect of a strategy, children can decide how to allocate their effort as they continue on the task. For example, if some but not all of the information has been learned, effort should be directed to the information that remains unlearned. Older children and adolescents usually allocate effort this way. Young children, in contrast, often continue to study information that they already know and disregard that which they have not yet learned. Similarly, only adolescents and older children typically will abandon an ineffective strategy and search for one that is more effective.

Knowledge and Memory

People often remember very accurately when the information to be recalled is from their area of expertise. Skilled bridge players can remember hands of cards much more accurately than bridge novices, just as chess experts can remember the positions of chess pieces on a board much more accurately than chess novices.

To explain results like these, psychologists believe that knowledge is represented in memory as a network in which similar entries are associated with one another. An example of a portion of such a network is shown in Figure 1. The network consists of nodes (the ellipses) linked by different types of associations: *isa* links denote category membership, *can* and *has* denote properties of the node.

Knowledge like that depicted in Figure 1 can aid memory because it provides special codes that simplify memorization. To illustrate, suppose that people were asked to remember a list of words like *collie, Doberman, Dalmatian, poodle. . . .* In this case, the category name, *dogs,* serves as a code for the list. People can recall the category name, then scan words associated with that name

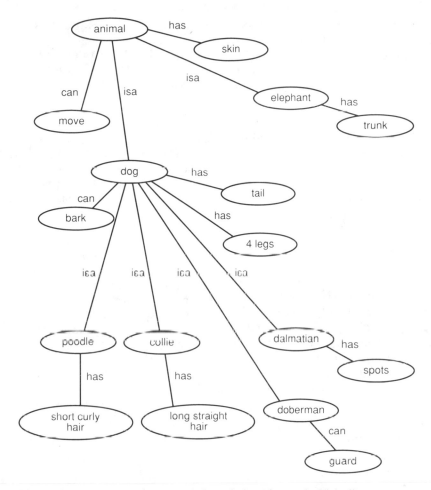

Figure 1. A portion of a person's knowledge of animals. The ellipses correspond to nodes in the network, linked by associations that denote membership in a category (*isa*) and properties (*has, can*).

and decide if they were presented. Thus, one benefit of greater knowledge is that a person is more likely to be able to provide a code that reduces the amount of material that must be remembered.

Another way that knowledge benefits memory is by providing more *retrieval* cues. Each of the links in Figure 1 provides an alternate way—a cue—to gain access to a word that was presented. Thus, the more links the better. When people are expert in some domain, their knowledge will be linked extensively; if they know little, their knowledge will have relatively few links. Consequently, experts will typically have more cues available to recall information.

Children usually acquire knowledge gradually as they develop, which means that the mnemonic benefits of greater knowledge are greater for adults and adolescents than for children. Illustrative results come from research with *incidental learning*

tasks. Because the aim of these experiments is to look at the impact of knowledge without the influence of memory strategies, at the beginning of these experiments, subjects are not told that they will be asked to remember words. Instead, words are presented and questions are asked that are designed to invoke the subject's knowledge of that word. For example, subjects might see *dachshund* and be asked, "Is this a dog?" Seeing *table*, they could be asked, "Is this a piece of furniture?" Later, subjects are asked to recall as many words as they can. Typically, the number of words recalled increases with age. This cannot reflect increased use of memory strategies with age, because subjects did not know that they were to remember the words. Instead, the results reflect increased task-relevant knowledge with age, which makes it easier for adolescents and adults to code and retrieve the words.

Of course, adults do not always have greater task-relevant knowledge than children. There are unusual instances in which children are more knowledgeable than adults, and the expected outcome here is that children should remember more effectively than adults. This was demonstrated in research by Chi (1978) that examined recall of digits and patterns by 10-year-olds and adults. Adults' recall of digits exceeded children's, but the reverse was true for patterns. Here children recalled approximately 9.5 arrays compared with 6 for adults. Two key details are that the "patterns" were chess pieces placed in realistic positions on chessboards and that the children (but not the adults) were chess experts. Thus, in recall of patterns, the child chess experts had much more knowledge than the adult chess novices about the information to be remembered. This knowledge simplified the task of remembering substantially. Whereas the adult novice had to remember the position of individual pieces, the child experts recognized the entire pattern of pieces and simply remembered the name of the pattern.

Knowledge is not always beneficial, because it can distort memories. Information to be remembered is often changed so that it conforms to our existing knowledge or stereotypes. For example, when children hear stories in which superheroes are said to be weak or ugly, they tend to recall the heroes as strong and attractive. Similarly, if asked to remember the actions of boys and girls whose behaviors violate sex-role stereotypes (e.g., a girl sawing wood), children will change the sex of the actor to make it consistent with sex-role knowledge. (see also EXPERTS' MEMORIES.)

Conclusions

At birth, human infants are able to remember. Memory processes improve rapidly through childhood and, less markedly, during adolescence. These changes reflect age-related increases in use of memory strategies, which are brought about because children diagnose memory problems more accurately and are better able to evaluate the effectiveness of the chosen strategy. Memory also improves because of age-related increases in knowledge, which allow more effective coding and retrieval of information.

REFERENCES

Bjorklund, D. F., ed. (1990). *Children's strategies: Contemporary views of cognitive development.* Hillsdale, N.J.: Erlbaum.

Brainerd, C. J., and Pressley, M., eds. (1985). *Basic processes in memory development.* New York: Springer-Verlag.

Chi, M. T. H. (1978). Knowledge structures and memory development. In R. S. Siegler, ed., *Children's thinking: What develops?*, pp. 73–96. Hillsdale, N.J.: Erlbaum.

Dempster, F. N. (1981). Memory span: Sources of individual and developmental differences. *Psychological Bulletin 89,* 63–100.

Kail, R. (1990). *The development of memory in children,* 3rd ed. New York: W. H. Freeman.

Moscovitch, M., ed. (1984). *Infant memory.* New York: Plenum.

Rovee-Collier, C. (1989). The joy of kicking: Memories, motives, and mobiles. In P. R. Solomon, G. R. Goethals, C. M. Kelley, and B. R. Stephens, eds., *Memory: Interdisciplinary approaches,* pp. 151–180. New York: Springer-Verlag.

Schneider, W., and Pressley, M. (1989). *Memory development between 2 and 20.* New York: Springer-Verlag.

Weinert, F. E., and Perlmutter, M., eds. (1988). *Memory development: Universal changes and individual differences.* Hillsdale, N.J.: Erlbaum.

Robert Kail

CODING PROCESSES

[Coding processes *refers to the ways that information may be represented in memory. Events in the world strike our senses and may be well perceived, but the mental operations that ensue determine whether the events will be remembered. These mental operations are referred to as coding processes and have been studied in several different ways. Three types of coding processes are discussed in the entries in this section. The first entry is on coding processes that involve mental* imagery. *People tend to remember information better if they convert the information to "mental pictures" while they study it. This technique is frequently used by experts who can memorize huge amounts of information (see* MNEMONISTS) *and by all people who employ effective memory strategies (see* MNEMONIC DEVICES). *In the* levels of processing *approach, people are directed to think about different aspects of events (attention is directed to superficial properties of events or their meaning) and memory is tested later. The "deeper" or more meaningful the level of processing, the better the later memory under most circumstances. The final topic in this section is more general, about organizing processes in memory. One effective strategy to code information is to organize it in terms of knowledge we already have. The study of memory organization is concerned both with how knowledge is organized and with how people use their knowledge to encode new information in memory. The study of coding processes is central to the study of human memory and ramifies through most other topics. For example, whether some bit of information can be retrieved from memory depends on how it was encoded when it was learned (see* RETRIEVAL PROCESSES*).]*

Imagery

According to Cicero, it was the poet Simonides who first recognized the utility of mental imagery for memory. During a brief absence from a banquet at which the poet recited the entertainment, the roof of the building caved in, mangling the guests so badly that recognition of the bodies was impossible. Simonides (who likely already had developed a fairly good memory in the context of his job) realized that he could remember the faces and clothing of the guests in various locations around the room; thus he was able to identify the corpses for their families. Secondarily, perhaps, the art of memory was born (see Yates, 1966, for full histories).

Image and *imagery* generally are used to refer to those concrete, perceptual, and usually visual modes of thought which appear to represent the physical world relatively directly. These are clearly distinguishable from verbal thought processes, which are arbitrary in the linguistic sense of there being no necessary relationship (other than social agreement) between words and their referents. Mental images of things we have experienced thus often appear to be fundamentally related to their meanings. It is difficult to think of a pizza without some olfactory or gustatory image of its taste or to think of your mother without experiencing a visual image of her face.

Consistent with our subjective impressions, a variety of studies have indicated that visual imagery and visual perception have some similar qualities. Several studies by Shepard and his colleagues, for example, have examined *mental rotation* (e.g., Cooper and Shepard, 1973). This paradigm typically involves asking people to judge whether two visually presented stimuli (e.g., letters or three-dimensional shapes) are identical or mirror reflections of each other. Shepard's results have consistently indicated that in order to decide on the possible identity of the two stimuli, subjects first mentally rotate one of them to the same orientation as the other. This is evidenced by the fact that reaction times to make the identity judgments increase regularly as the angular difference between the two stimuli increases from 0 to 180 degrees and then decreases to 360 degrees (as the rotation can be made "backwards").

Kosslyn and his colleagues have demonstrated similar findings in a series of studies on *mental scanning* (e.g., Kosslyn, 1973). In this paradigm, subjects memorize several landmarks on a simple map and then are asked to form an image of it. Consistently, the time required for subjects to scan from one location to another on their images is a direct function of the linear distance between the two locations on the original map, thus reflecting the analogue character of mental images. Further studies by Kosslyn, Finke, and others have shown that people can mentally construct two- and three-dimensional figures that have emergent properties not predictable from their component parts. Such findings indicate a perceptionlike quality of mental imagery that has been supported by some neurophysiological evidence (e.g., Farah, 1984).

Although the psychological processes underlying these phenomena may not be entirely clear, the utility of mental imagery and pictures to facilitate memory has been recognized for centuries. Simonides's *method of loci,* for example, in which successive items are imaged at specific locations along a familiar route, has long been used for learning ordered lists of unrelated items or remembering a series of points to be made during a speech. Imagery also can be helpful in learning foreign vocabulary, as in forming an image of a cadaver falling from a table for the Italian *cadere* (to fall) or someone harvesting cogs in a field for *cogliere* (to pick or gather). In addition, imagery seems central to the development of thinking and memory in children, and a progression from motor processes to visual images to verbal processes is

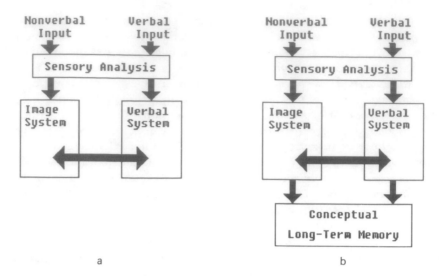

Figure 1. Schematic diagram of the dual coding model and one possible alternative.

assumed by most major theories of cognitive development.

In scientific studies of memory, there are several typical findings that indicate an important role of imagery: Words rated as referring to more concrete, highly imageable things are better remembered than words referring to abstract, nonimageable things—the *concreteness effect*; the use of imagery in learning (either by instruction or spontaneously) leads to better memory than nonimaginal strategies—the *imagery effect*; and pictures are better remembered than words—the *picture superiority effect*.

This apparent centrality of mental imagery in thinking and memory has led to several theoretical frameworks for studying human memory and cognition that give images an essential role. The most completely articulated of these, the *dual coding model* of Paivio (1971, 1986), is depicted in Figure 1(a). The model includes a verbal system specialized for dealing with sequential, especially linguistic information and an imagery system specialized for dealing with nonverbal, holistic information. It explicitly entails that concrete experiences generate perceptual memory traces (images) which preserve the structural attributes of the input. Those generated memory representations are assumed to be functionally equivalent to perceptual representations "in the sense that an image of an object generated to its name has the same mnemonic properties as the image evoked by the object itself" (Paivio, 1986, p. 144). Among other consequences, the storage of information-rich perceptual images is assumed to account for the findings that mental comparisons of things on physical dimensions (such as size) yield similar patterns of response times regardless of whether the objects, their pictures, or their printed names are presented.

The hypothesized existence of separate but interconnected verbal and imaginal systems in the dual coding model explains the concreteness effect in terms of *coding redundancy*: Concrete words usually result in dual verbal and imaginal memory codes (via the intersystem, referential crossover), whereas abstract words usually result in only a single, verbal code. Such redundancy provides two alternative "routes" to the traces for concrete words during recall and provides a "backup" if one code is forgotten. In learning of concrete word pairs (i.e., in *paired-associate learning*), imagery is assumed to provide a means of integrating the meanings of the two words into a single, imaginal unit that can be retrieved later in the context of one of the words as a cue. Integration of this sort is assumed to be unavailable for abstract word pairs, which must be stored as two-unit verbal strings. Finally, pictures are assumed by the dual code model to be better remembered than words in part because images may be inherently more memorable than verbal traces but primarily because pictures are likely to elicit verbal naming (and hence dual memory codes) with a somewhat higher probability than words elicit imagery.

One modified version of the dual coding model is depicted in Figure 1(b). In this alternative, dual verbal and imaginal processing systems are assumed to operate at a level akin to Baddeley's (1986) WORKING MEMORY, which has both visual and verbal components. The dual processing systems can account for most of the results concerning verbal processes and image manipulation and inspection. In contrast with the multiple, modality-specific memory codes of the original dual coding model, however, this version assumes that long-term memory involves some more generic, semantic, or propositional code common to both concrete and abstract information (Potter, 1979). Information is retrieved from this conceptual memory and images are constructed in visual working memory. Imagery is still invoked to explain the beneficial effects of imagery instructions, material concreteness, and picture presentation, but the locus of their effects on memory is placed on the *distinctiveness* of imaginally processed items within the encoding and retrieval contexts (Marschark et al., 1987). Interitem integration is assumed to be possible for abstract as well as concrete materials via conceptual relations.

One difficulty in explaining the effects of imageability on memory is that there are several other variables that co-occur with it. Dimensions such as concreteness and word frequency have been shown to be positively related to rated imagery values, whereas others, such as generality of reference and associative set size, have been shown to be negatively related to it. The effect of imagery can be empirically or statistically separated from all of those other variables, however, and remains a significant predictor of memory when the others are controlled (Paivio, 1986). Exceptions begin to occur only when memory for more complex materials like concrete and abstract texts are considered or when other meaningful contexts make the importance of imaginal processing less essential (Marschark and Cornoldi, 1990).

The precise role of imagery in language comprehension and problem solving remains unclear, although it clearly plays a role in visually and spatially oriented situations, such as route learning and chess playing, which seem to involve *analogue* mental manipulation. Distinguishing imagery from the nature of long-term memory codes highlights the role of *individual differences* in imagery ability. A variety of standardized and well-documented tests that involve tasks such as mental paper-folding, mental rotation, and mental scanning have provided evidence of large differences between individuals in the vividness, speed, and frequency of image generation. The imagery abilities tapped by these tests generally are not predictive of memory ability even for concrete materials. Nonetheless, it is clear that variability in some imagery abilities can have specific and marked effects in a variety of cognitive domains, including memory. Individuals who have suffered head injuries, for example, typically exhibit deficits in visual-spatial tasks such as finding hidden figures or reconstructing previously presented pictures. They may also fail to exhibit concreteness effects in memory and be particularly slow at making imaginal comparisons (see Richardson, 1990). People who score high on tests of image manipulation skill tend to be faster in comparing their images on particular dimensions, although they may be no faster in generating those images in the first place.

Among the more puzzling imagery findings yet to be explained is why people who are totally, congenitally blind still show apparent imagery and concreteness effects (DeBeni and Cornoldi, 1988). These effects appear not to be attributable to tactile knowledge, because they are just as readily obtained when the to-be-remembered items are things for which tactile experience is unlikely (e.g., *moon, tiger,* and *tower*). Clearly, imagery is a multidimensional construct that has great theoretical and practical utility but no simple psychological explanation.

REFERENCES

Baddeley, A. (1986). *Working memory.* Oxford: Clarendon Press.

Cooper, L. A., and Shepard, R. N. (1973). The time required to prepare for a rotated stimulus. *Memory and Cognition 1,* 246–250.

DeBeni, R., and Cornoldi, C. (1988). Imagery limitations in totally congenitally blind subjects. *Journal of Experimental Psychology: Learning, Memory, and Cognition 14,* 650–655.

Farah, M. J. (1984). The neurological basis of mental imagery: A componential analysis. *Cognition 18,* 245–272.

Kosslyn, S. M. (1973). Scanning visual images: Some structural implications. *Perception and Psychophysics 14,* 90–94.

Marschark, M., and Cornoldi, C. (1990). Imagery and verbal memory. In C. Cornoldi and M. A. McDaniel, eds., *Imagery and cognition,* pp. 133–182. New York: Springer-Verlag.

Marschark, M., Richman, C. L., Yuille, J. C., and Hunt, R. R. (1987). The role of imagery in memory: On shared and distinctive information. *Psychological Bulletin 102*, 28–41.

Paivio, A. ([1971] 1979). *Imagery and verbal processes.* New York: Holt, Rinehart, and Winston. Reprint. Hillsdale, N.J.: Erlbaum.

——— (1986). *Mental representations: A dual coding approach.* Oxford: Oxford University Press.

Potter, M. C. (1979). Mundane symbolism: The relations among objects, names, and ideas. In N. R. Smith and M. B. Franklin, eds., *Symbolic functioning in childhood,* pp. 41–65. Hillsdale, N.J.: Erlbaum.

Richardson, J. T. E. (1990). Imagery and the brain. In C. Cornoldi and M. A. McDaniel, eds., *Imagery and cognition,* pp. 1–45. New York: Springer-Verlag.

Yates, F. A. (1966). *The art of memory.* Chicago: University of Chicago Press.

Marc Marschark

Levels of Processing

Processing and Recall

The term "levels of processing" was introduced by Craik and Lockhart (1972) to describe the way in which the information contained in a stimulus can be analyzed at levels ranging from surface physical properties to deeper levels involving its meaning. Thus in reading the printed word "CLEVER," the reader might process *orthographic* features, such as its being in capital letters, or *phonemic* features, such as that it rhymes with "ever," or *semantic* features, such as that it is a synonym for "skilled."

The relevance of this concept to our understanding of memory is the well-documented fact (e.g., Craik and Tulving, 1975) that level of processing is a powerful determinant of how well an event will be remembered. A simple demonstration experiment illustrates this point. Subjects are presented with a sequence of common words and asked to make one of three possible judgments about each word. For some words subjects are asked to make a judgment at the orthographic level, such as whether the word is printed in capital letters; other words require a phonemic-level judgment, such as whether the word rhymes with a certain word; a third set of words requires a judgment involving meaning, such as whether the word is a synonym for a specified word. The assumption is that these three types of judgments require increasingly deep levels of processing. In a subse-

quent memory test in which subjects are asked to recall the words, deeper levels of processing are associated with higher levels of recall: those words which required a semantic-level judgment are best recalled, whereas those requiring orthographic processing yield the lowest recall level.

Craik and Lockhart (1972) proposed the general concept of levels of processing not as a theory of memory but rather as a framework for future research into the relationship between coding processes and memory. A retrospective commentary on the significance of this proposal is to be found in Lockhart and Craik (1990). The basic claim of levels of processing as a research framework is that a thorough understanding of remembering requires a careful analysis of the way in which (and the degree to which) coding processes involve the construction of meaning. According to this view there is no distinct coding process that can be identified as "committing to memory." Rather, memory coding—the memory trace—is constructed as a by-product of the everyday mental operations we perform as we interact with our environment and attempt to understand it. One implication of this claim is that a proper account of the relationship between coding processes and memory will involve an understanding of the broader issues of how we perceive and comprehend our world.

Orienting Tasks

Experimental conditions (termed "orienting tasks") such as those involving judgments of case, rhyme, or synonymity are but three examples of the large number of orienting tasks that have been used in experiments. Other examples are rating a word's pleasantness, deciding how many syllables it has, and whether it is spoken by a male or a female voice. Indeed, we can think of our everyday cognitive activity in terms of a continuous sequence of orienting tasks as our knowledge, goals, and needs interact with the circumstances of the moment. Our goals will influence our orientation toward a stimulus—the specific information that we selectively attend to and analyze—and the particular form of the analysis will strongly influence later remembering. In listening to a conversation, for example, our goal may be to comprehend what is being said, but it may also be to infer the speaker's intelligence, mood, intentions, or the origin of a distinctive accent. When we read a restaurant menu our goal may involve making judgments based on taste preference, cost, or nutritional value. As a research framework, levels of processing takes as its fundamental principle the claim that since the memory trace is the by-product of these analyses, the key to predicting subsequent memory performance is a matter of gaining increased understanding of the nature and level of these analyses. Orienting tasks used in experiments—tasks such as judging rhyme or synonymity (meaning)—are the scientist's effort to gain tight control over the processing that a subject applies to a stimulus in order to evaluate the specific impact that different processes have on memory.

Incidental Versus Intentional Processing

One important implication of the levels of processing framework that has great practical and theoretical significance concerns a distinction that can be made between *incidental* and *intentional* processing. We do not usually make an intentional effort to commit everyday experiences to memory; in this sense much of our normal remembering is *incidental.* You can probably recall what you were doing exactly twenty-four hours ago, even though at the time you were not making a conscious effort to commit the activity to memory. This aspect of everyday life can be captured in an experimental setting by using incidental orienting tasks in which subjects are not informed that they will receive a subsequent memory test. Thus in the demonstration experiment described above, subjects might perform the judgments believing that the only purpose of the experiment is to see how quickly they can respond. According to the levels of processing approach, such subjects should not be disadvantaged relative to subjects instructed to expect the memory test, *provided the level of processing for the two groups is comparable.* That is to say, the important determinant of remembering is not the conscious effort of committing something to memory but the level of processing that the orienting task induces. This conclusion is supported by experimental findings. For example, subjects who are asked to rate a word for pleasantness as an *incidental* orienting task perform as well on a subsequent unexpected memory test as subjects who are given prior warning of the test.

An Example of Deep Processing: The Self-Reference Effect

A further implication of levels of processing is that there is nothing to prevent incidental memory from being better than memory associated with a conscious effort to commit something to memory. This will happen whenever the incidental orienting task requires a deeper level of processing than the processing selected by a subject whose only instruction is to try to remember. A particularly well-documented example of this superiority of incidental over intentional instructions is a phenomenon known as the "self-reference" effect (Rogers, Kuiper, and Kirker, 1977). Suppose the incidental orienting task asks subjects to answer the question "How well does this adjective describe you?" Subjects who perform this task remember the adjectives better than subjects who have been instructed simply to try to remember them. The usual interpretation of this result is that the self-reference judgment involves the activation of the richly structured and highly meaningful self concept. By contrast, intentional subjects who do not perform this orienting task choose a form of processing that is less effective.

It is interesting to ask what subjects or students do when an experimenter or a class instructor simply exhorts them to "try to remember." Presumably they will process the material in whatever way they think will most effectively support later remembering. A common strategy with verbal material is to rehearse it by silently repeating a word or phrase over and over. Such a strategy is relatively ineffective for long-term remembering, since such repetitive processing typically involves no further analysis of meaning (no deeper-level processing) but consists of maintaining the material at a phonemic level. Again, the important point is that successful remembering is less a matter of conscious effort than of being led to perform an orienting task that demands deep levels of processing.

Skills and the Material to Be Remembered

Two further determinants of level of processing should be mentioned. One is the nature of the material to be remembered. Pictures and common words afford the rapid analysis of meaning. Other material, such as proper nouns, can pose greater difficulty. One reason for the common experience of rapidly forgetting names following introductions at a party is that proper nouns do not afford rapid deep processing. Hence most mnemonic techniques for remembering names are essentially strategies for converting proper names into a form of visual image that embodies deeper semantic-level processing. Interacting with the nature of the material is a second determinant: the skill of the rememberer. To the non-speaker of French the letter string *chien* is largely meaningless, as is a musical score to anyone who has not been trained to read music, or the game position of chess pieces to one who does not play chess. But to the speaker of French, to the trained musician, or to the skilled chess player, the word, the score, and the board position, respectively, afford deep processing and hence better remembering.

Summary

Levels of processing is a theoretical framework which claims that memory coding is to be understood as a by-product of cognitive processes which are used to interpret and comprehend our environment. Memory depends heavily on the degree to which the processing involves the construction and elaboration of meaning. Tasks such as judging case, rhyme, or synonymity provide a clear example of three distinct levels of processing, but, depending on the goals and skills of the rememberer in relation to material to be remembered, depth of processing can vary over a wide range. According to levels of processing as a research framework, the goal of research into coding processes is to provide a precise account of this variation and its impact on memory.

REFERENCES

Craik, F. I. M., and Lockhart, R. S. (1972). Levels of processing: A framework for memory research. *Journal of Verbal Learning and Verbal Behavior 11*, 671–684.

Craik, F. I. M., and Tulving, E. (1975). Depth of processing and the retention of words in episodic memory. *Journal of Experimental Psychology: General 104*, 268–294.

Lockhart, R. S., and Craik, F. I. M. (1990). Levels of processing: A retrospective commentary on a framework for memory research. *Canadian Journal of Psychology 44*, 87–112.

Rogers, T. B., Kuiper, N. A., and Kirker, W. S. (1977). Self reference and the encoding of personal information. *Journal of Personality and Social Psychology 35*, 677–688.

Robert S. Lockhart

Organization of Memory

Coding and Organization

Coding refers to the interpretations a person gives to experiences. The significance of experience for memory and action depends on the interpretation of the experience. Interpretations are influenced by knowledge and expectation to the extent that the same events can be interpreted in dramatically different ways depending on a person's knowledge and expectations. To understand coding we must understand how knowledge is organized in memory and how this knowledge is used in interpreting experience. The observation that ideas are interrelated is one of the most compelling facts of mental life. In personal memories, details of past experiences can be triggered by a single association with some present event. Psychology has developed several ideas about the nature of organization in memory.

Many facts lead to the conclusion that what we remember depends on the interpretation which occurs as we experience events. A simple illustration of the influence of coding can be seen by comparing the memories of two people with different knowledge. Suppose one person is very knowledgeable about cars (a car expert) and another one is not (a tyro). They both see the same small red car. The expert identifies it as a Miata; the tyro can identify it only as a small red car. Would it surprise you if later the expert was able to state with some confidence that a small red Triumph was not the car seen earlier, while the tyro had more difficulty in making this discrimination? Each individual's knowledge influences the coding of the experience, and that influence is reflected in what can be remembered about the experience. (See also EXPERT'S MEMORIES.)

A related fact about human memory is that we tend to impose organization on our experiences. Tulving (1962) and others have shown that when people learn a list of randomly selected words, they tend to impose some kind of organization on the words as the list is learned. This organization can be seen in the way the words are grouped together in the recall of the list. As the list is learned, there is more and more consistency in the grouping of the words in recall.

Bousfield (1953) showed that lists of words would be recalled as clusters of related words. For example, if the list contained some names of flowers, some names of people, some types of buildings, and so on, then the free recall of these words would group the similar items. This grouping occurs even though the words are presented in random order. Later Bower and his colleagues (see Bower, 1970) showed that theories about the structure of memory could provide reasonably detailed accounts of the organization of material to be learned. Bransford and Johnson (1972) studied certain passages that are very difficult to remember unless people are led to give them appropriate interpretations. Their work is an impressive demonstration of the role of interpretation in remembering.

Organization of Memory

What leads to the organization of memories? Most answers to this question refer to association as at least one fundamental process of organization (see ASSOCIATIONISM). Associations are formed when events are frequently experienced together in time. In the early part of the twentieth century, PAVLOV (1927) discovered classical conditioning. This discovery led to extensive investigations of the processes involved in the formation and maintenance of associations. Pavlov found that after frequently presenting a neutral stimulus (e.g., a tone) in close proximity to the presentation of food, a dog would salivate at the sound of the tone even in the absence of food. Thus, an association was formed between the tone and the food. Many years later, Garcia and Koelling (1966) found that some associations are learned more easily than others. Their laboratory rats learned to associate a novel taste with gastrointestinal illness much more easily than they learned the association between a flashing light and gastrointestinal illness. This result suggests that definite biological constraints operate to influence the formation of associations. The many associations we have between

ideas may result from co-occurrence of elements in experience. There are other ideas about the nature of memory organization as well.

In cognitive psychology, a great deal of effort has been devoted to the study of the acquisition and representation of knowledge. From this perspective, the basic notion of association has been extended in many directions. An important part of knowledge consists of concepts and the relations between concepts. Different theories about the representation of concepts in human memory make various claims about the basis of memory organization. (See also CONCEPTS AND CATEGORIES, LEARNING OF.)

Associative Networks

Perhaps the most basic idea about knowledge representation is the direct representation of associations in the form of a network. In this representation, concepts are shown as nodes and associations are shown by lines (or links) connecting the nodes. Schvaneveldt, Durso, and Dearholt (1989) presented a method of deriving such networks from judgments of relatedness among sets of concepts. One such network is shown in Figure 1, which was derived from the judgments of university students. The figure shows several of the salient associations among the concepts. Cooke, Durso, and Schvaneveldt (1986) found that the network in Figure 1 predicts the way people organize the concepts when they learn a list of the words shown in the network. Goldsmith and Johnson (1990) were able to predict students' grades from the similarity of student and instructor networks of important concepts in a course on experimental methods.

Semantic Networks

Another related idea about the organization of concepts in memory also uses network representations, but semantic networks specify more about the relations between concepts using labeled links (Collins and Loftus, 1975; Collins and Quillian, 1969; Meyer and Schvaneveldt, 1976; Quillian, 1969). For example, such a network would show that *robin* is a member of the class *bird* with an "isa" link (*A robin is a bird*). It would also show

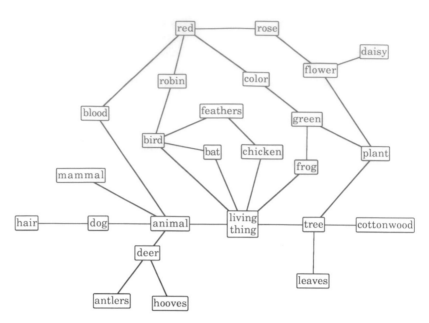

Figure 1. An associative network of some common concepts.

that a *deer has antlers,* and so on. Such networks can also support inferences such as concluding that *a robin is an animal* by retrieving *a robin is a bird* and *a bird is an animal.* Semantic networks have been used to explain experimental data from studies in language understanding and category judgments. Such networks are also frequently encountered in computer programs designed to exhibit artificial intelligence (details are available in the references cited above).

Semantic Features

Other theories propose that concepts consist of collections of features that serve to define the concepts (for an overview of feature theories, see Smith and Medin, 1981). The concept *bird,* for example, might consist of features such as *has wings, flies, lays eggs, has feathers,* and so on. According to feature theories, when people reason about concepts, features of the concepts are retrieved from memory and used to draw conclusions. For example, we know that *robin* is a member of the class *bird* because *robin* has the necessary features of the class *bird.* In contrast, semantic networks directly store information such as *a robin is a bird.* Some experimental results can be nicely explained with feature theory, while other results are better explained by network theo-

ries. There are other proposals about memory organization as well.

Scripts and Schemata

Some theories propose even larger units of memory organization on the basis of familiar experiences. Such familiar activities as going to a restaurant, visiting the doctor, going to the library, riding in a car, and so on are experienced often enough that we may form representations of these experiences as a whole. These representations are known as *scripts.* Scripts support certain kinds of inferences. For example, if we know that someone went to a restaurant, we presume that the person ate a meal, spoke with a waiter or a waitress, and paid for the meal (among other things). When we hear something that reminds us of a familiar experience, we may mistakenly believe that we also hear about activities commonly associated with that experience.

Scripts are examples of even more general organizational structures known as *schemata* (Bartlett, 1932; Minsky, 1975). Schemata are general representations of several different items of information together with the specification of the relations among the items. For example, the schema for a room might specify that it must have a floor, a ceiling, walls, and a door. Optionally, it might have additional doors and windows. Just as with scripts, schemata invite inferences. Several studies suggest that memory includes inferred information in addition to what we actually experience. For example, if we hear the sentence "Fred drove the nail into the board," we are likely to infer that he used a hammer even though the sentence does not mention a hammer.

Chase and Simon (1973) reported a classic demonstration of the power of schemata in memory, using memory for the positions of pieces on a chess board. They found that chess masters were no better than novices at reconstructing a board with randomly placed pieces, but the masters were far superior in recalling the positions of pieces from the middle of an actual chess game. The experts presumably had elaborate schemata that could be used to code the positions of the pieces on the board when the positions made sense.

Summary

Coding is the process of interpreting events in light of what we know. Such interpretation can have beneficial consequences, as in the superiority of the memory of chess masters for real board positions. Sometimes interpretation leads to the inclusion in memory of related information that was not actually experienced. To understand memory of an event, we must understand coding, which in turn reflects knowledge stored in memory prior to the event.

REFERENCES

Bartlett, F. C. (1932). *Remembering: A study in experimental and social psychology.* Cambridge: Cambridge University Press.

Bousfield, W. A. (1953). The occurrence of clustering in the recall of randomly arranged associates. *Journal of General Psychology 49,* 229–240.

Bower, G. H. (1970). Organizational factors in memory. *Cognitive Psychology 1,* 18–46.

Bransford, J. D., and Johnson, M. K. (1972). Contextual prerequisites for understanding: Some investigations of comprehension and recall. *Journal of Verbal Learning and Verbal Behavior, 11,* 717–726.

Chase, W. G., and Simon, H. A. (1973). Perception in chess. *Cognitive Psychology 4,* 55–81.

Collins, A. M., and Loftus, E. F. (1975). A spreading activation theory of semantic processing. *Psychological Review 82,* 407–428.

Collins, A. M., and Quillian, M. R. (1969). Retrieval time from semantic memory. *Journal of Verbal Learning and Verbal Behavior 8,* 240–247.

Cooke, N. M., Durso, F. T., and Schvaneveldt, R. W. (1986). Recall and measures of memory organization. *Journal of Experimental Psychology: Learning, Memory, and Cognition 12,* 538–549.

Garcia, J., and Koelling, R. A. (1966). Relation of cue to consequence in avoidance learning. *Psychonomic Science 4,* 123–124.

Goldsmith, T. E., and Johnson, P. J. (1990). A structural assessment of classroom learning. In R. Schvaneveldt, ed., *Pathfinder associative networks: Studies in knowledge organization.* Norwood, N.J.: Ablex.

Meyer, D. E., and Schvaneveldt, R. W. (1976). Meaning, memory structure and mental processes. In C. N. Cofer, ed., *The structure of human memory,* pp. 54–89. San Francisco: W. H. Freeman.

Minsky, M. (1975). A framework for representing knowledge. In P. Winston, ed., *The psychology of computer vision.* New York: McGraw-Hill.

Murphy, G. L., and Medin, D. L. (1985). The role of theories in conceptual coherence. *Psychological Review 92,* 289–316.

Pavlov, I. P. (1927). *Conditioned reflexes,* trans. by G. V. Anrep. London: Oxford University Press.

Quillian, M. R. (1969). The teachable language comprehender. *Communications of the ACM 12,* 459–476.

Schvaneveldt, R. W., Durso, F. T., and Dearholt, D. W. (1989). Network structures in proximity data. In G. H. Bower, ed., *The psychology of learning and motivation: Advances in research and theory,* vol. 24, pp. 249–284. New York: Academic Press.

Smith, E. E., and Medin, D. L. (1981). *Categories and concepts.* Cambridge, Mass.: Harvard University Press.

Tulving, E. (1962). Subjective organization in free recall of "unrelated" words. *Psychological Review 69,* 344–354.

Roger W. Schvaneveldt

COMPARATIVE COGNITION

Comparative cognition is the study of the minds of organisms and the ways in which those minds produce adaptive behaviors. It is an approach to understanding behavior that emphasizes what an animal knows and how it uses its knowledge. Investigations of learning and memory across a range of species can provide information about basic biological functions, the mechanisms that produce those functions, and their evolution. These investigations reveal that animal cognition employs a rich and varied set of mechanisms that has far more structure than the simple stimulus-response (S-R) systems that were formerly believed to be their basis (see Roitblat, 1987).

Learning

Learning in Invertebrates

Learning is widespread among animals, but most studies have concerned only a limited range of species. Comparisons across species are particularly important for discovering the basic units of learning and their evolution. For this purpose, investigations of learning in invertebrates are particularly important. Invertebrate brains are substantially different in structure from those of vertebrates but seem to function in similar ways at the micro level of the individual neuron and at the macro level of the whole organism (e.g., Hawkins and Kandel, 1984). Bitterman and his colleagues, for example, have found substantial similarity between the learning abilities of honeybees and vertebrates, and no important differences. Every phenomenon of vertebrate learning that has been investigated has been found in identical form in bees (Bitterman, 1988; Bitterman and Couvillon, 1991). The similarity across species may be the result of using similar brain mechanisms, or it may be a result of the basic ecological patterns of causation. Causation takes essentially the same form across species, whatever the signal or the event being caused, and different species contain neurons with essentially the same functional characteristics. (See also INVERTEBRATE LEARNING.)

Learning Abstract Concepts

In addition to general elementary learning processes, many animals learn and use abstract concepts such as similarity, and form abstract representations of categories of objects.

In the matching-to-sample task, an animal must choose the comparison stimulus (from among two or more items) that is the same as a designated sample. In an oddity task, the animal must choose the comparison stimulus that does not match the sample. An animal may learn to perform such conditional discriminations by learning an abstract

similarity concept or by learning specific responses to specific sets of stimuli. Discriminating between these alternatives is often difficult and controversial. Demonstration of the use of an abstract matching concept requires that the animal be able to generalize performance to a novel set of stimuli that cannot be explained either by stimulus-specific factors (e.g., stimulus generalization; see DISCRIMINATION AND GENERALIZATION) or metalearning factors (e.g., learning-to-learn).

One way stimulus-specific and metalearning factors can be controlled is by using *rule-congruent* versus *rule-incongruent* transfer tests. For a rule-congruent transfer test, the subject is trained and tested with the same task but with different stimuli. For example, the subject could be trained on a matching task and then tested on a matching task with a novel set of stimuli. For a rule-incongruent transfer test, the subject is trained on one task (e.g., matching) and then tested with the other task (e.g., oddity), again with novel stimuli. Animals generally perform more accurately on congruent than on incongruent transfer tests (Wilson, Mackintosh, and Boakes, 1985a; Zentall, Edwards, and Hogan, 1984).

The degree to which pigeons use a generalized matching concept depends on the number of stimuli in the training set (Lombardi, Fachinelli, and Delius, 1984; Wright et al., 1988). One group of pigeons, trained with 152 stimuli, did not show any decline in their performance when confronted with novel trial-unique test stimuli. Another group of pigeons, trained with only two stimuli, showed no evidence of transfer. Although these data support the use of a generalized matching concept by pigeons, this form of concept learning does not appear to be the pigeon's preferred strategy (Wright et al., 1988). Rather, pigeons seem to rely primarily on stimulus-specific rules unless the situation demands that they employ a more abstract concept.

Other bird species seem more likely to employ a generalized matching concept. Jackdaws (*Corvus monedula*), jays (*Garrulus glandarius*), and rooks (*Corvus frugilegus*) all showed positive transfer to novel stimuli when the transfer task employed the same rule as the training task (Wilson, Mackintosh, and Boakes, 1985b). An African gray parrot (*Psittacus erithacus*) was able to identify correctly the dimension of pairs of objects that was the same or different (Pepperberg, 1987).

Among mammals, rats showed no evidence of

oddity transfer using either visual or olfactory stimuli (Thomas and Noble, 1988), but California sea lions (*Zalophus californianus*) and bottle-nosed dolphins (*Tursiops truncatus*) did. One sea lion trained on an oddity problem reached 90 percent correct performance following 120 trials with trial unique stimuli (Hille, 1988). Another sea lion generalized its performance to novel stimuli in a rule-congruent matching task (Pack, Herman, and Roitblat, 1991). Similar results were obtained with bottle-nosed dolphins matching auditory (Herman and Gordon, 1974) as well as visual stimuli (Herman et al., 1989).

Monkeys and chimpanzees also show evidence of using a generalized similarity concept. Monkeys trained with an initial set of thirty-eight sounds selected the matching sound with 77.3 percent accuracy. Performance on a subsequent transfer test with ninety-two trial-unique stimuli was 78.8 percent accurate (Shyan et al., 1987; Wright, Shyan, and Jitsumori, 1990). Chimpanzees spontaneously transferred matching performance to a novel set of stimuli following training with only one pair of familiar objects (Oden, Thompson, and Premack, 1988). These data suggest that many animals can use a generalized similarity or matching concept to control their behavior, and thus are not limited to learning stimulus-specific rules.

Categorization

Another form of abstract concept demonstrated by a number of animals involves categorization. The basis for categorization may be as simple as perceptual similarity, such as was described above, or it may depend on such abstract relations as functional similarity. Categorization, thus, spans a class of mechanisms. Even perceptual similarity, however, is not as simple as it might appear. For example, it is far easier to claim that two slides resemble one another because they look similar than it is to specify the mechanism by which that judgment is made (Cerella, 1986; Duda and Hart, 1973; Biederman, 1990). Categorization has been studied in many species, including pigeons (Herrnstein, 1985). For example, Japanese macaques discriminate categorically between classes of macaque vocalization (May, Moody, and Stebbins, 1988), and vervet monkeys (*Cercopithecus aethiops*) discriminate between multiple synthesized examples of two of their alarm calls (Owren, 1990).

Visuospatial Representation

Imagery

Imagery is a controversial topic in many areas of cognitive science, but it is centrally concerned with the kind of representations organisms use (see Finke, 1985; Kosslyn, 1983). Because of the controversy, it is not entirely clear what approach to take to claims of imagery in animals. Animals clearly have perceptual and representational mechanisms to obtain, store, and process information about visuospatial properties of their environment (Gallistel, 1989). This information can be represented in a number of different forms. According to some investigators, images are the simplest form of representation (e.g., Premack, 1983), and so one would need special data to infer any other form. In contrast, some investigators (e.g., Pylyshyn, 1981) argue that because at least some representations must be propositionally encoded (by humans), images may be an unnecessary duplication of theoretical entities. Still others (e.g., Skinner, 1984) argue that animals do not use images, because the use of images implies a level of mentalism that stretches the bounds of parsimony.

Images are analog representations of the items they represent. One system is an analog representation of another when (a) continuous changes in the represented item produce continuous changes in the representation and (b) the similarity between codes corresponds to the similarity between the items they represent. A traditional clock is an analogue for the passage of time because continuous changes in the time of day correspond to continuous changes in the position of the hands. A digital clock is not an analog representation, because intermediate times correspond to symbolically intermediate representations, but the representation itself does not share the similarity structure. For example, the digital representation of 9:59 shares many features with the digital representation of 9:58 (two of the digits are the same) but very few features with the digital representation of 10:00 (none of the digits are the same). Hence, two pairs of times that are equally different from one another do not correspond to two representations that are equally different from one another. Therefore, the digital clock is not an analogue of time.

Studies of human imagery, particularly mental rotation experiments, find that people can perform transformations of represented objects that correspond to transformations that could be performed on real objects (e.g., Shepard and Metzler, 1971). Similar data are available from animal studies (e.g., Neiworth, 1992; cf. Hollard and Delius, 1982). Pigeons were trained to discriminate a computer-displayed clock hand that revolved at a constant velocity from one that moved at a nonconstant velocity. Three types of simulated movement were investigated. In the perceptual condition, the clock hand moved from its starting position at 12:00 to a position of 135° (4:00) or 180° (6:00) at a constant velocity of 90°/second. On imagery trials, the hand moved from its 0° vertical position to 90° (3:00), at which point it disappeared. After an appropriate amount of time (0.5 second for the 135° position and 1.0 second for the 180° position) it reappeared at a position of 135° or 180°. Hence, on imagery trials the hand disappeared at one point and reappeared in the position it would hold following the corresponding amount of time on a perceptual trial. On violation trials the hand also disappeared at 90°, then reappeared an inappropriate amount of time later in one of the two positions (1.0 second for the 135° position and 0.5 second for the 180° position). The discrimination of primary interest in this experiment is that between the imagery condition and the violation condition. In both cases, the simulated clock hand disappeared at the 3:00 position, then reappeared at either the 4:00 or the 6:00 position. Hence, the discrimination had to be based on the bird's estimate of the time that passed while the hand was invisible and the location at which it reappeared. The birds accurately discriminated these two conditions.

The continuity of the putative analog representation was demonstrated using a generalization test. In this test, the hand reappeared at the 158° position after 0.75 second during imagery trials and appeared at the same position after 0.5 or 1.0 second on violation trials. The pigeons were able to discriminate constant velocity imagery trials from nonconstant velocity violation trials even at the new intermediate position. This result demonstrated that the birds' representations preserved the analog position of the hand during the interval. (See also CODING PROCESSES: IMAGERY.)

Cognitive Maps

Images or imagelike analog representations may also be used by animals to represent larger portions of their environment (see Gallistel, 1989). The use of such representations is especially evident among the food-caching birds. Food storage is found in twelve families of birds (Sherry, 1985), but data are primarily available from two of these, the Corvidae and the Paridae. Clark's nutcracker (*Nucifraga columbiana*) is a corvid species that lives in high mountain coniferous forests of western North America. These birds harvest pine seeds during the late summer and conceal them in thousands of discrete caches. Both field studies and laboratory experiments support the claim that these birds recover their own caches by remembering their location (Balda et al., 1987). For example, Kamil and Balda (1985) found that nutcrackers could recover pine seeds that the birds had cached in randomly preselected locations after a retention interval of 10–15 days. The birds selectively searched holes in which seeds had been placed, whether the seeds were still there or had been removed by the experimenters.

Several parid species, including marsh tits (*Parus palustris*), have also demonstrated good memory for cache locations over delays measured in hours or days (Stevens and Krebs, 1986). As in the corvids (Balda and Kamil, 1989), the ability to remember cache sites in which food has been stored is correlated with the species dependence on cached food for survival in the field (Krebs, Healy, and Shettleworth, 1990; cf. Hilton and Krebs, 1990).

Conclusions

In contrast with the historic view of animals as passive responders to environmental change, the experiments reviewed above clearly show that animals are active processors of information about their environment. They form and use relatively sophisticated representations of their environment and events within it.

There is a growing body of evidence demonstrating good continuity among the processes of animals and humans. Space limitations have prevented discussion of a substantial body of work concerning languagelike processes in animals. Considerable progress has been made in recent years in the investigation of grammatical (Greenfield and Savage-Rumbaugh, 1990) and symbolic processes (Savage-Rumbaugh, 1986; Savage-Rumbaugh, et al., 1990) in chimpanzees (*Pan troglodytes*) and bonobos (*Pan paniscus*). These studies suggest that these animals are capable of extremely sophisticated representational systems similar to those in human language. (See also LANGUAGE LEARNING: NONHUMAN PRIMATES.)

REFERENCES

Balda, R. P., Bunch, K. G., Kamil, A. C., Sherry, D. F., and Tomback, D. F. (1987). Cache site memory in birds. In A. C. Kamil, J. R. Krebs, and H. R. Pulliam, eds., *Foraging behavior,* pp. 645–666. New York: Plenum.

Balda, R. P., and Kamil, A. C. (1989). A comparative study of cache recovery by three corvid species *Animal Behavior 38,* 486–495.

Biederman, I. (1990). Higher level vision. In D. N. Osherson, S. M. Kosslyn, and J. M. Hollerbach, eds., *Visual cognition and action: An invitation to cognitive science,* pp. 41–72. Cambridge, Mass.: MIT Press.

Bitterman, M. E. (1988). Vertebrate-invertebrate comparisons. In H. J. Jerison and I. Jerison, eds., *Intelligence and evolutionary biology,* pp. 251–275. New York: Springer-Verlag.

Bitterman, M. E., and Couvillon, P. A. (1991). Failures to find evidence of adaptive specialization in the learning of honeybees. In L. J. Goodman and R. C. Fischer, eds., *The behaviour and physiology of bees.* Wallingford, England: CAB International.

Cerella, J. (1986). Pigeons and perceptrons. *Pattern Recognition 19,* 431–438.

Duda, R. O., and Hart, P. E. (1973). *Pattern classification and scene analysis.* New York: Wiley.

Finke, R. A. (1985). Theories relating mental imagery to perception. *Psychological Bulletin 98,* 236–259.

Gallistel, C. R. (1989). Animal cognition: The representation of space time and number. *Annual Review of Psychology 40,* 155–190.

Greenfield, P. M., and Savage-Rumbaugh, E. S. (1990). Grammatical combination in *Pan paniscus:* Processes of learning and invention. In S. T. Parker and K. R. Gibson, eds., *"Language" and intelligence in monkeys and apes: Comparative developmental perspectives.* New York: Cambridge University Press.

Hawkins, R. D., and Kandel, E. R. (1984). Is there a cell biological alphabet for simple forms of learning? *Psychological Review 91,* 375–391.

Herman, L. M., and Gordon, J. A. (1974). Auditory delayed matching in the bottlenose dolphin. *Journal of the Experimental Analysis of Behavior 21,* 19–26.

Herman, L. M., Hovancik, J. R., Gory, J. D., and Bradshaw, G. L. (1989). Generalization of matching by a bottle-nosed dolphin (*Tursiops truncatus*): Evidence for invariance of cognitive performance with visual and

auditory materials. *Journal of Experimental Psychology: Animal Behavior Processes, 15,* 124–136.

Herrnstein, R. J. (1985). Riddles of natural categorization. *Philosophical Transactions of the Royal Society of London B308,* 129–144.

Hille, P. (1988). Versuche zur Ungleicherkennung beim kalifornischen Seelöwen (*Zalophus californianus*) unter besonderer Berücksichtigung der Begriffsbildung. Unpublished MS thesis, Westfälische Wilhelms-Universität, Münster, Germany.

Hilton, S. C., and Krebs, J. R. (1990). Spatial memory of four species of *Parus:* Performance in an open-field analogue of a radial maze. *Quarterly Journal of Experimental Psychology 42B,* 345–368.

Hollard, V. D., and Delius, J. D. (1982). Rotational invariance in visual pattern recognition by pigeons and humans. *Science 218,* 802–804.

Kamil, A. C., and Balda, R. P. (1985). Cache recovery and spatial memory in Clark's nutcrackers (*Nucifraga columbiana*). *Journal of Experimental Psychology: Animal Behavior Process 11,* 95–111.

Kosslyn, S. M. (1983). *Ghosts in the mind's machine.* New York: Norton.

Krebs, J. R., Healy, S. D., and Shettleworth, S. J. (1990). Spatial memory of Paridae: Comparison of a storing and a non-storing species, the coal tit, *Parus ater,* and the great tit, *P. major. Animal Behavior 39,* 1127–1137.

Lombardi, C., Fachinelli, C., and Delius, J. D. (1984). Oddity of visual patterns conceptualized by pigeons. *Animal Learning Behavior 12,* 2–6.

May, B., Moody, D. B., and Stebbins, W. C. (1988). The significant features of Japanese macaque coo sounds: A psychological study. *Animal Behavior 36,* 1432–1444.

Neiworth, J. J. (1992). Cognitive aspects of movement estimation: A test of imagery in animals. In W. K. Honig and G. Fetterman, eds., *Cognitive aspects of stimulus control.* Hillsdale, N.J.: Erlbaum.

Oden, D. L., Thompson, R. K. R., and Premack, D. (1988). Spontaneous transfer of matching by infant chimpanzees. *Journal of Experimental Psychology: Animal Behavior Process 14,* 140–145.

Owren, M. J. (1990). Acoustic classification of alarm calls by vervet monkeys (*Cercopithecus aethiops*) and humans (*Homo sapiens*): I. Natural calls. *Journal of Comparative Psychology 104,* 20–28.

Pack, A. A., Herman, L. M., and Roitblat, H. L. (1991). Generalization of visual matching and delayed matching by a California sea lion (*Zalophus californianus*). *Animal Learning and Behavior 19,* 37–48.

Pepperberg, I. (1987). Acquisition of the same/different concept by an African grey parrot (*Psittacus erithacus*): Learning with respect to categories of color, shape, and material. *Animal Learning and Behavior 15,* 423–432.

Premack, D. (1983). The codes of man and beasts. *Behavior and Brain Science 6,* 125–167.

Pylyshyn, Z. W. (1981). The imagery debate: Analogue media versus tacit knowledge. *Psychological Review 88*, 16–45.

Roitblat, H. L. (1987). *Introduction to comparative cognition.* New York: Freeman.

Savage-Rumbaugh, E. S. (1986). *Ape language: From conditioned response to symbols.* New York: Columbia University Press.

Savage-Rumbaugh, E. S., Sevcik, R. A., Brakke, K. E., Rumbaugh, D. M., and Greenfield, P. M. (1990). Symbols. Their communicative use, comprehension, and combination by bonobos (*Pan paniscus*). In C. Rovee-Collier and L. P. Lipsitt, eds., *Advances in infancy research,* vol. 6, pp. 221–271. Norwood, N.J.: Ablex.

Shepard, R. N., and Metzler, J. (1971). Mental rotation of three-dimensional objects. *Science 171,* 701–703.

Sherry, D. F. 1985. Food storage by birds and mammals. *Advances in the Study of Behavior 15,* 153–188.

Shyan, M. R., Wright, A., Cook, R., and Jitsumori, M. (1987). Acquisition of the auditory same/different task in a rhesus monkey. *Bulletin of the Psychonomic Society 25,* 1–4.

Skinner, B. F. (1984). The canonical papers of B. F. Skinner. *Behavior and Brain Science 7,* 473–764.

Stevens, T. A., and Krebs, J. R. (1986). Retrieval of stored seeds by marsh tits *Parus palustris* in the field *Ibis 128,* 513–525.

Thomas, R. K., and Noble, L. M. (1988). Visual and olfactory oddity learning in rats: What evidence is necessary to show conceptual behavior? *Animal Learning Behavior 16,* 157–163.

Wilson, B., Mackintosh, N. J., and Boakes, R. A. (1985a). Matching and oddity learning in the pigeon: Transfer effects and the absence of relational learning. *Quarterly Journal of Experimental Psychology 37B,* 295–311.

——— (1985b). Transfer of relational rules in matching and oddity learning by pigeons and corvids. *Quarterly Journal of Experimental Psychology 37B,* 313–332.

Wright, A. A., Cook, R., Rivera, J., Sands, S., and Delius, J. D. (1988). Concept learning by pigeons: Matching-to-sample with trial-unique video picture stimuli. *Animal Learning and Behavior 16,* 436–444.

Wright, A. A., Shyan, M. R., and Jitsumori, M. (1990). Auditory same/different concept learning by monkeys. *Animal Learning and Behavior 18,* 287–294.

Zentall, T. R., Hogan, D. E., and Edwards, C. A. (1984). Cognitive factors in conditional learning by pigeons. In H. Roitblat, T. G. Bever, and H. S. Terrace, eds., *Animal cognition,* pp. 389–408. Hillsdale, N.J.: Erlbaum.

Herbert L. Roitblat

CONCEPTS AND CATEGORIES, LEARNING OF

A concept is a mental representation that includes a description of important properties of a category. A category is a partitioning of examples referred to by a concept. One of the most fundamental questions about how the mind works is the nature of the processes by which we acquire, refine, and differentiate concepts and categories. The problem of concept formation can be broken down into subquestions concerning the what, how, and why of learning. Most attention has been directed at the *what* question, probably on the belief that if we can specify what is learned, it may tell us something about the how and the why.

What Is Learned

Classical vs. Probabilistic View

The classical view argues that concepts are structured around defining features (Bruner, Goodnow, and Austin, 1956). Defining features are features that are singly necessary and jointly sufficient to define the concept. For example, the concept "bachelor" has the defining features "unmarried" and "male."

The classical view, however, appears to have a number of serious problems. First, if concepts have defining features, then one ought to be able to specify what they are. But many common concepts, such as "game" or "chair," seem to have no defining features. Instances of these concepts are connected by characteristic features that are neither necessary nor sufficient for category membership (e.g., for "chairs," characteristic features are "have four legs," "have a back," etc.). Another serious problem is the observation that not all instances of a concept are equally good examples of it. People judge robins to be better examples of the concept "bird" than ostriches, for instance (see SEMANTIC MEMORY). These and other problems (see Smith and Medin, 1981) have led to a shift in attention from the classical view to the probabilistic view.

The probabilistic view argues that most concepts do not have defining features and instead are organized around properties that are only characteristic or typical of a category. A summary representation that indicates what is, on the average, true of a category is known as a prototype. The probabilistic view readily handles goodness-of-example effects; the more similar an item is to the concept's prototype, the more typical it will be of the concept (e.g., robins would be more similar to the bird prototype than are ostriches because they have more features that are generally true for birds).

The idea that concepts are organized around prototypes is not without problems of its own. Prototype representations alone are not rich enough to capture people's conceptual knowledge. People are sensitive to the number of instances that make up a concept, the variability of features (e.g., the size of quarters varies less widely than the size of pizzas), the correlations between features (e.g., wooden spoons tend to be big whereas metal spoons tend to be small), and the particular instances used. One explanation for these findings is that either in addition to, or instead of, abstract category-level information such as a prototype, people may simply store instances or examples of items in the category and reason with them (Brooks, 1978).

Concepts as Theory-Dependent

The shift from the classical view to the probabilistic view was motivated by a detailed analysis of natural object categories. Associated with this analysis has been the idea that mental representations of categories closely mirror the structure afforded by properties of category members. It seems almost a tautology that if the structure of examples does not have potential defining features, then the corresponding mental representations cannot conform to the classical view. Similarly, a probabilistic category structure seems to dictate a probabilistic concept representation. In brief, it has been common practice to assume that mental representations are determined by the structure of examples in the world. One should note, however, that the learner may impose structure as well as mirror it.

The idea that learners impose structure on their environment has been put forward by a number of researchers who have suggested that concepts are based on general knowledge and theories of the world that constrain the construction and organization of concepts (Carey, 1985; Murphy and Medin, 1985; Rips, 1989). For example, Susan Carey has shown that children's biological theories influence their patterns of inductions at a very early age. To illustrate, a mechanical monkey is rated by both children and adults to be more similar to a human being than is a worm, yet even young children make the inference that worms rather than toy monkeys have a spleen after being told that people have a spleen, "a round and green [thing] . . . in the person's body." While the classical and the probabilistic views did not constrain the features or relations that are important for a concept, the knowledge-guided view claims that a property is important for a concept to the extent that it fits into the theories concerning the concept.

Theories themselves may be anchored by how well the predictions derived from them receive support from the world. Murphy and Medin (1985) suggest that the relation between concept and examples is like that between theory and data. Mental representation of concepts would, therefore, not necessarily consist of features that are also in examples; rather, the constituents of examples would only need to "support" the more abstract constituents of concepts. For example, we may infer that a man is drunk because we see him jump into a pool fully clothed. If we do so, it is probably not because the feature "jumps into pools, clothed" is listed with the concept "drunk." Rather, it is because part of our concept of "drunk" involves a theory of impaired judgment that serves to explain the man's behavior.

Relation between Structure and Concept Learning: The How of Concept Learning

According to the classical view, the process of concept formation is one of discovering the necessary and sufficient attributes by observing which attributes occur in all members and only in members of the category. Research associated with the classical view has been directed at investigating hypothesis testing strategies, with each hypothesis being a guess as to which features are part of the definition (Levine, 1971). In contrast, according to the probabilistic view, concept learning occurs by averaging values of members (Posner and Keele, 1968), by attending to features commonly shared by members and discarding features varying among members (Elio and Anderson, 1981), or by noting the most common value on each dimension. The basic idea behind these models can be traced back to Galton's "composite photograph" theory (Galton, 1879). Galton superimposed several faces to make a composite photograph in which the common properties were accentuated and variant properties were attenuated. Such a process is assumed in prototype theories. On the other hand, exemplar models assume that category instances are stored but so far have been weak on specifying detailed learning mechanisms.

The theory-based view of concepts takes a different perspective on concept formation. Several researchers have proposed that humans may be born with a naive physics and a naive biology or psychology (e.g., Carey, 1985; Keil, 1989) that act as initial theories to organize conceptual knowledge. A major implication of the theory-based view is that concept learning involves integrating new examples with prior knowledge and that concepts should be easy to acquire to the extent that they fit with what we already know.

Taking the theory-based view, a group of researchers in artificial intelligence (an area in computer science the goal of which is to develop computers to do intelligent things) have developed models of concept formation called explanation-based learning (Mitchell, Keller, and Kedar-Cabelli, 1986; DeJong and Mooney, 1986). These models suggest that the most important aspect of concept learning is to explain why a given example is an instance of the concept. Construction of the explanation is carried out by causally connecting known concepts. For example, suppose a computer is to learn a concept "cup" and it already knows such concepts as "liftable," "handle," "liquid-container," and "stable." Seeing an object that is liftable, has a handle, contains liquid, and is stable, the system constructs an explanation for why this object is "drinkable from." Then it generalizes this explanation to develop its concept of "cupness."

Background knowledge also allows one to draw inferences about new concepts based on their context. Suppose one is learning a foreign language and knows that "wog" means "run." When one hears "Glug wog," she or he can at least assume that "glug" is animate (Sternberg, Powell, and Kaye, 1983).

Learning by analogy is another form of knowledge-driven learning in which a known similar concept is modified. For example, one can learn about the internal structure of atoms by applying one's knowledge of solar system (e.g., electrons revolve around the nucleus as planets revolve around the sun; Gentner, 1989). One can also discover new features through analogy or metaphors (e.g., given "a smile is like a magnet," one can learn that a smile attracts).

The Why of Concept Learning

The purpose of learning is an important issue because the learning process may be constrained by how concepts are to be used. Anderson (1990) has developed a categorization theory assuming that the goal of classification is to predict features of objects from knowledge of category membership (e.g., predicting whether a creature will be dangerous). Others have suggested other functions of categorization, including explanation (e.g., the concept "introvert" might help to explain why some person did not attend a party), reasoning (deriving knowledge from the stored information), communication, and conceptual combination (e.g., from the concepts "paper" and "bee" one might construct the combined concept "paper bee"). More work needs to be done in relating how different functions of categorization might affect learning processes.

Summary

We have described three aspects of concept learning: what, how, and why. The traditional approaches on conceptual structure (the classical, the probabilistic, and the exemplar) are based on the idea that our concepts are determined by the structure of examples in the world. That is, we have the concepts we have because of the way the world is. In contrast, the theory-driven approach argues that conceptual structures may be at least partially imposed by the human mind. According to this approach, we have the concepts we have because of the way humans interact with the world and attempt to understand it. In that sense, the concept formation process is more like developing theories from data than accumulating facts.

REFERENCES

Anderson, J. R. (1990). *The adaptive characteristic of thought.* Hillsdale, N.J.: Lawrence Erlbaum Associates.

Brooks, L. R. (1978). Non-analytic concept formation and memory for instances. In E. Rosch and B. Lloyd, eds., *Cognition and categorization.* Hillsdale, N.J.: Erlbaum.

Bruner, J. S., Goodnow, J. J., and Austin, G. A. (1956). *A study of thinking.* New York: Wiley.

Carey, S. (1985). *Conceptual change in childhood.* Cambridge, Mass.: MIT Press.

DeJong, G. F., and Mooney, R. J. (1986). Explanation-based learning: An alternative view. *Machine Learning 1, 2.*

Elio, R., and Anderson, J. R. (1981). The effects of category generalizations and instance similarity on schema abstraction. *Journal of Experimental Psychology: Human Learning and Memory 7,* 397–417.

Galton, F. (1879). Composite portraits, made by combining those of many different persons into a single, resultant figure. *Journal of the Anthropological Institute 8,* 132–144.

Gentner, D. (1989). The mechanisms of analogical learning. In S. Vosniadou and A. Ortony, eds., *Similarity and analogical reasoning.* Cambridge: Cambridge University Press.

Katz, J. J. (1972). *Semantic theory.* New York: Harper & Row.

Keil, F. C. (1989). *Concepts, kinds, and cognitive development.* Cambridge, Mass.: MIT Press.

Levine, M. (1971). Hypothesis theory and non-learning despite ideal S-R reinforcement contingencies. *Psychological Review 45,* 626–632.

Mitchell, T. M., Keller, R. M., and Kedar-Cabelli, S. T. (1986). Explanation-based generalization: A unifying view. *Machine Learning 1,* 47–80.

Murphy, G. L., and Medin, D. L. (1985). The role of theories in conceptual coherence. *Psychological Review 92,* 289–316.

Posner, M. I., and Keele, S. W. (1968). On the genesis of abstract ideas. *Journal of Experimental Psychology 77,* 353–363.

Rips, L. J. (1989). Similarity, typicality, and categorization. In S. Vosniadou and A. Ortony, eds., *Similarity and analogical reasoning.* Cambridge: Cambridge University Press.

Smith, E. E., and Medin, D. L. (1981). *Categories and concepts.* Cambridge, Mass.: Harvard University Press.

Sternberg, R. J., Powell, J. S., and Kaye, D. B. (1983). Teaching vocabulary-building skills: A contextual approach. In A. C. Wilkinson, ed., *Classroom computers and cognitive science.* New York: Academic Press.

Douglas L. Medin
Woo-Kyoung Ahn

CONDITIONING

[*A survey of the forms of learning called* conditioning *will be found under* CONDITIONING, CLASSICAL AND INSTRUMENTAL. *The following articles discuss specific aspects of the classical conditioning paradigm in greater detail:*

Behavioral Phenomena: Classical Conditioning
Conditioning, Cellular and Network Schemes for Higher-Order Features of Classical
Neural Substrates of Classical Conditioning

A particular type of instrumental conditioning is more closely examined under OPERANT BEHAVIOR.]

CONDITIONING, CELLULAR AND NETWORK SCHEMES FOR HIGHER-ORDER FEATURES OF CLASSICAL

Considerable progress has been made in elucidating the neural mechanisms of a number of simple forms of nonassociative learning in the marine mollusk *Aplysia*, including habituation, dishabituation, and sensitization. A neural mechanism for classical conditioning, known as activity-dependent neuromodulation, has also been identified in *Aplysia* (see APLYSIA: CLASSICAL CONDITIONING AND OPERANT CONDITIONING). This form of associative plasticity appears to be an elaboration of the form of nonassociative plasticity, known as heterosynaptic (presynaptic) facilitation, which is thought to contribute to sensitization and dishabituation (see APLYSIA: MOLECULAR BASIS OF LONG-TERM SENSITIZATION).

Given that the mechanism of classical conditioning in *Aplysia* is an elaboration of the mechanism of more simple forms of learning, the possibility arises that the mechanisms of even more complex forms of learning may be elaborations of the relatively simple mechanisms of classical conditioning and nonassociative learning. Behavioral studies indicate that *Aplysia* can exhibit higher-order features of classical conditioning. While the neural mechanisms of these more complex forms of learning have not yet been determined empirically, a number of theoretical studies have addressed the question of whether the forms of synaptic plasticity and the neural circuitry for the relatively simple forms of learning in *Aplysia* may also support higher-order features of learning, or whether these complex features of learning may require entirely novel cellular mechanisms.

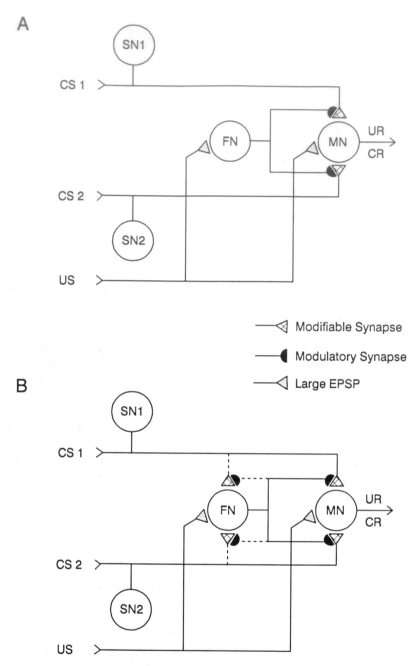

Figure 1. Simplified schematics of the type of neural circuit that mediates defensive withdrawal reflexes in *Aplysia.* (*A*) Conditioned stimuli (CS1 and CS2) activate sensory neurons (SN1 and SN2). The SNs make excitatory monosynaptic connections onto a motor neuron (MN) that produces the withdrawal response (unconditioned response, UR, or conditioned response, CR). The unconditioned stimulus (US) directly activates the MN and a facilitatory neuron (FN). The FN modulates the strength of the SN-to-MN synapses. (*B*) The broken lines represent additional circuit properties that could contribute to higher-order features of learning. These include excitatory connections between the SNs and the FN, and the ability of the FN to modulate these SN-to-FN synapses.

Neural Circuit for Withdrawal Reflexes in *Aplysia*

Studies of learning in *Aplysia* have focused largely on the defensive withdrawal reflexes. Figure 1A is a simplified schematic of the type of neural circuit that mediates these reflexes. It illustrates how activity-dependent neuromodulation contributes to classical conditioning.

Two sensory neurons (SN1 and SN2) constitute separate pathways for conditioned stimuli (CS1 and CS2). The SNs produce excitatory postsynaptic potentials (EPSPs) in a motor neuron (MN), which mediates the unconditioned response (UR). The reinforcing, or unconditioned, stimulus (US) has two effects. First, it activates the MN and produces the UR. Second, it activates the facilitatory neuron (FN), which produces heterosynaptic facilitation in all of the SNs. In SNs that were active just prior to the US, the facilitation produced by the FN is enhanced via activity-dependent neuromodulation. This amplification of the effects of the US in a paired SN underlies classical conditioning, or the enhanced ability of that SN to activate the MN and produce the conditioned response (CR).

Sensitivity to Contingency in *Aplysia*

One higher-order feature of classical conditioning for which there is evidence in *Aplysia* is sensitivity to the contingency between the CS and the US. Rescorla (1968) suggested that not just the number of CS-US pairings but also the correlation between the CS and the US, or the ability of the CS to predict the US, could affect conditioning. One way to reduce contingency is to present extra, unpaired USs during conditioning. Hawkins et al. (1986) used this manipulation to demonstrate sensitivity to contingency in *Aplysia*. They reported that classical conditioning of the siphon-withdrawal reflex was reduced when the contingency between the CS and the US was reduced by presenting extra unpaired USs during training. Hawkins et al. suggest that their behavioral results could be supported by a circuit like that in Figure 1A if there was "habituation" of the US. US habituation could be mediated by spike-frequency accommodation or homosynaptic depression in the FN. These forms of neuronal plasticity have been reported in the SNs of *Aplysia*, and homosynaptic depression is a neural correlate of habituation.

In a circuit like that in Figure 1A, extra USs would cause additional nonassociative heterosynaptic facilitation of all of the SNs during training. If these extra USs also caused accommodation or synaptic depression in the FN, then there would be a reduction in the amount of facilitatory transmitter released by the FN during paired (CS-US) trials and, hence, a reduction in the activity-dependent neuromodulation of the SN that is paired with the US. Taken together, these two effects would result in a decrease in the relative strength of the connections of paired versus unpaired SNs, which amounts to a reduction in associative conditioning. Thus, one plausible mechanism for contingency effects is simply a combination of the mechanisms of classical conditioning and habituation. Specifically, sensitivity to contingency could result from activity-dependent neuromodulation in the CS pathway in combination with accommodation and/or homosynaptic depression in the US pathway.

Theoretical Studies of Two Higher-Order Features of Classical Conditioning

Second-order conditioning and blocking are two higher-order features of classical conditioning that have been demonstrated in many vertebrates and invertebrates, including the terrestrial mollusk *Limax* (see INVERTEBRATE LEARNING: ASSOCIATIVE LEARNING IN LIMAX). While neither second-order conditioning nor blocking has been examined behaviorally in *Aplysia*, theoretical and modeling studies have tested the hypothesis that the simple forms of synaptic plasticity and the simple neural circuitry for the withdrawal reflexes in *Aplysia* could support these higher-order features of learning (Buonomano et al., 1990; Gluck and Thompson, 1987; Hawkins, 1989; Hawkins and Kandel, 1984).

Second-Order Conditioning

In second-order conditioning, a CS comes to produce a conditioned response without being directly paired with the US, but by being paired with another CS that has previously been paired with the US. The training protocol for second-order conditioning proceeds in two phases. During phase I, CS1 is paired with the US. During phase II, the presentation of the US is terminated, and CS2 is paired with CS1. The defining feature of second-order conditioning is that a conditioned stimulus

(CS1), as the result of previous pairing with the US, comes to function as a reinforcing stimulus for the conditioning of a second conditioned stimulus (CS2). If CS1 acts as a secondary reinforcer, then CS2 undergoes associative enhancement during phase II of training. This associative enhancement is called second-order conditioning.

Theoretical and modeling studies suggest that a CS could act as a secondary reinforcer if there were plastic excitatory connections between the SNs and the FN, and if the FN could facilitate such connections of the SNs onto itself (Figure 1B). At the start of training, the SN-to-FN connections would be weak, and the FN would be active only during presentations of the US. However, as the result of pairing CS1 with the US during phase I of training, the SN1-to-MN and SN1-to-FN connections would undergo significant associative enhancement. Eventually the connections of SN1 would be strong enough to activate the MN and FN. Hence, in phase II of training, when CS2 was paired with CS1, the CS1 pathway, due to its ability to activate the FN, would function as a secondary reinforcer for CS2. SN2 would undergo significant associative enhancement, even though it was never paired with an explicit US. Thus, in this model, second-order conditioning results directly from activity-dependent neuromodulation of the connections of an SN to two different follower cells, a MN and a FN.

Blocking

Blocking is a feature of classical conditioning in which a previously conditioned CS (CS1) prevents the conditioning of a new CS (CS2) when the two stimuli are paired as a compound CS (CS1/CS2) with the US. A blocking paradigm consists of two phases. During phase I, CS1 is paired with the US. During phase II, CS1 and CS2 are presented simultaneously, and this compound is paired with the US. Blocking is said to occur if the conditioning of CS1 during phase I of training reduces the associative enhancement of CS2 during phase II of training, even though CS2 is paired with the US.

The theoretical and modeling studies predict that, like second-order conditioning, blocking could arise from the ability of a previously conditioned CS (SN) to "take control" of the FN. During phase I of training, the synaptic strength of SN1 would, due to activity-dependent neuromodulation, increase and become strong enough to activate the FN. There are two consequences of this

CS1-induced activity in the FN that would contribute to blocking. First, during the compound CS1/CS2 stimuli in phase II of training, the FN would be activated approximately 0 millisecond after the onset of CS1/CS2. Activation of the FN in this temporal relation to activity in SN2 would not result in effective associative plasticity in SN2, since the optimal interstimulus interval (ISI) for associative plasticity is approximately 500 milliseconds after the onset of activity in SN2. Second, if the FN exhibited accommodation or synaptic depression in response to activation by CS1, then the output of the FN in response to a US that followed CS1/CS2 would be small or zero, and would not support associative conditioning of SN2.

Therefore, although CS2 would be paired with the US during phase II of training, prior conditioning of CS1 would block associative enhancement of SN2. Thus, blocking could, in theory, be supported by activity-dependent neuromodulation (the mechanism of classical conditioning) in combination with synaptic depression (the mechanism of habituation) in *Aplysia*. Specifically, blocking could arise from the ability of an SN that has previously undergone activity-dependent neuromodulation to "take control" of an FN and cause accommodation or synaptic depression in the FN.

Discussion

The neural mechanisms of higher-order features of conditioning are not known. However, the theoretical studies described above indicate that contingency effects, second-order conditioning, and blocking could, at least in principle, result from the simple associative and nonassociative learning rules that have been empirically derived from studies of habituation, dishabituation, sensitization, and classical conditioning in *Aplysia*. Additional features of learning also emerge readily from the circuit in Figure 1B. These include extinction and spontaneous recovery, stimulus specificity and generalization, US preexposure effects, and latent inhibition (Hawkins, 1989; Hawkins and Kandel, 1984). This leads to the suggestion that the relatively simple learning rules which seem to guide associative and nonassociative plasticity in *Aplysia* can serve as building blocks for higher-order features of classical conditioning. According to this hypothesis, higher-order features of conditioning emerge from the combinatorial interaction of a small number of neurons with a few simple forms of synaptic plasticity.

The theoretical studies have several limitations that should be considered. Some of the forms of learning that theoretically could emerge from the circuitry and plasticity rules of *Aplysia* have not yet been demonstrated behaviorally in this animal. Furthermore, additional empirical studies are required to determine whether the circuit properties and loci of plasticity that are assumed in Figure 1B actually exist in the *Aplysia* nervous system. Finally, some forms of learning, including context conditioning, which has been demonstrated in *Aplysia* (Colwill et al., 1988), cannot be readily supported by the circuit in Figure 1B. These forms of learning may require that the known forms of synaptic plasticity be embedded in more complex circuits. Alternatively, they may require novel forms of synaptic plasticity or further elaboration of the known forms of plasticity.

From the results of both empirical and theoretical studies, it is clear that at least two factors determine the ability of a neural circuit to support various features of learning. These are (1) the forms of synaptic plasticity and (2) the details of the circuit in which those forms of plasticity are embedded. Therefore, complex forms of learning may differ from simple forms of learning in either the form(s) of cellular plasticity involved or the properties of the circuit connectivity.

REFERENCES

Buonomano, D. V., Baxter, D. A., and Byrne, J. H. (1990). Small networks of empirically derived adaptive elements simulate higher-order features of classical conditioning. *Neural Networks 3*, 507–523.

Colwill, R. M., Absher, R. A., and Roberts, M. L. (1988). Context-US learning in *Aplysia californica*. *Journal of Neuroscience 8*, 4434–4439.

Gluck, M. A., and Thompson, R. F. (1987). Modeling the neural substrates of associative learning and memory: A computational approach. *Psychological Review 94*, 176–191.

Hawkins, R. D. (1989). A simple circuit model for higher-order features of classical conditioning. In J. H. Byrne and W. O. Berry, eds., *Neural models of plasticity*, pp. 73–93. San Diego: Academic.

Hawkins, R. D., Carew, T. J., and Kandel, E. R. (1986). Effects of interstimulus interval and contingency on classical conditioning of the *Aplysia* siphon withdrawal reflex. *Journal of Neuroscience 6*, 1695–1701.

Hawkins, R. D., and Kandel, E. R. (1984). Is there a cell-biological alphabet for simple forms of learning? *Psychological Review 91*, 376–391.

Rescorla, R. A. (1968). Probability of shock in the presence and absence of CS in fear conditioning. *Journal of Comparative and Physiological Psychology 66* 1–5.

Jennifer L. Raymond
John H. Byrne

CONDITIONING, CLASSICAL AND INSTRUMENTAL

Classical (Pavlovian) and instrumental (Thorndikian) conditioning are the two most widely employed paradigms for studying simple, associative learning resulting from the organism's exposure to the temporal conjunction of two or more events. The fully specified classical conditioning paradigm consists of a set of operations involving an *unconditioned stimulus* (US) reliably producing an *unconditioned response* (UR) and a *conditioned stimulus* (CS) initially shown not to produce a response resembling the UR. The CS and US are then presented repeatedly to the organism in a specified order and temporal spacing, and a response similar to the UR develops to the CS that is called the *conditioned response* (CR), that is, *CS-CR* functions are obtained. Control over the temporal conjunction of the CS, US, and UR makes classical conditioning preparations ideal vehicles for studying associative learning because they can uniquely specify stimulus antecedents to the target response. Various temporal arrangements of the CS and US give rise to different forms of classical conditioning (e.g., *delay, trace, simultaneous*). Classical conditioning is called *classical reward* conditioning if the US is a positive stimulus and *classical defense* conditioning if it is negative stimulus. The positive or negative designation depends on the independent demonstration of the organism's performing instrumental responses necessary to obtain the US or to remove itself from the US, respectively. What distinguishes classical from instrumental conditioning is that (a) presentation or omission of the US is independent of CR occurrence and (b) the definition of a CR is restricted to a target response selected from among those effector systems elicited as URs by the US. Adherence to both components of the definition of classical conditioning avoids common confusions and ambiguities with other associative learning paradigms commonly designated as "classical conditioning."

Stimulus-Stimulus Paradigms

In recent years, the designation "classical conditioning" has been applied to paradigms meeting only the requirement that CS and US be administered independent of the target response, ignoring selection of the UR. As a consequence, the term "classical conditioning" has been extended from Pavlov's *CS-CR* to stimulus-stimulus (*S-S*) conditioning paradigms involving principally conditioned stimulus–instrumental response (*CS-IR*) and *autoshaping* procedures. The *CS-IR* paradigms include *conditioned suppression* and other *classical-instrumental transfer* procedures in which the stimulus-stimulus pairings of classical conditioning are conducted with a CS and a biologically significant event (e.g., shock) but without measurement of a UR or CR. The CS is then presented during ongoing instrumental behavior and its facilitory or disruptive effect on responding is measured; therefore CS-IR functions are obtained. *Autoshaping* consists of response-independent presentations of a lighted manipulandum (e.g., lighted key) as a CS and activation of a food magazine as the US; the target response is contact with the manipulandum (e.g., key pecking). Key pecking is not an instrumental response, nor is it a UR appearing in the constellation of URs to food in the mouth (Woodruff and Williams, 1976). Hence, acquisition of a response in an effector system not elicited by the US qualifies autoshaping as a "new" associative learning paradigm.

Some *discriminative approach* procedures have been designated as "Pavlovian" simply because an explicit cue (CS) is presented and food or water, designated the US, is made available at a fixed time following CS onset (e.g., Holland and Rescorla, 1975) and the approach behavior, by definition instrumental to receipt of the reinforcing event, has been erroneously designated a CR. At present, the preceding paradigms are widely employed in the study of associative learning, but whether they will converge with the empirical laws of CS-CR paradigms has yet to be determined systematically. The S-S and discriminative approach paradigms lack the capability of CS-CR paradigms (a) to exer-

cise absolute control over the timing and sequencing of stimulus events, and (b) to identify the stimulus antecedents to the target response from the outset of training. In addition, with CS-IR and discriminative approach procedures, the target response is instrumentally conditioned. Consequently, these paradigms might be expected to be even less likely to display convergence with the empirical laws of CS-CR paradigms. In any event, despite the greater technical demands of measuring URs and CRs in CS-CR research, their methodological characteristics favor their use in the study of associative learning.

Biological Substrates

The CS-CR paradigms are ideally suited for the study of the biological substrates of associative learning because the target response is defined anatomically by a set of movements or secretions. The UCS's elicitation of the UCR permits identification of the target response's final common neural pathway(s) outside the conditioning situation and, thereby, affords the opportunity to observe changes in its activity from the start of conditioning (see Thompson, 1976). In contrast, S-S contingency and discriminative approach paradigms are inherently unsuitable for studying the biological basis of learning. First, in CS-IR paradigms, changes in the instrumental target response are not the consequences of its participation in the learning process. Rather, the changes are the result of interactions of hypothetical (unobserved) CRs with the CS that are governed by prior CS-US pairings. As a consequence, any neural analysis of learning that is directed at changes in the target response is pointless. Second, since the target response in the discriminative approach paradigm is outcome-defined, a wide variety of different body movements can yield the required outcome. Therefore, it is virtually impossible to identify a final common pathway for the movements that make up the response.

Control Methodology

The associative nature of a conditioning preparation has come to be determined by the contiguous occurrence of the CS and US and a set of control operations intended to estimate the contribution of other possible processes to responding. All response systems show some level of baseline activity, often raised by UCS presentations, which can produce an accidental coincidence of the CS and target response. Moreover, the likelihood of a target response to the CS may be systematically affected by (a) *alpha responses,* which are URs to the CS in the same effector system as the target response, and (b) *pseudo-conditioned* and *sensitized* responses established on the basis of prior US-alone presentations. A detailing of the latency, duration, amplitude, and course of habituation of the alpha response with a control group given CS-alone presentations can provide a basis for eliminating alphas from consideration as a CR, since they are usually of a shorter latency than CRs. Hence, if a sufficiently long CS-US interval is employed, both alphas and CRs can be observed in the interval and scored accordingly (Gormezano, 1966; Gormezano et al., 1983).

The reinstatement or augmentation of alphas to the CS through US-alone or CS-US pairings is referred to as *sensitization.* After eliminating alphas from consideration, the contribution of *pseudo-CRs* to CR measurement can be assessed by presentations of the US one or more times prior to CS presentations. The procedure frequently results in responses to the CS, labeled pseudo-CRs, which are treated separately from CRs because of their occurrence in the absence of CS-US pairings. However, the US-alone procedure precludes trial-by-trial assessment of pseudo-CRs for comparison with CRs. Accordingly, a single *unpaired control* procedure has evolved in which CS-alone and US-alone trials are presented randomly the same number of times as the paired CS-US group, but at variable CS-US intervals exceeding those effective for CR acquisition. Under the unpaired control, responses on CS trials (excluding alphas) provide a summative measure of pseudo-CRs and baseline responses.

Use of the unpaired control is based on associative assumptions that (a) temporal contiguity of the CS and US is necessary for CR acquisition and (b) responding produced by the unpaired control is nonassociative, since the randomized sequencing of CSs and USs at exceedingly long, random intervals prevents any CS-US contiguity effects. However, associative theory and its unpaired control methodology have been challenged by a *con-tingency hypothesis* (Prokasy, 1965; Rescorla, 1967) which asserts that associative learning in classical conditioning can be viewed as determined by the statistical relationship between the CS and US. The hypothesis assumes that if US probability is greater in the presence of the CS than in its absence, a *positive contingency* prevails and *excitatory* associative effects would accrue to the CS; and, conversely, if US probability is higher in the absence than in the presence of the CS, the *negative contingency* would yield *inhibitory* associative effects. Moreover, the contingency hypothesis assumes the unpaired control's perfectly negative contingency would lead the CS to acquire inhibitory associative effects. Hence, Rescorla (1967) proposed a *truly random control* to provide an associatively neutral condition for assessing excitatory and inhibitory conditioning.

Rescorla (1967) specified the truly random control as involving independent programming of the CS and US or equal US probabilities in the presence and absence of the CS. However, delineating pairing/unpairing cannot be determined a priori but only empirically. CS-US pairing is specified by the CS-US intervals demonstrated to produce CR acquisition for a specific preparation, while "explicitly unpaired" denotes the use of stimulus intervals outside the effective CS-US intervals. Consequently, in the absence of an empirically derived metric (i.e., effective CS-US conditioning intervals) to designate paired and unpaired conditions, it is virtually impossible to program an associatively neutral truly random control or predictable excitatory or inhibitory conditioning groups. Rescorla, seeking to validate the truly random control, reported its CS had no effect upon avoidance conditioning (Rescorla, 1966) or upon responding in a CS-IR study where shock-US probability in the presence and absence of the CS were equal (Rescorla, 1968). However, these findings were challenged by CS-IR studies revealing that trial number and frequency of chance CS-US pairings under a truly random control could substantially affect (excitatory) conditioning (see Gormezano and Kehoe, 1975). Subsequently, Rescorla (1972) disavowed the contingency hypothesis and truly random control, and reverted to the use of the unpaired control. Nevertheless, the truly random control is still widely employed despite the detailing of additional methodological limitations (Papini and Bitterman, 1990; Wasserman, 1989).

Instrumental Conditioning

Instrumental conditioning procedures are all characterized by a contingent relationship between the organism's response and a stimulus. Typically, if the stimulus increases, decreases, or leaves unaffected the probability of the response, it is identified as positive, negative, or neutral, respectively. Although such labeling appears to be circular, Thorndike's (1913) characterizations of stimuli as "satisfying" (positive) and "annoying" (negative) were not circular because they were specified by behavior changes independent of the target response. Noncircularity can also be achieved by demonstrating transitivity of stimulus effects on the target response to other (new) responses.

A positive or negative contingency between the target response and reinforcing stimulus gives rise to a variety of instrumental conditioning paradigms. The five most extensively studied are *reward, punishment, omission, escape,* and *avoidance,* which derive from responses producing a positive (*reward*) or a negative (*punishment*) stimulus; preventing a positive (*omission*) or negative (*avoidance*) stimulus from occurring; and terminating a negative stimulus (*escape*). Woods (1974), employing a classification schema that includes *operant conditioning* and presence or absence of a discriminative stimulus, enumerated sixteen instrumental conditioning paradigms. However, despite repeated attempts at conceptual clarification, the operant remains devoid of causal stimulus antecedents (Coleman, 1981) and, consequently, it cannot be employed to study associative learning. The operant is applicable only to the study of performance variables affecting postasymptotic or steady-state responding. Aside from the study of discrimination learning processes, *discriminative instrumental conditioning* paradigms are widely employed to assess the effects of concurrent classical conditioning of "fear" or "incentive motivation" to the discriminative stimulus upon the instrumental target response.

Control Methodology

Any occurrence of the target response without prior conjunction with the reinforcing stimulus is designated a *nonassociative* response attributable to (a) base rate; (b) independent presentations of the reinforcing stimulus; and (c) presentations of the reinforcing stimulus independent of the target response. Implementing controls for the first two factors are self-evident, and achieving a control for the third factor has been essentially limited to the *yoked-control* design. In the design, pairs of subjects are selected and one of them is randomly designated the experimental and the other the control subject. During conditioning, when the experimental subject performs the target response, the contingent event is received by both subjects. Therefore, both members of the pair receive the same number and temporal distribution of stimulus events; the only difference is that the experimental but not the control subject always receives the reinforcing event after execution of the target response, while the yoked partner receives the reinforcing event independent of execution of the response.

Thus, the yoked-control design appears to be admirably suited to test the (null) hypothesis that the temporal relationship between the response and subsequent stimulus event is irrelevant to the observed behavior change. Unfortunately, the design confounds within-subject sources of random error with the treatment effect: Control of stimulus events by experimental subjects can allow for systematic differences in the number of experimental subjects that are more affected by the stimulus event than their yoked partners. The possibility of such confounding has rendered the results of yoked-control designs necessarily ambiguous (see Church, 1964). As a consequence, a means for assessing the contribution of the third nonassociative factor to instrumental conditioning has not yet been achieved.

(see also PAVLOV, IVAN; THORNDIKE, EDWARD; OPERANT BEHAVIOR.)

REFERENCES

Coleman, S. R. (1981). Historical context and systematic functions of the concept of the operant. *Behaviorism* 9, 207–226.

Gormezano, I. (1966). Classical conditioning. In J. B. Sidowski, ed., *Experimental methods and instrumentation in psychology.* New York: McGraw-Hill.

Gormezano, I., and Kehoe, E. J. (1975). Classical conditioning: Some methodological-conceptual issues. In

W. K. Estes, ed., *Handbook of learning and cognitive processes,* vol. 2, *Conditioning and behavior theory.* Hillsdale, N.J.: Erlbaum.

Gormezano, I., Kehoe, E. J., and Marshall, B. S. (1983). Twenty years of classical conditioning research with the rabbit. In J. M. Sprague and A. N. Epstein, eds., *Progress in psychobiology and physiological psychology,* vol. 10. New York: Academic Press.

Holland, P. C., and Rescorla, R. A. (1975). Second-order conditioning with food unconditioned stimulus. *Journal of Comparative and Physiological Psychology 88,* 459–467.

Papini, M. R., and Bitterman, M. E. (1990). The role of contingency in classical conditioning. *Psychological Review 97,* 396–403.

Prokasy, W. F. (1965). Classical eyelid conditioning. Experimenter operations, task demands, and response shaping. In W. F. Prokasy, ed., *Classical conditioning: A symposium.* New York: Appleton-Century-Crofts.

Rescorla, R. A. (1966). Predictability and number of pairings in Pavlovian fear conditioning. *Psychonomic Science 4,* 383–384.

——— (1967). Pavlovian conditioning and its proper control procedures. *Psychological Review 74,* 71–80.

——— (1968). Probability of shock in the presence and absence of CS in fear conditioning. *Journal of Comparative and Physiological Psychology 66,* 1–5.

——— (1972). Informational variables in Pavlovian conditioning. In G. H. Bower and J. T. Spence, eds., *Psychology of learning and motivation.* New York: Academic Press.

Thompson, R. F. (1976). The search for the engram. *American Psychologist 31,* 209–227.

Thorndike, E. L. (1913). *Educational Psychology.* New York: Teachers College, Columbia University.

Wasserman, E. A. (1989). Pavlovian conditioning: Is contiguity irrelevant? *American Psychologist 44,* 1550–1551.

Woodruff, G., and Williams, D. R. (1976). The associative relation underlying autoshaping in the pigeon. *Journal of the Experimental Analysis of Behavior 26,* 1–13.

Woods, P. J. (1974). A taxonomy of instrumental conditioning. *American Psychologist 29,* 584–597.

I. Gormezano

CONSOLIDATION

See Amnesia, Organic; Electroconvulsive Therapy and Memory Loss; Memory Consolidation

CURIOSITY AND EXPLORATION

When placed in new situations or situations with novel elements, animals typically engage in *exploration,* a pattern of behavior that enables them to gather and store information about the situation for future use. This form of learning is crucial to *adaptive behavior* but appears on its surface to follow somewhat different rules than many other forms of learning, which are related to standard rewards such as food, water, and safety. The study of exploration played a major role in the abandonment of traditional learning theories that emphasized the essential role of these obvious biological rewards. This entry will trace some of the history of the study of exploration, describe the phenomena of which it is made up, and evaluate what we currently know about it.

Curiosity in humans and animals has been reported through history, and research interest in curiosity predates the formal founding of the discipline of psychology in 1879. For example, in *The Descent of Man* (1871), Darwin recounts his experience of taking a live snake in a burlap bag and placing the bag into the monkey cage at the London zoo. The monkeys were horrified by the snake but could not seem to resist peeking into the bag to look at it. Evidence of apparent curiosity is robust: Animals display curiosity by moving into and around novel environments, and by investigating and manipulating objects. In research settings, interest in curiosity is typically expressed in studies of exploration.

The first peak of empirical interest in exploration, from the late 1940s to the early 1960s, resulted from its role as an embarrassment to theories of behavior that relied on hypothetical psychological drives, tied to physical needs, to explain behavior. In an animal whose basic needs (e.g., for food or water) are unmet, exploration might easily be explained as a search for the necessities of life; this is often studied in contemporary psychology as FORAGING. However, exploratory behaviors also occur at times when the animal is not in need: Animals will leave shelter to explore, and exploration is displayed by animals who are neither hungry nor thirsty (and may in fact be displayed more by satiated animals). Exploration in this context is more difficult to explain, and these apparently unmotivated behaviors offer a challenge that *drive-reduction theories* were ultimately unable to meet.

Exploration does not lead directly to reduction of any physical need, yet animals will suffer discomfort (such as crossing an electrified grid that delivers a mild shock to the feet) for an opportunity to engage in it, and it can serve as enough reward to motivate other behaviors. In the 1940s through the 1960s, as drive-reduction theories lost favor, the primary motivation for studying exploration disappeared, and so did studies of exploration. When this occurred, the important conceptual questions raised by exploration were left unanswered.

A resurgence of interest in curiosity and exploration has come, in part, from increased awareness that exploration is a situation where learning occurs outside the context of specific goal-oriented tasks, and this type of learning may be important in developing a complete understanding of learning and memory. Curiosity is found widely in the animal kingdom; exploration has been observed in all vertebrate species that have been studied. Exploration does involve costs and risks, however; animals that are exploring are using energy and are exposed to predators, and thus it seems reasonable that exploring must serve some function or provide some benefit, or evolution would have selected against it. The prevalent explanation is that curiosity, expressed as exploration, helps animals discover useful information and resources. Experimental evidence suggests that the behaviors used in exploration are partly a product of learning, and there is a wealth of evidence that exploration results in learning of both spatial (e.g., Blodgett, 1929) and nonspatial (e.g., Renner, 1988) components. (See also SPATIAL LEARNING.)

A difficulty in studying exploration is that it is not a single behavior but a complex collection of behaviors: Berlyne (1963) classified exploratory behaviors into two types, *diversive exploration* (*stimulus-seeking* behaviors) and *specific exploration* (reactions to and investigation of particular stimuli). Diversive exploration would involve spatial memory, arousal (which may be tied to detection of novelty), and locomotion. Most previous studies of exploration, including studies of patrolling from the ecological literature, would be included under this type of exploration (Archer and Birke, 1983, contains chapters by several authors on this type of exploration).

Besides the components described above, specific exploration might involve memories for specific features of environmental stimuli and the mechanics of interacting with stimuli. It is this specific investigation aspect of exploration about which we know the least. The influence of specific stimulus characteristics on these behaviors is unknown, as are the motivational components (e.g., rewards) governing these behaviors (see Butler, 1954). It seems clear that the initial character of object investigation would be related to the species' ecological niche (Glickman and Sroges, 1966), but its connection to feeding and associated behaviors is not known (see Renner, 1990, for additional discussion).

Studies have provided support for the distinction between diversive and specific exploration, showing that the different components of exploratory behaviors are not expressions of the same underlying process (Renner, 1990). Some forms of experience alter one component, such as object investigation, without affecting others, such as the amount of locomotion. In spite of the prima facie validity of this distinction, a single variable (such as locomotion in an open field) is usually reported to represent exploration.

Probably because of its makeup as a complex combination of behaviors, there is little consistency from one study to the next in the way exploration is defined. This is an important point, because the connection between the construct of curiosity and what is reported as exploration is not always clear. Dependent variables are often labeled "measures of exploration," although the situation used for measuring it would obviously have the effect of suppressing a natural, unstressed curiosity. For example, rats are sometimes placed in an unfamiliar box from which they cannot escape, and observed under bright lights; the amount they move around in this context is reported as exploration. This may be because studies of the phenomenon of exploration for its own sake, or other studies of curiosity, are rare. Most studies reporting exploration use it as a dependent variable; as such, it is interesting only as an indication of the effect of some experimental manipulation rather than as the focus of the experiment.

It is often said of psychology that it tried to skip the descriptive phase that occupied much of the history of other sciences, and immediately began testing hypotheses about particular explanations of behavior. The phenomenon of exploration is an excellent case in point. Basic descriptive data about the character of exploration have not been available, and fundamental questions, such as the stimuli influencing exploration, have not been addressed. Understanding this behavior system will require extensive descriptive studies in order to identify the components of exploration and their interrelations, and comparative (cross-species) studies to explain what part exploration plays within each species' behavioral ecology and adaptations to its niche.

The nature of exploration as behavior for which some components necessarily make extensive use of spatial memory suggests that the hippocampus (SEE GUIDE TO THE ANATOMY OF THE BRAIN) is an important part of its neural foundation. The research literature on this question (reviewed in Renner, 1990) is mixed, with several studies supporting this hypothesis and others refuting it. The puzzling question of the source of reinforcement or reward of exploration has led to speculation about the possible involvement of the dopamine neurotransmitter system, particularly the nucleus accumbens, but so far all the evidence addressing this suggestion is based entirely on spatial and locomotor measures. This limited evidence does not answer the question of whether the various components of exploration rely on the same or different neural systems: The question of which neural systems underlie other components of curiosity, such as detection of novelty, arousal, and interaction with objects, is completely unexamined.

Exploratory behavior and curiosity remain one of the great unsolved puzzles in the field of learning and memory. Although obviously connected with learning and memory, a convincing empirical account of the nature of exploration is not yet available.

REFERENCES

Archer, J., and Birke, L. I. A., eds. (1983). *Exploration in animals and humans.* New York: Van Nostrand Reinhold.

Berlyne, D. E. (1963). Motivational problems raised by exploratory and epistemic behavior. In S. Koch, ed., *Psychology: A study of a science,* vol. 5. New York: McGraw-Hill.

Blodgett, H. C. (1929). The effect of the introduction of reward upon maze performance of rats. *University of California Publications in Psychology 4*, 113–134.

Butler, R. A. (1954). Incentive conditions which influence visual exploration. *Journal of Comparative and Physiological Psychology 48*, 19–23.

Glickman, S. E., and Sroges, R. W. (1966). Curiosity in zoo animals. *Behaviour 26*, 151–188.

Renner, M. J. (1988). Learning during exploration: The role of behavioral topography during exploration in determining subsequent adaptive behavior. *International Journal of Comparative Psychology 2*, 43–56.

——— (1990). Neglected aspects of exploratory and investigatory behavior. *Psychobiology 18*, 16–22.

Michael J. Renner

D

DEMENTIA

The term *dementia* refers to an acquired, relatively global impairment of cognitive (intellectual) functioning in the setting of clear consciousness. The absence of disordered consciousness distinguishes dementia from *delirium*. Generally, impairment in memory and at least one other cognitive function is required for the diagnosis of dementia to be made. Patients with memory deficits exclusively are usually described as suffering from *amnesia* (see AMNESIA, ORGANIC).

In addition to their intellectual losses, demented patients often have disturbances of emotional functioning, changes in personality, and/or behavioral disturbances. Common noncognitive symptoms are depression, irritability, behavioral disinhibition (e.g., taking desired objects from others without asking), and impaired social behavior (e.g., swearing in public).

Varieties of Dementia

There are many causes of dementia, some treatable and some not (Chui, 1989). Metabolic and nutritional disorders, for example, can cause dementia syndromes that remit with effective treatment of the underlying disorder. Major depression is a common cause of dementia, especially among the elderly. While this syndrome was formerly called *pseudo-dementia* because of the absence of an easily identifiable organic cause, it is actually a genuine dementia (Folstein and McHugh, 1978). However, the dementia of depression can be re-versed with successful treatment of the depression.

Primary degenerative dementia is the formal psychiatric diagnosis given to the progressive loss of cognitive functioning due to brain disease. By far the most common cause of primary degenerative dementia is ALZHEIMER'S DISEASE (AD). Patients with this brain disease undergo a progressive decline in cognitive function in which difficulty learning new information and retrieving old memories are typically among the first symptoms. Other early symptoms include disorientation to date, deterioration of work habits, and word-finding problems. In the later stages of AD, patients exhibit severe deficits in language (e.g., inability to name common objects) and in visuospatial abilities (e.g., getting lost, misidentifying family members), and a global impairment in activities of daily life.

The major neuropathological features of AD are neurofibrillary tangles (small, contorted, thickened fibers in the cytoplasm of nerve cells) and neuritic plaques (small patches of degenerated nerve cells). These are most abundant in the *hippocampus* (a critical memory structure in the medial temporal lobe) and the cerebral cortex. Early in the illness, the temporal and parietal cortices are most markedly affected. In later stages, all the association areas of the brain are involved.

The second most common cause of dementia is cerebrovascular disease. Dementia associated with cerebrovascular disease goes by many names, most commonly *multi-infarct dementia*. When large blood vessels in the brain are occluded, causing cerebrovascular accidents (strokes), specific deficits in cognition may result. In many patients, however, multiple small blood vessels become blocked, resulting in numerous, small brain lesions.

The heterogeneity of lesion size and location in multi-infarct dementia makes it difficult to discern any clear neuropsychological patterns in this illness.

Pick's disease is a much rarer degenerative brain disorder that causes dementia. As in AD, the association areas of the cerebral cortex are the major site of pathology. In Pick's disease, however, the prefrontal cortex is affected earliest and most prominently. As a result, problems in reasoning and social behavior (e.g., impulsivity, social disinhibition) are typically the earliest symptoms. Although few memory studies have been conducted with Pick's disease patients, it appears that memory is better preserved in Pick's disease than in AD (Knopman et al., 1989).

There are many dementia-producing diseases that affect the basal ganglia, cerebral white matter, brain stem, or other subcortical brain structures. Among the most frequently studied are *Huntington's disease (HD)*, where the neostriatum (caudate nucleus and putamen) are most significantly affected, and *Parkinson's disease (PD)*, where the primary pathology is in the substantia nigra. Collectively, these disorders have been described as *subcortical dementias*. Patients with subcortical dementias do not have the severe disorders of language (APHASIA), perception (agnosia), skilled movement (apraxia), and memory (amnesia) seen in AD. Instead, they suffer from a slowing and overall inefficiency of mental processes, resulting in impaired abstract reasoning, poor planning and judgment, and selective memory difficulties (Cummings, 1990). The dementia of depression is now widely regarded as a form of subcortical dementia, although the precise brain mechanism has yet to be firmly established. The cognitive disorders often seen in multiple sclerosis and acquired immune deficiency syndrome (AIDS) are also considered subcortical dementias.

Varieties of Memory Impairment in Patients with Dementia

Primary Memory

Primary memory, also known as short-term or working memory, refers to a system of limited capacity that maintains information in awareness before it is fully encoded and transferred to long-term storage. This system is engaged when one is asked, for example, to repeat a short series of digits. Secondary, or long-term, memory is required when information is stored and then retrieved after a period of other cognitive activity, thereby preventing conscious rehearsal of the information.

Research indicates that patients with cortical dementias such as AD are typically impaired on measures of primary memory, such as digit span and the Brown-Peterson task (recall of three letters after a few seconds of distraction by counting backward). When asked to remember lists of words (free recall), AD patients have difficulty recalling even the last words of the list, thought to reflect a defect in primary memory. In contrast, patients with subcortical dementias, such as HD and PD, have been found to perform near normal on many primary memory tasks (Brandt, 1991; Sullivan et al., 1989).

Episodic Memory

Secondary, or long-term, memory is frequently separated into episodic memory and semantic memory. Episodic memory refers to an individual's record of events that are encoded along with the particular time and place in which they occurred. Common tests of episodic memory involve the retelling of stories after a delay period and the learning over trials of word pairs or other paired associates.

Virtually every patient with dementia has some impairment in episodic memory. In general, AD patients display severely impaired recall, poor recognition (either yes/no or multiple-choice), and abnormally rapid forgetting, regardless of the type of material. However, some studies show that when AD patients are allowed a sufficient number of trials so that their immediate recall approximates that of normal subjects, their forgetting over time is reduced to near normal (Kopelman, 1985). A defect in the initial encoding of the to-be-remembered material appears to be prominent in AD.

In addition to having poor recall, AD patients are also prone to errors of *intrusion*. When asked to recall a list of words, for example, these patients often report words that were not on the list. Frequently these intrusion errors are semantically related to the target words, so that the patient might report the word *tuna* instead of the actual word *salmon*. While number of intrusion errors is significantly correlated with density of neuritic plaques in AD (Fuld et al., 1982), these errors are by no means unique to this disorder.

Patients with subcortical dementias often display near-normal recognition and normal rates of forgetting-on episodic memory tasks, in spite of poor immediate recall (Brandt, 1991; Flowers et al., 1984). Their episodic memory performance appears to be hampered most by inefficient strategies for retrieving information. HD patients, for example, can have very impaired free recall but near-normal multiple-choice recognition. They also display less forgetting over time (Moss et al., 1986) and make many fewer errors of intrusion (Kramer et al., 1988) than AD patients. Even among the subcortical dementias, there is significant variability in episodic memory abilities. Patients with HD, for example, appear to be more deficient in their immediate recall of a word list than PD patients, as well as in their rate of improvement over trials (Massman et al., 1990).

Semantic Memory

Semantic memory refers to that component of secondary or long-term memory where word meanings and general knowledge are organized according to relationships among concepts. Examination of semantic memory often involves asking subjects to name pictures of objects, generate lists of items belonging to a particular category (e.g., animals), or define words.

Many researchers consider an impairment in semantic memory to be a core defect in AD (Bayles and Kaszniak, 1987; Weingartner et al., 1983). When asked to provide the names of common objects, for example, AD patients often substitute items of the same class, or provide the name of the higher-order category (e.g., saying "a bird" for a picture of a pelican; Martin and Fedio, 1983). This naming deficit likely reflects a deterioration of semantic representations of concepts, thought to depend on the functioning of the temporoparietal region of the dominant (usually left) cerebral hemisphere. Other researchers maintain that AD patients have normal semantic memories but are impaired in their ability to access them (Nebes, 1989).

Semantic memory is widely regarded as relatively intact in the subcortical dementias. Although patients with HD and PD may perform below the level of healthy subjects on semantic memory tasks, they perform much better than AD patients and typically do not make the errors characteristic of

AD. In general, their performance is slow and retrieval is inconsistent.

Implicit Memory

Many brain-damaged patients can display significant learning and retention as long as they are not required to recollect particular learning episodes. This type of memory, known as *implicit memory*, consists of the acquisition of perceptual, motor, and cognitive skills, as well as the "priming" of specific responses through repetition or exposure to associated items.

Patterns of implicit memory differ among patients with dementias of different etiologies. For example, patients with AD typically produce normal learning curves on motor skill learning tasks, such as mirror-drawing or the pursuit rotor task. However, they are typically impaired on semantic priming tasks, where verbal responses are "primed" by words related in meaning. This deficit in semantic priming in AD may be highly dependent on the type of priming task employed (Nebes, 1989). In contrast, patients with HD and PD are very impaired on skill learning tasks. However, they perform normally, or nearly so, on semantic priming tasks. This double dissociation between skill acquisition and semantic priming in AD and HD suggests that these forms of implicit memory are dependent on different neuroanatomical systems (Heindel et al., 1989). It is likely that motor skill learning is mediated, at least in part, by the basal ganglia, while semantic priming requires that the cerebral cortex be intact.

Retrograde Amnesia

In addition to their deficits in new learning, demented patients are impaired in their ability to retrieve information acquired before the onset of illness. This deficit is known as *retrograde amnesia*. Two general patterns of retrograde amnesia have been identified: impaired memory for information from all time periods of the past, and severe impairment for recent events with relative sparing of remote events. Patients with the amnesia of *alcoholic Korsakoff's syndrome* display this latter pattern (i.e., a gradient of retrograde amnesia) most clearly.

Early studies suggested that all demented patients display "flat" retrograde amnesia, with equally poor recollection from all periods of the past. More recent research has found AD patients to be severely impaired on tests requiring the recognition of public events and people from the past, but with greatest impairment for the most recent past. HD patients, although impaired, typically outperform AD patients and display an equivalent degree of impairment across all periods. Thus, AD patients, like alcoholic Korsakoff patients, display a gradient of retrograde amnesia.

Conclusions

Memory impairment is one of the most debilitating aspects of dementia syndromes. The cortical/subcortical distinction may provide a useful way of conceptualizing the results of memory research with demented patients. Patients with AD, where the primary damage is to the hippocampus and cerebral cortex, have difficulty maintaining information in primary memory, encoding it "deeply," and transferring it to more permanent storage. As a result, they retain little after even a very brief delay, and are also impaired when tested with recognition procedures. Their impaired semantic memory makes it impossible for them to store or access information in an effective way.

Patients with subcortical dementias typically perform much better than do those with cortical dementias on most explicit tests of memory. These patients do not have the severe impairment in semantic associations and, as a result, are able to encode and store material more effectively, albeit slowly. They tend, however, to be very inconsistent in their ability to retrieve information from long-term storage. This impairment, as well as severe impairment in skill learning, is consistent with their known neuropathology of the striatum and associated subcortical nuclei.

REFERENCES

Bayles, K. A., and Kaszniak, A. W. (1987). *Communication and cognition in normal aging and dementia.* Boston: College-Hill Press.

Becker, J. T. (1988). Working memory and secondary memory in Alzheimer's disease. *Journal of Clinical and Experimental Neuropsychology 10,* 739–753.

Brandt, J. (1991). Cognitive impairments in Huntington's disease: Insights into the neuropsychology of the striatum. In F. Boller and J. Grafman, eds., *Handbook of*

neuropsychology, vol. 5, pp. 241–264. Amsterdam: Elsevier Science Publishers.

Chui, H. C. (1989). Dementia: A review emphasizing clinicopathologic correlation and brain-behavior relationships. *Archives of Neurology 46,* 806–814.

Cummings, J. L., ed. (1990). *Subcortical dementia.* New York: Oxford University Press.

Flowers, K. A., Pearce, I., and Pearce, J. M. S. (1984). Recognition memory in Parkinson's disease. *Journal of Neurology, Neurosurgery, and Psychiatry 47,* 1174–1181.

Folstein, M. F., and McHugh, P. R. (1978). Dementia syndrome of depression. In R. Katzman, R. D. Terry, and K. L. Bick, eds., *Alzheimer's disease: Senile dementia and related disorders,* pp. 87–93. New York: Raven Press.

Fuld, P., Katzman, R., Davies, P., and Terry, R. D. (1982). Intrusions as a sign of Alzheimer dementia: Chemical and pathological verification. *Annals of Neurology 11,* 155–159.

Heindel, W. C., Salmon, D. P., Shults, C. W., Walicke, P. A., and Butters, N. (1989). Neuropsychological evidence for multiple implicit memory systems: A comparison of Alzheimer's, Huntington's, and Parkinson's disease patients. *Journal of Neuroscience 9,* 582–587.

Knopman, D. S., Christensen, K. J., Schut, L. J., Harbaugh, R. E., Reeder, T., Ngo, T., and Frey, W. (1989). The spectrum of imaging and neuropsychological findings in Pick's disease. *Neurology 39,* 362–368.

Kopelman, M. D. (1985). Rates of forgetting in Alzheimer-type dementia and Korsakoff's syndrome. *Neuropsychologia 23,* 623–638.

Kramer, J. H., Delis, D. C., Blusewicz, M. J., Brandt, J., Ober, B. A., and Strauss, M. (1988). Verbal memory errors in Alzheimer's disease and Huntington's dementias. *Developmental Neuropsychology 4,* 1–15.

Martin, A., and Fedio, P. (1983). Word production and comprehension in Alzheimer's disease: The breakdown of semantic knowledge. *Brain and Language 19,* 124–141.

Massman, P. J., Delis, D. C., Butters, N., Levin, B. E., and Salmon, D. P. (1990). Are all subcortical dementias alike?: Verbal learning and memory in Parkinson's and Huntington's disease patients. *Journal of Clinical and Experimental Neuropsychology 12,* 729–744.

Moss, M. B., Albert, M. S., Butters, N., and Payne, M. (1986). Differential patterns of memory loss among patients with Alzheimer's disease, Huntington's disease, and alcoholic Korsakoff's syndrome. *Archives of Neurology 43,* 239–246.

Nebes, R. D. (1989). Semantic memory in Alzheimer's disease. *Psychological Bulletin 106,* 377–394.

Sullivan, E. V., Sagar, H. J., Gabrieli, J. D. E., Corkin, S., and Growdon, J. H. (1989). Different cognitive profiles on standard behavioral tests in Parkinson's disease and Alzheimer's disease. *Journal of Clinical and Experimental Neuropsychology 11,* 799–820.

Weingartner, H., Grafman, J., Boutelle, W., Kaye, W., and Martin, P. R. (1983). Forms of memory failure. *Science 221,* 380–383.

Jason Brandt
Ralph H. B. Benedict

DIENCEPHALON

See Amnesia, Organic

DISCRIMINATION AND GENERALIZATION

When individuals learn to respond to a particular stimulus, they also typically respond to other (similar) stimuli, a phenomenon called *stimulus generalization.* Generalization is adaptive because organisms rarely experience the exact same stimulus twice; even a light will appear different depending on the distance or angle from which it is viewed. Some stimulus differences, however, are significant; an animal's survival in the wild may depend on its ability to distinguish friend from foe. Responding differently to different stimuli is called *discrimination.* The term *stimulus control* is used to describe the relationship between stimulus change and response change; thus it encompasses both generalization and discrimination.

Normally, a change from the training stimulus to a similar (but not identical) test stimulus yields evidence of both generalization and discrimination. The subject responds less, thereby demonstrating discrimination, and the reduction is called *generalization decrement.* The fact that it responds at all to a nontraining value demonstrates generalization.

When experimental subjects are tested for generalization to several test stimuli that differ from the training stimulus along a single dimension such as brightness or tone frequency, the result is a *generalization gradient,* that is, the greater the change from the training value, the lower the tendency to respond. If the test stimulus differs from the training stimulus along two dimensions (for instance, in color and in brightness), the two decrements will summate and responding will be reduced even further.

In order to respond differently to different stimuli, the subject must detect a difference between them. On the other hand, the failure to respond differently does not necessarily indicate an inability to distinguish between the stimuli. The subject may have failed to notice the stimulus during training, or may have failed to notice that attribute of the stimulus that is varied during generalization testing.

Stimulus Generalization Test Procedures

Generalization gradients can be obtained in several different ways. Different groups of subjects can be trained to respond to a particular stimulus, and each group may be tested for response strength to a different value on the test dimension. More commonly the same subjects are tested for generalization to several different stimuli. This is more efficient, but there can be a problem with sequence effects—that is, subjects may respond differently to a given test stimulus depending upon which test stimulus or test stimuli were previously experienced. In order to minimize sequence effects, the test stimuli are usually arranged in blocks and each block contains a random ordering of all test stimuli. Furthermore, generalization testing is usually carried out without REINFORCEMENT. If in training a reinforcement schedule was used that delivered reinforcers only occasionally and unpredictably, the subject will continue responding long enough without reinforcement for a reliable generalization gradient to be obtained. The gradient will tend to sharpen during testing because responding to stimuli far removed from the training value will be the first to cease. Sometimes a *maintained generalization test procedure* is used, in which subjects are reinforced for responding either to the training value only or to all test stimuli including the training stimulus. The former procedure tends to sharpen the generalization gradient, whereas the latter procedure tends to flatten it.

Generalization gradients can be plotted in several ways. An absolute gradient is based upon an absolute measure of response strength in the presence of each stimulus (e.g., number of responses).

A relative gradient may be plotted in two ways. The measure of response strength (say, number of responses) to each stimulus may be computed as the percentage of total responses made during testing, or as the percentage of the number of responses made to the training stimulus value. Relative generalization gradients are often used in research because they minimize the effect of individual differences in response strength that are often considerable, particularly in operant experiments. Thus a group average based on relative generalization gradients is likely to be more representative of the performance of the individual subjects than one based on absolute gradients.

Training stimuli are multidimensional. A tone stimulus, for example, will have pitch, loudness, quality, and other attributes. Any or all of these attributes may be noticed by the subject and may come to exert control over learned responding. The obtaining of a decremental gradient, with maximal responding to the training value, indicates that the varied attribute was noticed or attended to during training. Furthermore, the greater the decrement (i.e., the sharper the gradient), the more the subject is presumed to have attended to that stimulus attribute during training.

It is commonly observed that subjects do not attend equally to all attributes of a training stimulus; their behavior is more controlled by some attributes than by others. In this sense, attention is a process of *stimulus selection*. Limitations of the subjects' sensory apparatus sometimes account for this. The stimulus attributes that come to control behavior may also differ based on whether appetitive or aversive reinforcers are employed or based on the subjects' past experience with different stimuli. The assumption is sometimes made that because subjects have a limited capacity to attend to different stimuli, or to different attributes of a single stimulus, there is a trade-off; the more attention paid to one stimulus attribute, the less attention necessarily paid to others. The strongest evidence for such an effect has come from experiments in which stimuli are presented for very brief periods, making it difficult or impossible for subjects to attend sequentially to different stimulus attributes (see Maki and Leith, 1973). When this is not done, it has often been shown that training in which one stimulus attribute is relevant may enhance attention to (i.e., control by) attributes that were irrelevant during training (see Thomas, 1970).

The trade-off that may occur in attention to different stimulus attributes during training may also occur at the time of testing for stimulus control. Suppose that a pigeon subject has been trained to respond to a white vertical line on a green background and we wish to determine whether (or how much) the subject attended to the line angle. To accomplish this, we would test for stimulus generalization along the line angle dimension. During testing, if we vary the line angle but retain the green background, the line angle gradient obtained will be much flatter than if the line were presented against a dark background. This indicates a *masking* effect; attention paid to the color (highly salient for pigeons) reduced attention paid to the line angle during testing. Thus the most sensitive way to test for attention paid to a stimulus attribute during training is to isolate and then vary that element during testing.

Discrimination Training Procedures

As pointed out earlier, whenever a training stimulus is changed, responding normally decreases, demonstrating discrimination. Different training procedures may enhance discrimination or, conversely, enhance generalization. *Discrimination training* enhances stimulus control (i.e., increases discrimination), whereas *equivalence training* reduces it. Discrimination training procedures can be characterized in several different ways. One basic distinction is between simultaneous and successive stimulus presentations. Subjects may be required to choose between two stimuli that are presented at the same time, with responding to one of them reinforced and to the other not reinforced (or both reinforced but with different frequency, amount, or delay). Alternatively, stimuli may be presented successively, with reinforcement available in the presence of only one of them. Discrimination training may also be categorized on the basis of the relationship between the training stimuli. Intradimensional training refers to a situation in which positive and negative stimuli differ in a single attribute, say wavelength or intensity of light. Such procedures focus attention on the relevant attribute of the training stimuli. In interdimensional training the stimuli differ in more than one attribute; thus a tone might signal availability of reinforcement and silence might signal its absence. This would call attention to the presence of the tone but not necessarily to its pitch.

Both intradimensional and interdimensional discrimination training were shown by Jenkins and Harrison (1960) to produce stimulus control by tonal frequency in pigeons, whereas without discrimination training, this dimension was essentially ignored by the subjects. Furthermore, intradimensional training was more effective than interdimensional training.

While interdimensional discrimination training has typically been employed to study attentional processes, intradimensional discrimination training has historically been used to study transposition and related phenomena. Kohler (1938) observed that chickens and chimpanzees trained to choose the larger of two squares or the brighter of two grays would avoid that stimulus in favor of a larger or brighter one on a choice trial. This finding, called *transposition,* was taken to indicate that the subjects' behavior was controlled by the (larger-than or brighter-than) relationship between the training stimuli. Kenneth SPENCE (1937) offered an alternative interpretation that explained transposition as a consequence of the summation of a generalization gradient of *excitation* centered on the S+ (reinforced stimulus) and a gradient of *inhibition* centered on the S− (extinguished stimulus). Spence's theory predicts that following intradimensional discrimination training, if subjects are tested with one stimulus at a time, they will show maximum responding to a stimulus removed from S+ in the opposite direction from S−. This *peak shift* has been observed in many experiments with many different stimulus dimensions. On the other hand, several lines of evidence suggest that animals may learn a discrimination in a relational manner. For example, when subjects are trained to respond to the intermediate of three stimuli on the same dimension, they continue to do so with a new set of three stimuli, a result that is inconsistent with Spence's "absolute" approach. Thus evidence exists that animals may learn both the absolute values of the training stimuli and the relationship between them. The manner of testing for stimulus control (e.g., a choice test or a generalization test in which stimuli are presented one at a time) may determine whether absolute or relative stimulus properties are reflected in performance.

A particularly interesting form of successive discrimination training requires explicit relational learning. In *matching-to-sample* procedures a trial begins with the presentation of a stimulus, called a sample. After this stimulus has been presented, two other (comparison) stimuli are presented, one of which is identical to (matches) the sample, and the subjects are rewarded for choosing the matching stimulus. Since the sample stimulus changes randomly from trial to trial and the correct comparison stimulus varies randomly between two locations, correct responding requires the use of a matching rule. A question of theoretical interest is whether the matching rule is restricted to the stimuli used in training or can be applied to novel stimuli not previously seen. Recent evidence with pigeons indicates that these animals can learn a generalized matching rule (a matching "concept") if trained with a very large number of different sample stimuli (see Wright et al., 1988).

A useful variation of the matching-to-sample procedure requires the subject to select a comparison stimulus that is not identical to the sample but is arbitrarily associated with it. Thus pigeons might be trained to select a vertical line comparison stimulus when the sample is green and a horizontal line comparison stimulus when the sample is red. This procedure is called symbolic matching-to-sample.

Probably the most frequent use of the matching-to-sample paradigm is in the study of short-term memory in animals. If the sample stimulus is terminated and a delay period intervenes before the comparison stimuli are presented, correct performance requires that the subjects remember what the sample was at the time that they choose between the two comparison stimuli. A delay of but a few seconds may disrupt matching performance substantially (i.e., cause a loss of stimulus control), although with extensive training, subjects may improve their ability to perform under conditions of delay.

Equivalence Training Procedures

Equivalence training refers to a procedure in which particular stimuli become somewhat interchangeable (i.e., generalization between them is enhanced) by virtue of a common mediating link. Suppose that in a symbolic matching-to-sample task two different sample stimuli are both associated with the same comparison stimulus. If one of those samples is trained in conjunction with a new comparison stimulus, the other sample stimulus may, when tested, result in the same choice.

Another example of stimulus equivalence is the

phenomenon of *semantic generalization*. If human subjects are trained to respond to a meaningful word, say *crow*, they will show generalized responding to a word that sounds very different but has a related meaning, say *robin*. Thus stimulus generalization is based on similarity between stimuli, but the similarity can be based upon physical characteristics or on mediating links, which in the case of human subjects are typically semantic.

It was pointed out earlier that stimulus control techniques are used not only to study learning but also to study memory (for stimuli). Delayed matching-to-sample is the most common procedure for investigating short-term memory in animals. Long-term memory can be investigated by testing for stimulus generalization following delay periods of days or weeks. As the value of the training stimulus is forgotten, obtained generalization gradients become flatter—that is, responding to a nontraining value increases relative to responding to the training value (see Thomas, 1981).

The techniques of stimulus control of learned behavior can also be used to investigate sensory and perceptual processes. Blough (1956) developed a "tracking" procedure for determining absolute and difference thresholds for visual intensity. To determine the absolute threshold, the pigeon subjects are trained to make one response when they see a stimulus light and to make another response when they do not. Each response causes an adjustment of the intensity in the opposite direction (down when they see the light, up when they do not), and the intensity at which the subjects switch between the two responses defines the threshold. This technique has been successfully applied to several different species and different sensory continua, and has generated a field of research called comparative psychophysics.

Stimulus control techniques are frequently used to study the formation of *perceptual concepts* in animals that are trained to respond differently to slides on which pictures of different exemplars of particular categories of objects are presented, such as cats, flowers, or fish. The field of COMPARATIVE COGNITION is one of the most active areas of stimulus control research today.

REFERENCES

Blough, D. S. (1956). Tracing dark adaptation in the pigeon. *Journal of Comparative and Physiological Psychology 49*, 425–430.

Jenkins, H. M., and Harrison, R. H. (1960). Effect of discrimination training on auditory generalization. *Journal of Experimental Psychology 59*, 246–253.

Kohler, W. (1938). Simple structural functions in the chimpanzee and in the chicken. In W. D. Ellis, ed., *A source book of Gestalt psychology*. New York: Harcourt, Brace.

Mackintosh, N. J. (1977). Stimulus control: Attentional factors. In W. K. Honig and J. E. R. Staddon, eds., *Handbook of operant behavior*. Englewood Cliffs, N.J.: Prentice-Hall.

Maki, W. S., and Leith, C. R. (1973). Shared attention in pigeons. *Journal of the Experimental Analysis of Behavior 19*, 345–349.

Rilling, M. (1977). Stimulus control and inhibitory processes. In W. K. Honig and J. E. R. Staddon, eds., *Handbook of operant behavior*. Englewood Cliffs, N.J.: Prentice-Hall.

Roitblat, H. L. (1987). *Introduction to comparative cognition*. Hillsdale, N.J.: Erlbaum.

Spence, K. W. (1937). The differential response to stimuli varying within a single dimension. *Psychological Review 44*, 430–444.

Thomas, D. R. (1970). Stimulus selection, attention, and related matters. In J. H. Reynierse, ed., *Current issues in animal learning*. Lincoln: University of Nebraska Press.

——— (1981). Studies of long-term memory in the pigeon. In N. E. Spear and R. R. Miller, eds., *Information processing in animals: Memory mechanisms*. Hillsdale, N.J.: Erlbaum.

Wright, A. A., Cook, R. G., Rivera, J. J., Sands, S. F., and Delius, J. D. (1988). Concept learning by pigeons: Matching-to-sample with trial-unique video picture stimuli. *Animal Learning and Behavior 16*, 436–444.

David R. Thomas

DISTRIBUTED PRACTICE EFFECTS

Repetition helps. If you want to memorize a fact or learn a skill, one way of doing so is to repeat it. That is not surprising (see REPETITION AND LEARNING).

Distributed repetitions help even more. Repetitions are distributed when the two (or more) presentations are separated in time rather than contiguous (or massed) in time. Under an extraordinarily wide variety of circumstances, distributed repetitions produce better learning and memory than do massed repetitions. Sometimes distributed repetitions produce two or three times the retention of massed repetitions. That is surprising (and useful).

Distributed practice effects are as venerable as the scientific study of learning and memory itself. Hermann EBBINGHAUS (1885), who seems to have observed just about every important mnemonic phenomenon, discussed distributed practice effects in Chapter 7 of his monograph on memory. Not long after, Jost (1897) formulated two laws, the second of which was "If two associations are of equal strength and different ages, further study has greater value for the older one" (quoted from Woodworth, 1938). That is, a second presentation will be of greater benefit if it is distributed (the first presentation is old) than if the second presentation is massed (the first presentation is recent). Jost's finding that the greater the temporal separation of the repetitions (the lag), the greater the learning, is often called the Melton lag effect, after Arthur Melton, who vigorously investigated the phenomenon (e.g., Melton, 1970). The finding is also called the spacing effect.

The remainder of this article is divided into three sections. The first will illustrate the generality of the distributed practice effect (and a few cases where it is not found). The second section contains a discussion of theories that have been used to account for the effect. The final section is a brief review of research on how the distributed practice effect can be useful in everyday situations.

Generality of the Effect

Most people, or at least most college students, don't appreciate that distributed practice leads to better memory than does massed practice (Zechmeister and Shaughnessy, 1980). This too is surprising, because the effect is amazingly general. For starters, the effect can be found in memory for lists of unrelated words (see Glenberg, 1979, or Greene, 1989, for reviews of this extensive literature), sentences, and chapters (Reder and Anderson, 1982). The effect is found for memorizing telephone numbers (Landauer and Ross, 1977) and multiplication facts (Rea and Modigliani, 1985). Baddeley (1990) notes that distributed practice helps in learning skills as varied as "archery to maze-learning in the dancing mouse" (quoted from Woodworth, 1938). Somewhere between archery and maze learning is the finding that distributed practice (1 hour per day compared with 2 or 4 hours per day) enhances the typing skill of British postal workers (Baddeley and Longman, 1978).

Not only are distributed practice effects found for many types of materials, they are also found for virtually all types of memory tests. Standard, explicit memory tests, such as free recall, cued recall, recognition, and frequency estimation, require a conscious experience of remembering. All of these types of memory tests are sensitive to distributed practice (see Glenberg, 1979; Greene 1989). Greene (1990) has shown that implicit (unaware) memory tests are also sensitive to distributed practice. For example, in one of Greene's experiments, a relatively uncommon form of a homophone (e.g., *fare*) was repeated using distributed presentations or using massed presentations. Later, a spelling test (an implicit memory test) was given, and Greene found that the distributed repetitions produced a greater bias toward the uncommon spelling than did the massed repetitions. (See also IMPLICIT MEMORY).

Distributed practice effects are found when learners are older adults (Balota, Duchek, and Paullin, 1989), college-age students (Glenberg, 1979; Greene, 1989), children (Rea and Modigliani, 1985, 1987), learning-disabled children (Gettinger, Bryant, and Mayne, 1982), and even infants (Cornell, 1980). Infants like to look at pictures of new faces when given a choice between pictures of old and new faces. In Cornell's experiment, infants between 5 and 6 months old were repeatedly shown pictures of faces with either 1 minute (distributed practice) or 3 seconds (massed practice) between repetitions. The infants were then shown an old picture paired with a new picture. They spent more time looking at the new picture when it was paired with an old picture given distributed practice than when the new picture was paired with an old picture given massed practice. Apparently, the infants remembered the picture presented using distributed practice and chose to look at the new picture.

As a general rule, increasing the lag or spacing between presentations leads to better memory (the Melton lag effect). There is an exception to this rule, however. When the memory test is shortly after the last presentation, then massing presentations produces better memory than spacing presentations (Balota, Duchek, and Paullin, 1989; Cornell, 1980; Glenberg, 1976, 1977, 1979). In practical terms, when studying for an exam, cramming immediately before the exam may result in slightly better performance than distributed practice (that's the exception to the rule), but distributed practice results in better long-term retention (that's the rule).

The Ranschburg effect (see Jahnke, 1969) is another exception to the distributed practice rule. Consider trying to recall a telephone number that has a repetition of one of the numbers. When the presentations of the repeated digit are contiguous (e.g., 233–7194), recall is more accurate than when the presentations are separated (e.g., 237–3194). The Ranschburg effect is found when the memorized sequences are constructed from a limited set of elements, such as digits or letters. When the size of the set is increased, the Ranschburg effect is eliminated (Greene, 1991; Jahnke, 1974).

In most of the work described so far, "distribution" in the distributed practice condition corresponded to the amount of time between successive presentations of individual, to-be-remembered *items,* such as words or pictures. In contrast with the reliable effects for this sort of distribution, there is little mnemonic benefit in the distributed repetition of whole *lists* of verbal items (e.g., Underwood 1961; but see Bahrick and Phelps, 1987, for an impressive counterexample). Why might this be? Even when successive presentations of a list are massed, successive presentations of a particular item on the list are distributed, because the item's presentations are separated by other items on the list.

Theories of the Distributed Practice Effect

Everyone agrees that there is a distributed practice effect and that we should try to understand why it occurs. There is little agreement, however, as to what causes the effect. Reviews of different theories may be found in Greene (1989) and Hintzman (1976).

Given that the distributed practice effect is so commonplace, perhaps the processes that produce it are also commonplace, or at least do not require any special effort on the part of the learner. Hintzman (1976) proposed that the distributed practice effect reflects a type of habituation (see HABITUATION AND SENSITIZATION IN VERTEBRATES). When a repetition follows within 15 seconds (or so) of the event's first presentation, the internal representation of the event is habituated so that the repetition is not thoroughly processed. Because habituation is involuntary, this account predicts that distributed practice effects will be commonplace. However, the size of the distributed practice effect can be changed by instructions (see Greene, 1989), so habituation cannot be the only explanation (if it

is correct at all). Also, the habituation account cannot explain improvements in memory when the lag between repetitions is increased well beyond 15 seconds (e.g., Baddeley and Longman, 1978; Bahrick and Phelps, 1987; Glenberg and Lehmann, 1981). An explanation related to the habituation account was proposed by Jacoby (1978; Cuddy and Jacoby, 1982; but see Glenberg and Smith, 1981).

Another account that invokes involuntary mechanisms is based on encoding variability. The term "encoding variability" derives from the assumption that what is remembered about each presentation of a repeated event may change from presentation to presentation, that is, what is encoded in memory is variable. One type of encoding variability is contextual variability. Supposedly, memory for focal events, such as vocabulary words, includes memory for the context, such as when and where the words were studied. As the lag between repetitions increases, there is usually a corresponding increase in contextual change, and hence an increase in the amount of new contextual information encoded in memory. Furthermore, it is proposed that contextual information helps people to remember focal events. Thus, increasing the lag between repetitions of a focal event (a) increases contextual change, (b) increases the amount of contextual information stored with the focal event, and (c) increases memory for the focal event. Explanations along these lines have been proposed by Glenberg (1979), Landauer (1976), Melton (1970), and others. Like the habituation theory, encoding variability theories run into difficulties when we note that voluntary activities can influence the spacing effect. These theories also run afoul of a rather technical prediction: Because context is supposed to change whether or not there are repetitions, the theories predict that memory for either of two once-presented events will increase with the spacing between the once-presented events. This is not the case, however (Glenberg and Lehmann, 1981; Ross and Landauer, 1978).

Other theories suggest that distributed practice effects result from voluntary activity. For example, Rundus (1971) found that learners spend more time rehearsing (vocalizing either out loud or to themselves) words given distributed practice than words given massed practice. Another explanation based on voluntary activity is that people choose to attend more carefully to the second of two distributed presentations than to the second of two massed presentations. A critical problem with these accounts is that strong distributed practice effects can be found even when the amounts of rehearsal and attention are equated in distributed and massed practice conditions (Glenberg and Smith, 1981; Hintzman et al., 1975).

If neither the voluntary nor the involuntary accounts will do alone, perhaps a combination of the two will be successful. In fact, that is just what Greene (1989) has proposed. The voluntary component of Greene's theory is that people choose not to rehearse the second of two massed presentations because the repeated event seems familiar and memorable, but that people do rehearse the second of two distributed presentations. The involuntary component of Greene's theory is called the *study-phase retrieval subtheory*. Study-phase retrieval occurs when the second presentation of an event reminds the person of the first presentation. According to Greene, study-phase retrieval is accompanied by the involuntary storage of changes in the context between the first and second presentations. (Because changes in the context are stored only after successful study-phase retrieval, this version of encoding variability is spared several of the embarrassments associated with versions discussed earlier.) Greene (1989) described how his theory can account for much of the literature that is problematic for other theories of the distributed practice effect.

Practical Applications

Because distributed practice leads to much better memory than does massed practice, the effect should be important in everyday memory. Rea and Modigliani (1988) reviewed research on educational implications of distributed practice effects. The flavor of that research will be illustrated with a few examples. Reder and Anderson (1982) demonstrated distributed practice effects in memory for textbooklike information. Charney and Reder (1986) found that distributed practice helped people to learn how to use a computer spreadsheet program. Rea and Modigliani (1985) used distributed practice to enhance retention of spelling and multiplication facts. In one of the most impressive studies of the long-term effects of distributed practice, Bahrick and Phelps (1987) had people study fifty pairs of English-Spanish translations. For the massed practice group, all study sessions were held on the same day. Another group studied the fifty

pairs on successive days, and a third group studied the pairs in sessions 30 days apart. *Eight years later*, the 30-day group remembered more than twice as many pairs as did the massed group.

Landauer and Bjork (1978) invented a method for effectively using distributed practice to learn names (and other facts). Suppose that you are at a party and you have just been introduced to someone whose name you wish to remember. You could try repeating the name over and over to yourself, but that sort of massed practice will not be very helpful. You could try to use distributed practice and repeat the name after a few minutes, but you may forget the name before you have a chance to repeat it. Landauer and Bjork suggest an expanding rehearsal pattern: Repeat the name a few times soon after hearing it; repeat the name again a few moments later; wait for a longer interval and repeat the name another time. Practice the name after successively longer intervals . . . and you've got it!

REFERENCES

Baddeley, A. (1990). *Human memory*. Boston: Allyn and Bacon.

Baddeley, A., and Longman, D. J. A. (1978). The influence of length and frequency of training sessions on the rate of learning to type. *Ergonomics 21*, 627–635.

Bahrick, H. P., and Phelps, E. (1987). Retention of Spanish vocabulary over 8 years. *Journal of Experimental Psychology: Learning, Memory, and Cognition 13*, 344–349.

Balota, D. A., Duchek, J. M., and Paullin, R. (1989). Age-related differences in the impact of spacing, lag, and retention interval. *Psychology and Aging 4*, 3–9.

Charney, D. H., and Reder, L. M. (1986). *Designing interactive tutorials for computer users: Effects of the form and spacing of practice on skill learning* (Tech. Rep. no. ONR-86-3). Pittsburgh: Carnegie Mellon University, Department of Psychology.

Cornell, E. H. (1980). Distributed study facilitates infants' delayed recognition memory. *Memory & Cognition 8*, 539–542.

Cuddy, L. J., and Jacoby, L. L. (1982). When forgetting helps memory: An analysis of repetition effects. *Journal of Verbal Learning and Verbal Behavior 21*, 451–467.

Ebbinghaus, H. (1885). *Über das Gedächtnis: Untersuchungen zur experimentellen Psychologie*. Leipzig: Duncker & Humblot. Trans. 1913 by H. A. Ruger and C. E. Bussenius as *Memory: A contribution to experimental psychology*. New York: Teachers College, Columbia University. Reprint, 1964. New York: Dover.

Gettinger, M., Bryant, N. D., and Mayne, H. R. (1982). Designing spelling instructions for learning disabled children: An emphasis on unit size, distributed practice, and training for transfer. *Journal of Special Education 16*, 439–448.

Glenberg, A. M. (1976). Monotonic and nonmonotonic lag effects in paired-associate and recognition memory paradigms. *Journal of Verbal Learning and Verbal Behavior 15*, 1–15.

Glenberg, A. M. (1977). The influence of retrieval processes on the spacing effect in free recall. *Journal of Experimental Psychology: Human Learning and Memory 3*, 282–294.

Glenberg, A. M. (1979). Component-level theory of the effects of spacing of repetitions on recall and recognition. *Memory & Cognition 7*, 95–112.

Glenberg, A. M., and Lehmann, T. (1981). Spacing repetitions over a week. *Memory & Cognition 7*, 475–479.

Glenberg, A. M., and Smith, S. M. (1981). Spacing repetitions and solving problems are not the same. *Journal of Verbal Learning and Verbal Behavior 20*, 110–119.

Greene, R. L. (1989). Spacing effects in memory: Evidence for a two-process account. *Journal of Experimental Psychology: Learning, Memory, and Cognition 15*, 371–377.

Greene, R. L. (1990). Spacing effects on implicit memory tests. *Journal of Experimental Psychology: Learning, Memory, and Cognition 16*, 1004–1011.

Greene, R. L. (1991). The Ranschburg effect: The role of guessing strategies. *Memory & Cognition 19*, 313–317.

Hintzman, D. L. (1976). Repetition and memory. In G. H. Bower, ed., *The psychology of learning and memory*, vol. 11, pp. 47–91. New York: Academic Press.

Hintzman, D. L., Summers, J. J., Eki, N. T., and Moore, M. D. (1975). Voluntary attention and the spacing effect. *Memory & Cognition 3*, 576–580.

Jacoby, L. L. (1978). On interpreting the effects of repetition: Solving a problem versus remembering a solution. *Journal of Verbal Learning and Verbal Behavior 17*, 649–667.

Jahnke, J. C. (1969). The Ranschburg effect. *Psychological Review 76*, 592–605.

Jahnke, J. C. (1974). Restrictions on the Ranschburg effect. *Journal of Experimental Psychology 103*, 183–185.

Jost, A. (1897). Die Assoziationsfestigkeit in ihrer Abhängigkeit von der Verteilung der Wiederholungen. *Zeitschrift für Psychologie 14*, 436–472.

Landauer, T. K. (1976). Memory without organization: Properties of a model with random storage and undirected retrieval. *Cognitive Psychology 7*, 495–531.

Landauer, T. K., and Bjork, R. A. (1978). Optimum rehearsal patterns and name learning. In M. M. Gruneberg, P. E. Morris, and R. N. Sykes, eds., *Practical aspects of memory*. New York: Academic Press.

Landauer, T. K., and Ross, B. H. (1977). Can simple instructions to use spaced practice improve ability to remember a fact?: An experimental test using telephone numbers. *Bulletin of the Psychonomic Society 10*, 215–218.

Melton, A. W. (1970). The situation with respect to the spacing of repetition and memory. *Journal of Verbal Learning and Verbal Behavior 9*, 596–606.

Rea, C. P., and Modigliani, V. (1985). The effect of expanded versus massed practice on the retention of multiplication facts and spelling lists. *Human Learning 4*, 11–18.

Rea, C. P., and Modigliani, V. (1987). The spacing effect in 4- to 9-year-old children. *Memory & Cognition 15*, 436–443.

Rea, C. P., and Modigliani, V. (1988). Educational implications of the spacing effect. In M. M. Gruneberg, P. E. Morris, and R. N. Sykes, eds., *Practical aspects of memory: Current research and issues*, vol. 1, pp. 402–406. Chichester, England: Wiley.

Reder, L. M., and Anderson, J. P. (1982). Effects of spacing and embellishment on memory for the main points of a text. *Memory & Cognition 10*, 97–102.

Ross, B. H., and Landauer, T. K. (1978). Memory for at least one of two items: Test and failure of several theories of spacing effects. *Journal of Verbal Learning and Verbal Behavior 17*, 669–680.

Rundus, D. (1971). Analysis of rehearsal processes in free recall. *Journal of Experimental Psychology 89*, 63–77.

Underwood, B. J. (1961). Ten years of massed practice on distributed practice. *Psychological Review 4*, 229–247.

Woodworth, R. S. (1938). *Experimental psychology*. New York: Holt.

Zechmeister, E. B., and Shaughnessy, J. J. (1980). When you know that you know and when you think that you know but you don't. *Bulletin of the Psychonomic Society 15*, 41–44.

Arthur M. Glenberg

DRUGS

See Drugs and Memory; Electroconvulsive Therapy and Memory Loss; Pharmacological Treatment of Memory Deficits

DRUGS AND MEMORY

The psychopharmacological approach to the study of cognition involves a systematic examination of the behavioral changes that occur following the administration of psychoactive drugs. It complements the neuropsychological approach to the study of learning and memory in that it attempts to understand cognition from a neurobiological perspective. Although we shall focus attention on experiments in humans, there is an extensive literature on the effects of drugs on learning and memory in lower animals (e.g., McGaugh, 1990; see also AGING ANIMALS, PHARMACOLOGICAL MANIPULATIONS OF MEMORY IN). Most psychoactive drugs produce reversible effects in the central nervous system. They are generally eliminated from the body relatively rapidly, and in some cases specific antagonists exist that allow a drug effect to be reversed almost immediately. This reversibility of drug effects allows subjects to be used as their own controls. That is, cognitive functions can be tested and contrasted in both a drugged and an undrugged state. This offers an advantage over neuropsychological studies of impaired cognition in patient populations. The lesions that are present in most patients are not reversible, and it therefore can be very difficult to obtain appropriate control data. In addition, it is possible to compare and contrast the effects of different drugs in the same subject.

Drug effects can be considered from a number of perspectives. First, knowledge of the basic neuropharmacology of the drug may yield information about specific sites where the drug acts, the distribution of these sites in the brain, and the neurochemical systems affected by the interaction of the drug with these sites. Some drugs that have profound effects on learning and memory, such as scopolamine and benzodiazepines, have fairly specific (although quite different) effects at the neurochemical level of analysis. Scopolamine acts as an antagonist at acetylcholine receptors, while benzodiazepines act at benzodiazepine receptors to facilitate the effects of the inhibitory neurotransmitter GABA (γ-aminobutyric acid). Other drugs, such as alcohol, appear to act rather less specifically.

Second, drugs that alter learning and memory generally have effects on behaviors that include more than just cognition. Drugs often alter mood and motivation. For example, alcohol, opiates, and benzodiazepines are sedatives, whereas cocaine and amphetamine are stimulants. It is important to consider whether these effects are responsible for these drugs' actions on learning and memory. The cognitive effects of alterations in mood and motivation have not been extensively investigated by cognitive psychologists (but see EMOTION, MOOD, AND MEMORY).

Third, the specificity of the drugs' effects within the cognitive domain must also be considered. For example, at perhaps the simplest level, a drug might alter the acquisition of information or its retrieval. The clearest and most frequently documented effects of drugs on learning and memory can be accounted for by changes in acquisition, as defined by alterations in learning curves. Alcohol, anticholinergics (such as scopolamine), marijuana, and benzodiazepines are some of the drugs that can produce impairments in how rapidly subjects acquire information. All these impairments appear to be dose-related. That is, greater impairments are observed with increasing doses. However, there is still considerable doubt about how these drugs impair acquisition. One of the possibilities that has been considered is that these drugs alter attentional mechanisms.

While drug effects on acquisition are clear and replicable, effects on retrieval appear to be more subtle. Perhaps the best-known example of drug-induced alterations in retrieval comes from the literature on state-dependency. State-dependent retrieval is the phenomenon in which subjects are able to retrieve information better when they are in the same state as they were when the material was acquired. For example, if material was learned under the influence of a drug such as alcohol, retrieval under sober conditions is often worse than if the subject is again intoxicated. Generally such effects have been observed following high doses of drugs, which also affect acquisition functions. The effects are critically dependent on the nature of the retrieval test, and not all information appears to be subject to state-dependent effects (see Eich, 1980, for an extensive review).

Many other distinctions have been made between different learning and memory processes. Evidence to support the distinctions has come from various sources, including studies in (undrugged) normal subjects and different patient populations. Drug studies have also provided some convergent support for some of the commonly accepted distinctions. One distinction that has been discussed for many years is that between short-term and long-term memory. Short-term memory is assessed using tests such as digit span and memory for the most recently presented items from a word list. Drugs such as alcohol and benzodiazepines exert their major effects on long-term memory, leaving short-term memory relatively unaffected (Lister, Eckardt, and Weingartner, 1987; Lister et al., 1988; Weingartner, 1985).

Another currently popular distinction is between implicit and explicit memory. These terms refer to subjects' conscious experience at the time of retrieval. In explicit tests (such as tests of free recall or recognition) subjects are aware that their memory is being assessed. Memory can be assessed indirectly (implicitly) by examining how a subject's previous exposure to some material affects performance on some task (e.g., solving a word puzzle; see IMPLICIT MEMORY). For example, facilitation in problem solving can occur without the subject's awareness of prior relevant experience. Benzodiazepines and alcohol both cause marked impairments when memory is tested explicitly. However, there is evidence that in some implicit tests of memory (e.g., tests of perceptual identification and word completion), these drugs fail to cause impairments (Danion et al., 1989; Weingartner et al., 1991).

Yet another distinction is between cognitive processes that can be accomplished relatively automatically and those that require considerable cognitive capacity and effort. Some drugs, particularly stimulants such as amphetamines and cocaine, selectively affect those cognitive processes that require sustained effort and concentration (Weingartner et al., 1984). In contrast, automatic cognitive operations are not affected by these drugs.

A major goal in psychopharmacology is to link the neurochemical and behavioral levels of analysis described above. This means providing a complete description of a drug's effects, from its initial interaction at its primary site of action in the brain to the functional consequences at the neurochemical and neurophysiological levels of analysis, to the specific effects on cognitive processes. However, this analysis has not yet approached completion for any drug.

The psychopharmacological approach to the study of cognition has several important clinical applications. One involves using drugs to model the learning and memory impairments that are expressed in different neuropsychiatric disorders. Another uses drugs to diagnose and treat the memory impairments seen in many patient groups. In both these cases a detailed knowledge of the neuropathology of the disorder that is being modeled or treated is invaluable. An appreciation of the neurobiological and psychobiological mechanisms of learning and memory is also helpful. There has been considerable interest in the possibility of using drugs in normal subjects to model clinical amnesias such as Korsakoff's disease and ALZHEIMER'S DISEASE. Knowledge of the neuropharmacology of a drug that modeled an amnesia might suggest useful treatment strategies and also pharmacological methods that might be useful in diagnosis.

The specific impairments seen in normal subjects treated with alcohol resemble those of patients with Korsakoff's disease, and it has been suggested that scopolamine mimics some of the features of the cognitive impairments seen in DEMENTIA patients (Sunderland et al., 1987; Weingartner, 1985.) However, to date, the drugs that produce the most marked cognitive impairments all appear to selectively impair acquisition rather than retrieval mechanisms. These results contrast with most of the literature on clinical amnesias. In many amnesic patients retrograde amnesia (amnesia for information acquired prior to the clinical syndrome) is frequently observed. The failure of drugs to produce a retrograde amnesia, therefore, limits their utility in modeling clinical amnesias.

Given the enormous number of people with cognitive disorders, it is not surprising that there is a very active search for drugs that may be useful in the treatment of impaired learning and memory. Therapies have been targeted for several populations of patients. Of particular note is the search for drugs that might lessen the changes in memory often observed in association with normal aging as well as the pathological and dramatic impairments in memory associated with Alzheimer's disease. The development of drugs that can improve attention and learning in hyperactive children (see LEARNING DISABILITIES), agents that can reverse the acute cognitive effects of some environmental stressors (e.g., sleep deprivation), and treatments for cognitive impairments that are associated with various lesions in the central nervous system have also received considerable attention.

Strategies for improving memory function often begin with studies testing the ability of some agent to reverse a laboratory-induced memory impairment (perhaps resulting from a surgical lesion in a rodent). A similar type of approach is one in which a normal control is administered a drug with known memory-impairing effects; then the ability of a second agent to reverse this impairment is examined.

Another important foundation for programmatic research for a drug that might improve memory functions begins with an appreciation of the neuropathological mechanisms that are responsible for the observed impairments in memory in some neuropsychiatric disorder. For example, we have learned a great deal about the neuropathology of Alzheimer's disease that should prove helpful in the development of treatments that can facilitate memory. This progressive disease alters both the structural and the neurochemical integrity of the central nervous system. One of the neurochemical systems that is particularly affected in Alzheimer's disease is the cholinergic nervous system. For that reason, many of the drugs currently being developed and evaluated in clinical trials are designed to activate this system in several ways. These include providing neurons with the chemical material for making more of the neurotransmitter, blocking the metabolism or deactivation of the neurotransmitter, and delivering drugs that can act directly to stimulate the neurons in the cholinergic nervous system. Other strategies are based on the use of drug combinations that are likely to affect not only the cholinergic nervous system but also other neurochemical systems that are known to be affected in Alzheimer patients. Our rapidly expanding knowledge of neural mechanisms of normal and impaired memory functions will eventually provide us with therapeutic tools for treating impaired memory. At present, however, we are still quite limited in our ability to treat memory impairments such as those expressed in dementing illness.

Before treating a cognitive dysfunction, it is highly desirable to make an accurate diagnosis. This can be very difficult, especially if the impairment is a subtle one or if many factors in a patient's life may have contributed to his or her memory difficulties. Attempts are being made to use psychopharmacological methods to assist in diagnosis. For example, we know that the cholinergic nervous system is damaged in Alzheimer's disease, and it appears that Alzheimer patients may be even more susceptible to the memory-impairing effects of the anticholinergic drug scopolamine than are elderly normal controls or young subjects.

In conclusion, drugs are useful tools for exploring processes that are involved in learning and remembering. Likewise, what we have learned about memory in the human learning laboratory has begun to be put to good use in defining how drugs alter memory and learning. Both of these approaches, along with a knowledge of the neurobiology of impaired memory, are used as a basis for the development of drugs that can be helpful for memory-impaired patients.

REFERENCES

Danion, J.-M., Zimmermann, M.-A., Willard-Schroeder, D., Grange, D., and Singer, L. (1989). Diazepam induces a dissociation between explicit and implicit memory. *Psychopharmacology 99*, 238–243.

Eich, J. E. (1980). The cue-dependent nature of state-dependent retrieval. *Memory and Cognition 8*, 157–173.

Lister, R. G., Eckardt, M. J., and Weingartner, H. (1987). Ethanol intoxication and memory: Recent developments and new directions. In M. Galanter, ed., *Recent developments in alcoholism*, vol. 5, pp. 111–126. New York: Plenum.

Lister, R. G., and Weingartner, H. J. (1987). Neuropharmacological strategies for understanding psychobiological determinants of cognition. *Human Neurobiology 6*, 119–127.

Lister, R. G., Weingartner, H., Eckardt, M. J., and Linnoila, M. (1988). Clinical relevance of effects of benzodiazepines on learning and memory. In I. Hindmarch and H. Ott, eds., *Benzodiazepine receptor ligands, memory and information processing*, pp. 117–127. Berlin: Springer.

McGaugh, J. L. (1990). Significance and remembrance: The role of neuromodulatory systems. *Psychological Science 1*, 15–25.

Newman, R. P., Weingartner, H., Smallberg, S., and Calne, D. (1984). Effortful and automatic memory processes: Effects of dopamine. *Neurology 34* (6), 805–807.

Sunderland, T., Tariot, P. N., Weingartner, H., Mueller, E. A., and Murphy, D. L. (1987). Anticholinergic sensitivity in patients with dementia of the Alzheimer type and age-matched controls. *Archives of General Psychiatry 44*, 418–426.

Weingartner, H. (1985). Models of memory dysfunctions. *Annals of the New York Academy of Science 444*, 359–369.

Weingartner, H. J., Eckardt, M., Hommer, D., and Wolowitz, O. (1991). Selective effects of triazolam on memory. *Lancet 338,* 883–884.

Richard G. Lister
Herbert J. Weingartner

DYSLEXIA

See Learning Disabilities

witz, O. (1991). Selective effects of triazolam on memory. *Lancet 338,* 883–884.

DYSLEXIA

E

EARLY EXPERIENCE AND LEARNING

The brain of the developing organism is a unique and dynamic system. During the prenatal and postnatal periods the brain differs dramatically from that of the adult. For example, it contains more synapses early in development than it does at any other stage in life (Purves and Lichtman, 1980). Receptors for a number of neuropeptides (e.g., oxytocin) are found in higher concentrations early in development than later in life (Shapiro and Insel, 1989). In certain brain areas (e.g., the suprachiasmatic nucleus of the hypothalamus), glucocorticoid receptors are found in high concentrations only during early ontogeny (Van Eekelen et al., 1987). These are but a few examples that attest to the differences in the brain during development. For the most part, the functional significance of these neuronal features of the newborn brain has not been determined.

One of the critical aspects of the developing brain is its plasticity. Both physiological and environmental stimuli have been shown to profoundly, and often permanently, influence the functional capacities of the organism (see Levine, 1966, for review). Neonatal disturbance of the normal hormonal milieu leads to some of the best-known cases of permanent alterations of function induced by early manipulations of physiological events. Neonatal exposure to heterotypical gonadal hormones, for example, results in a permanently altered reproductive physiology and behavior (Yahr, 1988). Both over- and underexposure to thyroid hormone during early development cause changes in the brain that produce learning disabilities (Eayrs and Levine, 1963).

The purpose of this entry is to illustrate the effects of alterations in early environments on learning capacity in the adult organism. Several areas of investigation have demonstrated the importance of early experience for later behavior, using a number of different models to examine this issue. Thus, deprivation of visual experience early in development has been shown to markedly affect adult vision; needless to say, this also affects the animal's behavior (Hyvarinen and Hyvarinen, 1979). There is an extensive literature on the effects of "enriched environments" on subsequent learning ability (see Rosenzweig, 1984, for review). We have chosen to examine the role of early handling as a model of infantile stimulation on learning in the adult.

In 1956 Levine et al. reported that neonatal manipulations have profound effects on later behavior. In essence, their study showed that neonatal handling (i.e., removing rat pups from their mother for a few minutes and returning them to their mother), or electric shock during the same time period, markedly improved the animals' capacity to learn a conditioned avoidance response when tested as adults.

The conditioned avoidance response was first developed by Miller (1948) as a presumed measure of learned fear or anxiety. This procedure involves placing the animal in a two-compartment chamber. Both sides of the chamber contain grid floors that can be electrified. The animal is presented with a signal, the conditioned stimulus, which is followed after a brief time by an electric shock. The animal is required to cross from the electrified side of the chamber to the safe side. If it crosses within the interval between the onset of the signal and the onset of shock, it avoids the shock (conditioned avoidance). However, if the animal fails to cross during this interval and the shock is delivered, this response is considered an escape response. There are many parameters that can be manipulated within this paradigm (e.g., shock intensity, intertrial interval, length of the conditioned signal). Variations of these parameters influence the rapidity of learning.

Following the initial observations demonstrating these marked differences between manipulated and nonmanipulated pups, a number of subsequent studies were conducted. In order to verify whether the effects of early handling were age-dependent, early-handled pups were compared with non-handled pups and with animals that were handled as adults. Pups manipulated as infants were found to show avoidance learning superior to that of nonhandled pups. Adult-handled animals were more similar to nonhandled rats (Levine, 1956).

Although it was clear that early handling improved avoidance learning, the underlying causes of this improvement remained to be determined. One possible explanation for these findings is that emotional reactivity was modified as a function of these early experiences. The more efficient avoidance learning may therefore be a consequence of reduced arousal levels. Levine (1966) showed that increasing arousal levels can, in fact, interfere with avoidance conditioning. Increasing the shock levels during avoidance conditioning results in an inverted U-shaped function with regard to acquisition of the conditioned avoidance response. Thus, acquisition is improved by very low levels of shock but impaired by very high levels (Levine, 1966).

There are numerous reports that early handling reduces emotional reactivity (Denenberg, 1964; Denenberg, 1969; Whimbey and Denenberg, 1967). This reduced reactivity is demonstrable using both behavioral and physiological indices. Activity levels and defecation in the open field differ between handled and nonhandled subjects. Handled animals explore more actively (i.e., show less freezing) and defecate less in the open field (Levine et al., 1967), are less neophobic (Weinberg, Smotherman, and Levine, 1978), and are less reactive to human handling as adults (Ader, 1965). One of the more sensitive physiological indices of arousal is the activation of the hypothalamic-pituitary-adrenal (HPA) system (Hennessy and Levine, 1978). Following stress, nonhandled animals show plasma corticosterone (the primary glucocorticoid secreted by the rodent) elevations that are both larger and more persistent than those found in animals handled during infancy (Hess et al., 1969).

These differences in emotionality are consistently found using a variety of different testing paradigms. However, the effects of early handling on avoidance conditioning appear to vary when the parameters are different from those used in the original studies. Both Ader (1965) and Weinberg and Levine (1977) failed to find differences in conditioned avoidance response, although differences in emotional reactivity were clearly present. The question of whether early handling influences associative learning therefore still remained unanswered.

In order to address this question, Denenberg and Morton (1962) studied the effect of early handling on the ability of rats to learn tasks that did not involve noxious stimuli. These investigators examined the interaction between early handling and environmental enrichment on the ability of adult rats to solve a Hebb-Williams maze. After weaning, handled and nonhandled rats were reared in a neutral, restricted, or enriched environment. The animals were then required to solve a sequence of twelve test problems (Rabinovitch and Rosvold, 1951). The results indicated that the animals' behavior was affected by the postweaning, but not by the preweaning, manipulation. Thus, rats reared in an enriched environment made significantly fewer errors than those reared in neutral or restricted environments. Based on these results, Rabinovitch and Rosvold concluded that preweaning handling affected emotional processes but not learning ability.

In 1972 Wong attempted to clarify the issue of whether early handling directly affects associative learning or whether the improvement in learning is due mainly to differences in emotional reactivity. An experiment was conducted that presumably could discriminate these two processes. Thus, subjects were trained to reach a criterion of stable performance on a positive reinforcement task (food), and then punished with an aversive stimulus (shock) for making the reinforced response. Comparisons could then be made in terms of (1) the degree of response suppression following the presentation of the aversive event and (2) the rate of recovery after removal of the aversive stimulus. Wong argued that if handled animals showed greater response suppression and a slower recovery than nonhandled animals, this would indicate a direct effect of handling on learning. If the contrary occurred, it could be assumed that the primary influence on the behavior was attributable to differences in emotionality. Animals were trained to alternate goal boxes in a T-maze to obtain food. Once criterion had been reached, they were given a shock in the goal box where they had obtained positive reinforcement (S+ box). Testing began 1 day after the punished trial. The animals were placed in the maze and received food only in the S+ box. During the acquisition phase the handled group made more correct responses (alternations) than the nonhandled group, indicating superior learning on a positive reinforcement task. Following the shock exposure, handled rats made fewer choices to the food reward box (S+) than nonhandled animals, suggesting that handled animals had superior associative learning.

In most of the studies described above, learning was investigated using behavioral situations in which a motivational component was present, making it difficult to dismiss entirely the effects of emotional reactivity on learning. Latent inhibition, a behavioral paradigm that avoids some of these problems, has recently been used to examine the relationship between handling and learning. This paradigm was described in the context of classical conditioning. Ivan PAVLOV was the first to demonstrate that repeated exposure to a conditioned stimulus (CS), prior to pairing this stimulus with an unconditioned stimulus (UCS), impairs the rate of conditioning that subsequently occurs (Pavlov, 1927). Thus, repeated exposure to a stimulus that is not followed by meaningful consequences renders this stimulus ineffective for subsequent learning (Lubow, 1973).

Weiner et al. (1985) employed the latent inhibition paradigm to study the question of early handling and learning. The experiment was conducted in two phases. During the first phase (preexposure) members of one group were placed in a shuttle box and presented with sixty 5-second tones. Members of the second group were placed in the shuttle box for an equivalent time without exposure to the tones. In the second phase the animals were presented with 100 tone (CS) and shock (UCS) pairings and the number of conditioned avoidance responses was recorded. The results showed that nonpreexposed handled animals exhibited better avoidance learning than nonhandled rats, thus replicating earlier findings. However, preexposed han-

dled animals performed more poorly than non-preexposed handled rats. The findings were to some extent sex-dependent: Whereas preexposed handled males and females and preexposed non-handled females exhibited the latent inhibition (i.e., performed more poorly than nonpreexposed animals), the nonhandled males did not show any effect of preexposure on the conditioned avoidance response.

In a further study, latent inhibition was investigated using a conditioned emotional response (CER) to test the influence of early handling (Weiner, Feldon, and Ziv-Harris, 1987). The CER procedure was conducted in three phases: (1) preexposure; (2) acquisition, in which the preexposed tone was paired with shock; and (3) testing, during which latent inhibition was indexed by the animals' suppression of licking during tone presentation. As in the previous experiment, latent inhibition was observed in the handled males and females and in nonhandled females, but not in the nonhandled males. Based on both of these studies, the conclusion was that early handling exerts a beneficial influence on learning capacity in the adult animal.

Only a very limited literature has attempted to examine the neural substrates of the early handling phenomenon. Meaney et al. (1988) studied the long-term influence of early handling on the neuroendocrine regulation of the HPA system. They reported a long-term downregulation of Type 2 glucocorticoid receptors (GR) in the hippocampus of nonhandled, but not of handled, aged animals. They further reported that spatial learning, a hippocampus-dependent process, is significantly improved in aging animals that had undergone early handling. However, the aged nonhandled animals appeared to have suffered hippocampal cell loss. The differences in spatial learning may thus be due to the prevention of this cell loss by early handling. These studies demonstrate the long-term consequences of early handling for at least one aspect of neural regulation. Although the implications of this downregulation of GRs for learning have not been extensively investigated, there is some evidence that administering specific GR antagonists interferes with the acquisition of a spatial learning task (Oitzl, Sutanto, and de Kloet, 1990). Other aspects of the HPA system also seem to be involved in learning and memory (van Wimersma Greidanus, 1982).

We have chosen to present the evidence concerning the effects of early handling on subsequent learning capacity. Although there are many examples in the literature on long-term consequences of manipulations during infancy that affect learning and memory, most of these studies have utilized toxic agents resulting in permanent and irreversible morphological and physiological changes in the central nervous system that are later reflected as impairments in the adult organism's ability to learn (for review, see Grimm, 1987). Environmental enrichment (Gardner et al., 1975; Krech, Rosenzweig, and Bennett, 1962) and early handling constitute the only available examples of subtle environmental manipulations that cause permanent alterations in adult function that facilitate rather than impair adult learning abilities.

(See also CHILDREN, DEVELOPMENT OF MEMORY IN; EMOTION, MOOD, AND MEMORY.)

REFERENCES

Ader, R. (1965). Effects of early experience and differential housing on behavior and susceptibility to gastric erosions in the rat. *Journal of Comparative and Physiological Psychology 60,* 233–238.

Denenberg, V. H. (1964). Critical periods, stimulus input, and emotional reactivity: A theory of infantile stimulation. *Psychological Review 55,* 813–815.

———— (1969). Open-field behavior in the rat: What does it mean? *Annals of the New York Academy of Sciences 159,* 852–859.

Denenberg, V. H., and Morton, J. R. C. (1962). Effects of preweaning and postweaning manipulations upon problem-solving behavior. *Journal of Comparative and Physiological Psychology 55,* 1096–1098.

Eayrs, J. T., and Levine, S. (1963). Influence of thyroidectomy and subsequent replacement therapy upon conditioned avoidance learning in the rat. *Journal of Endocrinology 25,* 505–513.

Gardner, E. B., Boitano, J. J., Mancino, N. S., and D'Amico, D. P. (1975). Environmental enrichment and deprivation: Effects on learning, memory and exploration. *Physiology and Behavior 14,* 321–327.

Grimm, V. E. (1987). Effects of teratogenic exposure on the developing brain: Research strategies and possible mechanisms. *Developmental and Pharmacology Therapeutics 10,* 328–345.

Hennessy, M. B., and Levine, S. (1978). Sensitive pituitary-adrenal responsiveness to varying intensities of psychological stimulation. *Physiology and Behavior 21,* 295–297.

Hess, J. L., Denenberg, V. H., Zarrow, M. X., and Pfeifer, W. D. (1969). Modification of the corticosterone response curve as a function of handling in infancy. *Physiology and Behavior 4,* 109–111.

Hyvarinen, J., and Hyvarinen, L. (1979). Blindness and modification of association by early binocular deprivation in monkeys. *Child Care and Health Development 5,* 385–387.

Krech, D., Rosenzweig, M. R., and Bennett, E. L. (1962). Relations between brain chemistry and problem-solving among rats raised in enriched and impoverished environments. *Journal of Comparative and Physiological Psychology 55,* 801–807.

Levine, S. (1956). A further study of infantile handling and adult avoidance learning. *Journal of Personality 25,* 70–80.

———— (1966). UCS intensity and avoidance learning. *Journal of Experimental Psychology 71,* 163–164.

Levine, S., Chevalier, J. A., and Korchin, S. (1956). The effects of early shock and handling on later avoidance. *Journal of Personality 24,* 475–493.

Levine, S., Haltmeyer, G. C., Karas, G. G., and Denenberg, V. H. (1967). Physiological and behavioral effects of infantile stimulation. *Physiology and Behavior 2,* 55–59.

Levine, S., and Mullins, R. F. (1966). Hormonal influences on brain organization in infant rats. *Science 152,* 1585–1592.

Lubow, R. E. (1973). Latent inhibition. *Psychological Bulletin 79,* 398–407.

Meaney, M. J., Aitken, D. H., van Berkel, C., Bhatnagar, S., and Sapolsky, R. M. (1988). Effects of neonatal handling on age-related impairments associated with the hippocampus. *Science 239,* 766–768.

Miller, N. E. (1948). Studies of fear as an acquirable drive: I. Fear as a motivation and fear reduction as a reinforcement in the learning of new responses. *Journal of Experimental Psychology 38,* 89–101.

Oitzl, M. S., Sutanto, W., and de Kloet, E. R. (1990). Mineralocorticoid and glucocorticoid function in a spatial orientation task. *Journal of Steroid Biochemistry supp. 36,* 72.

Pavlov, I. P. (1927). *Conditioned reflexes,* G. V. Arenp, trans. London: Oxford University Press.

Purves, D., and Lichtman, J. W. (1980). Elimination of synapses in the developing nervous system. *Science 210,* 153–157.

Rabinovitch, M. S., and Rosvold, H. E. (1951). A closed-field intelligence test for rats. *Canadian Journal of Psychology 5,* 122–128.

Rosenzweig, M. R. (1984). Experience, memory, and the brain. *American Psychologist 39,* 365–376.

Shapiro, L. E., and Insel, T. R. (1989). Ontogeny of oxytocin receptors in the rat forebrain: A quantitative study. *Synapse 4,* 259–266.

Van Eekelen, J. A. M., Rosenfeld, P., Levine, S., Westphal, H. M., and de Kloet, E. R. (1987). Post-natal disappearance of glucocorticoid receptor immunoreactivity in the suprachiasmatic nucleus of the rat. *Neuroscience Research Communications 1*, 129–133.

van Wimersma Greidanus, T. B. Disturbed behavior and memory in the Brattleboro rat. *Annals of the New York Academy of Sciences 394*, 655–662.

Weinberg, J., and Levine, S. (1977). Early handling influences on behavioral and physiological responses during active avoidance. *Developmental Psychobiology 10*, 161–169.

Weinberg, J., Smotherman, W. P., and Levine, S. (1978). Early handling effects on neophobia and conditioned taste aversion. *Physiology and Behavior 20*, 589–596.

Weiner, I., Feldon, J., and Ziv-Harris, D. (1987). Early handling and latent inhibition in the conditioned suppression paradigm. *Developmental Psychobiology 20*, 233–240.

Weiner, I., Schnabel, I., Lubow, R. E., and Feldon, J. (1985). The effects of early handling on latent inhibition in male and female rats. *Developmental Psychobiology 18*, 291–297.

Whimbey, A. E., and Denenberg, V. H. (1967). Experimental programming of life histories: The factor structure underlying experimentally created individual differences. *Behavior 29*, 296–314.

Wong, R. (1972). Infantile handling and associative processes of rats. *British Journal of Psychology 63*, 101–108.

Yahr, P. (1988). Sexual differentiation of behavior in the context of developmental psychobiology. In E. M. Blass, ed., *Handbook of behavioral neurobiology*, vol 9. New York: Plenum.

Seymour Levine
Deborah Suchecki

EBBINGHAUS, HERMANN

Hermann Ebbinghaus (1850–1909) was the founder of the experimental psychology of memory. He laid the foundation for the scientific study of memory in a monograph entitled *Über das Gedächtnis* (1885). The little book, whose appearance belies its impact, was translated into English in 1913 under the title *Memory: A Contribution to Experimental Psychology.*

Life

Ebbinghaus was born on January 23, 1850, at Barmen, near Bonn, Germany. His father was a well- to-do merchant. As the University of Bonn he studied languages and philosophy. He served in the army during the Franco-Prussian War of 1870–1871, and upon returning to the university completed his doctoral dissertation in 1873. Ebbinghaus then spent some five years traveling in France and England. He began his research on memory at Berlin in 1878, spending over a year on the initial set of experiments. Upon completing these studies he became a private lecturer at the University of Berlin in 1880, and continued his studies of memory. He repeated many of the original experiments from 1879/1880 in 1883/1884 and added new ones. He published the report on both series in his 1885 monograph.

Ebbinghaus's life after he published his epoch-making study was active and productive. He was appointed a professor at the University of Berlin in 1886, remaining there until 1894, when he moved to the University of Breslau. He stayed at Breslau for eleven years and then accepted an ap-

Figure 1. Hermann Ebbinghaus.

pointment at the University of Halle. Over the years he became known as a prominent and respected member of the new scientific discipline of experimental psychology. A major source of his renown lay in his textbook of general psychology, *Grundzüge der Psychologie* (1897). It went through many subsequent revisions and editions, and became the most widely read psychology text in Germany. Because of his administrative responsibilities and the time spent in writing and revising his textbook, Ebbinghaus did relatively little original research, and what he did was not comparable in impact with his 1885 monograph. He died of pneumonia at Halle on February 26, 1909.

Ebbinghaus's Approach to Memory

Before Ebbinghaus, the study of memory consisted of philosophical "armchair speculation" concerning remembering and forgetting in everyday life, and clinical observations of patients with memory disorders. The philosophical approach of the day is beautifully reflected in William JAMES's *Principles of Psychology* (1890). The clinical approach is well illustrated by the work of Théodule RIBOT. Both lines of thought produced many insights into the nature and workings of normal and impaired memory. However, there were also curious gaps; not surprisingly, the contemporary thinkers were unaware of many of them. There was, for instance, the widely held view that memory could not be studied by strict scientific methods. Although methods of science had been applied to the "lower" mental processes, such as sensation and perception, under the general rubric of psychophysics, the "higher" mental processes such as memory were regarded as being beyond the pale of such methods. Another, tacit, idea was that remembering and forgetting occur in an all-or-none fashion: A person either does or does not remember a fact, a thought, a name, and the like. The possibility that nonrecoverable mental contents could exist at different levels of strength was discussed neither by philosophers nor by students of memory pathology.

Ebbinghaus's work changed all that. In his now-classic monograph he introduced the general approach to the study and measurement of learning and memory by psychological means, outlined the appropriate methodology, and reported a number of experiments illustrating the power of his methods. All of this was highly original.

The general strategy that Ebbinghaus adopted can be summarized in terms of three simple principles for the scientific study of mental processes that are not directly observable. These principles are as valid today as they were when Ebbinghaus first made use of them. First, it is necessary to find a way of converting the unobservable mental processes into observable behavior. Second, it is necessary to be able to measure this observable behavior reliably. Third, it is necessary that the behavior thus quantified by shown to vary systematically with other variables and experimental conditions.

The unobservable mental processes that Ebbinghaus wanted to study and measure were *associations* between ideas. Like almost all of his contemporaries, he assumed that memory reflects the existence of associations between ideas. He also thought that learning consists in the acquisition of associations, whereas forgetting reflects their loss. Ebbinghaus decided that the study of the acquisition and loss of associations would be best undertaken in a situation in which the associations to be learned were initially nonexistent. To that end he invented the nonsense syllable as a basic idea unit to be used in experiments on memory. A nonsense syllable is a meaningless single syllable consisting of two consonants separated by a vowel or a diphthong. When he composed a number of randomly chosen syllables into a series—the "lesson" to be learned and remembered—no associations existed between and among the members of the series. Learning the series therefore would involve the formation and strengthening of associations. The process could be captured by observing and measuring some behavior that could be assumed to be closely correlated with changes in the associations.

Methods and Results

In all his experiments Ebbinghaus was his sole subject. In numerous different studies, in which he varied the conditions of learning and retention, he would learn and then test himself with a large number of different series of syllables. He would learn a given series by first reading and then repeating the sequence of syllables aloud to the beating of a metronome, at the rate of two and a half syllables per second, until he could produce the series faultlessly. The amount of effort required to master the series provided measures of both original learning and subsequent retention (or forgetting, the opposite of retention.) Ebbinghaus adopted the number of readings, or the amount of time required for the learning of the series, as the *measure of learning.* Some time later he would *relearn* the same series, using the same method of reading and repeating the syllables. The comparison of initial learning and relearning scores provided a measure of *savings.* Ebbinghaus took savings to represent a measure of retention of the original learning.

Using these methods of measurement of memory, Ebbinghaus investigated a number of basic phenomena of learning and retention. The results of his experiments, concerning things such as the relation between the length of the series and the difficulty of learning it, the effects of the original overlearning of a series on its subsequent relearning, the advantages of distributed over massed practice, and the shape of the forgetting curve, turned out to be highly regular and lawful. The underlying relations are in fact orderly, and Ebbinghaus exercised meticulous care in carrying out his experiments. Among other things, he went to the trouble of performing numerous replications of individual experiments. The resulting regularity and lawfulness of his findings greatly impressed other scientists.

In one particularly ingenious set of experiments Ebbinghaus measured and compared three kinds of associations: forward associations, backward associations, and remote associations. In order to measure remote associations he would initially learn a series of syllables in a particular order, and subsequently relearn various series systematically *derived* from the original one. In these derived series the originally learned syllables were separated by a certain number of other syllables. For instance, if the original series is symbolized by A B C D E F . . . (. . . designating other syllables), then the derived series "skipping one syllable" would consist of A C E . . . B D F . . . , and the derived series "skipping two syllables" would consist of A D . . . B E . . . C F . . . . Ebbinghaus found that the savings in learning these derived series varied regularly with the remoteness of the members of the derived series from one another in the originally learned series. These data suggested that in the course of learning a series of syllables, associations are formed not only between immediately adjacent syllables but also among remote ones, the strength of the remote associations between any two members of a series varying with the degree of their remoteness in the original series.

Influence

Ebbinghaus's work proved to be highly influential for a number of reasons. Despite the pioneering nature of his work, he did just about everything right by the standards of science. He replaced philosophical discussions about memory and its phenomena with tightly controlled experimental demonstrations of how memory could be measured, and how memory performance could be found to be related to and determined by various independent variables. He discussed the sources of error and the problems of unreliability of measurement. He explained and demonstrated how one could measure fine gradations in mental processes that until then were thought to be scientifically intractable. He showed how the "higher" mental processes seemed to obey the same general kinds of laws that governed the "lower" processes. He explicitly and forcefully pointed out the intimate connection that exists between learning and memory, a realization that guides the study of memory. Like many other novel ideas introduced by Ebbinghaus, the connection between learning and memory is terribly obvious in our day, but it had been overlooked by most thinkers before Ebbinghaus. Ebbinghaus's adoption of the basic study/test paradigm in which a subject learns some previously unknown material and is subsequently tested for retention of the material contrasted sharply with the then current philosophical practice of discussing problems and phenomena of memory from the vantage point of *existing* associations.

Three particular features of Ebbinghaus's ground-breaking work that are most frequently mentioned in textbooks—his invention of the nonsense syllable, his serial learning task, and his adoption of the savings method as a measure of strength of associations—have had little direct influence on succeeding generations of memory researchers, who even shortly after 1885 rapidly adopted other methods and techniques of studying and measuring memory. Nonsense syllables turned out to vary greatly in meaningfulness, and thus lost the advantage of homogeneity. The serial learning task did not allow independent manipulation or assessment of stimulus and response functions in learning and retention. And the originally ingenious savings method was replaced with more direct methods of measuring retention and forgetting.

Ebbinghaus's most important single achievement consisted in his highly convincing demonstration that it is possible to reliably measure aspects of complex mental processes that are not directly observable. Next to that, it was his general orientation and approach, and his attitude and spirit in the matter of applying the methods of science to the study of the human mind, that were embraced by succeeding generations of psychology students interested in learning and memory.

Ebbinghaus's pioneering role in the founding of the field of research on human learning and memory is universally acknowledged. Just about everyone agrees that *Über das Gedächtnis* represented a truly remarkable achievement of a great scientist, one that has left an indelible stamp on the study of one of the most fascinating problems of the human brain/mind.

(See also ASSOCIATIONISM.)

REFERENCES

Ebbinghaus, H. (1885). *Über das Gedächtnis: Untersuchungen zur experimentellen Psychologie.* Leipzig: Duncker & Humblot. Trans. (1913 by H. A. Ruger and C. E. Bussenius as *Memory: A contribution to experimental psychology.* New York: Teachers College, Columbia University. Reprint, 1964. New York: Dover.

———— (1897). *Grundzüge der Psychologie.* Leipzig: Veit.

Hoffman, R. R., Bringmann, W., Bamberg, M., and Klein, R. (1987). Some historical observations on Ebbinghaus. In D. S. Gorfein and R. R. Hoffman, eds., *Memory and learning: The Ebbinghaus centennial conference.* Hillsdale, N.J.: Erlbaum.

Postman, L. (1968). Hermann Ebbinghaus. *American Psychologist 23,* 149–157.

Roediger, H. L. (1985). Remembering Ebbinghaus. *Contemporary Psychology 30,* 519–523.

Slamecka, N. J. (1985). Ebbinghaus: Some associations. *Journal of Experimental Psychology: Learning, Memory, and Cognition 11,* 414–435.

Endel Tulving

ECOLOGICAL MEMORY

See Natural Settings, Memory in

EIDETIC IMAGERY

Nothing captures better the popular belief in "photographic memory" than the term *eidetic imagery,* although the latter hardly supports the exaggerated claims made for the former capacity. Photographic memory is the general claim that people can "still see in front of them" things that were experienced in the past. Eidetic imagery, on the other hand, is more closely tied to objective experimental criteria.

A generation of German investigations of eidetic imagery in the early years of the century (see Woodworth, 1938, p. 45) was largely ignored at midcentury when American psychology was dominated by theoretical behaviorism and had, at best, no use for the concept of imagery. The silence was broken in 1964 by publication of a paper by R. N. Haber and R. B. Haber (see also later summaries in Haber, 1979, and accompanying commentaries). Their report launched modern research on eidetic imagery and largely sustained conclusions from the continental work of a generation earlier.

Haber and Haber (1964) studied 150 elementary-school children in a standardized testing situation. The children were shown a set of four coherent pictures for 30 seconds apiece and interviewed immediately after each as to what they "saw" on a blank easel in the same location as the picture had been. Eight measures were collected, such as whether they saw an image, how long it lasted, whether the image description used positive coloration (rather than complementary colors, as in afterimages), whether it was described in the present tense, and so on. Although over half the children (84/150) reported at least some kind of imagery for the presented picture, there was considerable variability in scores on these eight measures: In particular, a group of twelve children was easily distinguished from the other seventy-two who had indicated some imagery. These twelve children were discontinuous with their classmates in the presence of positive coloration, duration of the images, use of the present tense to describe images, and visual scanning (of the blank surface) during the interview after each picture. For example, positive coloration was an average of 90 percent in the group of twelve but an average of only 34 percent in the remaining seventy-two children. In visual scanning (eye movements across the blank easel where the eidetic image was "projected"), the difference was even larger (100 percent versus 2 percent). Thus, the incidence of eidetic skill in the original survey was 8 percent (12/150). A survey using similar criteria by Paivio and Cohen (1979), on 242 second- and third-grade children, gave excellent agreement on the incidence of eidetic imagery in normal schoolchildren—8.6 percent (21/242).

In subsequent work (Leask et al., 1969) the "fusion method" was used to identify eidetic imagers. This method presents two, individually meaningless, pictures successively. After display of the first, the second picture is presented on the same surface, with the subject instructed to superimpose his or her image of the first picture upon the second. The pictures are designed so that this superposition yields a meaningful picture. Children identified by the criteria above to be possessors of eidetic imagery could perform this task, whereas normal children could not.

Age

Giray et al. (1976) examined 280 children, 20 at every age from 5 to 18 years old, using the Habers' (Haber and Haber, 1964) criteria. Fifteen children (5.6 percent) were identified as eidetic, but a clear relation to age emerged: Nine of these fifteen were either five or six years old, and only a single subject was over ten. The decline in eidetic skills with age is well documented (Haber, 1979; Leask et al., 1969; Richardson and Harris, 1986); they are apparently virtually absent among adults.

Recent evidence (Giray et al., 1985; Zelhart et al., 1985) suggests that the eidetic skill increases in geriatric populations and that the true relation between age and the incidence of eidetic imagery should be U-shaped. This possibility places the interpretation of high eidetic skill among young children in a different light: These young individuals might be especially likely to show eidetic imagery not because of their age but because of the functional level of their brains.

Brain Damage

The suggestion that eidetic imagery varies inversely with age (up to the college years) suggested that it might be a marker for retarded development *within* any age group. Although Haber (1979) had been unimpressed with the evidence favoring such a view, the many peer commentaries following his article demonstrate that the point is at least controversial. Leask et al. (1969) showed no evidence for mental retardation among their eidetic children, but they did observe more minor visual defects (wearing glasses) among the eidetic than among the noneidetic children. Siipola and Hayden (1965) tested mentally retarded children and found incidence rates of about 50 percent, a strikingly higher figure than among the comparable nonretarded population. Furthermore, eidetic imagery was a marker, among these children, for "organic" as opposed to "familial" diagnoses of retardation. Other investigators (Gummerman et al., 1972; Richardson and Cant, 1970; Symmes, 1971) have, however, reported many fewer cases among retardates of all types. But Giray et al. (1976) found even a higher incidence (78.5 percent of fourteen cases) in hydrocephalic children and only a "normal" rate (5 percent to 10 percent) among children with other forms of mental retardation. The force of these tantalizing observations is not yet clear.

Cross-Cultural Approaches

In the context of eidetic imagery as a developmentally primitive information storage mode, Doob (1966) supposed that primitive, illiterate societies might show a higher incidence of it, even among adults. An initial report did, as expected from this reasoning, show a high incidence using the Habers' criteria among the Ibo of Nigeria. However, Doob's further research was disappointing: He had expected that within the Ibo population, the incidence of eidetic imagery would be greater in truly remote, agrarian settlements than in more modern, urbanized population centers, but this was not the case.

Comment

The most important conclusion about eidetic imagery is that it is a genuine phenomenon, capable of objective measurement and study. Moreover, the skill has been distinguished from such related phenomena as iconic memory, sensory afterimages, and extremely accurate memory (but see Gray and Gummerman, 1975, for reservations on this last point). Eidetic imagery is characteristic of a minority of young children and is probably related to some forms of brain disorders. It is rather certainly not the agency for good memory of detail, as the Habers (1964) showed originally. Thus, systematic work on eidetic imagery indicates that it shares practically nothing with the popular concept of photographic memory. The apparent absence of eidetic imagery among adults and the fact that it is not predictive of particularly good memory for detail make it a poor basis for claims of photographic memory.

(See also CODING PROCESSES: IMAGERY.)

REFERENCES

Doob, L. W. (1966). Eidetic imagery: A crosscultural will-o'-the-wisp? *Journal of Psychology 63,* 13–34.

Giray, E. F., Altkin, W. M., and Barclay, A. G. (1976). Frequency of eidetic imagery among hydrocephalic children. *Perceptual and Motor Skills 43,* 187–194.

Giray, E. F., Altkin, W. M., Vaught, G. M., and Roodin, P. A. (1976). The incidence of eidetic imagery as a function of age. *Child Development 47,* 1107–1210.

——— (1985). A life span approach to the study of eidetic imagery. *Journal of Mental Imagery 9,* 21–32.

Gray, C. R., and Gummerman, K. (1975). The enigmatic eidetic image: A critical examination of methods, data, and theories. *Psychological Bulletin 82,* 383–407.

Gummerman, K., Gray, C. R., and Wilson, J. M. (1972). An attempt to assess eidetic imagery objectively. *Bulletin of the Psychonomic Society 28,* 115–118.

Haber, R. N. (1979). Twenty years of haunting eidetic imagery: Where's the ghost? *Behavioral and Brain Sciences 2,* 583–629.

Haber, R. N., and Haber, R. B. (1964). Eidetic imagery: I. Frequency. *Perceptual and Motor Skills 19,* 131–138.

Leask, J., Haber, R. N., and Haber, R. B. (1969). Eidetic imagery in children: II. Longitudinal and experimental results. *Psychological Monograph Supplements 3,* no. 3 (whole no. 35).

Paivio, A., and Cohen, M. (1979). Eidetic imagery and cognitive abilities. *Journal of Mental Imagery 3,* 53–64.

Richardson, A., and Cant, R. (1970). Eidetic imagery and brain damage. *Australian Journal of Psychology 22,* 47–54.

Richardson, A., and Harris, L. J. (1986). Age trends in eidetikers. *Journal of Genetic Psychology 147,* 303–308.

Siipola, E. M., and Hayden, S. D. (1965). Exploring eidetic imagery among the retarded. *Perceptual and Motor Skills 21,* 275–286.

Symmes, J. S. (1971). Visual imagery in brain injured children. *Perceptual and Motor Skills 21,* 507–514.

Woodworth, R. S. (1938). *Experimental psychology.* New York: Holt.

Zelhart, P. F., Markley, R. B., and Bieker, L. (1985). Eidetic imagery in elderly persons. *Perceptual and Motor Skills 60,* 445–446.

Robert G. Crowder

ELECTROCONVULSIVE THERAPY AND MEMORY LOSS

Electroconvulsive therapy (ECT) was developed in the 1930s as an alternative to psychiatric treatments that depended on inducing a *convulsion.* More recently, ECT has been reviewed and evaluated by scientific groups in several countries, and has been found to be a safe and effective treatment for severe and disabling *depression.* The therapeutic effect is caused by a brain seizure, not a convulsion visible in the limbs. In contemporary practice, ECT is administered in conjunction with a short-acting general anesthetic and a muscle relaxant. As a result, the seizure is most easily detected by recording brain waves during treatment. ECT can be either *bilateral,* in which case one electrode is applied to each side of the head, or *unilateral,* in which case two electrodes are applied to the right side of the head. The benefit of ECT is evaluated by considering both its effectiveness for treating depression and the adverse effects of treatment. The most prominent of the adverse effects is impaired memory. The extent of the memory impairment varies depending on how ECT is administered. Memory impairment is greater after bilateral ECT than after unilateral ECT, and it is greater when ECT is administered using machines that deliver *sine-wave current* rather than *brief pulses* of current.

Studies of the memory impairment associated with ECT suggest that memory is affected only temporarily. After a course of treatment, which typically involves six to twelve treatments given over a period of two to four weeks, the ability to learn new material is reduced and access to some memories that were formed prior to ECT is lost. *Anterograde amnesia* refers to the difficulty that patients have in remembering events that occur after treatment begins. This difficulty persists for many weeks after treatment, gradually resolving as the capacity for new learning recovers. *Retrograde amnesia*, the loss of memories acquired prior to treatment, can initially involve memories acquired many years earlier. Access to these memories gradually recovers as time passes after treatment.

It should be emphasized that memory for the time period surrounding the treatment period itself does not recover after ECT. For example, when patients were asked three years after treatment to identify what past time periods they had difficulty remembering, the average patient reported difficulty remembering the time during ECT, the two months after treatment, and the six months prior to treatment. Thus, except for this lacuna around the time of ECT, formal memory testing suggests that patients eventually recover their capacity for learning and memory. At the same time, absence of evidence for a lasting memory problem is not the same as proving that no such problem exists. It is possible that more sensitive tests could be developed that would detect persisting impairment. It is always difficult to prove that something does not exist. However, memory tests sensitive enough to show differences between the memory abilities of healthy forty-year-olds and healthy fifty-year-olds (some decline in memory ability does occur with normal aging) do not detect lasting memory problems in patients who have received ECT.

In contrast with the findings from memory tests, it is noteworthy that some patients do report, even long after ECT, that their memory is not as good as it used to be. Although it is possible that the patients have a degree of sensitivity about their own memory problems beyond what can be detected by memory tests, there are a number of other possibilities. One possibility is that, having recovered gradually from a period of rather severe and easily documented memory impairment, it is difficult for a person to know when memory abilities have recovered to what they should be. People who lead active lives use their memories many times each day to recall past events and previously acquired knowledge. It is commonplace for recall

to be incomplete or inaccurate, especially for information that lies at the fringes of our stored knowledge, such as information that was encountered only once or material that was not fully attended to when it was first encountered. Sometimes memory fails altogether. If someone has had ECT, how can he or she know whether any particular failure of memory is normal or whether it might be due to ECT? To the extent that ECT does lead many patients to doubt the integrity of their own memories, it is possible that this effect of treatment could be attenuated or eliminated by sympathetic and informed counseling during the period immediately following ECT.

REFERENCES

American Psychiatric Association. (1990). *The practice of ECT: Recommendations for treatment, training and privileging.* Washington, D.C.: APA.

Consensus Conference. (1985). Electroconvulsive therapy. *Journal of the American Medical Association 251,* 2103–2108.

D'Elia, G., Ottosson, J. O., and Stromgren, L. S. (1983). Present practice of electroconvulsive therapy in Scandinavia. *Archives of General Psychiatry 40,* 577–581.

Fink, M. (1979). *Convulsive therapy: Theory and practice,* pp. 203–204. New York: Raven Press.

Malitz, S., and Sackeim, H., eds. (1986). *Electroconvulsive therapy: Clinical and basic research issues.* Annals of the New York Academy of Sciences 462.

Royal College of Psychiatrists. (1989). *The practical administration of electroconvulsive therapy (ECT).* London: Gaskell.

Larry R. Squire

EMOTION, MOOD, AND MEMORY

The ways in which we attend, learn, and remember are related to our transitory moods and to our enduring emotional states. This assertion is based on research performed by experimental and clinical psychologists who use a variety of methods. In some studies, psychologists measure differences in emotional states and determine whether those differences are associated with differences in the ways that the participants perform cognitive tasks. These studies usually focus on unpleasant emotions and moods, such as depression and anxiety. In other studies, psychologists attempt to induce either unpleasant or pleasant moods in the participants (perhaps by having them listen to different types of music) and then examine how performance is affected by these manipulations. Both types of research have tried to answer three major questions about the interaction of mood and memory: (a) Do depressed and anxious moods hinder performance on cognitive tasks? (b) Do people remember events that are emotionally consistent with their moods better than other events? (c) Is performance improved if the same mood exists on the occasions of the original experience and the attempt to remember it? The ensuing summary suggests answers to the questions in the context of theoretical frameworks for understanding the relationships between mood and memory.

Mood-Related Impairments in Learning and Memory

Cognitive tasks vary according to the degree to which they require our attention. Some tasks require little attentional control for successful performance; many of the cognitive processes involved in these tasks are relatively automatic, which means that they are well practiced and can occur simultaneously with other cognitive processes. Other tasks require a more effortful and deliberate focus of attention if good performance is to be achieved. The degree to which focused attention is required for good performance is a characteristic of tasks that are performed during initial exposure or learning and tasks that reveal memory for past events. Reading a long list of unrelated words for the first time, for example, requires little attentional control by fluent readers, but organizing them in ways that will be useful during later attempts to remember them clearly requires more effortful and deliberate focus. Similarly, tests of memory for those words vary in the degree of focused attention that they require. Rereading the same words is one index of memory (in that the old words can be read faster than new words) that involves processes which are relatively automatic. In contrast, trying to recall the words on the list is a deliberate task that can benefit from a great deal of attention and the use of special strategies. (See also ATTENTION AND MEMORY.)

Separate assessments of learning and memory are not possible; any index of learning involves memory and vice vera. It *is* possible, however, to emphasize variations in one type of task by examining research in which the other type of task is held constant. When that is done, a pattern emerges: The learning and memory tasks that benefit from attentional control are the tasks that present difficulties to depressed and anxious people; they perform less well than people who are not mood-impaired. Weingartner and his colleagues (1981), for example, discovered that clinically depressed patients could learn lists of words organized into simple categories as well as could nondepressed people, but when the same words were unorganized, the depressed patients learned less well. Similarly, college students who are experimentally induced to feel depressed do not learn words presented in the context of more elaborate or distinctive sentences as well as do students in neutral moods, but the two groups perform similarly when the contexts are less elaborate or distinctive (Ellis et al., 1984). Williams and his colleagues (1988) reviewed similar findings in the literature on anxiety and cognition. If people approach these types of learning tasks by providing their own organization (a deliberate strategy) or by focusing attention on elaborations and distinctions, they learn at higher levels. Depressed and anxious people do not seem to attend in these ways.

Similar conclusions can be reached in examining different types of memory tests. Hertel and Hardin (1990), for example, found that depressed college students performed as well as nondepressed students when the test did not involve attentional focus on a past event, but when the test required such focus, depressed students did not spontaneously use strategies for recognition that characterized the performance of the nondepressed students.

Why do mood-impaired people experience attentional difficulties of the type just described? Some theoretical frameworks for understanding depression and anxiety emphasize capacity limitations. Although the capacity to allocate attention is normally limited in human beings, depression and anxiety may impose further limitations. These further limitations may be biochemically induced, or they may be a reflection of mood-impaired people's enduring concern with mood-related aspects of their experience—aspects that are often irrelevant to the task at hand. These task-irrelevant thoughts can distract attention when participants are left to their own devices (i.e., when they are told to learn a list of words). Yet when learning or memory tasks are devised in ways that constrain attention to materials or build in appropriate strategies, mood-impaired people may perform as well as others (Hertel and Rude, 1991).

Mood-Congruent Memory

People pay attention to and subsequently remember episodes and materials that are consistent (or congruent) with their moods more often than they attend to and remember other occurrences. Mood-congruent attention characterizes the performance of anxious people in particular. To the extent that anxiety is similar to a more general state of physiological arousal (or alertness), attention to threat-related events can be understood from an evolutionary perspective. Research conducted by Eysenck et al. (1987) illustrates anxiety-congruent attention. In that experiment anxious participants, more often than nonanxious participants, spelled spoken homophones (such as *die/dye*) to coincide with the more threatening concept. The results of another experiment by Mathews et al. (1989) showed similar mood-congruent attention on a test of memory. In this test, the participants were shown the first three letters of words and asked to complete them to form the first word that came to mind. The anxious subjects completed the stems of threat-related words that they had encountered in an earlier task more often than other types of old and new words; nonanxious subjects did not show this bias.

On more traditional tests of memory, such as tests of deliberate recall, anxious people do not always remember anxiety-related episodes better than other episodes (see Williams et al., 1988, for a review and possible explanation). Yet research concerned with other emotional states (including depression, happiness, and anger) shows more consistent evidence of mood-congruent recall. Separate investigations by many researchers have revealed mood-congruent recall of personal events from the participants' past, as well as materials provided in experimental settings. For depressed people, these findings are consistent with explanations of their poor performance on typically neutral tasks. If the conditions of the task permit it, depressed people focus on aspects of experience that are relevant to their emotional states; if those emotional aspects are tapped by the test, they are well remembered, but if they are not, performance on the mood incongruent aspects suffers because the latter received less attention.

Some theorists understand mood-congruent recall by constructing models of the mind, or internal representations of experience. Bower's (1981) network model of mood and memory, for example, represents emotional states as nodes that are connected to representations of events experienced in their context. A simple analogy can be achieved by thinking about nodes as hubs of wheels; spokes for one hub connect at the other end to other hubs and form a "Tinkertoy" network of interconnected nodes. When a mood is felt, the corresponding emotion node is activated, and that activation spreads along the preestablished pathways (spokes) to representations of mood-congruent experiences (such as adjectives with similar emotional tone). In this way, mood-congruent information is brought to mind (activated) at the time of a recall test.

The phenomena of mood-congruent memory and their interpretation are qualified by a number of considerations (Blaney, 1986). For example, depressed moods are often associated with a reduction in the recall of positively toned events rather than with increased recall of negative events. Isen (1984) interpreted these findings and other asymmetries to mean that attempts at mood control inhibit the recall of sad events. However, to the extent that mood-congruent memory is observed, it plays an important role in maintaining emotional states (see Teasdale, 1983).

Mood-Dependent Memory

Is there evidence of better memory when one's mood at the time of remembering is the same as one's mood during the original encounter? Initial research on this topic supported this claim for mood-dependent memory. Mood dependency and mood congruency have much in common in theory (as in Bower's network model) and in practice: Remembering mood-congruent events is often a matter of being in the same mood as when those events were encountered previously. Recent research, however, has frequently failed to produce evidence for mood dependency when mood congruency is not involved—when the materials are not inherently related to the mood. Bower and Mayer (1989) concluded that this type of mood dependency occurs only when other aspects of the context for remembering do not provide strong cues for recalling the material. In other words, a consistent emotional state by itself is a weak basis for retrieving memories of past experience (see Eich and Metcalfe, 1989). Moreover, researchers sometimes ignore possible differences in arousal on the two occasions of learning and remembering (Revelle and Loftus, 1990); because physiological arousal mediates attentional processes, differences in arousal might conceal regularities in mood-dependent memory.

Summary

Individual differences in emotional states and transitory moods correspond to differences in learning and remembering. To date, research findings are consistent with a theoretical framework that emphasizes attentional processes: Attentional deficits or attentional biases toward mood-related aspects of experience are possible sources for difficulties in remembering emotionally irrelevant events.

REFERENCES

Blaney, P. H. (1986). Affect and memory: A review. *Psychological Bulletin 99*, 229–246. A superb review and critique of issues and findings on mood-congruent and mood-dependent memory for the more advanced reader.

Bower, G. H. (1981). Mood and memory. *American Psychologist 36*, 129–148. A review of early research on mood-congruent and mood-dependent memory, with a description of Bower's network model of emotion and memory.

Bower, G. H., and Mayer, J. D. (1989). In search of mood-dependent retrieval. *Journal of Social Behavior and Personality 4*, 121–156.

Eich, E., and Metcalfe, J. (1989). Mood-dependent memory for internal versus external events. *Journal of Experimental Psychology: Learning, Memory, and Cognition 15*, 443–455.

Ellis, H. C., and Ashbrook, P. W. (1988). Resource-allocation model of the effects of depressed mood states on memory. In K. Fiedler and J. Forgus, eds., *Affect, cognition, and social behavior*, pp. 25–43. Toronto: Hogrefe. A cogent description of attentional difficulties associated with depressive memory performance.

Ellis, H. C., Thomas, R. L., and Rodriguez, I. A. (1984). Emotional mood states and memory: Elaborative encoding, semantic processing, and cognitive effort. *Journal of Experimental Psychology: Learning, Memory, and Cognition 10*, 470–482.

Eysenck, M. W. (1982). *Attention and arousal: Cognition and performance.* New York: Springer-Verlag. Theory and research on the relationships among anxiety, arousal, and cognitive performance.

Eysenck, M. W., MacLeod, C., and Mathews, A. (1987). Cognitive functioning in anxiety. *Psychological Research 49*, 189–195.

Hasher, L., and Zacks, R. T. (1979). Automatic and effortful processes in memory. *Journal of Experimental Psychology: General 108*, 356–388. Attentional deficits in depression are discussed in the context of the authors' general framework for understanding the relationship between attention and memory.

Hertel, P. T., and Hardin, T. S. (1990). Remembering with and without awareness in a depressed mood: Evidence for deficits in initiative. *Journal of Experimental Psychology: General 119*, 45–59.

Hertel, P. T., and Rude, S. S. (1991). Depressive deficits in memory: Focusing attention improves subsequent recall. *Journal of Experimental Psychology: General 120*, 301–309.

Ingram, R. E. (1990). Self-focused attention in clinical disorders: Review and a conceptual model. *Psychological Bulletin 107*, 156–176. An excellent review of the clinical literature related to mood-impaired focus on mood-congruent experience.

Isen, A. M. (1984). Toward understanding the role of affect in cognition. In R. Wyer and T. Srull, eds., *Handbook of social cognition*, vol. 3, pp. 179–236. Hillsdale, N.J.: Erlbaum.

Johnson, M. H., and Magaro, P. A. (1987). Effects of mood and severity on memory processes in depression and mania. *Psychological Bulletin 101*, 28–40. A review of memory research that is restricted to the clinical disorders of depression and mania.

Mathews, A., Mogg, K., May, J., and Eysenck, M. (1989). Implicit and explicit memory bias in anxiety. *Journal of Abnormal Psychology 98*, 236–240.

Revelle, W., and Loftus, D. A. (1990). Individual differences and arousal: Implications for the study of mood and memory. *Cognition and Emotion 4*, 209–237.

Teasdale, J. D. (1983). Negative thinking in depression: Cause, effect, or reciprocal relationship? *Advances in Behaviour Research and Therapy 5*, 27–49.

Teasdale, J. D., and Fogarty, S. J. (1979). Differential effects of induced mood on retrieval of pleasant and unpleasant events from episodic memory. *Journal of Abnormal Psychology 88*, 248–257.

Weingartner, H., Cohen, R. M., Murphy, D. L., Martello, J., and Gerdt, C. (1981). Cognitive processes in depression. *Archives of General Psychiatry 38,* 42–47.

Williams, J. M. G., Watts, F. N., MacLeod, C., and Mathews, A. (1988). *Cognitive psychology and emotional disorders.* New York: Wiley. An excellent review of cognitive phenomena associated with depression and anxiety.

Wine, J. D. (1980). Cognitive-attentional theory of test anxiety. In I. G. Sarason, ed., *Test anxiety: Theory, research, and applications,* pp. 349–385. Hillsdale, N.J.: Erlbaum.

Paula Hertel

EPISODIC MEMORY

Episodic memory is the form of memory that allows an individual to recollect happenings from his or her past. It is sometimes referred to as autobiographical memory.

The concept of episodic memory has undergone considerable changes since its introduction by Tulving in 1972, and is now used in different senses by different writers and in different contexts. The two principal meanings are (1) episodic memory as a type of memory task and memory performance, and (2) episodic memory as a distinct neurocognitive system. These two principal senses of the term are discussed here.

Episodic Memory Tasks

Episodic memory in the first sense manifests itself in situations in which a person remembers some information acquired on a particular occasion. Although episodic memory experiments have been concerned with a large variety of different kinds of information—words, names, faces, pictures, facts, sentences, paragraphs, stories, and the like—much of the basic knowledge we have gained about episodic memory comes from various *list learning* experiments in which the to-be-remembered items are familiar words, and in which the acquired information concerns the appearance of particular words in particular lists.

The use of words in episodic memory experiments is a matter of convenience: Words themselves are of no more intrinsic interest to the students of memory than fruit flies are to the scientists investigating the mechanisms of heredity. Many facts and phenomena of memory that have emerged from research with lists of words also hold for other types of information and materials. Words represent convenient units of to-be-remembered information, because the appearance of each word in a list is an event with well-defined temporal and spatial boundaries. Such an event is readily perceived and can be readily described by the learner. Also helpful is the fact that words have numerous and varied properties, many of which are systematically related to the words' memorability.

A prototypical laboratory experiment on episodic memory consists of (1) an original study experience during which individual items, such as words, are *encoded* and *stored* by the learner, and (2) a subsequent test during which some aspect of the experience is *retrieved.* Tests of different aspects of the original experience define different episodic memory tasks. (These tasks can also be referred to as *explicit* memory tasks.) They include but are not limited to the following (see also MEASUREMENT OF MEMORY):

1. Free recall task—Name the items in the study set or list, regardless of their order.

2. Serial recall, or serial reproduction, task—Name the items in the list in their proper order.

3. Paired-associate task—Name the item that appeared together with Item X.

4. Cued recall task—Name the item in the study list that represented an instance of Category C (or one that rhymes with Word W, or fits into the sentence frame S).

5. Free-choice (or Yes/No) recognition task—Did Item X appear in the study set?

6. Two-alternative forced-choice recognition task—Which of these two items, X or Y, appeared in the study set?

7. (Absolute) Frequency estimation task—How many times did item I occur in the study list?

8. (Relative) Recency judgment task—Which of these two items, X or Y, appeared earlier (or later) in the study list?

Each of these tasks can be described in terms of the subject's earlier personal experience. This is why they are classified as episodic memory tasks.

For example: Which items do *you* remember *seeing* in the list? Do *you* remember *hearing* Word X in the list? Which of these two items, X or Y, did *you encounter* earlier in the list?

Many variables are known to affect performance on episodic memory tasks. They include ability differences among subjects, the type of information presented for study, the amount of time and effort devoted to learning, subjects' previous knowledge of the material they are to learn, and the length of the retention interval between study and test. Especially important determinants of the accuracy of reproduction of materials studied in episodic memory experiments include the way subjects think about the to-be-remembered material at study, the so-called *encoding operations.* (These operations, which include levels of processing and organization, are discussed elsewhere in this volume, under the heading of CODING PROCESSES.) Also very important are the conditions under which RETRIEVAL PROCESSES occur or are attempted, as well as the relation between encoding and retrieval conditions.

Episodic Memory System

The second sense of the term *episodic memory* is that of a hypothetical neurocognitive system that differs from the other major memory systems for which evidence exists. These other systems include SEMANTIC MEMORY, procedural memory, short-term memory (see WORKING MEMORY IN HUMANS), and the perceptual representation system that subserves perceptual priming (discussed elsewhere in this volume under the heading of IMPLICIT MEMORY). The postulation of episodic memory as a separable memory system is part of the enterprise of the *classification* of natural phenomena of memory. Classification is a necessary prerequisite for the study of memory mechanisms and processes.

According to this second sense of episodic memory, the ability of an individual to *consciously recollect* personally experienced past events, that is, to become aware again of some aspect or some part of a previous experience, is possible only by virtue of an intact brain system specialized for that purpose. The retrieval of a great variety of general information about the world, the kind of information that other people also may possess, can be accomplished by the semantic memory system alone.

The evidence in support of such a separable episodic system is still fragmentary, and the issue is being widely debated. The principal observations of interest have been provided by the study of brain-damaged patients suffering from amnesia (see AMNESIA, ORGANIC). Some brain-damaged patients who suffer from a severe memory disorder are capable of slowly acquiring certain kinds of new factual (semantic) information even though they are completely incapable of remembering the learning episodes. For instance, Freed and his colleagues (1987) have shown that even the world's best-known and most thoroughly studied amnesic patient, H. M., can perform quite adequately in an episodic (in the first sense of the term) picture-recognition task, displaying a forgetting rate indistinguishable from that of normal control subjects, provided he is given a great deal of study time. But nothing can be done to make him remember that he ever participated in such a recognition experiment.

Such a *dissociation* between the ability to identify recently seen pictures and the inability to remember equally recent personal happenings serves as evidence that acquisition of knowledge and recollection of life events are subserved by different regions of the brain. Another category of relevant evidence is labeled *source amnesia:* Individuals with impaired or frail memories, such as amnesic patients and elderly people, do much better in recalling recently learned facts than they do in consciously recollecting the learning episode as the source of these facts.

Relation between Tasks and System

The two senses of *episodic memory*—type of memory tasks and performance on these tasks, on the one hand, and a distinct neurocognitive system, on the other—are related. But the two senses cannot be equated. A person's ability to retrieve information presented in an episodic memory task clearly depends on his or her episodic memory system. But it also depends on other systems. For instance, there is evidence that *recognition* of previously studied items involves two different sets of processes, one of which can be hypothetically identified with episodic retrieval of information about the study episode, and the other with processes that seem to be related to those underlying implicit memory. Thus, typical episodic memory experiments frequently yield evidence about the joint contributions of episodic and semantic memory systems, and perhaps even some others, in a manner that can be uncovered only through experimental analysis. Performance on other tasks depends on both the episodic and semantic systems. Furthermore, episodic tasks used in the laboratory do not assess the subject's ability to recollect the learning episode as such, but require only that the subject reproduce or otherwise indicate his or her knowledge of the semantic contents of the learning episode. Such lack of complete correlation between episodic memory tasks and the episodic memory system suggests that episodic memory defined in one sense cannot routinely be substituted for episodic memory in the other sense.

REFERENCES

Freed, D. M., Corkin, S., and Cohen, N. J. (1987). Forgetting in H. M.: A second look. *Neuropsychologia 25,* 461–471.

Mandler, G. (1980). Recognizing: The judgment of previous occurrence. *Psychological Review 87,* 252–271.

Shimamura, A. P., and Squire, L. R. (1987'0. A neuropsychological study of fact memory and source amnesia. *Journal of Experimental Psychology: Learning, Memory, and Cognition 13,* 464–473,

Tulving, E. (1972). Episodic and semantic memory. In E. Tulving and W. Donaldson, eds., *Organization of memory,* pp. 381–403. New York: Academic Press.

—— (1983). *Elements of episodic memory.* New York: Oxford University Press.

—— (1987). Multiple memory systems and consciousness. *Human Neurobiology 6,* 67–80.

Endel Tulving

EVERYDAY MEMORY

See Natural Settings, Memory in

EVOLUTION AND LEARNING

Learning, like all other biological phenomena, has undergone evolutionary change. Evolution by natural selection can take place whenever members of a population differ in reproductive success and the basis for this difference is inherited. A difference in reproductive success is critical for natural selection because other differences—for example, in survival—matter only if they ultimately cause some individuals to leave more surviving offspring than others. Some of the ways in which learning can affect reproductive success through its role in foraging, predator avoidance, navigation, mating, and other behaviors are described here and in the articles on FORAGING and on MIGRATION, NAVIGATION, AND HOMING.

Genetically inherited features are important for natural selection because only these features are passed on to offspring. Thus, for evolutionary change to occur in learning, the process of learning itself must be genetically inherited. This simply means that there must exist some differences between members of a population of animals in how learning occurs, and that these differences have a genetic basis. The evidence that genetic differences in learning exist is described in the following section. Genetic differences in learning do not preclude differences in learning that are caused by experience or by the environment—indeed, all aspects of behavior are ultimately the outcome of an interaction between genes and the environment.

Evolution by natural selection has a number of effects. First, fossils show that animal species change over long periods of time. Second, living species of animals are related by descent from common ancestors. Finally, structure and behavior consist of adaptations, features that serve important functions and promote reproductive success. The fossil record shows enormous change in animal life, but unfortunately learning leaves little fossil evidence. Some inferences about learning can, however, be drawn from fossil evidence of evolutionary change in neuroanatomy. Comparisons of learning among living animals, related to each other to a greater or lesser degree, can be made.

These comparisons serve two purposes. First, they can be used to reconstruct the evolutionary history of learning. If, for example, distantly related animals like sea slugs and mammals possess the same neurochemical learning mechanism, it is likely that this mechanism arose very early in evolution, in a common ancestor of sea slugs and mammals, and has been retained while these animals changed in other ways. Comparisons between living animals can also be used to study adaptation.

Adaptations are features of animals that serve a function, like the eye or the immune system. Learning, too, is an adaptation. Comparisons of learning among different species of animals can identify features of learning that are adaptations to the way of life of these animals. If two closely related species of animals live similar lives but differ in an important feature of their environment, then differences in their modes of learning may be adaptations to this environmental feature. Diet, predators, nest site, migration, and social behavior can all affect how learning occurs in various species of animals. This has been one of the most active areas of research into the evolution of learning.

The Genetics of Learning

Two methods are used to examine the inheritance of learning: selection for learning ability in rats and mice, and induced mutations of learning in the fruit fly *Drosophila*. As early as the 1920s it had been shown that by selecting mice which performed well on mazes and breeding them (and by selecting mice which performed poorly on mazes and breeding them), strains of mice could be established with a heritable ability to perform well (or poorly) on a maze. More recent research has confirmed this result with a wide range of learning tasks. Selection experiments of this kind, however, generally find that the ability to perform well on one learning task does not transfer to other learning tasks. The improvement in performance that results from selection is specific to the particular task. Even when it can be shown that this effect is not due to inadvertently selecting for some trait that has little direct connection with learning, such as activity or motivation, the change in learning still tends to be specific to the task learned. This may mean one of two things. It may be extremely difficult to select for general learning ability because every learning task must necessarily have unique properties. This interpretation would mean that selection for general learning ability is possible, but there are so many other ways to favor or interfere with learning that it is difficult to make general learning ability the target of selection. The alternative interpretation is that general learning ability simply does not exist. Learning instead consists of a large collection of learning abilities of greater or lesser specificity. Whatever the correct

conclusion to be drawn from selection experiments with learning, they do show that there is a great deal of heritable variation in learning on which natural selection can act.

In fruit flies, chemically induced mutations have many effects on behavior, and some of these are specific to learning. Although these mutations are induced by chemical agents, and thus do not indicate natural heritable variation in learning, as do selection experiments, they do show that change in a single gene can change how learning occurs. The effects of these mutations have been carefully observed, as described by Tully (1987), and their route of action can be followed from the initial change in DNA to its effects on the biochemistry of the neuron, the nervous system, and learning. Single gene mutations can have highly specific effects on the learning process. Several mutants, with whimsical names like *amnesiac, dunce, rutabaga,* and *turnip,* cause fruit flies that can normally learn an association between odor and food to acquire this association but then forget it very quickly. The biochemical effects of these mutations have been traced to alterations in the chemical signaling system within neurons that controls the cell's response to stimulation by other neurons.

Learning and Reproductive Success

Learning contributes directly and indirectly to reproductive success in many ways. Bumblebees learn how to reach floral nectar. Colonial swallows learn to recognize their young, and young herring gulls learn to recognize their parents. Most animals must learn what is edible and what is toxic; others learn migration routes, how to identify predators, how to defend a territory, and how to attract a mate. In all of these cases, any heritable change in learning that makes the animal slightly more successful at the task will make it slightly more successful at reproducing itself, and hence more likely to pass on the inherited modification of learning to its offspring. As a consequence of natural selection favoring different variations on learning, learning comes to differ between species and to possess specialized adaptive properties that make learning more effective. Learned food aversions illustrate this kind of specialization. Animals sometimes eat food that makes them ill, either because the food is contaminated or because what they have eaten produces toxins to discourage its consumption. Animals can clearly benefit from learning which foods are edible and which are not, but the natural situation presents them with a problem. Toxic food may not take effect until several hours after it is eaten. Animals usually have great difficulty in learning that two events are related if they are separated in time by more than a few minutes. Experiments with rats show that they can associate illness with food, even if the food was eaten several hours previously, and require only a single experience with the food to form a strong aversion to it. Furthermore, they associate the taste and odor of the food, not its appearance, with illness. Selectivity in what is learned and the ability to associate events separated in time are distinctive features of taste aversion learning (see TASTE AVERSION AND PREFERENCE LEARNING IN ANIMALS.)

Songbirds exhibit specialized learning in the way they acquire their songs. The songs that male passerine birds use to advertise territory ownership and to attract a mate are learned. This song-learning system possesses a number of unusual features. Most species learn only the songs of their own species, even if they are experimentally exposed to songs of other species for an equal period of time. In addition, the young of many birds have a "sensitive period" during which they learn songs most readily. Before and after this period they are less likely to learn new songs. Songs are not learned by singing them. Instead, songs heard during the sensitive period are remembered until they are first sung many months later, when the breeding season begins. Finally, there are specialized nuclei in the avian brain that are responsible for acquisition and production of song. Restrictions on what is learned, a sensitive period, separation in time of learning and performance, and specialized neural structures make the song learning system very different from other kinds of learning, but very effective for learning songs (see BIRD SONG LEARNING).

Evolution of Learning and the Brain

Evolutionary change in learning requires evolutionary change in the neural apparatus of learning. The song control nuclei of species of birds with large song repertoires are larger than the nuclei of birds with smaller repertoires. An increase in

the size of neural structures that participate in learning has been found for a number of other kinds of learning. Some species of birds, notably chickadees, nuthatches, and jays, store food. They make hundreds of caches of food and return several days to many months later to collect and consume their stored food. The caches are widely scattered and contain only a few food items each. Remarkably, these birds remember precisely where they have placed each cache (see SPATIAL LEARNING).

The avian hippocampus plays an important role in memory, as it does in mammals (see GUIDE TO THE ANATOMY OF THE BRAIN: HIPPOCAMPUS), and the hippocampus of food-storing birds is over twice the size of the hippocampus of closely related birds that do not store food (Sherry et al., 1989). Comparative studies of this kind show that adaptive evolutionary change occurs in brain regions involved in learning. A further example illustrates that such adaptive change can occur within a species. Most voles (rodents in the family Cricetidae) are polygynous: One male has several mates. Male home ranges are larger than female home ranges, and the home range of a polygynous male may encompass the home ranges of several females. Some species of vole, however, are monogamous, and male and female home ranges are of equal size in these species. Laboratory experiments have found that males of polygynous species perform better on spatial memory problems than do females, but in monogamous species males and females perform equally well. The sex difference in spatial ability in polygynous species is an adaptation to their breeding system and to the sex difference in home range size. As with food-storing birds, the consequences of natural selection for learning ability can be seen in the brain. Jacobs et al. (1990) found that the hippocampus of male polygynous voles is larger than that of females, while in monogamous voles there is no sex difference in the size of the hippocampus (see SEX DIFFERENCES IN LEARNING IN ANIMALS).

The Effect of Learning on Evolutionary Change

Evolutionary change has certainly occurred in learning, but learning can, in turn, affect the course of evolution. Many species of animals do things that are culturally determined. Behaviors that are traditional within a population of animals are learned from other members of the group, either directly or simply by associating with other group members. Migration routes, learned songs, and food preferences can all be transmitted culturally. Experiments by Curio (1988) have shown that European blackbirds learn to recognize predators by a cultural learning process. A blackbird that spots a predator such as an owl will make loud calls and attack the owl, a behavior called mobbing. Mobbing attracts other birds that join in the attack. It is possible to arrange things in the laboratory so that the bird initiating the mobbing sees a stuffed owl, while a bird in a neighboring cage sees only a stuffed model of a harmless bird. It will join in mobbing nonetheless, and eventually comes to treat the model of the harmless bird as a dangerous predator. This blackbird can then induce other blackbirds to mob the harmless model, and so a cultural tradition of treating certain other animals as predators can be established. The effect of such culturally transmitted behavior on biological evolution is not fully understood, though it is clear that learned behavior, such as a migration route or food preference, can consistently expose animals to a new environment and new sources of natural selection.

Conclusions

Learning exhibits genetic variation and is affected by single gene mutations. Learning also makes an important contribution to the ability of animals to reproduce themselves. These two properties together have the result that learning evolves by natural selection. Learning has changed over the course of evolution, and the learning abilities of different animals are related, because animals are related by descent from common ancestors. But these two effects can be difficult to observe or measure. The most obvious result of evolutionary change in learning is the occurrence of adaptations in learning. Food aversion learning and bird song learning provide examples of specialized learning abilities that serve particular functions. The effects of such evolutionary adaptation in learning can also be observed in brain areas such as the hippocampus that play an important role in learning. Not only has evolution affected learning, but learning can affect evolution, by exposing animals to selective pressures they would not otherwise encounter.

REFERENCES

Curio, E. (1988). Cultural transmission of enemy recognition by birds. In T. R. Zentall and B. G. Galef, Jr., eds., *Social learning*. Hillsdale, NJ: Erlbaum.

Jacobs, L. F., Gaulin, S. J. C., Sherry, D. F., and Hoffman, G. E. (1990). Evolution of spatial cognition: Sex-specific patterns of spatial behavior predict hippocampal size. *Proceedings of the National Academy of Sciences 87,* 6349–6352.

Sherry, D. F., Vaccarino, A. L., Buckenham, K., and Herz, R. S. (1989). The hippocampal complex of food-storing birds. *Brain Behavior and Evolution 34,* 308–317.

Tully, T. (1987). *Drosophila* learning and memory revisited. *Trends in Neurosciences 10,* 330–335.

David F. Sherry

EXPERTS' MEMORIES

An expert is a person who is very knowledgeable as well as very able in a given domain of activity, such as medicine or chess. This means that experts have acquired a vast body of knowledge and experience about their domain of expertise, which by definition makes them different from other individuals. The acquisition and retention of the enormous knowledge of experts is impressive. Furthermore, experts are often found to have remarkably accurate memory for their experiences. An elite athlete can, after a sports event, discuss the play-by-play action. Expert chess players can readily recall details of chess positions in all their matches in tournaments. Early in the twentieth century it was believed that experts and other unusually successful individuals are born with a superior general memory ability. Numerous anecdotes were collected as evidence of an unusual ability to store presented information rapidly. For example, Mozart was supposed to be able to reproduce a presented piece of music after hearing it a single time. However, more recent research has rejected the hypothesis of a generally superior memory in experts and has demonstrated that experts' superior memory is limited to meaningful information from their domains of expertise and can be viewed as the result of acquired skills and knowledge specific to each domain.

The Specificity of Experts' Superior Memory

The most influential early research was done with chess experts. In their pioneering studies Chase and Simon (1973) showed superior memory for chess positions by chess experts. Chess players ranging from beginners to international masters were shown a position from an actual chess game (such as the one illustrated in panel A of Figure 1) for a brief time (normally 5 seconds) and then asked to recall the location of all the chess pieces. The ability to recall increased as a function of chess skill. Beginners at chess were able to recall the correct location of about four pieces, whereas

international-level players recalled virtually all of the more than twenty pieces.

To rule out that the superior memory of chess experts reflects a general superior ability to store any kind of visual information, Chase and Simon (1973) had chess players recall chessboards with randomly placed pieces (as illustrated in Panel B of Figure 1). With briefly presented random chessboards, players at all levels of skill had the same poor recall performance and were able to recall the correct location of only about four pieces—a performance comparable with that of chess beginners for actual positions from chess games. Further, Chase and Simon (1973) showed that when an actual chess position was shown using an unfamiliar notation (see Panel C in Figure 1), the chess expert was able to display a similar level of superior memory performance after a brief period of adjustment. This result implies that the superior memory of experts is not photographic and requires arrangements of chess pieces that are meaningful

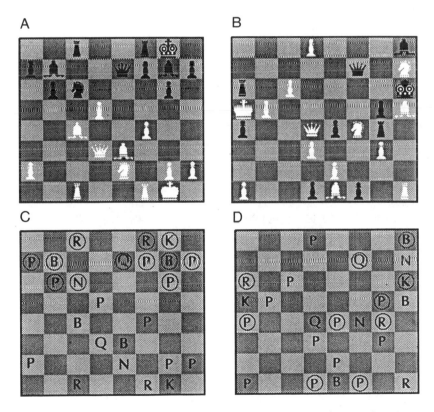

Figure 1. Standard diagrams of an actual chess position (Panel A) and a chessboard with randomly arranged pieces (Panel B). A nonstandard representation of the same information using the first letter of the names of the pieces is shown in Panels C and D.

in relation to the experts' extensive knowledge of chess. Since Chase and Simon's classic study, investigators have shown that level of expertise is related to superior memory performance for representative stimuli in many different domains, such as bridge, electronics, basketball, and field hockey, but that there is no memory superiority for random arrangements of the same stimuli (for a more recent review, see Ericsson and Smith, 1991).

The Role of Meaningfulness in Superior Memory Performance

Unless one has the knowledge of the expert, it is difficult—indeed, impossible—to grasp the meaningful relations perceived by the expert in panels A and C of Figure 1. If the availability of knowledge providing meaning to a stimulus is critical to superior memory, it should be possible to demonstrate the same effect in a domain where all adults are proficient, such as language. Human adults are able to recall verbatim meaningful sentences of twenty or more words after a brief presentation (Chase and Ericsson, 1982). An example of such a sentence would be THE WOMAN IN FRONT OF HIM WAS EATING PEANUTS THAT SMELLED SO GOOD THAT HE COULD BARELY CONTAIN HIS HUNGER. If the words of the sentence are randomly rearranged (analogous to Chase and Simon's procedure for generating random chessboards), accurate verbatim recall drops to around six words. An example of a random rearrangement of the above sentence would be WAS SMELLED FRONT THAT HIS THE PEANUTS HE GOOD HUNGER EATING BARELY WOMAN OF SO IN COULD THAT HIM CONTAIN. For random lists of words the recall of subjects is limited by the small number of words they can keep rehearsing (see REPETITION AND MEMORY; WORKING MEMORY IN HUMANS), and once they stop rehearsal, the words are quickly forgotten. In contrast, once meaningful sentences are understood, their meaning is well retained in long-term memory. The meaningfulness of the material influences both the amount of recall and the processes mediating storage in memory.

Stimuli from an unfamiliar domain of expertise, such as diagrams of chess positions and medical terms, are about as meaningless to most adults as random lists of words and digits. Recent studies have shown that memory for meaningless informa-tion can be dramatically improved through training by actively seeking out meaningful associations for the meaningless material. For example, the sequence 671945 can be remembered as 67 being the retirement age and 1945 being the year of the end of World War II (see MNEMONIC DEVICES). Through extended training individuals can acquire memory skills allowing them to memorize briefly presented lists of over 100 random digits. In fact, in some domains of expertise the memory performance of experts can be matched and even surpassed by students who train on the appropriate memory task for 50 to 100 hours. As is the case in the superior memory of experts, though, the memory improvement is limited to the specific types of material used in training (Ericsson, 1985).

The Acquisition of Expert Memory and Expertise

The acquisition of a vast body of knowledge in a given domain may be within the reach of average college students. Biographical analysis of the lives of international-level performers and experts shows that these individuals get involved in the domain relatively early. In many different domains, such as sports, chess, bridge, music, arts, and sciences, elite performers are found to have spent more than ten years of intense preparation before reaching the status of expert or attaining an internationally recognized performance (Bloom, 1985). Hence it appears to be not the speed of acquiring knowledge but the extended commitment to a single domain of expertise that makes experts different from normal adults.

An analysis of expert performance shows that it is not sufficient to have stored the knowledge in memory; it is also critical that relevant knowledge be well organized and capable of efficient retrieval when needed. Studies of solving physics problems show that novice college students have all the prerequisite knowledge necessary for generating a solution, but this knowledge has to be retrieved piece by piece, starting with the statement of the problem. If a problem asks for the velocity of an object, a novice starts to retrieve formulas yielding velocity and then checks whether each formula is consistent with the given information. This method of starting with the question is called backward reasoning. In contrast, physics experts proceed by forward reasoning and, as part of the comprehension of the physics problem, generate a representation of the problem with a plan for solving it. When physics experts categorize problems, they do it by the underlying physical principles (e.g., Newton's second law and conservation of energy), whereas novices categorize problems by surface features, such as problems involving pulleys. This finding suggests that experts form immediate representations of problems that integrate their relevant knowledge, whereas novices do not have this kind of access to their knowledge (Chi et al., 1981). The rapid formation of a representation that integrates presented information and relevant knowledge appears to be a general characteristic of experts in chess, medicine, and sports (Patel and Groen, 1991). With the superior organization of knowledge, a chess expert can rapidly perceive a promising move, or a medical expert can rapidly notice an inconsistency in a suggested diagnosis.

The superior memory performance of experts appears to be a direct consequence of their normal meaningful encoding of information in their domain. For example, when chess experts analyze a position to find the best move, their memory of the position is just as good whether they were informed about a subsequent memory test or not. The experts can also recall most of the important features of the presented information. In contrast, when subjects, after training based on mnemonics and knowledge unrelated to chess, attain a recall performance comparable with that of the chess experts, they still lack the ability to extract the information important for selecting the best move. Hence, the remarkable characteristic of expert memory is not the amount recalled, which can be matched by training, but the rapid extraction and storage of important patterns and information.

As their level of expertise increases, experts become able to engage in complex reasoning and planning. Mental exploration of alternative sequences of actions requires the expert to keep a great deal of information in working memory. A chess expert is able to plan longer sequences of future moves than are less experienced players (Charness, 1989). Chess masters are even able to play games without seeing the chessboard, mentally representing the locations of all the pieces on the board. Expert bridge players and medical doctors have also been found to engage in extensive planning and reasoning. Analyses of the superior ability to plan suggest that experts acquire memory skills which allow them to rely on long-

term memory for storage of generated information (Ericsson and Staszewski, 1989). Recent research on expertise is making it increasingly clear that the vast knowledge of experts has to be well organized and supplemented with special memory skills so as to support memory-demanding planning, design, and reasoning.

Conclusion

Experts have acquired a large body of knowledge and experience during many years of study and practice. Their memory performance is superior only for meaningful information in their domain of expertise. Through extensive experience, experts have organized their knowledge to make retrieval of relevant information efficient. Many types of experts have acquired memory skill that enhance their performance of such memory-demanding activities as planning and reasoning.

(See also CODING PROCESSES: ORGANIZATION OF MEMORY.)

REFERENCES

Bloom, B. S., ed. (1985). *Developing talent in young people.* New York: Ballantine Books.

Charness, N. (1989). Expertise in chess and bridge. In D. Klahr and K. Kotovsky, eds., *Complex information processing: The impact of Herbert A. Simon,* pp. 183–208. Hillsdale, N.J.: Erlbaum.

Chase, W. G., and Ericsson, K. A. (1982). Skill and working memory. In G. H. Bower, ed., *The psychology of learning and motivation,* vol. 16, pp. 1–58. New York: Academic Press.

Chase, W. G., and Simon, H. A. (1973). The mind's eye in chess. In W. G. Chase, ed., *Visual information processing,* pp. 215–281. New York: Academic Press.

Chi, M. T. H., Feltovich, P. J., and Glaser, R. (1981). Categorization and representation of physics problems by experts and novices. *Cognitive Science 5,* 121–152.

Ericsson, K. A. (1985). Memory skill. *Canadian Journal of Psychology 39,* 188–231.

Ericsson, K. A., and Smith, J. (1991). Prospects and limits in the empirical study of expertise: An introduction. In K. A. Ericsson and J. Smith, eds., *Toward a general theory of expertise: Prospects and limits.* New York: Cambridge University Press.

Ericsson, K. A., and Staszewski, J. (1989). Skilled memory and expertise: Mechanisms of exceptional performance. In D. Klahr and K. Kotovsky, eds., *Complex information processing: The impact of Herbert A. Simon*, pp. 235–267. Hillsdale, N.J.: Erlbaum.

Patel, V. L., and Groen, G. G. (1991). The general and specific nature of medical expertise: A critical look. In K. A. Ericsson and J. Smith, eds., *Toward a general theory of expertise: Prospects and limits.* New York: Cambridge University Press.

K. Anders Ericsson

F

FOOD AVERSION AND PREFERENCE LEARNING IN HUMANS

The need to obtain adequate nutrition involves selection, from all of the possible things that could go into the mouth, of those that are both nutritive and free of toxins. For an animal that eats only one kind of food, such as a frog that eats only insects, it is possible to program sense organs innately so that items of food can be specifically identified (e.g., food for an insect-eating frog is a small, moving, dark spot). However, for animals that eat a wide range of foods (generalists), there is no simple way to prespecify what is food and what is not; this must be learned. The problem is especially difficult because the effects of toxins or nutrients occur many minutes or hours after ingestion. Many animals, including humans, have a special type of long-delay classical conditioning that can bridge the gap (see TASTE AVERSION AND PREFERENCE LEARNING IN ANIMALS).

Humans differ from all other animals in that they have cuisines, systems for selecting and processing foods that incorporate the nutritional wisdom of past generations. Young humans may be the only animals that are explicitly taught what foods to eat and what things to avoid, as well as the social and sometimes moral significance of foods.

Humans accept or reject foods for one of three reasons: (1) liking or disliking the sensory qualities (e.g., flavor); (2) anticipated consequences of ingestion; and (3) the nature and origin of the food. Considering these three motivations, human food rejections fall into four categories (with overlaps): (1) *distaste*—foods rejected primarily because they have undesirable sensory properties; (2) *danger*—rejection based primarily on anticipation of negative consequences of ingestion (e.g., a food containing carcinogens or a food to which one has an allergic reaction); (3) *inappropriate*—items that one learns, on the basis of their origin, are not food (e.g., paper, stones); and (4) *disgust*—items that are rejected on the basis of their nature or origin but are also offensive, and are presumed to taste bad (for Americans, this would include insects, rotted meat). On the positive side, there are usually only two categories: (1) good taste—items consumed primarily because they have positive sensory properties (e.g., diet soda); and (2) beneficials—items consumed primarily because they are believed to produce positive consequences (e.g., health foods, medicines).

People learn about dangerous, inappropriate, and beneficial items in large part because information about these items is conveyed to them by others. This is not conditioning. We will focus on how foods come to be liked (good taste) or disliked (distaste, disgust).

In general, for both animals and humans, gradual exposure to a food with no obvious positive or negative consequences ("mere" exposure) tends to produce increased liking. However, if there is a great deal of exposure over a short period of time, there may be a temporary decline in liking for the food (sensory-specific satiety). We do not know how these experiential effects are produced.

The other documented means of changing the liking for a food involves classical conditioning (evaluative conditioning): the pairing of a food (CS) with a significant negative or positive event (US). (See CONDITIONING, CLASSICAL AND INSTRUMENTAL.) The best-documented change of this sort is called conditioned taste aversion, a phenomenon first described in rats. When a human ingests a relatively novel food, and within a few hours experiences nausea, there is a strong tendency for the ingested food to become bad tasting (a distaste). The disliked CS is usually a taste. This effect seems to be irrational in some cases, in the sense that a person may know that the food in question did not cause the illness (for example, it might clearly be a case of the flu). This type of evaluative conditioning differs markedly from a seemingly similar situation, in which ingestion of a food is followed by a negative consequence other than nausea, such as skin eruptions (as in an allergy) or cramps. Here people learn that the item in question is dangerous and should not be eaten, but the actual taste does not become unpleasant. A person who eats shrimp and becomes nauseated tends to come to dislike shrimp, whereas someone with a shrimp allergy who experiences serious respiratory distress after eating shrimp comes to fear shrimp but not to dislike the taste. Hence nausea serves as a sort of "magic bullet" US that, when paired with foods in only a single experience, produces a distaste.

There is no positive event (US) that has anything like the potency on the positive side that nausea has on the negative side. When a relatively neutral flavor (CS) is simultaneously paired with an already desirable flavor (US), some enhancement has been observed in humans' liking for the neutral flavor (flavor-flavor pairing). As with animals, another classical conditioning paradigm that can produce liking in hungry humans is association of a flavor with arrival of calories or nutrients in the body. Like the flavor-flavor pairing, this flavor–energy repletion pairing produces modest effects in comparison with conditioned taste aversions.

It seems that for humans, the most powerful events that cause changes in liking or disliking (other than nausea) are social. The approval/liking or disapproval/disliking of a food by respected others seems, by a mechanism not yet fully understood, to influence liking. The process could be cognitive, or involve social learning and imitation, or be a form of social classical conditioning. In the latter case, the food is the CS and the social display (e.g., facial expression) of another person while consuming the food is the US. Or it is possible that the social display (whether of pleasure, displeasure, or disgust) by another induces the same emotion or expression in the observer, and this event in the observer becomes the US. Foods associated with positive social regard or displays by significant others show increased liking by children over a period of at least months. In conjunction with what, in social psychology, is called the principle of minimal sufficiency, such changes seem to occur primarily when the observer does not feel forced or "bribed" to consume the food in question. Thus, when children are rewarded for eating a target food, they do not tend to increase liking for it, but when that food is used as a reward or is seen to be enjoyed by others, the food does tend to become more liked. (See also OBSERVATIONAL LEARNING.)

Social factors are almost surely involved in the development of disgusts, as when children observe the negative displays by their parents in response to body wastes, but this process has not been investigated. Social factors are also of importance in the development of animal food preferences. When a domestic rat (observer) simply interacts with another rat who has just eaten a specific food (a demonstrator rat), the observer rat develops a preference for the food in question. This may be mediated by the pairing of the food odor on the demonstrator rat with an odorant on the breath of the demonstrator rat.

A distinctive feature of human food likes is that they include many substances that are innately aversive to humans and other animals, such as bitter items like coffee, quinine water, and tobacco, and irritants like chili pepper and horseradish. These preferences may well be learned in the social setting of eating with family and friends, or they may involve special types of learning that are based on the initial negativity of these substances (compensatory conditioning).

The focus in this article has been on simple processes that are involved in the learning of likes and dislikes by humans. Of course, humans learn a great deal about foods (their origins, health values, costs, appropriate times for ingestion) that seems best described as acquisition of information (memories), just like the acquisition of other information. What is special about food, and hence the focus of this article, is that much of the learning has a strong affective (like/dislike) component, and sometimes involves relation of events (e.g., food and its subsequent effects) that span a period of hours. At this time, we really do not know enough about the acquisition of food likes and dislikes in humans to give good advice to a parent who wishes to change a child's food preferences. Indeed, one of the most surprising facts about human food preferences is that there is only a very low correlation between the food preferences of parents and those of their mature children.

REFERENCES

Birch, L. L. (1986). Children's food preferences: Developmental patterns and environmental influences. In G. Whitehurst and R. Vasta, eds., *Annals of child development*, vol. 4. Greenwich, Conn.: JAI Press.

Booth, D. A. (1982). Normal control of omnivore intake by taste and smell. In J. Steiner and J. Ganchrow, eds., *The determination of behavior by chemical stimuli. ECRO symposium*, pp. 233–243. London: Information Retrieval.

Galef, B. G., Jr. (1988). Communication of information concerning distant diets in a social central-place foraging species: *Rattus norvegicus*. In T. Zentall and B. G. Galef, Jr., eds., *Social learning: A comparative approach*, pp. 119–140. Hillsdale, N.J.: Erlbaum.

Garcia, J., Hankins, W. G., and Rusiniak, K. W. (1974). Behavioral regulation of the milieu interne in man and rat. *Science 185*, 824–831.

Logue, A. W. (1991). *The psychology of eating and drinking*, 2nd ed. New York: W. H. Freeman.

Martin, I., and Levey, A. B. (1978). Evaluative conditioning. *Advances in Behavior Research and Therapy 1*, 57–102.

Rozin, P. (1988). Social learning about foods by humans. In T. Zentall and B. G. Galef, Jr., eds., *Social learning: A comparative approach*, pp. 165–187. Hillsdale, N.J.: Erlbaum.

Rozin, P., and Vollmecke, T. A. (1986). Food likes and dislikes. *Annual Review of Nutrition 6*, 433–456.

Rozin, P., and Zellner, D. A. (1985). The role of Pavlovian conditioning in the acquisition of food likes and dislikes. *Annals of the New York Academy of Sciences 443*, 189–202.

Paul Rozin

FORAGING

Foraging, the search for food, is a fundamental part of behavior. All animals, from the simplest invertebrate to the most highly evolved primate, have to take in food. Since appropriate food may be more abundant at some times and places than at others, an animal that can learn about the characteristics of its food supply is likely to be able to forage more efficiently than one that cannot learn. Indeed, the need for efficient foraging creates a strong selection pressure for the evolution of learning and memory (see EVOLUTION AND LEARNING).

In recent years, the study of foraging behavior has been stimulated and guided by optimal foraging theory, a body of mathematical models specifying how animals should behave so as to maximize foraging efficiency. After briefly introducing this framework, this article describes some of the ways in which animals use learning and memory in foraging.

Optimal Foraging Theory

Optimal foraging theory is a topic in behavioral ecology, the field of zoology dealing with how behavior contributes to an animal's reproductive success, or fitness. Many aspects of foraging can be understood by assuming that animals have evolved to maximize the rate at which they take in energy while foraging. An animal that can forage efficiently will have more time for other important activities like finding a mate or defending a territory. If the economics of a particular foraging situation are understood well enough, it is possible to make a mathematical model that specifies what the animal should do in order to maximize its energy intake while foraging. Stephens and Krebs (1986) describe this approach in some detail. However, some examples are easy to understand intuitively without any mathematics.

Consider a small bird in the spring collecting food to bring back to the young in its nest. In order to feed the hungry nestlings it must spend a good part of the day making trips out from the nest, searching for food, and carrying it back home. How far should it travel and how much should it collect on each trip? It might seem obvious that the bird should load up as much as it can each time, but this suggestion overlooks the fact that as the bird loads its beak with food items like grubs or caterpillars, increasing the load becomes harder and harder. In addition, more energy is needed to fly back to the nest with more prey items in the beak, because they increase weight and wind resistance. On the other hand, if the bird has had to fly some distance from the nest in order to find suitable prey, it is worth its while to collect as many items as possible. This informal argument suggests that there should be a direct relationship between the size of the bird's load and the distance it has traveled: Bigger loads should be collected when the bird is farther from the nest.

Kacelnik and Cuthill (1987) studied this problem of central-place foraging with starlings nesting around a farm. They trained the birds to visit a feeder and collect mealworms that the experimenter dropped down a pipe. By placing the feeder at different distances from the starlings' nests while keeping constant the rate of dropping mealworms, Kacelnik and Cuthill were able to obtain clear evidence of the predicted relationship. With further experiments in both the field and the laboratory they were able to account for many of its details.

Implicit in this example are a number of uses of learning and memory. To return straight home with its prey, a starling had to learn the location of its nest. On each trip it had to remember where it was in relation to the nest. The birds also had to learn how often worms were available at the experimental feeder and how valuable they were.

Prey Selection

An animal encountering a potential prey item may accept it or go on searching for alternative prey. Again, what it should do to maximize its rate of energy intake can be understood intuitively. If it can expect to find a bigger or more quickly consumed item soon enough, the forager should reject the item at hand and go on searching; otherwise it should take the encountered item. This foraging problem has been studied with many different species in both the laboratory and the field. To solve it as efficiently as they do, animals must be able to learn about the value of potential prey and their abundance, and to adjust their behavior as the environment changes. Some studies of prey selection reviewed by Shettleworth (1988) have emphasized how the learning mechanisms animals use in such situations may be the same as those revealed in experiments on operant conditioning (see OPERANT BEHAVIOR).

Learning to Find Cryptic Prey

Many animals that are potential prey for other animals have evolved to look like their surroundings so they are harder for predators to see. For example, some moths preyed on by birds resemble the bark of the trees on which they rest. Caterpillars that live on green plants are likely to be green. In turn, predators have evolved the ability to learn how to discriminate such cryptic prey from their backgrounds. It has been suggested that predators may form a specific search image for, or "learn to see," a common cryptic prey. Laboratory studies using bluejays, chicks, and pigeons searching for grains or for images on slides under controlled conditions have provided evidence for this notion. (Some of this research is described by Krebs and Davies, 1987). When a bird encounters several cryptic prey items in a row, it becomes better at detecting them. It may be paying more attention to subtle details that differentiate the prey items from their background, or it may be learning to search more slowly when prey are difficult to detect. Quite possibly both kinds of learning contribute to improving the efficiency of prey capture.

Learning About Patches of Food

Not only do animals have to detect and capture prey efficiently, they have to find the areas where appropriate prey can be encountered. Food generally occurs in patches. For example, a freshly watered lawn is a good place for a robin to look for worms, but lawns may be separated by roads and sidewalks that do not provide very good foraging for a robin. Clearly, at any given time it is best to be in the patch with the most abundant prey, the freshly watered lawn with worms close to the surface rather than the dried-up lawn next door. For this an efficient forager needs a cognitive map of its environment in which it stores information about location of suitable foraging areas and the density of prey in each. This information has to be constantly updated as the environment changes. Thus animals should sample the environment, sometimes exploring new patches or patches that were not very good the last time they were tried in order to discover whether they have changed for the better.

The aspect of patch choice that has been studied most is how animals should respond to depletion of foraging patches. In our example, as the robin hops around the lawn finding worms, its own foraging activity (and perhaps that of other birds) will reduce the density of worms in the patch. Some are eaten and others burrow down into the soil at the birds' approach. When should the robin leave this patch and look for another? The foraging theorist's answer to this question takes into account two features of the environment other than the density of prey in the current patch. These are the density of prey in other patches and how long the predator would have to travel to get to those patches. The greater the average density of prey in alternative patches and the shorter the trip required, the sooner the predator should leave the current depleting patch. Experiments in laboratory and field with a wide range of species have shown that animals can respond very efficiently to depletion. Some of the laboratory studies reviewed by Shettleworth (1988) have begun to analyze what information animals use to do this.

Some Special Problems for Foragers: Nectar-Feeding and Food-Storing

Learning where to search for prey and detecting and selecting it once a suitable patch is found are problems for virtually any forager. Some animals face additional special problems that may require highly developed capacities for learning and memory. One set of problems, related to the patch-depletion problem just discussed, is faced by animals like bees and hummingbirds that suck nectar from flowers. A flower that has been depleted of nectar will produce more nectar again at a rate that depends on factors like what kind of flower it is. The efficient forager will time its visits so as to return at long enough intervals to find the flower full, but not so long that some other forager will have depleted the flower. One way to ensure this is to travel a fixed route among a number of plants. Some nectar-feeding animals do forage in this way. The learning of bees has been studied in the most detail. Gould (1982) describes how they learn the features of flowers and the times and places at which nectar could be found.

Another specialized foraging problem requiring memory is faced by some birds that spend the winter in a harsh climate. To have enough to eat at such times, birds such as chickadees, nuthatches, and jays store food when it is abundant. The Clark's nutcracker, a bird of the American Southwest, buries thousands of pine seeds in the late summer and recovers them up to six months later. Since each cache is in a different place, the birds must use memory to recover the food. Experiments in the laboratory with nutcrackers and chickadees, described by VanderWall (1990), have shown that these birds can indeed remember the locations

of their stores and do not need to use other cues. Some research suggests that they have evolved a better spatial memory than birds that do not store food. This suggestion is supported by evidence that relative to body size, food-storing birds have a larger hippocampus (the brain area necessary for spatial memory) than other birds. (See also SPATIAL LEARNING.)

Conclusions

The analysis of foraging is one of the best illustrations of how observations and theories about animals' behavior in the wild can provide valuable information about learning and memory. Considering how animals must learn and remember to forage efficiently can help us to understand why the principles of learning are as they are and suggest new ideas to be tested experimentally.

REFERENCES

Gould, J. L. (1982). *Ethology.* New York: W. W. Norton.

Kacelnik, A., and Cuthill, I. C. (1987). Starlings and optimal foraging theory: Modelling in a fractal world. In A. C. Kamil, J. R. Krebs, and H. R. Pulliam, eds., *Foraging behavior.* New York: Plenum Press.

Krebs, J. R., and Davies, N. B. (1987). *An introduction to behavioral ecology,* 2nd ed. Oxford: Blackwell Scientific.

Shettleworth, S. J. (1988). Foraging as operant behavior and operant behavior as foraging: What have we learned? *The Psychology of Learning and Motivation* 22, 1–49.

Stephens, D. W., and Krebs, J. R. (1986). *Foraging theory.* Princeton, N.J.: Princeton University Press.

VanderWall, S. B. (1990). *Food hoarding in animals.* Chicago: University of Chicago Press.

Sara J. Shettleworth

FORGETTING

Everyone is personally familiar with the phenomenon of forgetting. It is a common experience to be unable to remember something previously learned. Generally, there is a progressive, quantitative decline in the ability to remember as the retention interval lengthens. The retention interval is the amount of time that has elapsed since the material was last studied or thought about. A graph of the amount remembered (as measured by tests of recall or recognition or relearning) as a function of increasing retention intervals produces what is known as a forgetting curve, the slope of which represents the overall rate of forgetting. The first forgetting curve was published in 1885 by Hermann EBBINGHAUS, who was the pioneer in the scientific study of memory. His curve showed the now-familiar monotonic and negatively accelerated form, where the momentary rate of forgetting continually decreases over time.

Trace Decay Theory

Perhaps the earliest and simplest attempt to account for forgetting was the trace decay theory, which postulated that memorizing something lays down a neurochemical imprint or record in the brain, called a memory trace or engram, whose later reactivation is responsible for the experience of remembering. This trace was assumed to fade away spontaneously over time if it was not refreshed by some reacquaintance with the learned material; hence forgetting would occur. Today, with the possible exception of a pro forma decay parameter in some abstract mathematical models of memory, trace decay theory has been largely abandoned. This is not only because the hypothetical memory trace itself has never been identified, but also because of subsequent findings the theory could not handle gracefully. Among these latter are that forgetting is influenced by other activities taking place both before and after the original learning, and that it is affected by the kinds of cues given at the time of test. Thus, although forgetting takes place over time, it is probably not be-

cause of some inexorable autonomous fading of a memory trace.

Interference Theory

The one theoretical approach to forgetting that has inspired the greatest amount of experimental effort over several decades is interference theory. As the name implies, it focuses upon forgetting due to interference. It did not spring forth in finished form but evolved gradually into its present description. Among its beginnings was the influential demonstration by Jenkins and Dallenbach (1924) that the forgetting of a list of verbal items was markedly reduced if subjects passed the retention interval in sleep, rather than in their usual waking activities. This suggested that experiences comprising daily life somehow interfered with memory for the original material. Eventually, interest narrowed upon other specific learning experiences as the sources of that interference.

The empirical cornerstones of interference theory are to be found in two kinds of laboratory-produced forgetting. These are schematized in Table 1, and each defines a source of interference by comparing the memory performance of an experimental group which acquires two lists in succession against that of a control group which acquires only one (see also INTERFERENCE AND FORGETTING). Retroactive inhibition is the forgetting of the first set of materials, which is caused by the subsequent learning of a second set during the retention interval. Proactive inhibition is the forgetting of the second set, which is caused by the prior learning of a first set. It may seem strange that a preceding list would reduce the memory for a subsequently acquired one, but it can, especially when there is a retention interval before testing. Interference theory construes retroactive

Table 1. Retroactive and Proactive Inhibition

	Retroactive Inhibition				Proactive Inhibition			
Experimental group	Learn List 1	Learn List 2	Recall List 1	Less recall	Learn List 1	Learn List 2	Recall List 2	Less recall
Control group	Learn List 1	No	Recall List 1	More recall	No	Learn List 2	Recall List 2	More recall

and proactive inhibition to be the basic models for its approach to forgetting, whether inside or outside of the laboratory. It is the task of the theory to devise an experimentally testable description of the processes of retroactive and proactive inhibition. The present form of this account is essentially as follows.

Whenever two sets of materials are acquired in succession, two processes can occur that impair memory for them. One process is the dynamic competition of responses for emergence at time of test. To the extent that both sets of materials are activated, a response from the first list may be blocked from consciousness by a stronger competing response from the second list, or vice versa. Two competing responses of equal strength may even block each other. This process is set into motion by the demands of the memory test, and it reduces performances on both lists compared with the single-list control condition. The other process takes place during the learning of the second list, and consists of the unlearning or suppression of the contents of the first list, to the extent that they conflict with new response requirements. For example, if the first set of materials contains an A-B association while the second set requires an A-C association, then A-B may be suppressed. Taking both factors into consideration, the memory situation immediately after second-list acquisition is that of a suppressed first list competing against a dominant second list. This correctly predicts that retroactive inhibition will be much stronger than proactive inhibition. Another important observation to be explained is that with a delayed memory test, proactive inhibition increases in magnitude. This fact is handled by postulating a gradual dissipation of first-list suppression, wherein the list regains its strength and competes more effectively, producing increased interference. This implies that a suppressed set of materials should be better recalled after some time has passed, which is the opposite of forgetting. Such an effect has been experimentally verified.

An attempt to apply interference theory to normal forgetting, where only a single set of materials is learned in the laboratory and later recalled, was made by Underwood and Postman (1960). In place of the now-absent second list, interference was postulated to arise from one's preexisting repertoire of natural language habits developed over the years. The mechanism is that for proactive inhibition. It was proposed that language habits which conflicted with the associations to be learned in the list would be suppressed. For example, learning "table-robin" would tend to suppress the preexperimentally stronger association "table-chair." Over the retention interval this suppression would dissipate and permit the original association to interfere with memory of the prescribed one. In contrast, a list that did not offend language sequences would trigger no suppression and would therefore be better remembered. This account clearly predicts that the forgetting rate will be greater for materials which oppose language habits than for materials which do not. Suffice it to say that numerous experiments have failed to verify this prediction. Surprisingly, forgetting rates are constant despite large variations in the materials to be learned. Thus, although interference theory has given a credible explanation of laboratory-produced forgetting, it has not yet identified the extraexperimental sources and mechanisms that are responsible for normal forgetting.

Cue-Dependency Theory

A more recent alternative approach to forgetting is called cue-dependency theory. It is quite different from interference theory, but should not be seen as supplanting it so much as supplementing it. Cue-dependency stresses the importance of the reminders, or retrieval cues, that are operative at the time of test (see also RETRIEVAL PROCESSES). It emphasizes that the act of remembering requires not only the stored products of original learning but also an appropriate testing environment to make contact with that learning. The successful interaction of stored information and retrieval information produces the recollective experience. To the extent that adequate retrieval cues are not accessible, there will be forgetting. It further insists that the only useful memory aids are those features which were part of the original encoding or perceptual context of the materials when they were being studied. Not even the strongest preexperimental stimulus for an item can be an effective retrieval cue unless it was part of the original learning episode. This expresses the principle of encoding specificity. For example, it has been shown that if one studies *glue-chair*, *glue* is a good cue for recalling *chair* but *table* is not, even though it is a strong preexperimental stimulus for it, be-

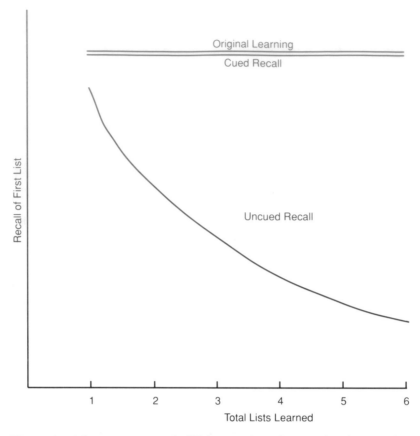

Figure 1. Schematic portrayal of Tulving and Psotka's results, showing that the impaired recall of the first list under uncued conditions was restored to its original level under cued conditions in all cases.

cause it was not encoded during the study episode.

The best demonstration of the force of cue-dependency is an experiment by Tulving and Psotka (1971). Six groups of subjects learned from one to six categorized lists, each consisting of words from various familiar conceptual categories such as fruits, countries, and metals (orange, apple, pear; Italy, Canada, Japan; copper, iron, aluminum; etc.). No lists had any category or word in common. Immediately after each list was studied, an uncued recall test measured its original learning level. After the assigned number of lists had been learned, there was an uncued recall test of all materials studied. The final phase was a cued recall of all materials studied, with the cues being category names. Figure 1 schematizes the recall pattern found for the first list learned by each group. Clearly, the more lists acquired, the greater the forgetting of the first one on the uncued test. Equally clearly, the cued test instantly reinstated all performances to their original learning levels. This dramatic reversal strongly suggests that the forgetting was due to the absence of adequate retrieval cues in the test environment, because when those cues were later supplied (in the form of category reminders), the forgetting was abolished. It should be noted that cue-dependency theory does not explain the findings of interference theory. Experiments in the latter tradition typically assign a different retrieval cue to each response word of the list, and always provide it during both original learning and the memory test. It is fairer to say that cue-dependency theory has identified another mechanism of forgetting in addition to response competition and suppression.

Normal Forgetting

One important research need is to establish whether there are any conditions of original learning that influence the rate of forgetting of a single set of materials learned in the laboratory. As mentioned previously, normal forgetting rates appear to be independent of the particular materials memorized. They also seem impervious to the levels of processing (superficial versus meaningful) employed at study. There is little evidence that they yield to deliberate mnemonic strategies. There is even serious doubt about whether the degree of original learning has any effect upon the rate of loss. The present picture suggests a remarkable resistance to experimental manipulation. Surely, no theory or model of memory can be expected to account satisfactorily for normal forgetting until more closure on this question is achieved.

REFERENCES

Baddeley, A. (1990). *Human memory,* Ch. 10. Needham Heights, Mass.: Allyn and Bacon.

Ebbinghaus, H. (1885/1913). *Memory: A contribution to experimental psychology* (H. A. Ruger and C. E. Bussenius, trans.). New York: Columbia University, Teacher's College. (Reprinted 1964, New York, Dover.)

Jenkins, J. G., and Dallenbach, K. M. (1924). Obliviscence during sleep and waking. *American Journal of Psychology 35,* 605–612.

Postman, L., and Underwood, B. J. (1973). Critical issues in interference theory. *Memory and Cognition 1,* 19–40.

Slamecka, N. J. (1985). Ebbinghaus: Some associations. *Journal of Experimental Psychology: Learning, Memory, and Cognition 11,* 414–435.

Slamecka, N. J., and McElree, B. (1983). Normal forgetting of verbal lists as a function of their degree of learning. *Journal of Experimental Psychology: Learning, Memory, and Cognition 9,* 384–397.

Tulving, E. (1974). Cue-dependent forgetting. *American Scientist 62,* 74–82.

Tulving, E., and Psotka, J. (1971). Retroactive inhibition in free recall: Inaccessibility of information available in the memory store. *Journal of Experimental Psychology 87,* 1–8.

Underwood, B. J., and Postman, L. (1960). Extra-experimental sources of interference in forgetting. *Psychological Review 67,* 73–95.

Norman J. Slamecka

FREUD, SIGMUND

Sigmund Freud (1856–1939) was the founder of psychoanalysis, a system of psychological therapy and personality theory that continues to be one of the most influential as well as controversial in psychology. Born in Freiberg, Moravia (then a province of the Austro-Hungarian Empire and today a part of Czechoslovakia), he was the first son of Jakob Freud, a wool merchant, and of Amalie Nathansohn Freud, Jakob's third wife.

Freud's background was Jewish, a fact that figured importantly in his life and work, although he himself was an atheist—in his words, "a Godless Jew"—and was to write withering critiques of religion, which he considered a "psychological narcotic" (see, e.g., Freud, 1927, 1930).

Notwithstanding his birthplace, Freud for all intents and purposes was a Viennese. His family moved to Vienna when he was 4, and he remained there until about a year before his death, when he fled Nazi Austria to settle with his family in London. His four sisters, who stayed behind, perished in the Holocaust. In 1886 Freud had married Martha Bernays. They had three sons and three daughters, the youngest of whom, Anna, was to become a prominent figure in the psychoanalytic movement.

Freud, a heavy cigar smoker, tried several times to give up his "vice" but found that he could not

Figure 1. Sigmund Freud. *Courtesy National Library of Medicine.*

write without smoking. He was found to have cancer of the mouth in 1923 and endured more than thirty operations before his death in 1939. He remained a prolific writer until the end, leaving some two dozen volumes of psychological works.

For the last six of his eight years in *Gymnasium* (the European equivalent of high school), Freud was at the top of his grade. He claimed to have a photographic memory, and he possessed a powerful, brilliant writing style. In 1930 he received the Goethe Prize, a literary award. He had less of a bent for the hard sciences and mathematics; after an initial inclination toward a career in law or politics, Freud decided upon the natural sciences and at 17 enrolled in the medical school of the University of Vienna, where he conducted research in anatomy and physiology.

After some dawdling, Freud obtained his M.D. degree in 1881, at the age of 25. He hoped to remain a research scientist at the university, but after realizing that he was not apt to receive a permanent university appointment (there were no likely openings soon, and his Jewish background also worked against him), he reluctantly opted for medical practice, training at the Vienna General Hospital (1882–1885) and, after a stint as an army doctor, assuming the directorship of the neurological department of a hospital for children while he established a private practice. In this period Freud published some papers on neurology, among them articles on children's paralyses, and a book on aphasia (1891). He also experimented on himself with the then exotic drug cocaine. Enthusiastic over its enhancing effects on energy and creativity, he was soon urging it upon his fiancée and family members. This cocaine phase came to an abrupt end when a friend of his whom he was trying to wean from a heroin addiction with cocaine overdosed and died. The episode may have hurt Freud's medical reputation in Vienna though it did, indirectly, lead to the successful use of cocaine as a local anesthetic in ophthalmology.

In 1885, while at the Vienna General Hospital, Freud won a 4-month grant to study with the world's preeminent neurologist, Jean Charcot, in Paris, who at this time was pursuing research on hysteria and hypnosis. Four years later Freud also visited the great center of hypnotic research and therapy, headed by Hippolyte Bernheim, at Nancy, France. Freud was much taken by demonstrations there of posthypnotic suggestion with amnesia, in which subjects carried out hypnotic suggestions after awakening from their trance without being aware of the reason for their actions. Beyond their therapeutic import, Freud saw such demonstrations as laboratory confirmations of the power of the unconscious to affect behavior.

In keeping with his background in neurology, many of the patients referred to Freud suffered from neurological symptoms such as paralysis, tic, or amnesia. However, it became clear that many of these patients were not actually afflicted with organic disorders but were suffering from psychological conditions that mimicked neurological symptoms. Such patients were often referred to as "neurotics" or "hysterics." Psychoanalysis was born in the effort to devise psychological treatment for these psychological afflictions.

An important partner in Freud's early psychotherapeutic research was his older friend and mentor, Josef Breuer, an eminent Viennese physician. Breuer had experimented with hypnotic suggestion therapy, a technique in which the hysteric patient, under hypnosis, is given the suggestion that his or her symptoms will disappear. With his famous patient Anna O., Breuer varied on the procedure and stumbled on a striking discovery: When the patient was able to recollect and report the painful events that had brought about her symptoms, the symptoms permanently disappeared. Breuer came to call the procedure the *cathartic* technique. Freud experimented with and extended the hypnotic and cathartic techniques, and in 1895 he and Breuer published what may be considered the founding work in psychoanalysis, *Studies on Hysteria.*

The central idea of the *Studies* was that "hysterics suffer mainly from reminiscences," which are not accessible to their consciousness but are expressed in the recondite dialect of body language as hysterical symptoms. The cathartic strategy was to recover the pathogenic idea and its associated affect into awareness. Freud gradually dropped hypnosis as his hypermnesic (memory-enhancing) agent, though he retained the couch on which hypnotized patients used to recline. Eventually he adopted psychoanalysis's free-association technique, in which the patient is committed to the "basic rule" of saying anything that comes to mind, without censorship. Freud, an ardent determinist, believed that the superficially haphazard approach would willy-nilly lead back to the pathogenic trauma or conflict. He found that the problematical mental contents often originated in childhood sexual and aggressive feelings, especially those arising from the "Oedipus Complex" (around the age of

5 or 6) when, Freud claimed, the child develops overtly erotic desires for the parent of the opposite sex and hateful feelings toward the parent of the same sex.

A prominent yield of the free-association procedure, considered within psychoanalysis a "microscope" of the mind, was that the basic rule was psychologically impossible to honor. Freud came to realize that certain thoughts and wishes were too disturbing to communicate to another person—even to oneself. This inward dishonesty led to the fundamental concept of *defense mechanisms,* psychological processes deployed to distort or exclude from consciousness thoughts and desires that are too anxiety producing. Ultimately (e.g., *The Ego and the Id,* 1923), Freud was to view the mind as divided into three often conflicting subsystems: an executive, reality-oriented component, the *ego;* a primitive, passion-controlled subsystem, the *id;* and a moral subsystem, the *superego.*

In addition to the publication of *Studies on Hysteria,* the year 1895 was a watershed in another way. Freud feverishly attempted to create a neurological model of basic psychological processes— "Psychology for Neurologists"—but by the end of the year concluded that the effort was a failure and withheld it from publication. In effect, he abandoned neurology and became a full-fledged psychologist. His followers published the manuscript posthumously under the title *Project for a Scientific Psychology.* It is a convoluted and often impenetrable monograph some 100 pages in length. It does, however, contain some remarkably prescient neurological intuitions about learning and memory, among them the notion that the neurological basis of learning and memory is the selective facilitation and inhibition of the flow of excitation across the "contact barriers"—*synapses,* in modern parlance—between neurons (see GUIDE TO THE ANATOMY OF THE BRAIN) resulting in the gradual differentiation of functional neural units or systems within broader neural networks. Freud's speculative neuropsychology foreshadowed many key notions in contemporary neuroscience, including today's influential "parallel distributed processing" models of learning, perception, and memory (see PARALLEL DISTRIBUTED PROCESSING MODELS OF MEMORY).

In 1900, following a "self-analysis" initiated in 1895, Freud published his epochal *Interpretation of Dreams.* If free associations were a microscope of the mind, dreams to Freud were the "royal road" to the unconscious. During sleep, defenses are weakened and the primitive drives and primitive modes of cognition—*primary processes thinking*—come to the fore. Like any complex mental product, dreams have multiple levels of meaning. The surface meaning, which Freud called the *manifest content,* often makes no sense; the deep or *latent content,* which requires interpretation, carries the important meaning. In dreams, the latent content is often unconscious to the subject. Thus, like a hysteric symptom, a dream involves a meaningful communication of which the patient is not aware.

Dream analysis, along with the free-association method, became an integral feature of psychoanalytic therapy. To these, later on, was added the analysis of *transference.* Freud found that in the course of therapy, patients developed passionate feelings for the therapist of both a loving and a hating character. Since these were not realistically warranted, Freud took the transference manifestations to be reenactments of past significant relations, especially between the patient and his or her parents. The "transference neurosis," then, was a profound form of remembering, involving not conscious recollection but reliving of problematic themes from the past. The goal of psychoanalysis was always in some sense "the education of conciousness." Through self-knowledge, the patient was thought to gain mastery over the irrational determinants of his or her pathological symptoms and behavior.

Freud always insisted on the scientific status of his creation, although his practices were often unscientific. Disagreements with his colleagues—figures such as Josef Breuer, Carl Gustav Jung, Alfred Adler—led to personal and professional ruptures. There was little if any true experimentation, and the empirical anchoring of the "science" was clinical observation, which often amounted to all-too-fallible interpretation. Probably for this reason, more than resistance to supposedly unpalatable claims (such as the doctrine of infantile sexuality), mainstream scientific psychology has maintained a suspicious, ambivalent stance toward psychoanalysis. Nevertheless, for all his great flaws, Freud had his great insights, among them the concept of unconscious mentation; the notion of remembering without awareness through behavior and other indirect channels; the meaningfulness of dreams; the therapeutic value of talking and of the interpersonal relation in therapy; and the pervasiveness of biased, often defensive, reconstructions of memory. These themes, some of them proposed almost a century ago, have only recently become mainstream notions in modern psychology.

Freud may be regarded as a towering figure in scientific psychology, but a transitional figure—a sort of Moses, who achieved great things but was not himself destined to reach the promised land.

REFERENCES

Breuer, J., and Freud, S. (1895). *Studies on hysteria,* A. Strachey and J. Strachey, trans. In J. Strachey, ed., *The standard edition of the complete psychological works of Sigmund Freud,* vol. 2. London: Hogarth Press, 1955.

Freud, S. (1891). *On aphasia.* New York: International Universities Press, 1953.

———— (1895). *Project for a scientific psychology.* In J. A. Strachey, ed., *The standard edition of the complete psychological works of Sigmund Freud,* vol. 1. London: Hogarth Press, 1966.

———— (1900). *The interpretation of dreams.* In J. A. Strachey, ed., *The standard edition of the complete psychological works of Sigmund Freud,* vols. 4 and 5. London: Hogarth Press, 1953.

———— (1914). Remembering, repeating, and working through: Further recommendations in the technique of psychoanalysis, II, J. Riviere and J. Strachey, trans. In J. Strachey, ed., *The standard edition of the complete psychological works of Sigmund Freud,* vol. 12. London: Hogarth Press, 1958.

———— (1917). *A general introduction to psychoanalysis,* J. Riviere, trans. New York: Liveright.

———— (1923). *The ego and the id,* J. Riviere and J. Strachey, trans. In J. Strachey, ed., *The standard edition of the complete psychological works of Sigmund Freud,* vol. 19. London: Hogarth Press, 1961.

———— (1926). *Inhibitions, symptoms, and anxiety,* A. Strachey and J. Strachey, trans. In J. Strachey, ed., *The standard edition of the complete psychological works of Sigmund Freud,* vol. 20. London: Hogarth Press, 1959.

———— (1927). *The future of an illusion,* W. D. Robson-Scott and J. Strachey, trans. In J. Strachey, ed., *The standard edition of the complete psychological works of Sigmund Freud,* vol. 21. London: Hogarth Press, 1961.

———— (1930). *Civilization and its discontents,* J. Riviere and J. Strachey, trans. In J. Strachey, ed., *The standard edition of the complete psychological works of Sigmund Freud,* vol. 21. London: Hogarth Press, 1961.

Matthew Hugh Erdelyi

FRONTAL LOBES AND MEMORY

The idea that the frontal lobes are implicated in memory has a long and controversial history (see Luria, 1980; Teuber, 1964). Damage to the frontal lobes was known to produce memory impairment, and sometimes even severe memory loss, but it was difficult to specify the nature of the disorder. It is now generally conceded that frontal lobe damage does not lead to memory disorders that involve deficits in consolidation, storage, and retention of newly acquired information. Such disorders, which in their most extreme form lead to a profound, global amnesia, are associated with damage to the medial temporal lobes, particularly the hippocampus and related structures (see GUIDE TO THE ANATOMY OF THE BRAIN), and to midline thalamic nuclei (Milner, 1966). Instead, a consensus is emerging that memory loss following frontal lobe lesions involves organizational or strategic aspects of memory that are necessary for devising strategies for encoding, for guiding search at retrieval, for placing retrieved memories in their proper spatial and temporal contexts, and for using mnemonic information to direct thought and plan future actions. In other words, the frontal lobe's function with respect to memory is consistent with its functions in other domains. It organizes the raw material that is made available by other structures so that thought and behavior can be goal directed. If the hippocampus and its related structures can be considered "raw" memory structures, then the frontal lobes are "working-with-memory" structures that operate on the input and output of the hippocampal circuit (see Figure 1). The present writers prefer the descriptive term "working-with-memory" to the more theoretically loaded term "working memory" or "executive function" favored by others (Baddeley, 1986; Goldman-Rakic, 1987); this term captures the essence of frontal-lobe contribution to memory but does not commit the user to endorse a "working memory" theory that may be flawed or inappropriate (see Moscovitch and Winocur, 1992).

One can best appreciate the contribution of the frontal lobes to memory by comparing the effects of frontal damage on various memory tests with effects of damage to the hippocampus and midline thalamic nuclei. Recognition and recall of isolated random words or pictures are typically normal in patients with frontal lesions but impaired in

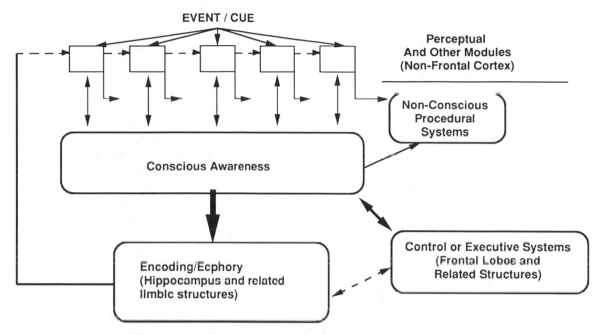

Figure 1. A schematic model of memory. Information delivered to consciousness by cortical modules is picked up automatically by the hippocampus. The hippocampus then binds the information, which is probably stored in the modules, to form a memory trace that can be accessed via a file or index (code) that is formed in the hippocampus. Conscious recollection involves the automatic reactivation of aspects of the memory trace by a retrieval cue that interacts with the hippocampal code. The reactivated trace is delivered to consciousness and is experienced as a memory. The frontal lobes are involved in setting goals for memory tasks, in organizing information that is made available to the hippocampus, in evaluating or monitoring the output from the hippocampus to consciousness, and in directing further searches should the retrieved memories prove not to be veridical (e.g., in contradiction with other knowledge) or to be inconsistent with the goals of the task. *Reproduced with permission from Moscovitch, 1989.*

patients with hippocampal or diencephalic damage (Mayes, 1988, chap. 8; Milner, Petrides, and Smith, 1985). Recall of categorized lists or of logical stories, however, is impaired in frontal patients, presumably because they cannot take advantage of the organizational structure inherent in that material (Incissa della Rochetta, 1986). Deficits may also be noted in free recall if normal performance depends on strategic search or retrieval (Janowsky et al., 1989).

In contrast with memory for target items or facts that can be elicited by cues directly associated with them, memory for spatiotemporal context often requires strategic search. Consider introspectively the difference in the processes involved in answering these two questions: Have you seen *Gone with the Wind?* What did you do two week-

ends ago? The first elicits an immediate, automatic reply; the second typically initiates a labored, strategic search. As expected, memory for spatiotemporal context, but not for targets, is impaired after frontal lesions, whereas the reverse is true after hippocampal or midline diencephalic lesions.

Memory for temporal order is poor in frontal patients when it is tested by asking patients to judge the relative recency of a pair of items or to arrange a set of items in the order in which they were presented (Milner, Petrides, and Smith, 1985; Shimamura, Janowsky, and Squire, 1990). The deficit also extends to remote memories that were acquired long before lesion onset. Defective memory for sources of facts they had learned has also been observed in patients with frontal lesions or frontal dysfunction. They erroneously ascribe the factual information to an incorrect source on tests of source recall and source recognition (Schacter, Harbluk, and McLachlan, 1984; Janowsky, Shimamura, and Squire, 1989b). On the other hand, hippocampal or diencephalic damage leads to deficient memory for targets or facts at long delays but not for their temporal order or for sources at delays in which the facts can be remembered. In other words, their memory for temporal order is no more impaired than, and may be superior to, their memory for facts (Milner, Petrides, and Smith, 1985; Shimamura, Janowsky, and Squire, 1990). (See also SERIAL ORGANIZATION.)

Poor memory for spatiotemporal context that results from impaired strategic processes may also underlie the frontal patient's deficits on a variety of other tests, such as delayed alternation, delayed response, and delayed match-to-sample with a small, repeated set of items (Freedman and Oscar-Berman, 1986; Prisko, 1963, cited in Milner, Petrides, and Smith, 1985). On delayed response, after a short delay the subject must choose one of the items that had been designated as the target. On delayed alternation, the designated target alternates on every trial. In delayed match-to-sample, the subject chooses from a small set of items the one that matches a target that was inspected earlier. On all these tests, frontal patients fail not because they cannot remember the target, but because they cannot segregate the current trial (keep the spatiotemporal context distinct) from preceding ones.

Impaired performance by frontal patients on self-ordered pointing tests may have a similar cause (Petrides and Milner, 1982). In these tests, subjects are required to point to one of a set of words, line drawings, or designs that appear on a sheet of paper. On each subsequent trial, new sheets are presented with the same items arranged differently and the subject is required to point to a different item each time. There are as many trials as there are items. Apart from remembering the items and keeping spatiotemporal context distinct, subjects performing this test need to monitor their responses and use their memory of them to plan future actions. Monitoring and planning are both prototypical frontal functions that are applied to memory and may be impaired following frontal lesions.

Impaired estimation of frequency of occurrence is also associated with frontal lesions (Smith and Milner, 1988). In this test, items are repeated a number of times and the subject's task is to estimate the number of repetitions. It is not clear whether the deficit on this test is a symptom of a general deficit in cognitive estimation that accompanies frontal damage (Shallice and Evans, 1978) or whether it also results from a failure to search memory strategically.

Although the formation and retrieval of new associations are not dependent on the frontal lobes, learning conditional associations is (Petrides and Milner, 1982). The difference between the two tests highlights the distinction between memories elicited directly by cues associated with them, a process that involves the hippocampus, and memories for which additional extra-cue, strategic processes are necessary and involve the frontal lobes. In learning new associations a single cue, such as a light, is paired with a unique response, such as an arm movement, which it eventually elicits. In conditional associative learning, all cues and potential responses are present in the situation and typically resemble each other. For example, a set of six lights is presented, each of which needs to be associated with one of six movements that the subject has mastered. The cue, one of the lights, does not elicit the response, the designated movement, but only provides the occasion for the subject to select from among potential responses the one that is appropriate for one particular cue, another one for another cue, and so on. That is, the subject must determine, by trial and error, which light is associated with which movement. Response selection and monitoring, both strategic frontal functions, are key elements of this task. Patients with frontal lesions have difficulty learning only conditional associations, whereas patients with hippocampal lesions have difficulty forming new associations.

Less consistent effects of frontal lesions are found on other memory tests, such as release from proactive inhibition (PI) and "feeling-of-knowing" judgments. In release from PI, four different lists of words from the same semantic category are presented, followed by a list from a different category. Recall, which is tested after each list, declines from the first to the fourth list as PI builds up, but recall recovers to baseline levels on the fifth trial. Release from PI occurs at retrieval. It is not surprising, therefore, that deficits in release from PI have been reported in patients with frontal lesions (Moscovitch, 1982); these are most reliable, however, when a severe memory disorder accompanies frontal dysfunction (Freedman and Cermak, 1986; Janowsky et al., 1989).

"Feeling of knowing" is an aspect of META-MEMORY, the knowledge about one's own memory. It refers to a person's belief that he or she would know the correct answer to a memory question. In testing the accuracy of "feeling of knowing" judgments, Janowsky, Shimamura, and Squire (1989a) gave subjects a cued recall test for information they had learned earlier. For those items they failed to recall, subjects were asked to rate their "feeling of knowing," their likelihood of recognizing the correct answer among a number of alternatives. Because this metamemory test involves goal-directed search and monitoring, it was expected that patients with frontal lesions would perform poorly on it. Although some deficits were found, the impairment, as in release from PI, was most reliable and far-reaching in patients who had severe memory problems in addition to frontal dysfunction.

Defective performance on memory tests sensitive to frontal lesions is noted in people with neurological conditions associated with frontal dysfunction, that is, with signs of impaired frontal functions though there is no evidence of direct frontal damage. Among those are patients with Parkinson's and Huntington's diseases, the neuropathology of which affects basal ganglia structures that are part of the "complex loop" that connects them to the frontal lobes (Brown and Marsden, 1990; Saint-Cyr, Taylor, and Lang, 1988). Declines in performance on frontal-sensitive tests are also observed in the elderly, presumably because their frontal lobes deteriorate with age (Moscovitch and Winocur, 1992).

Even normal young adults may show deficits on frontal tests under conditions that deplete cognitive resources. Because frontal functions are strategic—which implies that voluntary, often conscious, control is an integral part of them—they demand substantial cognitive, attentional resources if they are to operate effectively (Moscovitch and Umilta, 1990, 1991). In contrast, the operations of the hippocampus can be run off relatively automatically once the appropriate input is received. Experiments reported in the literature suggest that interference at the time of retrieval affects primarily performance on tests that are sensitive to frontal function, such as word fluency, recall of categorized lists, and list differentiation. A series of experiments designed to test this hypothesis further has confirmed that a sequential, finger-tapping task at encoding and retrieval interfered with performance on frontal-sensitive tests,

such as recall of categorized lists, release from PI, and phonemic fluency.

All the memory tests mentioned so far can be classified as explicit tests that require conscious recollection of the past for successful performance. In contrast, on implicit tests, memory is inferred from the effects of experience or practice on performance without requiring the individual to refer to the past. Since the frontal lobes are working-with-memory structures, they should be implicated on tests of implicit memory. Indeed, frontal lesions or dysfunctions lead to impaired performance on those tests that are not simply stimulus driven but require strategic search or application of organized rules or procedures. Thus, patients with frontal lesions or dysfunction have difficulty mastering the Tower of Hanoi, a cognitive puzzle whose solution depends on the application of a sequential, iterative rule (Owen et al., 1990; Shallice, 1982; St. Cyr, Taylor, and Lang, 1988). Frontal patients may also be impaired on other implicit tests, such as learning to read geometrically transformed script and completing word stems after being exposed to target words. More work is needed to determine the extent of frontal involvement on implicit tests. By comparison, a great deal of work has been conducted on amnesic patients with hippocampal or diencephalic lesions. Their performance on a variety of implicit tests appears to be relatively spared, indicating that these structures are involved only with conscious recollection (Moscovitch, 1982; Moscovitch and Umilta, 1991).

Many of the features of frontal-lobe memory disorders are observable in an especially severe and striking form in confabulating patients (see below) with aneurysms or infarcts of the anterior communicating artery. Admittedly, the lesions that typically affect the ventromedial and orbital regions of the frontal lobes also involve other structures in the basal forebrain (see GUIDE TO THE ANATOMY OF THE BRAIN), such as the anterior cingulate, the septum, and the anterior hypothalamus. Nonetheless, the memory symptoms displayed by these patients are indicative more of frontal than of hippocampal circuit damage. When tested formally, their recognition on tests that do not involve strategic search is relatively preserved, which distinguishes them from amnesic patients with hippocampal damage. However, their ability to search memory and to place events in a proper spatiotemporal context is virtually lost. That loss likely accounts for their tendency to confabulate or make up stories that are patently untruthful, often contradictory, and occasionally bizarre or fantastic. For example, one patient who had been in hospital for months claimed he was still at his office. When asked to account for the beds in his room, he suggested that they were brought in to deal with an epidemic. When such patients confabulate, they do not intentionally lie, but inadvertently combine true memories whose spatiotemporal context they have lost. It is as if the nonfrontal memory system, in response to situational cues, spews out loosely associated memories in a quasi-ordered fashion. Lacking intact frontal lobes, these patients cannot evaluate this output or impose a sensible organization on it. Their memory deficits, therefore, are not restricted to recently acquired memories but extend to remote, personal memories and even to historical information on events that occurred before they were born. Their memory is intact only for events and activities, such as their job routines, that are stored as self-organized and self-contained schemata that depend little on supervision by the frontal lobes for their operation (Moscovitch, 1989).

Though we have paid little attention to localization within the frontal lobes, we do not wish to leave the reader with the impression that the prefrontal cortex is a homogeneous structure. On the contrary, prefrontal cortex is a heterogeneous structure consisting of a number of distinct areas with unique projections to and from other brain regions, and with different phylogenetic and ontogenetic histories (Figure 2) (Pandya and Barnes, 1986). Whereas it has been known for some time

that two large subdivisions of the prefrontal cortex, the orbital and dorsolateral regions, have different functions (see Milner, Petrides, and Smith, 1985), only recently have we begun to appreciate that even smaller regions within these subdivisions have specialized functions that can be distinguished from each other (Goldman-Rakic, 1987; Petrides, 1989). Unfortunately, the evidence for microspecialization comes primarily from studies with monkeys. Evidence in humans will have to await findings that result from recent advances in functional neuroimaging techniques, such as POSITRON EMISSION TOMOGRAPHY scans, as well as from studies on patients with serendipitously located, small, focal lesions. As such data become available, perhaps we will be closer to distinguishing between two opposing views of frontal function that have dominated recent theories. One view holds that a common function underlies the operation of all regions in the frontal lobes, but that the function expresses itself in diverse ways determined by each region's unique anatomical connections. The other view does not assume a functional link among various regions but argues for true functional independence between them. Which view predominates will determine our conception of the mechanisms underlying memory, consciousness, and volitional behavior.

(See also WORKING MEMORY.)

REFERENCES

Baddeley, A. D. (1986). *Working memory.* Oxford: Oxford University Press.

Brown, R. G., and Marden, C. D. (1990). Cognitive function in Parkinson's disease: From description to theory. *Trends in Neurosciences 13,* 21–29.

Freedman, M., and Cermak, L. S. (1986). Semantic encoding deficits in frontal lobe disease and amnesia. *Brain and Cognition 5,* 108–114.

Freedman, M., and Oscar-Berman, M. (1986). Bilateral frontal lobe disease and selective delayed response deficits in humans. *Behavioral Neuroscience 100,* 337–342.

Goldman-Rakic, P. S. (1987). Circuitry of primate prefrontal cortex and regulation of behavior by representational memory. In F. Plum, ed., *Handbook of physiology—the nervous system,* vol. 5. Bethesda, Md.: American Physiological Society. An excellent and thorough review of behavioral, neuroanatomical, and physiological work in primates, including a little on humans.

Incissa della Rochetta, A. I. (1986). Classification and

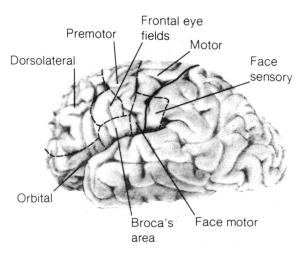

Figure 2. Approximate boundaries of functional zones of the frontal lobes. *Reproduced with permission from Kolb and Whishaw, 1989.*

recall of pictures after unilateral frontal or temporal lobectomy. *Cortex 22,* 189–211.

Janowsky, J. S., Shimamura, A. P., Kritchevsky, M., and Squire, L. R. (1989). Cognitive impairment following frontal lobe damage and its relevance to human amnesia. *Behavioral Neuroscience 103,* 548–560.

Janowsky, J. S., Shimamura, A. P., and Squire, L. R. (1989a). Memory and metamemory: Comparison between patients with frontal lobe lesions and amnesic patients. *Psychobiology 17,* 3–11.

——— (1989b). Source memory impairment in patients with frontal lobe lesions. *Neuropsychologia 27,* 1043–1056.

Kolb, B., and Whishaw, I. Q. (1990). *Fundamentals of human neuropsychology,* 3rd ed. New York: Freeman.

Luria, A. R. (1980). *Higher cortical functions in man,* 2nd ed , pp. 246–257. New York: Basic Books.

Mayes, A. R. (1988). *Human organic memory disorders,* Cambridge: Cambridge University Press.

Milner, B. (1966). Amnesia following operation on the temporal lobe. In C. W. M. Whitty and O. L. Zangwill, eds., *Amnesia.* London: Butterworth.

Milner, B., Petrides, M., and Smith, M. L. (1985). Frontal lobes and the temporal organization of memory. *Human Neurobiology 4,* 137–142. An excellent review of work on humans from Milner and her students, the leading researchers on the topic.

Moscovitch, M. (1982). Multiple dissociations of function in amnesia. In L. S. Cermak, ed., *Human memory and amnesia.* Hillsdale, N.J.: Erlbaum.

——— (1989). Confabulation and the frontal system: Strategic versus associative retrieval in neuropsychological theories of memory. In H. L. Roediger and F. I. M. Craik, eds., *Varieties of memory and consciousness: Essays in honor of Endel Tulving.* Hillsdale, N.J.: Erlbaum.

Moscovitch, M., and Umilta, C. (1990). Modularity and neuropsychology: Implications for the organization of attention and memory in normal and brain-damaged people. In M. E. Schwartz, ed., *Modular processes in dementia.* Cambridge, Mass.: MIT/Bradford.

——— (1991). Conscious and nonconscious aspects of memory: A neuropsychological framework of modules and central systems. In H. J. Weingartner and R. G. Lister, eds., *Perspectives in cognitive neuroscience.* Oxford: Oxford University Press.

Moscovitch, M., and Winocur, G. (1992). The neuropsychology of memory in the elderly: The hippocampus and frontal lobes. In T. Salthouse and F. I. M. Craik, eds., *The handbook of cognition and aging.* New York: Academic Press.

Owen, A. M., Downes, J. J., Sahakian, B. J., Polkeg, C. E., and Robbins, T. W. (1990). Planning and spatial working memory following frontal lobe lesions in man. *Neuropsychologia 28,* 1021–1034.

Pandya, D., and Barnes, C. L. (1986). Architecture and connections of the frontal lobes. In E. Perleman, ed., *The frontal lobes revisited.* New York: IRBN Press.

Petrides, M. (1989). Frontal lobes and memory. In F Boller and J. Grafman, eds., *Handbook of neuropsychology,* vol. 3. Amsterdam: Elsevier. A simpler, more accessible review of work on primates with some coverage of humans.

Petrides, M., and Milner, B. (1982). Deficits on subject-ordered tasks after frontal and temporal-lobe lesions in man. *Neuropsychologia 20,* 249–262.

Prisko, L. (1963). Short-term memory in focal cerebral damage. Unpublished Ph.D. thesis, McGill University, Montreal, Canada.

Saint-Cyr, J. A., Taylor, A., and Lang, A. (1988). Procedural learning and neostriatal dysfunction in man. *Brain 111,* 941–959.

Schacter, D. L., Harbluk, J. L., and McLachlan, D. R. (1984). Retrieval without recollection: An experimental analysis of source amnesia. *Journal of Verbal Learning and Verbal Behavior 23,* 593–611.

Shallice, T. (1982). Specific impairments of planning. *Philosophical Transactions of the Royal Society of London B298,* 199–209.

Shallice, T., and Evans, M. D. (1978). The involvement of the frontal lobes in cognitive estimation. *Cortex 14,* 294–303.

Shimamura, A. P., Janowsky, J. S., and Squire, L. R. (1990). Memory for temporal order in patients with frontal lobe lesions and patients with amnesia. *Neuropsychologia 28,* 803–813.

Smith, M. L., and Milner, B. (1988). Estimation of frequency of occurrence of abstract designs after frontal or temporal lobectomy. *Neuropsychologia 26,* 297–306.

Stuss, D. T., and Benson, D. F. (1986). *The frontal lobes.* New York: Raven Press.

Teuber, H.-L. (1964). The riddle of frontal lobe function in man. In J. M. Warren and K. Akert, eds., *The frontal granular cortex and behavior.* New York: McGraw-Hill.

Morris Moscovitch
Gordon Winocur

FUGUE STATE

See Amnesia, Functional

G

GENERALIZATION

See Discrimination and Generalization

GLUTAMATE RECEPTORS AND THEIR CHARACTERIZATION

The amino acids *l*-glutamate and *l*-aspartate are thought to be the major excitatory neurotransmitters in the mammalian central nervous system (CNS). These excitatory amino acids (EAAs) mediate their effects by interacting with a series of receptor macromolecules that have been defined by pharmacological, physiological, anatomical, and molecular genetic criteria. The interaction of EAAs with these receptors is thought to underlie many normal physiological phenomena, from rapid synaptic signaling and information transfer to longer-lasting changes in synaptic efficacy that are thought to be the cellular basis of learning and memory. In addition, EAAs and EAA receptors have been implicated in a variety of CNS pathologies, including epilepsy, cell death due to excitotoxicity and ischemia, and ALZHEIMER'S DISEASE. This article will review the general characteristics of EAA receptors, including pharmacological specificity, ion selectivity, and modulation by other compounds.

Excitatory Amino Acid Receptor Classes

EAA receptors can be divided into two major classes. One class appears to be directly associated with a cation (positive ion) channel, such that the receptor and the cation channel are part of a single transmembrane receptor/ion channel macromolecule. At least three pharmacologically distinct EAA receptor subclasses of this ionotropic type are known, named after their selective agonists: the *n*-methyl-*d*-aspartate (NMDA), 2-amino-3-hydroxy-5-methyl-4-isoxazolepropionate (AMPA), and kainate (KA) receptor ionophores. The AMPA and KA subclasses are frequently referred to as non-NMDA receptors.

A second major class of EAA receptors has been described in which the receptor is indirectly coupled to second messenger systems via guanine nucleotide-binding proteins (G-proteins) (see SECOND MESSENGER SYSTEMS; MEMBRANE CHANNELS AND THEIR MODULATION IN LEARNING AND MEMORY). In this case, the binding of an EAA to these metabotropic receptors induces secondary changes that are mediated by molecules distinct from the receptor itself. One such G-protein-coupled EAA receptor is coupled to the phosphoinositide (PI) second messenger system and is named after its selective agonist, trans-1-amino-1,3-cyclopentanedicarboxylic acid (trans-ACPD). A second G-protein-coupled EAA receptor named after its selective agonist, *l*-2-amino-4-phosphonobutanoic acid (L-AP4), may exist in the retina. And a distinct L-AP4-sensitive receptor type that functions as a presynaptic inhibitory autoreceptor has been described in select CNS pathways.

It has been shown that more than one receptor subclass may be present in any given excitatory synapse, working in concert to yield a complex transsynaptic response that depends on the number and location of individual receptors within the synapse and extrasynaptically.

Non-NMDA Receptors

The AMPA receptor ionophore is thought to mediate the rapid on-off type of synaptic signaling that underlies the fast excitatory postsynaptic potential (EPSP) at EAA synapses. Binding of an EAA to these receptor ionophores opens a cation channel that is permeable to Na^+ and K^+, inducing the rapid on-off depolarizing currents characteristic of these receptors. It has been shown that in some cases these receptors desensitize rapidly.

AMPA receptors are selectively activated by the nonendogenous agonists AMPA and quisqualate (QA), and other structurally related compounds. (Historically the AMPA receptor was commonly referred to as the QA receptor, but in view of the overlapping actions of QA at other EAA receptors [e.g., the KA and trans-ACPD receptors], it is more accurate to refer to this site as the AMPA or AMPA/QA receptor.) The delineation of potent and selective antagonists for the AMPA/QA receptor has proven problematic. Currently a series of quinoxaline derivatives (6-cyano-7-nitroquinoxaline-2,3-dione [CNQX]; 6,7-dinitroquinoxaline-2,3-dione [DNQX]; and 6-nitro-7-sulfamoyl-benzo(f)quinoxaline-2,3-dione [NBQX]) are the most selective known AMPA/QA antagonists, but they also act as KA antagonists.

KA has been shown to be both a potent excitant and a potent excitotoxin. The case for a KA receptor that is distinct from AMPA/QA receptors stems from pharmacological studies in which KA responses were inhibited by select antagonists more potently than were AMPA/QA or NMDA responses, and from anatomical studies in which KA and AMPA/QA receptors displayed distinct anatomical localizations. However, even considering the quinoxaline antagonists, accurate distinction of KA from AMPA/QA receptors remains difficult because of their similar pharmacological profiles. Localization of AMPA/QA and KA receptors by autoradiographic techniques demonstrates a differential distribution of these two types. For example, [^{3}H]AMPA binding sites are concentrated in the hippocampal CA1 region, outer cortical layers, lateral septum, and the molecular layer of the cerebellum, while [^{3}H]KA binding sites are concentrated in the hippocampal mossy fibers, deep cortical layers, and the granule cell layer of the cerebellum.

Recent advances in molecular genetic techniques have led to the identification of a series of complementary DNA (cDNA) clones derived from rat brain that encode for a family of non-NMDA-type EAA receptors. Thus, injection of messenger RNA derived from these cDNA sequences into oocytes (egg cells) of the African aquatic frog *Xenopus* results in electrophysiological responses to KA, QA, and AMPA, but not to NMDA or *dl*-2-amino-4-phosphonobutanoate (DL-AP4). At least five different clones of this type have been described to date, each having an approximate molecular weight of 100 kilodaltons. Functional receptors are formed following injection of single clone sequences or of combinations of clones. It remains to be determined how the subunits combine to form a functional receptor/channel. Such structural complexity may help to explain the difficulty in distinguishing AMPA/QA from KA responses, if these pharmacological distinctions are simply a matter of subunit composition. In situ hybridization studies demonstrate a diverse and complex anatomical distribution of these clone subtypes that in general overlaps with non-NMDA receptor distributions observed in more conventional ligand-binding autoradiography.

NMDA Receptors

The NMDA receptor ionophore is pharmacologically and functionally more complex than AMPA/QA and KA receptors. For example, binding of an EAA to the transmitter recognition site of the NMDA receptor will open the ion channel only if the membrane is depolarized and if glycine is present. Since NMDA receptors open as a function of the extent of membrane depolarization, they are described as voltage dependent, and are thus sensitive to postsynaptic activity. Therefore, the NMDA receptor complex provides an example of a conditional logic gate where Hebb-like conditions are realized at a single synapse (see LONG-TERM POTENTIATION; HEBB, DONALD). Furthermore, the ion channel is permeable to Ca^{++} in addition to Na^+ and K^+, resulting in the influx of Ca^{++} that induces a variety of secondary phenomena.

NMDA receptors have been shown to be involved in several physiological phenomena that appear to be Ca^{++} dependent. These include (1) the induction of long-term potentiation (LTP), which is regarded as a cellular model of memory analogous to Hebb-type synaptic plasticity; (2) learning and memory in animal models; (3) the pathophysiology of epilepsy; and (4) some forms of excitotoxicity.

The NMDA receptor appears to be regulated by a variety of endogenous and exogenous compounds that act at distinct binding sites to modify the function of the receptor. Thus, the NMDA receptor is frequently referred to as the NMDA receptor complex. The first of these binding sites is the transmitter recognition site, which binds *l*-glutamate, the nonendogenous ligand NMDA, and other agonists. It can be selectively and competitively antagonized by a series of compounds, including D-2-amino-5-phosphonopentanoate (D-AP5) and 3-(2-carboxypiperazin-4-yl)propyl-1-phosphate (CPP). This is the site that triggers channel opening if other conditions are met (see below). Second is the glycine allosteric site, which binds *l*-glycine and other structurally related compounds. This site must be occupied by glycine in order for the channel to be gated by an agonist bound to the transmitter recognition site. The pharmacology of this site is distinct from that of the inhibitory glycine receptor in the spinal cord and brain stem, in that the NMDA receptor glycine modulatory site is insensitive to strychnine but is antagonized by kynurenate, 7-chlorokynurenate, and other compounds. Although this site may always be saturated in vivo, glycine is often referred to as a cotransmitter. Third is a site within the ion channel that binds Mg^{++}. Binding of Mg^{++} at this site appears to block current flow through the channel when the membrane is at hyperpolarized potentials. This block is removed under depolarizing conditions, such that NMDA currents are voltage dependent. Fourth is a site at which Zn^{++} acts as an NMDA antagonist. Fifth is a site within the ion channel that binds PCP, dibenzocyclohepteneimine (MK-801), and other compounds, causing blockage of ion flow through the channel. Binding of these compounds is increased in the presence of glutamate and glycine site agonists, which suggests that this channel site is more accessible when the channel is in the open state. Finally, a variety of polyamines have been shown to be modulators of the NMDA receptor. For example, spermine and spermidine increase MK-801 binding to the NMDA complex and NMDA-evoked currents in cell culture and *Xenopus* oocyte preparations.

Localization of NMDA receptors by autoradiographic techniques demonstrates an anatomical distribution that in general parallels the distribution of AMPA/QA receptors, further supporting the idea that these two receptors work in concert in many synapses. Thus, NMDA receptors are found in the CA1 region of the hippocampus, throughout the cortex (particularly in outer cortical layers), and in striatum. However, specific localization of binding shows a very different distribution of NMDA agonist- and antagonist-preferring binding sites, suggesting that subpopulations of NMDA receptors may exist in different brain areas.

The NMDA receptor has been successfully isolated and characterized, and one subunit of this receptor complex has been cloned.

G-Protein-Coupled Receptors

A G-protein coupled EAA receptor has been identified that is coupled to the PI second messenger system via the interaction of a G-protein and can be activated by the selective agonist trans-ACPD. Activation of this receptor has been shown to stimulate the turnover of inositol phospholipids, increase intracellular Ca^{++} concentrations via release of Ca^{++} from intracellular sites, and block the slow afterhyperpolarization (AHP) current that normally serves to hyperpolarize neurons following a train of action potentials. The ability of this receptor to activate PI metabolism appears to be greater in neonatal rats than in adults, suggesting a role in growth and plasticity.

The trans-ACPD receptor can be activated by trans-ACPD, QA, ibotenate, and glutamate but not by AMPA, NMDA, or KA. Activation of the trans-ACPD receptor is not antagonized by CNQX or by other non-NMDA and NMDA antagonists. The stimulation of PI hydrolysis by EAA agonists in biochemical experiments can be antagonized by high concentrations of DL-AP3, but careful analysis suggests that this antagonism is not competitive, thus raising the question as to the site and mechanism of antagonism.

A cDNA clone has been identified that appears to encode a polypeptide receptor that exhibits the pharmacological and physiological characteristics of the metabotropic trans-ACPD receptor and has a molecular weight of approximately 130 kilodaltons. This clone shows little sequence homology to other known G-protein-coupled receptors, suggesting that it may represent a novel receptor family. In situ hybridization studies show that this receptor is expressed abundantly in the hippocampal dentate gyrus, CA2 and CA3 regions, and cerebellar Purkinje cells. (see GUIDE TO THE ANATOMY OF THE BRAIN).

L-AP4 Receptors

A receptor at which L-AP4 acts as an agonist has been described in studies of depolarizing bipolar cells (DBPs) of the retina. In these cells, L-AP4 mimics the action of the endogenous transmitter, *l*-glutamate, to hyperpolarize DBPs by decreasing a tonically active inward current in a G-protein-dependent fashion. Thus, this receptor appears to be very different from the depolarizing EAA receptors above.

Electrophysiological evidence has shown that L-AP4 is a potent inhibitor of synaptic transmission in a few select neural pathways, including the lateral perforant path, the lateral olfactory tract, and the dorsal horn of the spinal cord of the rat. This antagonism appears to be mediated by a presynaptic mechanism, such that L-AP4 is acting as an agonist at a presynaptic autoreceptor. At present there are no known antagonists for this receptor or for the retinal L-AP4 receptor described above. The relationship between this presynaptic L-AP4 receptor and the retinal L-AP4 receptor remains unclear.

In addition to these effects, L-AP4 acts as a weak agonist in some systems. However, it acts as a potent agonist following exposure of hippocampal and cortical slices to QA but not to AMPA, NMDA, or KA. This sensitization to L-AP4 may be mediated by activation of the trans-ACPD receptor.

Conclusion

The function of EAA synapses depends on the combination of the above-mentioned receptor subtypes within a given synapse (e.g., non-NMDA and NMDA, non-NMDA and L-AP4, non-NMDA and trans-ACPD, etc.). Since it is clear that these subtypes serve distinct functions, precise manipulation of individual subtypes is critical to understanding the role of a subtype in a normal physiological event or in the etiology of a given EAA-linked disease. The advent of more potent and selective drugs for each receptor subclass will allow for more precise experimental and clinical manipulation of these receptors. Similarly, molecular genetic approaches to both the structure and the regulation of these receptors and their genes have far-reaching implications for the basic science of EAA receptors and for a variety of EAA-linked human diseases.

(See also NEUROTRANSMITTER SYSTEMS AND MEMORY; GUIDE TO THE ANATOMY OF THE BRAIN: SYNAPSE.)

REFERENCES

Barnard, E. A., and Henley, J. M. (1990). The non-NMDA receptors: Types, protein structure and molecular biology. *Trends in Pharmacological Sciences 11,* 500–507.

Cotman, C. W., Monaghan, D. T., and Ganong, A. H. (1988). Excitatory amino acid neurotransmission: NMDA receptors and Hebb-type synaptic plasticity. *Annual Review of Neuroscience 11,* 61–80.

Cotman, C. W., Monaghan, D. T., Ottersen, O. P., and Storm-Mathisen, J. (1987). Anatomical organization of excitatory amino acid receptors and their pathways. *Trends in Neurosciences 10,* 273–280.

Hollmann, M., O'Shea-Greenfield, A., Rogers, S. W., and Heinemann, S. (1989). Cloning by functional expression of the glutamate receptor family. *Nature 342,* 643–648.

Johnson, R. L., and Koerner, J. F. (1988). Excitatory amino acid neurotransmission. *Journal of Medicinal Chemistry 31,* 2057–2066.

Masu, M., Tanabe, Y., Tsuchida, K., Shigemoto, R., and Nakanishi, S. (1991). Sequence and expression of a metabotropic glutamate receptor. *Nature 349,* 760–765.

Mayer, M. L., and Miller, R. J. (1990). Excitatory amino acid receptors, second messengers and regulation of intracellular Ca^{2+} in mammalian neurons. *Trends in Pharmacological Sciences 11,* 254–260.

Monaghan, D. T., Bridges, R. J., and Cotman, C. W. (1989). The excitatory amino acid receptors: Their classes, pharmacology, and distinct properties in the function of the central nervous system. *Annual Review of Pharmacology and Toxicology 29,* 365–402.

Watkins, J. C., Krogsgaard-Larsen, P., and Honore, T. (1990). Structure-activity relationships in the development of excitatory amino acid receptor agonists and competitive antagonists. *Trends in Pharmacological Sciences 11,* 25–33.

C. W. Cotman
E. R. Whittemore

GUIDE TO THE ANATOMY OF THE BRAIN

[*This entry consists of an* Overview *followed by nine articles on various features of the brain:*

Amygdala
Basal Forebrain
Basal Ganglia
Cerebellum
Cerebral Neocortex
Hippocampus
Neuron
Olfactory Cortex
Synapse]

Overview

The anatomy of the brain can be described at three increasingly complex levels. At the simplest level (cellular anatomy), we can describe the different cell types found throughout the brain. What do these cells look like? What do they do? Do they differ in the way they operate within different parts of the brain? What aspects of their biochemistry give them their unique properties?

At the next level (regional anatomy) we can look at the way cells are grouped in particular regions. Are the cells arranged in layers (as in the mammalian neocortex), or are they found in aggregations (as in many other regions of the brain)? Are cells densely or loosely packed? Are all the cells in a region of one type, or are different types present? An examination of these types of features may help us determine how a particular region may perform a task or communicate within itself and with other regions. It is on this level that the classic regions of the brain may be described—for example, how the hippocampus, neocortex, or basal ganglia are organized.

The final level, systems anatomy, looks at how the different regions are arranged relative to each other and, perhaps more important, describes how different regions communicate. Now we may begin to understand how particular regions combine to give the human brain the staggering ability to perform simultaneously such diverse operations as controlling the heart rate, driving a car, and remembering and organizing tasks to perform at a later time. Thus, by considering the anatomy of the brain at this level we can begin to describe the organization of the control of the cardiovascular system, the organization of the motor control of voluntary muscles, and the systems involved in learning and memory.

Cellular Anatomy

The vast majority of cells found within the central nervous system (CNS) fall into two categories; neurons and glial cells. Although glial cells are the most numerous cells in the brain—they outnumber neurons by about twenty-five to one—the processes most commonly associated with nervous activity are performed by neurons. In terms of shape and size no other cell type in the body shows as great a diversity as the neurons. Although they operate by using structural, biochemical, and metabolic principles common to many other cells in the body, neurons possess a number of features that set them apart from other cells. First, neuronal membranes are assembled so as to allow the specialized transmembrane transport of small ions, thus conferring on neurons the ability to generate and relay trains of electrical impulses (*action potentials*). The electrical excitability of neurons is a fundamental principle governing the operation of the central nervous system. In order to transmit action potentials over great distances, neurons have extended cytoplasmic processes (*axons*) that, for some spinal motor neurons of large mammals, may have lengths on the order of meters. Second, since neurons usually do not communicate by direct contact—each neuron operates as an independent metabolic unit—they have evolved highly specialized structures (*synapses*) at points of interaction in order to transmit the information contained within the patterns of action potentials. Synapses are essentially clefts between neurons. They are asymmetrically flanked by structures that release specialized chemicals (*neurotransmitters*) from one (*presynaptic*) neuron in response to the presence of action potentials. The response of the recipient (*postsynaptic*) neuron is determined by highly specific detectors (*receptors*) found on the postsynaptic membrane. The structure of the synapse allows information to flow in one direction only. Throughout the nervous system different neurons utilize a multiplicity of both neurotransmitters and other neurochemicals (*neuromodulators*) that may modify the biochemical processes occurring within the synapse.

Glial cells are the most numerous cells in the central nervous system. In terms of their morphology they are less complex than neurons, and they also show less structural diversity. Unlike neurons, they retain the ability to divide, a facility they utilize in their participation in the reaction of nervous tissue to injury. Two types of glial cells are found in the CNS: oligodendrocytes and astrocytes. The peripheral nervous system contains a related cell type, the Schwann cell, crucial to the formation and maintenance of the myelin sheaths of peripheral nerves. Within the brain, glial cells are involved with structural and metabolic maintenance of neuronal function and the blood-brain barrier. During development glial cells play a role in axon guidance and the correct arrangement of neural patterns.

An overview of the cellular anatomy of the brain is completed with reference to the ependymal cells lining the cerebral ventricles, the meningeal membranes surrounding and physically supporting the brain, and the network of blood vessels that form the vascular supply to the brain. Unlike neurons and glial cells, these elements are not exclusive to the nervous system. They share many common structural and functional features with other support cells found throughout the body.

Considering the vast number of neurons and glial cells in the brain, there is a bewildering variety of combinations of electrical excitability and chemical communication available for nervous function. This variety forms the basis of information processing within nervous tissue and, as can be imagined, the ordered grouping of the brain's cellular components (axons, synapses, glial cells) is the crux of how the CNS operates. Describing the anatomy of the brain at this next level is a major goal of neuroanatomical science. It is briefly summarized in the next section.

Regional Anatomy

At the regional level of analysis we can describe how the cellular elements outlined above are assembled into the functional areas usually associated with the anatomy of the brain. The arrangement of neurons can be relatively simple, as in the cerebellum or the hippocampus, where three or four neuronal types are arranged in a laminar pattern. Other regions of the brain contain a greater number of neuronal types that may (e.g., the neocortex, some parts of the thalamus) or may not

(e.g., basal ganglia, hypothalamus, many midbrain and brain stem regions) be arranged in a laminar manner.

The study and description of how the various regions of the brain are organized forms the basis of what may be regarded as neuroanatomy. The modern discipline of neuroanatomy has developed over the past 400 years through the descriptive studies of workers such as Vesalius (sixteenth century), Willis (seventeenth century), Retzius and Purkinje (nineteenth century), and Brodmann, Campbell, Ramón y CAJAL, and Golgi (nineteenth–twentieth centuries). Today, neuroanatomists can use a great number of sophisticated techniques to help them describe not only the fine cellular structure of different brain areas but also the biochemical and molecular components that contribute to the characteristic features and functions of different cells.

At the simplest level the brain can be thought of as a tube of neural tissue that surrounds a ventricular system containing cerebrospinal fluid. The brain is divided into three basic parts: the *hindbrain* (or rhombencephalon), the *midbrain* (or mesencephalon), and *forebrain* (or prosencephalon). The hindbrain can be further subdivided into the *pons, medulla oblongata,* and *cerebellum,* and the forebrain into the *telencephalon* and *diencephalon.*

Hindbrain: Medulla Oblongata, Pons, Cerebellum

The hindbrain (or brain stem) is that part of the brain contiguous to the uppermost part of the spinal cord. The *medulla oblongata* contains many of the neuronal groups concerned with controlling the autonomic nervous system, those functions normally considered "unconscious," such as respiration and control of the cardiovascular system. It also contains the motor neurons of some cranial nerves and major fiber tracts connecting many parts of the brain with the spinal cord.

The hindbrain contains the *cerebellum,* a large, prominent structure with a simple laminated cellular organization, situated immediately dorsal to the hindbrain. Through its extensive connections with the spinal cord, thalamus, and *pons,* the cerebellum is thought to be concerned with the coordination of motor function.

Within the hindbrain is part of the complex of cell groups that make up the *reticular formation.* This system projects to and receives information from much of the brain and spinal cord, and is involved with many aspects of brain function, including the control of the level of arousal and the processing of information used in pain perception and in regulating sexual behavior. Some groups of reticular neurons have axons that ramify extensively throughout the brain and are characterized by their use of aromatic amino acid–derived neurotransmitters (catecholamine and indoleamines).

Midbrain

The midbrain includes an extension of the brain stem reticular formation. These cell groups (collectively called the *periaqueductal gray*) are located in a central core of tissue surrounding the midbrain ventricular canal and contribute to the functions of the reticular formation described above.

Two midbrain regions are concerned with processing sensory information within the visual (*superior colliculus*) and auditory (*inferior colliculus*) systems. They are both important components of the system that processes sensory information from the retina and the cochlea, before it is projected onto the appropriate parts of the neocortex.

A prominent group of cells (the *substantia nigra*) in the ventral midbrain is concerned with motor coordination. It has extensive connections with the thalamus and basal ganglia, and is the region that is severely affected in patients with Parkinsonism. The *red nucleus* is another conspicuous midbrain cell group involved with motor coordination. The cerebellum and neocortex provide its major inputs, while the spinal cord and cell groups in the brain stem are the major recipients of information from the red nucleus.

Forebrain: Diencephalon, Telencephalon

The diencephalon contains the *hypothalamus* and the *thalamus*. The hypothalamus is part of the limbic system and consists of a number of poorly differentiated cell groups that are generally concerned with controlling growth, reproductive function, thirst, feeding and metabolism, temperature regulation, and sleep. A number of hypothalamic cells release their neurochemicals from axon terminals directly into the bloodstream rather than into a synaptic cleft (the process of *neurosecretion*). By this means the hypothalamus is able to control the secretions of the pituitary gland and, thus, many parts of the endocrine system. Other hypothalamic cells project toward the brain stem and spinal cord in order to modulate autonomic function. The hypothalamus receives information from the brain stem and from other regions of the limbic system, including the amygdala, hippocampus, and septal nuclei.

The *neocortex* (part of the telencephalon) is perhaps the most prominent feature of the mammalian brain. In all mammals the cortex consists of six laminae of varying thickness and cellular composition that overlie the dorsal (or upper) surface of the brain. In humans and other primates the surface of the neocortex consists of a series of folds (*gyri*) and fissures (*sulci*) that increase its total volume. Other mammals (e.g., rodents) have a much less convoluted cortical surface. During mammalian evolution the neocortex has progressively increased in size relative to the remainder of the brain. Consequently, in primates it is so enlarged that it wraps around the forebrain and midbrain, and extends back to the cerebellum. The neocortex is divided into four lobes: *frontal, temporal, parietal,* and *occipital.*

Adjacent to the temporal lobe are two nonneocortical structures: the *hippocampus,* a laminated structure that receives major inputs from many regions of the neocortex and has been implicated in the mechanisms of memory, and the *amygdala,* a complex collection of cell groups with connections to the cortex, hippocampus, hypothalamus, midbrain, and brain stem that has been associated with assigning emotional significance to sensory events.

Two regions of the forebrain are closely associated with the neocortex in terms of connections: the *basal ganglia* (part of the telencephalon) and the *thalamus* (part of the diencephalon). The basal ganglia consist of a number of nonlaminated areas and are one of the major systems through which the motor output of the neocortex is processed before it goes to the spinal cord. The thalamus is a collection of cell groups of varying shapes and neuronal composition located behind the basal ganglia and dorsal to the hypothalamus. Its various cell groups receive and process the information from peripheral sense organs (e.g., the retina, ear, somatosensory receptors). Much of the output of the thalamus is directed to the neocortex.

Systems Anatomy

At the systems level we can introduce a functional aspect to structural neuroanatomy. By this means we can begin to address which regions are involved with which function, and determine those aspects of cellular and regional anatomy which contribute to specialized function. For example, in the visual system the sensory part is made up of a sensory transducer (the retina) and a sensory nerve (the optic nerve). After some initial processing, these components transmit visual information into two structures in the thalamus and midbrain (the lateral geniculate nucleus and then the superior colliculus) for further processing. Visual information is then projected to the visual regions of the neocortex (in the occipital lobes) for final assessment. Cellular and regional neuroanatomy can tell us the detailed structure of each component, but at the systems level we want to know how the components interact: which neurotransmitters are used in which connections, which cells receive which type of information, what routes are used between the various structures.

Many of the pioneer neurophysiologists (e.g., David Ferrier, Charles Sherrington) who provided the seminal experimental observations regarding the functions of the nervous system appreciated the contributions that neuroanatomy made to the interpretation of their findings. Since the same strategy is still a prerequisite for the neuroscience of today, a great deal of current research concentrates on describing the direction and the biochemical and molecular composition of the neurons connecting different neural systems. When this anatomical approach is combined with data from experiments that investigate specific functions (e.g., lesion studies, electrophysiology), we have a very powerful procedure for determining brain function and for thinking about why the brain's collective structure endows it with unique properties.

REFERENCES

Brodal, A. (1981). *Neurological anatomy*. New York: Oxford University Press.

Nauta, W. J. H., and Feirtag, M. (1986). *Fundamental neuroanatomy*. New York: W. H. Freeman.

Nieuwenhuys, R., Voogd, J., and van Huijzen, C. (1988). *The human central nervous system*. New York: Springer.

Alan G. Watts

Amygdala

The amygdala is a complex of several nuclei located in the anteromedial part of the temporal lobe. It was named in the nineteenth century for a supposed resemblance to an almond (Latin, *amygdalum*) embedded in the temporal lobe. Although the amygdala is often considered part of the basal ganglia, it is distinctly different in structure, connections, and function from the caudate nucleus and putamen, which are contiguous to it. In fact, the cells of the amygdala are often compared with the pyramidal and other cells of the cerebral cortex. Perhaps most important, the amygdala is generally recognized as part of the *limbic system,* which also includes the hippocampus and parahippocampal cortical areas, and has been implicated in visceral control, emotional expression, and memory processing.

Bilateral damage to the amygdaloid nuclei in monkeys produces the *Kluver-Bucy syndrome,* in which the animal is unable to appreciate the significance of sensory stimuli ("psychic blindness"). This and other observations (see LeDoux, 1987) suggest that the amygdala is an important nodal point in the adaptive emotional or *affective* response of individuals to a constantly changing environment. This role appears to involve the interpretation of incoming sensory information in the context of species-specific objectives or emotional significance, and the subsequent elicitation of appropriate behavioral and visceral changes. Such a role requires access to integrated sensory information about current experience, as well as some connection with memory of past experience. A processing mechanism is also needed by which current experience can be labeled as aversive or rewarding. Finally, outputs are required that can evoke or potentiate appropriate visceral and behavioral responses. Possible channels for each of these functions can be recognized in the anatomical organization and connections of the amygdala. (For references and more extensive descriptions of the structure and connections of the amygdala, see Price, Russchen, and Amaral, 1987; Amaral et al., 1992.)

Intrinsic Structure and Connections

The amygdaloid complex consists of cortical areas on the medial surface of the temporal lobe, and

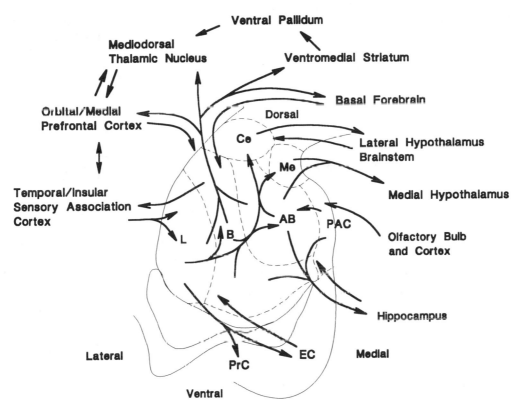

Figure 1. A schematic representation of the amygdaloid nuclei and their major axonal associations, both within the amygdala and with other parts of the brain, as described in the text. Abbreviations: AB, accessory basal nucleus; B, basal nucleus; Ce, central nucleus; EC, entorhinal cortex; L, lateral nucleus; Me, medial nucleus; PAC, periamygdaloid cortex; PrC, perirhinal cortex.

several deep nuclei. Many of the surface areas (cortical nuclei and periamygdaloid cortex) interact with the olfactory system. The deep nuclei include the lateral, basal, and accessory basal nuclei, which interact with several parts of the cerebral cortex. In the dorsal part of the amygdala are the central and medial nuclei, which interact with autonomic or endocrine-related areas of the hypothalamus and brain stem (Figure 1).

There are extensive connections within and between the amygdaloid nuclei. The major axonal systems between nuclei arise in the lateral, basal, and accessory basal nuclei and terminate in successively more dorsomedial parts of the amygdala. In contrast, there are only weak projections in the opposite direction. Many of the intra-amygdaloid connections are inhibitory; the amygdala has high levels of γ-aminobutyric acid (GABA) and of GABA receptors (especially the $GABA_A$ receptors that are closely related to the anxiolytic benzo-

diazepine drugs). The central and medial nuclei also have relatively high concentrations of neuropeptide-containing neurons and axons.

Sensory Inputs

Electrophysiological recordings from the amygdala indicate that the cells respond to visual, auditory, and gustatory/olfactory stimuli, as well as to mixed stimuli. In many cases the effective stimuli are relatively complex, such as a face, or both the sight and ingestion of a slice of watermelon. The response may change depending on the novelty of the stimulus and whether it is aversive or rewarding (Nishijo, Ono, and Nishino, 1988). The bulk of this sensory information reaches the amygdala by way of axons from sensory association areas in the temporal and insular cortex. For example, there is a substantial input to the amygdala from the visual association areas in the rostral inferior temporal cortex. Auditory inputs originate in the superior temporal cortex, and there apparently are somatic sensory inputs from the caudal insula. These axonal projections terminate primarily in the lateral amygdaloid nucleus, and to a lesser extent in the basal or accessory basal nuclei. There are also inputs to the lateral amygdaloid nucleus from nuclei in the thalamus (including the magnocellular part of the medial geniculate nucleus) that may provide a short-latency "alerting" signal in relation to fearful noises or other arousing stimuli.

In addition, olfactory inputs reach the amygdala through direct projections from the olfactory bulb or primary olfactory cortex to the cortical nuclei and the periamygdaloid cortex. The central amygdaloid nucleus receives taste and other visceral afferents from relay nuclei in the brain stem (especially the parabrachial nucleus).

The amygdala also sends axons back to the sensory cortical areas. Many of these projections are more extensive than the projections to the amygdala. For example, the dorsal part of the basal nucleus projects not only to the rostral inferior temporal cortex but also to more caudal areas, including the primary visual cortex. There are also amygdaloid projections to the primary olfactory cortex and to taste relay nuclei. Thus, the amygdala not only receives diverse sensory inputs but also may influence activity in the sensory areas themselves.

Outputs to the Hypothalamus and Brain Stem

Both the medial and the lateral hypothalamus receive substantial amygdaloid outputs, and there are also return axonal projections from the hypothalamus to the amygdala. The axons to the medial hypothalamus arise primarily from the medial and accessory basal nuclei, while the axons to the lateral hypothalamus arise predominantly from the central nucleus. Most of the amygdaloid nuclei also project through the stria terminalis to the bed nucleus of the stria terminalis, which in turn provides a relay to both the medial and the lateral hypothalamus. These projections allow the amygdala to influence hypothalamic control of both endocrine functions (through the anterior and posterior pituitary) and autonomic mechanisms (through descending projections to the sympathetic and parasympathetic systems).

The axonal projection from the central nucleus continues caudally from the hypothalamus through the ventral midbrain and brain stem reticular formation to reach a number of the brain stem nuclei directly involved in autonomic control and other visceral functions. These include the substantia nigra, the periaqueductal gray, the parabrachial nucleus, the dorsal vagal nucleus and nucleus of the solitary tract, and the lateral reticular formation. Electrical stimulation of either the amygdala or points along this pathway produce the *defense reaction,* an integrated response that includes cardiovascular, respiratory, and other visceral changes as well as overt behavioral actions that are apparently preparatory for "fight or flight" (see Kaada, 1972).

Associative Interactions with Other Forebrain Structures

The basal and accessory basal amygdaloid nuclei, and to a lesser extent the lateral nucleus, have connections to and from a number of other forebrain cortical and subcortical structures that have been implicated in affective behavior or memory. These connections cannot be considered either inputs or outputs of the amygdala but presumably form part of an associative axonal network.

The axonal projections to the cortex are distributed mainly to the medial and ventral (or orbital) parts of the frontal lobe (*prefrontal* cortex). These projections continue posteriorly onto the cortex of the insula and the anterior pole of the temporal lobe. All of these areas send axons back to the amygdala. The amygdala is also connected to the same prefrontal cortical areas through axonal projections to the mediodorsal nucleus of the thalamus, and reciprocal axonal connections between this thalamic nucleus and the frontal cortex. In addition, the amygdala has a substantial projection to the ventromedial part of the corpus striatum, especially the nucleus accumbens, the medial part of the caudate nucleus, and the ventral part of the putamen. This part of the striatum projects to a ventral extension of the globus pallidus (the *ventral pallidum*), which in turn sends axons to the mediodorsal thalamic nucleus.

Therefore, there are several direct and indirect pathways by which the amygdala can interact with the prefrontal cortex. It is likely that these form a functional circuit that is important for analyzing the psychic or emotional significance of stimuli, and is also involved in the regulation of emotional behavior. Indeed, POSITRON EMISSION TOMOGRAPHY (PET) imaging of brain activity suggests that all of these structures show abnormal activity in patients with severe unipolar depression.

The amygdala also provides a major part of the afferent input to the nucleus basalis of Meynert and other cholinergic nuclei of the basal forebrain, and receives a substantial cholinergic projection from the same nuclei. Other inputs to the basal forebrain nuclei come from the same orbital, insular, and temporal polar cortical areas that are interconnected with the amygdala. Because the cholinergic nuclei have a modulatory influence over the entire cerebral cortex, this system may allow the amygdala and related structures to influence very diverse brain functions.

Finally, there are several interconnections between the amygdala and the hippocampal formation. The most substantial of these link the lateral, basal, and accessory basal nuclei in the amygdala with the entorhinal and perirhinal cortex of the parahippocampal gyrus, and the subiculum/CA1 region of the hippocampus proper. These represent important input/output regions of the hippocampus, suggesting that activity in the two major limbic structures is correlated at key processing points.

REFERENCES

Amaral, D. G., Price, J. L., Pitkanen, A., and Carmichael, S. T. (1992). Anatomical organization of the primate amygdaloid complex. In J. P. Aggleton, ed., *The amygdala*. New York: Wiley-Liss. See also other chapters in this volume.

Kaada, B. (1972). Stimulation and regional ablation of the amygdaloid complex with reference to functional representation. In B. E. Eleftheriou, ed., *The neurobiology of the amygdala*, pp. 145–204. New York: Plenum Press. A good review of much of the earlier work on amygdaloid stimulation. See also the other chapters for reviews of anatomical and behavioral studies up to 1972.

LeDoux, J. (1987). Emotion. In F. Plum, ed., *Handbook of physiology*, vol. 5, *Higher function*, pp. 419–459. Washington, D.C.: American Physiological Society. An extended review of the neural basis of emotion, including the role of the amygdala.

Nishijo, H., Ono, T., and Nishino, H. (1988). Single neuron responses in amygdala of alert monkey during complex sensory stimulation of affective significance. *Journal of Neuroscience 8*, 139–151. A study of amygdaloid responses to sensory stimuli in awake monkeys.

Price, J. L., Russchen, F. T., and Amaral, D. G. (1987). The limbic region: II. The amygdaloid complex. In A. Bjorkland, T. Hokfelt, and L. W. Swanson, eds., *Handbook of chemical neuroanatomy*, vol. 5, *Integrated systems in the CNS, part I*, Amsterdam: Elsevier. pp. 279–381. Amsterdam: Elsevier. A comprehensive review of the neuroanatomy of the amygdala, with comparisons of rat, cat, and monkey.

Joseph L. Price

Basal Forebrain

A heterogeneous set of telencephalic structures on the medial and ventral aspects of the cerebral hemispheres collectively make up the basal forebrain. Although there is no consensus on exact boundaries, the septal area, the diagonal band nuclei, and the substantia innominata are usually included within its confines. These structures lack a true cortical organization but are located on the hemispheric surface and have therefore been described as having a "corticoid" architecture. This section will focus on the cholinergic efferents that emanate from this region of the brain.

The basal forebrain contains four overlapping constellations of cholinergic cell groups located in the medial septum, vertical and horizontal nuclei of the diagonal band, and the nucleus basalis of Meynert. These four cell groups provide the major source of cholinergic innervation for all limbic, olfactory, and neocortical structures (Figure 1). The cholinergic nature of these neurons has been established by showing that they are immunoreactive for choline acetyltransferase, and their connections have been analyzed with the help of axonally transported tracer substances (Mesulam, 1988).

The septal area is usually subdivided into dorsal, lateral, and medial nuclei. The medial septal nucleus of the primate brain is an inconspicuous structure containing relatively small (25–30 by 25–30 microns in the monkey), round neurons. Less than half of the medial septal neurons are cholinergic and correspond to the Ch1 sector of the basal forebrain. A second group of somewhat larger (20–25 by 30–40 microns) cholinergic neu-

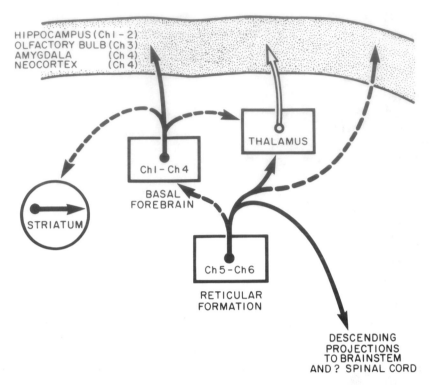

Figure 1. Diagrammatic representation of central cholinergic pathways in the primate brain. Solid arrows indicate major pathways and broken arrows, minor pathways. The open circle and arrow indicate that the thalamocortical pathway is noncholinergic. *From Mesulam, 1990a, with the permission of the publishers.*

rons is embedded within the vertical nucleus of the diagonal band of Broca, a nucleus that is usually considered a component of the septal complex. Approximately three-quarters of the neurons of the vertical limb nucleus are cholinergic and constitute the Ch2 sector. The substantia innominata (or the subcommissural gray) is a complex region composed of the ventral globus pallidus, the nucleus basalis of Meynert, and the horizontal nucleus of the diagonal band. A small minority (a tenth or less) of the neurons in the horizontal limb nucleus are cholinergic and constitute the Ch3 sector. These neurons tend to be hypochromic on Nissl stains and are shaped like a spindle (15–20 by 40–50 microns).

The largest group of cholinergic neurons in the primate brain is found within the nucleus basalis of Meynert. Approximately 90 percent of the larger neurons in the nucleus basalis of the monkey and human brain are cholinergic and constitute the Ch4 sector. These neurons are generally larger than the other basal forebrain cholinergic cells (40–50 by 60–70 microns). In the human brain,

each hemisphere may contain approximately 200,000 nucleus basalis neurons, about 90 percent of which belong to Ch4 (Arendt et al., 1985). The anteroposterior extent of the human Ch4 complex is 1.5–2 centimeters. In addition to the cholinergic neurons within the cytoarchitectonic confines of the nucleus basalis, there are interstitial cholinergic neurons embedded within the anterior commissure, the ansa peduncularis, the ansa lenticularis, and the internal capsule. These neurons can be considered part of the Ch4 complex on the basis of morphological, cytochemical, and hodological criteria. Furthermore, the nucleus basalis contains cholinergic as well as noncholinergic neurons. According to these observations, not all Ch4 neurons are located within the nucleus basalis and not all nucleus basalis neurons belong to Ch4. The designations "Ch4" and "nucleus basalis" are therefore not equivalent. The Ch designations for the other cholinergic cell groups in the basal forebrain and brain stem are based on similar considerations.

Gorry (1963) pointed out that the nucleus basalis (and therefore the Ch4 complex) displays a progressive evolutionary trend, becoming more and more extensive and differentiated in more highly evolved species, especially in primates and cetaceans. Our observations in the brains of turtles, mice, rats, squirrel monkeys, rhesus monkeys, and humans are consistent with this general view.

The Ch4 complex has been designated an "open" nucleus. There is a certain overlap with surrounding cell groups such as the olfactory tubercle, preoptic area, hypothalamic nuclei, striatal structures,

nuclei of the diagonal band, amygdaloid nuclei, and globus pallidus. There is no strict delineation between nuclear aggregates and passing fiber tracts. As noted previously, many Ch4 neurons are embedded within the internal capsule, the diagonal bands of Broca, the anterior commissure, the ansa peduncularis (inferior thalamic peduncle), and the ansa lenticularis. In fact, previous designations for the nucleus basalis included "nucleus of the ansa peduncularis" and "nucleus of the ansa

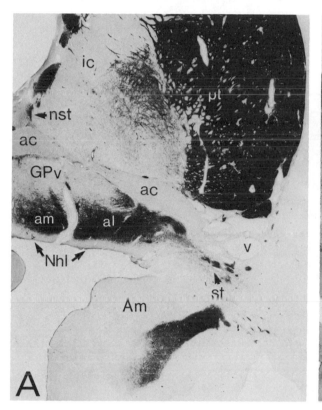
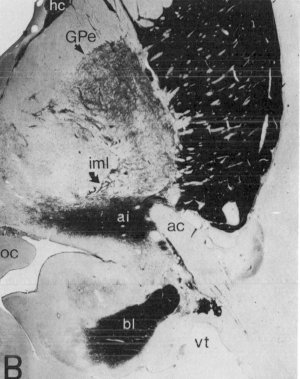

Figure 2. A. Acetylcholinesterase (AChE) histochemistry of a coronal section through the anterior sector of the nucleus basalis and of Ch4 (NB-Ch4) in a normal human brain, showing its anteromedial (am) and anterolateral (al) subsectors. Medial is to the left, dorsal to the top. This level is characterized by the crossing of the anterior commissure (ac) through the basal forebrain. The more laterally placed AChE-rich patches under the ac are striatal islands (st) not related to NB-Ch4. The subcommissural part of the basal forebrain is also known as the substantia innominata and contains the ventral globus pallidus (GPv), the NB-Ch4 (am and al), and the horizontal limb nucleus of the diagonal band (Nhl). Abbreviations: ic, internal capsule; nst, nucleus of the stria terminalis. **B.** A more caudal coronal section showing the anterointermediate (ai) sector of NB-Ch4. The ac is receding laterally. Note that the NB-Ch4 stands out from adjacent structures by an intense AChE reaction. A band of interstitial Ch4 neurons extends into the internal medullary lamina (iml) of the globus pallidus. Original magnification ×5. Abbreviations: bl, basolateral nucleus of the amygdala; hc, head of the caudate; oc, optic chiasm; Vt, temporal horn of the lateral ventricle. *From Mesulam and Geula, 1988, with the permission of the publishers.*

lenticularis." The physiological implication of this intimate association with fiber bundles is unknown. Conceivably, the Ch4 complex could monitor and perhaps influence the electrical activity along these fiber tracts. In addition to this open nuclear structure, the neurons of Ch4 are heteromorphic and have an isodendritic morphology with overlapping dendritic fields. These characteristics, also present in the nuclei of the brain-stem reticular formation, have led to the suggestion that the Ch4 complex could be conceptualized as a telencephalic extension of the brain-stem reticular core (Ramon-Moliner and Nauta, 1966).

Studies in the monkey (based on the concurrent demonstration of perikaryal cholinergic markers and retrograde transport) have shown that each group of cholinergic cells projects widely but also with some degree of topographical specificity. According to these studies, Ch1 and Ch2 collectively provide the major source of cholinergic input for the hippocampal formation, Ch3 provides the major cholinergic input to the olfactory bulb, and Ch4 provides the major cholinergic innervation for the amygdala and all neocortical regions. The primate Ch4 can be divided into anteromedial (Ch4am), anterolateral (Ch4al), intermediate (Ch4id, Ch4iv, Ch4ai), and posterior (Ch4p) subsectors (Figures 2 and 3). Each cortical area receives its cholinergic input primarily (but not exclusively) from a specific subsector of Ch4. For example, Ch4am is the major source of cholinergic innervation for the cingulate gyrus and adjacent

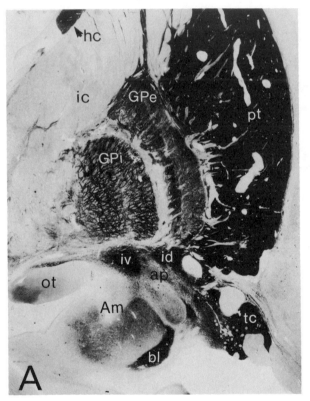

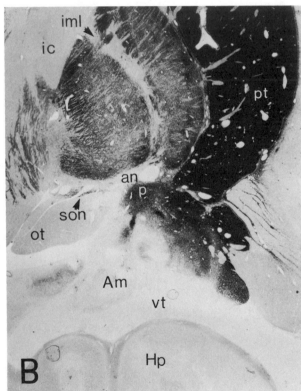

Figure 3. A.   A level more caudal than that shown in Figure 2B. Medial is to the left, dorsal to the top. The ac has completed its crossing. The ansa peduncularis (ap) passes through the NB-Ch4 region and divides it into intermedioventral (iv) and intermediodorsal (id) subsectors. Abbreviations: ot, optic tract; tc, tail of the caudate nucleus. **B.** A coronal section at a level more caudal than Figure 3A. Medial to the left, dorsal to the top. The posterior sector of NB-Ch4 (p) abuts upon the putamen (pt) and amygdala (Am). Note that the iv, id, and p sectors are delineated from the globus pallidus (GPi and GPe) by the ansa lenticularis (an). Original magnification ×5. Abbreviations: Hp, hippocampal formation; son, supraoptic nucleus. *From Mesulam and Geula, 1988, with the permission of the publishers.*

medial cortical areas; the Ch4al subsector is the major source of cortical innervation for the amygdala and the frontoparietal operculum; the Ch4i subsectors provide the major cholinergic innervation for peristriate, inferotemporal, and lateral frontoparietal cortex; and the Ch4p subsector provides the major source of cholinergic innervation for the superior temporal gyrus and the temporopolar area.

Not all cortical areas receive an equal density of cholinergic fibers. There is a much more intense cholinergic innervation in limbic and paralimbic areas than in association and primary sensory-motor areas. Cholinergic drugs may therefore be expected to have their greatest impact on limbic and paralimbic areas. This may explain why cholinergic agents seem to have relatively selective behavioral effects on mood and memory.

The acetylcholine that is released by cortical cholinergic fibers reduces the potassium conductance of the postsynaptic membrane and promotes the activation of cholinoceptive neurons by other excitatory inputs (Krnjevic, 1981). These physiological properties have led to the designation of acetylcholine as an excitatory neuromodulator. Limbic and cortical areas of the primate brain contain several different types of postsynaptic muscarinic and nicotinic receptors. The dominant species is the pirenzepine-sensitive M1 subtype of muscarinic receptor. The regional distribution of this receptor subtype shows a relatively good agreement with the regional distribution of presynaptic cholinergic fibers (Mash, White, and Mesulam, 1988).

All cortical areas receive cholinergic input, but only limbic paralimbic areas send substantial neural projections back to Ch4. This anatomical arrangement indicates that most cortical areas have no direct feedback control over the cholinergic innervation that they receive, whereas limbic and paralimbic areas have powerful feedback control over the cholinergic input that they receive and over the cholinergic input directed to other parts of cortex. The Ch4 complex may thus act as a cholinergic relay for rapidly shifting cortical activation in a way that reflects the emotional-motivational state encoded by the limbic system. A restricted corticofugal control of widely distributed corticopetal pathways appears to be a feature common to other transmitter-specific systems (e.g., monoaminergic) that are also implicated in setting global behavioral states.

Single-unit studies indicate that neurons in the nucleus basalis of the rhesus monkey are sensitive to sensory information that signals the delivery of reward (Wilson, 1990). Cortical cholinergic activity (with a density gradient that increases from sensory to limbic areas) is therefore expected to vary in a way that reflects the motivational relevance of extrapersonal sensory events. The response contingencies of cholinergic fibers and their regional density gradients suggest that they may provide a gating system for channeling motivationally relevant sensory information into and out of the limbic system. These projections may also participate in the temporospatial binding of distributed neural activity into coherent memory templates, especially when the corresponding event is motivationally relevant (Mesulam, 1990b). The memory impairments seen after experimental lesions in the nucleus basalis or after the administration of cholinergic antagonists such as scopolamine may therefore reflect a perturbation in sensory-limbic interactions and in the temporospatial binding of distributed memory traces.

REFERENCES

Arendt, T., Bigl, V., Tennstedt, A., and Arendt, A. (1985). Neuronal loss in different parts of the nucleus basalis is related to neuritic plaque formation in cortical target areas in Alzheimer's disease. *Neuroscience 14*, 1–14.

Gorry, J. D. (1963). Studies on the comparative anatomy of the ganglion basale of Meynert. *Acta Anatomica 55*, 51–104.

Krnjevic, K. (1981). Acetylcholine as a modulator of amino acid mediated synaptic transmission. In J. B. Lombardini and A. D. Kenny, eds., *The role of peptides and amino acids as neurotransmitters.* New York: Liss.

Mash, D. C., White, W. F., and Mesulam, M.-M. (1988). Distribution of muscarinic receptor subtypes within architectonic subregions of the primate cerebral cortex. *Journal of Comparative Neurology 278*, 265–274.

Mesulam, M.-M. (1988). Central cholinergic pathways: Neuroanatomy and some behavioral implications. In M. Avoli, T. Reader, R. Dykes, and P. Gloor, eds., *Neurotransmitters and cortical function.* New York: Plenum Press.

——— (1990a). Human brain cholinergic pathways. *Progress in Brain Research 84*, 231–241.

——— (1990b). Large scale neurocognitive networks and distributed processing for attention, language and memory. *Annals of Neurology 28*, 597–613.

Mesulam, M.-M., and Geula, C. (1988). Nucleus basalis (Ch4) and cortical cholinergic innervation of the human brain: Morphology, cytochemistry, connectivity and some behavioral implications. *Journal of Comparative Neurology 275,* 216–240.

Mesulam, M.-M., Geula, C., Bothwell, M. A., and Hersh, L. B. (1989). Human reticular formation: Cholinergic neurons of the pedunculopontine and laterodorsal tegmental nuclei and some cytochemical comparisons to the forebrain cholinergic neurons. *Journal of Comparative Neurology 281,* 611–633.

Ramon-Moliner, E., and Nauta, W. J. H. (1966). The isodendritic core of the brain stem. *Journal of Comparative Neurology 126,* 311–336.

Wilson, F. A. W. (1990). The relationship between learning, memory and neuronal responses in the primate basal forebrain. In T. C. Napier, P. W. Kalivos, and I. Hanin, eds., *The basal forebrain: Anatomy to function.* New York: Plenum Press.

M-Marsel Mesulam

Basal Ganglia

The telencephalon or endbrain in mammals is made up of the cerebral cortex, which forms the outer sheet of the endbrain, and subcortical structures, of which the *basal ganglia* form the largest group (see Figure 1). The basal ganglia include two well-known parts of the extrapyramidal motor system (the *striatum* and the *pallidum*) and also the amygdala (see "Amygdala" above). Most introductory treatments of the basal ganglia do not include a detailed consideration of the amygdala, for it forms a functional system quite different from the striatopallidal complex. These structures do, however, have direct and indirect interconnections with one another. Functionally, the basal ganglia are best known by the defects associated with basal ganglia disorders such as Parkinson's disease and Huntington's disease. These are movement disorders but have cognitive aspects as well. Indeed, abnormalities in the basal ganglia may contribute to some forms of neuropsychiatric disorder.

The striatopallidal complex operates as part of a system that receives inputs from the cortex (and thalamus), processes that information, interacts with modulatory loop-circuits, and passes the processed information on to the frontal cortex (via the thalamus) and to brainstem targets such as the superior colliculus and reticular formation. The main input side of the striatopallidal system is the striatum. For example, nearly the entire cortex projects to the striatum. The main output side of

the system is the pallidum, which gives rise to the system's outflow to the thalamus and has some descending connections as well. The most striking characteristic of these outputs is that they are inhibitory. The striatum-to-pallidum path also is inhibitory, however, so that activation of the striatum can *release* the thalamus and other output targets.

As the input side of this massive forebrain system, the striatum sets up some of the important functional subdivisions of the basal ganglia. The striatum has three anatomical subdivisions that roughly correspond to functional parts: the *caudate nucleus,* the *putamen,* and the *ventral striatum.* The caudate nucleus makes up the largest part of the striatum at anterior levels and receives strong inputs from the frontal cortex and some other areas of association cortex. The putamen is the large laterally placed nucleus of the striatum, and receives most of the input from the somatic sensory and motor cortex. The ventral striatum, which, as its name implies, lies at the base of the striatum, receives inputs particularly related to the limbic system (including direct projections from the hippocampal formation and amygdala). All three of these large subdivisions of the striatum project to the pallidum and substantia nigra, and there is considerable evidence that their projections are fairly separate so that channels set up in the striatum are maintained in the pallidum and substantia nigra and in their outflow pathways as well.

The striatum and pallidum act in close cooperation with two other nuclei, the *subthalamic nucleus* and the *substantia nigra.* First, the subthalamic nucleus (part of the subthalamic territory, which lies just underneath the thalamus) receives projections from the pallidum and sends projections back to the pallidum. The subthalamic nucleus is thought to be part of a powerful excitatory side-loop that increases pallidal outflow. This nucleus is damaged in the extrapyramidal disorder known clinically as *ballism.* The second nucleus allied with the striatopallidal complex is the substantia nigra, which lies in the midbrain and attains a very large size in the human brain. The substantia nigra has two parts, one of which, called the *pars reticulata,* is very much like the pallidum. The nigral pars reticulata is, in fact, judged by some authorities to be a differentiated extra part of the pallidum displaced caudally into the midbrain. The pars reticulata of the substantia nigra, like the pallidum, receives nearly all of its input from the striatum and the subthalamic loop, and projects strongly to the thalamus. An important difference

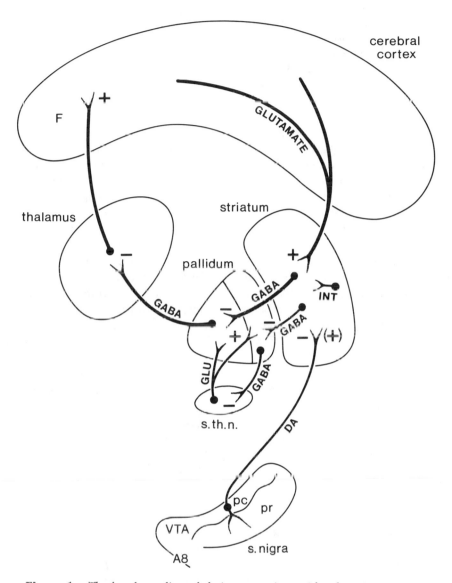

Figure 1. The basal ganglia and their connections with other structures. +, excitatory path; −, inhibitory path; GABA, γ-aminobutyric acid; GLU, glutamate; DA, dopamine; s.th.n., subthalamic nucleus; s. nigra, substantia nigra; pc, pars compacta, pr, pars reticulata, VTA, ventral tegmental area; F, frontal lobe; A8, cell group A8 (retrorubral area); INT, interneuron.

is that it also projects to the superior colliculus, a structure involved in controlling eye movements (especially saccadic eye movements).

The *pars compacta* of the substantia nigra is made up of neurons containing the neurotransmitter dopamine. In the normal brain, the nigral pars compacta neurons have long axons that ascend to the striatopallidal complex, where they principally innervate the striatum and release dopamine. In Parkinson's disease, these neurons degen-

erate, and dopamine is lost from the striatum. Near the nigral pars compacta proper there are other dopamine-containing neurons. In and near the midline are neurons of the *ventral tegmental area*, a region that innervates the ventral striatum. These neurons mostly survive in Parkinson's disease, but they have been implicated in reward circuits of the brain and are thought to be involved in some forms of drug addiction (e.g., to cocaine and amphetamine). There are also caudally situated dopamine-containing neurons (in the retrorubral region); much less is known about their connections. Serotonin-containing neurons also are present in the midbrain (in the raphe nuclei), and they send quite sizable projections to the basal ganglia and their allied nuclei.

Disorders affecting the basal ganglia are associated with major changes in neurotransmitter systems in basal ganglia circuits. Drugs affecting these systems include not only levodopa, given to Parkinson's patients as a "replacement therapy" for the lost dopamine, but also agents with powerful effects on mental activity and behavior, including antipsychotics such as haloperidol and psychoactive drugs such as marijuana. This broad range fits with evidence that the basal ganglia are not exclusively motor structures. The caudate nucleus, with its close ties to the frontal lobes, and the ventral striatum, with its ties to the limbic system, may be abnormal in such nonmotor disorders as obsessive-compulsive disorder and even psychoses.

Aspects of WORKING MEMORY and MOTOR SKILLS memory have been linked to basal ganglia function. The anatomical links of the basal ganglia with areas of the premotor and prefrontal cortex for which mnemonic functions have been suggested may support this view. Also compatible with this idea is the fact that the basal ganglia receive considerable input from each of the two main forebrain circuits implicated in memory functions of the forebrain: the hippocampus (see "Hippocampus" below) and the amygdala. The substantia nigra pars compacta (in addition to the ventral tegmental area) receives inputs from structures in the limbic system. The ventral tegmental area is known to function in relation to neural circuits mediating affect and motivation. The substantia nigra pars compacta may operate in relation to conditional aspects of movement, and may thus provide a bias mechanism acting on the striatopallidal complex.

REFERENCES

Evered, D., and O'Connor, M., eds. 1984. *Functions of the basal ganglia*. Ciba Foundation Symposium 107. London: Pitman.

Trends in Neurosciences (1990). Special issue on basal ganglia research. *Trends in Neurosciences 13* (7).

Ann M. Graybiel

Cerebellum

The cerebellum is absolutely essential for all normal sensorimotor activities. It participates in all organized postural and behavioral acts. Also, there is evidence that the cerebellum plays a crucial role in the learning of simple and complex acts and skills. If the cerebellum develops abnormally, or is injured or disabled (either experimentally or by disease), many striking behavioral abnormalities occur. For example, normal, everyday movements become incoordinated and clumsy, and they exhibit errors in direction, rate, amplitude, sequence, and precision. In addition, fine exploratory movements and simple, as well as complex, coordinated act sequences are drastically impaired or lost. Moreover, habitual postural adjustments deteriorate. How the machinery of the cerebellum contributes to normal, adaptive, coordinated behavioral sequences is not well understood. In searching for clues as to how the cerebellum works, it is essential to grasp rudimentary anatomical and connectional features such as are outlined below.

All vertebrates have a cerebellum (Figure 1). It lies behind the forebrain and on top of the hindbrain. It is a small, smooth protuberance in most fish, amphibians, and reptiles, but in birds and mammals it develops into a relatively large, folded structure. In birds and mammals, the surface of the cerebellum is folded into a complex arrangement of thin, elongated folia. Several folia are grouped into lobules that, in turn, assemble into larger lobes. The size, shape, and complexity of the cerebellum vary widely in different mammals, and it appears that the number, size, length, and grouping of folia are related to adaptive sensorimotor capability in some way. Thus, animals that have more complex behavioral repertoires that are modifiable by learning are likely to have a larger and more complexly convoluted cerebellum.

The cerebellum of the domestic cat is used in Figure 2 to illustrate some of the unique anatomical features of the cerebellum. A stained section just lateral to the midline reveals the highly folded cerebellar *cortex,* which consists of a three-layer sheet of neurons. Near the base of the cerebellum are several clusters of neurons of the *deep nuclei.* The *white matter* beneath the cortex and around the deep nuclei consists of numerous axon connections between the cortex, deep nuclei, and other parts of the central nervous system.

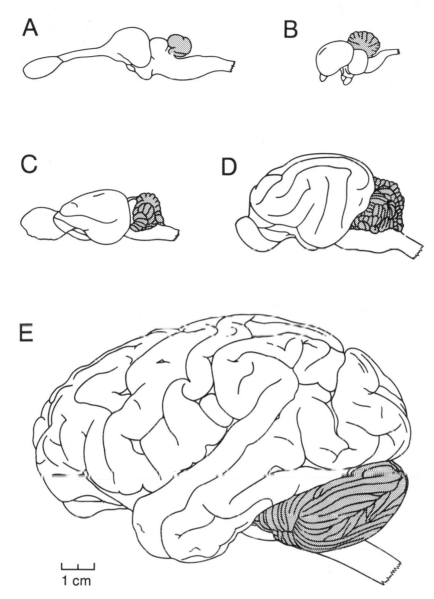

Figure 1. The cerebellum (in gray) varies widely in relative size, shape, and folding pattern in different animals: A, alligator; B, pigeon; C, opossum; D, domestic cat; E, chimpanzee. All brains are viewed from the left side and are drawn to the same scale. In the larger animals (cat and chimp), the cerebral cortex extends backward over the top of the cerebellum, concealing its greater size and complexity.

The cerebellar cortex is about 1 millimeter thick in all mammals. The total surface area of cerebellar cortex in humans is about 30 times greater than that of cats and about 200 times that of rats (Ito, 1984). The cerebellar cortex contains five types of neurons interconnected in highly organized, specific and stereotypic ways (Figure 3). The *Purkinje neurons* have the largest cell bodies and are distributed in a single layer (Figure 2) just beneath the outer fiber layer (*molecular layer*). Their axons are the only outputs of all integrative operations of cerebellar cortex. The thick dendrites of each Purkinje cell ascend and fan out in a flattened vertical plane into the molecular layer (Figure 3). These flattened dendrites are arranged at right angles to the long axis of each folium and thus also to the direction of parallel fiber axons in the molecular layer (see below). The *granule cells* are small,

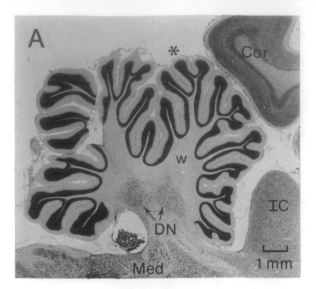
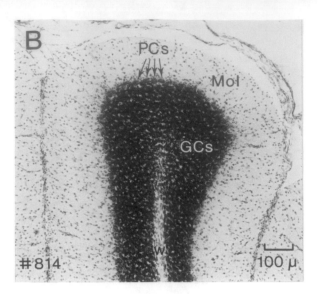

Figure 2. Stained 30-micron section through the whole cerebellum (A) and through a single fold or folium (B) of a domestic cat. In A the front of the brain is to the right, where cerebral cortex (Cor) overlies a portion of the cerebellum and an auditory center (inferior colliculus, IC) protrudes up in front of the cerebellum at the anterior part of the medulla (Med) of the brainstem. Abbreviations: DN, deep cerebellar nuclei; Mol, molecular layer; W, white matter (axons). The asterisk (*) in A indicates the folium that is enlarged in B. In B, the molecular layer consists mostly of parallel fibers as well as the dendrites (not stained) of Purkinje, Golgi, basket, and stellate cells. The large Purkinje cells (PCs) lie in a row just above the densely packed tiny granule cells (GCs). Magnification of each photograph is indicated by the scale bars.

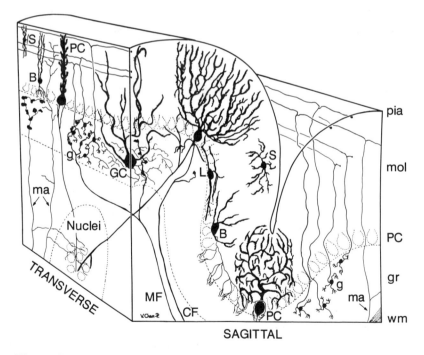

Figure 3. Schematic drawing of the major cell and axon types and their connections in a portion of cerebellar cortex. Connections to the deep nuclei (Nuclei) are also shown. Abbreviations: PC, Purkinje cell and Purkinje cell layer; B, basket cell; g, granule cell; S, stellate cell; GC, Golgi cell; L, cell of Lugaro; ma, monoamine axons; mol, molecular layer; gr, region of granule-cell layer; wm, white matter; pia, pia-arachnoid layer covering the cerebellar surface; MF, mossy-fiber input from brain-stem sources projecting into the granule cell layer; CF, climbing fiber input from the inferior olivary nucleus of the brain stem to a Purkinje cell. "Transverse" means a cross section and "Sagittal" means the plane from front to back. *Reprinted with permission from Chan-Palay, 1977, Fig. 15–22a; and from Palay and Chan-Palay, 1974, Fig. 5.*

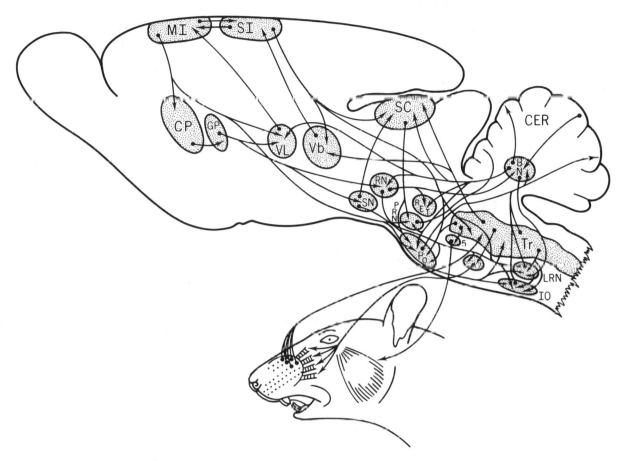

Figure 4. Schematic diagram of major (not all) somatosensory and motor circuits with which the cerebellum is directly or indirectly connected; shown on outline of parasagittal section of rat brain. This figure hints at the complexity of the systems and networks that are likely to be involved in relatively simple exploratory actions by the rat's face, mouth, and head. Most nuclei that project to the cerebellum receive inputs from the cerebellum, either directly or indirectly. For pictorial simplicity, many lines are drawn as diverging from a single source. These are not meant to signify collaterals. Abbreviations: 5, trigeminal (fifth) motor nucleus; 7, facial (seventh) motor nucleus, BN, deep (basal) nuclei of the cerebellum; CP, caudate-putamen nuclear complex; GP, globus pallidus; IO, inferior olive; LRN, lateral reticular nucleus; MI, primary motor cerebral cortex, PO, pons; PRN, pontine reticular nucleus; Ret, reticular nuclear complex; RN, red nuclear complex; SC, superior colliculus, SI, primary somatosensory cerebral cortex; SN, substantia nigra; Tr, trigeminal complex of the medulla; Vb, ventrobasal complex of the thalamus; VL, ventrolateral thalamic nucleus. Bottom drawing of rat's head depicts facial vibrissae pad as dots. Lines from the caudal vibrissae to Tr signifiy somatosensory afferents. Lines to the four striated bands at rear of vibrissae signify facial motor innervation from the seventh motor nucleus. Line to striped zone over the mandible signifies trigeminal motor innervation from the fifth motor nucleus. *Reprinted with permission from Welker, 1987.*

densely packed, and more numerous than all the rest of the neurons of the nervous system combined. These tiny cells form the thick *granule cell layer,* and their dendrites receive most of the pro-

jections to the cerebellum from many different sources in the forebrain, midbrain, medulla, and spinal cord (Figure 4). The axon of each granule cell ascends vertically, giving off synaptic connec-

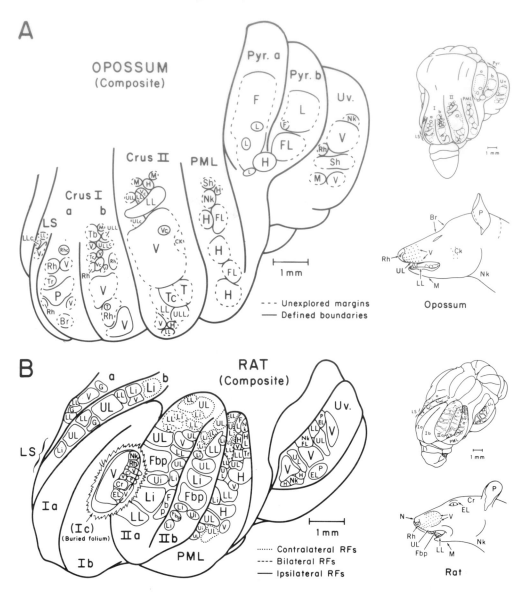

Figure 5. Schematic diagrams of fractured patchy somatosensory projections to the granule cell (GC) layer showing species differences as well as folial differences in mosaic projection patterns. The four brain diagrams portray composite patchy mosaic projections to the GC layer for A: a North American opossum (*Didelphis virginiana*); B: albino rat (*Rattus rattus*); C: domestic cat (*Felis domesticus*); and D: giant galago (*Galago crassicaudatus*). Note that the opossum (A) has tactile projections to all posterior-lobe hemispheric folia, including those of Crus I, whereas in the rat (B) two of three Crus I folia do not have tactile projections. In the cat (C), the folia of Crus I and most folia of Crus II do not have tactile projections, and in the galago (D), Crus I not only does not have somatosensory projections, but there are gaps between tactile projections in both of the Crus II lobules. Abbreviations of somatosensory projections: A, arm; Br, brow; Ck, cheek; Cr, crown; C, upper and lower canines; EL, eyelid; Fbp, furry buccal pad; F, foot; Fa, face; FL, forelimb; G, gingiva; H, hand; HL, hindlimb; L, leg; LC, lower canine; Li, lower incisors; LL, lower lip; LLc, contralateral lower lip; M, mandible; N, nose; Nk, neck; P, pinna; Rh, rhinarium; Rhc, contralateral rhinarium; Sh, shoulder; T, multiple teeth; Tc, contralateral multiple teeth; Tr, trunk; UC, upper canine; Ui, upper incisor; UL, upper lip; ULc, contralateral upper lip; V, mystacial vibrissae; Vc, contralateral vibrissae pad. Abbreviations of cerebellar folds: A_1, A_{2a}, A_{2b}, B_1, B_2, C, folia of paramedian lobule (PML) in cat; C_1,

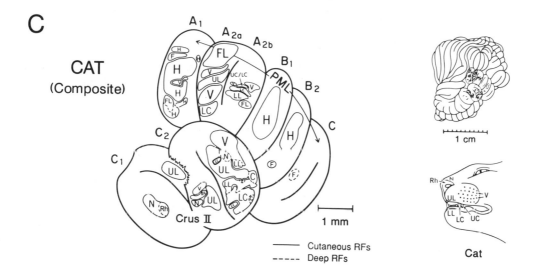

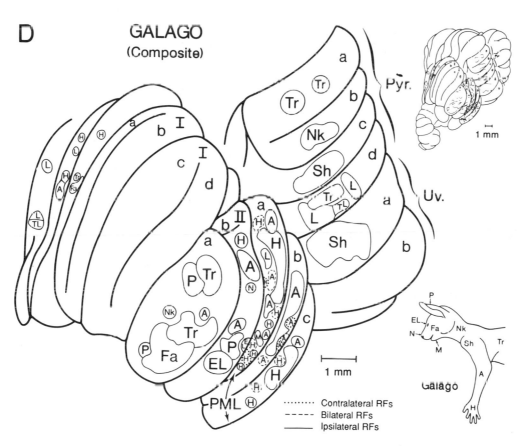

C_2, medial folia of Crus II in cat; Crus Ia, Ib, Ic, Id, folia of Crus I; LSa, b, folia of lobulus simplex; PML, paramedian lobule or its homologue; Pyr, a, b, c, d, four folia of the pyramidal lobule; Uv, uvula in galago. *Opossum composite (A) reproduced with permission from Welker and Shambes (1985, Fig. 3). Rat composite (B) reproduced with permission from Shambes et al. (1978, Figs. 2 and 6), Joseph et al. (1978, Fig. 4), and Bower and Woolston (1983, Fig. 1). Cat composite (C) reproduced with permission from Kassel et al. (1984, Fig. 6). Galago composite (D) reproduced with permission from Welker et al. (1988, Figs. 3, 5, 6, 7).*

tions to Purkinje cells. In the molecular layer, all granule-cell axons bifurcate and travel horizontally within the molecular layer in both directions along the long axis of the folium. These granule-cell fibers are called *parallel fibers* because they all lie in the same direction. The parallel fibers travel for variable distances, and in their course they make synaptic contact with dendrites of Purkinje cells, as well as with stellate cells, basket cells, and Golgi cells, all of which have their dendrites within this layer of parallel fibers.

Three major groups of inputs to cerebellar cortex exist: mossy fibers, climbing fibers, and monoaminergic fibers. *Mossy fiber* inputs to the enormous population of granule cells of the cerebellar cortex carry information from sensory receptors, but most originate from other parts of the brain, including some from the cerebellar deep nuclei. The peripheral circuits carry information from skin, muscles, tendons, joints, and other deep tissues throughout the body. Vestibular, auditory, and visual inputs also exist. In mammals with simple behavioral repertoires, the dominant mossy-fiber inputs to cerebellar cortex derive from sensory systems, but in behaviorally more complex mammals, the cerebral cortex contributes a greater number of cerebellar projections via the brain stem.

The pattern of organization of sensory inputs to the granule-cell layer of cerebellar cortex is organized into patterns of patchy mosaics in which different body parts send inputs to different spatially segregated patches (Figures 5 and 6). The patterns of somatosensory inputs to the granule-cell layer of cerebellar cortex that was defined in four different mammals are shown in Figure 5. All mossy-fiber inputs to cerebellar granule cells are excitatory, as are the outputs of these cells. The little that is already known reveals that the patterns of ascending and parallel fiber axons of granule cells are probably also patchy, highly specific, and localized. Inputs to granule-cell cortex from other parts of the brain also appear to be organized into patchy mosaics.

Another major source of excitatory inputs to the cerebellar cortex, the *climbing fibers*, arises from a single nuclear complex in the medulla called the *inferior olive*. These inputs are unique in that they make contact only with the flattened dendrites of Purkinje cells (Figures 3 and 6). These inputs align in sagittal strips on each folium, but they, too, contain patchy representations of different sensory surfaces. Activity of climbing fibers pro-

duces a short-lasting modification of the excitability of localized strips of Purkinje cells. These modifications are believed to be functionally important in the adaptive integration of sensorimotor activities (see below).

A third set of inputs to the cerebellar cortex arise from neurochemically specialized brain-stem cell groups. These inputs project diffusely and widely into the cerebellar cortex (Figure 3). They are *monoaminergic fibers,* which are capable of releasing specialized transmitters that probably modulate the activities of all cortical neurons in both excitatory and inhibitory fashion. They likely play a role in regulating levels of excitability or arousal within the cerebellum.

The large sheet of cerebellar cortex contains numerous specialized anatomical arrangements and connections of all its neurons (Figure 3). These orderly patterns of connections reveal that the cerebellar cortex is the major structure for integrating information arriving over a large number of different sensorimotor circuits. It is important to note that the granule cells are the only *excitatory neurons* within the cerebellar cortex. All others—the Golgi cells, stellate cells, basket cells, and the large Purkinje cells—are solely *inhibitory neurons.* The basket cells and the stellate cells send their axons into side loops that tend to inhibit adjacent Purkinje cells, but they do so in different spatial patterns. In addition, the Golgi cells exert feedback inhibition on localized patches of granule cells. Because of their interconnections, these different neurons selectively and differentially modulate one another's firing patterns in spatially discrete patterns. Moreover, because the cerebellar cortex is constantly being bombarded by mossy-fiber inputs to the cortical network, and because of the patterned geometric arrangement of afferents and efferents of the cortical circuits, complex ongoing patterns of activity are distributed throughout the cerebellar cortex in shifting spatial and temporal patterns, even during sleep.

The large Purkinje cells are the sole output of the cerebellar cortex and, being inhibitory, they tend to modulate the ongoing excitatory activities of neurons in the deep cerebellar nuclei, as well as of neurons of a vestibular nucleus of the medulla. The excitatory activity of these deep nuclear neurons is projected to several thalamic and brain-stem nuclear groups that are involved in sensorimotor networks (Figure 4). Since the large spatial array of Purkinje cells receives a constantly changing spatiotemporal array of excitation and inhibi-

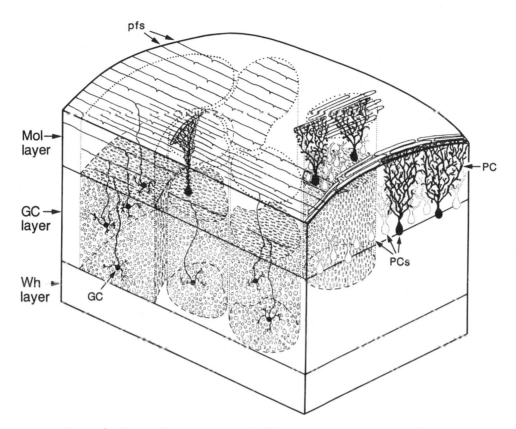

Figure 6.   Three-dimensional sketch of the conception that the uniform-appearing cerebellar cortex may be organized as patchy, columnar modules. This has been demonstrated for granule cells (GCs) and their overlying Purkinje cells (PCs). However, there is evidence that functionally distinct inputs from other sources may arrive within cerebellar cortex in patchy modular patterns. Although the interconnections among GCs, PCs, and the other cell types (not shown) may also be organized in restricted patchy patterns, very little is known about such functionally important possibilities. Abbreviations: Mol layer, molecular layer containing parallel fibers (pfs) of granule cells; GC layer, granule cell layer (only a few GCs are drawn, the remainder are shown as stippled circles); Wh layer, white layer containing arriving and departing axons.

tion of the kinds described above, the Purkinje cell sheet will deliver similarly complex inhibitory patterns to the deep nuclei and vestibular nuclei. There is accumulating evidence that spatially focused climbing fiber activity selectively modulates these shifting activity patterns of Purkinje cells in ways that promote the learned integration of motor activities. A great deal is already known about the anatomical circuitry of the cerebellum and of some of its major physiological attributes. Much additional research is needed, however, to disclose exactly how the cerebellum contributes to the smooth and orderly generation and maintenance of simple as well as complex performances.

REFERENCES

Bloedel, J. R., Dichgans, J., and Precht, W., eds. (1985). *Cerebellar functions.* New York: Springer-Verlag.

Bower, J. M., and Woolston, D. C. (1983). Congruence of spatial organization of tactile projections to granule cell and Purkinje cell layers of cerebellar cortex. *Journal of Neurophysiology 49,* 745–766.

Chan-Palay, V. (1977). *Cerebellar dentate nucleus: Organization, cytology and transmitters.* New York: Springer-Verlag.

Glickstein, M., Yeo, C., and Stein, J., eds. (1987). *Cerebellum and neuronal plasticity.* New York: Plenum Press.

Ito, M. 1984. *The cerebellum and neural control.* New York: Raven Press.

Joseph, J. W., Shambes, G. M., Gibson, J. M., and Welker, W. I. (1978). Tactile projections to granule cells in the caudal vermis of the rat's cerebellum. *Brain, Behavior and Evolution 15,* 141–149.

Kassel, J., Shambes, G. M., and Welker, W. (1984). Fractured cutaneous projections to the granule cell layer of the posterior cerebellar hemisphere of the domestic cat. *Journal of Comparative Neurology 225,* 458–468.

King, J. S., ed. (1987). *New concepts in cerebellar neurobiology.* New York: Liss.

Palay, S. L., and Chan-Palay, V. (1974). *Cerebellar cortex. Cytology and organization.* New York: Springer-Verlag.

Shambes, G. M., Beermann, D. H., and Welker, W. I. (1978). Multiple tactile areas in cerebellar cortex: Another patchy cutaneous projection to granule cell columns in rats. *Brain Research 157,* 123–128.

Shambes, G. M., Gibson, J. M., and Welker, W. I. (1978). Fractured somatotopy in granule cell tactile areas of rat cerebellar hemispheres revealed by micromapping. *Brain, Behavior and Evolution 15,* 94–140.

Welker, W. (1987). Spatial organization of somatosensory projections to granule cell cerebellar cortex: Functional and connectional implications of fractured somatotopy (summary of Wisconsin studies). In J. S. King, ed., *New Concepts in Cerebellar Neurobiology,* pp. 239–280. New York: Liss.

Welker, W., Blair, C., and Shambes, G. M. (1988). Somatosensory projections to cerebellar granule cell layer of giant bushbaby *Galago crassicaudatus. Brain, Behavior and Evolution 31,* 150–160.

Welker, W., and Shambes, G. M. (1985). Tactile cutaneous representation in cerebellar granule cell layer in opossum *Didelphis virginiana. Brain, Behavior and Evolution 27,* 57–79.

W. I. Welker

Cerebral Neocortex

The cerebral neocortex is the large overgrowth of the mammalian forebrain, the great complexity of which results from its division into many compartments of different sizes. These compartments are apparent at the grossest level, with the division of the cerebral neocortex into four large *lobes.* In the human brain, just behind the forehead and above the eyes is the frontal lobe, and at the back of the head is the occipital lobe. Between them are the parietal lobe, near the top of the head, and the temporal lobe, along the sides of the head. These lobes are easiest to locate in the brains of humans and other primates, where elongated crevices, referred to as sulci, divide the cortex into lobes, and the lobes into smaller units, called lobules.

Even at the very gross level of lobes one can make the powerful generalization that regions of distinct anatomy in the cerebral neocortex are sites of distinct physiology. Thus, exclusively within the frontal lobes are specific motor regions devoted to the planning and execution of movements; within the parietal lobe, regions devoted to the specific sense of touch; within the occipital lobe, regions devoted to vision, and within the temporal lobe, regions devoted to the sense of hearing. Each lobe also includes regions that are not specifically sensory or motor, referred to as association regions, which analyze sensory information to a greater degree or combine information from two or more senses. For example, in the frontal lobe is a region, the prefrontal cortex, which is closely associated with control of social behavior (see also PREFRONTAL CORTEX AND MEMORY IN PRIMATES).

The localization of function in the cerebral neocortex reaches an extreme in the human brain, where one region at the junction of the frontal and temporal lobes, known as Broca's area, serves to coordinate the movements of the mouth and tongue to produce speech ("motor speech"), while a second region at the junction of the parietal and temporal lobes, known as Wernicke's area, serves in the comprehension of spoken and written words ("sensory speech"). Destruction of either leaves a person incapable of speech (Geschwind, 1979).

All cortical lobes are further divided into anatomically and physiologically distinct *areas* or fields. Each cortical area is defined by the unique organization and physiology of the cells within it and by the unique set of connections the area has with other parts of the brain. All of these features may be specified early in development (Rakic, 1988). By even the most conservative estimates, some sixty areas of cortex can be recognized; they are usually designated by a numbering scheme. For example, the primary area of cortex devoted to vision is most often designated area 17.

The various areas of the cerebral neocortex receive and send connections to many parts of the brain. A two-way communication link exists between the cortex and a region beneath the cortex, the thalamus (Jones, 1985). This reciprocal link is very precise, so that one area of the cortex communicates with only one or two of the many

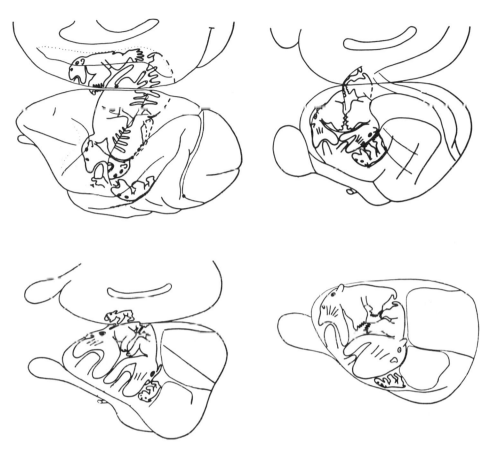

Figure 1. Sensory and motor maps of the cerebral cortex from monkeys (upper left), cats (upper right), rabbits (lower left) and rats (lower right) The drawings indicate the representation of the body surface in somatic sensory and motor areas. Note the large amount of cortex devoted to the face, particularly in rats and rabbits, and to the hand in monkeys. The brains of the different species are not drawn to scale. *Adapted from Harlan, C. F., and Woolsey, C. N., eds. (1958). Biological and biochemical bases of behavior. Madison: University of Wisconsin Press.*

collections of cells in the thalamus. In addition, each cortical area on one side of the brain has some connections with the same area on the opposite side. The connections to the opposite side are made by the axonal processes of cortical cells, which form bundles called the corpus callosum and the anterior commissure. Other, precise connections exist between cortical areas on the same side of the brain. Each of the precise connections with the thalamus, opposite cortex, and cortex of the same side helps to determine the unique physiological characteristics of a cortical area. More diffuse connections that go to all areas of cortex come from cells beneath the cortex that use the chemicals dopamine, norepinephrine, serotonin, and acetylcholine as neurotransmitters (see

also NEUROTRANSMITTER SYSTEMS AND MEMORY). These connections appear responsible for setting the overall level of activity in the cortex (Foote and Morrison, 1987).

A typical area of the cerebral neocortex is divided horizontally into six *layers*. As with layers in other parts of the brain, those in the cortex exist because cells of similar structure, function, and connections are grouped together and are segregated from cells with different properties. Areas of the cortex are also divided vertically into compartments that do not differ from one another in their structures but do differ markedly in connections and physiology. These vertical compartments are cortical *columns*. The key to the cortical column is that the cells within a single column are

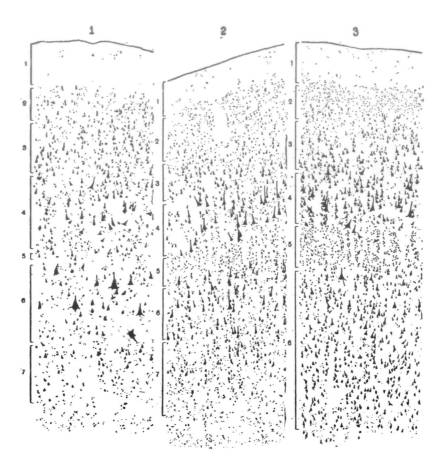

Figure 2. Drawings of cell structure and organization in three areas of the human cerebral cortex, including the areas primarily responsible for directing movements (numbered 1 at top) and for the analysis of touch (2) and audition (3). The dark shapes are cell bodies. In drawings 1 and 2, seven layers are designated (small numbers to the left of each drawing); more modern work shows that the ones designated 3 and 4 are parts of a single group, so that most areas of cortex have six layers. *Source: Campbell, A. W. (1905). Histological studies on the localisation of cerebral function. Cambridge: Cambridge University Press.*

interconnected so that all its cells exhibit a common physiological property, while cells in neighboring columns exhibit different properties. For example, in the visual area of primate cortex, cells that analyze signals from one eye make up one set of columns, 0.5–1.0 millimeters wide, and these interdigitate with a second set of columns containing cells that analyze signals from the other eye. Thus, cells in different columns are dominated by one eye or the other. These and other types of columns are the fundamental units of organization and function in the cerebral neocortex (Hubel and Wiesel, 1977).

The correlation of function with structure continues to the single cell in the cortex. Two general types of cells are present in all layers and columns. One, which has a triangular cell body, is called a *pyramidal cell.* This type is the principal source of axons that leave an area of cortex, carrying information to other cortical areas or to regions outside the cortex, while also communicating with other cells within the cortex. The second cell type has a rounded cell body and is called *nonpyramidal* or stellate. These are the major type of neuron concerned exclusively with local communication. The nonpyramidal cells are a very heterogeneous group and include one or two types of excitatory cells and several types of inhibitory cells. All of the inhibitory cells appear to use γ-aminobutyric acid as a neurotransmitter. From these excitatory and inhibitory cells and the interconnections they make arise physiological properties unique to the cerebral neocortex (Peters and Jones, 1984).

Although extraordinarily complex, then, the cerebral neocortex is understandable in terms of a general plan of organization, in which the great diversity of function is built up from the physiology of single cells to progressively larger compartments, including columns, layers, areas, and lobes.

REFERENCES

Geschwind, N. (1979). Specializations of the human brain. *Scientific American 241*, 180–199.

Rakic, P. (1988). Specification of cerebral cortical areas *Science 241*, 170–176.

Jones, E. G. (1985). *The thalamus.* New York: Plenum.

Foote, S. L., and Morrison, J. H. (1987). Extrathalamic modulation of cortical function. *Annual Review of Neuroscience 10*, 67–95.

Hubel, D. H., and Wiesel, T. N. (1977). Ferrier Lecture: Functional architecture of macaque monkey visual cortex. *Proceedings of the Royal Society of London B 198*, 1–59.

Peters, A., and Jones, E. G., eds. (1984). *Cerebral cortex*, vol. 1, *Cellular components of the cerebral cortex.* New York: Plenum.

Stewart Hendry

Hippocampus

The hippocampus, the most medial component of the cerebral cortex, is distinguished by the contrast between its relatively simple morphology and the complexity of information processing that goes on within it. This functional complexity is a reflection of the fact that activity associated with most, if not all, of the various sensory modalities converges upon the hippocampus, making it *polymodal association cortex* par excellence. From this perspective alone it should not be surprising that recent conjectures about hippocampal function tend to emphasize an important role in the formation of cognitive maps and/or the encoding of recent experiences in short-term memory and their possible transfer to more permanent storage in other cortical regions. Earlier suggestions that the hippocampus is an integral part of the olfactory system, as parts of the occipital lobe are an integral part of the visual system, have not survived experimental scrutiny.

Today's understanding of information processing in the hippocampus is based largely on the organization of the *trisynaptic circuit,* the anatomy of which was so clearly described by Ramón y Cajal toward the end of the nineteenth century. However, before outlining what is now known about this intrinsic circuit, or loop, and how it interacts with other parts of the brain, it will be useful to discuss the identity and topographical arrangement of the cortical fields most closely associated with the hippocampus.

Although opinions about nomenclature inevitably differ somewhat, for present purposes it is safe to say that the trisynaptic circuit serves to define the *hippocampal formation,* which can be divided into two major parts: the hippocampus proper and the *parahippocampal region.* The hippocampus in turn may be divided into the *dentate gyrus* and *Ammon's horn* (Lorente de Nó's fields CA_1, CA_2, and CA_3); the parahippocampal region contains the *subicular region* (*subiculum, presubiculum,* and *parasubiculum*) and the *entorhinal area.* In short, the hippocampal formation consists of at least eight distinct cortical fields. From a topographic point of view, it is important to appreciate that each field is, at a first level of analysis, a longitudinal strip of cortex and that these strips are aligned adjacent to each other like eight vertical boards in a wooden fence. In addition, the longitudinal axis of the strips has a roughly dorsoventral or septotemporal orientation, the precise orientation and curvature of which are species-dependent and related to the extent of temporal lobe development.

The transverse axis of each field, and of the hippocampal formation as a whole, is important because it is in this direction that the various axonal pathways associated with the trisynaptic circuit are rather strictly oriented. Beginning with Ramón y Cajal, the trisynaptic circuit was understood to consist of a pathway (the *perforant path* that cuts through the pyramidal layer of the subiculum, an unusual course for a cortical association pathway) from the entorhinal area to the distal dendrites of dentate gyrus granule (simple pyramidal) cells, which is relayed by the *mossy fiber* axons of these neurons to the proximal part of the apical dendrite of field CA_3 pyramidal cells, which send their *Schaffer* axon *collaterals* to the apical and basal dendrites of field CA_1 *pyramidal cells.* Ramón y Cajal emphasized that even for cortical structures, these

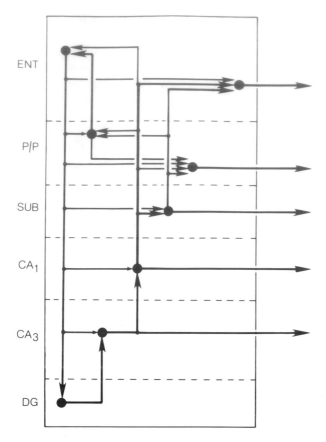

Figure 1. Schematic representation of the major features of the introhippocampal circuit on one side of the brain in rats. Abbreviations: DG, dentate gyrus; ENT, entorhinal area; P/P, pre- and parasubiculum; SUB, subiculum. CA1 and CA3 are two adjacent regions of the hippocampus. *Reproduced with permission from Swanson, Köhler, and Björklund, 1987, p. 247.*

and other hippocampal pathways demonstrate an unusually high degree of lamination along the dendrites of the projection neurons, and that the density of particular classes of terminals must be very great within particular zones; this has been amply confirmed by more recent work. For example, electron microscopic analysis suggests that perforant path terminals account for about 95 percent of the synapses on the outer two-thirds of dentate granule cell dendrites.

It should be obvious that the trisynaptic circuit is by itself an isolated chain of three pathways and that it must be embedded in a larger neural system. A useful view of the organization and functional significance of that system has only begun to emerge since the 1970s.

This breakthrough was initiated by the morphological demonstration of extensive bidirectional

connections between the retrohippocampal region and the cerebral hemispheres or isocortex, thus providing a sound anatomical framework for beginning to understand physiological demonstrations that hippocampal neurons may respond to information from each sensory modality. This isocortical information reaches all parts of the presubiculum and parasubiculum, as well as the entorhinal area, and clarifies one enigmatic feature of hippocampal anatomy: the major extrinsic input to the entorhinal area is from the presubiculum and parasubiculum. Until recently buried in absolute obscurity, the latter have emerged as a major relay for isocortical information to the entorhinal area, and as the origin of the fornix input to the mammillary body that had erroneously been ascribed to Ammon's horn for centuries.

Thus, the entorhinal area, the first link in the trisynaptic circuit, appears to act as a funnel for isocortical information to the hippocampus. The other end of the trisynaptic circuit, field CA_1, is now known to give rise to a dual output—one to the adjacent subiculum and entorhinal area, and another through the fornix to the *septal region*. The projection to the retrohippocampal region is interesting because it probably underlies the transfer of hippocampal information back out to the isocortex, while the descending projection to the septum feeds into the *ascending cholinergic system* as well as the descending *medial forebrain bundle* system (which may well play a critical role in REINFORCEMENT mechanisms).

In the broadest sense, then, the hippocampus may be viewed as lying between, and sharing bidirectional connections with, the isocortex on the one side and the septal region on the other. There can be no doubt that connections between the hippocampus and the isocortex are involved in the transfer and processing of cognitive information. The functional significance of massive connections between the hippocampus and septum is more problematic, but there is reason to suspect that they are related to the affective side of behavior—for example, in the reinforcement associated with the consequences of behavior.

REFERENCE

Swanson, L. W., Köhler, C., and Björklund, A. (1987). The limbic region. I: The septohippocampal system. In T. Hökfelt, A. Björklund, and L. W. Swanson, eds.,

Handbook of chemical neuroanatomy, vol. 5, *Integrated systems of the CNS,* pt. 1, pp. 125–277. Amsterdam: Elsevier.

Larry W. Swanson

Neuron

Cells of the central nervous system are divided into two categories, neurons and glial cells. The present paper deals with the characteristics of neurons in the vertebrate central nervous system. Neurons are independent morphological, trophic, and functional entities; they develop from the *neural plate of the ectoderm.* They differ from glial cells in their ability to generate propagated *action potentials* (spikes), in the release of neuroactive substances called *neurotransmitters,* and in their ability to communicate with other cells through specialized membrane junctions called *synapses.* There was a long debate in the first half of the twentieth century between those who maintained that the brain was a continuous reticulum of fibers and those who proposed that elements of the nervous system were discrete cells (for a historical account see Peters, Palay, and Webster, 1991). The first electron microscopic studies decisively resolved the issue by showing that each neuron is delineated by a continuous *plasma membrane* and is separated from other cells by a gap. However, like other cells of the body, neurons in some parts of the nervous system are interconnected through continuous cytoplasmic bridges organized into *gap junctions* that are permeable to ions and small molecules.

Neurons are polarized cells receiving information at certain locations on their plasma membrane and releasing neurotransmitters to other cells, usually from other sites (Kandel and Schwartz, 1985; Peters, Palay, and Webster, 1991; Shepherd, 1990). They emit several processes originating from the *cell body* or *soma.* One (occasionally two or three) of the processes is an *axon* propagating the action potential to the transmitter-releasing nerve terminals. The other processes are called *dendrites* and are usually shorter and branch less frequently than the axon. The shape and three-dimensional distribution of the processes are characteristic for each category of neuron and reflect their connections with other cells and, ultimately, the neuron's place in the neuronal network. The general arrangement is that information arrives through afferent (i.e., inward—transmitting) synapses on the dendritic processes and the cell body, and is transmitted to other cells through axonal enlargements, also called *boutons,* present on the axonal arborization. However, significant exceptions to this rule occur in some parts of the brain (see below). Neurons in invertebrates usually have only one process originating from the cell body that gives rise to branches, all of them both receiving and giving information and involved in different operations.

The Soma

The soma has a diameter of 5–50 microns and contains the nucleus and the usual cell organelles present in most cells, with great similarity to those present in secretory cells. This is in line with the observation that most neurons secrete proteins and peptides in addition to small transmitter molecules. For example, the rough endoplasmic reticulum (ER), the site of protein synthesis, is often highly developed and is organized into parallel lamellae forming large *Nissl bodies.* The *Golgi apparatus* is similarly highly developed and often extends into the proximal dendritic processes, which also contain ER and ribosomes. The axons are usually devoid of ribosomes and, together with the nerve terminals, lack the ability for significant protein synthesis. Thus the neuron is also a polarized biochemical machine where protein and other components synthesized in the cell body are transported through the axon to the nerve terminals.

The transport of molecules and organelles between the processes and the soma is bidirectional and is supported by the cytoskeleton, which also maintains the shape of the processes (see Kandel and Schwartz, 1985). The cytoskeleton consists of *microtubules* (polymers of *tubulin* dimers, external diameter 25–28 nanometers), *neurofilaments* (polymers of *cytokeratins,* diameter 10 nanometers), and *microfilaments* (polymers of *actin,* diameter 5–7 nanometers).

In addition to rough ER, many neurons are rich in smooth ER that is involved in intracellular Ca_2+ storage and release. Cysternae of the ER are often closely aligned with the plasma membrane of both the soma and dendrites forming *subsurface cysternae.*

Lysosomes are found in all neurons. Secondary lysosomes accumulate throughout the life of the

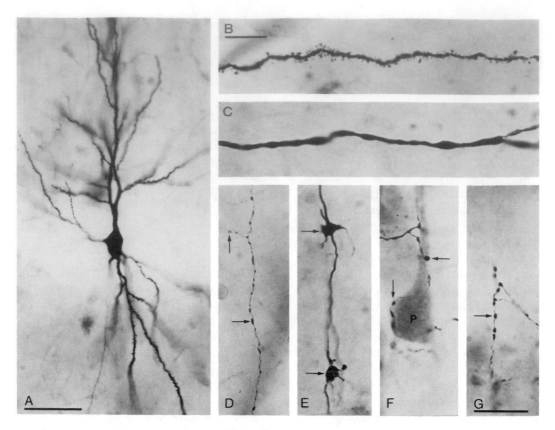

Figure 1. Parts of different neurons in the rat hippocampus shown in light microscopic photographs. The hippocampal formation is involved in memory formation. All cells were marked by intracellular injection of a marker molecule through a fine glass micropipette. The marker was transported to all the processes of the living cells. *Z.-S. Han, E. Buhl, and P. Somogyi, unpublished material.*

A. *Pyramidal cell* in the CA1 region emitting dendrites into two different layers toward the top and bottom of the picture; the two sets of dendrites sample different inputs coming from different sources. The light band in the middle contains the cell bodies of many more unmarked pyramidal cells. The rightmost dendrite is shown at higher magnification (rotated) in B, illustrating the large number of dendritic spines typical of these cells. C. Another type of cell, the *basket cell,* which has its cell body and dendrites in the same layers as the pyramidal cells, has smooth dendrites. Such dendrites have integrative properties different from spiny dendrites.

D–G. Terminal axonal segments of four different neuronal types, showing the differences in transmitter-releasing terminals (arrows) reflecting the specializations in synaptic connections. D. Axon collateral of a CA1 *pyramidal cell* similar to that shown in A. E. Two terminals of a mossy fiber originating from a *granule cell* in the dentate gyrus and making synapses with the apical dendrites of hippocampal pyramidal cells (not marked). F. Terminals of a *basket cell* surround the cell body and the main apical dendrite of a pyramidal cell (P), seen as a pale silhouette. G. The vertically aligned boutons of a *chandelier cell* form multiple synaptic contacts with the axon initial segment (not marked) of a pyramidal cell. Basket and chandelier cells release the inhibitory neurotransmitter GABA, but to different parts of the same postsynaptic cell. The pyramidal and granule cell terminals release the excitatory amino acid glutamate.

Scales: A, 50 microns; B and C, 10 microns; D–G, 20 microns.

cell and coalesce into *lipofuscin granules* showing characteristic distribution for each neuronal type.

The Dendrites

The dendrites are rarely longer than 1 millimeter and can be as short as 10–50 microns with a diameter of 3–0.05 microns, tapering toward their tip and decreasing in diameter at branching points. The main criterion that differentiates them from the axon is that dendrites lack the morphologically distinct initial segment (see below) at their origin from the soma. With the exception of peripheral sensory neurons, all neurons have dendrites. They are generally postsynaptic to axon terminals; from scores to tens of thousands of synapses converge on the dendritic tree of a single neuron.

In some parts of the nervous system, most prominently in the retina (amacrine cells), the olfactory bulb, the thalamus, the substantia gelatinosa of the brain stem and spinal cord, and the superior colliculus, dendrites of some classes of cells can be both pre- and postsynaptic. In these cases the dendrite at the presynaptic site contains synaptic vesicles and presynaptic membrane specialization as well as nearby postsynaptic membrane specializations at synapses received by the neuron. Often these combined pre- and postsynaptic sites are located on protrusions, grapelike clusters or gemmules, isolating the formations from each other on the same cell, and providing a basis for independent action. Synapses between two dendrites can be reciprocal, each partner receiving as well as giving synapses to the other at closely located sites.

Dendrites have various short postsynaptic extrusions, the best-known of them being *dendritic spines* (Figure 1). Spines are particularly prominent and numerous on cortical pyramidal and spiny stellate cells, on Purkinje cells, and on the spiny neurons of the neostriatum. Spines frequently contain a specialized organelle, the spine apparatus, consisting of parallel membrane saccules and continuous with the smooth ER of the dendritic shaft. The spine apparatus is thought to be involved in Ca^{2+} sequestration. Spines usually receive excitatory synaptic input and occasionally an additional inhibitory input. Numerous theories have been put forward for the role of spines. Of these, the formation of a biochemical compartment, semi-independent from the dendritic shaft and from other spines, seems the most attractive. The integrative proper-

ties of dendrites are determined by (1) their shape; (2) their intrinsic membrane properties, underlined by the presence and distribution of different *ion channels*; and (3) the location of synaptic inputs and their relationship to other inputs (for more detail, see Shepherd, 1990).

In addition to receiving and sometimes giving synaptic junctions, dendrites can also be connected to other dendrites and nerve terminals through small cytoplasmic bridges forming *gap junctions*. Gap junctions are sites of electrotonic transmission because they are permeable to ions and can facilitate the synchronization of neurons.

The Axon

Most neurons have axons; the few exceptions are retinal amacrine cells and granule cells of the olfactory bulb (Shepherd, 1990). Axons usually originate from the soma, rarely from a major dendrite, and begin with the axon hillock. A specialized trilaminar inner coat of the membrane, recognizable with the electron microscope, identifies the *axon initial segment*, which has the highest density of voltage-sensitive sodium channels. It is thought to be the site of the generation of the propagated action potential. Similar membrane undercoating is found in the axon at *nodes of Ranvier* between myelin segments. The other unique feature of the initial segment is the presence of interconnected microtubules organized into fascicles. In some regions of the brain the axon initial segment can receive numerous synapses. Such synapses are provided by the *chandelier cell*, a specialized inhibitory neuron unique to cortex, which makes synapses exclusively on the axon initial segment of pyramidal and spiny stellate neurons (Figure 2). Most axons emit several collaterals along their course addressing particular brain areas or groups of cells in the same brain area (Figure 3).

Myelin Sheath

The axons of neurons in the brain can be myelinated for part or for the whole of their course, or can be completely unmyelinated (Peters, Palay, and Webster, 1991). Some types of neurons, such as corticospinal cells and Purkinje cells, always have myelinated axons. The myelin is segmented, and each segment is formed by the plasma membrane of an *oligodendroglial cell*. Segments are

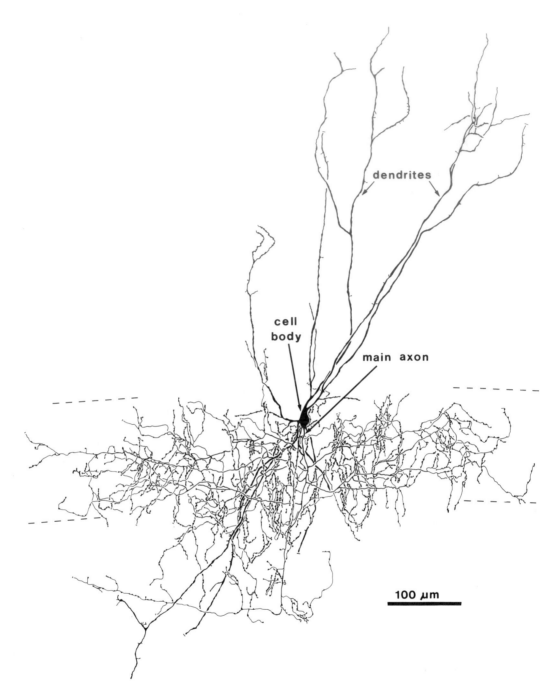

Figure 2.   Tracing of the processes of a local circuit inhibitory neuron, the *chandelier cell,* from the hippocampus of the cat. The terminals of this cell make synapses exclusively with the axon initial segment of pyramidal cells; therefore, the axon is localized mainly to the layer of pyramidal cell bodies enclosed by broken lines. Each vertically oriented terminal axon segment targets one initial segment; thus from this partial reconstruction it can be established that this single chandelier cell makes synapses with at least 320 pyramidal cells. The dendrites of the cell occupy the same layers as the pyramidal cell dendrites, so the cell has access to all the information pyramidal cells receive. The cell was visualized by Golgi impregnation. *Based on data in Somogyi et al., 1985.*

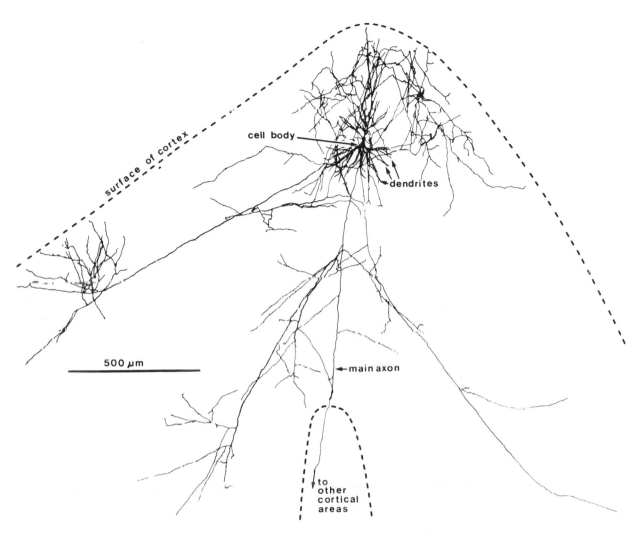

Figure 3. Tracing of the processes of a *pyramidal cell* in the visual cortex of cat. The cell body is in the superficial layer and emits dendrites reaching a few hundred microns. The main axon descends to the white matter (lower broken line) and proceeds to innervate other cortical areas. On its way through the gray matter it gives rise to several axon collaterals traveling for several millimeters within the same cortical area and addressing groups of cells with local ramifications while ignoring other groups of cells. The axon also richly supplies neurons in the vicinity of the cell body. Such selective connections enable effective coordination of neurons with similar properties. Having both a local axon arborization and a distant one gives the neuron both a local circuit role and a role in connecting different areas of the brain. The cell was visualized by the intracellular injection of a marker molecule. *Based on data from Kisvarday et al., 1986.*

interrupted by nodes of Ranvier, where axon collaterals often originate. The axons may acquire myelin for part of their course as they traverse a particularly heavily myelinated part of the brain. Axons may contain synaptic vesicles at nodes of Ranvier, and they may be presynaptic to neighboring dendrites.

Nerve Terminals

The terminal axon arborizations are characteristic of each cell type. The transmitter-releasing sites are bulbs or varicose enlargements having a diameter usually of 0.5–3 microns; they may have a position on the end of axon branches as *boutons termi-*

naux, or may be varicosities along the axon forming *boutons en passant* (Figure 1D–G). Many terminal boutons sit on the ends of short stalks branching off from main axon collaterals (Figure 1D, vertical arrow). Specialized formations of nerve terminals evolved, such as large mossy fiber terminals providing multiple localized input to the same target (Figure 1E), and climbing fibers providing multiple synapses distributed over the postsynaptic dendritic tree of the same target dendrite or cell. Boutons form *synaptic junctions* (see "Synapse" below). Boutons are usually only presynaptic to other cells, but terminals of a few cell types, most prominently the primary sensory afferents in the brain stem and spinal cord, may receive synapses and are postsynaptic to inhibitory terminals. One bouton may make synaptic junctions with only one postsynaptic element or may provide input to up to about ten different postsynaptic targets originating from about the same number of individual neurons. In some cases almost every bouton of the same axon establishes synapses with a different cell, providing a large degree of divergence in information transfer. Cortical cells, for example, may make synapses with thousands of other cortical neurons in a given area (Figure 3).

The boutons contain *synaptic vesicles,* which are membrane-delineated discrete structures. The morphology of the vesicles is characteristic to cell types and to some degree correlates with the chemistry of their neurotransmitter content. The two most common families of vesicles are the *small clear vesicles* with a diameter of 30–50 nanometers and the *large granulated vesicles* with a fine electron dense core and a diameter of about 80–200 nanometers. Boutons are also rich in mitochondria.

The synaptic vesicle–containing varicosities of some neurons do not establish morphologically recognizable synaptic junctions at all of their boutons. This applies in particular to neurons that use monoamines as transmitters.

Analysis of Neuronal Circuits

Connectivity patterns of morphologically identified neurons can be traced via the transport of marker molecules through the processes (see Heimer and Zaborszky, 1989). The active transport in the living cell can be exploited by introducing suitable tracers into the neuron that are carried to the dendritic and axonal processes (Figures 1,

3). Tracer molecules can be introduced directly into the cell or into the surrounding extracellular space from which the cell can take them up by an active process. It is also possible to label the processes of neurons that have been fixed with chemical agents (Figure 2). The visualization of processes makes it possible to identify the connections of particular types of neurons in the same area of the brain or between different brain regions. The morphological appearance of neurons reflects their patterns of connections. In many cases synapses from a given source terminate on certain parts of the neuron because the operation that the given input provides is best carried out in that part of the cell (Figures 1E–G, 2). Homologous parts of numerous postsynaptic cells in a given area of the brain tend to align with inputs arriving at that part of the cell, and this leads to the development of laminated structures. For example, axons originating from the CA3 region of the hippocampus terminate mainly on the main *apical dendrites* of pyramidal cells in the CA1 region, and the local recurrent collaterals of pyramidal cells in the CA1 sector address the *basal dendritic* region of the pyramidal cells (Figure 1A). The separation of inputs and the minimum amount of axon necessary to achieve addressing is ensured by the alignment of pyramidal cells.

The terminals of some neurons are all localized in the same brain area where the cell body is located. These cells play a role in the local processing of information and are called *local circuit neurons* (Figure 2). Other cells connect different brain regions or supply the periphery with their axons; these are called *projection neurons.* Many projection neurons also have axon collaterals within the same brain area where the cell is located, and thus play both a local circuit and a projection role (Figure 3). Accurate knowledge of the connectivity, especially in quantitative terms, is a prerequisite of establishing the operations taking place in real neural networks.

(See also MEMBRANE CHANNELS AND THEIR MODULATION IN LEARNING AND MEMORY; NEUROTRANSMITTER SYSTEMS AND MEMORY.)

REFERENCES

Heimer, L., and Zaborszky, L., eds. (1989). *Neuroanatomical tract-tracing methods,* vol. 2, *Recent progress.* New York: Plenum Press.

Kandel, E. R., and Schwartz, J. H., eds. (1985). *Principles of neural science,* 2nd ed. New York: Elsevier.

Kisvarday, Z. F., Martin, K. A. C., Freund, T. F., Magloczky, Z., Whitteridge, D., and Somogyi, P. (1986). Synaptic targets of HRP-filled layer III pyramidal cells in the cat striate cortex. *Experimental Brain Research 64,* 541–552.

Peters, A., Palay, S. L., and Webster, H. deF., eds. (1991). *The fine structure of the nervous system, neurons and their supporting cells,* 3rd ed. New York: Oxford University Press.

Shepherd, G. M., ed. (1990). *The synaptic organization of the brain,* 3rd ed. New York: Oxford University Press.

Somogyi, P., Freund, T. F., Hodgson, A. J., Somogyi, J., Beroukas, D., and Chubb, I. W. (1985). Identified axo-axonic cells are immunoreactive for GABA in the hippocampus and visual cortex of the cat. *Brain Research 332,* 143–149.

Peter Somogyi

Olfactory Cortex

The olfactory cortex is of interest to students of the brain for several reasons. It is the only part of the vertebrate forebrain to receive a direct sensory input. It is present in even the most primitive fish, retaining its place and form throughout the vertebrate series, thus suggesting that it is a core element in the basic plan of the vertebrate forebrain. Since olfaction is the dominant sensory modality in most vertebrate species, an understanding of olfactory cortical mechanisms can give insight into basic behavioral patterns underlying much of mammalian and primate behavior. The olfactory system is also one of the first sensory systems to differentiate and become functional during fetal life, so that it plays an important role during development.

Overall Structure

For an understanding of the olfactory cortex, we must have a clear view of its place in the olfactory pathway. This pathway and its constituent neurons was first revealed by the use of the Golgi stain in the later part of the nineteenth century. The pathway consists of three main parts (Figure 1). First is the olfactory sensory epithelium in the nose, containing the olfactory sensory neurons. These neurons transduce the stimulating odor molecules into impulses, which are sent over their axons in the olfactory nerve to the olfactory bulb, the second main structure of the olfactory pathway. Here the axons make synapses onto the dendrites of relay neurons, the large mitral cells and smaller tufted cells. These cells interact with interneurons in the olfactory bulb and send the processed information by means of impulse discharges in their axons in the lateral olfactory tract (LOT) on the ventrolateral surface of the brain. The axons give rise to numerous collaterals, which terminate in the third main region, the olfactory cortex, to make synapses on the dendrites of cortical pyramidal neurons.

The olfactory cortex is usually defined as the area of cortex in the vertebrate forebrain that receives direct input form the olfactory bulb. In most mammals, this cortex can be divided into six main regions (Figure 2). The main region is the *piriform* cortex (PC) (meaning "pear-shaped"; originally termed "prepyriform," and sometimes spelled "pyriform"). In most mammalian brains it extends over much of the ventrolateral surface of the brain dorsal to the LOT. The piriform cortex sends its output axons to several areas. One target area is the mediodorsal nucleus of the thalamus, which has connections to the prefrontal areas of the neocortex. This pathway is believed to be involved in conscious perception of odors. It is often claimed that the olfactory pathway is the only sensory pathway with direct input to the cortex, but it should be noted that this claim applies only to olfactory cortex; the relay through the thalamus to neocortex follows the rule for the other sensory modalities. Depending on the species, the piriform cortex also sends fibers to other cortical areas, such as the insula, where odor information may be combined with taste information to give the overall perception of flavor. Subcortical connections are made to parts of the limbic system, including the hypothalamus, hippocampus, and basal ganglia.

The other olfactory cortical areas include the following. The anterior olfactory nucleus (AON) is located just posterior to the olfactory bulb. It is a major station for integrating activity of the olfactory bulb with that of olfactory cortical areas on the same side of the brain, as well as of these regions on both sides of the brain, by means of fiber connections through the anterior commissure. This is an important point when studying split-brain patients, who can transfer olfactory in-

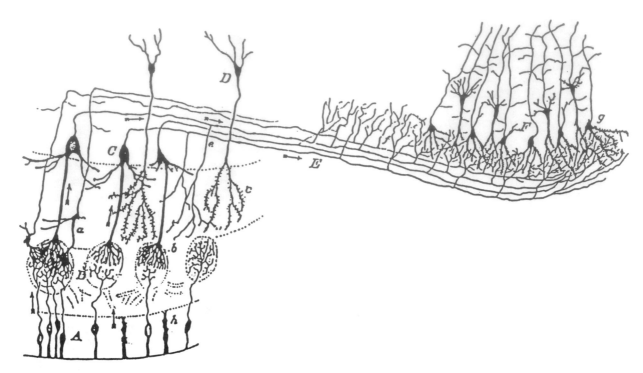

Figure 1. The main types of neurons and their connections in the olfactory pathway in the mammal. Relevant abbreviations: C, mitral; a, tufted; A, olfactory receptor neuron; F, olfactory cortical pyramidal neuron. *From Ramón y Cajal, 1894.*

formation by means of the anterior commissure. The olfactory tubercle (OT) in rodents lies on the most ventral surface of the forebrain, medial to the LOT. It is notable for containing clusters of cells called islets of Calleja and for receiving a heavy input of dopaminergic axons from the midbrain. Because of the implication of dopamine systems in various types of mental disorders (depression, sleep disturbances, schizophrenia), the olfactory tubercle has been studied intensively in rodents for its possible role in these types of disorders. Another target for olfactory bulb neurons is the amygdala. These fibers come mainly from the accessory olfactory bulb (AOB), which receives its input from the vomeronasal organ in the nose and is believed to relay information about chemical signals involved in mating in many vertebrate species. The AOB projects specifically to the corticomedial nuclei within the amygdalar complex, which in turn project to the hypothalamus, where they presumably activate some of the behavioral patterns in mating. The nucleus of the lateral olfactory tract (NLOT) is closely related to these amygdalar groups. Finally, there is the lateral entorhinal cortex (LEC). The entorhinal cortex is a major

region for multimodal integration of olfactory, visual, auditory, and somatosensory inputs; the output of this region is carried in fibers of the perforant pathway to the hippocampus, which is a critical region for storage and retrieval of information of behavioral significance.

Human Olfactory Cortical Areas

The regions of the rodent brain described above are similar in the brains of other mammals and some lower primates; in higher primates, including humans, there is sufficient modification in the forms and relations of the olfactory cortical areas to merit a separate brief description. In the monkey brain, the olfactory pathway appears much reduced in relative terms compared with the large forebrain, reflecting, it is believed, the reduced importance of the sense of smell. However, absolute numbers of neurons or fibers are not a reliable guide to the behavioral importance of a particular system; for example, the LOT contains many more fibers

A. Olfactory areas

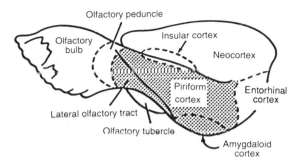

B. Olfactory bulb input

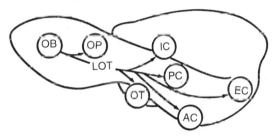

Figure 2. Schematic drawing of the main subdivisions of the olfactory cortex and their relative relations in the rodent. Not shown is the fact that different proportions of mitral and tufted cells innervate different subdivisions, and that connections between the subdivisions differ in extensiveness. Abbreviations: OB, olfactory bulb; OP, olfactory peduncle; LOT, lateral olfactory tract; IC, insular cortex; PC, piriform cortex; OT, olfactory tubercle; AC, amygdaloid cortex; EC, entorhinal cortex. Synthesis of studies by Price, Macrides, Haberly, and Shepherd. *From Haberly, 1990.*

than the auditory nerve, yet no one would say that hearing is unimportant in human life.

As a result of the overgrowth of the forebrain in primates, the olfactory pathway is entirely limited to the ventral surface of the brain (Figure 3). The olfactory bulbs give rise to a long LOT, which divides into three roots as it enters the brain. The lateral root goes to a cortical area at the junction of the frontal and temporal cortexes, which seems to be the homologue of the piriform cortex. From here there are connections to the prefrontal cortex, called the orbital cortex because it is on the surface of the brain facing the orbit of the eye. The medial root dives into a small area that, being pockmarked with many penetrating blood vessels, is called the perforated substance. This is more or less the homologue of the olfactory tubercle. The medial root includes fibers

that project toward or into the hypothalamus, whence there is a projection to the orbital cortex complementary to that from the piriform cortex. There are thus several routes over which information can be processed, through different olfactory cortical regions, to both cortical and subcortical regions.

The Basic Cortical Circuit

The main regions and pathways described above are like cities and motor routes on a map; however, in order to understand the basis of information processing, we need to analyze the structures within each region. A traditional way to characterize the organization of the olfactory cortex is by its layers. The olfactory cortex is the prototypical three-layer cortex, consisting of an outer "molecular layer" of incoming fibers and apical dendrites; a middle layer of pyramidal cell bodies; and an inner plexiform or polymorphic layer of basal dendrites, fibers, and interneurons. This three-layer organization is shared with the hippocampus, and

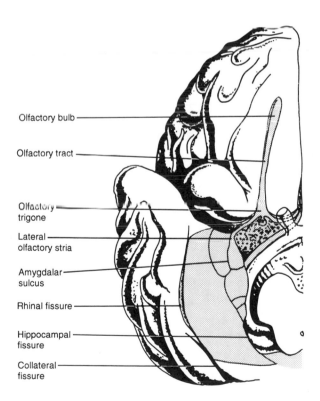

Figure 3. View of the basal surface of the human brain, with the olfactory cortex indicated by shading.

is traditionally contrasted with the six-layer construction of the neocortex (see "Cerebral Neocortex" above).

Research has enabled us to characterize these cortical regions in terms of their synaptic circuits; pursuing our analogy with a map, it is like going into the city streets, factories, and offices to find out how things are actually done. This information can be summarized by a basic circuit, which is defined as the minimum types of input fibers, output neurons, intrinsic neurons, and their connections sufficient to represent the most important functional circuits for information processing by a given region. For the olfactory cortex (see Figure 4), the main input elements are obviously the fibers from the LOT, which make excitatory synapses on the spines of the distal dendrites of the pyramidal neurons. The main output elements are the pyramidal neurons, each consisting of apical and basal dendrites, receiving excitatory synapses on their dendritic spines and inhibitory synapses on their dendritic shafts and cell bodies. The main intrinsic elements are two types of interneurons that make the inhibitory connections onto the pyramidal neurons. There are two main types of intrinsic circuits: a reexcitatory feedback circuit through long axon collaterals of the pyramidal neurons, and inhibitory circuits for feedforward and feedback inhibition of the pyramidal neurons.

This basic circuit not only summarizes the main anatomical circuits within the piriform cortex but also, with minor variations, applies to the other olfactory cortical areas; in addition, it is very similar to the basic circuit for the hippocampus. Moreover, it bears a strong resemblance to the basic circuit for the neocortex, particularly its superficial layers, as well as to the "canonical circuit" proposed for the neocortex on the basis of recent research. Thus, the basic circuit for the olfactory cortex is a useful model for correlating the general properties of all types of forebrain cortex.

Current studies are directed to characterizing

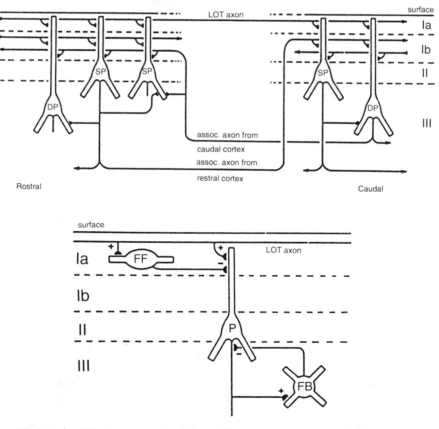

Figure 4.   The basic circuit of the piriform cortex. P, pyramidal neuron (DP, deep; SP, shallow); FF, feedforward; FB, feedback; LOT, lateral olfactory tubercle. Ia, Ib, II, and III are standard designations for layers of cortex. *From Haberly, 1990.*

the functional properties of each type of cortical element and synaptic circuit. Studies of development are aimed at identifying the stages at which different circuit components and types of excitatory, inhibitory, and modulatory neurotransmitters are expressed, in order to correlate them with the developing behavior of the fetus and the neonate. Studies of plasticity have indicated that the properties of the excitatory synapses made by the sensory input fibers from the LOT are different from those of the intrinsic reexcitatory collateral system; the latter give evidence of n-methyl-d-aspartate (NMDA) receptors, and are thus strong candidates for mediating the LONG-TERM POTENTIATION that is found in the piriform cortex. Computational networks based on the basic circuit model suggest that sensory inputs and reexcitatory feedback interact over extensive areas of olfactory cortex to provide a distributed parallel system; this gives insight into the mechanisms of odor discrimination, and may constitute a model for related types of pattern recognition by other cortical systems. Further knowledge of the structural organization of the olfactory cortex should provide a better basis for understanding these and other important aspects of olfactory function and behavior.

REFERENCES

Haberly, L. B. (1990). Olfactory cortex. In G. M. Shepherd, ed., *The synaptic organization of the brain*, pp. 317–345. New York: Oxford University Press.

Ramón y Cajal, S. (1894). *Les nouvelles idées sur la structure du système nerveux chez l'homme et chez les vertébrés*. Paris: Reinwald.

Shepherd, G. M. (1989). A basic circuit for cortical organization. In M. C. Gazzaniga, ed., *Perspectives on memory research*, pp. 93–134. Cambridge, Mass.: MIT Press.

Shepherd, G. M., and Stewart, W. B. (1985). The chemical senses: Taste and smell. In M. Swash and C. Kennard, eds., *Scientific basis of clinical neurology*, pp. 214–224. London: Churchill Livingstone.

Gordon M. Shepherd

Synapse

The nervous system is made up of billions of individual cells called neurons (see "Neuron" above), whose axons and dendrites form a complex fibrous network that permits the transfer of information in the form of electrical impulses between cells. The concept that nerve cells are independent functional units in the brain, and must form physical contacts to facilitate intercellular communication, was first proposed by neurohistologists at the turn of the twentieth century and is termed the neuron theory of brain organization. Implicit in the neuron theory is the assumption that neuronal processes do not form an uninterrupted labyrinth of intertwining nerves; instead, individual processes enter into close functional contacts to permit the transfer of information from one neuron to another. The site at which this transfer takes place is called the synapse. The term *synapse* is derived from the Greek word meaning "to clasp or fasten together" and was first used by Sir Charles Sherrington in 1897 to describe the specialized regions of neuronal membranes that are responsible for the transmission of information between neurons.

Before describing the detailed neuroanatomical features of the synapse, the following two paragraphs are included to provide a brief summary of the physiological characteristics of synaptic transmission in order to facilitate a better understanding of the structural-functional integration of individual synaptic structures.

In the central nervous system (CNS), the most common type of synapse is the chemical synapse. The distinctive feature of the chemical synapse is that information carried as an electrical impulse by an axon (presynaptic cell) is converted into a chemical signal at the axon terminal. The chemical signal, the neurotransmitter, is released from small membrane-bounded vesicles (synaptic vesicles) at the axon terminal and crosses a physical space or gap (about 20 nanometers) between the two neurons, called the synaptic cleft. The transport of the neurotransmitter across the synaptic cleft occurs by simple diffusion and does not require the use of an energy-dependent cellular mechanism. Upon arrival at the postsynaptic cell, the neurotransmitter combines with a protein embedded in the cell membrane that is specifically designed to bind with that neurotransmitter. This protein, or receptor, induces an electrical signal in the target cell (postsynaptic potential) as long as the neurotransmitter remains bound to the receptor. Subsequently, the neurotransmitter is deactivated by a degrading enzyme or taken back up into the presynaptic nerve terminal. In this way the transfer of information between cells is carried out through unidirectional electrochemical transduction between the presynaptic and postsynaptic cell and does not involve the direct transfer of an electrical signal from one cell to another.

Besides the unidirectional transfer of information, the chemical synapse has another characteristic that is fundamental to its physiological role. Chemical synapses may be either excitatory or inhibitory, that is, the neurotransmitter-receptor interaction either increases or decreases the electrical response of the postsynaptic cell. The terms *excitatory postsynaptic potential* (EPSP) and *inhibitory postsynaptic potential* (IPSP) are used to describe these events. Importantly, neither of these two postsynaptic potentials is sufficient to induce or extinguish an action potential in the postsynaptic cell. Rather, it is the sum of the postsynaptic potentials over a given period of time (temporal summation), from all the synapses on the cell (spatial summation), that will determine whether an action potential will be generated. Thus, information is passed on by an individual cell based on its total postsynaptic potential at any particular point in time. This signal integration by the postsynaptic cell constitutes the physiological basis of the neuron theory of brain organization.

In the CNS, the chemical synapse anatomically identifies the site where the neuritic process from one neuron comes into functional contact with a second cell and can be formed between any part of two neurons. The most common types of chemical synapses found in the CNS are between the axon of one neuron and the cell soma (axosomatic), dendrite (axodendritic), or dendritic spine (axospinous) of a second neuron. Alternatively, chemical synapses can be formed between two axons (axoaxonic), two dendrites (dendrodendritic) or the cell somata of two adjacent neurons (somasomatic). However, these types of synapses are less common in the brain and are not routinely found within the CNS.

Viewed through the light microscope, the number of synapses found on individual neurons can be examined by using silver staining techniques that outline the profile of the axon terminal adjacent to the dendrite or cell body of the target neuron. The number of axon terminals that synapse on an individual target neuron is not uniform across all areas of the brain but varies according to the brain region and cell type examined. For example, while granule cells of the cerebellum have only a few synapses, Purkinje cells of the cerebellum have several hundred thousand axon terminals

ending on their dendrites. Synapses on a single cell vary as to the origin of their presynaptic axon as well as the anatomical localization of the synapse on the target neuron. In addition, presynaptic fibers from specific regions of the brain may preferentially form synapses with specific parts of the target cell (soma, dendrite, or dendritic spine). For example, in the striatum 60 percent of all dopamine-containing axons from the midbrain (substantia nigra) form axospinous synapses with target neurons, while only 6 percent of the dopaminergic synapses are formed between the axon and the cell soma. In contrast, cholinergic neurons primarily form axosomatic synapses with striatal cells and rarely form synapses with dendritic spines. This differential distribution of a neuron's synaptic input influences how the synaptic input from one source will be integrated with the synaptic input from other sources. Thus, the anatomical distribution of presynaptic axons at various locations on the target cell, in conjunction with the summation of the excitatory and inhibitory postsynaptic potentials generated by these synapses, will determine the final effect individual presynaptic axons have on the target neuron.

Anatomically, the chemical synapse is composed of three elements: (1) the presynaptic element, formed as part of the presynaptic axon; (2) the synaptic cleft, ranging from 10 to 20 nanometers in width, which separates the plasma membrane of the presynaptic axon from the membrane of the postsynaptic neuron; and (3) the postsynaptic element, the specialized membrane component of the postsynaptic cell that contains the receptor protein. Both presynaptic and postsynaptic membranes have specializations or densities on their cytoplasmic surfaces that, together with the synaptic cleft, are defined as the synaptic junction. Based on the morphological characteristics of the synaptic junction, chemical synapses can be classified into two general types. Asymmetric synapses have a prominent postsynaptic density, giving them their characteristic asymmetric appearance; a widened synaptic cleft (20–30 nanometers), separating the two faces of the pre- and postsynaptic elements; and a synaptic cleft filled with amorphous dense material that binds the pre- and postsynaptic membranes together. Asymmetric synapses are also referred to as Gray type I synapses (named after E. G. Gray, who characterized them) and are often thought to be excitatory based on their electrophysiological effect on the postsynaptic membrane. In contrast, symmetric synapses have a narrower synaptic cleft, about 10–15 nanometers in width; relatively small amounts of dense material in the synaptic cleft; and a modest postsynaptic density that is approximately equivalent to its counterpart on the presynaptic side. Symmetrical synapses are also referred to as Gray type II synapses and are thought to be inhibitory in regard to their electrophysiological effect on the postsynaptic membrane of target neurons.

At the electron microscope level, the presynaptic element is seen as part of the presynaptic axon and represents that part of the presynaptic membrane which is juxtaposed to the postsynaptic cell. Presynaptic elements are usually formed as part of the rounded expansion of the tip of the terminal axon called the terminal bouton. However, presynaptic elements can also be formed by swollen expansions along the length of the axon, termed varicosities. In these cases the presynaptic terminal is termed a *bouton en passant* to denote the formation of a synapse between an axon varicosity and a neighboring target neuron as it courses through the neuropil to its final destination. In addition, presynaptic densities are arranged in hexagonal arrays that are spaced far enough apart for the small vesicles containing neurotransmitters to pass between them to fuse with the presynaptic membrane for the release of their neurotransmitter contents into the synaptic cleft. It is thought that this specialized arrangement allows the synaptic vesicles of the presynaptic terminal to adhere to these hexagonal arrays prior to the release of their neurotransmitter while the neuron is at rest.

In electron micrographs, presynaptic terminals are readily recognizable by the presence of mitochondria and numerous vesicles of various shapes and sizes (Figure 1). Mitochondria are thought to provide the energy necessary for synaptic transmission, and synaptic vesicles are considered the storage site for neurotransmitters in the presynaptic axon that are released from the terminal bouton in small quanta upon the arrival of the action potential. Synaptic vesicles range in size from 200 to 650 angstroms in diameter and are usually concentrated along the inner surface of the presynaptic terminal in association with the presynaptic density. Together, the presynaptic density and its accumulation of synaptic vesicles are referred to as the synaptic complex. Neurofilaments and microtubules are usually absent from the terminal bouton of most presynaptic neurons, and thus anatomically distinguish terminal boutons from small dendrites or glia processes. However, in *boutons*

en passant, neurofilaments and microtubules fill the central axis of the axon shaft or are concentrated to one side of the axon, away from the synaptic junction.

Because of the variation in the size, shape, and electron density of synaptic vesicles, numerous studies have attempted to correlate the neurotransmitter content of a particular terminal bouton with the shape and size of its vesicular content. However, while it is possible to make general categorical statements regarding the neurotransmitter content of a specific type of synaptic vesicle, it is impossible to identify specifically the neurotransmitter content of a particular terminal bouton based solely on the size or shape of its synaptic vesicles. For example, it is generally accepted that small, clear synaptic vesicles, ranging from 30 to 50 nanometers in diameter, contain one of several possible neurotransmitters—acetycholine, glycine, glutamate, or GABA—while terminal boutons that contain large vesicles, ranging from 40 to 60 nanometers in diameter, with a dense core, most likely contain one of the catecholamines—dopamine, norepinephrine, or epinephrine. In addition, presynaptic axon terminals that secrete neuropeptides have a heterogeneous population of vesicles, including large vesicles with electron-dense cores as well as smaller vesicles with varying electron density. It is believed that this mixed population of vesicles in some terminal boutons reflects the coexistence of two or more neurotransmitters or peptides in the same axon terminal that has been described in many parts of the nervous system. However, the functional significance for the coexistence of multiple neurotransmitter molecules in a single axon terminal is still unclear.

In contrast with the chemical synapse, an electrotonic synapse, also referred to as a gap junction, directly transfers electrical information via a nerve impulse between cells without the need for a chemical intermediary. These specialized synapses can occur between both neurons and glia and serve important modes of intercellular communication in the CNS. Morphologically, gap junction differs significantly from the chemical synapse in that the plasma membranes of the two cells are closely apposed to each other with only a gap of about 2 nanometers between them. In addition, gap junctions display little evidence of the dense membrane pre- and postsynaptic specializations characteristic of the chemical synapse and do not contain synaptic vesicles.

Physiologically, gap junctions differ significantly

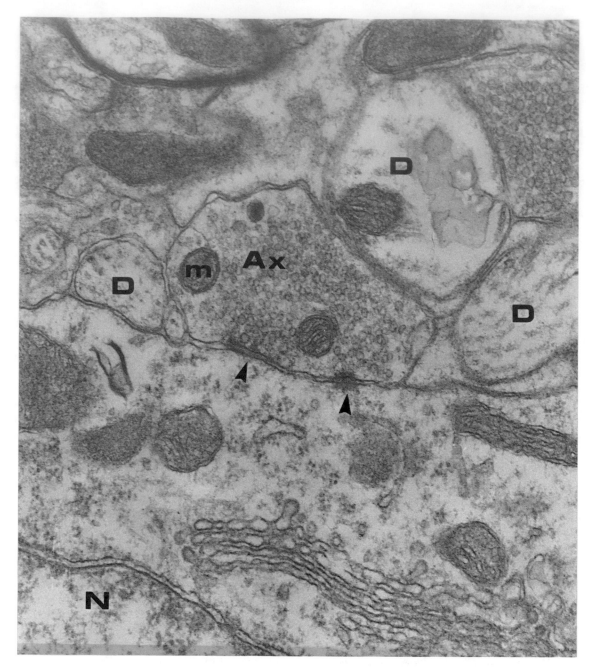

Figure 1.   High-magnification electron micrograph showing a presynaptic axon terminal (Ax) forming a symmetric synapse (*arrowheads*) with the cell body of a dopaminergic neuron from the pars compacta of the substantia nigra. The presynaptic terminal is filled with small clear synaptic vesicles and two mitochondria (m). N, nucleus; D, dendrite. Original magnification × 75,000.

from chemical synapses. Gap junctions are not uni-directional, in that an impulse can travel either way across the synapse. Also, the nature of the electrical potential induced in the postsynaptic cell does not depend upon the type of neuro-transmitter released from the synaptic vesicles because the potential of the presynaptic cell is transmitted directly to the postsynaptic cell across a region of low electrical resistance.

(See also NEUROTRANSMITTER SYSTEMS AND MEMORY.)

REFERENCES

Kandel, E. R., and Schwartz, J. H. (1985). *Principles of neuroscience,* 2nd ed. New York: Elsevier.

Kuffler, S. W., Nicholls, J. B., and Martin, A. R. (1984). *From neuron to brain: A cellular approach to the function of the nervous system.* 2nd ed. Sunderland, Mass.: Sinauer.

Shepherd, B. M. (1978). Microcircuits in the nervous system. *Scientific American 238,* 92–103.

———— (1979). *The synaptic organization of the brain,* 2nd ed. New York: Oxford University Press.

Peters, A., Palay, S. L., and Webster, H. deF. (1976). *The fine structure of the nervous system: The neurons and supporting cells.* Philadelphia: Saunders.

Thomas H. McNeill
Jonathan R. Day

Figure 1. Edwin R. Guthrie.

GUTHRIE, EDWIN R.

Edwin Ray Guthrie (1886–1959), a distinguished psychologist, spent most of his professional career at the University of Washington, where he served as an instructor in philosophy from 1914 to 1918 and as an assistant professor for a year, before he joined the department of psychology as an assistant professor. He was promoted to associate professor in 1925 and was made a professor in 1928. During World War II he served in Washington, D.C., as chief (civilian) consultant to the overseas branch of the general staff in 1941, and as chief psychologist of the overseas branch of the Office of War Information in 1942. Upon his return to the University of Washington he was named dean of the graduate school from 1943 until he reached retirement age in 1951. He was honored by having a campus building named for him while he was still alive. Among his other honors was an honorary LL.D. from his alma mater, the University of Nebraska, where he had received his A.B. in 1907, his A.M. in 1910, and his Ph.D. in 1912 (under Edgar A. Singer, a philosopher whom he much admired and whose views continued to influence his thinking). In 1945, the year he received the LL.D., Guthrie was elected president of the American Psychological Association. In 1958, the year before his death, he received the Gold Medal of the American Psychological Foundation, awarded for "outstanding lifetime contribution to psychology."

Guthrie was born December 9, 1886, in Lincoln, Nebraska, the eldest of five children of Edwin R. Guthrie and Harriett Pickett Guthrie. His father, the son of a clergyman, managed a piano store; his mother, the daughter of a newspaperman, taught elementary school prior to her marriage. In 1920 Edwin married Helen Macdonald, who helped him translate Pierre Janet's *Principles of Psychotherapy* (1924). Their son, Peter M. Guthrie (b. 1926), followed in his father's footsteps and became a professor of psychology (and department head) at Carleton College.

Although Guthrie had already published two short philosophical papers in the *Midwest Quarterly,* his first major publication was his Ph.D. dissertation on Bertrand Russell, which appeared as a monograph (Guthrie, 1915). Once he became a psychologist, he published chiefly in outlets for psychology, although some aspects of his psychological work appeared in *Journal of Philosophy* (e.g., Guthrie, 1924) and in a collection of philosophical essays (Guthrie, 1942). In other words, he never forgot his affiliation with philosophy. Because of his primary interest in learning and motivation, he had a scientific interest in education (Guthrie, 1945, 1949, 1959a; Guthrie and Powers, 1950).

Guthrie's philosophy mentor, Edgar Singer, had written an article titled "Mind as an Observable Object" (Singer, 1911). His point of view prepared Guthrie for a behaviorist orientation prior to John B. WATSON's announcement of BEHAVIORISM (Watson, 1913). It was not too surprising, therefore, that his early text *General Psychology in Terms of Behavior,* written in collaboration with Stevenson Smith, his senior colleague and friend at the University of Washington (Smith and Guthrie, 1921), should have stressed behavior and introduced to a wider audience the type of CONDITIONING as an interpretation of learning that was carried on particularly by Guthrie (e.g., Guthrie, 1930, 1960). At least among later students at the University of Washington, the theory was known as Guthrie's, regardless of whatever role Smith may have played earlier.

Guthrie's students became *imprinted* with this theory, and its influence upon them is recalled to this day. Guthrie developed his theory through a charming writing style, with an emphasis upon convincing examples rather than experimental demonstration. The most convincing experimental demonstration took place many years after the theory was first announced (Guthrie and Horton, 1946), and 11 years after the first edition of his *Psychology of Learning* (1935). But this gets ahead of the story.

Much of American psychology had long emphasized learning as a fundamental psychological process. What we are competent to do or learn may be considered a combination of what we are born with and capacities that develop as a matter of natural growth processes. Children all over the world, if given the opportunity, learn to crawl before they learn to walk, but healthy children require little instruction to achieve this skill. Other things they have to learn with assistance. While there is doubtless some natural tendency to babble, and hence to speak, in order to speak the artificial language that their home environment demands, children obviously have to learn the words that they hear and gradually to understand and talk in sentences. So the problem for the psychology of learning is how they acquire speech, reading, writing, and arithmetic. These cannot be entirely inborn, although one child may have more potential—that is, may be brighter—than another, and hence a more accomplished learner.

One of the early and persistent theories of learning was known as the doctrine of association: that one word (or one idea) became associated with another, just as the name becomes associated with the object named or a skilled action becomes associated with the task performed, as when a hammer is used to pound a nail. (See also ASSOCIATIONISM.)

There developed theories of how such associations came about. One widespread theory assumed that there were three laws of association: the laws of similarity, contrast, and contiguity. These are familiar enough. Many animals are four-footed, so the child easily learns to group a cat, a dog, and a cow as animals through their similarities. At first the class is narrow, and the first lamb observed may be thought to be a different kind of dog. But associations get to be corrected, both by discrimination and by generalization over a wider range. A fish and a duck do not at first seem to be like other animals—at least they do not have four feet—but they are alive and breathe and move about, and similarities such as these permit them eventually to be included as animals.

The law of contrast operates in a corresponding way, and the child soon learns that day contrasts with night, up with down, and large with small. Thus the contrasting pairs become associated, and one may suggest the other: day-night, up-down, large-small, and many other such pairs.

The third law of association in this scheme is that things that occur together—that is, in contiguity—become associated. Hence a color name may suggest an object often of that color—a red apple or a red tomato, or the contiguity may be more emphasized, as in an orange orange, where name and object are kept together.

Another idea that entered into early learning theory was that the consequences of an act, either pleasurable or painful, would affect the associations formed, as in "The burned child fears the fire" or "Nothing succeeds like success."

This particular kind of theory was further extended by assuming that a child would develop certain preferences (hence activities to be enjoyed) and also some annoyances (to be avoided). These were elaborated into theories of motivation—how our goals affect what we do, and how they are tied to theories of learning based on the sensible notions that we learn what gives us pleasure by satisfying our wants and that we hesitate to learn tasks that lead to results that we dislike.

A new theory came along when the Russian scientist Ivan PAVLOV introduced the idea of a *conditioned reflex* (CR). The standard experiment was to present a *conditioned stimulus* (CS) to a dog, say the turning on of a light. This was indifferent to the dog in that it did not start the flow of saliva, which was to become the *conditioned reflex* (CR). Following the CS, the flow of saliva was produced as an unconditioned reflex (UR) by a natural *unconditioned stimulus* (US), such as some meat powder in a dish accessible to the dog and attached to an apparatus designed to measure the flow of saliva. After the two stimuli (CS) and (US) were repeated several times, the CS would yield the original UR as a newly learned CR. It is easy to see that the CR can also be described as a form of associative learning, but the experimental setting in which it was achieved gave rather good controls over some circumstances favorable to learning.

It soon became clear that all that gets conditioned is *not* simple reflexes, such as the salivary reflex to food in the mouth, and many psychologists began talking about conditioned responses instead of conditioned reflexes (Hilgard and Marquis, 1940). This is where Guthrie came in. He had some disagreements with Pavlov that need not concern us here, and proposed his own interpretation of conditioning.

Guthrie proposed to reduce the laws of association (and the other theories of learning) to a single law of association by contiguity. He pointed out that similarity and contrast were effective only because of their occurrence together, and then interpreted the other theories of motivated learning and of conditioned response by his one principle appropriate to all instances of learning: "A combination of stimuli which has accompanied a movement will on its recurrence tend to be followed by that movement." [Note that Guthrie does not limit the stimulating condition to a single stimulus (S), nor the movement to a precise reflex as a response (R).] A slight revision was introduced later, to give some credit to attentive processes. Guthrie suggested that his basic law might alternatively be stated as "What is being noticed becomes a signal for what is being done" (Guthrie, 1959b).

A second statement is needed before his theory can be understood: "A stimulus pattern gains its full associative strength on its first pairing with a response." This is a remarkably parsimonious basic theory. Guthrie elaborated it to explain many puzzling problems of learning and forgetting.

Learning with repetition leads to the usual "learning curve" because a skilled response becomes conditioned to a variety of cues, so that as learning proceeds, the proportion of cues—internal and external—that have become conditioned, each on a single trial, increases the probability that the intended responses will occur, but a limit is approached as nearly all the cues become conditioned. (See also REPETITION AND LEARNING.)

Guthrie gave a cogent analogy of how the probability model works. He told of an artist whose meager income derived sporadically from the sale of his pictures. In order not to live beyond his means, he converted his cash to dimes that he scattered about the messy floor of his studio. When he needed money for a meal, he could at first easily find enough dimes; but as the dimes became used up, it was harder and harder to find more than enough for a very modest meal. The difficulty became greater and greater as the dimes were used up, but by diligent searching he could find enough to keep him going until he made another sale.

Much later, Estes (1950) developed a stimulus sampling mathematical theory of learning that followed much the same logic of one-trial learning leading to higher achievement as stimuli were assimilated to response, but again approaching an asymptote after most available stimuli had been used up.

Guthrie's theory was given a more formal statement by his student V. W. Voeks (1950), and in the area of learning theory and experimentation others of his students have shown the direct influence of what they learned from him (e.g., Sheffield, 1961).

REFERENCES

Estes, W. K. (1950). Toward a statistical theory of learning. *Psychological Review 57,* 94–107.

Guthrie, E. R. (1915). *The paradoxes of Mr. Russell: With a brief account of their history.* Lancaster, Pa.: New Era Printing.

———— (1924). Purpose and mechanism in psychology. *Journal of Philosophy 21,* 673–682.

———— (1930). Conditioning as a principle of learning. *Psychological Review 37,* 412–428.

———— (1942). Conditioning: A theory of learning in terms of stimulus, response, and association. *Yearbook, National Society for the Study of Education 41,* pt. 2, 17–60.

———— (1945). The evaluation of faculty service. *Bulletin. American Association of University Professors 31,* 255–262.

———— (1949). The evaluation of teaching. *Educational Record 30,* 109–115.

———— (1959a). *The state university: Its function and its future.* Seattle: University of Washington Press.

———— (1959b). Association by contiguity. In S. Koch, ed., *Psychology: A study of a science,* vol. 2, pp. 158–195. New York: McGraw-Hill.

———— (1960). *The psychology of learning,* rev. ed. Gloucester, Mass.: Smith. (Originally published 1935).

Guthrie, E. R., and Horton, G. P. (1946). *Cats in a puzzle box.* New York: Rinehart.

Guthrie, E. R., and Powers, F. F. (1950). *Educational psychology.* New York: Ronald Press.

Hilgard, E. R., and Marquis, D. G. (1940). *Conditioning and learning.* New York: Appleton-Century.

Janet, P. (1924). *Principles of psychotherapy,* trans. H. M. Guthrie and E. R. Guthrie. New York: Macmillan.

Sheffield, F. D. (1961). "Theoretical considerations in the learning of complex sequential tasks from demonstration and practice. In A. A. Lumsdaine, ed., *Student expectations in programmed instruction,* pp. 13–32. Washington, D.C.: National Academy of Sciences/National Research Council.

Singer, E. A. (1911). Mind as an observable object. *Journal of Philosophy, Psychology and Scientific Method 8,* 180–186.

Smith, S., and Guthrie, E. R. (1921). *General psychology in terms of behavior.* New York: Appleton.

Voeks, V. W. (1950). Formalization and clarification of a theory of learning. *Journal of Psychology 30,* 341–362.

Watson, J. B. (1913). Psychology as the behaviorist views it. *Psychological Review 20,* 158–177.

Ernest R. Hilgard

HABITUATION AND SENSITIZATION IN VERTEBRATES

When a ringing bell is presented to a cat, it may evoke a turning of the head toward the sound source. If that same stimulus is repeated over and over again, the probability and magnitude of this orienting response decrease. This phenomenon is called *habituation*. If a mouse now runs in front of the cat and then the bell is presented again, the cat may reorient to the bell. This phenomenon is called *dishabituation*. By recording electrical activity in the first central synapse in the auditory system, or by using another stimulus that elicits an orienting response of the same size, it can be shown that habituation cannot be explained by either sensory adaptation or muscle fatigue (cf. Thompson and Spencer, 1966). Thus, even though the original response no longer occurs, the stimulus still evokes the same electrical activity in early auditory structures as it did before and the original response can be fully elicited by a different stimulus or the same stimulus following dishabituation (e.g., the bell after the mouse ran by). Hence, the decrement in response strength must result from a synaptic change somewhere within the nervous system, and this change is specific to the stimulus that was presented repetitively.

Habituation has been the subject of a great deal of empirical investigation because practically every organism displays habituation, even those with very primitive nervous systems (Harris, 1943). In reviewing this literature, Thompson and Spencer (1966, pp. 18–19) enumerated nine parametric features of habituation and dishabituation that can be seen in a variety of organisms:

1. Given that a particular stimulus elicits a response, repeated applications of the stimulus result in decreased response (habituation). The decrease is usually a negative exponential function of the number of stimulus presentations.

2. If the stimulus is withheld, the response tends to recover over time (spontaneous recovery).

3. If repeated series of habituation training and spontaneous recovery are given, habituation becomes successively more rapid (this might be called potentiation of habituation).

4. Other things being equal, the more rapid the frequency of stimulation, the more rapid and/or more pronounced is habituation.

5. The weaker the stimulus, the more rapid and/or more pronounced is habituation. Strong stimuli may yield no significant habituation.

6. The effects of habituation training may proceed beyond the zero or asymptotic response level [i.e., additional habituation training given after the response has disappeared or reached asymptote will result in slower recovery].

7. Habituation of response to a given stimulus exhibits stimulus generalization to other stimuli.

8. Presentation of another (usually strong) stimulus results in recovery of the habituated response (dishabituation).

9. Upon repeated application of the dishabituatory stimulus, the amount of dishabituation produced habituates (this might be called habituation of dishabituation).

Thompson and Spencer's extremely influential review gave investigators working in diverse areas an explicit operational definition of habituation against which to test plasticity (change in response output with experience) in their particular preparations. In addition, it led to the general belief that habituation might be mediated by a single, fundamental mechanism inherent to most organisms across the phylogenetic scale.

Other experiments indicated, however, that the way in which one interrogates an animal can determine these parametric relationships. For example, the probability or amplitude of response is generally larger, the higher the intensity of the eliciting stimulus. It is not surprising, therefore, that it takes longer to reach a low level of response with intense, as opposed to weak, stimulus intensities. However, if the effects of prior exposure to strong and weak stimuli are subsequently evaluated, when all animals are tested with a common stimulus intensity, the magnitude of response change is actually greater following strong, as opposed to weak, stimuli (Davis and Wagner, 1968). Similarly, the probability of response is generally lower, the shorter the interval from an immediately prior stimulus. This leads to a rapid rate of response decrement when stimuli are presented at short, rather than long, interstimulus intervals. However, when animals are subsequently tested under conditions where the interstimulus interval is *identical* for all animals, prior exposure with long interstimulus intervals actually produces a greater decrease in response strength (Davis, 1970). On the one hand, habituation (i.e., the change in response during stimulus repetition) seems to be greater with weak stimuli presented at short intervals (e.g., Thompson and Spencer, 1966), but on the other, habituation (i.e., the change in response strength following stimulus repetition) seems to be greater with strong stimuli presented at long intervals (Davis, 1970; Davis and Wagner, 1968).

These disparities illustrate how the term habituation has been used to denote the empirical observation of response decrement with stimulus repetition as well as a theoretical construct to describe the underlying process that accounts for the observed response decrement. However, the two terms may not be isomorphic, so that it is just as necessary to apply a distinction between performance and learning within the study of habituation as it is with other forms of learning such as classical and instrumental conditioning.

The Dual-Process Theory of Habituation

On the basis of the observation that dishabituation appeared to result from a facilitatory effect superimposed on the habituation process (Humphrey,

1933; Sharpless and Jasper, 1956; Thompson and Spencer, 1966) and of some unusual results when stimulus intensity was used to study habituation (Davis and Wagner, 1969), Groves and Thompson (1970) proposed that novel and especially intense stimuli activate two hypothetical processes: habituation, which decreases response strength, and sensitization, which increases response strength. The final response output is then the net result of these two opposing influences. With strong stimuli, the underlying habituation process may be masked by a competing sensitization process that tends to decrease the rate of response decrement during stimulus repetition. However, because sensitization may not last as long as habituation, subsequent test sessions may be used to evaluate the effects of prior habituation, somewhat less contaminated by sensitization (e.g., Davis, 1972). The Groves and Thompson dual-process theory received wide empirical support and provided a fundamental theoretical base upon which to study the neural mechanisms of response change during iterative stimulus presentation, in both invertebrates and simple mammalian systems.

Mechanisms of Habituation and Sensitization in Vertebrates

Because of the ubiquity of habituation, many believe it is the simplest form of learning. The most definitive analysis of the cellular mechanisms of habituation and sensitization has been done in invertebrates (see INVERTEBRATE LEARNING). In vertebrates, the cellular mechanisms of habituation and sensitization are poorly understood. In broad terms, habituation could be mediated by some neural process intrinsic to the neural pathway in the reflex circuit under study or by activation of other neural circuits extrinsic to, but impinging on, the reflex pathway. Much of the literature on humans has assumed the latter mechanism, probably because of the influential theory of E. N. Sokolov (1960), who proposed a brain comparator process whereby higher brain centers form a neuronal model of incoming stimuli and actively inhibit response output when subsequent stimuli match the neuronal model.

Many animal experiments have attempted to prevent habituation by making lesions of brain areas extrinsic to the reflex circuits under study, or by giving drugs that might prevent these systems from inhibiting the reflex pathway. On balance, however, there are very few behavioral experiments that clearly show that habituation within a single test session is actually prevented by lesions or drugs. When effects are reported, they generally result from a change in overall response levels that does not affect the slope of response decrement (provided the manipulations do not push the initial response levels to the ceiling or floor of the response scale and that measures such as percent decrement or trials to criterion, which depend heavily on changes in overall response level, are not used). Moreover, when effects on the slope of the response decrement curve are found, it is not clear whether this is due to a change in the underlying process of habituation or of sensitization. In actuality, therefore, it has been extremely difficult to study in whole organisms how various manipulations affect the process of habituation, since the change in behavioral output may well be the product of two underlying processes, which cannot be distinguished with a single measure.

Habituation and Sensitization in the Spinal Cord

As illustrated by the landmark studies of Spencer, Thompson, and Neilson (1966a, 1966b), the most definitive work on the mechanism of habituation and sensitization in vertebrates has been done in the spinal cord, because this is one of the few places where the underlying neural circuitry of the reflexes being studied is reasonably well understood. Habituation and sensitization have been investigated in centrally projecting sensory fibers and in the interneurons and motoneurons to which they project. The reflexes most studied include the monosynaptic stretch reflex, the oligosynaptic plantar cushion reflex (Egger, Bishop, and Cone, 1976; Egger, 1978), the polysynaptic flexion reflex in the cat (see Mendell, 1984); and the lateral column–motoneuron pathway in the frog (Farel, Glanzman, and Thompson, 1973). Mammalian monosynaptic stretch reflexes (activated by primary afferents from muscle spindles that project directly to motoneurons) typically do not demonstrate marked habituation or sensitization, in contrast to reflexes involving interneurons, which typically do. Current evidence indicates that habituation and sensitization are mediated by synaptic changes intrinsic to interneurons within the reflex pathways being studied (depression or facilitation of transmitter release). To date, there is no direct evidence that interneuronal networks extrinsic to the reflex pathway account for habituation and sensitization by actively inhibiting or facilitating transmission (see Mendell, 1984), although such mechanisms cannot be entirely ruled out.

Habituation and Sensitization of the Startle Reflex

In complex mammalian systems habituation and sensitization of the acoustic startle reflex have been studied by eliciting startlelike responses at different points along the neural pathway believed to mediate the very-short-latency (8 milliseconds) startle reflex in rats, with a high level of background noise used to sensitize startle (Davis et al., 1982). Startle elicited by electrical stimulation in the early part of the pathway was increased by the noise but then decreased with repeated elicitations. Startle elicited by stimulation of the part of the pathway that projected directly to the spinal cord was also increased by noise, but did *not* decrease with stimulus repetition. In humans, the R1 component of the eyeblink reflex (latency = 10 milliseconds), elicited by electrical stimulation of the facial nerve, which is mediated by a disynaptic circuit, shows a net increase in response amplitude with stimulus repetition. However, the R2 component (latency = 25–40 milliseconds) elicited by the same stimulus, which involves a polysynaptic pathway, shows a net decrease in response strength (Sanes and Ison, 1983). Taken together, the data suggest that sensitization tends to act on the motor side of reflex arcs, whereas habituation tends to act on earlier parts of the circuitry. This suggestion is consistent with data from Thompson and Spencer (1966) on spinal preparations.

The best evidence for extrinsic control of habituation and sensitization has been gathered by looking at between-session or long-term habituation of the startle reflex. Leaton and Supple (1986) have shown that lesions of the cerebellar vermis, which is not part of the acoustic startle pathway, significantly attenuate the decrease in startle amplitude seen across daily test sessions, without affecting the rate of response decrement within test sessions. This blockade of long-term habituation was observed with two different stimulus intensities and cannot be explained by ceiling or floor effects caused by the cerebellar lesions. This effect has been replicated when the lesion was made before habituation training, but not when the lesion was made afterwards (Lopiano, DeSperati, and Montarolo, 1990). Hence, the cerebellar vermis appears to be necessary for the acquisition but not the retention of long-term habituation. In contrast, lesions of the mesencephalic reticular formation, which again is not itself part of the acoustic startle pathway, block both the acquisition (Jordan and Leaton, 1982) and the expression (Jordan, 1989) of long-term habituation. In other studies Borszcz, Cranney, and Leaton (1989) have shown that loud startle stimuli produce sensitization that can best be described as fear of the experimental context in which startle is measured. Reintroducing animals into this context produces a good deal of freezing, a reliable index of fear. Fear of the context elevates startle on subsequent test sessions, leading to a reduction in the amount of long-term response decrement. Treatments such as lesions of the ventral central gray matter (Borszcz, Cranney, and Leaton, 1989) that are known to reduce freezing, and treatments such as lesions of the amygdala or drugs such as diazepam, which reduce fear in many situations, facilitate the degree of long-term response decrement, presumably by blocking sensitization and hence allowing long-term habituation to be revealed. Taken together, these data provide some of the best evidence that extrinsic systems may be involved in both long-term habituation and sensitization of the startle reflex elicited by intense auditory stimuli.

Conclusions

Because habituation could be observed at all levels of the phylogenetic scale, there was great hope that its analysis would lead to fundamental insights into the neural mechanisms of learning and memory. Moreover, because habituation was such a basic mechanism, deficits in habituation might allow one to understand complex cognitive disturbances such as schizophrenia or mental retardation. These hopes have stimulated a great deal of research. Curiously, however, insights gained from this experience have not been as profound as anticipated. In the only systems where habituation could be analyzed at the cellular level (e.g., invertebrates and short-term spinal preparations), the decrease in response output seemed to result from a relatively short-term decrease in transmitter release. However, the actual cellular mechanism that mediates this effect is still unknown. Long-term habituation seems to be a more interesting phenomenon with respect to learning and memory, yet it has been much more difficult to study. Theories to account for enduring, long-term habituation (e.g., Wagner, 1976) or sensitization (Borszcz, Cranney, and Leaton, 1989) inevitably appeal to an associative process, that of classical conditioning. As a result, research on the neural mechanisms of habituation and sensitization has been largely replaced by research on the neural mechanisms of classical conditioning.

(See also ORIENTING REFLEX HABITUATION.)

REFERENCES

Borszcz, G. S., Cranney, J., and Leaton, R. N. (1989). Influence of long-term sensitization on long-term habituation of the acoustic startle response in rats: central gray lesions, preexposure, and extinction. *Journal of Experimental Psychology and Animal Behavior Processes 15,* 54–64.

Davis, M. (1970). Effects of interstimulus interval length and variability on startle response habituation in the rat. *Journal of Comparative Physiology and Psychology 72,* 177–192.

Davis, M. (1972). Differential rates of decay of sensitization and habituation of the startle response in the rat. *Journal of Comparative Physiology and Psychology 78,* 260–267.

Davis, M., Parisi, T., Gendelman, D. S., Tischler, M. D., and Kehne, J. H. (1982). Habituation and sensitization of "startle" responses elicited electrically from the brainstem. *Science 218,* 688–690.

Davis, M., and Wagner, A. R. (1968). Startle responsiveness following habituation to different intensities of tone. *Psychonomic Science 12,* 337–338.

Davis, M., and Wagner, A. R. (1969). Habituation of the startle response under an incremental sequence of stimulus intensities. *Journal of Comparative Physiology and Psychology 67,* 486–492.

Egger, M. D. (1978). Sensitization and habituation of dorsal horn cells in cats. *Journal of Physiology 279,* 153–166.

Egger, M. D., Bishop, J. W., and Cone, C. H. (1976). Sensitization and habituation of the plantar cushion reflex in cats. *Brain Research 103,* 215–228.

Farel, P. B., Glanzman, D. L., and Thompson, R. L. (1973). Habituation of a monosynaptic response in vertebrate central nervous system: lateral column–motoneuron pathway in isolated frog spinal cord. *Journal of Neurophysiology 36,* 1117–1130.

Groves, P. M., and Thompson, R. F. (1970). Habituation:

a dual process theory. *Psychological Review 77,* 419–450.

Harris, J. D. (1943). Habituatory response decrement in the intact organism. *Psychological Bulletin 40,* 385–422.

Humphrey, G. (1933). *The nature of learning.* New York: Harcourt, Brace.

Jordan, W. P. (1989). Mesencephalic reticular formation lesions made after habituation training abolish long-term habituation of the acoustic startle response. *Behavioral Neuroscience 4,* 805–815.

Jordan, W. P., and Leaton, R. N. (1983). Habituation of the acoustic startle response in rats after lesions in the mesencephalic reticular formation or in the inferior colliculus. *Behavioral Neuroscience 97,* 710–724.

Leaton, R. N., and Supple, W. F. (1986). Cerebellar vermis: essential for long-term habituation of the acoustic startle response. *Science 232,* 513–515.

Lopiano, L., DeSperati, C., and Montarolo, P. G. (1990). Long-term habituation of the acoustic startle response: role of the cerebellar vermis. *Neuroscience 35,* 79–84.

Mendell, L. M. (1984). Modifiability of spinal synapses. *Physiological Review 64,* 260–324.

Sanes, J. N., and Ison, J. R. (1983). Habituation and sensitization of components of the human eyeblink reflex. *Behavioral Neuroscience 97,* 833–836.

Sharpless, S., and Jasper, H. (1956). Habituation of the arousal reaction. *Brain 79,* 655–682.

Sokolov, E. N. (1960). Neuronal models and the orienting reflex. In M. A. B. Brazier, ed., *The central nervous system and behavior. III.* New York: Josiah Macy Foundation.

Spencer, W. A., Thompson, R. F., and Neilson, D. R. (1966a). Response decrement of the flexion reflex in the acute spinal cat and transient restoration by strong stimuli. *Journal of Neurophysiology 29,* 221–239.

Spencer, W. A., Thompson, R. F., and Neilson, D. R. (1966b). Alterations in responsiveness of ascending and reflex pathways activated by iterated cutaneous afferent volleys. *Journal of Neurophysiology 29,* 240–252.

Thompson, R. F., and Spencer, W. A. (1966). Habituation: a model phenomenon for the study of the neuronal substrates of behavior. *Psychological Review 73,* 16–43.

Wagner, A. R. (1976). Priming in STM: An information processing mechanism for self-generated or retrieval-generated depression. In T. N. Tighe and R. L. Leaton, eds., *Habituation: Perspectives from Child Development, Animal Behavior, and Neurophysiology.* Hillsdale, N.J.: Erlbaum.

Michael Davis

M. David Egger

HARLOW, HARRY F.

Harry Harlow was born in Fairview, Iowa, on October 31, 1905, and died on December 6, 1981. He attended Reed College in 1923 before transferring to Stanford, where he received his Ph.D. in 1930 under the supervision of C. P. Stone. Harlow's first appointment was at the University of Wisconsin, where he later established the Wisconsin Primate Laboratory. Except for the period 1949–1951, when he was chief psychologist for the U.S. Army, he remained at Wisconsin until his formal retirement in 1974, when he moved to the University of Arizona. Harlow's research, characterized by imaginative methods of studying cognition and motivation, led to important discoveries. He was elected president of the American Psychological Association and received its Distinguished Scientific Contribution Award. He also received awards from the Society for Research in Child Development and the Kittay International Scientific Foundation Award, the Gold Medal Award of the American Psychological Foundation, and the U.S. National Medal of Science.

Harlow was primarily interested in the cortical localization of intellectual functions such as learn-

Figure 1.   Harry F. Harlow.

ing and memory, and decided to work with primates because of their obvious cognitive capacities. As he approached this problem, he was convinced that the contemporary learning systems were fundamentally limited because they were based upon inadequate information, and he set out to collect such information from his monkeys in a systematic manner. One of the most important innovations that Harlow introduced was the study of transfer of training. Although there was a long history in the study of this general issue, previous workers had studied interproblem learning over a narrow range of problems in which subjects were trained to mastery on a given problem before being shifted to new ones. Harlow departed radically from this approach by training animals on individual problems for a small number of trials before shifting to new problems. He showed that on the initial training trials animals worked largely by trial and error, but at some point they began to catch on to a general principle that could be used to successfully solve problems in a single trial. That is, the animals had learned how to learn, a process that he called the development of a "learning set." This simple observation was important for theoretical reasons, but it had another important impact: It could be used to study the organization of cortical processes related to learning and memory. This represented another major breakthrough, and this type of behavioral analysis still represents a major tool in studies of neural mechanisms underlying learning and memory processes.

Harlow was convinced that many of the shortcomings of the contemporary theoretical systems stemmed from the fact that there were practically no data on the ontogenetic development of learning, perception, and motivation. In an effort to determine how and when different learning and perceptual processes developed, he and colleagues began a major program in which infant monkeys were separated from their mothers at birth and then studied intensively over the ensuing years. While the contributions of these experiments go far beyond the questions of learning and memory, it was clear from these studies that there were major maturational changes in the performance of monkeys on different learning tests. These changes could not be accounted for by traditional learning theories and thus led to a new field of inquiry in learning and memory research.

Finally, Harlow was a major advocate of the use of the comparative method in studies of learning and memory: "Basically the problems of generalization of behavioral data between species are sim-ple—one cannot generalize, but one must. If the competent do not wish to generalize, the incompetent will fill the field" (Harlow et al., 1972). The comparative studies of Harlow and those which followed were based upon the concepts related to learning sets, which led in turn to major advances in our understanding of the phylogenetic changes in learning and memory abilities. (See also COMPARATIVE COGNITION.)

Harry Harlow thus made a unique and long-lasting contribution not only to the way in which learning and memory are now studied but also to the development of psychological theory regarding learning and memory. His work helped shape the nature of the questions that are now being addressed.

REFERENCES

Harlow, H. F. (1956). Learning set and error factor theory. In S. Koch, ed., *Psychology: A study of a science*, vol. 2, pp. 492–537. New York: McGraw-Hill.

Harlow, H. F., Gluck, J. P., and Suomi, S. J. (1972). Generalization of behavioral data between nonhuman and human animals. *American Psychologist, 27,* 709–716.

Sears, R. R. (1982). Harry Frederick Harlow (1905–1981). *American Psychologist 37,* 1280–1281.

Bryan Kolb

HEAD INJURY

Memory deficit is one of the most characteristic features of closed head injury (CHI; head injury produced by sudden acceleration/deceleration, as in motor vehicle crashes), involving both amnesia for events shortly after (and often before) the insult and residual difficulty in learning and retaining information (Levin, 1989). Systematic studies reported over more than a 30-year span by the British neurologist Ritchie Russell showed that posttraumatic amnesia (PTA; failure to store information about events for varying periods after injury) was common in CHI patients (Russell, 1971). In contrast with the duration of PTA, which exceeded a week after severe CHI, retrograde amnesia (RA) typically extended over brief periods (e.g., minutes) into the past. However, Russell (1971) ob-

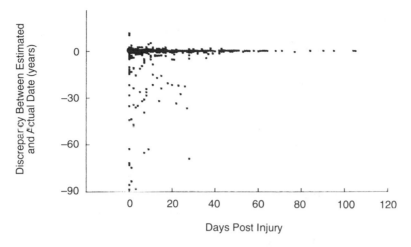

Figure 1. Scatterplot of the discrepancy between estimated and actual date and days post injury: All patients (N = 84). *Reproduced from High et al., 1990, Figure 2, p. 707, with permission.*

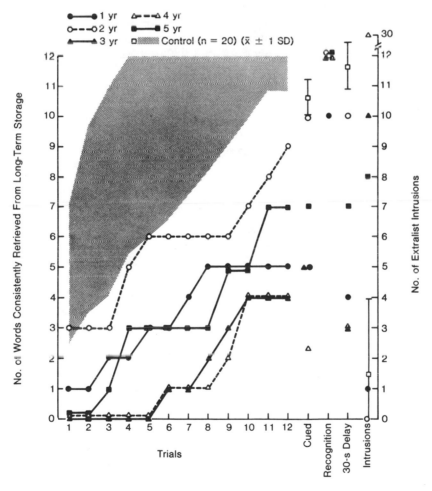

Figure 2. Consistent retrieval of words from long-term storage plotted against trials on Selective Reminding Test. Hatched area corresponds to mean +/− SD in twenty women similar to patient in age and education. There is no progressive improvement in memory retrieval during serial examinations beginning 1 year after injury. Despite persistent difficulties in cued and delayed recall, forced-choice recognition of test words was relatively preserved. Note highly variable number of extralist intrusions. *Reproduced from Levin et al. 1985, Figure 4, p. 967, with permission. Copyright 1985 American Medical Association.*

served that the duration of RA often shrank from a long interval (e.g., several months) to a brief period (e.g., minutes or seconds before injury) during the early stages of recovery. RA is reflected by a tendency of CHI patients initially to displace their temporal orientation into the past. High, Levin, and Gary (1990) reported the results of serial examinations of CHI patients during their acute hospitalization. Figure 1 shows that backward displacement of temporal orientation initially extended far into the past and gradually receded to the present.

Of the neurobehavioral sequelae which persist after PTA resolves, memory deficit (manifested primarily by difficulty remembering new information such as recent events, names, locations of objects, and duties to be performed at work or school) is one of the most frequent problems reported by patients and their families (Oddy et al., 1985). Although Russell (1971) estimated that about one-fourth of CHI patients exhibit residual memory disturbance, his estimate increased to 50 percent for patients who sustained severe CHI. As illustrated in Figure 2, recall of a word list (or other material, such as short stories or complex visual designs) is often chronically impaired after a severe CHI. Despite intellectual functioning that recovered to the average level, this young woman continued to exhibit impaired memory for both verbal and relatively nonverbal material.

To examine the specificity of memory disturbance after CHI, Levin et al. (1988) compared residual memory and intellectual functioning of patients who sustained CHI of varying severity against the results obtained from normal subjects of similar demographic background. The investigators transformed the memory test scores to standard scores to facilitate comparison. As depicted in Figure 3, the intellectual functioning of the patients closely approximated the level of control subjects. In contrast, patients who had sustained severe CHI exhibited unequivocal memory impairment after a long postinjury interval.

Investigators have identified indices of acute CHI that are related to persistent memory disturbance. The injury variables that are most predictive of residual memory deficit include the depth and duration of coma and pupillary reactivity, the latter often reflecting neurologic deterioration (Levin et al. 1990).

Relatively few studies have addressed the qualitative features of memory deficit following CHI.

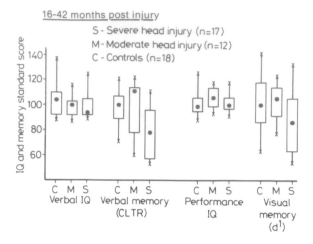

Figure 3. Box plots depicting the distribution of IQ and transformed memory scores for controls and moderately and severely head-injured patients who obtained IQ scores in the preserved range (> 85) at 16–42 months post injury. Each asterisk signifies the median; the upper and lower horizontal lines of each bar indicate the seventy-fifth and twenty-fifth percentile scores. The maximum and minimum scores are marked by X. *Reproduced from Levin et al. 1988, Figure 3, p. 1297, with permission.*

Levin and Goldstein (1986) found that survivors of severe CHI had difficulty imposing semantic organization on words that were drawn from three categories (e.g., parts of a house, fruits) and presented in a random sequence for recall. This deficiency in categorical clustering contrasted with the performance by normal control subjects who typically exhausted their recall of words in one category before beginning to recall words from another category. Richardson (1979) has shown that memory dysfunction after CHI is characterized by difficulty in utilizing visual imagery as a mnemonic. Diminished capacity for sustained cognitive effort is a plausible explanation for the qualitative changes in memory following severe CHI.

Apart from the aforementioned indices of acute head injury, the relationship between morphologic features of brain damage and residual memory disturbance awaits detailed analysis. At this stage of research, the most impressive relationship is between memory deficit and the degree of cerebral atrophy. Measurement of the area of the lateral ventricles and derivation of a ratio to the total intracranial area was employed by Levin et al. (1981) as an index of cerebral atrophy. Figure 4 shows that recognition memory for a series of pic-

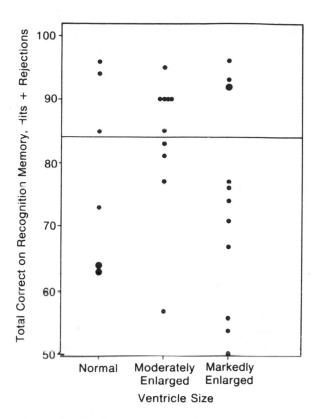

Figure 4. Total correct recognition memory score plotted according to extent of ventricular enlargement. Horizontal line indicates cutoff for defective scores that fall below 84. Larger circles denote patients in whom duration of coma and ventricle-brain percent ratio (VBR) were incongruous (e.g., normal VBR despite long period of coma). *Reproduced from Levin et al., 1981, Figure 4, p. 627, with permission. Copyright 1981 American Medical Association.*

tures was impaired in patients who had larger ventricle-brain ratios, which were interpreted as indicative of more severe cerebral atrophy (reflecting degeneration of the periventricular white matter). More recent studies have used magnetic resonance imaging (MRI) to characterize focal lesions persisting in survivors of CHI (Levin et al. 1985). Although chronic MRI abnormalities tend to be more closely related to residual memory disturbance than early MRI findings, the relationship between site of lesion and performance is variable.

Investigators have postulated that frontal lobe injury may underlie deficient use of memory strategies by CHI patients (see FRONTAL LOBES AND MEMORY), but there is no compelling neuroimaging evidence to support this assertion. Future research involving measurement of cerebral metabolism could potentially advance our understanding of the pathophysiology of posttraumatic memory disorder.

REFERENCES

High, W. M., Jr., Levin, H. S., and Gary, H. E., Jr. (1990). Recovery of orientation following closed-head injury. *Journal of Clinical and Experimental Neuropsychology 12,* 703–714.

Levin, H. S. (1989). Memory deficit after closed-head injury. *Journal of Clinical and Experimental Neuropsychology 12,* 129–153.

Levin, H. S., and Goldstein, F. C. (1986). Organization of verbal memory after severe closed head injury. *Journal of Clinical and Experimental Neuropsychology 8,* 643–656.

Levin, H. S., Meyers, C. A., Grossman, R. G., and Sarwar, M. (1981). Ventricular enlargement after closed head injury. *Archives of Neurology 38,* 623–629.

Levin, H. S., Handel, S. F., Goldman, A. M., Eisenberg, H. M., and Guinto, F. C., Jr. (1985). Magnetic resonance imaging after "diffuse" nonmissile head injury: A neurobehavioral study. *Archives of Neurology 42,* 963–968.

Levin, H. S., Goldstein, F. C., High, W. M., Jr., and Eisenberg, H. M. (1988). Disproportionately severe memory deficit in relation to normal intellectual functioning after closed head injury. *Journal of Neurology, Neurosurgery and Psychiatry 51,* 1294–1301.

Levin, H. S., Gary, H. E., Jr., Eisenberg, H. M., Ruff, R. M., Barth, J. T., Kreutzer, J., High, W. M., Jr., Portman, S., Foulkes, M. A., Jane, J. A., Marmarou, A., and Marshall, L. F. (1990). Neurobehavioral outcome 1 year after severe head injury: Experience of the Traumatic Coma Data Bank. *Journal of Neurosurgery 73,* 699–709.

Oddy, M., Coughlan, T., Tyerman, A., and Jenkins, D. (1985). Social adjustment after closed head injury: A further follow-up seven years after injury. *Journal of Neurology, Neurosurgery and Psychiatry 48,* 564–568.

Richardson, J. T. E. (1979). Mental imagery, human memory, and the effects of closed head injury. *British Journal of Social and Clinical Psychology 18,* 319–327.

Russell, W. R. (1971). *The traumatic amnesias.* New York: Oxford University Press.

Russell, W. R., and Smith, A. (1961). Post-traumatic amnesia in closed head injury. *Archives of Neurology 5,* 4–17.

Harvey S. Levin

HEBB, DONALD

Donald Olding Hebb (1904–1985) was born July 22, 1904, in Chester Basin, a small community on the Atlantic coast of Nova Scotia, Canada. Both his parents were physicians, his two brothers followed in their footsteps, and his sister Catherine became a well-known neurophysiologist after receiving her medical degree. Donald, ever the nonconformist, decided to be a novelist and in 1925 graduated from Dalhousie University with a degree in English. He spent the next 2 years teaching and traveling. Hebb never completed his novel, but he did write an autobiography (Hebb, 1980). He also taught numerous students how to communicate clearly. In 1927 Hebb enrolled as a part-time graduate student in psychology at McGill University and supported himself as a teacher and later principal of a local elementary school. He experimented with teaching methods in his school, and at McGill he developed an interest in the "nature-nurture" question.

At this stage, newly married, Hebb almost decided to make a career in education, but illness and tragedy diverted his course. He was immobilized by tuberculosis of the hip for more than a

Figure 1.   Donald O. Hebb. *Courtesy Peter M. Milner.*

year, and his wife was killed in a motor accident. During his illness he wrote a theoretical thesis on the role of Pavlovian conditioning in development. It was read by Prof. Boris Babkin, a McGill physiologist and former student of PAVLOV, and when Hebb was mobile again, Babkin encouraged him to embark on a conditioning experiment. This type of research soon palled, however, and after the death of his wife Hebb decided to leave Montreal. He was offered an assistantship at Yale, but Babkin recommended that he apply to study with Karl LASHLEY, which he did. In view of Lashley's harsh criticism of Pavlov's theories, Babkin's advice was surprisingly broad-minded; it also was crucial to Hebb's future. At the University of Chicago, Hebb came under the influence of L. L. Thurstone, C. Judson Herrick, Nathaniel Kleitman, Wolfgang Köhler, and, of course, Lashley himself. Lashley believed that the goal of psychology was to discover how the brain determines behavior, so the questions he asked were very different from those arising at the time in mainstream BEHAVIORISM.

After a year Lashley moved to Harvard and Hebb went with him, completing his experiments on the effect of dark-rearing on rat visual perception there. After receiving the doctorate, he remained at Harvard for a postdoctoral year and then returned to Montreal to study Wilder Penfield's patients at the newly established Montreal Neurological Institute (MNI). A major project was to determine the effect of frontal-lobe removal on measures of intelligence. Hebb found that extensive damage to that area had negligible effect on standard intelligence test scores, which pleased Penfield and gave Hebb much to think about. Another of his discoveries was that large right temporal-lobe ablations impaired visual perception.

At the end of his 2-year fellowship at the MNI Hebb went to Queen's University, in Kingston, Ontario, where he taught and followed up his work at the Neurological Institute with research on rats. He devised a rat intelligence test (Hebb and Williams, 1946) that he considered analogous to the tests used on human patients and, on the basis of his experiments, concluded that early experience had a significant effect on intelligence. Hebb developed this theme and used it to explain the lack of effect of large frontal-lobe lesions in adults (Hebb, 1942).

In 1942 Lashley was appointed director of the Yerkes Laboratories of Primate Biology in Orange Park, Florida, and invited Hebb to join the staff. The opportunity to work with Lashley again easily outweighed Hebb's reservations about chimpanzee experiments, and he seized the opportunity. Lashley intended to develop tests of learning and problem solving while Hebb worked on tests of temperament and emotionality. The effects of brain lesions on these tests would then be studied. In fact no operations were performed until after Hebb left 5 years later, largely because Lashley's experience with rats did not adequately prepare him for a battle of wits with chimpanzees. In the meantime Hebb made some interesting discoveries about the causes of fear, and accumulated a fund of chimpanzee anecdotes that enlivened his writing and lectures for the next 40 years. But it was the time he spent pondering the neurophysiology of thought and intelligence, and discussing his ideas with Lashley and other members of the staff, that Hebb valued most. In 1944 a paper by Lorente de Nó on neuronal loops and recurrent circuits came to Hebb's attention and restructured his conception of the brain. Strangely, although many psychological phenomena cried out for explanations in terms of feedback, and neurophysiologists had known about recurrent circuits for some time, the idea of one-way sensory-to-motor paths was so deeply ingrained among psychologists that before Hebb the only feedback route proposed was through the environment via the effects of responses on sensory input.

Of the many questions raised by Lashley's experiments, one of the most important was why the connections established during learning could not be localized by brain lesions. Another topic that must have been discussed at length by Lashley's circle was stimulus generalization: why changes in the size of a visual stimulus, for example, did not disturb learned recognition. These questions concern the nature of the representation of objects in the brain. Behaviorists were inhibited in their treatment of this problem because they considered any representation of a stimulus object to be dangerously close to an *idea*. For the nonphysiological behavior theorist an idea was a mentalistic phenomenon, and hence outside the scope of psychological inquiry. Hebb thought that neural loops would provide answers to these long-standing problems.

The theory that finally emerged (Hebb, 1949) was that initially random connections between cortical cells become organized by sensory input into massively interconnected groups that he called cell assemblies. Hebb's answer to Lashley's localization problem was that the cells of each assembly are dispersed over a large area of the cortex so that enough interconnected cells survive any but the largest lesion to ensure that objects continue to be represented. Hebb explained generalization by stipulating that during the initial investigations of an object, many different sensory patterns contribute inputs that are incorporated into, or closely linked to, a single cell assembly representing the object. The dense intrinsic connections ensure that the whole assembly fires when only partial input is presented. Cell assemblies that are active successively acquire connections with each other, which explains expectancy and the association of ideas. What Hebb did, in effect, was to sketch a neural model for the idea, rescuing it from the obloquy of mentalism under which it had languished for almost half a century. Many psychologists were chafing under the narrow constraints and dogmas of behaviorism, and they received Hebb's liberating ideas with enthusiasm.

The establishment of cell assemblies and the connections between them requires neural plasticity. The mechanism Hebb proposed was that if an axon terminal and its postsynaptic neuron were active at about the same time, the effectiveness of the synapse would increase. This model of synaptic change is now known as the "Hebb synapse," and a generation may be growing up to think of Hebb as a neurophysiologist. If so, this would be a pity; Hebb's attempt to explain how the brain represents the outside world, in which the Hebb synapse was a secondary step, was a far more original contribution and, by illustrating the power of neurological models, of more far-reaching influence. Although Hebb made no attempt to test a computer or mathematical model of the cell assembly, such an attempt was made at IBM shortly after his book appeared (Rochester et al., 1956), and the idea has influenced all subsequent network models of learning, from the Perceptron (Rosenblatt, 1962) to the Parallel Distributed Processing models of Rumelhart and McClelland (1986; see also PARALLEL DISTRIBUTED PROCESSING MODELS OF MEMORY). "Hebb nerve nets" would be a more fitting memorial to his name than "Hebb synapses."

Hebb returned to the McGill department of psychology in 1947 and became chairman a year later. He studied the effects of rearing environment in rats and dogs, obtaining results that were influential in shaping programs for providing more stimulating surroundings for disadvantaged infants. Later he measured effects of prolonged sensory deprivation on human subjects and probed the cell assembly more directly by studying the patterns of breakdown of perception of stabilized retinal images. Hebb was elected president of the Canadian Psychological Association in 1952 and of the American Psychological Association in 1960. In 1966 he was made a fellow of the Royal Society, and in 1979 a foreign associate of the National Academy of Sciences (USA). He was chancellor of McGill University from 1970 to 1974. Hebb retired to his birthplace in 1977 and died there in August 1985.

REFERENCES

Hebb, D. O. (1942). The effect of early and late brain injury upon test scores, and the nature of normal adult intelligence. *Proceedings of the American Philosophical Society 85,* 275–292.
———— (1949). *The organization of behavior.* New York: Wiley.
———— (1980). D. O. Hebb. In G. Lindzey, ed, *A history of psychology in autobiography,* vol. 7, pp. 273–303. San Francisco: Freeman.
Hebb, D. O., and Williams, K. (1946). A method of rating animal intelligence. *Journal of General Psychology 34,* 59–65.
Rochester, N., Holland, J. H., Haibt, L. H., and Duda, W. L. (1956). Tests on a cell assembly theory of action of the brain, using a large digital computer. *IRE Transactions. Information Theory IT-2,* 80–93.
Rosenblatt, F. (1962). *Principles of neurodynamics: Perceptrons and the theory of brain mechanisms.* Washington, D.C.: Spartan Books.
Rumelhart, D. E., and McClelland, J. L. (1986). *Parallel distributed processing,* vol. 1, *Foundations.* Cambridge, Mass.: MIT Press.

Peter M. Milner

HIPPOCAMPUS

See Amnesia, Organic; Guide to the Anatomy of the Brain; Neural Computation

HORMONES AND MEMORY

Hormones influence many physiological systems that are involved in regulating adaptation to environmental changes. In addition to their many other influences, hormones appear to serve an adaptive role in regulating the neurobiological process underlying memory storage. Extensive evidence indicates that, in laboratory animals, injections of hormones administered shortly after training influence retention of the recently acquired information. Hormones can produce enhancement as well as impairment of retention, depending upon the dose and other experimental conditions. Mildly stimulating experiences are known to release a variety of hormones into the blood and brain. Such findings suggest that endogenous hormones released by the training influence memory by modulating memory storage processes.

Although many hormones either enhance or impair long-term retention when administered shortly after training, the most extensive evidence has been obtained in studies of the effects of hormones, including epinephrine (adrenalin), ACTH (adrenocorticotropin), vasopressin, and opioid peptides, that are released by mildly stressful stimulation of the kinds typically used in studies of learning and memory in laboratory animals.

The peptide hormone ACTH is secreted from the anterior pituitary. Early studies investigating the influence of hormones on learning and memory indicated that hypophysectomy produces impairment of learning and memory and that the impairment is attenuated by injections of ACTH. Many subsequent experiments found that in normal animals memory is enhanced by low doses of ACTH and impaired by high doses. Findings that retention is affected by fragments of the ACTH peptide that do not induce the release of glucocorticoids from the adrenal medulla indicate that ACTH effects on memory are not mediated by glucocorticoids. However, there is also evidence that injections of glucocorticoids can influence memory when administered after training.

Vasopressin, a peptide hormone that is secreted from the posterior pituitary, also affects learning and memory. Early findings showed that damage to the posterior pituitary impaired rats' learning performance and that injections of an extract containing vasopressin attenuated the impairment. Recent experimental findings indicate that vasopressin administered after training enhances rats' retention in many types of learning tasks. Some evidence suggests that the memory-enhancing effects of vasopressin may be mediated, in part, by influences on blood pressure. However, in view of other evidence indicating that retention enhancement is induced by vasopressin peptide metabolites that do not affect blood pressure, it seems likely that vasopressin directly affects brain processes involved in memory storage. This conclusion is further supported by evidence that retention is enhanced by injections of vasopressin directly into the brain as well as findings indicating that injections of a vasopressin antagonist into the cerebral ventricles prevent the retention enhancement produced by vasopressin but do not block the effects on blood pressure.

The adrenergic catecholamine epinephrine is released into the blood from the adrenal medulla following arousing or stressful stimulation. Systemic injections of epinephrine administered after training produce dose-dependent effects on subsequent retention: Low doses enhance retention and high doses impair retention. Plasma epinephrine levels assessed following injections of memory-enhancing doses of epinephrine are comparable to those seen following training stimulation that produces good retention. Findings that epinephrine passes the blood-brain barrier poorly suggest that epinephrine effects on memory are initiated by activation of peripheral adrenergic receptors. This view is supported by research indicating that drugs which selectively block peripheral beta-adrenergic receptors (when administered peripherally) block the memory-enhancing effects of epinephrine. Epinephrine acts on receptors in the liver to initiate the release of glucose. Research findings indicating that glucose can enhance memory suggest that epinephrine-induced glycogenolysis may mediate, in part, epinephrine influences on memory. Other findings indicate that epinephrine stimulates the release of the noradrenergic neuromodulator norepinephrine (NE) in the brain. Extensive evidence suggests that the memory-enhancing effects involve activation of beta-adrenergic receptors within a specific brain region, the amygdaloid complex: Microinjections of beta-adrenergic antagonists into this brain region block the memory-modulating effects of peripherally administered epinephrine.

Research findings indicating that the opiate drug morphine impairs memory when injected after training suggest that endogenous opioid peptides may play a role in the regulation of memory storage. Beta-endorphin is released within the brain and also from the anterior pituitary into the blood along with ACTH. Enkephalin is released from the adrenal medulla together with epinephrine. Ex-

perimental findings indicating that effects of these opioid peptides on memory are similar to those of morphine suggest that endogenously released opioid peptides regulate memory storage. Studies of the effects of opiate antagonists provide additional support for this view: Opiate antagonists enhance retention when administered after training. Opioid peptide influences on learning, like those of epinephrine, appear to involve the amygdala. Injections of opiate agonists and antagonists administered directly into the amygdala after training produce effects on memory highly comparable to those seen following systemic injections. Such effects also appear to involve the noradrenergic system. Beta-adrenergic blockers injected into the amygdala block the memory-enhancing effects of the opiate antagonist naloxone. Such findings agree with the evidence that opioid peptides inhibit the release of NE.

Retention can be influenced by a number of peptide hormones, including substance P, neuropeptide Y, somatostatin, and cholecystokinin (CCK), that are not generally thought to be stress related. CCK, for example, is a peptide hormone found in the gastrointestinal tract as well as the brain and is involved in regulating food intake by signaling satiation. There is also evidence that CCK released by feeding enhances memory. Peripheral injections of CCK administered after training induce memory-enhancing effects comparable with those of epinephrine and ACTH. Evidence indicating that lesions of the vagus nerve block the memory-modulating effects of CCK strongly suggests that such effects are initiated at peripheral receptors located on neurons which project to the brain via the vagus. Although the central target of such influences has not been determined, it is noteworthy that the vagus projects to the nucleus of the solitary tract, which in turn projects to the amygdala. Thus, the anatomical as well as the pharmacological evidence suggests that the influences of several hormonal systems on memory storage may be integrated within the amygdala.

The extensive evidence that hormones can enhance memory in animals suggests that hormones might be effective in the treatment of disorders of human memory. As yet, however, there has not been extensive investigation of the effects of hormones on memory in humans. The available evidence, which is based on but a few studies, is conflicting.

(See also DRUGS AND MEMORY.)

REFERENCES

De Wied, D. (1991). The effects of neurohypophyseal hormones and related peptides on learning and memory processes. In R. C. A. Frederickson, J. L. McGaugh, and D. L. Felten, eds., *Peripheral signaling of the brain.* Toronto: Hogrefe and Huber.

Koob, G. F. (1987). Neuropeptides and memory. In L. L. Iversen and S. H. Snyder, eds., *Handbook of psychopharmacology,* vol. 19, *Behavioral pharmacology, an update.* New York: Plenum Press.

McGaugh, J. L. (1989). Involvement of hormonal and neuromodulatory systems in the regulation of memory storage. *Annual Review of Neuroscience 12,* 255–287.

McGaugh, J. L., and Gold, P. E. (1989). Hormonal modulation of memory. In R. B. Brush and S. Levine, eds., *Psychoendocrinology.* New York: Academic Press.

Morley, J. E., and Flood, J. F. (1991). Gut peptides as modulators of memory. In R. C. A. Frederickson, J. L. McGaugh, and D. L. Felten, eds., *Peripheral signaling of the brain.* Toronto: Hogrefe and Huber.

James L. McGaugh

HULL, CLARK L.

Clark Leonard Hull was born in Akron, New York, on May 24, 1884, and died in New Haven, Connecticut, on May 10, 1952. He earned the bachelor's degree from the University of Michigan in 1913, and the master's degree in 1915 and the Ph.D. in experimental psychology in 1918 from the University of Wisconsin. His graduate work was done primarily under the direction of Joseph Jastrow, Daniel Starch, and Vivian A. C. Henmon.

Hull recorded some of his earliest career plans in his Idea Books. "It seems," he wrote, "that the greatest need in the science at present is to create an *experimental* and a *scientific* knowledge of higher mental processes" (Ammons, 1962, p. 814). He planned to become the "supreme authority" in the psychology of abstraction, concept formation, and, possibly, reasoning—to "both know the literature and create the literature on the subject." His doctoral dissertation, *Quantitative Aspects of the Evolution of Concepts,* was published in *Psychological Monographs* (1920).

Hull was afflicted with a variety of health problems, and his relatively late entry into the field was another threat to his long-range goal. In 1930, at the age of 46, he wrote: "Sometimes I have been depressed and discouraged in my hope to achieve a major contribution to the theory of knowledge by the fact of my age. Recently, however, the examination of the ages at which several of the great critics have produced their best works has shown that I have by no means reason to be depressed" (Ammons, 1962, p. 836). The list included Hobbes, sixty-three; Spinoza, forty-five; Leibnitz, sixty-eight; Locke, fifty-eight; Kant, fifty-seven. (He could have added that Pavlov was fifty-six years old when he first proposed the principle of the conditioned reflex.)

Hull was elected to the American Academy of Arts and Sciences in 1935 and to the National Academy of Sciences in 1936, and to the presidency of the American Psychological Association 1935. He received the Warren Medal of the Society of Experimental Psychologists in 1945. A measure of his influence is that during the decade 1941–1950 approximately 40 percent of all experimental articles published in the *Journal of Experimental Psychology* and the *Journal of Comparative and Physiological Psychology* included references to his work (Spence, 1952). Today Hull is best remembered for one theoretical book on learning theory, *Principles of Behavior* (1943). However,

Figure 1.   Clark L. Hull. *Courtesy Archives of the History of American Psychology.*

a case has been made that the twenty-one theoretical articles he published in the *Psychological Review* between 1929 and 1950, the earliest of which introduced the Pavlovian construct, the *fractional anticipatory goal response* (r_G-s_G), represent at least as important a contribution to learning theory. (For an extensive account of Hull's work and influence, see Amsel and Rashotte, 1984.)

After receiving his doctorate, Hull stayed in the Psychology Department at the University of Wisconsin, where he became director of the laboratory in 1925. During these years, his projects included the effects of tobacco smoking on mental and motor efficiency; the definitive books of the time in aptitude testing and hypnosis; and, as forerunners of the computer age, a logic machine, a machine that automatically computed correlations, and a robot that learned.

For Hull, PAVLOV's conditioning identified the principle by which an event in one subsystem could come to influence functioning in remote parts of such machines, and THORNDIKE's law of effect, the principle whereby originally random movements could be selected and be linked as responses to specific stimulus patterns (trial-and-error learning and the principle of the habit-family hierarchy). The design of a machine that learned, he thought, should allow for common reactions to stimuli with sensory similarity (generalization), for the learning of common reactions to stimuli with quite different sensory qualities (discrimination), and for the possibility of differential responding to minute differences in stimulus pattern (afferent neural interaction). These became central principles in his papers and in his later formal writings (Hull, 1943, 1952).

In 1929, Hull accepted the position of research professor of psychology at the Institute of Psychology (later the Institute of Human Relations) at Yale University, where he remained for the rest of his career. When he arrived at Yale, aged forty-five, he made this entry in his Idea Books, which seems prophetic in the light of the computer age in which we now live:

> Just as the correlation machine has been intimately associated with the testing program, so it appears that the design and construction of automatic physical machines will be intimately associated with my attempts to work out my program involving the higher mental processes. . . . I am pretty certain to be criticized and called a trifle insane at the very least. But whatever genius I have quite evidently lies in this direction. I can do no less than make the best of it—let the tendency have free rein and go as far as it possibly can. . . . It may lead to real insight into the higher mental processes. . . . It may [on the other hand] possibly serve as the final *reductio ad absurdum* of a mechanistic psychology. If it does, well and good. But even if this should take place, it may at the same time result in such a development in psychic machines displaying an utterly new and different order of automaticity that mechanical engineering of automatic machines will be revolutionized to a degree similar to the introduction of steam engines and electricity. (Ammons, 1962, pp. 828–829)

As research professor at Yale, Hull had no formal teaching assignment, but he engaged in graduate instruction through a weekly seminar that attracted students and faculty of the institute for discussion of a variety of issues in behavior theory.

By Hull's own account, the Institute of Human Relations was a loose organization of behavioral scientists from various fields: mainly psychologists, sociologists, and cultural anthropologists. However, the conceptual framework for the unified contribution it provided was Hull's theoretical system, and it seems fairly clear, in retrospect, that this conceptual framework was an amalgam of influences from Darwin, Pavlov, and FREUD. Their influences, filtered through Hull's own, are evident in several important publications written by members of the institute, all of which featured stimulus-response analyses of complex learning. Books in this genre include *Frustration and Aggression* (Dollard et al., 1939), *Social Learning and Imitation* (Miller and Dollard, 1941), and *Personality and Psychotherapy* (Dollard and Miller, 1950).

Even before going to Yale, Hull had planned to prepare a magnum opus on the scientific (mechanistic) analysis of higher mental processes. The earliest titles he considered for his work, listed in his Idea Books in 1928 (Ammons, 1962, pp. 824–825), indicate this intended focus and the mechanistic emphasis: Mechanisms of Thought, Mechanisms of Mind, Mental Mechanisms, Mechanisms of Mental Life, Psychology from the Standpoint of a Mechanist.

Hull's plan was to invert the direction taken by the great philosophers—Hume, Locke, Kant, and Hobbes—who had attempted to construct a theory of knowledge, thought, and reason on the basis of conscious experience but who, in Hull's eyes, had failed. He planned to attack the same problem using the opposite strategy. He wrote, "I shall start with action—habit—and proceed to deduce all the rest, including conscious experience, from action, i.e., habit" (Ammons, 1962, p. 837).

To carry out this task, Hull planned a three-volume work. The first volume was intended mainly to present a set of formal axioms that constituted a logical system from which hypotheses about mammalian adaptive behavior could be deduced. Completed in Hull's fifty-eighth year, this volume appeared in 1943 and was titled *Principles of Behavior: An Introduction to Behavior Theory.* The orientation of the second volume, based on the principles set down in the first, was toward specific instances of more complex adaptive behavior, such as maze learning and problem solving. Completed in Hull's sixty-eighth year, it appeared shortly after his death in 1952, and was titled *A Behavior System: An Introduction to Behavior Theory Concerning the Individual Organism.* The third volume, which Hull thought would be the most important, was to have applied the system to some elementary phenomena of social mammalian behavior. It was never completed.

The basic formal structure of the theorizing in Hull's *Principles,* as revised in *Essentials of Behavior* (1951), was an intervening variable approach borrowed from Edward TOLMAN (e.g., 1938). It involved antecedent, manipulable environmental conditions (independent variables), consequent behavioral conditions (dependent variables), and a bridge of lower- and higher-level constructs connecting the two (the intervening variables). Hull's final version of the theory is summarized in the first chapter of *A Behavior System* as a set of postulates and corollaries, most are which are restated in mathematical form. Examples are Postulate II, relating the strength of an intervening variable, the "molar stimulus trace" S^1, to the independent variables, the physical stimulus (S), as a power function of time since the beginning of the stimulus; and Postulates XIV, XV, and XVI, in which the momentary effective reaction potential $_S\dot{E}_R$, which already takes into account the behavioral oscillation $_SO_R$ and the threshold for responding $_SL_R$, is related to four response measures—response latency, response amplitude, response frequency, and resistance to experimental extinction—by negatively accelerated functions in the first, third, and fourth cases, and by a linear function in the second. This is the nature of Hull's formal theorizing.

These later, more formal portions of Hull's theorizing were not taken up after his death except by Kenneth SPENCE (e.g., 1954, 1956) and a few of Spence's students (e.g., Grice, 1968; Logan, 1960). One reason was the advent of the *cognitive revolution* in psychology, which was for the most part a reaction against B. F. SKINNER'S BEHAVIORISM, but also against Hull's stimulus-response associationism, his hypothetico-deductive version of it in particular (see Amsel, 1989). Many thought that such a formal Newtonian treatment was both too general in scope and premature. However, more recent mathematical models of associative learning, greatly influenced by Hull but more restricted in explanatory scope (e.g., Rescorla and Wagner, 1972), continue to be very influential. Still very important in learning theory is the general approach, taken from Hull's earlier work, of employing hypothetical constructs derived from Pavlovian conditioning in the explanation of instrumental behavior. Hull (1931) regarded this work as stimulus-response analyses of "goal attraction" and "directing ideas," and called the mechanism the *fractional anticipatory goal response* (r_G-s_G). An extensive treatment of such a mechanism in appetitive learning occurs in frustration theory (Amsel, 1962).

The similarity of Hull's theorizing in the 1930s and 1940s to recent computer-generated models of learning and memory has been noted by Hintzman (1992) in an article with the subtitle "Was the Cognitive Revolution a Mistake?" Hintzman, himself a product of the cognitive revolution, asserts that "Key ideas of the cognitive revolution, including cognitive organization and the computer metaphor, have been largely abandoned; and basic concepts from the era of behaviorism and functionalism, such as association, inhibition, similarity, unconscious learning, and transfer, have reemerged." He points particularly to the similarity of "Hullian theories of 50 years ago" to connectionist and production-system models of today's cognitivists. Much the same can be said about the approaches to theory based on neural networks that often depend on what is called the Hebbian synapse (see HEBB, DONALD). The proposition here is that the efficiency of cell A in firing cell B is increased as a function of a growth process that takes place at the synapse between cell A and cell B. As a principle of association, this is not greatly removed from Hull's reinforcement postulate. In short, it appears that a part of Clark Hull's lasting contribution will be to modern theories of the neurobiology of learning and memory, an ironic outcome considering the criticisms Hull suffered for what was called his "neurologizing."

REFERENCES

Ammons, R. B. (1962). Psychology of the scientist: IV. Passages from the Idea Books of Clark L. Hull. *Perceptual and Motor Skills 15*, 807–882.

Amsel, A. (1962). Frustrative nonreward in partial reinforcement and discrimination learning: Some recent history and theoretical extension. *Psychological Review 69*, 306–328.

———— (1989). *Behaviorism, neobehaviorism, and cognitivism in learning theory*. Hillsdale, N.J.: Erlbaum.

Amsel, A., and Rashotte, M. E. (1984). *Mechanisms of adaptive behavior: Clark L. Hull's theoretical papers with commentary*. New York: Columbia University Press.

Dollard, J., and Miller, N. E. (1950). *Personality and psychotherapy*. New York: McGraw-Hill.

Dollard, J., Dooh, I. W., Miller, N. E., Mowrer, O. H., and Sears, R. R. (1939). *Frustration and aggression*. New Haven: Yale University Press.

Grice, G. R. (1968). Stimulus intensity in response evocation. *Psychological Review 75*, 359–373.

Hintzman, D. L. (1992). 25 years of learning and memory: Was the cognitive revolution a mistake? In D. E. Meyer and S. Kornblum, eds., *Attention and performance XIV*, Hillsdale, N.J.: Lawrence Erlbaum Associates.

Hull, C. L. (1920). *Quantitative aspects of the evolution of concepts. Psychological Monographs 28*, whole no. 123.

———— (1931). Goal attraction and directing ideas conceived as habit phenomena. *Psychological Review 38*, 487–506.

———— (1943). *Principles of behavior: An introduction to behavior theory*. New York: Appleton-Century-Crofts.

———— (1951). *Essentials of behavior*. New Haven: Yale University Press.

———— (1952). *A behavior system: An introduction to behavior theory concerning the individual organism*. New Haven: Yale University Press.

Logan, F. A. (1960). *Incentive*. New Haven: Yale University Press.

Logan, F. A. (1979). Hybrid theory of operant conditioning." *Psychological Review 86*, 507–541.

Miller, N. E., and Dollard, J. (1941). *Social learning and imitation*. New Haven: Yale University Press.

Rescorla, R. A., and Wagner, A. R. (1972). A theory of Pavlovian conditioning: Variations in the effectiveness of reinforcement and nonreinforcement. In A. H. Black and W. F. Prokasy, eds., *Classical conditioning II: Current research and theory*. New York: Appleton-Century-Crofts.

Spence, K. W. (1952). Clark Leonard Hull: 1884–1952." *American Journal of Psychology 65*, 639–646.

———— (1954). The relation of response latency and speed to the intervening variables and N in S-R theory. *Psychological Review 61*, 209–216.

———— (1956). *Behavior theory and conditioning*. New Haven: Yale University Press.

Tolman, E. C. (1938). The determiners of behavior at a choice point. *Psychological Review 45*, 1–41.

Abram Amsel

HUNTER, WALTER S.

Scientists studying learning and memory know Walter S. Hunter (1889–1954) best for his analytical application of a device for assessing short-term retention, the delayed-response task. But his contributions to psychology were much more broad, and deep, than that. He was an influential and moderating force in the behaviorist movement; his thoughts and experiments included topics that remain issues of mainstream interest today, such as the nature of an animal's representation for memory, consciousness, and genetic influences on intellectual achievement; and he was a significant applied psychologist with the military.

When Walter Samuel Hunter was born, in 1889, it had been about a century since his Scotch-Irish

Figure 1.   Walter S. Hunter. *Courtesy Brown University Archives.*

ancestors had come to the United States. Born in Decatur, Illinois, within a year of the births of Dwight D. Eisenhower, Charles de Gaulle, Adolf Hitler, Charles Chaplin, and T.S. Eliot, Hunter spent his early adolescence working on his father's farm near Fort Worth, Texas. His intellectual interests emerged early. In the first stages of his adolescence he purchased and read Darwin's *Origin of Species* and *Descent of Man,* and by age 15 he had developed an active interest in a career in electrical engineering (Hunt, 1956). He attended Polytechnic College at Fort Worth with this objective in mind, but psychology attracted his attention through his reading of William JAMES's textbooks and he transferred to the University of Texas in 1908 to study it (Hunt, 1956).

After graduating from the University of Texas in 1910, he pursued his graduate work at the University of Chicago. Within only 2 years he completed his doctorate and returned as an instructor to the University of Texas. But these 2 years at Chicago must have been a concentrated experience indeed, in view of two particularly substantial outcomes. First, his thinking as a scientist was shaped by two of his professors, James Angell and Harvey Carr, who were among the leading functionalists of the day. Their influence undoubtedly helped form Hunter's favorable view of BEHAVIORISM, which had close links to functionalism (an orientation that emphasized the relationships between environmental or task variables and learning, rather than theories of how hypothetical processes determine the occurrence of learning). In addition, Angell had directed the Ph.D. dissertation of John WATSON at the University of Chicago a few years earlier. He undoubtedly maintained sufficient contact with Watson to transmit the latter's ideas to his own students. It is likely that in this way, Hunter was exposed early to the notions set forth by Watson in his *Psychological Review* paper mapping out the elements of behaviorism just 1 year after Hunter received his Ph.D.

Undeterred by a teaching load of four courses per semester, Hunter was productive in his research at the University of Texas, and after 4 years was appointed professor and head of the department of psychology at the University of Kansas (at age 27). Soon afterward, World War I required that Hunter work in the military service. As a psychological examiner he helped illustrate the predictive value of simply administered psychological tests, and in World War II he served as one of the military's leading administrators of such testing.

In 1925 Hunter became the first G. Stanley Hall Professor of Genetic Psychology at Clark, and in 1936 he was named head of the department at Brown University, where he remained until his death in 1954 (Carmichael, 1954). Hunter worked influentially in the editing of several journals (*Psychological Bulletin, Comparative Psychology Monographs, Behavior Monographs,* and *Journal of Animal Behavior*), and he created *Psychological Abstracts* and edited it for a period of 20 years. His several, and diverse, honors included membership in the National Research Council and the National Academy of Sciences, posts as president of several professional research societies including the American Psychological Association, and receipt of the U.S. President's Medal for Merit for his service as chairman of the Applied Psychology Panel of the National Defense Research Council during World War II (Schlosberg, 1954).

Hunter's scientific contributions are equally impressive and diverse, including his study of visual afterimages, auditory discriminations (see DISCRIMINATION AND GENERALIZATION), and issues of social psychology, consciousness, and thinking, but his most lasting contributions dealt with the topic that pervaded his writing in all other respects, memory. This is despite the fact that Hunter himself assiduously avoided reference to "memories" or a "memory process" in animals. To describe how a horse seemed to remember the route home, Hunter preferred instead of memory the concept of "sensory recognition," which, he felt, avoided attributing ideation to animals.

Hunter's Ph.D. thesis was intended to test the animal's behavior in the absence of an eliciting stimulus, the sort of circumstance that might be thought to require a memory system of some sort. He chose a test of retention that had been tried out by two of Carr's students, Haugh and Reed. Whatever its origin, Hunter adapted the delayed-response task in a fashion sufficiently convincing to persuade others to use it as the dominant task for short-term retention over the next 50 years, until delayed matching-to-sample came to be more effectively applied through the use of computers.

In his first version of this task Hunter trained hungry animals initially to obtain food by entering the lighted door of three possible doors (in a later version, no light was used and only the location of the door indicated the reward site). After the animal had perfected this discrimination, Hunter began trials in which the light was shown in the same way but turned off before the animal was allowed to choose a door. For the animal to reach this point required hundreds of training trials. Yet, because responding was permitted only in the absence of the stimulus, at specified intervals after taking it away, reliable correct responding hardly could be caused by sensory recognition; there were no sensory events to be recognized. So long as he could discount "overt orienting attitudes" of the sort that a hunting dog might use when indicating the location of a bird in the field, accurate choice could apparently be attributed to control by an internal representational response, or some other form of ideation. Hunter reasoned that the efficiency of ideation could be compared across various species of animals or even between animals and humans by increasing the interval between the offset of the light and the opportunity to respond.

Hunter estimated the longest retention interval that each of his subjects could tolerate before retention no longer was significant. For rats he estimated this to be about 10 seconds, for raccoons 25 seconds, for dogs 5 minutes, for his 13-month-old daughter Thayer about 24 seconds, for 2½-year old children 50 seconds, and for a 6-year-old child 20 minutes. Hunter judged that the rats were solving the problem by using the overt orienting attitudes of the pointer, but this did not seem necessary for the raccoons and children and so Hunter entertained the possibility that "sensory thought" might be involved for these subjects. He supposed that the critical stimulus—the position of the light or the location of the exit holding the reward—might be represented within the animal as an intraorganic cue, probably of a kinesthetic nature.

Hunter's research stimulated a number of studies by other scientists directed at one of two issues of phylogeny: (1) which animals can perform such a delayed response task without the use of physical orientation and thus reveal a capacity for internal ideation of the "sensory thought" type suggested by Hunter; and (2) how animals are ordered phylogenetically in terms of their capacity for such ideation, which was presumed to be tapped by the degree to which correct responding occurred after a long delay interval. Hunter later argued that correct performance of the double alternation task also could reveal a capacity for ideation. Hunter made substantial contributions to psychology throughout his 42 years in the field and his ideas in a variety of areas within psychology were influential, but it can be argued that none of his subsequent experiments had the impact of his Ph.D. thesis.

Some intriguing paradoxes of Hunter's career have been described by Hunt (1956) and are paraphrased here. Despite Hunter's success in avoiding serving in university administration, for which he was frequently sought, he was obviously a successful administrator, as indicated by the strength of the department he built at Brown and his work in the military. Despite his sympathy with and support of behaviorism, some of his most important research seemed more clearly understandable in terms of the use of symbolic processes by animals. Although he was one of the most influential experimental psychologists of the first half of the twentieth century, he spent the last 10 years of his life focusing on psychology's applications. Finally, Hunt notes two paradoxes of Hunter's personal life: despite a high rate of professional productivity, Hunter always seemed relaxed and with time to spare, and despite his emphasis on being impersonal and objective as a scientist, he was warm in his relationships with others.

Hunter's primary contribution to the field of learning and memory was to implement two tasks, the delayed response and the double alternation task, which provided a metric for discussing animal memory in an objective fashion and a forum for considering the use of representation in memory by animals

REFERENCES

Carmichael, H. (1954). Walter Samuel Hunter: 1889–1954. *American Journal of Psychology 67*, 732–734.

Hunt, J. McV. (1956). Walter Samuel Hunter. *Psychological Review 63*, 213–217.

Schlosberg, H. (1954). Walter S. Hunter: Pioneer objectivist in psychology. *Science 120*, 441–442.

Tinklepaugh, O. L. (1928). An experimental study of representative factors in monkeys. *Journal of Comparative Psychology 8*, 197.

Norman E. Spear

HYPNOSIS AND MEMORY

For many years, scholars, clinicians, and law enforcement professionals have attempted to enhance memory with hypnosis. The results of these attempts have been inconsistent. Some have reported great success with hypnosis (Reiser and Nielsen, 1980), while others have cautioned that a hypnotized person is likely to make more errors and to give inaccurate reports under hypnosis (Orne, 1979).

Hypnosis has been useful in some criminal investigations, especially when trauma to the witness or victim was involved (Reiser and Nielsen, 1980). Enhanced memory under hypnosis also has been found in some controlled laboratory experiments (Stager and Lundy, 1985). On the whole, though, the evidence about memory under hypnosis is mixed; many studies find no memory enhancement with hypnosis. Of greater practical consequence, hypnosis may distort the memory process. It has been suggested that hypnotized subjects (a) introduce fabrications into their reports and exhibit increased error rates (Orne, 1979); (b) are more susceptible to leading questions (Sanders and Simmons, 1983); and (c) are more likely to view distorted memories as being accurate (Sheehan and Tilden, 1984). In addition, the accuracy of information generated under hypnosis typically is unrelated to the confidence of the witness in the information recalled (Zelig and Beidleman, 1981).

Yet the case against hypnosis also is equivocal because some researchers have found hypnosis to improve memory without showing increased errors or greater susceptibility to misleading questions (Stager and Lundy, 1985). Furthermore, even unhypnotized witnesses are highly subject to memory alterations (Loftus, 1979), and unhypnotized witnesses are often inaccurate about the quality of their reports (Wells and Lindsay, 1983). Nevertheless, as a general safeguard against the potential problems encountered with memory under hypnosis, several states have placed some restrictions on the admissibility of recall under hypnosis in a court of law.

Retrieval Inhibition and Hypnosis

Evidence supporting the use of hypnosis to recover "lost" memories was found in an experiment by Geiselman et al. (1983) in which people participated in two sessions designed to compare amnesias created with and without hypnosis. In the session without hypnosis, the participants were told to forget certain items immediately after they were presented. The stated purpose of the experiment was to determine whether people could remember some information better if they were allowed to forget other information. At test, the subjects were asked to recall both the to-be-remembered items and the to-be-forgotten items. In the second session, the same people were given a command under hypnosis to forget certain items that were well learned in the second session (retrieval inhibition). After an attempt to recall the items, they were given a countermand to release the hypnotically induced amnesia (memory retrieval inhibition release). A second recall attempt for the previously unrecalled items was then recorded.

It was found that forgetting in the nonhypnotic session was related to the extent of retrieval inhibition and inhibition release observed in the hypnotic session. Therefore, it was concluded that the mechanisms of forgetting involved in the two laboratory demonstrations of hypnotic and nonhypnotic amnesia were related; the implication was that some of them were the same: retrieval inhibition and inhibition release. Thus, these results lend support to the claim by Reiser and Nielsen (1980) that hypnosis has the potential to recover "inhibited" memories.

Nonhypnotic Retrieval Techniques Versus Hypnosis

Research by Geiselman, Fisher, MacKinnon, and Holland (1985) compared the effectiveness of three interview procedures for optimizing eyewitness memory performance: (a) the *cognitive interview* based on memory-retrieval techniques from current memory research, (b) the controversial *hypnosis interview,* and (c) the *standard (control) police interview.* The standard interview consisted of the a narrative report of the witness, followed by specific questions from the interviewer. The cognitive interview included methods for jogging memory recall, such as reconstructing the circumstances that existed when the to-be-remembered event occurred, and recalling the event in a variety of orders and from different perspectives.

The cognitive, hypnosis, and standard interviews were evaluated experimentally in a controlled yet realistic setting. People viewed police training films of simulated violent crimes and were questioned individually in interactive interviews 48 hours later by experienced law enforcement personnel. Both the cognitive and the hypnosis procedures elicited a significantly greater number of correct items of information from the "witnesses" than did the standard interview (35 percent increase). These results held even for the most critical facts from the films and for crime scenarios in which the density of events was high. The number of incorrect items of information generated did not differ across the three interview conditions, so the subjects apparently did not generate inaccurate reports under hypnosis.

Based on analyses of the interview transcripts, it was speculated that the hypnosis interviews may have been effective because of factors related to side effects of hypnosis, such as memory guidance techniques. That is, some of the memory-jogging methods from the cognitive interview were used spontaneously by the hypnotists. Whether cognitive interviewing is as effective as hypnosis with traumatized witnesses (Reiser and Nielsen, 1980) remains to be determined in future research.

Comparison of Experimental Methods

Geiselman and Machlovitz (1987) surveyed the literature on hypnosis memory recall to determine whether differences in methodology can explain the failure versus the success of hypnosis as a memory recall aid. The methodological factors examined were the nature of the to-be-remembered stimulus materials, the nature of the memory interview, the retention interval, and the number of participant observers studied. The survey was restricted to experiments described in published journal articles. The experimental designs that were used in these studies included (a) a hypnosis condition compared with a control (no hypnosis induction) condition, (b) a prehypnosis recall attempt compared with a hypnosis-aided recall attempt by the same person, and (c) a recall attempt under hypnosis by people classified as highly hypnotizable versus people classified as unhypnotizable.

Of the thirty-eight experiments, twenty-one reported significantly more correct information with hypnosis, thirteen reported no effect of hypnosis, and four reported significantly less correct information with hypnosis. Thus, there was a split between studies finding memory facilitation with hypnosis versus no effect or negative effects. With respect to incorrect information generated under hypno-

sis, eight experiments showed a significant increase in errors with hypnosis, while ten showed no effect of hypnosis. The remaining twenty experiments either did not present an analysis of error data or the designs did not permit an error analysis. For those eighteen studies where error rates were provided, five experiments showed memory facilitation with hypnosis without a significant increase in errors, and an equal number showed a significant increase in errors with hypnosis without memory facilitation. In sum, the effect of hypnosis on memory recall performance clearly is mixed.

The typical methodology employed in the experiments that were included in the Geiselman and Machlovitz survey consists of relatively artificial materials to be remembered (lists of words, pictures, stories) and static, predetermined questions to test memory rather than interactive interviews of the "witnesses" about live or filmed events. Thus, the typical experiment bears little resemblance to the use of hypnosis in the everyday forensic setting.

The five experiments that showed memory enhancement with hypnosis without an increase in errors generally made greater use of live events or films, interactive interviews, retention intervals of days to weeks, and larger sample sizes of observers than most of the other studies that were examined. The probability of obtaining this pattern of results by chance in this sample was quite low. Thus, the equivocal nature of the results of experiments on recall under hypnosis may be linked, in part, to methodological differences between the experiments. That is, the typical methodology may not capture critical factors in the forensic use of hypnosis.

These results are also interesting because it is usually more difficult to observe a phenomenon under natural conditions, where many factors are uncontrolled, than under conditions of rigorous experimental control. Therefore, some speculation is in order regarding why recall under hypnosis should be more successful when forensic-type conditions exist. An argument can be made that interactive interviews, long retention intervals, and arousing crimelike materials should increase the chance for success of any memory enhancement tool, including hypnosis.

First, an interactive interview gives the interviewer the opportunity to ask questions that build upon what the "witness" initially reports, whereas no such opportunity exists with fixed, prearranged questions. Thus, a memory recall aid, such as hypnosis, would have a greater opportunity for success in an interactive interview because any enhanced recall would likely lead to further recall.

Second, recall on long-delay tests logically would require greater focused attention for MEMORY SEARCH, as might be achieved with hypnosis, than would recall on immediate or minute-delay tests. There is experimental evidence that active memory search plays an increasingly important role in memory recall with longer time delays (Smith and Graesser, 1981).

Third, more realistic materials (live events or films) are (a) more arousing, and hypnosis has been claimed to relieve memory blockage caused by high levels of arousal (Reiser and Nielsen, 1980); and (b) more imageable, and hypnosis relies in large part on the use of mental imagery.

Conclusion

Some laboratory research on the usefulness of hypnosis as a memory aid has shown that the recovery of unrecalled (inhibited) memories can be achieved with the use of hypnosis. A survey of thirty-eight experiments on the enhancement of recall with hypnosis showed that success was most likely when hypnotists questioned observers interactively about natural events that occurred days to weeks earlier. However, research conducted under similar circumstances has shown that non-hypnotic memory-jogging techniques can enhance memory to the same extent as hypnosis without the use of hypnosis.

Still other research has shown hypnosis either to be ineffective or to produce inaccurate reports. On the basis of these results, several state supreme courts have been concerned about the increase in incorrect information that sometimes accompanies the increase in correct information gained from eyewitnesses with hypnosis. However, the relevance of many of those studies to the real-world use of hypnosis must be questioned, given that the experimental methodologies typically bear little resemblance to everyday conditions. Thus, the scientific jury is still out regarding the usefulness of hypnosis to enhance memory recall.

REFERENCES

Geiselman, R. E., Fisher, R. P., MacKinnon, D. P., and Holland, H. L. (1985). Eyewitness memory enhancement in the police interview: Cognitive retrieval mnemonics versus hypnosis. *Journal of Applied Psychology 70,* 401–412.

Geiselman, R. E., and Machlovitz, H. (1987). Hypnosis memory recall: Implications for forensic use. *American Journal of Forensic Psychology 1,* 37–47.

Geiselman, R. E., MacKinnon, D. P., Fishman, D. L., Jaenicke, C., Larner, B. R., Schoenberg, S., and Swartz, S. (1983). Mechanisms of hypnotic and nonhypnotic forgetting. *Journal of Experimental Psychology: Learning, Memory, and Cognition 9,* 626–635.

Loftus, E. F. (1979). *Eyewitness testimony.* Cambridge, Mass.: Harvard University Press.

Orne, M. T. (1979). The use and misuse of hypnosis in court. *International Journal of Clinical and Experimental Hypnosis 27,* 311–341.

Reiser, M., and Nielsen, M. (1980). Investigative hypnosis: A developing specialty. *American Journal of Clinical Hypnosis 23,* 75–84.

Sanders, G. S., and Simmons, W. L. (1983). Use of hypnosis to enhance eyewitness accuracy: Does it work? *Journal of Applied Psychology 68,* 70–77.

Sheehan, P. W., and Tilden, J. (1984). Real and simulated occurrences of memory distortion in hypnosis. *Journal of Abnormal Psychology 93,* 47–57.

Smith, D. A., and Graesser, A. C. (1981). Memory for actions in scripted activities as a function of typicality, retention interval, and retrieval task. *Memory and Cognition 9,* 550–559.

Stager, G. L., and Lundy, R. M. (1985). Hypnosis and the learning and recall of visually presented material. *International Journal of Clinical and Experimental Hypnosis 33,* 27–39.

Wells, G. L., and Lindsay, C. C. L. (1983). How do people infer accuracy? In S. M. A. Lloyd-Bostock and B. R. Clifford, eds., *Evaluating witness memory.* New York: Wiley.

Zelig, M., and Beidleman, W. B. (1981). The investigative use hypnosis: A word of caution. *The International Journal of Clinical and Experimental Hypnosis 29,* 401–412.

R. Edward Geiselman

I

IMPLICIT MEMORY

Psychological investigations of human memory have traditionally been concerned with conscious recollection or explicit memory for specific facts and episodes. During the 1980s, however, there was growing interest in a nonconscious form of memory, referred to as *implicit memory* (Schacter, 1987), that does not require any explicit recollection for specific episodes. Recent experimental investigations have revealed dramatic differences between implicit and explicit memory, and these differences have had a major impact on psychological theories of the processes and systems involved in human memory.

To understand the nature and significance of implicit memory, it is necessary first to consider the types of experimental paradigms that are used to assess both explicit and implicit memory. In a traditional explicit memory paradigm, there are three main phases: (1) a *study episode* in which people are exposed to a set of target materials, such as a list of words or a set of pictures; (2) a *retention interval,* which typically lasts for several minutes or hours, during which people perform tasks unrelated to the study phase; and (3) a *memory test* in which people are asked to think back to the study phase and either produce the target materials (recall) or discriminate the targets from items that were not presented during the study phase (recognition).

The typical implicit memory experiment includes a study phase and a retention interval that are similar to those used in studies of explicit memory. The critical difference between implicit and explicit memory experiments is observed during the test phase. Instead of being asked to try to remember previously studied items, people are simply instructed to perform a perceptual or cognitive task, such as identifying a word from a brief exposure or rating how much they like a face or an object; no reference is made to the prior study episode. However, some of the test items represent previously exposed target items—that is, words, faces, or objects that have been presented during the study episode; other test items represent novel or nonstudied words, faces, or objects that have not been presented during the study phase. Implicit memory for a previously studied item is inferred when it can be shown that subjects' task performance is influenced by prior exposure to studied items. For example, the probability of identifying previously studied items on the basis of a brief exposure may be increased relative to the accuracy of identifying nonstudied items, or subjects may indicate that they prefer or like previously exposed faces relative to nonexposed faces.

The hallmark of implicit memory, then, is a facilitation of performance that is attributable to information acquired during a specific episode, on a test that does not require conscious recollection of the episode. This facilitation of performance is often referred to as direct or repetition *priming.* Examples of tests used to assess priming include *stem* or *fragment completion* tasks, in which people are asked to complete word stems or fragments (e.g., TAB__) with the first word that comes to mind (e.g., TABLE), and priming is inferred from an enhanced tendency to complete the stems with previously studied words relative to nonstudied words; and *perceptual identification* tasks, in which people try to identify a word or object from a brief (e.g., 50 milliseconds) perceptual exposure, and priming is indicated by more accurate identification of recently studied items than of new, non-studied items.

Although it has been studied quite extensively in recent years, priming is not the only type of implicit memory. For instance, tasks in which people learn motor or cognitive skills may involve implicit memory, in the sense that skill acquisition does not require explicit recollection of a specific previous episode but does depend on information acquired during such episodes (see also MOTOR SKILLS). Similarly, tasks in which people are required to make various kinds of cognitive judgments (e.g., judging whether a name is famous or how much they like a face) can be influenced by implicit memory, in the sense that the cognitive judgment may be altered by information acquired during a study episode, even in the absence of conscious recollection of the episode.

Dissociations Between Implicit and Explicit Memory

One of the most fascinating aspects of implicit memory is that it can be separated or *dissociated* from explicit memory—that is, there are various experimental manipulations that affect implicit and explicit memory differently, and there are neurological conditions in which explicit memory is impaired while implicit memory is spared.

Perhaps the most dramatic dissociation between implicit and explicit memory has been provided by studies of brain-damaged patients with organic amnesia (see AMNESIA, ORGANIC). Amnesic patients are characterized by a severe impairment of explicit memory for recent events, although intelligence, perception, and language are relatively normal. This memory deficit is typically produced by lesions to either medial temporal or diencephalic brain regions. In contrast, a number of studies have demonstrated that amnesic patients show intact implicit memory. For example, it has been found repeatedly that amnesic patients show just as much priming as do normal subjects on stem completion and similar tasks, despite their inability to remember explicitly the target items or the study episode in which the items were encountered (see Shimamura, 1986). In addition, it has been demonstrated that amnesic patients often show normal or near-normal learning of motor and perceptual skills, and that their cognitive judgments can be biased by information acquired during specific episodes—episodes that the amnesic patient cannot remember explicitly (see Squire, 1987). Similarly, the administration of various drugs (e.g., anesthetic agents) that seem to eliminate explicit memory entirely may spare implicit memory (for review, see Kihlstrom and Schacter, 1990). These observations suggest that implicit memory is supported by different brain structures than is explicit memory, because normal implicit memory can occur in the absence of explicit memory.

Although the dissociation between implicit and explicit memory is highlighted most dramatically by studies of organic and drug-induced amnesia, similar dissociations have been produced in experiments with normal subjects who do not have any brain damage. Much of this work has focused on priming effects. For example, one important dissociation has been observed in experiments that have compared the effects of *semantic* and *nonsemantic* study tasks on implicit and explicit memory. It has been well established that performance on explicit recall and recognition tests is higher following semantic than nonsemantic study of an item—the *levels of processing* effect (see CODING PROCESSES: LEVELS OF PROCESSING). For example, when subjects perform a semantic encoding task during the study phase of an experiment (e.g., rate the pleasantness of a word or provide a definition of the word), subsequent probability of explicitly remembering the word is much higher than if subjects perform a nonsemantic encoding task during the study phase (e.g., count the number of vowels and consonants in the word). In contrast, however, it has been shown that the magnitude of priming on a stem completion task or perceptual identification task is less affected, or even unaffected, by the same manipulation: Priming effects do not differ significantly following semantic and nonsemantic encoding (cf. Jacoby, 1983; Roediger, Weldon, and Challis, 1989; Schacter, 1990).

The finding that priming is little affected by varying levels of processing at the time of encoding was reported initially in experiments that used familiar words as target materials. More recently, the same pattern of results has been observed in studies with visual objects. For example, in one experiment subjects were shown line drawings of common objects during the study phase, and performed either a semantic encoding task (think of functions that the object can be used to perform) or a nonsemantic encoding task (count the number of vertices in the object). Priming was later assessed with an object completion test in which subjects were shown perceptual fragments of studied and nonstudied objects, and provided the first object that came to mind in response to the perceptual fragment. The magnitude of priming on this test was identical following the semantic and nonsemantic encoding tasks, even though explicit memory for studied objects was considerably higher following the semantic study task than the nonsemantic study task (see Schacter, Delaney, and Merikle, 1990).

Several studies have shown that priming effects on a number of implicit memory tasks are frequently influenced by the physical form of a stimulus at study and test. For example, priming on visual implicit tests such as perceptual identification, stem completion, and fragment completion can be reduced substantially by presenting target words auditorily, thereby indicating that the phenomenon is to a large degree modality specific. Explicit memory, by contrast, tends to be less affected by such study/test modality shifts. There is also some evidence that priming can be reduced by changing the specific surface features of an item between study and test (e.g., if a word is studied in handwritten form and tested in typewritten form, there may be less priming than if the word is studied and tested in the same surface form), although the patterns of results are rather complex and such specificity effects are not always observed (cf. Graf and Ryan, 1990; Roediger, Weldon, and Challis, 1989; Schacter, 1990).

The foregoing does not constitute an exhaustive list of dissociations between implicit and explicit memory. For example, evidence exists that implicit memory is not influenced by presentation of interfering material during a retention interval, even though explicit memory is highly sensitive to such interference effects (see INTERFERENCE AND FORGETTING); and several studies have shown that forgetting over time can proceed differently for implicit and explicit memory (for further review, see Richardson-Klavehn and Bjork, 1988; Roediger, 1990; Schacter, 1987).

Dissociations between skill learning and explicit remembering have also been documented. The initial evidence was provided by neuropsychological studies which demonstrated that amnesic patients could acquire motor and perceptual skills in tasks that involve multiple learning trials and sessions, even though patients could not explicitly remember that they had acquired a new skill. More recent neuropsychological studies with patients suffering from different forms of dementia suggest that priming and skill learning are dissociable forms of implicit memory: Patients with Alzheimer's dementia show impaired priming on stem completion tasks yet show normal learning of motor skills, whereas patients with Huntington's disease show normal stem completion priming together with impaired learning of motor skills (see DEMENTIA).

Similarities between implicit and explicit memory have also been observed; this is to be expected, because both are forms of memory and hence presumably share some common characteristics. However, the differences between the two are most revealing theoretically and have led to a variety of proposals concerning the nature of implicit memory.

Theoretical Accounts of Implicit Memory

Most theoretical accounts of implicit memory have tended to focus heavily or exclusively on priming phenomena. It is important to keep in mind, however, that priming is only one type of implicit memory and that an adequate theory of implicit memory will ultimately have to come to grips with phenomena other than priming.

An early theoretical view held that implicit memory is attributable to the temporary activation of preexisting units or nodes in memory: Exposure to a word or object automatically activates a memory representation of it, and this activation subsides rather rapidly. Although able to accommodate some experimental results, this general idea has difficulty accounting for the finding that priming can be surprisingly long-lived—under certain conditions lasting weeks and months—and also fails to explain the fact that priming has been observed following exposure to unfamiliar materials, such as nonsense words or novel patterns and objects, that do not have any preexisting representation in memory as a unit (cf. Roediger, 1990; Schacter, 1987).

A rather different view holds that both implicit and explicit memory are based on newly created memory representations in a single episodic memory system, and that experimental dissociations can be attributed to the differing demands of the tests used to assess implicit and explicit memory. The general idea here is that dissociations between implicit and explicit memory are special cases of the general principles of transfer-appropriate processing and encoding specificity, which hold that memory performance is best when encoding and retrieval processes match. Specifically, it is held that most standard explicit memory tests require a good deal of *conceptually driven* processing: semantically based, subject-initiated attempts to recollect the study episode. By contrast, performance on such implicit memory tests as word completion and perceptual identification is held to be largely dependent on *data-driven* processing—processing that is determined largely by the physical characteristics of test cues. It thus follows that explicit memory—but not priming—should benefit from semantic study processing (which is thought to support conceptually driven processing) more than from nonsemantic study processing, whereas priming should be strongly dependent on matching of surface features between study and test (Jacoby, 1983; Roediger, Weldon, and Challis, 1989). However, it is possible to devise implicit tests that entail conceptually driven processing, and the transfer-appropriate processing view has led to predictions and corresponding demonstrations of dissociations *between* implicit tests, by contrasting implicit tasks that draw primarily on data-driven processing with implicit tasks that draw primarily on conceptually driven processing (see Roediger, 1990). However, a major problem for this view is that it does not provide a satisfying explanation of why priming is preserved in amnesic patients.

To accommodate the data on both amnesic patients and normal subjects, a number of investigators have proposed that priming depends on a memory system that is neuroanatomically distinct from the limbic structures—most important, the hippocampus (see GUIDE TO THE ANATOMY OF THE BRAIN)—that are damaged in amnesia and are necessary for explicit memory. A recent version of this hypothesis holds that priming depends on a *perceptual representation system* (PRS): a presemantic system composed of several interacting subsystems that handles information about the form and structure, but not the meaning, of words and objects (Schacter, 1990; Tulving and Schacter, 1990). Independent evidence for the existence of PRS has been provided by neuropsychological studies of patients with certain types of perceptual deficits. These studies have shown that for both words and objects, access to semantic and structural knowledge can be dissociated, thus suggesting that the two kinds of knowledge are represented separately; in addition, studies of lexical processing

using the neuroimaging technique of POSITRON EMISSION TOMOGRAPHY lead to the same conclusion (Schacter, 1990).

In view of the previously discussed evidence that many priming effects are largely independent of semantic study processing and dependent on structural information, there are grounds for hypothesizing that a presemantic system such as PRS is critically involved in priming. In addition, there is no reason to believe that PRS is impaired in amnesic patients, so the fact that amnesics generally show intact priming can be accommodated.

The PRS account, however, applies only to priming effects that are observed on such data-driven tests as word completion and identification. Priming in both normal subjects and amnesic patients has been observed on implicit memory tests that are primarily conceptually driven, such as producing members of a category in response to a category name. According to the PRS hypothesis, priming on conceptually driven tests has a different basis than does data-driven priming, and likely depends on semantic memory.

Concluding Comments

A great deal remains to be learned about implicit memory. Research concerning the phenomenon is in its infancy, and none of the major theoretical approaches outlined above is entirely satisfactory. Little is known about the manifestations and functions of implicit memory in everyday life, understanding of the neural basis of the phenomenon is limited, and questions are just beginning to be posed about the developmental course of implicit memory. Nevertheless, the discovery and exploration of implicit memory phenomena have already opened up some new vistas for memory research, and it seems likely that further empirical study and theoretical analysis of these phenomena will continue to pay handsome dividends in the future.

(See also EPISODIC MEMORY; SEMANTIC MEMORY.)

REFERENCES

Graf, P., and Ryan, L. (1990). Transfer-appropriate processing for implicit and explicit memory. *Journal of Experimental Psychology: Learning, Memory, Cognition 16,* 978–992.

Jacoby, L. L. (1983). Remembering the data: Analyzing

interactive processes in reading. *Journal of Verbal Learning and Verbal Behavior 22,* 485–508.

Kihlstrom, J. F., and Schacter, D. L. (1990). Anesthesia, amnesia, and the cognitive unconscious. In B. Bonke, W. Fitch, and K. Millar, eds., *Memory and awareness in anesthesia,* pp. 21–44. Amsterdam: Swets & Zeitlinger.

Richardson-Klavehn, A., and Bjork, R. A. (1988). Measures of memory. *Annual Review of Psychology 36,* 475–543.

Roediger, H. L. III (1990). Implicit memory: Retention without remembering. *American Psychologist 45,* 1043–1056.

Roediger, H. L. III, Weldon, M. S., and Challis, B. (1989). Explaining dissociations between implicit and explicit measures of retention: A processing account. In F. I. M. Craik and H. L. Roediger III, eds., *Varieties of memory and consciousness: Essays in honor of Endel Tulving,* pp. 3–42. Hillsdale, N.J.: Erlbaum.

Schacter, D. L. (1987). Implicit memory: History and current status. *Journal of Experimental Psychology: Learning, Memory, Cognition 13,* 501–518.

——— (1990). Perceptual representation systems and implicit memory: Toward a resolution of the multiple memory systems debate. *Annals of the New York Academy of Sciences 608,* 543–571.

Schacter, D. L., Delaney, S. M., and Merikle, E. P. (1990). Priming of nonverbal information and the nature of implicit memory. In G. H. Bower, ed., *Psychology of learning and motivation, vol. 26,* pp. 83–123. San Diego: Academic.

Shimamura, A. (1986). Priming effects in amnesia: Evidence for a dissociable memory function. *Quarterly Journal of Experimental Psychology 38A,* 619–644.

Squire, L. R. (1987). *Memory and brain.* New York: Oxford University Press.

Tulving, E., and Schacter, D. L. (1990). Priming and human memory systems. *Science 247,* 301–306.

Daniel L. Schacter

IMPRINTING

[*This composite entry consists of two articles,* Behavioral Aspects *by Johan J. Bolhuis and Gabriel Horn, and* Neural Substrates *by Gabriel Horn.*]

Behavioral Aspects

Imprinting is the learning process through which the social preferences of animals of certain species become restricted to a particular object or class of objects. A distinction is made between filial and sexual imprinting. *Filial imprinting* is involved in the formation, in young animals, of an attachment to, and a preference for, the parent, parent surrogate, or siblings. *Sexual imprinting* is involved in the formation of mating preferences that are expressed in later life. The phenomenon of filial imprinting has been known for a long time and was described as early as 1518 by Sir Thomas More in his *Utopia.* However, imprinting was investigated experimentally much later, by Spalding in 1873 and by Heinroth in 1911. Konrad LORENZ subsequently provided a detailed description of imprinting in a number of bird species in an influential work published in 1935.

Filial Imprinting

Although filial imprinting may occur in mammals (Sluckin, 1972), it has been studied mostly in precocial birds such as ducklings and chicks. These birds can move about shortly after hatching, and they approach and follow an object to which they are exposed. In a natural situation the first object the young bird encounters is usually its mother. In the absence of the mother, inanimate mother surrogates are effective in eliciting filial behavior (Bateson, 1966; Sluckin, 1972; Horn, 1985). When the chick or duckling is close to an appropriate object, it will attempt to snuggle up to it, frequently emitting soft twitters. Initially the young bird approaches a wide range of objects, though some are more attractive to it than others. After the bird has been exposed to one object long enough, it remains close to this object and may run away from novel ones. If the familiar object is removed, the bird becomes restless and emits shrill calls. When given a choice between the familiar stimulus and a novel one, the bird shows a preference for the familiar stimulus. Thus, filial imprinting refers to the acquisition of a social preference and not just an increase in following (Sluckin, 1972).

Conditions for Imprinting

To study visual imprinting in the laboratory, chicks or ducklings may be hatched in darkness, and exposed for a period of 1 to 2 hours to a conspicuous object when they are about 24 hours old. The animals are then returned to a dark incubator and kept there until their preferences are tested by exposing them to the familiar object and a novel object. A widely used measure of filial preference is approach to the familiar object relative to approach to a novel object. Another measure takes advantage of the fact that an imprinted chick emits distress calls in the presence of a novel object and does not do so, or does so less frequently, in the presence of the familiar. The effectiveness of imprinting stimuli varies. For example, young ducklings approach and follow objects larger than a matchbox, but peck at smaller objects. For chicks, red and blue objects are more effective imprinting stimuli than yellow and green objects. Movement, brightness, and contrast all enhance the attractiveness of an imprinting stimulus, as does the presentation of an auditory stimulus with a visual stimulus.

Imprinting and Learning

Filial imprinting has been regarded as different from other forms of learning because it proceeds without any obvious reinforcement such as food or warmth (see Bolhuis, De Vos, and Kruijt, 1990, for a discussion of these issues). However, an imprinting object may itself be a reinforcer, that is, a stimulus which an animal finds rewarding (see REINFORCEMENT). Just as a rat learns to press a pedal to receive a reward of food, so a visually naive chick learns to press a pedal to see an imprinting object. The ability to learn and remember the characteristics of objects to which an animal is exposed may be a very common form of learning.

Reversibility and Sensitive Periods

Imprinting was thought to be irreversible and to occur during a "sensitive period" (or "critical period"). Numerous studies have demonstrated that filial preferences can in fact be reversed when the original object is removed and the animal is exposed to a novel object. Evidence suggests that there is a difference between the memory of the first stimulus and that of subsequent stimuli to which the animal is exposed. Under certain circumstances the preference for the first object may return (Bolhuis, 1991). The ability to form filial attachments has been shown to depend on both developmental age and time since hatching. The ability to imprint is related to the development of the animal's sensorimotor abilities. The sensitive period is brought to an end by the learning experience (imprinting) itself: Once the bird has formed a preference for a particular object, it avoids novel objects. Consequently it tends not to be exposed to them for long, and so may learn little about them. When the bird is left in its cage, it may form an attachment to features of its rearing environment. Rearing the bird in a visually impoverished environment (in darkness or deprived of patterned light) extends the period during which it forms an attachment to a conspicuous object (see Bateson, 1966). The sensitive period pertains to filial attachment and may relate to the link formed between the (neural) representation of the imprinted object and approach behavior. While the formation of this link may have a sensitive period, there is no reason to suppose that the learning and recognition processes have one.

Auditory Imprinting

In the natural context auditory stimuli play an important role in the formation of filial preferences (Gottlieb, 1971). Numerous studies have failed to show that auditory preferences are formed in the same way as visual preferences (i.e., learning as a result of exposure). Preferences resulting from exposure to an auditory stimulus only, whether before or after the birds have hatched, are relatively weak and short-lived. Such preferences can be strengthened when the young bird is simultaneously exposed to an auditory stimulus and a visual stimulus during auditory training. Thus, strictly speaking, early auditory learning may not be a form of imprinting in the sense of learning through exposure.

Sexual Imprinting

It has been suggested that one of the consequences of filial imprinting is the determination of adult sexual preferences. Recent research suggests that filial imprinting and sexual imprinting are two separate (although perhaps partially overlapping) processes. Not only is the time of expression of the preferences different, but so is the period of time during which experience affects preferences. Sexual preferences continue to be affected by experience up to the time of mating. Furthermore, filial preferences may be formed after a relatively short period of exposure to an object. In contrast, sexual preferences develop as the result of a long period of exposure to, and social interaction with, the parents as well as the siblings. In zebra finches (*Taeniopygia guttata*) the amount of social interaction with the parents and the number of siblings with which the young bird is reared significantly affect later sexual preferences. Normally, sexual imprinting ensures that the bird will mate with a member of its own strain or species. When the young bird is cross-fostered, that is, reared with adults of a different species, it develops a sexual preference for the foster species. More specifically, in Japanese quail (*Coturnix coturnix japonica*) and domestic chickens, mating preferences are for individual members of the opposite sex that are different, but not too different, from individuals with which the young bird was reared (Bateson, 1978).

Predispositions

Research shows that filial preferences not only are formed as a result of learning through exposure but also are influenced by a specific predisposition (Horn, 1985; Johnson and Bolhuis, 1991; Bolhuis, 1991). This predisposition may be measured in the laboratory by giving chicks (*Gallus gallus domesticus*) a choice between a rotating stuffed jungle fowl and (for instance) a rotating red box. Under some conditions the two stimuli are equally attractive. But if the young chick is given a certain amount of nonspecific experience, such as being handled and allowed to run, the chick prefers the fowl to the box when tested 24 hours later. In order to be effective, this nonspecific experience must occur within a "sensitive period" (about 20 to 40 hours after hatching). It appears that the "target" stimuli of the predisposition are in the head and neck region but are not species-specific. Once the predisposition has developed, it does not function as a filter that prevents the chick from learning about objects that do not resemble conspecifics; such chicks can learn about other objects by being exposed to them. Thus, it is likely that the mechanisms underlying the predisposition and those underlying learning influence behavior independently.

REFERENCES

Bateson, P. P. G. (1966). The characteristics and context of imprinting. *Biological Reviews 41,* 177–220.

———— (1978). Sexual imprinting and optimal outbreeding. *Nature 273,* 659–660.

Bolhuis, J. J. (1991). Mechanisms of avian imprinting: A review. *Biological Reviews 66,* 303–345.

Bolhuis, J. J., De Vos, G. J., and Kruijt, J. P. (1990). Filial imprinting and associative learning. *Quarterly Journal of Experimental Psychology 42B,* 313–329.

Gottlieb, G. (1971). *Development of species identification in birds.* Chicago: University of Chicago Press.

Heinroth, O. (1911). Beiträge zur Biologie, namentlich Ethologie und Psychologie der Anatiden. In *Verhandlungen des 5. Internationaler Ornithologischer Kongress Berlin,* pp. 589–702.

Horn, G. (1985). *Memory, imprinting, and the brain.* Oxford: Clarendon Press.

Johnson, M. H., and Bolhuis, J. J. (1991). Imprinting, predispositions and filial preference in the chick. In R. J. Andrew, ed., *Neural and behavioural plasticity.* Oxford: Oxford University Press.

Lorenz, K. (1935). Der Kumpan in der Umwelt des Vogels. *Journal für Ornithologie 83,* 137–213, 289–413.

Sluckin, W. (1972). *Imprinting and early learning.* London: Methuen.

Spalding, D. A. (1873). Instinct, with original observations on young animals. *Macmillan's Magazine 27,* 282–293.

Johan J. Bolhuis
Gabriel Horn

Neural Substrates

Filial imprinting is a process by which the young of precocial animals learn the characteristics of certain objects by being exposed to them. Through this process the young animal comes to recognize an object and to prefer it to novel objects. The neural basis of the underlying recognition memory has been studied most extensively in the domestic chick (Horn, 1985, 1990). When dark-reared chicks are trained by exposing them to an imprinting object for approximately 1 to 2 hours, metabolic changes occur in the dorsal part of the cerebral hemispheres. Specifically, there is an increase in the incorporation of radioactively tagged uracil into RNA in this brain region of trained chicks compared with control chicks (dark-reared chicks or chicks that have merely been exposed to overhead light). There are several reasons for believing that the biochemical changes are related to learning rather than to various side effects of training (e.g., to differences in movement, excitement, sensory stimulation between the trained chicks and their controls): (1) when visual input is restricted to one hemisphere, incorporation of radioactive uracil into RNA is higher in the trained than in the untrained hemisphere; (2) the amount incorporated is related to how much the chicks learn and not to various other measures of behavior; (3) the increase is not related to short-term effects of sensory stimulation.

Biochemical Changes Localized to Specific Brain Regions

Imprinting leads to changes in the incorporation of radioactive uracil into RNA in a restricted brain region, the intermediate and medial part of the hyperstriatum ventrale (IMHV), a sheet of cells in the cerebral hemispheres (see Figure 1). Further evidence that the region is crucially involved in learning is the following: (4) destruction of IMHV before training prevents imprinting; (5) if the region is destroyed immediately after training, chicks do not prefer the training object, though for chicks with lesions of IMHV an imprinting object still elicits approach behavior but the chicks appear incapable of learning its characteristics; (6) it is possible to bias chicks' preferences by delivering trains of short pulses of electric current to IMHV through electrodes that have been implanted into the region. At the end of the period of electrical stimulation, the chicks were shown two lights, one flashing at the rate of 4.5 per second and the other at 1.5 per second. If the IMHV region had been stimulated at 4.5 trains per second, the chicks preferred the light flashing at this frequency. In contrast, chicks that had received electrical stimulation of IMHV at the rate of 1.5 trains per second preferred the light flashing at this rate. Electrical stimulation of two visual receiving areas of the forebrain did not influence the chicks' preferences. Taken together, these results strongly suggest that the IMHV region is involved in the recognition memory of imprinting, probably storing information.

Neuronal Mechanisms of Memory

Imprinting leads to changes in the structure of synapses in IMHV, in particular to an increase in the area of thickened membrane on the postsynaptic side of certain synapses. This area of membrane is known as the postsynaptic density. The changes are restricted to synapses on the spines of dendrites (axospinous synapses) and are found in the left, not in the right, IMHV. Certain spine synapses in the mammalian brain are excitatory and possess, in the postsynaptic density, receptors for the excitatory neurotransmitter l-glutamate. Does the increased area of the postsynaptic density of axospinous synapses imply that imprinting leads to an increase in the number of receptors for l-glutamate? It appears that it does. After chicks have been trained, there is an increase in the number of a certain type of receptors for l-glutamate in the left IMHV, but not in the right. The increased number of receptors is related to the amount the chicks have learned about the imprinting object. One consequence of this change may be that after training, the release of a given amount of l-glutamate from a presynaptic ending may exert a greater excitatory action on the postsynaptic cell than before training. That is, as many hypotheses have suggested, learning leads to an increased efficacy of synaptic transmission. Training also leads to specific changes in the responses of neurons in the left IMHV, changes that depend on the nature of the training object (McLennan and Horn, 1991).

We still do not know, however, whether the changes in synaptic organization that follow exposure to an imprinting object occur at all synapses in IMHV or to a restricted population of them; and if the latter is the case, whether and how the neurons bearing the modified synapses are interconnected. The particular l-glutamate receptors shown to be affected by imprinting are those of the n-methyl-d-aspartate (NMDA) variety. In mammals, these receptors are involved in other forms of synaptic plasticity. Thus the cellular mechanisms of synaptic plasticity may be similar in diverse systems though the functions of the synaptic change may be different: In circuits involved in learning, the synaptic changes may play a part in information storage. In other systems, these changes may be a response to either physical damage or physiological dysfunction. (See also GLUTAMATE RECEPTORS AND THEIR CHARACTERIZATION.)

Cerebral Asymmetry and Imprinting

Studies in which the left or right IMHV region has been surgically damaged suggest that, in accord

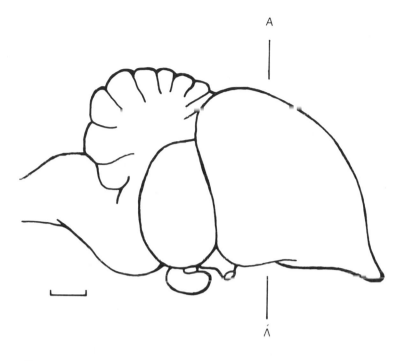

a

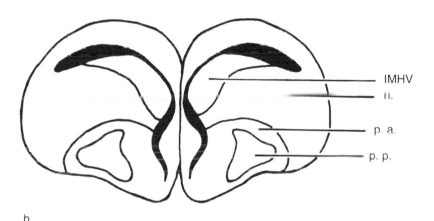

b

Figure 1.   Outline drawing of the chick brain. The vertical lines AA' above and below the drawing of the lateral aspect (**a**) indicate the plane of the transverse section outline (**b**) of the brain. IMHV extends approximately 2.5 millimeters from front to back of the cerebral hemisphere. Abbreviations: IMHV, the intermediate and medial part of the hyperstriatum ventrale; n., neostriatum; p.a., paleostriatum augmentatum; p.p., paleostriatum primitivum. Scale bar: 2 millimeters. *Reproduced with permission from G. Horn and M. H. Johnson, Memory systems in the chick: Dissociations and neuronal analysis. Neuropsychologia 27:1–22. Copyright 1989, Pergamon Press PLC.*

with the data on synaptic changes, the left IMHV functions as a long-term store. However, during the first day after imprinting another memory system, referred to as S^1, is established outside IMHV. S^1 is formed under the influence of the right IMHV:

If this region is absent, S^1 is not formed. It has been suggested that the right IMHV functions as a temporary store, transferring information to S^1. Hence there is a dynamic element to memory formation; and the left IMHV store and S^1 appear to be independent and to work in parallel. As a result, after both stores have been formed, chicks are still able to recognize the familiar object even if the left IMHV is removed. It seems unlikely that the left IMHV and S[1] are exact duplicates, but we do not yet know in what ways their storage functions differ. Thus, even in the case of the recognition memory of imprinting, more than one memory system is formed. Further evidence that several memory systems exist in the young chick is that chicks with lesions of IMHV (placed before S[1] has been formed), while being severely impaired in their ability to imprint, are nevertheless able to learn certain other tasks. Multiple memory systems therefore not only are found in mammalian brains but also may be a fundamental part of the design of the vertebrate brain.

On the basis of its connections and developmental history IMHV has been compared to the prefrontal lobes of primates (Horn, 1985). Evidence from humans suggests that this region plays a crucial role in the organization of memory (Janowsky, Shimamura, and Squire, 1989).

REFERENCES

Horn, G. (1985). *Memory, imprinting and the brain.* Oxford: Clarendon Press.
———— (1990). Neural bases of recognition memory investigated through an analysis of imprinting. *Philosophical Transactions of the Royal Society of London 329,* 35–44.
Janowsky, J. S., Shimamura, A. P., and Squire, L. R. (1989). Source and impairment in patients with frontal lobe lesions. *Neuropsychologia 27,* 1043–1056.
McLennan, J. G., and Horn, G., (1991). Learning-dependent responses to imprinting stimuli of units in a recognition memory system. *European Journal of Neuroscience suppl. 4,* 61.

Gabriel Horn

INDIVIDUAL DIFFERENCES IN LEARNING AND MEMORY

Individual differences in learning and memory abilities have fascinated people since they began to think about the operation of mind. In discussing his wax metaphor of memory, Plato noted that memories made of "pure and clear [wax]. . . easily learn and easily retain," whereas those made of "muddy and of impure wax [have] . . . a corresponding defect in the mind." Like most of us, Plato realized that people differ in what they learn and remember and in how well they do both. This is certainly true at the extremes (see AMNESIA, FUNCTIONAL; AMNESIA, ORGANIC; MNEMONISTS), but how relevant is it over the normal range of memory abilities?

The psychological research supports five main conclusions about individual differences in learning and memory (see, e.g., Hunt, 1978; MacLeod, 1979). First—and most obvious—people differ in what they know, their *knowledge base.* Second, people differ in their *capacity* to hold information in consciously accessible memory. Third, people possess and invoke different *strategies* for learning. Fourth, people differ in the *retrieval efficiency* with which they can summon information from more permanent, long-term memory. Fifth, there do not appear to be any consistent *sex differences* in learning and memory ability, although women and men may choose to learn different information (which relates to the first issue, knowledge base). Let us consider the first four claims in more detail, beginning with knowledge differences.

Knowledge Differences

Standard intelligence tests measure two aspects of memory, the first being general knowledge and vocabulary. People differ in the breadth and depth of their knowledge. Consider the "paradox of the expert": A simple theory of FORGETTING might claim that forgetting is caused by *interference* among related concepts in memory (see INTERFERENCE AND FORGETTING). This implies that someone who knows more about a particular topic should be more subject to forgetting in that domain. But if this is true, how does one ever become an expert in a domain? One resolution is to argue that we integrate our knowledge so that related ideas are joined and therefore support rather than compete with each other (Smith, Adams, and Schorr, 1978).

Indeed, those with high knowledge in a domain learn and retain new facts in that domain more easily than do those with low knowledge (Voss, Vesonder, and Spilich, 1980). Furthermore, the experts seem especially superior in remembering the important information (see EXPERTS' MEMORIES). Popular memory metaphors of libraries or warehouses do not fit comfortably here. Instead, think of memory as a scaffolding: The more memories are attached to the basic structure, the more places there are to attach new memories. The scaffolding may even guide us to where it would be best to attach each new memory.

People differ not only in what they know and how much they know, but also in how that knowledge is organized (Coltheart and Evans, 1981). Because retrieval relies heavily on the *association* between facts and ideas, *organization* influences how we retrieve our knowledge. An individual who has two facts directly connected in memory should be able to get from one to the other much more quickly than someone who must go through multiple "way stations." Part of coming to understand a domain better is, no doubt, reorganizing one's knowledge more appropriately.

Each of us is unique in large part because what we know is unique, both in terms of autobiographical knowledge (see EPISODIC MEMORY) and in terms of general world knowledge (see SEMANTIC MEMORY). Thus, the content of our memories is one major source of individual differences. The other three differences to be examined all have to do more with how we acquire, store, transform, and use that knowledge—with cognitive processes.

Capacity Differences

Probably the best-known individual differences dimension in learning and memory is that of the capacity of conscious memory (see WORKING MEMORY). This is the other aspect of memory that is directly measured in standard intelligence tests. Here a person must repeat back digits in the same order that they were read by the tester. We all have a sharp limitation on how much we can consciously think about at one time—our MEMORY SPAN (Dempster, 1981). But even in the normal range of intelligence, not everyone's span is the same. What causes these differences? There seem to be two main mechanisms underlying the span of working memory—ability to identify the specific elements to be held and ability to retain the order of information (Humphreys et al., 1983). Interestingly, speed of scanning through the information held in working memory does not seem to differ reliably across individuals (Hunt, 1978).

It is tempting to set aside data like those on span differences as irrelevant to the "real world."

After all, how often do we listen to a long string of items and then repeat them back to someone? In fact, though, holding information in working memory is something we do constantly and upon which we rely heavily. This is true not only in remembering a new phone number or several unfamiliar names. Daneman and Carpenter (1980) have shown that span differences have powerful implications for how successfully people read. Those with larger spans in reading (or in listening) show better comprehension of what they read. Apparently, people with a larger working memory capacity can hold previous sentences in mind more easily, and thus assemble the overall meaning of what they read more effectively.

Learning Strategy Differences

There are many different ways to learn (see CODING PROCESSES), from rote repetition to complex mnemonics. All learning involves *recoding;* information must be transformed from its perceived form into a form suitable for remembering. It is well established that people differ in their speed and in their efficiency of recoding (Gagné, 1967). What may be less obvious is that people also differ in which processes they use and in when they use them.

Studies of *learning style* converge on this point (Schmeck, 1983). At a global level, learners emphasize either overall comprehension or specific detail, appearing to be either conclusion-oriented or description-oriented. Those who emphasize overall comprehension engage in deeper processing, while those concerned with specific detail focus more on surface processing. Ordinarily, such a strategic difference will favor those who undertake deeper processing. Thus, note taking in a classroom setting induces deeper processing and better retention of important information.

Another illustration is individual differences in reported *imagery ability.* People vary in whether they use more language-based or picture-based strategies to learn and remember. Indeed, research suggests that visual memory can be quite independent of verbal memory. People who recognize faces or pictures well will not necessarily remember what they read better than will people with poorer visual memory. Yet although visual and *verbal* memory appear to be quite independent, the widely held belief that some people learn best visually and others learn best *auditorily* has not been supported experimentally. We can make sense of this by realizing that skills that are verbal need not be auditory in character.

There are many other different techniques and strategies for learning. Thus it seems quite reasonable to suppose that different individuals learn most effectively using different strategies. However, the evidence to support this intuition has been notoriously difficult to obtain. Usually a strategy that improves one person's learning also improves another person's learning. What may differ, then, is the choices that people make, a metacognitive issue (see METAMEMORY). How we select the optimal process(es) for a particular learning situation from among our repertoire of processes may be one of the most critical differences of all.

Retrieval Speed Differences

We saw above that *retrieval time* for information in working memory is not a reliable source of individual differences. Given the sharp capacity limitation, the small contents of working memory are easily searched. But the same is not true of long-term memory, where all of our knowledge is stored. If we know upward of 10 billion facts, as some speculations have it, how are we able to find any one of them quickly? Even searching at the impossibly fast rate of 1 millisecond per fact, it would take us months to find any single fact.

Extensive research (Hunt, 1978) has shown that people retrieve information from long-term memory at different rates. Consider a very simple retrieval: You see two letters, and you must ascertain if they have the same name. We know that it takes longer to determine the answer if the two letters are "Aa" than if they are "aa" or "AA." Presumably this is because long-term memory access is required only for the first letter pair, where the two are not physically identical. On average, this retrieval time is about 80 milliseconds, but high-ability individuals are faster than low-ability individuals by about 30–50 milliseconds.

A naive critic might say, "But this is a tiny difference." Now consider reading. If one were to lose 50 milliseconds for every letter read in an article, this would quickly add up. And this is just for such highly learned facts as the twenty-six letters of the alphabet. The problem must be vastly greater when we begin to consider words and other more complex types of knowledge. If the elementary

processes are not executed as efficiently in one individual as they are in another, the cost for learning and memory as a whole can be large indeed.

The goal of this brief sketch has been to localize four of the more crucial individual differences in learning and memory, and to provide some of the evidence for these differences. Of course, there are many other differences in how people learn and remember, but these are usually more isolated and less characteristic of the memory system as a whole. In years to come, we hope to find ways of recognizing these differences in our educational system and of assisting in improving skills to their optimal level. As always, though, we will have to understand before we can modify.

REFERENCES

Coltheart, V., and Evans, J. S. B. T. (1981). An investigation of semantic memory in individuals. *Memory and Cognition 9*, 524–532.

Daneman, M., and Carpenter, P. A. (1980). Individual differences in working memory and reading. *Journal of Verbal Learning and Verbal Behavior 19*, 450–466.

Dempster, F. N. (1981). Memory span: Sources of individual and developmental differences. *Psychological Bulletin 89*, 63–100.

Gagné, R. M., ed. (1967). *Learning and individual differences.* Columbus, Ohio: Charles E. Merrill.

Humphreys, M. S., Lynch, M. J., Revelle, W., and Hall, J. W. (1983). Individual differences in short-term memory. In R. F. Dillon and R. R. Schmeck, eds., *Individual differences in cognition*, vol. 1, pp. 35–64. New York: Academic Press.

Hunt, E. (1978). Mechanics of verbal ability. *Psychological Review 85*, 109–130.

MacLeod, C. M. (1979). Individual differences in learning and memory: A unitary information processing approach. *Journal of Research in Personality 13*, 530–545.

Schmeck, R. R. (1983). Learning styles of college students. In R. F. Dillon and R. R. Schmeck, eds., *Individual differences in cognition*, vol. 1, pp. 233–279. New York: Academic Press.

Smith, E. E., Adams, N., and Schorr, D. (1978). Fact retrieval and the paradox of interference. *Cognitive Psychology 10*, 438–464.

Voss, J. F., Vesonder, G. T., and Spilich, G. J. (1980). Text generation and recall by high-knowledge and low-knowledge individuals. *Journal of Verbal Learning and Verbal Behavior 19*, 651–667.

Colin M. MacLeod

INFANCY, MEMORY IN

According to classic developmental theory, infants operate in the present, without thoughts of the past or anticipations of the future. Adults cannot remember events from infancy (see AMNESIA, INFANTILE), a fact sometimes cited to corroborate the notion that memories are not formed during the preverbal period. Recent experimental studies demonstrate that young infants have more robust memories than heretofore believed. Indeed, modern theorists are focused on the different *types* of memory infants might have. Infants seem to remember particular things under certain conditions and not others; they may also have privileged memory for biologically relevant signals such as faces and speech sounds.

Three experimental procedures have been developed to probe infant preverbal memory: (1) visual preference tests, (2) CONDITIONING procedures, and (3) deferred imitation. Each approach measures a different type of memory capacity of the infant, as described below. (A fourth technique can also be used, the so-called object permanence test, which is reviewed elsewhere in this volume; see OBJECT CONCEPT, ACQUISITION OF).

Recent Work on Infant Memory

Infant Visual Recognition Memory

The procedures used to evaluate infant visual recognition rely on infants' curiosity in exploring novel visual patterns (Fagan, 1990; Cohen and Gelber, 1975). Infants are shown a visual pattern for a certain length of time. A delay is imposed, and then they are presented with the old visual pattern and a new one. If infants devote more looking time to the new pattern than to the old one, this is taken as evidence that they have some memory of the previously exposed target. Two specific techniques use this underlying principle: the *habituation-dishabituation* technique and the *paired-comparison* technique. For habituation-dishabituation, infants are repeatedly exposed to the initial target until they become bored with it (habituated). The new pattern is then introduced, and if looking time increases significantly (dishabituation), this shows that the infants recognize the pattern as being different from the one in memory. For the paired-comparison technique, infants are initially shown two identical patterns side by side for a certain familiarization period. It is not required that the infants habituate, only that they visually examine the display (usually 30 seconds to 2 minutes). Then a delay is imposed, and two patterns (the old one and a new one) are again presented. The index of memory is their preference for the novel pattern.

Age-Related Findings. Initially, studies found visual recognition memory in infants older than about 10–12 weeks of age, but no recognition memory in younger babies. This made some intuitive sense, because it coincided with the age at which infants first react to mothers with a smile of recognition. However, researchers soon discovered that if the length of time infants studied the to-be-remembered stimuli was increased (up to 5 minutes) and the patterns were made very different from one another, even newborn infants could retain information in the visual recognition paradigm, at least for delays of a few seconds. Research then shifted to (1) the effect of study time on memory and (2) the length of retention interval that can be tolerated by infants.

Study Time (Length of the "Encoding" Phase). Young infants require shorter study times to demonstrate the novelty preference (the measure of memory) when the choice stimuli are vastly different than when the stimuli are similar. This was illustrated in a study by Fagan (1990) using the paired-comparison technique. He tested 5-month-old infants using pairs of patterns that were graded in the degree to which they were discriminable from one another. The results showed that when the easiest pair was used, infants needed only about 5 seconds of study time to demonstrate the novelty preference; when the pair of medium discriminability was used, they needed about 20 seconds; and when the least discriminable pair was used, they required about 30 seconds. The inference that can be drawn is that infants, like students studying for an exam, need relatively more time to study material if they are asked to remember subtle differences between things.

Length of Retention Interval. Fagan showed visual patterns to 5-month-olds and then imposed delays of 3 hours and 1, 2, 7, and 14 days. The results revealed that infants could recognize which target they had previously seen even after the 14-day delay. What makes babies forget? Results from a variety of studies show that young infants will forget if they are shown highly related and distracting material during the retention interval. For example, if infants study photographs of faces and then are shown other face photographs during the retention interval, their subsequent memory performance will be poorer. The two factors that lead to maximum interference are (1) stimuli that closely resemble the to-be-remembered material and (2) stimuli presented soon after the initial exposure. This is reminiscent of adult memory, inasmuch as interference with remembering, say, a telephone number is maximized by hearing other numbers soon after the initial information is delivered (see INTERFERENCE AND FORGETTING). Another factor that influences the length of infant retention is the temporal spacing of the initial studying time. In one study, two groups of infants were given the same length of time to study a face photograph (20 seconds). However, for one group this study time was *massed,* meaning it consisted of four 5-second intervals with only a few seconds separating each interval. For the other group this experience was *distributed,* meaning there were much longer pauses between the four 5-second intervals. Both groups demonstrated immediate recognition memory; however, only the group that received the distributed exposure remembered over longer delays. This effect of distributed study is also a well-documented aspect of adult memory (see DISTRIBUTED PRACTICE EFFECTS).

Retention of a Conditioned Response

The second approach to evaluating infant memory was developed by Watson (1984) and Rovee-Collier (1990). It involves training infants to produce a footkick response to a mobile hanging in their cribs. The mobile is often attached by a ribbon to one of the infant's ankles, so that the frequency and intensity of the movement mimics that of the infant (conjugate reinforcement; see REINFORCEMENT). Infants as young as 2 to 3 months rapidly learn the contingency, doubling or tripling their baseline rates during the 9-minute training period. Once the infant has learned the response, a delay period can be inserted between the initial training period and the reintroduction of the mobile into the crib. Memory for the learned response is indexed by an increase in kicking over baseline rates, even after this delay interval.

Age-Related Findings. With this technique, long-term memory has been demonstrated at even earlier ages than with the visual recognition techniques. For example, Rovee-Collier (1990) and colleagues found that 2-month-olds remember the response after a delay of about 1–3 days; 3-month-olds remember for as long as 1 week; and 6-month-olds for 2 weeks.

Retrieving Infant Memories that Were Once Forgotten. One remarkable discovery made using this conditioning technique is that infants can be "reminded" about a past event that they have otherwise forgotten. This reminder stirs (reactivates) a previously inaccessible memory. Rovee-Collier's (1990) classic demonstration involved 3-month-old infants who had forgotten the learned response after a retention interval of 2 weeks or longer. These infants were then exposed to a brief reminder (the mobile, which was being moved surreptitiously by the experimenter). Then the infant was given another 24-hour delay period; finally, the stationary mobile was reintroduced to assess memory. The results showed that infants administered the reminder had their memories "reactivated" and kicked vigorously when the mobile was reintroduced. Control infants who were not given the reminder did not show any memory under the same circumstance.

Memory Specificity and the Importance of Context. In the first 6 months of life, infants are extremely sensitive to the context in which a behavior is acquired and show better memory if the test occurs in the same context as the learning episode. In one study, 6-month-olds were given footkick training in a specially decorated crib (the *context*). As long as these infants were tested in the same context as the original training, they would remember to kick when they saw the mobile again, even after a 14-day delay. However, if the crib decoration changed, the infants could not access their memories, even after a 1-day delay.

Imitation from Memory (Deferred Imitation)

The third procedure for testing infant memory is *deferred imitation,* that is, imitation after a delay (Mandler, 1990; Meltzoff, 1990). This technique capitalizes on the fact that preverbal infants enjoy imitating the actions of adults. To test memory, the infant is shown the to-be-imitated event, and then a delay is inserted before the infant is allowed to demonstrate the response. Memory is indexed by accurate reproduction of the target behavior after the delay. Control groups are tested to ensure that the production of the target behavior would not have occurred spontaneously, in infants not exposed to the initial modeling.

Age-Related Findings. Classic developmental theories (e.g., Piaget and Inhelder, 1973) had supposed that imitation from memory was a cognitive achievement that first emerged at about 18 months of age. Recent research has revised the classic view by showing that infants can perform deferred imitation after a 24-hour delay as early as 9 months of age (Meltzoff, 1988), with substantial implications for theories of memory development. The number of acts that can be kept in mind and imitated after a delay has also been explored. The results show that 14-month-old infants can keep in mind and imitate as many as three to five separate behaviors after a delay, again showing robust deferred imitation younger than the predicted age.

Imitative Learning and Length of Retention Interval. Scientists have been interested in whether infants can learn novel material through observation. Meltzoff (1990) showed infants a novel act that had not occurred in the baseline behavior of infants, and tested their memory for this act after a 1-week delay. The act consisted of bending forward from the waist and tapping the top surface of a box with the top of one's forehead. Fourteen-month-old infants were shown this novel act on one day but were not allowed to touch or handle the box. After a 1-week delay, the infants were brought back to the laboratory and presented with the object. Sixty-seven percent of the infants immediately bent forward from the waist and touched their head to the panel, thus demonstrating long-term memory for a novel act. Mandler (1990) assessed memory for temporal order by presenting a sequence of behaviors that could be performed in one order or another. Both the 16- and 20-month-olds showed immediate memory for the temporal order of these arbitrary sequences; the groups differed, however, on their long-term memory performance. The 20-month-olds still showed memory for temporal order after a 2-week delay, whereas the 16-month-olds were at chance levels. Long-term memory for the novel and arbitrary sequencing of events is something that may develop toward the second half of the second year, and perhaps is aided by the emergence of language during this time.

Real-World Implications of Imitation from Memory. Infants remember what they see on televi-

sion. In one study infants were shown how to manipulate a new toy by an experimenter who appeared on television. The infants were not allowed to handle the real toy, but the next day the real toy was presented on the table. The results showed that infants accurately imitated the television-presented actions they had seen 1 day earlier. Another study examined whether 14-month-olds could remember actions performed by other infants. A "tutor infant" was taught how to perform a series of particular acts. This tutor infant was then brought to day-care centers where he demonstrated the acts to "naive infants." After a 48-hour delay, the naive infants were visited at their homes by a researcher who laid out the toys on the floor. The results showed that the infants imitated what they had seen their peer do 2 days earlier. A general implication of this work is that imitation and memory are robust enough to play a significant role in the social and personality development of the preverbal infant. It is of adaptive significance that human beings are the most proficient imitators in the animal kingdom; before verbal pedagogy is possible, infants imitatively learn and remember many of the skills and customs of the adult culture.

Conclusions and a Look to the Future

Comparing Three Techniques for Testing Infant Memory

The three techniques used to explore infant memory complement each other but do not address precisely the same aspects of infant memory. The distinctions are important for theory.

Recognition Versus Recall. In deferred imitation, infants go beyond the regulation of attention; they do more than react to the "newness" of a pattern. They must *produce* an absent act without now seeing it and without having previously imitated it. Deferred imitation taps something more than visual recognition memory and provides a measure of recall memory prior to language.

Imitative Learning Versus Conditioning. Like the deferred imitation technique, the conditioned footkick technique also goes beyond visual recognition memory, because the infants do more than recognize the familiar mobile; they also retrieve from memory *what* to do (kick). However, the conditioning procedure and the deferred imitation task differ in other ways, primarily in terms of

Figure 1. A 14-month-old infant learning from television and imitating after a delay. (A) The infant leans forward to watch a television display. (B) After a short delay, the real toy is placed on the table and the infant picks it up. This is the first time the infant has seen the real toy. (C) The infant duplicates the action that was modeled by the adult, showing that information learned through television can be used by the infant to control real-world actions. *Courtesy A. N. Meltzoff.*

the type of information retained. Deferred imitation is based not on an incrementally learned procedure (as in the case of conditioned footkicks) but on the performance of an act that was simply perceived during a brief previous episode. The deferred imitation test does not involve any motor practice during acquisition of the to-be-remembered event (no immediate imitation is allowed). The two tests also differ because the link between the stimulus and the infant's response is not forged through conditioning in deferred imitation. These distinctions between the conditioning and imitation techniques may be important for theories of memory and its development. Work with both adult amnesic patients and experimental animals shows they can retain incrementally learned motor skills. This has led some theorists to suggest that the retention demonstrated in infant conditioning paradigms is the same kind of memory that is spared in amnesia (Moscovitch, 1984; see AMNESIA, ORGANIC). However, it seems likely that amnesic adults would fail on some of the other tests of infant memory using the deferred imitation and recognition memory techniques. Studies directly comparing infants and amnesic adults remain a rich area for future exploration.

Relations between Infant Memory and Childhood IQ

Do scores on infant memory tests predict later cognitive performance? Recent work demonstrates that infants who perform better on tests of memory at 2–9 months of age score higher on IQ tests given later in childhood (*Human Development,* 1989). Fagan (1990) argues that tests of preverbal

memory and information processing may eventually have some clinical utility. He tested infants known to be at risk for MENTAL RETARDATION on visual recognition memory. The children were subsequently given IQ tests at 3 years of age. Low infant memory scores correctly predicted about 80 percent of the children who would eventually be classified as retarded (IQ ≤ 70) while misclassifying only 11 percent of the children who would eventually achieve normal IQ scores. There is a (heated) social policy debate as to whether tests of early memory should be advertised as "infant intelligence tests." This healthy debate should not mask the scientific discovery that there is continuity or predictability between the mental performance of infants, as measured by their performance on tests of memory, and childhood IQ scores.

Early and Rapid Memory Formation for Biologically Relevant Signals

The newborn infant is predisposed to encode and remember biologically important signals such as facial and speech signals. The smile of recognition to the mother that emerges at about 10 weeks profoundly underestimates infant learning and memory for her face. Newborn infants, with only a few hours of exposure to the mother, look longer at their own mother's face than at a stranger's face (Field et al., 1984; Walton et al., 1992). Auditory signals of biological importance are also learned quite early, perhaps prenatally. DeCasper and Fifer (1980) demonstrated that newborn infants prefer to listen to the voice of their own mother versus a strange female talker. Finally, recent discoveries show that infants' early experience with their native language causes them to respond differently to native-language as opposed to foreign-language speech sounds. Kuhl and colleagues (1992) conducted a study with 6-month-old infants from the United States and Sweden, and showed that these prelinguistic infants had already committed certain native language phonetic units to memory. (See also LANGUAGE LEARNING: HUMANS.)

Infantile Amnesia Revisited

The research has taught us that infants have far more robust and complex memories than predicted by classic theories. The puzzling phenomenon of infantile amnesia becomes more of a mystery when considered in light of this modern infancy research, because it can no longer be thought that infants do not form memories, or are confined to sensorimotor skill routines, during the preverbal period. It is possible that the amnesia adults experience about their own infancy is due to the extreme mismatch between the cognitive, emotional, and physical context of the initial learning and the adult's present state. It is sometimes reported that adults can gain access to "lost" childhood memories by immersing themselves in unique situations they have not encountered since childhood.

(See also CHILDREN, DEVELOPMENT OF MEMORY IN.)

REFERENCES

Cohen, L. B., and Gelber, E. R. (1975). Infant visual memory. In L. B. Cohen and P. Salapatek, eds., *Infant perception: From sensation to cognition*, pp. 347–403. New York: Academic Press. Extensive analysis of research using the habituation-dishabituation technique for evaluating infant memory.

DeCasper, A. J., and Fifer, W. P. (1980). Of human bonding: Newborns prefer their mothers' voices. *Science 208*, 1174–1176.

Fagan, J. F. (1990). The paired-comparison paradigm and infant intelligence. *Annals of the New York Academy of Sciences 608*, 337–364. Comprehensive review and extensive bibliography on research using the paired-comparison technique for evaluating infant memory. Also contains a useful discussion by the pioneering researcher linking infant memory and later IQ.

Field, T. M., Cohen, D., Garcia, R., and Greenberg, R. (1984). Mother-stranger face discrimination by the newborn. *Infant Behavior and Development 7*, 19–25.

Human Development (1989). Special topic: Continuity in early cognitive development—Conceptual and methodological challenges *32*, 129–186. This special issue of the journal contains reviews by several investigators concerning the predictability of childhood IQ from tests of infant memory and information processing.

Kuhl, P. K., Williams, K. A., Lacerda, F., Stevens, K. N., and Lindblom, B. (1992). Linguistic experience alters phonetic perception in infants by 6 months of age. *Science 255*, 606–608.

Mandler, J. M. (1990). Recall of events by preverbal children. *Annals of the New York Academy of Sciences 608*, 485–516. Analysis of infant recall memory using the deferred imitation technique.

Meltzoff, A. N. (1988). Infant imitation and memory: Nine month-olds in immediate and deferred tests. *Child Development 59*, 217–225.

———— (1990). Towards a developmental cognitive science: The implications of cross-modal matching and imitation for the development of representation and memory in infancy. *Annals of the New York Academy of Sciences 608*, 1–37. Comprehensive review and extensive bibliography on research using the deferred imitation technique for evaluating infant memory. Places early memory capacities within a larger context of infant mental development. Connects infant work to the "multiple memory systems" debate in adults, and analyzes possible connections between memory in infants, amnesic patients, and animals.

Moscovitch, M. (1984). *Infant memory: Its relation to normal and pathological memory in humans and other animals*. New York: Plenum Press. Contains chapters by leading researchers analyzing similarities and differences between infant and animal memory and disordered memory in adults.

Piaget, J., and Inhelder, B. (1973). *Memory and intelligence*. New York: Basic Books. Presents a highly original and unique theory of memory development from the special viewpoint of Piagetian psychology.

Rovee-Collier, C. R. (1990). The "memory system" of prelinguistic infants. *Annals of the New York Academy of Sciences 608*, 517–542. Extensive bibliography and discussion of the conditioning technique for evaluating infant memory.

Walton, G. E., Bower, N. J. A., and Bower, T. G. R. (1992). Recognition of familiar faces by newborns. *Infant Behavior and Development 15*, 265–269.

Watson, J. S. (1984). Memory in learning: Analysis of three momentary reactions of infants. In R. Kail and N. E. Spear, eds., *Comparative perspectives on the development of memory*, pp. 159–179. Hillsdale, N.J.: Erlbaum.

Andrew N. Meltzoff

INSECT LEARNING

Why study learning in insects? What can it contribute to a general knowledge of how learning takes place in a wide variety of animals? There are many potential answers to these questions. This review will focus on the general contribution that can be made to systematic understanding of how learning has evolved and is controlled in a wide variety of vertebrate and invertebrate species. Any systematic study must begin with a well-defined phylogenetic lineage. Insects are in the phylum Arthropoda, which contains animals that have jointed exoskeletons (e.g., insects, ticks, crabs, lobsters, spiders, etc.). With at least 2 million extant species (some estimates range as high as 30–50 million), the arthropod class Insecta comprises the most diverse group of multicellular organisms (Borror, DeLong, and Triplehorn, 1976). Insects have adapted to a wide array of living conditions, ranging from most terrestrial to many aquatic environments. The diverse insect species found in these environments must solve the basic problems inherent in locating resources such as food or mates and avoiding threats from predation or environmental hazards. Learning abilities observed in any laboratory situation probably evolved to solve these problems.

Because of this species and habitat diversity, insects provide an excellent means of testing patterns of phylogenetic emergence of different learning mechanisms. In doing so one must carefully distinguish phylogenetically *homologous* traits from *analogous* ones (Mayr, 1969). *Homology* refers to traits that arise from a common ancestral condition. A monophyletic group of animals that possesses homologous traits is called a *clade,* and the process of modification of those traits is *cladogenesis* (Wiley, 1981). Through a comparison of traits that in their expression may appear dissimilar, and thus unrelated, in several closely related, extant species, it is possible to obtain a picture of which traits are ancestral (plesiomorphic) and which are derived. For example, are nonassociative learning mechanisms homologous to associative mechanisms? That is, did ancestral species possess the ability to modify behavior through habituation and sensitization prior to the ability to express associative conditioning? Were changes in the evolution of learning abilities gradual, adaptive alterations or the result of rapid, discontinuous changes resulting from dramatic reorganization of neural tissue (Wyers, Peeke, and Herz, 1973)? Through a study of insect species whose phylogenies with respect to other characters (e.g., morphological, physiological) are known, such hypotheses can be tested. (See also EVOLUTION AND LEARNING.)

Analogous traits are physically similar but have arisen independently; that is, they have been derived from very different ancestral conditions. For example, the expression of operant conditioning of leg movement in an insect might most likely be analogous to operant conditioning of leg movement in a vertebrate (see OPERANT BEHAVIOR). Insect legs and vertebrate legs are certainly not homologous structures, but both enable animals to move throughout their environment and the rules for operant conditioning of each may be the same. Analogous traits associated with complex learning abilities arise through convergent evolution, perhaps due to similar environmental problems that require one or more ways to modify behavior based on experience. This process of describing analogous learning abilities in terms of the complexity of the ability is termed *anagenesis* (Demarest, 1983). Through a comparative study of potentially analogous learning mechanisms in such phylogenetically diverse groups as insects and vertebrates, hypotheses regarding the conditions that give rise to analogous learning abilities can be tested. Thus learning abilities studied in insects have an important value for deriving hypotheses that can be tested in vertebrates. Even if learning traits do not have a common phylogenetic origin, working out mechanisms in one species can generate conceptual advances in understanding a similar learning ability in another species.

In addition to phylogenetic perspectives on the evolution of learning, there are other advantages to using insects for learning research. The variety of insect species makes it easy to find an animal suited for a particular experimental design (e.g., the fruit fly *Drosophila* is ideal for studies of the genetic bases of learning). Insects, like other invertebrates, are very convenient because many species can be studied in controlled laboratory situations and in natural environments. It is possible to apply biochemical and neurophysiological techniques to nervous systems (Mobbs, 1985) that are simpler than those of most vertebrates.

The remaining portion of this entry is organized along phylogenetic lines. We have restricted ourselves to cases where learning mechanisms have been worked out from a behavioral standpoint by using traditional methods for the study of learning.

Established learning paradigms have been applied to studies in only three of about thirty extant insect orders, and then only to one or a few species in each order. We do not provide a comprehensive review of the literature. Instead, we hope to impart an impression of learning abilities of various insects.

Orthoptera

The order Orthoptera comprises cockroaches, grasshoppers, and locusts. Horridge (1962) published results of an experiment in which headless cockroaches and locusts learned to keep one leg raised to terminate a series of electric shocks. This experiment generated considerable interest because it was one of the first to suggest that an insect can be used to explore the physiology of learning and memory. Subsequently, leg position learning, or the *Horridge paradigm,* has been used to demonstrate learning in a wide variety of experimental situations ranging from the use of intact animals to a single ganglion. This latter information demonstrated that learning need not be confined to a single area of the central nervous system (e.g., the brain) but can be distributed throughout several stimulus and motor processing pathways in a nervous system.

The Horridge paradigm also brought into focus the adequacy of the yoked control design in separating learning from nonassociative effects. In the original Horridge experiment, learning was inferred from a difference in the number of shocks received by experimental subjects and by their yoked controls. The experimental subjects were shocked contingent on leg position; control subjects were yoked in such a way that they received shock whenever the experimental subjects did, but independent of their own behavior. The yoked paradigm has been extensively criticized in the literature. Church (1964), for instance, pointed out that because of the nature of the yoked paradigm, random differences in inherent responsiveness will lead to artifactual learning in the population. Applying this criticism to the Horridge paradigm, Church and Lerner (1976) derived a mathematical model that accounts for differences between experimental and control subjects without learning taking place. Moreover, Willner (1978) suggested that the position of the legs at the start of training is a critical factor and that

such learning, if it indeed occurs, is not retained very long. (For an alternative explanation of the Church interpretation, see Buerger, Eisenstein, and Reep, 1981).

To answer such criticisms, a new experimental design was developed for training leg position in the locust (Forman and Hoyle, 1978; Forman, 1984). Rather than simply requiring the animal to raise a leg to terminate a series of shocks, Forman required his locust to maintain a particular range of leg movement arbitrarily selected by the experimenter. After a few minutes of training, the animal learns to shift its leg position to an angle that terminates aversive heat to the head or, alternatively, produces access to food. Locusts can also be trained to manipulate leg position to produce heat to the head in a cold environment. The task can be made more complex by narrowing or shifting the range of leg movement necessary to control the heat stimulus. The Forman experiment is important because it represents the first significant improvement in the Horridge paradigm, in that both the response and the reinforcer are arbitrary, and learning can be identified in an individual animal. This procedure has the additional advantage of eliminating shock as the aversive stimulus. Shock reflexively elicits leg flexion and stimulates a variety of receptors, thereby making the identification of the underlying physiological changes associated with learning difficult. Moreover, Forman was able to restrict learning to a single segment of the locust leg (the femorotibial joint). In previous experiments of the Horridge type, in which a leg simply moves up or down, as many as fifteen different leg segments may be involved in learning.

The rationale for developing the Forman paradigm is to obtain data on the cellular mechanisms underlying operant behavior. By using electromyograms and intracellular techniques, the motor neurons involved in learning have been found and characterized (Hoyle, 1979, 1980; Zill and Forman, 1983; Forman, 1984). Forman and Zill (1984), for example, identified three separate motor strategies utilized by the locusts during training ("kicking," changes in muscle tonus, and tonic slow excitor motor neuron activity). Each of these strategies can be selectively trained. It is also possible to use the Forman paradigm to manipulate directly the firing rate of the motoneuron responsible for leg position (Tosney and Hoyle, 1977). An exciting application of the technique and a fine example of the comparative method is an analysis of the similarities and differences in response strategies between locusts and the weta, a primitive New Zealand insect related to the locust (Hoyle and Field, 1983).

Diptera

The order Diptera comprises all flies. Fly species that have been extensively used in studies of learning include *Phormia regina* (blowflies) and *Drosophila melanogaster* (fruit flies). Research interest in flies was generated by the extreme ease of maintaining populations under controlled mating conditions over generations that cover only weeks rather than years. Through controlled breeding experiments a large number of studies have characterized the behavioral, genetic, and biochemical bases of different learning mechanisms (see INVERTEBRATE LEARNING: NEUROGENETIC ANALYSIS OF LEARNING IN DROSOPHILA). As Holliday and Hirsch (1986a, p. 131) have noted, *D. melanogaster* is an ideal species for learning research "because the well understood genetic system of this species makes it unique among the metazoa for use in the analysis of the genetic correlates of relatively simple learning processes."

Some of the first comprehensive studies of learning behavior in flies began with the pioneering work of Dethier and colleagues (see review in Dethier, 1990; see also Dethier, Salomon, and Turner, 1965) in which they worked out in considerable detail the stimulus control of feeding reflexes in *Phormia regina*. They described a procedure in which the tarsal (leg) receptors that mediate sucrose taste sensation were stimulated to elicit extension of a subject's proboscis (the sucking mouthparts) through which it feeds on the sucrose-water droplet. They found that prior exposure to sucrose greatly increased the probability that a fly would extend its proboscis to the presentation of water alone, that is, when no feeding stimulus was present. The motivational state that was modulated by the sucrose exposure was termed *central excitatory state* (CES), which describes a nonassociative (sensitization) modification of the probability of proboscis extension to a neutral stimulus such as water. CES can be characterized by at least three factors: (1) There is a decay over time between the sensitizing and test stimuli; (2) Increased sucrose concentrations lead to increases in CES; (3) Food deprivation leads

to increased levels of CES for any given sucrose concentration.

Tully and Hirsch's studies (1982a, 1982b, 1983) have documented genetic bases for CES effects in *P. regina,* and other studies extended the results on the genetic basis for CES effects to *D. melanogaster* (Vargo and Hirsch, 1982, 1985a, 1985b). Bidirectional selection for high and low CES lines in *P. regina* has shown that the response to selection is rapid and may reach asymptotic levels in one or a few generations. Hybridization of the different lines indicated that one major gene segregated in the selected lines was responsible for producing most of the variability in CES effect. Selection for CES effects in *D. melanogaster* has shown a slightly different genetic basis. Sometimes a low but not a high line was produced, or vice versa. These data indicate that several genes may be involved in regulating CES in fruit flies. Further studies have shown that genes reside on at least two chromosomes, and heritable cytoplasmic factors may be involved as well (Vargo and Hirsch, 1986).

Theories of anagenesis predict that as metazoan life becomes physically more complex, then more complex learning abilities will emerge (Demarest, 1983). Thus associative learning mechanisms may be mechanistically related to simpler nonassociative processes. Accordingly, more recent interest in learning studies with both *P. regina* and *D. melanogaster* has focused on developing associative conditioning paradigms and testing for genetic correlates with nonassociative processes. By associating either a saline or a water conditioned stimulus (CS) with sucrose, *P. regina* can learn to extend their proboscises to the CS (Nelson, 1971). McGuire and Hirsch (1977), McGuire (1983), and Tully, Zawistowski, and Hirsch et al. (1982) selected for high and low learning lines of blowflies. These lines showed a positive correlation between CES levels and asymptotic levels of learning performance. Therefore, CES and associative conditioning appear to have at least some common genetic bases, which might include pleiotropic genetic effects.

However, as with leg position learning in locusts, this work is not immune to controversy. Holliday and Hirsch (1986a, 1986b) have described control procedures for evaluating associative conditioning in flies that separate associative conditioning from nonassociative CES effects. They state that care must be taken in selecting the behavioral response measure and to use responses of individuals rather than mean responding in populations. These control procedures have been used to measure conditioned *suppression* of proboscis extension by associating response to sucrose with a bitter taste such as quinine (DeJianne, McGuire, and Pruzan-Hotchkiss, 1985). Flies that extended their proboscises when sucrose was applied to their foreleg sucrose taste receptors were exposed to a brief quinine aversive stimulus. Many flies could learn to withhold proboscis extension to the sucrose in order to avoid the aversive stimulus.

Another aversive conditioning assay has been widely used to select large numbers of *D. melanogaster* in order to rapidly isolate mutant strains that show deficiencies in learning and/or memory. The basic instrumental conditioning procedure (Quinn, Harris, and Benzer, 1974), which has been modified into a Pavlovian procedure (Tully and Quinn, 1985; see also PAVLOV, IVAN), involves exposing flies sequentially to two odors while they walk across a metal grid. While they are exposed to one odor, they receive shocks through the grid. Flies are then presented with a sequence of new "collection" tubes that contain either the odor paired with shock (S+) or the odor that was not paired with shock (S−). The response measure is the number of flies that enter a new tube that contains the S+ odor versus the number that enter a tube containing the S− odor. Decreased entries into the tube with the S+ odor relative to the tube with the S− odor indicates learning, given that several controls are run (Tully, 1984).

Note that the response measure in this procedure is a mean population response. At every test a fraction of the total number of flies enters the collection tube. Several controls have been run to test whether the response measure indicates a subpopulation of flies that always respond to the odor, or whether the response is a probabilistic measure associated with each fly. Furthermore, other types of learning experiments, such as proboscis extension conditioning or leg position learning (Booker and Quinn, 1981), can be run to test individual response measures once mutant lines have been isolated. Therefore, although this mass training procedure has been criticized (Holliday and Hirsch, 1986b), it is difficult to ignore the advances made with this procedure in isolating several learning mutants that show poor acquisition and/or poor memory retention (Heisenberg, et al., 1985; Dudai, 1983).

Hymenoptera

The order Hymenoptera contains a diverse group of insects commonly referred to as sawflies, ants, wasps, and bees. Hymenopterans such as ants and honeybees have been widely utilized to document learning abilities related directly to learning problems in the animal's natural environment. Furthermore, experiments with ants and bees in laboratory learning paradigms have demonstrated that these abilities conform to standard definitions of learning. But an ant's or a bee's learning ability may be less complex and/or less generalizable to new situations than that of animals with larger, more elaborate nervous systems (Demarest, 1983). Indeed, the crucial question is how complex these abilities are and to what natural situations they can be applied.

Learning in ants was first brought into the laboratory by Fielde (1901), who reported that ants can successfully negotiate a simple maze. Schnierla (1946) described the chemical, visual, and kinesthetic cues used by ants in solving a more complex maze. More recently, DeCarlo and Abramson (1989) used a different procedure to extend vertebrate learning paradigms to ants. They demonstrated an ant's ability to choose one compartment of a two-compartment chamber based on rates of stimulus delivery.

The honeybee (*Apis mellifera*) is an ideal species with which to research similar questions. On warm, sunny days worker bees regularly depart from the colony on foraging trips during which they collect resources (e.g., nectar, pollen, water; Winston, 1987) crucial for survival and reproduction of the colony. Beginning with the pioneering studies of Karl von Frisch (see 1967 review), a large number of studies have documented the abilities of freely flying honeybees to learn the relationships of visual, tactile, and olfactory cues to appetitive and aversive stimuli (see review in Menzel, 1990). For example, forager bees learn the association of nectar, which for most conditioning studies is replaced with a sucrose-water mixture, and floral color (Menzel, 1968), shape (Gould, 1985), odor (Frisch, 1967), and the time of day that floral rewards are available (Koltermann, 1974). Other work has documented the honeybee's ability to learn compounds of stimuli (Bogdany, 1978; Bitterman and Couvillon, 1982). Phenomena such as the unconditioned stimulus-preexposure effect and latent inhibition have also been studied

(Abramson and Bitterman, 1986a, 1986b). For studies of aversive learning, Abramson (1986) has demonstrated the ability of freely flying bees to use certain stimuli as a means to avoid exposure to an aversive shock stimulus. The learned avoidance ability of the honeybee may have evolved as a means to cope with bitter and even toxic nectars found in some flowers (Winston, 1987).

Proboscis extension conditioning of honeybees has been widely utilized to study learning under conditions in which stimulation parameters can be easily controlled (Menzel, Erber, and Masuhr, 1974; Menzel and Bitterman, 1983; Bitterman et al., 1983; see INVERTEBRATE LEARNING: ASSOCIATIVE LEARNING IN BEES). Honeybees restrained individually in harnesses can be readily conditioned to extend their proboscises upon presentation of a floral odor. After one or a few pairings of an odor conditioned stimulus with a sucrose unconditioned stimulus, 40–90 percent of the subjects will extend their proboscises (conditioned response) to the odor alone. Enhancement of a background rate of proboscis extension to odor is specific to situations in which the CS precedes the US (forward pairing) and is sensitive to latency of onset of odor relative to sucrose (Bitterman et al., 1983). Proboscis extension conditioning has been used to study a variety of phenomena in honeybees, such as sensory discrimination (Vareschi, 1971; Smith and Menzel, 1989a; Getz and Smith, 1987); control of motor systems (Smith and Menzel, 1989b); memory consolidation (Erber, Masuhr, and Menzel, 1980; Menzel, 1983); and the pharmacology of memory processing (Menzel et al., 1988). More recent work by the present writers has extended Abramson's (1986) study of aversive conditioning in freely flying bees to restrained bees. The majority of subjects that received a shock contingent upon their response to sucrose in the context of a particular odor learned to withhold proboscis extension to sucrose in order to avoid shock.

In a broader sense, ants and bees perform navigational tasks by using series of spatial references during regular trips from the colony (Dyer and Gould, 1983; Wehner and Menzel, 1990). The position of the sun serves as a reference to the most direct compass direction on the way to and from resource location. In the absence of the sun, patterns of light polarization in the sky are used to predict the current position of the sun and compensate for its movement. Prominent landmarks are also crucial for directing paths. In honeybees, it has been shown that foragers learn the position of landmarks relative to the sun's movement. Thus, on a completely overcast day they can reference the position of the sun by a circadian clock and the positions of landmarks in the locale of the colony.

A variety of tools can be used to navigate throughout the environment (see review in Wehner and Menzel, 1990). While searching in a new location, bees and ants keep track of their location relative to the colony by monitoring turning angles and distances traveled. This information can be used to calculate a fairly direct return path to the colony at any given time (*path integration*). Once they are in the vicinity of the colony, the positions of nearby landmarks are matched to relative positions in memory in order to locate the colony entrance more effectively (*goal localization*). Finally, if all else fails, systematic searching behaviors help to locate the goal.

The question whether bees and ants have a *cognitive map* has generated controversy. That is, do they have a "mental analogy of a topographic map, i.e., an internal representation of the geometric relations among noticeable points in the animal's environment" (Wehner and Menzel, 1990, p. 403)? Gould (1986) reports an experiment in which foragers displaced from their feeding station appeared to calculate a novel route based on such a maplike representation. However, several experiments have failed to replicate these data (see Wehner and Menzel, 1990), and Dyer (1991) has shown how Gould's data may have been a result of the training locale rather than of a cognitive map. Therefore, evidence to date points to a vector-based navigation system combined with memory matching of relative positions of landmarks (Cartwright and Collett, 1987) rather than to a more complex topographic representation (O'Keefe and Nadel, 1978). (See also SPATIAL LEARNING.)

REFERENCES

Abramson, C. I. (1986). Aversive conditioning in honey bees (*Apis mellifera*). *Journal of Comparative Psychology 100*, 108–116.

Abramson, C. I., and Bitterman, M. E. (1986a). Latent inhibition in honey bees. *Animal Learning and Behavior 14*, 184–189.

——— (1986b). The US-preexposure effect in honey bees. *Animal Learning and Behavior 14*, 374–379.

Bitterman, M. E., and Couvillon, P. (1982). Compound

conditioning in honey bees. *Journal of Comparative Physiology and Psychology 96,* 192–199.

Bitterman, M. E., Menzel, R., Fietz, A., and Schäfer, S. (1983). Classical conditioning of proboscis extension in honey bees *Apis mellifera. Journal of Comparative Psychology 97,* 107–119.

Bogdany, F. J. (1978). Linking of learning signals in honey bee orientation. *Behavioral Ecology and Sociobiology 3,* 323–336.

Booker, R., and Quinn, W. G. (1981). Conditioning of leg position in normal and mutant *Drosophila. Proceedings of the National Academy of Sciences (USA) 78,* 3940–3944.

Borror, D. J., DeLong, D. M., and Triplehorn, C. A. (1976). *An introduction to the study of insects,* 4th ed. New York: Holt.

Buerger, A. A., Eisenstein, E. M., and Reep, R. L. (1981). The yoked control in instrumental avoidance conditioning. An empirical and methodological analysis. *Physiological Psychology 9,* 351–353.

Cartwright, B. A., and Collett, T. S. (1987). Landmark maps for honey bees. *Biological Cybernetics 57,* 85–93.

Church, R. M. (1964). Systematic effect of random error in the yoked control design. *Psychological Bulletin 62,* 122–131.

Church, R. M., and Lerner, N. D. (1976). Does the headless roach learn to avoid? *Physiological Psychology 4,* 439–442.

DeCarlo, L. T., and Abramson, C. I. (1989). Time allocation in the carpenter ant (*Camponotus herculeanus*). *Journal of Comparative Psychology 103,* 389–400.

DeJianne, D., McGuire, T. R., and Pruzan-Hotchkiss, A. (1985). Conditioned suppression of proboscis extension in *Drosophila melanogaster. Journal of Comparative Physiology and Psychology 99,* 74–80.

Demarest, J. (1983). The ideas of change, progress, and continuity in the comparative psychology of learning. In D. W. Rajecki, ed., *Comparing behavior: Studying man studying animals.* Hillsdale, N.J.: Erlbaum.

Dethier, V. G. (1990). Chemosensory physiology in an age of transition. *Annual Review of Neuroscience 13,* 1–13.

Dethier, V. G., Solomon, R. L., and Turner, L. H. (1965). Sensory input and central excitation in the blowfly. *Journal of Comparative Physiology and Psychology 60,* 303–313.

Dudai, Y. (1983). Mutations affect storage and use of memory differentially in *Drosophila. Proceedings of the National Academy of Sciences (USA) 80,* 5445–5448.

Dyer, F. C. (1991). Bees acquire route-based memories but not cognitive maps in a familiar landscape. *Animal Behaviour 41,* 239–246.

Dyer, F. C., and Gould, J. L. (1983). Honey bee navigation. *American Scientist 71,* 587–597.

Eisenstein, E. M., and Reep, R. L. (1985). Behavioral and cellular studies of learning and memory in insects.

In G. A. Kerkut and L. I. Gilbert, eds., *Comprehensive insect physiology, biochemistry and pharmacology,* vol. 5, *Nervous system: Structure and function.* New York: Pergamon Press.

Erber, J., Masuhr, T., and Menzel, R. (1980). Localization of short-term memory in the brain of the bee. *Physiological Entomology 5,* 343–358.

Fielde, A. (1901). A further study of an ant. *Proceedings of the National Academy of Sciences (USA) 53,* 521–544.

Forman, R. R. (1984). Leg position learning by an insect. I. A heat avoidance learning paradigm. *Journal of Neurobiology 15,* 127–140.

Forman, R. R., and Hoyle, G. (1978). Position learning in behaviorally appropriate situations. *Society for Neuroscience Abstracts 4,* 193.

Forman, R. R., and Zill, S. N. (1984). Leg position learning by an insect. II. Motor strategies underlying learned leg extension. *Journal of Neurobiology 15,* 221–237.

Frisch, K. von (1967). *The dance language and orientation of bees.* Cambridge, Mass.: Belknap/Harvard University Press.

Gallistel, C. R. (1990). *The organization of learning.* Cambridge, Mass.: MIT Press.

Getz, W. M., and Smith, K. B. (1987). Olfactory sensitivity and discrimination of mixtures in the honeybee *Apis mellifera. Journal of Comparative Physiology A160,* 239–246.

Gould, J. L. (1985). How bees remember flower shapes. *Science 277,* 1492–1494.

——— (1986). The locale map of the honey bee. Do insects have cognitive maps? *Science 282,* 861–863.

Heisenberg, M., Borst, A., Wagner, S., and Byers, D. (1985). *Drosophila* mushroom body mutants are deficient in olfactory learning. *Journal of Neurogenetics 2,* 1–30.

Holliday, M., and Hirsch, J. (1986a). Excitatory conditioning of *Drosophila melanogaster. Journal of Experimental Psychology: Animal Behavior, Proceedings 12,* 131–142.

——— (1986b). A comment on the evidence for learning in diptera. *Behavior Genetics 16,* 439–447.

Horridge, G. A. (1962). Learning of leg position by headless insects. *Nature 193,* 697–698.

Hoyle, G. (1979). Instrumental conditioning of the leg lift in the locusts. *Neuroscience Research Progress Bulletin 17,* 577–586.

——— (1980). Learning using natural reinforcements, in insect preparations that permit cellular neuronal analysis. *Journal of Neurobiology 11,* 323–354.

Hoyle, G., and Field, L. H. (1983). Elicitation and abrupt termination of behaviorally significant catchlike tension in a primitive insect. *Journal of Neurobiology 14,* 299–312.

Koltermann, R. (1974). Periodicity in the activity and learning performance of the honey bee. In L. Barton Browne, ed., *Experimental analysis of insect behavior.* New York: Springer-Verlag.

Mayr, E. (1969). *Principles of systematic zoology.* New York: McGraw-Hill.

McGuire, T. R. (1983). Further evidence for a relationship between the central excitatory state and classical conditioning in the blow fly *Phormia regina. Behavior Genetics 13,* 509–515.

McGuire, T. R., and Hirsch, J. (1977). Behavior-genetic analysis of *Phormia regina:* Conditioning, reliable individual differences, and selection. *Proceedings of the National Academy of Sciences 74,* 5193–5197.

Menzel, R. (1968). Das Gedächtnis der Honigbiene für Spektralfarben. I. Kurzzeitiges und langzeitiges Behalten. *Zeitschrift für vergleichende Physiologie 60,* 82–102.

—— (1983). Neurobiology of learning and memory: The honey bee as a model system. *Naturwissenschaften 70,* 504–511.

—— (1990). Learning, memory, and "cognition" in honey bees. In R. P. Kesner and D. S. Olton, eds., *Neurobiology of comparative cognition.* Hillsdale, N.J.: Erlbaum.

Menzel, R., and Bitterman, M. E. (1983). Learning by honey bees in an unnatural situation. In F. Huber and H. Markl, eds., *Neuroethology and behavioral physiology.* New York: Springer-Verlag.

Menzel, R., Erber, J., and Masuhr, T. (1974). Learning and memory in the honey bee. In L. Barton Browne, ed., *Experimental analysis of insect behavior.* New York: Springer-Verlag.

Menzel, R., Michelson, B., Rüffer, P., and Sugawa, M. (1988). Neuropharmacology of learning and memory in honey bees. In G. Herting and H. C. Spatz, eds., *Synaptic transmission and plasticity in nervous systems.* Berlin: Springer-Verlag.

Mobbs, P. G. (1985). Brain structure. In G. A. Kerkut and L. I. Gilbert, eds., *Comprehensive insect physiology, biochemistry and pharmacology,* vol. 5, *Nervous system: Structure and function.* New York: Pergamon Press.

Nelson, M. C. (1971). Classical conditioning in the blowfly (*Phormia regina*): Associative and excitatory factors. *Journal of Comparative Physiology and Psychology 77,* 353–368.

O'Keefe, J., and Nadel, L. (1978). *The hippocampus as a cognitive map.* Oxford: Clarendon Press.

Quinn, W. G., Harris, W. A., and Benzer, S. (1974). Conditioned behavior in *Drosophila melanogaster. Proceedings of the National Academy of Sciences (USA) 71,* 708–712.

Schnierla, T. C. (1946). Ant learning as a problem in comparative psychology. In P. Harriman, ed., *Twentieth-century psychology.* New York: Philosophical Library.

Smith, B. H., and Menzel, R. (1989a). The use of electromyogram recordings to quantify odor discrimination in the honeybee. *Journal of Insect Physiology 35,* 369–375.

—— (1989b). An analysis of variability in the feeding motor program of the honey bee: The role of learning in releasing a modal action pattern. *Ethology 82,* 68–81.

Tosney, T., and Hoyle, G. (1977). Computer-controlled learning in a simple system. *Proceedings of the Royal Society of London B195,* 365–393.

Tully, T. (1984). *Drosophila* learning: Behavior and biochemistry. *Behavior Genetics 14,* 527–557.

—— (1987). *Drosophila* learning and memory revisited. *Trends in Neurosciences 10,* 330–335.

Tully, T., and Hirsch, J. (1982a). Behavior-genetic analysis of *Phormia regina:* I. Isolation of purebreeding lines for high and low levels of the central excitatory state (CES) from an unselected population. *Behavior Genetics 12,* 395–416.

—— (1982b). Behavior-genetic analysis of *Phormia regina:* II. Detection of single-major-gene effect from behavioral variation for central excitatory state (CES) using hybrid crosses. *Animal Behavior 30,* 1193–1202.

—— (1983). Two non-associative components of the proboscis extension reflex in the blow fly, *Phormia regina,* which may affect measures of conditioning and of the central excitatory state. *Behavioral Neuroscience 97,* 146–153.

Tully, T., and Quinn, W. G. (1985). Classical conditioning and retention in normal and mutant *Drosophila melanogaster. Journal of Comparative Physiology 157,* 263–277.

Tully, T., Zawistowski, S., and Hirsch, J. (1982). Behavior-genetic analysis of *Phormia regina:* III. A phenotypic correlation between the central excitatory state (CES) and conditioning remains in replicate F$_2$ generations of hybrid crosses. *Behavior Genetics 12,* 181–191.

Vareschi, E. (1971). Duftunterscheidung bei der Honigbiene—Einzelzellableitungen und Verhaltensreaktionen. *Zeitschrift für vergleichende Physiologie 75,* 143–173.

Vargo, M., and Hirsch, J. (1982). Central excitation in the fruit fly (*Drosophila melanogaster*). *Journal of Comparative Physiology and Psychology 96,* 452–459.

—— (1985a). Behavioral assessment of lines of *Drosophila melanogaster* selected for central excitation. *Behavioral Neuroscience 99,* 323–332.

—— (1985b). Selection for central excitation in *Drosophila melanogaster. Journal of Comparative Psychology 99,* 81–86.

—— (1986). Biometrical and chromosome analyses of lines of *Drosophila melanogaster* selected for central excitation. *Heredity 56,* 19–24.

Wehner, R., and Menzel, R. (1990). Do insects have cognitive maps? *Annual Review of Neuroscience 13,* 403–404.

Wiley, E. O. (1981). *Phylogenetics: The theory and practice of phylogenetic systematics.* New York: Wiley.

Willner, P. (1978). What does the headless cockroach remember? *Animal Learning and Behavior 6*, 249–257.

Winston, M. L. (1987). *The biology of the honey bee.* Cambridge, Mass.: Harvard University Press.

Wyers, E. J., Peeke, H. V. S., and Herz, M. J. (1973). Behavioral habituation in invertebrates. In H. V. S. Peeke and M. J. Herz, eds., *Habituation*, vol. 1. New York: Academic Press.

Zill, S. N., and Forman, R. R. (1983). Proprioceptive reflexes change when an insect assumes an active, learned posture. *Journal of Experimental Biology 107*, 385–390.

Brian H. Smith
Charles I. Abramson

INTERFERENCE AND FORGETTING

Human long-term memory is characterized by a storage capacity that is, for all practical purposes, unlimited. At any one point in time, however, much—probably most—of the information in long term memory (names, numbers, facts, procedures, events, and so forth) is not recallable. Why do we forget information that was once recallable? The principal answer to that question is that access to information in memory is subject to interference from competing information in memory. Before characterizing such interference processes in more detail, it is necessary to introduce some terminology.

First is *transfer.* The process of learning—that is, adding knowledge and skills to our memories—does not take place in a vacuum. After some early point in our lives we rarely, if ever, learn anything that is entirely new. We bring to any "new" learning process an accumulation of related knowledge, skills, and habits from our past. Such prior learning influences the qualitative and quantitative character of the new learning process. We refer to these influences as *transfer effects.* Such effects may be positive or negative, depending on whether our prior experiences facilitate or impair our new learning.

Second is *retroactive interference.* Whereas transfer, as defined above, refers to the effect of earlier learning on later learning, retroaction refers to an effect in the opposite direction: the impact of some *interpolated* (intervening) learning experience on one's memory for something learned earlier. Once again, such effects may be positive or negative (*retroactive facilitation* and *interference,* respectively), depending on the similarity of the original and interpolated learning tasks. It is the negative case—where retroactive interference causes forgetting—that concerns us here. Thus, if our ability to recall the maiden name of a woman friend is impaired by virtue of having learned her married name, we are suffering—by definition—retroactive interference.

Third is *proactive interference.* It is also the case that something learned earlier may impair our ability to recall something learned more recently. If, for example, we are less able to recall a woman friend's married name by virtue of having learned her maiden name at an earlier time, we are suffering—by definition—proactive interference.

Research on Forgetting: A Brief History

Rigorous research on the possible causes of forgetting dates back to the turn of the century when two German researchers, Müller and Pilzecker (1900), first demonstrated retroactive interference under controlled conditions. The history of that research is interesting, partly because it is a history where intuition served as a poor guide to theorizing.

Early Theories That Proved Inadequate

Consolidation. Müller and Pilzecker (1900) found that subjects' memory for a series of nonsense syllables (consonant-vowel-consonant nonword syllables, such as DAX) was impaired by subsequent activity, such as learning a new series of nonsense syllables (compared with a condition where subjects simply rested for a similar period of time). They put forward a *perseveration-consolidation hypothesis* to explain their results. They argued that the changes in the nervous system that result in true learning were not complete by the end of training—that activity in the brain perseverated after learning, and that during that perseveration the memory traces corresponding to learning were consolidated. A subsequent activity, particularly if demanding and close in time to the original learning task, could produce retroactive interference by disrupting the perseveration-consolidation process. (See MEMORY CONSOLIDATION.)

That subsequent activity could cause forgetting by disrupting a consolidation process seems plausible, especially given the evidence that certain traumas, such as electroconvulsive shock or a head injury, can produce retrograde amnesia (loss of memory for events occurring just prior to the injury), and that a period of sleep after a learning session produces less forgetting than does a comparable period of waking activity. The consolidation idea proved unsatisfactory, however, as an explanation of most, if not all, forgetting. Among its inadequacies are the following: (1) It cannot explain why, even long after the perseveration-consolidation process should be complete, interpolated learning nonetheless produces substantial retroactive interference; (2) it cannot explain why increasing the intensity of entirely unrelated interpolated activity results in little or no increase in forgetting; (3) it does not provide a natural account of the important role of intertask similarity in forgetting; and (4) it does not explain proactive interference.

Decay. An explanation of forgetting that seems particularly plausible was put forth by Edward THORNDIKE (1914) as his so-called *law of disuse.* The thrust of his "law" is straightforward: Unless we continue to access and use the memory representations corresponding to skills and information, those representations decay. Learning processes create memory representations, and practice maintains those representations; they fade with disuse.

However much the decay theory is in general agreement with our introspections as to how memories are formed and lost, it proved entirely inadequate as a theory of forgetting. Thorndike's law was thoroughly discredited in a devastating critique by John MCGEOCH (1932). Among the problems with the theory are (1) that forgetting is a function not simply of disuse across some retention interval but also of the nature of the activity in that interval (particularly its similarity to what is being remembered); (2) that information appears not to be lost from memory in some absolute sense, as implied by the theory, but, rather, becomes nonrecallable except under special circumstances; and (3) that it does not account for proactive interference.

The Emergence of Interference Theory

As an alternative to the consolidation and decay ideas, McGeoch (1932, 1942) put forth the initial version of what came to be called *interference theory.* That theoretical framework, as modified and refined over subsequent decades, constitutes the most significant and systematic theoretical formulation in the field of human learning and memory.

Reproductive Inhibition. McGeoch argued that human memory is fundamentally associative—that recall is guided by *cues* or *stimuli* to which items in memory are associated. As a consequence of a given individual's various experiences, however, multiple items in memory (responses) may become associated to the same cue. Recall of a given target response to a given cue, then, can suffer competition from other responses associated to that cue. Such competition, according to McGeoch, produces forgetting through *reproductive inhibition:* Recall of the target response is blocked or inhibited by the retrieval of other responses associated with that cue. Those other responses may have been learned before or after the response in question (proactive and retroactive interference, respectively), and—as observed—such interference should be a function of intertask similarity across learning episodes.

Another factor in forgetting, according to McGeoch, is that the stimulus conditions existing at the time recall is tested will differ to some extent from the conditions that existed during training. Such differences are likely to increase as the interval from training to test grows longer; and to the degree the stimulus conditions at test *do* differ, they will become less effective as cues for the response that was the target of training.

Unlearning and Spontaneous Recovery. In a pivotal study, Melton and Irwin (1940) took issue with McGeoch's analysis of retroactive interference. In their experiment, subjects learned two similar lists of verbal items and then were asked to relearn the first list. They found that the retroactive interference caused by the second list was, as predicted, an increasing function of the number of learning trials on the second list, but that the frequency of overt intrusions of second-list items during the relearning of the first list (a measure of response competition) actually *decreased,* given high levels of training on the second list. They argued that response competition at the time of test could not be the sole factor contributing to retroactive interference. They proposed a second factor: *unlearning* of first-list responses during second-list learning. Their (somewhat bizarre) idea was analogous to a basic result in the animal-learning literature: that learned responses are gradually extinguished when no longer reinforced by a reward of some kind. From that perspective, intrusions of first-list responses during second-list learning constitute unreinforced errors.

As if the unlearning idea were not strange enough by itself, it had an additional counterintuitive implication. Responses that are extinguished in animals show *spontaneous recovery* over time. To the degree that unlearning is truly like the extinction of learned responses in animals, unlearned responses should recover—become more available in memory—as time passes following the retroactive learning episode. Such an implication seems to violate a law of memory: that items in memory become less available with time. However unintuitive the unlearning/spontaneous recovery idea may seem, research carried out over the 20 years or so following the Melton and Irwin (1940) paper provided unambiguous support for the basic idea (see, in particular, Barnes and Underwood, 1959; Briggs, 1954; Underwood, 1957).

By the late 1960s the basic interplay of proactive and retroactive interference had become clear. The dynamics of that interplay are summarized below. More complete versions of the history and final state of "classical" research on interference and forgetting are available in Klatzky (1980), Bower and Hilgard (1981), Crowder (1976), and Postman (1971). In that order, those chapters are appropriate for the increasingly ambitious reader.

The Dynamics of Interference and Forgetting

Figure 1 summarizes the dynamics of interference and forgetting as presently understood. Assume that the original learning episode involves learning to associate each member, B, of a set of responses with a particular member, A, of a set of stimuli. Assume further that the new (interpolated) learning episode involves associating each member, D, of a different set of responses with a particular member, A', of a set of stimuli that may vary from being only generally similar to the A stimuli to being essentially identical. At the time memory is tested, assume that a given member of stimulus set A or A' is presented as a cue for the associated B or D response.

The A-B, A'-D notation is meant to be interpreted quite broadly. A given stimulus might be a person's face and the response that person's name, for example, and the number of A-B and A'-D pairings to be learned might vary from one of each to some large number (as in the case of a grade-school teacher learning the names of the students in each year's class). In certain cases the stimulus might actually correspond to a configuration of stimuli and the response might be a coordinated set of verbal or motor responses (A-B and A'-D, e.g., could refer to learning to operate two different automobiles, the first in the United States and the second in England). The time course of the A-B and A'-D learning episodes might vary from brief to very extended (as would be the case if A-B denotes learning to label objects in a first language and A'-D denotes learning to label those same objects in a second language).

Unlearning

During the new learning episode (A'-D), competing responses from the original learning episode (A-B) are gradually suppressed or extinguished. Such suppression facilitates A'-D learning by reducing the negative transfer from competing B responses, but it also impairs any subsequent efforts to recall B responses. On the basis of a considerable body of research (particularly McGovern, 1964; Postman et al., 1968), it appears that—depending on the relationship of the stimulus-response pairings in the two learning episodes—one or more of three distinct types of unlearning may take place. Forward associations (from A to B) can be unlearned (which facilitates A'-D learning), backward associations (from B to A) can be unlearned (which would, e.g., facilitate C-B learning, where C denotes stimuli that are not similar to A), and the entire set of B responses can be suppressed (which would aid A'-D or C-D learning).

Spontaneous Recovery

During the retention interval following A'-D learning (typically filled with other real-world activities

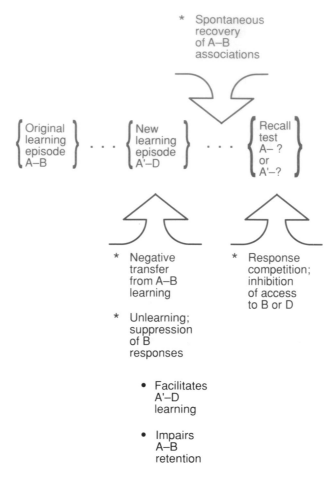

Figure 1. Summary of the processes underlying proactive and retroactive interference; A-B and A'-D denote associative learning tasks in which A and A' are similar or identical stimuli and B and D are different responses.

on the part of the learner) the A-B associations that were suppressed during A'-D learning gradually recover in strength. Any other preexperimental associations to a given A or A' stimulus that may have been learned prior to A-B or A'-D learning will recover in strength as well.

Thus, at the end of A'-D learning, the D responses will be highly accessible in memory and the B responses will be relatively inaccessible (the exact ratio of B and D strengths will depend, of course, on the initial levels of A-B and A'-D learning, and on the overlap of the A and A' stimuli). As the retention interval from the end of A'-D learning increases, however, the pattern changes: The D responses become less recallable as the interval increases, and the B responses become relatively or absolutely more recallable. Whether the B responses themselves become more recallable in *absolute* terms appears to depend on whether those responses are also in competition with other (recovering) responses learned prior to the A-B episode. If a given A-B association is itself subject to proactive interference from one or more prior associations (A-E, A-F, and so forth), recall of the B response will tend to decrease, not increase, as the retention interval increases.

As the B responses (and any other prior associations to a given A' stimulus) recover, recall of the D responses will suffer increasing proactive interference. One implication of such recovery is that the rate of forgetting of D responses after A'-D training should be a function of the number of preceding similar lists a subject has learned. In an analysis of the results of many experiments reported in the literature, Underwood (1957) found striking support for that prediction.

Response Competition

At the time a given A or A' stimulus is presented as a cue for recall of the appropriate B or D response learned earlier, that target response will be in competition with any other responses associated to that stimulus. The impact of that competition is to inhibit access to the target response in memory. In general, recall of a given target response will decrease as the number and strength of competing responses increases. That generalization, in more modern terms, is the *cue-overload principle* (Watkins and Watkins, 1975). In the analysis of such response competition, however, an important distinction is relevant. It is the *functional* stimulus, not the *nominal* stimulus, that cues the retrieval of items in memory. Thus, A and A' may be nominally identical or highly similar stimuli, but if the learning episodes involving those stimuli differ substantially—in terms of the environmental, temporal, or social context, or even in terms of the learner's emotional or physical state—the functional encoding of those stimuli may differ markedly. Thus, any stimulus, together with the context in which it is embedded, offers the learner a variety of aspects that may be "sampled" (Estes, 1955) or attended to, and that process determines the functional encoding of a given stimulus.

Consistent with the foregoing analysis, the degree to which different learning episodes result in later response competition depends on how discriminable—on one basis or another—those episodes are from each other at the time of test. The more such episodes are separated from each other temporally, for example, the less they will interfere with each other (Underwood and Ekstrand, 1967).

Output Interference

The results of somewhat more recent research add to the picture sketched above. There is abundant evidence that the recall process alters the relative accessibility of items in memory. The act of recall is itself a learning event in the sense that an item recalled in response to a given cue becomes more recallable in the future. One consequence of such response-produced strengthening of future access to recalled items, however, is that other items associated with that cue may become less recallable. That is, the recall process can alter the pattern of relative access strengths across the set of items associated to a given cue.

Consistent with the foregoing argument, there is evidence that recall is a "self-limiting process" (Roediger, 1978). When we attempt to recall the members of a category or list of items, we have difficulty recalling all the items in that set that actually exist in memory because the early items we recall impede the recall of subsequent items; by virtue of their having been recalled, the early items become more accessible in memory and block access to yet-to-be-recalled items.

Similar dynamics are probably at work in the inhibitory consequences of *part-list cuing*. When some members of a list or category of items are presented to subjects as cues to aid their recall of the remaining items, the recall of those remaining items is typically hindered rather than helped. Such inhibitory effects, considered an "enigma" in memory research (Nickerson, 1984), are at least in part a consequence of the cued items becoming *too* available in memory.

Concluding Comments

The processes of interference and transfer are fundamental to human learning, memory, and performance. After a period of almost 20 years during which research on interference and forgetting was not a dominant theme in experimental psychology, there has been a striking resurgence of interest in such phenomena over the last several years. Several contributing factors in that resurgence can be mentioned. First, there is renewed evidence of and appreciation for the role inhibitory processes play in human cognition. Second, in certain applied fields, such as research on memory factors in advertising and witness testimony, there is a need to understand how successive inputs to memory compete and interact. In research on witness memory, for example, an issue of intense current concern is how memory representations are modified by misleading postevent information (see RECONSTRUCTIVE MEMORY). Third, among researchers who are working to implement and test various types of mathematical and computer models of human memory, there is a growing realization that any plausible model must account for the basic patterns of proactive and retroactive interference (see, e.g., Mensink and Raaijmakers, 1988).

As a final comment, it is important to emphasize that forgetting is not simply a failure or weakness of the memory system. In terms of the overall functioning of the system, there must be some means to restrict what is retrieved in response to a given cue: Information that is out of date or inappropriate needs to be suppressed, or segregated, or eliminated in some fashion. During the attempt to recall one's home phone number, or where one left the car, for example, it is not useful to retrieve one's prior home phone number, or where one left the car yesterday or a week ago. In short, in terms of speed and accuracy of the recall process, we do not want *everything* that exists in our memories to be accessible, especially given the essentially unlimited capacity of human memory.

From that perspective, there are clearly some adaptive functions of the interference mechanisms that underlie forgetting. As we learn and continue to use new information, for example, access to the out-of-date information it replaces is inhibited. Such retrieval inhibition has several advantages over the kind of destructive updating of memory characteristic of computers (see Bjork, 1989). Because the old information is inhibited, it will tend not to interfere with the recall of the new information; because that information still exists in memory, however, it will tend to be recognizable and readily relearned should the need arise. And should we stop using the new information (e.g., how to drive in Britain), there will be some recovery of the old information (e.g., how to drive in the United States), which will often be adaptive as well.

In general, it appears that differences in accessibility across the vast number of items in memory acts as a kind of filter. The information and skills most readily accessible in our memories will tend to be those we have been using in the recent past. On a statistical basis, those are the same skills and knowledge we will tend to need in the near future.

(See also FORGETTING.)

REFERENCES

Barnes, J. M., and Underwood, B. J. (1959). Fate of first-list associations in transfer theory. *Journal of Experimental Psychology 58*, 97–105.

Bjork, R. A. (1989). Retrieval inhibition as an adaptive mechanism in human memory. In H. L. Roediger and F. I. M. Craik, eds., *Varieties of memory and con-*

sciousness: Essays in honor of Endel Tulving, pp. 309–330. Hillsdale, N.J.: Erlbaum.

Bower, G. H., and Hilgard, E. R. (1981). *Theories of learning*, 5th ed. Englewood Cliffs, N.J.: Prentice-Hall.

Briggs, G. E. (1954). Acquisition, extinction and recovery functions in retroactive inhibition. *Journal of Experimental Psychology 47*, 285–293.

Crowder, R. G. (1976). *Principles of learning and memory*. Hillsdale, N.J.: Erlbaum.

Estes, W. K. (1955). Statistical theory of spontaneous recovery and regression. *Psychological Review 62*, 145–154.

Klatzky, R. L. (1980). *Human memory: Structures and processes*, 2nd ed. San Francisco: Freeman.

McGeoch, J. A. (1932). Forgetting and the law of disuse. *Psychological Review 39*, 352–370.

——— (1942). *The psychology of human learning*. New York: Longmans, Green.

McGovern, J. B. (1964). Extinction of associations in four transfer paradigms. *Psychological Monographs 78* (16, whole no. 593).

Melton, A. W., and Irwin, J. M. (1940). The influence of degree of interpolated learning on retroactive inhibition and the overt transfer of specific responses. *American Journal of Psychology 53*, 173–203.

Mensink, G. J., and Raaijmakers, J. G. W. (1988). A model for interference and forgetting. *Psychological Review 93*, 434–455.

Müller, G. E., and Pilzecker, A. (1900). Experimentelle Beiträge zur Lehre von Gedächtnis. *Zeitschrift für Psychologie 1*, 1–300.

Nickerson, R. S. (1984). Retrieval inhibition from part-list cuing: A persisting enigma in memory research. *Memory and Cognition 12*, 531–552.

Postman, L. (1971). Transfer, interference, and forgetting. In J. W. Kling and L. A. Riggs, eds., *Woodworth and Schlosberg's experimental psychology*, 3rd ed. New York: Holt, Rinehart and Winston.

Postman, L., Stark, K., and Fraser, J. (1968). Temporal changes in interference. *Journal of Verbal Learning and Verbal Behavior 7*, 672–694.

Roediger, H. L. (1978). Recall as a self-limiting process. *Memory and Cognition 6*, 54–63.

Thorndike, E. L. (1914). *The psychology of learning*. New York: Teachers College Press.

Underwood, B. J. (1957). Interference and forgetting. *Psychological Review 64*, 49–60.

Underwood, B. J., and Ekstrand, B. R. (1967). Studies of distributed practice: XXIV. Differentiation and proactive inhibition. *Journal of Experimental Psychology 74*, 574–580.

Watkins, O. C., and Watkins, M. J. (1975). Buildup of proactive inhibition as a cue-overload effect. *Journal of Experimental Psychology: Human Learning and Memory 104*, 442–452.

Robert A. Bjork

INVERTEBRATE LEARNING

[Invertebrates are particularly useful for analyzing the neural and molecular events underlying learning and memory. The nervous systems of many invertebrates contain only several thousand cells (compared with the billions of cells in the vertebrate nervous system). Despite the small number of cells, an invertebrate ganglion can control a variety of different behaviors. A given behavior may therefore be mediated by 100 or fewer neurons, and this small size of the circuit makes complete description easier. Moreover, many neurons are relatively large and can be repeatedly identified as unique individuals, permitting one to examine the functional properties of an individual cell and to relate those properties to a specific behavior mediated by the cell. Changes in cellular properties that occur when a behavior is modified by learning can then be related to specific changes in behavior. Molecular and biophysical events underlying the changes in cellular properties can then be determined. This approach has been particularly successful with the crayfish, the bee, and the mollusks Aplysia, Hermissenda, Limax, Pleurobranchaea, and Tritonia.

Invertebrates are also excellent subjects for a genetic dissection of behavior and learning and memory. One animal that has been particularly useful is the fruit fly Drosophila. The basic strategy is to alter the genotype with a mutagen and test for specific defects in the ability of the animals to learn or remember. The role of individual biochemical processes and genes can then be related to specific aspects of learning and memory.

The entry that follows includes sections on each of these invertebrates except Aplysia, which is the subject of a separate entry. For additional information on insect species, see INSECT LEARNING.]

Associative Learning in Bees

The social life of the honeybee colony forms the evolutionary framework for the behavior of the individual animal and is crucial for the survival of each bee, as the individual bee cannot exist independently (Frisch, 1967; Lindauer, 1967; see also INSECT LEARNING).

The study of learning in bees has focused on operant learning (see OPERANT BEHAVIOR) in the context of food collection. When a searching bee discovers a source of sweet solution, it quickly learns to associate the surrounding visual and olfactory signals with the reward. Acquisition functions indicate that olfactory stimuli (e.g., floral odorants) are learned within one to two learning trials, colors within one to five learning trials, and black and white patterns from the fifth learning trial onward. Most of this learning is forward conditioning, because signals perceived before the reward are associated, whereas those perceived during the reward or departure flight are associated less effectively or not at all.

Reversal learning, overlearning, and multireversal learning are effective learning phenomena in the bee (Menzel, 1990). The experimental procedures that test the ability of an animal to adapt its performance to reward schedules are B. F. SKINNER's (1938) continuous, fixed-ratio, and fixed-interval REINFORCEMENT schedules (CR, FR, and FI, respectively). Bees develop a higher resistance to extinction in an FR than in a CR schedule. In an FI schedule of reinforcement, bees exhibit lower response rates than in an FR schedule. FR schedules of up to one reinforcement out of thirty trials, and FI schedules with up to 90 seconds between reinforcements, are reached after several days of training (Grossmann, 1973). Additional operant learning phenomena in honeybees have been studied in the tradition of experimental psychology and are reported by Bitterman (1988).

Reflex Conditioning

Classical conditioning of reflexes is a most convenient way to study the behavioral and neural mechanisms of associative learning (see CONDITIONING, CLASSICAL AND INSTRUMENTAL). In the honeybee, the proboscis extension reflex (PER) to a sucrose stimulus at the antennae is a reliable reflex in the context of feeding. The bee will extend its proboscis (tongue) reflexively when the antennae are touched with a drop of sucrose solution. It can be conditioned to an olfactory or mechanical stimulus (conditioned stimulus, CS), even under conditions in which the animal is harnessed in a tube (Kuwabara, 1957) or being prepared for physiological studies (Menzel, Erber, and Masuhr, 1974;

Menzel, 1990). The PER and its conditioning to a CS are highly dependent on the hunger-induced motivation.

The associative nature of PER conditioning has been established by demonstrating that only forward pairing of CS-US sequences is effective, by various control groups (unpaired CS and US, CS- or US-only presentations), and by differential conditioning of the two olfactory stimuli (Bitterman et al., 1983). The predictive value of the CS depends on the reliability with which it is causally related to the US. In differential conditioning, the reversal to the initially unpaired stimulus is slower after more frequent unreinforced preexposures than after a lesser number of preexposures. The same applies for US-only preexposures in an otherwise reinforced context. Partial reinforcement schedules have little effect on the acquisition function, because extinction trials do not alter the CR probability, but increase the resistance to extinction and other measures of learning.

Blocking and overshadowing experiments are used to characterize the informational content of the CS (Rescorla, 1988; see also BEHAVIORAL PHENOMENA: CONDITIONING, CLASSICAL). In PER conditioning, olfactory stimuli overshadow mechanical stimuli and blocking effects are not found. This indicates that attentiveness is not a limiting factor, and that the salience or associability of a stimulus (olfactory over mechanical) is an important factor. Second-order conditioning is a procedure that tests whether a CS can acquire the potential of an US. This has also been demonstrated for olfactory PER conditioning (Bitterman et al., 1983; Menzel, 1990). The strength of the effect is highly dependent on the CS used. Citral, a particularly salient CS and a chemical component of an attraction pheromone produced by bees to mark food sources, has strong potential as an acquired US; more neutral odors (e.g., octanal) have a weak potential for second-order conditioning.

Sequential Memory Processing

A stable, lifelong memory is formed even after only a few learning trials. Harnessed bees prepared for olfactory PER conditioning do not survive long enough to allow testing of their memory over periods of more than 2–3 days, but retention remains high during this period, even after only one to three conditioning trials. After a single learning

trial, the retention curve follows a biphasic time course, which indicates that memory and retrieval is at first very high, fades to a minimum 2–3 minutes after learning, rises again within the following 20 minutes, and stays high for a number of hours. The early memory phase in the minute range is particularly susceptible to both extinction and reversal learning, whereas the consolidated memory is much more resistant. The sensitizing effect of the appetitive stimulus (sucrose solution) overlaps with the early high response level, indicating that,

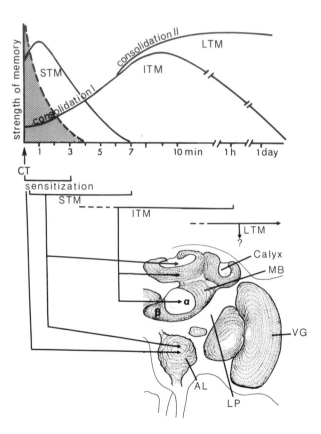

Figure 1. Model of memory phases and their respective localizations in the bee brain. The shaded area represents the time course of the nonassociative US sensitization effect. CT, conditioning trial; STM, short-term memory; ITM, intermediate-term memory; LTM, long-term memory. The diagram below shows half a bee brain with the major neuropils. The antennal lobe (AL) is the primary afferent neuropil; the mushroom bodies (MB) are the second- to higher-order multisensory neuropils with their input regions (calyxes) and output regions (α- and β-lobes); the lateral protocerebrum (LP) is the major output region of the brain to premotor pathways in the ventral chord; the two visual ganglia (VG) are not involved in olfactory processing.

at least in PER conditioning, the nonassociative memory initiated by the US contributes substantially to the response probability immediately after the single learning trial.

Amnestic treatments (cooling, narcosis, weak electroconvulsive brain stimulation), if applied within 2–3 minutes after the single-trial learning, erase the memory trace; this fact indicates a susceptible short-term memory (STM). Several conditioning trials within the STM make the memory trace immune to amnestic treatment. The memory initiated by a single conditioning trial consolidates within a few minutes so that it becomes resistant to retrograde amnestic treatments. The time course of retrograde amnestic sensitivity is independent of the kind of learning (opcrant color learning, olfactory PER conditioning), but depends on the particular structure of the brain to which the treatment is applied.

The model arising from these results (Figure 1) interprets the temporal dynamics of the retention function and the local amnestic phenomena as the dynamics of internal, automatic memory-processing mechanisms that pass through several consecutive memory traces and involve different brain structures. The nonassociative memory is thought to reside predominantly in the antennal lobes, the primary afferent neuropils, but may also include premotor and motor components because the response is strengthened during the period of sensitization. The STM is a joint function of the antennal lobes and the mushroom bodies. Intermediate-term memory (ITM) is established during the process of consolidation within the mushroom

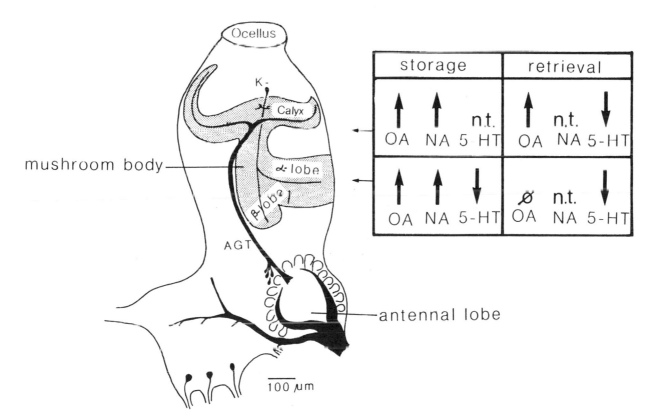

Figure 2. A summary of the pharmacological effects of octopamine (OA), norepinephrine (NA), and serotonin (5-HT) when injected locally in small quantities (2–8 nanoliters) in each of the paired structures of the mushroom bodies. Two series of experiments were performed, the storage test (injections before the one-trial PER conditioning) and the retrieval test (injection after conditioning). Arrows pointing upwards indicate an enhancement of the storage or retrieval, arrows pointing downwards a reduction of storage and retrieval. The diagram shows a side view of the brain. K, Kenyon cells; AGT, antennoglomerular tract; n.t., not tested. Scale bar, 100 microns. *After Bicker and Menzel, 1989.*

bodies. The mushroom bodies in the bee protocerebrum are paired structures each made up of 170,000 densely packed neurons. They receive multisensory inputs in the cup-shaped calyxes (two in each mushroom body), and communicate with the output region of the brain via extrinsic neurons in the α- and β-lobes. The localization of the long-term memory is unknown and may not be identical with that of the ITM in the mushroom bodies. Since the reflex pathway involves only the antennal lobe and the subesophageal ganglion (SEG; the motor center), associative memory does not appear to be a property of the reflex pathway alone, but rather of parallel pathways (Menzel et al., 1991).

(See also MEMORY CONSOLIDATION.)

Neurophysiology and Behavioral Neuropharmacology

The concept of functionally and anatomically separated memory traces is supported by single-cell recordings. Sucrose (US) induces sensitization effects in neurons at all levels (e.g., intrinsic antennal-lobe neurons, relay neurons to the mushroom lobes, projection neurons from the mushroom bodies to the ganglia in the ventral cord, SEG neurons, intrinsic premotor and motor neurons). Correlates of associative memory are found in neurons downstream from the neurons of the central brain. Mushroom-body extrinsic neurons have properties compatible with the neural plasticity underlying associative learning. They are multimodal, have long-lasting stimulus aftereffects that outlive a stimulus by many seconds, and change their response properties in an associative learning situation (Erber, 1981).

Learning behavior can be manipulated pharmacologically by injecting small amounts (a few nanoliters) of drugs or transmitters into different regions of the brain before or after single trials of olfactory PER conditioning (Menzel et al., 1988, 1991; Menzel, Wittstock, and Sugawa, 1990; Bicker and Menzel, 1989). As the conditioning trial lasts only a few seconds and the drugs take several minutes to act, the processes underlying memory storage and memory retrieval can be separated. Figure 2 gives a summary of the effects. Octopamine and norepinephrine appear to be involved in facilitating the storage and retrieval of the memory, whereas serotonin (5-HT) reduces both memory functions. The specific reinforcement function of the US is represented in an identified neuron, which projects from the SEG into the brain and arborizes, particularly in those neuropils (antennal lobe, calyxes of the mushroom bodies, lateral protocerebrum) where it converges with the CS-representing neurons (Hammer, 1991).

Conclusions

The effective learning behavior of honeybees in the context of feeding and the clear separation between memory processes have helped us to approach basic questions of memory research. The findings on the location of the olfactory memory engram in the bee brain suggest a working hypothesis, which localizes different forms of behavioral plasticities and the sequential memory phases in different regions of the brain. In essence, the hypothesis states that transient and nonassociatively modifiable pathways run parallel to pathways modified by associative learning processes. Pathways including the mushroom bodies are considered to change their properties specifically during associative memory formation, whereas direct connections involving the sensory motor centers or the sensory neuropil of the antennal lobes alone do not contain all the necessary components for an associative memory trace. Behavioral pharmacology clearly indicates that neuroactive substances, such as biogenic amines, exert general and selective actions on the different forms of memory.

REFERENCES

Bicker, G., and Menzel, R. (1989). Chemical codes for the control of behaviour in arthropods. *Nature 337,* 33–39.

Bitterman, M. E. (1988). Vertebrate-invertebrate comparisons. *NATO ASI Series—Intelligence and Evolutionary Biology 17,* 251–275.

Bitterman, M. E., Menzel, R., Fietz, A., and Schäfer, S. (1983). Classical conditioning of proboscis extension in honeybees (*Apis millifera*). *Journal of Comparative Psychology 97,* 107–119.

Erber, J. (1981). Neural correlates of learning in the honeybee. *Trends in Neurosciences 4,* 270–272.

Frisch, K. von (1967). *The dance language and orientation of bees.* Cambridge, Mass.: Harvard University Press.

Grossmann, K. E. (1973). Continuous, fixed-ratio and fixed-interval reinforcement in honey bees. *Journal of the Experimental Analysis of Behavior 20,* 105–109.

Hammer, M. (1991). A ventral unpaired median (VUM) neuron of the suboesophageal ganglion mediates the reinforcer function of the US in olfactory conditioning of the honeybee. In H. Penzlin and N. Elsner, eds., *Synapse, transmission, modulation.* Stuttgart: Thieme.

Kuwabara, M. (1957). Bildung des bedingten Reflexes von Pavlovs Typus bei der Honigbiene, *Apis mellifica. Journal of the Faculty of Science of Hokkaido University, Series VI: Zoology 13,* 458–464.

Lindauer, M. (1967). Recent advances in bee communication and orientation. *Annual Review of Entomology 12,* 439–470.

Menzel, R. (1990). Learning, memory and "cognition" in honey bees. In R. P. Kesner and D. S. Olten, eds., *Neurobiology of comparative cognition,* pp. 237–292. Hillsdale, N.J.: Erlbaum.

Menzel, R., Erber, J., and Masuhr, T. (1974). Learning and memory in the honeybee. In L. Barton-Browne, ed., *Experimental analysis of insect behaviour,* pp. 195–217. Berlin: Springer.

Menzel, R., Michelsen, B., Füffer, P., and Sugawa, M. (1988). Neuropharmacology of learning and memory in honey bees. In G. Herting and H. C. Spatz, eds., *Synaptic transmission and plasticity in nervous systems,* pp. 335–350. Berlin: Springer.

Menzel, R., Wittstock, S., and Sugawa, M. (1990). Chemical codes of learning and memory in the honey bees. In L. Squire and K. Lindenlaub, eds., *The biology of memory,* pp. 335–360. Stuttgart; Schattauer.

Menzel, R., Manner, M., Braun, G., Mauelshagen, J., and Sugawa, M. (1991). Neurobiology of learning and memory in honeybees. In L. J. Goodman and R. C. Fisher (eds.): *The behaviour and physiology of bees.* Wallingford, England: CAB International.

Rescorla, R. A. (1988). Behavioral studies of Pavlovian conditioning. *Annual Review of Neuroscience 11,* 329–352.

Skinner, B. F. (1938). *The behavior of organisms.* New York: Appleton.

Randolf Menzel

Associative Learning in *Hermissenda*

There are few features of conscious experience that have captured the human imagination more than the proclivity of animals to learn and to retain the consequences of experience in memory. Learning not only provides for the adaptation of organisms to changing environmental demands, but also, and more important, the persistence of learning, termed long-term memory, provides us with a history of human experience. In spite of the widespread interest in learning and memory, their basic mechanisms remain among the least thoroughly understood areas of physiology. An attractive experimental approach to this problem at a fundamental level is the analysis of learning in the less complex central nervous system of invertebrates. One animal that has contributed to the physiological study of learning and memory is the nudibranch mollusk *Hermissenda crassicornis,* whose behavior can be modified by a classical conditioning procedure. The *Hermissenda* central nervous system is relatively simple, consisting of many identifiable neurons that can be studied in detail using biochemical, biophysical, and molecular techniques. Cellular correlates of learning have been identified and have been the focus of physiological analysis.

Classical Conditioning

Hermissenda normally exhibits a positive phototaxis when stimulated with light. The phototactic response is expressed behaviorally by various measures of visually influenced locomotion (for a review see Crow, 1988). The conditioning procedure used to modify phototactic behavior consists of pairing the conditioned stimulus (CS), light, with the unconditioned stimulus (US), high-speed rotation. Crow and colleagues demonstrated that stimulation of the animal's visual and vestibular systems with paired light and rotation produces a long-term suppression, lasting days to weeks, of the normal positive phototactic response evoked by light. Results of behavioral studies have shown that the suppression of phototactic behavior by the conditioning procedure produces most of the features of classical conditioning as described for vertebrates. The change in phototactic behavior is dependent upon the temporal association of the two sensory stimuli. Animals that received the CS and US paired exhibited significant phototactic suppression compared with the groups that received the CS and US programmed on independent random schedules, or explicitly unpaired. The suppression of phototactic behavior is also specific to the presentation of the CS. Crow and Offenbach (1983) reported that conditioned animals show suppressed locomotor behavior in the presence of the CS; however, their locomotor behavior in the dark is not significantly changed. (See also CONDITIONING, CLASSICAL AND INSTRUMENTAL.)

Why should paired stimulation of the animal's visual and vestibular systems produce suppression of phototactic behavior? A clue to the nature of the motor response modified by CS-US pairings that may help explain phototactic suppression was provided by a study of the effect of conditioning upon the shape of the animal's foot by Lederhendler, Gart, and Alkon (1986). Before conditioning, animals moving in the dark respond to the onset of the CS by lengthening the foot. Rotation elicits a shortening of the foot of animals moving in the dark. Following three days of training consisting of fifty pairings of the CS and US each day, the CS elicited a shortening of the foot, a response similar to the response elicited by the US. These behavioral results may explain suppression of a number of components of phototaxis produced by conditioning.

Cellular Correlates of Classical Conditioning

An essential step in the analysis of conditioning is the search for the loci in the animal's nervous system where memories of the associative experience are stored. Crow and Alkon (1980) identified the primary sensory neurons (photoreceptors) of the pathway mediating the CS as one site for memory storage. Cellular correlates have been detected in surgically isolated photoreceptors from conditioned and random control animals following training. Cellular correlates that have been observed following conditioning involve an enhancement of the excitability of type B photoreceptors. One correlate of conditioning that has received a considerable amount of attention is the decreased membrane conductance found in the type B photoreceptors. Biophysical studies by Alkon et al. (1985) revealed that at least two K^+ currents are reduced in B photoreceptors following conditions. One K^+ current (I_A) is similar to the A current described previously in mollusks. The second K^+ current is primarily activated by intracellular Ca^{2+} ($I_{K,Ca}$). One hypothesis that has been proposed to explain the reduction in I_A and $I_{K,Ca}$ following conditioning involves the phosphorylation of K^+ channels. Support for this hypothesis came from the finding by Neary, Crow, and Alkon (1981)

that there is a change in the level of phosphate incorporation into a specific phosphoprotein band in the eyes of conditioned *Hermissenda*.

Mechanisms of Classical Conditioning

What are the mechanisms responsible for the reduction in K^+ currents of B photoreceptors observed after conditioning of *Hermissenda*? An attractive hypothesis involves the activation of protein kinases by second messenger systems (see SECOND MESSENGER SYSTEMS). To test this hypothesis, Alkon et al. (1983) injected protein kinases into B photoreceptors in an attempt to mimic conditioning effects on both the generator potential evoked by light and the reduction of K^+ currents. Iontophoresis of the catalytic subunit of cAMP-dependent protein kinase into B photoreceptors decreased both I_A and a slower delayed K^+ current called I_B. I_B consists of both $I_{K,Ca}$ and the voltage-dependent delayed rectifier $I_{K,V}$, and in the initial study no attempts were made to separate the two currents experimentally. These observations suggested that the cAMP system may contribute to the reductions in K^+ currents observed in conditioned animals. It has been proposed that $Ca^{2+}/$ calmodulin-dependent protein kinase and the phosphoinositide system may be involved in the phosphorylation of proteins associated with K^+ channels. Acosta-Urquidi, Alkon, and Neary (1984) reported that injections of phosphorylase kinase into B photoreceptors results in an increase in the input resistance of the photoreceptor and a reduction in I_A and I_B, as well as an enhanced light response.

Farley and Auerbach (1986) reported that activation of protein kinase C (PKC) by phorbol esters and intracellular injection of protein kinase C into B photoreceptors reduced both I_A and $I_{K,Ca}$. The essential feature of the proposed mechanism for associative memory is that PKC activation occurs together with elevated intracellular Ca^{2+}. Support for the proposed mechanism comes from a study by Falk-Vairant and Crow (1992) showing that the injection of the Ca^{2+} chelator BAPTA into B photoreceptors blocked the induction of short-term memory. As shown in Figure 1, activation of PKC could be initiated by a transmitter such as serotonin. The possible roles of PKC and $Ca^{2+}/$ calmodulin-dependent protein kinase are not mutually exclusive, since $Ca^{2+}/$calmodulin-depen-

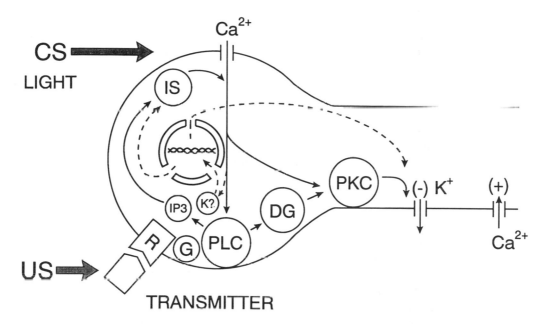

Figure 1. A cellular model for associative memory in B photoreceptors of *Hermissenda*. Short-term enhancement produced by one-trial conditioning involves activation and amplification of protein kinase C (PKC). Transmitter released by stimulation of the US pathway binds to a specific receptor (R). The receptor-activated signal is transmitted through a G protein to the enzyme phospholipase C (PLC). PLC splits PIP_2 (not shown) into inositol trisphosphate (IP3) and diacylglycerol (DG). The DG, Ca^{2+} influx produced by the conditioned stimulus (CS), and Ca^{2+} released by inositol trisphosphate from internal stores (IS) activate PLC and PKC, which reduces K^+ currents and results in enhanced excitability of the photoreceptors. The presentation of the CS results in increased levels of intracellular Ca^{2+} produced by the depolarizing generator potential activating voltage-dependent Ca^{2+} channels and light-induced release of Ca^{2+} from IS. Pairing specificity results from the amplification provided by Ca^{2+} acting on PLC and PKC. Long-term memory in this model is dependent upon protein synthesis and gene products dependent upon Ca^{2+} activating an unidentified kinase (K?) or long-term changes in Ca^{2+} buffering. The evidence suggests that short-term and long-term memory in this system involves independent parallel pathways (see text).

dent protein kinase may act synergistically with protein kinase C to produce changes in K^+ channels. Moreover, the cAMP cell-signaling system may also interact with both protein kinase C and Ca^{2+}/calmodulin-dependent kinases to produce reductions in the K^+ currents of B photoreceptors observed in conditioned animals.

One-Trial In Vivo Conditioning

Since all of the second-messenger pathways described above can be activated by transmitters in other systems, an obvious question is whether there is evidence that a transmitter or neuromodulator is involved in producing long-lasting changes in the photoreceptors of conditioned *Hermissenda*. Results by Crow and Bridge (1985) suggest a possible role for a modulatory transmitter, since the action of a number of biogenic amines can mimic some of the correlates observed in B photoreceptors following conditioning. A potential serotonergic pathway for direct interaction with photoreceptors has been identified by Land and Crow (1985). Their immunohistochemical study revealed serotonergic immunoreactive fibers and varicosities on the optic nerve and in the synaptic region of the neuropil near the synaptic terminals of the photoreceptors.

If a modulatory transmitter is released by stimulation of the US pathway, and is involved in conditioned modification of phototactic behavior, then substituting the direct application of the modulatory transmitter for stimulation of the US pathway should produce similar changes in behavior. To test this hypothesis, a one-trial in vivo conditioning procedure was developed by Crow and Forrester (1986). Light (CS) was paired with direct application of several modulatory transmitters (dopamine, octopamine, serotonin) to the exposed nervous system of otherwise intact *Hermissenda*. One 5-minute training session, consisting of the CS paired with 5-HT (serotonin), produced significant suppression of phototactic behavior when the animals were tested 24 hours after the end of the training session. The two other putative neuromodulators, dopamine and octopamine, did not produce significant suppression of phototactic behavior when paired with the CS. If the CS and 5-HT pairings are analogous to the conditioning procedure used to modify phototactic behavior, then the change in behavior should be dependent upon the temporal pairing of the CS and 5-HT. Pairing specificity was shown by comparing the group that received the CS paired with 5-HT to a group that received the CS and 5-HT unpaired, and a group that received only 5-HT. The group that received the CS paired with 5-HT showed phototactic suppression compared with the two control groups when tested the next day. As an additional control, one control group that had initially received the unpaired CS with 5-HT was tested again after receiving the CS paired with 5-HT. Following the paired procedure, the animals showed behavioral suppression when tested 24 hours later.

(See also NEUROTRANSMITTER SYSTEMS AND MEMORY.)

Cellular Correlates of One-Trial In Vivo Conditioning

In addition to the change in phototactic behavior produced by one-trial in vivo conditioning, cellular correlates were detected in identified B photoreceptors. Animals were trained with the one-trial in vivo conditioning procedure (see above), and neural correlates were examined in isolated B photoreceptors at 1 hour and 24 hours after training. Crow and Forrester (1991) found that pairing light (CS) with 5-HT produced both a short-term non-pairing-specific enhancement and a long-term pairing-specific enhancement of the generator potentials recorded from different identified B photoreceptors.

Crow et al. (1991) found that the induction of short-term enhancement is due to activation of PKC since kinase inhibitors and downregulation of PKC block short-term enhancement. Interestingly, the conditions that are sufficient to block short-term enhancement do not block long-term enhancement, indicating that independent parallel pathways may be involved in the induction of short- and long-term memory.

Role of Protein Synthesis in One-Trial In Vivo Conditioning

The finding that one-trial in vivo conditioning produces both suppression of phototaxis and short- and long-term correlates in identified B photoreceptors has provided a convenient tool to study the cellular mechanisms of time-dependent processes that may be related to both short- and long-term memory. The hypothesized mechanisms for associative interactions in the B photoreceptors, as summarized in Figure 1, may account for the short-term reductions of K^+ currents observed in conditioned animals. However, it is attractive to propose a role for protein synthesis in the induction of long-term cellular correlates produced by conditioning. Historically, it has been proposed that short- and long-term memory represent different components of memory with distinct qualitative and quantitative features. Previous studies of memory in vertebrates suggested that long-term memory requires the synthesis of new protein, whereas short-term memory does not (see PROTEIN SYNTHESIS IN LONG-TERM MEMORY IN VERTEBRATES). In *Hermissenda*, Crow and Forrester (1990) found that in vivo conditioning in the presence of the protein synthesis inhibitor anisomycin did not block short-term enhancement. In contrast, long-term enhancement of the generator potential was blocked if the one-trial in vivo conditioning procedure was applied in the presence of anisomycin. Moreover, inhibition of protein synthesis was effective only when applied during the presentation of the conditioning trial. For example, when anisomycin was applied 1 hour after the conditioning trial, long-term enhancement was not blocked. A derivative of anisomycin, deacetylanisomycin, which is inactive in inhibiting protein synthesis, also failed to block long-term enhancement produced by in vivo conditioning. In addition, anisomycin by itself did not cause any change in the amplitude of generator potentials. These findings indicate that ongoing protein synthesis is necessary for the induction and maintenance of long-term enhancement, but it is also likely that this process requires transcription.

Conclusions

Taken collectively, the electrophysiological and behavioral results suggest that a neuromodulator such as 5-HT may play a role in learning in *Hermissenda*. However, it has not been demonstrated that endogenous release of 5-HT is produced by activation of the US pathway. Moreover, it is not known if the same mechanism is responsible for both the cellular correlates produced by one-trial in vivo conditioning and correlates detected after classical conditioning of phototactic behavior. A modulator such as 5-HT may operate in parallel with the previously identified CS and US pathways to amplify conditioning-induced changes in membrane currents that have been previously identified. Alternatively, a modulatory transmitter such as 5-HT may activate second-messenger systems that interact with light- and/or voltage-dependent processes activated by the CS to induce short- and long-term changes in membrane conductances produced by in vivo conditioning.

The issue of whether short-term and long-term memory occur in series or in parallel has not yet been resolved. The further study of short-term and long-term enhancement produced by one-trial conditioning of *Hermissenda* provides an opportunity to examine this issue.

Long-term enhancement may depend upon an independent and parallel signaling system or, alternatively, both short- and long-term enhancement may depend upon the same steps for induction. However, the finding that the conditions sufficient to block short-term enhancement do not block long-term enhancement indicates that different pathways and different mechanisms may be involved in the induction of short-term and long-term memory.

REFERENCES

Acosta-Urquidi, J., Alkon, D. L., and Neary, J. T. (1984). Ca^{2+}-dependent protein kinase injection in a photoreceptor mimics biophysical effects of associative learning. *Science 224*, 1254–1257.

Alkon, D. L., Acosta-Urquidi, J., Olds, J., Kuzma, G., and Neary, J. T. (1983). Protein kinase activity reduces voltage-dependent K^+ current. *Science 219*, 303–306.

Alkon, D. L., Sakakibara, M., Forman, R., Harrigan, J., Lederhendler, I., and Farley, J. (1985). Reduction of two voltage-dependent K^+ currents mediates retention of a learned association. *Behavioral and Neural Biology 44*, 278–300.

Crow, T. (1988). Cellular and molecular analysis of associative learning and memory in *Hermissenda*. *Trends in Neurosciences 11*, 136–142.

Crow, T., and Alkon, D. L. (1978). Retention of an associative behavioral change in *Hermissenda*. *Science 201*, 1239–1241.

——— (1980). Associative behavioral modification in *Hermissenda*: Cellular correlates. *Science 209*, 412–414.

Crow, T., and Bridge, M. S. (1985). Serotonin modulates photoresponses in *Hermissenda* type-B photoreceptors. *Neuroscience Letters 60*, 83–88.

Crow, T., and Forrester, J. (1986). Light paired with serotonin mimics the effects of conditioning on phototactic behavior in *Hermissenda*. *Proceedings of the National Academy of Sciences 83*, 7975–7978.

——— (1990). Inhibition of protein synthesis blocks long-term enhancement of generator potentials produced by one-trial *in vivo* conditioning in *Hermissenda*. *Proceedings of the National Academy of Sciences 87*, 4490–4494.

——— (1991). Light paired with serotonin *in vivo* produces both short- and long-term enhancement of generator potentials of identified B-photoreceptors in *Hermissenda*. *Journal of Neuroscience 11*, 608–617.

Crow, T., Forrester, J., Williams, M., Waxham, N., and Neary, J. (1991). Down regulation of protein kinase C blocks 5-HT-induced enhancement in *Hermissenda* B photoreceptors. *Neuroscience Letters 121*, 107–110.

Crow, T., and Offenbach, N. (1983). Modification of the initiation of locomotion in *Hermissenda*: Behavioral analysis. *Brain Research 271*, 301–310.

Falk-Vairant, J., and Crow, T. (1992). Enhancement in type B photoreceptors of *Hermissenda* is blocked by injection of a Ca^{2+} chelator. *Biophysical Journal 61*, 520.

Farley, J., and Auerbach, S. (1986). Protein kinase C activation induces conductance changes in *Hermissenda* photoreceptors like those seen in associative learning. *Nature 319*, 220–223.

Land, P. W., and Crow, T. (1985). Serotonin immunoreactivity in the circumesophageal nervous system of *Hermissenda crassicornis. Neuroscience Letters 63,* 199–205.

Lederhendler, I., Gart, S., and Alkon, D. L. (1986). Classical conditioning of *Hermissenda:* Origin of a new response. *Journal of Neuroscience 6,* 1325–1331.

Neary, J. T., Crow, T. J., and Alkon, D. L. (1981). Changes in a specific phosphoprotein band following associative learning in *Hermissenda. Nature 293,* 658–660.

Terry J. Crow

Associative Learning in *Limax*

A phenomenon should be studied in its simplest possible form, but no simpler. (A. Einstein)

The model systems approach to questions of learning and memory mechanisms is based on the premise that the cellular and network properties that optimize information storage in the nervous sytem may be universal across the major animal phyla, given that properties of cells and synapses are very similar across the major animal groups. Specialized learning mechanisms have arisen as efficient solutions to information-processing problems in all major animal phyla (Corning, Dyal, and Willows, 1973), so it is natural to speculate that phylogenetically diverse species solving the same type of adaptive challenge with a learning mechanism having the same formal properties either may have converged on a similar mechanistic solution or may have retrained the same basic mechanism from a remote common ancestor. Ultimately these mechanistic speculations will be tested when, for example, mammalian and molluscan memory storage mechanisms for computationally equivalent learning tasks are sufficiently defined for detailed comparisons to be made (Byrne, 1987; Carew and Sahley, 1986).

The terrestrial slug *Limax maximus* has a highly developed associative learning ability in the domain of associative conditioning (see CONDITIONING, CLASSICAL AND INSTRUMENTAL) using odors as conditioned stimuli (CS). *Limax* associative learning about odors may be computationally equivalent to analogous mammalian learning, given the remarkable similarities between *Limax* and vertebrate conditioning phenomena (Gelperin, 1989; Sahley, 1990). Slugs show one-trial food avoidance conditioning with long delay when ingestion of a highly preferred food is paired with CO_2 applica-

tion as the aversive unconditioned stimulus (US) (Gelperin, 1975). One-trial odor aversion learning is obtained by pairing initially attractive food odors with the bitter taste of quinidine sulfate as the US (Sahley, Gelperin, and Rudy, 1981a). Several higher-order logic operations, such as second-order conditioning, blocking, and a US preexposure effect, also are readily demonstrated using odor aversion training (Sahley, Rudy, and Gelperin, 1981b).

Conditioning Odor Aversions

Although the first demonstration of odor-aversion conditioning in *Limax* used the amount of food consumed as the dependent measure, subsequent systematic explorations of higher-order properties of odor-aversion conditioning used a measure of directed locomotion in the presence of odor gradients to determine the consequences of exposing slugs to a variety of CS-US predictive relationships. The basic training protocol is applied to food-deprived animals to ensure their responsiveness to food odors. Typically slugs are given a 2-minute exposure to the odor of a highly preferred food plant, such as potato, carrot, or mushroom; then quinidine sulfate is applied to the circumoral taste receptors for 2 minutes. Control groups are given either explicitly unpaired presentations of the CS and US or random presentations of the CS and US. One day after training, testing is conducted in a chamber with perforated flooring. One test odor source is placed under the floor on one side of the test chamber, and a second test odor source is placed under the floor of the other side. Testing is started by placing the animal in a neutral zone between the two odor areas and measuring the percent of the total test time spent over each odor source during a 3-minute observation period. During testing, one odor is the CS odor and the other odor is derived from rat chow, which is the maintenance diet. Single CS–US pairings can reduce the time over the CS odor from 80 percent for controls receiving unpaired presentations of the CS and US to 20 percent for animals receiving paired presentations of the CS and US (Sahley, Gelperin, and Rudy, 1981a).

Various US treatments have been used to promote odor-aversion conditioning, including CO_2 or quinidine sulfate application, shock (Delaney and Gelperin, 1984), and the postingestive consequences of eating a diet devoid of an amino acid essential for growth (Delaney and Gelperin, 1986). Although these treatments are all effective in producing odor-aversion conditioning, they differ in the extent to which they support long-delay conditioning, one of the most distinctive aspects of taste-aversion conditioning in vertebrates (Domjan, 1980; Garcia, Ervin, and Koelling, 1966). Using CO_2 application as the aversive US, even if the US was delayed by 1 hour from the cessation of CS exposure, significant associative conditioning occurred (Gelperin, 1975). This experiment demonstrates that some form of central representation of the CS odor is retained in the CNS for periods of at least tens of minutes in a form which can be modified by subsequent US application.

Limax Logic Functions

The question of what is learned during odor conditioning was explored using the second-order conditioning paradigm. Second-order conditioning involves two phases of training. During the first phase, one odor (CS_1) is paired with the taste of quinidine (US). During the second phase, the animal learns to associate a new odor (CS_2) with the odor previously associated with the US (CS_1). During the second phase of training, are odor-odor connections (S-S learning) formed, or does each odor make independent connections with the US (S-R learning)? The robust nature of the second-order odor-aversion conditioning effect allowed exploration of this question in *Limax* using the postconditioning treatment strategy of Rescorla (Rescorla, 1980). If second-order conditioning depends on a CS_1-CS_2 linkage for its expression, then extinguishing the learned aversion to CS_1 after the second phase of conditioning should result in the loss of aversion to CS_2. Alternatively, if second-order conditioning leads to a CS_2-US association independent of the CS_1-US association, then extinguishing the learned aversion to CS_1 should have no effect on the CS_2 aversion. In vertebrate systems, the effect of the postconditioning extinction of CS_1 on responding to CS_2 depends critically on the timing of the presentation of CS_1 relative to CS_2 during the second phase of second-order conditioning. If CS_1 and CS_2 are presented simultaneously during the second phase of second-order conditioning, then CS_1-CS_2 associations are favored (Rescorla, 1982). If CS_1 and CS_2 are presented

sequentially during the second phase of conditioning, then independent CS_2-US associations are favored.

The results obtained with second-order conditioning followed by CS_1 extinction in *Limax* showed a striking parallel with previous results in vertebrate systems. Slugs given simultaneous CS_1-CS_2 presentations during the second phase of second-order conditioning and then given CS_1 extinction trials lost the learned aversion to both CS_1 and CS_2, whereas animals given sequential CS_2-CS_1 presentations during the second phase of conditioning, and then CS_1 extinction, retained the learned aversion to CS_2 (Sahley, 1990). These results provide a particularly clear example of how small differences in the timing of stimuli can lead to dramatic differences in the way stimulus associations are represented in the brain. The nature of the learned association is critically dependent on the relative timing between stimuli.

The predictive power or informational content of conditioned stimuli is another key concept in Pavlovian conditioning (Rescorla, 1988). A particularly compelling example of an experimental outcome that illustrates this concept is provided by the phenomenon of blocking (Kamin, 1968, 1969). To determine whether odor-aversion conditioning in *Limax* shows the blocking phenomenon, slugs were given two phases of odor-aversion conditioning. In the first phase CS_1-US pairings were given, while in the second phase CS_2-CS_1-US pairings were given. As expected from results with vertebrate preparations (Holland, 1977), the CS_2 was not associated with the US and hence was not avoided (Sahley, Rudy, and Gelperin, 1981b). In the second phase of conditioning, the exposure to CS_1 fully predicts the subsequent appearance of the US. The CS_2 provides no new information and hence is not associated with the US. This formulation emphasizing the informational content of stimuli also predicts that if some aspect of either the CS_1 or the US is changed during the second phase conditioning trials when the CS_2 is first introduced, then conditioning to CS_2 will occur. This has been observed in experiments with vertebrate preparations, for example, when a second brief US is presented shortly after the first US (Dickinson and Mackintosh, 1979; Flaherty, 1985).

Numerous studies have shown that the form of memory storage changes with time after conditioning, from a short-term disruption-sensitive form to a long-term disruption-insensitive form. Global neural disruptions such as electroconvulsive shock, drug treatments, or cooling delivered at various times after training have been used to probe temporal changes in the disruption sensitivity of the engram (Erber, 1976; Quinn and Dudai, 1976; Squire, 1987). The time course of odor-aversion memory storage in *Limax flavus* has been investigated using whole-body cooling to induce retrograde amnesia (Sekiguchi et al., 1991). Significant odor-aversion conditioning was found with single carrot odor-quinidine pairings. Testing was conducted in a two-choice chamber much like the testing chamber of Sahley, Gelperin, and Rudy (1981a). A short-term memory phase in which the memory of odor-aversion conditioning is disrupted by cooling was found to last for about 1 minute before transition to a long-term memory phase in which the memory was immune to cooling-induced amnesia. The network and biochemical storage schemes constructed to account for associative conditioning phenomena must have a number of overlapping processes with different time constants to match the number and variety of memory phases demonstrated in the behavioral work. (See also MEMORY CONSOLIDATION.)

Postingestive Conditioning

Another type of behavioral plasticity shown by *Limax* revealed that the long-term memory for food aversions can last for more than 110 days (Delaney and Gelperin, 1986). This result emerged from studies of feeding responses of slugs fed artificial diets that were either nutritionally complete or lacking one of the amino acids essential for growth, such as methionine. Slugs fed the complete diet ate it readily upon first encounter, although some neophobia was evident in that the second meal was consistently larger than the first. Slugs fed the methionine-deficient diet ate a first meal of the same size as slugs fed the complete diet but subsequently greatly reduced their intake of the methionine-deficient diet. When the size of each meal was measured, it was evident that the aversion to the methionine-deficient diet developed after the first meal. In these experiments animals were not given a choice of simultaneously present diets—only one diet was present during a given feeding test. In this no-choice situation, if animals previously fed the deficient diet were switched to the complete diet, they avoided it until they chanced to take a small sample meal.

After the small sample meal of the complete diet, their intake increased dramatically. This indicates that the odor and taste of the complete and deficient diets are most likely not discriminable. Evidence that the aversion to the deficient diet is due to the lack of methionine results from the observation that postprandial injections of methionine into the blood of slugs feeding on the methionine-deficient diet block the development of the aversion to the deficient diet (Delaney and Gelperin, 1986). Work in the terrestrial slug *Incilaria fruhstorferi daiseniana* has shown that most of the essential amino acids, including histidine, tryptophan, phenylalanine, leucine, isoleucine, and valine, can mediate postingestive conditioning in slugs (Lee and Chang, 1986).

Circuitry for Odor Learning

To understand how *Limax* learns to alter its behavior responses to odors, we must first understand how odor information is decoded and stored. A neural network model for the storage of patterns of olfactory receptor input in *Limax* (Gelperin, Hopfield, and Tank, 1986; Gelperin, Tank, and Tesauro, 1989) suggested that the procerebral lobe (PC) of the cerebral ganglion was a likely candidate for odor processing and perhaps for odor memory storage. The PC has direct access to olfactory input and uses extensive local feedback interactions to process its inputs, based on the anatomy of its synaptic interconnections. The PC displays a 0.7-hertz oscillation in its local field potential (Gelperin and Tank, 1990) that arises from coherent activity of at least two classes of rhythmically active interneurons, called E cells and I cells. The oscillation is dramatically modulated by olfactory input, as shown by puffing natural odors on the nose while recording the PC oscillation (Gelperin and Tank, 1990). Linking this physiological observation with the odor-aversion learning will require understanding how innately attractive and repellent odors differ in their effects on the PC lobe oscillation and how the effects of a given odor are changed when its behavioral meaning is reversed by learning.

The biochemical mechanisms for changing synaptic efficacy as a function of particular patterns of past usage have been most clearly revealed in the withdrawal circuitry of *Aplysia* (see APLYSIA: CLASSICAL CONDITIONING AND OPERANT CONDITIONING).

Second-messenger-mediated changes in conductance of specific subsets of ion channels can account for many aspects of activity-dependent changes in transmitter liberation at presynaptic terminals. Biochemical studies of transmitter-stimulated increases in cAMP levels in PC neurons (Yamane and Gelperin, 1987) and of aminergic alteration of protein synthesis (Yamane, Oesterricher, and Gelperin, 1989) encourage the view that *Aplysia*-like synaptic hardware may be used in the *Limax* PC lobe to change synaptic strengths during odor processing and perhaps during odor learning. Transmitter-evoked changes in patterns of protein synthesis are particularly relevant to models of how short-term memory storage is converted to a long-term storage form (Castellucci et al., 1989; Eskin, Garcia, and Byrne, 1989).

REFERENCES

Byrne, J. H. (1987). Cellular analysis of associative learning. *Physiological Reviews 67*, 329–439.

Carew, T. J., and Sahley, C. L. (1986). Invertebrate learning and memory: From behavior to molecules. *Annual Review of Neuroscience 9*, 435–487.

Castellucci, V. F., Blumenfeld, H., Goelet, P., and Kandel, E. R. (1989). Inhibitor of protein synthesis blocks long-term behavioral sensitization in the isolated gill-withdrawal reflex of *Aplysia. Journal of Neurobiology 20*, 1–9.

Corning, W. C., Dyal, J. A., and Willows, A. O. D. (1973). *Invertebrate learning,* vol. 2, *Arthropods and gastropod molluscs.* New York: Plenum Press.

Delaney, K., and Gelperin, A. (1984). Rapid food-aversion learning with shock as the UCS in *Limax maximus. Society for Neuroscience Abstracts 10*, 509.

———— (1986). Post-ingestive food-aversion learning to amino acid deficient diets by the terrestrial slug *Limax maximus. Journal of Comparative Physiology A 159*, 281–295.

Dickinson, A., and Mackintosh, N. J. (1979). Reinforcer specificity in the enhancement of conditioning by posttrial events. *Journal of Experimental Psychology: Animal Behavior Processes 5*, 162–177.

Domjan, M. (1980). Ingestional aversion learning: Unique and general processes. *Advances in the Study of Behavior 11*, 275–336.

Erber, J. (1976). Retrograde amnesia in honeybees (*Apis mellifera carnica*). *Journal of Comparative and Physiological Psychology 90*, 41–46.

Eskin, A., Garcia, K. S., and Byrne, J. H. (1989). Information storage in the nervous system of *Aplysia:* Specific proteins affected by serotonin and cAMP. *Proceedings of the National Academy of Sciences 86*, 2458–2462.

Flaherty, C. F. (1985). *Animal learning and cognition.* New York: Knopf.

Garcia, J., Ervin, F. R., and Koelling, R. A. (1966). Learning with prolonged delay of reinforcement. *Psychonomic Science 5*, 121–122.

Gelperin, A. (1975). Rapid food-aversion learning by a terrestrial mollusk. *Science 189*, 567–570.

———— (1989). Neurons and networks for learning about odors. In T. Carew and D. Kelley, eds., *Perspectives in neural systems and behavior,* pp. 121–136. New York: Liss.

Gelperin, A., Hopfield, J. J., and Tank, D. W. (1986). The logic of *Limax* learning. In A. I. Selverston, ed., *Model neural networks and behavior,* pp. 237–261. New York: Plenum Press.

Gelperin, A., and Tank, D. W. (1990). Odor-modulated collective network oscillations of olfactory interneurons in a terrestrial mollusc. *Nature 345*, 437–440.

Gelperin, A., Tank, D. W., and Tesauro, G. (1989). Olfactory processing and associative memory: Cellular and modeling studies. In J. W. Byrne and W. O. Berry, eds., *Neural models of plasticity,* pp. 133–159. New York: Academic Press.

Holland, P. C. (1977). Conditioned stimulus as a determinant of the form of the Pavlovian conditioned response. *Journal of Experimental Psychology: Animal Behavior Processes 3*, 77–104.

Kamin, L. J. (1968). Attention-like processes in classical conditioning. In M. R. Jones, ed., *Miami symposium on predictability, behavior and aversive stimulation,* pp. 9–32. Miami: University of Miami Press.

———— (1969). Predictability, surprise, attention and conditioning. In B. A. Campbell and R. M. Church, eds., *Punishment and aversive behavior,* pp. 279–296. New York: Appleton-Century-Crofts.

Lee, J. H., and Chang, J. J. (1986). Learning of post-ingestive food-aversion by the land slug, *Incilaria fruhstorferi daiseniana,* to amino acid deficient diets. *Society for Neuroscience Abstracts 12*, 39.

Quinn, W. G., and Dudai, Y. (1976). Memory phases in *Drosophila. Nature 262*, 576–577.

Rescorla, R. A. (1980). *Pavlovian second-order conditioning: Studies in associative learning.* Hillsdale, N.J.: Erlbaum.

———— (1982). Simultaneous second-order conditioning produces S-S learning in conditioned suppression. *Journal of Experimental Psychology: Animal Behavior Processes 8*, 23–32.

———— (1988). Behavioral studies of Pavlovian conditioning. *Annual Review of Neuroscience 11*, 329–352.

Sahley, C. L. (1990). The behavioral analysis of associative learning in the terrestrial mollusc *Limax maximus:* The importance of interevent relationships. In S. Hanson and C. Olson, eds., *Connectionist modeling and brain function: The developing interface,* pp. 36–73. Cambridge, Mass.: MIT Press.

Sahley, C., Gelperin, A., and Rudy, J. W. (1981a). One-trial associative learning modifies food odor preferences of a terrestrial mollusc. *Proceedings of the National Academy of Sciences 78,* 640–642.

Sahley, C., Rudy, J. W., and Gelperin, A. (1981b). An analysis of associative learning in a terrestrial mollusc: Higher-order conditioning, blocking and a transient US pre-exposure effect. *Journal of Comparative Physiology A 144,* 1–8.

Sekiguchi, T., Yamada, A., Suzuki, H., and Mizukami, A. (1991). Temporal analysis of the retention of a food-aversion conditioning in *Limax flavus. Zoological Science* (Tokyo) *8,* 103–112.

Squire, L. R. (1987). *Memory and brain.* New York: Oxford University Press.

Yamane, T., and Gelperin, A. (1987). Aminergic and peptidergic amplification of intracellular cyclic AMP levels in a molluscan neural network. *Cellular and Molecular Neurobiology 7,* 291–301.

Yamane, T., Oestericher, A. B., and Gelperin, A. (1989). Serotonin-stimulated biochemical events in the procerebrum of *Limax. Cellular and molecular neurobiology 9,* 447–459.

A. Gelperin

Associative Learning in *Pleurobranchaea*

Pleurobranchaea californica is a foraging predator that learns through experience to discriminate among food items and to recognize potentially dangerous prey. In the laboratory it exhibits a number of easily identifiable behaviors whose expression is organized by motivational state and learning processes. Its robust ability for associative learning and its simple nervous system have made the snail a useful model system for the study of how behavior is organized (Davis and Mpitsos, 1971; Mpitsos and Davis, 1973).

The context in which the learning and behavior of *Pleurobranchaea* are best approached is its natural history. The animal is one of the notaspidean opisthobranch gastropods, a shell-less sea slug with a true gill. It is obtained from deep Pacific waters (20–300 meters) off the coast of California, where it is caught in bottom trawl nets, or sometimes collected by divers, for shipment to the laboratory. *Pleurobranchaea* actively hunts small animals and swallows them whole, subduing their struggles in a bath of sulfuric acid secreted into the mouth cavity. Observations in the wild and analysis of stomach contents indicate that the diet of *Pleurobranchaea* is quite varied, including jellyfish, sea anemones, ectoprocts, other sea slugs, and the car-

rion of squid and fish. A reflection of the animal's voraciousness may be that many North American coastal invertebrates recognize the animal with vigorous, stereotyped escape behaviors. Stomach content evidence and laboratory observations show that the animal is frequently cannibalistic. However, ignoring cannibalism, no major predators of *Pleurobranchaea* have been identified.

The lack of predators on *Pleurobranchaea* may be a result of the animal's ability to secrete sulfuric acid from its skin when molested, dropping skin pH to 1–2 (Gillette, Saeki, and Huang, 1990; cf. Thompson, 1988). *Pleurobranchaea* also responds to its own acid skin secretions with enhanced avoidance behavior (Gillette, Saeki, and Huang, 1990). The sensory pathways mediating this effect are of experimental interest because of their resemblance to primitive pain pathways, and because of their possible roles in food-avoidance learning.

A simple nervous system and simple behavior facilitate the study of *Pleurobranchaea*. Although its foraging strategies are generally similar to those of vertebrate predators, it is less complex than vertebrate predators because the animal uses fewer behavioral subroutines and has a simple, unjointed body. These and other factors relieve the nervous system of the need for appreciable complexity to perform the chores of sensorimotor integration. There is little complexity in sensory structures—the eyes are reduced, internalized, and of uncertain function, and the statocyst organs of equilibrium are most simple. Locomotion is by means of myriad sweeping cilia on the foot that pull the animal forward. Simplicity also attends the animal's soft body; without jointed appendages to keep track of, to make an orienting or aversive turn, it needs only to shorten one side of its body while locomotor cilia pull it around. To right itself when placed on its back, a half-twist of the body suffices. Moreover, control of the periphery is simplified by an extensive peripheral nervous system that performs a good deal of local sensorimotor integration. These characteristics make a rather modest central nervous system (several tens of thousands of neurons) suffice for the major decisions of daily living and for retaining the memories needed to adapt behavior to the predictions of experience.

Another experimental advantage of *Pleurobranchaea* is that the neurons of the central nervous system are relatively quite large. This is probably because, like some other opisthobranch snails, the animal grows to a relatively large size (the largest recorded weighed over 3.1 kilograms). The enlarged body demands increased innervation for control by the nervous system; however, instead of simply increasing the number of central neurons proportionately, many opisthobranchs apparently enlarge peripheral effector neurons (motor neurons, neurons driving skin secretion, etc.) to innervate larger expanses, and enlarge sensory neurons and interneurons to drive adequately the now-giant effector neurons (Gillette, 1990, 1991). Neuron cell body diameters can be several hundred microns in diameter, and in *Pleurobranchaea* they are bright orange. These factors facilitate electrical recordings with microelectrodes. Thus, both the smallness of the nervous system and enhanced neuron sizes contribute to the ease with which the circuitry of behavior is analyzed.

For all animals, an analysis of behavior predicts the nature of the underlying neural mechanisms and circuitry. In the hungry *Pleurobranchaea*, feeding dominates the structural organization of behavior. Thus, in the presence of a feeding stimulus (e.g., a homogenate of squid flesh), an animal placed upside down suppresses its normal righting reflexes; when an animal is feeding, it suppresses its normal local withdrawal response to a light poke on the oral veil (Davis and Mpitsos, 1971). The underlying mechanisms arise in interactions between the neural networks. Kovac and Davis (1980) showed that when the neural network of feeding generated its cyclic motor output of biting and swallowing, it actively suppressed the excitation of oral veil withdrawal motor neurons by sensory inputs. Specific neurons were identified in the feeding network whose outputs presynaptically suppressed the inputs to the motor neurons. Similar neural mechanisms may account for most of the interactions of feeding and other behaviors.

Motivational processes regulate an animal's exploitation of its environment. For *Pleurobranchaea*, the motivation driving feeding behavior (hunger) can be experimentally quantitated by finding the threshold dilution of a feeding stimulus that initiates feeding behavior. Very hungry animals respond with bite/strikes to millionfold dilutions of squid homogenate, while totally satiated subjects suppress feeding and may show aversive behavior to full-strength homogenate.

Examining the sequences and alternative paths in the feeding behavior reveals how it is organized by sensory inputs, motivation processes, and learning mechanisms. Feeding behavior is initiated by a weak food stimulus eliciting locomotion and orienting turns toward the stimulus. The appetitive

phase culminates in the presence of a strong food stimulus that causes proboscis extension and the bite/strike, in which prey is seized by the hooked denticles of the radula. An item brought into the buccal cavity is swallowed if it has the proper chemosensory sign; if inert or noxious, it is rejected. The animal remains in place feeding until the food stimulus disappears or satiation occurs. An alternative behavior the animal can express upon food stimulation is active avoidance behavior: The animal makes aversive turns instead of orienting, and flees the stimulus source. Active avoidance can also occur when *Pleurobranchaea* attacks an animal with a noxious defense, such as the Spanish Shawl nudibranch, *Flabellinopsis iodinea*, a small sea slug that stores the stinging cells of its hydroid prey for its own use (Figure 1).

Food avoidance behavior is most notable in animals that have learned to associate a food with a punishing stimulus. A naturally adaptive function of food-avoidance learning must be the learned avoidance of potentially harmful prey; one to several exposures to *Flabellinopsis* is all it takes to instill a long-lasting aversion in *Pleurobranchaea*. The analogous laboratory paradigm of classical conditioning pairs electrical shock with a food stimulus (Mpitsos and Davis, 1973; Mpitsos and

Figure 1. An attack by *Pleurobranchaea* on the stinging Spanish Shawl nudibranch is followed by expulsion of the snail and aversive behavior. The photograph shows *Pleurobranchaea* with extended proboscis making rejection movements and beginning an aversive turn.

Collins, 1975). Learning is selective; the animal is able to discriminate different feeding stimuli, such as squid, sea anemone, and beer extract (Davis et al., 1980; Mpitsos and Cohan, 1986).

In the nervous system, learning mechanisms are expressed at the level of the neural network of feeding. Active feeding is a cycle of rhythmic biting and swallowing, driven by a network oscillator. The oscillator generates phases of protraction and retraction motor activity in the feeding apparatus (the buccal mass) during which the radula rocks to and fro in the movements of feeding. In the food-avoidance trained animal, a food stimulus causes the oscillator effectively to lock in a retraction-like state, as if the retraction neurons have become hyperexcitable or are receiving more sensory excitation (London and Gillette, 1986). Thus, a simple type of plasticity expressed in the pattern-generating circuitry appears to be at the heart of much of the adaptive organization of relatively complex behavior in *Pleurobranchaea*.

In drawing a predictive model of the organiza-

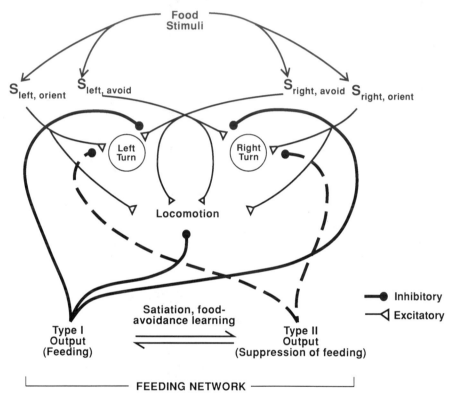

Figure 2. A simple model of functional connections that could organize interactions of feeding and food-avoidance behavior in *Pleurobranchaea*. The model is based on output of two different types of activity from the feeding network. The type of feeding network output modulates sensorimotor pathways to left and right "turn" motor neurons and regulates activity in locomotor effectors.

Food stimuli excite chemosensory (S) pathways conveying excitation to locomotor neurons, activating locomotion. Orientation to food is performed by ipsilateral stimulation of left- and right-turn motor neurons through sensory pathways from left ($S_{Left,Orient}$) and right ($S_{Right,Orient}$) sides. Crossed sensory pathways ($S_{Left,Avoid}$, and $S_{Right,Avoid}$) stimulating contralateral (aversive) turns are inhibited by feeding (type I) output from the motor network. Stronger type I output inhibits locomotor neurons, overcoming food-induced excitation, while the animal feeds.

Avoidance behavior is stimulated by type II output, which inhibits ipsilateral sensory stimulation of turn neurons, and disinhibits locomotion and contralateral stimulation of turn neurons.

tion of feeding and avoidance behaviors by learning and motivation, two principles are lent to the design from the existing knowledge of physiology and behavior. The first is the observation that the feeding network can suppress neural pathways and behavior incompatible with feeding by active inhibition (Kovac and Davis, 1980). The second is the inference that there must be two distinct sensorimotor pathways mediating responsiveness to food: one causing orienting turns (by muscular shortening of the ipsilateral body side), and another causing aversive turns (by contralateral body shortening). With these relationships, the general circuit of Figure 2 can account for the major aspects of the organization of *Pleurobranchaea*'s foraging behavior. In the model, the feeding network may transit between two states, depending on the animal's hunger state and learning experience. In one state (feeding) it suppresses the aversive sensorimotor pathway; in the other state (locked in a retractionlike phase) it suppresses orienting behavior, releases aversive turns, and disinhibits locomotion.

Many potential analogies to vertebrate systems heighten the interest in the neuroethology of *Pleurobranchaea*. Considerations such as those above suggest that the organization of seemingly complex behavior may have simple bases in interactions among sensory pathways and motor network interactions.

(See also TASTE AVERSION AND PREFERENCE LEARNING IN ANIMALS).

REFERENCES

Davis, W. J. and Gillette, R. (1978). Neural correlate of behavioral plasticity on command neurons of *Pleurobranchaea*. *Science* 199, 801–804.

Davis, W. J., and Mpitsos, G. J. (1971). Behavioral choice and habituation in the marine mollusk *Pleurobranchaea californica*. *Zeitschrift für Vergleichende Physiologie* 75, 207–232.

Davis, W. J., Villet, J., Lee, D., Rigler, M., Gillette, R., and Prince, E. (1980). Selective and differential avoidance learning in the feeding and withdrawal behavior of *Pleurobranchaea californica*. *Journal of Comparative Physiology* 138, 157–165.

Gillette, R. (1990). The molluscan nervous system. In L. Prosser, ed., *Comparative physiology*, 4th ed., pp. 574–611. New York: Wiley-Liss.

——— (1991). On the significance of neuron giantism in gastropods. *Biological Bulletin 180*, 234–240.

Gillette, R., Saeki, M., and Huang, R.-C. (1990). Defense mechanisms in notaspidean snails: Acid humor and evasiveness. *Journal of Experimental Biology*, 156, 335–347 (1991).

Kovac, M. P., and Davis, W. J. (1980). Neural mechanism underlying behavioral choice in *Pleurobranchaea*. *Journal of Neurophysiology 43*, 469–487.

London, J. A., and Gillette, R. (1986). Mechanism for food avoidance learning in the central pattern generator of feeding behavior of *Pleurobranchaea californica*. *Proceedings of the National Academy of Sciences 83*, 4058–4062.

Mpitsos, G. J., and Cohan, C. S. (1986). Differential pavlovian conditioning in the mollusc *Pleurobranchaea*. *Journal of Neurobiology 17*, 487–497.

Mpitsos, G. J., and Collins, S. D. (1975). Learning: Rapid aversion conditioning in the gastropod mollusk *Pleurobranchaea californica*. *Science 188*, 954–957.

Mpitsos, G. J., and Davis, W. J. (1973). Learning: Classical and avoidance conditioning in the mollusk *Pleurobranchaea*. *Science 180*, 317–320.

Thompson, T. E. (1988). Acidic allomones in marine organisms. *Journal of the Marine Biological Association of the United Kingdom 68*, 499–517.

Rhanor Gillette

Habituation and Sensitization in *Tritonia*

When animals learn, they store their memories as anatomically distributed sets of circuit modifications. While such circuit modifications can be mapped with precision, and the biophysical and molecular mechanisms underlying each locus of plasticity can often be identified, it has proven difficult to determine how the information acquired in learning corresponds to these sites of circuit modification. To address this aspect of the physiology of memory, the marine mollusk *Tritonia* has been used.

Tritonia was one of the first preparations in which it was demonstrated that individual neurons can have major roles in the behavior of an animal (Willows, 1967). Subsequent work by Willows, Getting, and their colleagues identified the neural circuit for the *Tritonia* escape swim (Getting, 1983). This circuit consists of several dozen neurons that are grouped into seven cell types (see Figure 1). The central pattern generator—the neurons that generate the oscillatory timing pattern underlying the swim—consists of just six cells (three cell types) on each side of the brain. The

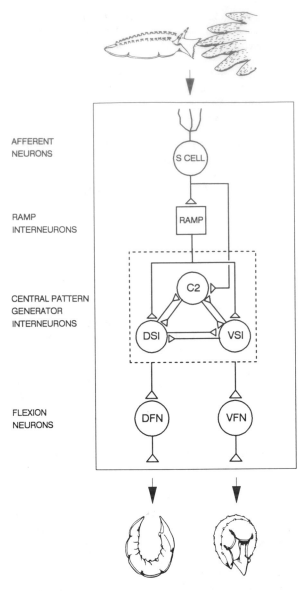

AFFERENT
NEURONS

RAMP
INTERNEURONS

CENTRAL PATTERN
GENERATOR
INTERNEURONS

FLEXION
NEURONS

Figure 1. The *Tritonia* escape swim is triggered by contact with predatory starfish. The circuit mediating this response consists of seven cell types. The S cells conduct the stimulus from the periphery to the brain. There they excite the RAMP interneurons, which activate the central pattern generator—the group of three neuronal types (C2, DSI, VSI) that generate the oscillatory neural pattern driving the swim. The output of the central pattern generator activates two groups of flexion neurons (DFN, VFN), which send axons to the periphery and whose activity elicits the alternating dorsal and ventral whole-body contractions of the swim. A single escape swim may last two minutes, and consist of up to eighteen flexion cycles.

small size of this circuit makes it a very attractive model system for studies of how the information acquired in learning is organized in nervous systems. This issue is being explored in *Tritonia* using a three-step procedure.

Behavioral Studies: How Does Training Modify Behavior? *Tritonia* shows two very robust forms of nonassociative learning: habituation and sensitization. *Habituation* refers to the gradual decrease in responsiveness shown by all animals to repetitive innocuous stimuli. *Sensitization* refers to the sudden increase in responsiveness that often follows a single unexpected, and therefore potentially dangerous, stimulus. In both habituation and sensitization, several aspects of the *Tritonia* escape swim are modified. Habituation training produces four behavioral changes, all of which reduce the vigor of the response: (1) fewer cycles per swim, (2) longer cycle period, (3) higher swim threshold, and (4) reduced swim flexion strength. Sensitization training produces four changes that increase response vigor: (1) more cycles per swim, (2) shorter cycle period, (3) lower swim threshold, and (4) shorter swim onset latency. These sets of behavioral changes serve as indicators of what the animal has learned.

Electrophysiological Studies: What Circuit Modifications Occur as a Result of Training? Several circuit modifications produced by habituation and sensitization training have been identified. In habituation, three circuit synapses have been found to decrease in strength with repeated stimulation—in effect, storing a record of their recent degree of activation (Frost and Getting, 1987). Other synapses are unaltered by such stimulation. In sensitization, one set of synapses increases in efficacy. In addition, one of the central pattern generator interneurons undergoes a long-lasting increase in excitability (Frost, Brown, and Getting, 1988). These findings indicate that in *Tritonia*, as in other animals that have been examined, individual memories are stored in the form of distributed sets of circuit modifications.

Computer Modeling Studies: What is the Functional Significance of Each of the Different Circuit Modifications? Determining how each circuit modification relates to the behavioral changes produced by training is a difficult problem (see NEURAL COMPUTATION). In *Tritonia*, an approach that has been used is to introduce each modification, one at a time, into a realistic computer model of the circuit. One finding has been that individual circuit modifications encode a subset of the behavioral changes acquired in learning. For example, the increase in C2 excitability seen in sensitization appears to contribute to the changes in swim cycle number and cycle period, but it has little effect on swim latency or threshold (Frost, Brown, and Getting, 1988). Presumably the latter two behavioral changes are encoded by other circuit modifications.

The parallel use of vertebrate and invertebrate preparations, each with unique advantages, is beginning to shed light on the network organization of memory in nervous systems.

REFERENCES

Frost, W. N., Brown, G., and Getting, P. A. (1988). Sensitization of the *Tritonia* escape swim involves multiple behavioral modifications. *Society of Neuroscience Abstracts 14,* 607.

Frost, W. N., and Getting, P. A. (1987). Habituation of escape swimming in *Tritonia* appears to involve multiple sites of circuit modification. *Society of Neuroscience Abstracts 13,* 815.

Getting, P. A. (1983). Neural control of swimming in *Tritonia.* In A. Roberts and B. L. Roberts, eds., *Neural origins of rhythmic movements,* pp. 89–128. London: Cambridge University Press.

Willows, A. O. D. (1967). Behavioral acts elicited by stimulation of single, identifiable brain cells. *Science 157,* 570–574.

William Frost

Neurogenetic Analysis of Learning in *Drosophila*

Neurogenetic analysis of learning identifies genes whose products are essential for normal learning and memory, and proposes function in learning and memory for the macromolecules so identified. The rationale underlying this experimental approach is straightforward: The basic ability of organisms to acquire, store, and retrieve information in the nervous system should be coded by genes. By isolating and analyzing the appropriate mutants, one might identify these genes and hence elucidate the molecular and cellular mechanisms that render

learning and memory possible. An additional, implicit pragmatic assumption is that some gene products play a relatively specific role in learning and memory; mutations that disrupt behavioral plasticity because they cripple sensory or motor capabilities are not of great interest in this context. Analysis of the effect of single gene mutants on learning is currently possible only in the fruit fly *Drosophila melanogaster,* because this organism fulfills two fundamental requirements: It is readily amenable to sophisticated genetic analysis, and it can learn a variety of nonassociative and associative tasks (reviewed in Aceves-Pina et al., 1983; Tully, 1987; Dudai, 1988).

The search for genes that affect memory in *Drosophila* originated in the laboratory of Seymour Benzer at the California Institute of Technology. It was there that the first reliable learning paradigm for *Drosophila* was developed (Quinn, Harris, and Benzer, 1974) and the first learning mutant identified (Dudai et al., 1976). This line of research has since been pursued and expanded in several other laboratories. To date, about half a dozen single-gene learning mutants have been identified in deliberate screens for "stupid flies" among the progeny of mutagenized *Drosophila.* In addition, several existing *Drosophila* mutants that were originally isolated due to other phenotypic abnormalities were later found to have some interesting defects in their learning capabilities. The search for additional learning mutants is under way.

So far, only a few learning mutants have been subjected to extensive behavioral, genetic, and molecular analysis. The most thoroughly investigated ones are *dunce* (*dnc*) and *rutabaga* (*rut*). *dnc* lesions a structural locus for an isozyme (enzyme form) of cAMP-phosphodiesterase, and *rut*, a locus for a form of the enzyme adenylate cyclase. Thus, both mutations affect enzymes that operate in the ubiquitous cyclic adenosine monophosphate (cAMP) signal-transduction cascade (see SECOND MESSENGER SYSTEMS). Both genes have been analyzed at the DNA level (Chen et al., 1987; Krupinski et al., 1989). An additional mutant, *turnip* (*tur*), affects a gene product that is involved in the operation of Ca^{2+}-phospholipid signal-transduction cascade, but probably also plays a role in other second-messenger cascades, including the cAMP cascade. In general, it was concluded that the learning impairment caused by these mutations, as well as by additional ones like *amnesiac* (*amn*), is "general" (i.e., the mutations impair learning in both nonassociative and associative situations, and in paradigms based on different sensory modalities). The effect of these mutations on nonlearned behavior is small and does not explain the failure to behave properly in a variety of learning tests. In most mutants, careful analysis of olfactory, gustatory, or mechanosensory learning reveals a substantial degree of learning capacity followed, however, by a remarkably abnormal, feeble memory, thus resulting in very poor performance upon testing minutes or hours after training.

Neurogenetic analysis of learning in *Drosophila* pinpoints potential molecular components of biological learning and memory systems (e.g., enzymes participating in the cAMP cascade), but the correlation of genetic and molecular damage with behavioral dysfunctions does not suffice to generate specific and robust cellular models of learning. For this purpose, cellular analysis of the effect of the mutation is required. Unfortunately, the central nervous system of *Drosophila* does not easily yield to cellular analysis. Therefore, although some progress has been made in recent years in the cellular analysis of *Drosophila* learning mutants (see below), most of the data obtained from those mutants has until now been interpreted in the context of cellular models of learning that emerge from investigations of other systems, especially APLYSIA.

Indeed, current data on *Drosophila* learning mutants seem at first sight to fit rather well with a simplified cellular model of learning proposed for *Aplysia*. The latter model is detailed elsewhere in this volume. Suffice it to mention here that cellular analysis of experience-dependent modifications of defensive reflexes in *Aplysia* suggests that acquisition and short-term memory involve cAMP-mediated phosphorylation of neuronal proteins, such as K^+ channels, which leads to persistently altered excitability of critical nodes in the neuronal network that encodes the behavioral information. As noted above, some *Drosophila* mutants with impaired learning and memory are directly or indirectly defective in the operation of the cAMP cascade. The *Aplysia* data also suggest that in the networks that subserve the associative modification of the gill-and-siphon-withdrawal or the tail-withdrawal reflexes, Ca^{2+} is a cellular code of the conditioned stimulus and a modulatory transmitter is a cellular code of the unconditioned stimulus. A Ca^{2+}/calmodulin-activated form of adenylate cyclase was proposed to serve as a convergence locus for these two molecular signals. This form of the enzyme is exactly the form abolished by the *rut* mutation in *Drosophila*. However, the fit

between the *Drosophila* data and the *Aplysia* model is far from ideal. For example, data from *Aplysia* offer no critical role for Ca^{2+}/calmodulin activation of adenylate cyclase in nonassociative learning, whereas *rut* displays abnormal memory of habituation and sensitization. Therefore, all one can state at present is that the data from neurogenetic analysis of learning in *Drosophila* are in partial agreement with the picture portrayed by the data from *Aplysia*, but they do not contradict other models that implicate second messenger cascades in learning and memory (for further discussion see Dudai, 1989).

The isolation of the first learning and memory mutants in *Drosophila* proved that the neurogenetic analysis of learning is indeed possible, and the identification of the molecular defects in these first mutants was undoubtedly a very rewarding development. But, as noted above, supplementary concepts and methodologies had to be recruited for further meaningful progress. In addition to conducting a search for additional mutants that affect either short- or long-term memory, research groups in this field pursue the following lines of investigation:

1. Detailed behavioral analysis of the mutants, aimed at fine dissection of the various phases of acquisition, consolidation, and memory. Various learning paradigms are used, including some that take advantage of ecological situations such as the experience-dependent modification of courtship (Hall, 1986). Generally speaking, the assumption here is that behavioral analysis of the mutants may cast light on the intricacies of memory phases, in a way similar to the use of mutants in unveiling and unraveling discrete metabolic steps in complicated biochemical cascades (for an example of this approach, see Dudai, 1983).

2. Molecular biology of the mutated genes. So far, the most scrutinized locus is *dnc*. This chromosomal locus has proved to be extraordinarily complex, coding for multiple, developmentally regulated transcripts (Chen et al., 1987). Other learning mutants still await careful structural analysis at the DNA level.

3. Identification of biochemical defects secondary to the defective gene product, which might pinpoint additional fragments of the molecular machinery that is essential for nor-

mal learning. For example, attempts are being made to identify abnormal phosphoproteins in the nervous systems of *dnc, rut,* and *tur,* in the hope that some of these protein kinase substrates are causally relevant to the impaired behavioral plasticity (an example of this line of investigation is provided in Devay and Friedrich, 1987).

4. Construction of molecular models for acquisition, association, and short- and long-term retention of neuronal information, based on biochemical cascades that include the gene products impaired in learning mutants. These projects involve, for example, proposing and testing properties of adenylate cyclase that enable it to serve as a cellular convergence locus for ions and transmitter, or proposing and testing kinetic models that explain how cAMP-dependent protein kinase, either per se or in conjunction with protein phosphatases and proteases, can serve as a molecular memory device by remaining active for minutes or hours following a brief pulse of cAMP. (Examples of theoretical and experimental approaches to these problems are provided in Buxbaum and Dudai, 1989; Muller and Spatz, 1989; Friedrich, 1990.)

5. LOCALIZATION OF MEMORY TRACES *Drosophila*-style, that is, pinpointing anatomical brain loci in which the mutations exert their effects. Plausible candidates are the mushroom bodies, prominent integrative centers in the insect brain (Balling, Technau, and Heisenberg, 1987; see "Associative Learning in Bees" above).

6. Cellular analysis of the effect of learning mutations. The brain of *Drosophila* is tiny and compact, rendering it unfavorable for neurophysiological analysis. Yet, without electrophysiological analysis to reveal neuronal abnormalities in networks that subserve learning and memory, interpretation of the results obtained from the neurogenetic dissection of learning in the fruit fly is bound either to remain phenomenological or to rely on models generated by research on other species that are more amenable to cellular electrophysiology. This evidently weakens the power of neurogenetics.

In recent years, several groups of investigators have set out to circumvent the problem partially by looking at the effect of learning mutations on excitable cells in the periphery rather than in the central nervous system. These peripheral cells, either sensory neurons, motoneurons, or muscle cells, lend themselves more easily to classical electrophysiological and neuroanatomical investigations. The assumption here is that cellular dysfunction revealed in the periphery may attest to cellular dysfunction in the central nervous system, which is expected to be the site of the engram.

This approach has already yielded novel information on the cellular dysfunction caused by the cAMP mutants *rut* and *dnc.* Corfas and Dudai (1990) found that both mutations lead to abnormal sensory habituation (or "fatigue") in mechanosensory neurons, that is, they modify the normal decrement observed in neuronal response following repetitive monotonous stimuli. Thus *dnc* accelerates sensory fatigue, whereas *rut* retards it. Delgado et al. (1991) have identified in *Drosophila* muscle a K^+ channel that is directly and reversibly activated by cAMP, and have found that in *dnc,* which has an increased level of cAMP (due to the defective cAMP-phosphodiesterase), this same channel displays an increased probability of opening. Zhong and Wu (1991) examined synaptic transmission in the neuromuscular junction of *Drosophila* larva, and found that *dnc* and *rut* cause impaired facilitation and POSTTETANIC POTENTIATION, as well as a shift in the Ca^{2+} dependence of transmitter release in *dnc.* All these results imply that some elementary properties of neuronal excitability and modifiability are impaired by the cAMP-cascade mutations.

It remains to be seen how, and if, all these abnormalities relate to learning and memory. Nevertheless, the findings obtained by cellular analysis of neuronal function in *Drosophila* learning mutants already show that the physiology of these flies is altered not only in the brain but probably in all excitable cells, and possibly in other types of cells as well. The results also call for caution in attempts to propose mechanistic models to account for the mutants' stupidity. For example, it is tempting to explain the learning defects in *dnc* and *rut* (and possibly *tur*) in the context of the *Aplysia* model (see above), but it is also possible that abnormal levels of cAMP in *Drosophila* interfere with metabolic events that are not included in this model (e.g., gating of cAMP-activated ion channels). It is also still unclear why *rut* and *dnc,* which exert opposite effects on cAMP level, also have opposite effects on sensory fatigue but similar effects on learning and memory. In addition, the fine behavioral abnormalities in the mutants must be further scrutinized, so as to eliminate the contribution of sensory and motor defects to the learning deficits observed.

In conclusion, the neurogenetic dissection of learning in *Drosophila* has yielded several intriguing mutants with relatively specific defects in the initial phases of memory formation. Some of these mutants are characterized by abnormal operation of second messenger cascades, mainly the cAMP cascade. All this attests to the specific role of ubiquitous signal-transduction and modulation cascades in elementary learning and memory processes. Additional mutants still await behavioral, anatomical, and molecular characterization; and many more, probably, await isolation. The combination of sophisticated genetics and molecular biology, so characteristics of *Drosophila*, with fine behavioral tests and electrophysiological analysis of fruit fly neurons, may disclose novel, unexpected facets of learning and memory mechanisms in the near future.

REFERENCES

Aceves-Pina, E. O., Booker, R., Duerr, J. S., Livingstone, M. S., Quinn, W. G., Smith, R. F., Sziber, P. P., Tempel, B. L., and Tully, T. (1983). Learning and memory in *Drosophila*, studied with mutants. *Cold Spring Harbor Symposia in Quantitative Biology 48,* 831–840.

Balling, A., Technau, G. M., and Heisenberg, M. (1987). Are the structural changes in adult *Drosophila* mushroom bodies memory traces? Studies on biochemical learning mutants. *Journal of Neurogenetics 4,* 65–73.

Buxbaum, J., and Dudai, Y. (1989). A quantitative model for the kinetics of cAMP-dependent protein kinase (type II) activity: Long-term inactivation of the kinase and its possible relevance to learning and memory. *Journal of Biological Chemistry 264,* 9344–9351.

Chen, C.-N., Malone, T., Beckendorf, S. K., and Davis, R. L. (1987). At least two genes reside within a large intron of the *dunce* gene of *Drosophila. Nature 329,* 721–724.

Corfas, G., and Dudai, Y. (1990). Adaptation and fatigue of a mechanosensory neuron in wild-type *Drosophila* and in memory mutants. *Journal of Neuroscience 10,* 491–499.

Delgado, R., Hidalgo, P., Diaz, F., Latorre, R., and Labarca, P. (1991). A cyclic AMP-activated K^+ channel in *Drosophila* larval muscle is persistently activated in *dunce. Proceedings of the National Academy of Sciences 88,* 557–560.

Devay, P., and Friedrich, P. (1987). Cyclic AMP-induced phosphorylation of 27.5 kDa protein(s) in larval brains of normal and memory mutant *Drosophila melanogaster. Journal of Neurogenetics 4,* 275–284.

Dudai, Y. (1983). Mutations affect the storage and use of memory in *Drosophila* differentially. *Proceedings of the National Academy of Sciences 80,* 5445–5448.

———. (1988). Neurogenetic dissection of learning and short-term memory in *Drosophila. Annual Review of Neuroscience 11,* 537–563.

———. (1989). *The neurobiology of memory.* Oxford: Oxford University Press.

Dudai, Y., Jan, Y. N., Byers, D., Quinn, W. G., and Benzer, S. (1976). *Dunce,* a mutant of *Drosophila* deficient in learning. *Proceedings of the National Academy of Sciences 73,* 1684–1688.

Friedrich, P. (1990). Protein structure: The primary substrate for memory. *Neuroscience 35,* 1–7.

Hall, J. C. (1986). Learning and rhythms in courting, mutant *Drosophila. Trends in Neurosciences 9,* 414–418.

Krupinski, J., Coussen, F., Bakalyar, H. A., Tang, W.-J., Feinstein, P. G., Orth, K., Slaughter, C., Reed, R., and Gilman, A. G. (1989). Adenylyl cyclase amino acid sequence: Possible channel- or transporter-like structure. *Science 244,* 1558–1564.

Muller, U., and Spatz, H.-C. (1989). Ca^{2+}-dependent proteolytic modification of the cAMP-dependent protein kinase in *Drosophila* wild-type and in *dunce* memory mutants. *Journal of Neurogenetics 6,* 95–114.

Quinn, W. G., Harris, W. A., and Benzer, S. (1974). Conditioned behavior in *Drosophila melanogaster. Proceedings of the National Academy of Sciences 71,* 708–712.

Tully, T. (1987). *Drosophila* learning and memory revisited. *Trends in Neurosciences 10,* 330–335.

Zhong, Y., and Wu, C.-F. (1991). Altered synaptic plasticity in *Drosophila* memory mutants with a defective cyclic AMP cascade. *Science 251,* 198–201.

Yadin Dudai

Nonassociative Learning in Crayfish

Like most arthropods, freshwater crayfish are capable of many kinds of learning. They can master mazes or learn that an arbitrary stimulus signals food or danger just as a vertebrate can, though the accuracy of their performance seldom equals that seen in higher animals. However, the particular importance of crayfish for the study of learning comes from their having an escape behavior, the lateral giant escape reaction, that is subject to several kinds of nonassociative learning and is produced by a relatively simple and well-analyzed neural circuit. Thus, the nervous system changes responsible for the learning can be located and analyzed.

Lateral giant escape is a more or less upward thrust through the water caused by a powerful flexion of the abdomen. It is caused by sudden stimulation of abdominal mechanoreceptors by water currents or contact. At the center of the neural circuit that mediates the response is the *lateral giant command neuron;* when it fires, it reliably recruits a motor pattern-generating circuit that produces the tail flip. The mechanoreceptors excite the lateral giants both monosynaptically and via a tier of interneurons, with both the direct and indirect input being needed to cause firing of the command neurons. The ability of mechanical stimuli to cause firing of the command neuron is variable and depends in various ways on past experience.

Repetition of a stimulus causes a gradual decrease in probability of response (*habituation*) due to diminished release of chemical transmitter at synapses between the stimulated mechanoreceptor neurons and sensory interneurons. Other synapses of the circuit, including those on the lateral giants themselves, operate electrically and are not thought to be subject to change. With rest, recovery of normal excitability occurs within a day or less. When animals make tail flips, the self-produced mechanical stimulation associated with their movements does not promote habituation because the motor system generates an input to sensory nerve terminals that nullifies the effects of stimuli occurring during the response.

While habituation in the laboratory is due to intrinsic changes at mechanoreceptor synapses, a powerful inhibitory pathway directed to the lateral giants descends from higher centers and also appears to be involved in experience-produced reductions of reactivity; however, the circumstances leading to such reductions remain undefined.

Traumatic stimulation of crayfish causes an increased tendency to escape from mechanical stimulation (*sensitization*). Sensitization is due at least in part to an increase in effectiveness of mechanoreceptor-sensory interneuron synapses. The induction of sensitization depends on a neural pathway that descends into the abdomen from higher centers. Effects similar to those seen in sensitization are produced by injections of the naturally occurring neuromodulator octopamine, which has sometimes been likened to the vertebrate "fight or flight" hormone, adrenalin. However, it is not known whether octopamine is involved in producing sensitization naturally.

REFERENCES

Glanzman, D. L., and Krasne, F. B. (1983). Serotonin and octopamine have opposite modulatory effects on the crayfish's lateral giant escape reaction. *Journal of Neuroscience 3*, 2263–2269.

Krasne, F. B. (1973). Learning in crustacea. In W. C. Corning, J. A. Dyal, and A. O. D. Willows, eds., *Invertebrate learning*, pp. 49–130. New York: Plenum Press.

Krasne, F. B., and Glanzman, D. L. (1986). Sensitization of the crayfish lateral giant escape reaction. *Journal of Neuroscience 6*, 1013–1020.

Krasne, F. B., and Wine, J. J. (1977). Control of crayfish escape behavior. In G. Hoyle, ed., *Identified neurons and behavior of arthropods*, pp. 275–292. New York: Plenum Press.

Wine, J. J., and Krasne, F. B. (1982). The cellular organization of crayfish escape behavior. In D. C. Sandeman and H. L. Atwood, eds., *The biology of crustacea*, vol. 4, pp. 241–292. New York: Academic Press.

Franklin B. Krasne

J

JAMES, WILLIAM

William James (1842–1910) was born in New York City in 1842, the oldest of five children (his brother Henry was to be a famous novelist) His father was a man of leisure who gave his children an unusual and rich education based on large amounts of travel and instruction in Europe. Young William set out to be an artist, apprenticing with William Morris Hunt for a year, but then turned toward science. He entered Harvard's Lawrence Scientific School in 1861 and worked with Charles William Eliot in chemistry and Jeffries Wyman in comparative anatomy. He then entered Harvard Medical School, took a year off to go with Louis Agassiz on an expedition to the Amazon, and eventually received his M.D. in 1869.

James never practiced medicine but pursued an academic career at Harvard. In 1872 he was appointed instructor in physiology and anatomy. He became assistant professor of philosophy in 1880 and full professor in 1885. In 1889 he was named professor of psychology, returning to philosophy in 1892 when Hugo Münsterberg came from Germany to take charge of Harvard's psychological laboratory. James retired in 1907 and spent his last years writing out his systematic philosophy.

Like most people of his time, James saw psychology as part of philosophy, an empirical avenue toward certain philosophical questions. Findings in science and medicine stimulated a vision of a physiological psychology. People like Wilhelm Wundt, Ivan Sechenov, John Hughlings Jackson, Henry Maudsley, and Theodor Meynert wrote about this vision, which inspired James. His varied academic appointments reflect his efforts, at first, to establish a "new psychology" in philosophy, and then, skeptical about much of the "normal science" that began growing up around him, to seek a more meaningful inquiry into psychic life through spiritualism and the study of exceptional mental states.

The culmination of James's first efforts and still his major contribution to psychology was his 1890 *Principles of Psychology,* an enormously popular and influential work that brought some people into "new psychology" and induced many others to accept it as a possibility. The two volumes are a delight to read today—full of life, ideas, and insights.

James defines psychology as "the Science of Men-

Figure 1. William James. *Courtesy Indiana University Psychology Department.*

tal Life, both of phenomena and their conditions" (p. 1). *Principles* explores the psyche using a mixture of introspective, physiological, medical, comparative, and experimental observations. The first six chapters are given to "the physiological preliminaries," a psychobiology of mind. "Both the anatomy and the detailed physiology of the brain are achievements of the present generation, or rather we may say (beginning with Meynert) the last twenty years" (p. 14). James sets forth a picture of a hierarchically organized brain and mind, one that remains today, with amplifications and amendments, a framing conception of contemporary neuropsychology. There are levels of behavioral organization: first reflexes and automatisms, then instincts, then habits, then finally voluntary and planned activity. Lower levels are more mechanical and sense-driven; higher centers are the seat of spontaneity and intellectual control. "In all ages the man whose determinations are swayed by reference to the most distant ends has been held to possess the highest intelligence" (p. 23).

In Chapter 7, James turns to psychological inquiry, which, he says, uses three methods: introspection, experiment, and the comparative approach. Introspection is the foundation, "what we have to remember first and foremost and always" (p. 185). The experimental method had been developed in Germany. "[It] taxes patience to the utmost, and could hardly have arisen in a country whose natives could be *bored*" (p. 192). Experimental psychology explores psychophysics, sensation and perception, attention span, and rote memory. The comparative method is loosest, "wild work," and includes psychological observations of the behavior of animals, mental patients, children, and people of other cultures, as well as inferences about mind drawn from artifacts such as human languages, customs, and social and political institutions.

James's discussions of learning and memory are not well integrated. His discussion of learning rests largely on comparative observations, while memory is approached introspectively. *Principles* appeared, it must be remembered, only 5 years after Hermann EBBINGHAUS launched the systematic study of human memory. James discusses Ebbinghaus's work in his chapter on memory, but the discussion is clearly an appendage. It took some years for an integrated discussion of human learning and memory to be fully elaborated.

A Parliamentary Theory of Learning

Like all evolutionary writers, James addresses the problem of the instinctual and the learned in the organization of human activity. Contrary to most writers, he argues that humans have many instincts and that instincts play a large role in the behavior of higher organisms.

> Nature [in the lower wild animals] has made them act *always* in the manner which would be *oftenest* right. There are more worms unattached to hooks than impaled upon them; therefore, on the whole, says Nature to her fishy children, bite at *every* worm and take your chances. But as her children get higher, and their lives more precious, she reduces the risks. . . . *Nature implants contrary impulses to act on many classes of things,* and leaves it to slight alterations in the conditions of the individual case to decide which impulse shall carry the day. (Pp. 1012–1013)

The proliferation of instincts in the higher animals leads to the beginnings of deliberation and choice. In higher animals, instincts do not remain fixed action patterns. Once an instinct is exercised, it produces consequences, and anticipations of those consequences henceforth accompany instinctive impulses. The experienced organism more and more faces new situations armed with a number of impulses; the organism is not a slave to any one instinct; and there are rational anticipations of the consequences various courses of action might bring. James's parliamentary theory of the inner competition among impulses and their anticipated consequences foreshadows twentieth-century behaviorism. Edward L. THORNDIKE, James's student, was the bridging figure. His connectionism built the parliamentary theory into a logic of response choice in problem-solving situations; that connectionism, in turn, has been recognized as the nuclear theoretical architecture of all subsequent learning theories.

Optimal human development, James argued, implies the fruition of as many instinctive tendencies as possible. After attributing to humans a large set of instincts (more, he says, than any animal), James says:

> In a perfectly-rounded development every one of these instincts would start a habit towards certain objects and inhibit a habit towards others. Usually this is the case; but, in the one-sided development of civilized life, it happens that the timely age goes by in a sort of starvation of objects, and the individual

then grows up with gaps in his psychic constitution which future experiences can never fill. Compare the accomplished gentleman with the poor artisan or tradesman of a city: during the adolescence of the former, objects appropriate to his growing interests, bodily and mental, were offered as fast as his interests awoke, and, as a consequence, he is armed and equipped at every angle to meet the world. . . . Over the city poor boy's youth no such golden opportunities were hung, and in his manhood no desires for most of them exist. Fortunate it is for him if gaps are the only anomalies his instinctive life presents; perversions are too often the fruit of his unnatural bringing-up. (Pp. 1056–1057)

Memories as Beliefs

James approaches the phenomena of human memory introspectively, though his conception of the presenting phenomena of mental life differs radically from previous psychological writings. Beginning with John Locke, and continuing through the research programs of nineteenth-century brass-instruments laboratories, psychologists have again and again said that human experience begins with simple sensations and ideas. James argues that this is false to experience. "Simple" sensations and ideas are, in fact, highly contrived and rationalized abstractions from experience. What presents itself to the mind is an always dynamic, often inchoate, moving flow—a fluidity that in the *Principles* he calls the "stream of consciousness," and in later writings he calls "pure experience." Redefining the mental life with which the psychologist must deal, James at once sets aside the traditional denizens of that mental life—sensations, ideas, faculties. In return, he has the obligation and the opportunity to ask in a very wide-open way where in the fluidity one may locate the conventional chapter headings: Attention, Conception, Discrimination and Comparison, Memory, and so on.

In older writings, memories are referred to as returns or reinstatements of experiences of the past; James, looking at mental life with a fresh eye, argues there must be more to the experience of a memory than that. "Memory," he says, "is the knowledge of an event, or fact, of which meantime we have not been thinking, *with the additional consciousness that we have thought or experienced it before*" (p. 610). It is not enough to see or hear something that one has seen or heard before. There must be some aspect of the experi-

ence that says the event has occurred before, not in just any past but in the person's past. "It must have that 'warmth and intimacy' which were so often spoken of in the chapter on the self, as characterizing all experiences 'appropriated by the thinker as his own.' " In the end, James concludes that a memory is far more than an image or copy of a fact in the mind, that it is in fact a very complex representation with objective, personal, and metacognitive components. What we usually refer to as memory, James argues, is a form of belief.

James's analyses of habit, as we have seen, had an immediate and large influence on the development of psychology in subsequent decades. His discussions of memory and other cognitive phenomena were out of step with the elementistic introspectionism of his time. It seems very likely that contemporary cognitive psychology—in particular, the study of personal, narrative memories—is picking up the thread of William James's thought.

REFERENCES

Bjork, D. W. (1983). *The compromised scientist: William James in the development of American psychology.* New York: Columbia University Press.

Feinstein, H. M. (1984). *Becoming William James.* Ithaca: Cornell University Press.

James, W. (1899). *Talks to teachers on psychology: And to students on some of life's ideals.* New York: Holt.

——— (1902). *The varieties of religious experience: A study in human nature.* New York: Longmans, Green.

——— (1890). *The Principles of Psychology.* 2 vols. Reprinted (1981) in F. H. Burkhardt, F. Bowers, and I. K. Skrupskelis, eds, *The works of William James.* Cambridge, Mass.: Harvard University Press.

——— (1983). *Essays in psychology.* Vol. 13 in F. H. Burkhardt, F. Bowers, and I. K. Skrupskelis, eds., *The works of William James.* Cambridge, Mass.: Harvard University Press.

Perry, R. B. (1935). *The thought and character of William James, as revealed in unpublished correspondence and notes, together with his published writings.* 2 vols. Boston: Little, Brown.

Taylor, E. (1983). *William James on exceptional mental states: The 1896 Lowell Lectures.* New York: Charles Scribner's Sons.

Sheldon H. White

KINDLING

Kindling may be viewed as an experimental model of the formation of a memory trace (Goddard, 1967). It differs from all other models of synaptic plasticity (or neuronal models of memory) by reason of its extraordinary duration. After only a few exposures to a low-level, localized electrical stimulus, the synaptic responsiveness of the stimulated circuit undergoes an augmentation that persists, without further reinforcement, for many years, perhaps for the life of the animal.

In the kindling paradigm, a subthreshold electrical stimulus is repeatedly delivered to a local brain area once or twice a day for a duration of 1–2 seconds. When first applied, the electrical stimulation results in only brief afterdischarge (AD) and no behavioral alteration. Without any change in stimulus parameters, the AD gradually increases in duration and spreads from the stimulated area to increasingly distant, though synaptically connected, brain regions. A progressive alteration of behavior is also seen, beginning with a momentary arrest of ongoing locomotor activity and proceeding through localized twitching to a generalized seizure. Once generalized seizures have occurred, cessation of stimulation for weeks, months, or even years does not result in loss of the newly acquired, electrophysiologically and behaviorally defined change. Reintroduction of the original stimulus, which was behaviorally ineffective to begin with, reliably causes a generalized seizure.

The gradual lengthening of AD and the incremental acquisition of a new behavior at the level of both nerve cell and the whole animal is an example of "learning," albeit, in this case, the learning of an abnormal cellular behavior that culminates in seizures. It occurs as a consequence of the repeated experience of the stimulation. A chart of the AD duration as a function of stimulation trials (Figure 1) would be generally accepted as a reasonable facsimile, in any behavioral study, of a typical learning curve. The persistence of the altered synaptic excitability in the absence of reinforcement may be viewed as an example of memory, as evidence that the altered neuronal properties eventually become self-sustained and permanent.

In addition to being a robust neuronal model of synaptic plasticity, kindling has also been extensively employed as a model of focal epilepsy. The bulk of this literature, which will not be dealt with here, relates to the use of kindling to study the pathophysiology of epilepsy or the mechanism of action of anticonvulsant drugs. Here we will emphasize only those particular features of the phenomenon that make it attractive for analysis of neuronal mechanisms in learning and memory.

Kindling may be elicited by stimulation of almost any site in the cortex and diencephalon, but the most effective areas (i.e., those where the fewest stimuli are required to establish the phenomenon) are those related to the limbic system—amygdala, hippocampus, pyriform cortex, entorhinal cortex, and septal region. These latter anatomical regions are also the areas most prominently implicated in the establishment of memory traces in behaving animals including man. Some of these same circuits, the hippocampus in particular, are also the areas most prominently involved in LONG-TERM POTENTIATION (LTP)—another favorite neurophysiological model of synaptic plasticity.

Long-term potentiation is the long-lasting enhancement of synaptic transmission observed following brief trains of high-frequency stimulation. Because of its associative property, its persistent nature, and the fact that it is especially prominent in hippocampal circuits, LTP is also widely viewed as a neuronal model of learning and memory. However, LTP has a duration of days to weeks (i.e., it is much less enduring than kindling) and is confined to the first synaptic relay in the stimulated circuit. Nevertheless, LTP is an early and invariant feature of the kindling process; its prior induction in a pathway subsequently stimulated to evoked kindling results in more rapid kindling of that circuit. One may consider kindling as an outgrowth of LTP, a manifestation of augmented synaptic efficacy that is not confined to the first synaptic relay (as is LTP) but that extends gradually and successively to other synaptic stations in the stimulated circuit.

There are many other similarities between behavioral manifestations of learning and memory on the one hand, and kindling and LTP on the other. These include the fact that inhibition of protein synthesis, which is known to interfere with long-term memory, also blocks LTP and hippocampal kindling. Enhanced synaptic responsiveness is characteristic not only of LTP and kindling, but also of nerve cells that have specifically participated in the process of behavioral learning. *n*-Methyl-*d*-aspartate antagonists that block spatial memory also impair kindling and LTP at least in some circuits.

Kindling is one example of the more general phenomenon of the "mirror focus" or secondary epileptogenesis, which has long been viewed as a model of neural learning. Secondary epileptogenesis may be defined as the sum total of the series of events by means of which an initially normal neuronal network, as a consequence of its chronic exposure to the activity of a primary epileptogenic lesion, develops epileptogenic properties of its own. In the human, the primary epileptogenic lesion may be the consequence of many different pathological processes. Regardless of cause, the nature of the primary focus is that abnormal electrical impulses, very similar to those produced by the stimulating electrode in the kindling paradigm (Racine, Tuff, and Zaide, 1975), are generated in a localized, chronic, and recurrent fashion. These impulses produce synchronous neuronal bombardment of distant but synaptically related networks. Ultimately, the neural elements of these "target" networks acquire the excessive discharge characteristics of the parent or primary focus. This pro-

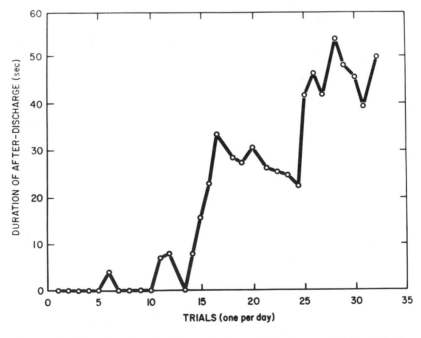

Figure 1.   Duration of epileptiform discharge following each daily trial of electrical stimulation of amygdala in the cat. *Source: Goddard and Morrell, unpublished data.*

cess, discovered in the study of a human disease, is an example of the acquisition and retention of abnormal cellular behavior. Nevertheless, it utilizes mechanisms relevant to understanding the neuronal basis of normal learning and memory mechanisms that are most effectively explored through the experimental model of kindling.

Kindling is, furthermore, not simply a consequence of electrical brain stimulation. Kindling can equally well be induced by repeated systemic injection of subconvulsant doses of excitatory agents such as pentylenetetrazol and picrotoxin, as well as by intracerebral injection of excitatory neurotransmitters such as carbachol or kainate. This chemical kindling demonstrates the generality of the phenomenon, namely, that repeated administration of an initially ineffective dose of an excitatory agent, electrical or chemical, results in a gradual acquisition of a state of increased excitatory responsiveness.

Several features of the kindling-induced enhancement of synaptic efficacy suggest that kindling may be associated with morphological alteration of the synapse itself. These features include the extreme durability of the effect, the fact that the process propagates only along synaptically linked stations of the stimulated circuit, and the fact that it is dependent on ongoing protein synthesis and intact axonal transport mechanisms. Although early morphological examinations carried out before the availability of modern quantitative stereological techniques were unrevealing, more recent investigations (Geinisman, Morrell, and deToledo-Morrell, 1988; Geinisman, deToledo-Morrell, and Morrell, 1990) have demonstrated that kindling is associated with a clear remodeling of synaptic architecture. These results have shown that the proportion of so-called perforated synapses to nonperforated ones in the field of termination of stimulated axons is increased in kindled rats compared with controls. The synaptic remodeling was not seen in a different segment of the dendrite of the same cell, a segment receiving input from a nonstimulated pathway. The so-called perforated synapses are large in size, have a discontinuous postsynaptic density, and are considered to be more efficacious with respect to synaptic transmission. A similar increase in the proportion of "perforated" synapses has also been demonstrated in other circumstances associated with storage of information or plasticity such as visual discrimination training and rearing in enriched environments. In addition to synaptic remodeling,

kindling is associated with a selective enlargement of the active zones of perforated synapses formed by stimulated axons. The synaptic active zone is a specialized region within the synapse where presynaptic secretion and postsynaptic reception of chemicals mediating impulse transmission take place. Enlargement of active zones in presumably more efficacious perforated synapses may represent a mechanism for an extensive amplification of impulse transmission within the polysynaptic circuit involved in the kindling process. (See also GUIDE TO THE ANATOMY OF THE BRAIN: SYNAPSE.)

It must be stressed that the relevance of any model for mechanisms of memory is substantially enhanced if it can be shown to correlate directly with a behaviorally measured mnemonic function. Such a correlation was demonstrated in an experiment designed to examine the relation between age-dependent alterations in mnemonic function and in hippocampal synaptic efficacy as measured by rate of kindling (deToledo-Morrell, Geinisman, and Morrell, 1988). Spatial memory function in young and old rats was tested in an eight-arm radial maze task. Performance in this task is severely compromised in lower mammals by bilateral hippocampal damage or dysfunction. The hippocampal formation is not only critically involved in the acquisition of certain kinds of new information, but is also a brain region most vulnerable to the aging process. In general, hippocampal kindling was much slower in aged rats (approximately 70 percent of which show a memory dysfunction; see also AGING AND MEMORY IN ANIMALS) than in young ones. The more important finding was a striking relationship between performance in the eight-arm maze (as determined by the number of trials to reach a criterion of three consecutive trials without errors) and speed of kindling for both young and old rats. Old animals with poor spatial memory kindled slowly, whereas those with good memory kindled as fast as young ones. Conversely, young animals that failed to reach criterion in the maze kindled more slowly than those that reached criterion. Interestingly, memory-impaired aged animals also showed a selective loss of perforated synapses in the hippocampus that was not due to age alone, but was closely related to the extent of memory loss. It is pertinent to recall that in young rats, kindling itself is associated with a selective *increase* in these perforated synapses. Thus, it appears that the impairment in hippocampal function as measured by spatial memory is related to a systematic, quantitative *diminution* of exactly those structural elements that increase with potentiation of the same synaptic system. Analogous morphological observations have been made with respect to LTP.

In summary, kindling provides a robust model of use-dependent facilitation of synaptic transmission. In contrast to some other candidate models of memory, such as LTP, one may cite the particularly long duration of the kindling effect and the fact that the modification of synaptic action induced by this experimental paradigm is not limited to the first synaptic relay but, like behavioral learning, extends through major sections of the interconnected network. The process, nevertheless, abides by the same constraints as apply to the dissemination of the normal everyday memory trace both in anatomical and temporal characteristics. An important feature of the kindling model is that the critical modification must have a postsynaptic locus, since it survives the complete destruction of the stimulation site and degeneration of all the axons emanating from it.

Finally, it is important to emphasize that, as a pathological phenomenon, kindling is not likely to be quantitatively comparable to the events that underlie normal learning and memory. Yet the power of the model may consist precisely in the fact that it represents an exaggeration of normal mechanisms that brings them into bolder relief and, thereby, facilitates recognition and allows more fundamental analysis.

REFERENCES

deToledo-Morrell, L., Geinisman, Y., and Morrell, F. (1988). Age-dependent alterations in hippocampal synaptic plasticity: Relation to memory disorders. *Neurobiology of Aging 9,* 581–590.

Geinisman, Y., deToledo-Morrell, L., and Morrell, F. (1990). The brain's record of experience: Kindling-induced enlargement of the active zone in hippocampal perforated synapses. *Brain Research 513,* 175–179.

Geinisman, Y., Morrell, F., and deToledo-Morrell, L. (1988). Remodeling of synaptic architecture during hippocampal "kindling." *National Academy of Sciences Proceedings 85,* 3260–3264.

Goddard, G. V. (1967). The development of epileptic seizures through brain stimulation at low intensity. *Nature 214,* 1020–1021.

Goddard, G. V., and Douglas, R. M. (1975). Does the engram of kindling model the engram of normal long term memory? *Canadian Journal of Neurological Sciences 2,* 385–394.

Morrell, F. (1959/1960). Secondary epileptogenic lesions. *Epilepsia 1,* 538–560.

——— (1961). Lasting changes in synaptic organization produced by continuous neuronal bombardment. In J. F. Delafresnaye, A. Fessard, R. W. Gerard, and J. Konorski, eds., *Brain mechanisms and learning.* Oxford: Blackwell Scientific.

——— (1985). Secondary epileptogenesis in man. *Archives of Neurology 42,* 318–335.

Morrell, F., and deToledo-Morrell, L. (1986). Kindling as a model of neuronal plasticity. In J. A. Wada, ed., *Kindling 3,* New York: Raven.

Morrell, F., Sandler, B., and Ross, G. (1959). The mirror focus as a model of neural learning. In *Proceedings of the 21st International Congress of the Physiological Sciences, Buenos Aires.*

Racine, R., Tuff, L., and Zaide, J. (1975). Kindling, unit discharge and neural plasticity. *Canadian Journal of Neurological Sciences 2,* 395.

Frank Morrell

KNOWLEDGE SYSTEMS

Studies of disrupted cognition enhance our understanding of normal cognitive functions. Structure of knowledge representation in the brain is elucidated by the studies of specific dissociations of knowledge loss in brain disease. The question whether there is one or several memory stores is of the foremost interest. Studies of amnesias are particularly illuminating in this respect. In most amnesic syndromes, skills are better preserved than facts. Within the declarative domain, context-free information is usually better preserved than context-dependent information. Generic information is better preserved than singular information. Generally, the patient's ability to give a conscious account of previously acquired knowledge is more likely to be impaired than the ability to benefit from this knowledge in various behavioral situations. These observations have been interpreted to indicate the neuropsychological reality of the distinctions between procedural knowledge (skills) and declarative knowledge (facts) (Cohen and Squire, 1980), SEMANTIC MEMORY (for general facts) and EPISODIC MEMORY (for personal facts) (Tulving, 1983; Kinsbourne and Wood, 1975), generic knowledge (referring to large classes of equivalent objects) and singular knowledge (referring to unique entities), and explicit knowledge (demonstrated through conscious reports) and IMPLICIT KNOWLEDGE (demonstrated through behavioral gains) (Schacter, 1987; Tulving and Schacter, 1990).

While the phenomenal distinctness of these knowledge categories is widely accepted, consensus is lacking as to whether these knowledge types are mediated by neurally distinct stores. Robustness and uniformity of the dissociations are often mentioned as the arguments in favor of separate stores (Schacter, 1985). An alternative hypothesis is that the difference between procedural and declarative, semantic and episodic, generic and singular, and explicit and implicit knowledge types reflects different degrees of accessibility of engrams that are part of the same store. This position suggests that the differences between components of the above dichotomies are quantitative rather than qualitative, and that the dichotomies themselves are but discrete approximations of continuous variations in the degree of engram accessibility.

Two additional types of knowledge base dissociations have been described: by sensory modalities and by semantic categories. Modality-specific knowledge loss is exemplified by associative agnosias and modality-specific aphasias (see APHASIA). In associative agnosias, the subject loses the ability to identify objects as members of generic categories (Warrington, 1975; Goldberg, 1990). The deficit may be isolated, in that it may be present without sensory or language impairment, and without dementia. Most important in the context of this analysis, the deficit is modality-specific, and at least three types of associative agnosias have been identified: VISUAL OBJECT AGNOSIA (McCarthy and Warrington, 1986), pure astereognosis (Hecaen and Albert, 1978), and auditory associative agnosia (Vignolo, 1982).

In each of these agnosias, the ability to interpret object meaning is impaired with respect to a distinct input modality. A patient can see that a watch is round and flat but does not recognize it as a watch in visual object agnosia; a patient can feel that it has a smooth, glassy surface and a small bump on the side, but does not recognize it as a watch in pure astereognosis; and a patient can hear it tick but does not recognize it as a watch in auditory associative agnosia. The knowledge-base impairment in associative agnosias is evident both in patients' inability to correctly name the object and in their inability to signal its correct meaning through nonverbal means, such as pantomime. However, successful object identification, both verbal and nonverbal, will be accomplished in each of these three conditions with reliance on other sensory modalities. The existence of modality-specific associative agnosias has led to the hypothesis that the nonverbal knowledge base is dimensionalized at least in part by sensory modalities (Warrington, 1975; Goldberg, 1990; Damasio, 1990; Shallice, 1987). This hypothesis is strengthened by the presence of double dissociations between any two types of associative agnosia.

In modality-specific aphasias, the patient can correctly identify the object meaning through nonverbal means (e.g., pantomime) but cannot come up with a correct name (Beauvois, 1982). However, the name is easily retrieved when the patient is allowed to resort to other sensory input modalities. The existence of sense-specific aphasias further supports the notion of modality-specific knowledge stores, by suggesting that each of them has a separate access to an amodal lexical store (Beauvois, 1982).

Modality-specific associative agnosias are distinct not only phenomenally but also neuroanatomically. Each type of agnosia has a distinct cortical territory that is consistent across patients. This observation lends further support to the notion of multiple, neurally distinct, modality-specific knowledge stores. It has been suggested that the modality-specific associative agnosias are all linked predominantly to the left hemisphere (Warrington, 1975; Goldberg, 1990). If this assertion is true, then the left hemisphere emerges as the repository of multiple knowledge systems, verbal and nonverbal alike. It has been further suggested that the neocortical functional organization within the posterior portion of a hemisphere is characterized by continuous, gradiental distributions of cognitive functions. The geometry of the cognitive gradients is determined by the sensory cortices (Goldberg, 1989). This position is highly consistent with the notion that representations are dimensionalized in terms of sensory modalities.

Category-specific knowledge loss has also been reported (Damasio, 1990; Warrington and Shallice, 1990; Hart, Berndt, and Caramazza, 1985). In the lexical domain, this pertains to the double dissociation of comprehension and naming of object names and action names (Goodglass et al., 1966; Miceli et al., 1984). Further fractionation of noun loss has also been reported (Warrington and Shallice, 1990; Hart, Berndt, and Caramazza, 1985; McKenna and Warrington, 1980).

Category-specific knowledge loss may also manifest as a selective inability to describe objects or elicit their mental images (Warrington and Shallice, 1984), or as selective agnosia for certain categories of objects but not for others (Nielsen, 1946). The most common and consistent observation of category-specific knowledge loss is that the knowledge of living objects or foods is more impaired than the knowledge of inanimate objects (Vignolo, 1982; Goldberg, 1989; Hart, Berndt, and Caramazza, 1985; Goodglass et al., 1986). However, the opposite pattern has also been reported (Warrington and McCarthy, 1983, 1987).

To account for the overwhelming unidirectionality of dissociation, with most studies reporting greater preservation of knowledge about inanimate than living things, and very few reporting the opposite pattern, it has been proposed that the difference may reflect inherently greater perceptual similarities, and therefore confusability, within the living domain than within the inanimate domain (Riddoch et al., 1988). Alternatively, it has been proposed that the category-specific knowledge loss may reflect different patterns of relative salience of different sensory modalities for different categories (Goldberg, 1989; Warrington and McCarthy, 1987). The latter position is particularly well suited to account for category-specific double dissociations. It also interrelates category- and sense-specific aspects of mental representations.

The inanimate objects used in most studies are in fact man-made objects or tools. Therefore, it is difficult to know which of the two distinctions, living versus inanimate or man-made versus natural, best captures the observed differences. The latter distinction emphasizes the secondary nature of category-specific aspects relative to modality-specific aspects of knowledge representations. This is due to the fact that man-made tools have mandatory somatosensory and motor representations in the brain, which are absent for most natural objects or foods. Therefore, tools are encoded with reliance on more sensory dimensions compared with most natural objects, which would make the corresponding engrams more robust.

In considering the more esoteric types of category-specific knowledge loss or knowledge preservation (Hart, Berndt, and Caramazza, 1985; Yamadori and Albert, 1973; McKenna and Warrington, 1978), one must also take into account the possible premorbid idiosyncrasies of individual lexical strengths and weaknesses. This may be a potent source of artifact in analyzing postmorbid performance.

Finally, combined category- and modality-specific knowledge loss has been reported in a patient who had a selective loss of living things but not objects in the verbal but not visual domain (McCarthy and Warrington, 1988). Warrington and Shallice (1984) conclude that knowledge is organized along both sensory and category dimensions.

Knowledge of the object's superordinate category is relatively well preserved in modality-specific, category-specific, and combined knowledge loss (Warrington, 1975; McCarthy and Warrington, 1988). This very pervasive observation has lent support to the hypothesis that knowledge about things is in some sense hierarchic. It has even been proposed that the access to a specific category member invariably begins with accessing a superordinate category (Warrington, 1975). While this may be true in some cases, the observation of the relative preservation of superordinate knowledge does not in itself necessitate this conclusion. In fact, a different route of object identification has also been proposed, from the basic category to superordinate and subordinate categories (Rosch, 1978).

Both degraded-store (Warrington and Shallice, 1984) and impaired-access (Humphreys, Riddoch, and Quinlan, 1988) hypotheses have been evoked to account for category- and modality-specific memory loss. It has been suggested that degraded store is characterized by the uniformity of responses across recall trials, and impaired access by their variability (Warrington and Shallice, 1984; Cermak and O'Connor, 1983; Shallice, 1988). The possible neuroanatomical basis for this distinction may be related to whether the critical lesion affects neocortical sites where representations are distributed, thus resulting in degraded store, or subcortical structures involved in various aspects of activation and arousal, thus resulting in impaired access.

(See also CONCEPTS AND CATEGORIES, LEARNING OF; MODALITY EFFECTS.)

REFERENCES

Beauvois, M.-F. (1982). Optic aphasia: A process of interaction between vision and language. *Philosophical*

Transactions of the Royal Society (London) *B298,* 35–47.

Cermak, L. S., and O'Connor, M. (1983). The retrieval capacity of a patient with amnesia due to encephalitis. *Neuropsychologia 21,* 213–234.

Cohen, N. J., and Squire, L. R. (1980). Preserved learning and retention of pattern-analyzing skill in amnesia: Dissociation of "knowing how" and "knowing that." *Science 210,* 207–209.

Damasio, A. R. (1990). Category related recognition defects as a clue to the neural substrates of knowledge. *Trends in Neurosciences 13,* 95–98.

Goldberg, E. (1989). Gradiental approach to the neocortical functional organization. *Journal of Clinical and Experimental Neuropsychology 11,* 489–517.

—— (1990). Associative agnosias and the functions of the left hemisphere. *Journal of Clinical and Experimental Neuropsychology 12,* 467–484.

Goodglass, H., Klein, B., Carey, P., and Jones, K. (1966). Specific semantic word categories in aphasia. *Cortex 2,* 74–89.

Hart, J., Berndt, R. S., and Caramazza, A. (1985). Category-specific naming deficit following cerebral infarction. *Nature 316,* 439–440.

Hecaen, H., and Albert, M. L. (1978). *Human neuropsychology.* New York: Wiley.

Humphreys, G. W., Riddoch, M. J., and Quinlan, P. T. (1988). Cascade processes in picture identification. *Cognitive Neuropsychology 5,* 67–103.

Kinsbourne, M., and Wood, F. (1975). Short-term memory processes and the amnestic syndrome. In D. Deutsch and J. A. Deutsch, eds., *Short-term memory.* New York: Academic Press.

McCarthy, R. A., and Warrington, E. K. (1986). Visual associative agnosia: A clinico-anatomical study of a single case. *Journal of Neurology, Neurosurgery and Psychiatry 49,* 1233–1240.

—— (1988). Evidence for modality-specific meaning systems in the brain. *Nature 334,* 428–430.

McKenna, P., and Warrington, E. K. (1978). Category-specific naming preservation: A single case study. *Journal of Neurology, Neurosurgery and Psychiatry 41,* 571–574.

—— (1980). Testing for nominal dysphasia. *Journal of Neurology, Neurosurgery and Psychiatry 43,* 781–788.

Miceli, G., Silveri, M. C., Villa, G., and Caramazza, A. (1984). On the basis for the agrammatic's difficulty in producing main verbs. *Cortex 20,* 207–220.

Nielsen, J. M. (1946). *Agnosia, apraxia, aphasia: Their value in cerebral localization,* 2nd ed. New York: Hoeber.

Riddoch, M. J., Humphreys, G. W., Coltheart, M., and Funnell, E. (1988). Semantic systems or system? Neuropsychological evidence re-examined. *Cognitive Neuropsychology 5,* 3–25.

Rosch, E. (1978). Principles of categorization. In E. Rosch and B. B. Lloyd, eds., *Principles of categorization.* Hillsdale, N.J.: Erlbaum.

Schacter, D. L. (1985). Multiple forms of memory in humans and animals. In N. M. Weinberger, J. L. McGaugh, and G. Lynch, eds., *Memory systems of the brain.* New York: Guilford Press.

—— (1987). Implicit memory: History and current status. *Journal of Experimental Psychology: Learning, Memory, and Cognition 13,* 501–518.

Shallice, T. (1987). Impairments of semantic processing: Multiple dissociations. In M. Coltheart, G. Santori, and R. J. Job, eds., *The cognitive neuropsychology of language.* Hilldale, N.J.: Erlbaum.

—— (1988). *From neuropsychology to mental structure.* Cambridge: Cambridge University Press.

Tulving, E. (1983). *Elements of episodic memory.* Oxford: Oxford University Press.

Tulving, E., and Schacter, D. L. (1990). Priming and human memory systems. *Science 247,* 301–306.

Vignolo, L. A. (1982). Auditory agnosia. *Philosophical Transactions of the Royal Society* (London) *B298,* 16–33.

Warrington, E. K. (1975). The selective impairment of semantic memory. *Quarterly Journal of Experimental Psychology 27,* 635–657.

Warrington, E. K., and McCarthy, R. A. (1983). Category specific access dysphasia. *Brain 106,* 859–878.

—— (1987). Categories of knowledge: Further fractionations and an attempted integration. *Brain 110,* 1273–1296.

Warrington, E. K., and Shallice, T. (1984). Category specific semantic impairments. *Brain 107,* 829–853.

Yamadori, A., and Albert, M. L. (1973). Word category aphasia. *Cortex 9,* 112–125.

Elkhonon Goldberg
William B. Barr

KONORSKI, JERZY

Although Jerzy Konorski (1903–1973) always regarded himself as a neurophysiologist, his empirical and theoretical legacy has been in psychology. Like those of Ivan PAVLOV, his theories, although expressed in terms of speculative physiology, were largely based on behavioral experiments and are readily recast into psychological concepts. And it is in this form that his ideas have come to exert a preeminent influence over the contemporary study of associative learning through conditioning.

Jerzy Konorski was born in the Polish city of Lódź. From his earliest student days, he was fascinated by brain function, and while studying medicine at Warsaw University, he came into contact with Pavlov's work. Although inspired by Pavlov's ideas, he doubted that Pavlovian mechanisms could explain all forms of acquired behavior—specifically, what we should now call instrumental or operant conditioning. Along with a fellow student, Stephan Miller, he set up a makeshift conditioning laboratory to investigate whether instrumental and classical (Pavlovian) conditioning obey the same principles of reinforcement. On the basis of this work, Miller and Konorski (1969) published the first statement of the distinction between the two forms of conditioning in 1928, while they were still students. The existence and importance of this distinction was not realized in the West until Konorski and Miller entered into a published debate with Skinner on the matter in the next decade.

Their subsequent work on instrumental conditioning, conducted in Pavlov's laboratory between 1931 and 1933, and subsequently at the Nencki Institute of Experimental Biology in Warsaw, was unknown in the West before World War II. Their studies of both modulatory and conditioned rein-

Figure 1. Jerzy Konorski. *Courtesy Professor B. Żernicki.*

forcing effects of Pavlovian stimuli on instrumental conditioning led them to a two-process theory, the like of which was not achieved in the West until the 1960s. Their analysis of avoidance conditioning still stands.

Ignorance of Konorski and Miller's work before World War II is understandable, for the presentation of this research in English had to await the publication of Konorski's monograph *Conditioned Reflexes and Neuron Organization* (1948). The neglect of this volume is less comprehensible, however, for in it Konorski presented the first detailed connectionist account of conditioning within the framework of a Sherringtonian conception of the central nervous system. Besides pioneering a connectionist approach to learning, two aspects of Konorski's 1948 theory deserve special mention. The first is his treatment of conditioned inhibition. Although inhibitory processes were studied intensively in Pavlov's laboratory, their importance was not recognized in the West until the 1960s. When research on this topic finally got under way in the West, Konorski's conception of an inhibitory connection was incorporated into current theories of conditioning.

The second notable feature of Konorski's theory, which has not yet received due recognition, is the rules that he outlined for changing connection weights. Konorski (1948, p. 106) suggested that a positive increment in an excitatory connection weight occurs when activity in an input element is paired with a rise in activity in the receptor element. Correspondingly, inhibitory connections are strengthened when input element activity is paired with a fall in the activation of the receptor element. The importance of these suggestions is that they provide a way of implementing in connectionist terms the error-correcting learning rules (e.g., the Rescorla-Wagner rule) that have come to dominate current theories of associative learning.

When Konorski returned to Poland immediately after World War II, he was instrumental in reestablishing the Nencki Institute, first as the head of the Department of Neurophysiology and later as its director. His enthusiasm and dedication to behavioral neuroscience are clear from the recollections of some of his students, published in his memorial issue of the Institute's journal, *Acta Neurobiologiae Experimentalis* (Żernicki, 1974), which contains a full bibliography. Unfortunately, his research activity was constrained at that time by the promulgation of Pavlovian orthodoxy in the later years of Stalin's reign, because his 1948 monograph was regarded as a revisionist text.

Stalin's death eventually loosened these intellectual shackles and allowed Konorski to establish contacts with American researchers. These contacts had a profound influence on him and culminated in the publication of *Integrative Activity of the Brain* (1967). The scope of this book was ambitious, attempting to describe the brain mechanisms subserving not just learning and conditioning but also perception, cognition, motivation, and emotion—indeed, the overall integration of these functions. Although replete with many interesting and perceptive ideas, this volume is less satisfactory than the first book. Its theoretical substance is too dependent upon the neuroscientific theories and claims of the time, many of which have suffered at the hands of subsequent research. Moreover, its scope precluded one of the most elegant and impressive features of the earlier book, the attempt to achieve a detailed concordance between theory and data.

When Konorski died in 1973, Western psychology had just begun to appreciate his legacy. Currently, his influence on research in conditioning and associative learning rivals that of Pavlov, let alone that of the neobehaviorists (see Dickinson and Boakes, 1979).

(See also CONDITIONING, CLASSICAL AND INSTRUMENTAL.)

REFERENCES

Dickinson, A., and Boakes, R. A., eds. (1979). *Mechanisms of learning and motivation: A memorial volume to Jerzy Konorski.* Hillsdale, N.J.: Erlbaum.

Konorski, J. (1948). *Conditioned reflexes and neuron organization.* Cambridge: Cambridge University Press.

——— (1967). *Integrative activity of the brain: An interdisciplinary approach.* Chicago: University of Chicago Press.

Miller, S., and Konorski, J. (1969). On a particular form of conditioned reflex. *Journal of the Experimental Analysis of Behavior 12,* 187–189. English translation by B. F. Skinner from the original French publication (1928).

Żernicki, B., ed. (1974). *Acta Neurobiologiae Experimentalis 34,* no. 6.

Anthony Dickinson

L

LANGUAGE

See Aphasia; Language Learning

LANGUAGE LEARNING

[This entry consists of two articles, Humans *by Peter W. Culicover and* Nonhuman Primates *by Duane M. Rumbaugh and E. Sue Savage-Rumbaugh. For another perspective on the relationship between language, learning, and memory, see* APHASIA.*]*

Humans

To understand language learning, we must understand three things: (1) what knowledge of language consists of, (2) what specific mechanisms are available for language learning, and (3) what the course of language development is. In general, we may distinguish two broad types of knowledge of language: grammatical knowledge, the nature of which is largely biologically determined, and experiential knowledge, the nature of which is largely determined by the learner's encounter with the world. (For a general introduction to the full scope of linguistic knowledge, see Akmajian et al., 1990).

Grammatical knowledge bears on rule-governed phenomena that can be given a precise formal description. A formal description of a language is called a *grammar* of the language. Typically, grammar consists of *phonology* (sound patterns), *morphology* (structure of words), *syntax* (structure of phrases and sentences), and *semantics* (meanings of words, phrases, and sentences). *Experiential knowledge* of language consists in part of the specific meanings and pronunciations of the individual words of a language. Such knowledge is more or less idiosyncratic, in that it must be acquired item by item and cannot be predicted by general rules. For example, the fact that the word *pig* is pronounced a certain way, and refers to a certain type of animal, is something that we must learn through experience. The totality of this knowledge constitutes the *lexicon* of a language.

Pragmatics concerns the relationships among the language, the speaker, and the speaker's knowledge of the real world. People employ knowledge of the world to infer the communicative intentions and expectations of other speakers and hearers (Bach and Harnish, 1979). For example, when someone says "What are you eating?" we might use our knowledge of the world to infer that they are possibly asking to share what we are eating. Our language may also encode aspects of the social relationships between speakers, knowledge of which is acquired through experience. For example, both an imperative sentence (e.g., "Give me a piece of pizza") and a question (e.g., "Could you give me a piece of pizza?") can be used to ask the hearer to do something. But it is part of the knowledge of how English is used that the imperative is much more direct and in many circumstances will be viewed as insufficiently polite.

Paralleling the distinction between grammatical and experiential knowledge of language are two broad areas of study: development of knowledge of formal structure of language (development of grammar) and language development (development of word meanings, and of the use of language to communicate ideas and intentions and to interact socially in other ways). This article focuses on the study of the relationship between the theory of grammar of natural language and the development of grammar, since it is this aspect of language learning that is least likely to prove to be merely a special case of a more general theory of knowledge acquisition.

The most influential (and controversial) view of the development of grammar is called *universal grammar,* or *UG* (Chomsky, 1975). The UG claim is, in effect, that linguistic knowledge consists of an inborn, universal, skeletal protolanguage, the details of which are elaborated in the course of learning. (A similar view has been proposed for the development of certain bird song systems; see BIRD SONG LEARNING: BEHAVIORAL ASPECTS). On this view, innate knowledge of language has two basic components: (1) a catalog of the fixed, universal set of possible grammatical categories along with a set of universal constraints on how these categories may combine to form phrases and sentences, and (2) a fixed set of specific, universal grammatical principles that determine in detail the well-formedness of linguistic phrasal structures. Typically, the constraints on possible structures and the universal principles are parameterized, in the sense that each constraint and principle may allow for some very limited range of variation.

The grammatical categories are assumed to be the familiar *lexical* categories of noun (e.g., *pig*), verb (e.g., *imagine*), adjective (e.g., *tall*), and preposition (e.g., *about*), and so on, as well as a set of *functional* categories whose members have formal grammatical functions and limited meaning, such as *that* in "I think that it is raining."

Here is an example of a constrained phrasal structure that allows for limited variation between languages. It is known that in natural languages there is a privileged relationship between the verb and its direct object such that the two form, or are *constituents* of, a verb phrase (VP), for example, "read the book." The verb and the direct object can thus be said to be *sisters* within VP. A native speaker of English knows that in VP, the verb (V) must precede its sister, the direct object noun phrase (NP), under normal circumstances. On the basis of this knowledge, the native speaker judges that "*the book read" is not a valid VP of English. (The asterisk indicates that a string of words does not constitute a grammatical sequence in the language.) But in a language such as Japanese, the proper order is the reverse of that in English: [$_{VP}$NP

V]. (Constituents within square brackets are sisters.)

On the UG approach to this phenomenon, language learners do not have to learn what the sisters in VP may be; they already know that the sisters in VP are V and NP. What learners *do* learn about their language is the proper order of the sisters inside VP. Learners of English learn that V precedes NP in VP, while learners of Japanese learn that V follows NP in VP.

Let us turn now to an example of a universal grammatical principle. Consider first the sentences in (1).

(1) a. [$_S$ [$_{NP}$ George] [$_{VP}$ loves himself]].
    b. [$_S$ [$_{NP}$ *George's mother] [$_{VP}$ loves himself]].
    c. [$_S$ [$_{NP}$ *Himself] [$_{VP}$ loves George]].

If two constituents, A and B, are sisters, then A is said to *c-command* B and the constituents of B. The subject NP *George* in (1a) is a sister of VP, and hence it c-commands *love* and *himself.* The c-command relation is illustrated in the tree diagram in (2), corresponding to the sentence (1a), where the NP *George* c-commands the circled constituents. Sisters are represented as branches from the same node.

(2)

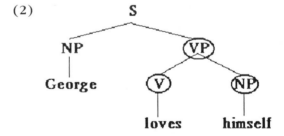

Examination of the sentences in (1) shows that a reflexive must be c-commanded by its antecedent. (This principle is part of what is called the *binding theory.*) In (1a), the antecedent *George* and the VP *loves himself* are sisters in S; thus *George* c-commands *himself.* In contrast, *George* does not c-command *himself* in (1b) or (1c). Again, the UG claim is that the knowledge of this principle is not acquired through experience but is part of the language learning mechanism.

Why is the UG view plausible? There are several reasons. Language apparently is learned almost entirely through exposure to examples of speech in a natural setting. That is, there is little or no explicit language instruction, and what instruction does take place is not in general perceived as such by learners. The spoken language to which the learner is exposed is not structured in the form of organized "language lessons" designed to reveal certain important properties of the language. Hence the learner is not systematically provided with information about what is grammatical and what is ungrammatical. In fact, while much of the speech encountered by learners is grammatical, much is not, yet all learners acquire the correct grammar of the language that they are exposed to. Many utterances are incomplete, which also constitutes a potentially confounding input to the learner. (See Newport et al., 1977, on all of these points.) There is little if any explicit correction by adults of learner's errors, especially grammatical errors (Brown and Hanlon, 1970; Wexler and Culicover, 1980). In fact, it is not clear that the learner would know what the correction is about, even if such correction occurred (Pinker, 1990).

In spite of all this, children make remarkably few errors in their acquisition of a grammar, and they have essentially completed the task within the first three years of life. The implication is that in order for learning to be accomplished so rapidly and under such unfavorable circumstances, much of what the learner knows must be known from the outset. There is also experimental evidence that certain aspects of children's knowledge of language are in place at the earliest stages of language use, before experience could have determined the form of this knowledge. For example, Crain and McKee (1985) have shown that children exhibit correct knowledge of aspects of the binding theory as early as age two (see Crain, 1991, for a review).

Further, there is the "argument from the poverty of the stimulus," which says that much of our linguistic knowledge could not be based on experience, since the crucial evidence for acquiring this knowledge does not exist in the discourse around us. One example is the binding theory outlined above. A very different example involves sentences that contain relative clauses such as (3).

(3) John knows [$_{NP}$ the man [$_S$ that loves Susan]].

It is well known that, in general, when a noun phrase is questioned in English, it must be located at the beginning of the sentence. Thus, if we replace *Susan* in "John said that the man loves Susan" with a question word like *who*, we have a sentence like "Who does John say that the man loves ___." The dash indicates the original position of the moved *who*.

Strikingly, it is impossible to perform the same sort of replacement on a noun phrase when the noun phrase is situated within a relative clause as in (4).

(4) *Who does John know [$_{NP}$ the man [$_S$ that loves ___]].

The question naturally arises as to how we know that this sentence is ungrammatical. The literature on language development provides no evidence that there is any stage at which children learning English treat (4) as grammatical. There is no evidence that children produce systematic errors of the form given in (4), and hence no evidence that children are explicitly corrected for producing such ungrammatical sentences. There is no evidence that children are instructed as to the ungrammaticality of (4). Thus, the claim of the UG approach is that the environment of the learner simply does not provide evidence, in the form of either instruction or correction, on the basis of which the ungrammaticality of (4) could be determined. The UG approach claims that what is going on here is that there is a universal, inborn principle of language that prevents interrogatives (and other types of phrases) from moving out of a relative clause, among other structures. This principle is called subjacency (Chomsky, 1973).

Finally, there are formal learnability considerations that support the UG view. It can be demonstrated that without severe constraints on rules, formal systems which have the essential properties of natural languages are not learnable under plausible definitions of what the input to the learner is, and of what constitutes "learning" (Wexler and Culicover, 1980). It is posited that the learner is exposed to examples of utterances in context from some language **L** and must acquire the grammar of **L**, call it $G(\textbf{L})$. Only if the learner has available a highly restricted set of possible hypotheses consistent with experience can the learner's hypothesis about the grammar to be learned converge rapidly to $G(\textbf{L})$. On this approach, universal principles such as the binding theory and subjacency exist precisely because they restrict the range of hypotheses available to the learner so that such rapid convergence is possible.

Let us turn briefly to the problem of acquiring

knowledge of the lexicon. For every word, the learner must learn at least the following:

- The *meaning* of the word. For a noun (e.g., *book, grandfather, happiness*) the meaning is tied intimately to its reference. For a verb (e.g., *read, eat, think, see*) the meaning is tied to a class of events or states of affairs (Dowty, 1979; Jackendoff, 1990).
- The *category* of the word (e.g., noun, verb, adjective).
- The *conceptual structure* of the word. Word meanings are composed of subtle and effectively arbitrary components (e.g., the difference between *hop* and *skip*, between *kill, murder,* and *assassinate,* or the difference between *broil* and *roast*). But some meaning components appear to have a privileged status, in that they are intimately tied to the structure of sentences in which they appear. Whether the subject of a verb is a causal agent (*John* in "John read the book" vs. *the bomb* in "The bomb exploded") is a more fundamental component of its meaning than is the manner of locomotion (e.g., *hop* and *skip*) (Jackendoff, 1990).

In acquiring the category and the conceptual structure of a word, the learner learns to link the word appropriately to the syntactic structures in which the word is used. Experimental evidence on lexical development suggests that acquisition of the linguistic properties of a word proceeds very rapidly; between the ages of one and a half and six years, a learner acquires about 14,000 words, which works out to about 9 words a day (Carey, 1977). Learning is "bootstrapped" by generalization of the conceptual structure of the word with that of words with similar meanings and grammatical functions (Pinker, 1990; Gleitman, 1990).

On the other hand, it can be seen that to acquire the meaning of a word, the learner must be able to link the word with the world. Full understanding of the word in a strict sense thus depends crucially on the learner's ability to interpret the fine detail of perceptual, cognitive, and social experience correctly. Experimental evidence on the acquisition of word meanings shows that this aspect of lexical development, not unexpectedly, is tightly yoked to perceptual, cognitive, and social development (e.g., Slobin, 1985; De Villiers and De Villiers, 1978; Bates, Bretherton, and Snyder, 1988).

In summary, then, two major types of linguistic knowledge are acquired in the course of language learning. The grammar of the language is acquired through a process in which the learner starts with a universal set of structures and constraints, and through experience fixes aspects of the grammar that the theory of grammar allows to vary from language to language. Within this category of learning is the fixing of the conceptual structures of the lexical items of the language. In addition, the learner acquires a vast array of knowledge of the individual properties of words and expressions, and learns how to use language to convey complex meanings.

REFERENCES

Akmajian, A., Demers, R., Farmer, A. K., and Harnish, R. M. (1990). *Linguistics: An introduction to language and communication,* 3rd ed. Cambridge, Mass.: MIT Press.

Bach, K., and Harnish, R. M. (1979). *Linguistic communication and speech acts.* Cambridge, Mass.: MIT Press.

Bates, E., Bretherton, I., and Snyder, L. (1988). *From first words to grammar.* Cambridge: Cambridge University Press.

Brown, R., and Hanlon, C. (1970). Derivational complexity and the order of acquisition in child speech. In J. R. Hayes, ed., *Cognition and the development of language.* New York: Wiley.

Carey, S. (1977). The child as word learner. In M. Halle, J. Bresnan, and G. A. Miller, eds., *Linguistic theory and psychological reality.* Cambridge, Mass.: MIT Press.

Chomsky, N. (1973). Conditions on transformations. In S. Anderson and P. Kiparsky, eds., *Festschrift for Morris Halle.* New York: Holt, Rinehart and Winston.

——— (1975). *Reflections on language.* New York: Pantheon.

Crain, S. R. (1991). Language acquisition in the absence of experience. *Brain and Behavioral Sciences 14,* 597–612.

Crain, S. R., and McKee, C. (1985). Acquisition of structural restrictions on anaphora. In *Proceedings of the Northeastern Linguistics Society 16.*

De Villiers, J. G., and De Villiers, P. A. (1978). *Language acquisition.* Cambridge, Mass.: Harvard University Press.

Dowty, D. R. (1979). *Word meaning and Montague grammar.* Dordrecht, The Netherlands: D. Reidel.

Gleitman, L. R. (1990). The structural sources of verb meanings. *Language Acquisition 1,* 3–55.

Jackendoff, R. S. (1990). *Semantic structures*. Cambridge, Mass.: MIT Press.

Marler, P., and Sherman, V. (1983). Song structure without auditory feedback: Emendations of the auditory template hypothesis. *Journal of Neuroscience 3*, 517–531.

Newport, E. I., Gleitman, H., and Gleitman, L. R. (1977). Mother I'd rather do it myself: Some effects and non-effects of maternal speech style. In C. E. Snow and C. A. Ferguson, eds., *Talking to children*. Cambridge: Cambridge University Press.

Pinker, S. (1990). *Learnability and cognition: The acquisition of argument structure*. Cambridge, Mass.: MIT Press.

Slobin, D. I., ed. (1985). *The crosslinguistic study of language acquisition*. Hillsdale, N.J.: Erlbaum.

Wexler, K., and Culicover, P. W. (1980). *Formal principles of language acquisition*. Cambridge, Mass.: MIT Press.

Peter W. Culicover

Nonhuman Primates

Darwin gave us a modern evolutionary perspective of the course whereby the morphology of the human body is as it is, but no one has accounted as satisfactorily for evolution of the human mind. Recently, however, comparative psychology has succeeded in finding the lodes that help clarify the biobehavioral origins of human language and symbolic competence through studies of our nearest living relatives—the Pongidae (chimpanzee, *Pan;* orangutan, *Pongo;* and gorilla, *Gorilla*). They are substantially more like humans than are the lesser apes, monkeys, or any other form of mammal. The similarities between human and chimpanzee DNA exceed 98 percent. Consequently, it is reasonable that we might expect to find traces of language and cognition in the ape—competencies for which humans are well known. Genetic relatedness enhances the probability that life forms will have similar psychology as well as appearance. (See also COMPARATIVE COGNITION.)

Even in the nineteenth century there was speculation that apes might be capable of language. Early in the twentieth century, occasional studies were undertaken to determine whether that might be true, but none succeeded. Efforts were renewed in the mid-1960s, with studies by the Gardners (Gardner and Gardner, 1969; Gardner, Gardner, and van Cantfort, 1989) and by Premack (1971;

1976). The Gardners used American Sign Language, and Premack used plastic tokens of different shapes and colors to function as words, with the aim of establishing two-way communication and an experimental analysis of language functions, respectively. Their chimpanzees, Washoe and Sarah, learned relatively large numbers of signs and tokens and, seemingly, their appropriate use.

In 1971, the LANA Project was initiated by Rumbaugh and his colleagues. A computer-based research system provided Lana, a chimpanzee, with a keyboard that held 125 keys, each embossed with a distinctive geometric symbol called a lexigram. Lexigrams functioned as words, and their concatenation was computer-monitored for correctness and for activation of a bank of devices, some of which delivered various foods and drinks, movies, slides, and music. Lana readily learned her lexigrams in order to request things and to give the names and colors of objects. Tests revealed that she saw Munsel color chips in a manner that resembles our own, an observation reaffirmed by Matsuzawa (1985) in Japan with his chimpanzee, Ai.

Within limits, Lana demonstrated her ability to modify her sentences so as to achieve ends other than the specific ones for which they were designated, such as using them to attract attention to malfunctioning food vendors and to the units that produced slides and music. A cucumber was innovatively called "banana which-is green," an overly ripe banana was called "banana which-is black," and an orange was called "apple which-is orange [colored]." Comprehensive analyses clearly indicated that Lana's productions could not be satisfactorily attributed either to rotely learned sequences or to imitation. Project LANA contributed what was perhaps the first successful application of a computer to a system for communicative research. Romski (1988) has demonstrated that keyboards similar to the one developed for LANA augment the communicative effectiveness of children with language deficits. Project LANA also affirmed the ability of the chimpanzee to learn large numbers of symbols, to use them in prescribed sequences, to alter use of those sequences creatively, and to use symbols so as to facilitate perceptions of sameness and difference between items when one was presented visually and the other by touch.

Terrace (1979) began Project Nim in the early 1970s. Nim learned signs, but Terrace reached the conclusion that not only Nim's signs but also those of the Gardners' Washoe were predomi-

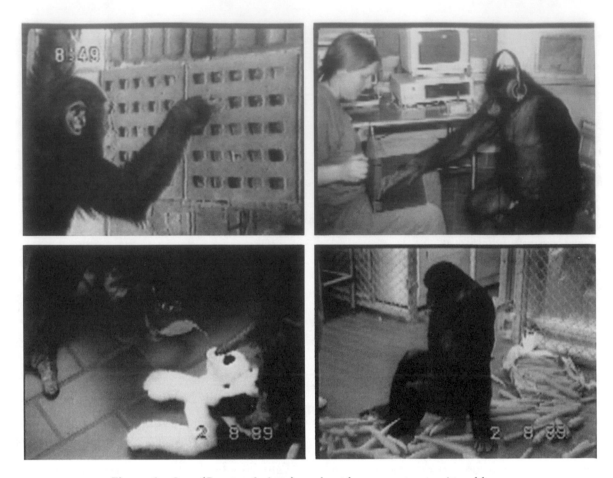

Figure 1. Lana (*Pan troglodytes*) works at her computer-monitored keyboard (upper left); Kanzi (*Pan paniscus*) indicates that he understands a word, which he hears through his headphones, by pointing to the appropriate word-lexigram or picture of an array presented in a test booklet—the experimenter knows neither when nor what word Kanzi hears (upper right); Kanzi indicates that he comprehends the request "Can you make the doggie bite the snake?" by opening the mouth of a stuffed dog and inserting the head of a rubber snake (lower left); and Kanzi pushes a bunch of carrots, extracted from a sack, to Rose upon being asked to "give Rose a carrot"—the sentences of request are given verbally by an experimenter located behind a one-way mirror, and Rose, one of three persons in the room, cannot hear what Kanzi is asked to do because of the loud music she hears through earphones.

nantly due to partial or complete imitation of what others working with their subjects had recently signed. (As noted, imitation was not an issue in the LANA Project.)

Also in the 1970s, Miles (1990) began Project Chantek. Chantek, an orangutan, was taught manual signs; Miles concluded that his signing was not confounded by or due to his imitation of human signers, as Terrace had claimed to be the case with Nim and Washoe.

Research of the mid- and late 1970s by Savage-

Rumbaugh and Rumbaugh with chimpanzees named Sherman and Austin used a variation of Lana's keyboard. These chimpanzees demonstrated their abilities to classify lexigrams, each of which represented a specific food or tool, through use of two other lexigrams, glossed as "food" and "tool," embedded with more than 100 other keys on their keyboard. That they could so categorize their lexigrams was strong evidence that each symbol did, in fact, represent an item to them and that they could use those representations, on trial-

1 test in controlled conditions, to classify almost errorlessly the symbols of their working vocabulary.

Research by Savage-Rumbaugh with the rare bonobo, a species (*Pan paniscus*) apart from the common chimpanzee (*P. troglodytes*), was the first to demonstrate the chimpanzee's ability to learn the meanings of symbols spontaneously. The bonobo came to comprehend the meanings of lexigrams, and even human speech, *prior* to developing competence in use of the keyboard. All previous apes had been able to "talk" (e.g., produce signs, use tokens, use lexigrams) as a result of specific training programs, but their comprehension skills were either deferred or never assessed. For the first time, then, we had a model of language learning in the ape that tracked or paralleled the course of language acquisition in the normal child. Early experience from birth has been critical for such observational learning of language to occur in the bonobo. The common chimpanzee also benefits similarly from such rearing, though possibly to a lesser degree than does the bonobo.

One bonobo, Kanzi, responded appropriately to about three-fourths of over 700 sentences of novel requests presented to him verbally under controlled test conditions to preclude cuing. His performance was generally comparable with that of a 2-year-old girl whose mental age was 2½ years. Neither Kanzi nor the girl had the benefit of people modeling the requests, nor had they been trained to do what was requested of them. The conclusion is, then, that they comprehended the syntax of the novel requests conveyed by normal human speech.

Language competence rests fundamentally in comprehension, not speech. Speech is an efficient mode for expressing language, but it does not ensure competence either in what is said or in comprehension of what is heard. Chimpanzees can comprehend language, but incomplete control of the larynx and the anatomy of their vocal tract deny them vocal speech. The "talking" of which they are capable is through the computer-based keyboard devised for Lana. Advances in keyboard technology might significantly escalate the ape's ability to "talk," for we now know that it has many topics about which to communicate.

Language is unique to humans primarily in that they alone can speak it and use it with seemingly infinite complexity for various purposes, including to insist endlessly upon the uniqueness and glory of their species. To continue doing so is no longer so reasonable—and reason, according to Descartes, should be humans' strongest suit.

REFERENCES

Gardner, B. T., and Gardner, R. A. (1969). Teaching sign language to a chimpanzee. *Science 162*, 664–672.

Gardner, R. A., Gardner, B. T., and van Cantfort, T. E. (1989). *Teaching sign language to chimpanzees.* Albany: State University of New York Press.

Greenfield, P. M., and Savage-Rumbaugh, E. S. (1990). Grammatical combination in *Pan paniscus*: Processes of learning and invention in the evolution and development of language. In S. T. Parker and K. R. Gibson, eds., *"Language" and intelligence in monkeys and apes: Comparative developmental perspectives,* pp. 540–578. New York: Cambridge University Press.

Matsuzawa, T. 1985. Color naming and classification in a chimpanzee (*Pan troglodytes*). *Journal of Human Evolution 14*, 283–291.

Miles, H. L. W. (1990). The cognitive foundations for reference in a signing orangutan. In S. T. Parker and K. R. Gibson, eds., *"Language" and intelligence in monkeys and apes: Comparative developmental perspectives,* pp. 511–539. New York: Cambridge University Press.

Premack, D. (1971). On the assessment of language competence in the chimpanzee. In A. M. Schrier and F. Stollnitz, eds., *Behavior of nonhuman primates,* vol. 4, pp. 186–228. New York: Academic Press.

——— (1976). *Language and intelligence in ape and man.* Hillsdale, N.J.: Erlbaum.

Romski, M. A., Sevcik, R. A., and Pate, J. L. (1988). The establishment of symbolic communication in persons with mental retardation. *Journal of Speech and Hearing Disorders 53*, 94–107.

Rumbaugh, D. M. (1977). *Language learning by a chimpanzee: The Lana Project.* New York: Academic Press.

Savage-Rumbaugh, E. S. (1986). *Ape language: From conditioned response to symbol.* New York: Columbia Univ. Press.

Terrace, H. S. (1979). *Nim.* New York: Knopf.

Duane M. Rumbaugh
E. Sue Savage-Rumbaugh

LASHLEY, KARL

Karl Spencer Lashley (1890–1958) pioneered the study of brain mechanisms of learning and memory. He was born in 1890 in Davis, West Virginia,

Figure 1. Karl S. Lashley.

and entered the University of West Virginia at the age of 15. As a freshman he signed up for a class in zoology under the distinguished neurologist John Black Johnston, and within a few weeks he "knew that I had found my life work." After graduation in 1910, he obtained a teaching fellowship at the University of Pittsburgh and received his M.S. there. Lashley then went to Johns Hopkins University to study for his doctorate in zoology under Herbert S. Jennings. He elected a minor in psychology with John B. WATSON, the founder of BEHAVIORISM. His work with Watson convinced him to make his career in psychology. This was the critical time in Lashley's development as a scientist. In his own words:

> In 1914, John Watson called attention to a seminar in the French edition of Pavlov's book on the conditioned reflex. In that winter the seminar was devoted to the translation and discussion of the book. In the spring I served as an unpaid assistant and we constructed apparatus and did experiments, repeating a number of Pavlov's experiments. Our whole program was then disrupted by the move to the lab in Meyer's Clinic. There were no adequate animal quarters there. Watson started work with infants as the next best material available. I tagged along for awhile but disliked the babies and found me a rat lab in another building. We accumulated a considerable amount of experimental material on the conditioned reflex that was never published. Watson sought the basis of a systematic psychology and was not greatly concerned with the reaction itself. (Letter from K. S. Lashley to Ernest Hilgard, ca. 1930; reprinted with the kind permission of Professor Hilgard.)

Ivan PAVLOV's conditioned reflex formed the basis of Watson's behaviorism. Lashley, on the other hand, became interested in the physiology of the reaction and the attempt to trace conditioned reflex paths through the central nervous system.

Over the next several years Lashley collaborated with Shepherd Franz, who was then at St. Elizabeth's Hospital in Washington, D.C. Their research, examining effects of lesions of the frontal cortex on learning abilities in the rat, set the tone of his major work. In 1920 Lashley accepted an assistant professorship at the University of Minnesota and began in earnest his search for the memory trace. He was made full professor at Minnesota in 1924, and in 1926 moved to the University of Chicago, where he became a professor in 1929. In this same year he was president of the American Psychological Association and published his monograph *Brain Mechanisms and Intelligence.* In 1935 Lashley accepted a professorship at Harvard, and in 1937 he was appointed research professor of neuropsychology with nominal teaching duties, which made it possible for him to accept the directorship of the Yerkes Laboratories of Primate Biology in Orange Park, Florida, in 1942. He held both these positions, spending only a few weeks a year at Harvard (he was not overly fond of formal teaching), until his death in 1958.

Lashley devoted many years to an analysis of brain mechanisms of learning, using the lesion-behavior method that he developed and elaborated from the work with Franz. During this period, Lashley's theoretical view of learning was heavily influenced by two widely held notions: localization of function in neurology and behaviorism in psychology.

Localization of function, the notion that each psychological "trait" or function has a specific locus of representation, a particular place, in the brain, was perhaps the major intellectual issue concerning brain organization at the beginning of the twentieth century. An extreme form of localization was popular early in the nineteenth century in "phrenology." The field of neurology then moved away from that position, though the discovery of a speech center began to move the pendulum back. Work in the last three decades of the nineteenth century identified the general locations of the motor, visual, and auditory regions of the cerebral cortex. Localization of function appeared to be winning the day.

In Watson's behaviorism, the learning of a particular response was held to involve the formation of a particular set of connections, a series set. Consequently, Lashley argued, it should be possible to localize the place in the cerebral cortex where that learned change in brain organization, the engram (memory trace), was stored. It was generally believed at the time, consistent with Pavlov's view, that learning was coded in the cerebral cortex. Thus, behaviorism and localization of function were very consistent; they supported the notion of an elaborate and complex switchboard on which specific and localized changes occurred in the cerebral cortex when specific habits were learned.

Lashley systematically set about finding the places in the cerebral cortex where learning occurred—the engrams—in an extensive series of studies culminating in his 1929 monograph. In this research he used mazes of differing difficulty and made lesions of varying sizes in different regions of the cerebral cortex of the rat. The results profoundly altered Lashley's view of brain organization and had an extraordinary impact on the young field of physiological psychology: The locus of the lesion was unimportant; the size was critically important, particularly for the difficult mazes. These findings led to Lashley's notions of *equipotentiality* (locus not important) and *mass action* (size critical). (See LOCALIZATION OF MEMORY TRACES.)

Subsequently, Lashley focused on a detailed analysis of the role of the cerebral cortex in vision and in visual discrimination learning and memory. But his interests and research included much more than this: classic work on the cytoarchitectonics (microscopic structure) of the cerebral cortex, a brilliant analysis of the problem of serial order in human language and thought, and a penetrating analysis of the biological substrates of motivation. Lashley, more than any other scientist, shaped and developed the field of physiological psychology.

It is fitting to close with Lashley's own summing up of the search for the memory trace, written in 1950:

This series of experiments has yielded a good bit of information about what and where the memory trace is not. It has discovered nothing directly of the real nature of the memory trace. I sometimes feel, in reviewing the evidence of the localization of the memory trace, that the necessary conclusion is that learning is just not possible. It is difficult to conceive of a mechanism that can satisfy the conditions set for it. Nevertheless, in spite of such evidence against it, learning sometimes does occur.

REFERENCES

Lashley, K. S. (1929). *Brain mechanisms and intelligence: A quantitative study of injuries to the brain.* Chicago: University of Chicago Press.

——— (1935). The mechanism of vision: XII. Nervous structures concerned in the acquisition and retention of habits based on reactions to light. *Comparative Psychology Monographs 11,* 43–79.

——— (1950). In search of the engram. *Society of Experimental Biology, Symposium 4,* 454–482.

Orbach, J., ed. (1982). *Neuropsychology after Lashley.* Hillsdale, N. J.: Erlbaum.

Richard F. Thompson

LEARNED HELPLESSNESS

The term *learned helplessness* is used to refer to any behavioral or physiological consequence of exposure to an aversive event that is produced not by the event itself but by the organism's *lack of behavioral control* over the event. By *behavioral control* is meant the organism's ability to alter the onset, termination, duration, intensity, or temporal pattern of the event. If the event (e.g., a loud noise, a painful electric shock, an attack by another animal or person) can be altered by some behavioral response, then the organism has some control over the event. If there is nothing that the organism can do to change the event, then the event is uncontrollable.

This concept has been studied using an experimental paradigm called the *triadic design.* Here one subject, say a rat, is given control over the event, say a mild electric shock, delivered to the rat's tail. The rat is exposed to a number of shocks, and performing some behavioral response, say pushing a lever with its paws, terminates each of the shocks. This rat thus has control over the termination of each shock. A second rat is placed in a similar apparatus, but this rat does not have control. Each shock begins for this rat at the same instant as it does for the rat with control, but for this second rat pushing the lever has no consequence. Each shock terminates whenever the rat with control presses the lever. Thus both rats receive identical shocks, but one has behavioral control and the other does not. A third rat is merely placed in the apparatus and receives no shock. Subsequent behavior and physiological functioning can be examined, and it is possible to determine which changes are caused by the stressor per se (here the animals with and without control would be identical and differ from the nonshocked controls), and which are a function of the controllability of the stressor (here the animals with and without control would differ).

The use of this sort of experimental design has revealed that many of the consequences which are normally thought to be produced by stressors are actually determined by the controllability/uncontrollability of the stressor rather than by mere exposure to the stressor. Three kinds of behavioral changes follow exposure to stressors, but only if they are uncontrollable.

The first type is *cognitive changes.* A particularly important consequence of exposure to uncontrollable aversive events has come to be called the *learned helplessness effect.* This refers to the fact that organisms ranging from fish to humans fail to learn to escape and avoid aversive events such as electric shocks, loud noises, and cold water after an initial exposure to aversive events that are uncontrollable (Overmier and Seligman, 1967). A great deal of research has been conducted to determine why this learning deficit occurs, and it has been found that at least part of the reason is cognitive. Uncontrollable aversive events interfere with some of the information-processing steps required to learn relationships between behavior and outcomes (Maier, 1989).

The second type is *motivational changes.* The motivation to obtain many of the reinforcers that are normally important for that organism is undermined. For example, a rat that is exposed to uncontrollable shock (but not to equal amounts of controllable shock) does not later compete for food, becomes inactive, and shows decreased sexual and maternal behavior.

The third type is *emotional changes.* Uncontrollable aversive events lead to increases in aspects of emotionality such as fear and anxiety. Physiological indicants of stress such as ulcer formation and blood pressure increases are similarly influenced by the controllability/uncontrollability dimension.

A considerable amount of research has been devoted to uncovering the behavioral and physiological mechanisms that produce these learned helplessness effects. This fact is at least in part attributable to the resemblance between the consequences of uncontrollable stressors in animals and human depression. Indeed, what is now known about the substrates of learned helplessness is remarkably similar to what is thought to underlie human depression (Weiss and Simson, 1986).

REFERENCES

Maier, S. F. (1989). Learned helplessness: Event co-variation and cognitive changes. In S. B. Klein and R. R. Mowrer, eds., *Contemporary learning theories,* pp. 73–109. Hillsdale, N.J.: Erlbaum.

Overmier, J. B., and Seligman, M. E. P. (1967). Effects of inescapable shock upon subsequent escape and avoidance behavior. *Journal of Comparative Physiology and Psychology 63,* 23–33.

Weiss, J. M., and Simson, P. G. (1986). Depression in an animal model: Focus on the locus coeruleus. In R. Porter, G. Bock, and S. Clark, eds., *Antidepressants and receptor function,* pp. 191–216. New York: Wiley.

Steven F. Maier

LEARNING CURVE

See Repetition and Learning

LEARNING DISABILITIES

[*The phase* learning disabilities *generally refers to difficulties with specific types of learning, as distinct from* MENTAL RETARDATION, *which is the subject of a separate article. This entry consists of two articles examining learning disabilities from different points of view:* Cognitive Aspects *and* Neurological Aspects.]

Cognitive Aspects

In 1896 Pringle Morgan reported the case of a 14-year-old boy who, despite normal intelligence, educational opportunity, and desire, appeared to have serious trouble learning to read. Morgan and his colleague James Hinshelwood (Hinshelwood, 1895, 1917) called this disorder *word blindness* and attributed the problem to neurologic impairments in a part of the left hemisphere of the cortex called the angular gyrus (see Figure 1), basing their ideas on contemporary studies of brain-damaged patients whose reading skills had been lost or impaired (Déjerine, 1892). Today most scientists and physicians use the term *dyslexia,* coined in 1887, instead of *word blindness* to describe severe reading problems, although some professionals prefer the term *specific reading disability.* When brain damage is known to exist, either through physical examination by a neurologist or by radiological evidence from a CT or MRI brain scan, the disorder is called *acquired dyslexia.* However, if no definitive neurological signs are found, the term *developmental dyslexia* is used, with the understanding that the individual was probably born with some neurological abnormality that cannot be identified but that nevertheless has a major effect on the ability to learn to read.

Since Morgan's time other disorders besides dyslexia have been recognized that affect the development of children's academic and social skills; they include *language disorders, developmental disabilities in writing and mathematics, social skill deficits,* and *attentional deficits/hyperactivity disorders (ADHD).* A child with a language disorder develops normally in all areas except language. Most develop academic problems including dyslexia when they reach school age (Tallal, 1988). Writing disabilities include problems with handwriting, spelling, written syntax, and the composition process itself, involving prewriting and revising activities. Studies of mathematical impairments have identified problems in logical reasoning, mathematical terminology, visual-spatial factors, and arithmetic strategies. Recently increased attention has been devoted to the study of how children learn to interact socially and to the identification of children who, because of learning problems, have social incompetencies. Children with ADHD have behavioral problems of inattention, impulsivity, and hyperactivity. Although ADHD is specifically considered not to be a learning problem, it is usually included in any discussion of school-related problems because it affects classroom performance and because there is substantial co-occurrence between ADHD and the other disorders already mentioned.

With the exception of ADHD all of these developmental problems collectively are called *learning disabilities,* a term that first gained popularity from a talk given by Samuel Kirk in 1963 (see Kirk and Becker, 1963). They are disorders that are considered to be congenital or intrinsic to the individual, probably the result of abnormal development in the central nervous system. It is no coincidence that the classification scheme for learning disabilities reflects the emphasis placed on reading, writing, arithmetic, and good behavior in school. If art, music, and physical education were the core subjects of the elementary school curriculum, we would undoubtedly be working with a different set of learning disabilities (Geschwind, 1984).

Diagnostic Considerations

Diagnosing learning disabilities in children is problematic for several reasons. First, no test exists that can positively identify each of the different disorders, and so the diagnosis is made by using exclusionary criteria, that is, ruling out other potential reasons for academic difficulties. In its report to Congress (Kavanagh and Truss, 1988), the National Conference on Learning Disabilities stated:

> Even though a learning disability may occur concomitantly with other handicapping conditions (e.g., sensory impairment, mental retardation, social and emotional disturbance), with socioenvironmental influences (e.g., cultural differences, insufficient or inappropriate instruction, psychogenic factors), and

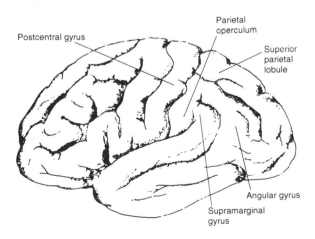

Figure 1. Diagram of the left hemisphere of the cortex.

especially with attention deficit disorder, all of which may cause learning problems, a learning disability is not the direct result of those conditions or influences. (pp. 550–551)

Second, the diagnosis of academic and linguistic disorders, such as dyslexia, is based upon how well a child does on various standardized tests of reading, arithmetic, or written and spoken language as compared with estimates of his or her general cognitive abilities. Although some have argued that intelligence is not a single entity to be measured (Gould, 1981), a commonly held view is that intelligence and other academic abilities are normally distributed throughout the population. A few people are very bright and excellent readers, most are average, and a few are mentally retarded and read poorly. If a child performs below average on an intelligence test, then reading problems are considered to be related to intelligence, an idea sometimes expressed in the phrase *backward reader*. In situations where the discrepancy between intelligence and reading scores is not severe (e.g., less than one and a half to two standard deviations), these children are considered to be *poor readers* who chance to fall at the lower end of the normal distribution of reading ability.

A final diagnostic problem concerns actual classroom performance. School districts adopt different expectations for academic achievement based on economic and social factors in the local community. Generally, a child will not be diagnosed by school personnel as having a learning disability if he or she is making adequate educational progress in the classroom. Consequently, a bright student who is performing below his or her intellectual potential in reading nevertheless may be making adequate progress when compared with other students of average ability. Even though such a child may be dyslexic, he or she is unlikely to be eligible for special educational services in most schools.

Such variable diagnostic criteria can lead to geographical and study-related differences in reporting the incidence of dyslexia. The public school systems reported almost 4 percent of school-aged children were diagnosed as learning disabled in 1982–1983 (Office of Special Education, 1984). However, there were big regional differences. For example, 63 percent of all educationally handicapped children in Rhode Island were classified as learning disabled, compared with only 26 percent in Alabama (Keogh, 1986). In contrast, a review of several comprehensive prevalence studies

suggests that about 15 percent of elementary school children are academically underachieving, and that about half of these children (roughly 7 percent) have some type of learning disability (Gaddes, 1985).

A related problem is found in the reporting of gender differences. Many studies have reported dyslexia to occur three to four times more frequently in boys than in girls (Johnson, 1988). However, other investigators (DeFries, 1989) have argued that large gender differences may be the result of sampling biases, suggesting that even in carefully controlled studies different selection criteria can have a profound effect on the characteristics of the study sample.

Cognitive Impairments in Dyslexia

The different types of learning disabilities are organized around general behavioral domains or specific academic skills. Space does not permit a description and analysis of the cognitive dysfunctions of each disorder. Historically, dyslexia has received the most attention, and so the focus of this section will be to review the cognitive skills involved in reading and those deficits associated with dyslexia. An excellent review of the other disorders can be found in Kavanagh and Truss (1988).

Reading is an extremely complicated behavior to learn, requiring years of formal instruction and practice. Despite some eloquent claims to the contrary (Goodman and Goodman, 1979), there is little evidence to suggest that reading comes naturally. The demands of the task vary depending upon the skill of the reader and the written material. Fluent readers spend most of their effort comprehending the text; novice readers spend their time sounding out words; and for prereaders the task is more perceptually oriented, involving the recognition of different visual patterns that make up the letters of the alphabet.

Many different cognitive skills are involved in these various tasks. Letter recognition requires developing a memory for the letter patterns and the ability to compare the text with the memory. Sounding out words requires learning the correct pronunciation for the letter sounds, called *phonemes*, and recognizing the different ways letters are pronounced in word contexts (e.g., the short vowel *i* in *mint* versus the long vowel *i* in *pint*). Some words are so distinctive that people must recognize them by sight and not by sound (e.g., yacht or colonel) and memorize a sight vocabulary. Sounding out words and comprehending text places demands on children's *short-term memory* skills to retain information as it is extracted from the text. Children's spoken vocabulary also is important. Their knowledge of the meanings of words and how they can be used, collectively called *lexical memory,* is very important to reading comprehension.

With so many different processing mechanisms involved, there are many possible ways for reading development to be disrupted. Although dyslexia historically has been considered to have a unitary cause (Hinshelwood, 1917), and many modern researchers have proposed their own unifying theories (e.g., Vellutino, 1979, Jorm, 1979), another approach has been to treat dyslexia as a heterogeneous group made up of several different subtypes (Malatesha and Dougan, 1982). Most of the subtyping research has focused either on the study of reading error patterns (Boder, 1973; Doehring and Hoshko, 1977; Temple, 1984) or on the analysis of neuropsychological correlations using test procedures derived from studies of brain-damaged patients (Mattis, French, and Rapin, 1975; Petrauskas and Rourke, 1979).

A review of the literature suggests that most studies have identified three subtypes of dyslexia (Malatesha and Dougan, 1982). Most of the studies reported a linguistic deficit subtype that includes a lack of awareness for phoneme segments, inability or slowness in accessing lexical memory, and problems with organizing verbal information in short-term memory (Liberman, 1983). Some dyslexic children also appear to suffer from *visual-spatial impairments,* although this type of problem appears to be more infrequent. Lovegrove and his colleagues (1986) reported two types of perceptual deficits for a selected dyslexic group: their processing speed is slower, so that it takes them longer to analyze visual features of letters; and the afterimage of a display, its *visual persistence,* lingers for a longer period of time, so that when their eyes move from one word to the next, there is perceptual interference. A third subtype found in several studies has articulation and motor problems affecting speech and handwriting. Many other subtypes have been proposed, including comparisons of acquired and developmental dyslexia (Marshall, 1989).

Most of these associated impairments are correlational, that is, there is no direct evidence to show

these cognitive deficits are producing the reading problems. Some studies, however, have demonstrated early phoneme awareness training to be effective in preventing reading problems (Ball and Blachman, 1988; Bradley and Bryant, 1983). The variety of cognitive impairments associated with dyslexia suggests that it may have many underlying causes, although without a theoretical framework that can relate these cognitive deficits to the reading process, we are not really sure of their significance.

Cognitive Models of Dyslexia

Several researchers have attempted to construct models that describe the way these cognitive processes work together in reading. Two kinds of reading models have been proposed. In one type, called the *serial box model,* each processing task is organized into separate and highly specialized subsystems (usually drawn as boxes in the model) that

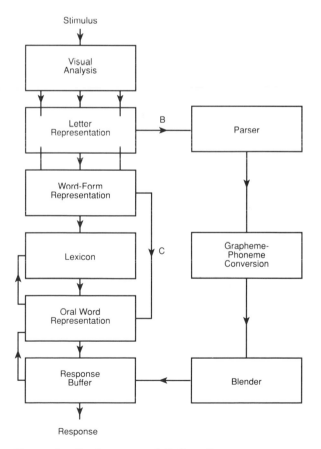

Figure 2. Dual-route model of reading.

work much like an assembly line. Information flows in one direction (illustrated by arrows); each subsystem waits its turn, taking the output from the unit upstream and passing its output to the next unit downstream. An example of this type is the *dual-route reading model* of Newcombe and Marshall (1984). This model (see Figure 2) has two ways in which the mind recognizes words. Familiar words are handled by a *lexical reading route* that retrieves from memory the correct pronunciation based on the way the word looks. Unfamiliar words are processed in a different system, called the *phonological reading route,* that breaks the word into phonemes and then sounds it out, using rules acquired from spelling experience. In this model,

dyslexic children with linguistic deficits affecting their phonemic awareness have phonologic deficits, whereas those who have visual-spatial problems or trouble accessing lexical information have abnormalities in the lexical system (Marshall, 1989).

An alternative modeling strategy employs very simple processing units that are highly interconnected. In these *connectionist models* processing is broadly distributed across many units, with information flowing upstream and downstream at the same time. An example of such a model, called the *interactive activation model of reading* (IA), is illustrated in Figure 3. Like the dual-route system, the IA model analyzes words by how they look

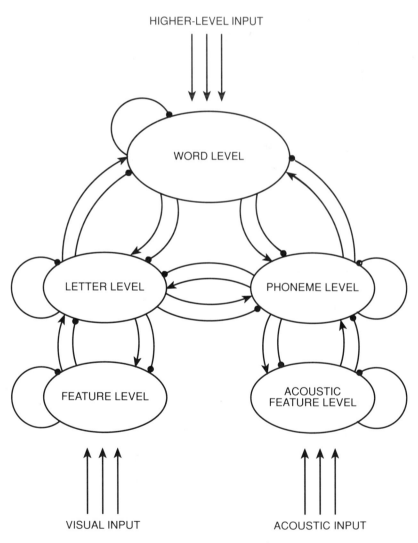

Figure 3. Interactive activation model of reading. Lines ending with arrows represent excitation and dots indicate inhibition. *Reproduced with permission from McClelland and Rumelhart, 1981.*

and sound; however, because information is distributed throughout the IA network, the system functions together as one unit. One advantage of the connectionist model is that sets of rules for decoding unfamiliar words are not necessary because cross talk between processing units creates patterns of activation that constrain the set of possible pronunciations, giving the appearance of rule-like behavior (see Van Orden, Pennington, and Stone, 1990). Understanding the nature of dyslexic impairments in connectionist models is somewhat complicated by the fact that much of the work is shared by the whole system, making it difficult to ascribe a dyslexic impairment to any one processing component. Two studies of connectionist models suggest that dyslexic children may have fewer processing units available (Seidenberg and McClelland, 1989), and that the degree of cross talk between units may be impaired (Chase and Tallal 1990).

(See also PARALLEL DISTRIBUTED PROCESSING MODELS OF MEMORY.)

Conclusion

Future research will continue to focus on identifying better diagnostic subtypes of the different learning disabilities, with particular emphasis on distinguishing the learning disabled from other underachievers. Working with models that are biologically more plausible also is an important goal. Without a theoretical framework to guide the interpretation of the data, it is difficult to build a bridge between our understanding of the structural abnormalities found in the dyslexic brain and the functional impairments associated with specific reading disabilities.

REFERENCES

Ball, E., and Blachman, B. (1988). Phoneme segmentation training: Effect on reading readiness. *Annals of Dyslexia 38,* 208–225.

Boder, E. (1973). Developmental dyslexia: A diagnostic based on three atypical reading-spelling patterns. *Development Medicine and Child Neurology 15,* 663–687.

Bradley, L., and Bryant, P. (1983). Categorizing sounds and learning to read—a causal connection. *Nature 301,* 419–421.

Chase, C. H., and Tallal, P. (1990). A developmental, interactive activation model of the word superiority effect. *Journal of Experimental Child Psychology 49,* 448–487.

DeFries, J. C. (1989). Gender ratios in children with reading disability and their affected relatives: A commentary. *Journal of Learning Disabilities 22,* 344–545.

Déjerine, J. (1892). Contribution à l'étude anatomoclinique et clinique des différentes variétés de cécité verbale. *Comptes Rendus des Séances de la Société de Biologie et de Ses Filiales 4,* 61–90.

Doehring, D. G., and Hoshko, I. M. (1977). Classification of reading problems by the Q-technique of factor analysis. *Cortex 13,* 281–294.

Gaddes, W. H. (1985). *Learning disabilities and brain function,* 2nd ed. New York: Springer-Verlag.

Geschwind, N. (1984). The brain of a learning-disabled individual. *Annals of Dyslexia 34,* 319–327.

Goodman, K. S., and Goodman, Y. M. (1979). Learning to read is natural. In L. B. Resnick and P. A. Weaver, eds., *Theory and practice of easy reading.* Hillsdale, N.J.: Erlbaum.

Gould, S. J. (1981). *The mismeasure of man.* New York: Norton.

Hinshelwood, J. (1895). Word-blindness and visual memory. *Lancet 2,* 1564–1570.

——— (1917). *Congenital word-blindness.* London: Lewis.

Johnson, D. (1988). Review of research on specific reading, writing, and mathematics disorders. In J. F. Kavanagh and T. J. Truss, eds., *Learning disabilities: Proceedings of the national conference.* Parkton, Md.: York Press.

Jorm, A. F. (1979). The cognitive and neurological basis of developmental dyslexia: A theoretical framework and review. *Cognition 7,* 19–33.

Kavanagh, J. F., and Truss, T. J., eds. (1988). *Learning disabilities: Proceedings of the national conference.* Parkton, Md.: York Press.

Keogh, B. (1986). Future of the LD field: Research and practice. *Journal of Learning Disabilities 19,* 455–460.

Kirk, S. A., and Becker, W., eds. (1963). *Conference on children with minimal brain impairment.* Urbana: University of Illinois Press.

Liberman, I. Y. (1983). "A language-oriented view of reading and its disabilities." In H. R. Myklebust, ed., *Progress in learning disabilities.* New York: Grune and Stratton.

Lovegrove, W., Martin, F., and Slaghuis, W. (1986). A theoretical and experimental case for a visual deficit in specific reading disability. *Cognitive Neuropsychology 3,* 225–267.

Malatesha, R. N., and Dougan, D. R. (1982). Clinical subtypes of developmental dyslexia: Resolution of an irresolute problem. In R. N. Malatesha and P. G. Aaron, eds., *Reading disorders.* New York: Academic Press.

Marshall, J. C. (1989). The description and interpretation of acquired and developmental reading disorders. In A. M. Galaburda, ed., *From reading to neurons.* Cambridge, Mass.: MIT Press.

Mattis, S., French, J. H., and Rapin, I. (1975). Dyslexia in children and young adults: Three independent neuropsychological syndromes. *Developmental Medicine and Child Neurology 17,* 150–163.

McClelland, J. L., and Rumelhart, D. E. (1981). An interactive activation model of context effects in letter perception: Part 1. An account of basic findings. *Psychological Review 88,* 375–407.

Morgan, W. P. (1896). A case of congenital word-blindness. *British Medical Journal 2,* 1378.

Newcombe, F., and Marshall, J. C. (1984). Varieties of acquired dyslexia: A linguistic approach. *Seminars in Neurology 4,* 181–195.

Office of Special Education (1984). *Sixth annual report to Congress on the implementation of the Education of the Handicapped Act.* Washington, D.C.: U.S. Department of Education.

Petrauskas, R., and Rourke, B. P. (1979). Identification of subgroups of retarded readers: A neuropsychological multivariate approach. *Journal of Clinical Neuropsychology 1,* 17–37.

Seidenberg, M. S., and McClelland, J. L. (1989). A distributed, developmental model of word recognition and naming. *Psychological Review 96,* 523–568.

Tallal, P. (1988). Developmental language disorders. In J. F. Kavanagh and T. J. Truss, eds., *Learning disabilities: Proceedings of the national conference.* Parkton, Md.: York Press.

Temple, C. M. (1984). New approaches to the developmental dyslexias. *Advances in Neurology 42,* 223–232.

Van Orden, G. C., Pennington, B. F., and Stone, G. O. (1990). Word identification in reading and the promise of subsymbolic psycholinguistics. *Psychological Review 97,* 488–522.

Vellutino, F. R. (1979). *Dyslexia: Theory and research.* Cambridge, Mass.: MIT Press.

Chris Chase
Paula A. Tallal

NEUROLOGICAL ASPECTS

The term *learning disabilities* typically describes disorders that interfere with academic success because of an underlying difficulty with one or more of the skills that support language functioning. Among early terms for learning disability were *minimal brain damage* and *minimal brain dysfunction.* The use of these terms reflected the belief that the behavioral deficits were due to a brain-based disorder. With the availability of noninvasive methods for studying the human brain, researchers have begun to explore the relation between behavior and neurobiology of learning disabilities. Recent investigations have provided evidence that the brains of learning-disabled individuals differ both structurally and functionally from those of individuals without the disorder.

Behavior and Neurobiology

Whatever their neurobiological correlates, learning disabilities are defined in terms of behavioral characteristics. The Education for All Handicapped Children Act (PL 94–142), which mandates identification and appropriate education for learning-disabled students in the United States, includes the following definition:

> "Specific learning disability" means a disorder in one or more of the basic psychological processes involved in understanding or in using language, spoken or written, which may manifest itself in an imperfect ability to listen, think, speak, read, write, spell, or to do mathematical calculations. The term includes such conditions as perceptual handicaps, brain injury, minimal brain dysfunction, dyslexia, and developmental aphasia. The term does not include children who have learning problems which are primarily the result of visual, hearing, or motor handicaps, of mental retardation, or emotional disturbance, or of environmental, cultural, or economic disadvantage. (Sec. 620, 89 Stat. 773, 794 [1975])

This definition includes children who carry a variety of labels that indicate the presence of language-based deficits. Groups of children who carry different labels within the learning disabilities spectrum do not necessarily represent different behavioral or biological groups. Indeed, a boy who is identified as "specifically language impaired" at age three is typically relabeled "learning disabled" by the public school system as language deficits impact on academic success after age six. If he later transfers to a private school that specializes in the remediation of reading difficulties, the same child may be relabeled "dyslexic." Because one child can carry multiple labels, the different labels do not necessarily reflect differences in either behavior or neurobiology.

The converse of this situation is that individuals with similar behavioral profiles, according to test scores, do not always represent the same biological group. Decker and Bender (1988) illustrated this principle by showing that reading deficits associated with a known genetic abnormality (Klinefelter syndrome) result in test scores similar to those associated with the reading deficits of learning-disabled individuals who lack the genetic abnormality. In addition, there was heterogeneity of test scores within each group, indicating that similar biological backgrounds can result in a range of skill levels. The sophisticated investigator acknowledges that the relation between the behavioral profiles and biological profiles is not one-to-one. Although there are a multitude of systems for subgrouping learning-disabled individuals, little information exists as to whether these classifications reflect distinct biological subgroups or one, more general biological effect that differs in its degree of severity.

Brain Anatomy and Learning Disabilities

Anatomical studies focus on the structure of the brain. The gross structure of the brain, as well as its microscopic, cellular structure, can be examined at autopsy. Although there have been only a handful of autopsy studies on individuals with learning disabilities (most recently Cohen, Campbell, and Yaghmai, 1989; Galaburda et al., 1985; Humphreys, Kaufmann, and Galaburda, 1990), some characteristic findings have emerged. Examination typically does not reveal brain damage that might have been caused by illness or injury during childhood. This "nonfinding" is important because it suggests that early notions that learning disabilities reflect overt or minimal brain *damage*, similar to acquired disorders in adults, must be revised. Instead, autopsy examinations have suggested an altered pattern of brain development. Across studies, microscopic abnormalities have been found in both cerebral hemispheres which suggest that neurons that typically develop and migrate to form the layers of the brain's cortex became misplaced during the prenatal period.

In addition to these cellular-level findings, there is a characteristic alteration of the brain's gross anatomy. Several anatomical regions in the left hemisphere support normal language functioning in most people. One of these regions, the planum

temporale, typically is larger in the left hemisphere than in the right (Geschwind and Levitsky, 1967). In the brains of individuals with learning disabilities examined at autopsy, these areas in the left and right hemispheres lacked the typical pattern of asymmetry. This is additional evidence for altered brain development, because asymmetries of the plana temporale are set before birth and remain constant across different ages through adulthood (Chi, Dooling, and Gilles, 1977a, 1977b; Wada, Clarke, and Hamm, 1975).

Autopsy studies are limited both by the few cases and by the typical paucity of behavioral information available for these cases. Both of these limitations can be addressed by brain imaging studies. Anatomical regions can be measured from the brain scans of individuals whose learning disabilities have been carefully documented. Currently, the best available images of brain anatomy are produced by magnetic resonance imaging (MRI). Several MRI studies (Hynd et al., 1990; Larsen et al., 1990; Plante et al., 1991) have demonstrated that children with learning disabilities have atypical asymmetries involving brain regions associated with language skills. Atypical asymmetries, along with language difficulties, occur in the parents and siblings of children with learning disabilities (Plante, 1991). This finding suggests that heritable factors, rather than poor rearing practices, account for the familial constellations of learning disabilities reported in several studies (e.g., DeFries et al., 1978; Tomblin, 1989; Tallal, Ross, and Curtiss, 1989).

Brain Physiology and Learning Disabilities

Physiological studies address the brain's functioning under different conditions. Brain functioning can be conceptualized as occurring along a continuum that ranges from basic, nonvolitional activity to complex, cognitive processing. The brain functioning of learning-disabled individuals has been sampled at several points along this continuum. At the basic end is the brain's ongoing pattern of activity "at rest." This has been studied by measuring cerebral blood flow (an indirect measure of brain metabolism) and electrical activity (an indirect measure of neural activation). In blood flow studies, children with language deficits, many of whom also had attentional problems, showed physiological differences from normally developing subjects in both hemispheres of the brain, including those regions associated with language functioning (Denays et al., 1989; Lou, Henriksen, and Bruhn, 1984). Electrophysiological studies of ongoing brain activity have found differences between learning-disabled and normally developing subjects (e.g., Ahn et al., 1980; Duffy and McAnulty, 1990; Pinkerton, Watson, and McClelland, 1989). Differences in brain wave activity can be recorded at many sites on the scalp of the resting individual. Some have taken this as an indication of widespread brain dysfunction. Such interpretations should be considered tentative because electrical activity can be measured at various scalp sites that are distant from the brain area generating that activity.

In addition to measures of resting state, responses to stimulation have been measured electrically from the early, automatic stages of processing in the brain stem to later stages that reflect cognitive, cortical-level processing. Early, brain-stem responses to auditory signals have been studied by several investigators (e.g., Grillon, Courchesne, and Akshoomoff, 1989; Marosi, Harmony, and Becker, 1990; Mason and Mellor, 1984). The auditory brain-stem response studies did not find differences in the amplitude (corresponding degree of synchronous electrical activity at a given point in time) and peak latency (time at which peaks of activity occur) in learning-disabled subjects compared with control subjects. One study (Marosi et al., 1990) found subtle differences between the learning-disabled subjects and control subjects in the way that several components of the brainstem response interrelated in a statistical factor analysis. Similarly, studies of the earliest cortical responses to auditory signals have not yet documented between-group differences in brain response (Grillon, Courchesne, and Akshoomoff, 1989; Mason and Mellor, 1984).

In contrast with the earlier components of brain response, differences between subject groups have been demonstrated for the later, more cognitively mediated components. When subjects are given tasks that involve attending to, anticipating, and selecting certain stimuli from a train of ongoing stimuli, a characteristic wave form can be recorded electrically. Several studies have found differences in this wave form in terms of its peak amplitude or its peak latency (e.g., Courchesne et al., 1989; Holcomb, Ackerman, and Dykman, 1985; Taylor and Keenan, 1990). These group differences have been elicited in response to a variety of stimuli, including pure tones, spoken words, written let-

ters, written words, and written nonletter symbols. The use of such diverse stimuli across studies illustrates that the altered brain physiology in groups of learning-disabled subjects is not specific to one sensory modality, or to language tasks alone. These individuals' brain responses appear altered even in response to relatively simple stimuli, in addition to the more complex, linguistic stimuli.

Conclusion

Across studies that vary in terms of method, stimuli, and level of processing some basic conclusions can be drawn. First, there is evidence that the brains of individuals with learning disabilities function differently than those of individuals without learning disabilities. To some extent, these functional differences probably relate to the underlying structural differences in the brains of learning-disabled individuals. Additional factors, such as the use of compensatory skills and experience-based neural reorganization, probably also play a role in producing differences in the patterns of brain activity. Brain structure, brain function, and behavior are interdependent, and each must be understood in order to appreciate fully the nature of learning disabilities.

REFERENCES

Ahn, H., Prichep, L., John, E. R., Baird, H., Trepetin, M., and Kaye, H. (1980). Developmental equations reflect brain function. *Science 210,* 1259–1262.

Chi, J. C., Dooling, E. C., and Gilles, F. H. (1977a). Left-right asymmetries of the temporal speech areas of the human fetus. *Archives of Neurology 34,* 346–348.

——— (1977b). Gyral development of the human brain. *Annals of Neurology 1,* 86–93.

Cohen, M., Campbell, R., and Yaghmai, F. (1989). Neuropathological abnormalities in developmental dysphasia. *Annals of Neurology 25,* 567–570.

Courchesne, E., Lincoln, A. J., Yeung-Courchesne, R., Elmasian, R., and Grillon, C. (1989). Pathophysiologic findings in nonretarded autism and receptive developmental language disorder. *Journal of Autism and Developmental Disorders 19,* 1–17.

Decker, S. N., and Bender, B. G. (1988). Converging evidence for multiple genetic forms of reading disability. *Brain and Language 33,* 197–215.

DeFries, J. C., Singer, S. M., Foch, T. T., and Lewitter,

F. I. (1978). Familial nature of reading disability. *British Journal of Psychiatry 132,* 361–367.

Denays, R., Tondeur, M., Foulon, M., Verstraeten, F., Ham, H., Piepsz, A., and Noel, P. (1989). Regional brain flow in congenital dysphasia: Studies with tecnetium-99m HM-PAO SPECT. *Journal of Nuclear Medicine 30,* 1825 1829.

Duffy, F. H., and McAnulty, G. (1990). Neurophysiological heterogeneity and the definition of dyslexia: Preliminary evidence for plasticity. *Neuropsychologia 28,* 555–571.

Galaburda, A. M., Sherman, G. F., Rosen, G. D., Aboitiz, F., and Geschwind, N. (1985). Developmental dyslexia: Four consecutive patients with cortical anomalies. *Annals of Neurology 18,* 222–233.

Geschwind, N., and Levitsky, W. (1967). Human brain: Asymmetries in temporal speech region. *Science 161,* 186–187.

Grillon, C., Courchesne, E., and Akshoomoff, N. (1989). Brainstem and middle latency auditory evoked potentials in autism and developmental language disorder. *Journal of Autism and Developmental Disorders 19,* 255–269.

Holcomb, P. J., Ackerman, P. T., and Dykman, R. A. (1985). Cognitive event-related brain potentials in children with attention and reading deficits. *Psychophysiology 22,* 656–667.

Humphreys, P., Kaufmann, W. E., and Galaburda, A. M. (1990). Developmental dyslexia in women: Neuropathological findings in three patients. *Annals of Neurology 28,* 727–738.

Hynd, G. W., Semrud-Clikeman, M., Lorys, A. R., Novey, E. S., and Eliopulos, D. (1990). Brain morphology in developmental dyslexia and attention deficit disorder/hyperactivity. *Archives of Neurology 47,* 919–926.

Larsen, J. P., Hoien, T., Lundberg, I., and Odegaard, H. (1990). MRI evaluation of the size and symmetry of the planum temporale in adolescents with developmental dyslexia. *Brain and Language 39,* 289–301.

Lou, H. C., Henriksen, L., and Bruhn, P. (1984). Focal cerebral hypoperfusion in children with dysphasia and/or attention deficit disorder. *Archives of Neurology 41,* 825–829.

Marosi, E., Harmony, T., and Becker, J. (1990). Brainstem evoked potentials in learning disabled children. *International Journal of Neuroscience 50,* 233–242.

Mason, S. M., and Mellor, D. H. (1984). Brainstem, middle latency and late cortical evoked potentials in children with speech and language disorders. *Electroencephalography and Clinical Neurophysiology 59,* 297–309.

Pinkerton, F., Watson, D. R., and McClelland, R. J. (1989). A neurophysiological study of children with reading, writing, and spelling difficulty. *Developmental Medicine and Child Neurology 31,* 569–581.

Plante, E. (1991). MRI findings in the parents and siblings of specifically language-impaired boys. *Brain and Language 41,* 67–80.

Plante, E., Swisher, L., Vance, R., and Rapcsak, S. (1991).

MRI findings in boys with specific language impairment. *Brain and Language 41,* 52–66.

Tallal, P., Ross, R., and Curtiss, S. (1989). Familial aggregation in specific language impairment. *Journal of Speech and Hearing Disorders 54,* 167–173.

Taylor, M. J., and Keenan, N. K. (1990). Event related potentials to visual and language stimuli in normal dyslexic children. *Psychophysiology 27,* 318–327.

Tomblin, B. (1989). Familial concentration of developmental language impairment. *Journal of Speech and Hearing Disorders 54,* 287–295

Wada, J. A., Clarke, R., and Hamm, A. (1975). Cerebral hemispheric asymmetry in humans. *Archives of Neurology 32,* 239–246.

Elena Plante

LEARNING THEORY

Even before psychology became an experimental science in the 1890s, learning was an important part of it. But there came a time in the 1910s when psychologists started to become fascinated by learning concepts and learning theories. The 1930s and 1940s are sometimes called the golden age of learning theory; that was when learning was the heart and soul of psychology. And then gradually the gold began to lose its glitter. The theorists did not seem able to settle their differences of opinion, psychologists began to think that the differences were only a matter of opinion with little empirical significance, and there emerged a growing distaste for the great debates over fundamental issues. In the 1960s new procedures and new phenomena were discovered that led psychologists away from the basic issues that the learning theorists had debated. Today learning remains an important part of psychology, but the issues are quite different from the classical ones and there is little theorizing in the grand style that characterized the golden age.

British empiricism culminated with the fourth edition of Alexander Bain's *The Senses and the Intellect* (1894). Everything psychological about humans is based on experience and is due to learning, he said. Bain argued that through association, sensations are linked with each other and with responses. He argued further that sensations can arouse ideas, and that when our ideas of pleasure and pain are aroused, they are particularly likely to produce responses. At the same time, Morgan

(1894) reported a number of rather casual learning experiments, interpreting his results very much as Bain had. Morgan had the same reliance upon associationist theory, empiricist philosophy, and the pleasure-pain principle. The difference was that Bain was a philosopher who thought about human knowledge, whereas Morgan was a naturalist who did research with animals. Looking back, it appears that Morgan's orientation was compelling because learning theory turned to the study of animals rather than of human learning, and to experimental studies rather than philosophical speculation.

The first systematic experimental study with animals was Edward THORNDIKE's (1898) puzzle-box experiment. Thorndike simply measured the time it took a cat to pull a string that opened the door of the box so that it could go out and eat. He was struck by the fact that the time scores decreased steadily and smoothly over trials; he never found a sudden improvement in performance. He therefore concluded that the cat was not learning anything about ideas but must be acquiring some sort of direct connection between the stimulus (S) that was present and the response (R) of pulling the string. It must be a direct neural connection between S and R. Thus, at the outset of learning experiments and learning theory, there was a strong commitment to the S-R concept of learning. One attraction of this approach was that it minimized all mentalist concepts; it took the mind out of the picture. It was "scientific."

Thorndike (1911) introduced what he called the Law of Effect, what we now call the law of REINFORCEMENT. Whether an S-R connection is strengthened on a particular trial depends, he argued, upon the environmental effect of the response. If the effect is positive, such as providing the hungry cat with food, then the connection gets stronger. Bain had a similar principle; he said the association will get stronger if the response produces pleasure. But pleasure is a mental concept, and so it had to go. Thorndike's version preserved the reinforcement mechanism but got rid of the mind and everything in it. It also took the control of the organism's behavior away from the organism and put it in the environment. The cat's behavior was totally controlled by the stimuli in the situation and the food.

John B. WATSON (1914) called this approach BEHAVIORISM; it was the ultimate mechanistic psychology. Everything remotely related to the mind was discarded. Even Thorndike's reinforcement mechanism was tainted because a positive effect looked too much like pleasure. In Watson's psychology just the stimulus and response occurring together would create a connection between them. Everything was habit, or what was called learning by contiguity. Thus began two long lines of theorists, the contiguity people and the reinforcement people. Watson also threw out all motivation concepts; hunger became just an internal stimulus, and emotion just a set of fixed responses to certain kinds of stimuli. Watson's behaviorism was appealing because it was so mechanistic and so conceptually simple. At the same time, Watson suggested that to understand anything and everything psychological, one had to start with learning. The description of the fear conditioning of Little Albert (Watson and Rayner, 1920) stated that that is how our personalities take shape. The message, which was believed by many, if not all, psychologists, was that wherever you wanted to go in the field, you had to start with learning theory.

There was, however, one problem that would be significant historically: In order to deal with certain cognitive-looking phenomena, Watson introduced some miniature responses, responses so small that they were basically unobservable. When we first learn to read, we read out loud. As we become practiced enough to read silently, we still move our lips. Ultimately nothing seems to move. But no, Watson asserted, there are still tiny responses in the mouth and throat. And it is the feedback from these small responses that mediates and controls what looks like intelligent or speech-related behavior. So Watson's learning theory, which was so elegantly simple, objective, and scientific, was obliged to hypothesize unobservable little responses.

Edwin GUTHRIE (1935) was a contiguity theorist who followed Watson in rejecting motivation and in other ways. He explained the great complexity and unpredictability of behavior in terms of the complexity of the stimulus situation. At any moment there are potentially millions of stimulus elements that one might respond to or have one's behavior conditioned to. Conditioning itself is simple and sudden, but the effective stimulus situation is impossible to control. So Guthrie's learning theory was forced to hypothesize unobservable little stimuli. The same problem in time caused the demise of Clark L. HULL's theory, which, in order to account for what looked like cognitive behavior, had to hypothesize unobservable little motivation terms, entities called r_G. The Skinnerians are no better off, for all their claims of objectivity and freedom from theory. They talk about self-reinforcement when the organism does something it is not supposed to, and they talk about conditioned (acquired) reinforcement when it does something that looks cognitive. Thus they are hypothesizing unobservable little reinforcers.

When Ivan PAVLOV's work finally became available in English translation in 1927, it seemed vaguely familiar. It reminded readers of Watson's. They shared the same view of how important learning is and how it should be studied. The theory included no motivation, no reinforcement, no mind, and it was all very scientific. Pavlov emphasized inhibition, something that American psychologists had largely ignored but in time found fascinating. What was new was the procedure, the pairing of two stimuli; the bell and the food had to occur together. The critical contingency the experimenter had to control was the timing of the stimuli. With Thorndike's procedure the critical contingency was the relationship between the response and its "effect." The procedural contrast was called by different people Pavlovian vs. trial and error, or classical conditioning vs. instrumental, or respondent vs. operant. There was always the uneasy feeling that while the two procedures were easily distinguished by their defining contingencies, perhaps there were not two separate underlying processes involved.

If there is a variable that one never varies, then one will never see its significance. Pavlov knew that his dogs had to be hungry or they would not salivate, so he always worked with hungry dogs. And so he never saw the significance of motivation. The first learning theorist to stress motivation was Edward TOLMAN (1932). He described a study by his student Tinklepaugh, who was studying monkeys and reinforcing their correct responses with pieces of banana. Occasionally Tinklepaugh would substitute lettuce for the banana; when this happened, the animals threw tantrums and became emotionally upset. Monkeys usually like lettuce and it can certainly be used as a reinforcer, so what had Tinklepaugh encountered here? First, he had the trivial finding that monkeys like banana better than lettuce. Second, he had discovered that monkeys can anticipate receiving, or expect to receive, a particular kind of food. Thus, he had discovered what we call incentive motivation, motivation that depends upon the expected

value of the outcome. Tolman's students also demonstrated effects of drive motivation, motivation that depends on the physiological state of the animal.

Thus, Tolman suddenly introduced two kinds of motivation, one psychological and one physiological, and he had abundant evidence for both kinds. He also challenged other conventional parts of Watsonian behaviorism, such as its mechanistic commitment. He introduced a cognitive language (e.g., "expectancies") in place of connections and neurons. Tolman maintained that animals learn not S-R connections but the predictive significance and value of environmental stimuli, sequences of events (what leads to what), and where things are located in space (a "map" of a maze). In the 1940s Tolman developed the theme that animals learn places rather than responses (see, e.g., Tolman, Ritchie, and Kalish, 1946).

Those were exciting times. There were two paradigms, Pavlovian and Thorndikian, to be organized. One could explain all learning with this one, or that one, or with some of each (Mowrer, 1947). Mowrer attributed emotional and motivational learning to Pavlovian mechanisms, and most other learned behavior to reinforcement. There were contiguity theorists and reinforcement theorists. Some people studied motivation and others ignored it. Some were mechanists, and others appeared very cognitive. Some believed in tiny stimuli or responses, twinkles and twitches, and others looked at behavior globally. And new behavioral phenomena were being discovered at an accelerated rate.

Could anyone put it all together? It seemed that Clark Hull and his dedicated followers might do it; they certainly tried. The great theory (Hull, 1943) was based on the reinforcement of S-R habits, but habits were only indirectly expressed in behavior. To be manifest, a habit had to be motivated by drive and/or incentive, and had to overcome the different kinds of inhibition that might be present. It was a very complex theory, but its virtue was that its complexity promised to match that of the empirical world. It was also a very explicit theory; everything was spelled out in detail. The theory even appeared to be able to explain away some of the mysterious things Tolman had reported. It was full of promise, and it gathered an enormous amount of attention.

Hull was fortunate to have a number of brilliant, energetic young associates who all agreed that this was the right kind of theory. Their disagreements were over details, and those differences called for further experiments to get everything straightened out. One could fuss over details, but all the Hullians endorsed the basic program. Miller and Dollard (1941) proposed a simpler model that anticipated many features of the great theory. Mowrer (1939) anticipated the all-important mechanism of reinforcement; he said a response is reinforced when it results in the reduction of some source of drive, such as fear. Kenneth SPENCE was another early associate of Hull's, and he had a multitude of graduate students who were proud to call themselves neo-Hullians and to work out different aspects of the theory. For them, the 1950s looked like the golden age because it was the time of awakening, the time of promise, and the time of payoff. Many of them moved away from animal learning and into human experimental, social, developmental, and clinical psychology. Learning was the center, but the time had come to apply the principles of behavior far and wide. Watson and Thorndike, the first learning theorists, had promised to build a better world with learning theory, and the neo-Hullians felt that the time had come to make good on that promise.

Two things went wrong. One, which should have been only a minor tactical setback, was that the drive-reduction hypothesis of reinforcement was wrong. That was discovered early on (Sheffield and Roby, 1950), and in his last written work Hull (1952) acknowledged the problem and said the hypothesis might have to be altered. The whole point of theory, according to Hull, is to use it to generate research and then use the research to modify the theory. So the loss of this particular hypothesis should not have hurt the basic Hullian program. But the neo-Hullians were severely wounded and badly discouraged. Furthermore, by about 1970, new difficulties had arisen with the concept of reinforcement itself (Bolles, 1975).

A second difficulty was that during the 1960s there were many problems with incentive motivation. It was based on the little response r_G, which had all the conceptual properties of a response (i.e., it was elicited by stimuli, it was conditionable, and it could be motivated). The problem was that it did not seem to be observable. The r_G concept was needed to account for Tolman's discovery that animals learn places (Hull held that it was elicited by spatial stimuli), and it was needed to explain a variety of other effects; but it was beginning to look like a fiction, a figment. The Hullians said

that when the animal looks to the left, it encounters stimuli that elicit r_G and so it moves in that direction. Tolman said that the animal expects food to be off to the west, and since it is hungry and values food, it moves in that direction. If you cannot measure r_G, then you have no way to test Hull's view against Tolman's view of the situation. Eventually psychologists figured out that Tolman's theory is untestable because one cannot measure expectancies or values, and that Hull's theory is untestable because one cannot measure r_G. Learning theories are basically untestable. The great promise of Hull's theory was slipping away. The golden age was ending.

Some found comfort in B. F. SKINNER's approach. It could have been an alternative learning theory but chose to present itself as theoretically neutral. Certainly Skinnerians did not worry about theoretical matters as such. And they were eager to leave learning behind and move into other areas of psychology and into applied problems. Others began to understand that there was something fundamentally flawed in the whole enterprise begun by Thorndike and Watson. Psychology did not become a science because it exorcised the mind and analyzed everything into atomic S-R units; it became a science as it looked systematically at psychological phenomena. If you want to understand a social phenomenon, then you do not need a basic learning theory; you need to look at social situations, social motivation, and social behavior strategies. And that is the sort of thing psychologists do now.

(See also ASSOCIATIONISM; MATHEMATICAL LEARNING THEORY.)

REFERENCES

Bain, A. (1894). *The senses and the intellect,* 4th ed. London: Longmans, Green.

Bolles, R. C. (1975). *Learning theory.* New York: Holt.

Guthrie, E. R. (1935). *The psychology of learning.* New York: Harper's.

Hull, C. L. (1943). *Principles of behavior.* New York: Appleton.

———— (1952). *A behavior system.* New Haven: Yale University Press.

Miller, N. E., and Dollard, J. (1941). *Social learning and imitation.* New Haven: Yale University Press.

Morgan, C. L. (1894). *An introduction to comparative psychology.* London: Scott.

Mowrer, O. H. (1939). A stimulus-response analysis of

anxiety and its role as a reinforcing agent. *Psychological Review 46*, 553–564.

——— (1947). On the dual nature of learning: A reinterpretation of "conditioning" and "problem-solving." *Harvard Educational Review 17*, 102–148.

Pavlov, I. P. (1927). *Conditioned reflexes*, trans. by G. V. Anrep. London: Oxford University Press.

Sheffield, F. D., and Roby, T. B. (1950). Reward value of a non-nutritive sweet taste. *Journal of Comparative and Physiological Psychology 43*, 461–481.

Thorndike, E. L. (1898). Animal intelligence: An experimental study of the associative processes in animals. *Psychological Review Monograph Supplement*, 2 (no. 8).

——— (1911). *Animal intelligence*. New York: Teachers College Press.

Tolman, E. C. (1932). *Purposive behavior in animals and men*. New York: Century.

Tolman, E. C., Ritchie, B. F., and Kalish, D. (1946). Studies in spatial learning: II. Place learning versus response learning. *Journal of Experimental Psychology 36*, 221–229.

Watson, J. B. (1914). *Behavior: An introduction to comparative psychology*. New York: Holt.

Watson, J. B., and Rayner, R. (1920). Conditioned emotional reactions. *Journal of Experimental Psychology 3*, 1–14.

Robert C. Bolles

LEFT HEMISPHERE

See Material-Specific Memory Deficits

LOCALIZATION OF MEMORY TRACES

The *memory trace*, also termed the *engram*, is the change in the brain that serves to store a memory. As of this writing, the memory trace remains hypothetical, none having been conclusively identified in the human or mammalian brain. Yet all scientists working in the field agree that memory traces must exist. *Learning* refers to changes in behavior as a result of experience. *Memory* refers to the persistence of such changes, which can range from Ivan PAVLOV's dog who learned to salivate at the sound of a bell, to one's memory of a poem, to one's memories of life experiences. The brain consists of a vastly complex set of interconnections among its elements, the neurons. Memory, the result of learning, is expressed in behavioral terms as a *change* in behavior, a change in output to the same sensory input. The bell, the conditioned stimulus, does not initially cause the dog to salivate. After the bell is repeatedly followed by meat powder in the mouth, the bell alone elicits the conditioned response of salivation (classical or Pavlovian conditioning). There must be relatively long-lasting changes in the interconnections or interactions among the neurons in the brain between the auditory input (sound) and the behavioral output (salivation).

In the early days of BEHAVIORISM it was thought that each memory was represented as a change in the brain at one particular place. Karl LASHLEY began the search for the memory trace, stressing the now obvious point that in order to analyze the nature of memory traces, it is necessary to find them. In his classical 1929 monograph, *Brain Mechanisms and Intelligence*, he concluded that memories, at least memories for complex mazes in rats, did not have any particular locus in the cerebral cortex (equipotentiality); the more cortex removed, the more the impairment in memory (mass action). Walter HUNTER was quick to point out that removing more cerebral cortex removed more sensory information (visual, auditory, kinesthetic, etc.), in effect reducing the number of available cues (e.g., animals that are blind do not learn mazes very well). This issue has never really been resolved, at least for complex maze learning in the rat, although we now know that the hippocampus is important for such memories.

Following Lashley's failure to localize memory traces, some scientists adopted the view that they were distributed either widely throughout the brain or widely within certain brain structures like the cerebral cortex. But as more was learned about the anatomical and functional organization of the brain, it became clear that the brain does not have a diffusely distributed organization; instead, it has a highly structured organization. Thus, there are a number of different areas in the posterior region of the cerebral cortex that receive visual information, but each is highly localized and organized. Donald HEBB, in his important and influential book *The Organization of Behavior* (1949), proposed a resolution of this dilemma by assuming that the organization of a memory trace can be complex and involve a number of brain areas but that the trace can involve specific connections in particular areas. This remains a common view today. Hebb also proposed a possible mechanism of memory trace formation that has come to be known as the Hebb synapse. In brief, he argued that at neurons where traces are formed, there must be active input from a to-be-learned source (e.g., conditioned stimulus in Pavlovian terms) at the same time the neuron is firing action potentials. Currently, the Hebb synapse is viewed more generally as a strengthening or weakening of one input (synapses) to a neuron if this input is active concurrent with activation from another input to the neuron. Since no memory traces have been localized definitively in the mammalian brain, the Hebb synapse remains a hypothetical idea.

In recent times, the focus has shifted away from memory traces in complex tasks to more specific and discrete learning and memory tasks, and the emphasis is on identifying the entire circuitries essential (necessary and sufficient) for particular forms of memory. Only after this has been accomplished can the memory traces be localized and analyzed. A great deal of progress has been achieved in the identification of essential memory circuits in the brain. The well-established methods of lesions, electrical recording of neuronal activity, and electrical stimulation of brain tissue, together with anatomical tracing of pathways in the brain, are sufficient to accomplish this task, at least for simpler forms of learning, although the experimental difficulties are formidable. Having accomplished this for a particular form of learning, the next step of localizing the memory trace(s) is orders of magnitude more difficult. Indeed, there are no universally agreed upon methods for doing so. This aspect of the search for memory traces is the conceptual center of the field today.

A distinction is often made between two general categories of memory: declarative (learning "what") and procedural (learning "how") (see CODING PROCESSES: ORGANIZATION OF MEMORY). Many other terms have been suggested for this dichotomy; extreme examples of the two types of memory are your memory of your own recent experiences (declarative) and classical or Pavlovian conditioning, where a specific conditioned response like salivation or eyeblink is learned to a particular conditioned stimulus (procedural). Although both types of memory formation involve many regions of the brain, the brain structures and systems essential for the two types of memories are quite different. Indeed, it is now clear that there are several different memory circuits and systems in the mammalian brain. Some of these

will be noted here; each is treated in a separate article in this volume.

In humans, the hippocampus appears to play a key role in recent experiential memory (declarative). Extensive damage to the hippocampus can markedly impair recent memory in humans and monkeys (see MATERIAL-SPECIFIC MEMORY DEFICITS; AMNESIA, ORGANIC). Current evidence suggests that the impairment is more in the establishing of memories—a process that appears to take weeks in monkeys and may take years in humans—than in their retrieval. In rodents, recent "working" memory and spatial memory are impaired by hippocampal lesions (see WORKING MEMORY: ANIMALS; SPATIAL LEARNING). Very recent or short-term memory in monkeys also involves the prefrontal areas of the cerebral cortex (see PREFRONTAL CORTEX AND MEMORY IN PRIMATES). The thalamus, the largest subdivision of the diencephalon, also plays a role in recent memory in humans. However, long-term permanent memories, for our knowledge and life experiences, are not stored in the hippocampus, prefrontal cortex, or thalamus—and thus are not impaired by damage to these structures. As of this writing we do not know where these long-term memories are stored in the brain; the cerebral cortex is often suggested as the storage site, but there is little evidence.

In contrast with recent visual memory, well-established memories for visual patterns in monkeys are not impaired by hippocampal damage; instead, lesions of visual and visual association areas of the cerebral cortex markedly impair such memories (see PRIMATES, VISUAL PERCEPTION AND MEMORY IN NONHUMAN). But we do not yet know whether these areas simply convey visual information to some other storage sites or are themselves the sites of storage.

Fear conditioning, as in conditioned changes in heart rate and blood pressure following pairing of a tone or light with a painful electric shock, critically involves the hypothalamus and amygdala (see GUIDE TO THE ANATOMY OF THE BRAIN: AMYGDALA; EMOTION, MOOD, AND MEMORY; NEURAL SUBSTRATES OF CLASSICAL CONDITIONING: CARDIOVASCULAR RESPONSES). Much of the circuitry essential for one aspect of learned fear, conditioned potentiation of startle, has been identified; it also includes the amygdala. It is not yet known whether such memories are stored in the amygdala. The amygdala is also critically involved in hormonal modulation of memory storage (see MEMORY CONSOLIDATION; HORMONES AND MEMORY). Most of the circuitry essential for classical conditioning of discrete behavioral responses (e.g., eyeblink, leg flexion) has been identified: It includes the cerebellum and associated brain-stem circuitry (see NEURAL SUBSTRATES OF CLASSICAL CONDITIONING: DISCRETE BEHAVIORAL RESPONSES).

At present the clearest evidence for a high degree of localization of a memory trace exists for classical conditioning of discrete behavioral responses. Evidence grows that for eyeblink conditioning, a particular small region of the interpositus nucleus in the cerebellum appears to be a site of trace formation. But even here there appear to be additional storage sites in the cerebellar cortex (in lobule HVI), and these sites certainly are distributed, in the sense that many thousands of neurons are involved. It is conceivable that the memory traces for procedural learning tasks are relatively localized but that declarative memories are much more widely distributed. On the other hand, the fact that damage to speech areas in the human cerebral cortex appears to abolish memory for language suggests that this complex learning and memory process, perhaps the most complex yet evolved in nature, may have a considerable degree of localization.

A somewhat different approach has been taken in the study of "simplified" neuronal circuits in certain invertebrate preparations where the number of neurons is small, their sizes are large, and their interconnections are well specified (see INVERTEBRATE LEARNING). Here, simplified neural circuits containing only a few identified neurons can be isolated and particular training procedures, usually classical conditioning, can result in the circuits' showing changes in activity that can be long-lasting and can closely resemble similar associative learning in mammals. In these preparations it is possible to localize the learning-induced changes in the activities of the neurons and analyze the underlying mechanisms in some detail. These mechanisms can then provide models of putative mechanisms of memory storage in the mammalian brain.

There are many theories regarding the nature of memory traces, that is, the mechanisms of memory trace formation. One early notion held that each memory was stored in a particular protein molecule. This view is no longer tenable, but proteins of course play key roles in the structure and functioning of nerve cells. Another early view was that the brain grew new pathways; thus, in Pavlovian conditioning a new pathway would grow to connect the conditioned stimulus region of the brain to the unconditioned stimulus or response region. This does not occur. Instead, all current evidence is now consistent with the more modest view that there are changes in the actions of the synapses that are the sites of the interconnections and interactions among the neurons of the brain (see GUIDE TO THE ANATOMY OF THE BRAIN: SYNAPSE). Changes in synaptic actions can occur in many ways: changes in amount of neurotransmitter release, changes in receptor molecules, and a variety of other biochemical processes, ranging from calcium entry into neurons to second messenger systems (cyclic AMP, cyclic GNP, protein kinases, etc.) to changes in gene expression (see PROTEIN SYNTHESIS IN LONG-TERM MEMORY IN VERTEBRATES; SECOND MESSENGER SYSTEMS; NEUROTRANSMITTER SYSTEMS AND MEMORY).

Perhaps the clearest evidence to date for a biological substrate of long-term memory storage concerns long-lasting structural changes in the synaptic interconnections among neurons (see MORPHOLOGICAL BASIS OF LEARNING AND MEMORY). Enriched environments and even particular learning experiences can result in changes in the numbers and distributions of spine synapses on neuron dendrites, and even in changes in the number of dendritic branches in certain types of neurons. Equally clear are certain physiological mechanisms that produce long-lasting changes in neuron and synapse excitability (see LONG-TERM POTENTIATION; LONG-TERM DEPRESSION IN THE CEREBELLUM, NEOCORTEX, AND HIPPOCAMPUS). It is possible that all these processes and many more are involved in memory formation. The search for the memory trace is one of the most active and exciting fields in neuroscience and psychology today.

REFERENCES

Hebb, D. O. (1949). *The organization of behavior*. New York: John Wiley and Sons.

Lashley, K. S. (1929). *Brain mechanisms and intelligence*. Chicago: University of Chicago Press.

Squire, L. R. (1986). Mechanisms of memory. *Science* 232, 1612–1619.

Thompson, R. F. (1990). The neurobiology of learning and memory. In K. L. Kelner and D. E. Koshland, Jr., eds., *Molecules to models—advances in neuroscience*, pp. 219–234. Washington, D.C.: AAAS.

Richard F. Thompson

LONG-TERM DEPRESSION IN THE CEREBELLUM, HIPPOCAMPUS, AND NEOCORTEX

Long-term depression (LTD) is a type of synaptic plasticity in which the efficacy of signal transmission across a synapse (see GUIDE TO THE ANATOMY OF THE BRAIN) is persistently reduced after a certain triggering activity. The simple case in which repeated activation of a synapse alone leads to an enduring decrease of strength of that synapse, somewhat like fatigue, is called posttetanic depression and usually is distinguished from LTD. In a proper sense, LTD is induced at a synapse repeatedly activated in a certain relationship with activity at (an)other synapse(s) on the same neuron. LTD is of particular interest as a device for weakening or functionally interrupting synaptic connections between neurons, and may be a neuronal counterpart of wiping out useless or erroneous memory or forgetting. Its roles as a memory device have been assumed in nerve-net theories of cerebellar neuronal circuitry formulated by Marr (1969), Albus (1971), and Fujita (1982). The occurrence of LTD was first found in the cerebellum by Ito et al. (1982), and its wide occurrence in the hippocampus and neocortex has been revealed more recently. It is to be noted, though, that LTD in the cerebellum and cerebrum occurs in different manners. This heterogeneity of LTD requires special caution in exploring its molecular and cellular mechanisms and in interpreting its functional implications.

Induction and Observation of LTD

Cerebellar LTD

In the cerebellar cortex each Purkinje cell receives two distinct types of excitatory synapses, one from numerous (some 10,000) parallel fibers, axons of granule cells in the cerebellar cortex, and the other from a (normally single) climbing fiber, the axon of a neuron located in the inferior olive of the medulla oblongata (Figure 1A). LTD occurs when these two types of synapses are activated repeatedly in approximate synchrony, leading to an enduring decrease of synaptic strength of the parallel fibers. As reviewed by Ito (1989), LTD is typically induced by conjunctive stimulation at 4 hertz for 25 seconds (100 stimuli), which reduces the transmission efficacy by 30 percent in terms of the magnitude of synaptic potentials induced by stimulation of the parallel fibers (Figure 2) or by 50–90 percent in terms of the probability of firing thereby evoked in a Purkinje cell. LTD so induced has been followed for 1–3 hours without sign of recovery. LTD is input-specific and associative; it occurs only in those parallel fiber synapses activated in conjunction with a climbing fiber impinging on the same Purkinje cell. Activation of parallel fibers alone induces potentiation instead of LTD, and activation of climbing fibers alone causes neither of these effects.

Hippocampal LTD

Pyramidal cells in the hippocampus receive excitatory inputs from numerous (some thousand) presynaptic fibers (Figure 1B). When a bundle of presynaptic fibers is stimulated with high-frequency stimulus trains (for example, bursts with 5 stimuli at 100 hertz repeated at 200-millisecond intervals for 2 seconds), long-term potentiation (LTP) takes place in the stimulated synapses (homosynaptic LTP); but when the bundle is stimulated with a low-frequency repetition of single stimuli (5 hertz), no LTP is induced. Nevertheless, when the low-frequency stimulation of a testing bundle (AF_t in Figure 1B) is paired with the high-frequency train stimulation of another conditioning bundle (AF_c), heterosynaptic LTP takes place in the testing bundle. Stanton and Sejnowski (1989) demonstrated that LTD occurs when the two bundles are stimulated out of phase in the manner of antiassociation, each testing stimulus (AF_c) falling between two successive conditioning stimuli. LTD so induced lasted for some hours.

Neocortical LTD

In the visual cortex, tetanic stimulation of an optic nerve induces LTP in those synapses supplied by the stimulated optic nerve to cortical cells. Tsumoto and Suda (1979) observed that the same stimuli induced LTD in those synapses derived from another optic nerve for up to 9 hours. The occurrence of the LTD is less frequent when the nontetanized optic nerve is deprived of spontaneous activity by intraocular injection of tetrodotoxin. Hence, spontaneous activity out of phase with tetanus stimuli seems to facilitate LTD. LTD has also been observed in the sensorimotor cortex

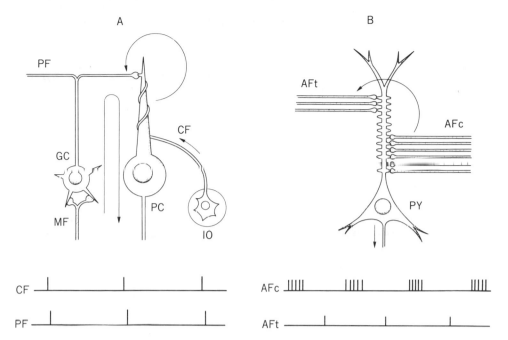

Figure 1. Occurrence of LTD: (A), in cerebellar Purkinje cell. PC, Purkinje cell; GC, granule cell; MF, mossy fiber; PF, parallel fiber; CF, climbing fiber originating from cell body in the inferior olive (IO). Arrows indicate the direction of impulse propagation. (B), in cerebral pyramidal cell. PY, pyramidal cell; AF_c, AF_t, bundles of presynaptic fibers for conditioning and testing, respectively. Stimulus paradigms effective in inducing LTD are indicated.

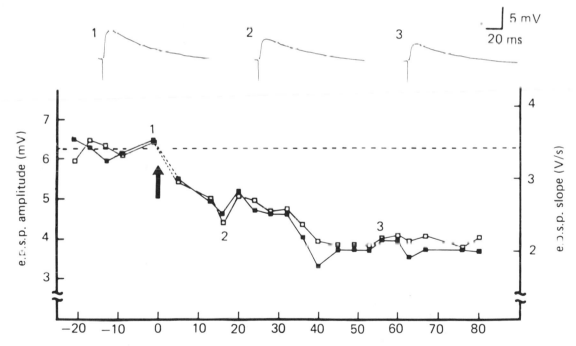

Figure 2. LTD in a Purkinje cell. Intracellular recording from a Purkinje cell in in vitro slice preparation of guinea pig cerebellum. 1–3, excitatory postsynaptic potentials (e.p.s.p.) evoked by stimulation of parallel fibers and recorded at the moments indicated in the graph. Conjunctive stimulation of parallel fibers and a climbing fiber converging onto the cell was performed at the moment indicated by an arrow. Time scale is in minutes. Solid squares, e.p.s.p. amplitude; open squares, e.p.s.p. slope. *Reproduced with permission from Sakurai, 1987.*

by Bindman and colleagues (1988) and in the prefrontal cortex by Hirsch and Crepel (1990).

Involvement of Calcium Ions

Impulses of climbing fibers evoke entry of Ca^{2+} (calcium) ions into Purkinje cell dendrites through voltage-sensitive Ca^{2+} channels, as demonstrated by W. N. Ross and colleagues (1990) with imaging techniques. This Ca^{2+} entry is an essential step of induction of LTD (Figure 3) since, according to Sakurai (1990), LTD is prevented by injection of the Ca^{2+} chelator EGTA into Purkinje cell dendrites.

In hippocampal pyramidal cells, excitatory postsynaptic potentials induced by conditioning stimuli (to AF_c) are followed by membrane hyperpolarization (increase of membrane potential) due to inhibitory postsynaptic potentials and afterhyperpolarization from mechanisms intrinsic to pyramidal neurons. The hyperpolarization prevails between conditioning stimulations. Stanton and Sejnowski (1989) reported that when membrane was hyperpolarized by passage of currents through an impaled microelectrode in conjunction with testing stimuli (to AF_t), LTD occurred. By contrast,

when the membrane was depolarized, LTP, instead of LTD, emerged. Hence, membrane potential critically governs induction of LTP and LTD. In the visual cortex as well, postsynaptic hyperpolarization induces LTD when paired with afferent stimulation. Artola and colleagues (1990), however, observed that LTD occurred when the depolarization exceeded a critical level but remained below a higher level above which LTP was induced.

The dependence of hippocampal and neocortical LTD on membrane potential may also indicate involvement of Ca^{2+} ions. This is because Ca^{2+} ions enter hippocampal and neocortical neurons through channels associated with a particular (*n*-methyl-*d*-aspartate-selective) subtype of glutamate receptors under influences of membrane potential. These channels are normally blocked by Mg^{2+} (magnesium) ions that are removed at a depolarized membrane potential level. At a hyperpolarized or less depolarized level, these channels are closed, so that intracellular Ca^{2+} concentration would be reduced by action of Ca^{2+}-binding proteins or accumulation into intracellular stores. In fact, Kimura et al. (1990) converted LTP to LTD by injecting EGTA into neocortical neurons. It is an interesting contrast that whereas cerebellar LTD requires an enhanced Ca^{2+} level, hippocampal and neocortical LTD is presumed to require a lowered Ca^{2+} level.

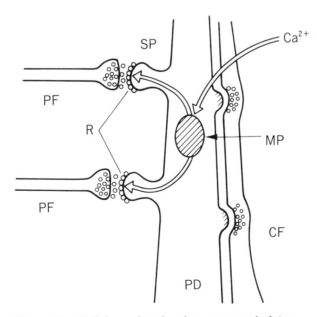

Figure 3. Cellular and molecular events underlying LTD in Purkinje cells. PD, Purkinje cell dendrite; PF, parallel fibers; CF, climbing fibers; SP, spine; R, Qi receptor; MP, intracellular messenger processes illustrated in Figure 4.

Desensitization of Glutamate Receptors

Cerebellar LTD can be accounted for by reduced sensitivity of glutamate receptors that mediate parallel fiber–Purkinje cell transmission. When a Purkinje cell was activated by iontophoretic application of *l*-glutamate through a micropipette in conjunction with stimulation of climbing fibers, as reported by Ito, Sakurai, and Tongroach (1982), or with induction of Ca^{2+} spikes by passage of depolarizing currents, as reported by Crepel and Krupa (1988), a long-lasting reduction occurred in the glutamate sensitivity of that Purkinje cell. At the same time, transmission from parallel fibers to the Purkinje cell was persistently depressed, as reported by Kano and Kato (1987). These observations disclose that glutamate receptors mediating parallel fiber–Purkinje cell synapses are desensitized when exposed to glutamate released from parallel fibers in conjunction with entry of Ca^{2+} ions into Purkinje cell dendrites.

Glutamate receptors involved in the cerebellar LTD are the ionotropic subtype activated by quisqualate and more specifically by AMPA (α-amino-3-hydroxy-5-methyl-4-isoxazole-propionic acid) as shown by Kano and Kato (1987; see GLUTAMATE RECEPTORS AND THEIR CHARACTERIZATION). Ito and Karachot (1990) found that these AMPA receptors in Purkinje cells were persistently desensitized following a brief (1–4 minutes) exposure to quisqualate. Quisqualate stimulates not only AMPA receptors but also the metabotropic subtype of glutamate receptors, which are linked with the metabolism yielding release of Ca^{2+} ions from intracellular stores. Conjunctive activation of AMPA receptors and metabotropic glutamate receptors is requisite for induction of the desensitization. The quisqualate-induced desensitization apparently differs from cerebellar LTD as to whether intradendritic Ca^{2+} concentration is enhanced through activation of metabotropic receptors or voltage-sensitive Ca^{2+} channels (Figure 4), but later processes are commonly shared by them (see below). How metabotropic receptors are activated under normal functional conditions is unclear.

Messenger Processes Underlying LTD

Studies have revealed intricate messenger processes in cerebellar tissues, as reviewed by C. A. Ross and colleagues (1990). There is evidence suggesting that Ca^{2+} ions activate calmodulin, which triggers the formation of nitric oxide (NO), that NO in turn accelerates guanylate cyclase to enhance the level of cyclic guanosine monophosphate (cGMP), and that cGMP eventually activates cGMP-dependent protein kinase (Figure 4). The

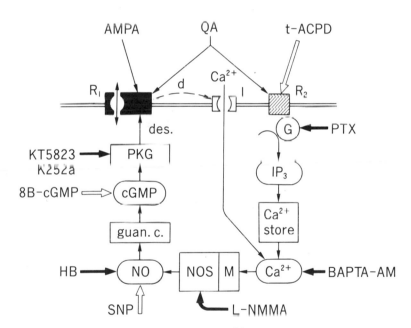

Figure 4. Chain of reactions driven by Ca^{2+} ions and leading to activation of cGMP-dependent protein kinase (PKG), which is proposed as the mechanism for MP in Figure 3. Two pathways for elevation of Ca^{2+} ions are indicated: entry through a voltage-sensitive channel (I) and release from intracellular stores by activation of metabotropic receptors (R_2), which are coupled through GTP-binding protein (G) to inositol-1,4,5-triphosphate (IP_3) production. t-ACPD, trans-1-amino-cyclopentyl-1,3-dicarboxylic acid; QA, quisqualate (stimulates both ionotropic receptors [R_1] and R_2); M, calmodulin; NOS, NO synthase; guan.c., guanylate cyclase; SNP, sodium nitroprusside; 8B-cGMP, 8-gromo-cGMP; PTX, pertussis toxin; BAPTA-AM, tetraacetocymethyl-(bis-aminophenoxy)ethane-tetra-acetic acid; L-NMMA, N^G-monomethyl l-arginine; HB, hemoglobin; KT5823, specific inhibitor of PKG; K252A, nonspecific inhibitor of protein kinases. *Reproduced with permission from Ito and Karachot, 1990.*

quisqualate-induced desensitization can be blocked by the membrane-soluble Ca^{2+} chelator BAPTA-AM, by the inhibitor of NO synthase L-NMMA, by hemoglobin (HB), which absorbs NO, and by the inhibitor of protein kinase G KT5823, as reported by Ito and Karachot (1990). Further, sodium nitroprusside, which releases NO, and a membrane-soluble derivative of cGMP are able to replace agonists of metabotropic receptors in inducing desensitization. Likewise, LTD can be manipulated effectively by using these agents, as reported by Crepel and Jaillard (1990) and Shibuki and Okada (1991). It is probable that AMPA receptors are finally phosphorylated, and that when they are further bound with agonist molecules, they fall into a stably desensitized state in which ion channels are kept closed.

Roles of LTD in Cerebellar Function

The prevalence of LTD in the cerebellum is in accordance with the fact that climbing fibers convey signals representing control errors involved in performance of a motor system. Those parallel fiber–Purkinje cell synapses acting during misperformance will be depressed by conjunction with error signals of climbing fibers. Since these synapses should be responsible for the misperformance, their functional removal by LTD would lead to improved performance. This view may match the major principle of motor learning in which skills are acquired by repeated practice of error-correcting trials.

The vestibulo-ocular reflex (VOR) is under control of the cerebellar flocculus, to which climbing fibers convey retinal error signals arising from inaccurate performance of VOR. It may be that LTD depresses those parallel fiber–Purkinje cell synapses erroneously acting on VOR through Purkinje cell projection to relay cells of VOR in vestibular nuclei. This proposition is supported by the finding that subdural application of hemoglobin to the flocculus in rabbits and a monkey abolished adaptive modification of VOR, which normally is induced by sustained imposition with artificially amplified retinal errors (Nagao and Ito, 1991).

The classical conditioning of eyeblinking with auditory or visual stimuli in rabbits has its central mechanisms in the interpositus nucleus of the cerebellum, as shown by Thompson (1986) and others (see NEURAL SUBSTRATES OF CLASSICAL CONDITIONING: DIS-CRETE BEHAVIORAL RESPONSES; LOCALIZATION OF MEMORY TRACES). Unconditioned corneal stimuli evoke climbing fiber signals that will induce LTD in those parallel fiber–Purkinje cell synapses conveying conditioned stimuli. If eyeblinking to be evoked via an interpositus pathway has been inhibited by Purkinje cells driven by the conditioned stimuli, LTD will release the reflex from the inhibition. There is evidence supporting this view, but more information is needed to account for details of the mechanisms of the classical conditioning.

Conclusion

Associative LTD is a major form of synaptic plasticity characteristic of the cerebellum. It is underlaid by intricate messenger processes including Ca^{2+} ions, NO, cGMP and protein kinase G, and is effected through desensitization of AMPA-selective glutamate receptors. LTD apparently serves as a mechanism for procedural memory as defined by Squire (1987). Whether LTD serves as a permanent memory or acts merely as a transient memory needs to be clarified.

The antiassociative LTD prevailing in the hippocampus and neocortex appears to involve Ca^{2+} ions, but further details of underlying messenger processes are unknown. This type of LTD is the obverse of associative LTP, and may represent the neuronal counterpart of forgetfulness, in contrast with acquisition of cognitive memory that may be underlaid by associative LTP. Whether the associative LTD in the cerebellum is likewise coupled with antiassociative LTP is unclear, even though Sakurai (1987) has recognized potentiation of parallel fiber–Purkinje cell transmission after tetanic stimulation of parallel fibers.

REFERENCES

Albus, J. S. (1971). A theory of cerebellar function. *Mathematical Biosciences 10,* 25–61.

Artola, A., Brocher, S., and Singer, W. (1990). Different voltage-dependent thresholds for inducing long-term depression and long-term potentiation in slices of rat visual cortex. *Nature 347,* 69–72.

Bindman, L. J., Murphy, K. P. S., and Pockett, S. (1988). Postsynaptic control of the induction of long-term changes in efficacy of transmission at neocortical synapses in slices of rat brain. *Journal of Neurophysiology 60*, 1053–1065.

Crepel, F., and Jaillard, D. (1990). Protein kinases, nitric oxide and long-term depression of synapses in the cerebellum. *NeuroReport 1*, 133–136.

Crepel, F., and Krupa, M. (1988). Activation of protein kinase C induces a long-term depression of glutamate sensitivity of cerebellar Purkinje cells. *Brain Research 458*, 397–401.

Fujita, M. (1982). Adaptive filter model of the cerebellum. *Biological Cybernetics 45*, 195–206.

Hirsch, J. C., and Crepel, F. (1990). Use-dependent changes in synaptic efficacy in rat prefrontal neurons in vitro. *Journal of Physiology* (London) *427*, 31–49.

Ito, M. (1989). Long-term depression. *Annual Review of Neuroscience 12*, 85–102.

Ito, M., and Karachot, L. (1990). Messengers mediating long-term desensitization in cerebellar Purkinje cells. *NeuroReport 1*, 129–132.

Ito, M., Sakurai, M., and Tongroach, P. (1982). Climbing fibre induced depression of both mossy fibre responsiveness and glutamate sensitivity of cerebellar Purkinje cells. *Journal of Physiology* (London) *324*, 113–134.

Kano, M., and Kato, M. (1987). Quisqualate receptors are specifically involved in cerebellar synaptic plasticity. *Nature 325*, 276–279.

Kimura, F., Tsumoto, T., Nishigori, A., and Yoshimura, Y. (1990). Long-term depression but not potentiation is induced in Ca^{2+}-chelated visual cortex neurons. *NeuroReport 1*, 65–68.

Marr, D. (1969). A theory of cerebellar cortex. *Journal of Physiology* (London) *202*, 437–470.

Nagao, S., and Ito, M. (1991). Subdural application of hemoglobin to cerebellar flocculus blocks adaptation of the vestibuloocular reflex. *NeuroReport 2*, 193–196.

Ross, C. A., Bredt, D., and Snyder, S. H. (1990). Messenger molecules in the cerebellum. *Trends in Neurosciences 13*, 216–222.

Ross, W.N., Lasse-Ross, N., and Werman, R. (1990). Spatial and temporal analysis of calcium-dependent electrical activity in guinea pig Purkinje cell dendrites. *Proceedings of the Royal Society of London B240*, 173–185.

Sakurai, M. (1987). Synaptic modification of parallel fiber–Purkinje cell transmission in *in vitro* guinea pig cerebellar slices. *Journal of Physiology* (London) *394*, 463–480.

———— (1990). Calcium is an intracellular mediator of the climbing fiber in induction of cerebellar long-term depression. *Proceedings of the National Academy of Sciences 87*, 3383–3385.

Shibuki, K., and Okada, D. (1991). Endogenous nitric oxide release required for long-term synaptic depression in the cerebellum. *Nature 349*, 326–328.

Squire, L. R. (1987). *Memory and brain.* New York: Oxford University Press.

Stanton, P. K., and Sejnowski, T. J. (1989). Associative long-term depression in the hippocampus induced by Hebbian covariance. *Nature 339*, 215–217.

Thompson, R. F. (1986). The neurophysiology of learning and memory. *Science 233*, 941–947.

Tsumoto, T., and Suda, K. (1979). Cross-depression: An electrophysiological manifestation of binocular competition in the developing visual cortex. *Brain Research 168*, 190–194.

Masao Ito

LONG-TERM MEMORY

See Knowledge Systems

LONG-TERM POTENTIATION

[*This entry consists of four articles:*

Overview; Cooperativity and Associativity
Signal Transduction Mechanisms and Early
  Events
Maintenance
Behavioral Role]

Overview; Cooperativity and Associativity

Long-term potentiation (LTP) is the collective name for synaptic plasticity processes in which a brief burst of high-frequency activation of presynaptic fibers leads to an enhancement of excitatory synaptic efficacy lasting hours to weeks, or longer. Some authors use other names: long-lasting potentiation, long-term enhancement, postactivation potentiation, long-term facilitation. It was first described in the rabbit hippocampal formation and later in a variety of pathways in the brain of vertebrates including man, in the peripheral nervous system, and in invertebrates. LTP has been most extensively studied in synaptic pathways in the hippocampal formation of the rodent brain. In this region, LTP has associative induction properties, implying coincident presynaptic and postsynaptic activity. This condition is similar to that suggested on theoretical grounds by Donald HEBB (1949) for a synaptic modification involved in learning and memory (Hebb synapse). Although the same condition appears to hold for LTP in other cortical regions of the vertebrate brain, not all forms have such properties.

LTP can be divided into *induction,* denoting the detection of certain stimulus conditions that lead to a trigger signal, and *maintenance* process(es) underlying the upkeep of the *expression* mechanism(s) responsible for the enhanced synaptic efficacy. This article deals with the induction of LTP in various brain regions, particularly in the hippocampus.

Hippocampus

Lømo (1966) reported in a short note that a few seconds of repetitive activation (10–15 hertz) of afferents led to a prolonged potentiation (LTP) of their monosynaptic excitatory action on granule cells in the dentate gyrus of the hippocampus. Later, Bliss and Gardner-Medwin (1973) reported that LTP could last for weeks and that its induction appeared to depend on the number of activated presynaptic fibers. The dependence of LTP induction on the coactivation of afferent fibers (cooperativity), and the restriction of LTP to the synapses of the activated afferents (input specificity), were demonstrated by several laboratories in the late 1970s. LTP induction was found to be associative: A repetitive activation of a weak input that did not induce LTP by itself did so when occurring in close temporal contiguity with repetitive activation of a separate strong input to the same cellular region. Thus, LTP can form an associative connection between a weak input and a strong one or, alternatively seen, an association between a weak input and the response elicited by the strong one. In the mid-1980s several groups showed, using intracellular recording technique, that LTP induction requires coincident presynaptic activity and depolarization of the postsynaptic membrane; this property is the essential factor accounting for cooperativity and associativity.

The excitatory postsynaptic potential (EPSP) measured in hippocampal LTP studies is mediated by the non-NMDA type of glutamate receptor channel (see GLUTAMATE RECEPTORS AND THEIR CHARACTERIZATION). Collingridge, Kehl, and McLennan (1983) showed that an antagonist to the NMDA type of glutamate receptor prevents the induction of LTP, and Lynch et al. (1983) showed that LTP cannot

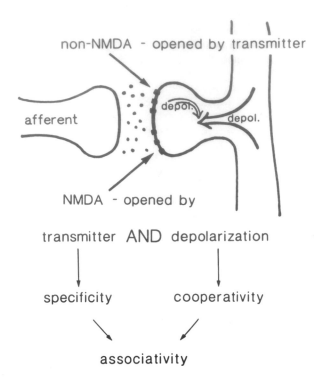

Figure 1. Schematic representation of the model for LTP induction in the hippocampus. A presynaptic terminal (left) releases transmitter (dots) onto a spine of a pyramidal cell dendrite. Non-NMDA and NMDA types of glutamate receptor channels are located in the spine membrane.

be induced after injection of a calcium chelator into the postsynaptic cell. These results, together with the dependence of the induction on coincident presynaptic and postsynaptic activity, led to the idea that LTP is initiated as a consequence of calcium influx through postsynaptic NMDA receptor channels. These act as coincidence detectors because their activation needs both transmitter binding and membrane depolarization. The colocalization of the NMDA and the non-NMDA receptor channels on the membrane of the postsynaptic spine, together with the restricting influence of the spine on calcium diffusion, secures input specificity of LTP. Except for the mossy fiber projection to CA3 pyramidal cells, this induction model is generally accepted for hippocampal LTP. Data suggesting a presynaptic locus for LTP expression have prompted consideration of retrograde messengers in LTP induction, such as arachidonic acid and/or nitric oxide produced by the rise in calcium postsynaptically and passing to the presynapse. Further mechanisms implementing input specificity are then needed. An unresolved problem is whether the increase in calcium is enough to initiate long-lasting LTP. For the mossy fiber-CA3 pyramidal cell synapse some data point to a postsynaptic induction mediated via calcium influx through nonsynaptic voltage-dependent calcium channels (Jaffe and Johnston, 1990), whereas other data point to a presynaptic induction (Zalutsky and Nicoll, 1990).

Induction Stimulation Paradigms

Although in many studies unnatural stimulus conditions, such as synchronous activation of afferents at 5–100 hertz for a few seconds, are used to evoke LTP, physiological stimulus patterns have been shown to be effective in inducing LTP. Burst stimulation that simulates the 5-to-7-hertz hippocampal EEG wave activity (theta rhythm) produces LTP that is stable for recording periods of several weeks. "Primed burst" stimulation, in which a single afferent stimulus precedes a brief burst by about 200 milliseconds, is also effective. These patterns produce LTP efficiently because they depress inhibitory circuits and thereby enable an afferent burst to produce more postsynaptic depolarization. LTP is even evoked in synapses of afferents subjected to a single stimulus if this activation is associated with sufficient postsynaptic depolarization.

Modulation of LTP Induction

LTP induction is modulated by substances that interfere with the opening of NMDA receptor channels, either directly or indirectly, by affecting pre- and/or postsynaptic activity. NMDA receptor antagonists effectively prevent LTP induction, and GABA receptor antagonists facilitate it. Concurrent activity in excitatory pathways (cooperativity) and in inhibitory ones have a decisive role in allowing LTP to occur. Neuromodulators, such as norepinephrine and acetylcholine, affect LTP induction by modifying the responses of pre- and/or postsynaptic channels and/or receptors.

Time Course of LTP

After a latency of a few seconds, LTP develops toward a peak value within a minute. LTP then decays for 10–30 minutes before attaining a more stable level. Several reports describe a subsequent decay of LTP with time constants of hours to days, but LTP induced by theta-rhythm stimulation may remain stable for weeks. LTP at a single synaptic site may be heterogeneous with respect to maintenance and expression mechanisms. Matthies (1989) suggests that LTP in the CA1 region consists of three phases: an early transient one (1–2 hours), a later transient one (5–6 hours), and a late, more stable one. These phases are supposed to be maintained by different biochemical processes, and possibly associated with different expression mechanisms.

Nonhippocampal Brain Structures

LTP is observed in a number of other limbic forebrain pathways, in neocortex, and in subtelencephalic structures such as the medial geniculate nucleus and the superior colliculus. In the neocortex one form of LTP resembles the hippocampal one, with an associative induction dependent on coincident presynaptic and postsynaptic activity and NMDA receptor activation. There are other forms of LTP, including enhancement of NMDA-mediated EPSPs, but the complex circuitry of the neocortex makes it uncertain which cells and synapses express these LTPs. Neocortical LTPs are reported to have slower kinetics of development and decay, and may be mechanisms for more permanent alterations in synaptic efficacy.

The heterogeneity of LTP is further indicated by studies of synaptic plasticity in the superior colliculus (Miyamoto, Sakurai, and Okada, 1990). LTP in this nucleus is most efficiently induced by prolonged high-frequency activation (50 hertz for 20 seconds), and its expression, but not induction, is masked by NMDA receptor antagonists. Whether it has associative induction properties is not known.

LTPs with associative and nonassociative induction have been described for EPSPs mediated by muscarinic and nicotinic types of acetylcholine receptor, respectively. Libet (1984) studied LTP of a slow muscarinic EPSP produced by prolonged (minutes), low-frequency (3–20 hertz) repetitive activation of preganglionic pathways; the induction depends on an interaction between the activation of the muscarinic receptor and the release of dopamine (and possibly peptides) from an interposed interneuron. There is also LTP of a fast nicotinic EPSP. Its induction results from a presynaptic calcium accumulation caused by the repetitive activation of the presynaptic fibers and is nonassociative.

Invertebrates

LTP is described in the neuromuscular junction of crayfish and in sensory neuron-motor neuron synapses in the snail APLYSIA. In the crayfish, LTP resembles the nonassociative one in sympathetic ganglia. Walters and Byrne (1985) described an associatively induced LTP in *Aplysia*. In this case, release of a transmitter from a modulatory pathway interacts with the presynaptic calcium influx in activated sensory axon terminals.

Conclusions

LTP denotes forms of synaptic plasticity with associative as well as nonassociative induction (i.e., they depend on temporal contiguity between activity in different pathways and on activity in a single pathway, respectively). Nonassociative LTP will allow for a more efficient transmission in pathways that are intensely used. Among associative LTPs, hippocampal and neocortical ones have induction of the Hebbian type, which relies on contiguity of activity in those neuronal elements which are connected via the modifiable synapse. The Hebbian modification rule is a powerful device used in neural network models of nonsupervised learning to produce, for example, self-organizing capabilities. Other forms of associative LTP, including those present in the nervous system of invertebrates, are non-Hebbian; they rely on activity in specific modulatory pathways, usually in combination with activity in the presynaptic element of the modifiable synapse. Non-Hebbian associative LTP is involved in learning and memory in invertebrates, and it is an open question to what extent such mechanisms have been preserved during evolution to be used in the vertebrate brain (Hawkins and Kandel, 1990).

REFERENCES

Bliss, T. V. P., Clements, M. P., Errington M. L., Lynch, M. A., and Williams, J. H. 1990). Presynaptic changes associated with long-term potentiation in the dentate gyrus. *Seminars in the Neurosciences 2,* 345–354. Discusses presynaptic locus and retrograde messengers.

Bliss, T. V. P., and Gardner-Medwin, A. R. (1973). Long-lasting potentiation of synaptic transmission in the dentate area of the unanaesthetized rabbit following stimulation of the perforant path. *Journal of Physiology 232,* 357–374.

Byrne, J. H. (1987). Cellular analysis of associative learning. *Physiological Reviews 67,* 329–439. Includes invertebrate LTP.

Collingridge, G. L., Kehl, S. J., and McLennan, H. (1983). Excitatory amino acids in synaptic transmission in the Schaffer collateral-commissural pathway of the rat hippocampus. *Journal of Physiology 334,* 33–46.

Gustafsson, B., and Wigström, H. (1988). Physiological mechanisms underlying long-term potentiation. *Trends in Neurosciences 11,* 156–162. Discusses LTP induction.

—————— (1990). Basic features of hippocampal long-term potentiation. *Seminars in the Neurosciences 2,* 321–333. Discusses LTP induction and onset.

Hawkins, R. D., and Kandel, E. R. (1990). Hippocampal LTP and synaptic plasticity in *Aplysia:* Possible relationship of associative cellular mechanisms. *Seminars in the Neurosciences 2,* 391–401.

Hebb, D. O. (1949). *The organization of behavior.* New York: John Wiley and Sons.

Hinton, G. E., and Anderson, J. A., eds. (1981). *Parallel models of associative memory.* Hillsdale, N.J.: Erlbaum.

Jaffe, D., and Johnston, D. (1990). Induction of long-term potentiation at hippocampal mossy-fiber synapses follows a hebbian rule. *Journal of Neurophysiology 64,* 948–960.

Kuba, K., and Kumamoto, E. (1990). Long-term potentiations in vertebrate synapses: A variety of cascades with common subprocesses. *Progress in Neurobiology 34,* 197–269. Extensive review of LTPs, including those in sympathetic ganglia. Also discusses modulation of LTP induction.

Landfield, P., and Deadwyler, S. A., eds. (1988). *Long-term potentiation: From biophysics to behavior.* New York: Liss. Contains several extensive review articles that deal with many aspects of hippocampal LTP; articles by Bliss and Lynch, Wigström and Gustafsson for history, and cooperativity and associativity.

Libet, B. (1984). Heterosynaptic interaction at a sympathetic neuron as a model for induction and storage of a postsynaptic memory trace. In G. Lynch, J. L. McGaugh, and N. M. Weinberger, eds., *Neurobiology of learning and memory.* New York: Guilford Press.

Lømo, T. (1966). Frequency potentiation of excitatory synaptic activity in the dentate area of the hippocampal formation. *Acta Physiologica Scandinavica 68,* Suppl. 277, 128.

Lynch, G., Kessler, M., Arai, A., and Larson, J. (1990). The nature and causes of hippocampal long-term potentiation. In J. Storm-Mathisen, J. Zimmer, and O. P. Ottersen, eds., Understanding the brain through the hippocampus. *Progress in Brain Research 83.* Discusses stimulus induction paradigms.

Lynch, G., Larson, J., Kelso, S., Barrionuevo, G., and Schottler, F. (1983). Intracellular injections of EGTA block induction of hippocampal long-term potentiation. *Nature 305*, 719–721.

Matthies, H. (1989). In search of cellular mechanisms of memory. *Progress in Neurobiology 32*, 277–349.

Miyamoto, T., Sakurai, T., and Okada, Y. (1990). Masking effect of NMDA receptor antagonists on the formation of long-term potentiation (LTP) in superior colliculus slices from the guinea pig. *Brain Research 518*, 166–172.

Teyler, T., Aroniadou, V., Berry, R. L., Borroni, A., DiScenna, P., Grover, L., and Lambert, N. (1990). LTP in neocortex. *Seminars in the Neurosciences 2*, 365–379.

Walters, E. T., and Byrne, J. H. (1985). Long-term enhancement produced by activity-dependent modulation of *Aplysia* sensory neurons. *Journal of Neuroscience 5*, 662–672.

Zalutsky, R. A., and Nicoll, R. A. (1990). Comparison of two forms of long-term potentiation in single hippocampal neurons. *Science 248*, 1619–1624.

Holger Wigström
Bengt Gustafsson

Signal Transduction Mechanisms and Early Events

Long-lasting changes in synaptic function are thought to be essential for learning and memory in the mammalian brain. A widely studied example of such synaptic plasticity is long-term potentiation (LTP). The remarkable feature of LTP is that a short burst of synaptic activity can trigger persistent enhancement of synaptic transmission lasting for at least several hours, and possibly weeks or longer. There is great interest in understanding the cellular and molecular mechanisms that underlie this form of synaptic plasticity. First found in the hippocampus (see GUIDE TO THE ANATOMY OF THE BRAIN), this phenomenon is now known to exist in cerebral cortex and other areas of the mammalian central nervous system. Indeed, damage to the hippocampus can result in certain defects in memory acquisition (see Squire and Lindenlaub, 1990).

Most studies on LTP focus on the synapse between Schaffer collaterals and hippocampal CA1 neurons. In this system, a brief burst of afferent stimulation leads to induction of LTP in postsynaptic CA1 cells through a combination of (1) membrane depolarization and (2) activation of

glutamate receptors of the NMDA type (e.g., Collingridge, Kehl, and McLennan, 1983; Wigström et al., 1986; Malinow and Miller, 1986) (see "Overview" above). It is generally agreed that the depolarization relieves Mg^{2+} (magnesium ion) block of NMDA receptor channels and allows a Ca^{2+} (calcium ion) influx into dendritic spines that somehow triggers LTP (see, e.g., Nicoll, Kauer, and Malenka, 1988; Cotman et al., 1989).

Importance of a Rise in Postsynaptic $[Ca^{2+}]_i$

The $[Ca^{2+}]_i$ transient has been measured by the use of fluorescent Ca^{2+} indicator dyes in pyramidal cell dendrites within hippocampal slices (Regehr and Tank, 1990; Collingridge et al., 1991). Under conditions of voltage clamp in the cell soma, the free Ca^{2+} concentration ($[Ca^{2+}]_i$) within the dendrite rises quickly during a train of action potentials and falls with a half-time of about 5 seconds after afferent stimulation has ceased; the $[Ca^{2+}]_i$ transient displays voltage dependence and pharmacology consistent with Ca^{2+} entry through NMDA receptor channels (Collingridge et al., 1991).

The importance of the rise in $[Ca^{2+}]_i$ for LTP has been demonstrated by a variety of experiments. Ca^{2+} buffers such as EGTA or BAPTA have been introduced with the aim of suppressing the Ca^{2+} transient; such maneuvers are effective in preventing the induction of LTP (Lynch et al., 1983; Malenka et al., 1988). Moreover, a rise in postsynaptic Ca^{2+}, independent of glutamate receptors, has been imposed by photoactivation of a caged Ca^{2+} compound, nitr-5; this method for Ca^{2+} delivery causes a sustained synaptic potentiation (Malenka et al., 1988).

Possible Involvement of Protein Kinases

The key question at this point is how a relatively brief rise in $[Ca^{2+}]_i$ can lead to a long-lasting enhancement of synaptic function. One popular hypothesis is that Ca^{2+} acts through a signal transduction pathway that somehow requires the function of a Ca^{2+}-dependent protein kinase such as protein kinase C (PKC) or multifunctional Ca/calmodulin-dependent protein kinase (CaMKII) (for reviews, see Lisman, 1985; Cotman et al., 1989; Kennedy, 1989; Malenka et al., 1989; Stevens, 1989).

Involvement of Ca^{2+}-dependent protein kinases has been tested by intracellular injection of peptides that are potent and selective inhibitors of either PKC or CaMKII (Malinow, Schulman, and Tsien, 1989). Peptide fragments of pseudosubstrate region of the PKC regulatory domain (PKC(19–31) or PKC(19–36); House and Kemp, 1987) are more than 600-fold more potent as blockers of PKC than as blockers of CaMK. The results of intracellular injection of peptides are illustrated in Figure 1. PKC(19–31) or PKC(19–36) blocked LTP when delivered to the postsynaptic cell with the recording intracellular microelectrode (Figure 1A). In contrast, the glu^{27} derivative of PKC(19–31), which is relatively inactive against either kinase, failed to block LTP (Figure 1B). These results are compatible with effects of injecting PKC or PKC inhibitory peptides (e.g., Hu et al., 1987).

Participation of postsynaptic CaMKII has been investigated by use of the pseudosubstrate peptide CaMKII(273–302), which inhibits CaMKII at much lower concentrations than PKC. A control was provided by CaMKII(284–302), a shorter peptide that is much less effective in blocking CaMKII and, if anything, shows opposite selectivity. When delivered to postsynaptic cells through the recording microelectrode, CaMKII(273–302) prevents sustained synaptic potentiation (Figure 1C), while CaMKII(284–302) does not (Figure 1D).

Similar blocking effects have been obtained with a calmodulin-blocking peptide (Malenka et al., 1989; Malinow, Schulman, and Tsien, 1989). This would be consistent with participation of either CaMKII or some other calmodulin-dependent enzyme (see below).

The period of susceptibility to postsynaptic kinase inhibition seems limited to a critical period associated with induction of LTP. When postsynaptic cells were impaled with microelectrodes containing protein kinase inhibitors shortly *after* the high-frequency stimulation, previously established LTP was *not* suppressed. This holds for introduction of the combination of PKC(19–31) and CaMKII(273–302), or for intracellular postsynaptic injection of H-7, a rather general protein kinase inhibitor that blocks catalytic effects of PKC and CaMKII (Malinow, Schulman, and Tsien, 1989). Control procedures showed that the agents were successfully delivered and that LTP had indeed been established before the impalement. Thus, once established, the persistent signal is inaccessible to postsynaptic delivery of PKC/CaMKII peptides or to H-7. However, established LTP remains sensitive to bath application of H-7 (Malinow, Madison, and Tsien, 1988).

The participation of tyrosine kinases in LTP has been tested, and the pattern of response is very much like that found with inhibitors of serine/threonine kinases. In the presence of lavendustin A and genistein, relatively selective inhibitors of tyrosine kinase, tetanic stimulation produces only slowly decaying potentiation.

The results obtained with postsynaptic inhibition of PKC, CaMKII, and tyrosine kinase can be interpreted in terms of a network of protein kinases, with protein phosphorylation as a link between the rise in $[Ca^{2+}]_i$ and the eventual expression of enhanced synaptic function. However, the topology of the network and the nature of the interactions remain undefined. Indeed, there is no evidence to date to exclude the idea that one or more of these enzymes act in a merely permissive way. At one extreme, background activity of a particular kinase might be necessary only *prior to* induction, to set the stage for some other signaling mechanism triggered by Ca^{2+} (see below).

Evidence for Presynaptic Expression of LTP

The question of how the kinases act leads to consideration of ongoing debate about the nature of the maintained synaptic enhancement in LTP (see "Maintenance" below). There is growing evidence to support the view that increased presynaptic transmitter release is a predominant mechanism. For example, whole-cell recordings of synaptic transmission in conventional hippocampal slices show a large trial-to-trial variability during stimulation of single afferents, reflecting the probabilistic nature of transmitter release (Malinow and Tsien, 1990; Bekkers and Stevens, 1990; Malinow, 1991). Changes in the synaptic variability after LTP show an increase in quantal content, indicating that the characteristics of presynaptic transmitter release are significantly modified (Malinow and Tsien, 1990; Bekkers and Stevens, 1990). On the other hand, the quantal amplitude is little changed (Malgaroli et al., 1991). This electrophysiological evidence seems qualitatively consistent with earlier inferences from other methods (e.g., Dolphin, Errington, and Bliss, 1982; Malenka, Ayoub, and Nicoll, 1987). The results support the idea of a retro-

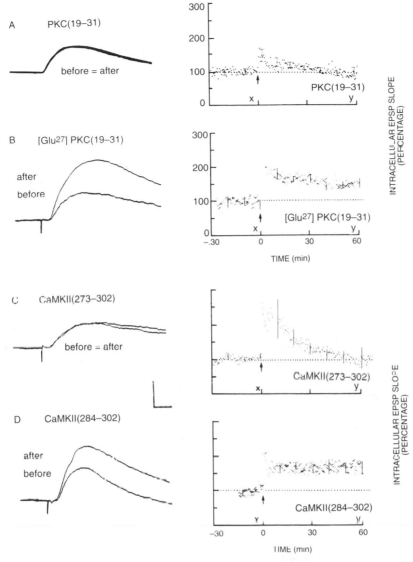

Figure 1. Selective postsynaptic block of PKC or CaMKII prevents LTP. (A) Synaptic potentials monitored with an intracellular microelectrode whose tip is filled with 3 millimolar PKC(19–31) (n = 8). Following the tetanus there is no persistent potentiation. Transmission in a nontetanized pathway, monitored through the same PKC(19–31)-containing electrode, is constant throughout the experiment, indicating no nonspecific depressant effect on basal synaptic transmission; extracellular monitoring shows LTP after tetanic stimulation from synapses on neighboring cells (data not shown). (B) Transmission monitored in a different set of slices with 3 millimolar [Glu^{27}]PKC(19–31) in the intracellular electrode shows LTP after a conditioning tetanus (n = 6 pathways from three slices). (C) Synaptic potentials monitored with intracellular electrode containing 1.1 millimolar CaMKII(273–302) shows no persistent potentiation after tetanic conditioning. Transmission in a non-tetanized pathway, monitored with the same CaMKII(273–302)-containing electrode, is constant throughout the experiment; extracellular monitoring shows LTP after tetanic stimulation from synapses on neighboring cells (data not shown). (D) Transmission monitored in a different set of slices, using 1.1 millimolar CaMKII(284–302) in the intracellular electrode, shows LTP after a tetanus (n = 5 pathways from three slices). Error bars indicate standard errors of measurement for representative time points. Insets: average of ten consecutive potentials obtained at the times designated on time axis. Scale bars 5 millivolts and 12.5 milliseconds. *Reproduced with permission from Malinow, Schulman, and Tsien, 1989.*

grade signal that travels from the postsynaptic cell back to the presynaptic terminal. Increases in quantal content and decreases in the proportion of synaptic failures are prominent within the first minute following the procedure for induction of LTP, suggesting that retrosignaling begins early (Malinow and Tsien, 1990; Malinow, 1991).

Retrograde Messenger Candidates

This line of reasoning has led to a search for specific compounds that might act as the retrograde messenger, with arachidonic acid and nitric oxide (NO) the most widely considered possibilities (see Bliss et al., 1991, for review). Application of bromphenacylbromide or nordihydroguaieretic acid, agents that inhibit phospholipase A_2 and thereby prevent arachidonate production, appears to block LTP. However, effects of exogenous arachidonate are too slow to account for the early manifestations of LTP. This has led Bliss et al. (1991) and others to consider other possible retrograde messengers, including NO, which appears to act as a diffusible messenger in the cerebellum. It is formed as a product of the breakdown of arginine to citrulline, a reaction catalyzed by nitric oxide synthase (NOS). This enzyme is calmodulin-activated and may be found at significant levels in the hippocampus (Bredt et al., 1991a). Schumann and Madison (1991) have found that LTP can be inhibited by intracellular l-N^6-monomethylarginine, a blocker of NOS, but not its d-isomer, which is ineffective against NOS (see also O'Dell et al., 1991). Furthermore, synaptic potentiation can be prevented by extracellular hemoglobin (known to sequester NO). Thus, the available evidence is consistent with the hypothesis that retrograde signaling in LTP involves NO production in the postsynaptic cell and diffusion across the synaptic cleft.

It seems possible that activity of NOS may depend on protein phosphorylation, since the primary amino acid sequence of NOS shows several consensus sites for serine/threonine phosphorylation (Bredt et al., 1991b). Thus, one might suppose either that serine/threonine kinases such as PKC or CaMKII help activate NOS, or that such phosphorylation merely maintains availability of NOS for activation by Ca^{2+}/calmodulin. Studies of the functional effects of NOS phosphorylation would be informative.

Possible Presynaptic Signaling Mechanisms

Little is known for certain about possible presynaptic mechanisms that might be set in motion by putative retrograde messengers such as arachidonate or NO. A widely considered mechanism for synaptic potentiation involves a persistent enhancement of a presynaptic protein kinase, such as PKC (see Linden and Routtenberg, 1989, for review). Presynaptic terminals in the CA1 region of the hippocampus contain the α and β subtypes of PKC, but not PKCγ, the PKC isotype that is directly activated by arachidonate (Kose et al., 1990). The maintained expression of LTP can be reversibly blocked by bath application of a relatively nonspecific kinase inhibitor, H-7 (Malinow, Madison, and Tsien, 1988), but not by its intracellular delivery in the postsynaptic cell (Malinow, Schulman, and Tsien, 1989). Biochemical measurements show a sustained enhancement of PKC in hippocampal slices. PKC is known to increase the efficiency of excitation-secretion coupling in many systems, including chromaffin cells, motor nerve terminals, and cultured hippocampal neurons. Further exploration of presynaptic mechanisms is needed to determine which steps leading to exocytosis are enhanced in LTP.

REFERENCES

Bekkers, J., and Stevens, C. F. 1990. Presynaptic mechanism for long-term potentiation in the hippocampus. *Nature 346,* 724–729.

Bliss, T. V. P., Errington, M. L., Lynch, M. A., and Williams, J. H. 1991. Presynaptic mechanisms in hippocampal long-term potentiation. *Cold Spring Harbor Symposium in Quantitative Biology 55,* 119–129.

Bredt, D. S., Glatt, C. E., Hwang, P. M., Fotuhi, M., Dawson, T. M., and Snyder, S. H. 1991a. Nitric oxide synthase protein and mRNA are discretely localized in neuronal populations of the mammalian CNS together with NADPH diaphorase. *Neuron 7,* 615–624.

Bredt, D. S., Hwang, P. M., Glatt, C. E., Lowenstein, C., Reed, R. R., and Snyder, S. H. 1991b. Cloned and expressed nitric oxide synthase structurally resembles cytochrome c. *Nature 351,* 714–718.

Collingridge, G. L., Kehl, S. J., and McLennan, H. 1983. Excitatory amino acids in synaptic transmission in the Schaffer collateral-commissural pathway of the rat hippocampus. *Journal of Physiology 334,* 33–46.

Collingridge, G. L., Randall, A. D., Davies, C. H., and Alfred, S. 1991. Interactions among cell signalling systems: The synaptic activation of NMDA receptors and Ca^{2+} signalling in neurons. In *Ciba Foundation Symposium 164.* West Sussex, England: Wiley.

Cotman, C. W., Bridges, R. J., Taube, J. S., Clark, A. S., Geddes, J. W., and Monaghan, D. T. 1989. The role of the NMDA receptor in central nervous system plasticity and pathology. *Journal of NIH Research 1 (?)*, 65–74.

Dolphin, A. C., Errington, M. L., and Bliss, T. V. P. 1982. Long-term potentiation of the perforant path *in vivo* is associated with increased glutamate release. *Nature 297*, 496–498.

House, C., and Kemp, B. E. 1987. Protein kinase C contains a pseudosubstrate prototype in its regulatory domain. *Science 238*, 1726–1728.

Hu, G. Y., Hvalby, O., Walaas, S. I., Albert, K. A., Skjelfo, P., Andersen, P., and Greengard, P. 1987. Protein kinase C injection into hippocampal pyramidal cells elicits features of long term potentiation. *Nature 328*, 426–429.

Kennedy, M. B. 1989. Regulation of synaptic transmission in the central nervous system: Long-term potentiation. *Cell 59*, 777–787.

Kose, A., Ito, A., Saito, N., and Tanaka, C. 1990. Electron microscope localization of γ- and βII-subspecies of protein kinase C in rat hippocampus. *Brain Research 518*, 209–217.

Linden, D. J., and Routtenberg, A. 1989. The role of protein kinase C in long-term potentiation: A testable model. *Brain Research Reviews 14*, 279–296.

Lisman, J. E. 1985. A mechanism for memory storage insensitive to molecular turnover: A bistable autophosphorylating kinase. *Proceedings of the National Academy of Sciences 82*, 3055–3057.

Lynch, G., Larson, J., Kelso, S., Barrionuevo, G., and Schottler, F. 1983. Intracellular injections of EGTA block induction of hippocampal long-term potentiation. *Nature 305*, 719–721.

Malenka, R. C., Ayoub, G. S., and Nicoll, R. A. 1987. Phorbol esters enhance transmitter release in rat hippocampal slices. *Brain Research 403*, 198–203.

Malenka, R. C., Kauer, J. A., Perkel, D. J., and Nicoll, R. A. 1989. The impact of postsynaptic calcium on synaptic transmission—its role in long-term potentiation. *Trends in Neurosciences 12*, 444–450.

Malenka, R. C., Kauer, J. A., Zucker, R. S., and Nicoll, R. A. 1988. Postsynaptic calcium is sufficient for potentiation of hippocampal synaptic transmission. *Science 242*, 81–84.

Malgaroli, A., Malinow, R., Schulman, H., and Tsien, R. W. 1991. Interactions among cell signalling systems: Persistent signalling and changes in presynaptic function in long-term potentiation. In *Ciba Foundation Symposium 164.* West Sussex, England: Wiley.

Malinow, R. 1991. Synaptic transmission between individual hippocampal slice neurons shows quantal levels, oscillations and LTP. *Science 252*, 722–724.

Malinow, R., Madison, D. V., and Tsien, R. W. 1988.

Persistent protein kinase activity underlying long-term potentiation. *Nature 335*, 820–824.

Malinow, R., and Miller, J. P. 1986. Postsynaptic hyperpolarization during conditioning reversibly blocks induction of long-term potentiation. *Nature 320*, 529–530.

Malinow, R., Schulman, H., and Tsien, R. W. 1989. Inhibition of postsynaptic PKC or CaMKII blocks induction but not expression of LTP. *Science 245*, 862–866.

Malinow, R., and Tsien, R. W. 1990. Presynaptic changes revealed by whole-cell recordings of long-term potentiation in rat hippocampal slices. *Nature 346*, 177–180.

Nelson, R. B., Hyman, C., Pfenninger, K. H., and Routtenberg, A. 1989. The two major phosphoproteins in growth cones are probably identical to two protein kinase C substrates correlated with persistence of long-term potentiation. *Journal of Neuroscience 9*, 381–389.

Nicoll, R. A., Kauer, J. A., and Malenka, R. C. 1988. The current excitement in long-term potentiation. *Neuron 1*, 97–103.

O'Dell, T. J., Hawkins, R. D., Kandel, E. R., and Arancio, () 1991. Tests of the roles of two diffusible substances in long-term potentiation: Evidence for nitric oxide as a possible early retrograde messenger. *Proceedings of the National Academy of Sciences 88*, 11285–11289.

Regehr, W. G., and Tank, D. W. 1990. Postsynaptic NMDA receptor-mediated calcium accumulation in hippocampal CA1 pyramidal cell dendrites. *Nature 345*, 807–810.

Schuman, E. M., and Madison, D. V. 1991. A requirement for the intercellular messenger nitric oxide in long-term potentiation. *Science 254*, 1503–1506.

Squire, L. R., and Lindenlaub, E., eds. 1990. *The biology of memory.* Stuttgart: Schattauer.

Stevens, C. F. 1989. Strengthening the synapses [News]. *Nature 338*, 460–461.

Wigström, H., Gustafsson, B., Huang, Y.-Y., and Abraham, W. C. 1986. Hippocampal long-term potentiation is induced by pairing single afferent volleys with intracellularly injected depolarizing current pulses. *Acta Physiologica Scandinavica 126*, 317–319.

Richard W. Tsien

Maintenance

One of the most striking properties of memory is its extreme duration; we all have memories dating as far back as 20 years or more. Similarly, one of the features of long-term potentiation or LTP (at least in certain brain structures) is its duration; it has been a major challenge for neurobiology to provide a cellular mechanism for long-lasting changes in synaptic transmission that outlast protein turnover. The discovery of the critical role of the NMDA receptors in triggering LTP indicated the existence of distinct stages in the establishment of LTP, which are generally defined as induction and maintenance (Bliss and Lynch, 1988). The former refers to events activated during the high-frequency stimulation, whereas the latter designates the processes that are responsible for the long-term changes in synaptic transmission that underlie LTP. In general, three types of mechanisms have been proposed as maintenance mechanisms: (1) those producing increased transmitter release, (2) those resulting in changes in spine electrical properties, and (3) those implicated in regulating receptor properties (Landfield and Deadwyler, 1988). Since the 1980s evidence against and for each of these mechanisms has been obtained, and the most salient features of the arguments will be presented below. Despite the ever-growing number of studies devoted to LTP, the exact mechanisms involved in LTP maintenance remain elusive. The difficulties encountered in the search for them may simply reflect the existence of multiple forms of synaptic plasticity that are differentially expressed across various brain structures.

Presynaptic Mechanisms

An *increase in transmitter release* obviously could account for an increase in synaptic transmission; it is generally admitted, for instance, that short-term potentiation is due to increased transmitter release (Zucker, 1989; see also POSTTETANIC POTENTIATION). Biochemical and electrophysiological evidence has been obtained in support of the hypothesis that increased transmitter release accounts for LTP. Glutamate is likely to be the neurotransmitter used by the synapses exhibiting LTP in various hippocampal pathways (Cotman et al., 1989; see also GLUTAMATE RECEPTORS AND THEIR CHARACTERIZATION), and increased glutamate levels have been found after LTP induction in perfusates obtained with push-pull cannulas implanted in the dentate gyrus (Dolphin, Errington, and Bliss, 1982). Increased glutamate release also was found after LTP induction in hippocampal slices and in synaptosomes prepared from hippocampus of rats in which

LTP had been induced. Since the induction of LTP involves the postsynaptic activation of NMDA receptors, a retrograde signal has been postulated that relays the postsynaptic activation to the presynaptic terminal. Current evidence suggests that arachidonic acid is the *retrograde signal* since activation of NMDA receptors stimulates phospholipase A_2 (PLA_2) and PLA_2 inhibitors prevent LTP formation (Bliss and Lynch, 1988). Moreover, arachidonic acid in conjunction with levels of electrical stimulation not sufficient to produce LTP alone induces LTP (Williams et al., 1989). Arachidonic acid could also provide a link with the presynaptic machinery involved in the regulation of transmitter release because it activates protein kinases that have been shown to participate in phosphorylation reactions important for transmitter release (Hemmings et al., 1989). While this mechanism could provide a satisfactory explanation for a short-lasting enhancement of transmitter release, in its present version it does not account for a long-lasting increase.

Quantal analysis of synaptic transmission (Martin, 1966) is an approach that, in principle, could provide an unambiguous answer to the question of the locus of the changes underlying LTP. It uses the intrinsic variability of transmitter release and statistical methods to determine the parameters generally thought to govern synaptic transmission, the probability of release, the number of release sites, and the elementary size of a postsynaptic response elicited by a quantum of neurotransmitter. Three groups have reported results obtained with quantal analysis in field CA_1 before and after LTP induction in hippocampal slices. Two groups observed an increase in quantal content (Malinow and Tsien, 1990; Bekkers and Stevens, 1990), whereas one group observed an increase in quantal size (Foster and McNaughton, 1991). In addition to this ambiguity in the results, it should be pointed out that quantal analysis requires a number of assumptions that might not be satisfied at hippocampal synapses.

Finally, increased transmitter release could be accounted for by an increase in the *number of synapses*. Anatomical studies using quantitative electron microscopy have provided evidence that the number of certain categories of synapses, in particular sessile synapses, is increased in field CA_1 following LTP induction (Lee et al., 1980; Chang and Greenough, 1984; see also MORPHOLOGICAL BASIS OF LEARNING AND MEMORY: VERTEBRATES). Although an increased number of synapses could explain the duration of LTP and account for its maintenance, it is not yet clear whether the increase in sessile synapses represents the formation of new synapses or the transformation of existing synapses by shape modification.

Changes in Spine Electrical Properties

Since their discovery, there has been much speculation concerning the roles of dendritic spines in synaptic transmission and the possibilities that synaptic plasticity could be due to alterations in their electrical properties (Rall, 1978; Coss and Perkel, 1985). Because of their shape—large heads relative to long, narrow necks—they are considered to be high-resistance elements coupling voltage changes at the synapses with voltage changes in dendritic shafts. In view of the technical difficulties in obtaining experimental data concerning the parameters of these elements, much of the work has been obtained by calculation and computer simulation using realistic values for these parameters. Based upon these calculations, it has been proposed that decreased neck resistance could account for an increased synaptic response (Wilson, 1988), which could affect the non-NMDA receptors component more specifically than the NMDA receptor component (Lynch and Baudry, 1991). Such a decrease in spine resistance could be due to an increase in neck dimension, and anatomical evidence indicates that LTP is accompanied by an increase in spines with wider and shorter necks. (See GUIDE TO THE ANATOMY OF THE BRAIN: NEURON.)

A major difficulty with this hypothesis arises when comparing spine morphology and LTP properties in hippocampus of adult and young animals. LTP is regularly detected after postnatal day 10 in field CA_1 and is maximal at about postnatal day 16 (Teyler, Perkins, and Harris, 1989). However, the morphology of spines at this stage of development is very different from the one seen in adults, with a majority of spines exhibiting short and wide necks. It would thus seem very unlikely that LTP would be due to a similar biophysical modification resulting from alterations of very different structures.

It should be added that very little is known concerning the existence of active elements (channels or pumps) in dendritic spines that could provide alternative means of modifying their electrical properties.

Changes in Receptor Properties

One of the most important characteristics of LTP is that it is expressed by an increase in the component of the synaptic response resulting from the activation of the AMPA subclass of glutamate receptors without changes in the component generated by the activation of NMDA receptors. Thus an alteration of the properties of the glutamate receptors has been proposed as a potential maintenance mechanism. Early experiments failed to detect changes in the responses to iontophoretically applied glutamate, but more recent experiments have shown an increased responsiveness to AMPA following LTP induction in field CA_1 in hippocampal slices. Several studies have shown that both the ligand binding and the ionic conductance properties of the *AMPA receptors* are affected by a variety of manipulations. In particular, changes in the lipid environment of the AMPA receptors modify its affinity for agonists, an observation that could account for the involvement of PLA_2 in LTP. More recently, the molecular biology of the AMPA receptors has provided exciting results concerning the nature and properties of these receptors. It appears that AMPA receptors belong to a family of receptors encoded by at least four related genes, each existing in two closely similar versions generated by alternative splicing of the genes, and designated *flip and flop*. It has been proposed that AMPA receptors exist as oligomers composed of any possible arrangement of flip and flop elements, and it has been shown that the flip elements provide larger currents than do the flop (Sommer et al., 1990). It is thus conceivable that LTP maintenance is the result of either a rearrangement of receptor configuration or a modification in gene expression (Massicotte and Baudry, 1991).

Conclusion

Although several mechanisms discussed above could account for some characteristics of LTP, most of them run into difficulties when they have to explain its stability. This feature is almost certain to eliminate most mechanisms, however attractive they might appear, that are based solely on conformational or posttranslational changes in proteins. In particular, several speculative mechanisms of LTP maintenance have been based on the idea of *biochemical switches*, constituted of biochemical reactions involving positive feedback. The most popular of these biochemical switches is derived from the properties of autophosphorylation of calcium calmodulin kinase type II, which is a very prominent protein in postsynaptic densities and especially in hippocampus (Crick, 1984). The mechanism involved in LTP maintenance therefore will probably require structural modifications that can confer lasting stability to biochemical modifications responsible for changes in synaptic transmission. Meanwhile, the various mechanisms described above underline the richness of mechanisms that have evolved to produce synaptic plasticity and that are likely to contribute to the multiple forms of potentiation that are being uncovered at a variety of central synapses.

REFERENCES

Bekkers, J. M., and Stevens, C. F. (1990). Presynaptic mechanism for long-term potentiation in the hippocampus. *Nature 346*, 724–729.

Bliss, T. V. P., and Lynch, M. A. (1988). Long-term potentiation: Mechanisms and properties. In P. W. Landfield and S. A. Deadwyler, eds., *Long-term potentiation: From biophysics to behavior*, pp. 3–72. New York: Liss.

Chang, F., and Greenough, W. T. (1984). Transient and enduring morphological correlates of synaptic activity and efficacy change in the rat hippocampal slice. *Brain Research 309*, 35–46.

Coss, R. G., and Perkel, D. H. (1985). The function of dendritic spines: A review of theoretical issues. *Behavior, Neurology, and Biology 44*, 151–185.

Cotman, C. W., Bridges, R. J., Taube, A. S., Clar, A. S., Geddes, J. W., and Monaghan, D. T. (1989). The role of the NMDA receptor in central nervous system plasticity and pathology. *Journal of NIH Research 1*, 65–74.

Crick, F. (1984). Memory and molecular turn-over. *Nature 312*, 101.

Dolphin, A. C., Errington, M. L., and Bliss, T. V. P. (1982). Long-term potentiation of the perforant path in vivo is associated with increased glutamate release. *Nature 297*, 496–498.

Foster, T. C., and McNaughton, B. L. (1991). Long-term synaptic enhancement in CA1 is due to increased quantal size, not quantal content. *Hippocampus 1*, 79–91.

Hemmings, H. C., Nairn, A. C., McGuiness, T. L., Huganir, R. L., and Greengard, P. (1989). Role of protein phosphorylation in neuronal signal transduction. *FASEB Journal 3*, 1583–1592.

Landfield, P. W., and Deadwyler, S. A., eds. (1988). Long-term potentiation: From biophysics to behavior. New York: Liss.

Lee, K., Schottler, F., Oliver, M., and Lynch, G. (1980). Brief bursts of high frequency stimulation produce two types of structural changes in rat hippocampus. *Journal of Neurophysiology 44*, 247–258.

Lynch, G., and Baudry, M. (1991). Re-evaluating the constraints on hypotheses regarding LTP expression. *Hippocampus 1*, 9–14.

Malinow, R., and Tsien, R. W. (1990). Presynaptic enhancement shown by whole-cell recordings of long-term potentiation in hippocampal slices. *Nature 346*, 177–180.

Martin, A. R. (1966). Quantal nature of synaptic transmission. *Physiological Review 46*, 51–66.

Massicotte, G., and Baudry, M. (1991). Triggers and substrates of hippocampal synaptic plasticity. *Neuroscience and Biobehavioral Review 15*, 415–423.

Rall, W. (1978). Dendritic spines and synaptic potency. In R. Porter, ed., *Studies in neurophysiology*, pp. 203–209. Cambridge: Cambridge University Press.

Sommer, B., Keinanen, K., Verdoorn, T. A., Wisden, W., Burnashev, N., Herb, A., Kohler, M., Takagi, T., Sakmann, B., and Seeburg, P. H. (1990). Flip and flop: A cell-specific functional switch in glutamate-operated channels of the CNS. *Science 249*, 1580–1585.

Teyler, T. J., Perkins, A. T., and Harris, K. M. (1989). The development of long-term potentiation in hippocampus and neocortex. *Neuropsychologia 27* (1), 31–39.

Williams, H. H., Errington, M. L., Lynch, M. A., and Bliss, T. V. (1989). Arachidonic acid induces a long-term activity-dependent enhancement of synaptic transmission in the hippocampus. *Nature 341*, 739–742.

Wilson, C. J. (1988). Cellular mechanisms controlling the strength of synapses. *Journal of Electron Microscope Technology 10*, 293–313.

Zucker, R. S. (1989). Short-term synaptic plasticity. *Annual Review of Neuroscience 12*, 13–22.

Michel Baudry
Gary Lynch

Behavioral Role

The long-lasting nature of the synaptic change induced in long-term potentiation (LTP) has fueled speculation that its underlying mechanisms may occur during, and be necessary for, certain kinds of learning. The gist of the idea is as follows: Suppose an animal wanted to remember where its burrow was located. Different views of the surrounding environment would presumably be represented in the brain as distinct patterns of neural activity, as the animal scanned the scene. Views in the immediate neighborhood of the burrow would occur at closely related points in time and, through the properties of cooperativity and associativity (see "Overview" above), result in strengthened synapses between coactive neurons in that brain area. While the functional effect of these changes would, of course, depend very much on the exact neural circuitry in which they occurred, it is not difficult to imagine that one consequence would be that the animal would now be able to retrieve a memory of the scene around its burrow from some distance away. This capacity to remember what something looks like in the absence of the immediate visual stimuli of which that scene is composed is a crucial constituent of memory, and one part of the system that the animal could use to navigate back home accurately.

Working out whether and what exact role LTP might play in learning and memory is a very active field of research. Three strategies have been pursued: (1) Is there overlap between the behavioral characteristics of certain kinds of learning and the known physiological properties of LTP? (2) Can learning be impeded when LTP is blocked selectively? (3) Do LTP-like changes occur when animals learn?

Is There Overlap Between the Characteristics of Learning and the Physiological Properties of LTP?

One important characteristic of memory is FORGETTING. LTP also decays to its nominal baseline over time. If LTP is the basis of memory, does its decay underlie the forgetting of information? Barnes (1979) carried out a laboratory study remarkably similar to the problem faced by the animal trying to remember the location of its burrow. Rats were placed once a day on a large circular table illuminated by fairly bright lights and given an opportunity to find a burrow hidden just underneath the edge of the table, from which they could escape

into the darkness. For an individual rat, the burrow might be at (say) the 8 o'clock position. Initially, this rat would search all over the table until eventually finding and entering the burrow, but after a few days, it would run straight to the 8 o'clock location. All of the rats had previously been implanted with indwelling electrodes in order to induce and record LTP in the dentate gyrus of the hippocampus (see GUIDE TO THE ANATOMY OF THE BRAIN). Barnes found that the rats which showed LTP that lasted for a long time (a day or more) learned the task faster and better than rats whose LTP was less persistent.

Another important characteristic of learning is that often we can only learn so much at one sitting—after a while we saturate and can take in no more. McNaughton et al. (1986) have described experiments suggesting that this phenomenon might be explained in terms of LTP. They also prepared animals with indwelling stimulating and recording electrodes and then trained them on the Barnes tabletop task. Once all the animals were finding the burrow quickly, they induced LTP physiologically to its asymptote (to the point where no more synaptic increase could be obtained). They then moved the burrow to a new hidden location under the tabletop (e.g., from the 8 o'clock to the 12 o'clock position) and continued training the animals. A control group also received stimulation of the dentate gyrus but using patterns that did not induce LTP. The experimenters found that the rats which had their synapses saturated had great difficulty in learning the new location of the burrow. In an ingenious follow-up, Castro et al. (1989) found that if a two-week period intervenes between the saturation of LTP and the retraining phase of a spatial task, learning proceeds normally. They believe the crucial variable is allowing sufficient time for the saturated synapses to decay back to baseline.

McNaughton et al. (1986) obtained a further puzzling finding. The rats that had LTP induced to asymptote were not lost in space on the tabletop—they persisted in going straight to the former location of the burrow. This indicates that the pattern of synaptic weights in the hippocampus itself cannot be the only, or even the major, site of long-term storage of spatial information. Perhaps hippocampal LTP is involved in processing and storing information for a short period (e.g., a few days), but this pattern then enables information to be laid down in a cortical storage site through a process of consolidation.

Can Learning Be Impeded When LTP Is Blocked Selectively?

The main physiological type of LTP is known to require the activation of NMDA receptors for its induction (see "Signal Transduction Mechanisms and Early Events" above). This finding suggests a further avenue for investigating whether LTP is necessary for learning. Is learning blocked by NMDA antagonists?

Morris et al. (1986) examined this issue, using the drug 2-amino-5-phosphonovalerate (AP5), a potent and highly selective antagonist of NMDA receptors. Unfortunately, AP5 does not cross the blood-brain barrier (membranes surrounding blood vessels throughout the brain that prevent toxic substances in the bloodstream from gaining access). However, by implanting osmotic mini-pumps containing AP5 under the skin of a rat and leading a small delivery tube to the lateral ventricle of the brain, they were able to create a situation in which neural activity in brain regions such as the hippocampus was normal except for its being unable to alter synaptic efficacy. The experimenters then attempted to train these rats in a simple spatial learning task in which the animals have to swim through cold water in search of a hidden escape platform located at one spot just under the surface. Normal and control rats learn this water maze task very rapidly, swimming from any starting position directly to the location of the platform. Rats treated with AP5 are impaired. Morris, Davis, and Butcher (1990) checked the physiological and behavioral selectivity of this AP5-induced impairment in various ways. For example, if the dose of AP5 is varied, the deficit is found only if a dose sufficient to block LTP is used. In addition, AP5 does not impair all learning tasks and, specifically, fails to affect visual discrimination learning. This finding implies that the drug is not impairing the animals' ability to see or to move around properly. It also means that LTP may be involved only in selected types of learning.

Not all experiments have looked at spatial learning. Miserendino et al. (1990) have examined a phenomenon called "fear-potentiated startle" that is known to depend on circuitry through the amygdala and brain stem. Rats show a pronounced startle reaction to loud sounds. This reaction is amplified if the sound is presented at a time when the rat has otherwise been made fearful, such as by the immediately prior presentation of a second stimulus, such as a light previously paired with weak electric shock. These experimenters wondered if the NMDA receptors found in certain regions of the amygdala were responsible for learning this fear-potentiating effect. In a series of studies, they first demonstrated that an NMDA antagonist would impair the task, then examined whether this was due to a direct effect upon the learning process or to various nonassociative processes. The results were clear-cut: The drug had no effect on sensitivity to light, sound, or shock but selectively impaired learning.

Pharmacological studies have several drawbacks. Despite everyone's best efforts to control for them, there are always side effects that could be contributing to the behavioral changes observed. This is particularly problematic with NMDA antagonists because of the presence of NMDA receptors in many circuits throughout the brain, where they are surely involved in myriad different functions in addition to any role they have in learning. The use of other pharmacological routes to impairing or improving LTP (e.g., glycine antagonists, inhibitors of selected protein kinases, calpain inhibitors) is clearly desirable. If drugs could be found to improve LTP, and if these also improved memory, it might be possible to use these clinically to alleviate at least some of the progressive memory loss seen in such crippling conditions as ALZHEIMER'S DISEASE.

Do LTP-like Changes Occur When Animals Learn?

If learning naturally causes LTP-like changes in brain areas such as the hippocampus and the cortex, it should be possible to see and measure them. Unfortunately, matters are not quite so straightforward. One problem is that if the storage capacity of these areas is anything appreciable, which we know it must be to hold a lifetime's worth of information, searching for the synaptic changes caused by a limited set of training experiences in an individual animal is a bit like searching for a needle in a haystack. Several experimenters have claimed to find dramatic changes in neural excitability in hippocampus following learning, but such changes can be explained without reference to mechanisms of synaptic plasticity. McNaughton and Morris (1987) have gone further and dubbed this puzzle the "Catch-22" problem of learning, teasing that if a dramatic change is found in the adult brain of vertebrates—if the experiment appears to work—it cannot be memory! There are other problems, too. One is that there have been reports that, in addition to the increases in synaptic strength characteristic of LTP, synaptic weakening may occur with certain patterns of stimulation (Stanton and Sejnowski, 1989). If this is true, finding specific changes in selected synapses using such gross indicators as extracellularly recorded field potentials looks remote.

However, an analogy might be helpful. The use of an extracellular recording electrode to record selected synaptic changes is a bit like placing a microphone at the center of the crowd at a Superbowl game to record conversations. It won't work. But what it will do, and do very well, is give an overall impression of the level of excitement in the crowd—after a spectacularly good play, for instance. The life of a laboratory rat is not, shall we say, very exciting, but it does have its moments. And one such moment for one set of experimental animals was a daily opportunity to visit a triangular tabletop stocked with interesting toys, smells, and things to climb on. Sharp, McNaughton, and Barnes (1989) examined what happened to field potentials during exploratory incidents like this and found a gradual short-term increase in the size of the synaptic component of field potentials in the dentate gyrus that then declined to baseline over the next 30 minutes or so. Interestingly, they also found a decrease in the size and latency of cell firing, indicating that whatever the basis of this change, it is probably not a change in neural excitability. Follow-up studies have also shown that this short-term increase is specifically related to exploratory rather than just any movements, suggesting that it may indeed be connected to the acquisition and processing of information about the novel objects on the platform.

Another way of trying to get at the issue is to examine, through single-unit recording studies, whether patterns of activity that are known from physiological work to be capable of inducing LTP are actually observed. Although it is not possible to examine the specific synaptic consequences of these patterns, their existence would imply that sufficient conditions for LTP to occur would have been met. Otto et al. (1991) have found that single units in the CA_1 region of the hippocampus display short patterns of burst firing during learning, spaced at what we know to be exactly optimum intervals for inducing LTP. Pavlides and Winson (1989) saw similar patterns in animals exposed for long periods to areas of a familiar environment: Cells responsive to features of that environment fired frequently. Interestingly, they also found that these cells fired more often than cells which were responsive only in other areas of the environment during periods, later on, of REM (rapid eye movement) sleep. This extraordinary finding hints at the possibility that the burst firing is consolidating information in long-term memory (see MEMORY CONSOLIDATION) and that even rats dream about the places they have recently been.

Conclusion

The underlying synaptic mechanisms of LTP may be activated during certain forms of learning, and their activation appears to be necessary for learning to occur. One obstacle to current research is that we are still very ignorant about how information is represented as spatiotemporal patterns of neural activity in the vertebrate brain, and how synaptic plasticity interacts with activity in different neural circuitry to realize the particular types of information processing that then occur. Computational models of how neurons, neural architecture, and mechanisms of synaptic plasticity interact (see NEURAL COMPUTATION) will be an important complement to experimental work of the kind summarized above.

REFERENCES

Barnes, C. A. (1979). Memory deficits associated with senescence: A neurophysiological and behavioral study in the rat. *Journal of Comparative Physiology and Psychology 93*, 74–104.

Castro, C. A., Silbert, L. H., McNaughton, B. L., and Barnes, C. A. (1989). Recovery of spatial learning following decay of experimental saturation of LTE at perforant path synapses. *Nature 342*, 545–548.

McNaughton, B. L., Barnes, C. A., Rao, G., Baldwin, J., and Rasmussen, M. (1986). Long-term enhancement of hippocampal synaptic transmission and the acquisition of spatial information. *Journal of Neuroscience 6*, 563–571.

McNaughton, B. L., and Morris, R. G. M. (1987). Hippocampal synaptic enhancement and information storage within a distributed memory system. *Trends in Neuroscience 10*, 408–415.

Miserendino, M. J. D., Sananes, C. B., Melia, K. R., and

Davis, M. (1990). Blockade of acquisition but not expression of conditioned fear-potentiated startle by NMDA in the amygdala. *Nature 345,* 716–718.

Morris, R. G. M., Anderson, E., Lynch, G. S., and Baudry, M. (1986). Selective impairment of learning and blockade of long term potentiation by an N-methyl-D-aspartate receptor antagonist. *Nature 319,* 774–776.

Morris, R. G. M., Davis, S., and Butcher, S. P. (1990). Hippocampal synaptic plasticity and NMDA receptors: A role in information storage? *Philosophical Transactions of the Royal Society of London B329,* 187–204.

Otto, T., Eichenbaum, H., Wiener, S. I., and Wible, C. G. (1991). Learning-related patterns of CA1 spike trains parallel stimulation parameters optimal for inducing hippocampal long-term potentiation. *Hippocampus 1,* 181–192.

Pavlides, C., and Winson, J. (1989). Influences of hippocampal place cell firing in the awake state on the activity of these cells during subsequent sleep episodes. *Journal of Neuroscience 9,* 2907–2918.

Sharp, P. E., McNaughton, B. L., and Barnes, C. A. (1989). Exploration-dependent modulation of evoked responses in fascia dentata: Fundamental observations and time course. *Psychobiology 17,* 257–269.

Stanton, P., and Sejnowski, T. J. (1989). Associative long-term depression in the hippocampus induced by hebbian covariance. *Nature 339,* 215–218.

R. G. M. Morris

LORENZ, KONRAD

Konrad Zacharias Lorenz was born November 7, 1903, in Vienna and died February 27, 1989, in Altenberg, Austria. By his own account he was fascinated from an early age with keeping and observing animals. He attended Columbia University in New York for one term in 1922, received an M.D. from the University of Vienna in 1928, and was awarded a Ph.D. in zoology by the same university in 1933. His first professional appointment was at the Anatomical Institute in Vienna (1928–1935); later he became professor of psychology at the University of Königsberg (1940–1942). Lorenz's brush with Nazism permanently tarnished his scientific reputation, especially in the United States and Great Britain. In a 1940 paper he mixed Nazi jargon into a discussion of one of his favorite themes, the destructive effects of domestication on animals and humans. Although he later repudiated this paper, his ideas sat well with Nazi theoreticians. During World War II he was an army physi-

cian on the eastern front and was a Russian prisoner of war in Armenia from 1944 to 1948.

With Erich von Holst, Lorenz was a founder in 1958 of the Max-Planck-Institut für Verhaltensphysiologie at Seewiesen, West Germany, where he remained as director until his retirement in 1973. Following his retirement, the Austrian Academy of Sciences created for Lorenz the Institute of Comparative Ethology based at his family home in Altenberg, where he served as director of the department of animal sociology until his death. In 1973 Lorenz, Niko Tinbergen, and Karl von Frisch shared the Nobel Prize in Physiology or Medicine for their pioneering work in ethology, the scientific study of animal behavior. In addition to his many scientific papers and books, Lorenz reached a wide audience with two popular books, *King Solomon's Ring* (1952), a reminiscence on the delights of animal study, and the more controversial *On Aggression* (1966), a discussion of the origins of animal and human aggression.

Lorenz's contribution to the study of animal behavior was the recognition that behavior is as much a property of biological organization as is anatomy. In this, Lorenz always acknowledged his debt to

Figure 1.   Konrad Lorenz. *Courtesy Dr. Richard I. Evans.*

two early students of animal behavior, Oskar Heinroth and Charles O. Whitman. Behavior, Lorenz asserted, can be described with the same precision as anatomy, and the causes of behavior can be analyzed by the methods of the natural sciences. Furthermore, the comparative study of different species reveals the effects of evolutionary adaptation on behavior. Behavior differs between species because it has been molded by natural selection to serve specific functions in the physical and social environments of different animals.

Lorenz's influence on contemporary research in learning and memory comes from two sources: his work on imprinting and his ideas about the interplay between the learned and the innate in behavior. The popular image of Lorenz usually places him at the head of a straggling line of imprinted goslings following him through the Austrian countryside. Imprinting is the formation of attachment between young precocial birds and their parents. Once formed, the bond is not easily broken. Viewed from the operant perspective that once dominated the study of animal learning, especially in the United States, imprinting seemed a very puzzling form of learning. Research findings on imprinting, song learning by birds, and other specialized forms of learning contributed to the decline of the strict operant reinforcement approach to learning. The time course of imprinting, the range of stimuli to which young birds will imprint, the neural basis of imprinting, and its later effects on mate choice have been extensively studied in the years since Lorenz first drew attention to the importance of the phenomenon. (See also IMPRINTING; OPERANT BEHAVIOR.)

The second source of Lorenz's influence on current research in learning and memory was his debate with the American psychologist Daniel S. Lehrman during the 1960s on the relative importance of nature and nurture in the development of behavior. Much of Lorenz's scientific work is an analysis of instinct. He regarded instinctive behavior as the expression of information accumulated in the genome over evolutionary time. Animals could thus produce appropriate responses to food, mates, offspring, or predators without having to learn how to respond. Behavior that was appropriate to the context could appear in its full form on the first performance of the behavior. Lorenz further regarded such instinctive behavior as under strict genetic control, in contrast with other behavior in which developmental plasticity and learning played a role. He saw behavior as consisting of sequences of actions in which the learned and the innate were intercalated. This view was criticized for ignoring important findings about the development of behavior. In his theory of instinct, Lorenz conflated a number of very different ideas about innate behavior, genetics, and evolution. The debate between Lorenz and Lehrman led to a clarification and revision of both positions (Lorenz, 1965; see also EVOLUTION AND LEARNING).

The modern view of the matter preserves some of Lorenz's ideas, particularly that animals can exhibit behavior that is innate in the sense that it occurs in a functional form in the absence of prior relevant experience. It is not correct, however, to regard such behavior as any more "genetic" than anything else animals do, or to suppose that such behavior is developmentally inflexible. Genetic differences can produce differences in behavior between animals, as can environmental differences. Other of Lorenz's views about learning have retained their currency, however, such as his insistence that learning cannot be simply open-ended plasticity in behavior, but consists of evolved rules for acquiring information and modifying behavior.

Although he performed little empirical work, preferring to draw on his enormous store of personal observation of animals, and although many of his pronouncements on human behavior were more folk psychology than science, Lorenz had a profound influence on transforming the study of animal behavior into a natural science.

REFERENCES

Lorenz, K. (1940). Durch Domestikation verursachte Störungen arteigenen Verhalten. *Zeitschrift für angewandte Psychologie und Characterkunde 59*, 1–81.
——— (1952). *King Solomon's ring.* London: Methuen.
——— (1965). *Evolution and modification of behavior.* Chicago: University of Chicago Press.
——— (1966). *On aggression.* London: Methuen.

David F. Sherry

LURIA, A. R.

The Soviet psychologist Alexandr Romanovich Luria (1902–1977) is best known for his work in neuropsychology but contributed also to develop-

Figure 1.   A. R. Luria. *Courtesy Elena A. Luria.*

mental and crosscultural psychology. The son of a prominent physician, Luria graduated from the University of Kazan in 1921 and joined the staff of the Moscow Institute of Psychology in 1923. His very early interest in psychoanalysis was tempered by his awareness of the need for objective methods. His attempts to study the subconscious by means of objective methods resulted in the book *The Nature of Human Conflicts* (1932). In 1924 Luria met Lev Vigotsky, and their subsequent collaboration until Vigotsky's premature death in 1934 was to have a lifelong influence on Luria's work. Together they developed the concept of historicocultural psychology, in which they argued that higher cognitive functions are determined by culture and arise as the end products of the internalization of external cultural devices and codes. Vigotsky and Luria embarked on two lines of research driven by the historicocultural theory: developmental studies of language acquisition and the regulatory role of language in behavior, and cross-cultural studies of modes of inference among the tribes of Central Asia. Eventually both lines of research ran afoul of the Marxist ideological doctrine, and Luria was forced to terminate his developmental and cross-cultural work.

Luria's scientific interests were gradually evolving toward more biological aspects of psychology, and ultimately neuropsychology. In the early 1930s Luria turned his attention to the "nature-nurture" debate and embarked on a series of studies of cognitive processes in identical and fraternal twins. In the late 1930s, by then professor of psychology, he earned a medical degree. The extent to which this shift of interests reflected a natural intellectual evolution as opposed to an escape from the more ideologically charged, and therefore more personally dangerous, areas of psychology in the context of the Soviet ideological terror of the times, is a matter for speculation. Luria's turning toward neuropsychology was facilitated by World War II, when he was called upon to develop remedial procedures for head-injured soldiers.

Regardless of the actual impact of his writings, the intellectual drive behind Luria's work was primarily to understand the fundamental aspects of brain-behavioral relations and to develop a comprehensive theory of those relations, and only secondarily to describe clinical syndromes and develop diagnostic and remedial techniques. His early eclectic interests shaped his brand of neuropsychology. Luria entered the field at the time of the raging debate between "narrow localizationism" and "equipotentialism." He went beyond this simplistic dilemma and formulated his concept of "dynamic functional systems," which captures the relationship between the localizable dimensions of cognition and complex traits, skills, and behaviors as they are manifested in everyday life. Although certain basic cognitive dimensions were thought by Luria to be localized in invariant ways, the dimensional composition of the "functional systems" corresponding to complex processes was thought to be predicated on cultural and developmental factors.

Given Luria's cultural-developmental interests, it is not surprising that the neuropsychology of language was foremost on his agenda, as reflected in the major monographs *Traumatic Aphasia* ([1947] 1970), *The Role of Speech in the Regulation of Normal and Abnormal Behavior* ([1955] 1961), and *The Higher Cortical Functions in Man* ([1962] 1966). Luria's distinct taxonomy of aphasias reflects his interest in fine linguistic operational analysis. The frontal lobes were another major interest of Luria's, a continuation of his earlier interest in self-regulation and consciousness. Here, the theme of the hierarchic nature of cognitive control was prominent, undoubtedly reflecting Luria's interactions with Nicholas Bernstein, a Soviet physiologist and mathematician who foreshadowed some of the basic concepts of cybernetics but shared Vigotsky's fate of being ostracized for deviation from the Pavlovian doctrine. In the later part of his career, Luria became deeply interested in memory. His attempts to identify distinct amnesic syndromes on the basis of the underlying subcortical neuroanatomy are described in the monograph *Neuropsychology of Memory* ([1974] 1976). He distinguished the "midline" amnesic syndromes (curiously, without further distinguishing between the diencephalic and mesiotemporal variants), pituitary, mesiofrontal, "massive prefrontal," and cortical memory deficits. He was particularly interested in the relationship between consolidation and executive functions.

Although Luria is widely known in the West for various adaptations of his diagnostic approaches, he never bothered to compile them into a battery. In fact, the notion of a battery was abhorrent to him, and he always advocated a flexible, hypothesis-testing approach. The notion of instrument standardization was also abhorrent to him. Although Luria's bias against quantification is often cast in East-West terms, it is probably a generational phenomenon. After all, Luria the clinician was descended from the lineage of the great turn-of-the-century European neurologist-phenomenologists. What makes his diagnostic approach singularly attractive is that every procedure targets a cognitive dimension accounted for in his brain-behavioral theory.

During the later part of his career, Luria was professor of psychology at Moscow State University, where he held the chair of neuropsychology, and director of the Neuropsychology Laboratory at the Bourdenko Institute of Neurosurgery in Moscow. He received numerous awards and was elected member of various academies and learned societies in the Soviet Union and in the West.

(See also AMNESIA, ORGANIC; APHASIA; MEMORY CONSOLIDATION; MNEMONISTS.)

REFERENCES

Luria, A. R. (1932). *The nature of human conflicts.* New York: Liveright.

——— [1947] (1970). *Traumatic aphasia.* Trans. D. Bowden. The Hague: Mouton.

——— [1955] (1961). *The role of speech in the regulation of normal and abnormal behavior.* Ed. J. Tizard. London: Pergamon.

——— [1962] (1966; 2nd ed., 1980). *The higher cortical functions in man.* Trans. B. Haigh. New York: Basic Books.

——— [1974] (1976). *Neuropsychology of memory.* Trans. B. Haigh. Washington, D.C.: Winston.

Elkhonon Goldberg

M

MATERIAL-SPECIFIC MEMORY DISORDERS

Throughout the history of neuropsychology, researchers have attempted to understand the relationship between brain and behavior through the localization of function. In the nineteenth century, much of the effort was devoted to correlating aphasic symptoms with anatomical sites. The result of this endeavor was the emergence of the concept of cerebral dominance, referring to lateralization of language in the left hemisphere. It has largely been over the past 50 years that the cognitive functions of the right hemisphere have become recognized, and there has been a gradual switch from the notion of cerebral dominance to that of complementary specialization of function.

The complementary specialization of function of the human brain is perhaps best illustrated by studies of the effects on memory of unilateral, focal lesions, particularly lesions involving the temporal lobes and underlying structures of the limbic system (amygdala and hippocampus). In 1955, Meyer and Yates showed that lesions of the left temporal lobe impaired verbal associative learning; they termed this phenomenon an impairment of auditory learning. Milner (1978) was able to extend this finding by demonstrating that left temporal-lobe lesions impair recall of the content of short prose passages as well as the learning of word pairs. Importantly, she also demonstrated that this deficit was present under conditions of visual presentation as well as auditory presentation of the target information, and thus she interpreted the impairment as a verbal one. The verbal memory deficit resulting from left temporal-lobe lesions has been elicited with other story learning tasks, with

learning and recalling lists of words, and with the recall of the names of pictured objects or the names of toy models of objects. These verbal memory deficits are not due to underlying impairments in cognitive organization, integration of information, WORKING MEMORY, or rate of processing of information, or to an impairment of the SEMANTIC MEMORY system (see Smith, 1989, for a more complete review).

Verbal learning and verbal memory tasks on which performance is so sensitive to the effects of left temporal lobe lesions are performed normally by patients with comparable lesions in the right temporal lobe. The right, nondominant temporal lobe is also specialized in function for memory, but unlike the left, it is specialized for information that is not easily verbalized or coded into words. Similarly, the memory deficits associated with right temporal-lobe lesions are not modality specific, but are evident regardless of whether the information is presented via the auditory, visual, or tactile senses. Right temporal-lobe lesions impair the recall and recognition of abstract designs, spatial information, and unfamiliar tonal melodies.

On certain of the memory tasks on which deficits are observed after temporal-lobe lesions, it has been found that the severity of the deficit is related to the extent to which the lesion encroaches upon the hippocampal region (hippocampus and parahippocampal gyrus), which Mishkin (1982) has identified as part of a memory circuit involving widespread cortical systems. In terms of specialization of function, the nature of the impairments seen after hippocampal lesions is a function of the specialization of the neocortex of the same hemisphere.

The contrasting effects of left and right temporal-lobe lesions on verbal and nonverbal memory are illustrated well in experiments utilizing materials that can be encoded with either a visual or a verbal code. Jaccarino (1975) presented subjects with line drawings of common objects; immediately after viewing the drawings, and again 24 hours later, the subjects were required to name from memory as many of the pictures as possible. In immediate recall, a mild impairment was seen in patients with left temporal-lobe lesions, whereas, as expected on this verbal memory task, patients with right temporal-lobe lesions performed normally. Twenty-four hours later, however, both patient groups showed a severe deficit in recall. Jaccarino interpreted these results as indicating the duality of memory processing, relying on the idea put forth by Paivio (1971) that both a verbal and an imaginal code can be used to mediate memory performance. In this experiment, Jaccarino assumed that the verbal code was sufficient for the initial recall, but the visual code was more important for recall after the delay. Further evidence for the duality of memory processing from the study of material-specific memory disorders is found in Jones-Gotman's (1979) work on image-mediated verbal learning. She found that severity of the verbal memory deficits of patients with left temporal-lobe lesions can be lessened by the use of visual imagery to mediate learning, and that impairments in verbal learning can be elicited in patients with right temporal-lobe lesions by imposing the use of visual imagery as a learning strategy.

Material-specific memory disorders have also been documented as a consequence of lesions outside the temporal lobes. For example, Habib and Sirigu (1987) have determined that the critical lesion for producing topographical memory loss involves the right posterior medial area. Warrington (1984) has shown that recognition memory for words and faces can be impaired following unilateral lesions of the frontal or parietal lobes, as well as the temporal lobes; in these cases, whether the deficit involves words or faces depends on the hemisphere of the lesion. In their review of impairments in short-term memory span, McCarthy and Warrington (1990) note that these deficits are dissociable with respect to their nature and anatomical correlates; deficits in visuospatial span are found after right posterior lesions, and deficits in visuoverbal span after left posterior lesions.

One of the long-standing debates in cognitive psychology has focused on whether or not memory should be subdivided into different stores or systems. This is not a new issue; as long ago as the 1930s, psychologists were questioning whether or not there exists a separate system underlying memory for visual material that operates independently of a verbal processing system. The material-specific memory disorders, together with the evidence of dual encoding by normal subjects, imply that such theoretical accounts must allow for separate processing systems for verbal and nonverbal material.

REFERENCES

Habib, M., and Sirigu, A. (1987). Pure topographical disorientation: A definition and anatomical basis. *Cortex 23,* 73–85.

Jaccarino, G. (1975). Dual encoding in memory: Evidence from temporal-lobe lesions in man. Unpublished M.A. thesis, McGill University, Montreal. Also see Milner (1978) for a description of Jaccarino's work.

Jones, M. K. (1974). Imagery as mnemonic aid after left temporal lobectomy: Contrast between material-specific and generalized memory disorders. *Neuropsychologia 12,* 21–30.

Jones-Gotman, M. (1979). Incidental learning of image-mediated or pronounced words after right temporal lobectomy. *Cortex 15,* 187–197.

Jones-Gotman, M., and Milner, B. (1978). Right temporal-lobe contribution to image-mediated verbal learning. *Neuropsychologia 16,* 61–71.

Meyer, V., and Yates, A. J. (1955). Intellectual changes following temporal lobectomy for psychomotor epilepsy. *Journal of Neurology, Neurosurgery and Psychiatry 18,* 44–52.

McCarthy, R. A., and Warrington, E. K. (1990). *Cognitive neuropsychology.* New York: Academic Press.

Milner, B. (1978). Clues to the cerebral organization of memory. In P. Buser and A. Rougeul-Buser, eds., *Cerebral correlates of conscious experience,* pp. 139–153. Amsterdam: Elsevier.

——— (1980). Complementary functional specializations of the human cerebral hemispheres. In R. Levi-Montalcini, ed., *Nerve cells, transmitters and behaviour,* pp. 601–625. Vatican City: Pontificia Academia Scientiarum.

Mishkin, M. (1982). A memory system in the monkey. *Philosophical Transactions of the Royal Society* (London) *B298,* 85–95.

Paivio, A. (1971). *Imagery and verbal processes.* New York: Holt.

Smith, M. L. (1989). Memory disorders associated with temporal-lobe lesions. In F. Boller and J. Grafman, eds., *Handbook of neuropsychology,* vol. 3, pp. 91–106. Amsterdam: Elsevier.

Warrington, E. K. (1984). *Recognition memory test.* Windsor, Canada: Nelson.

Mary Lou Smith

MATHEMATICAL LEARNING THEORY

Theories of learning were enormously visible and influential in psychology from 1930 to 1950, but dropped precipitously from view during the next two decades while the information-processing approach to cognition based on a computer metaphor gained ascendancy. The groundwork for a resurgence of learning theory in the context of cognitive psychology was laid during the earlier period by the development of a subspecialty that may be termed *mathematical learning theory.*

In psychology, just as in physical and biological sciences, mathematical theories should be expected to aid in the analysis of complex systems whose behavior depends on many interacting factors and to bring out causal relationships that would not be apparent to unaided empirical observation. Mathematical reasoning was part and parcel of theory construction from the beginnings of experimental psychology in some research areas, notably the measurement of sensation, but came on the scene much later in the study of learning, and then got off to an inauspicious start. By the 1930s, laboratory investigation of conditioning and learning at both the animal and the human level had accumulated ample quantitative data to invite mathematical analysis. However, the early efforts were confined to the routine exercise of finding equations that could provide compact descriptions of the average course of improvement with practice in simple laboratory tasks (Gulliksen, 1934). Unfortunately, these efforts yielded no harvest of new insights into the nature of learning and did not enter into the design of research.

The agenda for a new approach that might more nearly justify the label *mathematical learning theory* was set by Clark L. HULL, who distilled much of the learning theory extant at the end of the 1930s into a system of axioms from which theorems might be derived to predict aspects of conditioning and simple learning in a wide variety of experimental situations (Hull, 1943). One of the central ideas was a hypothetical measure of the degree of learning of any stimulus-response rela-

tionship. This measure, termed *habit strength (H),* was assumed to grow during learning of the association between any stimulus and response according to the quantitative law

$$H = M(1 - e^{cN}), \qquad (1)$$

where N denotes number of learning experiences, M is the maximum value of H, and c is a constant representing speed of learning. Thus, H should increase from an initial value of zero to its maximum as a smooth "diminishing returns" function of trials. However, knowing the value of H does not enable prediction of what the learner will do at any point in practice for two reasons. First, a test for learning may be given in a situation different from that in which practice occurred (as when a student studies at home but is tested in a classroom), and according to Hull's principle of *stimulus generalization,* the effective habit strength on the test is assumed to be some reduced value H' that differs from H as a function of the difference between the two situations. But, further, motivation must be taken into account. If the student in the example studies in a relaxed mood but arrives at the test situation in a state of anxiety, performance may be affected and fail to mirror the actual level of learning. In Hull's theory, it is assumed that the strength of the tendency to perform a learned act, termed *excitatory potential* (E), is determined by habit strength and level of motivation or emotion (denoted D) acting jointly according to the multiplicative relation

$$E = H \times D. \qquad (2)$$

These conceptions were implemented in vigorous research programs mounted by Kenneth W. SPENCE, one analyzing the relation between anxiety and learning in human beings and the other producing the first quantitative accounts of the ability of some animals to exhibit transposition (i.e., to generalize from learning experiences in terms of relationships such as brighter than or larger than, as distinguished from absolute values of stimulus magnitude).

Hull's theory as a whole did not prove viable. It depended on too many assumptions and was too loose-jointed in structure to be readily testable, and its deterministic axioms lacked the flexibility needed to interpret varieties of learning more complex than simple conditioning. However, some components have survived to reappear as constituents of new theories. A notable instance is the law of habit growth. An implication of Equation 1 is that the change in habit strength, ΔH, on any trial can be expressed as

$$\Delta H = c(M - H), \qquad (3)$$

in which form it is apparent that learning is fastest when the difference between current habit strength and its maximum is large, and slow when the difference is small. According to Hull's assumptions, and indeed nearly all learning theories of his time, the function should be applicable on any trial when the response undergoing learning occurs in temporal contiguity to reinforcement (that is, a positive incentive such as food for a hungry animal or a to-be-feared event such as an electric shock). In the course of research over the next two decades, it became apparent that learning depends also on the degree to which an experience provides the learner with new information. If, for example, an animal has already learned that a particular stimulus, S1, predicts the occurrence of shock, then on a trial when S1 and another stimulus, S2, precede shock in combination, the animal may learn nothing about S2 (Kamin, 1969). This observation and many related ones can be explained by a new theory that can be viewed as a refinement and extension of one component of Hull's axiom about habit growth. In the new version, the change in habit strength on any learning trial is described by the function

$$\Delta H = c(M - H_T), \qquad (4)$$

where H denotes strength of a particular habit undergoing acquisition—for example, the relation between S2 and shock in the illustration—and H_T denotes the sum of strengths of all habits active in the situation—for example, the habits relating both S1 and S2 to shock in the illustration (Rescorla and Wagner, 1972). Studying the new learning function, one can see that if habit strength for S1 is large enough so that H_T is equal to M, then there will be no increment in habit strength for S2. The prediction that learning about S2 is blocked by the previous learning about S1 has been borne out by many experiments. This success, and others like it, in dealing with novel and sometimes surprising findings has put the body of theory built by Rescorla and Wagner and others on the groundwork of Hull's system into a commanding position in present-day research on animal learning.

At one time it appeared that the basic ingredients of Hull's theory could be adapted in a straightforward and simple way to apply to human learning. In the early 1950s, a physicist converted to mathematical psychology, in collaboration with an eminent statistician, arrived at the idea that the hypothetical notion of habit strength could be dispensed with so that learning functions like Equation 3 would be expressed in terms of changes in response probabilities (Bush and Mosteller, 1955). If, for example, a rat was learning to go to the correct (rewarded) side of a simple T maze, they assumed that when a choice of one side led to reward, the probability, p, of that choice would increase in accord with the function

$$\Delta p = c(1 - p), \qquad (5)$$

and when it led to nonreward, p would decrease in accord with

$$\Delta p = -cp, \qquad (6)$$

where c is a constant reflecting speed of learning. By a simple derivation it can be shown that if reward on one side of the maze has some fixed probability (0, 1, or some intermediate value), Equations 5 and 6, taken together, imply a learning function of the same form as Hull's function for growth of habit strength. Also, the prediction can be derived that the final level of the learning function will be such that, on the average, the probability of choosing a given side is equal to the probability of reward on that side, as illustrated in Figure 1. This prediction of *probability matching* has been confirmed (under some especially simplified experimental conditions) in a number of studies. In an elegant series of elaborations and applications of this simple model, Bush and Mosteller (1955) showed that it could be carried over to human learning in situations requiring repeated choices between alternatives associated with different magnitudes and probabilities of reward, as in some forms of gambling.

However, only a few such applications appeared, and in time it became apparent that although Bush and Mosteller's methods proved widely useful, neither their approach nor others building on Hull's system could be extended to account for many forms of human learning.

The limitations of models based on conceptions of habit growth or similarly gradual changes in response probabilities were anticipated by the

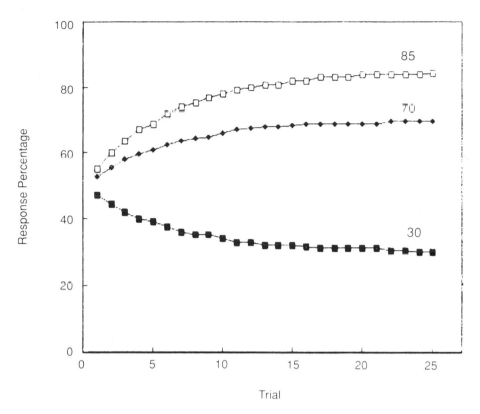

Figure 1. Theoretical predictions of percentages of responses to a given side of a choice point on each trial of an illustrative experiment for groups of learners who had different probabilities of reward (.85, .70, or .30) on that side. Details of the model are given in the text.

great pioneer of modern neuroscience D. O. HEBB. In a seminal monograph, Hebb (1949) noted that whereas slow and gradual learning characterizes animals low on the phylogenetic scale and immature organisms higher on the scale, the learning of the higher forms, most conspicuously human beings, as adults is normally much faster, and often takes the form of abrupt reorganizations of the products of previous learning (as when a person trying to master a technique of computer programming suddenly grasps a key relationship).

A theoretical approach that would prove more adaptable to the treatment of human learning appeared in the 1950s, contemporaneously with the work of Bush and Mosteller, in the development of statistical learning theory, also known as stimulus sampling theory (Estes, 1950). This approach is based on the ideas that even apparently simple forms of learning entail the formation of associations among representations in memory of many aspects of the situation confronting the learner, and that more complex forms are largely a matter

of classifying or reclassifying already existing associations (now more often termed *memory elements*). In the earliest versions of the theory, the associations simply related stimuli and responses. If, say, a rat was learning the correct turn in a T maze, then on any trial associations would be formed between the response made, together with the ensuing reward or nonreward, and whatever aspects of the choice situation the animal happened to attend to (the notion of sampling).

An interesting mathematical property of this model is that for simple learning situations, if the total population of stimulus aspects available for sampling is large, the basic learning functions take a form identical to those of Bush and Mosteller's model (Equations 5 and 6), with the learning-rate parameter c interpreted as the proportion of stimulus aspects sampled on any trial. When the population is not large, however, the model is better treated as a type of probabilistic process (technically, a Markov chain) in which learning is conceived in terms of discrete transitions between states. A state is defined by the way the total set of memory elements is classified with respect to alternative responses. The model is thus able to handle the fact that learning is under some conditions slow and gradual but under other conditions fast and discontinuous. In a special case of the model, it is assumed that the learner perceives the entire stimulus pattern present on a trial as a unit, so that the system has only two states, one in which the unit is associated with the correct response and one in which it is not. Surprisingly at the time, this ultrasimplified model was found to account in detail for the data of experiments on the learning of elementary associations (as between faces and names) and concept identification, even for human learners (Bower, 1961).

The stimulus sampling model automatically accounts for the phenomenon of generalization, which required a special postulate in Hull's system. If learning has occurred in one situation, the probability that the learned response will transfer to a new situation is equal to the proportion of aspects of the second situation that were sampled in the first. The sampling model has the serious limitation that it cannot explain how perfect discriminations can be learned between situations that have aspects in common. However, this deficiency was remedied in a new version formulated by Douglas L. Medin and his associates especially for the interpretation of discrimination and categorization (Medin and Schaffer, 1978). With a new rule for computing similarity between stimuli or situations, this formulation, generally known as the exemplar-memory model, has been shown to account for many properties of human category learning in simulated medical diagnosis and the like. (See also DISCRIMINATION AND GENERALIZATION.)

An interesting aspect of science is the way progress often occurs by seeing older theories in a new light. A striking instance is the observation that Rescorla and Wagner's extension of Hull's learning theory can be viewed as a special case of a type of adaptive network model that has been imported from engineering into the new branch of cognitive science known as *connectionism* (Rumelhart and McClelland, 1986). A connectionist network is composed of layers of elementary units (nodes) interconnected by pathways. When the network receives an input at the bottom layer, as from the stimulus display in a learning situation, activation is transmitted through the network to output nodes at the top layer that lead to response mechanisms. During learning, memories are stored not in individual units but as distributions of strengths of connections in groups of units. These strengths are modified during learning by a process that is driven by an overall tendency toward error correction. Connectionist models have been developed and applied for the most part in relation to complex cognitive activities such as speech perception and language acquisition (McClelland and Rumelhart, 1986), but it has also been discovered that the descendant of Hull's learning theory embodied in the Rescorla-Wagner model can be viewed as a special case of a connectionist network (Gluck and Bower, 1988). The consequence of this observation has been a wave of new work applying and extending what was originally conceived as a model of animal conditioning to a variety of work on human learning and categorization. Thus, by the recurring process of rediscovery and reinterpretation, mathematical learning theory has become active in a new guise as a component of the new discipline of cognitive science.

(See also LEARNING THEORY.)

REFERENCES

Bower, G. H. (1961). Application of a model to paired-associate learning. *Psychometrika 26,* 255–280.

Bush, R. R., and Mosteller, F. (1955). *Stochastic models for learning.* New York: Wiley.

Estes, W. K. (1950). Toward a statistical theory of learning. *Psychological Review 57,* 94–107.

Gluck, M. A., and Bower, G. H. (1988). From conditioning to category learning: An adaptive network model. *Journal of Experimental Psychology: General 117,* 225–244.

Gulliksen, H. A. (1934). A rational equation of the learning curve based on Thorndike's law of effect. *Journal of General Psychology 11,* 395–434.

Hebb, D. O. (1949). *Organization of behavior: A neurophysiological theory.* New York: Wiley.

Hull, C. L. (1943). *Principles of behavior.* New York: Appleton.

Kamin, L. J. (1969). Predictability, surprise, attention, and conditioning. In B. A. Campbell and R. M. Church, eds., *Punishment and aversive behavior.* New York: Appleton-Century-Crofts.

McClelland, J. L., and Rumelhart, D. E. (1986). *Parallel distributed processing: Explorations in the microstructure of cognition,* vol. 2. Cambridge, Mass.: MIT Press.

Medin, D. L., and Schaffer, M. M. (1978). Context theory of classification learning. *Psychological Review 85,* 207–238.

Rescorla, R. A., and Wagner, A. R. (1972). A theory of Pavlovian conditioning: Variations in the effectiveness of reinforcement and non-reinforcement. In A. H. Black and W. F. Prokasy, eds., *Classical Conditioning*, vol. 2, *Current research and theory*. New York: Appleton-Century-Crofts.

Rumelhart, D. E., and McClelland, J. L. (1986) *Parallel distributed processing*, vol. 1. Cambridge, Mass.: MIT Press.

W. K. Estes

McGEOCH, JOHN A.

John A. McGeoch (1897–1942) was the single most seminal figure in defining the research area known as verbal learning. Trained in the Chicago functionalist tradition by Harvey A. Carr, he received the Ph.D. in 1926 with a dissertation titled "A Study in the Psychology of Testimony." His professional career was notable for its meteoric advancement, its geographic mobility, and its massive research energy. After rising through the academic ranks at Washington University in St. Louis, he became professor at the University of Arkansas in 1928, at the age of 31. Two years later he went as chairman of the Psychology Department to the University of Missouri, a position he subsequently filled at Wesleyan University and at the University of Iowa (Pratt, 1943; Wolfle, 1943).

McGeoch's major work was *The Psychology of Human Learning: An Introduction* (1942). It was not intended as such: He had been at work, during the 1930s, with the collaboration of Carr, on a projected two-volume manual covering all published work on human learning. The first draft of the manual was about 80 percent complete in 1936, and had received chapter-by-chapter feedback from Carr (see Carr's introduction to McGeoch, 1942). After several years' delay, caused by ill health and frequent moves, McGeoch was persuaded by a publisher, on assuming the Iowa chairmanship, to write a digest of the manuscript, intended for use as a textbook. McGeoch's impact on the field has come through the comprehensiveness and authority of this book and its revision a decade later by his student Arthur L. Irion (McGeoch and Irion, 1952).

McGeoch's reputation rests additionally on a theoretical assertion and a related empirical corpus. The theoretical assertion is in a paper (McGeoch,

Figure 1. John A. McGeoch.

1932) that argues that the process of FORGETTING, which was by then his special commitment, could not in principle be explained by the mere passage of time, as was asserted by the decay theory of forgetting. Rather, he said, activities that occurred *during that time* must be responsible. It follows that to penetrate the mechanism of forgetting, one should study retroactive inhibition. McGeoch's most visible research activities respected that logical agenda. (See also INTERFERENCE AND FORGETTING.)

His scientific style remained close to the data and was conservative with respect to theoretical leaps. McGeoch believed that the psychology of human learning and memory was in a basically pretheoretical phase, in which the field was responsible for determining, first of all, what the data *were* before proposing elaborate explanations of them. Postman (1972) has described this and other characteristics of the functionalist attitude McGeoch received from such predecessors as Carr and J. R. Angell and passed along to such students as A. W. Melton (an undergraduate at Washington University) and B. J. Underwood (a graduate student at Iowa). The austerity of his book, the programmatic drive of his experiments on retroactive inhibition, and his atheoretical bias established McGeoch as an archetype for the contrived laboratory approach to human learning and memory. In the more recent days of cognitive psychology, neither McGeoch's reputation nor the reputation of verbal learning has fared well. The latter tradition is held up as an example of the sterility into which orthodox science can pass.

In the context of McGeoch's total career, this reputation is largely erroneous: His dissertation was a series of field studies on memory as *testimony* in which McGeoch tested children (ages 9 to 14) in intact classrooms within the East St. Louis school system (McGeoch, 1928a, 1928b, 1928c). Among many other comparisons, he was interested in the relation between accuracy and intelligence, which he operationalized by contrasting normal and institutionalized children and by the administration to each group of the Army Alpha test (McGeoch, 1928b). An earlier publication (McGeoch, 1925a) had compared (1) the staged event (eyewitness reality) with (2) objects or (3) words as stimuli. Thus, McGeoch may be among a handful of pioneers in developing the study of eyewitness testimony in American psychology (all but one of the references he cited in this work were from German laboratories). Nor was this work on practical aspects of memory isolated: Others of his early publications concerned memory for poetry (Whitely and McGeoch, 1928), emotional measurement (McGeoch and Bunch, 1930), and the relation between suggestibility and juvenile delinquency (McGeoch, 1925b). The catholicism of his original research interests is solidly within the functionalist tradition. One speculation is that McGeoch later turned to the precision and control of experimental studies *because of* his commitment to finding answers for everyday problems in human life, not in order to escape from them.

REFERENCES

McGeoch, J. A. (1925a). The fidelity of report of normal and subnormal children. *American Journal of Psychology 36,* 434–445.

——— (1925b). The relationship between suggestibility and intelligence in delinquents. *Psychological Clinic 6,* 133–134.

——— (1928a). The influence of sex and age upon the ability to report. *American Journal of Psychology 40,* 458–466.

——— (1928b). Intelligence and the ability to report. *American Journal of Psychology 40,* 596–599.

——— (1928c). The relation between different measures of the ability to report. *American Journal of Psychology 40,* 592–596.

——— (1932). Forgetting and the law of disuse. *Psychological Review 39,* 352–370.

——— (1942). *The psychology of human learning.* New York: Longmans, Green.

McGeoch, J. A., and Bunch, M. E. (1930). Scores in the Pressey X-O tests of emotion are influenced by courses in psychology. *Journal of Applied Psychology 14,* 150–159.

McGeoch, J. A., and Irion, A. L. (1952). *The psychology of human learning.* New York: Longmans, Green.

Postman, L. (1972). The experimental analysis of verbal learning and memory: Evolution and innovation. In C. P. Duncan, L. Seechrest, and A. W. Melton, eds., *Human memory: Festschrift for Benton J. Underwood,* pp. 1–23. New York: Appleton-Century-Crofts.

Pratt, C. C. (1943). John A. McGeoch: 1897–1942. *American Journal of Psychology 56,* 134–136.

Whitely, P. L., and McGeoch, J. (1928). The curve of retention for poetry. *Journal of Educational Psychology 19,* 471–479.

Wolfle, D. (1943). McGeoch's psychology of human learning: A special review. *Psychological Bulletin 40,* 350–353.

Robert G. Crowder

MEASUREMENT OF MEMORY

Since 1885, when Hermann EBBINGHAUS introduced the *method of savings,* the number and variety of techniques for measuring memory have increased enormously. Many are highly specialized, either for the purpose of addressing a particular research question or for diagnosing a specific memory dysfunction. However, most of the more specialized procedures are variants of the techniques described below. These techniques are based on the common forms of everyday remembering, the formal procedures having been appropriately standardized to provide the kind of comparability required of scientific and clinical data.

Measures of Recall

Immediate Serial Recall: Memory Span

In the most commonly used version of this task, a randomly ordered sequence of digits (e.g., 4-7-

8-2-5-9) is read once to the subject, who is required to repeat them in the same order. The measure obtained through this procedure is known as the digit span and is defined as the number of digits that can be repeated without error and in the correct order. An immediate difficulty is that a subject's performance may fluctuate slightly from one occasion to the next, six digits being correctly repeated on one occasion, for example, and seven on the next. The formal measurement of span is therefore usually taken as the number of digits that can be correctly recalled on 50 percent of occasions. The digit span test is found in such standard test batteries as the Wechsler Adult Intelligence Scale. Span can also be measured using items other than digits: letters or words, for example. However, it should be noted that the span measure obtained may vary with the kinds of items employed. Thus word span is typically somewhat shorter than digit span, and word span itself will vary depending on various features of the words, such as their length and familiarity. (See also MEMORY SPAN.)

Free Recall

In free recall, a list of items is presented and the subject is asked to recall them in any order. The measure of memory is the number (or proportion) of these items recalled. If subjects are allowed to begin recalling immediately after the presentation of the last item, this simple measure is subject to a strong recency effect: The last few items in the list will be recalled very well (and usually recalled first). There is also a weaker primacy effect: The first few items in the list will be better recalled than those in the middle positions. In some applications these serial position effects are eliminated by inserting "buffer" items at the beginning and end of the list that are not counted as part of the recall measure.

Cued Recall

In cued recall, the subject is asked to recall each item in response to a cue provided by the tester. This cue may have been presented along with the item at the time of study (an intra-list cue) or be an item not studied before (an extra-list cue). For example, the subject may study word pairs such as *dog-tail* and when tested be given the intra-list cue *dog* and asked to recall the word with which it was paired. Alternatively, subjects may study a list of single words (including *tail* but

not *dog*) and when tested be given the extra-list cue *dog* as a potential aid to recall. A special case of extra-list cuing is category cuing. If the list contained items from several different categories (fruits, animals, etc.), cued recall could take the form of providing the subject with the category labels as cues.

A potential difficulty in measuring cued recall is guessing. This problem arises when the items to be recalled have strong prior associations with the cue. For example, suppose the word *orange* was studied and at recall the extra-list cue *fruit* is provided. The subject may have forgotten the item *orange* but offer it merely because it is a plausible guess to the cue *fruit*. The usual solution to this difficulty is to obtain a baseline measure of how often the item is wrongly recalled in response to the cue when it was not on the study list. In this example, the control measure for the word *orange* would be its recall rate to the cue *fruit* when *orange* was not part of the study list.

Measures of Recognition Memory

Forced-Choice Recognition

In this procedure memory is measured by presenting each of the previously studied items (the "old" items) with one or more new items or "lures" and instructing the subject to choose which of these items is old. The measure is then the number or proportion of items correctly identified as old. There are two difficulties with this measure. Guessing poses an obvious problem because in the case of a two-alternative forced choice, a subject who remembered nothing at all could guess correctly half the time. Increasing the number of lures reduces the expected rate of correct guessing but does not eliminate the problem entirely. Various methods of "correcting for guessing" have been proposed but are rarely used, partly because the problem of guessing is not as serious as it may seem. Normally one is interested not in the absolute number of items recognized but in the comparison of recognition rates across different occasions or conditions. If the influence of guessing is the same across these conditions, then the *differences* in the recognition rates between conditions will provide an adequate comparative measure.

A second potential source of difficulty is the nature of the lures. A recognition test can be made more or less difficult by altering the degree of similarity between the correct ("old") items and the lures. Thus errors are more likely if the lure is a synonym of the old item than if it is an unrelated word chosen at random.

Single-Item (Yes/No) Recognition Tests

In what may seem the simplest form of recognition test, subjects are shown each test item in turn and asked to respond "yes" if they have seen it before (an old item) and "no" if they have not (a new item). The test list contains a mixture of old and new items. A possible measure of memory would be the proportion of items correctly identified as old, a measure referred to as the *hit rate*. This measure has a serious shortcoming, however; it will be influenced by the subject's criterion for saying "yes." Adopting a lax criterion (that is, saying "old" even if the item is only faintly familiar) can yield a high hit rate, usually at the expense of mistakenly saying "old" to a large number of new items. Such errors are termed "false positives" or "false alarms." Thus, from the subject's point of view, responding in a yes/no recognition test becomes a trade-off between hits and false alarms. The difficulty from a measurement point of view is that different subjects may adopt different criteria, so that comparing hit rates alone can be very misleading.

Clearly what is needed is some way of adjusting the hit rate to take into account criterion differences reflected in the false alarm rate. One method is to take as a score the difference between hits and false alarms, a procedure that has little theoretical justification but offers a simple, and in many circumstances adequate, measure. A more sophisticated method is to make use of a model known as the theory of signal detection, a decision model taken from psychophysics. The model yields a measure, termed d' (d-prime), that is independent of the subject's criterion and can be interpreted as a measure of the subject's ability to discriminate difference in subjective familiarity between the old and the new items.

Other Measures of Memory

Savings Measures

Savings was the method of measurement introduced by Ebbinghaus in 1885. He recorded the length of time necessary to learn a list of items, then after an interval of time (during which forget-ting had taken place) he recorded the length of time necessary to relearn the same material. Invariably this relearning took less time than the original learning, and Ebbinghaus used the difference between the two times as a measure of how much of the original material had been retained.

Measures of Implicit Memory

As with the method of savings, implicit measures are obtained through observing performance on a task that indirectly reveals the influence of past experience. A common example of an implicit memory test is word-fragment completion. Suppose a subject has seen a list that includes the word *assassin*. Some time later the subject is given a fragment completion test consisting of some but not all of the letters of the word (e.g., A--A--IN) and asked to find the word that could be formed by filling in the blanks. No reference is made to the prior list. The essential aspect of an implicit memory test is that subjects receive no instructions to remember items from the prior list, nor are they informed of the list's possible relevance. They may therefore be quite unaware that their performance is being influenced by a past experience. The measure of implicit memory is the improvement in performance on the word-fragment completion task. Improvement is measured relative to word-fragment performance obtained under control conditions in which the solution word (*assassin*) was not on the prior study list. Among the other tasks that can be used to measure implicit memory is stem completion. In this task subjects are given the initial letters of a word and asked to add letters to complete a word. The major difficulty with implicit measures is to ensure that the subject is not making use of explicit memory strategies. One way to achieve this is to prevent subjects from becoming aware of the relationship between the initial study and subsequent test phases of the procedure. Another is to instruct subjects that they should avoid conscious strategies by responding with the first thing that comes to mind. (See also IMPLICIT MEMORY.)

The Relationship among the Different Measures

It is important to realize that the various measurement procedures described above are not merely alternative ways of estimating a single "true" quantity that could be thought of as the "amount remembered." In this regard the measurement of memory is very different from the measurement of physical quantities such as length or weight. Various techniques for measuring the distance between two points should yield the same result, and any variation should be regarded as reflecting errors of measurement. The situation is quite different in the case of memory measurement. For example, in evaluating memory for an event, a recognition test and a recall test should not be thought of as alternative methods of measuring a single ideal quantity (the "amount" remembered) but as different measures of memory performance on two distinct, although possibly related, tasks. Much recent research suggests that under many circumstances different measures of memory are quite dissociated or uncorrelated, reflecting the fact that different measurement procedures tap different aspects of the memory system.

Robert S. Lockhart

MEMBRANE CHANNELS AND THEIR MODULATION IN LEARNING AND MEMORY

The electrical signaling of nerve cells depends on a class of integral membrane proteins called *ion channels* that form an aqueous pore through the cell membrane and facilitate the flow of ions across the membrane. One of the most intriguing features of ion channels is that their normal activity can be modulated by a variety of signals, including neurotransmitters, hormones, and even nerve activity itself. Such modulatory changes in ion channel function can cause profound, long-lasting changes in the electrical properties of neurons and can regulate the strength of their synaptic connections. Over the past several years, channel modulation has been implicated as a primary mechanism underlying the cellular and behavioral changes associated with certain simple models of learning and memory. This entry discusses some basic properties of ion channels, their modulation by neurotransmitters, and the role that such modulation may play in learning and memory.

Ion Channels

Our knowledge of ion channels has greatly expanded since 1980 with the introduction of the patch clamp technique by Neher, Sakmann, and their colleagues (Hamill et al., 1981), which allows one to record the small ionic currents that flow through a single open ion channel. Ion channels have two important properties: (1) They select for particular ionic species; (2) they open and close in response to different signals, a process termed *gating* (Figure 1). When open, a channel conducts ions at an extremely high rate, typically around 20 million ions per second. Ion channels can be classified by their ionic selectivity (e.g., sodium channels, potassium channels, calcium channels) and by the signals that regulate their opening and closing. So far, three major classes of signals have been identified that can gate channels: membrane voltage (the voltage gated channels), chemical ligands (the ligand-gated channels), and pressure or stretch (mechanically gated channels). Voltage-gated ion channels generate the all-or-none action potential, ligand-gated channels give rise to excitatory and inhibitory synaptic potentials, and mechanically gated channels play important roles in touch and hearing.

In 1952, Hodgkin and Huxley demonstrated that generation and conduction of an action potential depends on two types of ion channels: a voltage-gated, sodium (Na^+)-selective channel and a voltage-gated, potassium (K^+)-selective channel (Figure 2). The Na^+ channels are controlled by two gates: (1) an activation gate that is normally shut at the resting potential and opens rapidly upon depolarization, and (2) an inactivation gate that is normally open at the resting potential and closes after the activation gates open following a depolarization. Here the term *gate* is used to convey the notion of some process that regulates channel opening and closing and may not necessarily correspond to a physical gate. The Na^+ channels can conduct ions only when both activation and inactivation gates are open. The K^+ channels are controlled by a voltage-dependent activation gate that opens more slowly upon depolarization than the Na^+ channel activation gate.

How do the properties of these channels govern the firing of an action potential? At a neuron's normal resting potential of -80 millivolts (mV), where the inside of the cell is negative with respect to the outside, most of the Na^+ and K^+ channels

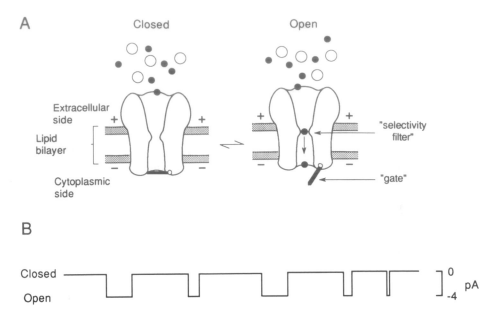

Figure 1. Ion channels facilitate the flow of ions across cell membranes. A. The channel is thought to have a specialized region in the pore, the "selectivity filter," that allows it to discriminate among different ionic species. Here the channel allows one ionic species (*filled circles*) but not another (*open circles*) to permeate. In addition, many channels open and close in response to different stimuli, a process termed gating. In some instances, a physical gate is believed to plug and unplug the channel, as illustrated here. In other cases, the channel protein is believed to undergo a more widespread conformational change. B. Channel opening and closing is associated with all-or-none steplike changes in unitary current flow through the pore. Each time this hypothetical channel opens it passes a unitary current of -4×10^{-12} amperes (or -4 picoamperes). According to standard convention, the negative sign means that the channel allows positive depolarizing charge to flow into the cell.

are closed. In response to an excitatory stimulus that depolarizes a cell past a threshold of around -60 to -40 mV, the voltage-gated Na^+ channels open rapidly. This allows positively charged Na^+ to enter the axon from the extracellular solution. Na^+ enters the axon because it flows down its chemical concentration gradient (there is about ten times more Na^+ outside the axon than inside) and down its voltage gradient (the internal negative voltage attracts external positively charged Na^+). This causes the membrane potential to become more positive, which results in the opening of more Na^+ channels and a greater depolarization until the membrane depolarizes to its peak value of around $+40$ mV (at which point there is little Na^+ entry because the positive voltage gradient nearly balances the chemical concentration gradient).

How does the membrane repolarize from this positive potential? Repolarization depends on two processes. First, the Na^+ channels that have opened during the depolarizing phase of the action potential begin to shut as the inactivation gates close. Second, the voltage-gated K^+ channels open. This allows positively charged K^+ to flow out of the cell (down *its* concentration and voltage gradients) so that the inside of the cell becomes more negative and the cell repolarizes to its normal resting potential.

We now know that nerve cells possess many more types of ion channels than originally described by Hodgkin and Huxley, as summarized by Hille (1991). Thus, neurons contain several varieties of K^+-selective channels. Some rapidly inactivate in a way similar to the Na^+ channel (e.g., the transient or A-type K^+ current), others are active around the resting potential and help control its level, and still others are activated by

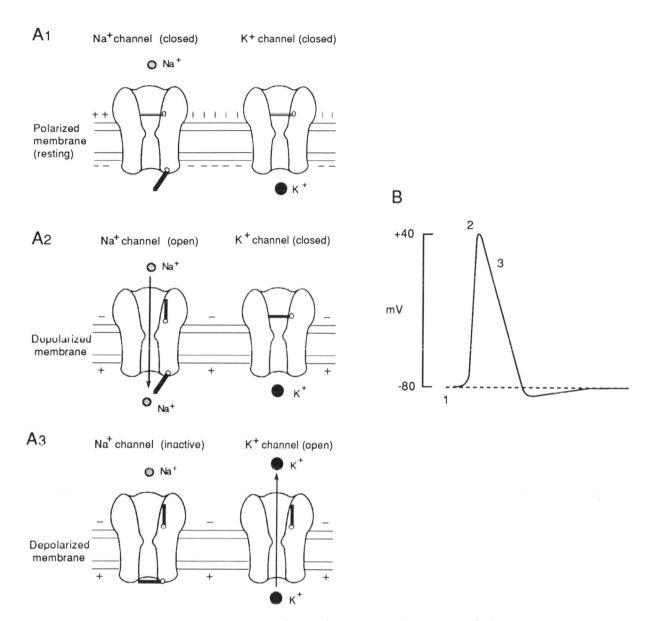

Figure 2. Voltage-gated Na^+ and K^+ channels. Voltage-gated Na^+ channels contain an "activation" gate that is closed at negative resting potentials and opens after a depolarization. They also contain an "inactivation" gate that is open at negative potentials and closes following depolarization. Since the activation gate opens more rapidly than the inactivation gate shuts, the Na^+ channels open transiently during an action potential. The K^+ channels have an activation gate that opens with a slight delay. A1. Channels at rest before eliciting an action potential. A2. During the rising phase of the action potential, Na^+ channels open before the K^+ channels, allowing for a net influx of positive charge. A3. During the repolarizing phase of the action potential, the Na^+ channels inactivate and the K^+ channels open. B. Typical action potential voltage waveform. The numbers correspond to the times illustrated in A1–A3.

a rise in the intracellular Ca^{2+} concentration. These different K^+ channels can be expressed differently in different cell types in the nervous system and are largely responsible for the variety of firing patterns observed in different nerve cells.

Another very important type of channel is the voltage-gated Ca^{2+} channel. Like the Na^+ channels, these channels contribute inward depolarizing current as they allow external Ca^{2+} to enter a cell (down its voltage and concentration gradients). However, Ca^{2+} channels play little role in axonal conduction. Rather, one of their main roles is to provide for Ca^{2+} influx into presynaptic terminals during an action potential and thus to regulate transmitter release. Several types of Ca^{2+} channels have been identified.

Channels Involved in Synaptic Transmission

At a synapse, the information from a presynaptic (transmitting) neuron must be communicated to a postsynaptic (receiving) neuron. Two major forms of synaptic transmission have been identified: electrical and chemical. At electrical synapses, ionic current flows directly between the presynaptic and postsynaptic cells through specialized channels, the gap junction channels, that span the pre- and postsynaptic cell membranes. These channels have been studied extensively in neurons by Michael Bennett and his colleagues (Bennett et al., 1991). At chemical synapses, there is no such direct pathway for current flow. Rather, as shown by Bernard Katz and his colleagues (Katz, 1969), synaptic transmission is mediated through the release of a chemical transmitter from the presynaptic neuron and the binding of the transmitter to receptors in the postsynaptic cell membrane. Since chemical synapses are by far the more common form of synaptic transmission and are the type most often (but not exclusively) associated with modulatory synaptic changes, the focus here is on this form of transmission.

As an action potential invades the presynaptic terminal at a chemical synapse, it opens voltage-gated Ca^{2+} channels in the presynaptic terminals, allowing calcium to enter (Figure 3). In response to the subsequent increase in cytoplasmic Ca^{2+} concentration, synaptic vesicles filled with neurotransmitter fuse with the presynaptic membrane at sites called active zones and release their contents into the synaptic cleft. The transmitter then

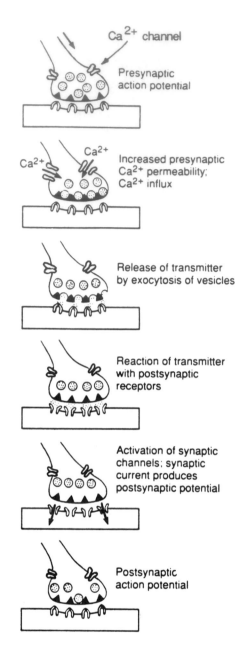

Figure 3. Chemical synaptic transmission. An action potential invades the presynaptic terminals, opens voltage-gated Ca^{2+} channels, and allows Ca^{2+} to enter the presynaptic terminal. The rise in internal Ca^{2+} causes presynaptic vesicles filled with transmitter to fuse with the presynaptic terminal membrane, causing the vesicles to release their contents into the synaptic cleft, a process termed exocytosis. The transmitter diffuses across the cleft to activate receptors in the postsynaptic membrane. At excitatory synapses, transmitter activates a channel that generates a depolarizing current in the postsynaptic membrane, leading to the generation of an excitatory postsynaptic potential (EPSP). If the EPSP is suprathreshold, the postsynaptic cell will fire an action potential. *Modified from Kandel, Schwartz, and Jessell, 1991.*

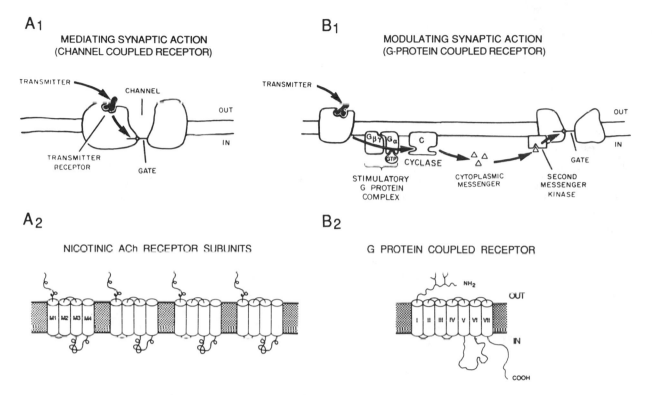

A1

MEDIATING SYNAPTIC ACTION
(CHANNEL COUPLED RECEPTOR)

B1

MODULATING SYNAPTIC ACTION
(G-PROTEIN COUPLED RECEPTOR)

A2

NICOTINIC ACh RECEPTOR SUBUNITS

B2

G PROTEIN COUPLED RECEPTOR

Figure 4. Two major classes of chemical transmitter actions. A. Directly gated receptor-channels. A1. Binding of transmitter to receptor opens a channel that is part of a single receptor-channel macromolecule. A2. The nicotinic ACh receptor-channel, present at the neuromuscular junction, is composed of five subunits: two identical alpha subunits that both bind ACh and one beta, one gamma, and one delta subunit. All four subunit genes code for distinct but related proteins, indicating that they are derived from a common ancestral gene. The entire protein has a molecular weight of around 250,000 daltons. Each subunit is thought to contain four membrane-spanning regions (M1–M4), one of which (M2) forms the lining of the pore. B. Modulatory transmitter actions. B1. The transmitter receptor and channel are distinct macromolecules. Binding of transmitter to its receptor activates a guanine nucleotide binding protein (G protein) that in turn activates an effector molecule. Here, the effector is the enzyme adenylate cyclase (C), leading to cAMP production, activation of the cAMP-dependent protein kinase, and phosphorylation of an ion channel. B2. The G protein–coupled receptors are composed of a single subunit with seven membrane-spanning segments (I–VII). *Modified from Hille, 1991.*

diffuses across the synaptic cleft to combine with specific receptors in the postsynaptic membrane, leading to changes in ion channel activity in the postsynaptic cell and the generation of postsynaptic potentials.

Two major types of postsynaptic neurotransmitter actions have been identified that depend on the activation of two very different classes of neurotransmitter receptor proteins: the ligand-gated receptor-channels and the G protein–coupled receptors (Figure 4).

Transmitter Actions via Ligand-Gated Receptor-Channels

The ligand-gated receptor-channels are responsible for rapid chemical transmission in the central and peripheral nervous system. In this type of transmitter action, the binding of transmitter to its receptor directly opens a channel that is part of a single channel-receptor macromolecule (Figure 4A). So far, all ligand-gated receptor-channels have been shown to be composed of four or five different protein subunits. The most thoroughly studied example of a ligand-gated receptor-channel is the nicotinic acetylcholine (ACh) receptor-channel at the neuromuscular junction. Here, ACh is released from a presynaptic motoneuron and then binds to its postsynaptic receptor, causing the receptor to undergo a rapid conformational change that leads to the opening of an ion channel that is permeable to most cations (e.g., Na^+, K^+, and Ca^{2+}) but not to anions. When this channel opens, it allows a net influx of positive charge into the muscle, leading to a quickly depolarizing postsynaptic potential.

Similar ligand-gated channels have been described at neuronal synapses. Inhibitory receptors for the amino acids GABA and glycine gate a chloride-selective channel, leading to an influx of Cl^- ions and a hyperpolarization of the cell (i.e., the potential becomes more negative). Excitatory receptors for the amino acid glutamate gate a cation-selective channel, which allows Na^+ (and in some cases Ca^{2+}) to enter a neuron and thus depolarizes the cell. (See also GLUTAMATE RECEPTORS AND THEIR CHARACTERIZATION.)

Transmitter Actions through Modulation of Channel Activity

The direct ligand-gated channels produce rapid postsynaptic potential changes that last only a few milliseconds. How can neuronal activity be regulated over the longer time periods of seconds, minutes, days, and years that we associate with short-term and long-term memory? One potential mechanism is through the long-term regulation of ion channel activity by a class of slow transmitter actions that depend on intracellular metabolic reactions (see Kaczmarek and Levitan, 1987). These slow, modulatory synaptic actions can produce changes in neuronal activity lasting for many minutes and even for hours. More permanent regulation of channel properties has been demonstrated during development where changes in gene expression can lead to insertion of new types of channels into the cell membrane.

With modulatory chemical transmitter actions, the receptor and channel are distinct macromolecules where binding of transmitter indirectly alters channel activity through a series of intracellular metabolic reactions (Figure 4B). Transmitters whose actions are mediated by such indirectly act-

ing receptors include the catecholamines, serotonin, histamine, neuropeptides, and ACh (acting through the muscarinic receptors). These receptor proteins are composed of a single subunit and are members of a large gene superfamily. The receptors act by stimulating a type of intracellular protein called guanine nucleotide binding proteins (or G proteins), studied extensively by Gilman (1987). The activated G proteins then couple to different types of effector proteins. Many effector proteins are enzymes that lead to the production of relatively low-molecular-weight metabolites called *second messengers* (see SECOND MESSENGER SYSTEMS). These second messengers often activate protein kinases, enzymes that catalyze the transfer of the terminal phosphate group from ATP to certain amino acid residues of various proteins.

Ion channels can serve as efficient substrates for many different protein kinases, and their resultant phosphorylation can dramatically alter their function, leading to either increases or decreases in channel activity (see Levitan, 1988). The relatively slow time course of these G protein–dependent synaptic actions is due to the relatively slow rates of phosphorylation and dephosphorylation reactions (requiring seconds to minutes). In addition to acting via second messenger production, some G proteins can directly interact with and regulate ion channels, leading to synaptic actions with an intermediate time course lasting hundreds of milliseconds (see Brown and Birnbaumer, 1990).

Channels that are the targets for modulatory transmitter actions include voltage-gated K^+, Ca^{2+}, and Na^+ channels and various ligand-gated receptor-channels. Modulatory changes in K^+ channel activity are among the most common G protein-coupled transmitter actions and often have a marked effect on the firing properties of neurons (Figure 5). Transmitters that decrease K^+ channel activity have a general excitatory effect on neuronal activity, leading to membrane depolarization, decreased threshold for action potential firing, increased action potential duration, and/or increased tendency to fire repetitively. Conversely, transmitters that increase K^+ channel activity have a general inhibitory effect on neuronal firing.

One of the most important functions of modulatory transmitter actions is to regulate synaptic function. By increasing or decreasing Ca^{2+} channel currents, modulatory transmitters can regulate Ca^{2+} influx into the presynaptic terminal and so

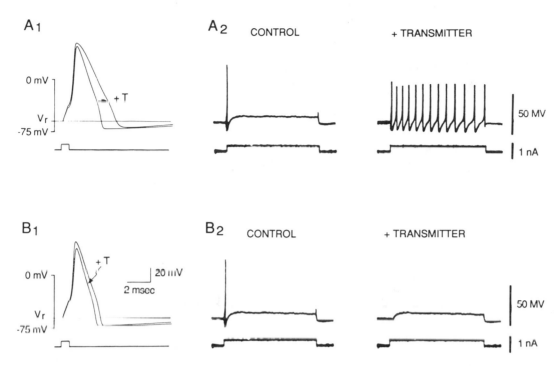

Figure 5. Effects of K$^+$ channel modulation on neuronal activity. A. Effects of a modulatory decrease in K$^+$ current. A1. The transmitter (+T) may increase action potential duration. A2. The transmitter may increase neuronal excitability. B. Effects of a modulatory increase in K$^+$ current. B1. An increase in K$^+$ channel current can lead to a decrease in action potential duration (+T). B2. An increase in K$^+$ current can increase threshold and inhibit firing of an action potential. *A2, B2 redrawn from Brown, 1982.*

increase or decrease transmitter release. By regulating action potential duration, changes in K$^+$ channel activity can also alter Ca^{2+} influx and thus transmitter release indirectly by causing the voltage-dependent-Ca^{2+} channels to stay open for longer or shorter times. Finally, transmitters can control the postsynaptic sensitivity of the membrane to transmitter by modulating the ligand-gated receptor-channels.

How do modulatory transmitters act to alter single channel function and thus regulate the macroscopic current carried by a large population of such channels? The mean current (I) carried by a population of channels is given by the product $I = N_f p_o i$, where N_f is the number of functional channels in the membrane, p_o is the probability that a given channel is open, and i is the size of the current that flows through a single open channel. In principle a modulatory transmitter could increase or decrease the size of the macroscopic

current by affecting any one of these three parameters. Figure 6 illustrates these possible modes of action on single channel currents in the case of a modulatory transmitter that decreases the macroscopic K$^+$ current.

Apart from their different time courses and molecular mechanisms of action, fast and slow synaptic actions have very different roles in controlling neuronal activity. The fast synaptic actions are ideally suited to the rapid transfer of information in the neuronal circuitry that mediates primary behaviors. In contrast, the slower modulatory transmitter actions are best suited for regulating the circuitry involved in the mediatory behaviors. Such regulation is often associated with general changes in arousal and is ideally suited to play a role in learning and memory. So far, channel modulation has been implicated in several simple models of learning and memory. Many of these are discussed in more detail elsewhere in this encyclopedia.

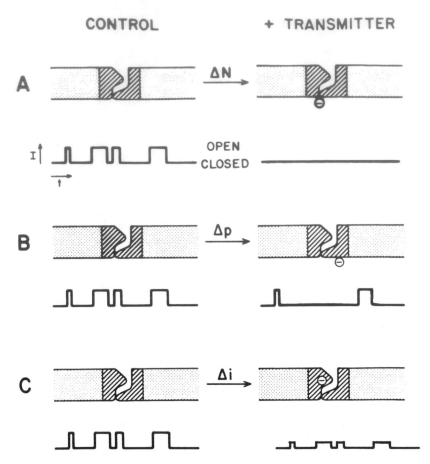

Figure 6. Modes of action of a modulatory transmitter on single channel function. A modulatory transmitter can decrease the total current carried by a population of channels by decreasing the number, N, of active channels (top trace); by decreasing the probability, p, that a channel is open (middle trace); or by decreasing the single channel current amplitude, i (bottom trace).

Conclusions

The modulation of ion channels plays an important role in controlling the activity of neurons. Channel modulation is especially important as a means of controlling the strength of synaptic connections in the brain. It generally depends on the actions of neurotransmitters and hormones that recruit intracellular second messengers and G proteins that regulate channel activity. Compared with transmitter actions mediated by the direct ligand-gated channels, modulatory transmitter actions are relatively slow and can produce changes in channel activity that persist for many minutes or longer. More permanent changes in channel activity are likely to involve different regulatory mechanisms that require changes in gene expression and protein synthesis.

(See also GUIDE TO THE ANATOMY OF THE BRAIN; NEUROTRANSMITTER SYSTEMS AND MEMORY.)

REFERENCES

Bennett, M. U. L., Barrio, L. C., Bargiello, T. A., Spray, D. C., Hertzberg, E., and Sáez, J. C. (1991). Gap junctions: New tools, new answers, new questions. *Neuron 6,* 305–320.

Brown, A. M., and Birnbaumer, L. (1990). Ionic channels and their regulation by G protein subunits. *Annual Review of Physiology 52,* 197–213.

Brown, D. A. (1982). Slow cholinergic excitation—a

mechanism for increasing neuronal excitability. *Trends in Neurosciences 6,* 302–307.

Gilman, A. G. (1987). G proteins: Transducers of receptor generated signals. *Annual Review of Biochemistry 56,* 615–649.

Hamill, O. P., Marty, A., Neher, E., Sakmann, B., and Sigworth, F. J. (1981). Improved patch-clamp techniques for recording from cells and cell-free membrane patches. *Pflügers Archiv 391,* 85–100.

Hille, B. (1991). *Ionic channels of excitable membranes,* 2nd ed. Sunderland, Mass.: Sinauer. An excellent in-depth treatment of ion channel biophysics.

Hodgkin, A. L., and Huxley, A. F. (1952). A quantitative description of membrane current and its application to conduction and excitation in nerve. *Journal of Physiology 117,* 500–544.

Kaczmarek, L. K., and Levitan, I. B. (1987). *Neuromodulation.* New York: Oxford University Press. Provides an overview of several examples of ion channel modulation.

Kandel, E. R., Schwartz, J. H., and Jessell, T. (1991). *Principles of neural science,* 3rd ed. New York: Elsevier. A background text covering basic principles of ion channels, transmitter actions, and learning and memory.

Katz, B. (1969). *The release of neural transmitter substances.* Springfield, Ill.: Thomas.

Levitan, I. B. (1988). Modulation of ion channels in neurons and other cells. *Annual Review of Neuroscience 11,* 119–136.

Steven A. Siegelbaum

MEMORY CONSOLIDATION

Almost a century ago, Müller and Pilzecker (1900) proposed that neural processes underlying newly formed memories initially perseverate in a labile form and then, over time, become consolidated into lasting neural traces. The "perseveration-consolidation" hypothesis was proposed as an explanation for retroactive interference, the forgetting of recently learned information induced by subsequent learning of other information. Subsequently, Donald HEBB (1949) proposed the "dual-trace" hypothesis as a more explicit form of the consolidation hypothesis. He suggested that learning induces reverberating activity in neural circuits and that such neural activity (1) serves as the basis of short-term memory and (2) produces changes at synapses of the neurons in the circuits, resulting in the consolidation or stabilization of long-term memory. The hypothesis that memory-storage processes are time-dependent has guided extensive research over the past several decades.

Clinical findings of retrograde amnesia (RA) and anterograde amnesia (AA) following HEAD INJURY provide strong support for the view that memory storage is based on time-dependent consolidation processes. From the perspective of the dual-trace consolidation hypothesis, head injury induces RA, the selective disruption of recent memories by conditions occurring after learning, because the memories were not fully consolidated at the time of the injury; AA, the impairment in retention of memories acquired after brain damage, is presumably due to impaired functioning of brain processes underlying memory consolidation.

After the introduction of electroconvulsive shock therapy (ECT) as a psychiatric treatment in the late 1930s, clinical findings indicating that such treatments produced RA (see ELECTROCONVULSIVE THERAPY AND MEMORY LOSS) triggered intensive investigation of experimentally induced RA in laboratory animals. It is now well established that electrical stimulation of the brain, as well as many other treatments affecting brain functioning, induces RA. The experimental findings support the view that such treatments administered after training impair memory by altering time-dependent neurobiological processes underlying memory consolidation. Furthermore, RA comparable to that seen in humans has been observed in studies of memory in monkeys, cats, rodents, birds, fish, insects, and mollusks. Evidence indicating that memory consolidation has been conserved in evolution clearly suggests that postlearning consolidation processes serve an adaptive function.

The conclusion that a treatment affecting brain functioning produces RA requires evidence of a gradient of the effect, that is, that the degree of alteration in memory decreases as the interval between the training and the posttraining treatment is lengthened. The shape of the RA gradient observed in clinical and experimental studies depends upon many factors. Under some experimental conditions the gradients are very short (less than a minute) and, as is indicated below, under other conditions memory is affected by treatments administered at long intervals following learning. In human patients, the degree and duration of RA following head injury are known to depend upon the severity of the trauma. In studies using laboratory animals, the degree of arousal or stress induced by the training, and the drug dose or intensity of brain stimulation, are particularly important factors influencing the degree of amnesia produced by treatments administered at different times following training. Thus, it is clear that studies of RA do not provide time constants for memory consolidation. Rather, the research findings indicate that memory storage processes remain susceptible to modulating influences following training and that the degree of susceptibility decreases over time. There is evidence that ECT treatments administered to human patients (for treatment of depression) can induce RA for events occurring a year or two prior to the onset of the treatments. The fact that several-year-old memories remain relatively intact is consistent with Théodule RIBOT's observation, made in 1882, that older memories are less fragile than recent ones. However, since the RA induced by ECT treatments administered 2 years after learning dissipates over time, it seems unlikely that the effects are due to the disruption of memory consolidation. Rather, it seems more likely that such changes in the stability of the memory trace at long intervals of time after learning are due to continuing reorganization of the neural substrate mediating stored information.

The experimental design used in studies of memory consolidation has proved to be extremely useful in examining the effects of treatments, such as drugs, on learning. In experiments in which treatments are administered prior to the training and/or the retention test session, it is difficult to distinguish effects on learning and memory from influences of the treatments on perceptual, attentional, motivational, and motor processes. In contrast, in studies of memory consolidation, the treatments are administered after training and the influences of the treatments on memory are typically assessed on retention tests administered after an interval of at least 24 hours. Thus, since the direct effects of the posttraining treatments typically dissipate well before the time of the retention test, any effects of the treatment on test performance can be attributed to effects on memory storage processes occurring shortly after the learning. Consequently, memory consolidation experiments are used extensively in studies attempting to distinguish drug effects on memory from other effects of drugs on performance.

There is extensive evidence indicating that memory can be enhanced, as well as impaired, by posttraining treatments. In laboratory animals, retention of newly acquired information is enhanced by posttraining administration of drugs that stimulate brain activity, as well as by low-intensity electrical stimulation of specific brain regions, including the mesencephalic reticular formation and the amygdala. The effects of memory-enhancing treatments, like those of memory-impairing treatments, are time-dependent: Effects of such posttraining treatments are greatest when the treatments are administered shortly after training. Such findings strongly suggest that the treatments enhance memory by modulating memory consolidation processes.

The dose-response effects of posttraining memory-enhancing drugs are generally in the form of an inverted U: The greatest memory-enhancing effects are obtained with moderate doses and memory impairment is often seen at high doses. Furthermore, the effect of a particular dose depends upon the degree of arousal or stress induced by the training conditions. Lower doses produce optimal enhancement when arousing or stressful stimulation is used in training. Thus, the effects of the drug treatments summate with endogenous physiological responses induced by the training stimulation. There is extensive evidence suggesting that hormones released by arousing stimulation modulate memory storage. Studies using laboratory animals indicate that the retention of newly learned information can be influenced by posttraining administration of a number of hormones (including epinephrine, adrenocorticotropin, vasopressin, and β-endorphin) that are known to be released into the brain and blood by mildly arousing or stressful stimulation. For example, epinephrine administered post training generally produces an inverted-U, dose-dependent effect on retention (i.e., enhancement at low doses and impairment at high doses), and β-endorphin and opiate drugs generally produce RA. Opiate receptor antagonists typically produce memory enhancement. The posttraining susceptibility of memory storage processes to modulating influences thus appears to provide the opportunity for hormonal consequences of experiences to regulate the strength of memory of the experiences. Viewed from this perspective, postlearning memory consolidation processes serve an important adaptive function in providing a mechanism by which the importance of experiences influences their remembrance. And, in this regard, it is of interest that memory consolidation appears to have been conserved in evolution.

There is also much evidence suggesting that many of the posttraining treatments known to affect memory may act through influences involving hormonal modulation of memory consolidation. The effects of brain stimulation on memory, for example, are attenuated by removal of the adrenal medulla, the major source of epinephrine (adrenaline), and by administration of drugs that block adrenergic receptors. Such evidence suggests that the modulating effects of brain stimulation on memory consolidation involve adrenergic hormonal systems, particularly epinephrine released from the adrenal medulla. Increases in blood glucose levels after epinephrine release or administration may contribute to the memory-modulating effects of epinephrine. While a wide range of hormonal and pharmacological treatments are known to affect memory storage, there is general agreement that activation of peripheral and central adrenergic systems and central cholinergic systems enhances memory, whereas activation of opiate and GABAergic systems impairs memory. Conversely, adrenergic and cholinergic antagonists impair memory storage, whereas opiate and GABA antagonists enhance memory storage. Such findings suggest that hormonal and neurotransmitter systems interact in their influences on memory consolidation.

The findings of some experiments with laboratory animals have suggested that states induced by hormones may serve as contextual cues that affect the retrieval of information. Thus, in addition to influencing memory storage, neuroendocrine systems may modulate memory retrieval mechanisms. For example, the amnesia produced by posttraining administration of some hormones is attenuated by administration of the same hormones prior to the retention test. Such findings suggest that under some conditions, RA may be due to differences in the hormonal states following training and during testing rather than to interference with the storage of information. Memory enhancement, however, is readily obtained when the treatments are administered only following training, and the degree of enhancement is not influenced by administration of the same treatments prior to the retention test. Thus, state-dependent effects seem not to be involved in retrograde enhancement of memory.

Studies of humans, monkeys, and rats suggest that medial temporal brain structures are involved in memory consolidation. In humans and monkeys, damage to the hippocampus and amygdala produces AA as well as RA. In rats, amygdala or hippocampal lesions produce RA, and memory is enhanced or impaired by posttraining electrical stimulation of these brain regions. Furthermore, retention is enhanced by posttraining intra-amygdala administration of adrenergic agonists and GABAergic and opioid antagonists. Evidence indicating that damage to the amygdala or hippocampus blocks neuromodulatory influences on memory suggests that hormones modulate memory through influences mediated by medial temporal brain systems. Indirect involvement of the hippocampus is shown by evidence indicating that memory is modulated by drugs infused into the medial septum, a brain region known to influence hippocampal activity via the septohippocampal path.

Furthermore, it is well established that LONG-TERM POTENTIATION (LTP, an increase in synaptic efficacy induced by activation of neuronal circuits) can be induced in both the hippocampus and the amygdala, among other brain areas. In some regions of the hippocampus, LTP is enhanced by some neuromodulators, including norepinephrine and acetylcholine, that are known to enhance memory. Norepinephrine and acetylcholine also appear to participate in modulation of neocortical plasticity, particularly during sensitive periods of development. Such findings indicating that neuromodulatory influences which promote memory consolidation also affect the development of LTP are consistent with the view that memory consolidation is based on LTP mechanisms.

In most studies of the effects of drugs and hormones on human memory, the treatments have been administered prior to the learning experience. Although the consolidation hypothesis has stimulated extensive research with laboratory animals, relatively few studies have investigated the effects of posttraining treatments on memory in human subjects. Thus, it is not yet known whether drugs and hormones found to modulate memory consolidation in animals have comparable influences on human memory. The extensive evidence suggesting that endogenous neuroendocrine responses induced by experiences can influence memory consolidation raises the possibility that diminished endogenous responses may contribute to minor memory deficits, such as those seen during normal aging, as well as to major memory pathologies as seen in DEMENTIA and after brain damage. Recent findings indicate that some pharmacological treatments, including epinephrine and glucose, which enhance memory in young animals also ameliorate memory deficits in aged animals. As in animals, glucose appears to enhance memory in elderly humans, suggesting that findings obtained from studies of memory consolidation in animals may contribute to an understanding of human memory dysfunction.

REFERENCES

Gold, P. E. (1975). An integrated memory regulation system: From blood to brain. In R. C. A. Frederickson, J. L. McGaugh, and D. L. Felten, eds., *Peripheral signaling of the brain: Role in neural-immune interactions, learning and memory*, pp. 391–419. Toronto: Hogrefe and Huber.

Gold, P. E., and McGaugh, J. L. (1975). A single-trace, two-process view of memory storage processes. In D. Deutsch and J. A. Deutsch, eds., *Short-term memory*, pp. 355–378. New York: Academic Press.

Hebb, D. O. (1949). *The organization of behavior.* New York: Wiley.

McGaugh, J. L. (1966). Time-dependent processes in memory storage. *Science 153*, 1351–1358.

———. (1989). Modulation of memory storage processes. In P. R. Solomon, G. R. Goethals, C. M. Kelley, and B. R. Stephens, eds., *Memory: Interdisciplinary approaches*, pp. 33–64. New York: Springer-Verlag.

McGaugh, J. L., and Herz, M. J. (1972). *Memory consolidation.* San Francisco: Albion.

Müller, G. E., and Pilzecker, A. (1900). Experimentelle Beiträge zur Lehre vom Gedächtnis. *Zeitschrift für Psychologie 1*, 1–288.

Ribot, T. (1881). *Les maladies de la mémoire.* Paris: Germer Baillère. Translated as *Diseases of memory.* New York: Appleton-Century-Crofts, 1882.

Squire, L. (1987). *Memory and brain.* New York: Oxford University Press.

Weingartner, H., and Parker, E., eds. (1984). *Memory consolidation.* Hillsdale, N.J.: Erlbaum.

James L. McGaugh
Paul E. Gold

MEMORY SEARCH

Encoding refers to the content or form in which information is stored in memory; FORGETTING is loss of the stored information with the passage of time or with exposure to interfering materials; and *retrieval* refers to accessing of information. Any observation of memory reflects all three components, but measurements of recognition time emphasize retrieval. Recognition time is usually operationalized as the time required to respond whether a visually presented test item was part of a previously studied list. For an example of a recognition test following a short-term memory list, see Figure 1. Recognition time and accuracy in both short-term and long-term memory are consistent with retrieval mechanisms involving parallel, or direct access, operations rather than unguided search through many memories. Some aspects of the increase in recognition time with the length of short (but not long) lists suggest a serial, or sequential, search of the list encoding. However, when list position effects, response-time distributions, and full retrieval functions are considered, serial search is ruled out as the sole mechanism of retrieval. Increases in response time are controlled by factors that covary with list length, such as average recency and primacy. These serve to mediate the strength or availability of information processed by parallel retrieval mechanisms.

Retrieval in Short- and Long-Term Memory

Primary, or short-term, memory (STM) for a few recently active concepts is almost certainly distinct from the secondary, or long-term, memory (LTM), which is the repository for all the varied information we retain over extended periods of time (James, 1890/1950). Retrieval from LTM during recognition (of a presented item) has many properties of direct access or content addressability (Gillund and Shiffrin, 1984; Murdock, 1982). Direct-access retrieval occurs when a cue or set of cues makes contact with memory in a unitary process without recourse to a sequence of searches through irrelevant memories (Kohonen, 1987). In contrast, recall, or production (of an unpresented item), may involve a series of retrieval operations resampling memory, possibly using modified sets of cues (Raaijmakers and Shiffrin, 1981).

In the 1960s, strong claims were made that access to STM was fundamentally different from the direct-access retrieval from LTM. STM retrieval was asserted to involve a series of comparisons to all currently active concepts (Sternberg, 1966). Although this view fails to give a full account of memory search, it is a useful starting point.

Recognition Time and STM

Anecdotal information about human memory largely reflects memory failures. Scientists use both memory failures (errors) and measures of retrieval

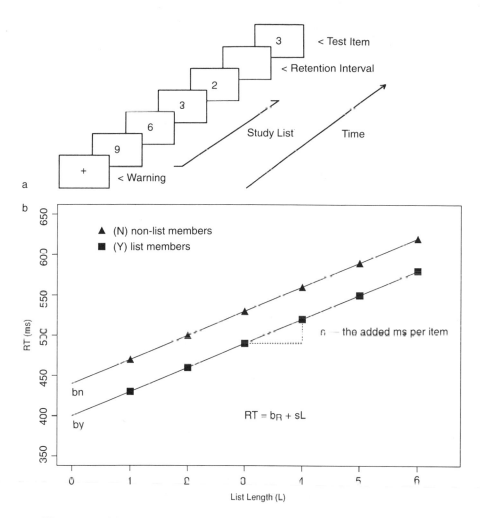

Figure 1. (a) A sample test sequence in an STM item recognition experiment (see, e.g., Sternberg, 1966). In this sample, the items are visually presented digits and the list length (4) is within the short-term range. Subjects press one of two keys to indicate whether or not the test item appeared on the current list. Time and accuracy of key presses are measured. (b) Typical results of the item recognition experiments, graphing the average (correct) response time (RT) as a function of the length of the list for list members (Y) and nonmembers (N). RT increases approximately linearly with list length, with roughly equal slopes for list members and nonmembers ($RT = b_R + sL, R = Y\,or\,N$). The slope, s, has been used as a measure of retrieval efficiency.

time to infer properties of memory. Retrievability of items in memory is often measured in terms of the average time to recognize (respond to) a test item (response time, RT). In Sternberg's classic experiments, subjects decided whether a displayed digit (or, in other studies, letter, word, syllable, outline shape, etc.) had appeared on a short study list of one to six items. One key-press indicated a yes response, another no (Figure 1a). RT increased approximately linearly for each additional

list item (Figure 1b): *mean RT = b_R + sL, R = Y or N,* where L is the list length, s is the additional average RT per list item, and b_R is a base time that depends on the response. This characteristic relationship holds for lists of up to six to nine items (Burrows and Okada, 1975), at which point the increment for additional items decreases sharply, reflecting a transition from list lengths within the capacity of STM to those exceeding that capacity.

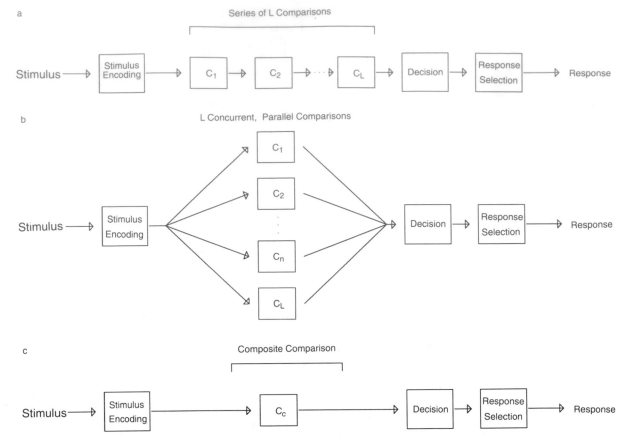

Figure 2. Schematics illustrating serial and parallel retrieval mechanisms for comparing a test item against the memory representation of the list. All these schematics distinguish nonretrieval processes (stimulus encoding, decision, response selection, and execution) from the retrieval processes or memory comparisons. Parallel retrieval mechanisms can mimic serial mechanisms in predicting average RT (see Townsend and Ashby, 1983). (a) Sternberg (1966) proposed that recognition following short memory lists of length L consisted of a serial and exhaustive sequence of comparisons of the test item against a representation of each list item in memory. The test item is compared with all list items regardless of whether a match is found, and a new comparison does not begin until the preceding one has been completed. (b) Recognition as a set of parallel, concurrent comparisons of the test item against representations of L list items (see, e.g., Murdock, 1971). Efficiency depends on the number of concurrent comparisons. (c) Recognition as direct access to a relevant list memory. Efficiency depends on familiarity (see McElree and Dosher, 1989).

Underlying Retrieval Mechanisms

The linear relation of mean RT to list length, where both positive (yes) and negative (no) test items frequently yield approximately the same slope, was interpreted by Sternberg as evidence for a *serial and exhaustive* set of comparisons between the test item and all items in the list representation in memory (Figure 2a). The slope s of the RT function (the added time for each additional list member) was identified as the time to compare the test item with each item on the list, one at a time, in series. The intercept b_R then reflects all the processing mechanisms (encoding of the test stimulus, organization and execution of the response, etc.) that do not depend on list length. If the list items were searched in series, equality of positive and negative slopes implies that the test item is compared exhaustively against all list items.

A search, or sequence of comparisons, that terminated upon finding a match would finish, on average, about halfway through the list when the test item was positive, but would go through the entire list when the test item was negative. The slope of the negative tests would then be twice that of the positives; the 2 : 1 slope ratio is a property of some searches of items in visible displays (Schneider and Shiffrin, 1977) but not of items in memory.

However, linear increases in mean RT with list length are also consistent with a parallel retrieval mechanism in which all comparisons take place at the same time, but with an efficiency that depends on the number of concurrent comparisons (Figure 2b). This is called *mechanism mimicry.* Mimicry of serial mechanisms by parallel mechanisms occurs when only simple measures such as the average RT are available (see Townsend and Ashby, 1983, for a mathematical treatment of this mimicry). Hence, the regularities noted by Sternberg (1969, 1975; see Figure 1a) may result from exhaustive and serial comparisons, or from a set of parallel comparisons whose efficiency is affected by the number of comparisons, or by a direct-access process (Figure 2c) whose efficiency is affected by other factors that covary with list length (see below). More detailed analyses discriminate the serial and parallel mechanisms. In either case, time to retrieve information from STM depends on the number of items currently being remembered.

Other Regularities: Recency, Primacy, RT Distributions

A serial exhaustive search mechanism has these properties: (1) linear increases in RT with list length where (2) slopes for positive and negative tests are equal; (3) RT should not depend on the position of a positive test item on the list; (4) the fastest (minimum) RTs should increase with the length of the list; and (5) the RT variance (a measure of variation from test to test) should increase linearly with list length for both positive and negative recognition tests. Over many variants of STM item recognition experiments, properties (1) and (2) hold approximately, although RT increases with list length may be more logarithmic than linear (Briggs, 1974). Properties (3) and (4), which require more detailed breakdowns of data, fail systematically.

RT, the time to recognize an item from STM,

depends strongly on its recency (property 3 fails). Test items experienced very recently yield fast RTs, with RT increases for each less recent item. There is also a small advantage for the first list item. Recency in the study list is the controlling factor whenever rehearsal is minimal or constrained to match study order. This is easily seen when the data are graphed appropriately (i.e., Monsell, 1978; see Figure 3a). Longer lists yield slower mean RTs because they include items of less recency. Averaging over list positions yields approximately linear (or logarithmic) increases in mean RT with list length. Failure of the prediction that the minimum RT should depend fairly strongly on list length (property 4) is implied by the recency data (Figure 3a): RT for the most recent items depends only weakly on the length of the list. Distributions of RTs from shortest to longest show only tiny shifts of the minimum with list length; average RT increases with list length largely reflect shifts in the longer RTs (Figure 3b) (Hockley, 1984). Predictions of linear increases in variability (property 5) also fail (Schneider and Shiffrin, 1977). Other findings that contradict the exhaustive serial search mechanism are decreases in RT when a stimulus is repeated (Baddeley and Ecob, 1973) and decreased RT for stimuli with high test probability, in situations where list items are the same over long sets of trials (Theios et al., 1973).

The list position effects and aspects of the RT distributions contradict properties 3–5 of the serial exhaustive scan. The approximate equality of positive and negative slopes (property 2) contradicts terminating (nonexhaustive) scan. All the data are consistent with a direct-access retrieval mechanism in which decreased availability of less recent items determines average RT for particular list positions and hence for different list lengths (McElree and Dosher, 1989).

Time Course of STM Retrieval

A direct-access retrieval mechanism is directly confirmed by more detailed RT methods, which allow inferences about the full time course of retrieval. These methods interrupt retrieval at various times after onset of the test display and observe the rate of increase in correct responding with additional retrieval time. McElree and Dosher (1989) showed that the rate of retrieval of items from lists of different length was fastest for the single most recent item—a case of an immediate match between the last item studied and the test item—but is other-

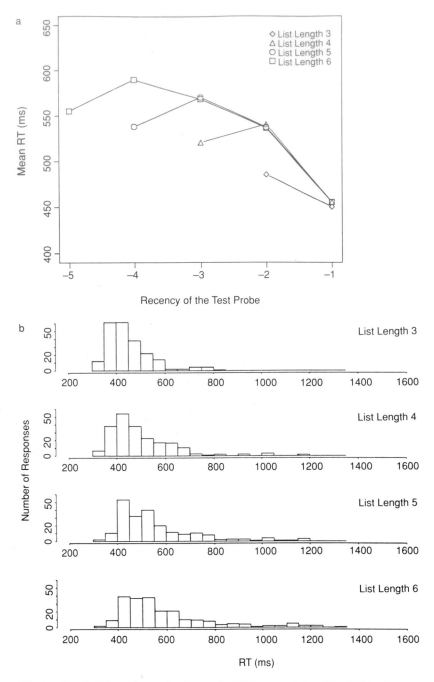

Figure 3. (a) Recency and primacy in STM recognition. The RT is shown for each list position for each of several list lengths. (List position is labeled in terms of recency, with -1 denoting the last item studied, -2 the next-to-last item studied, etc.). Recognition RT is fastest for items appearing closest to the *end* of short lists (right of graph), increasing as items become less recent, except for the first (primacy) item in each list (data from Monsell, 1978). Recency effects on RT of both list members and nonmembers are not predicted by serial exhaustive mechanisms. (b) Distributions of RT (the number of responses in each RT band) for lists of length 3–6 (data from Hockley, 1984). List length primarily affects the longest RTs. Serial mechanisms predict shifts in the entire distribution with list length.

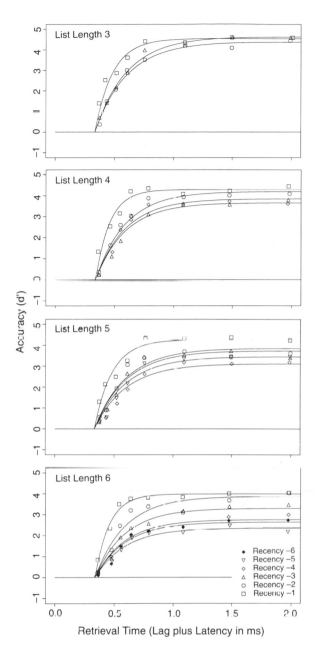

Figure 4. Full time course of STM retrieval for list positions is consistent with parallel, direct-access mechanisms. Time course is measured by examining accuracy after allowed recognition times between 0.1 second and 2 seconds for list lengths 3–6; *d'* is a bias-free measure of accuracy. Retrieval is fastest for the single most recent item in each list (labeled -1). Maximum accuracy late in retrieval varies with recency and primacy. Related effects on RT are shown in Figure 3a and Figure 3b.

wise unaffected by either list length or list position (Figure 4). Retrieval from STM was parallel or direct access, yet the ultimate success of retrieval

was limited by familiarity in memory. Recent items have been least affected by forgetting due to the passage of time or intervening items between study and test. The strength of items when measured by errors and the accessibility of items when measured by RT are both directly related to the recency of study, with a small additional advantage for the primary or first item on the list.

LTM Retrieval

Recognition of items presented in longer lists that exceed estimates of STM capacity shows many of the same properties as recognition of items from short, recent lists (Ratcliff and Murdock, 1976). Recognition from longer lists leads to more errors than for STM lists, where the error rates may be less than 5 percent. However, as in STM, list position is an important factor in LTM, affecting both RT and accuracy. As in shorter lists, items near the end of the list are recognized more quickly and accurately. When longer lists are used, study is usually followed by many test trials, and location in the test protocol also has a powerful effect. Earlier tests yield faster RT and accuracy. Later in the test sequence, additional time and materials are interpolated between encoding and retrieval; this is another manipulation of recency. As with the STM data, study and test position effects on average RT primarily reflect shifts in the long tail of the RT distributions (Ratcliff and Murdock, 1976). Full time course of recognition is fastest for the single most recent item, and otherwise equivalent but limited by familiarity (Wickelgren et al., 1980). These findings rule out recency-dependent serial comparisons that terminate on a match. The details of these data, when examined carefully, are accounted for by a parallel, direct-access retrieval process with shifts in estimated familiarity (Ratcliff, 1978).

Relation of STM Recognition to STM Recall

Another classic measure of STM is the ordered recall of all items on a short list. The list length at which ordered recall is perfect 50 percent of the time (usually an interpolated value) is called

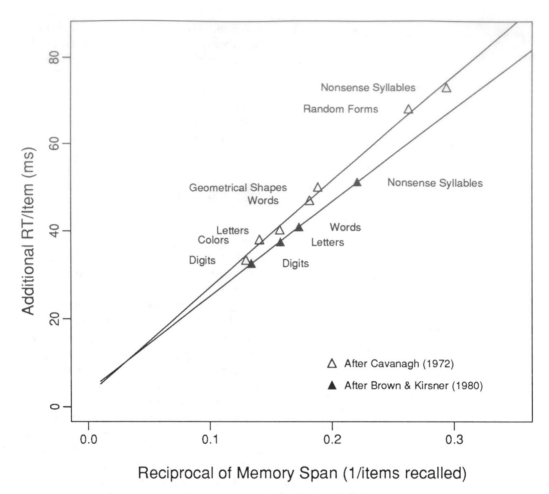

Figure 5.   STM recognition and STM recall are strongly coupled over study material. The additional recognition RT (milliseconds) for each additional list member (*s* in Fig. 1a) is correlated with the inverse of the longest list recalled in perfect order half the time, or memory span (items). RT per item is a measure of STM retrieval efficiency and span is a measure of STM capacity. Familiar materials such as digits or letters yield larger measured capacity and more efficient retrieval than unfamiliar materials such as nonsense syllables or random shapes.

the *span*. Span and the RT and accuracy for recognizing a single list member both measure aspects of STM function. Span is often taken as a measure of capacity (Miller, 1956; Baddeley, 1986), while recognition RT is often taken as a measure of retrieval efficiency (Hunt et al., 1973). Although, mysteriously, the two measures do not correlate strongly with each other across individuals (Brown and Kirsner, 1980; Puckett and Kaussler, 1984), they are related empirically in that they vary together across different to-be-remembered materials. Cavanaugh (1972) compared, via a survey of the literature, the memory spans and the RT list-length slopes of digits, letters, words, shapes, and nonsense materials. Materials yielding higher spans

(longer list lengths supporting 50 percent recall) exhibit relatively shallower slopes (less increase in average RT with increasing list length; see Figure 5). The primary factor producing differences in materials in both measures of STM may be overall familiarity (Puckett and Kausler, 1984; Sperling et al., 1984). (See also MEMORY SPAN.)

Relation to Other Abilities

The capacity of STM (or the closely related concept of WORKING MEMORY) has been viewed as an elementary information-handling process, related to efficiency in a variety of mental tasks (Baddeley, 1986). The speed of access to information in STM, defined as the slope of the dependence of RT on list length (s in the linear equation above), has been tested as a correlate of the quality of performance on general cognitive indices such as aptitude scores (Hunt et al., 1973). Correlations of capacity with psychometric measures are usually higher than those of retrieval time with psychometric measures (Hunt, 1978; Sternberg, 1975). However, various special populations, such as the young, the elderly, and the mentally retarded, have been shown to have characteristic increases in STM recognition times, either in base times or in slopes, compared with the performance of young adults (Sternberg, 1975). STM function is one of the important information-processing correlates with verbal intelligence (Hunt, 1978; Palmer et al., 1985).

(See also RETRIEVAL PROCESSES.)

REFERENCES

Baddeley, A. D. (1986). *Working memory.* New York: Oxford University Press.

Baddeley, A. D., and Ecob, J. R. (1973). Reaction time and short-term memory: Implications of repetition effects for the high-speed exhaustive scan hypothesis. *Quarterly Journal of Experimental Psychology 25,* 229–240.

Briggs, G. E. (1974). On the predictor variable for choice reaction time. *Memory and Cognition 2,* 575–580.

Brown, H. L., and Kirsner, K. (1980). A within-subjects analysis of the relationship between memory span and processing rate in short-term memory. *Cognitive Psychology 12,* 177–187.

Burrows, D., and Okada, R. (1975). Memory retrieval from long and short lists. *Science 188,* 1031–1033.

Cavanaugh, J. P. (1972). Relation between the immediate memory span and the memory search rate. *Psychological Review 79,* 525–530.

Gillund, G., and Shiffrin, R. M. (1984). A retrieval model for both recognition and recall. *Psychological Review 91,* 1–67.

Hockley, W. E. (1984). Analysis of response time distribution in the study of cognitive processes. *Journal of Experimental Psychology: Learning, Memory, and Cognition 10,* 598–615.

Hunt, E. (1978). Mechanics of verbal ability. *Psychological Review 85,* 109–130.

Hunt, E., Frost, N., and Lunneborg, C. (1973). Individual differences in cognition: A new approach to intelligence. In G. Bower, ed., *Advances in learning and motivation,* vol. 7, pp. 87–122, New York: Academic Press.

James, W. (1890/1950). *The principles of psychology.* New York: Dover.

Kohonen, T. (1987). *Content-addressable memories.* New York: Springer.

McElree, B., and Dosher, B. A. (1989). Serial position and set size in short-term memory: The time course of recognition. *Journal of Experimental Psychology: General 118,* 346–373.

Miller, G. E. (1956). The magic number seven, plus or minus two: Some limits of our capacity for processing information. *Psychological Review 63,* 81–97.

Monsell, S. (1978). Recency, immediate recognition memory, and reaction time. *Cognitive Psychology 10,* 465–501.

Murdock, B. B., Jr. (1971). A parallel processing model of scanning. *Perception and Psychophysics 10,* 289–291.

———— (1982). A theory for the storage and retrieval of item and associative information. *Psychological Review 89,* 609–626.

Palmer, J., MacLeod, C. M., Hunt, E., and Davidson, J. E. (1985). Information processing correlates of reading. *Journal of Memory and Language 24,* 59–88.

Puckett, J. M., and Kausler, D. H. (1984). Individual differences and models of memory span: A role for memory search rate? *Journal of Experimental Psychology: Learning, Memory, and Cognition 10,* 72–82.

Raaijmakers, J. G., and Shiffrin, R. M. (1981). Search of associative memory. *Psychological Review 88,* 93–134.

Ratcliff, R. (1978). A theory of memory retrieval. *Psychological Review 85,* 59–108.

Ratcliff, R., and Murdock, B. B. (1976). Retrieval processes in recognition memory. *Psychological Review 83,* 190–214.

Schneider, W., and Shiffrin, R. M. (1977). Controlled and automatic human information processing: 1. Detection, search, and attention. *Psychological Review 84,* 1–66.

Sperling, G., Parish, D., Pavel, M., and Desaulniers, H. (1984). Auditory list recall: Phonemic structure, acoustic confusability, and familiarity. *Bulletin of the Psychonomic Society 22(4),* 292.

Sternberg, S. (1966). High speed scanning in human memory. *Science 153,* 652–654.

———— (1969). Memory-scanning: Mental processes revealed by reaction-time experiments. *American Scientist 57,* 421–457.

———— (1975). Memory-scanning: New findings and current controversies. *Quarterly Journal of Experimental Psychology 27,* 1–32.

Theios, J., Smith, P. G., Haviland, S. E., Traupmann, J., and Moy, M. C. (1973). Memory scanning as a serial self-terminating process. *Journal of Experimental Psychology 97,* 323–336.

Townsend, J. T., and Ashby, F. G. (1983). *The stochastic modeling of elementary psychological processes.* New York: Cambridge University Press.

Wickelgren, W. A., Corbett, A. T., and Dosher, B. A. (1980). Priming and retrieval from short-term memory: A speed-accuracy tradeoff analysis. *Journal of Verbal Learning and Verbal Behavior 19*, 387–404.

Barbara Anne Dosher
Brian McElree

MEMORY SPAN

Memory span refers to the maximum length of a sequence of items that can be reproduced from memory following a single presentation. It has been of interest since the publication of the very first important study of memory, Hermann EBBINGHAUS's monograph in 1885. Using himself as his only subject, Ebbinghaus determined the number of presentations necessary for an error-free reproduction of a sequence of items; he found that this number decreased dramatically as the length of the sequence decreased until the sequence included only seven items, at which point only a single presentation was needed. Ebbinghaus showed no particular interest in this finding, but others did. Within 2 years memory span was shown to increase systematically during childhood, and to be appreciably shorter for the mentally impaired. Within a decade, memory span was firmly established in what was then an emerging field of mental abilities testing, where it has remained ever since.

Most often, the procedure for testing memory span calls for the recall of the items in the order in which they were presented. Sometimes the order in which the items have to be recalled is entirely unconstrained; sometimes the items have to be recalled in their reverse order of presentation. But only rarely does the procedure call for more difficult transformations, such as recall of the items in alphabetical or numerical order. Such transformations would draw on what is often referred to as WORKING MEMORY and, interestingly, would probably provide a more valid measure of mental ability.

The order of reproduction aside, there has always been considerable variation in how memory span is measured. An early review by Guilford and Dallenbach (1925) still gives a useful idea of the scope of this variation. In some cases the sequence of items is deliberately set somewhat too long for perfect reproduction, and memory span is defined as the number of items from this sequence that are recalled. This method is very quick to administer, but it is too problematic to be considered anything more than rough and ready. One problem is that the usual requirement that the items be recalled in their exact order of presentation has to be modified to allow for imperfect recall. Another is that, whatever the criterion regarding recall order, the number of items recalled is likely to vary according to the number presented, even in the supraspan range.

For such reasons, memory span is usually determined by presenting lists of several different lengths and ascertaining the maximum length for which there is perfect recall. In the procedure typical of most mental abilities tests, list length is at first so short that perfect reproduction is virtually certain, and then is gradually increased until errors are made. Like any other psychological measure, memory span is not entirely reliable, and is therefore a statistical concept—the sequence length for which there is an even chance of perfect reproduction. For this reason, most tests include two or three lists of each length, a specific stopping rule, and a specific averaging procedure. More precise estimates, as may be needed for certain research purposes, may be obtained with the staircase or the up-and-down method. This involves the presentation of a series of lists, with the length of any given list being one more than the length of the immediately preceding list if the latter was correctly reproduced and one less if it was not. Memory span is given by averaging the list lengths. In determining this average the first few lists should be disregarded because they will reflect the arbitrary length of the first list. Also, the length of what would have been the next list in the series, as given by the length and outcome for the final presented list, should be included.

Ebbinghaus's finding of seven items as the maximum length for a reproducible list provides a first approximation of memory span. Closer approximations will vary with the age of the rememberer, for span increases through childhood and declines in old age. Moreover, span varies among individuals of the same age.

In addition to varying among individuals, memory span varies for a given individual according to a considerable number of factors. For example, span can be increased by presenting the items at an irregular rate, so that they appear temporally grouped. Also, span for verbal items tends to be slightly greater with auditory presentation than with visual presentation. Of particular interest is the effect of the nature of the list item. The most common kind of item, especially in mental abilities testing, is the digit. *Digit span* is roughly one item greater than letter span, which in turn is roughly one item greater than word span. Also used as list items have been nonsense syllables (which is what Ebbinghaus used), geometric designs, and pictures of objects. One curious finding that has emerged from a comparison of memory span for different kinds of items is an impressive linear relation between memory span and a hypothetical "search rate," operationalized in terms of the slope of the roughly linear function that relates the time to decide whether a test, or probe, item was included in a just-presented short sequence to the length of the sequence. Specifically, a relatively small increment in decision time is incurred by increasing the length of a sequence of items of the kind that yields a relatively large memory span. Although the significance of this finding remains uncertain, it clearly raises the question of how memory span should be conceptualized.

One way of conceptualizing memory span is as a measure of the capacity of what William JAMES called *primary memory*. In other words, memory span can be considered as the number of items that can be held in conscious mind at any given instance. Aside from its intuitive appeal, this interpretation is supported by evidence that memory span varies according to certain characteristics of the list items that are salient in conscious experience during performance of the task. In particular, the representation of the list items in mind usually takes the form of inner speech, and memory span has been found to depend on factors that can reasonably be regarded as relevant to the spoken form of the items. Thus, span is shorter when the list items are phonemically similar to one another than when they are phonemically dissimilar (e.g., shorter for *GBVDPTZ* than for *GMRKSQY*), when the list items are phonemically lengthy than when they are phonemically short (e.g., shorter for lists of polysyllabic words than for lists of monosyllabic words), and when subjects engage in irrelevant vocalization during list presentation—an activity that is likely to suppress covert naming of the items. Other support for the idea of memory span as the product of primary memory derives from evidence that memory span for one kind of item predicts fairly well memory span for another kind

of item but is a poor predictor of performance on supraspan tasks that clearly cannot be performed on the basis of primary memory.

Such supportive evidence notwithstanding, the idea that memory span measures primary memory does little to shape current theorizing. One reason for this is that virtually all of today's memory theorists adopt an information-processing perspective, and they give little or no consideration to the conscious realization of the mechanisms they hypothesize. A more particular reason is that primary memory has been recast as a *short-term store*, the capacity of which has been estimated at three or four items. This estimate, which was based on the number of items recalled from toward the end of a supraspan sequence, is appreciably smaller than memory span. One way to account for the discrepancy is to make the plausible assumption that the capacity of primary memory varies with the nature of the task and that, unlike supraspan recall tasks, the memory span task stretches primary memory to its maximum. Another way is to assume that memory span represents primary memory supplemented by secondary memory, by items that have dropped out of conscious mind and have to be recollected.

A conception of memory span more in keeping with the zeitgeist, though not inherently incompatible with the primary memory interpretation, is that it represents the amount of information that can be articulated in a certain time, variously estimated as between 1.5 and 2.0 seconds. This notion accounts for much of the variation in memory span with type of item, in that items which yield long spans, such as digits, tend to be those which are articulated relatively quickly. The utility of this interpretation, and of the information-processing conception generally, must await the test of time.

REFERENCES

Brener, R. (1940). An experimental investigation of memory span. *Journal of Experimental Psychology, 26*, 467–482. Demonstrates variation of memory span with type of item.

Brooks, J. O., III, and Watkins, M. J. (1990). Further evidence of the intricacy of memory span. *Journal of Experimental Psychology: Learning, Memory, and Cognition, 16*, 1134–1141. Provides additional references for many of the issues touched on in this summary.

Cavanaugh, J. P. (1972). Relation between immediate memory span and the memory search rate. *Psychological Review, 79,* 525–530.

Dempster, F. N. (1981). Memory span: Sources of individual and developmental differences. *Psychological Bulletin, 89,* 63–100. Provides an exceptionally thorough and careful analysis of potential sources of individual differences in memory span from an information-processing viewpoint.

Guilford, J. P., and Dallenbach, K. M. (1925). The determination of memory span by the method of constant stimuli. *American Journal of Psychology, 36,* 621–628. Gives a comprehensive review of the methods for measuring memory span used in early studies.

Schiano, D. J., and Watkins, M. J. (1981). Speech-like coding of pictures in short-term memory. *Memory and Cognition, 9,* 110–114. Illustrates the effects of speech-related variables on memory span.

Schweikert, R., and Boruff, B. (1986). Short-term memory capacity: Magic number or magic spell? *Journal of Experimental Psychology: Learning, Memory, and Cognition, 12,* 419–425. Reviews evidence and provides additional support for the theory that memory span corresponds to the number of items that can be recited in 1.5–2.0 seconds.

Underwood, B. J., Boruch, R. F., and Malmi, R. A. (1978). Composition of episodic memory. *Journal of Experimental Psychology: General, 107,* 393–419. Shows that memory span is not a good predictor of performance in supraspan memory tasks.

Michael J. Watkins

MENTAL RETARDATION

It has long been recognized that a number of individuals in any society fail to make normal progress in intellectual, social, and linguistic growth and development, exhibiting marked difficulties in learning. The need to distinguish these individuals led directly to the development of intelligence tests, starting with the Binet-Simon around 1904, and to an operational definition little changed to this day. Mental retardation is currently defined as "significantly subaverage general intellectual functioning existing concurrently with deficits in adaptive behavior, and manifested during the developmental period." It is typically interpreted to include those individuals who obtain an I.Q. score two or more standard deviations below the mean (i.e., I.Q. < 70 or 65) on an intelligence measure such as the Stanford-Binet or the Wechsler Intelligence Scale. These same measures are used to indicate levels of retardation, including mild (I.Q. 55 to 69), moderate (40 to 54), severe (25 to 39), and profound (below 25). Because an I.Q. measure is based on a conception of normal functioning inevitably defined in terms of a culture and an age group, the further requirement that candidates must show evidence of impairments in adaptive functioning outside an academic context aids in combating the misapplication of this term to minority group children whose experience, knowledge base, and belief systems may differ from those of the dominant culture.

Although this behavioral definition is widely used for determining educational placement and providing social services, it has limited utility for understanding or treating the causes of mental retardation. In particular, an overreliance on an omnibus I.Q. score fails to acknowledge either the composite nature of this score or current perspectives on the multidimensional nature of intelligence, such as are espoused by Gardner (1983). In fact, a single I.Q. score (e.g., 50) may be associated with markedly different patterns of development, with one child failing to make progress on language and performing near age level on visuospatial tasks and another showing the exact opposite pattern. Some investigators, such as Baumeister (1987) and Burack, Hodapp, and Zigler (1988), note that mentally retarded subjects grouped homogeneously with respect to I.Q. exhibit significant individual differences on certain tasks, perhaps more so than similarly grouped nonretarded subjects. They note that retarded individuals are characterized by within-subject variability as well.

Such heterogeneity may arise, in part, because the causes of mental retardation are so many and varied. Using the American Association on Mental Deficiency definition of retardation presented above, we would expect 22.7 cases of mental retardation per 1,000 population, solely on the basis of normal variation in those environmental and multigenic factors assumed to underlie human intelligence. In fact, epidemiological studies find the overall number is somewhat higher than this, more like 25–30/1,000. One way to account for this "bulge" in the curve, proposed by Zigler, among others, has been to distinguish between *cultural-familial retardation,* which represents the low end of a normal distribution, and more clear-cut cases of *organic pathology.* Consistent with this account, familial retardation is reported to be mild in degree, to elude specific biological explanation, to run in families, and to be overrepresented in impoverished living conditions; it accounts for 75 percent of all cases of mental retardation. In contrast, more than 200 biological factors have been identified as leading to moderate, severe, or profound retardation.

Much progress in understanding and treating mental retardation has been made by focusing on well-defined organic syndromes, such as autism and Down syndrome. Recent research ties these and other forms of retardation both to specific forms of brain damage and, less robustly, to a particular complex of cognitive and behavioral deficits. This effort raises hopes that we will soon understand some of the causes of mental retardation while it provides insights into the structure of human intelligence. This, in turn, improves the possibility of eventual prevention and treatment of these disorders. Several of the major forms of retardation are discussed below, together with presenting symptoms, characteristic cognitive deficits, recent explorations of their neurobiological underpinnings, and attempts at treatment.

Chromosomal Disorders

Down syndrome (DS), trisomy 21, is the best-known form of mental retardation and the most prevalent form known to be associated with a chromosomal abnormality, occurring once in every 800 to 1,000 live births. The syndrome was identified and described in 1866 by Langdon Down, and the extra twenty-first chromosome was discovered in 1959. Since that time, Down syndrome has been the focus of intensive genetic research. Two less common forms have come to light, including *translocation DS,* which may be inherited, and *mosaic DS,* which is often associated with near normal intelligence. Children with DS usually have characteristic physical features including the epicanthic fold (leading to its original label, "mongolism"), a protruding tongue, short stature, and hypotonia (soft muscle tone). DS often occurs together with such medical conditions as heart defects, leukemia, and gut atresia. In addition, it is now known that neuropathological signs of ALZHEIMER'S DISEASE appear to be universal in individuals with DS by age thirty-five or forty. Geneticists continue to explore the connection with Alzheimer's, and to learn more about pathological segments of chromosome 21 involved in overlapping conditions. Although the degree of retardation in trisomy 21 varies from mild to profound, it is associated with a characteristic cognitive/behavioral pattern including a relative deficiency in language structure and verbal short-term memory, relative strengths in social adaptation, and a decline in I.Q. over early childhood. Although in the past individuals with DS had a short life span and were often institutionalized, medical treatments have improved their life span and they are now typically raised at home. They have received considerable recent attention for educational successes that have far outstripped earlier predictions. DS may be detected during pregnancy through chorionic villus sampling or amniocentesis; this is usually recommended in older women, who bear a substantially higher risk.

Fragile-X syndrome, caused by an abnormality on the X chromosome, is thought to be the most common genetic form of retardation after trisomy 21. It occurs in 1/1,000 births, accounting for 20 percent of severely impaired males. It is of particular interest because of the wide degree of cytogenetic and phenotypic variability present within the syndrome. For example, although most affected boys are intellectually impaired to some degree, 70 percent of the girls are unimpaired carriers. Fragile-X syndrome is associated with distinctive facial features, macroorchidism, cognitive and language impairments, and a decline in I.Q. during adolescence. Although the cognitive profile is variable, there is a high prevalence of associated attention deficit disorder and infantile autism; visuospatial function appears to be the area of greatest impairment.

Metabolic Disorders

PKU, or phenylketonuria, affecting 1/10,000 births, involves a failure to metabolize the amino acid phenylalanine, leading to a toxic condition that affects the brain and causes mental retardation. PKU can now be diagnosed immediately after birth and treated with a low-phenylalanine diet, preventing or reducing the mental retardation. A variety of other metabolic diseases lead to mental retardation, including *Tay-Sachs disease,* a fatal degenerative illness that has now been almost eradicated through carrier detection and prenatal screening among Ashkenazi Jews, the highest-risk group. Yet another metabolic disorder, involving calcium metabolism, is known as *Williams disease.* Children with this disorder, often only mildly retarded, have a distinctive cherubic face and a characteristic cardiac defect. With relatively intact structural language skills and dramatically impaired visuospatial function, they form an interesting contrast to individuals with Down syndrome.

Neural Tube Defects

Neural tube defects, such as anencephaly or spina bifida, result from a failure of the neural folds to fuse and form the neural tube; defects occur anywhere from the skull and brain down to the spinal cord and vertebrae. Children with neural tube defects may suffer from hydrocephalus (excessive accumulation of cerebrospinal fluid within the brain), which can be treated, even in pregnancy, through surgical drainage. A learning difficulty specific to some children with a history of hydrocephalus either with or without spina bifida is a curious language dysfunction termed the cocktail party syndrome, characterized by Tew (1979) and the topic of continuing interest. The cocktail party syndrome involves high verbal fluency but an apparent lack of comprehension, and good language structure with no apparent content. It is accompanied by low intelligence scores, very retarded social skills, and poor visuoperceptual abilities.

Autism

Autism, or *pervasive developmental disorders,* is now considered to be not a specific disease but a syndrome with multiple etiologies. Although it is generally believed to be organic in origin, rather than an environmentally caused syndrome, there are still major gaps in understanding its etiology. Associated with mental retardation in about 70 percent of the cases, the major features of autism include delay or deviance in social relatedness, qualitative impairments in verbal and nonverbal communication, a markedly restricted repertoire of stereotypic activities, and a severe restriction of imagination and imaginative play. Recent estimates of prevalence range from 6.6 to 13.6 cases per 10,000 population; autism can occur in conjunction with a wide range of biological syndromes including Fragile-X, PKU, Rett syndrome, and hy-

drocephalus. Although theories abound for the neurological bases of autism, with brain-stem pathology a common factor, the specific neural circuitry that must be dysfunctional for autism to occur has not yet been identified. Despite many positive effects of various treatments, there is not yet a cure.

Extrinsic Factors

The syndromes discussed thus far are primarily organic in nature, assumed to be a function of the child's genetic makeup. However, even after the genetic code has been laid out, growth and development of the human brain and nervous system can be harmed in numerous ways, frequently leading to mental retardation. Many causes of retardation can now be prevented or identified and treated. For example, it has long been recognized that exposure to *rubella* (German measles) during the third semester will lead to blindness and/or mental retardation; widespread vaccination of prepubescent girls has yielded drastic reductions in this incidence. Similarly, a bout of *meningitis* during childhood can cause severe retardation in the previously normal child; meningitis can be effectively treated, and now can be prevented through introduction of the vaccine against haemophilus B influenza. Other prenatal infections include *toxoplasmosis, herpes simplex, syphilis* (curable through early detection and treatment), and *AIDS.* In the fetus and newborn, AIDS leads to microcephaly, cerebral atrophy, seizures, and mental retardation.

Fetal development can also be affected by exposure to harmful drugs. The effects of fetal exposure to *thalidomide* have been identified and its use eradicated. Of great concern currently are the dramatic deleterious effects of alcohol (*fetal alcohol syndrome*) and other drugs during pregnancy. Of babies exposed to crack cocaine during fetal development, 25 percent develop microcephaly; it remains to see whether they become mentally retarded. Mental retardation can also result from high levels of exposure to *environmental poisons* such as lead, coal gas, mercury, and carbon monoxide. *Low birth weight* is now seen as an important predisposing factor toward mental retardation, and is often accompanied by such exacerbating factors as respiratory distress syndrome and neonatal seizures. Finally, it has long been observed that *severe environmental deprivation,* that is, lack of exposure to normal human contact or stimulus variety, may lead to arrest in intellectual development.

Familial Retardation

Although Zigler (1967) suggested that familial retardation is part of a normal continuum, more recently the familial account has been called into question. Rather, it is argued that mild retardation may result from an interaction of biological, familial, psychological, social, and environmental risks that put it on a continuum with more severe cases of retardation. In particular, multiple risks present in impoverished circumstances include malnutrition, exposure to toxic substances such as lead, hazardous environmental conditions, psychological stress (including substance abuse), inadequate hygiene, and lack of or inadequate medical care. Taking this perspective, prevention and treatment must be targeted toward at-risk populations where the mildly retarded are overrepresented.

Developmental Accounts of Mental Retardation

Despite the extreme variability of cause in retardation, analytic study of some of the affected cognitive structures has revealed development in well-defined domains to be normal in pattern, if extremely delayed in rate. Developmental studies indicate that syntactic structure, conceptual organization, and object permanence follow the normal sequence of acquisition, although knowledge acquired may be applied erratically and progress often ceases altogether at an early stage of development (refer to chapters in Nadel, 1988; Cicchetti and Beeghly, 1990). This developmental perspective leads to an approach to intervention that contrasts with the dominant behavior modification techniques developed in the 1950s. According to this approach, children should be treated in terms of their current mental age (or, more specifically, in terms of the developmental age for the particular domain of interest) and provided with developmentally appropriate opportunities to move forward.

Summary

In sum, the causes of mental retardation are legion. However, current analytic approaches toward both the causes of retardation and the character of specific cognitive disorders promise to improve prevention, diagnosis, and treatment while advancing our knowledge of genetics, neuropsychology, and cognition.

REFERENCES

Baumeister, A. A. (1987). Mental retardation: Some conceptions and dilemmas. *American Psychologist 42,* 796–800.

Burack, J. A., Hodapp, R. M., and Zigler, E. (1988). Issues in the classification of mental retardation: Differentiating among organic etiologies. *Journal of Child Psychology and Psychiatry and Allied Disciplines 29,* 765–779.

Cicchetti, D., and Beeghly, M., eds. (1990). *Children with Down syndrome: A developmental perspective.* Cambridge: Cambridge University Press.

Costeff, H., Cohen, B. E., and Weller, L. E. (1983). Biological factors in mild mental retardation. *Developmental Medicine and Child Neurology 25,* 580–587.

Gardner, H. (1983). *Frames of mind.* New York: Basic Books.

Gillberg, C. (1990). Autism and pervasive developmental disorders. *Journal of Child Psychology and Psychiatry and Allied Disciplines 31,* 99–119.

Grossman, H. J., ed. (1983). *Classification in mental retardation.* Washington, D.C.: American Association on Mental Deficiency.

Nadel, L., ed. (1988). *The psychobiology of Down syndrome.* Cambridge, Mass.: MIT Press. Excellent integration of neuropsychological, neurobiological, and cognitive perspectives on Down syndrome.

Stough, C., Nettelbeck, T., and Ireland, G. (1988). Objectively identifying the cocktail party syndrome among children with spina bifida. *The Exceptional Child 35,* 23–30.

Tew, B. (1979). The "cocktail party syndrome" in children with hydrocephalus and spina bifida. *British Journal of Disorders of Communication 14,* 89–101.

Thal, D., Bates, E., and Bellugi, U. (1989). Language and cognition in two children with Williams syndrome. *Journal of Speech and Hearing Research 32,* 489–500.

Valente, M. (1989). Etiologic factors in mental retardation. *Psychiatric Annals 19,* 179–183.

Zigler, E. (1967). Familial mental retardation: A continuing dilemma." *Science 155,* 292–298.

Anne Fowler

METAMEMORY

Metamemory refers to the *self-monitoring and self-control of one's own memory* during the learning of new information and during the retrieval of previously learned information. It is a relatively new topic, having been investigated by psychologists for less than thirty years. Prior to that time, researchers viewed people as blank slates, and the way that learning was assumed to occur was that new ideas were etched by repetition onto those slates, with the individual learner assumed to be passive and to have little or no control over his or her own learning. Subsequently, however, researchers have been viewing the individual as having substantial control over learning and as being active rather than passive, both during the learning of new information and during the retrieval of previously learned information. Moreover, researchers now know that people can monitor their progress during both learning and retrieval.

An example might help us to note the various aspects of metamemory that are involved during learning and retrieval. Imagine a student who is studying for an examination that will occur tomorrow in French class, say on French-English vocabulary such as *château*–castle and *rouge*–red. Let us keep that student in mind as we consider the monitoring processes and the control processes that occur as the student learns the new vocabulary and then attempts to retrieve the answers during the test the next day.

Various monitoring and control processes are discussed next. A theoretical framework that integrates all of these processes into an overall system can be found in Nelson and Narens (1990).

Monitoring

Different kinds of monitoring processes can be distinguished in terms of when they occur in the learning/retrieval sequence and whether they pertain to the person's future performance (in which case the focus is said to be on *prospective monitoring*) or to the person's past performance (in which case the focus is said to be on *retrospective monitoring*). Each kind of monitoring process will be discussed separately.

Prospective Monitoring

Ease-of-Learning Judgments. The first metamemory judgment made by someone who is getting ready to learn new information occurs prior to the beginning of learning. This *ease-of-learning judgment* is the person's judgment of how easy or difficult the items will be to learn. For instance, the person might believe that the overall set of items will take such-and-such amount of time to learn and that *château*–castle will be more difficult to learn than *rouge*–red. The psychologist Benton Underwood (1966) first showed that people are moderately accurate—not perfectly accurate but well above chance—at predicting which items will be easiest/hardest to learn. People's predictions of how easy it will be to learn each item, made in advance of learning, are moderately correlated (i.e., covaried) with their subsequent recall after a constant amount of study time on every item. Those items which people predict will be easiest to learn have a greater likelihood of being recalled than items predicted as hardest to learn.

Judgments of Learning. The next kind of monitoring occurs during and/or at the end of learning. The person's *judgment of learning* is the evaluation of how well he or she has learned a given item and, more precisely, is a prediction of the likelihood that the item will be recalled correctly on a future test. The psychologists Arbuckle and Cuddy (1969) first showed that the predictive accuracy of people's judgments of learning is above chance but far from perfect, not unlike the aforementioned situation for ease-of-learning judgments. However, research by Leonesio and Nelson (1990) has shown that judgments of learning are more accurate than ease-of-learning judgments for predicting eventual recall; this is probably because the judgments of learning—but not the ease-of-learning judgments—can be based in part on what the learner notices about how well he or she is mastering the items during learning.

Feeling-of-Knowing Judgments. These judgments are people's prediction of whether they will eventually remember an answer that they *currently do not recall*. Historically, this was the first kind of metamemory judgment to be examined in the laboratory. It was first investigated by Hart (1965), who found that these feeling-of-knowing judgments were somewhat accurate in predicting subsequent memory performance. The subsequent likelihood of correctly recognizing a nonrecalled answer was higher for nonrecalled items that people said were stored in their memory than for nonrecalled items that people said were not stored in their memory. However, as in the case of other metamemory judgments, the accuracy of this judgment was far from perfect; people often did not recognize answers they had claimed they would recognize, and people sometimes did recognize answers that they had claimed they wouldn't recognize. The accuracy of predicting other kinds of memory performance (e.g., ease of relearning) on nonrecalled items was subsequently reviewed and investigated by Nelson, Gerler, and Narens (1984), who also offered several theoretical explanations for how people might make their feeling-of-knowing judgments.

Retrospective Confidence Judgments

In contrast with the previous three kinds of metamemory monitoring judgments, which are attempts by people to predict their future memory performance, retrospective confidence judgments are made after a person recalls or recognizes an answer (either correctly or incorrectly) and are judgments of how confident the person is that his or her answer was correct. For instance, if our hypothetical student were asked to recall the English equivalent of *château*, the person might say "castle" (correct answer) or might say "red" (incorrect answer); then he or she would make a confidence judgment about the likelihood that the recalled answer was correct. Fischhoff, Slovic, and Lichtenstein (1977) investigated the accuracy of these retrospective confidence judgments and found that although people's retrospective confidence judgments had substantial accuracy, there was a strong tendency to be somewhat overconfident. For instance, for those items which people had given a confidence judgment of "80 percent likely to be correct," the actual percentage of correct recognition was much less.

Source Monitoring and Reality Monitoring

In addition to the aforementioned kinds of monitoring that pertain to a person's knowledge of a particular item, people also can monitor information about when and where they learned the item ("source information"; people who are unable to remember when/where the learning occurred are said to have *source amnesia*). One useful distinction in terms of the source of prior learning is whether the item occurred externally to the person and was perceived and then remembered by the person, or whether the item occurred internally in the person (e.g., in a dream). Being able to distinguish between those two possibilities is called *reality monitoring* and has been investigated by Johnson and Raye (1981).

Control

Not only can people monitor their progress during learning and retrieval, but they can also control many aspects of their learning and retrieval. First, we will consider aspects that people can control during self-paced learning, and then we will consider aspects they can control during retrieval.

Control During Self-Paced Learning

Allocation of Self-Paced Study Time During Learning. Our hypothetical student who is learning foreign-language vocabulary can choose to allocate large or small amounts of study time to each item and subsequently can allocate extra study time to some items. Moreover, as shown by Bisanz, Vesonder, and Voss (1978), the allocation of study time may be made in conjunction with the judgments of learning described above. In an investigation of learners of various ages, Bisanz et al. discovered that learners in the early years of primary school might make accurate judgments of learning but would not utilize those judgments when allocating additional study time across the items, whereas slightly older children would utilize those judgments when allocating additional study time. In particular, the older children allocated extra study time to items that were judged not to have been learned and did not allocate extra study time to items that were judged to have been learned. By contrast, the younger children were not systematic in allocating extra study time primarily to the unlearned items. For instance, if our hypothetical student judged his or her learning to be greater for *rouge*–red than for *château*–castle, then the utilization of that knowledge should result in extra self-paced study being more likely to be given to *château*–castle than to *rouge*–red.

Strategy Employed During Self-Paced Study. Not only can people control *how much* study time they allocate to various items (as discussed in the previous paragraph), they can also control *which particular strategy* they employ during that study time. For many kinds of learning, there are strategies that are much more effective than rote repetition. For instance, people's utilization of a mnemonic strategy for learning foreign-language vocabulary was investigated by Pressley, Levin, and Ghatala (1984). After people had learned some foreign-language vocabulary by rote and other foreign-language vocabulary by the mnemonic strategy, they were given a choice of using whichever strategy they wanted for a final trial of learning some additional foreign-language vocabulary.

If those people were adults, only 12 percent chose the mnemonic strategy if they had not received any test trials during the earlier learning phase, whereas 87 percent chose the mnemonic strategy if they had received test trials during the earlier learning phase. Apparently, people should have test trials to help them realize the effectiveness of different strategies for learning. Moreover, if those people were children instead of adults, then to get them to adopt the mnemonic strategy spontaneously, they not only had to have test trials during the earlier learning phase, but they also needed to have feedback after those test trials to tell them how well they had done on the rote-learned items versus the mnemonic-learned items.

Control During Retrieval

Control of Initiating One's Retrieval. Immediately after someone is asked a question and before he or she attempts to search memory for the answer, a metamemory decision is made about whether the answer is likely to be found in memory. For instance, if you were asked the telephone number of the president of the United States, you probably would decide immediately that the answer is not in your memory. Notice that you do not need to search through all the telephone numbers that you know, nor do you need to search through all the information you have stored in your memory about the president; you probably realize that the president does have a telephone number—but you know you don't know it, and therefore you don't initiate attempts to retrieve that answer. Consider how different that situation is from one in which you are asked the telephone number of one of your friends.

This initial feeling-of-knowing judgment that precedes an attempt to retrieve an answer was investigated by Reder (1987). She found that people were faster at making a feeling-of-knowing decision about whether they knew the answer to a general-information question (e.g., "What is the capital of Finland?") than they were at answering that question (e.g., saying "Helsinki"). This finding demonstrates that the metamemory decision is made prior to—not after—retrieving the answer. If and only if people feel that they know the answer will they initiate attempts to retrieve the answer from memory. When they feel that they do not know the answer, they don't even attempt to search memory (as in the example of the president's telephone number).

Control of the Termination of Extended Attempts at Retrieval. People may initially feel strongly enough that they know an answer to begin searching memory for it, but after extended attempts at retrieval without producing a potential answer, they will eventually terminate the search. The metamemory decision to terminate such an extended search of memory was investigated by Nelson, Gerler, and Narens (1984). They found that people would search longer for a sought-but-not-retrieved answer if they had a high feeling of knowing that they knew the answer. Put differently, the amount of time elapsing before someone gives up searching memory for a nonretrieved answer is greater when the person's ongoing feeling of knowing the answer is high rather than low.

As an example, our hypothetical student mentioned above might spend a long time during the examination attempting to retrieve the English equivalent of *château* (which the person had studied the night before) but little or no time attempting to retrieve the English equivalent of *cheval* (which the person did not study previously). The metamemory decision to continue versus terminate attempts at retrieving an answer from memory may also be affected by other factors, such as the total amount of time available during an examination.

REFERENCES

Arbuckle, T. Y., and Cuddy, L. L. (1969). Discrimination of item strength at time of presentation. *Journal of Experimental Psychology 81,* 126–131.

Bisanz, G. L., Vesonder, G. T., and Voss, J. F. (1978). Knowledge of one's own responding and the relation of such knowledge to learning. *Journal of Experimental Child Psychology 25,* 116–128.

Fischhoff, B., Slovic, P., and Lichtenstein, S. (1977). Knowing with certainty: The appropriateness of extreme confidence. *Journal of Experimental Psychology: Human Perception and Performance 3,* 552–564.

Hart, J. T. (1965). Memory and the feeling-of-knowing experience. *Journal of Educational Psychology 56,* 208–216.

Johnson, M. K., and Raye, C. L. (1981). Reality monitoring. *Psychological Review 88,* 67–85.

Leonesio, R. J., and Nelson, T. O. (1990). Do different measures of metamemory tap the same underlying aspects of memory? *Journal of Experimental Psychology: Learning, Memory, and Cognition 16,* 464–470.

Nelson, T. O., Gerler, D., and Narens, L. (1984). Accuracy of feeling-of-knowing judgments for predicting perceptual identification and relearning. *Journal of Experimental Psychology: General 113,* 282–300.

Nelson, T. O., and Narens, L. (1990). Metamemory: A theoretical framework and new findings. In G. H. Bower, ed., *The psychology of learning and motivation.* San Diego, Calif.: Academic Press.

Pressley, M., Levin, J. R., and Ghatala, E. (1984). Memory strategy monitoring in adults and children. *Journal of Verbal Learning and Verbal Behavior 23,* 270–288.

Reder, L. M. (1987). Strategy selection in question answering. *Cognitive Psychology 19,* 90–138.

Underwood, B. J. (1966). Individual and group predictions of item difficulty for free learning. *Journal of Experimental Psychology 71,* 673–679.

Thomas O. Nelson

MIGRATION, NAVIGATION, AND HOMING

The prevailing intellectual sentiment among behavioral biologists, or ethologists, of the 1950s was that the remarkable ability of migratory animals, foremost birds, to return to the same breeding and wintering area year after year is based on innate mechanisms of orientation and navigation. This emphasis on hereditary control has yielded to current conceptualizations of spatial behavior focusing on dynamic interactions with the environment that permit animals to modify their spatial behavior through learning, learning being defined broadly as an experience-dependent change in behavior.

Orientation refers to a heading or directed movement that bears a specific spatial relationship to some environmental or proprioceptive reference. It is typically discussed in terms of compass directions using the sun, stars, or earth's magnetic field as references. All three of these environmental stimuli are used by birds that migrate at night to orient their seasonal movements. From a learning perspective, what is interesting is that nocturnal migrants show an impressive ability to modify how they respond to a given environmental stimulus by forming a type of association between orientation responses to different stimuli. For example, several species of birds have been shown to change how they respond to stars based on experience with different ambient magnetic fields. Wiltschko and Wiltschko (1990) found that shifting the orientation of an ambient magnetic field resulted in birds' displaying a corresponding shift in their migratory orientation. What is important is that the birds displayed similarly shifted orientation with respect to the stars, which were not subjected to experimental shifting. This suggests that birds could learn a new orientation response to the stars, using the magnetic field as a calibrating reference. Bingman and Wiltschko (1988) described similar results in birds of another species that learned a new orientation response to the setting sun based on their experience with magnetic fields. Migratory orientation to the stars was also found to be modifiable based on experience with the sun. Moore (1987) found that shifting the apparent position of the setting sun with mirrors would cause birds to learn a new migratory orientation response to the stars. Collectively, these findings demonstrate that the migratory orientation of birds is to a large extent modifiable by experience, thereby emphasizing an important role for learning in this behavior.

The results described above were derived from experiments with birds that had already experienced at least one migration. Work with birds prior to their first migration has revealed that experience during their first summer may have an even larger effect on their subsequent migratory behavior. Evidence to date suggests that migrant birds are born with a disposition to orient in a particular direction with respect to the axis of celestial rotation and the earth's magnetic field. Emlen (1970) has shown that to learn a migratory orientation response to specific star patterns, birds rely on the rotation of the night sky about its axis as a directional reference. Once directional information from celestial rotation is transferred to the star patterns during their first summer, birds can use the patterns as an independent source of directional information.

Surprisingly, the presumably innate migratory orientation response to the earth's magnetic field is subject to change depending on a bird's first summer experience. Bingman (1983) found that different magnetic field experiences during summer resulted in birds' learning different autumn migratory orientation responses to the earth's magnetic field. The advantage of being able to learn a new orientation response to a magnetic field is that birds raised in different magnetic fields are still able to maintain the same seasonally appropriate migratory orientation with respect to geographic directions. Able and Able (1990) found that celestial rotation is the reference used by these birds to override their innate orientation response to the earth's magnetic field and learn a new response better suited for reaching their winter homes. As with experienced birds, changes in behavior based on learning the directional relationship among a variety of environmental stimuli are characteristic of young birds who have yet to engage in their first migration.

Birds are not the only animals that display highly directed movements, nor are they unique in being able to learn new responses. The beachhopper (*Talitrus saltator*) is a small crustacean that inhabits the shoreline of the Mediterranean. These animals are born displaying an orientation response to the sun that enables them to move quickly in a direction perpendicular to the shoreline axis in order to avoid danger. Ugolini and Macchi (1988) have shown that this innate orientation response can be modified by exposing young animals to a different environment. This is another example of altered orientation based on learning the spatial relationship among salient environmental stimuli, in this case sun and shoreline.

Homing is a phenomenon characterized by the ability of an animal to return to some goal location or "home." *Navigation* encompasses a set of spatial behavior mechanisms through which homing may be accomplished. Traditionally, true navigation implies both specification of one's location in space and the ability to determine a course to arrive at some undetectable goal. It is important to emphasize that spatial orientation, as displayed by migratory birds, does not necessarily imply spatial navigation. This is best illustrated by the experiments of Perdeck (1958).

Perdeck captured and marked thousands of starlings (*Sturnus vulgaris*) that were migrating

through the Netherlands in autumn. The birds were then transported to Switzerland and released. Looking at the locations where the birds were subsequently recaptured, an important difference emerged between adults that had already experienced one migration cycle and young birds that were migrating for the first time. Adult starlings were recovered primarily northwest of the release point. Northwesterly orientation corresponded to the direction in which they needed to fly if they were to arrive at their normal wintering homes near the northern coast of France. The adults displayed true navigational behavior. They succeeded in determining a course from an unfamiliar location that would bring them close to their goal. Young birds, in contrast, were recovered primarily southwest of the release point. Southwesterly orientation corresponds to the direction needed to fly if the birds were to arrive at their winter homes from the area where they were captured. Although displaying good orientation, the young birds failed to orient in a manner consistent with true navigation.

In addition to emphasizing the difference between orientation and navigation, the results of Perdeck demonstrate the importance of learning some characteristic(s) of the goal location for navigation to occur. Young birds that had never been to the wintering area could not navigate a course to it. Young birds on their first migration appear to possess an innate disposition to fly in a certain direction for a fixed period of time in order to arrive in the general vicinity of their population's wintering range. However, it is only after experiencing their winter home that they develop the ability to navigate to it from unfamiliar locations. It is believed that a similar learning process supports the ability of birds to navigate to and recognize the same breeding site year after year.

The importance of learning in the ability of salmon to return to breed in their natal stream has been well documented by Cooper et al. (1976). In an elegant experiment, young coho salmon (*Oncorhynchus kisutch*) were placed in a tank of water containing a specific odorant. The fish were marked and later released into Lake Michigan. The odorant was placed at the mouth of one stream that feeds into the lake. Sometime later, as the fish began to enter streams for breeding, it was found that fish that had been exposed to the odorant in the tank were much more likely to enter the stream where the odorant was placed. The fish apparently learn the characteristic odor of their stream during early development, and use that information to guide their return home.

Perhaps the best-studied navigational system in animals is that of the homing pigeon. Generally unappreciated is the fact that pigeon homing is supported by a number of distinct spatial behavior mechanisms. Regarding learning, all of the mechanisms have been shown to be dependent on experience with the environment. To orient in space, homing pigeons rely on the sun. Wiltschko and Wiltschko (1980) have shown that sun orientation is not innate but dependent upon a young bird's learning the path taken by the sun across the sky. Interestingly, experience limited to observing the sun before noon results in the ability to use the sun for orientation before noon but not after.

Pigeons rely on at least two navigational mechanisms: a *navigational map* that they can use from distant locations where they have never been before, and *landmark navigation*, which they can use when they are in sensory contact with familiar environmental stimuli. In some young pigeons learning a navigational map has been shown to be dependent on the opportunity to associate atmospheric odors with wind directions. Using fans to alter the relationship of wind direction and atmospheric odors experienced by different groups of young pigeons, Ioalé et al. (1978) succeeded in raising pigeons that learned different navigational maps which varied in accordance with a bird's experience with odors and wind direction. Landmark navigation has been shown to be similarly dependent on experience. Wallraff (1966) has shown that young birds held in an outdoor aviary but not permitted to fly outside it are able to learn a navigational map, as evidenced by their ability to orient toward home when released from a distant, unfamiliar location. Such birds are nonetheless impaired in returning home because of an inability to navigate in the vicinity of their home aviary. The lack of opportunity to fly outside their aviary renders them unable to build up their landmark navigational system, which is important for navigation near home. Although the two navigational systems discussed here are treated as being independent, both are learning based. Bingman et al. (1990) have shown that both are regulated in part by the same central forebrain structure, the hippocampus. Involvement of the same brain structure suggests that the two navigational systems share common features.

Like orientation, the importance for learning in navigation is not a uniquely vertebrate phenomenon. Gould (1986) has shown that honey bees (*Apis mellifera*) learn a familiar landmark map in a manner similar to homing pigeons, and that they are able to use this map from locations where they have never been before as long as sensory contact with the familiar landmarks can be maintained.

In the context of traditional psychological learning theory, what is remarkable about naturally occurring spatial learning is that it often occurs in the absence of any tangible external reward or reinforcement system. For example, what is rewarding about associating atmospheric odors with wind direction to a young pigeon locked in an aviary? What is rewarding about learning the path taken by the sun? It is difficult to explain such phenomena without assuming that animals are biologically predisposed to learn spatial relationships among stimuli in a rapid and efficient way without dependence on environmental reinforcement. Natural selection has seemingly endowed animals with nervous systems that predispose exploration, which in some way is intrinsically rewarding. Exploration would then form the basis of most learned spatial behavior.

(See also SPATIAL LEARNING.)

REFERENCES

Able, K., and Able, M. (1990). Calibration of the magnetic compass of a migratory bird by celestial rotation. *Nature 347*, 378–380.

Baker, R. (1984). *Bird navigation: The solution of a mystery*. London: Houder and Stoughton. An excellent review of spatial behavior mechanisms used by birds to navigate.

Bingman, V. (1983). Magnetic field orientation of migratory Savannah sparrows with different first summer experience. *Behaviour 87*, 43–53.

Bingman, V., Ioalé, P., Cashi, G., and Bagnoli, P. (1990). The avian hippocampus: Evidence for a role in the development of the homing pigeon navigational map. *Behavioral Neuroscience 104*, 906–911.

Bingman, V., and Wiltschko, W. (1988). Orientation of dunnocks (*Prunella modularis*) at sunset. *Ethology 77*, 1–9.

Cooper, J., Scholz, A., Horrall, R., Hasler, A., and Madison, D. (1976). Experimental confirmation of the olfactory hypothesis with artificially imprinted homing coho salmon (*Oncorhynchus kisutch*). *Journal of the Fisheries Resources Board of Canada 33*, 703–710.

Emlen, S. (1970). Celestial rotation: Its importance in the development of migratory orientation. *Science 170*, 1198–1201.

Gould, J. (1986). The local map of honeybees. Do insects have cognitive maps? *Science 232*, 861–863.

Ioalé, P., Papi, F., Fiaschi, V., and Baldaccini, N. (1978). Pigeon navigation: Effects upon homing behavior by reversing wind direction at the loft. *Journal of Comparative Physiology 128,* 285–295.

Kesner, R., and Olton D., eds. (1990). *Neurobiology of comparative cognition.* Hillsdale, N.J.: Erlbaum. Many chapters offer an excellent review of learning and spatial behavior, as well as its neural control, in a variety of species.

Moore, F. (1987). Sunset and the orientation behaviour of migrating birds. *Biological Review 62,* 65–86.

Perdeck, A. (1958). Two types of orientation in migrating starlings, *Sturnus vulgaris* L., and chaffinches, *Fringilla coelebs* L., as revealed by displacement experiments. *Ardea 55,* 194–202.

Ugolini, A., and Macchi, T. (1988). Learned component in the solar orientation of *Talitrus saltator* Montagu (Amphipoda: Talitridae). *Journal of Experimental Marine Biology and Ecology 121,* 79–87.

Wallraff, H. (1966). Über die Heimfindeleistungen von Brieftauben nach Haltung in verschiedenartig abgeschirmten Volieren. *Zeitschrift für vergleichende Physiologie 52,* 215–259.

Wiltschko, R., and Wiltschko, W. (1980). The development of sun compass orientation in young homing pigeons. *Behavioral Ecology and Sociobiology 9,* 135–141.

Wiltschko, W., and Wiltschko, R. (1990). Magnetic orientation and celestial cues in migratory orientation. *Experientia 46,* 343–351.

Verner P. Bingman

MNEMONIC DEVICES

Mnemonic devices are methods for memorizing. The ancient Greek poet Simonides of Ceos is the legendary discoverer of mnemonic devices. Pleased by Simonides's praise, the twin gods Castor and Pollux called him from a banquet just before the hall collapsed. The other guests were mangled beyond recognition, but Simonides remembered the places they had been sitting and so was able to identify the dead. Such was the discovery of the *method of loci* (or locations). It became so much a part of the study of rhetoric that the most venerable of the Roman orators used the method of loci for memorizing their speeches. Simonides remembered what his eyes had seen, but the mnemonists had to remember their speeches using their mind's eye. Their procedure was as follows: First, a series of locations (loci), such as those in a public building, were memorized. Second, some object was thought of to represent each important part of the oration, such as a spear to represent the tenth topic, war. Third, the image created for each topic was combined with the image of its corresponding location. The spear might be imaged as penetrating the tenth locus, a door. While making his speech, the orator thought of each location in turn and used the image seen in his mind's eye as the prompt for the next part of his address. After a few days, the images from the speech would fade from memory, but the more highly learned loci could be used to memorize a new speech.

During the Middle Ages and the Renaissance mnemonic devices were used not so much by orators for memorizing speeches as by scholars to classify and memorize all knowledge. This fascinating aspect of mnemonic devices is surveyed by Yates (1966).

Principles of Mnemonic Learning

Most mnemonic procedures utilize the three memory processes of *symbolizing, organizing,* and *associating.* Symbolizing is finding a memorable, preferably imageable, representation for what is to be learned. In the example above, a spear represents war. Organizing involves activating a knowledge structure in memory, such as a set of loci, to which new information can be associated. The new information must then be associated to components of the knowledge structure. These knowledge-structure components, labeled *mental cues,* must have certain properties for mnemonic learning to be effective. Designing a mnemonic device must take into account how easily mental cues can be reconstructed, as well as how easily they can be associated with new information and how easily they can be discriminated from other mental cues (Bellezza, 1981). Visual imagery is often used by the learner to create the association between the mental cue and the symbol to be remembered.

Types of Mnemonic Devices

Higbee (1988) discusses the wide variety of mnemonic procedures and some of the research done on them. I shall attempt only a brief overview here. Examples of some of the mnemonic devices mentioned appear in Table 1.

The process of organizing is particularly important when using a mnemonic technique such as the method of loci, the story mnemonic, or the link mnemonic. When using the story mnemonic, a list of words is memorized by creating a story from them. The words become organized in memory by the theme and context of the story. When the list words later have to be recalled, the story can be reviewed by the learner and the list words recognized.

The link mnemonic is somewhat different from the method of loci or the story mnemonic: The successive words forming a pair in a list are associated using a visual image. Each image can be distinct and separate from the other images. All the words end up joined together in memory by visual images like links in a chain.

In other mnemonic devices the memory process of symbolizing is paramount. When memorizing numbers, a system that goes back to the seventeenth century, the digit-consonant mnemonic, can be used. In this system numbers are changed to words because words are more easily memorized than numbers. The words can then be recalled and changed back into the numbers they represent.

One of the most useful mnemonics has been the *keyword mnemonic,* in which symbolizing processes play an important role. The keyword mnemonic is particularly useful for learning the meanings of words. For example, when learning the word *hegemony,* meaning authority of one nation over others, the word must first be correctly pronounced. It is pronounced something like he-GEM-oh-knee. Next, a keyword must be chosen that is familiar, meaningful, and sounds like the word to be learned. The keyword for hegemony

Table 1.   Examples of Mnemonics

Mnemonic	Example
Story mnemonic	Make up a story to remember the following grocery list: bread, paper plates, apples, broom, hamburger. Example: "When I tried to walk into the grocery store, my way was blocked by a giant *loaf* of bread. I made a path of *paper plates* and climbed over the bread. A little boy then hit me with an *apple.* I chased him with a *broom,* and when I caught him, he offered me a *hamburger.*" Later, when one goes into the grocery store, the story made up about the grocery store will be recalled along with the items that should be purchased there.
Link mnemonic	You have to remember the following list of items to be purchased from the hardware store: hammer, red paint, rope, pliers, and glue. First form a visual image of a hardware store and the first word, *hammer,* interacting in some way. The *hardware store* window was smashed by a *hammer.* Do the same for the hammer and red paint. A *hammer* smashed the can of *red paint.* Next, *red paint* was poured over a coil of *rope.* Then, a *rope* was cut with a pair of *pliers.* Finally, the jaws of the *pliers* were stuck together with *glue.* To recall the list, first think of the hardware store, and the visual images should pull one another from memory like links in a chain.
Digit-consonant mnemonic	When trying to memorize a number, consonant sounds are substituted for digits, using the following rules: $0 \rightarrow$ z, s, or soft c, $1 \rightarrow$ t or d,

(Continued on next page)

Table 1. Examples of Mnemonics (*Continued*)

	$2 \rightarrow$ n, $3 \rightarrow$ m, $4 \rightarrow$ r, $5 \rightarrow$ 1, $6 \rightarrow$ cj, j, sh, or soft g, $7 \rightarrow$ k, hard c, hard g, or qu, $8 \rightarrow$ f, v, or ph, $9 \rightarrow$ p or b. The vowels, the letters w-h-y, and unpronounced consonants have no digit equivalents and can be used as fillers when creating the words. The number 0123456789 can be transformed into *Satan may hurl a huge coffee pie*. Later, to remember the number, first recall the sentence and then transform the sounds in the sentence back into digits using the digit-consonant rules.
Keyword mnemonic	Learn the meaning of the word *jejune* (pronounced gee, JUNE), which means not of interest, insipid. A keyword mnemonic could be as follows: Jejune $\rightarrow$ "Gee, June" (keyword) $\rightarrow$ Gee, June is not an interesting person (mnemonic image).
Face-name mnemonic	Associate the name *Ms. Flanagan* with her face or figure. Replace the name Flanagan with the more meaningful keyword *flannel gown*. Perhaps Ms. Flanagan's most noticeable feature is that she looks like a model. A visual image should be formed of Ms. Flanagan modeling a flannel nightgown to help associate her appearance with a symbol for her name. The next time one sees Ms. Flanagan, one will think of her as a model, think of her modeling a flannel nightgown, remember the keyword *flannel gown*, and remember her name as *Flanagan*.

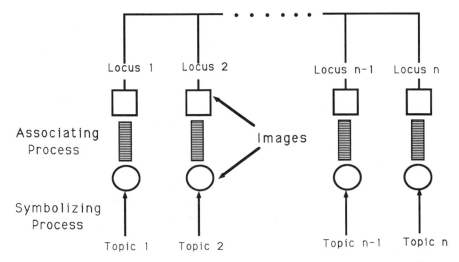

Figure 1. The processes organizing, symbolizing, and associating in the method of loci.

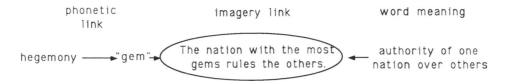

Figure 2. The phonetic and imagery links in the keyword mnemonic.

might be *gem.* Next, a visual image or sentence is formed that associates the key word with the meaning of the word to be learned. In this instance, the sentence might be *The nation with the most gems rules the others.* When coming across the word *hegemony* again, the learner must first think of the word *gem,* which then acts as a prompt for the mnemonic sentence containing the meaning of the word.

A useful but difficult variation of the keyword mnemonic is the face-name mnemonic used for associating names and faces. First, the person's name is transformed into a meaningful and concrete keyword, such as *Cushing* into *cushion.* The keyword then has to be associated to a salient bodily feature. In this example one might think of Mr. Cushing as having a cushion on his head because of his thick hair. When meeting Mr. Cushing again, one must recognize his hair as his critical physical feature. His hair should act as a cue for the word *cushion,* which in turn will act as a prompt for the name *Cushing.*

Practical Applications

The more complicated mnemonic devices, such as the digit-consonant mnemonic, the keyword mnemonic, and the face-name mnemonic, require study and practice in order to be effective. But little research has been performed to determine if the investment in time and effort to become proficient in these mnemonics results in improved performance in the classroom, in the workplace, in situations in which many people's names have to be remembered, and so on. However, interest in this topic seems to be growing. The keyword mnemonic has been shown to be useful to students learning classroom-type materials. This is true for both normal students and students with learning disabilities (Mastropieri et al., 1987).

(See also MNEMONISTS.)

REFERENCES

Bellezza, F. S. (1981). Mnemonic devices: Classification, characteristics, and criteria. *Review of Educational Research 51,* 247–275.

Higbee, K. L. (1988). *Your memory: How it works and how to improve it,* 2nd ed. New York: Prentice-Hall.

Mastropieri, M. A., Scruggs, T. E., and Levin, J. R. (1987). Mnemonic instruction in special education. In M. McDaniel and M. Pressley, eds., *Imaginal and mnemonic processes,* pp. 359–376. New York: Springer-Verlag.

Yates, F. A. (1966). *The art of memory.* London: Routledge and Kegan Paul.

Francis S. Bellezza

MNEMONISTS

The *Guinness Book of World Records* reports that in 1981 Rajan Srinavasen Mahadevan (known as Rajan) recited the first 31,811 digits of pi from memory and that in 1987 Hideaki Tomoyori broke that record by reciting the first 40,000 digits. People performing such feats of memory are called mnemonists or memorists. Although feats like these are rare, since the 1890s there have been several scientific accounts of people with prodigious memories. Starting with the pioneering work of Alfred Binet, the scientific literature describes over a dozen people showing exceptional memory for verbal materials. Brown and Deffenbacher (1988) give a comprehensive review of these studies. Studies of exceptional memory performance contribute to our understanding of memory both by describing the processes memorists use and by comparing them with processes used by people with ordinary memories.

Representative Case Studies

The studies on memorists have shown that they use a variety of techniques to remember material. Four memorists are presented here to demonstrate that variety in memory processes: Shereshevskii, Alexander Craig Aitken, VP, and Rajan.

Shereshevskii

A. R. LURIA (1968) has made Shereshevskii (S) the most famous mnemonist. (Luria referred to him only as S, but his real name later became known.) S was almost thirty when Luria began his studies, and the research continued for almost thirty years. Somewhat surprisingly, S was unaware that his memory was unusual until Luria began his investigations.

S used three basic processes, usually in combination, for remembering verbal material. The first was to generate rich visual images to represent information. When he became a stage performer, he trained himself to convert senseless words into meaningful images so that he could remember nonsense words or words from unfamiliar languages. The second process was to use familiar locations, such as stops on an oft-traveled street, to place the images mentally for later retrieval. This procedure is the method of locations (or loci) developed by the ancient Greek poet Simonides of Ceos about 500 B.C. The method of locations has been discussed by authors as diverse as Aristotle and Thomas Aquinas. S apparently developed the technique independently. The third process was to create a story with appropriate images to retrieve the information.

With these techniques, S was able to remember any information presented. Luria was unable to find any limit to the amount of material S could recall in this fashion. More surprisingly, there appeared to be no limit to the duration of S's memory. Luria reports a request for recall of a fifty-word list given without warning sixteen years after presentation of the list. That request, like all the others Luria reports, resulted in successful retrieval of the list.

S had strong synesthesia, which appears to be unique among the memorists who have been investigated. Synesthesia is said to occur when information coming into one sensory system (e.g., audition) produces an effect in another sensory system (e.g., vision). S once said to the Russian psychologist Vygotsky, "What a crumbly, yellow voice you have" (Luria, 1968, p. 24). On another occasion, Luria was concerned that S might not remember his way in an unfamiliar location. S replied that he couldn't possibly forget because "here's this fence. It has such a salty taste and feels so rough; furthermore, it has such a sharp, piercing sound . . ." (Luria, 1968, p. 38). Synesthesia interfered with the images S produced and presented an enduring problem for him. For example, S once noted that "Other times smoke or fog appears . . . and the more people talk, the harder it gets, until . . . I can't make anything out" (Luria, 1968, p. 39).

Professor Aitken

Many psychologists think that Professor Aitken, who lived from 1895 to 1967, was the best all-around mnemonist. That may be because they are also college professors.

In a summary of the work on Aitken, Hunter (1977) points out that he was a brilliant mathematician, an excellent mental calculator, and an accomplished violinist with an extraordinary memory. His primary method for learning was to search out meaningful relationships within the material and with previously learned information. Hunter provides a quote from Aitken that best captures his approach:

> Musical memory can . . . be developed to a more remarkable degree than any other, for we have a metre and a rhythm, a tune, or more than one, the harmony, the instrumental color, a particular emotion or sequence of emotion, a meaning, . . . in the executant an auditory, a rhythmic and a muscular and functional memory; and secondarily in my case, a visual image of the page . . . perhaps also a human interest in the composer, with whom one may identify oneself . . . and an esthetic interest in the form of the piece. They are so many, and they are so cumulative, that the development of musical memory, and appreciation, has a multitude of supports. (1977, p. 157)

Although Aitken's memory was prodigious, it was not infallible. For example, in 1936 he correctly recalled sixteen three-digit numbers after four presentations. Two days later, he recalled all but one of the numbers and, after an additional presentation, he recalled them all. In 1960, without further study, he recalled twelve of the numbers but also produced eight incorrect numbers.

VP

VP (identified only by these initials in the published report) is an excellent chess player whose memory has been investigated by Hunt and Love (1972). VP has an exceptional memory but, like Aitken's, it is not infallible. For example, Hunt and Love reproduced VP's recall of an Indian story after intervals of 1 hour and 6 weeks. Although there were small changes in both recalls, his overall accuracy was remarkable.

VP learned material by relating it to prior information. For example, he knew several languages and could associate any three-letter string with a word. He learned number matrices by rows and sometimes recoded the row as a date. It is also clear that he spent a great deal of time practicing memorizing so that he became very adept at recoding information.

Rajan

Rajan has an exceptional memory for digits but not for other material. A group of researchers from Kansas State University (Thompson et al., 1991) performed extensive tests on his memory.

Their studies showed that Rajan learned sets of digits more rapidly than VP or S. He used a procedure pairing locations and digits to learn the material. He also encoded the digits in chunks (such as a row in a matrix). Thus, he learned that the fifth digit in the fourth row was 3 rather than using preexisting knowledge to encode the information. He explicitly attached cues to the chunks for retrieval. For example, he learned the first column in a matrix as a cue for retrieving each row of the matrix.

Once the material was learned, Rajan's procedure allowed for extremely effective retrieval of information. Working in the first 10,000 decimal digits of pi, he could retrieve a digit at a specified location (e.g., digit 4765) in an average time of 12 seconds. He had the digits of pi chunked in groups of 10 digits. When he was given the first 5 digits of a 10-digit group in the first 10,000 digits of pi, he could give the next 5 digits in an average time of 7 seconds.

The Memorists and a Theory of Skilled Memory

In several papers, Ericsson and his colleagues (e.g., Ericsson and Chase, 1982) suggest three general principles for skilled memory and illustrate these principles with people skilled at some aspect of memory. The three principles they propose are meaningful encoding (the use of preexisting knowledge to store the presented information in memory), retrieval structure (explicitly attaching cues to the encoded material to allow efficient retrieval), and speedup (a reduction in study time with further practice). They claim that ordinary subjects, as well as skilled memorists, show these principles.

Consistent with this theory, all four mnemonists described here attach retrieval cues when learning material to ensure accurate and fast retrieval. Further, three of them show a reduction in study time with practice. There is no clear evidence available on this point for Professor Aitken. However, it seems likely that he would show a similar effect.

The data from these memorists suggest that the skilled memory theory founders on the third principle. All four memorists use procedures for encoding the material that are available to, and used by, people with ordinary memories. But, contrary to the theory, not all of them encode the material by relating it to preexisting knowledge. VP fits the theory because he encodes material by relating it to prior information. Aitken uses that technique and also searches for relationships within the material to be learned. S uses imagery and the classic method of locations as his primary means for learning material. Because Ericsson and his colleagues clearly refer to relating the material to preexisting verbal knowledge, S's procedures do not conform to their theory. Rajan also does not fit the theory at all. His procedure, pairing locations and digits, cannot be construed as encoding by relation to preexisting knowledge.

Conclusions

The four memorists use quite different techniques to remember information, some of which call into question a portion of the theory of skilled memory. Their memories are unusually good, but the processes they use to remember can all be used by people with ordinary memories. In short, their unusual memories are unusual in the amount they can remember but not in the processes they use to remember.

(See also EXPERTS' MEMORIES; MNEMONIC DEVICES.)

REFERENCES

Brown, E., and Deffenbacher, K. (1975). Forgotten mnemonists. *Journal of the History of the Behavioral Sciences 11,* 342–349.

——— (1988). Superior memory performance and mnemonic encoding. In L. K. Obler and D. Fein, eds., *The exceptional brain,* pp. 436–473. New York: Guilford Press. An excellent review of memorists with a complete set of references.

Ericsson, K. A., and Chase, W. G. (1982). Exceptional memory. *American Scientist 70,* 607–615.

Hunt, E., and Love, T. (1972). How good can memory be? In A. W. Melton and E. Martin, eds., *Coding processes in human memory.* Washington, D.C.: John Wiley & Sons. Describes VP.

Hunter, I. M. L. (1977). An exceptional memory. *British Journal of Psychology 68,* 155–164. Contains a review of the work on Professor Aitken.

Luria, A. R. (1968). *The mind of a mnemonist.* New York: Basic Books. Describes S.

Obler, L. K., and Fein, D. (1988). *The exceptional brain.* New York: Guilford Press. Contains contributed chapters on many types of exceptional performance.

Thompson, C. P., Cowan, T. M., Frieman, J., Mahadevan, R. S., Vogl, R. J., and Frieman, J. (1991). Rajan: A study of a memorist. *Journal of Memory and Language 30,* 702–724.

Charles P. Thompson

MODALITY EFFECTS

The classic modality effect is the finding that immediate recall of the last few items from a verbal sequence is more likely if the sequence is spoken aloud than if it is read silently. The effect can be readily understood phenomenologically. We are all familiar with the experience of briefly retaining speech in echoic form and occasionally using this "echo" to do a double take. This modality effect has been widely attributed to an echoic memory system that is necessary for speech perception and that stores raw acoustic information for up to roughly 2 seconds after its occurrence.

Recent evidence challenges this traditionally accepted view. Similar modality effects have been discovered with other modalities, such as lipreading and sign language. And modality effects have been discovered in long-term memory as well as in short-term memory. As a result, the term *modality effect* is increasingly used to refer to any differences in memory performance that are associated with differences in stimulus mode. Such modality effects are more pervasive, and of more fundamental importance, than had been thought.

The Classic Effect

The classic modality effect occurs in comparing the immediate recall of sequences of verbal items that are presented in written or in spoken form (see also MEMORY SPAN). It does not matter much whether it is the experimenter or the subject who reads the spoken sequences aloud. Recall performance is usually plotted as a function of each item's serial position in the sequence. The modality effect occurs both when recall itself is serial—that is, when the items have to be recalled in their order of occurrence—and when recall is free, in the sense that subjects are free to choose any order of recall. Two of the earliest demonstrations of this modality effect are reproduced in Figure 1 (serial recall) and Figure 2 (free recall).

As the figures show, in serial recall sequence length often only just exceeds memory span and performance is commonly scored in terms of errors, whereas in free recall sequence length is usually well above memory span and performance is scored in terms of the probability of recall. Digit sequences are frequently used for serial recall; sometimes letters or syllables are used, sometimes unrelated words. In free recall, the sequences are almost always unrelated words.

The modality effect is intimately bound up with two other effects, the recency effect and the suffix effect. The recency effect is the finding that the last few (or most recent) items from a sequence are more likely to be recalled than the preceding items. As Figures 1 and 2 illustrate, in serial recall there is little recency effect for the silent sequences, but in free recall both input modes show a large recency effect and the modality effect appears as an enhanced recency effect. The suffix effect is the finding that in serial recall, a single spoken item at the end of the sequence, such as a *zero* after the last to-be-recalled digit, essentially wipes out the modality effect. With the suffix, there is as little recency effect for spoken as for silent sequences.

By far the most influential theory proposed to account for these effects is Crowder and Morton's (1969) Precategorical Acoustic Storage (PAS)

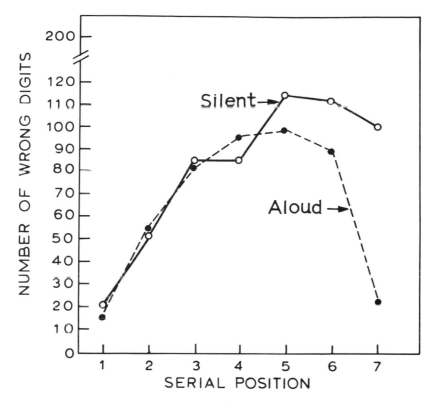

Figure 1. The modality effect in serial recall. *After Conrad and Hull (1968),
Fig. 1, p. 136. Reproduced with permission.*

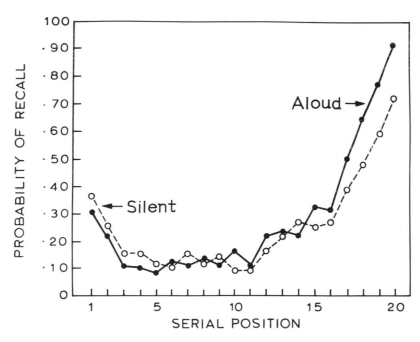

Figure 2. The modality effect in free recall. *After Murdock and Walker
(1969), Fig. 2, p. 668. Reproduced with permission.*

model. PAS is an auditory SENSORY MEMORY store, the echoic counterpart of the visual sensory store (iconic memory). Its function is to retain speech input at precategorical level—that is, prior to analysis of meaning—long enough to continue and complete processing shortly after stimulus offset. Information in PAS persists for roughly 2 seconds, but it is overwritten or erased by subsequent speech input. Thus the modality effect occurs because echoic memory, unlike iconic memory, persists long enough to contribute to immediate recall. The decay and overwriting characteristics of PAS explain why the modality effect is restricted to the most recent items in the sequence and why it is wiped out by the suffix effect.

This theory is elegant and powerful. One great strength lies in its ability to integrate modality, recency, and suffix effects. Another lies in its implications for understanding speech perception as well as short-term memory. No rival theory has been able to match both these accomplishments.

The PAS model of echoic memory inspired a great deal of subsequent research, particularly on the suffix effect in serial recall. Much of the earlier research provides impressive support for the model (e.g., Morton, Crowder, and Prussin, 1971). For example, there is evidence that the suffix effect is modality-specific—cross-modal effects do not occur; that the suffix effect depends on sensory, not semantic, factors; and that the sound of the suffix has to be speechlike. Indeed, both modality effects and suffix effects depend on the acoustic distinctiveness of the items. Neither effect occurs if the items differ only in their stop consonants. The modality effect in free recall, too, is vulnerable to suffixlike interference, especially with several successive suffixes. And modality effects in both free and serial recall depend in a similar way on acoustic distinctiveness (Watkins, Watkins, and Crowder, 1974).

Modality differences do occur in some other short-term memory tasks, but these effects have been relatively neglected.

Recent Developments

Among alternatives to the PAS model is a more phenomenological view of echoic memory, based partly on evidence that echoic memory persists for longer than had been assumed (Watkins and Watkins, 1980). But there are other recent developments that challenge not only the PAS model but also any echoic memory interpretation of modality effects.

Modality Effects in the Absence of Sound

It is now well established that modality and suffix effects in serial recall occur when the items are lip-read or mouthed silently instead of being spoken aloud (Campbell and Dodd, 1980; Nairne and Walters, 1983; Spoehr and Corin, 1978). Recent work suggests that though the silent and spoken effects are very similar—for example, like the spoken effect, the mouthed effect depends on acoustic distinctiveness—they are not entirely equivalent (see, e.g., Turner et al., 1987).

These findings led to a revision of the PAS model and to several other theoretical developments. The revised PAS model (Crowder, 1983; Greene and Crowder, 1984; see also Morton et al., 1981) assumes that information in PAS can also be activated by the facial-gestural features involved in lipreading and mouthing, on the grounds that these features are involved in speech perception.

Campbell and Dodd (1980) propose a changing-state hypothesis that attributes modality effects to the dynamic way stimuli in certain modes unfold over time, compared with their static nature in written or graphic form. However, modality and recency effects cannot easily be simulated by changing-state presentations of stimuli in written or graphic form, though changing-state effects may depend on whether the information that changes over time is critical in identifying the item (Kallman and Cameron, 1989). A related hypothesis takes a more sensory view of recency effects in general, including visual recency with graphic stimuli (Broadbent and Broadbent, 1981).

Evidence of modality and suffix effects with American Sign Language in the congenitally deaf led Shand and Klima (1981) to propose a primary linguistic coding hypothesis. This hypothesis assumes that such effects occur whenever the stimulus modality is compatible with the short-term memory code involved in a person's primary mode of communication.

These more recent hypotheses all have heuristic value, but they lack precision and are limited in scope. For instance, they do not explain other modality and suffix effects that have been discovered with tactile stimuli and with musical notes or rhythms. Nor can even the revised PAS model explain effects with such nonlinguistic items.

Modality Effects in Long-Term Memory

There are modality effects in long-term as well as short-term memory. Although the PAS model does not explain these effects, they are less directly relevant to it because they lie outside its domain. For example, a spoken modality effect occurs in a free recall task in which each word in the sequence is preceded and followed by lengthy periods of spoken distractor activity (Gardiner and Gregg, 1979; Glenberg, 1984; Greene, 1985). Such interference is assumed to eliminate any contribution from sensory or short-term memory because it wipes out modality and recency effects when it occurs only after the last word in the sequence. This long-term modality effect does not seem to depend on acoustic distinctiveness, nor does it occur in serial recall. But there is a similar long-term effect with silent mouthing.

This long-term modality effect led Glenberg and Swanson (1986) to propose a detailed model which assumes that temporal information is more finely represented in the auditory mode and that the modality effect reflects greater temporal distinctiveness (see also Gardiner, 1983). Since it is possible that temporal distinctiveness underlies the recency effect in both short-term and long-term memory, temporal distinctiveness theory can potentially provide a quite general account of modality and recency effects. A number of current studies have investigated temporal and ordinal factors, and though it is becoming clear that serial-order information is better retained in the auditory mode, it is less clear that the same is true for temporal information as such (Neath and Crowder, 1990).

A few modality effects have been discovered in other long-term memory tasks, including recognition memory, where the effect is found across all serial positions (Conway and Gathercole, 1987). Some of these effects are a reversal of the usual auditory superiority, and they seem to interact with other factors in ways that are as yet poorly understood. Finally, there are long-term modality effects of a rather different kind in implicit measures of retention (see IMPLICIT MEMORY).

Conclusion

Modality effects have a much broader empirical base than had been realized, and recent discoveries have led to fresh theoretical approaches, among which temporal distinctiveness theory perhaps is currently the most influential. In addition to the alternative hypotheses already mentioned, there are other suggestions that there has been less time to evaluate. Nairne (1988) suggests conceptualizing the memory trace in terms of modality-independent and modality-dependent features, which may or may not reflect sensory aspects of the stimulus. Penney (1989) develops a "separate streams" hypothesis which assumes that modality separation of verbal items is inherent to the structure of short-term memory. All these ideas assign modality effects to more fundamental, less peripheral, aspects of memory function than originally envisaged in echoic memory theory.

REFERENCES

Broadbent, D., and Broadbent, M. H. P. (1981). Recency effects in visual memory. *Quarterly Journal of Experimental Psychology A33,* 1–15.

Campbell, R., and Dodd, B. (1980). Hearing by eye. *Quarterly Journal of Experimental Psychology A32,* 85–99.

Conrad, R., and Hull, A. J. (1968). Input modality and the serial position curve in short-term memory. *Psychonomic Science 10,* 135–136.

Conway, M. A., and Gathercole, S. E. (1987). Modality and long-term memory. *Journal of Memory and Language 26,* 341–361.

Crowder, R. G. (1983). The purity of auditory memory. *Philosophical Transactions of the Royal Society of London B302,* 251–265.

Crowder, R. G., and Morton, J. (1969). Precategorical acoustic storage (PAS). *Perception and Psychophysics 5,* 365–373.

Gardiner, J. M. (1983). On recency and echoic memory. *Philosophical Transactions of the Royal Society of London B302,* 267–282.

Gardiner, J. M., and Gregg, V. H. (1979). When auditory memory is not overwritten. *Journal of Verbal Learning and Verbal Behavior 18,* 705–719.

Glenberg, A. M. (1984). A retrieval account of the long-term modality effect. *Journal of Experimental Psychology: Learning, Memory, and Cognition 10,* 16–31.

Glenberg, A. M., and Swanson, N. G. (1986). A temporal distinctiveness theory of recency and modality effects. *Journal of Experimental Psychology: Learning, Memory, and Cognition 12,* 3–15.

Greene, R. L. (1985). Constraints on the long-term modality effect. *Journal of Memory and Language 24,* 526–541.

Greene, R. L., and Crowder, R. G. (1984). Modality and suffix effects in the absence of auditory stimulation.

Journal of Verbal Learning and Verbal Behavior 23, 371–382.

Kallman, H. J., and Cameron, P. (1989). Enhanced recency effects with changing-state and primary-linguistic stimuli. *Memory and Cognition 17,* 318–328.

Morton, J., Crowder, R. G., and Prussin, H. A. (1971). Experiments with the stimulus suffix effect. *Journal of Experimental Psychology 91,* 169–190.

Morton, J., Marcus, S. M., and Ottley, P. (1981). The acoustic correlates of "speechlike": A use of the suffix effect. *Journal of Experimental Psychology: General 110,* 568–593.

Murdock, B. B., Jr., and Walker, K. D. (1969). Modality effects in free recall. *Journal of Verbal Learning and Verbal Behavior 8,* 665–676.

Nairne, J. S. (1988). A framework for interpreting recency effects in immediate serial recall. *Memory and Cognition 16,* 343–352.

Nairne, J. S., and Walters, V. L. (1983). Silent mouthing produces modality- and suffix-like effects. *Journal of Verbal Learning and Verbal Behavior 22,* 475–483.

Neath, I., and Crowder, R. G. (1990). Schedules of presentation and temporal distinctiveness in human memory. *Journal of Experimental Psychology: Learning, Memory, and Cognition 16,* 316–327.

Penney, C. G. (1989). Modality effects and the structure of short-term memory. *Memory and Cognition 17,* 398–422. An exceptionally comprehensive review and reference source.

Shand, M. A., and Klima, E. S. (1981). Nonauditory suffix effects in congenitally deaf signers of American Sign Language. *Journal of Experimental Psychology: Human Learning and Memory 7,* 464–474.

Spoehr, K. T., and Corin, W. J. (1978). The stimulus suffix effect as a memory coding phenomenon. *Memory and Cognition 6,* 583–589.

Turner, M. L., LaPointe, L. B., Cantor, J., Reeves, C. H., Griffith, R. H., and Engle, R. W. (1987). Recency and suffix effects found with auditory presentation and mouthed visual presentation: They're not the same thing. *Journal of Memory and Language 26,* 138–164.

Watkins, M. J., Watkins, O. C., and Crowder, R. G. (1974). The modality effect in free and serial recall as a function of phonological similarity. *Journal of Verbal Learning and Verbal Behavior 13,* 430–447.

Watkins, O. C., and Watkins, M. J. (1980). The modality effect and echoic persistence. *Journal of Experimental Psychology: General 109,* 251–278.

John M. Gardiner

MODELS OF MEMORY

Models of memory are theories of how information is represented in memory and the processes by which information is stored in and retrieved from memory. To develop a model that successfully accomplishes these goals is a daunting task. Thousands of experiments have been done to investigate memory, and there are hundreds of phenomena to explain. Theoretical progress in understanding memory is made by trying to map a wide range of phenomena onto a model that specifies what processes operate on what kinds of information for each phenomenon. So, for example, questions are asked like the following: Are the processes used in recognizing that a string of letters is a word the same processes that are used in recalling that the word appeared in a sentence? Do the processes operate on a common memory representation of the string of letters or on different representations? While progress can be made on such questions experimentally by using intuitive notions of process and structure, models provide more insightful ways of addressing these issues and integrate our understanding across different kinds of experiments.

The first issue is "Why develop models at all; are the data alone not enough?" Several papers have addressed the need to use theory in guiding research; here some major points are summarized (Estes, 1975; Hintzman, 1991). Models are useful because they bring out relationships among sets of data that would not otherwise have been apparent to us, because they allow reclassifications of phenomena that are not obvious in the data alone, and because they allow specific predictions about processing and representation to be formulated and tested against data. Both Estes and Hintzman provide excellent examples of these and other reasons for the use of models. In cognitive psychology, models usually are relatively simple in structure and make use of accessible and well-understood mathematics. Thus the domain is exciting for a researcher because it is possible to develop new models and to make major contributions in a relatively short time. This stands in contrast with many domains of research in the physical sciences.

Representation

The key to understanding and modeling human cognition is representing knowledge. While there has been a great deal of work on representation (e.g., see SEMANTIC MEMORY and CONCEPTS AND CATEGORIES, LEARNING OF), it is clear that definitive answers have not been found. One structure that has been proposed for representing knowledge is a semantic network (e.g., Anderson, 1983) in which each concept is a single node and relationships among concepts are shown by labeled links between nodes. Similarity between two concepts can be measured as the distance between the concepts in number of links or the number of common concepts directly linked to the two concepts. A second method for representing knowledge uses a feature representation in which each concept is made up of a number of semantic features, and similarity is measured by the number of features in common.

Most current memory models have less to say about representation than about processing. However, all the models make use of either semantic networks or feature representations, but without spelling out exactly what kinds of information are carried in the nodes, links, or features.

Process

Several memory models do a good job of explaining a number of phenomena from a number of different tasks, and of explaining multiple aspects of the data from each task. One model is presented in moderate detail and another is presented briefly.

The SAM (search of associative memory) model of Gillund and Shiffrin (1984) is designed to account for performance on recognition tasks and recall tasks. Subjects are presented with a list of words (or other materials) that they are to study. Then, in recall, they are asked to write down all of the words from the list that they can remember. In recognition, subjects are shown a list of test words and are asked to indicate which of the words on the test list were on the study list. For these tasks, the SAM model can predict the effects of a number of variables, such as presentation time per study word, number of repetitions of study words, forgetting over time or by interference from other learning, effects of rehearsal of the study words, effects of the context of other words in the test list, effects of the frequency with which the words occur in English, and so on. The aim is to explain how the accuracy of recognition and recall varies as a function of these variables. The model uses the same representation of the study words in memory for both tasks, and to account for the effects of all the variables. However, recall and recognition are assumed to employ different retrieval processes. The SAM model assumes that each study item is represented separately in mem-

ory. At encoding, a simple buffer model builds a retrieval structure that contains strengths of connections between cues (potential test items) and images (representations of items in memory). The parameters of this encoding process are expressed in terms of units per second, and measure the strength that accumulates per second. The parameter a refers to the strength built up between the context in which an item is presented and the item, b refers to interitem strengths (the strengths between the items that are in the buffer at the same time), c refers to the strength built up between an item as a cue and its own image in memory, and d refers to the residual strength that exists between any item as cue and any other item in memory independently of encoding.

The process that operates on information in memory for the recognition task is a global parallel matching process whereby the test word is compared against all words in memory. The test word is combined with the test context to be compared against memory; the result of this comparison is a match value, a number that indicates how well the test word matches memory. The value is calculated as the sum over all items in memory of the products of the strength between the test word (the cue) and each image in memory. If the value is large (larger than some criterion value), then the response to the test item will be that it is from the studied list; if the value is smaller than a criterion value, then the response will be that the word was not from the list. Consider a numerical example. If the strengths of connections between the test context and the test item (what memory is probed with) and each item in memory are as shown in Figure 1 (.2 for context to item 1, .9 for test item to item 1, etc.), then the value of the match is the sum of products as shown in the figure. Real subjects make errors in recognition; in the SAM model, these errors result from variability at encoding. During study, some words will be encoded extremely well, others not so well, and others very poorly. A poorly encoded word may have a small match value when presented as a test word, and so the response to it may be incorrect. Similarly, some words not on the list may match memory better than the criterion value, and so be responded to incorrectly. To model the time taken to make a response, the value of the match between test and memory can be used to determine the rate at which information is accumulated over time (Ratcliff, 1978). Such an evidence accumulation process predicts a range of phenomena including the behavior of the average response

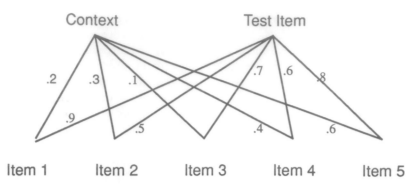

Figure 1.   Items 1–5 are in memory; the numbers represent the strengths between context and memory and between the test item and memory. The match between the test item plus context (familiarity) = .2 × .9 + .3 × .5 + .1 × .7 + .4 × .6 + .6 × .8 + ...

time, the shape of the response time distribution, and the average accuracy of responses.

In recall, a search process recovers items one after another. First, memory is probed with the test context in order to find an item. Then, if the strength is high enough, the item will be recovered (i.e., recalled). Then this item, along with context, probes memory again in an attempt to recover another item. This process is repeated until the process runs out of time or cannot recover any more items.

SAM represents memory as a network of strengths connecting items. A contrasting model is Hintzman's MINERVA2 model, in which items are represented in memory as sets of features (items are represented separately, i.e., an instance-based model; other models are composite, all items entering a common memory. See Murdock, 1982). For recognition, a test item (which is also represented as a list of features) is matched against all the items in memory. When a feature in the test item matches a feature in an item in memory, the match value is increased by 1; when they do not match, the match value is decreased by 1. All of these match values between the test and individual items in memory are then cubed and pooled to produce an overall match value. Hintzman's (1986, 1988) model has been applied successfully to a range of phenomena including recognition, cued recall, frequency judgments, and categorization.

Comparison of Models

What is interesting about current memory models is that although their structures are different in many ways, they make remarkably similar predictions in their common domains of application. In one sense, this should be expected; if they did not, one model would be right and another wrong. But in another sense, the question becomes "What are the mechanisms that give rise to similar predictions?" For example, to explain better accuracy in recognition as study time per word increases, the MINERVA2 model assumes an increase in the probability of a feature's being encoded into memory. Similarly, in the SAM model, greater retrieval strength is accumulated as a function of study time. The major characteristic that makes the models produce similar predictions in recognition is that they compute an overall match value between the test item and all items in memory.

Application to Other Phenomena

One important use of the global memory models is to serve as either a qualitative or a quantitative metaphor for processing, and thus to serve in other research domains. An example is the application of the models to priming. Priming occurs when one test item speeds responses to the next test item by virtue of the relation between them. The most popular current view of this phenomenon is that the first item sends spreading activation through a semantic network of concepts and the second item is responded to more quickly because it is partially activated before it is actually presented. Ratcliff and McKoon (1988) and Dosher and Rosedale (1989) developed an alternative, compound cue, model using the mechanisms that already existed in the global memory models.

These models emphasize parallel retrieval and have mechanisms for matching pairs of test items against memory in parallel. Thus the new compound cue model assumes that a test probe to be matched against all of memory consists of the first and second items together. If the two items are related in memory, then the value of the match will be larger than if they are not (through the standard mechanisms of the global models). This provides a counterinterpretation to the popular, spreading activation theory.

Connectionist Models

Many connectionist/neural network models are advertised as having associative memory, and many of these models can be successfully used to store and retrieve information from a content-addressable memory (see PARALLEL DISTRIBUTED PROCESSING MODELS OF MEMORY). Few of the models, however, have been seriously applied to the same range of experimental data in memory as the global memory models. It has been shown (e.g., McCloskey and Cohen, 1989, Ratcliff, 1990) that it is far from trivial to get models of this class to account for more than a few of the major trends in experimental data. However, the application of connectionist models to memory data is sure to be a major area of research in the future.

Conclusions

Models of memory have a number of uses and are an end in themselves. They attempt to organize and predict a large number of phenomena within their single framework. They also form the basis for developing new and different accounts of other phenomena in related domains. Finally, the models provide a basis for competition with connectionist models and an impetus for development of future models.

REFERENCES

Anderson, J. R. (1983). *The architecture of cognition.* Cambridge, Mass.: Harvard University Press.

Dosher, B. A., and Rosedale, G. (1989). Integrated re-trieval cues as a mechanism for priming in retrieval from memory. *Journal of Experimental Psychology: General 2,* 191–211.

Estes, W. K. (1975). Some targets for mathematical psychology. *Journal of Mathematical Psychology 12,* 263–282.

Gillund, G., and Shiffrin, R. M. (1984). A retrieval model for both recognition and recall. *Psychological Review 91,* 1–67.

Hintzman, D. (1986). "Schema abstraction" in a multiple-trace memory model. *Psychological Review 93,* 411–428.

——— (1988). Judgments of frequency and recognition memory in a multiple-trace memory model. *Psychological Review 95,* 528–551.

——— (1991). Why are formal models useful in psychology? In W. E. Hockley and S. Lewandowsky, eds., *Relating theory and data: Essays on human memory in honor of Bennet B. Murdock.* Hillsdale, N.J.: Erlbaum.

McCloskey, M., and Cohen, N. J. (1989). Catastrophic interference in connectionist networks: The sequential learning problem. In G. H. Bower, ed., *The psychology of learning and motivation.* New York: Academic Press.

Murdock, B. B. (1982). A theory for the storage and retrieval of item and associative information. *Psychological Review 89,* 609–626.

Ratcliff, R. (1978). A theory of memory retrieval. *Psychological Review 85,* 59–108.

——— (1990). Connectionist models of recognition memory: Constraints imposed by learning and forgetting functions. *Psychological Review 97,* 285–308.

Ratcliff, R., and McKoon, G. (1988). A retrieval theory of priming in memory. *Psychological Review 95,* 385–408.

Roger Ratcliff

MORPHOLOGICAL BASIS OF LEARNING AND MEMORY

[*This article consists of two sections,* Invertebrates *by Craig H. Bailey and* Vertebrates *by William T. Greenough.*]

Invertebrates

The idea that learning and memory might involve morphological changes within the nervous system was first suggested by the influential neuroanatomist Santiago Ramón y CAJAL at the beginning of the twentieth century. A basic tenet of this hypothesis was that the structure of the brain could be modified throughout life and that learning was capable of producing neuronal growth and differentiation, including the formation of new synaptic connections. This concept has been restated and refined by numerous contributors, and in modern terms has come to mean that learning in general and memory in particular are likely to involve a persistent change in synaptic function and form. However, prior to the last few decades there was little direct evidence either to support this hypothesis or to indicate precisely what aspects of synaptic change might be important for information storage.

Recent studies exploiting the experimental advantages of identified neurons in a variety of higher invertebrate preparations have begun to address these issues directly, and have enhanced our knowledge about the critical loci and mechanisms that underlie various forms of short- and long-term synaptic plasticity. This work has demonstrated that the cellular basis of learning and memory involves a family of biochemical, biophysical, and structural changes that are ultimately expressed at the level of the synapse. This review will focus on the morphological correlates of synaptic plasticity and, wherever possible, try to relate these structural changes to alterations in cellular function and behavior. Two general classes of identified synapses will be examined: peripheral and central.

Structural Plasticity at Identified Synapses

Peripheral Synapses

Perhaps the best-studied experimental model for correlating function and structure has been the peripheral nerve–muscle synapse. Several arthropod neuromuscular junctions have proven to be well-suited for examining activity-dependent and growth-dependent modifications of the synapse. In particular, crustacean motor terminals have provided a set of experimentally accessible synapses that have several plastic properties in common with central synaptic connections (Atwood and Wojtowicz, 1986; Atwood and Govind, 1990). Early studies of crustacean motor systems focused on a possible correlation between synaptic structure and transmitter output. The general picture that has emerged from this work suggests that terminals demonstrating high transmitter release following a single impulse have more and larger active

zones—those focal and highly modified regions of the presynaptic terminal where transmitter is thought to be released—than do low-output terminals. Similar findings have come from a variety of studies on the vertebrate neuromuscular junction that suggest a positive relationship between transmitter release and active zone morphology (Herrera et al., 1985).

One of the forms of prolonged synaptic plasticity that is exhibited by the crustacean neuromuscular junction is long-term facilitation (for review see Atwood, Dixon, and Wojtowicz, 1989). Long-term facilitation can be produced by repetitive stimulation of a motor neuron axon and is characterized by a progressive increase in the amplitude of evoked synaptic potentials followed by a long-lasting (several hours to 1 day) enhancement of transmission. Mathematical treatments predict that this increase in synaptic response could be explained by the appearance of additional transmitter-responding units on the nerve terminal. This model suggests that normally low or nontransmitting synapses are capable of being recruited to an active state by tetanic activity. Ultrastructural studies have provided some direct morphological support for these theoretical predictions (Wojtowicz, Marin, and Atwood, 1989). Complete serial sections of nerve terminals from preparations exhibiting long-term facilitation and from corresponding controls indicate an increase in the percentage of synapses exhibiting presynaptic active zones following training. Moreover, Mearow and Govind (1989) have found that repeated bouts of tetanic stimulation at the same neuromuscular terminals can lead to a long-lasting increase in the incidence of synaptic active zones. These observations suggest that alterations in neuronal activity can induce rapid structural transformations at the synapse that are reflected primarily by modulation of active zone morphology.

Another example of activity-dependent structural changes has been provided by studies of the phasic and tonic motor innervation of crayfish neuromuscular junctions. Tonic motor neurons typically display high levels of activity, and their terminals are characterized by large and abundant synaptic varicosities. By contrast, phasic motor neurons that have low levels of impulse activity do not develop clear varicose expansions but have thinner, more uniform terminals. During repetitive stimulation, tonic terminals show facilitation and no depression, whereas phasic terminals demonstrate synaptic fatigue. To determine the role that activity might play in this morphological differentiation, Lnenicka and colleagues (1986) produced in vivo tonic stimulation of a relatively silent phasic motor neuron over a period of 1 to 2 weeks. As a result of conditioning, the phasic terminals demonstrated both an increase in fatigue resistance and a change in structure to a more tonic phenotype. These morphological changes included both an increase in the number of synaptic varicosities and an increase in the size of mitochondria and individual synapses. These results indicate that the increased transmitter-releasing capabilities of tonic terminals compared with their phasic counterparts may be due to the presence of larger and more numerous synaptic varicosities. Moreover, the formation of these varicosities appears to be dependent upon some critical ongoing pattern of nerve impulse activity.

Central Synapses

Similar changes have been observed at identified synapses within the invertebrate central nervous system (CNS), and in many cases these alterations in function and structure can be directly correlated with behavioral learning. One such model system has been the gill- and siphon-withdrawal reflex in the marine mollusk *Aplysia californica*. This simple behavior is analogous to vertebrate defensive escape and withdrawal responses, and like them can be modified by several types of nonassociative and associative learning. Two elementary forms of nonassociative learning in *Aplysia* are habituation and sensitization, each capable of giving rise to a short-term memory lasting minutes to hours and a long-term memory that persists for several weeks. Several aspects of the cellular and molecular mechanisms that underlie habituation and sensitization are now particularly well understood and involve changes in synaptic effectiveness produced by modulation of the calcium current at a common locus, the synapses made by identified mechanoreceptor sensory neurons onto their follower cells (see APLYSIA: MOLECULAR BASIS OF LONG-TERM SENSITIZATION). Until recently, it was not known whether or not morphological mechanisms of the sort described in vertebrates (see "Vertebrates," below) accompany the biochemical and biophysical changes that have been described at identified sensory neuron synapses and whether or not such mechanisms might be involved in the expression of both short-term and long-term memory.

To address these issues, Bailey and Chen have combined selective intracellular labeling techniques with the analysis of serial sections to study complete reconstructions of identified sensory neuron synapses from both control and behaviorally modified animals. Their results indicate that learning in *Aplysia* produces morphological as well as functional changes at specific synaptic loci. Long-term memory (lasting several weeks) is accompanied by a family of alterations at identified sensory neuron synapses. These changes reflect structurally detectable modifications at two different levels of synaptic organization: (1) alterations in focal regions of membrane specialization—the number, size, and vesicle complement of sensory neuron active zones are larger in sensitized animals than in controls and are smaller in habituated animals (Bailey and Chen, 1983)—and (2) a parallel but more pronounced and widespread effect involving modulation of the total number of presynaptic varicosities per sensory neuron (Bailey and Chen, 1988a). Sensory neurons from long-term habituated animals had on average 35 percent fewer varicosities (compared with controls). By contrast, the morphological changes that accompany long-term sensitization involve an element of long-lasting growth reflected by a doubling in the total number of synaptic varicosities, as well as an increase in the size of each neuron's neuropil arbor. Quantitative analysis of the time course over which these anatomical changes occur during long-term sensitization has further demonstrated that only alterations in the number of sensory neuron varicosities and active zones persist in parallel with the behavioral retention of the memory (Bailey and Chen, 1989).

In contrast with these extensive anatomical changes following long-term training, the morphological correlates of short-term memory in *Aplysia* (lasting minutes to hours rather than days to weeks) are far less pronounced and are primarily restricted to shifts in the proximity of synaptic vesicles adjacent to sensory neuron active zones, a phenomenon that may reflect altered levels of transmitter mobilization (Bailey and Chen, 1988b). Altogether, these studies in *Aplysia* suggest a clear difference in the sequelae of structural events that underlie memories of differing durations. The transient duration of short-term memories probably involves the covalent modification of preexisting proteins (proteins that turn over slowly) and is accompanied by modest structural remodeling in the vicinity of the active zone, such as the transloca-

CONTROL   LONG-TERM SENSITIZATION

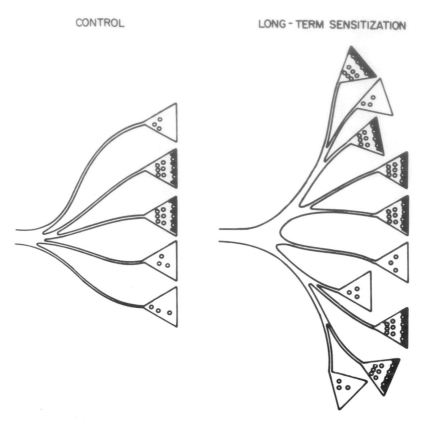

Figure 1.   Morphological basis of long-term memory in *Aplysia*. Long-term sensitization is characterized by a family of structural changes at identified sensory neuron synapses. These alterations include a remodeling of active zone morphology as well as an increase in the total number of presynaptic varicosities per sensory neuron. Similar changes occur at peripheral synapses following repetitive stimulation. Active zone = solid triangles, synaptic vesicles = open circles. *Reproduced with permission from Bailey and Chen, 1988a.*

tion of synaptic vesicles near the release site. The more prolonged duration of long-term memories is probably dependent upon new macromolecular synthesis (see PROTEIN SYNTHESIS IN LONG-TERM MEMORY IN VERTEBRATES) and is accompanied by substantial and potentially more enduring morphological transformations that are reflected by changes in both the number of synaptic contacts and their active zone morphology.

Data from central neurons in a number of other invertebrate systems have provided additional support for the idea that one mechanism for memory storage is an alteration in neuronal architecture. An early report by Brandon and Coss (1982) described a rapid shortening of dendritic spine stems in the honeybee's brain following one-trial learning, an observation related to those made on a number of vertebrate preparations during learning-

like phenomena (see "Vertebrates," below). Balling and colleagues (1987) have shown that in the mushroom bodies of *Drosophila*, a part of the fly's brain implicated in learning, the number of Kenyon cell fibers can be modulated by experience. More recently, Alkon et al. (1990) have examined the effects of associative training on the macroscopic structure of a single identified neuron, the medial type B photoreceptor cell in the mollusk *Hermissenda crassicornis*. Previous studies had demonstrated that associative memory can be correlated with a variety of biochemical and biophysical changes in this neuron. Four to five days following training, cells were labeled and the terminal arborizations measured. The branching volume of cells from conditioned animals was found to be reduced compared with naive animals or animals trained with unpaired stimuli, an observation that suggests some similarities with the phenomenon of synapse elimination that has been described during development. (See also INVERTEBRATE LEARNING.)

Several common themes have begun to emerge from these structural studies of synaptic plasticity. For example, the remodeling of transmitter release sites observed at CNS synapses during learning and memory is consistent with the reorganization of the neuromuscular junction reported in both vertebrates and invertebrates, suggesting that activity-dependent alterations in specific components of active zone morphology may function as good predictors of changes in synaptic effectiveness. Moreover, the increase in the number of synaptic varicosities that accompanies long-term sensitization in *Aplysia*, as well as prolonged repetitive stimulation at the crayfish neuromuscular junction, is similar to the reports of alterations in the number and/or pattern of synaptic connections in the vertebrate brain following environmental manipulation and training (see "Vertebrates," below). Unfortunately, the specific role that these structural changes at the synapse may play during long-term memory is still unknown. One potential clue comes from studies of both vertebrates and invertebrates indicating that long-term memory depends in part upon the synthesis of new proteins and RNA (see PROTEIN SYNTHESIS AND LONG-TERM MEMORY IN VERTEBRATES). These newly synthesized proteins induced during the training for long-term memory may contribute to the synaptic growth that seems to characterize various forms of long-lasting behavioral change.

The experimental advantage of identified neurons offered by invertebrates has made possible additional insights into the nature of the macromolecular candidates and signaling mechanisms that may underlie these structural changes. Glanzman, Kandel, and Schacher (1990), using cocultures of *Aplysia* sensory neurons and the identified gill motor neuron L7, have found that repeated exposure to the facilitating transmitter serotonin produces a long-term enhancement in the amplitude of the sensory-to-motor synaptic potential as well as a long-lasting increase in the number of sensory neuron varicosities. The increase in varicosity number appears to depend upon the presence of the postsynaptic neuron, because sensory neurons plated alone do not exhibit varicosity number changes in response to serotonin. Studies by Nazif, Byrne, and Cleary (1991) in the intact ganglion and by Montarolo et al. (1991) in dissociated cell culture have provided evidence for a second macromo-

lecular candidate for the structural changes underlying long-term sensitization in *Aplysia*. They have demonstrated that the intracellular injection of cAMP into identified pleural sensory neurons can mimic the increase in varicosity number and enlarged neuropil arbor that characterize long-term sensitization, suggesting a role for the cAMP cascade in shaping neuronal connectivity.

Conclusions

Since the early 1980s it has become increasingly apparent that the mature nervous system is endowed with a remarkable capacity to modify its anatomical circuitry. Studies of central and peripheral terminals of identified neurons from a wide range of invertebrates have provided an ample body of evidence that now clearly associates structural changes at the synapse with neuronal activity and learning. The increasing convergence of behavioral, molecular, and morphological techniques with simple system approaches promises to elucidate further the mechanisms that underlie these structural changes. The striking parallels in the response of both invertebrate and vertebrate neurons to behavioral training indicate that learning can produce changes in neuronal architecture across a broad segment of the animal kingdom and suggest that synaptic growth and synapse formation may be highly conserved mechanisms underlying long-term memory.

REFERENCES

Alkon, D. L., Ikeno, H., Dworkin, J., McPhie, D. L., Olds, J. L., Lederhendler, I., Matzel, L., Schreurs, B. G., Kuzirian, A., Collin, I., and Yamoah, E. (1990). Contraction of neuronal branching volume: An anatomical correlate of Pavlovian conditioning. *Proceedings of the National Academy of Sciences 87*, 1611–1614.

Atwood, H. L., Dixon, D., and Wojtowicz, J. M. (1989). Rapid introduction of long-lasting synaptic changes at crustacean neuromuscular junctions. *Journal of Neurobiology 20*, 373–385.

Atwood, H. L., and Govind, C. K. (1990). Activity-dependent and age-dependent recruitment and regulation of synapses in identified crustacean neurons. *Journal of Experimental Biology 153*, 105–127.

Atwood, H. L., and Wojtowicz, J. M. (1986). Short-term and long-term plasticity and physiological differentiation of crustacean motor synapses. *International Review of Neurobiology 28*, 275–362.

Bailey, C. H., and Chen, M. (1983). Morphological basis of long-term habituation and sensitization in *Aplysia. Science 220*, 91–93.

―――― (1988a). "Long-term memory in *Aplysia* modulates the total number of varicosities of single identified sensory neurons. *Proceedings of the National Academy of Sciences 85*, 2373–2377.

―――― (1988b). Morphological basis of short-term habituation in *Aplysia. Journal of Neuroscience 8*, 2452–2459.

―――― (1989). Time course of structural changes at identified sensory neuron synapses during long-term sensitization in *Aplysia. Journal of Neuroscience 9*, 1774–1780.

Balling, A., Technau, G. M., and Heisenberg, M. (1987). Are the structural changes in adult *Drosophila* mushroom bodies memory traces? Studies on biochemical mutants. *Journal of Neurogenetics 4*, 65–73.

Brandon, J. G., and Coss, R. G. (1982). Rapid dendritic spine shortening during one-trial learning: The honeybee's first orientation flight. *Brain Research 252*, 51–61.

Glanzman, D. L., Kandel, E. R., and Schacher, S. (1990). Target-dependent structural changes accompanying long-term synaptic facilitation in *Aplysia* neurons. *Science 249*, 799–802.

Herrera, A. A., Grinnell, A. P., and Wolowske, B. (1985). Ultrastructural correlates of naturally occurring differences in transmitter release efficacy in frog motor nerve terminals. *Journal of Neurocytology 14*, 193–202.

Lnenicka, G. A., Atwood, H. L., and Marin, L. (1986). Morphological transformation of synaptic terminals of a phasic motorneuron by long-term tonic stimulation. *Journal of Neuroscience 6*, 2252–2258.

Mearow, K. M., and Govind, C. K. (1989). Stimulation-induced changes at crayfish (*Procambarus clarkii*) neuromuscular terminals. *Cell Tissue Research 256*, 119–123.

Montarolo, P. G., Glanzoran, D. L., Kandel, E. K., and Schacher, S. (1991). cAMP and arachidonic acid induce opposite morphological changes with long-term presynaptic facilitation and inhibition in the sensory neurons of *Aplysia. Society of Neuroscience Abstracts 17*, 1591.

Nazif, F. A., Byrne, J. H., and Cleary, L. J. (1991). cAMP induces long-term morphological changes in sensory neurons of *Aplysia. Brain Research 539*, 324–327.

Craig H. Bailey

Vertebrates

The central issue in morphology of learning and memory is how memory is stored in the structure of the nervous system. The basic morphology of neurons and synapses is illustrated in Figure 1. In the late nineteenth century, the great neuroanatomist Santiago Ramón y CAJAL captured the thoughts of many predecessors by suggesting that learning might involve changes in the synaptic connections through which neurons communicate. Such synaptic change could take at least two possible forms. First, the pattern of functional connections could be altered by *forming new synapses or removing existing synapses.* There is very strong morphological evidence that this occurs during learning. Second, the pattern of functional connections could be altered by *selectively strengthening or weakening some synapses.* There is also strong evidence for this during learning, and in models of learning such as LONG-TERM POTENTIATION. Other hypotheses propose both changes in the nonsynaptic regions of neurons and changes in nonneural elements of the brain such as glial cells. Evidence on these points has been more difficult to gather, although it is now very clear that the astroglia can change their morphology in response to experience.

Two very general points should be made at the outset. First, the changes in connections described here occur in the context of an organized nervous system that has been laid down through prenatal and postnatal development. Changes brought about by learning in adulthood supplement, rather than supplant, that pattern of organization. Second, much of the research on structural bases of memory was conducted without benefit of modern stereological methodology, which allows one to measure various anatomical parameters in a manner that is unbiased by differences in the size, shape, or orientation of the structures of interest and is related to a specific reference volume (typically the volume of the brain region under consideration). Relevant component densities in the tissue are also considered in terms of its other components. Hence, for example, the number of synapses per neuron in a brain structure is a much more useful measure than the mere density of synapses in the tissue, which can be affected both by synapse number changes and by changes in other components of the tissue.

Changes in Synapse Number

Important roots of memory research lie in studies of the effects of experience upon brain development. For example, normal visual experience is necessary to develop normal visual ability in many mammals, including humans. Searching for a basis for this in brain anatomy, Cragg (1975) and others noted that animals deprived of visual experience had fewer synaptic connections per nerve cell in visual cortex. These studies profoundly influenced thinking about the processes by which the brain stores information, because they showed that (1) brain structure is malleable; (2) synaptic organization, the "wiring diagram" of the brain, can be orchestrated into different configurations by behavioral experience; (3) both the formation of new connections and the loss of existing connections are involved in altering brain organization; (4) differences in experience cause differences in the structure of synapses, suggesting that synaptic efficacy (or strength) also can change. This research is discussed separately below. The fact that synaptic connections are affected by experience during development led to proposals that such changes might underlie adult learning.

A separate developmental approach that was very fruitful in understanding brain substrates of learning and memory involved enriching young animals' lives with extra stimulation. Donald HEBB proposed ways in which synaptic change could be incorporated meaningfully into functional circuitry. With his students, he also showed that enriching the rearing environment of rats with cage-mates and toys improved the animals' ability to solve complex problems. Hebb concluded that behavior, and by implication brain organization, was permanently altered by this early experience. Subsequently, Rosenzweig et al. (1972) found that regions of the cerebral cortex became thicker and heavier in rats reared in enriched environments, compared with rats reared in solitary or group cages. Volkmar and Greenough (1972) followed up these findings, reporting that visual cortical neurons of rats reared in enriched environments had larger dendritic fields than did those of cage-housed rats. Dendrites are the regions of neurons that receive the bulk of their synaptic input (see Figure 1), so the implication was that new synapses formed. Similar findings were subsequently reported in other regions of the cerebral cortex and in other brain regions, such as the hippocampus (of female rats), the superior colliculus, and the cerebellar cortex. Of particular importance to learning and memory was that the enriched environment changed cortical thickness and dendritic field size in *adult* rats. As in the visual development

work, there were changes in the structure of synapses, which are discussed separately below.

The dendritic field measurements had been made upon neurons impregnated by Golgi procedures. Golgi procedures (1) impregnate only a small proportion of neurons, with the basis for selection of particular neurons over others not known, and (2) do not allow direct visualization of synapses. Thus it was not possible to conclude unequivocally that synaptic connections were altered in these animals because (1) the particular neurons impregnated might not have been representative and (2) the dendrites could have become elongated without adding new synapses. Using a combined light microscopic and electron microscopic procedure, Turner and Greenough (1985) found that rats reared in enriched environments had more synapses per neuron in the visual cortex, compared with rats reared alone or in pairs in standard laboratory cages. Hence the conclusion from the enriched environment studies is that when animals are placed in an environment in which they store information that affects later behavior, they form new synapses.

Direct follow-up studies have explored the effects of specific learning tasks upon these same measures. There is very compelling evidence that many kinds of learning change both the amount of dendrite per neuron and the number of synapses per neuron. Greenough and colleagues (1979) examined maze training. They found increases in dendritic branching in visual cortical neurons following 25 days' exposure to a series of maze problems. Subsequent work used "split-brain" rats, severing the nerve fibers that allow the right and left hemispheres to communicate, and opaque contact lenses that restricted visual input from training to one eye. In rats, unlike humans, each eye projects largely to the opposite hemisphere, so visual input from the training was restricted to one side of the brain. Neurons on the "trained" side of the brain exhibited dendritic field size increases. This study and others indicated that the altered dendritic fields were associated with neural input and output related to the training. The changes were not of the general sort that might be due to stress or arousal associated with the task, which should affect both sides of the brain equally.

Synaptogenesis is also implicated in associative learning. Tsukahara (1981) investigated associative limb flexion conditioning, using electrical stimulation to the cerebral peduncle as the conditioned stimulus and electric shock to the forelimb

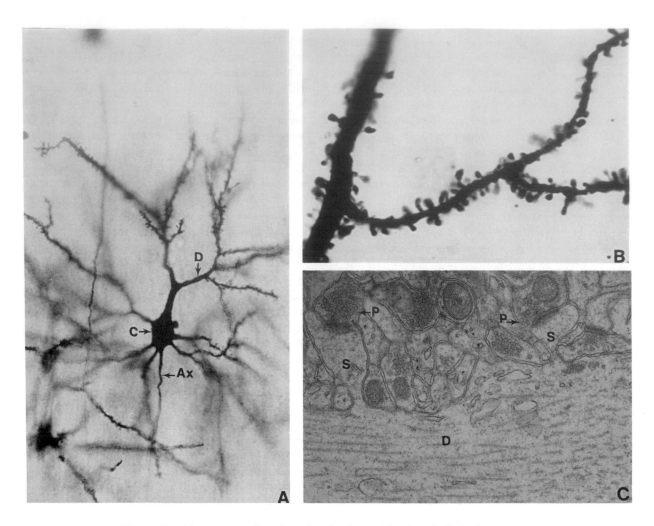

Figure 1. The nerve cell at three levels of magnification. A. Golgi-impregnated small pyramidal neuron from the upper visual cortex. C = soma or cell body, D = dendrites, Ax = axon. Input from other nerve cells arrives primarily on dendrites. Output of nerve cell is via the axon, to other neurons (original magnification 740×). B. Higher-magnification view of dendrite branches reveals fingerlike projections called spines (original magnification 2400×). C. Electron micrograph reveals that spines (S) are projections from dendrite (D) upon which presynaptic terminals (P) of axons terminate. The round, clear objects within the presynaptic terminal are vesicles, which are thought to contain the chemical neurotransmitter that is used for communication at the synapse (original magnification 28,000×).

as the unconditioned stimulus. Red nucleus lesions abolish the conditioned response, indicating the involvement of this structure. Electrophysiological studies following conditioning indicated increased input to the red nucleus from the cerebral cortex. Subsequently, Tsukahara's coworkers Murakami et al. (1987) reported morphological evidence for increased numbers of corticorubral synapses in conditioned animals, although no nonpaired stimulus presentation group was run.

Similar anatomical effects of training have been

observed in other behavioral tasks. Stewart (1991) examined day-old chicks that learned to avoid pecking a bad-tasting food particle. They found increases in the number of synapses in the paraolfactory lobe, a forebrain region previously shown to be involved in the learning. In another involved brain region, the intermediate and medial hyperstriatum ventrale, there were increases in the number of spines (see Figure 1), the dendritic component of one type of synapse. Two other paradigms in which similar synaptic changes have been observed are BIRD SONG LEARNING and IMPRINTING in birds. Finally, this discussion is confined to vertebrates; there is excellent evidence for comparable synaptic number changes in invertebrate plasticity paradigms (see "Invertebrates," above).

An issue that affects all of these studies is whether anatomical changes that are seen following training are merely a result of increased neural activity that results from performing the learned task. Muscles grow larger as a result of exercise; perhaps nerve cells do, too, such that these structural changes have nothing to do with learning or memory. (This issue is, of course, not unique to morphological studies; proposed molecular and other aspects of the cellular mechanisms of memory may similarly be artifacts of activity; see PROTEIN SYNTHESIS IN LONG-TERM MEMORY IN VERTEBRATES.)

There have been direct tests of the effects of neural activity versus learning on synapse change. Black et al. (1990), for example, compared a cerebellar cortical region in rats that had learned a complex series of motor tasks and in rats that experienced one of two forms of physical exertion involving little learning: running on a treadmill or in an activity wheel. The rats that had learned exhibited an increase in the number of synapses in the cerebellar cortex, whereas those which had exercised showed no change in synapse number. In contrast, the exercising rats had a higher density of blood vessels in this region, whereas the motor learning rats had the same blood vessel density as a control group that neither learned nor exercised. These results indicate that mere activity and learning have very different effects upon brain tissue.

Additional support for the role of synapse formation in plastic neural change has come from some of the studies of long-term potentiation. LTP, which is exhibited in many regions of the vertebrate nervous system (see below), involves an increase in the response of postsynaptic neurons following high-frequency bursts of presynaptic firing. In subfield CA1 of the hippocampus, Lee et al. (1981) reported formation of new synapses following LTP induction. This has been confirmed by others, and Chang and Greenough (1984) showed that the synapse formation was not the result of high-frequency stimulation alone, finding no synapse formation when they included a type of high-frequency stimulation that did not induce LTP. In contrast, induction of LTP in the dentate gyrus of the hippocampal formation apparently does not cause synapse formation but appears to change the structure of synapses (Geinisman, de Toledo-Morrell, and Morrell, 1991). This reinforces the view that a number of different cellular changes may be involved in learning and in other forms of neural plasticity.

Changes in Synapse Structure: Indications of Synapse Efficacy Change

Several structural features of synapses have been found to be altered by behavioral experience. One of the most obvious features is the *size* of synapses. Larger synapses may release more chemical neurotransmitter or have more neurotransmitter receptors, such that a size change could indicate a strength change. Some early reports indicated smaller synapses in visual cortex of animals visually deprived during development, and a more recent and specific report by Tieman (1985) indicates smaller geniculocortical synapses associated with monocularly deprived cats. Conversely, increased synapse size was reported following imprinting in day-old chicks, and similar size changes were found after chick avoidance learning. Larger synapses were also described in layer IV of visual cortex of rats reared in enriched environments, compared with individually caged controls. Changes in the size of synaptic spine heads and necks (see Figure 1) have been described by Van Harreveld and Fifkova (1975) following LTP induction in dentate gyrus. The larger spine components may have lower electrical resistance, facilitating the passage of synaptic current into the dendrite. Spine shape changes have not been found in behavioral paradigms such as environmental complexity.

Synaptic vesicle numbers have been reported to decrease with visual deprivation (e.g., Tieman, 1985) and to increase in rats reared in enriched environments (Sirevaag and Greenough, 1991). Synaptic vesicles are believed to contain the chemical neurotransmitter, and changes in their numbers could indicate changes in synapse strength. There have also been reports of both decreased vesicle density and altered vesicle location within the presynaptic terminal following LTP induction (e.g., Fifkova and Van Harreveld, 1977; Applegate, Kerr, and Landfield, 1987).

Shapes of various aspects of synapses have been reported to change with both different behavioral experiences and LTP. The curvature of the synaptic contact zone has been reported to change (possibly transiently) with both LTP induction and housing in an enriched environment.

Two other synapse features appear to be sensitive to experience. First, small discontinuities in the postsynaptic density termed *perforations* have been found to increase in number following enriched environment exposure and to decrease in synapses of a monocularly deprived eye (Greenough, West, and DeVoogd, 1978). Moreover, Vrensen and Cardozo (1981) found that perforated synapses increased in the visual cortex following visual discrimination learning. The function of these perforations is unknown. Second, the cellular organelles that synthesize protein, *polyribosomal aggregates,* are frequently found in the heads and necks of spines during periods of synapse formation (Steward and Falk, 1985). They are also found more frequently in spines of animals in complex environments, possibly reflecting greater rates of synapse formation.

Changes in Nonneural Elements

The enriched environment work indicated from its earliest days that the morphological changes were not restricted to those in synapses. Glial cells, supportive elements that maintain ionic, metabolic, and neurotransmitter homeostasis, also responded to increased environmental stimulation. Data of Sirevaag and Greenough (1991) indicate that astrocytes, the more metabolically active type of glia, grow larger, extending additional processes into the tissue, in the first phase of their response to the animal's housing in an enriched environment. In a second phase, astrocytes divide, increasing their numbers, and shrink, on average, toward their initial size. These stages are qualitatively comparable with those of gliosis, the glial reaction to injury, but they are much more protracted. Blood vessel density also increases in rats placed in an enriched environment at the age of weaning. In animals that are older at the time they are first exposed to enrichment, this blood vessel response diminishes with increasing age. With the exception of the motor learning study described above, these variables have not yet been examined in adult learning paradigms.

Conclusions

Morphological research has provided strong evidence for both forms of synaptic change that have been proposed to underlie learning and memory. Formation, and occasionally loss, of synapses occurs both during periods of development when the brain is storing information and during exposure to specific learning tasks. Various control procedures have largely ruled out the possibility that these synaptic changes are artifactual results arising from factors other than learning. Changes in the structure of synapses, such as in the size or shape of synaptic components, also occur during learning and in other situations in which functional brain organization is altered, such as LTP. Many of these structural changes have been associated with synapse strength differences in other research. Thus the weight of the evidence indicates that both synapse formation/removal and synapse strength change are involved in learning and memory.

REFERENCES

Applegate, M. D., Kerr, D. S., and Landfield, P. W. (1987). Redistribution of synaptic vesicles during long-term potentiation in the hippocampus. *Brain Research 401,* 401–406.

Black, J. E., Isaacs, K. R., Anderson, B. J., Alcantara, A. A., and Greenough, W. T. (1990). Learning causes synaptogenesis, whereas motor activity causes angiogenesis, in cerebellar cortex of adult rats. *Proceedings of the National Academy of Sciences 87,* 5568–5572.

Chang, F.-L. F., and Greenough, W. T. (1984). Transient and enduring morphological correlates of synaptic activity and efficacy change in the rat hippocampal slice. *Brain Research 309,* 35–46.

Cragg, B. G. (1975). The development of synapses in kitten visual cortex during visual deprivation. *Experimental Neurology 46,* 445–451.

Fifkova, E., and Van Harreveld, A. (1977). Long-lasting morphological changes in dendritic spines of dentate granular cells following stimulation of the entorhinal area. *Journal of Neurocytology 6,* 211–230.

Geinisman, Y., de Toledo-Morrell, L., and Morrell, F. (1991). Induction of long-term potentiation is associated with an increase in the number of axospinous synapses with segmented postsynaptic densities. *Brain Research 566,* 77–88.

Greenough, W. T., and Chang, F.-L. F., (1988). Plasticity of synapse structure and pattern in the cerebral cortex. In E. G. Jones, and A. Peters, eds., *Cerebral cortex,* vol. 7, pp. 391–440. New York: Plenum Press. This very comprehensive chapter covers both brain structure changes that arise from learning and other plastic changes in brain organization.

Greenough, W. T., Juraska, J. M., and Volkmar, F. R. (1979). Maze training effects on dendritic branching in occipital cortex of adult rats. *Behavioral and Neural Biology 26*, 287–297.

Greenough, W. T., West, R. W., and DeVoogd, T. J. (1978). Sub-synaptic plate perforations: Changes with age and experience in the rat. *Science 202*, 1096–1098.

Lee, K. S., Oliver, M., Schottler, F., and Lynch, G. (1981). Electron microscopic studies of brain slices: The effects of high-frequency stimulation on dendritic ultrastructure. In G. A. Kerkut, and H. V. Wheal, eds., *Electrophysiology of isolated mammalian CNS preparations*, pp. 189–211. New York: Academic Press.

Murakami, F., Higashi, S., Katsumaru, H., and Oda, Y. (1987). Formation of new corticorubral synapses as a mechanism for classical conditioning in the cat. *Brain Research 437*, 379–382. In this article Tsukahara's coworkers offer definitive evidence for the association of new synapse formation with learning.

Rosenzweig, M. R., Bennett, E. L., and Diamond, M. C. (1972). Chemical and anatomical plasticity of brain: Replications and extensions. In J. Gaito, ed., *Macromolecules and behavior*, 2nd ed., pp. 205–278. New York: Appleton-Century-Crofts. This is one of the best summaries of the work of this group, which began in the early 1960s.

Sirevaag, A. M., and Greenough, W. T. (1991). Plasticity of GFAP-immunoreactive astrocyte size and number in visual cortex of rats reared in complex environments. *Brain Research 540*, 273–278.

Steward, O., and Falk, P. M. (1985). Polyribosomes under developing spine synapses: Growth specializations of dendrites at sites of synaptogenesis. *Journal of Neuroscience Research 13*, 75–88.

Stewart, M. G. (1991). Changes in dendritic and synaptic structure in chick forebrain consequent on passive avoidance learning. In R. J. Andrew, ed., *Neural and behavioral plasticity*, pp. 305–328. London: Oxford University Press. Thorough review of this occasionally overlooked body of work.

Tieman, S. B. (1985). The anatomy of geniculocortical connections in monocularly deprived cats. *Cellular and Molecular Neurobiology 5*, 35–45. A very thorough and careful piece of work.

Tsukahara, N. (1981). Sprouting and the neuronal basis of learning. *Trends in Neurosciences 4*, 234–237.

Turner, A. M., and Greenough, W. T. (1985). Differential rearing effects on rat visual cortex synapses. I. Synaptic and neuronal density and synapses per neuron. *Brain Research 329*, 195–203.

Van Harreveld, A., and Fifkova, E. (1975). Swelling of dendritic spines in the fascia dentata after stimulation of the perforant fibers as a mechanism of post-tetanic potentiation. *Experimental Neurology 49*, 736–749. A classic that inspired both rapid freezing studies and much theoretical biophysical modeling regarding LTP mechanisms and the functions of dendritic spines.

Volkmar, F. R., and Greenough, W. T. (1972). Rearing complexity affects branching of dendrites in the visual cortex of the rat. *Science 176*, 1445–1447.

Vrensen, G., and Cardozo, J. N. (1981). Changes in size and shape of synaptic connections after visual training: An ultrastructural approach of synaptic plasticity. *Brain Research 218*, 79–97.

William T. Greenough

MOTOR SKILLS

The systematic study of the learning and retention of motor skills dates from the 1890s. The theoretical and operational emphases of this field of study have tended to parallel those in other subdomains of learning. This can be attributed in part to the fact that motor skills, perceptual skills, cognitive skills, and social skills are not mutually exclusive. Motor skills are usually set apart by their emphasis on the movement of the limbs and torso as well as on the outcome of movement in terms of the goal of the act. There are various categories of motor skills including those occurring in communication, dance, work, play, sport, music, and self-help endeavors.

How do people learn and remember how to dance, type, hop, play the piano, and tie their shoelaces? In discussing this challenging question, Bartlett (1932, p. 202) captured the essence of the problem when he said, in reference to the skilled tennis player, "When I make the stroke I do not, as a matter of fact, produce something absolutely new, and I never merely repeat something old." A central issue in the learning of motor skills is how the movement form is acquired through practice and retained over time. A related issue has been the role that variations of movement form play in realizing the goal of the act. These two issues, which have been labeled *movement invariance* and *motor equivalence*, respectively, have been the focus of the theorizing about the acquisition and retention of motor skills.

A moment's reflection will confirm that the acquisition and retention of skill in motor tasks is very task-dependent. Some function was to select and initiate the movement. The other state was the *perceptual trace,* which acted as the reference of correctness for the ongoing movement and was based on prior experience gained via the sensory consequences of the movement. The strength of both the memory and the perceptual traces was developed through practice and information feedback in the form of knowledge of results.

One-to-one memory accounts of movement representation were challenged by the emerging conceptions of cognitive psychology. An outgrowth of this trend was Schmidt's (1975) schema theory of motor learning. This theory promoted a one-to-many representational construct for both recall and recognition processes of movement. The representation for each memory state consisted of the relations between task, organism, and environmental variables rather than the absolute levels of the variables themselves. The schema was a generic rule for a given class of movements that allowed the generalization of movement outcome to a variety of task and environmental circumstances. Schema theory proposed that the more variable the practice within the potential class of movements (e.g., variations in the length, velocity, and/or angle of a forehand drive in tennis), the more general the schema rule would become for that activity.

The schema theory was seen to provide a solution to two enduring problems in motor skill acquisition and retention: the novelty problem and the limited storage capacity problem. The so-called novelty problem addresses the question of how the performer accommodates to novel task and environmental circumstances. The second problem is the limited storage capacity of the CNS that arises as a consequence of the many one-to-one representations that would be generated from an individual's lifetime movement experience. However, the Schmidt schema theory could not solve the novelty problem because it did not account for how the movement class was initially established. The theory only accounted for changes in the scaling of force, velocity, or position of a given action pattern (such as a tennis forehand drive) rather than the generation of the forehand drive movement pattern itself. Furthermore, the storage capacity problem is a hypothetical theoretical boundary that in practice may not be a problem at all for the movement system.

During the 1980s one-to-one and one-to-many prescriptive accounts of motor skill learning were challenged by the tenets of the ecological approach to perception and action (Fowler and Turvey, 1978; Kugler and Turvey, 1987). The ecological approach seeks the solution to motor learning through the mapping of perception and action with minimal appeal to representational processes typically posited by cognitive psychologists. A central concern has been the appropriateness of cognitive strategies proposed to map the emergent movement dynamics into a rule-based symbolic representation. For example, although there are invariant properties of the movement dynamics that arise from the variations of the act of producing a forehand drive, these persistent qualitative movement properties may not reflect a rule-based representation, as proposed by schema theory. Rather, the movement form may reflect emergent properties of the self-organizing biological system, in a fashion that is consistent with pattern formation principles of complex physical systems that drive, for example, cloud formations, sand-dune formations, and vortices in streams.

The emergent structure and variability of the movement sequence is currently being analyzed in terms of physical systems solutions to the mapping of the gradient and equilibrium regions of the perceptual and motor processes (Kugler and Turvey, 1987; Schoner and Kelso, 1988). A major challenge for a physical approach to the study of the learning and retention of motor skills is the question of how information and dynamics are related to the intention of the performer. Within this emergent orientation to motor skills, learning can be viewed as an exploratory activity with the performer searching for stable regions of the perceptual and motor dynamics that realize the goal of the act (Newell et al., 1989).

Conclusions

The traditional theories of motor learning and retention failed to capture many of the qualities of the stages of skill learning exhibited in the progression from novice to expert. Skill in a task is a reflection of a continuous exploratory activity and not the faithful reproduction of a static representation of action. Current cognitive models and the ecological approach to perception and action are beginning to capture some of the important invariant and changing qualities of the dynamics of motor skill acquisition and retention.

REFERENCES

Adams, J. A. (1971). A closed-loop theory of motor learning. *Journal of Motor Behavior 3,* 111–150.

Bartlett, F. C. (1932). *Remembering: A study of experimental and social psychology.* Cambridge: Cambridge University Press.

Bernstein, N. A. (1967). *The coordination and regulation of movements.* London: Pergamon.

Fowler, C. A., and Turvey, M. T. (1978). Skill acquisition: An event approach with special reference to searching for the optimum of a function of several variables. In G. E. Stelmach, ed., *Information processing and motor control.* New York: Academic Press.

Kugler, P. N., and Turvey, M. T. (1987). *Information, natural law, and the self-assembly of rhythmic movement.* Hillsdale, N.J.: Erlbaum.

Newell, K. M., Kugler, P. N., van Emmerik, R. E. A., and McDonald, P. V. (1989). Search strategies and the acquisition of coordination. In S. A. Wallace, ed., *Perspectives on the coordination of movement.* Amsterdam: North-Holland.

Schmidt, R. A. (1975). A schema theory of discrete motor skill learning. *Psychological Review 82,* 225–260.

Schöner, G., and Kelso, J. A. S. (1988). A dynamic theory of behavioral change. *Journal of Theoretical Biology 135,* 501–524.

Karl M. Newell

MULTIPLE PERSONALITY

See Amnesia, Functional

NATURAL SETTINGS, MEMORY IN

The systematic study of memory as it operates in everyday life is a relatively new enterprise. Naturalistic studies had no place in the classical psychology of memory, which aspired to the status of a laboratory science rather like chemistry or physics. In the century between 1880 and 1980, an emphasis on experimental control led most memory researchers to use specially prepared tasks and materials in their work, even if—as often happened—those tasks seemed meaningless to the subjects of their studies. The study of memory in natural settings was largely ignored.

There were a few exceptions to this principle. The most studied, because of its practical importance, was *eyewitness testimony*. William Stern, a German psychologist, published a journal devoted entirely to this problem soon after the turn of the century (*Beiträge zur Psychologie der Aussage*). In many of Stern's experiments, unexpected or dramatic events were staged in the presence of groups of people who were then interrogated as if they had witnessed a real crime. (An example appears in Neisser, 1982.) Such testimony is surprisingly unreliable. Witnesses often give highly confabulatory accounts of the event itself, and are rarely able to describe the individuals who participated in it. Moreover, confidence is no guarantee of accuracy: Eyewitnesses may be quite wrong even when they are absolutely sure that they are right. (See also RECONSTRUCTIVE MEMORY.)

Some other examples of early work on memory in natural settings are worth mentioning:

- Sigmund FREUD developed the concept of *repression* before the turn of the century, and continued to refine it for many years. Although the evidence for repression is primarily clinical (efforts to demonstrate it in the laboratory have not been very successful), there is no reason to doubt the existence and significance of unconsciously motivated forgetting. In everyday life, repression may reveal itself through meaningful errors or slips of the tongue.

- The study of ORAL TRADITION has typically been the province of humanistic scholars rather than psychologists. Nevertheless, the ability of non-literate singers and storytellers to remember enormous amounts of material (as in the epic poems of ancient Greece) is clearly relevant to the study of memory.

- Case studies of MNEMONISTS—people with outstanding memory ability—have appeared intermittently since the turn of the century. Some mnemonists' achievements are truly remarkable, but research in this area has had little theoretical impact.

- F. C. BARTLETT's 1932 book *Remembering* was the first extensive study of memory for stories, a field now included as part of PROSE RETENTION. His ideas, almost completely ignored until the late 1960s, are now widely cited. Bartlett's work was an important precursor of modern laboratory research on "schemata" and "scripts" as well as of the study of memory in natural settings.

Naturalistic vs. Laboratory Methods

In 1978, a conference at Cardiff, Wales, brought together many researchers with an interest in practical aspects of memory. In the opening address Ulric Neisser attacked the traditional study of memory as largely unproductive, and called for a new emphasis on more naturalistic studies. A great many such studies have been carried out since that time. A second conference on practical aspects of memory, held nine years later, provided an occasion to summarize some of these achievements (Gruneberg et al., 1978, 1988).

This work is not without its critics. Some proponents of more traditional memory research believe that naturalistic studies have little value. They argue that scientific progress can be based only on controlled laboratory experiments. In a 1989 article entitled "The Bankruptcy of Everyday Memory," Mahzarin Banaji and Robert Crowder asserted that a decade of such research had produced no important findings. A symposium including nine replies to Banaji and Crowder appeared in the January 1991 *American Psychologist.* Clearly, the issue is still controversial.

Recall of Life Events

A number of psychologists have studied their own memories by making notes of one or more events each day for a prolonged period. After delays of several months or years, they have tested their recall of the events in question. These studies show that although experiences judged to be "unusual" are remembered better than others, this variable is not always easy to assess. (The true importance of an event may not be apparent immediately.) They also show that pleasant life experiences are recalled better than unpleasant ones, just as Freud's repression hypothesis would suggest. Forgetting occurs regularly, but it is not an all-or-none matter. An event that seems completely forgotten at first may yet be retrieved if enough additional cues are given.

Another way to study autobiographical memory is to provide subjects with random words as cues, and ask for recall of whatever life event the cue brings to mind; the subject then assigns a date to each recalled event. When the frequency of memories thus retrieved is plotted on a log/log scale as a function of time since the events occurred, a linear forgetting function appears (see Figure 1). However, this function does not fit the first few years of life, from which very few events are recalled. The virtual absence of memories from early

childhood, often called *infantile amnesia,* has been the object of considerable theoretical interest in its own right (see AMNESIA, INFANTILE).

Bias in Personal Recollections

It has often been suggested that memory is vulnerable to egoistic bias, so that we recall our own actions as more important and more consonant with our self-image than they really were. (For an example, see "John Dean's Memory" in Neisser, 1982). Michael Ross (1989) has proposed a specific theory of one type of bias. His theory, which has a good deal of experimental support, concerns people's recall of their own traits at earlier points in time. (How bad were my headaches last month? How fast did I read before I took this study-skills course?) Rather than being based on direct recollection, such estimates are deduced from the trait's present value (my headache today, my reading speed now) together with an implicit theory of its stability or change. When there is no reason to think the trait has changed, one estimates it simply by referring to its present value. A person who has just been through a headache treatment program or a study-skills course, however, tends to remember a worse pain or a lower reading speed than the one that presently prevails: After all, the course must have done some good!

"Flashbulb" Memories

Some events seem unforgettable: We remember them so vividly and confidently that it seems almost as if the brain had taken a snapshot of the scene. Most "flashbulb" memories are of unique, personally significant experiences, but they can also arise from shared public events. For many Americans, hearing the news of President Kennedy's assassination in 1963 was such an event. A dozen years later, seventy-nine of eighty adults interviewed by Brown and Kulik (1977) still vividly remembered the moment when they first heard this news. The 1986 explosion of the space shuttle *Challenger* provided many people with "flashbulb" memories of the same kind, which have been explored in a number of systematic studies.

The mechanisms that underlie these vivid recollections are still in dispute. Some psychologists

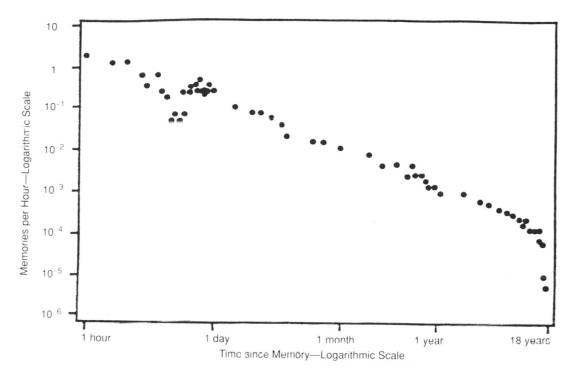

Figure 1. A forgetting function for autobiographical memory. Mean number of memories (plotted per hour of the 18-year-old subjects' lives up to the time of the experiment) retrieved by cuing in Rubin's experiment, as a function of the age of those memories. The vertical axis assumes a total of 100 reported memories. One point, zero memories per hour for events 18 years earlier, is not plotted. *From D. C. Rubin, On the retention function for autobiographical memory.* Journal of Verbal Learning and Verbal Behavior 21, *21–38 (1982).* *Reprinted by permission of the American Psychological Association*

have suggested that strong emotions directly increase the strength of stored memory traces; perhaps there is even a special neural system devoted to such memories. Others argue that these events are well remembered only because, being unusual, they are less vulnerable to interference from other memories. They have the further advantage of being often rehearsed and retold. Moreover, not all "flashbulb" memories are veridical: Despite the strong subjective conviction that accompanies them, many cases of substantial error have been documented. These complications show that the role of emotion in memory is still not well understood.

Eyewitness Memory Revisited

Recent studies have continued to show that confidence is no guarantee of accuracy. This is especially true when hypnosis has been used, often in a misguided attempt to "refresh" a witness's memory (see HYPNOSIS AND MEMORY). Because hypnosis typically produces confabulated (but very confident) memories, evidence produced by this means is no longer admissible in many states. Leading questions during an interrogation are also quite likely to produce false reports. A better method of improving eyewitness memory is Edward Geiselman's (1985) "cognitive interview," in which witnesses are asked to recall an event in several different orders and from several points of view.

There have been many recent studies of witnesses' ability to recognize and identify the perpetrators of crimes. These studies have shown (for example) that it is more difficult to identify a person of another race than of one's own race, that adults are better recognizers than children, and that it is far easier to identify a face as having been seen "somewhere" than to recall just where one saw it (e.g., at the crime scene). Attempts to train police officers in techniques of recognition and identification have been relatively unsuccessful to date.

Very Long-Term Memory

While the ability to recognize individuals who were seen only briefly under high-stress conditions is quite limited, recognition of familiar faces is excellent and long-lasting. Harry Bahrick and his collaborators (1975) have shown, for example, that the ability to recognize photographs of one's high school classmates remains very high even 35 years after graduation. In contrast, recall of the classmates' names drops steadily during the same period. This high level of recognition depends on depth of acquaintance: College professors' ability to identify the faces of students they had once taught fades much more quickly.

Bahrick (1984) has also studied very long-term memory for classroom material. In one study, individuals who had studied Spanish (in high school or college) from 1 to 50 years earlier were tested for retention of what they had learned. Much is forgotten in the first half-decade after learning, but performance seems to level off after that; little more is lost in the next 25 years or so. Those with more initial training, and those who had earned better grades, remember more at every delay interval. Other studies show that even "forgotten" academic material may have left some trace behind: It can often be relearned on the basis of brief reminders.

(See also FORGETTING.)

REFERENCES

Bahrick, H. P. (1984). Semantic memory content in permastore: Fifty years of memory for Spanish learned in school. *Journal of Experimental Psychology: General 117,* 1–29.

Bahrick, H. P., Bahrick, P. O., and Wittlinger, R. P. (1975). Fifty years of memory for names and faces: A cross-sectional approach. *Journal of Experimental Psychology: General 104,* 54–75.

Banaji, M. R., and Crowder, R. G. (1989). The bankruptcy of everyday memory. *American Psychologist 44,* 1185–1193.

Bartlett, F. C. (1932). *Remembering.* Cambridge: Cambridge University Press.

Brown, R., and Kulik, J. (1977). Flashbulb memories. *Cognition 5,* 73–99.

Cohen, G. (1989). *Memory in the real world.* Hillsdale, N.J.: Erlbaum. *A useful, up-to-date survey.*

Erdelyi, M. H., and Goldberg, B. (1979). Let's not sweep repression under the rug: Toward a cognitive psychology of repression. In J. F. Kihlstrom and F. J. Evans, eds., *Functional disorders of memory,* pp. 355–402. Hillsdale, N.J.: Erlbaum. *A good review of the status of repression research.*

Freud, S. (1914/1965). *The psychopathology of everyday life.* New York: Norton.

Geiselman, R. E., Fisher, R. P., MacKinnon, D. P., and Holland, H. L. (1985). Eyewitness memory enhancement in the police interview: Cognitive retrieval mnemonics versus hypnosis. *Journal of Applied Psychology 70,* 401–412.

Gruneberg, M. M., Morris, P. E., and Sykes, R. N., eds. (1978). *Practical aspects of memory.* Chichester, England: Wiley.

———, eds. (1988). *Practical aspects of memory: Current research and issues,* 2 vols. Chichester, England: Wiley.

Neisser, U., ed. (1982). *Memory observed: Remembering in natural contexts.* New York: Freeman. *An anthology of studies of memory in natural settings, from various periods and perspectives.*

Ross, M. (1989). Relation of implicit theories to the construction of personal histories. *Psychological Review 96,* 341–357.

Rubin, D. C., ed. (1986). *Autobiographical memory.* New York: Cambridge University Press. *The first collection of original papers on this topic.*

Ulric Neisser

NEOCORTICAL PLASTICITY

[*This composite article consists of the following sections:*

Development of the Visual System
Adult Visual Cortex—Adaptation and
   Reorganization
Adult Visual Cortex—Neural Conditioning and
   Map Rearrangement
Auditory Cortex
Somatosensory Cortex]

Development of the Visual System

The neocortex, or cerebral cortex, is a thick layer of cells (neurons) covering the outer surface of the forebrain (see GUIDE TO THE ANATOMY OF THE BRAIN). In humans and some other mammals it is wrinkled, with many folds separated by deep fissures. In humans about 75 percent of the neurons in the entire brain are contained in the cerebral cortex, a much higher proportion than is the case for other animals. Partly for this reason, and also because of clinical observations on people with brain damage, it is generally accepted that the cortex plays a significant role in behaviors that are uniquely human, such as highly complex learning and information processing.

Our knowledge of how the cortex works has grown enormously since the 1950s and 1960s, in very large measure through experiments in which the activity of cortical neurons is studied one neuron at a time. This may seem paradoxical, since there is great redundancy in the brain and the activity of any particular neuron cannot be crucially important. But through painstaking studies of hundreds of thousands of neurons in different cortical regions, a picture has emerged that allows us to understand many basic operating principles of the cortex.

An important function of the cortex is perception. Just about all the information we receive from the world around us, through our senses, arrives eventually in the cortex. The visual cortex is one of the best-understood cortical regions, in terms of how it works as a system. It has a complicated, elegant structural and functional organization that appears to underlie many processes of visual perception and recognition. David Hubel and Torsten Wiesel, who together have performed a great many pioneering experiments on the visual cortex, have written a thoughtful introduction that summarizes recent work (Hubel and Wiesel, 1979).

An intriguing question concerns the ways in which the brain develops these sophisticated mechanisms for analyzing and interpreting the visual world, and this has been the subject of much experimentation. It is now clear that visual experience early in life is extremely important: The system exhibits a high degree of malleability or plasticity in the sense that its development depends in specific ways on the type and amount of visual information the young, developing organism receives. It is altogether possible that this property of plasticity is related to the kind of plasticity seen in the adult brain when humans and other animals learn new behaviors.

Basic Properties of Visual Cortical Neurons

Information from the two eyes converges on individual neurons in the visual cortex; most of these neurons have the ability to respond to visual stimuli presented in either eye, and so are termed *binocular neurons*. Many cells, though, respond more strongly to stimulation of one eye than of the other; the term *ocular dominance* refers to the relative influence of the two eyes on a cell's response. Visual cortical neurons have another interesting property: They are feature detectors. Almost every neuron responds best to a very specific stimulus, usually a line, bar, or straight edge having a particular orientation (e.g., horizontal, vertical, diagonal) as well as a precise location in the visual field. A third principal characteristic of the responses of neurons in the visual cortex concerns the relationship between a binocular cell's preferred or optimal stimulus in each eye. Many cells show interocular matching; that is, the stimulus orientation that produces the best response is the same in both eyes and has the same location within the visual field. Many other cells have slightly different optimal stimulus orientations or locations in the two eyes. These small differences are called *interocular disparities*, and neurons that exhibit this property are termed *disparity detectors*.

Plasticity in Visual Development

The question of how this cortical system for the analysis of visual space develops early in life has been the subject of hundreds of experiments since the 1960s. An important overall conclusion is that many of the response characteristics of visual cortical neurons depend crucially on early visual experience for their normal development; these include binocularity and ocular dominance, orientation selectivity, and interocular matching of cells' optimal stimulus requirements, especially location and orientation (i.e., disparity detection). Typically, experiments of this sort involve raising young animals (usually kittens or monkeys, whose visual systems resemble humans') for a period of days or weeks during which visual experience is controlled or manipulated and differs from normal in specific ways, after which microelectrode studies are made in order to determine whether and how the activity of visual cortical cells has been altered by the abnormal experience.

During the first weeks or months of postnatal life, the developing mammal's visual system undergoes a period of special vulnerability or susceptibility to the effects of many altered rearing conditions, called the critical or sensitive period. After the critical period and continuing into adulthood, the same manipulations of the animal's visual experience generally do not affect the physiological organization of the visual cortex in terms of neurons' response characteristics (although some kinds of plasticity are definitely present later).

For instance, early studies examined the effects of completely depriving kittens of experience with visual form or pattern by closing both eyelids during the first few postnatal weeks. Initially it appeared that this manipulation does not produce major changes: Visual cortical cells' binocularity and the distribution of ocular dominance are unaffected, and these kittens' cells also show orientation selectivity resembling that of normally reared kittens, although the precision of orientation detection is slightly reduced. Subsequently, more detailed experiments showed that the system of disparity-detecting neurons does not develop normally in binocularly deprived kittens.

By contrast, kittens raised with just one eyelid closed (monocular deprivation) show dramatic changes in their visual cortical organization. Virtually all the cells are responsive only to stimulation of the eye that was open, and almost none to stimulation of the formerly closed eye. As might be expected, behavioral tests of visual acuity reveal deficits in the deprived eye.

This cortical ocular dominance shift is not due simply to the presence or absence of patterned visual input, but to the absence of simultaneous stimulation of both eyes, as shown by experiments in which kittens were raised with one eye closed for several days or a few weeks, after which that eye was opened and the opposite eye was closed for a comparable period (reverse suture), and also by experiments involving alternating daily monocular deprivation. Kittens raised using these methods experience the same amount of patterned visual input through both eyes, but at any given moment only one eye is receiving stimulation. When cortical ocular dominance and binocularity are studied in these kittens, it is found that almost all neurons are visually responsive, but each responds only to stimulation of one eye; there are almost none of the binocular cells that comprise 80–90 percent of the visual cortical neurons in normally reared kittens. Furthermore, if the relative amount (time) of stimulation given the two eyes is made unequal in these experiments, there is a corresponding change in the proportion of cells activated by stimulation of each eye.

Not only must patterned visual stimulation be temporally synchronized (simultaneous) between the two eyes in order for cortical binocularity to develop normally, it must also be spatially synchronous; that is, each part of the pattern must stimulate the same point on both retinas (corresponding points). Some humans exhibit an oculomotor disorder called strabismus, in which the two eyes are misaligned. People with this disorder often have poor visual acuity in one eye, and virtually always have deficient binocular depth perception. An animal model of strabismus, in which some of the muscles that control the position of the eyes are severed, has proved useful in studying the cortical effects of this disorder. Kittens raised with experimental strabismus show a marked loss of binocular neurons; in fact, the physiological organization of the visual cortex resembles that of kittens reared with alternating monocular deprivation.

The system of orientation-detecting neurons in the visual cortex is also susceptible to the effects of early visual experience. Kittens raised viewing contours or edges confined to a single orientation (e.g., vertical stripes) have a great preponderance of visual cortical cells whose preferred receptive fields are oriented at or near the experienced orientation; this finding is in marked contrast with the cortical organization seen in normally reared kittens, in which all possible orientations are represented about equally among cells' receptive fields.

In addition to the dramatic alterations in binocularity and orientation selectivity consequent upon experimental manipulations of early visual experience, there is also a degree of plasticity in the development of visual cortical cells specialized for disparity detection, especially interocular orientation disparity. For instance, changes are seen in the visual cortices of kittens raised wearing prism goggles that introduce rotations of the images seen by the left and right eyes. These rotations are around the visual axis (line of sight), and are opposite in the two eyes, producing a controlled amount of interocular orientation disparity; that is, an edge or contour in the field of view does not give rise to parallel images on the two retinas, as is normally the case, but instead is displaced clockwise in one eye and counterclockwise in the other. If these rotations are small (e.g., 8° in each eye), there is a corresponding shift in the average disparity of cortical neurons' preferred receptive-field orientations between the two eyes: Most cells show an interocular orientation disparity that matches the experienced image rotation. On the other hand, if the rotations are large (e.g., 16° or more in each eye), there is a disruption of binocularity: Most cells respond only to stimulation in one eye but not in both eyes. In this respect the effects of large interocular rotations are like those of strabismus or alternating monocular deprivation.

From an evolutionary standpoint, cortical plasticity in the development of interocular relationships has clear adaptive significance. The developing animal undergoes relatively rapid changes in height and in the lateral separation of the two eyes. There is thus a continually changing relation between the interocular image disparity of objects in the environment and the distance of those objects from the observer. The existence of neuronal disparity-detecting mechanisms able to adjust to these changes during early life provides an advantage in capturing prey, eluding predators, and so forth. Detailed reviews of the many studies on this issue have been written by Frégnac and Imbert (1984) and by Shinkman, Isley, and Rogers (1985).

Some Theoretical Considerations

There has been much discussion and more than a little controversy regarding the interpretation of this enormous body of experimental work. The problem of identifying underlying mechanisms responsible for plasticity in the developing visual system has been of particular interest. One appealing idea involves a process called *binocular competition*, in which fibers from the thalamus, some carrying information from one eye and some from the other, compete to form synapses on binocular cortical cells. When one eye is placed at a disadvantage during monocular deprivation, fibers representing the other eye are more successful at making cortical connections. This idea has received support from many experiments; one approach has been to raise kittens with monocular deprivation combined with damage to a small area of the retina in the open eye. Later, these kittens show the usual shift in ocular dominance toward the experienced eye, except that cortical cells that would otherwise have been responsive to stimulation of the damaged retinal area are instead responsive to stimulation of the deprived eye. An important role has also been shown for intracortical inhibitory mechanisms. For example, if a drug that blocks the action of inhibitory neurotransmitters is administered to a previously monocularly deprived kitten while

recordings from cells in the visual cortex are in progress, responsiveness to stimulation of the deprived eye increases immediately; this effect continues until the drug wears off, and then disappears.

What, exactly, is the role of visual experience in neocortical development? Does it serve simply to maintain the feature-detecting capabilities and the interocular relationships of visual cortical neurons, or does it actively sharpen and even alter these properties? Some writers have related this question to the age-old philosophical issue of nature versus nurture; however, we now understand quite clearly that both genetic influences (nature) and the influences of the individual's unique visual environment (nurture) are crucially important. The real question concerns the relative degree of these influences on the development of any particular aspect of the organization of our visual system and of our perceptual capacities. Many scientists are increasingly convinced that early visual experience can, at least within certain limits, directly modify connections being formed in the central nervous system, thereby exerting substantial control over the final outcome. This conclusion is borne out both by studies using experimental animals and by clinical observations on humans who have experienced visual disorders in early childhood.

Relation of Developmental Plasticity to Learning and Memory

We are now beginning to understand some mechanisms that may underlie both neural plasticity in early development and plasticity as manifested in adult learning and memory. These may include some dynamic aspects of the synaptic relations within neuronal networks of the cerebral cortex, and some chemical changes that accompany (and may ultimately be responsible for) some of the phenomena of neuronal plasticity described above.

For instance, the neurotransmitters noradrenalin (NA) and acetylcholine (ACh) have been demonstrated to play critical roles in the acquisition and storage of memories in adult mammals, using a wide variety of training procedures (see NEUROTRANSMITTER SYSTEMS AND MEMORY). In the late 1970s it was reported that monocular deprivation does not lead to a loss of binocularity in kittens subjected to depletion of neocortical NA; that is, plasticity depends on a normal level of NA. Subsequent experiments, however, using different methods for depleting cortical NA, failed to obtain this effect; it turns out that cortical levels of both NA and ACh must be greatly reduced in order to demonstrate a clear loss of plasticity in experiments on visual cortical binocularity.

Neurotransmitters exert many of their effects in the brain by acting on their receptors located on postsynaptic cells. There are numerous classes of receptors in the central nervous system; one type that has attracted a great deal of attention is known as the n-methyl-d-aspartate (NMDA) receptor. This receptor is particularly interesting because its action has been shown to be voltage-dependent; its properties come into play only when the postsynaptic cell is depolarized by a certain amount. It may therefore carry out a kind of gating function, permitting additional excitation only when some excitatory effects are already present in the postsynaptic neuron. Activation of the NMDA receptor may thus be thought of as a neurochemical analogue of the behavioral excitatory effects produced when a conditioned stimulus is combined with an unconditioned stimulus in a learning experiment. Indeed, drugs that block the NMDA receptor have been shown to interfere with, or even prevent, the normal acquisition of learned responses in experimental animals. As with NA and ACh depletion, this effect has been obtained using several different kinds of conditioning procedures.

It has recently been reported that in kittens, blocking NMDA receptors pharmacologically also blocks the neural plasticity shown in the loss of cortical binocular cells following monocular deprivation. Furthermore, plasticity due to the actions of neurotransmitters and to the activation of NMDA receptors has been demonstrated at the cellular level by recording from a single neuron while using minute electrical currents to eject small quantities of neurotransmitter substance or of NMDA from the electrode into the immediate vicinity of the neuron under study, a technique called *iontophoresis*. The responses of many visual cortical cells to a visual stimulus presented to the nondominant eye, or at a nonoptimal orientation, show a substantial temporary increase in strength when these stimuli are repeatedly paired with the iontophoretic application of NA and ACh, or of NMDA and glutamate (an excitatory transmitter that acts upon NMDA receptors). This effect is found in kittens but is absent in adult cats. Thus these neuro-

transmitter systems and the NMDA receptors have been clearly implicated in neuronal plasticity early in life and also in adult learning and memory.

Another phenomenon that may be related to both developmental plasticity and adult learning is known as LONG-TERM POTENTIATION (LTP). In a subcortical structure called the hippocampus (see GUIDE TO THE ANATOMY OF THE BRAIN), LTP is observed as an increase in responsiveness to an electrical stimulus following repeated activation of input pathways by high-frequency trains of impulses. This plastic change in a neural response has been proposed as a candidate mechanism underlying some forms of learning. Recently it has been found that LTP may also be induced in the visual cortex. LTP is more prominent in kittens during the critical period than in adult cats, and its production is blocked by drugs that prevent the activation of NMDA receptors. Studies are currently attempting to elucidate further the role of LTP in developmental plasticity and in adult conditioning and learning.

Conclusion

An exciting period is beginning, in which a new research area is emerging: the relation between brain mechanisms of developmental plasticity and of learning and memory. It seems safe to say that the search for general mechanisms of neural plasticity will occupy a prominent place in neuroscience for quite some time, and that studies of visual cortical neurons and neuronal networks will be especially fruitful in this regard.

REFERENCES

Frégnac, Y., and Imbert, M. (1984). Development of neuronal selectivity in primary visual cortex of cat. *Physiological Reviews 64,* 325–434.

Hubel, D. H., and Wiesel, T. N. (1979). Brain mechanisms of vision. *Scientific American 241,* 150–162.

Shinkman, P. G., Isley, M. R., and Rogers, D. C. (1985). Development of interocular relationships in visual cortex. In R. N. Aslin, ed., *Advances in neural and behavioral development,* vol. 1. Norwood, N.J.: Ablex.

Paul G. Shinkman

Adult Visual Cortex—Adaptation and Reorganization

Compared with the vast literature on use-dependent neuronal plasticity in the developing visual cortex, few studies address adaptivity of the adult visual cortex because it is commonly believed that primary sensory areas of neocortex show little plasticity in the adult. However, both psychophysical and neurobiological observations indicate the persistence of adaptivity in the mature visual cortex.

The perceptual phenomenon of *adaptation aftereffects* suggests the possibility of use-dependent and long-lasting (minutes to hours) modifications of responsiveness of feature-specific neurons in the visual cortex. Prolonged exposure to patterned stimuli leads to a feature-specific elevation of perceptual thresholds that lasts several minutes. Such adaptation has been shown for the movement and the orientation of contours, for the spatial frequency of gratings, and for color contrast. A related and very long-lasting (up to 24 hours) adaptation phenomenon is the McCulloch effect. After exposure to colored gratings of different orientation, black and white gratings appear to a subject to be tinted in complementary colors that remain associated with the respective orientations of the gratings. All these adaptation aftereffects show interocular transfer, indicating that adaptation has occurred at the cortical level. This notion is supported by recordings from single cells. Prolonged exposure to moving gratings induces orientation and direction-specific response adaptation that leads to a transitory change in the neurons' direction and orientation preference.

Profound modifications of neuronal response properties have been observed after pharmacological conditioning. When acetylcholine, noradrenaline, or potassium ions are applied to the recorded neuron in conjunction with repeated visual stimulation, both orientation and direction preferences can be altered.

Morphological changes and long-lasting response modifications also occur in response to manipulations of visual experience. If animals are transferred from an impoverished to an enriched visual environment, the density of dendritic spines increases in pyramidal cells of the visual cortex. This suggests that synaptic connections continue to be malleable in the adult. Likewise, long-lasting monocular deprivation (up to one year) leads to changes of ocular dominance similar to those occurring after brief monocular deprivation in young animals, in particular when the animals had no visual experience prior to monocular exposure. However, in adult animals these changes are restricted to modifications in nongranular layers, suggesting that adaptivity in the adult is preserved only for intracortical but not for thalamocortical connections. Another report describes a strong reduction of responsiveness and of feature selectivity of cortical neurons in adult cats whose visuomotor coordination had been disturbed by monocular eye rotation and restriction of vision to this eye. When these animals were again allowed to use their normal eye, visual functions recovered and so did the functional properties of cortical neurons. This recovery was associated with a significant shift of ocular dominance toward the normal eye.

Ocularity changes in response to monocular deprivation have further been observed in adult cats after transplantation of immature glial cells. This finding has been interpreted as evidence that glial factors promote neuronal plasticity.

Finally, there is evidence for functional reorganization after lesions. In patients suffering from visual field defects due to cortical lesions, intensive visual training can lead to a shrinkage of the scotoma. This suggests that cortical tissue adjacent to the zone of destruction can recover functions in a use-dependent manner. A functional reorganization has also been reported after circumscribed retinal lesions. Initially such lesions lead to a loss of visual responses in the corresponding cortical area. However, after several weeks neurons in this deafferented zone become responsive to input from the adjacent intact retinal areas.

A likely substrate of these modifications is use-dependent synaptic plasticity of intracortical connections. In vitro studies of slice preparations of rat visual cortex show that connections to cells in supragranular layers remain susceptible to use-dependent modifications in the adult. They can undergo both LONG-TERM POTENTIATION and depression, the requirements for the induction of these modifications being similar to those in the hippocampus and the cerebellum.

In conclusion, behavioral, electrophysiological, and morphological evidence confirms the persistence of use-dependent plasticity in the striate cortex of adult mammals and humans. This supports the notion that adaptivity is a constituent property of cortical networks.

REFERENCES

Rakic, P., and Singer, W., eds. (1988). *Neurobiology of neocortex.* Chichester, England: John Wiley.

Shaw, G. L., McGaugh, J. L., and Rose, S. P. R., eds. (1990). *Neurobiology of learning and memory.* Singapore: World Scientific.

Wolf Singer

Adult Visual Cortex—Neural Conditioning and Map Rearrangement

Many experimental manipulations that profoundly affect visual development in young experimental animals are generally ineffective in producing plastic changes in adult visual cortex. For instance, temporarily depriving young cats or monkeys of vision in one eye produces a change in binocularity whereby almost all visual cortical neurons are responsive to stimulation of the experienced (open) eye but not of the closed eye. In normally reared cats this monocular deprivation does not produce plastic changes in binocularity if instituted later than about 5 months of age; kittens raised in total darkness, however, are susceptible to the effects of monocular deprivation up to at least 10 months of age. By the same token, the interocular matching of visual cortical cells' preferred stimulus orientations is influenced by early visual experience in which prism goggles introduce a slight rotation (torsional disparity) between the images in the two eyes; susceptibility to this plastic modification of cortical neurons' receptive-field properties is prolonged in kittens raised for 3 months in complete darkness.

The basis for this effect is unclear at present; it may have to do with the fact that in some neurotransmitter systems normal development depends on a normal light-dark cycle. Indeed, local microperfusion of noradrenalin onto visual cortex, performed as late as 2 years of age, has been reported to restore neural plasticity as manifested in deprivation-induced changes in binocularity in normally reared adult cats. Furthermore, a provocative study has shown that neural plasticity is reinstated in adult visual cortex by transplantation of cultured astrocytes from the visual cortices of young kittens (Müller and Best, 1989). The results of this experiment, which also used the monocular deprivation method, emphasize the importance of the glial environment in promoting neocortical plasticity.

Training or Conditioning the Responses of Adult Visual Cortical Neurons

Most visual cortical neurons show considerable specificity with respect both to optimal stimulus requirements and to temporal pattern of response. These neuronal characteristics can be altered in adult cats by using procedures bearing a formal resemblance to classical (Pavlovian) and operant conditioning (see CONDITIONING, CLASSICAL AND INSTRUMENTAL.) In one such experiment, a cell's preferred stimulus requirements (which eye evokes a stronger response, what is the best stimulus orientation for an edge-detecting cell, and so forth) are determined as a baseline. Then a nonoptimal stimulus that initially elicits a much smaller response is paired with forced firing of cellular action potentials (evoked by minute electrical currents passed through the recording microelectrode). A large number of paired presentations (trials) is given during about an hour, after which it is often found that the cell's response to the nonpreferred stimulus shows a significant and persistent increase; this effect resembles the way an initially neutral stimulus elicits a conditioned response in Pavlovian conditioning.

In a similar type of experiment, analogous to behavioral operant conditioning, a baseline determination is made of a cell's pattern of firing in response to a visual stimulus. These patterns are usually quite stable: during 1–2 seconds after each stimulus presentation, a series of excitatory and inhibitory fluctuations in firing rate are seen, characteristic of each individual neuron and differing considerably among neurons. Arbitrary, experimenter-designated shifts in a cell's response pattern may be produced, however, if reinforcement, such as rewarding brain stimulation in the hypothalamus, is delivered contingent upon the occurrence of these specific changes. The cat learns to alter the brain's response to a visual stimulus at the cellular level, perhaps in the same way a human subject learns to alter brain waves in a biofeedback procedure.

Reorganization of Visual Cortex after Partial Deactivation

Another type of plasticity in visual cortex has been demonstrated in experiments by Kaas et al. (1990) in which parts of retinotopic maps in the visual cortex of adult cats are deprived of sources of activation by lesions of the retina. To avoid the complication that the visual cortex is normally activated by superimposed inputs from both eyes, inputs from one eye are removed so that the orderly retinotopic maps in the visual cortex are completely dependent on the other eye. In addition, a small laser lesion is placed in the retina of the functioning eye, thereby removing the sole remaining source of visual activation for small expanses of cortex in the first (V-I) and second (V-II) areas. After a month or more of recovery, neurons in the deprived zones of cortex in V-I and V-II that previously had receptive fields in the lesioned part of the retina have new receptive fields displaced to functioning parts of the retina immediately surrounding the lesion. Thus, the orderly maps of the retina in V-I and V-II are reorganized to replace the representation of the lesioned parts of the retina with an expanded representation of retina surrounding the lesion. Much less extensive reorganization occurs at the level of the lateral geniculate nucleus of cats, so the cortical reorganization may relate to changes in effectiveness of synapses within the arbors of thalamocortical and corticocortical neurons, which have greater potential for the retinotopic spread of information than do the more restricted arbors of retinogeniculate axons.

Similar reorganizations of V-I apparently occur after matched lesions of the retinas of both eyes in monkeys, and comparable reorganizations of somatosensory, auditory, and motor cortex have been reported. Together, these studies indicate that the effectiveness of previously existing connections in cortical structures can be modified by changes in activity patterns within the ascending afferent streams. Thus, changes in normal use may functionally reassign cortical neurons in ways that may enhance performance. But when more dramatic reorganizations follow retinal lesions, perceptual distortions could result from major increases in the cortical magnification of parts of the retina near the lesion. Overall, the evidence suggests that many features of cortical organization are dynamically maintained, and that alterations based on changes in use may relate to acquired individual differences in ability, and to recoveries and compensations after brain injury.

REFERENCES

Kaas, J. H., Krubitzer, L. A., Chino, Y. M., Langston, A. L., Polley, E. H., and Blair, N. (1990). Reorganization of retinotopic cortical maps in adult mammals after lesions of the retina. *Science 248,* 229–231.

Müller, C. M., and Best, J. (1989). Ocular dominance plasticity in adult cat visual cortex after transplantation of cultured astrocytes. *Nature 342,* 427–430.

Paul G. Shinkman
Jon H. Kaas

Auditory Cortex

Learning and memory involve the acquisition and storage of information. Acquired information can be used to produce new behaviors immediately or at a much later time (e.g., performance on a school test of assigned material). A common belief is that, among all brain systems, our sensory systems are not involved in learning but provide instantaneous knowledge of the world, like telephone or video systems. However, recent findings reveal that the actual sensory processing of stimuli is specifically modified as learning takes place. This article concerns such plasticity in the auditory cortex of adult animals, which provides most of the neurophysiological information on learning in the neocortex.

Issues and Findings

Early studies of the auditory cortex revealed increased magnitude of evoked field potentials (EP) during presentation of an acoustic stimulus when that stimulus (CS) was always followed by reinforcement (*associative classical conditioning*). Subsequent studies showed that both this effect and increased cellular discharges to the CS were reversed by removal of the reinforcer (*extinction*), were more likely to occur for pairing of the CS and reinforcement than for random presentation of these stimuli (*sensitization*), and were larger for a reinforced, compared with a nonreinforced, sound (*discrimination*). Moreover, when care was taken to ensure that such plasticity was not due to inadvertent increases in stimulus intensity (as when a subject moves closer to the source of a sound that signals reinforcement), no physiological plasticity developed at the cochlea, the acoustic receptor organ. Although these findings indicated that the facilitated responses involved central auditory processes and associative learning, some workers reported similar effects when animals were trained with a visual CS but tested with acoustic stimuli that were not involved in learning. This suggested that learning simply enhanced the processing of stimuli in all sensory systems and did not involve a specific change in the processing of information about the acquired significance of stimuli (for review, see Weinberger and Diamond, 1987).

Resolution of this important issue required that the effects of learning upon receptive fields (RF) be determined. The RF of a neuron is that part of the stimulus environment to which it is sensitive. In the auditory system, individual neurons are *tuned* to a small range of the acoustic frequency spectrum, with the whole range of audible frequencies covered by the overlapping frequency RF of the whole population of auditory neurons. To determine if learning involves a systematic change in the way acoustic information is processed, it would be necessary to show that the RF becomes *retuned* so as to favor the processing of the frequency of the CS relative to non-CS frequencies.

Recent studies have discovered that associative learning does indeed produce CS-specific plasticity of receptive fields, both in carnivores (cats) and in rodents (rats). RFs were obtained before and following classical conditioning (about thirty trials); postconditioning responses to the CS frequency were increased, whereas responses to other frequencies increased less or not at all, or even exhibited substantial decreased responses (Figure 1). Thus, the overall change was a retuning of the RF that favored processing of the CS. The retuning is stable, lasting at least 24 hours, but can be reversed by extinction training (Diamond

A: Pre-Conditioning

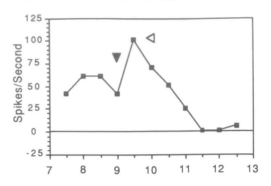

B: Post-Conditioning

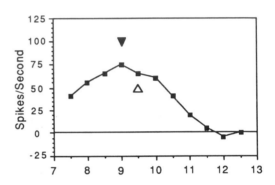

C: Post-Conditioning minus Pre-Conditioning

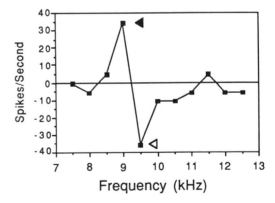

Figure 1.   Retuning of receptive fields in classical conditioning. **A:** Before training, the neuronal RF was best tuned to 9.5 kHz (white arrow). Following behavioral classical conditioning, there was a systematic modification of the RF. **B:** responses to the frequency of the CS (9.0 kHz, black arrow) were increased while responses to other frequencies were decreased or changed little. **C:** This is best seen in the panel **C**, in which the pre-RF has been subtracted from the post-RF.

and Weinberger, 1986; Bakin and Weinberger, 1990). Habituation (repeated presentation of one tone) produces an opposite effect, that is, a specific decreased response at the repeated frequency versus other frequencies (Condon and Weinberger, 1991).

Conclusions

The neuronal mechanisms of auditory cortical RF plasticity remain to be fully delineated. They do not seem merely to reflect plasticity at lower levels of the auditory system but may involve the action of the neuromodulator acetylcholine, released at the cortex during learning (Weinberger et al., 1990). Whatever the mechanisms, learning involves plasticity in the sensory processing and representation of information about environmental events. The extent to which sensory system plasticity in development and in recovery of function are related to learning remains to be elucidated.

(See also CONDITIONING, CLASSICAL AND INSTRUMENTAL; DISCRIMINATION AND GENERALIZATION.)

REFERENCES

Bakin, J. S., and Weinberger, N. M. (1990). Classical conditioning induces Cs-specific receptive field plasticity in the auditory cortex of the guinea pig. *Brain Research 536,* 271–286.

Condon, C. D., and Weinberger, N. M. (1991). Habituation produces frequency-specific plasticity of receptive fields in the auditory cortex. *Behavioral Neuroscience,* 416–430.

Diamond, D. M., and Weinberger, N. M. (1986). Classical conditioning rapidly induces specific changes in frequency receptive fields of single neurons in secondary and ventral ectosylvian auditory cortical fields. *Brain Research 372,* 357–360.

Weinberger, N. M., Ashe, J. H., Metherate, R., McKenna, T. M., Diamond, D. M., and Bakin, J. S. (1990). Retuning auditory cortex by learning: A preliminary model of receptive field plasticity. *Concepts in Neuroscience 1,* 91–132.

Weinberger, N. M., and Diamond, D. M. (1987). Physiological plasticity of single neurons in auditory cortex: Rapid induction by learning. *Progress in Neurobiology 29,* 1–55.

Norman M. Weinberger

Somatosensory Cortex

Somatosensory cortex of mammals consists of a number of subdivisions or processing areas. Although the number is species-variable, each cerebral hemisphere in all mammals contains at least two systematic representations of the tactile receptors of the contralateral body surface, the primary somatic area SI and the secondary somatic area SII. Neurons throughout these representations can be activated by stimuli on restricted portions of the body surface, the receptive fields of the neurons. Neurons in different parts of SI and SII relate to different body parts so that each area can be said to represent, in an orderly way, the contralateral body surface from tail to tongue. These two representations have fairly consistent organizations from individual to individual within a species, and conform to a general plan across species. Yet the organizations of the maps of the body surface can be altered in developing or adult mammals by removing or changing the significance of some of the inputs, or by damaging parts of maps. These changes in map organizations are the result of neurons losing their original receptive fields and acquiring new ones on different body parts. Thus, the organization of somatosensory cortex can change.

Plasticity in the somatosensory cortex may be important in development by allowing the sensory systems of individuals to adjust to bodily growth and to use information from the environment to adjust the system. Plasticity in adults may also be important in reassigning neurons to new roles after damage to the system in order to promote recovery, as well as in allowing adjustments in the neural network that may be critical in learning sensorimotor skills. However, there is little direct evidence about how plasticity relates to behavior.

Plasticity in somatosensory cortex has been demonstrated in a number of ways, including cutting the sensory nerve to part of the skin of the hand of a monkey. Over a period of weeks, neurons in somatosensory cortex formerly activated by inputs from the denervated skin of the hand acquire new receptive fields on adjoining parts of the hand with intact sensory afferents. Some reactivation may occur sooner, within seconds or hours of the nerve section. Thus, there are likely to be several different cellular mechanisms of change with different time courses. It is not certain how cortex does reorganize, but there are several obvious possibilities. In adults, all plasticity is thought to result from alterations in the effectiveness of existing anatomical connections, but in developing brains, the formation of new connections may provide an additional source of plasticity. Some immediate recovery of responsiveness might be due to a reduction in the lateral spread of ongoing inhibition of excitatory pathways, as a result removing a source of activation for the inhibitory neurons. Other changes might be due to a reduction in the production of inhibitory neurotransmitters in the deprived zones of cortex. Increases in the number, sizes, or strengths of excitatory synaptic contacts probably play a major role, and this could involve the formation of new synapses and the elaboration of axon arbors and dendrites.

The plasticity changes seen in cortex reflect, in part, adjustments made in the relays of sensory information in the brain stem and thalamus before they reach cortex. There is evidence for slight changes in the receptive fields of spinal cord neurons after the section or anesthetic block of peripheral nerves, but it is uncertain if these changes are effectively transmitted to cortex. Other changes undoubtedly occur in the important relay nuclei of the lower brain stem, but these structures have not been adequately studied. In the ventroposterior nucleus of the thalamus, however, clear changes in organization have been described after peripheral nerve section. For example, in monkeys, neurons throughout the subnucleus related to the glabrous hand become responsive to inputs related to the dorsal hairy skin of the hand after section of nerves to the glabrous hand.

The best evidence that the reorganization in cortex partly involves changes that occur in cortex rather than those relayed from the brain stem and thalamus comes from studies where the second somatosensory area, SII, was shown to reorganize after lesions to the first area, SI. In monkeys, neurons in SII depend on inputs from SI for activation. Thus, after complete lesions of SI, neurons in SII no longer respond to tactile stimuli. However, after partial lesions of the portion of SI devoted to the hand, the hand area of SII can no longer be activated from the hand, but it gradually becomes responsive to inputs from other body parts, largely the foot.

Plasticity of sensory representation in cortex has been most extensively studied for the somatosensory cortex, but reorganizations occur after partial removals of inputs for visual and auditory areas as well. Thus, plasticity is a basic feature of sensory systems.

REFERENCES

Kaas, J. H. (1983). The reorganization of somatosensory cortex following peripheral nerve damage in adult and developing mammals. *Annual Review of Neuroscience 6,* 325–356.

——— (1991). Plasticity of sensory and motor maps in adult mammals. *Annual Review of Neuroscience 14,* 137–167.

Jon H. Kaas

NEURAL COMPUTATION

[*In this five-part article,* Approaches to Learning—*an overview of biological neural networks and their relationship to artificial neural networks—is followed by examinations of neural computation as it is evidenced in the functioning of the cerebellum, the hippocampus, the neocortex, and the olfactory cortex.*]

Approaches to Learning

Nervous systems are capable of solving extraordinarily sophisticated computational problems. The visual or tactile recognition of an object in a cluttered scene is child's play, but well beyond the capability of the fastest digital computers. Most animals can navigate over rough surfaces with great agility, but present-day robots are limited in their movements to a very narrow range of terrains. We can learn to use language and to read and write, well beyond anything so far accomplished by artificial intelligence. We take all of these abilities for granted because we are so good at them; trying to duplicate them with machines has made their great difficulty more apparent.

Neural computation is the systematic study of the computational principles underlying the function of neural systems, from the level of molecular mechanisms to the organization of brain systems (Figure 1). This computational approach to neuroscience is still in its infancy (Sejnowski et al., 1988). There has been a recent emphasis on studying neural networks, small groups of highly connected neurons; however, as shown in Figure 1, neural networks are only one level of investigation in the nervous system, and neural computation depends on computational principles at each of these levels. A few general principles have emerged from the study of abstract models of neural systems

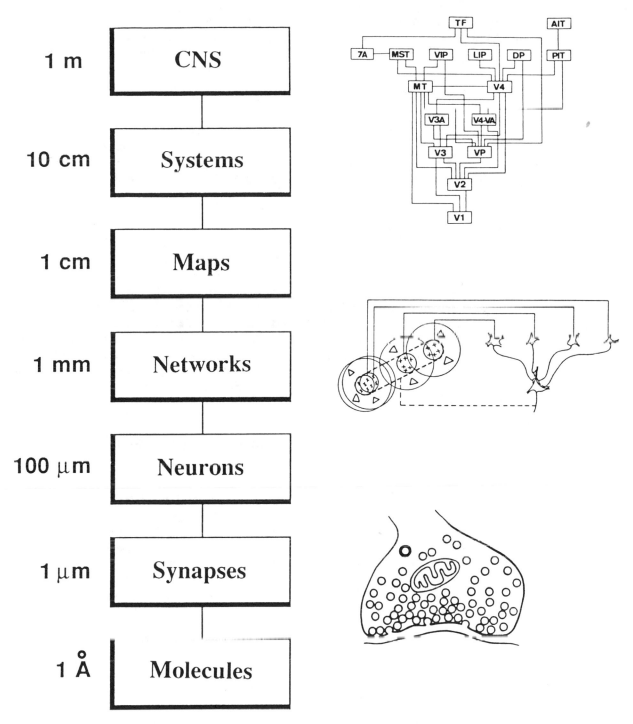

Figure 1. Structural levels of organization in the nervous system. The spatial scale at which anatomical organizations can be identified varies over many orders of magnitude.

that are likely to be important for the biological study of learning and memory.

Some Principles of Neural Computation

In the von Neumann architecture commonly used in digital computers, the memory and the processor are physically separated. This separation gives rise to a bottleneck in the flow of information between the two. In neural systems, memory and processing are intertwined; the same circuits that process sensory and motor information are involved in learning and the storage of new information. A unified processor-memory system allows many circuits to work together in parallel and, as a consequence, the solutions to many commonly occurring problems can be computed in only a few serial steps. The representation of sensations and memories in such an architecture is more difficult for us to imagine and to use than one in which the functions are segregated (Churchland and Sejnowski, 1992). The brain, however, did not evolve to make it easier for us to analyze.

Locality is an important constraint that arises when hardware for artificial neural networks is designed (Mead, 1989). Wires are expensive on computer chips, just as they are in the brain, so only limited connectivity is possible between processing elements. The organization of sensory processing into a hierarchy of maps and the laminar organization of cortical structures is wire-efficient. This also places constraints on the organization of learning systems, which share the same circuitry. In particular, the decision to store a piece of information at a particular location in the brain is a local one that depends on electrical and chemical signals which are spatially and temporally restricted. The Hebbian mechanism (see HEBB, DONALD) for synaptic plasticity that has been found in the hippocampus and neocortex obeys this principle of locality: The presynaptic release of neurotransmitter and the postsynaptic depolarization needed to trigger the long-term potentiation at these synapses are spatially contiguous, and there is a brief temporal window during which both signals must be present. Modulatory influences on learning may be more diffuse and widespread.

Neurons have limited dynamic range. Unlike digital systems, which are capable of accurately representing very large and very small numbers, the range of membrane potentials and firing rates found in neurons is limited. Also, the variability in the properties of neurons within the same population is significant, and the properties of the same neuron can vary with time. The same is true for analog VLSI (very-large-scale integration) circuits that are designed to mimic the processing which occurs in neurons (Mead, 1989). This variability and limited dynamical range have consequences for the way that information is coded and the way that neural circuits are designed. One way to preserve information is to process relative levels, or differences, rather than absolute levels. Thus, visual neurons are more sensitive to contrast (spatial differences) and changes (temporal differences) than to absolute intensity levels. Another mechanism for preserving information is dynamically altering baseline activity in neurons. Adaptive biochemical mechanisms inside cells, such as light adaptation in photoreceptors, allow neurons to remain in their most sensitive range. Adaptive mechanisms have been found for calibrating sensorimotor coordination, such as slow adaptation of the vestibulo-ocular reflex (VOR) to changes in the magnification of the lens (Lisberger, 1988).

Taxonomy of Learning Systems

Adaptation to ongoing sensory stimulation does not require an additional source of information outside the processing stream; this type of learning is called *unsupervised*. In contrast, the type of adaptation that occurs in response to sensorimotor mismatch does require an outside error signal; this is called *supervised* learning. In the case of VOR learning, the error signal is the slip of the image on the retina, and the gain of the reflex is changed to reduce the slip. The amount of supervision can vary from a crude good/bad reinforcement signal to very detailed feedback of information about complex sensory signals from the environment that might be termed a "teacher." Supervised learning is sometimes called *error-correction learning*.

It is not necessary for the error signal to come from outside the organism; important information about the proper operation of a circuit can be provided by another internal circuit, or even by internal consistency within the same circuit. For example, a sensory area that was trying to predict future inputs could compare its prediction against the next input to improve its performance. Such an unsupervised system with an internal measure of error is termed *monitored* (Churchland and Sejnowski, 1992). As shown in Figure 2, all possible combinations of supervised and unsupervised, monitored and unmonitored, learning systems are possible.

Selected Examples

An interesting example of a monitored system is song learning in the white-crowned sparrow. In this species of songbird, the male hears the local dialect after hatching but does not produce the song until the next spring. At first the song is imperfect, but with each repetition the details improve until it is a good reproduction of the original song heard the previous year, even though there is no external "teacher" during the refinement. The internally stored template is compared with the imperfect song production; the error between them drives learning mechanisms to improve the song. This learning is monitored because the error is derived from an internal template of the desired sound. We may use a similar strategy when learning to produce new sounds in a foreign language. (See also BIRD SONG LEARNING; LANGUAGE LEARNING.)

Transformations between two populations of neurons can be learned with Hebbian mechanisms at the synapses between the input fibers and the output neurons. The pattern of activity on the input fibers is matched with the desired pattern on the output neurons. In some models of the cerebellum, for example, associative motor learning is mediated by climbing fibers, which provide a teaching signal to the output Purkinje cells. By including feedback projections of the output neurons back onto themselves, a partial input cue can regenerate the entire stored pattern. In this mode, the system is unsupervised because the desired output pattern of activity during learning is the same as the input pattern. Such content-addressable recurrent networks have been suggested as models for the piriform cortex and area CA3 of the hippocampus. Some properties such as memory capacity of associative networks of simplified processing units have been well studied; the analysis of networks based on model neurons with more complex properties is just beginning.

Learning mechanisms have also been used to model the development of cortical systems. One of the best-explored areas of unsupervised learning in artificial networks is competitive learning, in which incoming sensory information is used to organize the internal connections of a sensory map. For example, the formation of ocular dominance columns in visual cortex of cats and monkeys during development (see NEOCORTICAL PLASTICITY) depends on competitive synaptic mechanisms. The development of ocular dominance columns can be mimicked in a computer model that uses Hebbian learning in the spatially restricted terminal arbors of axons projecting to the cortex from the lateral geniculate nucleus (Miller et al., 1989). Similar mechanisms can also be used in neural systems to learn more complex features that distinguish among different types of sensory inputs (Kohonen, 1984). It is also likely that other learning mechanisms are used to discover invariants of sensory patterns, which are often as important in pattern recognition as the distinctive features that separate classes (Churchland and Sejnowski, 1992).

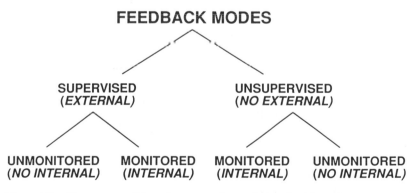

Figure 2. Taxonomy of learning procedures. Supervised learning occurs when there is feedback on the performance of the system from the external environment. If the feedback is a scalar reward, it is called reinforcement learning. The learning is called monitored if the system has an internal measure of error.

As computers grow more powerful, it will become possible to simulate more complex models of neural systems; however, even these simulations will fall short of the richness of real neural systems and the complex environments that confront biological creatures. Hardware emulations that interact with the real world in real time would greatly improve our ability to test hypotheses about the organization of neural systems (Mead, 1989). Ultimately we will need to study complete model systems in order to understand the multiple levels of adaptation and learning that provide flexibility and stability in a changing world.

REFERENCES

Churchland, P. S., and Sejnowski, T. J. (1992). *The computational brain*. Cambridge, Mass.: MIT Press.

Kohonen, T. (1984). *Self-organization and associative memory*. Berlin: Springer-Verlag.

Lisberger, S. G. (1988). The neural basis for motor learning in the vestibulo-ocular reflex in monkeys. *Science 242*, 728.

Mead, C. (1989). *Analog VLSI and neural systems*. Reading, Mass.: Addison-Wesley.

Miller, K. D., Keller, J. B., and Stryker, M. P. (1989). Ocular dominance column development: Analysis and simulation. *Science 245*, 605–615.

Sejnowski, T. J., Koch, C., and Churchland, P. S. (1988). Computational neuroscience. *Science 241*, 1299–1306.

Terrence J. Sejnowski

Cerebellum

The cerebellum is located at the rear of the brain and sits above the brain stem (see GUIDE TO THE ANATOMY OF THE BRAIN). It is richly interconnected with a wide range of sensory systems (somatosensory, auditory, visual, vestibular) as well as motor structures in the brain. Thus, it is a component of very complex sets of *brain systems* that are responsible for a wide range of motor behaviors, from "simple" reflexive behaviors to speech, playing a violin, or skiing a slalom course. The roles that the cerebellum plays—what computations it performs on its inputs and what functions its outputs control in this complex network—are not known. However, neuroscientists have been able to make educated guesses about its function on the basis of a broad range of findings that have come from fields as diverse as neurology and computer science. These guesses are currently the subject of lively debates in neuroscience.

Clinical findings show that people with cerebellar injuries experience a loss of coordination. They cannot execute well-timed movements or movements that require precise spatial coordination, such as playing the piano or smoothly threading a needle (see Brooks and Thach, 1985; Dow and Mourzzi, 1958; and Ito, 1984). Experimental work with animals has shown that certain simple forms of motor learning cannot occur if particular areas of the cerebellum are destroyed—for instance, Pavlovian conditioned defensive motor reflexes (e.g., McCormick and Thompson, 1983; Donegan et al., 1989) and adaptations required for the coordination of eye movement with head movement, such as changes in the vestibulo-ocular reflex, or VOR (Lisberger, 1988).

Our ideas about cerebellar function have been further sharpened by attempts to develop computational models of cerebellar function. A general heuristic is to work "down" from the level of behavioral analysis and "up" from the knowledge of the nervous system. This approach to model development acts to constrain the range of plausible forms that the model takes. Starting with behavior, such as picking up an object, we must acquire visual information about the location of the object and integrate it with information about the position of our body in relation to the object. The motor system must then integrate the information about the object's spatial position with our body position to compute a set of motor commands that select the appropriate sequence of movements—that is, the groups of muscles involved and the temporal pattern and force with which they will be called into play (see Churchland, 1989, pp. 77–108). The next step in model development is to specify what representations need to be acquired and how input to the system is transformed so that the desired output is generated. Thus, at the level of behavioral analysis there may be various ways of characterizing what is being computed and numerous algorithms for doing the computations (e.g., Jordan and Rosenbaum, 1990). At this point, thinking about what classes of computations the neural systems may or may not allow serves to constrain the range of algorithms to be considered.

In starting with a brain system, we can identify a range of functions in which it could, in principle, participate. We can then work "up" by making guesses about what kinds of computations are required and the algorithms the system may or may not be able to implement, given its physical properties. At this point, characterizing the nature of the computations that the system needs to perform, indicated by analysis of the *behavioral* task, can act to constrain the range of physiological properties that are incorporated into the model—these constraints indicate which set of components of the brain system are most promising for developing models of the behavioral capacities to be explained.

It is the structural properties of the cerebellum, in particular the cerebellar cortex, that have made it the most studied structure of the motor system. The cerebellum is made up of two principal structures, the overlying cortex and the deep nuclei, the latter providing the output from the cerebellum to other brain structures. The cortex is made up of five principal types of neurons that are arranged in a very uniform pattern. The cerebellum receives input from mossy fibers and climbing fibers. Input from the mossy fibers is relayed to the granule cells, which send out bifurcating axons, called parallel fibers, that run in "beams." The axons of the granule cells make synapses onto Purkinje cells, among the largest cells in the brain and the sole output of the cerebellar cortex. Each Purkinje cell receives as many as 200,000 inputs from granule cells and shows a wide dynamic range of firing "simple" spikes to this input. The Purkinje cells provide inhibitory input onto the deep nuclei. This throughput pathway, mossy fiber $\rightarrow$ granule cell $\rightarrow$ Purkinje cell, is modulated by three classes of inhibitory interneurons: Golgi, basket, and stellate cells. From their patterns of connectivity they can control the patterns of activity across particular spatial arrangements of Purkinje cells, although their functional significance is not well understood.

The second form of input to the cerebellum is through the climbing fibers, which come exclusively from the inferior olive. Climbing fibers send projections to the cerebellar cortex, forming strong synaptic connections on Purkinje cells, and send collaterals to the cerebellar deep nuclei. Climbing fiber input occurs at a relatively low frequency and over a narrow dynamic range but powerfully excites Purkinje cells, causing them to generate bursts of three to four high-frequency spikes (complex spikes). Functions attributed to the climbing fibers include (1) a teaching input that modifies parallel fiber $\rightarrow$ Purkinje cell synapses and allows for forms of motor learning, and (2) an

input for generating appropriate temporal patterns of activity in the cerebellar cortex that allow for the precise timing of motor responses.

Neuroscientists and computer scientists have used information about the anatomy and physiology of the cerebellum to develop mathematical and abstract neural network models of its function. Many of these models have focused on how particular patterns of activity in mossy fiber $\rightarrow$ parallel fiber pathways and from climbing fibers influence Purkinje cell activity, and thus the output of the cortex onto the deep nuclei (e.g., Ito, 1984, pp. 325–349). One class of models, starting from the seminal work of Albus (1971) and Marr, assumes that the cerebellum is involved in forms of MOTOR LEARNING. (Examples include Ito's corticonuclear microcomplexes and microzones, Houk's [1990] arrays of adjustable pattern generator modules; Fugita's [1982] control systems model of the cerebellum and VOR; the cerebellar and brain-stem model of eyeblink conditioning of Donegan et al. [1989]; the dynamical neural network models of Keeler [1990].) A form of associative learning is thought to be induced by mossy fiber activation of parallel fibers and activation of climbing fiber input onto Purkinje cells. This conjunction is thought to modify the strength of the parallel fiber and Purkinje cell synapse—a long-term depression (weakening) of synaptic strength (see LONG-TERM DEPRESSION IN THE CEREBELLUM, NEOCORTEX, AND HIPPOCAMPUS).

Keeler (1990) has presented an abstract neural network model inspired by cerebellar architecture (e.g., the relative size of cell layers and the fan in and fan out across layers). In each layer of the network, each processing unit sums the activation passed to it from active input units, transforms it, and passes this activity to the next layer. Learning rules of the model specify the conditions under which particular patterns of activity in the network can modify the strengths of the links between the processing units. From such analyses, it is proposed that the role of the cerebellar cortex is to develop a model of the dynamics of the external world and the sensorimotor system of the individual. Its function is to predict the dynamics of the system, using these computations to modulate activity in the deep cerebellar nuclei to achieve smooth, coordinated movements.

Other models of cerebellar function are purely dynamic models. For example, they see the primary role of the cerebellum as transforming representations in our spatial maps of our environment into representations in a motor "space" or map, but not as a site of learning. In Pellionisz's (1985) tensor model, the cerebellum takes complex arrays of sensory inputs (which can be conceptualized as input vectors) and transforms them into a series of vectors in the coordinates of the motor space, through a kind of matrix multiplication (see Churchland, 1989). However, due to a number of serious problems, tensor models are no longer taken seriously (e.g., see Arbib and Amari, 1985). In more recent dynamic models, the climbing fiber input is said to allow appropriate computations for the timing of movements.

One goal of these theoretical exercises is to determine the capacities to which particular network architectures and learning rules give rise in order to gain insights into the possible functions of the cerebellum. A constant problem that the theorist faces is knowing the level of analysis at which the critical computations are taking place, that is, knowing which properties of the neural system are important and which are not (e.g., properties of various ion channels, dendritic spines, the cell body, local circuits, and brain systems). Probably all are involved—the trick is to figure out the contributions of each to the overall function of the system. This is a daunting conceptual and computational challenge. With the synergistic interaction of experimental work, theory development, and faster, more sophisticated computers, we should see exciting developments in our understanding of cerebellar and motor system functioning in the near future.

REFERENCES

Albus, A. (1971). A theory of cerebellar function. *Mathematical Biosciences 10*, 25–61.

Arbib, J. M., and Amari, S. (1985). Sensorimotor transformations in the brain. *Journal of Theoretical Biology 112*, 123–155.

Brooks, B. B., and Thach, W. T. (1985). In V. B. B. J. M. Brookhart and S. R. Geiger, eds., *Handbook of physiology.* Bethesda, Md.: American Physiological Society.

Churchland, P. M. (1989). *A neurocomputational perspective.* Cambridge, Mass.: MIT Press.

Churchland, P. S. (1986). *Neurophilosophy.* Cambridge, Mass.: MIT Press.

Donegan, N. H., Gluck, M. A., and Thompson, R. F. (1989). Integrating behavioral and biological models of classical conditioning. In R. D. Hawkins and G. H. Bower, eds., *Computational models of learning in simple neural systems,* pp. 109–156. New York: Academic Press.

Dow, R. S., and Mourzzi, G. (1958). *The physiology and pathology of the cerebellum.* Minneapolis: University of Minnesota Press.

Fugita, M. (1982). Adaptive filter model of the cerebellum. *Biological Cybernetics 45*, 195–206.

Houk, J. C., Singh, S. P., Fisher, C., and Barto, A. G. (1990). An adaptive sensorimotor network inspired by the anatomy and physiology of the cerebellum. In R. S. Sutton, W. T. Miller, and P. J. Werbos, eds., *Neural networks for control,* pp. 301–348. Cambridge, Mass.: MIT Press.

Ito, M. (1984). *The cerebellum and neural control.* New York: Raven Press.

Jordan, M. I., and Rosenbaum, D. A. (1990). Action. In M. I. Posner, ed., *Foundations of cognitive science.* Cambridge, Mass.: MIT Press.

Keeler, J. D. (1990). A dynamical system view of cerebellar function. *Physica D42*, 396–410.

Lisberger, S. (1988). The neural basis for learning of simple motor skills. *Science 242*, 728–735.

Marr, D. (1969). A theory of cerebellar cortex. *Journal of Physiology 202*, 437–470.

——— (1982). *Vision.* San Francisco: W. H. Freeman.

McCormick, D. A., and Thompson, R. F. (1983). Cerebellum: Essential involvement in the classically conditioned eyelid response. *Science 223*, 296–299.

Pellionisz, A. J. (1985). Tensorial brain theory in cerebellar modelling. In J. D. J. R. Blodel and W. Precht, eds., *Cerebellar functions,* pp. 201–229. New York: Springer-Verlag.

Nelson Donegan

Hippocampus

Both clinical neuropsychological studies and animal experiments involving damage to the hippocampal formation indicate that this structure plays a fundamental role in at least the initial establishment of long-term associative memory; however, the exact role of the hippocampus in associative memory, and the physiological and computational mechanisms by which this role is accomplished, remain subjects of intense study and debate. Although by no means proven, evidence favors the hypothesis that the hippocampus acts as a simple interim repository for memories of certain kinds of events, and that other (neocortical) circuitry draws on this repository during a process known as memory consolidation (e.g., Zola-Morgan and Squire, 1990). The following is a brief overview of some current ideas about how the unique circuitry of the hippocampal formation might enable rapid associative memory, and why such an interim repository might be necessary.

Specific events are generally represented in the nervous system as *distributed* patterns of activity within rather large populations of cells, and rarely by the activity of single cells. The activity pattern may be thought of as a *vector,* that is, a list of ones and zeros, indicating which neurons are firing and which are silent, or as a list of positive real numbers indicating the firing rates of the neurons over some short interval. Associative recall, by its most general definition, is the ability of the brain to reconstruct the vector corresponding to a stored event when presented with a vector that is missing some of the original information, has been corrupted somehow by noise, or merely bears some

significant resemblance to the original. This ability is often called either *pattern completion* or *autoassociative recall.* Using the pre- and postsynaptic *conjunction* principle for modifying the connection strengths between neurons originally elaborated by Donald HEBB (1949), work in the 1960s and early 1970s by Kohonen (1972), Marr (1971), Steinbuch (1961), Willshaw and colleagues (1969), and others laid the theoretical foundations for how a simple pattern-completion network might operate. In particular, the work of Marr was seminal, because it outlined several clear principles as to how actual neural circuits might accomplish this.

The essence of these principles is illustrated in Figure 1, which may be thought of as an incomplete

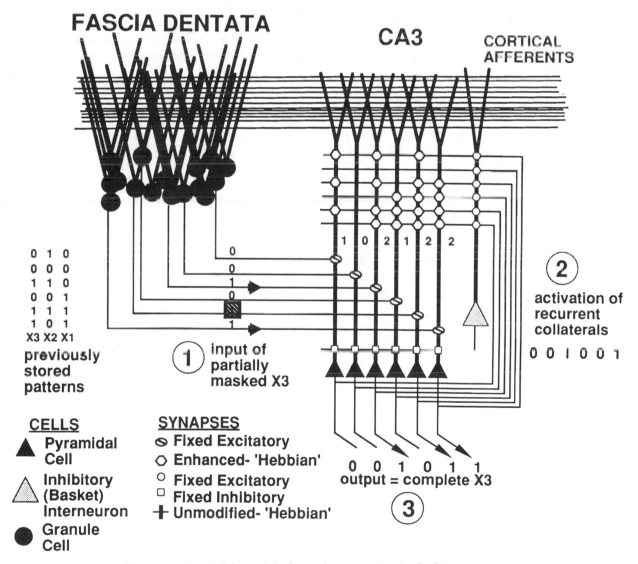

Figure 1. A possible model of neural computation in the hippocampus.

and crude model for hippocampal regions CA3 and fascia dentata, and their neocortical inputs. The axons from the granule cells of the fascia dentata make sparse but strong contacts with the CA3 pyramidal cells. The axons of the pyramidal cells feed back into the pyramidal layer, making contacts that are initially ineffective but can be made effective by implementing "Hebbian" synaptic enhancement. That is, whenever a pyramidal cell is strongly activated by its granule cell input, those synapses which it receives from other pyramidal cells that have been activated by the same input become strengthened (in this illustration, the strength goes from 0 to 1). By strengthening the connections among neurons that have been active together during an event, it becomes possible later to recall that event in its entirety, given only a fragment of it. One of Marr's important contributions was the idea that a small population of inhibitory interneurons plays the crucial role of assessing the total number of active inputs and adjusting the threshold of the memory (pyramidal) cells such that only a fixed proportion of them are allowed to fire. This adjustment is accomplished essentially by dividing the total excitation of a given cell by the total number of active inputs. In this way, when an incomplete event is presented, the effective threshold of the pyramidal cells is lowered (because there is less inhibition). If the reduced input is part of a stored event, all of the corresponding synapses will have been strengthened and the correct cells will fire. Incorrect cells will not fire because they will, on average, not have as many enhanced inputs in that particular event. Thus, provided it is unique, even a small fragment of a stored event will cause activation of the full event. The reader unfamiliar with these principles might benefit by working through the example in Figure 1. For more detailed discussion, see McNaughton and Nadel (1989) or McNaughton and Barnes (1990).

There are, of course, constraints on the amount (and kinds) of information that can be stored by such a memory, as can readily be understood by imagining the consequences of attempting to store so much information that all of the synapses have been enhanced. At this point no information is recoverable. One solution is to encode an event with the minimum number of fibers necessary to capture its vital features (sometimes called *redundancy removal*). The hippocampus constitutes the highest level of association cortex in the nervous system, receiving its input from polymodal associa-

tion cortex. Much of the processing that occurs in these areas can be thought of as redundancy removal or *feature extraction*. Moreover, hippocampal cells are often silent for prolonged periods, suggesting that rather few of them are active at any one time. Another solution is to make the patterns to be stored as different from each other as possible, a process known as *orthogonalization*, because orthogonal vectors are uncorrelated.

Although feature extraction is itself an orthogonalization process, sometimes it is necessary to store as separate, one-time events that may differ only in some arbitrary but important way. Because feature detector formation requires "knowledge" of the long-term statistical regularities in the input, this solution will not work. An alternative solution is to use an extra layer of very many cells between the input and the memory cells. By spreading the connections from the input to this layer more or less randomly, yet adjusting the thresholds so that about the *same total number* of intermediate cells as input cells are active, the degree of overlap between input events will be reduced. This is merely a consequence of the facts that, in the larger population, the probability that a given cell is active in any one event is reduced, and the probability of its being active in any two events is the square of the single-event probability. Marr called this solution *codon formation*. It is likely that the granule cells of the fascia dentata perform something like this function.

Although greatly oversimplified, models such as this go a long way toward accounting for the known anatomical and physiological organization of the hippocampal formation. Many theoretical and experimental neuroscientists believe that something like this process goes on in the hippocampus during the original encoding of long-term associative memory. One of the major outstanding questions in the field, however, is why the hippocampus, and presumably the information stored there, is necessary only for a limited period after the initial registration. Estimates of exactly how long vary from hours to years in different species, and for different kinds of memory. At present only educated guesses can be offered in answer to this question. The first is that it is probably both unnecessary and biologically expensive simply to store all experience; however, often it cannot be predicted at the time of an event whether the information is sufficiently important or reliable to be stored permanently. Second, if a set of events does contain some statistical regularity, it may be possible to generate a new "feature detector" for that regularity, and hence to achieve redundancy reduction in permanent memory. In order to assess this, however, some representation of the raw events must be stored for comparison. J. L. McClelland (personal communication) has proposed a somewhat related hypothesis, expressed in terms of the parallel distributed processing or connectionist models of cognitive psychology. Briefly, the argument is that learning appropriate and efficient internal representations for a particular problem or set of events generally requires multiple exposures to the events (at least with currently discovered algorithms). During these exposures a kind of global error term for the performance of the memory can be computed and used to correct (in small steps) the set of synaptic connection strengths (*weights*). The argument, then, is that the hippocampus makes use of many cells to store a set of memories that later can be "played back" to the neocortex for the purpose of computing an appropriate set of connection weights to store the information with the minimal number of units. Ideas such as these, it is hoped, will eventually provide a firm computational explanation for the process of memory consolidation and the crucial role of the hippocampal formation. (See also PARALLEL DISTRIBUTED PROCESSING MODELS OF MEMORY).

A simple (and incomplete) model for the fascia dentata and CA3 subfields of the hippocampus illustrates how this system may implement *autoassociation*, using simple "Hebbian" synaptic enhancement. Inputs from fascia dentata essentially impose output patterns in CA3. The synapses of the activated recurrent collaterals that terminate on active pyramidal cells are enhanced (in this simple illustration, the weights go from 0 to 1). Later, input of some fragment of a stored pattern (1) activates a corresponding subset of pyramidal cells and their recurrent collaterals (2). Each pyramidal cell then adds up how many of its currently active recurrent collateral synapses have previously been enhanced, and divides this by the total number of active inputs. If this is equal to or greater than threshold (i.e., 1), the unit fires. If not too many patterns are stored, the result will be the output of the complete original pattern (3). The inhibitory interneuron sums the total input and sets the divisor for the pyramidal cells accordingly. There is some evidence that something of this sort actually happens in the brain.

REFERENCES

Hebb, D. O. (1949). *The organization of behavior.* New York: Wiley.

Kohonen, T. (1972). Correlation matrix memories. *IEEE Transactions on Computers C-21,* 353–359.

Marr, D. (1971). Simple memory: A theory for archicortex. *Philosophical Transactions of the Royal Society of London B262,* 23–81.

McNaughton, B. L., and Barnes, C. A. (1990). From cooperative synaptic enhancement to associative memory: Bridging the abyss. *Seminars in the Neurosciences 2,* 403–416.

McNaughton, B. L., and Nadel, L. (1989). Hebb-Marr networks and the neurobiological representation of action in space. In M. A. Gluck and D. E. Rumelhart, eds., *Neuroscience and connectionist theory.* Hillsdale, N.J.: Erlbaum.

Steinbuch, K. (1961). Die Lernmatrix. *Kybernetik* 1:36–45.

Willshaw, D. J., Buneman, O. P., and Longuet-Higgins, H. C. (1969). Nonholographic associative memory. *Nature 222,* 960–962.

Zola-Morgan, S. M., and Squire, L. R. (1990). The primate hippocampal formation: Evidence for a time-limited role in memory formation. *Science 250,* 288–289.

Bruce L. McNaughton

Neocortex

One of the central goals of recent neuroscience research has been to understand the nature of the computations carried out in the *neocortex.* The neocortex is a thin sheet of roughly 10^{10} neurons and fibers that forms the external surface of much of the brain (see also GUIDE TO THE ANATOMY OF THE BRAIN). The neocortex arose relatively recently in evolution, around the time that mammals branched off from their reptilian precursor. Yet during that short evolutionary time the neocortex has shown the most dramatic expansion and elaboration of any brain system. In fact, changes in it constitute the most important distinction between the human brain and those of the other primates and mammals. As such, the neocortex is thought to be the site of higher perceptual and cognitive processing in the brain. The human neocortex contains areas that are specialized for vision, hearing, somatosensation, and generating movement, as well as areas for language and complex memory tasks.

From an anatomical, physiological, and pharmacological standpoint, individual neurons in the neocortex are qualitatively similar to those in other brain regions; thus the unique computational and information-processing capabilities of the neocortex must arise from the way its neurons are connected into circuits. Although much remains to be discovered about the structure and function of cortical circuits, there is reason to believe that the basic principles of cortical operation may be understood before all the details are forthcoming.

The functional properties of neocortex depend upon its structure, and four major principles of neocortical organization have been discovered. First, the cortex is organized vertically into six *layers,* each layer receiving and sending connections to specific brain sites. Second, there is a horizontal organization of the cortex into *columns,* such that neurons in a vertical column (of approximately 0.5 millimeter diameter) share particular physiological properties. Third, most cortical areas contain one or more *topographic* maps (in a topographic map, adjacent areas of the periphery are represented in adjacent areas of cortex. For example, in visual cortex, area V1 contains a map of the visual field; in somatosensory cortex, area SI contains four separate maps of the body surface.) Finally, cortical areas are *functionally segregated*—cells in each area are specialized for particular functional tasks (e.g., cells in visual area MT are specialized for *motion detection,* among other things; those in visual area V4 are specialized for color and *pattern analysis,* among other things). To complete matters, the maps in different cortical areas are interconnected in a vast and intricate scheme.

Insights have been gained from studying different areas of neocortex. For example, in somatosensory cortex (which mediates touch, temperature, and pain), maps have been found to be dynamically organized such that they change in an ongoing manner in response to skin stimulation (Merzenich et al., 1988; Finkel, 1990). However, visual neocortex has been the region most intensively studied and provides perhaps the clearest example of the kinds of computations the cortex must carry out.

Vision is a complex act that requires a parallel analysis of shape, motion, depth, color, texture and several other modalities leading to the discrimination and recognition of an object (Livingstone and Hubel, 1988). Each of these visual processes is complex in its own right. For example, the major cue to depth comes from *stereopsis,* essentially a process of triangulation in which the slightly dispa-

rate views of the world seen by the two eyes are compared, and from the shift in view, the distance of various objects is computed (Poggio and Poggio, 1984). *Perception of depth* thus results from a cortical computation. Computations in another set of cortical areas result in *perception of color.* Contrary to the implications of simple optics, our perceptions of color are not solely determined by the wavelengths of light reflected from an object. As Land (1983) has shown, color perception is determined by the *relative* amount of light of different wavelengths reflected by an object versus that reflected by its surrounding environment. Neurons in cortical area V4 have been found to respond to the "color" of an object as we perceive it; those in the more peripheral area V1 respond to the wavelength of the light, not the color (Zeki, 1980); thus, the color computation is probably carried out in area V4.

The analysis of motion is similarly carried out in several stages, and provides perhaps the best example of a cortical computation. In some species, such as the rabbit and the housefly, retinal neurons are capable of detecting motion. However, in most mammals, sophisticated motion detection first arises in the cortex. Cortical neurons each receive visual inputs from small regions of space, that is, they "see" only a limited visual field. As Marr (1982) and others have pointed out, this leads to the so-called *aperture problem* (see Figure 1). If you look at a moving line through a small aperture, you can determine only the component of motion perpendicular to the line because it is impossible to tell whether the line is moving along its own axis. Each neuron faces essentially the same problem. The problem is compounded by the fact that area V1 contains several different populations of cells, but most are both orientationally and directionally selective, which means that they respond only to lines and edges whose orientation falls within a certain narrow range (e.g., within 10 degrees of vertical) and that are moving within a narrow range of directions (usually perpendicular to the preferred orientation). The only way around the aperture problem is to combine information from cells with different directional selectivities. This "neural synthesis" probably occurs in area MT (a small region of visual neocortex), as was shown in an ingenious experiment on monkey cortex by Movshon et al. (1985).

The key to Movshon's experiment is the visual stimulus presented to the monkey. The stimulus, as shown in Figure 2, consisted of two gratings (arrays of parallel, evenly spaced, lines), oriented

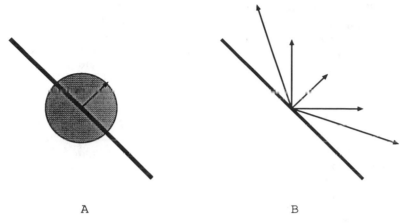

A   B

Figure 1.   Illustration of the aperture problem. (A) Cortical neurons receive inputs from spatially restricted regions of the world, depicted in the figure as the shaded circular region. If a long line is viewed as it moves through this region, only the component of motion perpendicular to the line can be detected, since motion along the line's axis is undetectable. (B) This leads to an indeterminacy in detecting the true direction of motion of the line, since all motions sharing the same perpendicular component will be treated as equal. [Adapted from Marr, 1982.]

at different angles, and each moving in a direction perpendicular to the orientation of their lines. If one draws two such gratings on transparent plastic sheets, superposes them, and moves them with

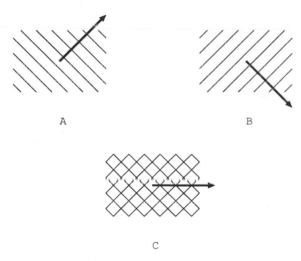

A   B

C

Figure 2.   The Movshon experiment (Movshon et al., 1985). (A) Two gratings are shown, oriented at different angles. Each grating is moved in a direction perpendicular to the orientation of its lines, as indicated by the arrow. (B) The two gratings are superposed and moved, as in (A). The resulting perception is of a checkerboard pattern moved in a third, unrelated direction (see text for details). This experiment illustrates how the cortex computes the direction of motion of an object from sets of indeterminate information (due to the aperture problem).

respect to each other, instead of two sets of moving lines, one sees what appears to be a checkerboard pattern moving in a third direction. This third direction is *not* the vector sum of the two component directions; rather, it is a more complicated function that reflects the intersection of the lines of uncertainty as specified by the constraints of the aperture problem (Movshon et al., 1985).

This stimulus was presented to alert, behaving monkeys, and the responses of neurons in areas V1 and MT were observed (V1 is the first visual neocortical area and provides input to MT). In area MT, neurons were found that responded to the direction of motion of the checkerboard. In V1, no such neurons were found; rather, neurons responded to the direction of motion of either one grating or the other. Thus, to speak somewhat broadly, V1 "sees" only the component gratings, whereas MT "sees" the checkerboard. This is a situation analogous to color vision in that a higher-level cortical area computes an object-related invariant based on variant information from a lower cortical area.

Most objects have edges arranged at different orientations. When viewing such an object as it moves, the nervous system is confronted with the constraints of the aperture problem—that is, the direction of motion of each edge is indeterminate. In order to discriminate the true direction of motion of the *object* correctly, the nervous system must be able to integrate and synthesize the analyses of each component motion. This is exactly what the Movshon experiment demonstrates is occurring in cortical area MT. Thus, the underlying neural computations are carrying out the fundamental steps for motion detection.

Several recent *models* of motion detection have been proposed that account for the Movshon experiment (see Hildreth and Koch, 1987). Most of these models use *neural networks* composed of simplified neuronlike units to carry out a series of functional processes such as comparing two inputs, one of which is temporally delayed. These models, in turn, have begun to be used as artificial vision systems for detecting motion.

In fact, most of the visual processes mentioned above have been modeled theoretically, and there has been significant interplay between modeling and experiment. As the stimuli used in physiological experiments become more complicated, and as the data base of neurobiological knowledge continues to increase rapidly, there is an ever more pressing need for models (from detailed *computer simulations* to broad conceptual frameworks) to serve as theoretical testing grounds. Indeed, one of the most exciting prospects for future research on neocortical computations is the growing synthesis of physiological, psychophysical, and modeling approaches.

REFERENCES

Finkel, L. H. (1990). A model of receptive field plasticity and topographic reorganization in somatosensory cortex. In S. J. Hanson and C. R. Olsen, eds., *Connectionist modeling and brain function: The developing interface,* pp. 164–192. Cambridge, Mass.: MIT Press.

Finkel, L. H., and Edelman, G. M. (1989). Interaction of distributed cortical systems by reentry: A computer simulation of interactive functionally segregated visual areas. *Journal of Neuroscience 9,* 3188–3208.

Hildreth, E. C., and Koch, C. (1987). The analysis of visual motion: From computational theory to neuronal mechanisms. *Annual Review of Neuroscience 10,* 477–533.

Land, E. H. (1983). Recent advances in retinex theory and some implications for cortical computations. *Proceedings of the National Academy of Sciences 80,* 5163–5169.

Livingstone, M., and Hubel, D. (1988). Segregation of form, color, movement, and depth: Anatomy, physiology, and perception. *Science 240,* 740–749.

Marr, D. (1982). *Vision: A computational investigation into the human representation and processing of visual information.* San Francisco: W. H. Freeman.

Merzenich, M., Recanzone, G., Jenkins, W. M., Allard, T. T., and Nudo, R. J. (1988). Cortical representational plasticity. In P. Rakic and W. Singer, eds., *Neurobiology of neocortex,* pp. 41–68. New York: John Wiley.

Movshon, J. A., Adelson, E. H., Grizzi, M. S., and Newsome, W. T. (1985). The analysis of moving visual patterns. In C. Chagas, R. Gattass, and C. Gross, eds., *Pattern recognition mechanisms, Experimental Brain Research Supp. 11,* 117–151.

Poggio, G. F., and Poggio, T. (1984). The analysis of stereopsis. *Annual Review of Neuroscience 7,* 379–412.

Zeki, S. M. (1980). The representation of colours in the cerebral cortex. *Nature 284,* 412–418.

Leif H. Finkel

Olfactory Cortex

The primary goal of computational neuroscience is the identification and computational characterization of functional properties of specific brain circuitry. Satisfaction of this goal has as prerequisites the specification of anatomical and physiological characteristics of neural circuits, and the integrative synthesis of these often disparate components into a coherent form. It is hoped that such analysis may provide insight into those simple circuit computations which underlie psychological and behavioral abilities. Indeed, in the absence of such bottom-up research, it is difficult to see how it is possible for psychological research alone to identify some processes as more fundamental than others. Only by careful characterization of the computational properties of basic circuits can we hope to compose an understanding of building blocks of psychological function and their interaction in more complex or cognitive processes. Recent analysis and simulation of anatomical circuitry and physiological adaptive processes in the olfactory system have revealed a way in which this system may store, organize, and retrieve memories of odors; the findings make specific predictions that have been tested, and suggest a new interpretation of how neurobiological operations may give rise to one kind of perceptual memory.

"Everyday Learning" and Long-Term Potentiation

A common form of learning that might be termed "everyday" human learning can be characterized as rapid, specific, and long-lasting; if you see a new piece of furniture or a new car only once, it can effortlessly be remembered and recognized. This kind of rapid, persistent learning contrasts with many other forms of learning that may require dozens to hundreds of trials in order to learn one or two items, as in many animal learning paradigms, and as humans learn MOTOR SKILLS such as bicycling or swimming. Until the 1970s, there were no candidate biological mechanisms that could underlie this rapid-learning ability (i.e., mechanisms that had the appropriate properties of being rapidly induced, specific, and extremely long-lasting). In 1973, Bliss and Lømo showed that brief electrical activation of synaptic connections between cells could cause a long-lasting increase in the effectiveness of those contacts: LONG-TERM POTENTIATION (LTP). A decade later, Gary Lynch and Michel Baudry (1984) put forward a candidate cascade of events that might underlie LTP, in which afferent activity at a target synapse initiated an influx of calcium into the postsynaptic spine, activating a calcium-activated protease (calpain) that caused structural changes in the cytoskeletal proteins anchoring the synaptic membrane, which in turn caused changes in glutamate receptors, making them more effective conductance conduits. The rapid onset, synapse specificity, and resulting permanent structural changes had the appropriate properties for a substrate of the type of memory under discussion. This hypothesis thus deserves consideration as a memory substrate; however, even if correct, it is difficult to see how a mechanism for changes in individual synapses could be related to behavioral memory. In the context of aggregates of neurons in networks, however, it is possible to create explanations of how many parallel changes in multiple synaptic connections could have the effect of storing and retrieving memories.

What Learning Computes in the Olfactory System

Under these guiding assumptions, mathematical models and computer simulations have been constructed based on the anatomical structure and physiological function of specific brain regions known to exhibit synaptic LTP. One such region is the primary olfactory cortex, a phylogenetically old structure that is a presumed precursor to the dominant structure in the human brain, the neocortex. A number of researchers have generated computational simulations of the olfactory system, primarily in attempts to understand how its physiological functioning might arise from its biophysical mechanisms, and how the circuitry might lead to coherent behavioral function (see, e.g., Freeman, 1975; Freeman and Skarda, 1985; Haberly, 1985; Haberly and Bower, 1989). These ongoing efforts in part raise the question of how the physiological function of the olfactory system, embedded in its anatomical architecture, might give rise to psychological or behavioral properties.

The beginnings of such a study rest first of all on the anatomical structure of the system. The olfactory cortex receives its primary afferent input from peripheral structures termed the olfactory bulbs, which are innervated directly by chemically activated receptor cells in the nasal epithelium. This entire system of brain structures and its target structures (entorhinal cortex and hippocampus) have been found to operate in tightly synchronous fashion during learning (Macrides, 1975; Macrides et al., 1982); moreover, the synchronous activity is time-locked to the behavioral sniffing activity of the animal, occurring about four to eight times per second. That is, with each inhalation or sniff, the entire set of olfactory-hippocampal brain structures exhibits a cascade of activity from the periphery inward. Computer simulation of the neuronal activity emerging from this synchronous behavior showed that, with synaptic enhancement via LTP, specific cortical target cells that initially responded to a particular odor would become increasingly responsive not only to that odor but also to a range of similar odors. This had the effect of clustering odors into groups based on their similarity: After LTP, cortical neuron responses corresponded to membership in such a group or cluster. For instance, if the network model was presented with patterns of input cell activity designed to correspond to a set of simulated floral odors, then after LTP, the olfactory cortical model would give a characteristic response to any floral odor, and would give different characteristic responses to members of other olfactory categories (e.g., smoky odors, meat odors, musk odors). Thus a given cortical response would convey information about what category an odor was in, without any more specific information (Granger et al., 1989).

Cortical neurons emit axons that flow back to their input structure, the olfactory bulb, and act to selectively inhibit the most active inputs in the bulb. This inhibitory corticobulbar feedback suppresses what was the predominant bulb input to cortex, thereby unmasking the remainder of the bulb's activity. This remainder becomes the next input to the cortx, and the same operations as before are performed. Thus, following the clustering response described above, the next cycle of activity is based on the bulb remainder response, which amplifies the differences among members of the category. For instance, after the first cycle of olfactory activity identifies an odor as floral, the shared chemical component of floral odors, which makes them floral, is inhibited by the inhibitory feedback from cortex to bulb. Inhibition of that primary component unmasks the odor components that are responsible for the differences among floral odors. These differences are then input to the cortex and give rise to subcategories of floral odors. Thus it is suggested that repeated cyclings of the olfactory cortex and bulb successively cluster and subcluster odors into categories and subcategories.

This successive subclustering activity turns out to be mathematically characterizable as a novel algorithm for the well-studied statistical task of hierarchical clustering, and in fact proves to be a more efficient mechanism for clustering than most of those in the (extensive) literature on such methods (Ambros-Ingerson et al., 1990). This unexpected finding gives hope to the idea that the computational functioning of brain circuitry may yield novel circuit designs with properties camparable with or even superior to those developed by engineers.

Implications for Perceptual Memory

Perhaps more important, these findings enable the formulation of hypotheses about fundamental psychological function. Once the function of a basic brain circuit is formally characterized, it can be strongly suggested that that functionality is a basic building block of mental operation, since it emerges directly from simple brain circuit functioning. Such elemental operations presumably act in combination to yield more complex psychological processes, in ways not yet understood. In the particular case at hand, the sequence of cortical responses to a stimulus yields successively finer-grained information about the stimulus, suggesting a purpose for repetitive perceptual sampling. Why is it that we "take a second glance"? What do we

glean from our second look that was lacking in the first? Visual, auditory, and somatosensory (touch) cortex have anatomical architectures containing arrangements strongly analogous to that in the olfactory system; in particular, the excitatory feedforward and inhibitory feedback pathways, and many specific elements of the arrangement and operation of the constituent networks, can be found in these other sensory cortical systems (see, e.g., Herkenham, 1986, for a review). The modeling work described here can thus be elaborated to make the specific suggestion that repeated perceptual samples may act to give coarse-grained category information at first glance, followed by increasingly more specific information on subsequent glances. In fact, human subjects in perceptual and conceptual studies robustly recognize objects first at categorical levels and subsequently at successively subordinate levels (Rosch and Lloyd, 1978), suggesting the presence of structured memories that are organized and searched hierarchically during recognition. The hypotheses arising from the computational neural circuit studies described here suggest that this prevalent effect may be due to fundamental operations of cortical circuitry, raising the possibility that this biologically generated mechanism for hierarchical clustering may be a routine part of perceptual recognition memory behavior in animals and humans.

REFERENCES

Ambros-Ingerson, J., Granger, R., and Lynch, G. (1990). Simulation of paleocortex performs hierarchical clustering. *Science 247,* 1344–1348.

Bliss, T. V. P., and Lømo, T. (1973). Long-lasting potentiation of synaptic transmission in the dentate area of the anesthetized rabbit following stimulation of the perforant path. *Journal of Physiology 232,* 331–356.

Freeman, W. (1975). *Mass action in the nervous system.* New York: Academic Press.

Freeman, W., and Skarda, C. (1985). Spatial EEG patterns, non-linear dynamics and perception: The neo-Sherringtonian view. *Brain Research Reviews 10,* 147–175.

Granger, R., Ambros-Ingerson, J., and Lynch, G. (1989). Derivation of encoding characteristics of layer II cerebral cortex. *Journal of Cognitive Neuroscience 1,* 61–87.

Haberly, L. (1985). Neuronal circuitry in olfactory cortex: Anatomy and functional implications. *Chemical Senses 10,* 219–238.

Haberly, L., and Bower, J. (1989). Olfactory cortex:

Model circuit for study of associative memory? *Trends in Neuroscience 17,* 258–264.

Herkenham, M. (1986). New perspectives on the organization and evolution of nonspecific thalamocortical projections. In E. Jones and A. Peters, eds., *Cerebral cortex,* vol. 5. New York: Plenum Press.

Lynch, G. (1986). *Synapses, circuits and the beginnings of memory.* Cambridge, Mass.: MIT Press.

Lynch, G., and Baudry, M. (1984). The biochemistry of memory: A new and specific hypothesis. *Science 224,* 1057–1063.

Macrides, F. (1975). Temporal relations between hippocampal slow waves and exploratory sniffing in hamsters. *Behavioral Biology 14,* 295–308.

Macrides, F., Eichenbaum, H. B., and Forbes, W. B. (1982). Temporal relationship between sniffing and the limbic (theta) rhythm during odor discrimination reversal learning. *Journal of Neuroscience 2,* 1705–1717.

Rosch, E., and Lloyd, B. B. (1978). *Cognition and categorization.* Hillsdale, N.J.: Erlbaum.

Richard Granger
Gary Lynch

NEURAL SUBSTRATES OF CLASSICAL CONDITIONING

[*Classical conditioning, a type of learning first investigated by Ivan* PAVLOV, *is described in the article* CONDITIONING, CLASSICAL AND INSTRUMENTAL. *The following composite article concerns what is known about the physical mechanisms that make Pavlovian learning possible. This article consists of the following sections:*

Cardiovascular Responses
Discrete Behavioral Responses
Fear-Potentiated Startle]

Cardiovascular Responses

Learning is a relatively permanent change in behavior due to experience, and this change results from experience-induced structural changes in the brain. For example, during Pavlovian aversive learning an organism learns that an auditory or visual stimulus (the conditioned stimulus, CS) which repeatedly precedes an electric shock (the unconditioned stimulus, UCS) predicts the occurrence of the shock. This learned association is reflected in a variety of adaptive cardiovascular responses that develop to the CS and are a specific consequence of the associative relationship between the CS and UCS. Guiding the search for the structural changes of Pavlovian learning is the assumption that if an association is to be made between the CS and the UCS, information concerning both must converge at a common brain structure or structures. It is this convergence that results in structural changes.

Researchers have used learned cardiovascular responses, particularly changes in heart rate in response to the CS during Pavlovian learning, as model responses to assess learning and to identify the brain regions where structural changes responsible for learning occur. The use of heart rate responses is particularly advantageous because the locations of the motor neurons that produce these responses are known. Consequently, central brain structures that activate these neurons leading to response expression can be identified. This identification, along with that of the pathways by which CS and UCS information converges upon these structures, exposes an entire circuit which contributes to learning. This then sets the stage for determining the specific location(s) and nature of the structural changes.

Learned Heart Rate Acceleration in the Pigeon: A Model to Assess the Neural Substrates of Learning

David Cohen and his associates (Cohen, 1984) have used this approach to identify such a circuit using learned heart rate acceleration (tachycardia) in the pigeon. This response develops to a visual CS that repeatedly precedes a footshock UCS. At the motor end of the circuit, the motor neurons that produced the response were identified. Recordings from these neurons revealed that the expression of the response could be attributed to changes in their activity. At the sensory end of the circuit, three pathways were identified that transmitted information about the visual CS from the retina to more central structures. Damage within all three was required to block the development of the learned response, suggesting that each was sufficient for learning to occur.

Cohen also identified several central structures interposed between sensory pathways and motor neurons that contribute to the development of the learned tachycardiac response. Most notable were the avian homologues of the mammalian visual cortex, amygdala, and medial hypothalamus. Destruction of each blocked the development of the learned response, and electrical stimulation of the latter two produced tachycardia, suggesting that when active, they exert a direct influence on the motor neurons.

Having identified some essential components of a circuit required for learning, Cohen and associates then sought to identify the site(s) of convergence of CS and UCS information. Their research suggested that sites of convergence are located along the CS pathways and that the avian equivalent of the mammalian lateral geniculate nucleus (LGNe) was one of these sites (Gibbs et al., 1986). It receives information about the CS directly from the retina and information about the UCS from the locus coeruleus (LC), a structure located in the brainstem. Indeed, the activity of LGNe neurons was altered by the CS and UCS, and their activity to the CS increased over repeated pairings of the CS and UCS with a time course similar to the development of the learned tachycardiac response. A similar increase also was observed when electrical stimulation of the LC was substituted for the UCS. The LGNe, therefore, is a site where changes in neuronal activity develop during learning, but changes in cellular structure responsible for the development of these activity changes have yet to be determined. Finally, central structures lying beyond traditional sensory structures (e.g., the amygdala and hypothalamus) of the circuit also may be sites of structural changes that form the substrate for learning. Although not investigated in the pigeon, research using mammals, as described below, suggests that such central structures are potential sites of structural change.

Learned Heart Rate Deceleration in the Rabbit: A Model to Assess the Neural Substrates of Learning in the Mammalian Brain

Heart rate slowing (bradycardia) in the rabbit during Pavlovian learning has been widely used to assess learning and its neural substrates in the mammalian brain (Schneiderman et al., 1987; Pascoe et al., 1991). Much of this research also has been devoted to identifying the components of the circuit that contributes to learning as reflected by this response. The motor neurons that produce

the response are located in the medulla, and their axons travel to the heart via the vagus nerves.

Pathways Transmitting CS Information

Investigations using this response generally have used auditory CSs that precede an electric shock UCS. The peripheral components of the CS pathway have not been investigated in the rabbit, but they most likely involve traditional auditory pathways. Indeed, research using an auditory CS in the rat during Pavlovian aversive learning has demonstrated that destruction of the inferior colliculus, a structure relaying auditory information from the most peripheral structures of the auditory system, blocks the expression of several learned responses (LeDoux et al., 1984).

The inferior colliculus projects to the medial geniculate nucleus, and lesions of its magnocellular component (MGm) produce deficits in the acquisition of the learned bradycardiac response in the rabbit (Schneiderman et al., 1988). Destruction of the auditory cortex, which receives projections from the MGm, does not interfere with the initial acquisition of the learned response (Teich et al., 1988). This suggests that the auditory cortex is not necessary for learning the relationship between the CS and the UCS, and that structures other than auditory cortex, but receiving MGm projections, may be essential components of the circuit (see also NEURAL SUBSTRATES OF EMOTIONAL MEMORY).

Central Structures Involved in Learned Bradycardia

One central structure recipient of projections from the MGm is the amygdala (LeDoux et al., 1990), and the contribution of its central nucleus (ACe) to learned bradycardia in the rabbit has been extensively investigated (Kapp et al., 1991). This nucleus receives input from the lateral amygdaloid nucleus, which in turn receives projections from the MGm. The ACe projects directly to the region of cardiodecelerative motor neurons within the medulla, and electrical stimulation of the ACe elicits vagal bradycardia and excitation of these neurons. Hence, the ACe is located between the CS pathway and the motor neurons that produce the response. Interference with its normal functioning markedly attenuates the learned response. Further, the activity of its neurons in response to the CS changes over repeated CS-UCS pairings; and for some neurons, the greater the neuron's excitatory response to the CS, the greater the conditioned bradycardiac response. These combined observations suggest that the ACe excites motor neurons leading to response expression.

While the ACe may be a critical structure within the circuit, other structures, including the cerebellar vermis and medial prefrontal cortex, also appear to be important (Supple et al., 1989; Gibbs and Powell, 1988). Lesions of either produce a marked attenuation of the response, and the activity of neurons to the CS in each region changes as a function of repeated CS-UCS pairings. As with the ACe, in each region it was found that increased neuronal responses to the CS were predictive of greater magnitudes of the bradycardiac response. Both regions are anatomically associated with the amygdala: the medial prefrontal cortex via a direct pathway, and the vermis via an indirect one. These three interconnected regions appear to be essential structures for the learning of the relationship be-

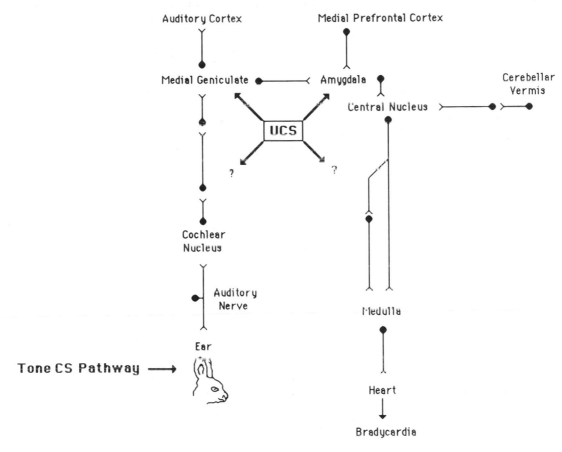

Figure 1. A schematic diagram of the components of the putative neural circuit mediating learned bradycardia in the rabbit. The left side shows auditory structures that carry information about the tone CS. Components are believed to include primary auditory relay nuclei from the ear to the medial geniculate nucleus. CS information diverges from the primary auditory pathway at the level of the medial geniculate and is carried to the amygdala. From the amygdala, the central nucleus exerts both direct and indirect influences on motor neurons in the medulla that decrease heart rate when activated. The cerebellar vermis and medial prefrontal cortex, both important in learned bradycardia, may influence the central nucleus through indirect routes. Evidence also suggests that information about the UCS may access the medial geniculate, amygdala, prefrontal cortex, cerebellar vermis, and perhaps other structures of the circuit. However, the pathways that transmit UCS information have not been extensively investigated. Nevertheless, there are multiple sites of CS and UCS convergence within the circuit, suggesting multiple potential sites of structural change.

tween the CS and UCS in the rabbit, as reflected in learned bradycardia (see Figure 1).

Where does the convergence of CS and UCS information, necessary for the structural changes responsible for learning, occur within the components of this circuit? The research to date suggests that multiple components may represent sites of structural change. On the sensory side, neurons within the MGm are responsive to both the CS and the UCS and, like more central structures, neuronal activity changes as a function of repeated CS-UCS pairings (Supple and Kapp, 1989). Likewise, neurons in the ACe, cerebellar vermis, and medial prefrontal cortex are responsive to the UCS, although the pathways by which the UCS is transmitted to these structures have not been extensively analyzed. The evidence therefore suggests that structural changes may occur at multiple sites along the critical circuit.

Conclusion

Research using avian and mammalian models of Pavlovian learning has led to an identification of major components of brain circuits critical to the formation of associations as reflected in learned changes in heart rate. This analysis has led to an identification of potential sites where structural changes forming the substrate for learning occur, setting the stage for future analyses aimed at identifying the exact nature of these changes.

REFERENCES

Cohen, D. H. (1984). Identification of vertebrate neurons modified during learning: An analysis of sensory pathways. In D. L. Alkon and J. Farley, eds., *Primary neural substrates of learning and behavioral change*, pp. 129–154. Cambridge: Cambridge University Press.

Gibbs, C. M., Cohen, D. H., and Broyles, J. L. (1986). Modification of the discharge of lateral geniculate neurons during visual learning. *Journal of Neuroscience 6*, 627–636.

Gibbs, C. M., and Powell, D. A. (1988). Neuronal correlates of classically conditioned bradycardia in the rabbit: Studies of the medial prefrontal cortex. *Brain Research 442*, 86–96.

Kapp, B. S., Markgraf, C. G., Wilson, A., Pascoe, J. P., and Supple, W. F. (1991). Contributions of the amygdala and anatomically-related structures to the acquisition and expression of aversively conditioned responses. In L. Dachowski and C. F. Flaherty, eds., *Current topics in animal learning: Brain, emotion and cognition*, pp. 311–346. Hillsdale, N.J.: Erlbaum.

LeDoux, J. E., Farb, C., and Ruggiero, D. A. (1990). Topographic organization of neurons in the acoustic thalamus that project to the amygdala. *Journal of Neuroscience 10*, 1043–1054.

LeDoux, J. E., Sakaguchi, A., and Reis, D. J. (1984). Subcortical efferent projections of the medial geniculate nucleus mediate emotional responses conditioned to acoustic stimuli. *Journal of Neuroscience 4*, 683–698.

Pascoe, J. P., Supple, W. F., and Kapp, B. S. (1991). Learning and memory: Vertebrate models. In J. L. Martinez and R. P. Kesner, eds., *Learning and memory: A biological view*. New York: Academic Press.

Schneiderman, N., Markgraf, C. G., McCabe, P. M., Liskowsky, D. R., and Winters, R. W. (1988). Ibotenic acid lesions in the magnocellular medial geniculate nucleus prevent the acquisition of classically conditioned bradycardia to single tones in rabbits. *Neuroscience Abstracts 14*, 784.

Schneiderman, N., McCabe, P. M., Haselton, J. R., Ellenberger, H. H., Jarrell, T. W., and Gentile, C. G. (1987). Neurobiological bases of conditioned bradycardia in rabbits. In I. Gormezano, W. F. Prokasy, and R. F. Thompson, eds., *Classical conditioning*, pp. 37–63. Hillsdale, N.J.: Erlbaum.

Supple, W. F., Archer, L., and Kapp, B. S. (1989). Lesions of the cerebellar vermis severely impair acquisition of Pavlovian conditioned bradycardic responses in the rabbit. *Neuroscience Abstracts 15*, 640.

Supple, W. F., and Kapp, B. S. (1989). Response characteristics of neurons in the medial component of the medial geniculate nucleus during Pavlovian differential fear conditioning in rabbits. *Behavioral Neuroscience 103*, 1276–1286.

Teich, A. H., McCabe, P. M., Gentile, C. G., Jarrell, T. W., Winters, R. W., Liskowsky, D. R., and Schneiderman, N. (1988). Role of auditory cortex in the acquisition of differential heart rate conditioning. *Physiology and Behavior 44*, 405–412.

Bruce S. Kapp
William F. Supple

Discrete Behavioral Responses

Over the years, a large proportion of research concerned with how the brain codes and interacts with behavior has included studies of the neural bases of learning and memory. Much of the progress in this research area has been made by physiological psychologists, neurophysiologists, neuroanatomists, and neuropsychologists who have used a variety of experimental techniques to provide an interdisciplinary study of brain processes involved in learning and memory.

One particular research strategy that has been

successful in generating data about learning-related phenomena in the nervous system is the use of simple mammalian models (see Kapp and Pascoe, 1986). Use of the model systems approach assumes that complex learning and memory phenomena associated with human behavior can eventually be understood by first studying neural processes associated with simple learning and memory tasks in nonhumans. In essence, the manner in which the brain codes learning and memory events is assumed to be less complex when simple learning tasks are presented than when relatively complex paradigms are used. This reduction in task complexity has made it possible to begin an analysis of brain pathways and structures involved in learning and memory processes.

A simple learning paradigm that has generated a great deal of data concerning brain substrates of learning is classical conditioning of discrete behavioral responses. Classical conditioning involves presenting a conditioned stimulus (the CS) just before a second stimulus called an unconditioned stimulus (the US). Before training, the CS typically elicits no overt response while the US reliably elicits a discrete, reflexive response called the unconditioned response (UR). After a number of CS-US pairings, however, the animal begins to execute the discrete response after presentation of the CS but before presentation of the US. This learned, anticipatory response is called the conditioned response (CR). Over the years, this simple learning paradigm, and variations of it, have been used to investigate the neural substrates of learning and memory. Three examples of the use of classical conditioning will be presented here: conditioned eyeblink in the cat, forelimb flexion conditioning in the cat, and nictitating membrane/eyeblink conditioning in the rabbit.

Conditioned Eyeblink in the Cat

Woody and associates performed an extensive series of studies aimed at delineating the brain correlates of a short-latency eyeblink conditioning task in cats (see Woody, 1988). These experiments normally involved pairing a tone CS with a glabellar tap US (i.e., a light tap to the forehead). Before training, the tone produced no overt response while the glabellar tap produced an eyeblink and sometimes a nose twitch. After three–six sessions of paired CS-US presentations, eyeblink CRs were consistently elicited by the tone CS. Woody and

associates have used this paradigm to define brain pathways involved in the learning of this discrete response and also to delineate cellular processes that are ongoing in structures involved in processing the CS and US.

Studies showed that the glabellar tap US caused the eyeblink UR via a direct brain-stem reflexive circuit involving the facial nucleus. Other studies showed that the tone CS activated the coronal pericruciate cortex, a rostral region of the cerebral cortex involved in motor control. The pericruciate area outputs to the facial nucleus in the brain stem, which activates the musculature responsible for the eyeblink CR. Woody's research group recorded activity from the pericruciate cortex before and after conditioning. Many neurons discharged when the auditory CS was presented. In addition, conditioning caused an increase in the activity of a specific subpopulation of pericruciate cells that sent output to neurons in the facial nucleus (i.e., neurons that generated the eyeblink CR). Analysis of unit activity in the facial nucleus demonstrated changes in neuronal excitability as a result of training as well as short-term changes after unpaired presentations of the CS and US. Lesions of the cerebral cortex provided additional evidence for its role in this conditioning paradigm. Reversible lesions involving the rostral cortex suppressed the CR but not the UR, while more extensive lesions encompassing caudal cortical areas impaired only acquisition of the CR. Finally, using microstimulation and intracellular recording techniques, Woody and associates provided evidence that conditioning produced long-lasting alterations in the membrane resistance of cortical cells, thereby affecting the flow of critical ions that contribute to altering the excitability of cortical neurons. These studies have provided interesting information about cellular and molecular events that may be associated with learning-related changes in cortical neurons.

Forelimb Flexion Conditioning in the Cat

A modification of a simple forelimb conditioning preparation has been used to study the role of the red nucleus, a midbrain region, in simple motor learning (see Murakami, Oda, and Tsukahara, 1988). A classically conditioned forelimb flexion response can be established in cats by pairing a tone CS with a shock US delivered to the forelimb. Instead of presenting a tone CS, Tsukahara and colleagues used electrical stimulation of a bundle of nerve fibers that connects the cerebral cortex with the red nucleus as a CS and a mild forelimb shock as a US. Before CS-US pairing, the corticorubral tract stimulation produced no forelimb flexion. However, after seven–ten days of paired training, a forelimb flexion CR was elicited by presentation of the corticorubral tract stimulation CS. Tsukahara and associates have used this paradigm to examine learning-related electrophysiological and structural changes at synapses located within the red nucleus. First, recording activity of red nucleus cells revealed training-related increases in firing rates in trained cats but not in untrained cats. Second, using histological methods, Tsukahara's group measured the diameters of dendrites of red nucleus neurons that received input from the axons of corticorubral neurons stimulated as a CS. Compared with untrained cats, the conditioned cats showed a larger proportion of axonal endings that synapsed on large-diameter dendrites. Because the diameters of dendrites of red nucleus cells decrease as the distance from the cell body increases, it was suggested that new synapses formed in the trained cats on the regions of the dendrites closest to the neuron's cell body. These results provide some evidence that, for at least this classical conditioning procedure, the sprouting of new synaptic contacts may be involved in the acquisition of conditioned responding seen with CS-US pairings.

Nictitating Membrane/Eyelid Conditioning in the Rabbit

In the early 1960s, Gormezano developed a classical conditioning preparation in rabbits that has proven valuable for the study of the neural bases of conditioning (see Gormezano, Kehoe, and Marshall, 1983). During simple classical delay conditioning, a tone or light CS is paired with a shock or air puff US. The CS initially causes no movement, while the US elicits movement of the nictitating membrane (the NM, a third eyelid found in some species) and closure of the outer eyelids. After 100–150 of these pairings, an NM or eyelid movement is elicited by the CS even on trials when the air puff or shock US is not presented. Because many of the parametric features of this behavioral paradigm have been well-documented by Gormezano and associates, it has been adopted by a number of laboratories for use as a model system for the study of the neural substrates of learning (see

Thompson, 1986; Thompson and Steinmetz, 1991).

Data from a variety of animal preparations as well as the human amnesia literature suggested that the hippocampus, a limbic system structure (see GUIDE TO THE ANATOMY OF THE BRAIN), was involved in coding learning and memory. Because of these observations, attempts were first made by Thompson and associates to assess hippocampal involvement in classical NM conditioning. Recordings from the hippocampus revealed neurons that altered their firing patterns during paired but not unpaired presentations of the CS and US. Even before CRs were observed, neurons in the hippocampus began discharging in a pattern that preceded and "modeled" the amplitude and time course of the learned behavioral response (i.e., the unit activity looked as if it could be producing the behavioral response). However, lesions of the hippocampus failed to abolish learning or retention of the simple motor response even when the lesions included all of the neocortex as well as the hippocampus. These data indicated that the hippocampus was probably involved in coding the classically conditioned NM response, but that it was not essential for producing CRs. More recent data suggest that in addition to possibly modulating the conditioning process during simple delay conditioning, an intact hippocampus may be necessary for more complex classical conditioning preparations like trace conditioning and discrimination-reversal conditioning.

One brain region that Thompson and associates have identified as essential for classical conditioning is the interpositus nucleus of the cerebellum. The cerebellum is a structure that is intricately involved in motor control. Recordings from the interpositus nucleus as well as portions of cerebellar cortex revealed populations of neurons that formed amplitude-time course models of the CR during paired CS-US presentations. Furthermore, electrolytic or chemical lesions of the interpositus nucleus (as small as 1 cubic millimeter) permanently abolished CRs in trained rabbits. Cerebellar lesions before training prevented the formation of CRs. The interpositus is known to output to the red nucleus, which in turn sends projections to brain-stem nuclei that control the musculature involved in generating NM movements and eyelid closure. Using brain stimulation, recording, and lesion methods, possible pathways involved in projecting the CS and US to the cerebellum have been delineated. It appears that an acoustic CS may be projected to a number of primary brain-stem auditory nuclei that, in turn, relay parallel projections to lateral regions of the pontine nuclei. Cells in the lateral pontine nuclear regions may then project axons to the cerebellum. The air puff US appears to be projected from the cornea of the eye to the trigeminal nucleus in the brain stem to the inferior olivary complex (also in the brain stem). Cells in the inferior olive then appear to send axons to regions of the cerebellum. If neuronal plasticity is indeed established in the cerebellum, it is reasonable to assume that it is established in cerebellar regions that receive convergent CS and US input and then relayed to brain-stem nuclei responsible for generating the motor response. Sites in the interpositus nucleus and discrete regions of the cerebellar cortex are candidates for this convergent input and are currently being investigated. Figure 1 shows a schematic diagram of neural circuitry hypothesized to be involved in classical eyelid conditioning.

Use of the rabbit classical NM conditioning para-digm has produced a wealth of data concerning the neural substrates of a simple form of motor learning. The careful control over stimulus presentation and response elicitation that is afforded by this learning preparation has allowed critical stimulus pathways and potential regions of stimulus convergence to be analyzed, thus advancing the study of the cellular bases of this form of learning.

Conclusions

Presented here are three different model systems that have been used to investigate the neural substrates of classical conditioning of discrete behavioral responses. These preparations have provided basic data concerning how the brain codes learning, including cellular and molecular mechanisms involved in establishing plasticity in cortical cells, anatomical changes seen in midbrain cells as a

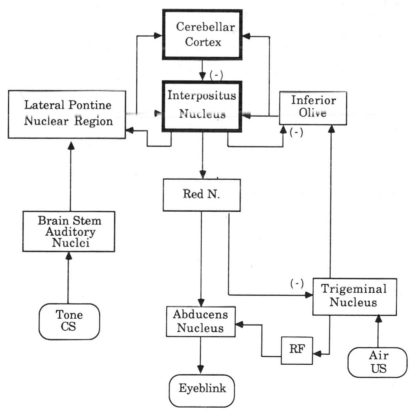

Figure 1. A schematic diagram depicting brain regions and circuitry proposed to be involved in classical eyelid conditioning. The (-) depicts synapses where inhibition occurs. All other synapses are thought to be excitatory. Note the proposed convergence of CS- and US-related information in the cerebellum. (CS, conditioned stimulus; US, unconditioned stimulus; N, nucleus; RF, reticular formation.)

result of conditioning, and the definition and analysis of essential circuits for classical conditioning that include brain-stem and cerebellar structures. Future work in this area will likely be in two directions: (1) further delineation of essential cellular processes that actually code the conditioning process (e.g., possible mechanisms in the cerebellum and brain stem that account for the conditioning) and (2) studies aimed at delineating the interactions that occur between higher (e.g., cerebral cortex) and lower (e.g., brain stem and cerebellum) brain areas during classical conditioning. Together, these approaches should provide interesting data about how the brain codes simple learning tasks like classical conditioning of discrete responses.

REFERENCES

Dudai, Y. (1989). *The neurobiology of memory.* New York: Oxford University Press.

Gormezano, I., Kehoe, E. J., and Marshall, B. S. (1983). Twenty years of classical conditioning research with the rabbit. In J. M. Sprague and A. N. Epstein, eds., *Progress in physiological psychology,* vol. 10, pp. 197–275. New York: Academic Press.

Gormezano, I., Prokasy, W. F., and Thompson, R. F. (1987). *Classical conditioning,* 3rd ed. Hillsdale, N.J.: Lawrence Erlbaum Associates.

Kapp, B. S., and Pascoe, J. P. (1986). Memory: Vertebrate model systems. In J. L. Martinez and R. P. Kesner, eds., *Learning and memory: A biological view,* pp. 299–340. New York: Academic Press.

Murakami, F., Oda, Y., and Tsukahara, N. (1988). Sprouting as a basis for classical conditioning in the cat. In C. D. Woody, D. L. Alkon, and J. L. McGaugh, eds., *Cellular mechanisms of conditioning and behavioral plasticity,* pp. 21–26. New York: Plenum Press.

Squire, L. R. (1987). *Memory and brain.* New York: Oxford University Press.

Thompson, R. F. (1986). The neurobiology of learning and memory. *Science, 233,* 941–947.

Thompson, R. F., and Steinmetz, J. E. (1991). Brain substrates of aversive classical conditioning. In J. M. Madden IV, ed., *Adaptation, learning and affect.* New York: Raven Press.

Woody, C. D. (1988). Is conditioning supported by modulation of an outward current in pyramidal cells of the motor cortex of cats? In C. D. Woody, D. L. Alkon, and J. L. McGaugh, eds., *Cellular mechanisms of conditioning and behavioral plasticity,* pp. 27–35. New York: Plenum Press.

Joseph E. Steinmetz

Fear-Potentiated Startle

When a stimulus, such as a light, that does not produce much of a behavioral effect before pairing, is paired with an aversive stimulus such as a foot-shock, the light (conditioned stimulus) can elicit a constellation of behaviors that are typically used to define a state of fear in animals. These include changes in the autonomic system, freezing, and an increase in the amplitude of the startle reflex elicited by an auditory stimulus in the presence of the light (Brown, Kalish, and Farber, 1951). This increased amplitude of startle has been termed the "fear-potentiated startle effect" and can occur with either an auditory or a visual conditioned stimulus under conditions where startle is elicited by either a loud sound or an air puff (cf. Davis, 1986). Fear-potentiated startle is a valid measure of classical conditioning because it occurs only following paired, rather than unpaired or "random," presentations of the conditioned stimulus (Davis and Astrachan, 1978). Potentiated startle shows considerable temporal specificity because its magnitude in testing is greatest at the interval after light onset that matches the light-shock interval in training (Davis, Schlesinger, and Sorenson, 1989). This paradigm offers a number of advantages as an alternative to most animal tests of fear or anxiety because it involves no operant and is reflected by an enhancement rather than a suppression of ongoing behavior. In fact, various drugs that reduce fear or anxiety in humans decrease the expression of potentiated startle in rats. Drugs like clonidine, morphine, diazepam, and buspirone, which differ considerably in their mechanism of action, all block potentiated startle. Conversely, drugs like yohimbine, piperoxane, and B-carbolines, which induce anxiety in normal people and exaggerate it in anxious people, increase the magnitude of potentiated startle in rats.

Neural Systems Involved in Fear-Potentiated Startle

A major advantage of the potentiated startle paradigm is that fear is measured by a change in a simple reflex. Hence, with potentiated startle, fear is expressed through some neural pathway(s) activated by the conditioned stimulus and ultimately impinges on the startle circuit. Figure 1 shows a schematic summary diagram of the convergence of the neural pathways we believe are required for fear-potentiated startle.

The Acoustic Startle Pathway

In the rat, the latency of acoustic startle is 6 milliseconds recorded electromyographically in the foreleg and 8 milliseconds in the hind leg (Ison et al., 1973). This very short latency indicates that only a few synapses can be involved in mediating acoustic startle. Using a variety of techniques (Davis et al., 1982; Cassella and Davis, 1986), we have shown that acoustic startle may be mediated by a pathway which includes the ventral cochlear nucleus; an area just medial to the ventral nucleus of the lateral lemniscus; an area just dorsal to the superior olives in the nucleus reticularis pontis caudalis; and motoneurons in the spinal cord. Bilateral lesions of these nuclei eliminate startle, whereas lesions in a variety of other auditory or motor areas do not. Startle-like responses can be elicited electrically from each of these nuclei, with progressively shorter latencies as the electrode is moved down the pathway.

Determining the Point in the Startle Pathway Where Conditioned Fear Alters Neural Transmission

By eliciting startle-like responses electrically from various points along the startle pathway in the presence and absence of a light previously paired with a shock, we have concluded that fear ultimately alters transmission at the nucleus reticularis pontis caudalis (Berg and Davis, 1985). Injection of retrograde tracers into this part of the startle pathway indicates that it receives direct projections from the central nucleus of the amygdala, an area of the brain long implicated in fear.

Lesions of the Amygdala Block Fear-Potentiated Startle

Lesions of the central nucleus of the amygdala following fear conditioning completely eliminate potentiated startle (Hitchcock and Davis, 1986). In contrast, lesions of a variety of other brain areas, including the frontal cortex, insular cortex, visual cortex, hippocampus, septal nuclei, superior colliculus, red nucleus, and cerebellum, do not. Low-level electrical stimulation of the amygdala markedly increases acoustic startle amplitude at stimulus currents and durations that do not produce any other signs of behavioral activation (Rosen and Davis, 1988a). By varying the interval between the onset of amygdala stimulation and the onset of the startle-eliciting stimulus, we have estimated that the transit time from the amygdala to the startle circuit is 4–5 milliseconds (Rosen and Davis, 1988b). This very rapid effect is consistent with a direct neural pathway from the amygdala to the startle circuit and indicates that the increase in startle is not secondary to autonomic or hormonal changes that might be produced by amygdala stimulation, which would have a much longer latency.

The Role of Different Amygdala Efferent Projections in Fear-Potentiated Startle

The pathway between the central nucleus of the amygdala and the part of the nucleus reticularis pontis caudalis critical for startle involves the caudal division of the ventral amygdalofugal pathway, which also sends collaterals to many brain-stem target areas involved in the somatic and autonomic symptoms of fear and anxiety (cf. Davis et al., 1987). Lesions at a variety of levels along this pathway completely block potentiated startle. In contrast, lesions of other major projections from the central nucleus of the amygdala do not.

Possible Convergence of Light and Shock at the Amygdala

Figure 1 shows the possible visual pathway that may carry visual information to the amygdala, thus allowing a visual conditioned stimulus to elevate startle. Although we are still unclear about the details of this pathway, we believe it involves a connection between the ventral lateral geniculate nucleus and the perirhinal cortex, which projects to the lateral and basolateral nuclei within the amygdala, which in turn project to the central nucleus. Lesions of each of these areas, but not other visual areas, block potentiated startle. In addition, footshock is known to elevate startle, and lesions of the amygdala or the pathway connecting the amygdala to the startle circuit block this effect (Hitchcock, Sananes, and Davis, 1989). Activation of the amygdala by footshock may be important for fear conditioning, and the amygdala may be the point of convergence of light and shock, and therefore a critical site of neural plasticity involved in fear conditioning. In fact, local infusion of

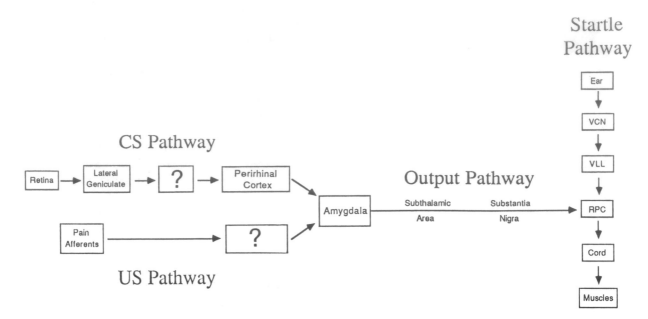

Figure 1.   Convergence of the neural pathways required for fear-potentiated startle.

n-methyl-*d*-aspartate (NMDA) antagonists into the amygdala blocks the acquisition but not the expression of fear-potentiated startle (Miserendino et al., 1990). Because these drugs block the formation of long-term potentiation, an activity-dependent modification of synaptic transmission that may be involved in memory, it is conceivable that an NMDA-sensitive form of long-term potentiation in the amygdala mediates fear conditioning.

Conclusions

The fear-potentiated startle paradigm has been useful for elucidating neural substrates of fear and anxiety. Conditioned fear appears to result when a formerly neutral stimulus comes to activate the amygdala after being paired with an aversive stimulus. Activation of the central nucleus of the amygdala increases startle via a direct connection between the amygdala and the startle pathway. More generally, the central nucleus of the amygdala and its efferent projections to the brain stem may constitute a central fear system that produces a constellation of behaviors used to define fear in animals and observed during a state of anxiety in people. Finally, the acquisition of conditioned fear may involve an NMDA-dependent process at the level of the amygdala.

REFERENCES

Berg, W. K., and Davis, M. (1985). Associative learning modifies startle at the lateral lemniscus. *Behavioral Neuroscience 99*, 191–199.

Brown, J. S., Kalish, H. I., and Farber, I. E. (1951). Conditioned fear as revealed by magnitude of startle response to an auditory stimulus. *Journal of Experimental Psychology 41*, 317–328.

Cassella, J. V., and Davis, M. (1986). Neural structures mediating acoustic and tactile startle reflexes and the acoustically-elicited pinna response in rats: Electrolytic and ibotenic acid studies. *Society for Neuroscience Abstracts 12*, 1273.

Davis, M. (1986). Pharmacological and anatomical analysis of fear conditioning using the fear-potentiated startle paradigm. *Behavioral Neuroscience 100*, 814–824.

Davis, M., and Astrachan, D. I. (1978). Conditioned fear and startle magnitude: Effects of different footshock or backshock intensities used in training. *Journal of Experimental Psychology: Animal Behavior Processes 4*, 95–103.

Davis, M., Gendelman, D. S., Tischler, M. D., and Gendelman, P. M. (1982). A primary acoustic startle circuit: Lesions and stimulation studies. *Journal of Neuroscience 6*, 791–805.

Davis, M., Hitchcock, J. M., and Rosen, J. B. (1987). Anxiety and the amygdala: Pharmacological and anatomical analysis of the fear-potentiated startle paradigm. In G. H. Bower, ed., *The psychology of learning and motivation*, pp. 263–305. San Diego, Academic Press.

Davis, M., Schlesinger, L. S., and Sorenson, C. A. (1989).

Temporal specificity of fear conditioning: Effects of different conditioned stimulus-unconditioned stimulus intervals on the fear-potentiated startle effect. *Journal of Experimental Psychology: Animal Behavior Processes 15*, 295–310.

Hitchcock, J. M., and Davis, M. (1986). Lesions of the amygdala, but not of the cerebellum or red nucleus, block conditioned fear as measured with the potentiated startle paradigm. *Behavioral Neuroscience 100*, 11–22.

Hitchcock, J. M., Sananes, C. B., and Davis, M. (1989). Sensitization of the startle reflex by footshock: Blockade by lesions of the central nucleus of the amygdala or its efferent pathway to the brainstem. *Behavioral Neuroscience 103*, 509–518.

Ison, J. R., McAdam, D. W., and Hammond, G. R. (1973). Latency and amplitude changes in the acoustic startle reflex of the rat produced by variation in auditory prestimulation. *Physiology and Behavior 10*, 1035–1039.

Miserendino, M. J. D., Sananes, C. B., Melia, K. R., and Davis, M. (1990). Blocking of acquisition but not expression of conditioned fear-potentiated startle by NMDA antagonists in the amygdala. *Nature 345*, 716–718.

Rosen, J. B., and Davis, M. (1988b). Temporal characteristics of enhancement of startle by stimulation of the amygdala. *Physiology and Behavior 44*, 117–123.

Rosen, J. B., and Davis, M. (1988a). Enhancement of acoustic startle by electrical stimulation of the amygdala. *Behavioral Neuroscience 102*, 195–202.

Michael Davis

NEURAL SUBSTRATES OF EMOTIONAL MEMORY

Emotion and *memory* are closely related processes. Emotion, for example, can enhance or inhibit the encoding and/or retrieval of memories. This notion is central to the psychoanalytic theory of repression (e.g., Freud, [1915] 1957; Rappaport, 1942; Erdelyi, 1985), learning theories that attribute hedonic properties to REINFORCEMENT (Hull, 1943; Konorski, 1948; Mowrer, 1960; Dollard and Miller, 1950; Olds, 1977), the flashbulb memory hypothesis (Christianson, 1989; Brown and Kulik, 1977), the Yerkes-Dobson law (Yerkes and Dobson, 1908), the mood-congruity hypothesis of memory retrieval (Bower, 1981), and certain MEMORY CONSOLIDATION hypotheses (McGaugh, 1990). But in addition to enhancing or inhibiting the remembrance of facts and episodes in our lives, emotion itself can be remembered.

Memory of the emotional significance of events is readily studied in the laboratory using *classical conditioning* techniques. For example, if an animal encounters a meaningless stimulus, such as a tone or a flashing light, in the presence of some aversive event, such as footshock, the tone or light, when presented alone, will itself evoke an emotional reaction. In the language of classical conditioning, the tone or light is the conditioned stimulus (CS) and the footshock is the unconditioned stimulus (US). With one or two pairings, the CS can acquire emotion-arousing properties that are difficult to extinguish. Classically conditioned emotional memories are thus rapidly learned and long-lasting. (See also CONDITIONING, CLASSICAL AND INSTRUMENTAL.)

Several studies have examined the brain mechanisms underlying the transformation of simple sensory stimuli into aversive events through studies of classical conditioning in the rat (LeDoux et al., 1983, 1984, 1985, 1986, 1987, 1988, 1989, 1990a, 1990b; Iwata et al., 1986, 1987). For training, auditory conditioned stimuli paired with footshock unconditioned stimuli have been used. As conditioned emotional responses changes in emotional behavior ("freezing") and autonomic activity (arterial pressure increases) evoked by the CS after conditioning have been measured. The strategy has been to identify, from sensory to motor neurons, the pathways in the brain through which the auditory stimulus gains control over the skeletal muscles and the autonomic nervous system.

Through a series of lesion experiments conducted in association with anatomical tracing studies, it has been possible to achieve the goal of mapping the emotional conditioning pathway from sensory to motor neurons (Figure 1). The pathway, as it is now understood, involves transmission through the auditory system to medial areas of the *medial geniculate body*. From there, the signal is transmitted directly to the *amygdala*. The lateral amygdaloid nucleus receives the thalamic sensory inputs and transmits to the central amygdaloid nucleus. The central nucleus, in turn, transmits to the lateral hypothalamus for the regulation of the autonomic changes and to the midbrain central gray area for the regulation of freezing. These latter structures, in turn, connect with the final common motor neurons controlling the autonomic nervous system and skeletal muscles.

These connections thus constitute an essential through-processing circuitry of emotional (fear) learning. The *fear* learning circuitry, though, does

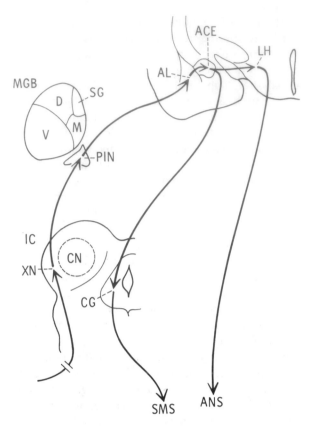

Figure 1. Neural circuitry of fear conditioning. The pathways mediating fear conditioning involve transmission of auditory conditioned stimulus (CS) information through the auditory system to the external (XN) shell region of the inferior colliculus (IC) to the medial areas of the medial geniculate body (MGB), especially to the posterior intralaminar nucleus (PIN) but also to the medial (M) and suprageniculate (SG) divisions of MGB. From there the CS is relayed to the lateral nucleus of the amygdala (AL), which in turn projects to the central nucleus of the amygdala (ACE). After ACE the pathway bifurcates, with projections to the lateral hypothalamic area (LH) mediating autonomic conditioned responses and with projections to the central gray region (CG) mediating somatomotor (freezing) conditioned responses. The amygdaloid areas are likely to be critical sites of plasticity because they are situated between sensory and motor processing areas. Other abbreviations: ANS, autonomic nervous system; CN, central nucleus of the inferior colliculus; D, dorsal division of MGB; SMS, somatomotor system; V, ventral division of MGB.

not stand alone. It receives inputs from many other systems in the brain, and these systems modulate the processing that occurs in the fear learning circuitry.

What is particularly significant about the fear conditioning circuitry is that it bypasses the neocortex and may therefore be involved in the acquisition and expression of emotional associations independent of the higher cognitive processes organized at the level of cortical systems. If so, this could help to explain why we seem to have so little volitional control over our moods and emotions.

The circuitry described has been identified through studies using simple stimulus events. While considerable evidence suggests that for emotional responses elicited by complex stimuli, cortical systems are required (Aggleton and Mishkin, 1986; Rolls, 1986; Jarrell et al., 1987), this should not diminish the potential significance of the subcortical input system. The subcortical system is likely to be of particular importance when rapid responses are required to potentially threatening stimuli (LeDoux, 1986, 1987). In such situations it is more important to respond quickly than it is to be certain that the stimulus is worthy of a response. This system may therefore be wired to respond on the basis of features and fragments of stimuli rather than on the basis of complete object representations, which can be achieved only at the level of the neocortex. This arrangement demands tight coupling between thalamo-amygdala and cortico-amygdala processing in order to maintain a sense of understanding of the origins of our emotions with respect to eliciting stimuli.

Recent studies have examined the capacity of the thalamo-amygdala system for experience-dependent modification of neural transmission (Clugnet and LeDoux, 1990). These studies have shown that high-frequency stimuli applied to the medial geniculate body produce long-lasting enhancements of synaptic transmission. Such changes, usually described as LONG-TERM POTENTIATION, are believed by many to be a possible mechanism for the rapid establishment of memories (Brown et al., 1988; Teyler and DiScenna, 1987; Cotman et al., 1988).

The circuits underlying the formation of emotional memories through simple classical conditioning procedures do not involve the *hippocampus* and related structures, which are known to be essential for the establishment of conscious or *declarative memories* for personal experiences and for factual information (Squire, 1987). For a given experience, the brain thus stores many kinds of information in parallel. Emotional influences on declarative memory are likely to involve interactions between the amygdala and the hippocampus.

Emotional memories established through thalamo-amygdala transmission last for long periods of time (LeDoux et al., 1989). With repeated nonreinforced presentations of the CS, the conditioned emotional responses do extinguish. However, if the responses are established following removal of the cortical sensory area of the CS sensory modality (visual cortex for a flashing light CS, auditory cortex for an acoustic CS), unreinforced presentations of the CS have little effect (LeDoux et al., 1989; Teich et al., 1989). In other words, in animals with such cortical lesions, extinction is greatly slowed and may in fact be eliminated. Lesions of the sensory cortex may interfere with *extinction* because they block the transmission of sensory input to other brain areas, such as the hippocampus or frontal cortex, that have been implicated in extinction. More to the point is the possibility that emotional memories, once established, may be more or less permanent and that extinction represents not the erasure of emotional memories but the inhibition, by behavioral and/or cognitive control systems, of these memories. This could explain why it is so hard to eliminate learned fears and PHOBIAS. Reasoning and behavioral desensitization are unlikely to erase emotional memories and can only help the individual control their expression.

(See also EMOTION, MOOD, AND MEMORY; GUIDE TO THE ANATOMY OF THE BRAIN. AMYGDALA.)

REFERENCES

Aggleton, J. P., and Mishkin, M. (1986). The amygdala: Sensory gateway to the emotions. In R. Plutchik and H. Kellerman, eds., *Emotion: Theory, research and experience, vol. 3*, pp. 281–299. Orlando, Fla.: Academic Press.

Bower, G. H. (1981). Mood and memory. *American Psychologist 36*, 129–148.

Brown, R., and Kulik, J. (1977). Flashbulb memories. *Cognition 5*, 73–99.

Brown, T. H., Chapman, P. F., Kairiss, E. W., and Keenan, C. L. (1988). Long-term synaptic potentiation. *Science 242*, 724–728.

Christianson, S. (1989). Flashbulb memories: Special but not so special. *Memory and Cognition 17*, 435–443.

Clugnet, M. C., and LeDoux, J. E. (1990). Synaptic plasticity in fear conditioning circuits: Induction of LTP in the lateral nucleus of the amygdala by stimulation of the medial geniculate body. *Journal of Neuroscience 10*, 2818–2824.

Cotman, C. W., Monaghan, D. T., and Ganong, A. H. (1988). Excitatory amino acid neurotransmission: NMDA receptors and Hebb-type synaptic plasticity. *Annual Review of Neuroscience 11*, 61–80.

Dollard, J. C., and Miller, N. E. (1950). *Personality and psychotherapy*. New York: McGraw-Hill.

Erdelyi, M. H. (1985). *Psychoanalysis: Freud's cognitive psychology*. New York: Freeman.

Fitzgerald, R. D., and Teyler, T. J. (1970). Trace and delayed heart rate conditioning in rats as a function of US intensity. *Journal of Comparative Physiology and Psychology 70*, 242–253.

Freud, S. [1915] (1957). Repression. Trans. C. M. Baines and J. Strachey. In J. Strachey, ed., *The Standard Edition of the Complete Works of Sigmund Freud*, vol. 14. London: Hogarth Press.

Hull, C. L. (1943). *Principles of behavior*. New York: Appleton-Century-Crofts.

Iwata, J., Chida, K., and LeDoux, J. E. (1987). Cardiovascular responses elicited by stimulation of neurons in the central amygdaloid nucleus in awake but not anesthetized rats resemble conditioned emotional responses. *Brain Research 418*, 183–188.

Iwata, J., LeDoux, J. E., Meeley, M. P., Arneric, S., and Reis, D. J. (1986). Intrinsic neurons in the amygdaloid field projected to by the medial geniculate body mediate emotional responses conditioned to acoustic stimuli. *Brain Research 383*, 195–214.

Jarrell, T. W., Gentile, C. G., Romanski, L. M., McCabe, P. M., and Schneiderman, N. (1987). Involvement of cortical and thalamic auditory regions in retention of differential brachycardia conditioning to acoustic conditioned stimuli in rabbits. *Brain Research 412*, 285–294.

Konorski, J. (1948). *Conditioned reflexes and neuron organization*. Cambridge: Cambridge University Press.

LeDoux, J. E. (1986). Sensory systems and emotion. *Integrative Psychiatry 4*, 237–248.

LeDoux, J. E. (1987). Emotion. In *Handbook of physiology, section 1: The nervous system*. Vol. 5, *Higher functions of the brain*, F. Plum, ed., pp. 419–460. Bethesda, Md.: American Physiological Society.

LeDoux, J. F., Iwata, J., Cicchetti, P., and Reis, D. J. (1988). Different projections of the central amygdaloid nucleus mediate autonomic and behavioral correlates of conditioned fear. *Journal of Neuroscience 8*, 2517–2529.

LeDoux, J. E., Romanski, L. M., and Xagoraris, A. E. (1989). Indelibility of subcortical emotional memories. *Journal of Cognitive Neuroscience 1*, 238–243.

LeDoux, J. E., Ruggiero, D. A., Forest, R., Stornetta, R., and Reis, D. J. (1987). Topographic organization of convergent projections to the thalamus from the inferior colliculus and spinal cord in the rat. *Journal of Comparative Neurology 264*, 123–146.

LeDoux, J. E., Ruggiero, D. A., and Reis, J. D. (1985). Projections to the subcortical forebrain from anatomically defined regions of the medial geniculate body in the rat. *Journal of Comparative Neurology 242,* 183–213.

LeDoux, J. E., Sakaguchi, A., Iwata, J., and Reis, D. J. (1986). Interruption of projections from the medial geniculate body to an archi-neostriatal field disrupts the classical conditioning of emotional responses to acoustic stimuli in the rat. *Neuroscience 17,* 615–627.

LeDoux, J. E., Sakaguchi, A., and Reis, J. D. (1984). Subcortical efferent projections of the medial geniculate nucleus mediate responses conditioned by acoustic stimuli. *Journal of Neuroscience 4* (3), 683–698.

LeDoux, J. E., Thompson, M. E., Iadecola, C., Tucker, L. W., and Reis, D. J. (1983). Local cerebral blood flow increases during auditory and emotional processing in the conscious rat. *Science 221,* 576–578.

LeDoux, J. E., Cicchetti, P., Xagoraris, A., and Romanski, L. M. (1990a). The lateral amygdaloid nucleus: Sensory interface of the amygdala in fear conditioning. *Journal of Neuroscience 10,* 1062–1069.

LeDoux, J. E., Farb, C. F., and Ruggiero, D. A. (1990b). Topographic organization of neurons in the acoustic thalamus that project to the amygdala. *Journal of Neuroscience 10,* 1043–1054.

McGaugh, J. L. (1990). Significance and remembrance: The role of neuromodulatory systems. *Psychological Science 1,* 15–25.

Mowrer, O. H. (1960). *Learning theory and behavior.* New York: Wiley.

Olds, J. (1977). *Drives and reinforcement.* New York: Raven.

Rappaport, D. (1942). *Emotions and memory.* New York: International Universities Press.

Rolls, E. T. (1986). A theory of emotion, and its application to understanding the neural basis of emotion. In Y. Oomur, ed., *Emotions: Neural and chemical control,* pp. 325–344. Tokyo: Japan Scientific Societies Press.

Squire, L. R. (1987). Memory: Neural organization and behavior. In *Handbook of Physiology, Section 1: The Nervous System.* Vol. 5, *Higher Functions of the Brain,* F. Plum, ed., pp. 295–371. Bethesda, Md.: American Physiological Society.

Teich, A. H., McCabe, P. M., Gentile, C. C., Schneiderman, L. S., Winters, R. W., Liskowsky, D. R., and Schneiderman, N. (1989). Auditory cortex lesions prevent the extinction of Pavlovian differential heart rate conditioning to tonal stimuli in rabbits. *Brain Research 480,* 210–218.

Teyler, T. J., and DiScenna, P. (1987). Long-term potentiation. *Annual Review of Neuroscience 10,* 131–161.

Yerkes, R. M., and Dobson, J. D. (1908). The relation of strength of stimulus to rapidity of habit-formation. *Journal of Comparative Neurology and Psychology 18,* 458–482.

Joseph E. LeDoux

NEURON

See Guide to the Anatomy of the Brain

NEUROTRANSMITTER SYSTEMS AND MEMORY

Ever since the discovery of the chemical nature of synaptic transmission, the role of neurotransmitters in the formation and retrieval of memories has been the subject of intense investigation. As the number of both neurotransmitters and different forms of memories have been steadily increased over the years, the task of uncovering general principles describing the involvement of neurotransmitter systems in memory has become extremely difficult. Furthermore, the lack of understanding of the molecular and cellular mechanisms of learning and memory has limited the experimental approaches to two general strategies: (1) an interventional strategy using pharmacological tools or lesion/stimulation of specific neurotransmitter systems and (2) a correlational strategy using "naturally" occurring conditions (neurological diseases, aging) affecting specific neurotransmitter systems. Based on these studies, a number of neurotransmitters have consistently demonstrated an important role in learning and memory (Chapoutier, 1989; Decker and McGaugh, 1991). That evidence will be summarized here.

Glutamate

Early work by Van Harreveld and Fifkova (1974) suggested a role for glutamate in learning and memory. Using an avian retina preparation, they showed that *l*-proline might prove to be a glutamate-release inhibitor. Building on these results, Cherkin and his colleagues (1976) published a series of articles demonstrating that various glutamate antagonists injected intracerebrally could retard memory consolidation in neonatal chicks, using a behavioral paradigm involving flavor aversion learning. The memory effects were dose-, time-, and isomer-dependent. More recently, the role of glutamate in learning and memory has received considerable support from two independent lines of research. Perhaps the most studied cellular models of learning and memory is the LONG-TERM POTEN-

TIATION (LTP) of synaptic transmission elicited by brief bursts of high-frequency electrical stimulation of the monosynaptic pathways using glutamate as their neurotransmitter (Bliss and Lomo, 1973). The relationships among LTP, learning and memory, and glutamatergic systems have been further established by the use of specific antagonists of different subtypes of glutamate receptors (Morris et al., 1990). Various human conditions associated with major disturbances of memory have been shown to exhibit marked degeneration of glutamatergic neurons. Thus, severe cases of *amnesia* are the result of loss of glutamatergic neurons in the *hippocampal formation* (Squire, 1986), and one of the hallmarks of ALZHEIMER'S DISEASE is a loss of glutamatergic neurons in the entorhinal cortex and hippocampus (Hyman et al., 1987) (See also GLUTAMATE RECEPTORS AND THEIR CHARACTERIZATION.)

GABA (γ-Aminobutyric Acid)

Historically, GABAergic neurons have been neglected as possible participants in memory processes. The discovery of the mode of action of benzodiazepines and the known effects of these compounds on memory (Lister, 1985) renewed the interest in the possible role of GABA in memory. Thus benzodiazepines, which potentiate the effect of GABA at the $GABA_A$ receptors (Tallman and Gallagher, 1985), generally produce an impairment of learning, whereas ligands acting at the benzodiazepine sites but producing an opposite effect (and therefore called reverse agonists) enhance learning in mice, chickens, and humans. Local administration of GABA agonists or antagonists in discrete brain regions have been effective in producing impairment or enhancement, respectively, in various learning tasks (McGaugh, 1989a).

Acetylcholine

There exists a very extensive literature describing the role of acetylcholine in learning and memory (Deutsch, 1983; Bartus et al., 1985; Hagan and Morris, 1988). Pharmacological studies using both acetylcholinesterase inhibitors (producing increased levels of acetylcholine at synapses) and blockers of acetylcholine receptors have been performed in numerous learning tasks and animal spe-

cies. The general conclusion is that impairment of cholinergic transmission produces cognitive impairment. This conclusion is reinforced by studies in humans with pathological alterations in cholinergic function. Thus, Alzheimer's disease is associated with loss of cholinergic neurons in the nucleus basalis of Meynert (Coyle et al., 1983). In Parkinson's disease, memory impairment is correlated with a decrease in cholinergic function in the frontal cortex (Chapoutier, 1989). A possible unifying mechanism for a role of cholinergic neurons in memory processes has been ascribed to the participation of these neurons in the generation of rhythmical brain activity (Θ *rhythm*) directly involved in information storage and in LTP (Winson, 1990).

Catecholamines and Serotonin

Although noradrenergic systems have often been implicated in learning and memory (Gold and Zornetser, 1983; Wenk et al., 1987), studies using pharmacological blockade of norepinephrine receptors or destruction of noradrenergic neurons indicate that these neurons do not participate in the learning of a variety of tasks (Pontecorvo et al., 1988). However, the situation is probably more complicated, for noradrenergic systems appear to participate in modulation of some memory processes (Decker and McGaugh, 1991). Similarly, serotonergic neurons have been involved in learning and memory, although the precise role of this system in memory processes has been quite elusive (Altman and Normile, 1988). Serotonergic function appears to be depressed in certain brain regions in patients with Alzheimer's disease.

Other Systems

Although not generally considered to be neurotransmitters, a growing number of peptides have been found colocalized within traditional neurotransmitters and have been assigned the role of neuromodulators. Their role in synaptic function is still a matter of debate, but it is impossible not to mention here the evidence implicating a number of neuropeptides in memory processes. In particular, ACTH and fragments of ACTH have repeatedly been shown to improve memory consolidation. Vasopressin has also been suggested as participating in memory formation, possibly through an interaction with noradrenergic systems (McGaugh, 1989b). Similarly, opioid peptides have been clearly implicated in memory processes, including the suggestion (Gallagher, 1985) that opioid peptide-containing neurons are part of a forgetting mechanism.

Conclusion

As it becomes more and more widely accepted that learning and memory reflect the existence of a variety of synaptic plasticity mechanisms occurring at numerous stages of information processing, it follows that several neurotransmitter systems participate directly or indirectly in the processes of information storage and retrieval. Correlating the roles of specific neurotransmitters to specific forms of learning and memory will await the development of ever more specific pharmacological tools and behavioral tests, but this strategy will result in the development of useful treatments capable of alleviating learning and memory disorders.

REFERENCES

Altman, H. J., and Normile, H. J. (1988). What is the nature of the role of the serotonergic system in learning and memory: Prospects for development of an effective treatment strategy for senile dementia. *Neurobiology of Aging 9*, 627–638.

Bartus, R. T., Dean, R. L., Pontecorvo, M. J., and Flicker, C. (1985). The cholinergic hypothesis: A historical overview, current perspective, and future directions. *Annals of the New York Academy of Sciences 444*, 332–358.

Bliss, T. V. P., and Lomo, T. (1973). Long-lasting potentiation of synaptic transmission in the dentate area of the anesthetized rabbit following stimulation of the perforant path. *Journal of Physiology 232*, 334–356.

Chapoutier, G. (1989). The search for a biochemistry of memory. *Archives of Gerontology and Geriatrics supp. 1*, 7–19.

Cherkin, A., Eckardt, M. J., and Gerbrandt, L. D. (1976). Memory: Proline induces retrograde amnesia in chicks. *Science 193*, 242–244.

Coyle, J. T., Price, D. L., and DeLong, M. R. (1983). Alzheimer's disease: A disorder of cortical cholinergic innervation. *Science 219*, 1184–1190.

Decker, M. W., and McGaugh, J. L. (1991). The role of interactions between the cholinergic systems and other neuromodulatory systems in learning and memory. *Synapse 7*, 151–168.

Deutsch, J. A. (1983). The cholinergic synapse and the site of memory. In *The physiological basis of memory*. J. A. Deutsch (ed.). New York: Academic Press.

Gallagher, M. (1985). Re-viewing modulation of learning and memory. In N. Weinberger, J. McGaugh, G. Lynch, eds., *Memory systems of the brain*, pp. 311–334. New York: Guilford Press.

Gold, P. E., and Zornetser, S. F. (1983). The mnemon and its juices. *Behavioral and Neural Biology 38*, 151–189.

Hagan, J. J., and Morris, R. G. M. (1988). The cholinergic hypothesis of memory: A review of animal experiments. In L. L. Iversen, S. D. Iversen and S. H. Snyder, eds., *Handbook of Psychopharmacology*, pp. 237–323. New York: Plenum Press.

Hyman, B. T., Van, H. G. W., and Damasio, A. R. (1987). Alzheimer's disease: Glutamate depletion in the hippocampal perforant pathway zone. *Annals of Neurology 22*(1), 37–40.

Lister, R. G. (1985). The amnesic action of benzodiazepines in man. *Neuroscience and Biobehavioral Review 9*, 87–94.

McGaugh, J. L. (1989a). Dissociating learning and performance: Drug and hormone enhancement of memory storage. *Brain Research Bulletin 23*, 339–345.

——— (1989b). Involvement of hormonal and neuromodulatory systems in the regulation of memory storage. *Annual Review of Neuroscience 12*, 255–287.

Morris, R. G. M., Davis, S., and Butcher, S. P. (1990). Hippocampal synaptic plasticity and NMDA receptors: A role in information storage. *Philosophical Transactions of the Royal Society of London B329*, 187–204.

Pontecorvo, M. J., Clissold, D. B., and Conti, L. H. (1988). Age-related cognitive impairments as assessed with an automated repeated measures memory task: Implications for the possible role of acetylcholine and norepinephrine in memory dysfunction. *Neurobiology of Aging 9*, 617–625.

Squire, L. R. (1986). Mechanisms of memory. *Science 232*, 1612–1619.

Tallman, J. F., and Gallagher, D. W. (1985). The GABAergic system: A locus of benzodiazepine action. *Annual Review of Neuroscience 8*, 21–42.

Van Harreveld, A., and Fifkova, E. (1974). Involvement of glutamate in memory formation. *Brain Research 81*, 455–467.

Wenk, G., Hughey, D., Boundy, V., and Kim, A. (1987). Neurotransmitters and memory: Role of cholinergic, serotonergic, and noradrenergic systems. *Behavioral Neuroscience 101*, 325–332.

Winson, J. (1990). The meaning of dreams. *Scientific American 263*, 86–96.

Michel Baudry
Joel L. Davis

OBJECT CONCEPT, ACQUISITION OF

Understanding the nature and properties of objects is central to understanding the world around us. While philosophers have long debated the nature of reality, it is psychologists who have demonstrated most clearly the problems faced by infants in understanding objects and the physical laws that govern interactions between objects.

Research with young infants has shown that learning to understand even simple events—for example, the momentary disappearance of an object behind a screen—entails a surprisingly long apprenticeship. The average human infant in fact takes between 18 months and 2 years to develop a fully fledged concept of objects. By then the child will have a working knowledge of the rules governing both interactions between himself/herself and objects in the immediate environment and also of the basic rules governing simple events involving one or more objects—the laws of space, time, and causality. During this apprenticeship, the child's understanding of objects passes through a series of well-defined stages. Lower species have been found to pass through the earlier steps in this developmental sequence more quickly than human infants, but few other species—some psychologists would maintain none—have shown themselves capable of achieving the final, most advanced stages in the development of a concept of objects.

Infants by definition have no language. They also have a very limited repertoire of behaviors. How, then, do we know what they do or do not understand of the world around them? It is surprisingly easy to demonstrate the primitive nature and inadequacies of the infant's early object knowledge. A 5-month-old infant, for example, will show no surprise when an object moves along a track, goes behind a screen, then emerges on the same path of movement at the appropriate time as a completely different object (Goldberg, 1976); at this age, we know that infants are capable of discriminating different colors, sizes, and shapes, but it seems that they disregard this information in favor of the constancy of the rate and path of the movements on either side of the screen. Similarly, if shown an attractive toy that is then put underneath a cup, a 4-to-6-month-old infant will typically act as if that toy no longer exists, unaware of the seemingly simple principle that the toy is still there even though it can no longer be seen. It takes more than a year, moreover, before that infant will also appreciate that if a toy is put inside something, say a box, and that container is then moved, the toy will also have moved but can be retrieved at the box's new position. Being able to understand invisible displacements such as these represents one of the final steps in object concept development.

The Classic Piagetian Analysis

It is now over 50 years since the Swiss psychologist Jean PIAGET observed that the understanding of objects in infancy goes through a regular, invariant sequence of development. Although Piaget was not the first psychologist to carry out research in this area, his careful observations of the early development of his own three children led to the three books that have been the starting point for almost all subsequent researchers in this area: *The Origins of Intelligence in Children* (1936), *The Construction of Reality in the Child* (1937), and *Play, Dreams and Imitation in Childhood* (1946).

489

When translated into English, these books generated a vast number of empirical studies of what became known as object permanence.

The term *object permanence* does little justice to the detail of Piaget's observations and to the complexity of his theory of how infants develop a working knowledge of objects. Piaget believed development of the object concept to be an essential prerequisite for the development of reasoning and logical thought at older ages, and to be prototypical of all cognitive development. According to his analysis, young infants are basically solipsists, failing to appreciate that objects persist independently in space, time, and form, regardless of whether they themselves are perceiving or acting upon them at any given moment. Piaget identified what he believed to be six clear stages in object concept development, each more advanced stage developing out of the preceding, less complex stage (for a summary of these stages, see Miller, 1989).

Piaget devised a number of hiding tasks to tap each stage in development of the object concept. These tasks are a remarkably simple route for revealing the limits on an infant's understanding at any given age. The first two stages, generally acquired by 4 months of age, are tested by tasks that require the infant to search visually for a disappearing object (e.g., a ball that drops out of sight). All subsequent stages require manual search for an object that has been hidden in some way, with the complexity of the hiding sequence increasing at each stage.

To adults, the solution to even the most advanced of these search tasks seems very obvious. Infants, however, very clearly do not think of objects in the way that adults do. Take, for instance, what has become one of the most researched cognitive tasks in developmental psychology, the AAB task. In this task, the infant is shown a small, attractive toy that is then hidden under one of two (usually identical) occluders, at position A (see Figure 1). If the child successfully retrieves the toy, it is again hidden at A. If the toy is recovered a second time from A, the experimenter then hides the same object at location, B.

Unless the infant understands that the toy will now be found where it was last seen to disappear rather than where it was found on the two previous occasions, he or she will not succeed on this task. Achievement of this level of understanding marks the transition from Piaget's Stage IV to Stage V, a transition usually made around 8 to 10 months. While still at the Stage IV level, the infant will typically return to search first at A; sometimes he or she will refuse to look at B even after search at A has failed to produce the toy—despite having carefully watched the toy being placed at B during the hiding sequence. (A number of trials of all object concept tasks are usually presented to rule out the possibility of chance success; in the AAB task, for instance, there is a 50/50 chance that

Figure 1. The AAB search task.

guessing could lead to success on any single trial.)

Piaget's descriptions of the AAB error and of the other errors characteristic of each of the six stages in object concept development have withstood the test of time and numerous replication studies (for overview, see Schuberth, 1982). Infants of virtually every culture and level of intelligence have been presented with these tasks, and although the rate at which individual infants may pass through the sequence can vary widely, the developmental sequence of errors and advances has generally proved to be invariant.

Piaget believed these errors indicated that the young infant is at first egocentric, initially unable to understand objects other than as extensions of himself/herself and his/her own activity. Until the infant's repertoire of behaviors in relation to objects becomes sufficiently large and flexible for object invariances to be recognized, there can be neither understanding of the independent existence of objects nor any differentiated awareness of the self as a distinct entity, according to Piaget. This means that neither objects nor events can be evoked in their absence, an ability that is a prerequisite for the development of more advanced cognitive skills such as symbolic play (e.g., games of pretend), drawing, mental imagery, and, most important of all, language. For many interpreters of Piaget's theory, this means that "out of sight" is "out of mind" for the infant, with early object understanding restricted to immediate perceptions and actions.

Alternative Explanations of Search Errors in Infancy

Although it is widely accepted that the average infant will show each of the errors described by Piaget at some point in his or her development, there is considerably less agreement about what these errors signify for cognitive development; indeed, many question Piaget's claim that these search errors reflect different stages in the development of a single underlying object concept. Certainly an "out of sight, out of mind" theory of early cognitive development would seem to be insufficient to explain the many other types of search errors that subsequent researchers have found to be common in infancy. Experiments have demonstrated, for instance, that infants produce Piagetian errors when transparent occluders are used to "hide" the toy in otherwise traditional object concept tasks (Nielson, 1982). It has also been shown that infants can successfully retrieve objects that have disappeared from sight as a result of the room lights being put out (Hood and Willatts, 1986). Clearly, out of sight is not always out of mind for the young infant. To be fair to Piaget, it should be pointed out that his interpretation of infants' search errors was far more complex than the accounts typically found in developmental textbooks would suggest. Nonetheless, many psychologists cannot accept his basic contention that the young infant cannot yet think and has no real understanding at any level of either the permanence of objects or the distinction between himself/herself and objects.

A considerable body of empirical evidence supports the view that the infant comes into the world capable of representation and with at least some basic understanding of objects and their physical properties (for review, see Gibson, 1988). This evidence, in conjunction with the types of search errors typically found in infancy, suggests that development consists of evolving a more complete and more powerful understanding of objects, one that will allow the infant to interact more efficiently and effectively with the people and objects in the surrounding world (people are subject to many of the same physical laws as objects, after all). For some researchers, the deficits in understanding revealed by object concept tasks reflect the infant's inadequate knowledge of object *identity* and of the spatiotemporal rules that determine, for instance, whether two objects that look identical are the same object seen in two different places at two different times or are two quite different objects that merely look the same. Other theorists see the problem as essentially one of *information processing*, with more complex search tasks making increasingly greater demands on the infant's ability to process the information required to keep track of an object throughout a hiding sequence. Yet others believe the basic problem to be one of *memory*, although studies that have varied the delay between hiding the object and allowing the infant to search would seem to indicate that memory is not always a major factor in determining success or failure on these tasks. *Spatial coding difficulties* and *motor skill problems* have also been put forward as possible explanations for the infant's early difficulties in finding hidden objects. A major weakness in alternative theories such as these, however, is that they can usually account for only some of the errors evidenced on search tasks during infancy. A different theory would have to be offered for each of the different errors seen at different points in development. This is hardly parsimonious, doing little to advance our understanding of the processes of cognitive development in infancy.

Conclusions

Although there is considerable theoretical disarray in object concept research, there is widespread acceptance that object concept-type tasks do tap early cognitive processes and can provide some indication of an infant's current stage of development. Most tests of infant "intelligence" have incorporated one or more hiding tasks into the test battery. In the course of normal everyday activity, even in the most impoverished surroundings, human infants will repeatedly be confronted with problems that will reveal the inadequacy of their current understanding of objects. It would appear that human infants are highly motivated to resolve the conflict that arises between their own limited conception of their world and the real world. Although the rate at which infants increase their understanding of objects has been shown to be highly susceptible to environmental influence, it would also appear that the object concept is a "buffered" area of development: All but the most underprivileged or most severely handicapped infants will have developed a functional concept of objects by the end of their second year of life.

REFERENCES

Gibson, E. J. (1988). Exploratory behavior in the development of perceiving, acting and the acquiring of knowledge. *Annual Review of Psychology 39*, 1–41.

Goldberg, S. (1976). Visual tracking and existence constancy in 5 month old infants. *Journal of Experimental Child Psychology 22*, 478–491.

Hood, B., and Willatts, P. (1986). Reaching in the dark to an object's remembered position: Evidence for object permanence in 5-month-old infants. *British Journal of Developmental Psychology 4*, 57–66.

Miller, P. H. (1989). *Theories of developmental psychology*, 2nd ed. New York: W. H. Freeman.

Neilson, I. E. (1982). An alternative explanation of the infant's difficulty in the Stage III, IV and V object concept tasks. *Perception 11*, 577–588.

Piaget, J. (1951). *Play, dreams and imitation in childhood*. Trans. G. Gattegno and F. M. Hodgson. New York: Norton. (Original French ed., 1946.)

——— (1953). *The origins of intelligence in children*. Trans. M. Cook. London: Routledge and Kegan Paul. (Original French ed., 1936.)

——— (1954). *The construction of reality in the child*. Trans. M. Cook. London: Routledge and Kegan Paul. (Original French ed., 1937.)

Schuberth, R. E. (1982). The infant's search for objects: Alternatives to Piaget's theory of object concept development. In L. P. Lipsitt, ed., *Advances in infancy research*, vol. 2. Norwood, N.J.: Ablex.

Jennifer G. Wishart

OBSERVATIONAL LEARNING

Psychological theories have traditionally emphasized learning from the effects of one's actions. If knowledge and skills could be acquired only by repeated trial and error, human development would be greatly retarded, not to mention exceedingly tedious and hazardous. Moreover, the constraints of time, resources, and mobility impose severe limits on the situations and activities that can be directly explored for the acquisition of new knowledge. However, humans have evolved an advanced cognitive capacity for observational learning that enables them to abbreviate the acquisition process by learning from the examples provided by others. Indeed, virtually all types of learning that result from direct experience can occur vicariously by observing people's behavior and its consequences for them (Bandura, 1986; Rosenthal and Zimmerman, 1978).

Much human learning occurs by observing the actual behavior of others and the outcomes they experience. A special power of psychological modeling is that it can transmit knowledge of wide applicability simultaneously to vast numbers of people in dispersed locales through symbolic modes of communication. By drawing on these modeled patterns of thought and behavior, observers can transcend the bounds of their immediate environment. With the advent of enormous advances in the technology of communication, observational learning from the symbolic environment is playing an increasingly powerful role in shaping thought patterns, attitudes, values, and styles of behavior.

Subfunctions Governing Observational Learning

Observational learning is governed by four subfunctions that are summarized in Figure 1. *Attentional processes* determine what people selectively observe in the profusion of modeling influences and what information they extract from ongoing modeled events. A number of factors influence what people choose to explore and how they perceive what is modeled in the social and symbolic environment. Some of these factors concern the cognitive skills, preconceptions, and value preferences of the observers. Others are related to the salience, attractiveness, and functional value of the modeled activities themselves. Still other factors relate to the structural arrangements of human interactions and social networks, which largely determine the types of models available for observation.

People cannot be much influenced by observed events if they do not remember them. A second subfunction governing observational learning concerns cognitive *representational processes*. Retention involves an active process of transforming and restructuring information about modeled events into rules and conceptions for generating new patterns of behavior. Preconceptions and

emotional states can bias how observed information is transformed into memory codes. Similarly, recall involves a process of reconstruction of past experiences rather than simply retrieval of registered past events.

In the third subfunction in observational learning—the *production process*—symbolic conceptions are transformed into appropriate courses of action. Conceptions are rarely translated into proficient action from the outset. Skills are usually perfected through a conception-matching process. Conceptions guide the construction and execution of behavior patterns, and the behavior is modified as necessary to achieve close correspondence between conception and action. The richer the repertoire of subskills that people possess, the easier it is to integrate them to produce the new behavior patterns.

The fourth subfunction in observational learning concerns *motivational processes*. People do not perform everything they learn. Performance of observationally learned behavior is influenced by three major types of incentive motivators: *direct, vicarious,* and *self-produced.* People are more likely to perform observationally learned behavior if it results in valued outcomes for them than if it has unrewarding or punishing effects. The observed detriments and benefits experienced by others influence the performance of modeled patterns much as directly experienced consequences do. People are motivated by the successes of others who are similar to themselves, but are discouraged from pursuing courses of behavior that they have

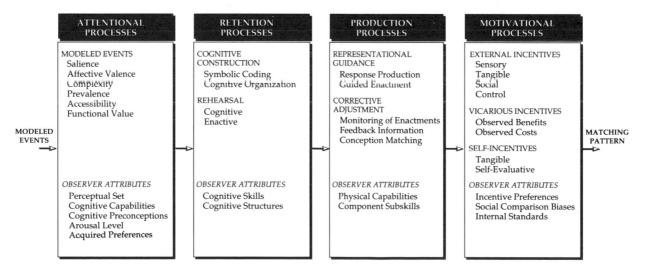

Figure 1. The four major subfunctions governing observational learning and the influential factors operating within each subfunction.

often seen result in adverse consequences. Personal standards of conduct provide a further source of incentive motivation. People pursue activities they find self-satisfying and give them a sense of self-worth but reject those they personally disapprove.

Abstract Observational Learning

Observational learning is not merely a process of behavioral mimicry. Highly functional patterns of behavior, which constitute the proven skills and established customs of a culture, may be adopted in essentially the same form as they are exemplified. There is little leeway for improvisation on how to drive automobiles or solve arithmetic problems. However, in many activities, subskills must be improvised to suit different situations. Modeling influences can convey rules for generative and innovative behavior as well. For example, an individual may see others confront moral conflicts involving different matters but apply the same moral standard to them. In abstract observational learning, observers extract the rules or standards embodied in the specific judgments or actions exhibited by others. Once they learn a rule, they can use it to generate new instances of behavior that go beyond what they have seen or heard. Thus, on the basis of modeled information, people acquire standards for categorizing and judging events, linguistic rules of communication (see LANGUAGE LEARNING), thinking skills on how to gain and use knowledge, and personal standards for regulating motivation and conduct (Bandura, 1986; Rosenthal and Zimmerman, 1978). Evidence that generative rules of thought and behavior can be created through abstract modeling attests to the broad scope of observational learning.

Multiple Effects of Observational Learning

So far the discussion has centered on the acquisition of knowledge, cognitive skills, and new styles of behavior through observational learning. In addition to creating new competencies, modeling influences can strengthen or weaken restraints over behavior that has previously been learned. The impact of observational learning on behavioral restraints depends on observers' judgments of their ability to perform the modeled behavior, their perceptions of the outcomes produced by the modeled forms of behavior, and their inferences that similar rewarding or punishing outcomes would result if they themselves were to behave in similar ways.

People are easily aroused by the emotional expressions of others. Therefore, observers can acquire lasting attitudes, values, and emotional reactions toward persons, places, or things that have been associated with modeled emotional experiences. They learn to fear the things that frightened others, to dislike what repulsed them, and to like what gratified them. Fears can be weakened or eliminated by modeling coping strategies for exercising control over the things that are feared (Rosenthal and Bandura, 1978). Values can similarly be developed and altered vicariously by repeated exposure to references exhibited by others.

During the course of their daily lives, people have direct contact with only a small sector of the physical and social environment. They inhabit a circumscribed locale, usually visit the same places, perform the same routines day in and day out, and interact with the same circle of friends and associates. Consequently, their conceptions of social reality with which they have little or no contact are greatly influenced by vicarious experiences—by what they see and hear—without direct experiential correctives (Gerbner, Morgan, and Signorielli, 1986). The more people's conceptions of reality depend upon the media's symbolic environment, the greater is the social impact of the media influences. Many of the shared misconceptions about occupational pursuits, ethnic groups, minorities, the elderly, social and gender roles, and other aspects of life are at least partly cultivated through symbolic modeling of stereotypes.

Social Diffusion through Symbolic Modeling

Much of the preceding discussion has been concerned mainly with observational learning at the individual level. Video systems feeding off telecommunications satellites have become the dominant vehicle for disseminating symbolic environments to vast populations. Social practices are being widely diffused within societies, and ideas, values, and styles of conduct are being modeled worldwide. Observational learning is thus coming to play an increasingly influential role in transcultural change. In this broader function of social diffusion, modeling through the mass media instructs people in new ideas and social practices. Positive and negative incentives determine which of the modeled innovations will be adopted. People are linked together by networks of social relationships. Social networks provide diffusion paths for the spread of new ideas and behavior (Rogers and Kincaid, 1981).

In sum, observational learning takes many forms and produces diverse outcomes. The modeling influences on which it draws serve as instructors, motivators, inhibitors, disinhibitors, social facilitators, emotion arousers and modifiers, constructors of subjective social realities, and transnational acculturators.

REFERENCES

Bandura, A. (1986). *Social foundations of thought and action: A social cognitive theory.* Englewood Cliffs, N.J.: Prentice-Hall. Provides a comprehensive review of the different forms of observational learning.

Gerbner, G., Morgan, M., and Signorielli, N. (1986). Living with television: The dynamics of the cultivation process. In J. Bryant and D. Zillman, eds., *Perspectives on media effects,* pp. 17–40. Hillsdale, N.J.: Erlbaum.

Rogers, E. M., and Kincaid, D. L. (1981). *Communication networks: Toward a new paradigm for research.* New York: Free Press.

Rosenthal, T. L., and Bandura, A. (1978). Psychological modeling: Theory and practice. In S. L. Garfield and A. E. Bergin, eds., *Handbook of psychotherapy and behavior change: An empirical analysis,* 2nd ed., pp. 621–658. New York: Wiley.

Rosenthal, T. L., and Zimmerman, B. J. (1978). *Social learning and cognition.* New York: Academic Press.

Albert Bandura

OLDS, JAMES

James Olds (1922–1973) became a prominent figure in the field of physiological psychology when he discovered in 1953 that rats could be trained to perform a variety of experimental tasks, some at very high rates, in order to obtain a very brief electrical shock applied to a discrete central nervous system site. This phenomenon is often referred to as self-stimulation or intracranial self-

stimulation and is intimately related to the brain pathways that mediate positive REINFORCEMENT. At the time of his sudden death, Olds was Bing Professor of Behavioral Biology at the California Institute of Technology (Caltech) in Pasadena, and a member of the National Academy of Sciences. The events leading up to the serendipitous discovery of pleasure centers in the brain were described both by Olds (1973b, 1975a, 1977) and by others (Miller, 1980; Milner, 1989).

Olds was born in Northbrook, Illinois, where his father, Leland, was industrial editor for the Federated Press. The family moved in 1931 to Nyack, New York, where Olds's father was head of the New York State Power Commission. In 1939 the family moved to Washington, D.C., where the elder Olds served as commissioner and then chairman of the Federal Power Commission until 1949. Olds began his college career as an undergraduate at the University of Wisconsin in Madison. He transferred to Saint John's College in Annapolis, Maryland, and spent a brief period working for the International News Service before being drafted into the army during World War II. He was trained in Arabic and spent most of his time overseas in Cairo, with the Persian Gulf Command. After returning

Figure 1. James Olds. *Courtesy Dr. M. E. Olds.*

to the United States at the end of the war, Olds transferred to Amherst College, of which his grandfather had been president, to finish his undergraduate studies.

Olds received his doctoral training in the department of social relations at Harvard University. This department was relatively new at that time and included social, experimental, and clinical psychology as well as sociology. Olds's mentor was Richard Solomon, who gave him thorough training in experimental psychology and exposed him to the current literature on physiological psychology. Olds had a part-time job as editor of a book by Talcott Parsons, chairman of the department, to supplement his graduate fellowship. Olds's contributions were so substantial that Parsons made him a coauthor, unique intellectual origins for an individual who made substantial contributions to understanding the neural substrates of reward learning during the substance of his career. Parsons's contact with Olds during subsequent years provided the biological perspective for his sociological theorizing.

Olds's thesis dealt with motivation and was influenced by Donald HEBB's landmark book, *The Organization of Behavior* (1949). He planned to train under Hebb as a first step toward developing a neural realization of a model of Edward TOLMAN's sign-Gestalt theory, by which ideas determine behavior (Olds, 1954). The basic conviction underlying his career plans at this stage was that behavior had to be explained in terms of underlying brain activity. Olds felt that the two principal problems of physiological psychology were motivation and learning, that these two problems were closely intertwined, and that their solution was dependent upon a detailed knowledge of the central nervous system. These basic ideas motivated Olds's entire professional career.

After completing his doctoral thesis, Olds spent a year as a lecturer at Harvard. For the next 2 years he was a postdoctoral trainee in the department of psychology under Hebb at McGill. During this period, Hebb's laboratory interacted extensively with the Wilder Penfield and Herbert Jasper groups at the Montreal Neurological Institute. When Olds arrived at McGill to begin his training, he was placed under the guidance of Peter Milner, who was then finishing his doctoral thesis. Milner taught him how to implant stimulating electrodes in the brain, and Olds prepared a rat with stimulating electrodes in what he presumed was the reticular formation, an area of considerable interest at

that time. The hypothesis to be tested was that the animal would avoid stimulation in the reticular formation (assumed to be the source of neural activity to be reduced by behavior). But when the rat received stimulation through the implanted electrode, quite the opposite effect occurred. The rat actually was attracted to those locations which were associated with the stimulation. This observation in the very first rat he studied turned Olds's initial hypothesis on its head and also suggested that the brain contains reward or pleasure centers that mammals seek to activate during goal-seeking behaviors.

Some unsuccessful attempts to replicate the original electrode placement led to the determination that the hypothalamus and septal regions supported self-stimulation. Olds and Milner described their landmark discovery in a paper that appeared in 1954. It is interesting to note Milner's description of the energy and organizational ability that Olds showed in fleshing out their original observation (Milner, 1989). Olds proceeded to do a large number of very systematic studies using a standard and sensitive technique to determine which portions of the brain supported self-stimulation. He also developed new technical approaches and took advantage of new developments from throughout the brain/behavioral sciences. This approach also characterized the contributions he made to the study of learning and memory.

A unique series of studies designed to "map the brain for learning" was done in Olds's laboratory at Caltech in the early 1970s (Disterhoft and Buchwald, 1980; Olds, 1973a). These studies utilized a technique he had perfected for recording small groups of neurons in the freely moving rat (Olds et al., 1972; Olds, 1975b). The basic concept was to determine how neurons in many brain regions in animals learning the same associative response compared in the time dimension. Those regions which changed earliest in this temporal map, by definition, made special contributions to the formation and readout of the learned response because of their sequential position.

Studies of how the auditory system might change its processing of the tone-conditioned stimulus demonstrated that neurons from the inferior colliculus up to the auditory cortex showed alterations in firing rate during differential auditory conditioning. Considerable effort was focused on the posterior nucleus of the thalamus, a region that receives multisensory afferent drive and showed large firing rate changes very early in the learning process. The involvement of the hippocampus (see GUIDE TO THE ANATOMY OF THE BRAIN), a region that Olds sometimes referred to as the "Rosetta Stone of the brain," also received considerable attention. Olds's previous mapping of the brain for self-stimulation had demonstrated that widely spread brain regions supported this phenomenon. In this tradition, neurons in many other regions throughout the brain, including the nonspecific thalamus, the basal ganglia, the reticular formation, and the hypothalamus, were studied and found to show altered firing rates during an important behavioral event such as auditory learning.

There were some general contributions to the study of learning and memory, in addition to the specific observations mentioned above, made during the series of studies done by Olds's group. First, the advantage of using an apparently simple task as a "model system" to study mechanisms of learning in the mammalian brain was delineated. Second, it was clearly demonstrated that many neurons in many brain regions do change during acquisition of even a simple learning task. This was firm support for the idea that learning is truly a distributed process in the brain. Third, the advantages of formulating temporal maps of alterations in the brain during learning as a way to determine where important alterations were occurring was demonstrated (Olds et al., 1972). The temporal maps were drawn in the two dimensions. (1) from conditioned stimulus onset through conditioned response performance, and (2) from the first training trial through acquisition and overlearning of the conditioned response. This approach gave a clear way to prioritize the relative importance of the many alterations in single-neuron activity observed during learning in widely scattered brain regions. Finally, the studies clearly emphasized the importance and strength of an approach that dissected individual subsystems for detailed analysis during learning the common task, whatever that task might be. Following subsystem analysis, the total system interactions are more amenable to delineation. (See also LOCALIZATION OF MEMORY TRACES.)

The approaches Olds designed and the studies he initiated may not have been unique, but the approach his group used to such obvious advantage was adapted by many laboratories and is still being profitably used in the continuing search for mechanisms of learning and memory. For example, Berger and Thompson (1978) used it in their analysis of hippocampal system activity during learning of the nictitating membrane response in the rabbit.

Woody (1974) had begun studies using temporal analysis of the motor side of the eyeblink pathways in overtrained cats at about the time the Olds group's mapping studies began. More recent approaches have combined in vitro analyses of hippocampal brain slices with in vivo recording to ensure that localized cellular and subcellular alterations in the hippocampus during eyeblink conditioning are being studied (Disterhoft, Coulter, and Alkon, 1986).

Olds spent considerable time and effort setting the stage for the work in which those in the laboratory were involved, but his colleagues had the opportunity to be intimately involved in the daily sequence of events that led to the important observations made during the studies. This is particularly true because Olds's approach to postdoctoral training was modeled after that of Donald Hebb—to learn by doing. His experience in Hebb's laboratory, where he discovered self-stimulation as a postdoctoral fellow, clearly impressed upon him the value of serendipity and the value of personal effort and scientific tinkering. The series of studies done to map the brain for learning used that general approach and are still considered one of the landmarks in the study of associative learning in mammalian brain.

Olds was immersed in his work and loved science, especially as it concerned the brain and how it functioned. If he had one frustration, it was that he had not spent enough of his life learning facts about the brain. He felt that the more facts he had with which to make associations, the more significant the insights that were possible from his theoretical speculations. He spent a good deal of time thinking, talking, and writing about how the brain worked (Olds, 1975a, 1977, 1980). Olds was also fascinated with computers and electronics. Many of his ideas about brain function, such as his speculations about memory storage function in the hippocampus, used computers and their memories as analogies (Olds, 1969). His laboratory was well equipped with computers, and much effort was spent on developing and testing software and hardware. His studies of associative learning utilized a combined hardware-software system simultaneously to study a large number of brain regions in animals engaged in learning the same relatively simple associative task.

The technical problem of developing better ways to study single neurons in conscious animals was one on which Olds expended considerable energy. One of the reasons that he had come to

Caltech was to take advantage of the possibilities for developing electronic gadgetry for his experiments. He was extremely excited when, in collaboration with an electrical engineer from the Jet Propulsion Laboratory, he designed and built what must have been one of the earliest telemetry systems for multiple single-neuron recording. The idea was to transmit signals from ten microwire electrodes simultaneously without danger of cable artifacts. The rat looked a little ungainly with the miniature transmitter on its head (considerably less miniature in 1971 than it would be today), but the system worked pretty well. Olds was always trying to come up with a better operational amplifier than the ones he was using—although it generally turned out that the old standbys worked better. He also was involved in troubleshooting things like electronic waveform identifiers—he wanted his to work better, to be simpler and more state of the art. He would hook up a rat, sit down in front of an oscilloscope, and run a new waveform identifier through its paces by himself. He knew from experience that often the product did not work precisely as intended by the engineer.

The portion of the laboratory used for the mapping of learning was set up with four training stations. Olds used a recording station of his own and carried on a series of experiments separate from those of the postdoctoral fellows and graduate students. He spent a fair amount of time traveling, but when he was in town, he came in every morning to check the rat that was being trained in his station and to check the setting of the waveform discriminators on the unit channels being used. Olds was very demanding about the quality of the data he and his group gathered. He was a firm believer that high-quality findings came from high-quality data. His system had numerous checks for electronic noise and other artifacts. He also took an intense interest in the experiments as they were being run. Those with freely moving rats ran from evening until early morning, the peak of the rats' diurnal cycle. A collaborator coming in during the evening to check experimental progress was likely to discover that Olds had been there shortly before. Almost invariably Olds was in the laboratory early on Sunday to make notes on the printout or adjustments to the computer.

Olds and his collaborators met in his office every afternoon to discuss the data and their interpretation. These meetings often included theoretical discussions that ranged far from the data at hand and discussions of appropriate strategies to use in ongoing or planned experiments. Descriptions of Olds's scientific activities by Neal Miller (1980) and Peter Milner (1989) suggest that his eagerness to share ideas with colleagues and students, and to approach brain function with novel perspectives, characterized his entire scientific career.

Olds was a gracious, urbane person with a good sense of humor. He was also a family man. His wife, Marianne, worked closely with him in the lab. He also lavished considerable attention on his son, also named James, who was in high school during the time Olds was on the Caltech faculty.

[*Acknowledgment.* Dr. M. E. Olds provided the photograph of James Olds and the details on his early years and family background.]

REFERENCES

Berger, T. W., and Thompson, R. F. (1978). Neuronal plasticity in the limbic system during classical conditioning of the rabbit nictitating membrane response. I. The hippocampus. *Brain Research 145,* 323–346.

Disterhoft, J. F., and Buchwald, J. S. (1980). Mapping learning in the brain. In A. Routtenberg, ed., *Biology of reinforcement,* pp. 53–80. New York: Academic Press.

Disterhoft, J. F., Coulter, D. A., and Alkon, D. L. (1986). Conditioning-specific membrane changes of rabbit hippocampal neurons measured *in vitro. Proceedings of the National Academy of Sciences 83,* 2733–2737.

Hebb, D. O. (1949). *The organization of behavior.* New York: John Wiley.

Miller, N. E. (1980). Introduction: Brain stimulation reward and theories of reinforcement. In A. Routtenberg, ed., *Biology of reinforcement,* pp. 1–7. New York: Academic Press.

Milner, P. M. (1989). The discovery of self-stimulation and other stories. *Neuroscience and Biobehavioral Reviews 13,* 61–67.

Olds, J. (1954). A neural model for sign-gestalt theory. *Psychological Review 61,* 59–72.

——— (1969). The central nervous system and the reinforcement of behavior. *American Psychologist 24,* 114–132.

——— (1973a). Brain mechanisms of reinforcement learning. In D. E. Berlyne and N. B. Madsen, eds., *Pleasure, reward, preference,* pp. 35–63. New York: Academic Press.

——— (1973b). Commentary on Olds and Milner's "Positive reinforcement produced by electrical stimulation of septal area and other regions of rat brain." In E. S. Valenstein, ed., *Brain stimulation and motivation: Research and commentary,* pp. 53–68. Glenview, Ill.: Scott, Foresman.

——— (1975a). Mapping the mind onto the brain. In F. G. Worden, J. P. Swazey, and G. Adelman, eds., *The neurosciences: Paths of discovery*, pp. 375–400. Cambridge, Mass.: MIT Press.

——— (1975b). Unit recordings during Pavlovian conditioning. In N. A. Buchwald and M. A. B. Brazier, eds., *Brain mechanisms in mental retardation* pp. 343–371. New York: Academic Press.

——— (1977). *Drives and reinforcements: Behavioral studies of hypothalamic functions*. New York: Raven Press.

——— (1980). Thoughts on cerebral functions: The cortex as an action system. In A. Routtenberg, ed., *Biology of Reinforcement*, pp. 149–167. New York: Academic Press.

Olds, J., Disterhoft, J. F., Segal, M., Kornblith, C. L., and Hirsh, R. (1972). Learning centers of rat brain mapped by measuring latencies of conditioned unit responses. *Journal of Neurophysiology* 35, 202 219.

Olds, J., and Milner, P. M. (1954). Positive reinforcement produced by electrical stimulation of septal area and other regions of rat brain. *Journal of Comparative and Physiological Psychology* 47, 419–427.

Woody, C. D. (1974). Aspects of the electrophysiology of cortical processes related to the development and performance of learned motor responses. *The Physiologist 17*, 49–69.

John F. Disterhoft

OLFACTORY CORTEX

See Guide to the Anatomy of the Brain; Neural Computation

OPERANT BEHAVIOR

In the 1930s B. F. Skinner developed a new methodology for the study of animal learning and behavior. He called it *operant behavior,* to reflect the fact that the animal "operated" on the environment to produce a reward, or *reinforcer. The Behavior of Organisms,* published in 1938, was the principal document in which he presented his findings and his conceptual approach to the study of animal learning and behavior.

In the method that Skinner developed, the animal (most often a rat, pigeon, or monkey) emits particular behaviors, called *instrumental responses* (or behaviors), to gain a reinforcer. Most often, these responses involve an *operandum* (for-

merly called manipulandum) that is suited to the subject's motor abilities. Rats, monkeys, and other mammals press a horizontal bar (or lever) in the experimental chamber (often called a *Skinner box*), while pigeons peck at a vertical disk (or key); fish can be taught to swim through a ring. Normally, the reinforcer immediately follows the response.

Animals learn to emit particular instrumental responses because the reinforcers *shape* behavior. Behaviors that are followed by a reinforcer increase in frequency, and behaviors that are not followed by a reinforcer decrease in frequency. For example, to train a rat to press a lever, the experimenter may first reinforce the animal every time it approaches the lever. When the rat is reliably approaching the lever, reinforcers are provided only if it actually touches the lever. Finally, only pressing the lever is reinforced. This shaping of behavior by progressively narrowing the range of behaviors that are reinforced (the *operant class*) is known as the method of *successive approximation.* If reinforcement for a behavior is discontinued, the behavior will decrease in frequency and may stop completely. This process is known as *extinction.*

In *discrete-trial* procedures, the trial ends with a single response, and the probability, latency, or force of that response is recorded as the measure of behavior. Skinner developed another method of studying behavior that he called *free-operant* procedures. Here, the subject has access to the operandum for extended periods—sometimes an extended trial, on other occasions an entire experimental session—and can respond repeatedly during that period. Therefore, the *rate of responding* becomes the primary measure of behavior. Skinner developed an ingenious method for displaying the rate with a *cumulative record* (see Figure 1). Each response displaces a pen upward by a small amount on a moving strip of paper. This makes the rate of responding immediately visible as the measure of behavior. The higher the rate of responding, the steeper the slope of the cumulative record. However, in most current experimental applications, counters and computers are used to record and analyze response output. These measures allow for more quantitative analyses of behavior.

Schedules of Reinforcement

The designated instrumental response is followed on at least some occasions by a *reinforcer* such

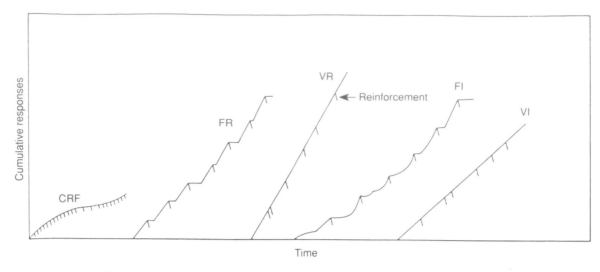

Figure 1. Sample cumulative records of lever pressing on various simple reinforcement schedules. Horizontal displacements in the records indicate passage of time. Vertical displacements indicate cumulative responses. Hatch marks indicate times when the reinforcer is delivered. CRF is continuous reinforcement; FR, fixed ratio; VR, variable ratio; FI, fixed interval; and VI, variable interval. (Hypothetical data.) *Adapted with permission from Domjan and Burkhard, 1985, p. 131.*

as a food pellet or liquid refreshment for the rat or monkey, grain for the bird, or money, tokens, or "points" for a human subject. Skinner designed *schedules of reinforcement* that provided reward only intermittently, in contrast with *continuous reinforcement,* where each response is reinforced. The subject may be reinforced only after emitting a number of responses, on a *ratio* schedule, or for a response after a period of time has elapsed, on an *interval* schedule. The required ratio may be constant on all occasions; this is a *fixed-ratio* schedule. Or it may vary from trial to trial; this is a *variable-ratio* schedule.

Likewise, in an interval schedule the interval may be fixed or variable. Skinner found that each of these schedules produced distinctive cumulative records. For example, in fixed-ratio schedules, animals frequently do not respond immediately after a reinforcer; this is called a *post-reinforcement pause.* Then they emit responses in a high-rate "burst" to obtain the reinforcer. In fixed-interval schedules, the subject typically does not respond immediately after the reinforcer, and the rate of responding steadily accelerates as the end of the interval approaches. Variable-interval and variable-ratio schedules usually generate steady rates of responding. Ratio schedules generally produce high rates of responding because the rate of reinforcement depends entirely on the rate of

responding. However, ratio schedules requiring a large number of responses for each reinforcer may induce *ratio strain* in the form of extended periods of no responding.

These simple schedules of reinforcement can be combined into more complex schedules. One schedule may produce yet another schedule before a reinforcer is given, a *chain schedule,* or two schedules may regularly alternate on one operandum, a *multiple schedule.* In these schedules, distinctive stimuli signal which particular schedule is currently in effect. In a *mixed schedule,* the component schedules alternate, but they are not signaled by an external cue.

In *concurrent schedules,* two (or more) schedules are simultaneously in effect and the subject can choose between them. These schedules can be arranged on separate operanda or on one operandum. In the latter procedure the subject can choose between schedules by performing a switching response to a different operandum. It has been found that animals distribute the time spent responding to each schedule in proportion to the rate of reinforcement obtained from each. This relation is known as the *matching law.* Type of schedule, magnitude of the reinforcers, and type of reinforcement are also important determinants of choice. For example, studies of *self-control* have shown that animals are "impulsive"; they choose small, immediate reinforcers over delayed, but much larger, reinforcers.

Stimulus Control

Discriminative stimuli can signal the effective schedule of reinforcement. For rats, these can be different tones or the presence or absence of a "house light" in the chamber. For pigeons, different colors or patterns may be projected onto the response key. Monkeys are often presented with complex visual patterns. The discriminative stimuli come to control the rates of responding. For example, a pigeon will respond at the same rate to a key lit red or green if both colors signal a variable-interval (VI) schedule. However, if the VI schedule during the green-light component is removed, then the rate of responding to this negative stimulus rapidly decreases. The response rate to the red light, the positive stimulus, will actually increase over its previous level, a phenomenon called *behavioral contrast*. New stimuli from the same *stimulus dimension* can be presented in a *generalization test*. For example, if the discriminative stimuli used in training are two tones, then a rat may be tested with a range of tonal frequencies. *Gradients of generalization* (or discrimination) are readily obtained; that is, the amount of responding to each new stimulus is an orderly function of its similarity to the positive training stimulus. (See also DISCRIMINATION AND GENERALIZATION.)

If the stimuli are more complex, such as pictures, this provides an opportunity for the study of *concept attainment* when the stimuli belong to different classes. Pigeons, for example, readily learn to discriminate between pictures containing images of one or more people and pictures without a person.

Stimulus control is also studied using discrete-trial choice procedures. A stimulus is presented as a sample, and then the animal must choose which of two response alternatives is correct for that particular stimulus. Correct choices are reinforced. Such methods are analogous to *signal detection* experiments with human subjects and have provided precise measurements of animal perception. If a delay intervenes between the sample stimulus and the choice, the short-term memory or WORKING MEMORY of animals can be studied. Generally, the accuracy of choice decreases markedly with delays of even a few seconds.

Control with Aversive Stimuli

Positive reinforcers are normally *appetitive* stimuli. *Aversive* stimuli, such as electric shock or loud noise, are also effective in the control of behavior. If aversive stimuli are consequences for responding, they are *punishers,* and they reduce the rate of responding, which is otherwise maintained by positive reinforcement. Animals are very sensitive to both the strength and the frequency of the punishers. Aversive stimuli are also used in the study of *escape* and *avoidance.* The latter is most often studied in a free-operant situation. The subject, most often a rat, is subjected to brief, intermittent shocks. By emitting a required response, such as bar pressing or crossing a hurdle, the subject can postpone or cancel the shock. This procedure generates consistent rates of avoidance behavior in rats, monkeys, and other organisms, especially when each response guarantees a shock-free interval.

Summary

Operant methodology has shown that animal behavior is an orderly function of its antecedents (discriminative stimuli) and its consequences (reinforcement and punishment). It has also enabled experimenters to explore various areas of animal perception, cognition, and choice. Furthermore, the principles of operant behavior have application to humans. Operant techniques have been employed in personal instruction and in the treatment of dysfunctional human behavior.

(See also REINFORCEMENT; CONDITIONING, CLASSICAL AND INSTRUMENTAL.)

REFERENCES

Catania, A. C. (1979). *Learning.* Englewood Cliffs, N.J.: Prentice-Hall.

Domjan, M. P., and Burkhard, B. (1985). *The principles of learning and behavior,* 2nd ed. San Francisco: Brooks/Cole.

Flaherty, C. F. (1985). *Animal learning and cognition.* New York: Knopf.

Schwartz, B., and Reisberg, D. (1991). *Learning and memory.* New York: Norton.

Skinner, B. F. (1938). *The behavior of organisms.* New York: Appleton-Century.

W. K. Honig
Brent Alsop

ORAL TRADITIONS

Oral traditions depend on human memory for their preservation. Songs or stories from a tradition must be stored in one person's memory and passed to another person who can also remember and retell them. All this must occur over many generations. For example, verses from versions of ballads collected in the 1600s in Great Britain are similar to versions more recently collected in North Carolina. Most of the words have changed, but the basic ideas and poetic structures have not. Similarly, the counting-out rhyme "eenie meenie" has remained stable, though with much less change, for a century. Rote memorization is not occurring. Rather, there is evidence that poetic and meaning rules are being transmitted. Oral traditions must, therefore, have forms of organization and modes of transmission to decrease the changes that human memory usually imposes on verbal material. The major forms of organization that contribute to stability of oral traditions include *imagery, gist, rhyme, alliteration, rhythm,* and *music.*

Imagery is perhaps the most powerful and widespread factor in mnemonic systems (see CODING PROCESSES: IMAGERY). As Paivio (1971) points out, imagery is most effective for concrete (versus abstract), parallel-spatial (versus sequential), and dynamic (versus static) processing. Oral traditions consist predominantly of sequences of concrete actions by active agents, not abstract principles (Havelock, 1978). In ballads, for example, verses that contain concrete, imageable actions are recalled better than ones that do not (Wallace and Rubin, 1988).

Meaning or thematic organization plays a large role in adult oral traditions. The cognitive psychologists' descriptions of such organization, including *schemas, scripts, story grammars,* and *causal chains,* can all be used to quantify and describe thematic organization, though the rules for these vary from tradition to tradition. For instance, common scripts in epic include arming a hero or the hero's horse, assembling an army, and joining battle. The scripts are at least as well-formed and strict as undergraduates' knowledge of going to the dentist's office or a fast-food restaurant. The forms of thematic organization allow singers to expand or contract their story at will, as is common in epic (Lord, 1960).

Poetics and music each add a unique contribution. When two words in a ballad are linked by rhyme or alliteration, undergraduates have a higher recall for them than when the poetics are broken. Furthermore, when ballad singers perform the same ballad twice, they are less likely to change poetically linked words (Wallace and Rubin, 1988). Some genres, such as counting-out rhymes, have nearly all their words poetically linked, whereas others have minimal poetics. We know from the extensive work by Nelson and McEvoy (e.g., Nelson, 1981) that rhyme cues function differently than meaning cues. It is as if rhyme cues a whole set, while meaning cues, when available, single out the target. Rhyme, as opposed to meaning cues, tends to work best with fast presentation rates, small set size, and strong cue strength, three conditions that tend to be present in the small world of oral traditions. Thus, rhymes have their own peculiar properties, which have been studied extensively and often are well suited to oral traditions. This is true even with subjects not trained to attend to rhyme the way users of many oral traditions are.

Oral traditions are rhythmic. Rhythm functions in at least four ways: (1) Rhythm is a constraint, like others, limiting word choice to words with the correct number of syllables and correct stress pattern. (2) Rhythm creates slots that need to be filled, producing a demand characteristic to recall, and thereby favors changes within a rhythmic unit rather than errors of omission. (3) Rhythm, like meaning, provides an organization, allowing singers to select, substitute, add, or delete whole rhythmic units, then continue. Such rhythmic units typically coincide with meaning units in oral traditions (Lord, 1960), as expected from laboratory studies. (4) Rhythm emphasizes certain locations within lines that facilitate other constraints, such as the placing of rhyme and alliteration on stressed syllables.

Imagery, meaning, poetics, and music all provide forms of organization or constraint. Once the properties of each form of organization are listed, it is easy to add the constraints together to produce an impressive total degree of constraint. However, more than additive effects are found. For example, although a rhyme or meaning cue by itself may not lead to recall of the last word of a line, when combined they can be effective because there is often only one word that fits them both (Rubin and Wallace, 1989).

Besides interaction effects that limit word choices, the specific properties of the various forms of organization complement each other. For instance, imagery leads to the original verbal stimulus being transformed into a nonverbal, atemporal representation. When a verbal output is needed, the original words and the order of presentation will not be available for retrieval and will be generated from the image, resulting in changes in wording and the order of ideas. Thematic organization, such as scripts, story grammars, and causal chains, however, functions to preserve the temporal order lost by imagery. Even so, in most models of memory, words are translated to and from a more abstract representation that contains none of the sound pattern, allowing for the possibility of translation errors. This remaining lack is remedied by poetics and music, which preserve the sound pattern.

Many strategies of transmission add to the stability provided by the organizational constraints outlined. Songs in an oral tradition are recalled repeatedly after they have been mastered, that is, they benefit from *overlearning*. Moreover, this overlearning is usually spaced over time, in some cases once a year, when the appropriate season arrives. Overlearning and *spaced practice* (see DISTRIBUTED PRACTICE EFFECTS) are two of the most powerful factors in maintaining material in memory for long periods. In addition, there are social supports aiding stability. In many genres, only experts who are suited by interest and ability are the active transmitters. They hear their songs from more than one source, which allows better variants to replace inferior ones. Their audience, though it may not be able to supply alternatives, can show approval or disapproval of what it hears.

REFERENCES

Foley, J. M. (1988). *The theory of oral composition: History and methodology.* Bloomington: Indiana University Press.

Havelock, E. A. (1978). *The Greek concept of justice: From its shadow in Homer to its substance in Plato.* Cambridge, Mass.: Harvard University Press.

Kelly, M. H., and Rubin, D. C. (1988). Natural rhythmic patterns in English verse: Evidence from child counting-out rhymes. *Journal of Memory and Language* 27, 718–740.

Lord, A. B. (1960). *The singer of tales.* Cambridge, Mass.: Harvard University Press.

Nelson, D. L. (1981). Many are called but few are chosen: The influence of context on the effects of category size. In G. H. Bower, ed., *The psychology of learning and motivation,* vol. 15. New York: Academic Press.

Paivio, A. (1971). *Imagery and verbal processes.* New York: Holt, Rinehart and Winston.

Rubin, D. C., and Wallace, W. T. (1989). Rhyme and reason: Analysis of dual cues. *Journal of Experimental Psychology: Learning, Memory, and Cognition* 15, 698–709.

Wallace, W. T., and Rubin, D. C. (1988). "The wreck of the old 97": A real event remembered in song. In U. Neisser and E. Winograd, eds., *Remembering reconsidered: Ecological and traditional approaches to the study of memory,* pp. 283–310. Cambridge: Cambridge University Press.

David C. Rubin

ORIENTING REFLEX HABITUATION

The orienting reflex (OR) is a complex response of the organism to a novel stimulus. It was discovered by IVAN PAVLOV ([1927] 1960) as an interruption of ongoing activity by presentation of an unexpected stimulus (external inhibition). This inhibition of the ongoing activity, accompanied by somatic, vegetative, electroencephalographic, humoral, and sensory manifestations, was termed the "what-is-it reflex." The OR is a set of components contributing to optimize the conditions of stimulus perception. A sequence of ORs directed toward new aspects of the environment constitutes an exploratory behavior. The somatic components of the OR are represented by eye and head targeting movements, perking of ears, and sniffing. The vasoconstriction of peripheral vessels and vasodilation of vessels of the head, heart rate deceleration, and skin galvanic response (SGR) constitute vegetative OR components. POSITRON EMISSION TOMOGRAPHY has demonstrated enhancement of blood supply in different brain areas during sensory stimulation. The electroencephalographic manifestation of OR is characterized by negative steady potential shift that parallels a transition from slow-wave brain activity to high-frequency oscillations, demonstrating an enhancement of the arousal level (Lindsley, 1961). Humoral components of OR are represented by β-endorphin and acetylcholine released within brain tissues. The sensory components of OR are expressed in a lowering of sensory thresholds and increase of fusion frequency.

The repeated presentation of a stimulus results in a gradual decrement of OR components, called *habituation* (see also HABITUATION AND SENSITIZATION IN VERTEBRATES). The process of habituation is stimulus-selective. That selectivity can be demonstrated with respect to elementary features (intensity, frequency, color, location, duration) as well as to complex aspects of stimuli (shape, accord, heteromodal structure). The habituation of the OR is also semantically selective, indicating a high level of abstraction in the OR control. In the process of habituation of OR, a neuronal model of the presented stimulus is elaborated in the brain. Any change of stimulus parameters with respect to the established neuronal model results in an elicitation of the OR. After a response to a novel stimulus, one sees the OR recover to a standard stimulus, a phenomenon called *dishabituation*. The OR is evoked by a mismatch signal resulting from the comparison of the presented stimulus with the established neuronal model. If the stimulus coincides with the neuronal model, no OR is generated. The neuronal model can be regarded as a multidimensional, self-adjustable filter shaped by a repeatedly presented stimulus. The magnitude of the OR depends on the degree of noncoincidence of the stimulus with the shape of the multidimensional filter. In accordance with the degree of spreading of excitation, local and generalized forms of ORs are distinguished. Short and long duration of excitation constitutes a basis for separation of phasic and tonic forms of ORs. In the process of habituation, tonic and generalized forms of OR are transformed into phasic and local ones (Sokolov, 1963).

The habituation of the OR can be studied using event-related potentials (ERPs) represented by a sequence of positive (P1, P2, P3) and negative (N1, N2) brain waves elicited by stimulus onset.

The computer-based isolation of separate ERPs evoked by rare stimuli demonstrates a partial habituation of vertex N1 that parallels the habituation of SGR. A novel stimulus results in an increase of N1 and evocation of SGR. Thus the stimulus deviating from the neuronal model triggers a modality-nonspecific negativity overlapping the stable part of N1 (Verbaten, 1988). The deviant stimuli following with short intervals among standard ones generate a modality-specific mismatch negativity overlapping N1-P2 components (Näätänen, 1990). The OR evoked by nonsignal stimuli is termed *involuntary OR*. It differs from an OR evoked by signal stimuli, which is termed *voluntary OR* (Maltzman, 1985). The OR habituated to a nonsignal stimulus is recovered under the influence of verbal instruction announcing that the stimulus is a target of the response. Such an enhancement of an OR due to verbal instruction is lacking in patients with frontal lobe lesions, whereas their ORs to nonsignal stimuli remain intact (Luria, 1973).

The verbal instruction actualizes a memory trace of the target stimulus. The presented stimuli are matched against the memory trace. The match signal is evident in brain ERPs as a processing negativity overlapping N1-N2. The processing negativity is the greater the more closely the stimulus matches the memory trace, which is activated by verbal instruction (Näätänen, 1990). Similar enhancement of OR can be observed in the process of elaboration of conditioned reflexes (see CONDITIONING, CLASSICAL AND INSTRUMENTAL). The nonsignal stimulus evoking no OR after habituation produces an OR again after its reinforcement. During conditioned reflex stabilization, OR is gradually extinguished, but more slowly than in response to a nonsignal stimulus. When a new nonreinforced differential stimulus is introduced into the experimental procedure, the OR is reestablished. The more difficult is the differentiation of signals, the greater the OR. Thus the magnitude and stability of ORs depend on novelty, significance, and task difficulty. Involuntary and voluntary ORs can be integrated within a common attentional process: A novel nonsignal stimulus triggering an involuntary OR followed by a voluntary OR constitutes sustained attention.

The OR has its own reinforcement value and can be used as a reinforcement in the elaboration of conditioned ORs. The β-endorphin released by novel stimulus presentation plays a role of positive reinforcement in a search for novelty. The OR can contribute as an exploratory drive in selection of new combinations of memory traces during creative activity.

The OR at the neuronal level is represented by several populations of cells. The most important are novelty detectors, represented by pyramidal hippocampal cells characterized by universally extended receptive fields. Being activated by novel stimuli, these cells demonstrate stimulus-selective habituation that parallels the OR habituation at the macro level. Any change of input stimulus results in their spiking again. Thus a multidimensional neuronal model of a stimulus is formed at a single pyramidal neuron of the hippocampus. The selectivity of the neuronal model is determined by specific neocortical feature detectors extracting different properties of the input signal in parallel. The feature detectors characterized by stable responses converge on novelty detectors through plastic (modifiable) synapses. The plasticity of synapses on novelty detectors is dependent on hippocampal dentate granule cells. A set of excitations generated in selective feature detectors reach pyramidal and dentate cells in parallel. The dentate cells have synapses on pyramidal cells controlling the habituation process. The synapses of feature detectors constitute a map of features on a single novelty detector.

The neuronal model is represented on such a feature map by a specific pattern of synapses depressed by repeated stimulus presentations. The output signals of novelty detectors are fed to activating brain-stem reticular formation neurons, generating an arousal reaction. The rest of the hippocampal pyramidal neurons are sameness detectors characterized by a background firing. A new stimulus results in an inhibition of their spiking. This inhibitory reaction is habituated by repeated stimulus presentation. The inhibitory response is evoked again by any stimulus change. The maximal firing rate is observed in sameness neurons under familiar surroundings. The output signals from sameness detectors are directed to inactivating reticular formation neurons, inducing drowsiness and sleep. The selective habituation of the pyramidal cell responses is based on the potentiation of synapses of dentate cells on pyramidal neurons. Under such potentiation of dentate synapses, the pyramidal cells stop responding to afferent stimuli. The injection of antibodies against hippocampal granule cells results in elimination of pyramidal cell habituation (Vinogradova, 1970).

Such are the neuronal mechanisms of involuntary OR habituation. The neuronal mechanisms of voluntary OR are more complex (Figure 1). The stimuli analyzed by feature detectors are recorded by memory units of the association cortex. The verbal instruction, through semantic units with the participation of frontal lobe mechanisms, selects a set of memory units as a template. The match signal generated by memory units of the template is recorded as processing negativity. The match signal is addressed to novelty detectors, resulting in an enhancement of OR to significant stimuli. Through novelty detectors and sensitization of activating units, novel stimulus results in an electroencephalographic arousal correlated

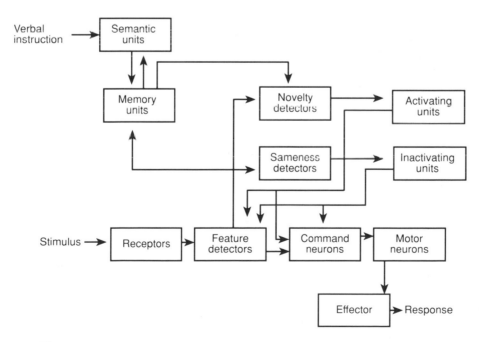

Figure 1. Neuronal mechanisms of the voluntary orienting reflex.

with sensitization of feature detectors and external inhibition of ongoing activity at the level of the command neurons. The repeated presentation of a stimulus switches on sameness neurons, which, with participation of inactivating units, induce lowering of the arousal level, expressed in drowsiness and sleep.

REFERENCES

Lindsley, D. B. (1961). The reticular activating system and perceptual integration. In D. E. Sheer, ed., *Electrical stimulation of the brain*. Austin: University of Texas Press.

Luria, A. R. (1973). The frontal lobes and the regulation of behavior. In K. H. Pribram and A. R. Luria, eds., *Psychophysiology of the frontal lobes*. New York: Academic Press.

Maltzman, I. (1985). Some characteristics of orienting reflexes. *Psychiatry 2,* 913–916.

Näätänen, R. (1990). The role of attention in auditory information processing as revealed by event-related potentials and other brain measures of cognitive function. *Behavioral and Brain Sciences 13,* 201–288.

Pavlov, I. P. [1927] (1960). *Conditioned reflexes: An investigation of the physiological activity of the cerebral cortex*. Trans. and ed. G. V. Anrep. New York: Dover.

Sokolov, E. N. (1963). *Perception and conditioned reflex*. Oxford: Pergamon Press.

——— (1975). The neuronal mechanisms of the orienting reflex. In E. N. Sokolov and O. S. Vinogradova, eds., *Neuronal mechanisms of the orienting reflex*. Hillsdale, N.J.: Erlbaum.

Verbaten, M. N. (1988). A model for the orienting response and its habituation. *Psychophysiology 25,* 487–488.

Vinogradova, O. S. (1970). Registration of information and the limbic system. In G. Horn and R. Hind, eds., *Short-term changes in neuronal activity and behavior*. Cambridge: Cambridge University Press.

E. N. Sokolov

P

PARALLEL DISTRIBUTED PROCESSING MODELS OF MEMORY

This article describes a class of computational models that help us understand some of the most important characteristics of human memory. The computational models are called *parallel distributed processing* (PDP) models because memories are stored and retrieved in a system consisting of a large number of simple computational elements, all working at the same time and all contributing to the outcome. They are sometimes also called *connectionist* models because the knowledge that governs retrieval is stored in the strengths of the connections among the elements.

The article begins with a common metaphor for human memory, and shows why it fails to capture several key characteristics of memory that are captured by the PDP approach. Then a brief statement of the general characteristics of PDP systems is given. Following this, two specific models are presented that capture key characteristics of memory in slightly different ways. Strengths and weaknesses of the two approaches are considered, and a synthesis is presented. The article ends with a brief discussion of the techniques that have been developed for adjusting connection strengths in PDP systems.

Characteristics of Memory

A common metaphor for human memory might be called the "computer file" metaphor. On this metaphor, we store a copy of an idea or experience in a file, which we can later retrieve and reexamine. There are several problems with this view.

Memories are accessed by content. First of all, the natural way of accessing records in a computer is by their address in the computer. However, what actually happens in human memory is that we access memories by their contents. Any description that uniquely identifies a memory is likely to be sufficient for recall. Even more interesting, each individual element of the description may be nearly useless by itself, if it applies to many memories; only the combination needs to be unique. Thus

He bet on sports.
He played baseball.

is enough for many people to identify Pete Rose, even through the cues about baseball and betting on sports would not generally be sufficient as cues individually, since each matches too many memories.

Memory fills in gaps. The computer-file metaphor also misses the fact that when we recall, we often fill in information that could not have been part of the original record. Pieces of information that were not part of the original experience intrude on our recollections. Sometimes these intrusions are misleading, but often enough they are in fact helpful reconstructions based on things we know about similar memories. For example, if we are told that someone has been shot by someone else from a distance of 300 yards, we are likely to recall later that a rifle was used, even though this was not mentioned when we heard about the original event. (See RECONSTRUCTIVE MEMORY.)

Memory generalizes over examples. A third crucial characteristic of memory is that it allows us to form generalizations. If every apricot we see is orange, we come to treat this as an inherent characteristic of apricots. But if cars come in many different colors, we come to treat the color as a freely varying property. So when we are asked to retrieve the common properties of apricots, the color is a prominent element of our recollection; but no color comes out when we are asked to retrieve the common properties of cars.

Proponents of the computer-file view of memory deal with these issues by adding special processes. Access by content is done by laborious sequential search. Reconstruction is done by applying inferential processes to the retrieved record. Generaliza-

tion occurs through a process of forming explicit records for the category (e.g., *car* or *apricot*).

In PDP systems, these three characteristics of memory are intrinsic to the operation of the memory system.

Characteristics of PDP Systems

A PDP system consists of a large number of neuron-like computing elements called *units*. Each unit can take on an activation value between some max-

Name	Gang	Age	Education	Marital status	Occupation
Art	Jets	40s	JH	single	pusher
Al	Jets	30s	JH	married	burglar
Sam	Jets	20s	college	single	bookie
Clyde	Jets	40s	JH	single	bookie
Mike	Jets	30s	JH	single	bookie
Jim	Jets	20s	JH	divorced	burglar
Greg	Jets	20s	HS	married	pusher
John	Jets	20s	JH	married	burglar
Doug	Jets	30s	HS	single	bookie
Lance	Jets	20s	JH	married	burglar
George	Jets	20s	JH	divorced	burglar
Pete	Jets	20s	HS	single	bookie
Fred	Jets	20s	HS	single	pusher
Gene	Jets	20s	college	single	pusher
Ralph	Jets	30s	JH	single	pusher
Phil	Sharks	30s	college	married	pusher
Ike	Sharks	30s	JH	single	bookie
Nick	Sharks	30s	HS	single	pusher
Don	Sharks	30s	college	married	burglar
Ned	Sharks	30s	college	married	bookie
Karl	Sharks	40s	HS	married	bookie
Ken	Sharks	20s	HS	single	burglar
Earl	Sharks	40s	HS	married	burglar
Rick	Sharks	30s	HS	divorced	burglar
Ol	Sharks	30s	college	married	pusher
Neal	Sharks	30s	HS	single	bookie

Figure 1. Characteristics of a number of individuals belonging to two gangs, the Jets and the Sharks. *Reprinted with permission from McClelland, 1981.*

imum and minimum values, often 1 and 0. In such systems, the representation of something that we are currently thinking about is a pattern of activation over the computing elements. Processing occurs by the propagation of activation from one unit to another via connections among the units. A connection may be excitatory (positive-valued) or inhibitory (negative-valued). If the connection from one unit to another is excitatory, then the activation of the receiving unit tends to increase whenever the sending unit is active. If the connection is inhibitory, then the activation of the receiving unit tends to decrease. But note that each unit may receive connections from many other units. The actual change in activation, then, is based on the net input, aggregated over all of the excitatory and inhibitory connections.

In a system like this, the knowledge that governs processing is stored in the connections among the units, for it is these connections that determine what pattern will result from the presentation of an input. Learning occurs through adjustments of connection strengths. Memory storage is just a form of learning, and also occurs by connection weight adjustment.

To make these ideas concrete, we now examine two PDP models of memory. The models differ in a crucial way. In the first, each individual computing element (henceforth called a unit) represents a separate cognitive unit, be it a feature (for example, the color of something), or a whole object, or the object's name. When we are remembering events, there is a unit for each event. Such models are called *localist* models. In the second type of model, cognitive units are not separately assigned to individual computing units. Rather, the representation of each cognitive unit is thought of as a pattern of activation over an ensemble of computing units. Alternative objects of thought are represented by alternative patterns of activation. This type of model is called a *distributed* model.

A Localist PDP Model of Memory

McClelland (1981) presented a PDP model that illustrates the properties of access by content, filling in of gaps, and generalization. The data base for the model is shown in Figure 1. The network is shown in Figure 2.

The data base consists of descriptions of a group of people who are members of two gangs, the

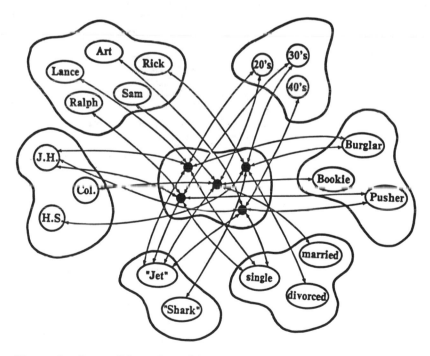

Figure 2. Some of the units and interconnections needed to represent the individuals shown in Figure 1. The units connected with double-headed arrows are mutually excitatory. All the units within the same cloud are mutually inhibitory. *Reprinted with permission from McClelland, 1981.*

Jets and the Sharks. Each person has a name, and the list specifies the age, marital status, and education of each person. Perusal of the list reveals that the Jets are, by and large, younger and less well educated than the Sharks, and tend to be single rather than married. However, these tendencies are not absolute and, furthermore, there is no single Jet who has all of the properties that tend to be typical of Jets.

The goal of the network is to allow retrieval of general and specific information about individuals in the data base. The network consists of a unit for each person (in the center of Figure 2) and a unit for each property (name, age, educational level, occupation, gang) that a person can have. Units are grouped into pools by type as shown, so that all the name units are in one pool, for instance. There is a bidirectional excitatory connection between each person's unit and the units for each of his properties; and there are bidirectional inhibitory connections between units that can be thought of as incompatible alternatives. Thus there is inhibition between the different occupation units, between the different age units, and so on. There is also inhibition between the different name units and between the units for different individuals.

In this network, units take on activation values between 1 and −0.2. The output is equal to the activation, unless the activation is less than 0; then there is no output. In the absence of input, the activations of all the units are set to a resting value of −0.1.

Retrieval by Name

Retrieval begins with the presentation of a probe, in the form of externally supplied input to one or more of the property units. To retrieve the properties of Lance, for example, we need only turn on the name unit for Lance. The activation process is gradual and builds up over time, eventually resulting in a stable pattern that in this case represents the properties of Lance. Activation spreads from the name unit to the property units by way of the instance unit. Feedback from activated properties tends to activate the instance units for other individuals, but because of the mutual inhibition, these activators are kept relatively low.

Retrieval by Content

It should be clear how we can access an individual by properties, as well as by name. As long as we present a set of properties that uniquely matches a single individual, retrieval of the rest of what is known of properties of that individual is quite good. Other similar individuals may become partially active, but the correct person unit will dominate the person pool, and the correct properties will be activated.

Filling in Gaps

Suppose that we delete the connection between Lance and *burglar*. This creates a gap in the data base. However, the model can fill in this gap, in the following way. As the other properties of Lance become active, they in turn feed back activation to units for other individuals similar to Lance. Since the instance unit for Lance himself is not specifying any activation for an occupation, the instance units for other, similar individuals conspire together to fill in the gap. In this case it turns out that there is a group of individuals who are very similar to Lance and who are all burglars. As a result, the network fills in *burglar* for Lance as well. One may view this as an example of guilt by association. In this case, it so happens that the model is correct in filling in *burglar,* but of course this kind of filling in is by no means guaranteed to be correct. Similarly, in human memory, our reconstructions of past events often blend in the contents of other, similar events.

Generalization

The model can be used to retrieve a generalization over a set of individuals who match a particular probe. For example, one can retrieve the typical properties of Jets simply by turning on the Jet unit and allowing the network to settle. The result is that the network activates *20's, junior high,* and *single* strongly. No name is strongly activated, and the three occupations are all activated about equally, reflecting the fact that all three occur with equal frequency among the Jets.

In summary, this simple model shows how retrieval by content, filling in gaps, and generalization are intrinsic to the process of retrieval in the PDP approach to memory.

A Distributed PDP Model of Memory

The second model to be considered is a distributed model. Many authors (e.g., Kohonen, 1977; Ander-

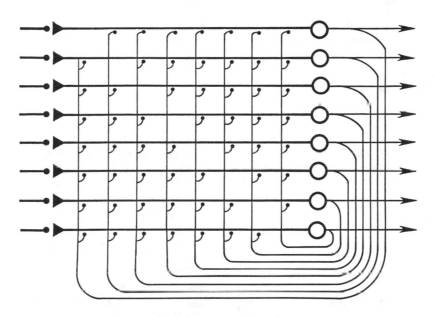

Figure 3. A simple distributed memory, consisting of a small ensemble of eight processing units. Each unit receives input from the left and sends its output to the right. Each unit also has a modifiable connection to all the other units in the memory, as indicated by the branches of the output lines that loop back onto the input lines leading into each unit. *Reprinted with permission from McClelland and Rumelhart, 1985.*

son et al., 1977) have proposed variants of such models. The one shown in Figure 3 is from McClelland and Rumelhart (1985). The model is called *distributed* because there are no single units for individuals or for properties. Instead, the representation to be stored is a distributed pattern over the entire set of units. Similar memories are represented by similar patterns, as before; but now each unit need not correspond to a specific feature or property, and there are no separate units for the item as a whole. Again, the knowledge is stored in the connections among the units.

Methods for training such networks will be considered in more detail below. Suffice it to note one simple method, called the Hebbian method (see HEBB, DONALD). According to this method, we increase the connection strength between two units if they are both active in a particular pattern at the same time.

Distributed networks trained with this Hebbian learning rule exhibit many of the properties of localist networks. They perform an operation, called pattern completion, that is similar to retrieval by content. In pattern completion, any part of the pattern can be used as a cue to retrieve the rest of the pattern, although there are limits to this that we will consider below. Because many memories are stored using the same connection weights, they have a very strong tendency to fill in gaps in one pattern with parts of other, similar patterns. These models also generalize. When similar patterns are stored, what is learned about one pattern will tend to transfer to those parts that it has in common with the other. When a set of similar patterns is stored, what is common to all of them will build up as each example is learned; what is different will cancel out.

There is a final important property of distributed memory models, and that is graceful degradation. The knowledge that governs the ability to reconstruct each pattern is distributed throughout the network, so if some of the connections are lost, it will not necessarily be catastrophic. In fact, the network can function quite well even when many of the units are destroyed, especially if it is relatively lightly loaded with memories.

A Synthesis

Each of the two models described above has some limitations. The localist model requires a special instance unit to be devoted to each memory trace;

this is inefficient, especially when there is redundancy across different memories in terms of what properties tend to concur in the same memory. On the other hand, the distributed model is limited because only a few distinct patterns can be stored in the direct connections among the members of a set of units.

The best of both worlds can be obtained in a hybrid system, in which the various parts of the representation of a memory are bound together by a set of superordinate units, as in the localist model, but each superordinate unit participates in the representation of many different memories, as in the distributed model.

(See also LOCALIZATION OF MEMORY TRACES.)

Learning Rules for PDP Systems

Several of the learning rules for PDP systems are reviewed in Rumelhart, Hinton, and McClelland (1986). Here we consider two main classes, *Hebbian* learning rules and *error-correcting* learning rules. We have already mentioned the Hebbian learning rule, which increases the strength of the connection between two units when both units are simultaneously active. In a common variant, the strength of the connection is decreased when one unit is active and the other is inactive.

These Hebbian learning rules are limited in what can be learned with them. Some of these limitations are overcome by what are called error-correcting learning rules. In such learning rules, the idea is that the pattern to be learned is treated not only as input but also as the target for learning. A pattern is presented, and the network is allowed to settle. Once it has done so, the discrepancies between the resulting pattern and the input pattern are used to determine what changes should be made in the connections. For example, if a unit is activated that should not be active, the connection weights coming into that unit from other active units will be reduced. Several very powerful learning procedures for adjusting connection weights that are based on the idea of reducing the discrepancy between output and target have been developed in recent years. The best-known is the back-propagation learning procedure (Rumelhart, Hinton, and Williams, 1986). Another important learning rule for PDP systems is the Boltzmann machine learning rule (Ackley, Hinton, and

Sejnowski, 1985). Both work well in training the hybrid systems described above.

(See also NEURAL COMPUTATION.)

REFERENCES

Ackley, D. H., Hinton, G. E., and Sejnowski, T. J. (1985). A learning algorithm for Boltzmann machines. *Cognitive Science 9*, 147–169.

Anderson, J. A., Silverstein, J. W., Ritz, S. A., and Jones, R. S. (1977). Distinctive features, categorical perception, and probability learning: Some applications of a neural model. *Psychological Review 84*, 413–451.

Hertz, J., Krogh, A., and Palmer, R. (1990). *Introduction to the theory of neural computation*. Redwood City, Calif.: Addison-Wesley.

Hinton, G. E., and Anderson J. A., eds. (1981). *Parallel models of associative memory*. Hillsdale, N.J.: Erlbaum.

Kohonen, T. (1977). *Associative memory: A system theoretical approach*. New York: Springer-Verlag.

McClelland, J. L. (1981). Retrieving general and specific information from stored knowledge of specifics. Paper presented at the third annual meeting of the Cognitive Science Society. Berkeley, Calif.

McClelland, J. L., and Rumelhart, D. E. (1985). Distributed memory and the representation of general and specific information. *Journal of Experimental Psychology: General 114*, 159–188.

Rumelhart, D. E., Hinton, G. E., and McClelland, J. L. (1986). A general framework for parallel distributed processing. In D. E. Rumelhart, J. L. McClelland, and the PDP Research Group, eds., *Parallel distributed processing: Explorations in the microstructures of cognition*, vol. 1. Cambridge, Mass.: MIT Press.

Rumelhart, D. E., Hinton, G. E., and Williams, R. J. (1986). Learning internal representations by error propagation. In D. E. Rumelhart, J. L. McClelland, and the PDP Research Group, eds., *Parallel distributed processing: Explorations in the microstructures of cognition*, vol. 1. Cambridge, Mass.: MIT Press.

Rumelhart, D. E., McClelland, J. L., and the PDP Research Group. (1986). *Parallel distributed processing: Explorations in the microstructure of cognition*, 2 vols. Cambridge, Mass.: MIT Press.

James L. McClelland

PAVLOV, IVAN

Ivan Petrovich Pavlov (1849–1936) is best known as the discoverer of the conditioned reflex (see

Figure 1. Ivan Pavlov. *Courtesy National Library of Medicine.*

CONDITIONING, CLASSICAL AND INSTRUMENTAL.) His motto, "Observation and Observation!," like that of Socrates ("The unexamined life is not worth living," or, more precisely, "The uninquiring life is not the life for man"), encapsulates the life and work of this Nobel laureate physiologist, whose influence on psychology in general, and on learning and memory in particular, has been enormous.

Pavlov's life may be viewed as a move from a religious to a scientific perspective. His ancestry can be traced to an illiterate eighteenth-century serf known only by his first name, Pavel (Anokhin, 1949). Pavel's son gained emancipation and became a member of the clerical estate; during the next two generations, the family head rose through the religious hierarchy from church sexton to deacon. The deacon was able to provide a seminary education for his sons, who became ordained priests. The youngest of his three sons, Pavlov's father, Petr Dmitrievich, became a priest in Riazan.

As Windholz's (1991) account indicates, Petr Pavlov, who had a library of his own, transmitted to his son a scholastic attitude toward knowledge. The father's advice to his children was that any book should be read at least twice, in order not to miss anything important and to recall it more accurately. His son Ivan took this advice to heart throughout his scientific career but could not accept his father's position on fundamental (including religious) issues. According to a later account by Ivan, "I had heated arguments with my father, which, because of my position, led to strong words and ended in serious disagreements" (Pavlov, 1952, p. 447). The exact nature of the disagreements is hard to specify, but Windholz's suggestion is probably correct—that significant components were Pavlov's loss of faith by the time he entered the seminary in Riazan and his decision to leave the seminary before completing his studies. In 1870, he entered the natural sciences section of the Faculty of Physics and Mathematics at St. Petersburg University. His father refused to support him financially, yet he had probably unwittingly set the stage for it by providing an intellectual oasis during Pavlov's seminary period. Unlike most seminary students, "Pavlov lived in his parents' home which gave him considerable freedom to pursue his own intellectual interests" by being "able to avoid the discipline imposed upon seminarians living in the dormitory and enjoy[ing] uninhibited reading in a small room over the family living quarters" (Windholz, 1991, p. 58).

For psychology, and for his later interests, perhaps the most important book that the young seminarian may have read in that small room was Ivan Sechenov's *Reflexes of the Brain* (1866). Sechenov had had a brush with the authorities (the government censor), who forced him to change the more explicit title *An Attempt to Place Psychical Processes on a Physiological Basis* to the more neutral published one (Koshotiants, 1945). Nevertheless, the idea that by studying behavior it is possible to give an account of subjective processes is evident in Sechenov's thought and constitutes Pavlov's objective method in psychology, that is, the objective study of mental processes. It is important to stress that in this method, the only restriction on "the levels of explanatory constructs that are used [is] that the evidence concerning those constructs be stated in an objective or scientifically communicable way" (Furedy, Heslegrave, and Scher, 1984, p. 182). Thus there are no Watsonian (e.g., Watson, 1913) or Skinnerian restrictions on the nature of theoretical concepts, but only on the mode of evaluation of the inferences about those concepts. (See WATSON, JOHN B.; SKINNER, B. F.)

Like Sechenov, Pavlov was a revolutionary thinker who, however, was able to deal with authority without either surrendering on vital points or being forced to oppose at the cost of personal ruin. An early instance of this flexibility is that a seminary inspector stated on a written certificate at the end of Pavlov's period of study that "thoughts contrary to the Christian religion . . . I never noticed in him" (cited in Windholz, 1991, p. 63), well after Pavlov's religious arguments with his father. Much later, after he had achieved the pinnacle of scientific status for his work on the physiology of digestion (the Nobel Prize, 1904), and had then turned to the study of the "psychic" salivary (digestive) reflex (i.e., Pavlovian conditioning), he was able to maintain an active laboratory throughout the reign of Stalin, a considerable testament to his political skills.

Yet Pavlov also showed great courage in challenging authority. Horsley Gantt, a young American scientist who was a visiting member of Pavlov's laboratory in the 1920s, recounts that in 1926 the minister of education and head of the department that supported Pavlov's laboratory came on a site visit, but Pavlov refused even to meet with him, much less show him his laboratory. His stated reason was that he disapproved of the minister's recent book, *The ABC of Communism* (Gantt, 1991, p. 68). The fact that Pavlov's laboratory survived and thrived following this piece of incredible political insolence suggests both his intellectual integrity and his skill in knowing just how far he could go in challenging authority. He shared with Socrates and other great thinkers the passion for inquiry and the world of the mind, but unlike Socrates he retained the practical skills necessary to survive in the political world.

One mark of Pavlov's fame is that he is one of the handful of modern thinkers whose name is used adjectivally to describe concepts. Pavlovian concepts in psychology are widely referred to and may be classified in three areas, the last of which is the most relevant to learning and memory. The first area is that of popular psychology, wherein the term *Pavlovian response* refers to automatic, nonreflective, reflexlike reactions. In this vein, the brainwashing activities of the Chinese and the North Koreans in the 1950s were considered to be "Pavlovian," and much of orthodox Marxist writings in psychology during the same period in the Soviet Union paid lip service to "Pavlovian principles."

Of general scientific interest for personality theory is the Pavlovian notion of differing strengths in the nervous system, a concept that arose from Pavlov's study of experimental neurosis occurring from the breakdown of conditional discrimination in dogs. In the West, Eysenck's work on extraversion and introversion draws heavily on these Pavlovian concepts. Detailed analysis of this psychological (and physiological) theorizing is not relevant here, but it is worth noting that the theoretical ideas and concepts involved are quite complex and go well beyond the observable data that Watson (1913) argued were the only proper subject matter of psychology.

For the psychology of learning, however, Pavlov's most important concept is indubitably that of the conditioned reflex, which is a form of learning resulting from "classical" or "Pavlovian" conditioning. In classical conditioning, a stimulus (e.g., food) that unconditionally elicits the to-be-learned response (e.g., salivation, the unconditioned response or UR) is paired with a "neutral" stimulus (e.g., bell) that, conditional on being paired repeatedly with the unconditioned stimulus (US), comes to elicit salivation as the conditioned reflex or response (CR). In Pavlov's view, the classical conditioning preparation was contrary to "subjective psychology [which] held that saliva flowed because the dog wished to receive a choice bit of meat" (Grigorian, 1974, p. 433). This sort of cognitive and purposive formulation is akin to interpretations of the Skinner-box bar press, instrumental conditioning in terms of bar-pressing being emitted by the rat "in order to get the food."

The conditioned reflex concept was of considerable theoretical importance in psychology during the heyday of LEARNING THEORY in the 1940s and 1950s. During this period, learning theory was viewed as primary, as illustrated by the dictum that learning theory *is* behavior theory. And classical conditioning was considered to be the basic building block that underlay all forms of learning and behavior. The dominant learning-theory approach was that of the stimulus-response (S-R) theorists like C. L. HULL (1943) and K. W. SPENCE (1956), and an important concern was the theoretical attempt to account for apparently cognitive, stimulus-stimulus behavior in terms of S-R principles, that is, through the learning of responses only. The fractional anticipatory goal response construct was the S-R theoretical concept of choice, and both Hull (1931) and Spence (1956) specifically asserted that this theoretical response mechanism was learned through classical conditioning.

In addition to such theoretical usage of classical conditioning, there was widespread empirical research directed at observing the acquisition and extinction of the CR as a phenomenon in its own right, although the dominant preparation under study was not the animal salivary one but the human eyelid conditioning experiment. In this preparation, an air puff to the eye served as the US, a blink as the UR and CR, and (usually) a tone as the CS (conditional stimulus). Consistent with the prevailing S-R emphasis, eyelid conditioning was found to be critically determined by various independent variable manipulations and dependent variable measurements. Concerning independent variables, the most important one was the period between CS and US onsets, the CS-US interval. The optimal CS-US interval was slightly less than 0.5 second, and CS-US intervals of 2 seconds or greater produced no conditioning at all (i.e., no increase in CS-elicited blinks as a function of paired CS-US trials). The CS-elicited response latency measurement was also found to be crucial: shorter-latency blinks (occurring within 150 milliseconds following CS onset) were found to decrease rather than increase as a function of repeated CS-US pairings, so that only longer-latency blinks (the frequency of occurrence of which did increase as a function of CS-US pairings) were classified as CRs.

The decline of the S-R approach in psychology and the "paradigm shift" to the cognitive, S-S approach resulted in a radical shift in theoretical perspective on Pavlovian conditioning. According to its most famous modern exponent, Pavlovian conditioning is "now described as the learning of relations among events so as to allow the organism to represent its environment" (Rescorla, 1988, p. 151). It is interesting to compare this cognitive ("relations between events") and purposive ("so as to allow") formulation with the "subjective psychology" account cited above, which Pavlov opposed. At a more empirical level, the 1970s and 1980s also saw the virtual abandonment of the eyelid preparation as a means of studying the Pavlovian (response) conditioning phenomenon. An improved form of the preparation (the rabbit nictitating membrane preparation developed in the 1960s) has been employed, but predominantly as a technique to study the effects of physiological manipulations rather than the phenomenon of conditioning itself. Consideration of the CS-US interval has essentially disappeared, to the extent that, in the currently dominant Rescorla-Wagner (1972) model of Pavlovian conditioning, the CS-US interval

does not appear as a parameter. Considering the fact that, as indicated above, the CS-US interval is crucial in preparations such as eyelid conditioning, this omission may seem strange. However, most of the evidence and experimental work of current cognitive S-S Pavlovian conditioners is based on preparations where conditioning is not measured directly through assessing the CR, but indirectly through assessing the effect of the CS on some instrumental indicator behavior, as in the conditioned emotional response preparation. Such indicator-behavior preparations are more likely to suggest that Pavlovian conditioning is the learning of "relations between events" (i.e., cognitive, S-S learning of CS/US contingency) rather than the learning of (conditional) responding (i.e., the CR) to the CS.

It is also interesting to note that not only during the current cognitive S-S phase, but also during the earlier S-R phase, of Western experimental psychology, no body of systematic reports of Pavlovian dog salivary conditioning emerged in the journal literature. Pavlov's methods were based on single case studies, and the dependent variable differences were reported quasi-anecdotally rather than with specified reliability in terms of the rules of statistical inference. Furthermore, his preparation is extremely difficult to work with. For example, the typical subject requires some 3 months of adaptation to the holding harness before the food reliably elicits salivation rather than competing struggling behavior. Still, the Pavlovian emphasis on using behavior as the objectively observed dependent variable has been retained by both the S-R experimentalists and their cognitive, S-S oriented successors.

The Pavlovian emphasis on observation has been carried on as an intellectual tradition by the Pavlovian Society. This international organization was founded in the United States in 1955 by Horsley Gantt, who, as noted above, worked in Pavlov's laboratory in the 1920s. The official journal of this society was first *Conditional Reflex,* then *Pavlovian Journal of Biological Science,* and, most recently (1991), *Integrative Behavioral and Physiological Science.* Although few members of this interdisciplinary group (whose backgrounds and interests range from single-cell physiology to psychoanalysis) specialize in classical-conditioning research, the common ground is provided by the society's motto ("Observation and Observation"). To them it means that whatever the differences may be between favored theoretical positions, the issues should be debated in the light of the observed evidence.

REFERENCES

Anokhin, P. K. (1949). *Ivan Petrovich Pavlov: Zhizn, deiatel'nost i nauchnaia shkola.* Moscow and Leningrad: Izdatel'stvo Akademii Nauk SSSR.

Furedy, J. J., Heslegrave, R. J., and Scher, H. (1984). Psychophysiological and physiological aspects of T-wave amplitude in the objective study of behavior. *Pavlovian Journal of Biological Science 19,* 182–194.

Gantt, W. H. (1991). Ideas are the golden coins of science. *Integrative Physiological and Behavioral Science 26,* 68–73.

Grigorian, N. A. (1974). Pavlov, Ivan Petrovich. In *Dictionary of scientific biography,* vol. 10, pp. 431–435. New York: Scribner.

Hull, C. L. (1931). Goal attraction and directing ideas conceived as habit phenomena. *Psychological Review 38,* 487–505.

———— (1943). *Principles of behavior: An introduction to behavior theory.* New York: Appleton-Century-Crofts.

Koshotiants, K. S. (1950). *I. M. Sechenov.* Moscow: Izdatel'stvo Akademii Nauk SSSR.

Pavlov, I. P. (1952). Ivan Petrovich Pavlov (avtobiografiia). In his *Polnoe sobranie sochinenii,* vol. 6. Moscow and Leningrad: Akademii Nauk SSSR.

Rescorla, R. A. (1988). Pavlovian conditioning: It's not what you think it is. *American Psychologist 43,* 151–160.

Rescorla, R. A., and Wagner, A. R. (1972). A theory of Pavlovian conditioning: Variations in the effectiveness of reinforcement and nonreinforcement. In A. H. Black and W. F. Prokasy, eds., *Classical conditioning,* vol. 2, *Current theory and research.* New York: Appleton-Century-Crofts.

Sechenov, I. (1866). *Refleksy golovnogo mozga.* St. Petersburg: Tipographiia A. Golovachova.

Spence, K. W. (1956). *Behavior theory and conditioning.* New Haven: Yale University Press.

Watson, J. B. (1913). Psychology as the behaviorist views it. *Psychological Review 20,* 158–177.

Windholz, G. (1991). I. P. Pavlov as a youth. *Integrative Physiological and Behavioral Science 26,* 51–67.

John J. Furedy

PERCEPTION

See Visual Object Agnosia

PHARMACOLOGIC TREATMENT OF MEMORY DEFICITS

Because memory loss is so debilitating, the search for possible pharmacologic treatments has been intensive. ALZHEIMER'S DISEASE (AD) is the most common disease responsible for memory loss, accounting for 50–70 percent of all cases. Other dementing disorders, including cerebrovascular disease, Parkinson's disease, and amnesic disorders such as Wernicke-Korsakoff syndrome and posttraumatic amnesia, are responsible for the remainder. Because of the prevalence of AD, it serves as the model for memory disorders, and most therapeutic trials and strategies for treatment have focused on elderly patients with AD.

Until recently, DEMENTIA was thought to be due to cerebrovascular disease, and early treatments for the symptoms of "senility" used vasodilators to improve the supply of blood to the brain, in an effort to relieve the symptoms. This assumption is now known to be erroneous as a result of major advances regarding the neurochemistry of AD. This, in turn, has provided researchers with information upon which to base a rational approach to pharmacological treatment of the dramatic cognitive decline seen in patients with AD.

There are many problems inherent in attempting to determine the efficacy of a compound designed to improve memory. First of all, there are many different kinds of memory and numerous ways of testing it, making it difficult to compare results of various studies. In addition, the choice of patients may greatly affect the outcome, since patients with different severity of dementia or differing etiologies, such as head trauma, may not respond equally to a given drug. Many drugs are poorly absorbed, have very short half-lives (thus requiring frequent administration), and do not cross the blood-brain barrier well. Finally, the design of the study and the optimum times for administering drug and testing must be considered. Double-blind trials comparing placebo against active drug are essential for objective evaluation of a candidate drug.

Alzheimer's Disease: Cholinergic Therapy

Considerable evidence supports an important role for neurons utilizing acetylcholine (ACh) in memory acquisition. ACh is made by neurons in a small subcortical area of the brain that connects to and activates widespread areas of the neocortex. In AD, one of the earliest abnormalities is a significant loss of brain choline acetyltransferase (CAT), a marker for intact cholinergic neurons, and a reduction in levels of ACh in the cortex. The loss of brain CAT activity can be correlated with the degree of dementia and the pathologic changes in brain tissue characteristic of AD. Though multiple neurotransmitter systems are affected in AD, attempts to enhance cholinergic transmission using four basic pharmacologic strategies have emerged.

First, *augmenting the synthesis of acetylcholine*. In an attempt to increase synthesis of ACh, precursors used by the enzyme CAT to make ACh—choline and lecithin—have been given to patients with AD. Results of placebo-controlled double-blind studies for both have been uniformly disappointing, however, despite increases in blood choline levels. This finding is not surprising because the pool of available precursors is not the rate-limiting step in ACh synthesis.

Second, *intensifying the release of acetylcholine*. 4-aminopyridine, a pyridine derivative that enhances acetylcholine release, has been tried with only limited success in patients with AD.

Third, *using drugs to stimulate the cholinergic receptor*. These drugs (which behave like the natural neurotransmitter and are called agonists)—such as arecoline, oxotremorine, RS-86, pilocarpine, and bethanechol—act directly at the postsynaptic muscarinic cholinergic receptor, which appears to be relatively spared in AD. Their use has often been impeded by peripheral side effects; many of them are extremely short-acting and do not appear to cross the blood-brain barrier. To circumvent the prominent peripheral side effects, administration of bethanechol directly into the ventricles of the brain has been attempted with AD patients; unfortunately, initial promising results have been overshadowed by a larger multicenter trial that failed to show improved cognition. Many clinically tested agonists are actually mixed agonists/antagonists. Whether agonist therapy can improve cognition in AD awaits the development of purer agonists with fewer peripheral side effects.

Fourth, *protecting acetylcholine from degradation*. After the nerve terminals release ACh, its action is terminated by the enzyme acetylcholinesterase. Agents known as cholinesterase inhibitors extend the action of ACh at the postsynaptic cholinergic receptor by preventing its breakdown.

The most widely studied acetylcholinesterase inhibitor has been physostigmine, a tertiary amine that crosses the blood-brain barrier but generally is poorly absorbed following oral administration. Many early intravenous physostigmine studies demonstrated some improvement in verbal and nonverbal memory in AD, especially in less severely demented patients where dose titration was attempted. Double-blind trials of oral physostigmine have largely shown only modest and short-lived improvements, even when physostigmine is combined with ACh precursors such as lecithin. Studies on the longer-acting cholinesterase inhibitor THA, also known as tacrine, have attracted considerable attention. Early reports of marked improvement of neuropsychological tests and global functioning in some THA-treated AD patients were followed by less successful studies from France, Canada, and Sweden.

In general, clinical efforts with cholinergic agents have met with only limited success. While these drugs are neither a cure nor a definitive treatment for AD, there does appear to be a suggestion of efficacy early in AD.

Alzheimer's Disease: Noncholinergic Agents

A large number of experimental noncholinergic agents have been tried in patients with AD, including a group referred to as "cognitive enhancers" that includes the vasodilators and a class of drugs called nootropics. The most familiar vasodilator, Hydergine, appears to exert a nonspecific alerting effect but has not been shown to influence memory. The word *nootropic* means "toward the mind," and the group of drugs bearing this name appears to alter brain functioning by unknown means, and without side effects. The results of therapeutic trials with nootropic agents, of which the best-known is piracetam, have been generally negative; most studies have found, at most, increased attention but little significant improvement on objective measures of cognition.

A number of studies have been carried out with neuropeptides, including the hypothalamic hormones, vasopressin, and ACTH. Overall, the therapeutic effect on memory and cognition in AD patients has been disappointing. In addition, though numerous studies have demonstrated a decrease in brain concentrations of a peptide called somatostatin in patients with AD, no effect on memory impairment was detected in a group of AD patients given a powerful analogue of somatostatin.

In a similar manner, multiple double-blind placebo-controlled studies and, more recently, a multicenter trial of several opiate antagonists (naloxone and its longer-acting relatives, naltrexone and nalmefene) have failed to provide evidence for a beneficial effect on cognitive performance.

Head Injury

Pharmacologic treatment of memory deficit after closed HEAD INJURY is complex because the injury usually causes more than isolated memory impairment. A wide range of brain damage is seen, with local lesions usually superimposed on extensive diffuse neuronal injury. In addition, secondary brain insult, as a result of hypoxia or shock, is not uncommon.

At present, there are no cogent studies demonstrating unambiguous memory improvement with drug therapy following head trauma. Most studies have been small and uncontrolled, with conflicting results. In general, compounds tested for posttraumatic amnesia are tried on empirical grounds alone, as there are no known neurochemical alterations in head trauma patients.

The most extensively tested agent, vasopressin, appears to produce modest improvement in attention, but not in memory, in closed head injury patients. Attempts to potentiate central cholinergic pathways with physostigmine and lecithin also have resulted in little significant improvement in memory deficit. A double-blind placebo-controlled trial of piracetam following concussion demonstrated subjective improvement of several postconcussive symptoms, but virtually no improvement in memory.

Wernicke-Korsakoff Syndrome

This amnesic syndrome, which usually occurs as a result of chronic alcoholism or malnutrition, is associated with thiamine deficiency. Chronic deficits are not likely to be reversed by administration of the vitamin, however. Prominent impairment of memory is the hallmark of this syndrome.

Only a small number of clinical trials have been carried out on patients with Wernicke-Korsakoff syndrome, and the results have been disappointing. Treatment with vasopressin failed to show improvement in short- or long-term memory in two small double-blind studies. More recently, clonidine, a drug active at certain receptors for the neurotransmitter norepinephrine, attracted attention following demonstration of a possible deficit in this transmitter system in patients with Wernicke-Korsakoff syndrome. Administration of clonidine in two small double-blind crossover trials, however, resulted in only modest improvement in short-term memory in these patients.

Future Prospects and Conclusion

There are at present no agents that unequivocally improve memory, though during the 1990s significant advances are likely. Strategies to deal with some of the problems of delivery of present agents will likely be developed, including alternative routes of administration, sustained-release formulations to maintain adequate blood levels of agents with short half-lives, and manipulation of the blood-brain barrier to allow better central nervous system (CNS) access.

In addition, new types of drugs will likely be investigated, with the aim of preserving vulnerable neurons rather than manipulating synaptic transmission. Nerve growth factor (NGF) has been shown to exert trophic effects on cholinergic neurons in the mammalian forebrain. Significantly, these are the same areas that degenerate in the brains of Alzheimer's patients. It is hoped that supplying exogenous NGF to patients with AD will increase cholinergic activity and inhibit further CNS degeneration. Other strategies to retard neuronal degeneration in AD are likely to include drugs that modulate excitatory amino acid neurotransmission, as well as membrane-stabilizing agents such as acetyl-*l*-carnitine and calcium channel blockers.

Though at present there are no agents that unequivocally improve memory, many avenues of research are currently being explored, and it appears almost certain that pharmacologic treatments will be developed to enhance memory in the near future.

(See also AGING ANIMALS, PHARMACOLOGICAL MANIPULATIONS OF MEMORY IN; DRUGS AND MEMORY.)

REFERENCES

Bartus, R. (1990). Drugs to treat age-related neurodegenerative problems. *Journal of the American Geriatric Society 38*, 680–695.

Davies, P. (1983). An update on the neurochemistry of Alzheimer's disease. In R. Mayeux and W. G. Rosen, eds., *The dementias*. New York: Raven Press.

Iverson, L. L., Iverson, S. D., and Snyder, S. H., eds. (1988). *Handbook of psychopharmacology*, vol. 20, *Psychopharmacology of the aging nervous system*. New York: Plenum Press.

Joyce, E. (1987). The neurochemistry of Korsakoff syndrome. In S. M. Stahl, S. D. Iverson, and E. C. Goodman, eds., *Cognitive neurochemistry*. Oxford: Oxford University Press.

Levin, H. (1989). Memory deficit after closed head injury. *Journal of Clinical and Experimental Neuropsychology 12* (1), 129–153.

Mayeux, R. (1990). Therapeutic strategies in Alzheimer's disease. *Neurology 40*, 175–180.

Thal, L. J. (1989). Pharmacologic treatment of memory disorders. In F. Boller and J. Grafman, eds., *Handbook of neuropsychology*, vol. 2. Amsterdam: Elsevier.

Jody Corey-Bloom
Leon J. Thal

PHOPIAS

Phobias are intense, persistent, unadaptive fears that are irrational/excessive. They are commonly classified into three groups: *complex phobias*, including agoraphobia (fear of public places, travel); *social phobias* (fear of social situations/scrutiny); and *circumscribed phobias*, including intense fears of insects, animals, heights, and enclosed spaces.

There are biological contributions to the development of some phobias, but the main determinants appear to be learned. Three main pathways to the acquisition of phobias have been identified. The conditioning acquisition of a phobia results from exposure to a traumatic stimulation or from repeated exposures to aversive sensitizing conditions. The second pathway is vicarious acquisition: direct or indirect observations of people, or of other animals, displaying fear. Among humans the transmission of fear-inducing verbal information is the third pathway. For a considerable time, explanations of the acquisition of phobias were dominated by the conditioning theory, which emphasized the importance of exposure to traumatic stimulation; recognition that fears can be acquired vicariously and/or by the direct transmission of information has led to a fuller account of the causes of phobias. (See also OBSERVATIONAL LEARNING.)

Important advances have been made in our ability to reduce phobias. Under controlled conditions, it is now possible to produce substantial and lasting reductions of phobias within a few sessions. It requires greater effort and far more time to reduce the complex and intense phobias, such as agoraphobia, but even these respond moderately well to treatment programs. There have been several attempts to explain how and when these methods of fear reduction achieve their effects, but each explanation has limitations.

Despite the many opportunities and circumstances in which phobias might develop, people acquire comparatively few; a satisfactory explanation of phobias must accommodate this fact as well as the appearance of phobias in a significant minority of the human population. It has also become apparent that people are more resilient than most psychologists have implied. Phobic patients who behave courageously during the course of treatment and soldiers who perform dangerous acts are notable examples of resilience.

Causes

The major features of the conditioning theory of phobias are as follows. Fears are acquired by a process of conditioning (see CONDITIONING, CLASSICAL AND INSTRUMENTAL). Neutral stimuli that often are associated with a fear-producing or pain-producing state of affairs develop fearful qualities. They become conditioned phobic stimuli. The strength of the phobia is determined by the number of repetitions of the association between the pain/fear experienced and the stimuli, and by the intensity of the pain or fear experienced in the presence of the stimuli. Stimuli that resemble the fear-evoking ones also acquire phobic properties; that is, they become secondary conditioned stimuli. The likelihood of a phobia's developing is increased by confinement, by exposure to intensely painful or frightening situations, and by frequent associations between the new conditioned stimulus and the pain/fear. In an important extension, it has also been proposed that once objects or situations acquire phobic qualities, they develop motivating properties. A secondary fear drive emerges. Behavior that successfully reduces fear, notably avoidance behavior, will increase in strength.

Supporting evidence for the theory was drawn from six sources: research on the induction of fear in laboratory animals, the development of anxiety states in combat soldiers, experiments on the induction of fear in a small number of children, clinical observations (e.g., dental phobias), incidental findings from the use of aversion therapy, and a few experiments on the effects of traumatic stimulation.

The strongest and most systematic evidence was drawn from a multitude of experiments on laboratory animals. It is easy to generate conditioned fear reactions in animals by exposing them to a conjunction of neutral and aversive stimuli, usually electric shock. These fear reactions can be intense and persistent. Phobias can result from traumatic experiences in combat. In clinical practice, it is not uncommon for patients to give an account of the development of their phobias that can be construed in conditioning terms, and sometimes they can date the onset of the phobias to a specific conditioning experience (e.g., Lautch, 1971, on thirty-four cases of dental phobia). Di Nardo et al. (1988) found that nearly two-thirds of their subjects who were phobic toward dogs had experienced a conditioning event in which a dog featured, and in over half the dog had inflicted pain. It is important, however, that over two-thirds of a comparable group of subjects who were not frightened of dogs reported that they, too, had experienced a conditioning event, and that in over half of these instances the animal had inflicted pain.

These reports provide some support for the conditioning theory but also illustrate the fact that conditioning experiences, even those of a painful nature, do not necessarily give rise to a phobia or even to fear. Here, as in other instances, there was less fear than an unqualified conditioning theory would lead us to expect. Presumably the people who experienced conditioning events but failed to acquire a fear or phobia were "protected" by a history of harmless contacts with dogs. The roles that phobic patients attribute to direct and indirect experiences in generating their phobias differ with the content of the phobia, and of course the accuracy of their reports cannot be assured. In their analysis of 183 phobic patients, divided into six groups, Ost and Hugdahl (1985) found a range of attributions. For example, 88 percent of the agoraphobic patients attributed the onset of the phobia to a conditioning experience, but only 50 percent of those who were frightened of animals attributed the onset of their phobias to such an experience. Among the animal phobics, 40 percent traced the origin of the phobia to indirect experiences; such attribution was uncommon among the agoraphobics.

Although the importance of the phenomenon of acquired food aversions was not made evident until 1966, it is sometimes used to buttress the conditioning theory. The findings on this aversion also served to prompt radical rethinking of the concept of conditioning. Garcia and his colleagues were the first to demonstrate that strong and lasting aversive reactions can be acquired with ease when the appropriate food stimulus is associated with illness, even if the illness occurs many hours after eating (Garcia, Ervin, and Koelling, 1966). Given that the genesis of food aversions is a form of conditioning, if we also allow an equation between the acquisition of a food aversion and the acquisition of a fear, this phenomenon may have a bearing on the effect of the phobias. (See TASTE AVERSION AND PREFERENCE LEARNING IN ANIMALS.)

If the acquisition of aversions is used to support the conditioning theory of phobias, it will have to take into account the temporal stretch of the phenomenon—that is, the delay that can intervene between the tasting of the food and the onset of the illness. Classical conditioning is expedited by temporal proximity between the stimuli, but food aversions can be easily and rapidly established even when there are long delays between the events. Hence, if the food aversion phenomenon provides support for a new or a revised conditioning theory of phobias, the temporal qualities of the conditioning processes must be deemphasized.

There are various arguments against acceptance of the conditioning theory of phobias as a comprehensive explanation. People fail to acquire phobias in what should be fear-conditioning situations, such as air raids. It is difficult to produce stable phobic or fear reactions in human subjects even under controlled laboratory conditions. The theory rests on the untenable equipotentiality premise (Seligman, 1972). The distribution of fears and phobias in normal and neurotic populations is difficult to reconcile with the theory. A significant number of people with phobias recount histories that cannot be accommodated by the theory. We also know that fears and phobias can be acquired vicariously, and that fears can be acquired by the reception of threatening verbal information. Fears, and possibly phobias as well, can be acquired even when the causal events are temporally separated (see Rachman, 1990).

Neoconditioning Concepts

The traditional insistence on the contiguity of the conditioned stimulus and the unconditioned stimulus as a necessary condition for the establishment of a conditioned response is mistaken. Rescorla has observed that "although conditioning can sometimes be slow, in fact most modern conditioning preparations routinely show rapid learning. One trial learning is not confined to flavor-aversion" (1988, p. 154). Apparently the associative span of animals "is capable of bridging long temporal intervals" (Mackintosh, 1983, p. 172). However, the learning must be selective; otherwise, animals would collect what Mackintosh has referred to as a "useless clutter of irrelevant associations." According to Mackintosh, the functioning of conditioning is to allow organisms to discover "probable causes of events of significance."

Given this new view, that conditioning is far more flexible and wide-ranging than was previously supposed, many of the objections to the conditioning theory of fear and phobias are weakened or eliminated. Although the application of neoconditioning concepts can shore up the conditioning theory, at the present stage the new view is too liberal. It lacks limits, and there is little left to disallow. In theory, almost any stimulus can become a conditioned signal for fear; but in practice people develop comparatively few phobias, and those we do acquire are confined to a limited range of stimuli. Phobias are not normally distributed.

Several sources of evidence suggest that phobias and fears can be acquired vicariously. Reports given by phobic patients, wartime observations, correlations between the phobias displayed by parents and children, laboratory demonstrations of conditioned fears, and research on animals have all provided some support for this view.

Verbal information can also generate a fear, and it is possible that in limited circumstances, it can even induce a phobia. Clinical evidence, especially that accumulating on the nature of panic disorders, suggests that phobias can be generated by information that is slightly or not at all threatening but is catastrophically misinterpreted by the recipient as being threatening.

Biological Determinants

The nonrandom distribution of human phobias, the high incidence of phobias of snakes and spiders and the low incidence of fears/phobias of motor travel, the remarkable speed with which certain objects can be transformed into objects of fear, and the common occurrence of irrational fears all point to the operation of nonlearned processes in the acquisition of fears and phobias. The main explanations fall into two classes: Some human fears and phobias are innately determined, or people are innately disposed rapidly to acquire phobias of certain specifiable objects or situations.

The most influential explanation is that set out by Martin Seligman, who argued that "The great majority of phobias are about objects of natural importance to the survival of the species . . . (human phobias are largely restricted to objects that have threatened survival, potential predators, unfamiliar places, and the dark)" (1972, p. 450). He postulates that certain kinds of fears are readily acquired because of an inherited biological preparedness. These phobias are highly prepared to be learned and, like other highly prepared relationships, "they are selective and resistant to extinction, and probably non-cognitive" (1972, p. 455).

The main features of prepared phobias are that they are very easily acquired (even by watered-down representations of the actual threat), selective, stable, biologically significant, and probably noncognitive. After some encouraging early laboratory demonstrations of fear preparedness in human subjects, subsequent research was disappointing because the phenomenon appeared to be too fragile. The laboratory effects appeared to be weak, transient, and difficult to reproduce. The plausibility of the concept has been weakened but not seriously damaged, and more powerful stimuli and more appropriate measures of fear responding are needed before the theory can be subjected to rigorous testing. The demonstration of preparedness in the development of phobias among laboratory monkeys encourages the belief that Seligman's theory retains considerable value. Mineka (1988) has shown that the fears induced in monkeys in laboratory conditions are intense, vivid, and lasting. The animals readily developed fears of snakes but showed little or no propensity to develop fears of biologically insignificant stimuli such as flowers.

Fear Reduction

Three powerful and dependable methods for reducing fear have been developed since the 1970s: desensitization, flooding, and therapeutic modeling. The common element in all three methods is the repeated and/or prolonged exposure of the fearful person to the stimulus or situation that provokes the fear (the exposure method). The selection of the appropriate fear-reducing technique depends on the nature of the phobia and the preference of the fearful subject, but all three methods are reliably robust. Fears of circumscribed stimuli, such as snakes or spiders, can be reduced fairly rapidly, even if they are intense and well established. The reduction or elimination of more complex fears, such as agoraphobia, requires greater effort and time. Despite these important practical advances, there still is no widely accepted explanation for the effects of these techniques. (See also BEHAVIOR THERAPY.)

REFERENCES

Di Nardo, P. A., Guzy, L. T., Jenkins, J. A., Bak, R. M., Tomasi, S. F., and Copland, M. (1988). Etiology and maintenance of dog fears. *Behaviour Research and Therapy 26*, 245–252.

Garcia, J., Ervin, F., and Koelling, R. (1966). Learning with prolonged delay of reinforcement. *Psychonomic Science 5*, 121–122.

Lautch, H. (1971). Dental phobia. *British Journal of Psychiatry 119*, 151–158.

Mackintosh, N. J. (1983). *Conditioning and associative learning.* New York: Oxford University Press.

Mineka, S. (1988). A primate model of phobic fears. In H. Eysenck and I. Martin, eds., *Theoretical foundations of behaviour therapy.* New York: Plenum Press.

Ost, L. G., and Hugdahl, K. (1985). Acquisition of blood and dental phobia and anxiety response patterns in clinical patients. *Behaviour Research and Therapy 23*, 27–34.

Rachman, S. J. (1990). *Fear and courage,* 2nd ed. New York: W. H. Freeman.

Rescorla, R. A. (1988). Pavlovian conditioning. *American Psychologist 43*, 151–160.

Seligman, M. E. P. (1972). Phobias and preparedness. *Behavior Therapy 2*, 307–320.

Stanley J. Rachman

PHOTOGRAPHIC MEMORY

See Eidetic Imagery

PIAGET, JEAN

Together with Sigmund FREUD and B. F. SKINNER, Jean Piaget (1896–1980) was one of the three most influential psychologists of the twentieth century. Among developmental psychologists he has had no equal or close second as to the volume, scope, and impact of his work. Yet he thought of his psychological work primarily as a tool for the creation of a new science, *genetic epistemology*— a new synthesis of logic, philosophy, history of science, biology, and psychology.

Life and Oeuvre

Piaget was born on August 9, 1896, in Neuchâtel, Switzerland, and died in Geneva, September 17, 1980. His father, Arthur Piaget, was a historian. Jean's first publication, a paragraph about sighting an albino sparrow, appeared in 1907, when he was 11 years old. He was active until the end of his life, and posthumous monographs continued to appear until 1990. The total oeuvre comprises over sixty books and monographs plus nearly a thousand articles.

During his long life Piaget held professorships at the University of Paris and at the Swiss universities of Neuchâtel, Lausanne, and Geneva. The chairs he held were in psychology, sociology, and the history and philosophy of science. His longest association was with the University of Geneva. Among his many honors were over thirty honorary doctorates from major universities (the first from Harvard, 1936) in a dozen countries; numerous awards, including the Distinguished Scientific Contribution Award of the American Psychological Association (1970); and the presidency of various scientific

Figure 1.   Jean Piaget. *Courtesy Professor Howard Gruber.*

it he introduced his conception of egocentrism, interpreting the world from one's own immediate perspective without adequately taking into account the existence of alternative perspectives. In three subsequent books during the 1920s Piaget showed how this egocentrism pervades the child's mentality from about the age of 5 to 10 in the domains of logic and reasoning, causal thinking, conceptions of the world, and (not published until 1932) moral judgment.

All of these works can be construed as studies of learning in a wide sense, since through its interaction with the world, the child's intelligence develops: Moving through several necessary stages, the child learns to think more and more like an adult. The same can be said of the trilogy Piaget wrote about his own three children in the first 2 years of life. These works, using the method of naturalistic observation, delineate the major stages in (a) the development of active, intelligent, inventive exploration of the world; (b) the child's own activity in the construction of reality (the permanent object, space, time, and causality); and (c) the emergence of language and the symbolic or representational function through play, dreams, and imitation.

associations. For many years he was director of the International Bureau of Education. His wife, Valentine Chatenay Piaget, was among his collaborators in the research for his first few books, and especially in the study of their three babies.

As an adolescent Piaget pursued malacology, the study of mollusks, and reached a professional level, publishing thirty-two papers in this field by 1916, his twentieth year. He continued this line of work in natural history for the rest of his life.

In 1918 Piaget received his doctorate in natural science from the University of Neuchâtel for a dissertation on the mollusks of the Valais, a region of Switzerland. By that time he had begun to move toward the study of psychology, which he pursued in Zurich and in Paris. In 1921 he published his first article on child logic and thought, a subject that grew to dominate his thinking throughout his later life.

Egocentrism

Piaget's first book in psychology, *The Language and Thought of the Child,* appeared in 1923. In

Assimilation and Accommodation

In the course of his work on infant development, Piaget introduced the twin concepts of assimilation and accommodation as tools for understanding cognitive growth. The infant is born with a few basic reflexes. Through its own activity novelties arise (for example, through the chance coincidence of events) that are assimilated into these initial schemes, giving rise to changing schemes of action. These schemes can assimilate external events or stimuli and, equally important, they can assimilate each other, giving rise to new adaptive organizations. Paired with the process of assimilation is that of accommodation, the way in which the set of schemes or cognitive organizations must change in response to the new inputs ("aliments," as Piaget sometimes called them, emphasizing the digestion metaphor).

Toward the end of the first year of life, as the child repeats its actions in order to make interesting events recur (e.g., the noise of a rattle), it notices variations in its own actions and their consequences. These variations and their consequences are, in their turn, assimilated into existing schemes, and thus these schemes grow. Piaget considered this analysis of infant cognitive growth to be germane to his analysis and descriptions of the growth of thought at other levels, including the history of science.

Stages of Development

In the 1930s and 1940s Piaget's main focus was on the stagewise progression of intelligence in infancy and childhood. He elaborated his idea of three great periods of intellectual growth: sensorimotor (0–2 years), preoperational (2–6 or 7 years), and concrete operational (7–11 or 12 years). In the 1950s, this model was expanded to include adolescent cognitive development in the period of formal operations.

Genetic Epistemology

In the late 1940s Piaget displayed increasing preoccupation with the further elaboration of ideas long held, the approach that has become known as *genetic epistemology*. Some of the most important components of this approach had been sketched in his religious prose poem *La mission de l'idée* (1915) and in his philosophical novel *Recherche* (1918).

This phase was most fully expressed in Piaget's three-volume work *Introduction à l'epistémologie génétique* (1950). In 1956 he organized the Centre International de l'Epistémologie Génétique, an interdisciplinary center for research and reflection on questions concerning the intersection of the natural sciences, psychology (especially developmental), and philosophy (especially epistemology). Rather than becoming a philosopher, Piaget hoped to transform one branch of philosophy, epistemology, into a new science. In 1957, the Centre turned its attention to the study of learning—both logical models of the learning process and the learning and development of logical reasoning by the child. Piaget and his collaborators published their theoretical and empirical findings in four monographs (1959).

Equilibration Model

In the 1960s and 1970s, without dropping any of his previous concerns, Piaget turned his attention to elaborating the "equilibration model," an attempt to specify the actual mechanisms by which intellectual growth and change come about.

Alternative Theoretical Approaches

Throughout his life Piaget was interested in the contrast between his own theoretical approach and two others. He was quite drawn toward Gestalt psychology, especially its emphasis on holism and self-regulating systems; but in the end he rejected it as relying too heavily on the analogy between perception and thought, and being consequently nondevelopmental. He was never drawn toward BEHAVIORISM (or its antecedent, ASSOCIATIONISM); he objected to the lack of any intrinsic structure in knowledge accrued as an arbitrary collection of chance associations. He summed all this up in a favorite aphorism: Gestalt psychology speaks of structure without development; behaviorism, of development without structure.

Method

Piaget relied mainly on two related methods for the exploration of the child's intellect. For his trilogy on the origins of intellect in babies, and also for his earlier *Language and Thought in the Child,* he relied on naturalistic observation. For most of his work, however, he stuck to the "clinical method" of extended interaction between child and investigator, with searching analysis of the protocols (i.e., of what the child said and did in reaction to the problems posed by the adult). The clinical method evolved into something approaching naturalistic observation in problem-solving situations. The problems were not construed as tasks having definite solutions to be sought by the child, but as occasions to provoke thought in the child, thus permitting the experimenter to observe the child's way of thinking.

Using different age groups, these methods permitted the study of the broad trajectory of cognitive development. By avoiding narrower experimental approaches, Piaget sacrificed the opportunity for what might be called microscopic analysis of the effects of specifiable variables on cognitive functioning. What he gained was a better picture of child mentality as a whole—first as a system of beliefs and later as a structured group of operations.

Development, Learning, and Structure

Although the development of cognition as depicted by Piaget resembles what other psychologists might call "learning," there are a number of important differences. First, changes in performance are seen as a function of developmental stage, not of repeated exposures and responses to the same stimulus. Second, the investigator analyzes broad strategic changes in approach rather than the correctness and incorrectness of solutions or memories. Third, what accrues over time is not a sum of associations but operative structures; thus, for Piaget the older subject does not necessarily know "more" than the younger but knows differently.

For Piaget a structure is not the momentarily given perceptual configuration of interest to Gestalt psychologists. A mental structure is a set of logicomathematical operations or mental acts, permitting the decomposition of wholes into parts and the recomposition of wholes from parts. To take a very simple example, the idea of the permanent object entails the recognition of the continued existence of an object as it moves around in space—the movements $AB + BC \rightarrow AC$, the movements $AB + BA \rightarrow 0$. Thus, the idea of the permanent object is an embodiment of the group of displacements. (See also OBJECT CONCEPT, ACQUISITION OF.)

Conservation of Matter

In a key and famous illustration of the mentality of the concrete operational child, Piaget discovered that the young child does not understand that a given amount of matter remains the same under transformations of shape; thus, if water is poured from a short, wide vessel into a long, thin tube, the child may believe that as the water level mounts higher and higher, the amount of water increases. The weight of experimental evidence shows that the child is relatively unaffected by repeated exposures to this event, because it can always map the results of direct observations onto the preexisting schema. The argument of reversibility—if the water is poured back into the first container, it regains the original level—will be a satisfying demonstration of conservation for the older child. The young child watching, or even pouring, the liquid can actually *see* the level mounting or falling but, because attention is centered on one dimension, does not yet grasp the idea of conservation that would lead to the coordination of changes of length and width.

In other words, direct teaching or learning is relatively ineffectual in modifying the growth of fundamental cognitive categories and operations, because these depend on the protracted, often slow, development of the knowing system as a whole through the self-regulated activity of that knowing system.

Memory

From 1921, when he published his first empirical study of child development, until the 1960s, Piaget did virtually no work on memory. A possible exception was his use of tasks involving memory but focusing on other problems. For example, in 1923, in *Language and Thought of the Child*, Piaget studied the way in which a child who has just been told a story repeats it to another child. This work could be considered a study of memory, but Piaget's interest was in the relation between the first child's comprehension of the story and the communication from the first child to the second. He was aware of the involvement of memory in this task but thought he could distinguish errors of memory from those of comprehension and communication. In his later work he took a very different tack, emphasizing the effect of changes in comprehension on memory.

For the most part, during a very long period Piaget's interest lay primarily in the general operations and structures of mental activity rather than in the contents of experience or the stuff of thought. But in a wider perspective Piaget believed that growth comes about through interaction with the world, and that this world must somehow be represented in the child's mind (and consequently in Piaget's theory). About 1942, Piaget began a systematic study of what he called the "figurative" aspects of thought—perception, imagery, and memory—as contrasted with the "operative" aspects of mental activity. By far the largest part of this effort was centered on the study of perception: some sixty experimental papers, brought together in *The Mechanisms of Perception* (1969). But he also studied mental imagery, which resulted in yet another volume, *Mental Imagery in the Child: A Study of the Development of Imaginal Representation* (Piaget and Inhelder, 1971).

The work on imagery led on to work on memory, resulting in the book *Memory and Intelligence* (Piaget, Inhelder, and Sinclair-De Zwart, 1973). Perhaps the most striking finding of this work is that rather than remaining stable or decaying, a memory can actually improve with time because its evolving structure depends on the child's maturing operativity. For example, a young child shown a series of rods arranged from short to long may remember them 1 week later as a dichotomy, short rods and long rods. But 6 months later, reflecting the child's growing mastery of the scheme of seriation, the child may remember the series as it was originally presented. In contrast with his position in the 1920s, when he tried to separate memory from understanding, Piaget now concluded that "The structure of memory appears to be partly dependent on the structure of the operations" (Piaget, 1970, p. 719).

Collaborators

The work we call Piaget's was really teamwork. Its scope and volume are so vast that it cannot be imagined without the skillful leadership necessary to generate enthusiasm and maintain a sense of direction. Piaget had many collaborators, ranging from student assistants to distinguished scientists and scholars in various fields. Besides psychologists there were mathematicians, logicians, philosophers and historians of science, biologists, physicists, and linguists. Almost everyone he worked with called him *patron* (boss). His longest collaboration (50 years), and the most important, was with Bärbel Inhelder, who began as his student and became a distinguished scientist in her own right, almost always working together or in close proximity—both spatially and intellectually—with Piaget.

Conclusion

Since about 1970 there have been numerous critical studies of Piaget's empirical findings and of his theoretical approach. By about 1990, much of the anti-Piagetian criticism had ebbed and had given way to neo-Piagetian efforts to assimilate Piaget's findings, correct some of his errors, and synthesize his work with newer developments in cognitive and social psychology. Most of his empirical findings have been verified by studies in many countries. Perhaps his most important contribution to developmental psychology was to reveal the child as a thinking being, and the child's intellect as growing through its own efforts in interaction with the physical and social world.

REFERENCES

Chapman, M. (1988). *Constructive evolution, origins and development of Piaget's thought.* New York: Cambridge University Press.

Gruber, H. E., and Vonèche, J. J. (1977). *The essential Piaget.* New York: Basic Books. A compendious anthology with explanatory comments.

Inhelder, B., Sinclair, H., and Bovet, M. (1974). *Learning and the development of cognition.* Cambridge, Mass.: Harvard University Press.

Kuhn, D., ed. (1989). *Human Development 32* (6), 325–387. A special issue devoted to reflections on the impact of Piaget's work.

Piaget, J. (1921). Essai sur quelques aspects du développement de la notion de partie chez l'enfant. *Journal de psychologie normale et pathologique 18,* 449–480.

——— [1961] (1969). *The mechanisms of perception.* Trans. G. N. Seagrim. New York: Basic Books.

——— (1970). Piaget's theory. In P. H. Mussen, ed., *Carmichael's manual of child psychology.* New York: Wiley.

——— [1967] (1971). *Biology and knowledge.* Trans. B. Walsh. Chicago: University of Chicago Press.

Piaget, J., and Inhelder, B. [1966] (1969). *The psychology of the child.* Trans. H. Weaver. New York: Basic Books. An excellent, readable introduction to the psychological work.

——— [1966] (1971). *Mental imagery in the child: A study of the development of imaginal representation.* Trans. P. A. Chilton. New York: Basic Books.

Piaget, J., Inhelder, B., and Sinclair-De Zwart, H. [1968] (1973). *Memory and intelligence.* Trans. A. J. Pomerans. New York: Basic Books.

Howard E. Gruber

POSITRON EMISSION TOMOGRAPHY

Positron emission tomography (PET) is a technology that creates images of the distribution of radioactivity within any tissue that is placed within the central opening of a doughnut-shaped PET camera. In the case of brain imaging, a small amount of radioactive substance, called a tracer, is given to a subject, usually by injection into the bloodstream or by inhalation of gas. Most tracers have short half-lives and must therefore be manufactured on site with a cyclotron. The tracers emit positrons, which travel a short distance within the tissue before encountering an electron. The annihilation event resulting from this encounter results in two photons, which travel from their source in precisely opposite directions. The ring of detectors surrounding the head is constructed to record an event only when two photons reach the detectors simultaneously. Computer algorithms are then applied to reconstruct a three-dimensional image of radioactivity.

The most commonly used tracer for cognitive studies is radioactively tagged water to measure brain blood flow. Because the tracer in this case is carried through the circulatory system, radioactivity will be high in those parts of the brain that have high local blood flow and low in those parts that have low local blood flow. The rationale behind imaging local regional blood flow is based on observations of higher blood flow in those parts of the brain that are "working harder" (i.e., those parts with high rates of neuronal activity).

An important feature of PET methodology, as it applies to the study of cognition in general and of memory in particular, is the use of subtraction techniques. If one simply recorded a PET image while a subject engaged in a task, many different areas of the brain would prove to be involved. However, one can potentially isolate specific components of cognition by imaging the brain on two occasions several minutes apart, while subjects engage successively in two closely related tasks. The subtraction of the first image from the second then identifies those areas of the brain that are active in the second task but not in the first.

In the case of studies of memory involving PET, the strategy is to ask subjects to engage in a memory task in which they attempt to recollect recent information, and a related task in which they read, process, and otherwise interact with the same stimuli but do not retrieve from recent memory. Studies of this kind have revealed activation of the hippocampal region and prefrontal cortex, areas known through studies of brain-damaged patients and of experimental animals to be associated with memory functions. Other information from these same studies illuminated the anatomical basis of word priming, a simple form of nonconscious memory in which the ability to detect or identify words is facilitated by their recent exposure. An area of decreased activation was observed in posterior visual cortex during priming, as compared with a similar condition when priming could not occur. These results suggest that when a word is presented visually, modifications occur along the visual pathways that process the word, so that on subsequent exposure less neural work is required to process the same word.

In another series of studies, PET has been used to gain insight into how subjects process single words that are presented visually. One important finding is the activation of an area in left posterior cortex by words and orthographically regular nonwords (e.g., *glone, stog*) but not by illegal nonwords (e.g., *glxqr, pntjk*). These findings thus identify an area of the brain that must be organized during normal development and that can achieve its final organization only after a person learns to read. These findings provide direct evidence for the long-term storage of memories in neocortex (in this case, memory for word forms that are legal in written English).

Studies of cognition with PET are just beginning. Much more can be expected to be learned about cognition and memory through use of this new technique.

Steven Petersen
Larry R. Squire

POSTTETANIC POTENTIATION

The synapse is the point of transmission of information between one neuron and another. Electrical activity in the presynaptic neuron influences electrical activity in the postsynaptic cell. This influence can be excitatory, in which case presynaptic action potentials trigger postsynaptic action potentials, or at least increase the probability of their occurrence in response to other inputs. Synaptic interactions can also be inhibitory, in which case presynaptic action potentials reduce the postsynaptic firing frequency or reduce the probability of firing action potentials in response to other excitatory inputs. *Posttetanic potentiation* is an increased effectiveness of synaptic transmission that lasts for minutes following high rates of neuronal activity.

Most synapses operate by means of an electrical-to-chemical transduction at the presynaptic neuron, followed by a chemical-to-electrical transduction at the postsynaptic cell. An action potential in the presynaptic neuron opens calcium channels in the membrane, and calcium rushes into the presynaptic terminal, the region of the presynaptic neuron that comes into contact, or synapses, with the postsynaptic cell. The rise in presynaptic calcium triggers the release of a chemical substance, called a transmitter, that diffuses across the synaptic cleft separating presynaptic from postsynaptic cells and binds to receptor proteins in the membrane of the postsynaptic cell. In fast-acting synapses, the activation of these receptors opens postsynaptic ion channels, and the flow of current through these channels makes the postsynaptic cell more electrically positive (depolarizes it) or more negative (hyperpolarizes it). Depolarization tends to trigger postsynaptic action potentials, exciting the postsynaptic cell, so the signal generated in the postsynaptic cell is called an excitatory postsynaptic potential (EPSP). Hyperpolarization blocks postsynaptic action potentials, inhibiting the postsynaptic cell; such a response is called an inhibitory postsynaptic potential (IPSP). (See also MEMBRANE CHANNELS AND THEIR MODULATION IN LEARNING AND MEMORY.)

Synaptic Plasticity

Synapses are not static in their transmission properties. Rather, the effectiveness of a presynaptic action potential depends on its proximity to prior activity. At some synapses, following a presynaptic action potential, a second action potential is likely to be more effective for about 1 second. This short-lasting increase in the size of the postsynaptic potential (PSP) is called synaptic facilitation. At many synapses, a slightly longer-lasting (several seconds) phase of increased transmission has been detected, which is called augmentation. At other synapses,

a second action potential will have less effect than the first for several seconds. The decrease in PSP amplitude is called synaptic depression. Although these effects can be observed following a single action potential, they accumulate or increase during repeated presynaptic activity. They are especially prominent during *tetanus*, high-frequency repetitive stimulation of the presynaptic neuron. Some synapses show a mixture of facilitation, augmentation, and depression, such that the first few PSPs in a tetanus grow for one or a few seconds due to facilitation and augmentation, while subsequent responses decline for several more seconds due to depression. These short-lived changes in the strength of synaptic transmission are collectively called short-term synaptic plasticity (Figure 1).

Another form of short-term synaptic plasticity is called synaptic potentiation. It is similar to synaptic facilitation or augmentation in that it consists of an increase in the strength or effectiveness of synaptic transmission, and is expressed as an increase in the size of the EPSP or IPSP. It differs in its kinetics. Potentiation is a slowly accumulating increase in PSP amplitude seen during a tetanus. It consists of a gradual growth in the PSPs over a period of minutes during continued presynaptic electrical activity. Tetanic potentiation therefore continues to grow long after facilitation has reached a steady state (usually about 1 second). However, it may be obscured by depression occurring simultaneously during a tetanus. Often depression is stronger than potentiation, so that the net effect of continued stimulation is reduction of the PSP. In that case, tetanic potentiation can be observed only when techniques are used to block the development of depression. One such technique is use of a low-calcium medium to reduce the amount of transmitter released by action potentials. This prevents the depletion of presynaptic transmitter stores during the tetanus, and avoids depression. Such a reduction in calcium has little effect on the opposing processes of synaptic facilitation and potentiation.

In normal medium, depression usually lasts for a few seconds or perhaps a minute after repetitive stimulation ceases, while the effect of potentiation lasts for tens of minutes. Thus, after a tetanus sufficiently long (usually several minutes) to initiate a significant degree of potentiation, and after the synapse has recovered from depression, single presynaptic test stimuli evoke PSPs that remain potentiated for minutes; that is, they are larger than

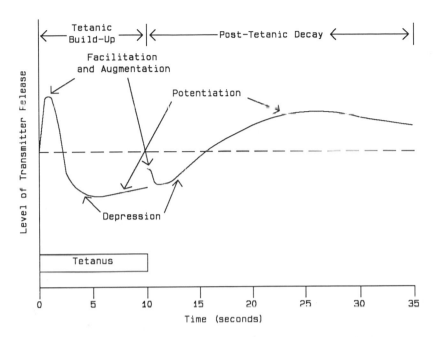

Figure 1. Changes in strength of synaptic transmission due to facilitation, augmentation, depression, and potentiation operating simultaneously, measured during a tetanus and as a function of time after a tetanus.

the original isolated PSP that follows a long period of silence. This phenomenon is called posttetanic potentiation, frequently abbreviated PTP. It is really the persistent effect of tetanic potentiation, observed most clearly after recovery from depression.

Presynaptic Locus

In principle, short-term synaptic plasticity could arise at either presynaptic or postsynaptic sites. Presynaptically, action potentials could evoke the release of more or less transmitter. Postsynaptically, the transmitter receptors could become more or less sensitive, or the electrical response of a neuron to the postsynaptic current could change. In fact, at almost all synapses that have been studied, short-term synaptic plasticity is due to changes in the amount of transmitter released by an action potential. Transmitter is released in small packages of about 5,000 molecules, probably by the fusion of membrane-bound transmitter-containing vesicles with the presynaptic membrane, followed by exocytosis of their contents. Facilitation, depression, and potentiation or PTP are all caused by changes in the number of these packages,

called quanta, that each action potential causes to be released at the presynaptic nerve terminals. The size of the quanta and their postsynaptic effectiveness change little during these processes.

Prevalence and Significance

Practically all chemically transmitting synapses that have been studied show a mixture of facilitation, depression, augmentation, and potentiation. This includes central synapses between neurons in the mammalian brain and spinal cord, sensory nerve synapses, peripheral synapses in the ganglia of the autonomic nervous system, release of transmitter from neurosecretory terminals in the pituitary, synapses between neurons in invertebrate ganglia (especially mollusks and annelids), and synapses from motor neurons onto muscles (neuromuscular junctions) in vertebrates, crustaceans, and insects.

The effect of these forms of short-term plasticity is to make synapses selective for certain patterns of presynaptic activity. Potentiation in particular causes only sustained and prolonged activity to be maximally effective in exciting or inhibiting the postsynaptic neuron. This can be important in extracting significant signals from noise. Differences in the mixture of plasticities can cause the various terminals of a neuron to select different patterns of activity for transmission to different postsynaptic targets. This adds greatly to the information-processing capabilities of synapses, and may allow certain pathways to respond only to specific patterns corresponding to particular significant stimuli. The ability to distinguish such patterns is an important aspect of many neural networks proposed as models of neural circuits capable of learning. These forms of plasticity are forms of synaptic modifiability, which plays an important role in most theoretical models of learning networks.

Role of Calcium

Calcium can be manipulated rapidly in the neighborhood of nerve terminals by ejecting it iontophoretically from a micropipette in a calcium-free medium. Such experiments show that facilitation, augmentation, and potentiation all require calcium to be present during the conditioning stimulation for the effects to be expressed by test stimuli. This has led to the hypothesis that all three effects require the entry and accumulation of presynaptic calcium during conditioning stimulation. Transmitter release by single action potentials depends in a highly nonlinear way on external calcium concentration and the influx of calcium during action potentials. When calcium-sensitive dyes are injected into nerves near their terminals, changes in external calcium relate nearly linearly to changes in influx and calcium accumulation. Thus there appears to be a highly cooperative action of calcium ions at their presynaptic receptor site in releasing transmitter. Roughly speaking, release is proportional to the fourth power of external calcium concentration, calcium influx, or calcium activity at presynaptic release sites.

One might imagine that a small residual amount ($R(t)$) of the calcium that enters during action potentials (E) remains at time t after one or more spikes. Then a single action potential will release T_1 quanta according to $T_1 = K(E)^n$, where K is a proportionality constant. A second action potential, or one following a tetanus, will release T_2 quanta according to $T_2 = K(E + R)^n$. Suppose that at time t, $R(t)$ is 10 percent of E. Then the degree of facilitation, augmentation, or potentia-

tion, T_2/T_1, will be $(1 + R(t)/E)^n$, which for $n = 4$ and $R(t)/E = 0.1$ comes to 1.46 (i.e., the second response will be 46 percent larger than the first). Meanwhile, transmitter release to the residual calcium itself will be negligible: $(R(t)/E)^n$, or 0.01. Finally, the ratio of T_2/T_1 will be independent of calcium concentration in the bath, because E and $R(t)$ are scaled by the same amount as calcium influx changes. These are all properties of facilitation, augmentation, and potentiation, and thus this is a very attractive explanation for these phenomena. Their different time courses would simply reflect the different phases for the accumulation of residual calcium during a tetanus, and of its removal afterward.

Qualitative evidence for such a critical role of residual calcium in potentiation has been obtained. The time course of PTP closely matches the time course of residual calcium actually measured in nerve terminals. In fact, the correspondence is better than expected. The above formulation predicts a nonlinear relationship between $R(t)$ and potentiation. PTP should decay faster than $R(t)$. The linear relation observed means that PTP was greater than expected from the simple hypothesis (Figure 2). Perhaps calcium acts at another site to potentiate the release of more transmitter than predicted by the above model. There is some evidence that calcium can bind to a calmodulin receptor on a kinase that phosphorylates a protein called synapsin I. Phosphorylated synapsin I may release synaptic vesicles from cytoskeletal attachment sites and allow them to move up to release sites, contributing to PTP. This mechanism, if present, acts in addition to the nonlinear summation of residual calcium with entering calcium postulated above, which may be more uniquely responsible for facilitation and augmentation. This would explain why potentiation does not simply summate with facilitation and augmentation but, rather, seems to interact with it multiplicatively. The exploration of these possibilities remains an active area of research.

Role of Sodium in PTP

In addition to calcium, sodium influx during a tetanus contributes to PTP. Action potentials are generated by a brief increase in nerve permeability to sodium ions. Sodium flows into nerves down its

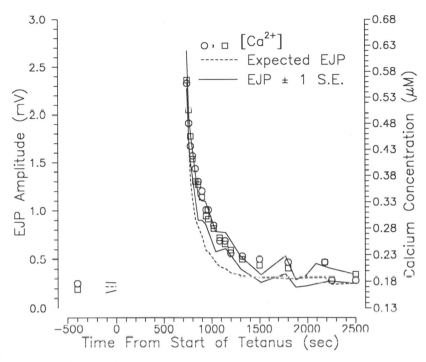

Figure 2. EPSPs from a crayfish muscle fiber (solid lines show average values ± one standard error) before and after a 20-hertz tetanus lasting 12 minutes closely follow the presynaptic calcium concentration measured in two presynaptic terminals using the indicator dye fura-2 (squares and circles). The dashed line is a prediction of the decay of the posttetanic potentiation of the EPSPs, calculated from the simple nonlinear residual calcium model described in the text, from the decay of posttetanic calcium concentration.

electrochemical gradient, briefly depolarizing the membrane before the sodium channels shut. During a tetanus, the presynaptic sodium concentration gradually rises. This accumulation of sodium can be augmented by blocking the sodium pump, which normally slowly restores intracellular sodium to its resting level, with ouabain. This treatment augments PTP and prolongs its decay. Moreover, injection of sodium directly into nerves near their terminals potentiates transmitter release. Conversely, sodium entry can be prevented with the sodium channel blocker tetrodotoxin, and transmitter release can be triggered by direct pulsed depolarization of the nerve terminals with electrodes placed next to them. Transmitter release to a tetanus of such pulses shows reduced PTP. How does sodium exert this influence on PTP? Normally, the calcium that accumulates presynaptically in a tetanus is extruded by a membrane transport pump that exchanges external sodium for internal calcium. Elevation of internal sodium in a tetanus retards this pump, so that more cal-

cium accumulates during the tetanus and its subsequent removal is retarded. Thus the time course of PTP is determined by the rate at which calcium is removed from the terminals, and this in turn depends on the accumulation of presynaptic sodium. Theoretical calculations of the extrusion of calcium from nerve terminals by such membrane pumps predict a late phase of decay of potentiated release similar to PTP (Figure 3).

PTP, then, is a fascinating property of chemical synaptic transmission. It contributes to the information-processing capabilities, temporal selectivity, and modifiability of synaptic transmission. It appears to be triggered by residual calcium remaining after action potentials. It may arise in part from the nonlinear dependence of transmitter release upon calcium, and in part from calcium acting independently to mobilize vesicles to release sites. Sodium accumulation contributes to PTP by impeding the removal of presynaptic calcium by sodium/calcium exchange. PTP is an entirely presynaptic process, and as such is distinct from the

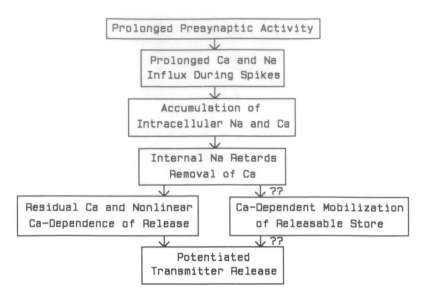

Figure 3. A block diagram of the roles of calcium and sodium in PTP.

much longer-lasting and more complex class of phenomena called LONG-TERM POTENTIATION.

REFERENCES

Atwood, H. L., and Wojtowicz, J. M. (1986). Short-term and long-term plasticity and physiological differentiation of crustacean motor synapses. *International Review of Neurobiology 28*, 275–362. Summarizes the evidence for roles for calcium and sodium in PTP.

Delaney, K. R., Zucker, R. S., and Tank, D. W. (1989). Calcium in motor nerve terminals associated with posttetanic potentiation. *Journal of Neuroscience 9*, 3558–3567. Describes experiments on the relationship between residual calcium and PTP.

Fogelson, A. L., and Zucker, R. S. (1985). Presynaptic calcium diffusion from various arrays of single channels: Implications for transmitter release and synaptic facilitation. *Biophysical Journal 48*, 1003–1017. Describes simulations of residual calcium underlying synaptic plasticity.

Katz, B. (1969). *The release of neural transmitter substances.* Springfield, Ill.: Charles C. Thomas. The classic treatise on transmitter release.

Magleby, K. L., and Zengel, J. E. (1982). A quantitative description of stimulation-induced changes in transmitter release at the frog neuromuscular junction. *Journal of General Physiology 80*, 613–638. Summarizes extensive work by these authors on the kinetics and interactions between the various phases of short-term synaptic plasticity.

McGuinness, T. L., Brady, S. T., Gruner, J. A., Sugimori, M., Llinas, R., and Greengard, P. (1989). Phosphorylation-dependent inhibition by synapsin I of organelle movement in squid axoplasm. *Journal of Neuroscience 9*, 4138–4149. Suggests that calcium-sensitive protein phosphorylation may contribute to PTP.

Smith, S. J., and Augustine, G. J. (1988). Calcium ions, active zones and synaptic transmitter release. *Trends in Neuroscience 11*, 458–464. A good discussion of calcium action in transmitter release.

Zucker, R. S. (1989). Short-term synaptic plasticity. *Annual Review of Neuroscience 12*, 13–31. A general review with many references.

Zucker, R. S., Delaney, K. R., Mulkey, R., and Tank, D. W. (1991). Presynaptic calcium in transmitter release and post-tetanic potentiation. *Annals of the New York Academy of Sciences 635*, 191–207. Includes recent results on sodium-calcium interactions in PTP.

Robert S. Zucker

PREFRONTAL CORTEX AND MEMORY IN PRIMATES

A primate needs its prefrontal cortex whenever and wherever it has to perform an action based on information that is not available at the time to act but has been available in the recent past. The prefrontal cortex is especially important if the information is new to the organism or is in conflict with prior cues or memories that call for different actions. Whether the information is new or old, it must be retained in memory until the time to act in accord with it. That is the kind of memory the prefrontal cortex supports. It is short-term memory (also called WORKING MEMORY) at the service of behavior. Prefrontal memory is defined not by content or by duration but by context, the context of action. Short-term memory is not the only function of the prefrontal cortex, nor is it exclusively the role of the prefrontal cortex. But, inasmuch as short-term memory is needed in and for action, the prefrontal cortex is needed. It follows that this part of the cortex is essential for the construction of sequential behaviors, especially if they are novel or require choices between competing alternatives. It is needed for the *syntax of the action,* including of course the syntax of the spoken language, particularly creative speech.

The prefrontal cortex is the cortex of the pole of the frontal lobe. It is conventionally defined as that part of the cerebral cortex to which the nucleus mediodorsalis of the thalamus projects. Phylogenetically, it is the neocortical region to undergo the greatest and latest expansion (Figure 1). It reaches maximum development in the brain of the human, where it occupies almost one-third of the totality of the neocortex. In the course of evolution, its dorsolateral aspect, that is, the cortex of the external convexity of the frontal lobe, develops relatively more than its medial and inferior aspects. This is an important consideration because the dorsolateral prefrontal cortex supports mainly cognitive functions, whereas the orbitomedial prefrontal cortex is involved predominantly in emotional and visceral functions.

Cytoarchitectonically, the prefrontal cortex of the primate (area FD of Von Bonin and Bailey, 1947) includes areas 9, 10, 11, 12, and 13 of Brodmann (1909). It is one of the best-connected of all neocortical regions; it is directly and reciprocally connected to the anterior and dorsal thalamus, the hypothalamus, and limbic structures, especially the amygdala and the hippocampus. It sends profuse efferent fibers to the basal ganglia. Dorsolateral prefrontal areas have rich reciprocal connections with many other neocortical areas of the frontal lobe and of the temporal and parietal lobes. (See GUIDE TO THE ANATOMY OF THE BRAIN.)

The first clear indication of the involvement of the prefrontal cortex in short-term memory was provided by Jacobsen in the early 1930s (Jacobsen, 1935). He showed that monkeys with lesions of the dorsolateral prefrontal cortex are impaired in the learning and performance of delayed response (DR) and delayed alternation (DA) tasks. These tasks fall within a general category of behavioral tasks—*delay tasks*—that demand from the animal the performance of motor acts in accord with sensory information presented a few seconds or minutes earlier. In other words, delay tasks demand short-term memory for the logical and consequent bridging of temporal gaps between perception and action, the mediation of cross-temporal contingencies of behavior. Primates deprived of substantial portions of dorsolateral prefrontal cortex cannot properly perform delay tasks, regardless of the nature of the sensory information that guides them, especially if a long lapse of time (delay) is interposed between sensory cue and motor response.

There appears, however, to be some specificity of prefrontal areas with regard to the type of sensory information they help retain. Lesions of the cortex of the sulcus principalis are most detrimental to performance of delay tasks with spatially defined sensory cues, such as DR and DA. However, time seems to override space on this matter. Those "spatial tasks" are impaired only *if* a temporal gap, a delay, is interposed between cue and response. The critical factor is time, the time during which the cue must be retained. Furthermore, dorsolateral prefrontal lesions also impair performance of delay tasks in which the sensory cue is not spatially defined. This has been demonstrated by local cortical cooling. The cryogenic depression of a large portion of dorsolateral cortex (area 9), including the sulcus principalis, induces a reversible deficit in performance of delay tasks, whether the cue is visual and spatially defined (as in DR) or not (as in delayed matching to sample). Furthermore, the cryogenic deficit also affects delayed matching tasks in which the cue (sample) is perceived by active touch (haptically).

Humans with dorsolateral prefrontal lesions also show impairments in delay tasks. Tasks in which the material to be retained can be verbally encoded are more affected by lesions of the left than of the right prefrontal cortex. They are impaired most of all by bilateral lesions. The human prefrontal syndrome is usually characterized by disorders of attention, planning, and language. Prefrontal patients have difficulty maintaining attention on internal cues or mental material to be retained for the short term. Their planning is poor for both the short and the long term; it is as if they lacked "memory of the future" in addition to memory of the recent past. Both retrospective and prospec-

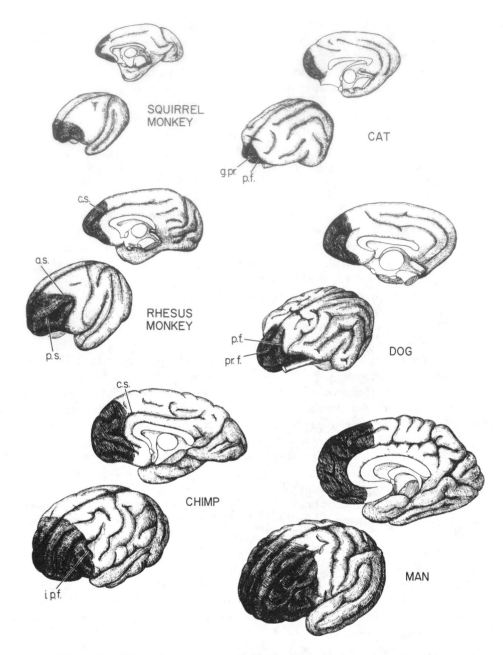

Figure 1. The prefrontal cortex, darkly shaded, in six animal species. Abbreviations: a.s., arcuate sulcus; c.s., cingulate sulcus; g. pr., gyrus proreus; i.p.f., inferior precentral fissure; p.f., presylvian fissure; p.s., principal sulcus; pr. f., proreal fissure.

tive representations are needed for the sequential construction not only of external motor action but also of "internal action," such as sequential logical thinking. Hence the trouble the patients have in this kind of activity, whether expressed in spoken language or not. Speech is most impaired if it requires the bridging of long intervals (cross-temporal contingencies) between subjects and

verbs, subjects and predicates, or logically interdependent sentences. The trouble is extreme in lesions of Broca's area, which is a part of the prefrontal cortex specialized in the most elementary aspects of linguistic syntax. In conclusion, animal and human neuropsychology suggests that the prefrontal cortex is essential for bridging cross-temporal contingencies of behavior, and that this is so

Figure 2. Discharge of a neuron in the prefrontal cortex of a monkey during five delayed-response trials. The cue period is marked by a horizontal bar and the response of the animal by an arrow. Note the sustained activation of the cell during the delay (the memory retention period, about 60 seconds long in the last two trials); note also that the cell reverts to the lower level of spontaneous discharge immediately after every trial.

at least in part because of its role in short-term memory.

Microelectrode recording in the monkey has substantiated the role of the prefrontal cortex in short-term memory. Prefrontal neurons show sustained activation of firing during the delay periods of delay tasks (Figure 2). Statistical analysis and control experiments indicate that this activation is (1) a result of learning the task, (2) dependent on the presence of a cross-temporal contingency between cue and motor response, (3) related in some cells to the particular property of the cue on which the response depends, (4) related in some cells to the particular response that the animal has to execute at the end of the delay, and (5) directly related to the efficacy with which the animal performs the task. All these indications are consistent with the presumption that prefrontal neurons participate in cortical networks that, by their sustained activation, retain sensory information as long as needed for prospective action.

The analysis of single-unit discharge in other areas of association cortex (inferotemporal and posterior parietal) during visual and haptic delay tasks has revealed sustained neuronal activations in those areas. This observation, in addition to the study of the effects of local cortical cooling on remote cortical cell discharge and delay-task performance, has led to the following inference: The prefrontal cortex exerts its role in short-term memory and preparation for action by close functional interplay with areas of posterior association cortex with which it is intimately and reciprocally connected. Thus, the activated cortical network that during behavior retains sensory information in short-term memory has several components. Posterior areas are involved in the network inas-

much as the information falls within their special modality (vision, audition, somesthesis, etc.). The prefrontal cortex is involved inasmuch as the information calls for prospective goal-directed action. The maintenance of activity in the network is assured by the continuous circulation of excitatory impulses within and between all contributing areas, including the prefrontal cortex if the outcome is to be a goal-directed action in accord with the sensory information.

In conclusion, the prefrontal cortex of the primate is a large and phylogenetically new part of the cerebral cortex that performs a critical function in short-term memory for action. Thus, it is critically important for sequential behaviors with cross-temporal contingencies. In the human, such behaviors include the spoken language and the logical thought process, which is a form of sequential "inner action." The memory function of the prefrontal cortex is one of several functions that this cortex supports in cooperation with other associative cortical areas. These functions are essential for the syntax of action, that is, for organization of behavior in the time domain.

REFERENCES

Bauer, R. H., and Fuster, J. M. (1976). Delayed-matching and delayed-response deficit from cooling dorsolateral prefrontal cortex in monkeys. *Journal of Comparative Physiology and Psychology 90*, 293–302.

Bonin, G. von, and Bailey, P. (1947). *The neocortex of Macaca mulatta.* Urbana, Ill.: University of Illinois Press.

Brodmann, K. (1909). *Vergleichende Lokalisationslehre*

der Grosshirnrinde in ihren Prinzipien dargestellt auf Grund des Zellenbaues. Leipzig: Barth.

Fuster, J. M. (1973). Unit activity in prefrontal cortex during delayed-response performance: Neuronal correlates of transient memory. *Journal of Neurophysiology 36*, 61–78.

Fuster, J. M. (1985a). The prefrontal cortex and temporal integration. In E. G. Jones and A. Peters, eds. *Cerebral cortex*, vol. 4, pp. 151–175. New York: Plenum Press.

Fuster, J. M. (1985b). The prefrontal cortex, mediator of cross-temporal contingencies. *Human Neurobiology 4*, 169–179.

Fuster, J. M. (1989). *The prefrontal cortex*, 2nd ed. New York: Raven Press.

Goldman-Rakic, P. S. (1987). Circuitry of primate prefrontal cortex and regulation of behavior by representational memory. In F. Plum, ed., *Handbook of physiology, Section 1: The Nervous System*, vol. 5, pp. 373–341. Bethesda, Md.: American Physiological Association.

Jacobsen, C. F. (1935). Functions of the frontal association area in primates. *Archives of Neurology and Psychiatry 33*, 558–569.

Joaquin M. Fuster

PRIMATES, VISUAL ATTENTION IN

The neural mechanisms for visual attention comprise a class of mechanisms that are not strictly sensory or motor but affect how information is processed within the visual system. These include mechanisms for arousal, alerting, vigilance, behavioral or motor "set," and selective attention for spatial location or visual features. Of these, the ones that most directly affect visual processing are selective attention to a location in space or to a particular visual feature of an object. These latter mechanisms help route selected visual inputs to visual processing structures in the brain and also to motor control systems, usually at the expense of nonselected inputs.

Why are selection mechanisms needed in visual processing? A simple answer is that the brain's ability to process incoming sensory information is limited. It is not possible, for example, to recognize within the same instant more than one or two objects in a typical complex scene. Thus, much of the information impinging on our retinas must ultimately be filtered out before reaching either conscious awareness or memory. Some filtering occurs largely automatically, or preattentively, because of separation of figures from their background ("pop-out") based on differences in color, contrast, motion, and so on. Yet, even after figure-ground separation, a typical visual scene will still contain many different figures, requiring a subsequent attentional stage of selection. The neural system that controls the eyes (oculomotor system) also requires a selection mechanism, as it is not possible to move the eyes to two different targets at once.

In neurobiological studies, it is useful to distinguish the mechanisms involved in the *control* of attention from the mechanisms that are *influenced* by attention. The control system for spatially directed attention is both widely distributed and closely associated with the oculomotor system, involving the posterior parietal cortex, parts of frontal cortex, the pulvinar nucleus of the thalamus, and possibly the superior colliculus. Within at least some of these structures, a given neuron responds to stimuli in a limited region of space (i.e., its receptive field), and this response is enhanced whenever the animal directs its attention into the region. Damage or dysfunction within any of these structures, particularly if unilateral, can cause a variety of attentional disorders, such as extinction, which is a difficulty in detecting or perceiving objects within the affected portion of the visual field when a competing object is located in intact portions of the field.

Neurons in extrastriate visual cortical areas that process information about object features such as color and shape probably do not directly control the locus of attention but, rather, receive attentional control signals. When more than one stimulus is located within the receptive field of a neuron in either cortical area V4 or the inferior temporal cortex, and a monkey attends to just one of them, the response of the neuron will be determined almost solely by the color, shape, or orientation of the attended stimulus. Neurons communicate little information about the features of ignored stimuli, explaining why we have little awareness of them. Neuronal responses in monkey extrastriate cortex are larger and more selective for a stimulus when an animal is challenged by a difficult discrimination task, compared with an easy one. Likewise, studies using POSITRON EMISSION TOMOGRAPHY in humans reveal that different portions of extrastriate cortex are activated when subjects focus their attention on different features of a complex stimulus. The neural circuitry by which the attentional control system exerts such a strong influence on the neurons that process sensory information in extrastriate cortex has yet to be established.

REFERENCES

Desimone, R., and Ungerleider, L. G. (1989). Neural mechanisms of visual processing in monkeys. In F. Boller and J. Grafman, eds., *Handbook of neuropsychology*, vol. 2. Amsterdam: Elsevier.

Goldberg, M. E., and Colby, C. L. (1989). The neurophysiology of spatial vision. In F. Boller and J. Grafman, eds., *Handbook of neuropsychology*, vol. 2. Amsterdam: Elsevier.

Posner, M. I., and Presti, D. E. (1987). Selective attention and cognitive control. *Trends in Neuroscience 10*, 13–17.

Wise, S., and Desimone, R. (1988). Behavioral neurophysiology: Insights into seeing and grasping. *Science 242*, 736–741.

Robert Desimone

PRIMATES, VISUAL PERCEPTION AND MEMORY IN NONHUMAN

Anatomical and physiological studies have revealed at least twenty separate areas with visual functions in the cortex of monkeys, and there could be an even greater number of visual areas in the cortex of humans. According to Ungerleider and Mishkin (1982), these multiple visual areas are organized into two major processing systems, or pathways, both of which originate within the primary visual cortex. One of the pathways is directed ventrally from the occipital lobe into the temporal lobe and is crucial for the visual recognition of objects (i.e., identifying *what* an object is). The other pathway is directed dorsally from the occipital lobe into the parietal lobe and is crucial for visuospatial localization (i.e., identifying *where* an object is). This article will focus on the ventrally directed, occipitotemporal processing stream and its role in object perception and memory.

The Occipitotemporal Pathway for Object Recognition

The occipitotemporal pathway begins with the projection from the striate cortex (the primary visual cortex, V1) to the second and third visual areas, V2 and V3, which in turn project to area V4 (see Figure 1). These three prestriate visual areas are arranged in adjacent cortical belts that nearly surround the striate cortex. The major output of area V4 is to a widespread region within the inferior temporal cortex, including area TEO posteriorly and area TE anteriorly. Area TE appears to be the last, or "highest-order," visual area in the cortical system for object recognition, as its principal cortical outputs are to areas in the temporal and frontal lobes that are not exclusively concerned with vision.

Like the striate cortex, each of the prestriate cortical belts contains a representation of the contralateral visual field. Area TEO also contains such a representation, although it is considerably coarser than that found in the prestriate areas posterior to it. By contrast, area TE has no discernible visuotopic organization. Rather, neurons in TE have very large receptive fields that nearly always include the center of gaze and frequently cross the midline to include large portions of the ipsilateral visual field. Thus, a single neuron in TE can "see" an object no matter where it occurs in the visual field.

Although much of the neural mechanism for object recognition can be viewed as a bottom-up process, in which low-level inputs are transformed into a more useful representation through successive stages of processing, anatomical studies have shown that each of the feedforward projections between successive pairs of areas in the occipitotemporal pathway is reciprocated by a feedback projection. Such projections from higher-order processing stations back to lower-order ones could mediate some top-down aspects of visual processing, such as the influence of selective attention (see also PRIMATES, VISUAL ATTENTION IN).

Neuronal Properties in the Visual Areas of the Occipitotemporal Pathway

Given the nearly sequential anatomical route to the inferior temporal cortex from V1, one would expect many types of visual information relevant to object recognition to be processed within each area along the route. Indeed, electrophysiological studies have shown that neurons in V1, V2, and V3 are sensitive to one or (usually) more stimulus qualities such as length, width, orientation, spatial

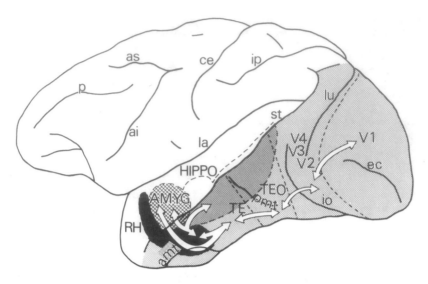

Figure 1. Diagram of the occipitotemporal visuolimbic pathway mediating object recognition. Arrows indicate two-way information flow from early (V1–V4) through late (TEO, TE) cortical visual stations, and then medially into the limbic system, including the amygdaloid complex (AMYG), hippocampal formation (HIPPO), and the rhinal cortex (RH). Interactions of visual cortex with the limbic system are presumably subserved by the projections from TE to the rhinal cortex, the amygdaloid complex (both directly and indirectly via the rhinal cortex), and the hippocampal formation (indirectly via the parahippocampal gyrus and rhinal cortex), as well as by projections from both the amygdaloid complex and the rhinal cortex back to TE. For ease in viewing the inferior temporal cortex, the hippocampus is shown slightly superior to its actual location. Sulcal abbreviations: ai, inferior arcuate; amt, anterior middle temporal; as, superior arcuate; ce, central; ec, external calcarine; io, inferior occipital; ip, intraparietal; lu, lunate; la, lateral; p, principal; pmt, posterior middle temporal; st, superior temporal. *Courtesy J. Bachevalier.*

frequency, texture, color, direction of motion, and binocular disparity. Although these earliest stations in the occipitotemporal pathway also participate in the occipitoparietal pathway, recent evidence has shown that many of the stimulus qualities analyzed in V1 and V2 are represented in separate columnar and laminar systems that project differentially to the two pathways. For example, the input to area V4, which plays a crucial link in the occipitotemporal pathway, is derived preferentially from subregions of V2 that contain neurons selective for either color or length and orientation. By contrast, the input to the middle temporal visual area, which plays a crucial link in the occipitoparietal pathway, is derived preferentially from a separate subregion of V2 that contains neurons selective for direction of stimulus motion. Thus, the anatomical pathway for object recognition appears to be specialized for analyzing color and form information, while a major component of the pathway for visuospatial perception is devoted to the analysis of motion.

It is possible to view the areas along the occipitotemporal pathway as forming a processing hierarchy. As one moves along the pathway from V1 to area TE, both neuronal response latencies and average receptive field size increase steadily, consistent with the notion that neuronal responses in later areas are built up from those in earlier areas. A hierarchical model further predicts that the product of visual processing will become progressively more complex at each successive stage in the pathway. So far, the results of electrophysiological studies in prestriate areas V2 and V4 and inferior temporal area TE support this prediction.

Emergent Properties of Neurons in V2

Although neurons in V2 have many properties similar to those of neurons in V1, two newly discovered properties suggest ways in which object features are coded more explicitly in V2 than in V1. The first is the ability of V2 but not V1 neurons to respond to illusory contours, that is, contours that are physically discontinuous but are "filled in" and thus perceived to be continuous. This finding suggests that V2 but not V1 neurons extract contours and provide an explicit representation of them. The second newly discovered property of V2 is evidenced by a type of neuron that is tuned to the color and size of small spots within a relatively large receptive field. Such cells thus combine color selectivity with a type of primitive shape selectivity and appear to maintain this selectivity over relatively large shifts in stimulus position, a property that seems to be further elaborated in areas beyond V2.

Emergent Properties of Neurons in V4

All of the stimulus qualities that are coded by neurons in V1, V2, and V3 also appear to be coded by neurons in V4. However, in addition to sensitivity to the contour, texture, and color of a stimulus, many V4 neurons respond to a stimulus only if it stands out from its background on the basis of a difference in color or form. This responsivity to stimulus differences is due to the unique receptive-field structure of V4 neurons: a small excitatory receptive field surrounded by a large, silent suppressive zone. Because the stimulus-selective properties of the excitatory receptive field and the suppressive surround are often matched (e.g., the orientation or color of the surround stimulus that elicits maximal suppression is the same that elicits maximal excitation inside the receptive field), the surround can suppress the responses to an excitatory-field stimulus if the two are stimulated in the same way. Neurons respond maximally when the receptive field stimulus is different from surrounding stimuli. Thus, V4 neurons may play a role in separating figure from ground, or "breaking camouflage," a basic requirement for object recognition.

Emergent Properties of Neurons in Area TE

Although early findings led some theorists to propose that TE neurons code specific objects within their large, bilateral receptive fields, the overwhelming evidence indicates that TE neurons respond selectively to object features such as shape, color, and texture, rather than to specific objects. Thus, the neural code for object recognition must

be a population code based on stimulus features. The only exception appears to be the small proportion of neurons selective for faces and, more rarely, hands. Why should the coding of faces be treated differently from the coding of other objects? One possibility is that faces are extremely important to primates not only for the recognition of individuals in the social group but also for social communication by facial expression. Thus, there may have been selective pressure to evolve specialized neural mechanisms for the analysis of faces and facial expression.

In summary, within each area along the occipitotemporal pathway, several different stimulus qualities related to object recognition are processed in parallel, but the type of analysis becomes more global at each successive stage of processing.

Effects of Lesions in the Visual Areas of the Occipitotemporal Pathway

Numerous studies have shown that lesions of V1 produce a scotoma, or blind spot, that corresponds to the part of the visual field represented in the damaged area. The effects of selective lesions of V2 and V3 on visual perception and memory have not yet been investigated. As described below, the impairments that follow lesions of areas V4, TEO, and TE are consistent with a contribution from these areas to the object-recognition process.

Lesions of Area V4

Several studies in monkeys have examined the contribution of V4 lesions to color and form vision. Although one reported that the lesion impaired color constancy but not hue or form discrimination (see DISCRIMINATION AND GENERALIZATION), subsequent studies found impairments in both hue and form discrimination, which is consistent with the notion that V4 processes both color and form information and relays this information to the inferior temporal cortex.

Lesions of Areas TEO and TE

It is well established that the visual discrimination learning impairment resulting from lesions of the inferior temporal cortex is not due to an impairment of basic sensory capacities such as visual acuity or color vision. Rather, the behavioral impairment seems to result from the loss of a "high-level" mechanism. If the lesion is confined to area TEO, there is a devastating effect on discrimination learning of two-dimensional patterns, which can be even more severe than the effects of lesions of area TE. The more similar the patterns are to one another, the more devastating the impairment. By contrast, lesions of area TE cause a greater impairment than TEO lesions on concurrent discrimination, that is, learning to discriminate among several object pairs at the same time. In concurrent object discrimination, the multiple objects can be easily distinguished from one another on the basis of simple object features; the task is difficult to learn because of the high memory load caused by proactive and retroactive interference. Thus, area TEO appears to be particularly important in tasks emphasizing fine discrimination, whereas TE appears to be particularly important in tasks taxing visual memory.

The precise nature of the visual impairment following TE lesions is controversial. One model, initially proposed by Dean (1982) and elaborated by Gaffan, Harrison, and Gaffan (1986), is that monkeys with TE lesions have fewer perceptual categories than normal. Thus, in a visual discrimination task, learning to associate one object with reward and another, very different object with nonreward might be as difficult for an animal with a TE lesion as a normal animal would find learning to discriminate between two highly similar objects. In contrast, Mishkin (1982) has argued that a reduction in the number of perceptual categories cannot explain the full range of impairments that follow TE lesions, which appear to cause a loss of certain perceptual constancies, a reduction in the visual inputs to a "habit" learning system involving the basal ganglia (see GUIDE TO THE ANATOMY OF THE BRAIN), and a profound loss of visual memories.

Visual Recognition Memory

In monkeys, the delayed nonmatching-to-sample (DNMS) task has proved to be a reliable way to measure visual recognition memory for objects. On each trial, the animal is shown a sample object, which it displaces in order to find a food reward underneath, and then, about 10 seconds later, is shown both the sample and a novel object for choice. The monkey can obtain another food reward by choosing the novel object. When the ani-

mal has learned the nonmatching rule, the task is made more difficult—either by increasing the delay between the sample presentation and the choice test or by increasing the number of items to be remembered—to tax the monkey's memory.

Lesions of area TE lead to severe deficits on DNMS. In general, the animals can perform the nonmatching task if the delay between the sample and the choice is short, but their performance falls nearly to chance levels when the delays are as long as a minute or two. Thus, the deficit is not with visual perception but appears to be specific to memory. On the basis of findings such as these, Mishkin (1982) has proposed that TE contains the "central representations" for visual objects, and that removal of TE leads to an inability to form new memories as well as the loss of old memories.

Interactions of the Occipitotemporal Pathway with the Limbic System

If visual memories are stored in area TE, the storage must occur through the interaction of visual cortex with medial temporal-lobe limbic structures (see Figure 1). This idea is supported by the finding that recognition deficits of the same magnitude as those caused by lesions of area TE result from combined lesions of the amygdala (AMYG), hippocampus (HIPPO), and rhinal cortex (RH, comprised of both the entorhinal and perirhinal cortical fields). However, because limbic system damage does not lead to the loss of previously stored information, the limbic system itself cannot be the site of memory storage. In this view, the role of the limbic system in visual memory is to facilitate the consolidation of new memories within area TE. The relative contributions of the structures within the medial temporal lobe to this consolidation process are currently under investigation.

Lesions of the medial temporal-lobe limbic structures in both monkeys and humans lead to memory deficits not only in vision but in other sensory modalities as well. Furthermore, given that the limbic structures receive information from the cortical sensory processing areas for each sensory modality (vision, touch, audition, etc.), it is likely that there are corticolimbic pathways subserving object recognition for other sensory modalities which parallel those for the visual system.

Further Stations in the Memory System

It has been proposed that the medial temporal lobe constitutes only one part of an anatomical circuit subserving recognition memory for all the sensory modalities. The medial temporal-lobe limbic structures are the source of direct projections to certain portions of the medial diencephalon, basal forebrain, and ventromedial prefrontal cortex; interruption of the limbic-diencephalic projections or direct damage to any one of these other stations also results in severe impairments in visual recognition memory in monkeys. Memory impairments are found in humans following damage to these same brain loci. For example, memory impairments are produced by damage to medial temporal lobe limbic structures as a result of either herpes encephalitis or ischemic episodes, to the medial diencephalon as a result of Korsakoff's disease, and to the basal forebrain and ventromedial prefrontal cortex as a result of aneurysms of the anterior communicating artery.

(See also VISUAL OBJECT AGNOSIA.)

REFERENCES

Dean, P. (1982). Visual behavior in monkeys with inferotemporal lesions. In D. J. Ingle, M. A. Goodale, and R. J. W. Mansfield, eds., *Analysis of visual behavior,* pp. 587–628. Cambridge, Mass.: MIT Press.

DeYoe, E. A., and Van Essen, D. C. (1988). Concurrent processing streams in monkey visual cortex. *Trends in Neuroscience 11,* 219–226.

Desimone, R., and Ungerleider, L. G. (1989). Neural mechanisms of visual perception in monkeys. In F. Boller and J. Grafman, eds., *Handbook of neuropsychology,* vol. 2, pp. 267–299. Amsterdam: Elsevier.

Gaffan, D., Harrison, S., and Gaffan, E. A. (1986). Visual identification following inferotemporal ablation in the monkey. *Quarterly Journal of Experimental Psychology 38B,* 5–30.

Gross, C. G. (1973). Visual functions of inferotemporal cortex. In R. Jung, ed., *Handbook of sensory physiology,* vol. VII/3B, pp. 451–482. Berlin: Springer-Verlag.

Maunsell, J. H. R., and Newsome, W. T. (1987). Visual processing in monkey extrastriate cortex. *Annual Review of Neuroscience 10,* 363–401.

Mishkin, M. (1979). Analogous neural models for tactual and visual learning. *Neuropsychologia 17,* 139–151.

——— (1982). A memory system in the monkey. *Philosophical Transactions of the Royal Society of London B298,* 85–95.

Mishkin, M., and Appenzeller, T. (1987). The anatomy of memory. *Scientific American 256,* 80–89.

Murray, E. A. (1990). Representational memory in nonhuman primates. In R. P. Kesner and D. S. Olton, eds., *Neurobiology of comparative cognition.* pp. 127–155. Hillsdale, N.J.: Erlbaum.

Squire, L. R. (1987). *Memory and brain.* New York: Oxford University Press.

Squire, L. R. and Zola-Morgan, S. (1983). The neurology of memory: The case for correspondence between the findings for human and nonhuman primate. In J. A. Deutsch, ed., *The physiological basis of memory,* 2nd ed., pp. 199–268. New York: Academic Press.

Ungerleider, L. G., and Mishkin, M. (1982). Two cortical visual systems. In D. J. Ingle, M. A. Goodale, and R. J. W. Mansfield, eds., *Analysis of visual behavior,* pp. 549–586. Cambridge, Mass.: MIT Press.

Leslie G. Underleider
Elisabeth A. Murray

PROBLEM SOLVING

Solving a problem can take many forms. Sometimes it can involve a small, rapidly concluded set of actions as simple as searching for the on-off switch on a new computer or determining how to pry open a balky window. At the other extreme, it can involve years of work at unraveling some scientific mystery: the structure of the DNA molecule, the cure for AIDS, how to design a human-powered airplane, or even how to construct models of the information-processing mechanisms people use to solve complex problems. Solving problems is clearly something people do in many different ways, in many different situations, and with many different outcomes. It is one of the major ways in which we use our minds, and as a result is a very important human activity and the object of much study by cognitive psychologists.

One definition of problem solving is that it is what occurs when you are in a situation where you want to get from one state of knowledge to another (much as a person lost on a branching path in the woods might want to get to some goal), and the way to proceed is not immediately obvious. Usually solving a problem involves the performance of a number of steps, although occasionally a problem can be solved in a single step. In the latter case, if the situation is challenging enough to be characterized as a real problem, the step is likely to be particularly hard to find or difficult to execute, and we often describe its discovery as an *insight*. This feeling or belief that we have attained an insight is particularly likely when the correct step is discovered suddenly, after a prolonged period of search.

Our current conceptualization of problem solving began to emerge in the late 1950s and early 1960s, a key event being the publication of a major text on problem solving by Allan Newell and Herbert A. Simon (1972). In that book, Newell and Simon introduced both a methodology for studying problem solving and the results of using those methods to understand people's behavior in solving a variety of problems. The methods that emerged from that work include the use of verbal protocols, which consist of people's verbalizations of what they are thinking while they work on a problem. These protocol data can be combined with records of the moves people make and the amount of time they take to make those moves to obtain an understanding of how people solve problems. This understanding can then be tested by constructing a model of problem solving. Modeling is done by writing a computer program that embodies the processes hypothesized to occur during problem solving and comparing the behavior of the model with that of human subjects to see if the model is an accurate portrayal of how people go about solving problems. This modeling technique has been used on problems ranging from very small and easily solved ones to models of scientific discovery that recapitulate historic scientific discoveries when presented with the data that the original scientist had (Simon et al., 1987).

A major result of this analysis is that problem solving can be viewed as search through a state space, or a set of all possible knowledge states a solver can be in when starting from some initial state and attempting to reach some goal by applying "move operators" that enable the solver to move from state to state. This is analogous to search through a maze to find the correct path. Move operators can range from very simple, easily executed actions, such as moving to a diagonally adjacent square in checkers, to executing a complex mathematical step in the derivation of a new theorem. While the "maze" or task environment in which the search is occurring has a certain structure, different problem solvers will often construct quite different internal representations of that space.

The understanding of problem solving that has developed from this work can be divided into categories based on type of problem, type of process used to solve the problem, and type of problem solver. Each of these will be examined in turn.

One way in which different problems can be categorized is based on the size of their state spaces. The state space can be conceptualized as a search tree, a set of pathways with branch points, one of which leads to the goal. The size is a function of how many choices there are at each branch point, and the number of such choices that have to be made. As an example, the state space for a simple three-step problem is presented in Figure 1. The number of possible moves is usually correlated with, although not identical to, the number of knowledge states in the space. (The two can differ due to the possibility of repeating moves—backtracking—and of circular and/or multiple pathways to a given point). Thus, for example, if a problem involves four sequential moves, each of which involves a choice from among three possibilities, the size of the state space (and the related number of possible moves) is relatively small, 4^3 states. This number grows rapidly with either increasing length of solution path (number of branch points) or number of branches at each such point. An average-length chess game has been estimated to involve approximately 10^{120} possible move choices, a number larger than the total number of atoms in the universe (about 10^{80}). Some problems have even larger state spaces. (Of course, not all possibilities are considered by the problem solver.) Other problems have quite small state spaces, yet they can be quite difficult. The difficulty in those cases is often due to either the nonobvious nature of a particular move (often true of insight problems) or the difficulty of applying the move operators (Kotovsky, Hayes, and Simon, 1985). Other ways in which problems can be categorized are based on whether the problem is *well defined*—whether there is a widely agreed-upon, unique, or precisely defined solution or goal (obtaining a driver's license, solving a math problem, finding your way to a concert hall)—or *ill defined* (designing a functional and beautiful house, composing a melodious piece of music, or planting a good garden).

On many problems, people know exactly what solution process to use, that is, what set of steps must be taken to achieve a solution. Such a "known" solution procedure can be very short (what one must do to look up a word in a dictionary) or very long (how to multiply 56,258,199 by 387,276), yet in both cases the application of

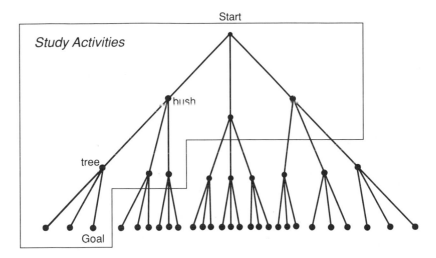

Figure 1. A state space with branching = 3 and depth = 3. The total number of possible end states is $3^3 = 27$. If we imagine that the search for the goal in the state space represents a search for the correct path through a woods and that we have been given subgoals of finding a distinctive bush at the first choice point we come to (after the start) and a distinctive tree at the next choice point, then the two subgoals reduce the search to one of examining at most the nine positions contained in the box, instead of the whole state space.

a known set of operators in a certain sequence will guarantee a solution. Such a well-defined, step-by-step process that guarantees a solution is termed an algorithm, and in cases where a problem solver possesses a known algorithm, problem solving is often relatively easy. On large search-space problems where the solution path is not known, solvers often use various general procedures, strategies, or rules of thumb to select moves in a manner that reduces the amount of the search space that must be explored to achieve a solution. These general strategies, termed heuristics, are crucially important in reducing the amount of search to the point where finding a solution becomes possible. The following are two examples of general heuristics that are used when a problem solver does not know what move or moves to choose next to proceed toward the goal.

1. Hill climbing: This heuristic selects moves by means of the criterion that a move will be made only if it takes the solver closer to the goal (much as a person lost and trying to find the top of a mountain at night might use the criterion of selecting each step on the basis of its moving the climber to a position higher than before). It does not work if the climber is on a foothill that has to be

climbed and then partially descended on the other side before going up the mountain. Thus it will not handle problems involving necessary detours, points where one must temporarily move away from the goal in order ultimately to reach it.

2. Generating subgoals: When a move operator cannot be applied, a solver can adopt as a goal making some move that will unblock the desired goal move. This method of selecting move operators that will move you closer to the goal, testing to see if the conditions for applying them are met, and, if they are not, adopting a subgoal, is known as means-ends analysis. Unlike hill climbing, it allows a problem solver to make a necessary detour on the way to a solution.

In addition to the use of heuristics that reduce the size of the external search space, another feature of problem solving that determines whether a problem will be solved and how difficult it will be to solve is the type of internal representation a person forms of that space. Research in which the same problem is embedded in different cover stories that elicit different representations has shown that problems possessing identical search spaces can vary widely in difficulty, with some versions of a problem being up to sixteen times harder than other versions (Hayes and Simon, 1977; Kotovsky, Hayes, and Simon, 1985). The difficulty differences in these cases often reside in the differing amounts of information that must be simultaneously kept in memory during the application of the move operators. As the move operators are learned, people become better able to plan and execute subgoals, and thus achieve the ability to solve the problem.

In addition to the role played by the nature of the problem and the type of solution processes that are useful or necessary for its solution, there are large differences in the experience or ability of the person solving the problem that play an important role in problem solution. Many studies have focused on the differences between novice and expert problem solvers in a number of domains. Much of the original work on this issue was performed by investigating people's performance on chess. In one set of experiments, expert chess players (masters and grand masters) and novices were briefly shown chess games and then asked to reconstruct the board positions of all the pieces from memory. The experts were usually able to reconstruct most of the entire board of twenty-four pieces, while the novices were able to place only about eight or nine (DeGroot, 1966). Further analysis showed that the performance difference was not due to the experts' having better memories; rather, they thought about and remembered the board in larger pieces ("chunks") than did the novices (Chase and Simon, 1973). Having spent a great deal of time studying chess, they saw the displayed game as being made up of sets of pieces in meaningful relationships to each other, whereas the novices remembered it piece by piece. This is similar to the way adult readers, who have had thousands of pages of practice, read whole words rather than "sounding out" individual letters the way beginning readers do. Storing these chunks of information is a time-consuming process that forms a basis of expertise. It has been estimated that a chess master has about 50,000 chunks of chess information stored away (Simon and Gilmartin, 1973). In studies of expertise in other domains (music composition, painting, mathematics, etc.), a similar process is suggested by the fact that it takes a minimum of about 10 years of full-time study or work to become a world-class expert across a wide variety of domains (Hayes, 1989). This work demonstrates that expert performance is based on the acquisition of a vast body of knowledge. Other studies of expert performance in a variety of domains have yielded additional information about expert-novice differences in categorizing problems and in their search strategies (Chi, Feltovich, and Glaser, 1981; Chi, Glaser, and Farr, 1989). (See also EXPERTS' MEMORIES.)

Studies of problem solving have yielded a rich body of information about the workings of the mind, the importance of knowledge and memory to problem solving, factors that make problems hard or easy to solve, and how people transfer what they have learned in one situation to another, similar situation. In addition, the study of problem solving has been one of the major sources of the new field of cognitive science that combines artificial intelligence and cognitive psychological studies with contributions from a number of other disciplines to form a new science of cognition. For further information about this and related developments, the book edited by Posner (1989) can be consulted. The book by Hayes (1989) is a good general introduction to the topic of problem solving, and the book by Newell and Simon (1972) is the classic advanced text in the field.

REFERENCES

Chase, W. G., and Simon, H. A. (1973). Perception in chess. *Cognitive Psychology 4,* 55–81.

Chi, M. T. H., Feltovich, P. J., and Glaser, R. (1981). Categorization and representation of physics problems by experts and novices. *Cognitive Science 5,* 121–152.

Chi, M. T. H., Glaser, R., and Farr, M. J. (1989). *The nature of expertise.* Hillsdale, N.J.: Erlbaum.

DeGroot, A. D. (1966). Perception and memory versus thought. In B. Kleinmuntz, eds., *Problem-solving.* New York: Wiley.

Hayes, J. R. (1989). *The complete problem solver.* Hillsdale, N.J.: Erlbaum.

Hayes, J. R., and Simon, H. A. (1977). Psychological differences among problem isomorphs. In N. J. Castellan, D. B. Pisoni, and G. R. Potts, eds., *Cognitive theory,* pp. 21–41. Hillsdale, N.J.: Erlbaum.

Kotovsky, K., Hayes, J. R., and Simon, H. A. (1985). Why are some problems hard?: Evidence from tower of Hanoi. *Cognitive Psychology 17,* 248–294.

Newell, A., and Simon, H. A. (1972). *Human problem solving.* Englewood Cliffs, N.J.: Prentice-Hall.

Posner, M. I. (1989). *Foundations of cognitive science.* Cambridge, Mass.: MIT Press.

Simon, H. A., and Gilmartin, K. (1973). A simulation of

memory for chess positions. *Cognitive Psychology* 5, 29–46.

Simon, H. A., Langley, P., Bradshaw, G., and Zytkow, J. (1987). *Scientific discovery: Explorations of the creative processes.* Cambridge, Mass.: MIT Press.

Kenneth Kotovsky

PROSE RETENTION

As with memory for other kinds of verbal material, memory for prose is a complex function of various factors. Some of the more important factors include (1) the kind of reading or studying activity in which the learner engages while processing a text, (2) the particular type of prose that is being remembered, (3) the kinds of information and events that intervene between the initial reading of the text and when remembering is attempted, and (4) the way in which memory is assessed (e.g., through recall, short-answer, multiple-choice, or true/false tests). For clarity of presentation, prose retention will be considered in terms of each of these factors separately. In reality, however, each of these factors does not operate in isolation; instead, they work together to influence memory for prose.

Influences of Encoding and Reading Processes

One of the dominant themes in contemporary memory research is that memory benefits to the extent that the material is processed for meaning. The same holds true for prose. For example, research has shown that readers who have been instructed to count the number of four-letter words in a passage do not remember the passage as well as readers who have been instructed to rate the paragraphs for ambiguity (Schallert, 1976). Similarly, if a text is written so that its topic is obfuscated, the degree to which meaningful processing can take place decreases, and this text is recalled less well than a text in which the topic is clearly stated (e.g., through an informative title or by reference to the topic throughout the text; Bransford and Johnson, 1972). The lesson here is straightforward: A prerequisite for remembering prose is extracting the meaning that is being conveyed. (See also CODING PROCESSES.)

On the assumption that readers typically are extracting meaning as they read, one can further analyze the components of that meaning which are retained. It is typically the case that people do not remember prose verbatim (except with concerted effort, and even then it is difficult; Sachs, 1967). Instead, prose retention is characterized by *memory for the ideas* that are captured by the particular words used. Further, memory for the ideas in a text generally conforms to the following function. The main or most important ideas are recalled best, followed by ideas of intermediate importance, with unimportant details usually recalled worst.

One of the interesting aspects of this function is that the importance of an idea in a text is not completely determined by the structure of the text. The reader's point of view or frame of reference also determines the importance of the ideas contained in the text. Different points of view adopted by different readers can result in the same ideas being assigned different levels of importance. Because an idea's level of importance determines its memorability, very different patterns of memory for the same text can be observed across readers. For example, a prose passage about a household and its daily activities will be remembered differently by a reader who adopts the perspective of a prospective home buyer compared with a reader who adopts the perspective of a burglar appraising particular properties for a clandestine visit (Fass and Schumacher, 1981). The differences in recall for these two readers will directly reflect the fact that the particular ideas in the passage differ in importance, depending on the perspective adopted while reading the passage.

Perspective is just one dimension of how the reader orients to text that can influence memory for text. In some cases, readers use selected study processes (e.g., outlining or underlining) to focus their attention on certain aspects of the information in the text. For simple verbal materials like word lists, it has been shown that attending well to each word and to the possible organizational links among the words produce the best recall. Prose recall appears to depend on the same kinds of attending, except that for prose, as already noted, the unit of memory is the ideas that appear in the passage. More specifically, reading or study strategies that ensure both attention to the individual ideas and to how these ideas are organized or related produce better recall for the text as a whole than reading or study strategies that focus

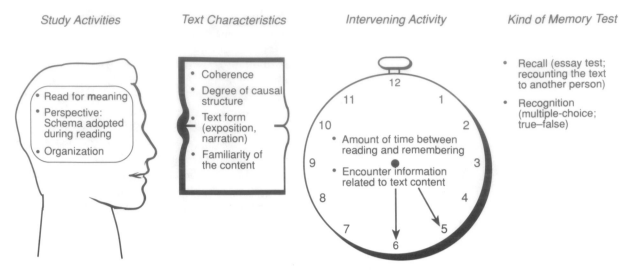

Figure 1. Factors influencing prose retention.

only on one or the other (McDaniel and Kerwin, 1987). One difference between prose memory and memory for word lists, however, is that prose may allow special forms of organization which are not operative with simpler materials. The varied kinds of organizational factors that can be influential in prose memory are best revealed by considering how the genre of the prose affects remembering.

Prose Organization and Prose Type

Generally, narrative prose (e.g., a story) is better remembered than expository prose (e.g., an essay or article). The superior memorability of narratives relative to expositions is probably due in large part to readers' better ability to organize and interrelate the ideas expressed in a narrative. There are a number of differentiating factors between narratives and expository prose that could underlie the extent to which the ideas expressed in the text are organized by the reader. Though it may ultimately turn out that not all of these factors are important in accounting specifically for the memory differences between narratives and expository text, these factors do seem to play a role in prose memory. Accordingly, they merit mention here.

One factor is that readers presumably activate relevant "packets" or structures of world knowledge when attempting to understand a text. These packets are usually termed *schemata* (singular, *schema*). In general, schemata are believed to influence the degree to which incoming text information is organized. Text content for which readers have a schema is believed to be better organized and elaborated, and thus better remembered, than text content for which readers have a poorly articulated or sketchy schema. For instance, researchers have shown that a narrative about a fictitious baseball game is better recalled by readers knowledgeable about baseball (i.e., readers who have a baseball schema) than readers who are not knowledgeable about baseball (Spilich et al., 1979). (See also EXPERTS' MEMORIES.)

In contrasting narratives and expository text, it is arguably the case that narratives have content for which most of the readers in the culture have relevant schemata, whereas for expository texts, the content articulates with schemata that only a subset of readers might possess. Narratives are about people or other animate objects, their goals and conflicts, and their other activities—concepts for which readers have schemata. Narratives frequently entail events that, if not directly experienced by the reader, relate to basic cultural values and goals (e.g., finding happiness, wealth, love, etc). The influence of schemata in organizing and guiding memory of narratives can be observed when readers try to recall narratives from a culture with which they have little familiarity. Recall of such narratives is characterized by the omission and transformation of ideas and details in the narrative that do not fit with the conventional schema of the reader's culture (Bartlett, 1932).

Prose can also be organized by linking the elements in terms of *causal relations*. Causal relations capture relations between events (described in a text) that involve motivation, psychological causation (e.g., greed causes certain behaviors), and physical causation (e.g., rain causes things to become slippery). Understanding a narrative seems to involve the formation of a sequence of causal relations into a chain that links the opening of the narrative to its outcome. In remembering a narrative, people tend to remember those parts of a narrative which fit into the causal chain and forget the parts which are not incorporated into it (Fletcher and Bloom, 1988). More generally, better memory for narrative prose may occur because causal sequences are more clearly defined in narratives than in expository passages.

A third factor that contributes to prose organization is the reader's knowledge about the *structure* of conventional text forms. That is, when reading a fairy tale, regardless of the particular content, we expect to see certain components: a setting, an initiating event posing a problem, an attempt at its solution by the protagonist, and a consequence. This knowledge presumably allows the reader to better organize the information found in the passage. (See also ORAL TRADITIONS.)

In contrast, expository prose does not seem to entail a consistent structure, thereby reducing the extent to which the reader has a prestored structure that facilitates organization. Recent research indicates, however, that if readers are explicitly trained to notice and utilize some conventional expository forms (e.g., argumentative structures), then memory for such material is improved. Further, this positive effect is obtained for older as well as younger adults (Meyer, Young, and Bartlett, 1990).

Remembering Prose over Time

The organizational processes outlined above seem to exert greater influence as the interval between reading and attempted remembering increases. If recall is attempted within minutes after reading, then information that does not fit an initial perspective or schema can be recovered. If recall is delayed for at least 1 day, however, then recall of information that does not fit the schema may drop substantially, whereas information that fits the schema will still be well recalled (Fass and Schumacher,

1981). Similarly, in some cases study strategies designed to increase organizational processing of a text (e.g., outlining) will not improve memory for a text (relative to reading alone, with no studying) when recall is tested immediately, but will increase recall when testing is delayed for several days (Einstein et al., 1990). This increasingly beneficial mnemonic effect of organization with longer retention intervals is another aspect of prose memory that parallels memory for simpler verbal material.

Another factor that affects memory for prose is information that the learner encounters between reading a text and trying to remember it. Such *intervening information* can have facilitative as well as interfering effects on retention. To illustrate both kinds of effects, consider a biography about a poet named Susan. In the biography it is stated that Susan's father was a servant who died of diphtheria when Susan was 5 years old. After reading this biography, another biography is encountered in which Ann's blacksmith father dies of lung cancer when Ann is 2 years old. Research has shown that readers who are given the two biographies and are then asked to recall the first biography, recall the theme of the first biography (e.g., "the main character's father died when she was young") better than readers who are not given the second biography. But readers given the second biography do *not* recall the specific details of the first biography (the father's occupation, what he died of, and when) as well as the readers not given the second biography (Bower, 1974).

Perhaps one of the more interesting features of prose recall is that intervening information, or even a long retention interval, can promote *reconstruction* in remembering. *Reconstruction* refers to the finding that memory of a text can be distorted by the inclusion of information consistent with the theme of the text but not actually mentioned in it. Reconstruction also includes alteration of information that was in the text to bring it more in line with information encountered subsequent to the text or with readers' schemata that were activated in comprehending the text. For instance, in one study (Spiro, 1980) participants read a narrative about two college students who started dating seriously but disagreed about their desires to have children. After the participants read the text, the experimenter casually mentioned that the students had ended up getting married. Several weeks later, the participants attempted to recall the narrative. Their recall included reconstructions and distortions consistent with the new information mentioned by the experimenter but not actually in the narrative (e.g., "The students underwent counseling to correct the major discrepancy"). (See also RECONSTRUCTIVE MEMORY.)

Prose recall need not always be reconstructive. If the reader expects a memory test on what has been read, then recall is more *reproductive*. That is, details are recalled more accurately, and there is very little inclusion of extra information not actually in the text. Also, in situations in which the reader's initial interpretative schema is invalidated at the time of recall, recall becomes more reproductive (Hasher and Griffin, 1978).

Assessing Prose Retention

In discussing prose retention, much of the focus has been on remembering as evidenced in recall. The influence of many of the factors mentioned above changes, however, if remembering is assessed with *recognition memory tests*. In recognition tests, the learner is presented with facts stated in the text and facts not stated in the text, and must determine which facts were presented and which were not. Common kinds of recognition tests include true/false and multiple-choice tests. In general, if prose memory is tested with recognition tests, the robust influence of organizational factors like those discussed earlier can be mitigated or eliminated. Thus, recognition is the same regardless of whether the text is written so that its overall theme can be clearly identified. Further, information that does not fit an encoding schema is recognized as well as information that does fit it, even if memory is tested 1 week after the text was read (McDaniel and Kerwin, 1987). Thus, as is the case with simple verbal materials, organizational factors play a prominent role when prose retention is measured with recall but not when recognition is considered.

REFERENCES

Bartlett, F. C. (1932). *Remembering*. Cambridge: Cambridge University Press.

Bower, G. H. (1974). Selective facilitation and interference in retention of prose. *Journal of Educational Psychology 66*, 1–8.

Bransford, J. D., and Johnson, M. K. (1972). Contextual prerequisites for understanding: Some investigations of comprehension and recall. *Journal of Verbal Learning and Verbal Behavior 11*, 717–726.

Einstein, G. O., McDaniel, M. A., Owen, P. D., and Coté, N. C. (1990). Encoding and recall of texts: The importance of material appropriate processing. *Journal of Memory and Language 29*, 566–581.

Fass, W., and Schumacher, G. M. (1981). Schema theory and prose retention: Boundary conditions for encoding and retrieval effects. *Discourse Processes 4*, 17–26.

Fletcher, C. R., and Bloom, C. P. (1988). Causal reasoning in the comprehension of simple narrative texts. *Journal of Memory and Language 27*, 235–244.

Hasher, L., and Griffin, M. (1978). Reconstructive and reproductive processes in memory. *Journal of Experimental Psychology: Human Learning and Memory 4*, 318–330.

McDaniel, M. A., and Kerwin, M. L. E. (1987). Long-term prose retention: Is an organizational schema sufficient? *Discourse Processes 10*, 237–252.

Meyer, B. J. F., Young, C. J., and Bartlett, B. J. (1990). *Memory improved: Reading and memory enhancement across the life span through strategic text structures.* Hillsdale, N.J.: Erlbaum.

Sachs, J. (1967). Recognition memory for syntactic and semantic aspects of connected discourse. *Perception and Psychophysics 2*, 437–442.

Schallert, D. L. (1976). Improving memory for prose: The relationship between depth of processing and context. *Journal of Verbal Learning and Verbal Behavior 15*, 621–632.

Spilich, G. J., Vesonder, G. T., Chiesi, H. L., and Voss, J. F. (1979). Text processing of domain-related information for individuals with high and low domain knowledge. *Journal of Verbal Learning and Verbal Behavior 18*, 275–290.

Spiro, R. J. (1980). Accommodative reconstruction in prose recall. *Journal of Verbal Learning and Verbal Behavior 19*, 84–95.

Mark A. McDaniel

PROTEIN SYNTHESIS IN LONG-TERM MEMORY IN VERTEBRATES

Most modern theories assume that memories are stored in the brain in the form of changed patterns of synaptic connections within ensembles of neurons. Any such lasting change will demand the growth or reorganization of synapses, and this in turn requires the synthesis of the molecules comprising them, especially the proteins and lipids of the synaptic and dendritic membranes. The idea that memory formation involves protein synthesis has been around for a long time—certainly since the days of Santiago Ramón y CAJAL at the beginning of the twentieth century—but serious experimental tests of the idea became possible only with techniques available beginning in the 1960s. The adult brain has one of the highest rates of protein synthesis of any body organ, and also shows the greatest diversity of protein molecules. Some 30,000 different proteins are synthesized in the primate brain, only a small fraction of which have been characterized or ascribed functional roles. It is perhaps this great diversity that led, during the 1960s, to ideas about the possible roles of proteins in memory becoming confused. Some theorists argued that because the amino acid sequences that compose proteins can form potentially many billions of unique molecules, the proteins themselves may in some way be "coded for" memory, with each memory being represented by one or more unique protein sequences. This idea is no longer regarded as credible; the working assumption is that the proteins whose synthesis is enhanced during memory formation are in some ways involved in reorganizing synaptic connections; what provides the specificity for the memory trace is not the particular protein but the new pattern of synapses it helps to construct.

It is one thing to speculate about possible roles for proteins in memory and quite another to be able (1) to prove that protein synthesis is necessary for long-term memory and (2) to identify the necessary proteins and their functions. Two general approaches have been used, sometimes described as *interventive* and *correlative*. In the first, the behavioral consequences of preventing protein synthesis from occurring during or after training an animal on a particular task have been studied. If protein synthesis is necessary for memory formation, animals in which the synthesis has been blocked at the time of training should be amnesic for the task when subsequently tested. The second approach attempts to measure an increase in the synthesis of particular proteins as a result of the training experience. Both approaches have methodological pitfalls. Drugs that block protein synthesis may have general effects on behavior, sensory or motor performance, or arousal, and therefore exert their effect on memory nonspecifically. Similarly, increases in protein synthesis following training could be the consequence of nonspecific behaviors such as the motor activity involved in

carrying out the training task. Ruling out such alternative explanations requires devising careful control experiments.

Evidence for the Role of Proteins in Memory

Interventive Strategies

Proteins are synthesized in a series of steps beginning with the copying of strands of DNA into messenger RNA (mRNA), after which the mRNA is translated into the sequence of amino acids that constitutes the protein. Many proteins, especially those of the cell and synaptic membranes, are further modified posttranslationally. For instance, to synthesize glycoproteins, which are key constituents of the cell membrane, it is necessary to add sugar molecules to the protein chains before transporting them to the cellular sites at which they will function. Inhibiting any one of the steps in this synthetic sequence from the DNA to the finished molecule may block the synthesis of a protein or render it nonfunctional, and hence interfere with memory formation. The first experiment of this sort was made in the mid-1960s, using an inhibitor of RNA synthesis, 8-azaguanine. Rats were trained to swim a water maze and then injected with the inhibitor. It had no effect on the performance of animals that had already learned the maze, or on their ability to swim in general. However, if the inhibitor was injected during the training trials, and the rats were tested the following day, they showed impaired memory for the maze.

In the decade that followed, experimenters employed various antibiotics that interfere with particular steps in protein synthesis: puromycin, cycloheximide, acetoxycycloheximide, and more recently anisomycin. The consensus observation, in a variety of appetitive and aversive paradigms and with several species including rats, mice, chicks, goldfish, and even humans, is that concentrations of antibiotic sufficient to inhibit more than 80 percent of all protein synthesis in the brain for several hours are, perhaps surprisingly, without effect on performance of already-learned tasks or other aspects of behavior. However, if the inhibitors are injected within the time window between an hour prior to training and an hour afterward, they will produce amnesia in animals tested 24 hours or more later. Behavioral controls rule out the possibility that these amnestic effects are due to some form of state dependency, and although the inhibitors have a variety of less specific biochemical effects (notably increasing the concentrations of intracellular amino acids, including several that are neurotransmitters and can be neurotoxic), it is generally agreed that they do indeed exert their amnestic effect by preventing the synthesis of proteins necessary for memory formation. Almost the only known exception to the rule that long-term memory formation is protein-synthesis-dependent comes not from studies of vertebrates but from studies of some forms of learning in insects, such as odor discrimination in bees and *Drosophila*. The reasons for and implications of these exceptions are unknown.

The demonstration of the time window during which the protein synthesis inhibitors are amnestic has been an important piece of evidence in developing stage theories of time-dependent processes in memory formation, notably in relation to the transition from short-term to long-term memory (see MEMORY CONSOLIDATION); but because protein synthesis is such a general cellular process, and its inhibition will in due course lead to widespread biochemical consequences, it has not been very helpful in identifying more precisely which proteins and which biochemical mechanisms may be involved. Some advances have been made in this direction by using more specific inhibitors of the posttranslational modification, packaging, or transport of particular proteins. Thus, in both rats and chicks, 2-deoxygalactose (a chemical analogue of fucose, one of the sugar constituents of glycoproteins), which inhibits synthesis of certain synaptic membrane glycoproteins, has been shown to be amnestic when injected during a time window comparable with that of the more general inhibitors. Even more specifically, particular antibodies have been shown to have amnestic effects. Thus a monoclonal antibody raised against a key synaptic membrane constituent, the neural cell adhesion molecule N-CAM, a central player in the processes of cell-cell recognition, is amnestic if injected into rats trained in a passive avoidance task some 6–8 hours after training. Similarly, colchicine, a molecule that binds to the ubiquitous microtubular protein tubulin and prevents axonal and dendritic transport without blocking protein synthesis, is also amnestic. It is likely that studies using such increasingly specific inhibitors will become important in the next few years.

Correlative Studies

Like the interventive approach, correlative studies began in the 1960s. Because it is not probable that there will be measurable increases in the total amount of proteins in general or of specific proteins in particular during memory formation, the approach has instead been to measure the rate of protein synthesis during training by the use of a radioactive precursor. A radioactively labeled amino acid, injected into the bloodstream, is taken into the brain and there becomes incorporated into protein. The amount of radioactivity found in the protein after a fixed time interval—generally an hour—then depends, among other factors (which need to be controlled for), on the rate of synthesis of the protein. If more radioactivity is found in brains of trained than of control animals, this is assumed to indicate that the training procedure has resulted in enhanced synthesis, and the behavioral question then becomes that of ensuring by appropriately designed experiments that it is memory formation rather than some other aspect of the task that has increased the synthesis.

Early experiments with this approach were often confounded by behavioral and/or biochemical artifacts, especially since the changes in synthesis in most learning paradigms were likely to be small and localized to specific brain regions, and therefore to be "swamped" if whole brain samples were analyzed. Some of the clearest evidence for enhanced protein synthesis by the correlative approach came from studies of early learning in the chick, especially IMPRINTING and one-trial passive avoidance training. These tasks involve strong and biologically programmed learning in an otherwise naive animal and therefore maximize the chance of finding changes. For example, training on the passive avoidance task results in an increase in incorporation of radioactive amino acids into the proteins of specific brain regions, an increase that persists for up to 24 hours after training.

To study such increases in more detail, it is necessary to know which brain regions might be involved. Here an autoradiographic mapping technique can be employed in which, after incorporation of the radioactivity, the brains are sectioned and apposed to X-ray film, and the specific regions showing training-related increases are identified by image analysis. This technique has located three nuclei of the left hemisphere of the chick forebrain that show training-related increases in protein synthesis; the proteins from these regions can then be studied in isolation from the rest of the brain.

The next task becomes that of identifying which of the many proteins are involved. Various approaches are possible. Subcellular fractionation can show in which cellular compartments the new proteins are most concentrated there are increases both in soluble proteins such as tubulin and in synaptic membrane constituents. If, instead of a radioactive amino acid, a radioactive sugar molecule (fucose) is used, synthesis of glycoproteins can be measured. In both rat and chick, synthesis of several glycoproteins of the synaptic and dendritic membranes increases in the hours following training.

Further identification of the proteins depends on separating them by standard biochemical procedures—for instance, by one- or two-dimensional electrophoresis, which enables several hundred different protein fractions to be distinguished and their molecular weights determined. By this means several research groups have reported increased synthesis of synaptic membrane glycoproteins, of molecular weights ranging from around 20 to 220 kilodaltons. In an unusual training task in goldfish—in which the animal has a float attached to its belly that inverts it, so that it has to learn to swim correctly once more—a different class of low-molecular-weight soluble glycoproteins, named ependymins, has been identified by similar techniques. This class of molecules has also been shown to be relevant in mammalian learning.

Once the proteins are identified and partially purified by such techniques, the next step is to endeavor to raise specific antibodies. This has two goals. First, if the proteins are indeed necessary for memory formation, then injection of antibodies to them should result in failure to learn or to remember, and will thus both confirm the behavioral role of the proteins and also, perhaps, point to their cellular functions. Second, the antibodies can be used to purify further the proteins by affinity-binding techniques. These approaches have so far been used most effectively with the ependymins.

Molecular Biological Approaches

As should be apparent, the research issue is no longer to demonstrate that both de novo protein synthesis and posttranslational modification are necessary steps in memory formation, but to identify the proteins and their cellular and subcellular localizations and functions. It is here that the techniques of molecular biology offer new prospects. The current working hypothesis is that the initial stages of memory formation involve transient synaptic membrane events (see MEMBRANE CHANNELS AND THEIR MODULATION IN LEARNING AND MEMORY). These events include the phosphorylation of membrane proteins (including the presynaptic protein known as B50 or GAP43) by a membrane-bound enzyme, protein kinase C. This phosphorylation step activates a cycle of intracellular second messengers, including calcium ions, which in turn trigger a genomic response in the neuronal cell nucleus. The initial genomic response is to switch on a family of specific "immediate early genes" whose protein products include in particular c-fos and c-jun. These proteins are expressed only during the early phases of neuronal plasticity, when neurons are growing or actively differentiating, and they have been shown to increase dramatically in concentration in a number of learning tasks, including brightness discrimination in the rat and passive avoidance in the chick, as well as hippocampal long-term potentiation. But rather than measuring the proteins themselves, molecular biological techniques enable probes to be synthesized that detect the mRNAs for the proteins, which can be located autoradiographically very precisely in specific brain regions. This technique enables a map of gene activation following training to be obtained, a map that can be followed in space to specific cell ensembles, and in time, showing how a wave of gene activation can pass through different cells during the minutes to hours after training.

But c-fos and c-jun, although they are excellent markers to show where in the brain neural plasticity is occurring, are themselves only intermediates; their production acts as a trigger for the activation of further genes ("late genes") whose products include the proteins and glycoproteins already mentioned.

Molecular biological techniques are beginning to be employed to identify these, too. The mRNAs for such proteins will be produced in tiny quantities in the specific cells involved in memory formation. A technique called subtractive hybridization should, in principle, enable these mRNAs to be purified from the general background level of nonspecific messages, and then "amplified" so that the proteins for which they code can be prepared in bulk and their properties studied. The stumbling block confronting research on the proteins involved in memory formation, their presence in small amounts against a large background, may thus be circumvented.

Conclusions

Protein synthesis is necessary for the formation of long-term vertebrate memory. The proteins involved are synthesized in increased amounts in specific cells in the hours following a training experience and during the period of memory consolidation. Different proteins are synthesized at different times after training in a time- and space-dependent sequence; in the first phase they include members of the "immediate-early" family, such as c-fos and c-jun. Later stages involve the synthesis of the microtubular protein tubulin and glycoprotein components of synaptic and dendritic membranes, although exactly which molecules are involved remains to be discovered. If their synthesis is prevented, amnesia results. These proteins are not, however, in themselves specific to the particular memory; what conveys specificity is the pattern of neurons whose connections are modified by the learning experience; the proteins are part of the "housekeeping processes" involved in modifying those connections. However, identifying more precisely the proteins involved, their locations, and their functions will help substantially in the development of theories of memory formation in addition to being of major intrinsic neurobiological interest.

REFERENCES

Agranoff, B. W., Burrell, H. R., Dokas, L. R., and Springer, A. D. (1976). Progress in biochemical approaches to learning and memory. In M. Lipton, A. De Mascio, and K. Killam, eds., *Psychopharmacology*, pp. 623–635. New York: Raven Press.

Andrew, R. J., ed. (1991). *Neural and behavioural plasticity*. Oxford: Oxford University Press.

Chiarugi, V. P., Ruggiero, M., and Corradetti, R. (1989). Oncogenes, protein kinase C, neuronal differentiation and memory. *Neurochemistry International 14*, 1–9.

Davis, H. P., and Squire, L. R. (1984). Protein synthesis and memory: A review. *Psychological Bulletin 96*, 518–559.

Dudai, Y. (1989). *Neurobiology of memory*. Oxford: Oxford University Press.

Dunn, A. (1980). Neurochemistry of learning and memory: An evaluation of recent data. *Annual Review of Psychology 31*, 343–390.

Matthies, H.-J. (1989). Neurobiological aspects of learning and memory. *Annual Review of Psychology 40*, 381–404.

Rahmann, H., ed. (1989). *Fundamentals of memory formation: Neuronal plasticity and brain function*. Stuttgart: Fischer Verlag.

Rose, S. P. R. (1981). What should a biochemistry of learning and memory be about? *Neuroscience 6*, 811–821.

——— (1989). Glycoprotein synthesis and post-translational remodeling in long-term memory. *Neurochemistry International 14*, 299–307.

——— (1992). *The making of memory*. London: Bantam.

Shashoua, V. E. (1985). The role of brain extracellular proteins in neuroplasticity and learning. *Cellular and Molecular Neurobiology 5*, 183–207.

Steven P. R. Rose

PSYCHOPHARMACOLOGY

See Drugs and Memory

R

RECONSTRUCTIVE MEMORY

Human memory is far from completely reliable. One reason is that memory does not function like a video camera. Video cameras record all information, which can later be played back almost verbatim. Human memory, on the other hand, is reconstructive in nature. Our memories are often the result of actively combining existing knowledge, beliefs, and expectations with new information to reconstruct memories that are consistent with our views. We form memories by filling in gaps, often sacrificing accuracy when we do so.

Studies on Reconstruction

Psychologists have studied reconstructive memory for over 50 years. One of the classic studies in this area is that of Frederic C. BARTLETT (1932), who presented subjects with a legend from Indian folklore entitled "The War of the Ghosts." This story tells of two young Indians who go down to a river to hunt, whereupon the weather becomes foggy and calm. Out of the fog appears a canoe with five men. The five urge the two to accompany them to a battle. One of the young Indians accepts, and the other declines. During the battle, the accompanying Indian is wounded but feels no pain or sickness. The young Indian then realizes that the men of the war party are ghosts. He returns home, telling his people what has happened to him, and dies the next day at sunrise.

After reading this story, subjects were instructed to retell the story to another subject who had not read the story. The second subject subsequently told the story to another subject, and so on, until the story had been told to ten subjects.

A major finding was that subjects deviated from the original story, systematically modifying the tale. But the deviations or changes were not haphazard. Rather, subjects tended to systematically delete details that were not consistent with their worldviews. For example, mystical references, such as ghosts, which are not part of Westerners' concepts of life, were dropped. Also, subjects tended to embellish details in the story. In the original story, for example, the second Indian declined to join the party because his relatives would not know where he had gone. By the tenth retelling of the story, the subject explained that the second Indian refused because his elderly mother was dependent on him, an embellishment consistent with Western concepts of a son's responsibilities in general and perhaps consistent with that particular subject's personal family situation. Another common change was that subjects tended to add a moral, possibly because stories told in our culture often end this way. Bartlett concluded that "Remembering is not re-excitation of innumerable fixed, lifeless, and fragmentary traces. It is an imaginative reconstruction, or construction, built out of the relation of our attitude towards a whole mass of organized past reactions or experiences . . ." (1932, p. 213).

Another widely cited study of reconstructive memory is that of Carmichael, Hagan, and Walter (1932). They briefly presented subjects with neutral drawings, ambiguous as to what they represented, and later told them to reproduce a drawing of a specific item. For example, one of the drawings was a sketch of two circles connected by a horizontal line. After the sketch was removed from the subjects' view, the subjects were asked to draw

Figure 1. Photographs used in an experiment to test accuracy of recollection in two groups of subjects. They are identical except that there is a stop sign in one and a yield sign in the other. *Courtesy Elizabeth F. Loftus.*

either a pair of eyeglasses or a set of dumbbells. In other words, for some subjects the drawing was called by one name (eyeglasses); for other subjects the drawing was called by another (dumbbells). A major finding was that the name used to refer to the original drawing significantly influenced the way that drawing was reproduced. These results have been used to support the notion that visual material is easily distorted by what we are later told we have seen. It is another classic demonstration of the reconstructive nature of memory.

More evidence on the ease with which recollection is influenced by information that a person acquires later can be found in the work of Elizabeth Loftus and colleagues (1979a; Loftus and Doyle, 1987; Loftus and Hoffman, 1989). In one study, subjects were shown a simulated automobile-pedestrian accident (Loftus, Miller, and Burns, 1978). In this scenario, a vehicle stops at an intersection, turns right, and then hits a pedestrian. For half of the subjects there was a stop sign at the intersection; for the other half, a yield sign. After viewing the entire scenario, the subjects answered questions about it. One question mentioned either a stop sign or a yield sign. In other words, half of the subjects in each group were asked a question that was consistent with the sign they saw; the other half were not. Finally, subjects were tested on their memory of the original accident. The results indicated that when the subjects had been asked a question consistent with what they had seen, they chose the correct sign 75 percent of the time. But when the subjects had been asked a question inconsistent with what they had seen, they chose the correct sign only 41 percent of the time. These investigators concluded that some subjects had initially encoded a stop sign in memory, but the subsequent mention of a yield sign caused a change in memory, and vice versa.

In a later study, Loftus and Greene (1980) tested whether misleading information affects memories of faces of people who had been seen earlier. Subjects were shown a 3-minute film in which a man parked his car on the street, entered a grocery store, bought a few items, and returned to his car. A young man was breaking into his car. The two argued for a few seconds, and then the young man ran off. Next, subjects were presented with a one-page description of the incident. Control subjects received a completely accurate description, and misinformed subjects were given a mostly accurate description except for one incorrect detail about the suspected thief's appearance. Finally, all subjects wrote their own descriptions of the incident and suspect. They were explicitly told to write down only what they themselves had seen, not details embodied in the one-page description that they had read. Nevertheless, 34 percent of the subjects included incorrect details from the one-page description in their own summaries. Apparently they were unable to distinguish their own perceptions from the one-page description. They reconstructed the event, blending their own firsthand memories with the inaccurate statement from the one-page description.

Real and Suggested Memories

Once a false memory has been implanted in a person's recollection, it is often difficult to tell whether the memory is real or suggested. People can give detailed descriptions of their false memories, which can lead others to think they are real. In one study (Schooler, Gerhard, and Loftus, 1986), some subjects viewed a simulated accident in which a car went through a yield sign. Other subjects did not see a sign, but it was suggested to them. Finally, all subjects were asked if they had seen the sign; and if they said "yes," they gave a description of it. Here are some examples: "As the car was approaching the intersection, I saw the yield sign at the corner." "It was on the corner, on the right of the street." "When the Datsun pulled up to the yield sign, it was there on the right corner. It was a red and white triangle, not yellow."

Judges who read these descriptions found it exceedingly difficult to tell which descriptions came from subjects who actually saw the sign and which came from subjects who had it suggested to them. In reality, the first and third examples came from subjects who saw the sign, while the second example came from a subject who had it created in his mind. Statistically there were some differences between real and suggested descriptions (e.g., real descriptions were more likely to mention sensory properties of the sign such as "red and white triangle"). But it was also true that many suggested memory descriptions looked similar to real memory descriptions.

Although the research indicates that our memories are malleable and easily manipulated, there are circumstances in which memory is relatively resistant to change. For example, if people publicly state that they remember a particular detail, subsequent suggestions are less likely to cause them to change their minds (Loftus, 1977). Second, if there are gross disparities between clearly perceived details and contradicting misinformation, people are resistant to changing their recollection (Loftus, 1979b). Finally, misinformation has a minimal effect on people who have been warned of the possibility of misleading messages. Thus, although our memory is reconstructive in nature, and errors in those reconstructions can occur when people are exposed to misleading information, people do not always succumb to that information.

The empirical findings on reconstructive memory suggest that recollections can be modified by subsequently introduced information. A fundamental issue that is still not resolved is whether the new information actually modifies the original memory traces or whether it coexists with the original information in memory (Belli, 1989; McCloskey and Zaragoza, 1985). The original information could reside somewhere in the recesses of the brain, awaiting the right retrieval cues to coax it to the surface. Some earlier research by brain surgeon Wilder Penfield suggested that the original memories might still exist. He found that people sometimes report vivid memories of apparently long-forgotten events when part of the cerebral cortex is electrically simulated (Penfield, 1969). For example, when a mild electrical current was passed through a region of one patient's brain, she claimed to relive the birth of her child. Penfield thought that the electrical stimulation made a former stream of consciousness flow again with all the clarity of the original experience. As compelling as Penfield's findings may seem, they can be explained in another way. Further analyses of Penfield's patient protocols suggest that the reports from patients did not involve accurate memory retrieval. Instead of reliving the past, they were reconstructing it. Patients and nonpatients alike often make an error called *confabulation*. When they are unable to retrieve a certain fact from memory, they sometimes manufacture another fact that seems appropriate. This is part of the inherent reconstructive nature of our memories.

(See also PROSE RETENTION.)

REFERENCES

Bartlett, F. C. (1932). *Remembering: A study in experimental and social psychology.* New York: Macmillan.

Belli, R. F. (1989). Influences of misleading postevent information: Misinformation interference and acceptance. *Journal of Experimental Psychology: General 118,* 72–85.

Carmichael, L., Hogan, H. P., and Walter, A. A. (1932). An experimental study of the effect of language on the reproduction of visually perceived form. *Journal of Experimental Psychology 15,* 73–86.

Loftus, E. F. (1977). Shifting human color memory. *Memory and Cognition 5,* 696–699.

—— (1979a). *Eyewitness testimony.* Cambridge, Mass.: Harvard University Press.

—— (1979b). Reactions to blatantly contradictory information. *Memory and Cognition 7,* 368–374.

Loftus, E. F., and Doyle, J. M. (1987). *Eyewitness testimony: Civil and criminal.* New York: Kluwer.

Loftus, E. F., and Greene, E. (1980). Warning: Even memory for faces may be contagious. *Law and Human Behavior 4,* 323–334.

Loftus, E. F., and Hoffman, H. G. (1989). Misinformation and memory: The creation of new memories. *Journal of Experimental Psychology: General 118,* 100–104.

Loftus, E. F., Miller, D. G., and Burns, H. J. (1978). Semantic integration of verbal information into a visual memory. *Journal of Experimental Psychology 4,* 19–31.

Luria, A. R. (1968). *The mind of a mnemonist.* New York: Basic Books.

McCloskey, M., and Zaragoza, M. (1985). Misleading postevent information and memory for events: Arguments and evidence against memory impairment hypotheses. *Journal of Experimental Psychology: General 114,* 1–16.

Penfield, W. (1969). Consciousness, memory, and man's conditioned reflexes. In K. H. Pribram, ed., *On the biology of learning,* pp. 127–168. New York: Harcourt Brace Jovanovich.

Schooler, J. W., Gerhard, D., and Loftus, E. F. (1986). Qualities of the unreal. *Journal of Experimental Psychology: Learning, Memory, and Cognition 12,* 171–181.

Elizabeth F. Loftus
Rick L. Leitner

REHABILITATION

See Electroconvulsive Therapy and Memory Loss; Head Injury; Pharmacological Treatment of Memory Deficits; Rehabilitation of Memory Disorders

REHABILITATION OF MEMORY DISORDERS

Associated with a number of neurological disturbances, including closed HEAD INJURY, aneurysm, stroke, tumor, encephalitis, ALZHEIMER'S DISEASE, and Korsakoff's syndrome, memory impairment constitutes one of the most pervasive and debilitating consequences of brain damage. The memory deficits that often accompany these various neurological disorders are typically characterized by an inability to remember recent experiences and to learn new information. Because memory and learning skills are required so ubiquitously in everyday life, patients afflicted with such disorders have great difficulty functioning on a day-to-day basis: They are unable to remember daily schedules, they forget appointments, they often lose their way when going from place to place, they cannot function adequately in school, and they are unable to learn new jobs. Even in familiar home and work situations, they cannot keep track of ongoing events and are often wholly dependent on others for their daily needs.

Approaches to rehabilitation have tended to be aligned with one of two objectives. On the one hand are methods that are aimed at *restoring* general memory function; on the other hand are approaches with the goal of *alleviating* specific problems associated with memory disorder. Different intervention strategies or techniques have emerged from each of these approaches. In general, evidence for restoration of function has been lacking. Recent research, however, has produced some promising findings concerning possibilities for alleviating problems of everyday living.

Four main methods of memory rehabilitation have dominated clinical and research interests in recent years. The first two—exercises and mnemonic strategies—have developed within the framework of a restoration approach; the second two—external aids and domain-specific learning—have been investigated within the context of an alleviation approach.

Exercises and Repetitive Drills

One of the oldest intervention strategies for the rehabilitation of memory disorders (as well as the rehabilitation of other neurological dysfunctions) is the establishment of exercise regimens. Consistent with the unfounded notion that memory is like a muscle, which must be exercised to maintain its strength, the use of repetitive drills continues in many clinical settings even today. With the ready availability of inexpensive computers, which are ideally suited for delivering repetitive exercises and which imply a high level of sophistication and expertise, attempts to restore damaged memories through drilling techniques have persisted despite lack of evidence of their effectiveness. Although there are clear benefits to practice, such benefits do not appear to apply in a general sense to memory capability. Practice in remembering one set of words, pictures, or shapes will increase the probability of remembering that particular set of studied items but will not improve one's ability to learn other unrelated materials. Advantages of practice, therefore, lie in its benefits for the acquisition of specific information.

Mnemonic Strategies

The teaching of mnemonic strategies has focused on three areas: visual imagery, verbal or semantic elaboration, and rehearsal. Visual imagery techniques involve teaching people how to construct vivid and distinctive mental images of things they are trying to remember. These methods have been used most successfully with patients who have damage only to the left hemisphere of the brain. In contrast, techniques that rely on verbal rather than visual cues, such as first-letter cuing, are most useful for patients with right hemisphere damage (see Wilson, 1987). More complex strategies, such as story mnemonics, word chaining, and PQRST (an organizational scheme for processing text), have proven beneficial primarily for individuals with relatively mild memory impairments who are otherwise high functioning. The generally limited applicability of these methods may be attributable to the considerable cognitive effort that they require, which may be beyond the capabilities of many brain-damaged persons. To the extent, however, that patients are able to master the techniques, they may be useful for learning specific pieces of information, such as people's names. Improvement in general memory ability as a result of learning mnemonic strategies is, however, unlikely. Even the use of simple rehearsal techniques has not been found to have long-term benefits. Although patients learn the strategies, they generally do not use them spontaneously in everyday life. (See also MNEMONIC DEVICES.)

External Aids

Attempts to facilitate daily living for memory-impaired individuals have frequently taken the form of providing external means for remembering, such as notebooks and diaries, bell timers and alarm watches, environmental labels and directions, and, most recently, microcomputers. Although these devices are potentially useful for brain-damaged patients, effective use often depends on specific training and extensive practice. Sohlberg and Mateer (1989) have demonstrated successful control of daily activities through the trained use of a notebook. Kirsch et al. (1987) have shown that memory-impaired individuals are capable of using a microcomputer to guide them through the steps of a cooking task or a janitorial job. Research in this area is just beginning. With advances in technology, the microcomputer will likely play an increasingly important role in the rehabilitation of brain-damaged patients.

Domain-Specific Learning

Although it has been known for some time that memory-impaired patients are capable of learning small amounts of information, recent developments suggest that the preserved learning capabilities of patients with organic memory disorders may permit, under appropriate training conditions, the acquisition of large amounts of complex knowledge relevant to important domains of everyday life. Glisky and Schacter (1989) have developed a training technique called the *method of vanishing cues* that capitalizes on patients' preserved abilities to retrieve previously presented information in response to fragment cues. This technique, which involves the gradual withdrawal of cues across learning trials, has enabled persons with memory disorders to acquire a variety of skills and knowledge applicable in their daily lives. These include computer language, computer operating procedures, vocational tasks such as data entry, microfilming, data-base management, and word processing.

Summary

Current understanding of memory disorders favors a rehabilitation strategy that focuses on alleviating problems of daily living rather than on restoring lost function. With the discovery of preserved memory and learning abilities in memory-impaired patients, the emphasis on rehabilitation has shifted toward finding ways to use patients' intact abilities to enable them to accomplish functional tasks. As the numbers of young survivors of head injury increase, efforts to identify jobs that exploit their preserved skills will also expand. Computer technology, which has just begun to impact on rehabilitation strategies, will play a more prominent role in terms of providing external aid and support, and also as a training and vocational adjunct. The trend in rehabilitation is toward the teaching of specific skills that can be applied directly in home and vocational contexts and toward greater exploitation of technology and of its interface with brain-damaged individuals.

REFERENCES

Bigler, E. D., ed. (1990). *Traumatic brain injury.* Austin, Tex.: Pro-Ed.

Glisky, E. L., and Schacter, D. L. (1989). Models and methods of memory rehabilitation. In F. Boller and J. Grafman, eds., *Handbook of neuropsychology,* vol. 3. Amsterdam: Elsevier.

Kirsch, N. L., Levine, S. P., Fallon-Kreuger, M., and Jaros, L. A. (1987). The microcomputer as an orthotic device for patients with cognitive deficits. *Journal of Head Trauma Rehabilitation 2,* 77–86.

Schacter, D. L., and Glisky, E. L. (1986). Memory remediation: Restoration, alleviation, and the acquisition of domain-specific knowledge. In B. Uzzell and Y. Gross, eds., *Clinical neuropsychology of intervention,* pp. 257–282. Boston: Martinus Nijhoff.

Sohlberg, M. M., and Mateer, C. A. (1989). *Introduction to cognitive rehabilitation.* New York: Guilford.

Wilson, B. (1987). *Rehabilitation of memory.* New York: Guilford.

Elizabeth L. Glisky

REINFORCEMENT

In its earliest technical usages, the term *reinforcement* implied strengthening, much as in its colloquial usage. It has been applied to a broad range of phenomena in learning, from the operant or instrumental behavior studied by B. F. SKINNER to the respondent or classical conditioning procedures of Ivan PAVLOV. The latter application has become largely obsolete, and the term now refers predominantly to cases in which responding has some consequences and, by virtue of doing so, occurs more often. The term *reward,* sometimes used as a nontechnical synonym, is not equivalent. For example, one can speak of delivering a reward even without evidence that the reward has an effect on behavior.

As an example of reinforcement, imagine a rat in a chamber with a lever and a cup into which food pellets can be delivered. If lever pressing does nothing, the rat presses only occasionally. If each press produces a food pellet, however, the rat presses the lever more often. The food is called a *reinforcer* and the rat's lever press is said to have been *reinforced*. The response that increases must be the one which produced the consequence. For example, if lever presses produce shock and only the rat's jumping increases, it would be inappropriate to speak of either lever pressing or jumping as reinforced.

An ambiguity of usage is that *reinforcement* sometimes refers to delivery of the reinforcer ("the lever press was reinforced" means that lever presses produced food) and sometimes to the resulting behavior change ("the lever press was reinforced" means that lever presses occurred more often because they produced food). The sense is usually clear from the context.

The Operant Nature of Reinforcement

Important early studies of reinforcement were Edward THORNDIKE's experiments with animals in problem boxes. Typically, a food-deprived animal was placed inside the box with food available outside. Sooner or later, typically by chance, the animal operated a device that released the door and freed it from the box. With repetition it operated the device more and more rapidly upon being placed in the box. To describe his findings, Thorndike formulated his *law of effect*. The law went through many revisions, but its essence was that responses can be made more probable by some consequences and less probable by others; in language closer to Thorndike's, responses with satisfying effects are *stamped in,* whereas those with annoying effects are *stamped out.*

Behavior that is modified by its consequences is called OPERANT BEHAVIOR or, in older and less common usages, *instrumental behavior;* it is behavior that operates on its environment. It corresponds closely to the behavior colloquially called *voluntary* or *purposive.* It is said to be *emitted* because it is primarily determined by its consequences; it does not require an eliciting stimulus, as in reflex relations (e.g., as when a puff of air to the eye produces a blink). *Operants* are classes of responses defined by their environmental effects rather than by their topography (their form or the particular muscle groups involved). For example, a rat might press a lever with its left paw, its right paw, or both paws; it might even depress the lever by biting or sitting on it. But similar

movements at the other end of the chamber, far from the lever, would not be lever presses no matter how closely they resembled the responses that operated the lever.

The analysis of reinforcement was significantly extended by Skinner. One of his critical contributions was to clarify the difference between operant learning and the classical or respondent learning that had been studied by Pavlov (in Pavlov's experiments, the organism's responses had no effect on the stimuli that were presented).

Consider the relation between a red traffic light and a driver's stepping on the brakes. The red light sets the occasion for stepping on the brakes; this response occurs at a red light and not at a green light because it has different consequences in the presence of each stimulus. A stimulus that signals or sets the occasion for different consequences of responding is said to be *discriminative.* Three terms are involved: the discriminative stimulus, the response, and the consequences of the response in the presence of that stimulus.

For example, imagine a pigeon in a chamber with a feeder; above the feeder is a small disk or key that can be lit from behind with lights of different colors. Suppose now that reinforcement of the pigeon's key peck depends on the presence of a green or a red light. If the peck produces food only when the key is green, the pigeon will come to peck in the presence of green but not red. Its pecking in the presence of green is called a *discriminated operant.* Discriminative stimuli correspond to the stimuli colloquially called *signals* or *cues.* They do not elicit responses; instead, they set the occasions on which responses have consequences.

The Relativity of Reinforcement

Reinforcement does not explain the increase in responding produced by the consequences of responding. Instead, it is a term that is appropriate when such an increase is caused by a reinforcement contingency (the relation between response and consequence). In a reinforcement relation, a response must have some consequence, it must increase in probability (i.e., it must occur more often than when it does not have this consequence), and the increase in probability must occur *because* the response had this consequence and not for some other reason. For example, it would not be appropriate to say that a response must have been reinforced simply because it has become more probable; the increase may have occurred for other reasons (e.g., the response may have been elicited by a stimulus).

Once a reinforcer has been identified, it cannot be assumed that it will continue to be effective in the future or that it will reinforce other responses in other situations. The effectiveness of reinforcers can change over time, and a given reinforcer may reinforce some responses but not others.

A formulation that defined reinforcers independently of their behavioral consequences was provided by Premack (1962), who noted that reinforcers typically provide the opportunity for other behavior. Food, for example, provides an opportunity for eating. Premack's principle stated that the effectiveness of a reinforcer is based on the relative probabilities of the responses for which it provides an opportunity and the responses to be reinforced. A less probable response can be reinforced by the opportunity to engage in a more probable response. These probabilities can be assessed by allowing the organism to choose between the responses and can be altered by limiting the organism's opportunities to engage in one or the other.

For example, imagine a rat in a chamber where it can either drink or run in an activity wheel. After it has been deprived of water but not of access to the wheel, drinking will be more probable than running. After it has been deprived of access to the wheel but not of water, running will be more probable than drinking. At times when the rat is more likely to drink than to run, an opportunity to drink will reinforce running. But when it is more likely to run than to drink, the opportunity to run will reinforce drinking.

These examples illustrate the *relativity of reinforcement*: The reinforcement relation is reversible, and it is inappropriate to classify events as reinforcers independently of the situations within which they are arranged. Whether any stimulus is a reinforcer depends on its context. For example, the opportunity to eat a good meal is often an effective reinforcer, but consider how often children are persuaded to finish their dinners by making other activities depend on that eating. Eating can reinforce, as when a child's snack depends on whether the child has completed homework, or it can be reinforced, as when the opportunity to play depends on whether the child has finished a meal. Reinforcers are not defined by common physical properties; they are defined by their effects on behavior.

Reinforcement and Extinction

The consequences of many responses remain reasonably constant throughout life. For example, a fairly reliable consequence of reaching for a nearby object is touching it. But for other responses, consequences change. Educational systems often arrange consequences such as praise or grades, but sooner or later these artificial consequences are discontinued (with the hope that other, more natural consequences take over when the student moves on to other settings). The increase in responding produced by reinforcement is not permanent; responding decreases to its earlier levels when reinforcement is discontinued.

The discontinuation of reinforcement is called *extinction,* and responding that decreases to its earlier level as a result is said to be *extinguished.* This does not mean, however, that the effects of reinforcement have been completely wiped out. For example, during reinforcement the lever-pressing rat may have learned more efficient ways to make the lever work, and these will not be erased by extinction. In addition, the rat had been eating frequently during reinforcement, and in extinction the eating necessarily ended. The termination of food alone, without regard to the relation between food and lever pressing, may have effects on the rat's behavior during extinction. For example, the rat may exhibit aggressive behavior such as biting at the lever.

Positive and Negative Reinforcement

A variety of consequences can be arranged as reinforcers, ranging from those of obvious biological significance, such as food or water or a sexual partner, to relatively minor changes in things seen or heard or touched. Consequences are not restricted merely to the production of stimuli. Responses can remove stimuli, as when operating a switch turns off a light; responses can prevent stimuli from occurring, as when unplugging a lamp before repairing it eliminates the possibility of a shock; and responses can even change the consequences of other responses, as when replacing a burned-out light bulb makes the previously ineffective response of operating the light switch an effective response again. Each type of consequence may affect later behavior.

A stimulus is a *positive reinforcer* if its presentation increases the likelihood of responses that produce it, and a *negative reinforcer* if its removal increases the likelihood of responses that terminate or prevent or postpone it. Negative reinforcers are sometimes called *aversive stimuli.* Responding that turns off an aversive stimulus (e.g., when a rat turns off a loud noise by pressing a lever) is called *escape responding.* Responding that prevents or postpones an aversive stimulus (e.g., when a rat's lever press prevents or postpones the delivery of an electric shock) is called *avoidance responding.* Positive reinforcement and negative reinforcement have many properties in common, but one distinction between them is that negative reinforcement procedures often produce behavior that is likely to interfere with the to-be-reinforced responding. For example, suppose a rat can turn off an electric shock by pressing a lever. Lever pressing may increase in the presence of shock, but the shock may also produce other behavior (e.g., jumping) that is likely to compete with lever pressing.

Reinforcement and Punishment

Consequences can reduce responding instead of increasing it. For example, if shock is delivered whenever a rat grooms its tail, the rat may groom its tail less often. Responding that is reduced by its consequences is said to be *punished.* Punishment, simply the inverse of reinforcement, has had a more controversial history. Thorndike's early versions of the law of effect argued that behavior could be stamped out by annoyers as well as stamped in by satisfiers, but he later withdrew the part that dealt with the stamping out of behavior.

A rat's reinforced lever pressing can be reduced when presses are punished by shock, but the responding recovers to earlier levels once punishment is discontinued. Because punishment suppresses responding only temporarily, the argument was offered that it is ineffective. Yet reinforcement would also have to be judged ineffective by this criterion. In early studies, standards for the effectiveness of punishment were different from those for the effectiveness of reinforcement. Investigations tended to concentrate on the recovery of responding after punishment was discontinued rather than on the reduction of responding during punishment.

Punishment is effective, but that does not recommend it. It is usually an undesirable method for eliminating behavior. Thorndike and his successors were probably right for the wrong reasons. For example, one major problem is that aversive stimuli used as punishers have side effects, such as eliciting aggressive behavior.

Biological Constraints

Many responses automatically have particular consequences. For example, to see something below eye level, we look down rather than up. Organisms may learn these consequences of responding, but such cases must be distinguished from those in which behavior has other sources (e.g., behavior determined by the evolutionary history of a species). Biological factors may constrain the behavior that can be reinforced and the events that will serve as effective reinforcers. For example, it is not necessary to teach a rat to avoid predators through negative reinforcement; appropriate behavior has been selected through evolutionary contingencies, and rats rarely have a chance to learn such behavior in natural habitats because their predators rarely give them a second chance. Studies of reinforcement must be alert to the interactions between the consequences of behavior and its evolutionary determinants.

Shaping and the Selection of Behavior

Reinforcement does not establish connections or associations between responses and stimuli. Rather, it changes the probability of classes of responses. Some responses become more likely and others, less likely. In other words, some responses survive in the organism's behavior and others do not. In this respect, reinforcement works by selection. It operates on populations of responses within the lifetime of the individual organism much as evolutionary selection operates on populations of organisms over successive generations.

The selective nature of reinforcement is best

illustrated by a procedure called *shaping,* which creates new responses through the successive reinforcement of other responses that more and more closely approximate it. For example, a rat may rarely if ever press a lever with a force that approximates its own body weight, but it can be brought to do so by selectively reinforcing stronger and stronger presses. Shaping begins with whatever behavior is available. At the start, most presses will probably be weak; but if the strongest of these are reinforced, the force of pressing will increase a little, and the criterion for reinforcement can then be moved up to the strongest of the new population of responses. This in turn produces another increase in force and a change in criterion, and so on, until the rat is pressing with a force that might never have been observed in the absence of the shaping procedure. Reinforcement has had many useful applications, and shaping has figured in a significant way in many of them, ranging from the training of animals to the production of speech in autistic children.

Conclusion

This article has treated some properties of the contemporary concept of reinforcement. The principle of reinforcement emerged as a descriptive term appropriate when responding increases because of its consequences. Reinforcement does not produce learning; it produces behavior. The rat that presses a lever when lever presses are reinforced, and not otherwise, has learned the consequences of its lever pressing. The consequences of responding are critical to learning not because learning follows from them but because they are what is learned.

REFERENCES

Estes, W. K. (1944). An experimental study of punishment. *Psychological Monographs 57,* no. 263.
Pavlov, I. P. (1927). *Conditioned reflexes,* trans. by G. V. Anrep. London: Oxford University Press.
Premack, D. (1962). Reversibility of the reinforcement relation. *Science 136,* 255–257.
Skinner, B. F. (1938). *The behavior of organisms.* New York: Appleton-Century-Crofts.
——— (1969). Contingencies of reinforcement. New York: Appleton-Century-Crofts.
——— (1981). Selection by consequences. *Science 213,* 501–504.
Thorndike, E. L. (1898). Animal intelligence: An experimental study of the associative processes in animals. *Psychological Review Monograph Supplements 2* (4), 109.

A. *Charles Catania*

REPETITION AND LEARNING

Sayings such as "Practice makes perfect" illustrate the well-known fact that repetition improves learning. This was discussed by numerous ancient and medieval thinkers and was demonstrated empirically by Hermann EBBINGHAUS, the first researcher to carry out a prolonged series of experiments on human memory. Ebbinghaus showed that retention of information improves as a function of the number of times the information has been studied.

The effects of repetition on learning and memory have been studied in two distinct ways. The first is to repeat the number of learning trials and observe the effects on performance. Such learning trials may commonly involve conditioning of humans or other animals, or may involve presentation of a list of to-be-remembered verbal material to humans. Alternatively, researchers investigating human memory have often presented subjects with a single list of verbal items but varied how often particular items occurred on the list.

The Effects of Repetition of Learning Trials

In a situation where an organism has been exposed to information on numerous occasions, one can keep track of how well it has learned the material as a function of number of exposures. A hypothetical but typical example of this learning curve is shown in Figure 1. The horizontal axis shows the number of trials, the opportunities that the organism has had for learning to occur. The vertical axis shows some measure of retention. This learning curve can be said to be a monotonic, negatively accelerated function. The term *monotonic function* refers to the fact that the curve is going in only one direction, higher. By *negatively acceler-*

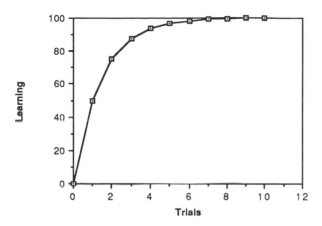

Figure 1. A hypothetical but typical learning curve.

ated, we mean that the rate of increase is always slowing down. The greatest amount of learning happens on the first trial, and all subsequent trials show smaller and smaller increases in learning. The curve levels off to an asymptote, a point where the amount being learned on each trial is too small to be detectable.

The monotonic, negatively accelerated learning curve can be demonstrated in a variety of learning situations. It illustrates that acquisition of information is typically gradual and continuous. However, numerous authors (e.g., Guthrie, 1935) have pointed out that the continuous nature of the learning curve does not necessarily mean that the learning process itself has to be either gradual or continuous. Most learning situations contain a number of smaller facets or subproblems that must be mastered before learning is complete. It is possible that each of these subproblems is mastered suddenly, perhaps through insight. However, the subproblems are learned at different times, with more and more of them mastered as the number of trials increases. This analysis proposes that the continuous nature of the learning curve does not reflect a gradual learning process but, rather, the accumulation of subproblems that have been mastered in a sudden fashion.

Distinguishing between a truly gradual learning process and the accumulation of small, sudden insights is difficult. A common assumption is that learning may be either gradual or sudden, depending on the background of the learner and the nature of the information to be learned. For example, Harry HARLOW (1949) showed that learning may occur in sudden flashes of insight when the organ-

ism has had experience in a number of similar situations. Thus, although the learning curve for a complex task tends to be gradual and continuous, determination of whether subcomponents of the task are learned gradually or suddenly is more difficult and requires careful analysis.

Repetition of Verbal Items on Lists

Researchers in human memory often present subjects with a list once and then give a test for its retention. Repetition effects have been studied by varying the frequency of presentation of the items on the list. Items may occur once, twice, or however many times the experimenter chooses When retention is measured as a function of item repetition, the results typically resemble the learning curve depicted in Figure 1. That is, increases in item frequency have their greatest effect at lower frequencies.

The procedure of repeating items varying numbers of times on a single list has been useful in studying the mechanisms through which repetition may influence learning. Ward (1893) discussed possible explanations for the beneficial effects of repetition. One class of explanations (commonly known as strength theory) claims that there is a single location in memory storage that corresponds to an event. Every time the event is repeated, that location (known as the memory trace) increases in effectiveness or strength. It is also assumed that stronger traces are easier to retrieve from memory than are weaker traces. Repetition thus improves learning by increasing the strength of a single memory trace.

A second class of explanation for the effects of repetition on memory is known as multiple-trace theory. This approach assumes that every occurrence of an event is a unique episode. Every time an event occurs, a separate, independent memory trace is formed. This trace contains information about the time and situation in which that occurrence happened. The more times an event occurs, the more traces of that event are placed in memory. According to this multiple-trace theory, repetition improves learning because finding at least one trace of an event becomes easier when there are more traces of that event in memory.

A fundamental difference between these two accounts concerns the representation of the individual occurrences of a repeated item. The strength theory claims that each occurrence of an event strengthens a single memory trace. Since each occurrence has the same effect, the specific details of individual occurrences are forgotten. In contrast, the multiple-trace theory claims that every occurrence produces its own trace. The individuality of specific occurrences is maintained.

Experiments distinguishing between these two accounts have often required subjects to remember a list of words. A word on the list may occur once or a varying number of times. After seeing the list, subjects are shown the list items again and asked to make some kind of judgment regarding how often each item occurred on the list. Even when they do not expect to be tested on the frequencies of the items, subjects are typically able to perform this task with considerable (but not perfect) accuracy. However, strength theory and multiple-trace theory make different proposals as to how subjects are able to make judgments about the frequency of occurrence of list items. Strength theory claims that subjects retrieve the memory trace corresponding to a test item and evaluate that trace's strength. They then use the strength to make a judgment of frequency. For example, if a memory trace is very strong, subjects will guess that the item occurred many times on the list. If a memory trace is weak, subjects may decide that the item occurred once (or possibly not at all) on the list. In contrast, the multiple-trace theory claims that subjects make judgments of frequency by retrieving as many traces as possible of that item occurring in the context of the list. Subjects then base their judgments on a count of the traces they found.

Numerous experiments have investigated whether a frequency judgment is based on a single trace or on the retrieval of many different traces. For example, Hintzman and Block (1971) showed subjects two lists of words, 5 minutes apart. Some words occurred on both lists. Each word occurred zero, two, or five times on List 1 and zero, two, or five times on List 2. After seeing both lists, subjects were asked to estimate frequency of occurrence separately for each list. They were quite accurate at this task; their estimates were chiefly influenced by the frequency of the item on the list being judged and were influenced little by the item's frequency on the other list. Such a finding is difficult for a strength theory to explain: If judgments of frequency were based simply on the overall strength of the trace of the word, subjects would not be able to make separate estimates for the frequency of an item on two lists. However, a multiple-trace theory would predict this finding because frequency judgments are seen as being based on a count of individual traces, each carrying information about its time of formation.

Subsequent studies have found further evidence in favor of a multiple-trace theory. For example, when some words are presented visually and others auditorily, subjects are able to give separate frequency judgments for each kind of presentation. Also, subjects are able to judge how often a word followed another word on a list. Such findings suggest that the individual identities of the occurrences of a repeated event are maintained in memory, as assumed by the multiple-trace theory.

Studies such as these suggest that a multiple-trace theory is necessary to account for the effects of repetition on memory. They do not show that such a theory is sufficient to account for all the effects of repetition. The question of whether repetition has other effects in addition to the creation of multiple memory traces has not been resolved. Moreover, there is little evidence that would allow one to determine whether the multiple-trace approach can be applied to situations in which learning trials (rather than items on a single list) are repeated.

When Is Repetition Ineffective in Increasing Learning?

Although the emphasis in this entry has necessarily been on the mechanisms through which repetition improves learning, one should not assume that repetition alone is always sufficient. For example, consider a common coin, such as the American penny. We have seen such coins countless times. Yet, as Nickerson and Adams (1979) showed, subjects can have quite poor memory for the details of a penny. They are often unable to remember exactly where such features as the date and the words "In God We Trust" are located. There is no need for people to attend to these features of a penny because pennies can easily be distinguished from other coins on the basis of their size and color. This suggests that attention to an event may be necessary before repetition of that event leads to noticeable improvements in memory. The generality of this claim has been established by studies demonstrating poor memory for other currencies, for the details of telephone dials, and for the messages of common advertisements.

Additional examples of ineffective rehearsal have come from experiments on rote rehearsal (e.g., Glenberg, Smith, and Green, 1977; Rundus, 1977). In these studies, subjects have repeated words aloud over and over. An unexpected memory test on the words is later given to the subjects. Memory performance is usually only slightly affected by the number of times that a person read each word aloud. On the other hand, if people are encouraged to carry out more active, effortful processing on the words, memory improves dramatically as study time is increased.

Thus, repetition need not lead to improved learning. Rather, repetition leads to increased opportunities for learning to occur. Whether such learning takes place will depend on the amount and nature of processing that a person carries out.

(See also ATTENTION AND MEMORY; DISTRIBUTED PRACTICE EFFECTS.)

REFERENCES

Ebbinghaus, H. (1964). *Memory: A contribution to experimental psychology.* New York: Dover. (Originally published 1885; translated 1913.)

Glenberg, A., Smith, S. M., and Green, C. (1977). Type 1 rehearsal: Maintenance and more. *Journal of Verbal Learning and Verbal Behavior 16,* 339–359.

Guthrie, E. R. (1935). *The psychology of learning.* New York: Harper.

Harlow, H. F. (1949). The formation of learning sets. *Psychological Review 56,* 51–65.

Hintzman, D. L., and Block, R. A. (1971). Repetition and memory: Evidence for a multiple-trace hypothesis. *Journal of Experimental Psychology 88,* 297–306.

Nickerson, R. S., and Adams, M. J. (1979). Long-term memory for a common object. *Cognitive Psychology 11,* 287–307.

Rundus, D. (1977). Maintenance rehearsal and single-level processing. *Journal of Verbal Learning and Verbal Behavior 16,* 665–681.

Ward, J. (1893). Assimilation and association. *Mind 2,* 347–362.

Robert L. Greene

RETRIEVAL PROCESSES IN MEMORY

The processes of learning and memory are often subdivided into stages of *encoding* (initial learning of information; see CODING PROCESSES), *storage* (maintaining information over time), and *retrieval* (using stored information). Processes of encoding establish some representation of experience in the nervous system, which is referred to as a *memory trace.* Memory traces certainly have physiological underpinnings, but cognitive psychologists use the construct as an abstraction to refer to the changed state of the cognitive system before and after some experience. *Retrieval processes* refers to the means of accessing stored information and can be affected by a variety of factors.

The division of processes into those affecting encoding, storage, or retrieval seems simple in concept but cannot be readily defended in practice. One reason is that it is impossible to distinguish cleanly between encoding and storage processes, because the two are inextricably connected. When does initial learning (encoding) end and maintenance of information over time (storage) begin? There is no clear answer to this question; suggestions provided by some theorists to cut this Gordian knot are relatively arbitrary. However, separation between the bundle of processes referred to as encoding and storage, on the one hand, and those involving retrieval, on the other, can be accomplished more directly.

The general logic of this separation is to hold conditions of encoding and storage constant and to manipulate only conditions of retrieval. For example, two groups of people could be presented with material (lists of words or sets of stories) to remember and could be treated identically until the time they are tested. Then one group of people might simply be given a blank sheet of paper and asked to recall all that they can of the material. Imagine that they recall 40 percent of the material under these *free recall* conditions (so called because they are given no external cues to aid recall and are free to recall material in any order). This measure might be thought to reflect the amount of information that people have encoded and stored—the amount they know—but this conclusion would ignore the possibility that the bottleneck in performance is at the retrieval stage. Perhaps the people really have encoded and stored much more, but have simply failed to retrieve the extra material. This possibility can be examined by testing another group of subjects who are given retrieval cues to prompt recall of the material. Often appropriate cues can produce great benefits relative to free recall (Mantylä, 1986).

The advantage of cued recall over free recall

indicates that more information is *available* (or is stored) in memory than is *accessible* (retrievable) on a particular test such as free recall (Tulving and Pearlstone, 1966). More generally, no test of memory provides a perfect measure of information stored in memory; the retrieval processes involved in any test filter the information. At best, we study the information that can be produced under a particular set of retrieval conditions. Although no test or set of retrieval conditions can ever provide a perfect window on the contents of memory, study of retrieval processes can proceed meaningfully in many different ways.

Repeated Testing

One straightforward way to study retrieval processes is to test people repeatedly on the same material, under the same or differing conditions. For example, people might study sixty pictures of easily named objects and then be tested on the names of those objects under conditions of free recall. After a first test, they would be given a second and then a third test under identical conditions without intervening study of the material. An almost universal finding in such experiments is that people will recall items on the second and third tests that they did not recall on the earlier tests, a phenomenon called *reminiscence* (Ballard, 1913). Of course, some pictures recalled on the first test might be forgotten on later tests, but surprisingly the reminiscence or recovery between tests often outweighs the interest forgetting. When total recall improves over tests, this phenomenon is called *hypermnesia* (Erdelyi and Becker, 1974). Whereas reminiscence (recall of items on a later test that could not be recalled on an earlier test) almost always occurs in experiments, hypermnesia is observed more rarely and usually under conditions where no retrieval cues are given. Under certain conditions the phenomenon is quite reliable, so the challenge is to specify the necessary conditions for its observation. It may be that hypermnesia occurs more regularly with materials that involve imagery (such as pictures); another proposal is that hypermnesia depends on the level of retention (regardless of type of material) and on retrieval dynamics across tests (Roediger and Challis, 1989). Whichever is the case—and some argue for a hybrid theory—the phenomena of reminiscence and hypermnesia point up again that a

single test of retention provides a faulty assessment of the amount of information stored in memory (Payne, 1987).

Testing with Retrieval Cues

The most popular method of studying retrieval processes is by manipulating the nature of the testing conditions, particularly the types of cues given to aid recollection. In a typical paradigm, people are given a list of words to remember that belong to common categories. The list might be composed of words such as *zebra, ocelot, sheep, beaver, desk, dresser, couch,* and *footstool,* representing the categories *four-footed animals* and *articles of furniture.* After receiving a long list, some people are tested under conditions of free recall (recall the words in any order) and some under conditions of cued recall (the same instruction, but now the names of the categories are provided as retrieval cues). The typical finding is that people tested with category names as retrieval cues recall many more items than those tested without cues, showing again the disparity between information that might be available in memory and that accessible on a particular test. The gains from cues are genuine and not due merely to guessing items belonging to the categories, because the items used are typically not the most likely to be guessed (*horse* and *dog* are avoided as study materials in favor of *ocelot* and *beaver*).

What causes retrieval cues to be effective? A primary consideration is what type of information was learned and how it was encoded—what information is stored in memory. The general principle governing retrieval of such stored information is called the *encoding specificity principle:* retrieval cues are effective to the extent that they help reinstate or re-create processes involved in original learning (Tulving, 1983). The idea is that events are encoded in specific ways—we retain specific coded features of our experiences that may comprise the memory traces of these experiences. Retrieval cues are then effective to the extent that they match or overlap the specific encoded features.

Consider a thought experiment to illustrate this point: You are asked to recall all the experiences you can from your year in the fifth grade, and are given half an hour to do so. You should include the names of your classmates and, if possible, the seating arrangement in your classroom. Presumably you could accomplish this task with a certain (low) level of performance. Now imagine a second phase to the experiment wherein you are actually taken to your elementary school, reenter your classroom, and squeeze into your little desk, to perform the task again under these new conditions. We might now assume (and experiments confirm) that powerful retrieval cues, such as the place in which an event occurred, would greatly increase your memory of your fifth grade year (Bjork and Richardson-Klavehn, 1989). The sights, sounds, and smells of your classroom would revive dormant memories that would otherwise be inaccessible.

Numerous laboratory experiments have confirmed the essence of the encoding specificity principle by showing that retrieval cues that match, or re-create, the original features of the learning experience promote better memory. This is not to say that all retrieval phenomena are well accounted for, because some empirical problems do exist. For example, certain types of cues that seem as if they should be effective are not; in some cases, seemingly "good" retrieval cues actually hinder rather than help recall. One example is the *part-list cuing phenomenon,* wherein giving people part of a list of items hurts recall relative to control conditions (Slamecka, 1968). For example, if people are given lists of words belonging to common categories (such as the examples used above) and then at test either are given only category names as cues or are given category names plus two items from the categories, recall of the remaining items from the categories will be better when only category names are given as cues. Providing some items from the category in addition to the category names will re-create the learning situation better than just giving the category names, but in fact such item cues hurt recall.

Explaining this retrieval inhibition has proved to be a challenge; much research has established the validity of the finding and eliminated many artifactual possibilities for the results (Nickerson, 1984). One interpretation links the part-list cuing effect to a *cue-overload principle:* a retrieval cue becomes less effective as more events are subsumed under the cue (Watkins, 1975). So, for example, a category name retrieval cue provides better recall of the studied members of a category if two items were given in each category of the list rather than six items. In the case of part-list cues, it may be assumed that presentation of the category members at test somehow adds to the number of items subsumed under the category name cue and thereby reduces recall. Numerous observations accord with the cue overload principle's interpretation of the part-list cuing effect, although other theories exist as well. The cue overload principle complements the encoding specificity principle in making sense of the variable effectiveness of retrieval cues.

State-Dependent Retrieval

Alcohol and other drugs having a depressing effect on the central nervous system are known to impair retention of information. The usual interpretation is that alcohol interferes with the neural processes which underlie encoding and storage of information, or the consolidation of information. This is likely true, but may not represent the whole story of drug-induced amnesia. Retrieval factors are at work, too. Clinicians working with alcoholic patients have observed that the patient may, for instance, hide a bottle while drunk and then not be able to remember where it is hidden when sober. However, the next time the patient gets drunk, the bottle may be recovered. The phenomenon suggests that successful retrieval of memories may depend on matching the pharmacological states in which information is learned and used.

This phenomenon of *state-dependent retrieval* (better recall when pharmacological states of learning and testing match rather than mismatch) has been verified in laboratory experiments. In one case (Eich et al., 1975) volunteer students smoked marijuana or a placebo cigarette before being exposed to a categorized word list. Four hours later the subjects again smoked either a marijuana cigarette or a placebo and then were tested on the material, first by free recall and then by cued recall in which category names served as the retrieval cues.

The results are shown in Table 1; first consider the free recall results, where the number of words recalled from the set of 48 are shown. If people were sober both when they studied the words and when they were tested on them, they performed best (11.5 words recalled). If they were under the influence of marijuana at study but sober at test, they recalled fewest (6.7). This condition represents the usual case of drug-induced amnesia, when people experience events under the drug

Table 1.   Results of the Experiment on State-Dependent Retrieval

Condition		Average Number of Words Recalled	
Study	**Test**	**Free Recall**	**Cued Recall**
Placebo	Placebo	11.5	24.0
Placebo	Drug	9.9	23.7
Drug	Placebo	6.7	22.6
Drug	Drug	10.5	22.3

but are sober when tested. Is this effect due only to encoding and storage factors, or are retrieval factors at work, too? This question can be answered by examining the last row: when people were drugged at both study and test, they recalled more words (10.5) than when they were drugged only during study (6.7). Just as in the anecdote about the alcoholics related above, retention improved when the pharmacological state at test matched that at study. Do not conclude from this experiment that drugs improve memory, because they usually do not. (When people learned the information sober but were tested under marijuana, they performed worse than when tested sober.)

Although state-dependent retrieval is a real phenomenon, it usually occurs only under free recall conditions, as can be verified by examining the cued recall results. The category names served as good retrieval cues, because cued recall was better than free recall in all four conditions. However, the state-dependent retrieval effect (better recall in the drug-drug study and test condition compared with the drug-sober condition) has vanished. These results are broadly consistent with the encoding specificity hypothesis. Under conditions of free recall, a person's pharmacological state can serve as a retrieval cue, and if the cues match between study and test conditions, performance is enhanced. However, when powerful external retrieval cues are provided, they overshadow the weak "state" cues and render them ineffective. This account explains the common finding that state-dependent retrieval effects are rarely found on tests employing cued recall (Eich, 1989). (See also DRUGS AND MEMORY.)

Do state-dependent retrieval phenomena exist with states other than drug states? The conditions most often investigated are moods, in studies where researchers induce happy or depressed moods in people by various means prior to study or test of material. The expected finding is that congruence of mood at study and test should produce better retention than when moods mismatch. This result has been reported in some studies, but there have been numerous failures to replicate it and the reasons for this state of affairs are not well understood at this point. (See also EMOTION, MOOD, AND MEMORY.)

Transfer-Appropriate Processing

A viewpoint related to the encoding specificity hypothesis, *transfer-appropriate processing*, emphasizes that all retention tests can be considered as cases of transfer of prior experience to the test situation. Depending on the nature of the task used to assess memory, some experiences will provide good transfer and others will provide poor transfer. Further, this approach emphasizes the relativity of memory tests: some methods of learning may prove superior for one type of test but disastrous for another. The phrase *transfer-appropriate processing* was first used to explain some results obtained in the *levels of processing* tradition (Morris, Bransford, and Franks, 1977). Under many conditions, if people study events while focusing on their meaning, they retain the events better later than if they had focused on other aspects of the events, such as what they look or sound like, while studying them. For words, retention is better on many tests after people have generated meaningful associations for the words (thus forcing attention to their meaning) than when rhyming words have been generated (causing attention to sounds or phonemes).

Most of the tests showing the superiority of meaningful encodings have been those, such as recall or recognition, that are thought to rely heavily on meaning (Craik and Tulving, 1975). But suppose a test were given for the sound of words following study experiences encouraging attention to either the meaning or the sound of words. When such tests were constructed, the results came out largely as expected: having people think about the rhyming aspects of words during study produced better performance on tests requiring knowledge of the sound of the words than did study experiences emphasizing the meaning of words. Therefore, the ways in which one studies events are not inherently good or bad for later retention; instead, whether study strategies are good or bad depends on their relation to the nature of the test. Learning experiences transfer well or poorly depending on the nature of the test and the type of knowledge it requires.

The ideas of transfer-appropriate processing have been applied to several different problems. One is the explanation of differences between explicit tests of memory (those in which people are told that their memories are being tested) and implicit tests of memory (those in which people are simply given a new task and retention is measured by how prior experiences transfer to the new task). Many implicit memory tests seem to involve perceptual components and to benefit from appropriate perceptual processing, whereas many explicit tests depend upon meaningful processing. Numerous experiments have confirmed that these two broad areas of experience (perceptual, conceptual) differentially affect certain tests in the predicted manner (Roediger, 1990). (See also IM-PLICIT MEMORY.)

Related Topics

Retrieval processes play a role in all memory phenomena, so the coverage here has perforce been selective. For example, the fact that distinctive events are well remembered may be interpreted in terms of the cue overload principle; the inhibition from part-list cues may be related to the TIP-OF-THE-TONGUE PHENOMENON wherein people are blocked from recalling well-known information by intrusion of related information. All memories depend not just on conditions of encoding and storage, but on myriad retrieval factors. Some retrieval processes seem reasonably well understood at this point, albeit at a general level, but others present problems whose solutions have not yet been attempted.

REFERENCES

Ballard, P. B. (1913). Oblivescence and reminiscence. *British Journal of Psychology Monograph Supplements 1*, 1–82.

Bjork, R. A., and Richardson-Klavehn, P. (1989). On the puzzling relationship between environmental context and human memory. In C. Izawa, ed., *Current issues in cognitive processes: The Tulane Floweree symposium on cognition*, pp. 373–344. Hillsdale, N.J.: Erlbaum.

Craik, F. I. M., and Tulving, E. (1975). Depth of processing and the retention of words in episodic memory. *Journal of Experimental Psychology: General 104*, 268–294.

Eich, E. (1989). Theoretical issues in state-dependent memory. In H. L. Roediger and F. I. M. Craik, eds., *Varieties of memory and consciousness. Essays in honour of Endel Tulving*. Hillsdale, N.J.: Erlbaum.

Eich, J. E., Weingartner, H., Stillman, R. C., and Gillin, J. C. (1975). State dependent accessibility of retrieval cues in the retention of a categorized list. *Journal of Verbal Learning and Verbal Behavior 14*, 408–417.

Erdelyi, M. H., and Becker, J. (1974). Hypermnesia for pictures: Incremental memory for pictures but not for words in multiple recall trials. *Cognitive Psychology 6*, 159–171.

Mantylä, T. (1986). Optimizing cue effectiveness: Recall of 500 and 600 incidentally learned words. *Journal of Experimental Psychology: Learning, Memory, and Cognition 12*, 66–71.

Morris, C. D., Bransford, J. D., and Franks, J. J. (1977). Levels of processing versus transfer appropriate processing. *Journal of Verbal Learning and Verbal Behavior 16*, 519–533.

Nickerson, R. S. (1984). Retrieval inhibition from part-set cuing: A persisting enigma in memory research. *Memory and Cognition 12*, 531–552.

Payne, D. G. (1987). Hypermnesia and reminiscence in recall: A historical and empirical review. *Psychological Bulletin 101*, 5–27.

Roediger, H. L. (1990). Implicit memory: Retention without remembering. *American Psychology 45*, 1043–1056.

Roediger, H. L., and Challis, B. H. (1989). Hypermnesia: Increased recall with repeated tests. In C. Izawa, ed., *Current issues in cognitive processes: The Tulane-Floweree symposium on cognition*, pp. 175–199. Hillsdale, N.J.: Erlbaum.

Slamecka, N. J. (1968). An examination of trace storage in free recall. *Journal of Experimental Psychology 76*, 504–513.

Tulving, E. (1983). *Elements of episodic memory*. New York: Oxford University Press.

Tulving, E., and Pearlstone, Z. (1966). Availability versus accessibility of information in memory for words.

Journal of Verbal Learning and Verbal Behavior 5, 381–391.

Watkins, M. J. (1975). Inhibition in recall with extralist "cues." *Journal of Verbal Learning and Verbal Behavior 14,* 294–303.

Henry L. Roediger III

RIBOT, THÉODULE

Théodule Armand Ribot (1839–1916) was born in Guingamp, Brittany. After attending lycée in Saint-Brieuc, he entered the Ecole Normale Supérieure at Paris in 1862. He received his degree in philosophy in 1865, and until 1872 he taught philosophy in the secondary schools of Vesoul and Laval. In 1870 Ribot published his first work, *La psychologie anglaise contemporaine.* Seven years later he gave up teaching so that he could concentrate on writing. He also attended clinical courses in psychiatry given by Valentin Magnan, Benjamin Ball, Jules Luys, Félix Voisin, and Jean-Martin Charcot, then defended his thesis, "L'hérédité psychologique." In 1876 Ribot and Hippolyte Taine founded the journal *Revue Philosophique,* which is still published.

In 1885, Ribot started a course in experimental psychology at the Sorbonne, and in 1888, through the influence of Ernest Renan, a chair of experimental and comparative psychology was created at the Collège de France that Ribot occupied until his retirement in 1901. Among Ribot's honors was his election to the Académie des Sciences Morales et Politiques (Section of Philosophy) in 1899.

Ribot was responsible for creating in France "scientific" psychology, rejecting a psychology that depended on spiritualism and introspection in favor of one that depends on facts and has to agree with known physiological and biological data. Ribot was interested in pathological psychology because it enabled one to understand normal psychological mechanisms by discovering the laws that govern facts. Influenced by Herbert Spencer's evolutionism, Ribot described, as did Hughlings Jackson, the law of regression (or of dissolution) that controls pathological mental phenomena, such as the amnesias. It is important to point out that Ribot was neither an experimenter nor a clinical observer. His contributions were purely intellectual and the result of personal reflection upon the

Figure 1. Théodule Ribot. *Photo by Harlingue-Viollet.*

events reported by others, which he categorized and regrouped. He never attempted to construct models. His work was empirical and rational rather than experimental.

Ribot is probably best known today for his law of regression in the amnesias, Ribot's Law. The law outlines in a logical fashion the progressive dysfunction of memory in disease. First to be affected are recent memories. Second, personal memories disappear, "going downward to the past." Third, things acquired intellectually are lost bit by bit; last to disappear are habits and emotional memories. Thus, Ribot's Law refers to progressive amnesia as a temporal gradient going from the most recent to the oldest memories. For Ribot this law implied that memory depends upon permanent modifications and organization of neurons, and it is their disorganization that leads to amnesia. Ribot's Law considers only one type of memory, defined by a double capacity of conservation and of reproduction of certain states (for example, a skill); the recognition and localization in the past that are carried by consciousness are exclusively psychological and do not constitute memory. Ribot applied his law to aphasias, which he regarded as partial amnesias.

Ribot's influence was significant because it represented the beginnings of pathological psychology, which included neuropsychology. Two of his students influenced psychology: Pierre Janet, who succeeded him at the Collège de France, and Alfred Binet. Ribot's biological concepts led the philosopher Henri Bergson to write *Matière et mémoire* (1896).

REFERENCES

Centenaire de Th. Ribot. Jubilé de la psychologie scientifique française 1839–1889–1939. (1939). Agen: Imprimerie Moderne.

Dugas, L. (1924). *Le philosophe Théodule Ribot.* Paris: Payot.

Gasser, J. (1988). La notion de mémoire organique dans l'oeuvre de T. Ribot. *History and Philosophy in Life Sciences 10,* 293–313.

Ribot, T. (1881). *Les maladies de la mémoire.* Paris: Baillière.

—— (1883). *Les maladies de la volonté.* Paris: Baillière.

—— (1885). *Les maladies de la personnalité.* Paris: Alcan.

—— (1889). *La psychologie de l'attention.* Paris: Alcan.

—— (1896). *La psychologie des sentiments.* Paris: Alcan.

—— (1897). *L'évolution des idées générales.* Paris: Alcan.

—— (1900). *L'imagination créatrice.* Paris: Alcan.

—— (1905). *La logique des sentiments.* Paris: Alcan.

—— (1907). *Essai sur les passions.* Paris: Alcan.

—— (1910). *Problèmes de psychologie affective.* Paris: Alcan.

—— (1914). *La vie inconsciente et les mouvements.* Paris: Alcan.

Jean-Louis Signoret

RIGHT HEMISPHERE

See Material-Specific Memory Deficits

S

SAVANT SYNDROME

Savant syndrome (formerly called idiot savant syndrome) refers to an exceedingly rare but remarkable condition in which persons with severe mental handicaps have some isolated but spectacular islands of genius or brilliance that stand in stark, incongruous contrast with the serious limitations of the overall handicaps. The mental handicap can be either autism or MENTAL RETARDATION. The skills, remarkable as they are, exist within a very narrow range of human abilities. They include music (usually piano); art (drawing or sculpting); calendar calculating (the ability to give the day of the week for any past or future date); lightning calculating (the ability to add, multiply, subtract, or divide complex numbers with lightning rapidity); and mechanical or spatial skills including map memorizing, visual measurement, unusual sensory discrimination such as enchanced sense of touch and smell, or perfect appreciation of time without knowledge of a clock. These skills, within these very narrow bands, are always linked to a spectacular memory.

In some persons (*talented savants*) the skills are remarkable simply in contrast with the handicap; in others (*prodigious savants*) the abilities are spectacular in contrast with the handicap and would be spectacular even if they occurred in normal persons. Savant syndrome can be hereditary or it can be acquired following central nervous system injury before, during, or after birth. It occurs in males approximately six times more frequently than in females. The skills can appear suddenly, without explanation, and can disappear just as suddenly.

The condition was first described in 1887 by J. Langdon Down (better known for having described Down syndrome). He was struck by the paradox of deficiency and superiority in a number of cases he saw as superintendent of a hospital in England. At that time in Britain the word *idiot* was an accepted legal classification for a severe degree of mental retardation and did not have the pejorative, comical connotation the term now has. Down combined that word with the term *savant*—knowledgeable person—derived from the French word *savoir* (to know), to denote these fascinating persons. The term is a misnomer in that almost all cases have an IQ of 40 or above, and thus have moderate rather than the severe mental retardation that now-archaic legal term *idiot* once defined.

Superior memory is a trait all savants share. It is a particular type of memory, however: very deep but within a very narrow area; concrete and not richly associative; direct and nonsymbolic; nonemotional and seemingly automatic or unconscious. This "memory without reckoning" may be akin to what Mishkin, Malamut, and Bachevalier (1984) refer to as "habit" memory, as opposed to "cognitive" memory; it relies on a brain circuitry that is more primitive and lower than the later-developed, higher brain circuitry of cognitive or associative memory. In the savant this unconscious memory presumably is relied upon as an alternative pathway to damaged higher-level cognitive memory circuitry.

There has been no well-designed study of the prevalence of savant syndrome, but it has been reported to occur in 1 out of 2,000 in an institutionalized mentally retarded population and in as many as 1 out of 10 autistic persons. Mental retardation and autism are both developmental disabilities, but since autism is so much less common than mental retardation, the number of savants is generally evenly divided between those with autism and those with mental retardation. In the movie *Rain Man,* the character Raymond Babbit (played by Dustin Hoffman) is the best-known portrayal of a savant, in that instance an autistic savant. It is important to remember, however, that not all autistic persons are savants and not all savants are autistic. The number of prodigious savants worldwide is estimated to be less than fifty as of 1991. Talented savants are, of course, more common; but the savant syndrome overall is still a rare condition.

REFERENCES

Mishkin, M., Malamut, B., and Bachevalier, J. (1984). Memories and habits: Two neural systems. In G. K. Lynch, J. L. McGaugh, and N. M. Weinberger, eds., *Neurobiology of learning and memory.* New York: Guilford Press.

Treffert, D. A. (1988). The idiot savant: A review of the syndrome. *American Journal of Psychiatry 145*(5), 563–572.

—— (1989). *Extraordinary people: Redefining the "idiot savant."* New York: Harper & Row.

—— (1990). *Extraordinary people: Understanding savant syndrome.* New York: Ballantine Books.

Darold A. Treffert

SCHOOL LEARNING

School learning is the process of acquiring knowledge, subject matter, organized information, understanding, and skill from teaching. Schools and teachers provide the conditions designed to foster the learning of these types of information.

Since Socrates tried to teach a slave boy the Pythagorean theorem (Plato, trans. 1924) by having him construct the theorem from his knowledge, rather than by telling him the theorem, teachers and researchers have studied how students acquire, remember, and use knowledge. Plato's emphasis on constructive learning closely resembles modern conceptions of how students learn in school, which emphasize the importance of having students construct meaning by relating new concepts to familiar ideas, called schemata, or to memories of experience, called scripts.

ARISTOTLE (trans. 1964) wrote that students learn information by forming relations or associations between new information and previously learned information or concepts, which are stored in memory as images. He believed that subject matter and other abstract information are logically organized in memory into hierarchies that consist of classes, or general concepts, that are divided into species, or smaller groups (Aristotle, trans. 1928; Kintsch, 1980). Aristotle's ideas about hierarchically organized abstract verbal information closely resemble modern understanding of the organization of SEMANTIC MEMORY. His ideas about associations underlie much of modern thinking about how to increase learning, retention, and understanding in schools through teaching students to associate new and old information using imagery and semantic (abstract-verbal) processes.

Aristotle's ideas influenced school learning in ancient times, when memory training systems (mnemonics) were taught to students, orators, and statesmen (Cicero, trans. 1967) to help them learn and remember concepts, much as they are still taught today in memory training courses. In the Middle Ages, Aristotle's ideas about forming associations between new and familiar concepts influenced the widespread use of statues, paintings, mosaics, and murals to relate different and abstract moral concepts to familiar contexts. Modern conceptions of school learning as association building, and knowledge acquisition as the construction of hierchically organized relations between new and old information, still reflect these ancient ideas of Aristotle. The modern conception of school learning as the process of learners generating these relations between new information presented in school and old information stored in students' memories shows the influence of Plato's writings about constructive learning and Aristotle's writings about association building.

How Students Learn in School

Recent research in educational psychology, cognitive psychology, and neuropsychology helps us to understand how memory, knowledge acquisition, attention, learning strategies, and metacognition (self-control of learning) influence school learning. This research shows the importance of getting students to attend to the information to be learned, to relate it actively to their knowledge and experience, and to use it to solve problems. The research also shows that students can learn "how to learn" (learning strategies) and can learn to control and to monitor their own learning (metacognitive strategies).

Memory

The information students have organized into schemata in their semantic (abstract and verbal) memory, and into scripts in their episodic (concrete and image) memory greatly influences their learning and comprehension. In schools, teaching procedures focus on building relations between these types of information in memory and the new information to be learned. These relations increase memory or comprehension or both.

Learning to Remember Facts

Dates, names, and places, along with other factual information, are often difficult to remember because they seem to have little relation to other information of interest or importance to students. Memory for factual information improves when learners construct relations, even arbitrary ones, between their semantic or episodic memories and the facts to be learned. Mnemonic systems are built on that principle. For example, lists of words can be remembered in order by forming images between the words on the list and mnemonic words organized into a series (e.g., one is a bun, two is a shoe). Capitals of states can be remembered by forming colorful or comic associations between the name of the state and its capital city. For example, to remember Annapolis as the capital of Maryland, picture an apple getting married. The word *Maryland* then cues the image of an apple, which helps one to recall the word *Annapolis*. Although these associations between schema (e.g., marriage) and new information (e.g., name of a capital) are arbitrary, they markedly improve memory of facts (Levin, 1981; 1985). (See also MNEMONIC DEVICES.)

Acquiring Knowledge in School

Knowledge acquisition requires understanding and comprehension of what one has learned. Research on reading comprehension and science learning shows the importance of schemata (Rumelhart, 1980) and student preconceptions (Osborne and Wittrock, 1983; 1985) in determining what students will understand and how their comprehension can be improved. For example, if students read a passage about a house as a home buyer would read it, their comprehension is different than if they read the same passage as a burglar would read it. (See also PROSE RETENTION.)

Elementary school students' preconceptions about how direct current (DC) flows in an electric circuit from a battery to a light bulb influence what they comprehend in science classes (Osborne and Wittrock, 1983). Students who believe there are two currents, one from each side of the battery, flowing in opposite directions to the light bulb, do not understand or believe the scientific explanation of DC current flow, even when ammeters indicate that only one current flows throughout the circuit. Their preconceptions greatly influence their comprehension.

Research on the teaching of comprehension and the acquisition of knowledge in schools shows that students in schools acquire knowledge and increase their comprehension when they generate meanings for information, such as subject matter, stories, and concepts (Wittrock, Marks, and Doctorow, 1975). The student construction of meaning involves associating or relating the new information in a personally meaningful, nonarbitrary way to knowledge and experience (Wittrock, 1990).

The generation of summaries, pictures, inferences, applications, and examples is an effective way to organize the parts of the information to be learned and to relate them to experience and to knowledge stored in memory. Comprehension and understanding seem best facilitated when students construct two types of relations: (1) among the parts of the subject matter and (2) between the subject matter and the learner's knowledge and experience (Wittrock, 1974; 1990). Both verbal processes (e.g., summaries and inferences) and imagery (pictures, graphs, and diagrams) enhance comprehension when students use them to construct these two types of relations.

As with the facilitation of memory of factual information, the student's building of relations between memory and new information enhances school learning. However, with comprehension and understanding, these relations are less arbitrary, more organized, more meaningful, and more integrated with schemata and scripts.

Attention

Recent research in neuropsychology and in cognitive psychology shows the importance of attention in learning in schools, especially of long-term, voluntary attention (i.e., ability to focus one's thoughts over time on themes or concepts, rather than attending short term to sudden, loud noises or flashing lights). Mentally retarded or learning-disabled children and some hyperactive children show problems in voluntary attention in school, where they have difficulty selectively attending to relevant information and ignoring irrelevant information (Hallahan and Reeve, 1980).

All students, however, need to learn to control their voluntary attention and to focus their thoughts upon relevant school learning tasks. Researchers have developed simple and effective strategies for teaching normal and learning-disabled students to control their voluntary attention in school (e.g., Meichenbaum and Goodman, 1971; Camp, 1980). These strategies teach children to use self-talk in school to control their impulses, to "stop, look and listen" before they act, and to ask themselves "What is my objective?" "Am I working toward my objective?" These attention-directing strategies increase performance of elementary school children on tests of planning, reading comprehension, and ability to control attention (Douglas et al., 1976).

In classrooms, teachers are now beginning to apply knowledge from research on attention to understand better how objectives, questions, and even praise function to increase learning. Objectives and questions direct student attention (Wittrock, 1986). Praise directs students who observe it to the teacher's objectives and desires (Brophy, 1981).

Research on attention has improved understanding of how students and teachers can direct learners' thoughts to the problems of constructing meaning from information presented in schools.

(See also ATTENTION AND MEMORY.)

Learning Strategies and Metacognition

Learning strategies are procedures for constructing relations across concepts and between new information and experience and knowledge (e.g., constructing summaries, inferences, and pictures). Metacognition is awareness of and control over one's thoughts (e.g., planning to use an attention strategy, or thinking about how you try to comprehend a subject and how you decide to use a better method of comprehension). Learning strategies and metacognition often produce large increases in comprehension and knowledge acquisition (Palincsar and Brown, 1984; Weinstein and Mayer,

1986; Wittrock, 1986). These increases occur when students learn to plan and to monitor their thinking and studying, to control their attention, and to use comprehension strategies, such as analogy building and summarization. Although these sophisticated self-control strategies are not yet widely used in schools, they offer promise for improving learning through teaching students effective ways to attend to subject matter and to construct meaning for it.

Summary

Modern research has greatly enhanced understanding of school learning. The cognitive processes involved in memory, attention, knowledge acquisition, learning strategies, and metacognition are being studied and their results applied to the improvement of school learning. Research in these areas demonstrates in laboratories and in schools the power and the utility of these ideas for improving teaching and learning.

Unfortunately, many of these ideas have only recently begun to influence teachers and teaching practices. Greater emphasis is needed in school learning on the teaching of comprehension through constructive learning processes, on the focusing of attention through strategies of attention control, and on the self-control of learning through strategies of metacognition.

Ancient writings of Plato and Aristotle about constructive learning and association building and modern scientific research on memory and knowledge acquisition complement each other. Both the ancient writings and the modern research indicate that school learning is the process of constructing meaning for new information by attending to it, organizing it, and relating it to one's knowledge and experience.

REFERENCES

Aristotle (1928). *The works of Aristotle,* vol. 1, W. D. Ross, ed. Oxford: Clarendon Press.

———— (1964). On memory and recollection. In *On the soul (De anima); Parva naturalia; and On breath,* W. S. Hett, trans. Cambridge, Mass.: Harvard University Press.

Brophy, J. E. (1981). Teacher praise: A functional analysis. *Review of Educational Research 51,* 5–32.

Camp, B. W. (1980). Two psychoeducational treatment programs for young aggressive boys. In C. K. Whalen and B. Henker, eds., *Hyperactive children, the social ecology of identification and treatment*, pp. 191–279. New York: Academic Press.

Cicero. (1967). *De oratore*, E. W. Sutton, ed. Cambridge, Mass.: Harvard University Press.

Douglas, V. I., Parry, P., Martin, P., and Garson, C. (1976). Assessment of a cognitive training program for hyperactive children. *Journal of Abnormal Child Psychology 4*, 389–410.

Hallahan, D. P., and Reeve, R. E. (1980). Selective attention and distractibility. In B. K. Keogh, ed., *Advances in special education*, pp. 141–181. Greenwich, Conn.: JAI Press.

Kintsch, W. (1980). Semantic memory: A tutorial. In R. S. Nickerson, ed., *Attention and performance*, vol. 8. Hillsdale, N.J.: Erlbaum.

Levin, J. R. (1981). On functions of pictures in prose. In F. J. Pirozzolo and M. C. Wittrock, eds., *Neuropsychological and cognitive processes of reading*. New York: Academic Press.

———— (1985). Educational applications of mnemonic pictures: Possibilities beyond your wildest imagination. In A. A. Sheikh and K. S. Sheikh, eds., *Imagery in education*. Farmingdale, N.Y.: Baywood.

Meichenbaum, D., and Goodman, J. (1971). Training impulsive children to talk to themselves: A means of developing self-control. *Journal of Abnormal Psychology 77*, 115–126.

Osborne, R. J., and Wittrock, M. C. (1983). Learning science: A generative process. *Science Education 67* (4), 489–504.

———— (1985). The generative learning model and its implications for science education. *Studies in Science Education 12*, 59–87.

Palincsar, A. S., and Brown, A. L. (1984). Reciprocal teaching of comprehension-fostering and monitoring activities. *Cognition and Instruction 1*, 117–175.

Plato (trans. 1924). Meno. In W. R. M. Lamb, ed., *Plato*, pp. 265–377. Loeb Classical Library. Cambridge, Mass.: Harvard University Press.

Rumelhart, D. E. (1980). Schemata: The building blocks of cognition. In R. J. Spiro, B. C. Bruce, and W. F. Brewer, eds., *Theoretical issues in reading comprehension*, pp. 33–59. Hillsdale, N.J.: Erlbaum.

Weinstein, C. E., and Mayer, R. (1986). The teaching of learning strategies. In M. C. Wittrock, ed., *Handbook of research on teaching*, 3rd ed., pp. 315–327. New York: Macmillan.

Wittrock, M. C. (1974). Learning as a generative process. *Educational Psychologist 11*, 87–95.

———— (1986). Students' thought processes. In M. C. Wittrock, ed., *Handbook of research on teaching*, 3rd ed., pp. 297–314. New York: Macmillan.

———— (1990). Generative processes of comprehension. *Educational Psychologist 24*, 345–376.

Wittrock, M. C., Marks, C. B., and Doctorow, M. J. (1975).

Reading as a generative process. *Journal of Educational Psychology 67*, 484–489.

M. C. Wittrock

SECOND MESSENGER SYSTEMS

All cells of the body respond to their environment. For most *mature* cell types, the responses can both be general and be related to the cell's particular function. A general response is to regulate the utilization of sugar: When sugar is plentiful, glucose is polymerized to glycogen, a storage form. When sugar is scarce, the biochemistry of the cells will be changed so that glycogen is broken down to make sugar available. Stimulation of gland cells to release their secretions is an example of a response related to a mature cell's specialized function. In *developing* cells, changes occur in rate of cell division, in motility, and in the formation of specific subcellular parts. These changes are also responses to signals from neighboring cells or from elsewhere in the environment. In neurons (see GUIDE TO THE ANATOMY OF THE BRAIN) the *specialized* functions changed are (1) properties of ion channels; (2) availability of synaptic vesicles for exocytosis, a process called *mobilization*; and (3) responsiveness of postsynaptic receptors.

In both mature and developing cells, many of these responses, both general and specialized, are produced by signal transduction, a process in which an extracellular stimulus activates a specific receptor on the surface of the responding cell. As a consequence, the receptor initiates changes in the biochemical state of the cell through the production of a substance that, in turn, causes the cell's responsiveness to be altered. This modulating substance is called a *second messenger* because it is evoked by an environmental cue (the first messenger). The process is called *signal transduction* because the external stimulus is recoded (transduced) into the change in biochemical state. Although ionized calcium (Ca^{2+}) is often thought of as a second messenger, it may be more instructive to call it a *primary regulator*. Along with membrane potential, it is the ultimate governor of neuronal excitability and synaptic transmission.

Historically, formulation of the concepts and principles for understanding second messenger systems arose from studies of two distinct physiological processes: regulation of sugar metabolism in muscle and fat cells and the conversion of light energy into nerve impulses in rod cells of the retina. In the 1950s, Sutherland and Rall (1957) discovered the first second messenger, cyclic adenosine monophosphate (cAMP), and he and his coworkers identified the enzymatic pathway by which cAMP is synthesized and how it brings about the changes in sugar metabolism. At about the same time, Wald (1959) investigated how rhodopsin converts the energy of a photon into a chemical signal; the enzymatic and electrophysiological events in phototransduction were then identified. We now know that both these processes are mediated by proteins encoded by genes that are closely related phylogenetically, and that operate by similar mechanisms.

Production of Second Messenger Molecules

Second messenger systems make use of similar protein constituents. They are initiated when an external cue—most often a neurotransmitter, a hormone, an odorant, a physical stimulus such as light, or a mechanical force—reacts with a receptor. These molecules, which are single polypeptide chains, characteristically have seven membrane-spanning domains. Although these receptors have several regions on the external surface of the responding cell, the actual binding site for the first messenger is slightly buried within the membrane. Some of the receptor is situated on the intracellular side of the membrane; a part of this intracellular domain associates with another protein, called a G-protein because it binds a guanosine nucleotide (GDP or GTP).

The receptors that usually mediate signal transduction are closely related members of a large gene family that, in addition to rhodopsin, contains adrenergic receptors, muscarinic acetylcholine receptors, and receptors for serotonin, dopamine, histamine, and all neuropeptides. G-proteins belong to another large gene family. They are made up of three subunits ($\alpha\beta\gamma$). The α subunit binds GDP when associated with a receptor that has not been activated by an external stimulus; it binds GTP when the receptor is activated. More than a dozen α subunits have been identified, each of which interacts with different receptors. There are fewer isoforms of the β and γ subunits.

When the α subunit binds GTP because of receptor activation, it dissociates from the $\beta\gamma$ portion of the protein. Depending on the particular combination of receptor and G-protein, the dissociated α subunit either activates or inhibits the next constituent of the second messenger system, which can be called a *primary effector*. If the α subunit is stimulatory, its association with the primary effector results in synthesis of a second messenger.

The cAMP system is the best-understood intracellular signaling pathway. Binding of a neurotransmitter—for example, norepinephrine to the β_1-adrenergic receptor—activates a stimulatory G-protein (G_s), which promotes the synthesis of cAMP from adenosine triphosphate (ATP) by adenylyl cyclase. This primary effector enzyme, which also is a complex membrane-spanning protein, operates only when associated with an α_s subunit with bound GTP.

The α_s-cyclase complex also acts as a GTPase, an enzymatic activity that hydrolyzes the bound GTP to GDP and P_i. When GTP is replaced by GDP, the α_s subunit dissociates from the cyclase and reassociates with the receptor, to be activated again. Some receptors—for example, the muscarinic acetylcholine receptor—interact with an inhibitory G-protein (G_i). The α_i subunit, when activated by the muscarinic receptor, associates with adenylyl cyclase to inhibit synthesis of cAMP. The opposing actions of norepinephrine and acetylcholine on the cyclase through G_s and G_i represent one form of second messenger interaction called *cross-talk*.

An important functional aspect of signal transduction pathways, inherent in the arithmetic of the relationships among these constituents (receptor/G-protein/primary effector), is amplification of the external stimulus. Amplification occurs because a neuron has far fewer receptors than G-proteins and primary effectors. It therefore takes relatively few stimulated receptors to activate many primary effectors. Since primary effectors are enzymes that produce the second messenger catalytically, this step amplifies the signal even further.

What Second Messengers Do

Second messengers activate *secondary effectors*, enzymes that are protein kinases in most instances. Typically these enzymes, which catalyze the transfer of the terminal (γ) phosphoryl group of ATP to hydroxyl groups of serine or threonine residues in proteins, are multifunctional: They can phosphorylate many different protein substrates. Phosphorylation of these proteins, which can be called *secondary regulators*, changes their properties either to stimulate or to inhibit their function. These changes in the activity of the substrates are the means by which the responses to the environmental stimulus are produced. For example, phosphorylation of a channel protein can alter the flux of ions into the neuron to raise or lower the membrane potential. Whether a substrate can be phosphorylated depends on the amino acid sequences around the serine and threonine residues in the protein: Each type of kinase prefers special sequences. Often more than one type of protein kinase phosphorylates the same protein. The phosphorylations then occur at different sites in the substrate molecule, however.

Serine/threonine protein kinases exist in several isoforms in the same neuron. For each second messenger, the isoforms of the kinase are closely related, some encoded by the same genes with diversity produced by alternative RNA splicing, and some encoded by distinct but closely related genes. The protein kinases for each of these second messenger systems are also related to the kinases for the others; these, in turn, are related to other protein kinases, including tyrosine-specific kinases, that phosphorylate proteins on the hydroxyl group of tyrosine residues. They also are related to many kinases that phosphorylate only a special protein substrate (for example, β-adrenergic receptor kinase) or kinases that are present in only a few kinds of neurons (for example, the cGMP-dependent protein kinase). The family of cAMP-dependent protein kinases (PKA) was the first to be described. These kinases consist of two regulatory (R) subunits and two catalytic (C) subunits. (There are two major types of R subunits, R^I and R^{II}, and several isoforms of C.) The PKAs illustrate how all second messenger kinases are regulated: The common mechanism of activation is through binding of the second messenger to the regulatory portions of the kinase.

With PKA, the inactive kinase is activated when the concentration of cAMP is elevated within the cell according to the reaction

$$R_2C_2 + 4\text{ cAMP} \rightleftarrows 2(R - 2\text{cAMP}) + 2C.$$

The two R subunits each bind two molecules of cAMP and dissociate from the C subunits, which then are free to phosphorylate protein substrates.

The free C subunits are enzymatically active until the concentration of cAMP within the cell falls, which results in the dissociation of the cAMP bound to the R subunits. Lacking cAMP, R subunits reassociate with C subunits, thereby inactivating the enzyme.

Inositol Polyphosphates and Diacylglycerol

Many receptors activate phospholipase C (PLC) through other G-proteins. PLC catalyzes the hydrolysis of phospholipids in the external membrane of the responding cell. Phospholipids consist of a glycerol moiety esterified at the first (*sn 1* position) and second (*sn 2*) hydroxyl groups to fatty acids, and at its third, to a diester of phosphoric acid and one of four special alcohols (inositol in phosphatidylinositol, PI; choline in PC; ethanolamine in PE; and serine in PS). In PI of nervous tissue, the fatty acid at the *sn 1* position is usually stearic (an 18-carbon saturated fatty acid); the second hydroxyl is usually esterified to arachidonic acid, an unsaturated 20-carbon fatty acid.

The PLC activated in this second messenger system is a diesterase that hydrolyzes PI to an inositol phosphate and diacylglycerol (DAG). Inositol is an unsaturated six-membered cyclic polyalcohol that, in addition to the phosphoryl linkage, can be phosphorylated at hydroxyl groups on the other five carbons. Most often the fourth and fifth hydroxyl groups are phosphorylated in the inositol moiety of nerve cells (PIP_2). When hydrolyzed by PLC, it is therefore called inositol 1,4,5-trisphosphate (IP_3), a water-soluble second messenger. Other inositol polyphosphates exist, but it is not yet certain whether they, too, act as second messengers. Diacylglycerol, which is soluble only in lipid, remains within the membrane and also serves as a second messenger.

Protein kinase C, another multifunctional enzyme, is activated by DAG. (Phorbol esters, cancer-promoting substances from plants, act as potent pharmacological analogues of DAG.) There now are eight isoforms of PKC known. All require the presence of membrane lipid, notably PS, to be active. The PKCs form two groups, Ca^{2+}-dependent (or *major*: α, $β_I$, b_{II}, and γ) and Ca^{2+}-independent (or *minor*: δ, ε, ζ, and η). The functional significance of this variety is not yet known, but structural diversity is presumed to cause differences in substrate specificity and subcellular localization. Unlike PKA, the regulatory and catalytic regions of PKCs are both parts of a single polypeptide chain.

The catalytic part is masked by the regulatory domain. When a lipid activator and membrane (and Ca^{2+} for the major forms) bind to the regulatory domain of the enzyme, its conformation changes, exposing the catalytic part of the kinase for action. The dependence of the major PKC isoforms on Ca^{2+} is an important instance of the complexity of regulation by second messengers. In the pathway involving PLC, both DAG *and* IP_3 are formed. The function of IP_3 as a second messenger is to bind an intracellular receptor that is located on the cytoplasmic surface of the endoplasmic reticulum. When this receptor is activated, stored Ca^{2+} is released, thereby raising the intracellular concentration of the free ion.

Ca^{2+} is required for the action of many enzymes in neurons, either as the free ion or complexed to calmodulin, a small protein that can bind four Ca^{2+} ions. In addition to the major forms of PKC, Ca^{2+} is required by some forms of adenylyl cyclase, guanylyl cyclase, PLC, phospholipase A_2 (PLA_2), 5-lipoxygenase, some protein phosphatases, and one other kinase, Ca^{2+}/calmodulin-dependent protein kinase II. This multifunctional kinase, like the PKCs, is a single polypeptide chain containing both regulatory and catalytic domains. Unlike either of the other kinases, however, it exists in the cell as a complex of several individual kinase molecules, the exact number varying with the type of cell and with the location within the neuron. This enzyme is quite abundant but is highly concentrated in the postsynaptic region of neurons that is called the *postsynaptic density*.

Arachidonic Acid

PLA_2, which hydrolyzes PI at the *sn 2* position to release arachidonic acid, also is activated by a G-protein-coupled receptor for histamine and other neurotransmitters.

The arachidonic acid produced by receptor-mediated activation of PLA_2 can serve as a second messenger in two systems: Arachidonic acid can replace DAG as a lipid activator of one isoform of PKC, PKC-γ. It also is converted into many metabolites, some of which alter synaptic transmission and neuronal excitability. For example, 12-lipoxygenase produces 12-hydroperoxyeicosanoic acid (12-HPETE), which is further metabolized to substances that can modulate the function of ion channels. These substances, called *eicosanoids,* have the interesting property of being able to cross the cell's membrane readily. It is attractive to think that some eicosanoids might act as transcellular or retrograde messengers.

Degradation of Second Messengers

cAMP and cGMP are rapidly degraded by several different phosphodiesterases. There are many phosphodiesterase inhibitors that prolong the action of these cyclic nucleotides, including the naturally occurring caffeine and theophylline. Some of these degradative enzymes can also be secondary effectors—for example, in rod cells, where receptor-activated G-proteins activate a cGMP-phosphodiesterase. The second messengers derived from membrane phospholipids are inactivated by being reincorporated into the membrane. IP_3 is dephosphorylated by several phosphatases, one of which is blocked by Li^+ ion. This inhibition is thought to be important for the effectiveness of Li^+ in the treatment of bipolar depression.

Although the individual protein substrates phosphorylated by the various protein kinases are discussed elsewhere (see MEMBRANE CHANNELS AND THEIR MODULATION IN LEARNING AND MEMORY), it is important to point out that they exist only transiently, since there are at least four different types of protein phosphatases that remove phosphoryl groups from the proteins.

Cross-Talk

Second messenger systems typically consist of a receptor coupled to a G-protein that activates a primary effector enzyme to produce the second messenger. Each second messenger activates a secondary effector enzyme, often a protein kinase, to phosphorylate protein substrates that can be called secondary regulators. The usual points of cross-talk are the actions of secondary effector enzymes on receptors, primary effector enzymes, and secondary regulators. For the most part, there is little cross-talk between primary effector enzymes.

Variations of Signal Transduction Pathways

Although the typical second messenger system consists of all of the constituents described, there are examples in which one or more of them is absent. In some instances the receptor-activated G-protein itself acts directly on a secondary regulator—for example, in heart muscle cells, where the G-protein modulates an ion channel without any intervening constituents. Guanylyl cyclase can be activated by nitric oxide, a short-lived substance that penetrates the membrane without using a receptor/G-protein complex. Nitric oxide is formed in one neuron from the amino acid arginine, as a consequence of the activation of the enzyme nitric oxide synthetase (which requires reduced nicotinamide adenine dinucleotide phosphate and Ca^{2+} ions) through a second messenger pathway. Nitric oxide is unusual because it does not act as a second messenger in the neuron in which it is synthesized, but in a neighboring nerve cell. The possibility that eicosanoids may act transcellularly as second messengers has already been mentioned; in this way they also would bypass receptor, G-protein, and primary effector enzyme. Finally, some secondary effector enzymes are linked directly to their own special receptor through the membrane; important examples of this kind of signaling are tyrosine-specific protein kinases.

(See also NEUROTRANSMITTER SYSTEMS AND MEMORY.)

REFERENCES

Casey, P. J., and Gilman, A. G. (1988). G protein involvement in receptor-effector coupling. *Journal of Biological Chemistry 263*, 2577–2580.

Colbran, R. J., and Soderling, T. R. (1990). Calcium/calmodulin-dependent protein kinase II. *Current Topics in Cellular Regulation 31*, 181–221.

Dennis, E. A., ed. (1991). *Methods in enzymology: Phospholipases.* New York: Academic Press.

Frielle, T., Kobilka, B., Dohlman, H., Caron, M. G., and Lefkowitz, R. J. (1989). The β-adrenergic receptor and other receptors coupled to guanine nucleotide regulatory proteins. In S. Chien, ed., *Molecular biology in physiology*, pp. 79–91. New York: Raven Press.

Kaczmarek, L. K., and Levitan, I. B. (1987). *Neuromodulation: The biochemical control of neuronal excitability.* New York: Oxford University Press.

Kikkawa, U., Kishimoto, A., and Nishizuka, Y. (1989). The protein kinase C family: Heterogeneity and its implications. *Annual Review of Biochemistry 58*, 31–44.

Majerus, P. W., Connolly, T. M., Bansal, V. S., Inhorn, R. C., Ross, T. S., and Lips, D. L. (1988). Inositol phosphates: Synthesis and degradation. *Journal of Biological Chemistry 263*, 3051–3054.

Nathanson, N. M., and Harden, T. K., eds. (1990). *G*

proteins and signal transduction. Society of General Physiologists Series, vol. 45. New York: Rockefeller University Press.

Nestler, E. J., and Greengard, P. (1984). *Protein phosphorylation in the nervous system.* New York: Wiley.

Role, L. W., and Schwartz, J. H. (1989). Cross-talk between signal transduction pathways. *Trends in Neuroscience 12*, centerfold.

Schwartz, J. H., and Kandel, E. R. (1991). Synaptic transmission mediated by second messengers. Chap. 12 in E. R. Kandel, J. H. Schwartz, and T. M. Jessell, eds., *Principles of neuroscience*, 3rd ed. New York: Elsevier.

Shapiro, E., Piomelli, D., Feinmark, S., Vogel, S. S., Chin, G. J., and Schwartz, J. H. (1988). The role of arachidonic acid metabolites in signal transduction in an identified neural network mediating presynaptic inhibition in *Aplysia. Cold Spring Harbor Symposia in Quantitative Biology 53*, 425–433.

Sutherland, E., and Rall, T. W. (1957). Isolation of cyclic AMP. *Journal of the American Chemical Society 79*, 3608.

Taylor, S. S., Buechler, J. A., and Yonemoto, W. (1990). cAMP-dependent protein kinase: Framework for a diverse family of regulatory enzymes. *Annual Review of Biochemistry 59*, 971–1005.

Wald, G. (1959). Life and light. *Scientific American 201*, 92–108.

James H. Schwartz

SEMANTIC MEMORY

Semantic memory is our knowledge of the world. It is contrasted with EPISODIC MEMORY, our knowledge of our personal experience (Tulving, 1983). Although semantic memory was originally conceptualized as our knowledge of the language (Tulving, 1972), it is now commonly used to refer to our everyday knowledge of the world and includes such facts as "Robins are birds," "Trolleys are larger than shoes," "Chairs have legs," and "Fireworks are dangerous." Semantic memory has been thought by some (Tulving and Schacter, 1990) to be a functionally separate memory system, distinct from episodic memory and perhaps from other types of memory. However, it appears that such a distinction is premature at this juncture (McKoon, Ratcliff, and Dell, 1986; Shoben and Ross, 1986). There is not sufficient evidence to conclude that we have more than one long-term memory system.

Research in semantic memory can be divided

into three categories concerning our knowledge of concepts: First, we know that concepts belong to various categories. Second, we know that concepts have certain properties and bear certain relations to other concepts. Third, we know that concepts can be combined with other concepts.

Categorical Knowledge

Categorical knowledge is the most studied area in semantic memory. As a consequence, there are a number of robust findings in this area. First, there is a *typicality* effect (Rosch, 1975). Items that are good examples of a category are more readily verified as members than are poor examples. For example, people decide that "robins are birds" more rapidly than they decide that "chickens are birds."

The typicality effect has its counterpart for false statements. The *relatedness* effect (Smith, Shoben, and Rips, 1974) is the finding that false statements are easier to disconfirm if subject and predicate are unrelated than if subject and predicate are related. Thus, for example, "A goose is a mammal" is more difficult to disconfirm than "A goose is a tool." Like the typicality effect, this finding is quite robust and exceptions to it are rare.

Other effects are more controversial and are reviewed in detail elsewhere (Chang, 1986). For example, it has often been argued that there is a *category size* effect (Wilkins, 1972) in semantic memory in which it is harder to confirm membership in a large category than it is in a smaller one. However, reversals of this finding do occur, so the effect appears weak, if it exists at all. Moreover, it is also usually the case that size is manipulated such that larger categories tend to be at a higher level of abstraction than smaller categories (for example, "tool" and "implement").

Many believe that there are effects of familiarity (McCloskey, 1980) on semantic memory decisions. Some early research demonstrated that people are faster at categorizing objects familiar to them. In fact, it was suggested that familiarity might underlie the effects of typicality. For example, North American subjects judge "robin" as much more typical than "lark" of the category "bird," although there is no reason why that would be so. However, subsequent work has demonstrated that familiarity cannot be the whole story (Malt and Smith, 1982).

Finally, it is clear that there are context effects in semantic memory. Some early findings indicated that the size of the typicality effect, for example, varies as a function of the proportion of related false statements among the test stimuli (McCloskey and Glucksberg, 1979). Other studies have shown that what is a typical member of a semantic category can vary, depending upon a variety of circumstances. For example, it appears that what is a typical bird to a resident of south Florida depends upon whether that resident is Hispanic (Schwanenflugel and Rey, 1986). Similarly, people are adept at adopting various points of view. People who are asked to take the perspective of a South American, for example, will judge the typicality of various birds quite differently than will people who have adopted their own perspective (Barsalou, 1987). Finally, specification of particular contexts will cause variations in typicality (Roth and Shoben, 1983). For example, people told that "Each morning the secretaries drank the beverage during their break" found "tea" a better example of "beverage" than "milk." However, "milk" was a better example than "tea" in the context "The truck driver liked the beverage with his donut."

Theoretical Concerns

The question of how this categorical information is represented in memory remains unresolved. Some early theorists suggested that semantic memory could be viewed as a hierarchical tree or semantic network (Collins and Quillian, 1969; Holyoak and Glass, 1975) in which concepts such as "robin" and "canary" would be represented at the bottom of the tree with links from both extending up to "bird." Others espoused a componential approach in which concepts were represented as sets of properties or semantic features. Semantic decisions were made by a comparison of these features or properties (Smith, Shoben, and Rips, 1974; McCloskey and Glucksberg, 1979). In fact, neither of these approaches is likely to account for all of the available data (Chang, 1986). Models based on semantic features, for example, have difficulty accounting for effects of familiarity, because if only features are compared, there is no reason why decisions about familiar concepts should be made more rapidly. Analogously, network models have trouble with the disconfirmation of false statements because the links in a network provide no information about whether a relation is false. More recent advances have demonstrated that retrieval of information occurs continuously in time as opposed to in discrete stages (Kounios, Osman, and Meyer, 1987), but the nature of the verification process remains unclear.

Judgments of Relative Magnitude

Although there have been some direct investigations of how people process information about properties of concepts, most of the work on this question has been concerned with how people make judgments of relative magnitude, such as "Are rabbits larger than mice?" This research has produced some solid empirical findings and some theoretical squabbles. In the study of categorical information, judgments of relative magnitude have received less attention, which is surprising because people probably know as much relational information as they do categorical information.

Empirical Findings

The oldest and most robust finding in the literature is the *symbolic distance effect*. Objects that are further apart on some dimension are more readily discriminated than objects that are closer together (Moyer, 1973). For example, it is easier to determine that "Desks are larger than strawberries" than that "Desks are larger than dogs."

A second finding is that judgments are easier when the form of the comparative matches the magnitude of the objects, small or large (Banks, 1977). An example of this *congruity effect* is that it is easier to determine that "Elephants are larger than rhinos" than to determine that "Rhinos are smaller than elephants." At the same time, it is easier to say that "Raspberries are smaller than passports" than to say that "Passports are larger than raspberries."

A more recent finding is the *bowed serial position effect*: objects of intermediate magnitude are more difficult to discriminate than objects of extreme magnitude (Shoben et al., 1989). For example, it is more difficult to select the larger of "wolf" and "pig" than to select the larger of either "toad"

and "snail" or of "bull" and "elephant." Obviously, experiments such as these must be done with symbolic distance held constant.

Like decisions about categorical information, judgments of relative magnitude are subject to context effects. In standard experiments, pairs such as "rabbit-beaver" are discriminated more readily under the instruction to select the smaller item than under the instruction to select the larger item. However, if the context is manipulated such that "rabbit" and "beaver" are the largest items in the study, then this pair is discriminated more rapidly under the instruction to select the *larger* item (Cech and Shoben, 1985). In the context of small items, these concepts suddenly behave as if they are large items.

It also appears that there are effects of categorization difficulty. Some items are difficult to classify as large or small, and others are relatively easy. In general, items of extreme magnitude are readily classified, and items of intermediate magnitude are relatively difficult to judge. This finding is not surprising; however, items of nearly equivalent magnitude can have varying classification times. For example, "raccoon" and "eagle" are nearly equivalent in the existing size norms, but "eagle" takes much longer to classify as small. These effects can be seen in an experiment in which people make judgments about relative magnitude. In one ordering, the items in the order displayed the usual pattern of classification times: extreme items were classified more readily than items of intermediate magnitude. In a second ordering, however, the classification times were nearly uniform across magnitude. For the first ordering with heterogeneous classification times, the usual bowed serial position effect was observed: Extreme pairs were discriminated more readily than intermediate pairs. For the second ordering with homogeneous classification times, however, no bowed serial position effect was found: Pairs of intermediate magnitude were discriminated as readily as pairs of extreme magnitude.

Finally, there are *reference point effects*. If people are asked to determine which of two objects is closer to a third, the task is more difficult if the items are far from the reference point (Holyoak, 1978). Thus, for example, it is easier to determine which is closer to 3, 4 or 5, than which is closer to 3, 6 or 7. Similar results have been obtained for judgments of geographical distance, although no report exists of reference point effects that have used words as stimuli. Thus, it is not clear how general these effects are.

Theories of Relational Information

None of the existing theories of relational information is adequate. Perhaps the most often cited theory is the discrete code model (Moyer, 1973). According to this proposal, people first determine if objects are large or small. These *codes* are then compared. If they are different, then a decision can be made immediately. If they are not, then one must return to memory and, by accessing additional information, fine-tune the codes to "large" and "larger" or "small" and "smaller," as appropriate. Although this model can deal with the symbolic distance, congruity, and categorization effects, it has difficulty with reference point effects and with the bowed serial position effect.

In contrast with this kind of linguistic account, there are analogical models (Moyer and Dumais, 1978). According to these models, magnitude information is represented directly, and comparisons are made using a kind of "internal psychophysics," in which the memorial judgment is "just like" one actually holding or seeing the items. Although such models do a good job of accounting for the symbolic distance effect, they do not have any way of dealing easily with the bowed serial position effect, the congruity effect, and others. Some recent formulations, such as the reference point model, do better with some effects, but no current model comes close to accounting for all of them.

Conceptual Combinations

A problem that has received some measure of recent attention is the study of how concepts are combined. Some of these combinations appear superficially simple, while others are clearly more complex. For example, "red ball" can readily be paraphrased as "a ball that is red," but "malarial mosquitos" cannot be paraphrased in similar form; instead, it must be paraphrased as "mosquitos that cause malaria." "Red ball" uses a *predicating* adjective, "red," while "malarial mosquitos" employs the *nonpredicating* adjective "malarial."

Most research on conceptual combinations has been done with predicating adjectives. One funda-

mental question is how people determine membership in combined categories. For example, "A cardinal is a red bird" is clearly true, because a cardinal is clearly both a red thing and a bird. At the same time, "A female cardinal is a red bird" is only partly true, because although a female cardinal is clearly a bird, it is only somewhat red. Such concerns might lead us to propose a *min rule:* An exemplar is a member of a combined category only to the minimum degree that it is a member of the category defined by the adjective and the category specified by the noun.

Although this rule makes intuitive sense at some level, there are counterexamples. For example, "A guppy is a pet fish" is clearly true; guppies are perhaps the paradigmatic example of the category "pet fish." At the same time, guppies are not good examples of pets, nor are they particularly good examples of fish. Besides this linguistic argument, empirical judgments of subjects also show clear violations of the min rule (Smith and Osherson, 1984).

In addition, there are clear indications that a simple model which assumes that combinations change only one value of one attribute of the noun will not work. For example, one might assume that the difference between "an apple" and "a red apple" is that the color dimension is unambiguously specified as "red" in the latter case, whereas "apple" may admit several values. However, one can demonstrate that such an approach will not work in many cases. For example, people regard "metal spoon," rather than "wooden spoon," as a better example of the category "spoon," suggesting that the materials dimension of "spoon" has more values indicating metal than wood. However, if we change the concept to "large spoon," this preference reverses; now "wooden spoon" is judged as more typical than "metal spoon." This pattern of preferences demonstrates that the representations for "spoon" and "large spoon" differ on more than the size dimension (Medin and Shoben, 1988).

It would thus appear that the representation for conceptual combinations must be relatively complicated. Such complexity is increased when one considers nonpredicating adjectives, such as "criminal lawyer." Phrases involving nonpredicating adjectives have been shown to be more difficult to comprehend (Murphy, 1990). Some work in linguistics (Levi, 1978) has attempted to classify these adjectives into various subcategories (such as causals, as in "malarial mosquitoes," or use relations, as in "oil lamp," or "is" relations, as in "servant girl," and so forth) but the psychological reality of these subcategories has yet to be demonstrated.

Broader Issues

This review has necessarily been selective, with many topics omitted. In closing, however, it should be noted that our knowledge of the world will influence most of the cognitive things that we do. Solving a problem, finding our way, or just reading involves our semantic memory. It is clearly one of the building blocks of cognition.

(See also CONCEPTS AND CATEGORIES, LEARNING OF.)

REFERENCES

Banks, W. P. (1977). Encoding and processing of symbolic information in comparative judgments. In G. H. Bower, ed., *The psychology of learning and motivation*, vol. 11. New York: Academic Press.

Barsalou, L. (1987). The instability of graded structure: Implications for the nature of concepts. In U. Neisser, ed., *Concepts and conceptual development: Ecological and intellectual factors in categorization*, pp. 101–140. Cambridge: Cambridge University Press.

Cech, C. G., and Shoben, E. J. (1985). Context effects in symbolic magnitude comparisons. *Journal of Experimental Psychology: Learning, Memory, and Cognition 11*, 299–315.

Chang, T. M. (1986). Semantic memory: Facts and models. *Psychological Bulletin 99*, 199–220.

Collins, A., and Quillian, M. R. (1969). Retrieval time from semantic memory. *Journal of Verbal Learning and Verbal Behavior 8*, 240–247.

Holyoak, K. J. (1978). Comparative judgments with numerical reference points. *Cognitive Psychology 10*, 203–243.

Holyoak, K. J., and Glass, A. L. (1975). The role of contradictions and counterexamples in the rejection of false sentences. *Journal of Verbal Learning and Verbal Behavior 14*, 215–239.

Kounios, J., Osman, A. M., and Meyer, D. E. (1987). Structure and process in semantic memory: New evidence based on speed-accuracy decomposition. *Journal of Experimental Psychology: General 116*, 3–25.

Levi, J. N. (1978). *The syntax and semantics of complex nominals*. New York: Academic Press.

Malt, B. C., and Smith, E. E. (1982). The role of familiarity in determining typicality. *Memory and Cognition 10*, 69–81.

McCloskey, M. (1980). The stimulus familiarity problem in semantic memory research. *Journal of Verbal Learning and Verbal Behavior 19*, 485–502.

McCloskey, M., and Glucksberg, S. (1979). Decision processes in verifying category membership statements: Implications for models of semantic memory. *Cognitive Psychology 11*, 1–37.

McKoon, G., Ratcliff, R., and Dell, G. S. (1986). A critical evaluation of the semantic-episodic distinction. *Journal of Experimental Psychology: Learning, Memory, and Cognition 12*, 295–306.

Medin, D. L., and Shoben, E. J. (1988). Context and structure in conceptual combination. *Cognitive Psychology 20*, 158–190.

Moyer, R. S. (1973). Comparing objects in memory: Evidence suggesting an internal psychophysics. *Perception and Psychophysics 13*, 180–184.

Moyer, R. S., and Dumais, S. T. (1978). Mental comparison. In G. H. Bower, ed., *The psychology of learning and motivation*, vol. 12. New York. Academic Press.

Murphy, G. L. (1990). Noun phrase interpretation and conceptual combination. *Journal of Memory and Language 29*, 259–288.

Rosch, E. H. (1975). Cognitive representations of semantic categories. *Journal of Experimental Psychology: General 104*, 192–233.

Roth, E. M., and Shoben, E. J. (1983). The effect of context on the structure of categories. *Cognitive Psychology 15*, 346–378.

Schwanenflugel, P. J., and Rey, M. (1986). The relationship between category typicality and concept familiarity: Evidence from Spanish- and English-speaking monolinguals. *Memory and Cognition 14*, 150–163.

Shoben, E. J., Cech, C. G., Schwanenflugel, P. J., and Sailor, K. M. (1989). Serial position effects in comparative judgments. *Journal of Experimental Psychology: Human Perception and Performance 15*, 273–286.

Shoben, E. J., and Ross, B. H. (1986). The crucial role of dissociations. *Behavioral and Brain Sciences 9*, 568–571.

Smith, E. E., and Osherson, D. N. (1984). Conceptual combination with prototype concepts. *Cognitive Science 12*, 485–527.

Smith, E. E., Shoben, E. J., and Rips, L. J. (1974). Structure and process in semantic memory: A featural model for semantic decisions. *Psychological Review 81*, 214–241.

Tulving, E. (1972). Episodic and semantic memory. In E. Tulving and W. Donaldson, eds., *Organization of memory*. New York: Academic Press.

——— (1983). *Elements of episodic memory*. Oxford: Oxford University Press.

Tulving, E., and Schacter, D. L. (1990). Priming and human memory systems. *Science 247*, 301–306.

Wilkins, A. T. (1972). Conjoint frequency, category size, and categorization time. *Journal of Verbal Learning and Verbal Behavior 11*, 382–385.

Edward J. Shoben

SEMON, RICHARD

Richard Wolfgang Semon (1859–1918) is a relatively unknown but nevertheless important figure in the history of research on learning and memory. Although he was little recognized by his contemporaries and is frequently overlooked by memory researchers today, Semon anticipated numerous modern theories and—perhaps ironically—created one of the best-known terms in the memory literature, *engram.*

Semon was born in Berlin on August 22, 1859. His father, Simon, was a stockbroker, and the Semon family became part of the upper echelon of Berlin Jewish society during Richard's childhood. Simon Semon suffered severe losses in the stock market crash of 1873, however, and the family was forced to adopt a much humbler life-style. Semon's older brother, Felix, left Germany after receiving a medical degree and practiced in England, where he became a pioneer of clinical and scientific laryngology.

Figure 1.   Richard Semon.

As a child, Richard Semon expressed strong interest in the study of biology and zoology. He attended the University of Jena, a major European center of biological research, where he received a doctorate in zoology in 1883 and a medical degree in 1886. While at Jena, Semon was strongly influenced by the evolutionary biologist Ernst Haeckel, whose monistic philosophy stressed the importance of attempting to unify diverse biological phenomena with a single set of theoretical principles.

Semon's career as an evolutionary biologist developed rapidly during the 1890s. Shortly after assuming an associate professorship at Jena in 1891, he led a major expedition to Australia in search of the "missing link." The expedition was responsible for the discovery of 207 new species and 24 new genera. After returning from Australia in 1893, Semon continued his research at Jena until 1897, when his life changed dramatically. He became involved with and eventually married Maria Krehl, who was then the wife of an eminent professor of pathology at Jena, Ludolph Krehl. Their relationship caused a scandal in Jena, and Semon resigned his position because of it. He and Maria moved to Munich, where he began working as a private scholar.

Semon wrote two major books on memory during the next 20 years: *Die Mneme* (1904) and *Die mnemischen Empfindungen* (1909). Psychologists paid little attention to his work, and Semon's acute dismay at his lack of recognition is evident in letters written to his colleague and ally, the Swiss psychiatrist August Forel (see Schacter, 1982, for a sampling of the letters and a detailed biography). By 1918, Semon was depressed over the neglect of his work, troubled by Germany's role in World War I, and shattered by his wife's death from cancer. He took his own life on December 27, 1918.

Theory of Memory

To appreciate fully Semon's ideas about human memory, it is necessary to understand the biological context from which they emerged. In his first book, *Die Mneme,* Semon's discussion of human memory was embedded in a more global theory that broadened the construct of memory to include more than simple remembering of facts, events, and the like. Semon argued that phenomena of heredity and reproduction could also be viewed as forms of memory that preserved the effects of experience across generations. He referred to the fundamental process that subserved both heredity and everyday memory with a term of his own creation, *mneme*. According to Semon, mneme is a fundamental organic plasticity that allows the effects of experience to be preserved over time; it is mneme "which in the organic world links the past and present in a living bond" (1921, p. 12).

Semon distinguished three aspects of the mnemic process that he believed are crucial to the analysis of both everyday memory and hereditary memory, and he described them with additional terms of his own invention in order to avoid the potentially misleading connotations of ordinary language: *engraphy, engram,* and *ecphory. Engraphy* refers to the process of encoding information into memory; *engram* refers to the change in the nervous system—the "memory trace"—that preserves the effects of experience over time; and *ecphory* refers to a retrieval process, "the influences which awaken the mnemic trace or engram out of its latent state into one of manifested activity" (Semon, 1921, p. 12). In attempting to apply these constructs to the analysis of hereditary memory—that is, how the experiences of one organism could somehow influence its progeny—Semon encountered a variety of biological phenomena that led him to place great emphasis on the process of ecphory as a crucial determinant of memory.

Semon's rather speculative ideas on hereditary memory were severely criticized because they relied heavily on the discredited doctrine of the inheritance of acquired characteristics, which had been developed by the French biologist Lamarck (Schacter, 1982). However, the concern with ecphoric processes that emerged from this analysis enabled Semon to develop new perspectives on human memory, and he elaborated these ideas without any reference to hereditary phenomena in his second book, *Die mnemischen Empfindungen.* At the time he wrote this book, memory researchers paid virtually no attention to the ecphoric or retrieval stage of memory; their attention was focused almost entirely on processes occurring at the time of engraphy (see Schacter, 1982; Schacter et al., 1978, for further discussion). By

contrast, Semon developed a detailed theory of ecphoric processes, and argued that successful ecphory requires that the conditions prevailing at the time of engraphy be partially reinstated at the time of ecphory. He laid great emphasis on this latter idea, elevating it to a "law of ecphory." This concern with the relation between conditions of engraphy and ecphory rather closely anticipated such modern notions as the encoding specificity principle and transfer-appropriate processing (see RETRIEVAL PROCESSES).

Semon also developed novel ideas about the beneficial effects of repetition on memory. In contrast with the then widely accepted idea that repetition of a stimulus improves memory by strengthening the preexisting engram of that stimulus, Semon argued that each repetition of a stimulus creates a unique, context-specific engram; at the time of ecphory the multiple, separate engrams are combined by a resonance process that Semon termed *homophony.* This multiple-engram approach to repetition effects, with its strong emphasis on ecphoric processes, anticipated a number of recently influential conceptualizations, such as the multiple-trace model developed by Hintzman and colleagues (see Schacter et al., 1978).

Although many of his ideas were prescient, Semon's contemporaries ignored his contributions. This neglect may be attributable partly to his theoretical emphasis on ecphoric processes at a time when few were interested, partly to his social isolation as a private scholar without institutional affiliation, and partly to the fact that his Lamarckian approach to hereditary memory had been belittled. Curiously, the one construct developed by Semon used by subsequent researchers—the engram—did not represent a novel contribution and was one of the less interesting parts of his otherwise innovative theoretical approach.

REFERENCES

Schacter, D. L. (1982). *Stranger behind the engram: Theories of memory and the psychology of science.* Hillsdale, N.J.: Erlbaum.

Schacter, D. L., Eich, J. E., and Tulving, E. (1978). Richard Semon's theory of memory. *Journal of Verbal Learning and Verbal Behavior 17,* 721–743.

Semon, R. (1921). *The mneme.* London: Allen and Unwin. Originally published 1904 as *Die Mneme* (Leipzig: Engelmann).

———— (1923). *Mnemic psychology.* London: Allen and Unwin. Originally published 1909 as *Die mnemischen Empfindungen* (Leipzig: Engelmann).

Daniel L. Schacter

SENILITY

See Alzheimer's Disease; Pharmacological Treatment of Memory Deficits

SENSORY MEMORY

Sensory memory is an agency of information storage that not only carries the mark of the sense modality in which the information originally arrived—*imagery* is the more general term for that—but also carries traces of the sensory processing that was engaged by the experience. Sensory memory is the brain's more or less detailed record of a sensory experience, after it happened. Thus, we can generate a visual image of an object without actually seeing it, but we cannot, thereby, have a sensory memory of it.

Because of the overwhelmingly verbal component of human cognition, a heavy emphasis has been placed on sensory processes that result from the auditory or visual exposure to language materials, perhaps to the neglect of sensory information for nonverbal experiences and for experiences in other modalities, such as nonverbal visual patterns (snowflakes or kaleidoscope designs), nonverbal auditory patterns (voice quality or naturalistic sounds), olfactory memory, or kinesthetic sensations. Each of these has been studied, and must carry a corresponding sensory memory persistence, but most data and theory are from the visual or auditory presentation of verbal materials.

Two theoretical perspectives animate work on memory in general and sensory memory in particular. The *storage position* is that retention of experiences (EPISODIC MEMORY) informs us about the existence of dedicated storage repositories. On this view, evidence for sensory memory in a particular modality defines a sensory store in that modality. Early evidence from the visual modality (Sperling, 1960) suggested such an *iconic store,* and evidence from the auditory modality, a corresponding *echoic store* (Crowder and Morton, 1969). Subsequent

evidence has shown that different techniques for measuring the presumed iconic and echoic stores yield importantly different storage properties. The response of the storage position is to postulate additional memory stores.

The *proceduralist position* (Kolers and Roediger, 1984; Crowder, 1989) denies that information is retained in memory stores as such. Instead, this view proposes that retention is a natural consequence of the information processing that was originally aroused by the experience in question. Accordingly, memory is not a faculty with dedicated stores but, rather, the lingering residue of operations that were engaged by the original event. If two visual experiences, for example, recruit two different kinds of information processing, by virtue of stimulus or task properties, then they may well show two different kinds of retention, not because they are served by different memory stores but because different portions of the nervous system, perhaps anatomically distinct (Farah, 1988), were active in processing the original information.

Thus, the evidence reviewed here may be attributed either to the properties of multiple sensory stores or to the principle that sensory aftereffects will be a function of the sensory machinery originally active. No decision on this question needs to be made beforehand.

Visual Sensory Memory

Iconic Memory

A single publication by Sperling (1960) may be said to have brought, abruptly, both the concept and the methods of visual sensory memory to modern attention. The subjects in Sperling's experiment saw twelve letters (three rows of four) in a brief flash. In a *whole-report* control condition, the subject was asked to report all twelve of the letters presented; in the *partial-report* conditions, a tone indicated which row was to be reported, the pitch of the tone corresponding to the row tested (high, medium, and low tones for first, second, and third rows, respectively). The results showed that subjects had about nine letters available to the visual system if the tone indicating which row to report sounded just as the display went off. People could report an average of three out of the four letters on any row. However, partial-report scores dropped to half that figure, almost exactly the level of whole report, if the cue tone was delayed by 1 second. Coltheart's (1983) review may be consulted for the extraordinary durability of Sperling's demonstration as well as for subsequent findings.

Subjective Persistence

Haber and Standing (1970) briefly showed subjects a 3 × 3 array much like those used in Sperling's experiments. However, the task was to adjust the timing of two auditory clicks to coincide with the apparent onset and offset of the display. The duration of the display varied from 100 to 1,000 milliseconds. By turning a knob, subjects could control the occurrences of two clicks relative to the visual exposure of the display. For a given objective duration, the mean onset adjustment can be subtracted from the mean offset adjustment to arrive at an estimate of how long the display seemed to last. Haber and Standing found that these subjective durations were longer than the objective durations. This is consistent with the suggestion that some form of visual storage follows the termination of the external display. By subtracting the subjective duration from the objective duration, it is possible to estimate the duration of visual sensory memory, and then to compare this estimate with that produced by Sperling's partial-report experiment. Efron (1970) and Di Lollo (1980) arranged alternative procedures to investigate subjective persistence, and arrived at estimates of about 100 milliseconds.

Sakitt (1976) argued that the source of at least some sensory memory in the visual system is in the rod photoreceptors on the retina, making those memories theoretically akin to visual aftereffects. Coltheart (1980) conducted a lengthy review and analysis of the evidence pertinent to Sakitt's proposal of a retinal locus for visual sensory memory. The resolution he proposed distinguishes two sorts of storage in this area, and his distinction has been respected in this review: One type of storage, *visible persistence,* refers to the subjective experience that the stimulus remains available to the visual system after stimulus offset, much in the manner of an afterimage. Coltheart concluded that visible persistence of this sort probably is associated with photoreceptor mechanisms at the retinal level, as Sakitt claimed.

A second kind of visual memory was termed *iconic memory* by Coltheart (1980). It refers to the formal availability of information from the stimulus as measured in Sperling's partial-report technique. The main support for Coltheart's distinction between visible persistence and iconic memory is that the two obey different empirical laws. Experiments on iconic memory show essentially no effect of initial stimulus duration within a reasonable range during the first few hundred milliseconds (Sperling, 1960). Likewise, in iconic memory experiments, the effect of stimulus luminance on performance is either positive or negligible. When techniques measuring visible persistence—subjective duration—are used, however, both display duration and luminance show an inverse effect on the length of persistence. That is, brighter and briefer displays seem to last longer than dimmer and longer ones. A retinal locus for part of visual memory is very consistent with proceduralist accounts of memory in general; presumably iconic memory, as Coltheart described it, occurs at a higher level of the visual system.

Auditory Sensory Memory

As in the visual modality, two major research programs have contributed the bulk of information on memory for auditory sensory memory. Several promising alternative approaches have been identified but have not received close experimental attention (Crowder, 1978).

Precategorical Acoustic Storage

Crowder and Morton (1969) proposed that auditory sensory (that is, precategorical) memory lies behind the consistent advantage of auditory over visual presentation in serial, immediate recall situations. They suggested that following a spoken stream of characters or words, people have access not only to the interpretations they have made of these items (categorical memory) but also to the actual sounds of the most recent item or items. This is why in modality comparisons the auditory presentation resulted in superior performance, but only for the last few positions in the list. Presentation of an extra item, called a stimulus suffix, posing no additional load on memory was shown to erase most or all of this auditory advantage. Subsequent experiments showed that the meaning of this suffix item had no effect on its tendency to reduce performance on the recency portion of an auditory list. However, differences between the list to be remembered and the redundant suffix had a large effect if they were changes in physical properties, such as spatial location or voice quality (male versus female). This sensitivity to physical attributes along with the insensitivity to conceptual attributes would be expected of a precategorical memory store (Crowder, 1976).

The modality-suffix findings on immediate memory were confidently attributed to precategorical acoustic storage until experiments by Spoehr and Corin (1978) and by Campbell and Dodd (1980) showed that the original hypothesis had been too simple. These authors demonstrated that silent lip-reading and related procedures produced results in immediate memory almost indistinguishable from auditory presentation and readily differentiated from visual presentation. One response has been to make revisions in the precategorical acoustic storage model that leave its essential features unchanged. Another option has been to seek a different interpretation of the suffix-modality results altogether, but so far no worthy candidate has emerged (Crowder and Greene, 1987).

Recognition Masking

Massaro (1972) delivered to subjects one of two possible pure tones, 20 milliseconds long and pitched at either 770 or 870 hertz. The main task was to identify which of the two tones had been presented. After this target, and at delays of from 0 to 500 milliseconds, a masking tone (820 hertz) was presented. In general, presentation of the masking tone reduced subjects' abilities to identify correctly, or to recognize, which of the two tones had come before, especially if the mask came within about 250 milliseconds of the target. The logic of this experiment is that if the original target tone had been fully processed before the mask arrived, there would have been no decrement in its identification. But if the target was still being processed when the mask arrived, there must have been a sensory trace of it still available somewhere in the auditory system. Comparable experiments with speech have given much the same result.

From a detailed review of results and models of auditory integration and auditory persistence, Cowan (1984) distinguished two types of auditory sensory memory, which he called short and long. The short auditory store is believed to have a useful life of about 250 milliseconds and is represented in the experiments on recognition masking and related techniques. The long auditory store may last as long as 2 to 10 seconds, roughly a logarithmic step longer, and underlies the suffix and modality comparisons.

Summary

Thus, research on vision has revealed two manifestations of sensory memory, both measured in hundreds of milliseconds. Auditory sensory memory also has shown two forms of sensory memory, one measured in milliseconds and the other in seconds. These may be viewed as distinct stores or as the residues of distinct kinds of information processing.

(See also CODING PROCESSES: IMAGERY.)

REFERENCES

Campbell, R., and Dodd, B. (1980). Hearing by eye. *Quarterly Journal of Experimental Psychology 32,* 85–99.

Coltheart, M. (1980). Iconic memory and visible persistence. *Perception and Psychophysics 27,* 183–228.

——— (1983). Iconic memory. *Philosophical Transactions of the Royal Society of London B302,* 283–294.

Cowan, N. (1984). On short and long auditory stores. *Psychological Bulletin 96,* 341–370.

Crowder, R. G. (1976). *Principles of learning and memory.* Hillsdale, N.J.: Erlbaum.

——— (1978). Sensory memory systems. In E. C. Carterette and M. P. Friedman, eds., *Handbook of perception,* vol. 9. New York: Academic Press.

——— (1989). Modularity and dissociations of memory systems. In H. L. Roediger III and F. I. M. Craik, eds., *Varieties of memory and consciousness: Essays in honor of Endel Tulving,* pp. 271–294. Hillsdale, N.J.: Erlbaum.

Crowder, R. G., and Greene, R. L. (1987). On the remembrance of times past: The irregular list technique. *Journal of Experimental Psychology: General 116,* 265–278.

Crowder, R. G., and Morton, J. (1969). Precategorical acoustic storage (PAS). *Perception and Psychophysics 5,* 365–373.

Di Lollo, V. (1980). Temporal integration in visual memory. *Journal of Experimental Psychology: General 109,* 75–97.

Efron, R. (1970). The minimum duration of a perception. *Neuropsychologia 8,* 57–63.

Farah, M. J. (1988). Is visual imagery really visual? Overlooked evidence from neuropsychology. *Psychological Review 95,* 307–317.

Haber, R. N., and Standing, L. (1970). Direct estimates of the apparent duration of a flash. *Canadian Journal of Psychology 24,* 216–229.

Kolers, P. A., and Roediger, H. L. III (1984). Procedures of mind. *Journal of Verbal Learning and Verbal Behavior 23,* 425–449.

Massaro, D. W. (1972). Preperceptual images, processing time, and perceptual units in auditory perception. *Psychological Review 79,* 124–145.

Sakitt, B. (1976). Iconic memory. *Psychological Review 83,* 257–276.

Sperling, G. (1960). The information available in brief visual presentations. *Psychological Monographs 74* (whole no. 498).

Spoehr, K. T., and Corin, W. J. (1978). The stimulus suffix effect as a memory coding phenomenon. *Memory and Cognition 6,* 583–589.

Robert G. Crowder

SERIAL ORGANIZATION

A critical form of memory organization, and one frequently used, is retention of events in the temporal order in which they occurred. Consider, for example, your memory for the events that occurred last summer. If someone asked you what you did during your summer vacation, most likely you would discuss the events in the sequence in which they occurred, beginning with those that occurred at the start of the summer and concluding with those that occurred at the summer's end. Of course other types of organization are possible. Alternatively, for example, you could report together all the parties you attended and report as another group all the times you went hiking or swimming. But retention in terms of temporal sequence, or serial order, is most common.

Definitions and Distinctions

To study the retention of serial order in the laboratory, the information pertaining to temporal sequence must be distinguished and isolated from other types of related information. The relevant distinctions can be made clear by considering the following hypothetical situation: Imagine a waiter in a restaurant who is taking dinner orders from the people sitting around a table. Usually in such a situation, the individuals make their requests in a temporal sequence that follows the spatial arrangement of the seats around the table—for example, beginning at the head of the table and moving clockwise around the table. However, in the present situation this ordinary practice is not observed. Instead, in accordance with some rules of etiquette, the waiter takes the requests in an order determined by the individuals' ages and genders, starting with the oldest woman and ending with the youngest man. This situation is illustrated in Figure 1. The first order is for ham, the second for liver, the third for steak, and the fourth for chicken. The temporal sequence of the requests is thus ham, liver, steak, and chicken, a sequence that does not correspond to the spatial arrangement around the table. Hence, the temporal and spatial orders are not the same. When the waiter returns to deliver the dinners, he serves the first person liver, the second turkey, the third steak, and the last chicken. The waiter thus makes two mistakes.

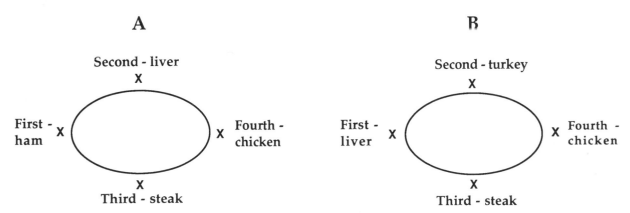

Figure 1. Arrangement of table when waiter takes dinner orders (A) and when dinner is served (B) in hypothetical restaurant situation.

In the case of the turkey, he brings a dinner requested by nobody, and in the case of the liver, he gives a dinner ordered by one person to another. The first type of mistake is called an *item error* because the identity of the dinner item is incorrect. The second type of mistake is called an *order error* because a correct item is brought but it is placed in the wrong position in the temporal sequence. For a discussion of laboratory methods used to distinguish between the retention of item, temporal order, and spatial order information, see Healy et al. (1991).

Another important distinction that must be made when studying the retention of temporal sequence information is the difference between the order of the items and their positions in the sequence. This distinction can be clarified by considering a related hypothetical situation with the same waiter and diners. In this case, the waiter returns to take the requests for dessert. The first person orders ice cream, the second nothing, the third cake, and the last pudding. When he returns, the waiter correctly brings the first person ice cream and the last pudding, but he gives the cake to the second person instead of the third. The waiter, therefore, correctly remembers the order of desserts—cake between ice cream and pudding—but he confuses the second and third temporal positions. An important investigation examining the distinction between memory for order and memory for position was reported by Lee and Estes (1977).

Empirical Results

Although a number of techniques have been used to study retention of serial order, two procedures have been most popular. Much of the early work on this topic used serial learning with the method of anticipation, and many of the more recent studies have used short-term serial recall with the distractor paradigm. In both methods, the results of primary interest have focused on the serial position curve, which reveals the proportion of correct responses as a function of the temporal position of each item on the list.

Serial Learning Method of Anticipation

In serial learning, subjects attempt to learn an ordered list of items (often nonsense syllables or words) across a number of successive trials. On each trial the list is presented and the subject tries to recall it. With the method of anticipation, the subjects are not required to recite the entire list at one time. Rather, each list item is presented in turn, and the subjects are required to anticipate (i.e., recall) each item before it is presented, in response to the item immediately preceding it on the list. A correct response is scored whenever the subject correctly anticipates an item, and the subject receives feedback (i.e., the subject is told the next item in the sequence) regardless of whether a correct response is made. Usually the experimental trials are continued until the subjects are able to anticipate every item with no errors. At that point, the investigator counts the number of correct responses made at each position in the list, and it becomes evident that the items in the different ordinal positions in the list are not learned with the same ease. Rather, items at the beginning and end of the list yield more correct responses than those in the middle. The point of maximum difficulty is somewhat beyond the center of the list.

Although the total number of correct responses on the list may decrease when the items are more difficult, as when nonsense syllables are used instead of words or when the rate of list presentation is faster, the serial position curve remains constant across such changes in the learning situation when it is plotted as the proportion of the total number of correct responses made at each position in the list. The constancy of the serial position curve when plotted in this manner is known as the Hunter-McCrary Law. A typical serial position curve for an eight-item list is shown in Figure 2, which presents data reported by Murdock (1960) in an important article relating the serial position function to results of experiments in domains of psychology outside of verbal learning. The serial position function is described as *bow shaped* because it resembles a bow used in archery. The large relative advantage for the items from the beginning of the list is known as the *primacy effect,* and the smaller relative advantage for the items from the end of the list is known as the *recency effect.*

Short-Term Serial Recall with the Distractor Paradigm

On a trial in the distractor paradigm used to study serial recall over a short time interval, subjects are given a short list of items to remember (typi-

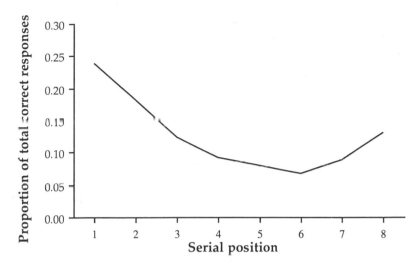

Figure 2. Typical serial position curve for an eight-item list learned under the serial method of anticipation. The data are plotted as the proportion of the total number of correct responses made at each serial position of the list. *Adapted from Murdock, 1960, p. 26.*

cally three to five letters), then are required to participate in an interpolated distractor task that is meant to prevent them from rehearsing the list (for example, they may be told to count backward from a random number), and finally they are asked to recall the list of items according to the order of presentation. The duration of the distractor task, or the length of the retention interval, varies from trial to trial but is usually quite short (no longer than 20 seconds). Also, the list of items to be

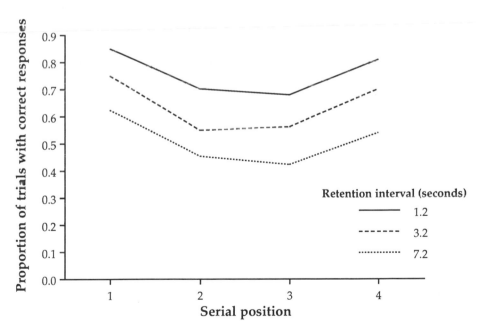

Figure 3. Typical serial position curves for a four-item list recalled under the distractor paradigm. The data are plotted as the proportion of trials on which correct responses were made at each retention interval and serial position of the list. *Adapted from Healy, 1974, p. 649.*

recalled changes from one trial to the next. A correct response is scored whenever the subject recalls an item that was shown and places it in the ordinal position in which it occurred on the list. The time course of forgetting the serial list is revealed by comparing the proportion of correct responses at each retention interval. The resulting retention function is usually very steep; forgetting is very rapid in this paradigm. A plot of the proportion of trials on which correct responses are made at each ordinal position in the list reveals a serial position curve that is usually bow shaped and nearly symmetrical; the primacy effect is approximately equal in magnitude to the recency effect. Typical serial position curves for three different retention intervals are shown in Figure 3, which presents data reported by Healy (1974). In Healy's study, order information was isolated from item information because the same four items were shown on every trial of the experiment; the subjects knew the identity of the items in advance and had to recall only the order in which they were shown on a particular trial.

Theoretical Models

Classic Models

Although many models of serial order retention have been proposed, two simple opposing models dominated the early research on this topic. Both of these models include associative mechanisms as the basis for retaining serial order information. According to the associative chaining model, item-to-item associations are constructed so that the first item in a serial list is linked to the second item as a stimulus-response pair, the second item is linked in the same way to the third item, and so on to form an associative stimulus-response chain of items. For example, given the list of dinner orders ham, liver, steak, and chicken in the hypothetical restaurant example discussed earlier, ham would be associated with liver, liver with steak, and steak with chicken. The second model to account for serial order retention involves positional associations. By this account, each item on the list is associated with the ordinal number corresponding to its serial position in the list. In our example, ham would be associated with the number 1, liver with 2, steak with 3, and chicken with

4. Experimental evidence has refuted both of these simple explanations for serial order retention.

Contemporary Models

Despite the problems with the simple associative models, two more complex contemporary models have been proposed that can be viewed as extensions of the earlier models. Both of these models have derived support from a wide range of experimental investigations and observations, including the pervasive serial position functions. According to the *theory of distributed associative memory* (TODAM), serial order information is represented in memory as a series of pairwise associations linking successively presented items. TODAM resembles the traditional chaining approach except that the items in the list and their associations are stored together in memory. Each item is represented as a list of features or a vector of numbers. Rather than simple links connecting the two items in a pair, the items are connected by means of "convolution," which is a mathematical operation that merges the separate vectors for the items into a single composite vector. The new vector formed in this way is an image that does not directly resemble either of its original constituents. The vectors for all the items in the list and for all the pairwise associations are superimposed on, or added to, a common memory vector. The mathematical details of TODAM and its ability to account for data from many serial order tasks are described in Lewandowsky and Murdock (1989).

In contrast with TODAM, a second influential model of serial order retention emphasizes positional information. According to this *perturbation* model, the representation of order information derives from the representation of position information, so that subjects can recall items in the temporal sequence exactly to the extent that the positional information they have stored in memory can adequately prescribe the order. Associations are included in the perturbation model. However, instead of associative bonds linking successive items on the list, there are associative bonds between each item and a single control element, which represents some aspect of the current context or environment in which the list is presented. For example, given two successively presented items X and Y, rather than an association of the form X-Y, the perturbation model includes associations of the form X-C-Y, where C represents the control element. This new associative mechanism has allowed for a powerful and elegant description of short-term serial order recall. For a lucid discussion of the perturbation model, see Estes (1972).

(See also MEMORY SPAN.)

REFERENCES

Estes, W. K. (1972). An associative basis for coding and organization in memory. In A. W. Melton and E. Martin, eds., *Coding processes in human memory*, pp. 161–190. Washington, D.C.: Winston.

Healy, A. F. (1974). Separating item from order information in short-term memory. *Journal of Verbal Learning and Verbal Behavior 13*, 644–655.

Healy, A. F., Cunningham, T. F., Gesi, A. T., Till, R. E., and Bourne, L. E. (1991). Comparing short-term recall of item, temporal, and spatial information in children and adults. In W. E. Hockley and S. Lewandowsky, eds., *Relating theory and data: Essays on human memory, in honor of Bennet B. Murdock*, pp. 127–154. Hillsdale, N.J.: Erlbaum.

Lee, C. L., and Estes, W. K. (1977). Order and position in primary memory for letter strings. *Journal of Verbal Learning and Verbal Behavior 16*, 395–418.

Lewandowsky, S., and Murdock, B. B. (1989). Memory for serial order. *Psychological Review 96*, 25–57.

Murdock, B. B. (1960). The distinctiveness of stimuli. *Psychological Review 67*, 16–31.

Alice F. Healy

SEX DIFFERENCES IN LEARNING IN ANIMALS

Findings in the field of neuroendocrinology, which explores the functional relationships between hormones and the brain, have indicated that the release of testicular (androgens) and ovarian (estrogens) hormones during critical periods of brain development exert a profound effect on the genesis and survival of neurons in specific brain areas, resulting in sex differences in reproductive behaviors. Sex differences are not restricted to the reproductive sphere, however. They are found in a broad range of nonreproductive behaviors such as aggression, locomotor activity, play behavior, and learning abilities. When sex differences in learning abilities of humans have been observed, they have been repeatedly interpreted as reflecting sex differences in early experience, training, and social expectations rather than in brain structures and functions. Yet there is now experimental evidence to indicate that sex differences in cognitive behaviors, more specifically learning and memory abilities, are the result of the action of gonadal steroid hormones on the morphology of brain areas related to these functions. Support for this conclusion is of four kinds. First, sex differences have been reported in various learning abilities that depend on neural structures other than those involved in reproductive functions. Second, there are sex differences in the morphology of neural structures mediating learning abilities. Third, lesions of neural structures underlying learning abilities can affect males and females differently. Finally, sex differences in learning abilities, brain morphology, and the effects of brain lesions can be reversed by early manipulations of gonadal steroid hormones.

Sexual Dimorphism in Learning Abilities

Although the majority of data pertaining to the effects of gonadal steroid hormones on learning abilities have been gathered in rodents, there is growing evidence for similar effects in nonhuman primates. In rodents (for review, see Beatty, 1979), mature male rats make fewer errors than females in learning complex mazes, and are faster learners in appetitive learning. Conversely, female rats outperform males in discrimination reversal learning and in the acquisition of active avoidance. In addition, the pattern of male and female performance in avoidance learning can be reversed by treating ovariectomized female rats with androgens (testosterone) and male rats with antiandrogens from birth to adulthood. That is, the avoidance performance of feminized male rats is hastened and that of masculinized female rats is delayed. Finally, lesions of brain areas known to be functionally involved in avoidance learning, such as the basal ganglia, do not impair performance of males and females equally. For example, small lesions of the globus pallidus impair acquisition of active avoidance in males but not in females. This sex difference in the effects of pallidal lesions can be reversed by androgenization of female rats and feminization of male rats. These data in rodents suggest that androgens are, at least in part, responsible for the sex differences in learning abilities. (See also AVOIDANCE LEARNING, NEURAL SUBSTRATES OF.)

In nonhuman primates (for review, see Mitchell, 1977), adult female rhesus monkeys outperform males in spatial memory, as measured by the delayed-response task. Similarly, adult female chimpanzees exhibit significantly superior short-term stimulus memory, as measured by the delayed matching-to-sample task. These studies in adult primates did not examine whether the sex differences in learning abilities could be reversed by perinatal gonadal steroid hormone treatments, but such evidence has been obtained in studies of infant primates.

Performance on an object discrimination reversal task, a task known to depend on the integrity of the orbital prefrontal cortex in the adult monkey, was studied in male and female infant rhesus monkeys (Clark and Goldman-Rakic, 1989). Male infant monkeys learned significantly more quickly than females of the same age, but postnatal injections of testosterone propionate in the females enhanced their performance to the level of the normal infant males. In addition, when orbital prefrontal cortex was removed in infancy, intact male monkeys and androgenized female monkeys were as impaired as adult monkeys with the same lesions, whereas untreated infant females did not differ from untreated age-matched females. The data suggest that the orbital prefrontal cortex matures earlier in male than in female monkeys, presumably due to the inductive role played by gonadal steroid hormones in the postnatal differentiation of cortical mechanisms.

Further evidence of sex differences in maturation of cortical structures was obtained in a study of concurrent visual discrimination learning (Bachevalier et al., 1989), an ability known to depend on the integrity of the inferior temporal cortex (area TE). In this task, 3-month-old female infants required fewer trials than age-matched males to reach the learning criterion, a sex difference that was absent in both 6-month-old monkeys and adults. The sex difference was positively correlated in 3-month-old male animals with circulating levels of testosterone but not with estradiol levels, such that the higher the level of testosterone, the poorer the score. In addition, neonatal orchiectomy, which reduced plasma testosterone levels, hastened performance on visual discrimination learning in male infant monkeys (Bachevalier and Hagger, 1991). By contrast, performance was delayed in neonatally ovariectomized female monkeys treated with androgens (dihydrotestosterone). Finally, early postnatal area TE lesions affected performance of female but not of male infant monkeys, though male and female adults with the same lesions were impaired equally. Thus, such lesions affect performance of infant female monkeys more than that of infant males, presumably because at that age, area TE is functionally more mature in females than in males (Bachevalier et al., 1990). Together with the neuroendocrinological findings, these data suggest that the high levels of androgens found in infant male monkeys before and shortly after birth retard the development of visual concurrent discrimination learning, presumably by slowing the maturation of cortical area TE, its projection targets to the striatum, or both. (See also DISCRIMINATION AND GENERALIZATION.)

Sex Differences in Brain Areas Related to Learning Abilities

Although no direct correlation has been established between sex differences in learning abilities and morphology of brain areas, sex differences in numerous neural structures related to learning abilities are well documented in rodents (for review, see Beatty, 1979; Juraska, 1984). In the limbic system (bed nucleus of the stria terminalis and hippocampus), the number and volume of neurons differ in male and female rats. These morphological differences are reversed after postnatal treatment with gonadal steroid hormones. Interestingly, the rate of neonatal cell proliferation has been shown to be slower in male than in female rats, indicating a delayed maturation of the neocortex in males compared with that of females. Similarly, the neurons in the somatosensory cortex of young male rats are larger than those of females, reflecting a cortical immaturity and, possibly, a less developed synaptic network in males than in females.

The question of precisely how and when in development androgen levels influence the maturation of brain areas related to learning abilities remains to be answered. There is, however, indirect evidence regarding the mechanism of their action on brain areas related to learning abilities (for review, see Luine and McEwen, 1985). For example, gonadal steroid hormones are known to act via intracellular receptors located in limbic structures and some parts of the neocortex. In the developing rhesus monkey, androgen metabolism has been observed in all cortical areas; this activity declines from prenatal to early postnatal life. Also, the presence of sex differences in neurochemical concentrations and regulatory processes suggests an influence of gonadal steroid hormones on the differentiation of neurochemical features of neurons. Finally, gonadal steroid hormones stimulate neurite outgrowth during the sensitive period of brain differentiation, presumably by increasing the competitive advantage of neurons to make connections with other neurons. The perinatal androgen surge seen in infant males could therefore affect the rate of brain maturation by influencing neuronal connectivity at the cortical level.

Conclusion

From the data available on sex differences in learning abilities, we are just beginning to assemble some of the pieces that constitute the puzzle of how sex differences in the development of learning abilities could be related to sex differences in the maturation of the brain. Interestingly, the experimental evidence gathered in nonhuman primates demonstrates that steroid gonadal hormones act not only on the organization of brain structures related to primary sex characteristics, such as the hypothalamus (accounting for sex differences in reproductive behaviors), but also on the organization of brain structures that are not so related, such as the orbital prefrontal and inferior temporal cortices (accounting for sex differences in learning abilities). Thus, it is becoming clear that sex differences in structure and function are likely to be a pervasive characteristic of brain organization and are mediated by gonadal steroid hormones. Presumably this action of gonadal hormones on brain maturation could explain sex differences in learning abilities in humans as well.

Yet many unanswered questions remain. What are the temporal limits of the period in development when steroid gonadal hormones influence the organization of behavioral and cognitive functions? Experimental evidence strongly suggests that this sensitive period extends postnatally, at least in nonhuman primates. In addition, the two sets of findings regarding sex differences in the development of learning abilities in infant rhesus monkeys lead to an intriguing conclusion. They indicate that the directionality of steroid hormonal influences on structure and function varies from one cortical area to the other. Specifically, whereas orbital prefrontal cortex appears to mature earlier in male than in female monkeys, inferior temporal cortical area TE appears to mature earlier in female than in male monkeys. These contradictory results could be explained by the metabolic action of androgens in the brain. It is known that androgens bind to both androgenic and estrogenic receptors, a property that may lead to functional differences in cortical areas. Finally, although the studies reported here indicate an action of androgens on brain maturation, this finding does not preclude a significant action of estrogens as well. Indeed, in light of the apparent equivalence of estrogen and androgen receptors in fetal and early postnatal neural structures, future studies should begin to examine the respective roles of these steroids during brain development in primates.

(See also HORMONES AND MEMORY.)

REFERENCES

Bachevalier, J., Brickson, M., Hagger, C., and Mishkin, M. (1990). Age and sex differences in the effects of selective temporal lobe lesion on the formation of visual discrimination habits in rhesus monkeys (*Macaca mulatta*). *Behavioral Neuroscience 104,* 885–899.

Bachevalier, J., and Hagger, C. (1991). Sex differences in the development of learning abilities in primates. *Psychoneuroendocrinology 16,* 179–190.

Bachevalier, J., Hagger, C., and Bercu, B. B. (1989). Gender differences in visual habit formation in 3-month-old rhesus monkeys. *Developmental Psychobiology 22,* 585–599.

Beatty, W. W. (1979). Gonadal hormones and sex differences in nonreproductive behaviors in rodents: Organizational and activational influences. *Hormones and Behavior 12,* 112–163.

Clark, A. S., and Goldman-Rakic, P. S. (1989). Gonadal hormones influence the emergence of cortical function in nonhuman primates. *Behavioral Neuroscience 103,* 1287–1295.

Juraska, J. M. (1984). Sex differences in developmental plasticity in the visual cortex and hippocampal dentate gyrus. In G. J. DeVries et al., eds., *Progress in brain research,* vol. 61. Amsterdam: Elsevier Science Publishers.

Luine, V. N., and McEwen, B. S. (1985). Steroid hormone receptors in brain and pituitary. In N. Adler, D. Pfaff, and R. W. Goy, eds., *Handbook of behavioral neurobiology,* vol. 7. New York: Plenum Press.

Mitchell, G. (1977). A note on sex differences in learning or motivation in nonhuman primates. *Laboratory Primate Newsletter 16,* 1–5.

Jocelyne Bachevalier
Corinne Hagger

SKINNER, B. F.

Burrhus Frederic Skinner, (1904–1990) best known as B. F. Skinner, was the older son of William Arthur Skinner and Grace Madge Burrhus Skinner, born March 20, 1904 in Susquehanna, Pennsylvania. His father was an attorney with some political aspirations. Skinner's younger brother died suddenly of a cerebral aneurysm at the age of 16. Skinner did his undergraduate work at Hamilton College in Clinton, New York, where he majored in English. During the summer before his senior year, he studied at the Bread Loaf School of English at Middlebury, Vermont. There he had the opportunity to have lunch with Robert Frost, who asked Skinner to send him some of his work. Frost's comments were encouraging and Skinner tried his hand at writing, at first in his parents' home and eventually in Greenwich Village in New York City. He

Figure 1.   B. F. Skinner. *Courtesy Dr. Julie Vargas.*

discovered that "I had nothing important to say" (Skinner, 1970, p. 7). With this failure of the literary method to satisfy his interest in human behavior, he turned to psychology and graduate work at Harvard University.

Skinner was drawn to psychology by several factors. First, his biology teacher directed him to Jacques Loeb's *Physiology of the Brain and Comparative Psychology* (1900) and PAVLOV's *Conditioned Reflexes* (1927). Then the writings of Bertrand Russell in *The Dial,* a literary magazine, and Russell's *Philosophy* (1927), which he read while trying out the role of writer in Greenwich Village, led him to J. B. WATSON's *Behaviorism* (1924). Skinner pointed out that whereas the Department of Psychology at Harvard did not strengthen his interest in BEHAVIORISM, Fred S. Keller, then a graduate student in the department, did. Keller is described by Skinner as "a sophisticated behaviorist in every sense of the word" (Skinner, 1970, p. 9). As for his thesis, it "had only the vaguest of Harvard connections" (Skinner, 1970, p. 10). It included his study of eating rate in the rat (which came to be the response rate of later work), two brief papers on the reflex and drive, and his paper on the concept of the reflex in psychology. That concept of the reflex was based on an operational analysis in which he insisted on defining it simply as an observed correlation of stimulus and response. He used the equation $R = f(S, A)$, where R stood for reflex strength, S stood for stimulus, and A stood for any condition affecting reflex strength, such as drive, which was specified in terms of the deprivation operation (Skinner, 1977).

After he received his Ph.D., Skinner served as a junior fellow in the Harvard Society of Fellows for 3 years; then he moved to the University of Minnesota, where during World War II he embarked on a project training pigeons to guide missiles. While at the University of Minnesota, he married Yvonne (Eve) Blue, with whom he had two children, Julie and Deborah. The older one (Julie) became an educational psychologist and the younger one (Deborah) an artist. In 1945 he moved to Indiana University, where he remained until 1947, when he returned to Harvard University. During that same year, he delivered his William James Lectures on Verbal Behavior, which evolved into his book on that subject in 1957.

As he himself implied, Skinner held on to the concept of "reflex" beyond its usefulness when he wrote his book *The Behavior of Organisms* in 1938. Not long after that, he gave up the concept because OPERANT BEHAVIOR is not elicited but emitted, and thus he ceased to be a stimulus-response psychologist. This means that Skinner did not conceive of human beings, or for that matter of any organism, as automatons waiting to have some behavior elicited. Rather, organisms were viewed in the following way: They emit behavior upon which the environment acts by selecting some of it through the provision of consequences. Also important in this context is the concept of *classes of behavior* and *classes of stimuli*—Skinner referred to this as the generic nature of stimulus and response (1935). Despite the fact that behavior analysis, a term now most often used to describe Skinner's concepts of learning, refers to classes and not to some hyperspecified atomistic stimulus and response, uninformed people continue to characterize Skinner's approach incorrectly as atomistic.

The fact that there is no reliable way of eliciting operant behavior necessitated the invention of a special procedure to produce "new" behavior. The concept of "shaping" by reinforcing successive approximations to the desired behavior resulted from that need. Critical in Skinner's approach to learning was the concept of the three-part REINFORCEMENT contingency, which states that behavior occurring on particular occasions and followed by certain consequences (reinforcers) will be strengthened by those consequences; that is, other members of the same response class will have a higher probability of occurring on similar occasions. Two different types of reinforcers exist, positive and negative. The former strengthens the behavior that produces it and the latter strengthens the behavior that avoids or eliminates it. Reinforcers are also divided into unconditioned (primary) and conditioned (secondary). The former act as reinforcers without any learning history, whereas the latter act as reinforcers due to their association with the unconditioned reinforcers. Skinner distinguished reinforcers from punishing stimuli, which weaken the behavior they produce.

Skinner's concept of operant behavior generated many experiments and continues to do so, including those on schedules of reinforcement in which the different intermittent patterns give rise to characteristic patterns of response rates (Ferster and Skinner, 1957). The concept of intermittent reinforcement was significant in a variety of ways, not least of which was its resemblance to the conditions of the natural environment, thus bringing basic learning research closer to the "real" world.

The number of different kinds of intermittent schedules that can be generated is limited only by the experimenter's imagination, but they generally fall into two broad classes, one in which reinforcement depends on the frequency or type of behavior and the other in which it depends on the occurrence of a response plus the passage of a certain period or periods of time.

Intermittent schedules of reinforcement produce behavior that is particularly resistant to extinction and thus gave rise to the study of maintenance of behavior, to which other learning approaches gave scant attention. Maintenance of behavior can be said to approximate memory, a concept Skinner avoided. Instead of viewing the process of recall as one of "searching a storehouse of memory," he considered the conditions, both external and response-produced, that increase "the probability of responses" (Skinner, 1974, pp. 109–110). Of special interest is the fact that Skinner did not limit his interest to basic research. With respect to memory, to take the area under consideration, he wrote a charming and informative book (Skinner and Vaughn, 1983) outlining a program of self-management in old age.

During the same year that Skinner's work on intermittent reinforcement was published, his book on verbal behavior appeared in print (Skinner, 1957). He considered it to be his most important contribution to psychology. He viewed verbal behavior as he did other behavior, not as standing for something else (Skinner, 1945) but as constituting the subject matter of interest. As a radical behaviorist, and in contrast with the methodological behaviorists, who must restrict their studies to currently measurable phenomena, he was able to extend his analysis to private events that do not yet have any way of being measured. In his book on verbal behavior and later in his *Contingencies of Reinforcement* (Skinner, 1969), Skinner explicitly recognized that not all behavior is produced through conditioning; rule-governed behavior is produced not through the exposure to the actual contingencies of reinforcement but to a verbal description of those contingencies. In what is no doubt one of his last papers, Skinner (1990) suggested that such rule-governed behavior might, in the words he attributed to Bertrand Russell as "knowledge by description," postpone the destruction of the earth. He died August 18, 1990.

Skinner applied his principles of behavior to many areas of functioning. In education, he invented programmed instruction, a form of learning in which students always make the "correct" response, thus having their correct responses immediately reinforced (Skinner, 1954a; 1968). He used the methods of shaping and stimulus fading to make that possible. In abnormal psychology, he first talked about behavior modification by applying reinforcement to psychotic patients' behavior (Skinner, 1954b). He applied behavior theory to the study of drugs (Skinner and Heron, 1937), thereby initiating an area of study still practiced and useful; and, as already mentioned, he applied it to old age.

Skinner's first excursion into the study of culture and what to do about it occurred when he wrote a novel, *Walden Two* (Skinner, 1948). He returned to that theme in *Science and Human Behavior* (Skinner, 1953), and even more so when he wrote *Beyond Freedom and Dignity* (Skinner, 1971). Always he managed to remain close to the principles of behavior analysis that he had discovered in his basic research.

Skinner has undoubtedly been one of the most influential psychologists of the twentieth century. A recent reconsideration of his basic papers, complete with comments by present-day psychologists both sympathetic and opposed to his approach, along with his response to those comments, is in Catania and Harnad (1984). Unlike any of the other learning psychologists who reached prominence, Skinner's systematization of behavior was never limited merely to learning, the acquisition of new behavior. Rather, his approach was applied by him and subsequently by many others to all areas of psychology.

REFERENCES

Catania, A. C., and Harnad, S., eds. (1984). Canonical papers of B. F. Skinner. *The Behavioral and Brain Sciences 7,* 473–724.

Ferster, C. F., and Skinner, B. F. (1957). *Schedules of reinforcement.* New York: Appleton-Century-Crofts.

Loeb, J. (1900). *Physiology of the brain and comparative psychology.* New York: Putnam.

Pavlov, I. (1927). *Conditioned reflexes.* London: Oxford University Press.

Russell, B. (1927). *Philosophy.* New York: Norton.

Skinner, B. F. (1935). The generic nature of the concepts of stimulus and response. *Journal of General Psychology 12,* 40–65.

———— (1938). *The behavior of organisms.* New York: Appleton-Century-Crofts.

———— (1945). The operational analysis of psychological terms. *Psychological Review 52,* 270–277.

———— (1948). *Walden two.* New York: Macmillan.

———— (1953). *Science and human behavior.* New York: Macmillan.

———— (1954a). The science of learning and the art of teaching. *Harvard Educational Review 24,* 86–97.

———— (1954b). A new method for the experimental analysis of the behavior of psychotic patients. *Journal of Nervous and Mental Diseases 120,* 403–406.

———— (1957). *Verbal behavior.* New York: Appleton-Century-Crofts.

———— (1968). *The technology of teaching.* New York: Appleton-Century-Crofts.

———— (1969). *Contingencies of reinforcement.* New York: Appleton-Century-Crofts.

———— (1970). B. F. Skinner . . . An autobiography. In P. B. Dews, ed., *Festschrift for B. F. Skinner.* New York: Appleton-Century-Crofts.

———— (1971). *Beyond freedom and dignity.* New York: Alfred A. Knopf.

———— (1974). *About behaviorism.* New York: Alfred A. Knopf.

———— (1976). *Particulars of my life.* New York: Alfred A. Knopf. First volume of Skinner's autobiography.

———— (1977). The experimental analysis of operant behavior. In R. W. Rieber and K. Salzinger, eds., *The roots of American psychology: Historical influences and implications for the future. Annals of the New York Academy of Sciences 291,* 374–385.

———— (1979). *The shaping of a behaviorist.* New York: Alfred A. Knopf. Second volume of Skinner's autobiography.

———— (1983). *A matter of consequences.* New York: Alfred A. Knopf. Third and final volume of Skinner's autobiography.

———— (1990). To know the future. *The Behavior Analyst 13,* 103–106.

Skinner, B. F., and Heron, W. T. (1937). Effects of caffeine and benzedrine upon conditioning and extinction. *Psychological Record 1,* 340–346.

Skinner, B. F., and Vaughn, M. E. (1983). *Enjoy old age.* New York: W. W. Norton.

Watson, J. B. (1924). *Behaviorism.* New York: W. W. Norton.

Kurt Salzinger

SPATIAL LEARNING

Most terrestrial animal species move extensively through space, searching for food, water, mates, and safety. The ability to acquire and remember the spatial layout of the environment, and where important things are located, is thus highly adaptive; it is therefore not surprising that spatial learning is extremely well developed in most animals.

Scientists have studied spatial learning in many species, and we now know a great deal about the ways in which it is similar to, yet different from, other kinds of learning. We also know much about how the brain manages such learning, although much more remains to be understood.

Spatial learning begins with exploratory behavior, during which the animal gathers information about the environment and commits it to memory. This kind of learning differs from most other forms of learning in that it does not appear to be based on the same kinds of motivations. Animals explore and learn about space even though they are not at the moment hungry, thirsty, in danger, or in search of a mate. The information they gather will be used when they do have some specific need.

The power of spatial learning is easily demonstrated in learning experiments by a wide variety of animals that show through their behavior that they can remember where they have been, and in general how to return to their home from their current location. Ants, for example, can apparently keep track of their movements with sufficient accuracy that they can return directly to the home nest, regardless of the zigzag nature of their outward path. It is assumed that they do this by maintaining a record of their movements and calculating, on a continuous basis, where those movements have taken them. This ability, known as *inertial navigation,* suffices to permit them to return home by the shortest route—unless they have been purposely moved (by an experimenter, for example) or have been blown off course by the elements. Many species of birds demonstrate considerable powers of spatial learning. In some cases this involves the ability to migrate over very long distances and to home in on their goal: the winter nesting ground or their summer home. In other cases this involves the ability to cache large numbers of seeds in a widely dispersed fashion, and to retrieve these seeds some time later with great accuracy. Rodents show their spatial abilities in situations where they must retrieve goal objects (typically food or water) from a variety of locations without returning to sites already visited. Rats learn to do this very quickly and with great accuracy.

Animals such as rats learn about space by attending to spatial cues, which provide information about various aspects of the external environment. The most common of such cues is a *landmark,* which is a fixed object or feature of the physical landscape that the animal can use for orientation. Some landmarks are close to the locations the animal seeks to approach, others are at a distance but still close enough to be of some value in determining the distance an animal must move to get where it wants, while still others, such as the stars, are so far away that their location and the spatial relations among them remain constant even as the animal moves around. This constancy allows such distal landmarks to provide useful information about directions, although not about distances.

Spatial learning is studied in the laboratory by setting up a problem-solving situation in which the animal must figure out where to go in order to obtain some reward. For example, rats must learn a number of things about space in solving the *radial maze* task (Olton and Samuelson, 1976). In this situation, rats are placed on a maze consisting of a central platform and a number of arms radiating outward. Typically eight arms have been used, but it is possible to use more or fewer. Some reward, say a food pellet, is placed at the end of each arm. The rat's task is to retrieve all the food pellets with the minimum number of arm entries. In order to do this, the animal must remember which arms it has already entered, so as to avoid entering them again. Research has shown that rats (and other animals) do this by learning about the entire environment, and by remembering which arms they have entered in terms of their location in the environment. Typically, they use distant extramaze cues to solve this task, much as birds use the stars to navigate.

Another frequently used spatial learning task involves a large water tank in which a submerged platform is located (Morris, 1981). The tank is filled with water made cloudy with white powder, and the rat must find the platform in order to escape from swimming. Since there are no local landmarks indicating the exact site of the submerged platform, the rat solves this task by learning about the distal extratank environment and navigating according to the directional information this environment provides. Rats can learn this task quite readily, and can swim directly to the submerged platform no matter where in the tank they are placed.

Much has been learned in recent years about the way in which spatial learning is mediated in the brain. The first indication of where "spatial maps" might be created in the brain came from studies by O'Keefe and his coworkers that demonstrated the presence of single neurons in the *hippo-*

campal formation (see GUIDE TO THE ANATOMY OF THE BRAIN: HIPPOCAMPUS) that seem to be coding the *place* where the animal is located (O'Keefe and Dostrovsky, 1971; O'Keefe, 1976, 1979; O'Keefe and Nadel, 1978). That is, these neurons are most active when the animal is in a certain part of the environment, and rather inactive at other locations. These results, which have been repeated in a number of other laboratories, led O'Keefe and Nadel to hypothesize that the hippocampal formation and its nearest neighbors provide the neural basis for place learning and the formation of internal representations of external environments. O'Keefe went on to show that these spatial neurons are part of a spatial memory circuit, in that they retain their spatially selective activity patterns even when all the spatial information has been removed from the environment, so long as the animal had an initial opportunity to get a fix on where it was located (O'Keefe and Speakman, 1987).

The role of the hippocampal formation in spatial learning has been confirmed in two other kinds of experiments. In the first type, animals are subjected to lesions in the hippocampus or related structures, and are tested on their ability to learn the kinds of spatial tasks noted above. With very few exceptions, these experiments have shown that damage in the hippocampus renders such learning impossible (see Barnes, 1988, for a review). For example, rats with hippocampal lesions cannot solve the water maze task (Morris et al., 1982). It is important to note that these learning failures relate directly to the spatial learning requirement of this task. It is possible to create "nonspatial" versions of the typical spatial mazes, where distinctive cues mark the locations of the rewards. In such mazes animals with hippocampal lesions are quite capable of learning normally. In the second type of experiment immature rats are tested on spatial and nonspatial versions of the water maze task; the ability to learn the spatial version appears only at that point in early life when the hippocampal formation becomes functional (Rudy, Stadler-Morris, and Albert, 1987).

In recent years, researchers have concentrated on how large collections of neurons in the hippocampal formation can act together to represent and store spatial information, and how these neural ensembles can generate spatially adaptive behavior (see NEURAL COMPUTATION: HIPPOCAMPUS). This pursuit should ultimately enable us to understand how the brain performs the calculations necessary to the kinds of spatial behaviors described earlier.

Some recent research has demonstrated a remarkable fact about the relation between the hippocampal formation and spatial learning: It has been shown that there is a correlation between the size of the hippocampus (or certain structural parameters of the hippocampus) and the spatial learning ability of the given species. Thus, if one looks at a number of bird species, and compares those that cache food in various locations with those that do not, the former have larger hippocampi. There appears to be some evolutionary pressure in these species favoring an increased hippocampal size (see EVOLUTION AND LEARNING). Much the same result has been reported in several mammalian species (Jacobs et al., 1990). In two closely related species of meadow voles, hippocampal size of males and females was compared. In one species, in which males and females had essentially the same space-use patterns, there were no size differences observed. In the other species, in which males roamed over much larger ranges than did the females, the males had a larger hippocampus than the females. These size differences were reflected in superior spatial learning. Similar advantages in spatial learning in males have been demonstrated in laboratory rats (Warren et al., 1990).

In discussing spatial learning, mention should be made of the extraordinary spatial learning skills demonstrated by humans from certain cultures. In the South Seas, open-sea navigation is a well-developed art, enabling those who acquire the skill to navigate, using sea, stars, and imaginary landmarks, across thousands of miles of open ocean. Such skill stands as a clear indication that spatial learning is not some specialized ability restricted to species such as birds and rats, but instead is widespread throughout the animal world.

(See also MIGRATION, NAVIGATION, AND HOMING.)

REFERENCES

Barnes, C. A. (1988). Spatial learning and memory processes: The search for their neurobiological mechanisms in the rat. *Trends in Neurosciences 11*, 163–169.

Jacobs, L. F., Gaulin, S. J. C., Sherry, D. F., and Hoffman, G. E. (1990). Evolution of spatial cognition: Sex-specific patterns of spatial behavior predict hippocampal size. *Proceedings of the National Academy of Sciences 87*, 6349–6352.

Morris, R. G. M. (1981). Spatial localization does not

require the presence of local cues. *Learning and Motivation 12,* 239–261.

Morris, R. G. M., Garrud, P., Rawlins, J. N. P., and O'Keefe, J. (1982). Place navigation in rats with hippocampal lesions. *Nature 297,* 681–683.

O'Keefe, J. (1976). Place units in the hippocampus of the freely moving rat. *Experimental Neurology 51,* 70–109.

——— (1979). A review of hippocampal place cells. *Progress in Neurobiology 13,* 419–439.

O'Keefe, J., and Dostrovsky, J. (1971). The hippocampus as a spatial map: Preliminary evidence from unit activity in the freely-moving rat. *Brain Research 31,* 171–175.

O'Keefe, J., and Nadel, L. (1978). *The hippocampus as a cognitive map.* Oxford: Clarendon Press.

O'Keefe, J., and Speakman, A. (1987). Single unit activity in the rat hippocampus during a spatial memory task. *Experimental Brain Research 68,* 1–27.

Olton, D. S., and Samuelson, R. J. (1976). Remembrance of places passed: Spatial memory in rats. *Journal of Experimental Psychology: Animal Behavior Processes 2,* 97–116.

Rudy, J. W., Stadler-Morris, S., and Albert, P. (1987). Ontogeny of spatial navigation behaviors in the rat: Dissociation of "proximal"- and "distal"-cue based behaviors. *Behavioral Neuroscience 101,* 62–73.

Warren, S. G., Wilson, L. A., and Nadel, L. (1990). Sexually dimorphic spatial abilities in the Morris water task. *Society for Neuroscience Abstracts 20,* 1321.

Lynn Nadel

SPENCE, KENNETH

Kenneth W. Spence (1907–1967) played a major role in psychology from the early 1930s until his untimely death. His impact is illustrated by the fact that from 1962 to 1967, he was the most cited author in a survey of the fourteen most prestigious psychological journals (Myers, 1970). Spence's influence resulted from achievements as experimentalist, theorist, methodologist, and teacher. In all of these roles, he operated as a natural science psychologist, one who believed that the science of psychology can employ the same methods of empirical inquiry and theory construction as physics, chemistry, and biology. In essence, he was asserting that psychology, in principle, is capable of producing a body of reliable scientific knowledge. To achieve this goal he deemed it necessary to conceptualize psychology as the science of behavior, not of the mind. That

is, the basic observations of the science of psychology are the behavior of organisms, not the direct examination of conscious experience. This methodological position, BEHAVIORISM, was initially expressed, in a radical form, by John B. WATSON (Kendler, 1987), but since has matured into a more sophisticated version known as *neobehaviorism.*

Spence was born May 6, 1907, in Chicago. When he was 4, Western Electric transferred his father, an electrical engineer, to Montreal. He majored in psychology at McGill University, receiving a B.A. in 1929 and an M.A. in 1930. His Ph.D. was granted in 1933 by Yale University, where he served as a research assistant to Robert M. Yerkes, under whose direction he completed a dissertation on the visual acuity of chimpanzees. The dominant intellectual influence during his Yale days evolved from the inspirational ideas of Clark L. HULL, who set as his goal the formulation of a theoretical interpretation of behavior that emulated the conceptual structure of Newtonian physics.

Hull's general approach was shaped by both Ivan PAVLOV and Edward THORNDIKE. Pavlovian conditioning, for Hull, was the simplest form of learning, and hence principles of conditioning could provide the premises from which more complex forms

Figure 1.   Kenneth W. Spence. *Courtesy Dr. Janet T. Spence.*

of behavior could be deduced (explained). Thorndike's *law of effect* represented, for Hull, another fundamental principle of behavior; rewards, technically known as *reinforcements*, are necessary for the formation and strengthening of a connection between a situation and behavior, or what became to be known as a *stimulus-response association* (e.g., in Pavlovian conditioning the sound of a tone became connected with salivation because it was reinforced by food).

While a graduate student, Spence prepared a paper (Spence, 1932) that illustrated Hull's general strategy. Based on assumptions about the effect of delayed reinforcement in conditioning, Spence predicted that in a complex maze, one with several successive choice points, entrances into blind alleys would be eliminated in a backward order, that is, the blinds are more difficult the farther they are from the goal. After completing his graduate work at Yale, Spence accepted a National Research Council fellowship to the Yale Laboratories of Primate Biology at Orange Park, Florida, where he published his classical theory of animal discrimination learning (Spence, 1936), a conception that is still influential (Kendler, 1992; see also DISCRIMINATION AND GENERALIZATION). In 1937 he moved to the University of Virginia as an assistant professor of psychology. The following year he was appointed associate professor at the University of Iowa, where, in 1942, he became professor and head of the Department of Psychology, a position he occupied until 1964, when he moved to the University of Texas.

Kenneth Spence's efforts in theoretical psychology are characterized by a consistent direction and a close relationship between facts and theory. He had (a) an ability to express ideas in a lucid prose that resulted from clear thinking and hard work; (b) a flair for designing clever experimental tests of competing hypotheses; (c) a knack for analyzing data so that their theoretical implications would become fully apparent; (d) an ingenious talent for theoretically integrating a range of experimental results with the added, and unusual, feature of being able to offer possible alternative explanations, even some from competing theories; and (e) a special aptitude, in spite of limited mathematical training, to coordinate his theoretical interpretation with a quantitative model that structured an empirical problem so that further theoretical clarification and empirical development could occur.

One excellent example of Spence's style of theoretical and empirical structuring is exhibited in his influential analysis of discrimination learning of animals (Spence, 1936), which contained one of the first mathematical simulations (without the aid of a computer!) of a theory. The model, which seeks to identify the psychological processes involved in how animals learn to choose between two stimuli when one is followed by reward and the other is not, postulates two basic theoretical mechanisms that Hull had employed in interpreting conditioning phenomena: excitation and inhibition. When the animal is reinforced for selecting one stimulus, that habit (stimulus-response association) is gradually strengthened; when a response to the other cue is not reinforced, that habit is gradually weakened. When the difference in strengths between the two competing habits reaches a certain value, the subject consistently chooses the reinforced stimulus. Spence had no illusion that his formulation represented a complete interpretation of the discrimination learning process. He readily acknowledged that certain fundamental processes, such as complex perceptual mechanisms, were ignored but insisted, as a matter of strategy, that discrimination learning, as well as all psychological problems, must be broken down into bare essentials to be investigated fruitfully. Reducing discrimination learning to the analysis of competing habits in a simple experimental situation was a fruitful strategy for dealing with fundamental principles of behavior.

Spence's theory of discrimination learning had many ramifications, including the formulation of an ingenious stimulus-response explanation (Spence, 1937) of the transposition phenomenon, the tendency for nonverbal organisms to transfer a relational choice from one problem to a subsequent one (e.g., after learning to choose a medium gray in preference to a lighter one, a rat will probably select a darker gray rather than the previously rewarded medium gray). In addition, his theory initiated a crucial controversy as to whether discrimination learning was a continuous or noncontinuous process, occurring gradually or suddenly (Kendler, 1987).

Although Spence's discrimination learning theory was designed for nonverbal organisms, he sought to discover how the acquisition of symbolic skills would influence discrimination learning. He encouraged a doctoral student, Margaret Kuenne (1946), to investigate this problem; she found that in a transposition problem the behavior of inarticulate youngsters was similar to that of rats, in that simple stimulus-response associations were formed but the acquisition of symbolic skills introduced a more complex pattern of stimulation and associative connections that enhanced relational responding. This led to a two-stage theory of discrimination learning (Kendler and Kendler, 1962, 1975) in which the lower stage (single unit), based upon Spence's continuity model, hypothesized that the responses of subhuman animals were directly linked (associated) to stimuli (e.g., black, white), whereas higher-level functioning (mediational model) suggested that incoming stimulation is transformed into some internal conceptual representation (e.g., brightness) that guides subsequent behavior. This model, which had its origins in Spence's discrimination learning theory, could account for developmental changes in the discrimination learning exhibited by humans.

From 1950 to the end of his life, classical (Pavlovian) eyeblink conditioning with human subjects occupied Spence's interest. His efforts revealed basic principles of habit formation and the interaction effects between habits and drives. With the collaboration of Janet A. Taylor, who later became his wife, the role of anxiety as a motivational mechanism was empirically and theoretically analyzed (e.g., Spence and Taylor, 1951; Spence, 1956). Spence (1966) was able, by clever experimental manipulations, to get human subjects to respond either in a simple associative manner analogous to subhuman behavior or in a cognitive (mediational) manner. This was another example of his effort, as well as that of several of his students, to gain an experimental grip on evolutionary processes in behavior theory (see also EVOLUTION AND LEARNING).

In 1955, Spence was invited to deliver the Silliman Lectures at Yale, a prestigious series that until then had been given by distinguished physical and biological scientists such as Ernest Rutherford, Enrico Fermi, and Charles Sherrington. The lectures, published under the title *Behavior Theory and Conditioning* (1956), can be characterized as a realistic and reasonable theoretical interpretation of a wide range of experimental data. Unlike many of the theoretical messiahs who have dotted the psychological landscape with grandiose theories, Spence's formulation was never far removed from experimental evidence. In essence, Spence was an experimental psychologist's theorist because his hypotheses were clearly testable.

Spence's skills as an experimentalist and theorist were matched by his talents as a methodologist.

With the collaboration of the philosopher of science Gustav Bergmann, Spence contributed to the clarification of the meaning of psychological concepts and the logic of psychological measurement (Bergmann and Spence, 1941, 1944). His greatest contribution as a methodologist was his clarification of issues in theoretical psychology, particularly in relation to the comparative analysis of competing learning theories. The competing theory to the Hull-Spence model that interested Spence the most was Edward TOLMAN's cognitive theory of animal learning. This formulation generated much confusion among both behaviorists and antibehaviorists; the former could not reconcile Tolman's hypothesized mentalistic processes with methodological behaviorism, and the latter denied that Tolman could be labeled a behaviorist if he employed phenomenological experience as a metaphor for his theoretical constructs. Spence clearly distinguished between the strategies employed for conceptualizing theoretical processes—mechanistic, phenomenological, mathematical, or some other—and the theory's deductive, empirical consequences. Unfortunately this distinction between a theorist's thinking style and the explicit theory with its deductive empirical implications was not fully appreciated at the time of the cognitive revolution, and as a result needless disputation and misunderstanding were encouraged. Many segments of the psychological community failed to appreciate the linkage between neobehaviorism in general, and Spence's theoretical efforts in particular, in attempting to understand the relationship between associative and cognitive processes (Kendler, 1984).

Spence's contributions to psychology cannot be limited to his own publications. His inspired teaching must also be considered. Many of his seventy-five doctoral students, too many to mention, made solid contributions to the science of psychology: "All of his doctoral students carry with them some of Spence's ideas and commitments and a desire to achieve a level of quality in their own work that would be acceptable to their Professor" (Kendler, 1967, p. 341).

In addition to being the first and only psychologist to give the Silliman Lectures, Spence received many other honors, including membership in the National Academy of Sciences, the Howard Crosby Warren Medal of the Society of Experimental Psychologists in 1953, and the American Psychological Association's Scientific Contribution Award in 1956, the first year that it was presented. But perhaps the greatest honor Spence aspired to was a place in the history of psychology. Although it is difficult to penetrate the haze of the future, especially in relation to psychology, a discipline that is conceptualized in many antithetical ways, it is likely that Spence will be remembered as a clear and sophisticated exponent of natural science psychology and as a theorist and empiricist who, while appreciating the immaturity of the science of psychology, was nevertheless able to advance it with fruitful conceptions of learning and motivation.

REFERENCES

Bergmann, G., and Spence, K. W. (1941). Operationism and theory construction. *Psychological Review 48*, 1–14.

——— (1944). The logic of psychological measurement. *Psychological Review 51*, 1–24.

Kendler, H. H. (1967). Kenneth W. Spence: 1907–1967. *Psychological Review 74*, 335–341.

——— (1984). Evolutions or revolutions? In K. M. B. Lagerspetz and P. Niemi, eds., *Psychology in the 1990's.* Amsterdam: North Holland.

——— (1987). *Historical foundations of modern psychology.* Pacific Grove, Calif.: Brooks/Cole.

Kendler, H. H., and Kendler, T. S. (1962). Vertical and horizontal processes in problem solving. *Psychological Review 69*, 1–16.

——— (1975). From discrimination learning to cognitive development: A neobehavioristic odyssey. In W. K. Estes, ed., *Handbook of learning and cognitive processes,* vol. 1. Hillsdale, N.J.: Erlbaum.

Kendler, T. S. (1992). *Levels of cognitive development.* Hillsdale, N.J.: Erlbaum.

Kuenne, M. R. (1946). Experimental investigation of the relation of language to transposition behavior in young children. *Journal of Experimental Psychology 36*, 471–490.

Myers, C. R. (1970). Journal citations and scientific eminence in contemporary psychology. *American Psychologist 25*, 1041–1048.

Spence, K. W. (1932). The order of eliminating blinds in maze learning by the rat. *Journal of Comparative Psychology 14*, 9–27.

——— (1936). The nature of discrimination learning in animals. *Psychological Review 43*, 427–429.

——— (1937). The differential response in animals to stimuli varying within a single dimension. *Psychological Review 44*, 430–444.

——— (1956). *Behavior theory and conditioning.* New Haven: Yale University Press.

——— (1966). Cognitive and drive factors in the extinction of the conditioned eye blink in human subjects. *Psychological Review 73*, 445–451.

Spence, K. W., and Taylor, J. A. (1951). Anxiety and strength of the UCS as determiners of the amount of eyelid conditioning. *Journal of Experimental Psychology 42*, 183–186.

Howard H. Kendler

SPINAL PLASTICITY

The mammalian spinal cord has long been recognized as a unique part of the central nervous system. It is usually viewed as a transmitter of information to and from the brain, with various reflex functions built in to allow automatic responding to stimuli impinging on the body. The reflex functions of the spinal cord are generally assumed to be unchanging entities whose excitabilities may be temporarily altered by descending activity from the brain or by repeated sensory input. In the 1930s, however, a body of work began to accumulate that now shows that the spinal reflex pathways can be altered in ways that have many characteristics of learning and memory in the intact mammal. This indicates that the relatively simple spinal reflex pathways may be actively involved in information processing and behavioral change.

Spinal Conditioning

Initial research on "learning" in the spinal cord began with attempts to determine the simplest part of the nervous system that could support learning. Classical conditioning operations were used (see CONDITIONING, CLASSICAL AND INSTRUMENTAL), in which a conditioned stimulus was followed by an unconditioned stimulus to the hind limb of an anesthetized subject with a spinal transection at the mid-back level, usually a dog. These studies appeared to show alterations in reflex excitability due exclusively to the pairing of the two stimuli, a conclusion soon challenged on grounds of both procedure and accuracy. It was not clear from the early studies whether the response alterations were actually due to the pairing or to other factors, such as general excitability changes or other nonspecific factors.

However, by the early 1970s, additional studies on the ability of the spinal reflexes to respond to classical conditioning procedures began to appear. These studies, using well-established control group technology, proved that spinal reflex excitability could be altered by classical conditioning procedures. The results showed that the pairing of two stimuli had effects on the response excitability not produced by presenting the same stimuli separately or in reverse order. Thus the effects of the response pairing were unique, as in classical conditioning. Spinal conditioning showed many other features of classical conditioning in the intact animal, although the spinal reflex system apparently could not learn to respond differentially. The learned changes did not spontaneously decay but showed the extinction decreases generally seen in classical conditioning. The effect also seemed to be heavily dependent on inputs from neural pathways that normally conduct noxious sensations to the cord and brain. Other studies demonstrated that reflex excitability alterations induced by classical conditioning procedures occurred in the interneurons of the reflex pathways rather than in the initial synapses of the sensory fibers into the cord or in the motoneurons.

Spinal Fixation

A second type of excitability alteration of spinal reflexes has become known as *spinal fixation*. Here, a fairly intense, 35–50 minute stimulus to the spinal cord can increase the excitability of the activated reflex pathways for hours or days. This increased excitability is like a memory trace in the spinal cord. The change is usually large enough to produce ongoing motoneuron output after the initiating stimulus is removed. In initial studies, the ongoing activity caused limb flexion in animals following complete spinal transection, when a flaccid paralysis would have been expected, leading to the term *fixation* of postural asymmetry. More recent studies have shown that fixation can be produced by stimulation or lesions of various brain regions, or by stimulation of the leg skin or a sensory nerve. Fixation intensity can be altered with stimulants and other drugs, and by protein synthesis inhibitors or enhancers. Physiological stress also seems to enhance the fixation process. A similar alteration of spinal reflex excitability has been demonstrated in intact monkeys that were taught to increase their leg muscle tone over many days. Here the change was gradual but also long lasting, and occurred in the spinal reflexes. As with spinal conditioning, fixation apparently occurs in the interneurons of the spinal cord. Fixation seems

similar to LONG-TERM POTENTIATION, a process that is hypothesized to be a part of learning and memory in intact animals.

Conclusions

The studies of spinal conditioning and fixation clearly show that the mammalian spinal cord contains reflex pathways that are subject to long-lasting excitability changes similar in many ways to learning and memory in the whole animal. With spinal conditioning, the alteration is produced uniquely by two stimuli delivered in a specific order and temporal sequence, while in fixation, one stimulus is sufficient. The fact that the conditioning stimuli are delivered to two separate sensory inputs to the cord means that the conditioning paradigm involves two sets of interacting synapses that must be activated sequentially but briefly to produce the reflex alterations, whereas the fixation process occurs within a single synaptic pathway that is strongly activated over a period of time. Thus, it is possible that the conditioning and fixation phenomena represent two distinct processes of excitability alteration in the cord. The evidence also shows that these changes can occur during the animal's day-to-day life, supporting the notion that the spinal cord actively processes information and that its response patterns may be altered by ongoing afferent inputs, rather than simply acting as a passive receiver and transmitter of information.

REFERENCES

Anderson, M. F., Mokler, D. J., and Winterson, B. J. (1991). Inhibition of chronic hindlimb flexion in rat: Evidence for mediation by 5-hydroxytryptamine. *Brain Research 541,* 216–224.

Beggs, A. L., Steinmetz, J. E., and Patterson, M. M. (1985). Classical conditioning of a flexor nerve response in spinal cats: Effects of tibial nerve CS and a differential conditioning paradigm. *Behavioral Neuroscience 99* (3), 496–508.

Durkovic, R. G. (1975). Classical conditioning, sensitization, and habituation of the flexion reflex of the spinal cat. *Physiology and Behavior 14,* 297–304.

——— (1985). Retention of a classically conditioned reflex response in spinal cat. *Behavioral and Neural Biology 43,* 12–20.

Patterson, M. M. (1976). Mechanisms of classical conditioning and fixation in spinal mammals. In A. H. Reisen and R. F. Thompson, eds., *Advances in psychobiology,* pp. 381–433. New York: Wiley. An exhaustive review to 1975.

Patterson, M. M., Cegavske, C. F., and Thompson, R. F. (1973). Effects of a classical conditioning paradigm on hind-limb flexor nerve response in immobilized spinal cats. *Journal of Comparative and Physiological Psychology* 84 (1), 88–97.

Steinmetz, J. E., and Patterson, M. M. (1985). Fixation of spinal reflex alterations in spinal rats by sensory nerve stimulation. *Behavioral Neuroscience* 99 (1), 97–108.

Wolpaw, J. R., and Carp, J. S. (1990). Memory traces in spinal cord. *Trends in Neuroscience* 13 (4), 137–142.

Michael M. Patterson
Michael J. Bartelt

STIMULUS CONTROL

See Discrimination and Generalization

STRESS AND MEMORY

Stress can have profound effects on learning and memory processes. These effects can be either positive or negative, and vary considerably depending on the type of learning that is being measured as well as on the specific characteristics of the stressor. Operationally, stress is the external condition that places demands on the organism, and the stress response is the organism's adaptive response to the stressor, typically measured as changes in performance or physiological or biochemical states. Most adaptive responses are crucial to an organism's capacity for survival and can be easily reconciled with theories of natural selection. For instance, the release of glucocorticoids from the adrenal glands directs glucose to the brain and musculature in preparation for "fight or flight," thereby eliminating unnecessary processing of ongoing vegetative functions such as digestion. One adaptation, however, is counterintuitive: loss of performance.

At first it seems reasonable to assume that stress is linearly related to performance such that the more stressful the experience the greater the detriment. In reality, animals (including humans) perform optimally at moderate levels of demand and performance is compromised at the extremes. In this context, the relationship between stress and performance is an inverted-U-shaped function: Performance is impaired equally at high levels of stress as at low levels (boredom or drowsiness), and at moderate levels, performance is facilitated. For example, exposure to a moderate stressor such as background noise can facilitate performance of a prolonged vigilance task. Substituting arousal for stress, Donald HEBB (1955) suggested that ongoing neural activity could provide a physiological means for describing such self-motivating phenomena as curiosity and exploration and their obvious contribution to learning. Moreover, he emphasized that without such an arousal foundation, no learning would occur. This relationship, in combination with the inverted-U relationship proposed between stress and performance, predicts a linear relationship between stress and arousal. Others, however, have reported that stress relates to arousal in an upright U-shaped manner, thus forecasting a monotonic relationship between stress and performance. Still others report that stress and arousal are independent. The burden of proof is on the neurophysiologists to establish whether, indeed, these phenomena are independent, and if so, how they interact.

The exact relationship between these concepts depends, presumably, on the significance of the information to be remembered, and therefore on the type of learning that is being tapped. In the case of one-trial learning, one highly stressful encounter can create a lifelong impression on the animal, thereby maximizing retention. One of the most salient characteristics is that of task difficulty. Autonomic tasks with a high degree of preparedness are less likely to be adversely affected than tasks requiring high cognitive capacity and concentration. These two extremes can be viewed as the ends of a continuum, with stress decreasing performance as task difficulty increases. This relationship is exemplified by the intense training and practice required of highly skilled professionals, such as military personnel who must perform optimally under high levels of stress and uncertainty.

The degree to which stress impinges on performance is highly susceptible to individual differences. Although there is a limit to the attentional capacity that can be allocated to a particular task, this capacity is not fixed and will vary from individual to individual and from day to day. On the evidence of human self-report scales, high-anxiety subjects tend to perform optimally on easy tasks, low-anxiety subjects perform optimally under

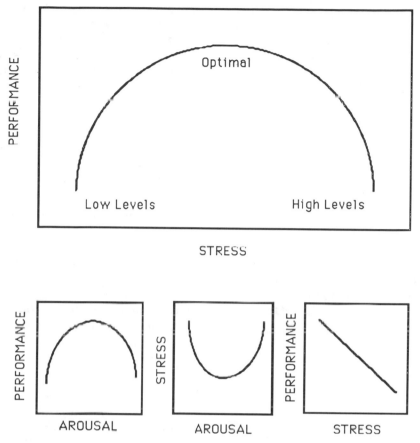

Figure 1. Performance versus stress, performance versus arousal, and stress versus arousal.

more demanding circumstances, and, within tasks, low-anxiety subjects perform better during early stages of learning and high anxiety facilitates the later stages. Additional sources of response variability include sociological factors, age, and disease. Perhaps the most significant source is past memories. The animal must not only calculate the imbalance between the perceived demand and the ability to cope with that demand, but must also incorporate this information into its previous experience.

In the early 1960s, J. B. Overmier and M. E. P. Seligman noticed that dogs exposed to inescapable shock were later impaired in their ability to perform a task where escape was possible. Proposing that the animals became helpless after learning that the aversive event and the ability to cope with that event were not contingent, they termed the phenomenon LEARNED HELPLESSNESS. Because the secondary characteristics that accompany helplessness—weight loss, sleep disturbances, decreased

activity, among others—resemble characteristics observed in depressed humans, the phenomenon evolved into one of the first experimental models of depression. It has been used successfully to demonstrate stress-induced effects on immune function, ulcer development, tumor growth, analgesia, aggression, and status within a dominance hierarchy. But over and above these effects has been the continued demonstration, under the appropriate conditions, of deficits in performance. However intuitively appealing, this paradigm of helplessness is constrained by more general theories of stress and learning and is, in fact, dependent on individual sex, species, and strain differences as well as specific task demands and task difficulty. For example, prior exposure to inescapable shock can, under certain conditions, greatly *facilitate* classical conditioning of the eyeblink response (i.e., a learned help*ful*ness phenomenon occurs).

In addition to its impact on behavior, exposure to inescapable shock has an equally extensive impact on neuronal plasticity, affecting synaptic morphology, receptor affinity and number, gene expression, and electrophysiological responsiveness. For example, the stressor induces immediate early gene (IEG) expression and impairs LONG-TERM POTENTIATION (LTP), both putative biological substrates for learning in the mammalian brain. Since most neurobiological theories of learning and memory presume underlying changes in neuronal plasticity, stress effects on learning are presumed, at least in part, to be mediated through such changes.

Although much has been written anecdotally on stress and the biological response to stress, the integration of these two approaches has been minimal. One of the first to do so was the eminent physiologist Hans Seyle, who wrote several books ranging in approach from the intimate to the mechanistic. Seyle put forth the notion that the stress response was the *nonspecific* response of the body to any demand placed upon it. What Seyle referred to was activation of the hypothalamic-pituitary-adrenal (HPA) axis. In this axis hypothalamic peptides activate adrenocorticotropin (ACTH) secretion from the anterior pituitary. ACTH induces the release of glucocorticoids from the adrenal cortex, and glucocorticoids, in turn, inhibit release of pituitary ACTH. Glucocorticoids are released peripherally into the blood upon most, if not all, stressful encounters, and are potentially damaging, especially in high concentrations and/or chronic conditions. What has not been fully appreciated in their necessary and vital role in bringing the system back to homeostasis, and more generally, the inherent *specificity* of the stress response.

In addition to glucocorticoids, many other stress-related neuromodulators are viable candidates for the behavioral response to stress and subsequent effects on mnemonic processes. The catecholamines, known for their critical role in learning, are released peripherally from the adrenal medulla as well as synthesized centrally, as are dopamine systems of mesocortical origin. Along with ACTH, β-lipocortin and β-endorphin are released from the pituitary in response to stress. Peptides, such as the opioids (the enkephalins) and vasopressin, are stress-induced and play a significant role in learning and memory processes. Most recently, evidence to support the involvement of the excitatory amino acid glutamate and its corresponding receptors, n-methyl-d-aspartate (NMDA) and α-amino-3-methylsoxazole-4-propionic acid (AMPA), has surfaced. Glutamate is one of the primary neurotransmitters in the brain, and activation of its receptors is critical to certain types of learning. Most of these stress-induced neuromodulators and their receptors are abundant in the hippocampus, the limbic structure long considered integral to the successful acquisition of various sorts of information.

Many of the aforementioned neuromodulatory systems are colocalized and codependent, making it difficult to interfere experimentally with one without affecting another. Furthermore, given the wide diversity of stressors and the inherent variance in individual responsiveness to the same stressor, it is probable that specific but overlapping circuits contribute to stress effects on learning. Finally, these stress-induced responses should not necessarily be viewed as detrimental to the physical and psychological well-being of the organism, but rather should be seen as contributing to reestablishment of homeostasis following the stressful encounter and appropriate consolidation of the experience.

REFERENCES

Cox, T. (1980). *Stress.* Baltimore: University Park Press.

Hasher, L., and Zacks, R. T. (1979). Autonomic and effortful processes in memory. *Journal of Experimental Psychology 108,* 356–388.

Hebb, D. (1955). Drives and the C.N.S. (conceptual nervous system). *Psychological Review 62,* 243–254.

Munck, A., Guyre, P. M., and Holbrook, N. J. (1984). Physiological functions of glucocorticoids in stress and their relation to pharmacological actions. *Endocrine Reviews 5,* 25–44.

Seyle, H. (1956). *The stress of life.* New York: McGraw-Hill.

Tracey J. Shors

STROKE

See Amnesia, Organic; Aphasia; Frontal Lobes and Memory; Knowledge Systems; Material-Specific Memory Deficits; Rehabilitation of Memory Disorders; Visual Object Agnosia

SYNAPSE

See Guide to the Anatomy of the Brain

T

TASTE AVERSION AND PREFERENCE LEARNING IN ANIMALS

Historically taste aversion learning arose as a problem in evolutionary biology. Darwin was puzzled by an incongruity: Some tender caterpillars were brightly colored and exposed themselves so that they caught the eye of every passing bird. Such behavior appeared maladaptive. A. R. Wallace suggested that brightly colored butterfly larva probably tasted bitter and might be poisonous; therefore the colors served to deter birds and other predators. Subsequent research supported Wallace's hypothesis. Consumption of the colorful insects causes gastric nausea and emesis, and after one or two trials, birds and other predators learn to avoid them. As larva, these insects feed on plants which evolved the bitter toxins as a defense against herbivores; the insects turned that defense to their own advantage.

Taste-aversion learning proved to be widespread in phylogeny and ontogeny. Taste-toxin conditioned aversions have been observed in snails, insects, fish, frogs and salamanders, lizards and snakes, domestic and wild birds and mammals, fetal and neonate rats, young children and adult humans. Even protozoans reject bitter, the natural taste of plant poisons. The ubiquity of the phenomenon indicates this mechanism to protect the gut must have evolved many millions of years ago.

It was known early on that toxic defenses of plants were only half of the coevolutionary story. Plants use sweet nectar and sweet fruit to entice animals to pollinate blossoms and to carry indigestible seeds in their gut and so disperse them in their droppings. Sweet is a natural signal for nutrients, and animals acquire preferences for flavors followed by nutritious aftereffects. Animals also demonstrate "specific hungers" that presumably reflect a dietary need. For example, thiamine-deficient rats will acquire preferences for flavors paired with thiamine injections. Rats also prefer flavors paired with recuperation from gastric nausea. In nature, animals have been observed eating materials such as clay, bones, or bitter leaves, presumably for "medicinal" or "dietary" purposes. For example, wild chimpanzees occasionally eat bitter aspelia leaves, which contain powerful antibiotic constituents. Thus palatability can be modulated positively as well as negatively.

Taste-aversion learning caught the attention of experimental psychologists in the 1960s when two factors became known. First, when an animal drinks tasty water marked by a bright-noisy signal, and is injected with a mild toxin, it will develop an aversion for the taste but not the bright-noisy signal. Conversely, if the animal is mildly shocked on the feet, it will avoid the bright-noisy signal but not the tasty water. Second and furthermore, the electrocutaneous shock must be applied immediately after the signal for effective learning, but the drug injection can be delayed hours after the tasty drink and the animal will still learn the taste aversion in one trial. These two factors, known as (1) selective association and (2) long-delay learning, respectively, caused a restructuring of learning theory beginning around 1970.

Both classical (Pavlovian) and instrumental (Thorndikian) systems must be expanded to handle taste-nausea learning. In classical food conditioning, a distal signal such as noise catching the attention of the animal is called the conditioned stimulus (CS). The taste of food or liquid contacting the mouth and evoking salivation is the unconditioned stimulus (US). Nausea is a third event that adjusts the palatability of the taste US by a feedback (FB) mechanism, hence the complete sequence is CS-US-FB (see Figure 1). Instrumental conditioning is basically similar except that a specific response emitted by the animal is designated as the CS to be followed by the food US and its subsequent FB. (See also CONDITIONING, CLASSICAL AND INSTRUMENTAL.)

The taste, US, plays a curious dual role in the CS-US-FB sequence. The CS-US phase is a cognitive process, that is, the alerted animal soon comes to recognize that the CS means food is coming soon, precisely timing the CS-US interval, its mouth watering in anticipation of the US. The US-FB phase is an entirely different matter. After consuming the food US, animals usually go to sleep; thus the FB must operate on the US in an unconscious animal. For example, a rat is given a drink of saccharin water and is put under deep anesthesia 15 minutes later. Then a nauseous drug is injected while the rat remains in deep sleep for an hour or two. Several days later, when saccharin water is offered again, the rat approaches the spout eagerly, but on tasting, it reels backward in surprise, mouth gaping as if to eject the flavor of the saccharin US from its mouth. This effect has been demonstrated with various anesthetic, soporific, tranquilizing, and neurologic treatments.

There are other peculiarities in prolonged US-FB learning that distinguish it from the crisp clarity of the traditional CS-US association. An animal on a diet that is inadequate or contains a low-grade toxin may take weeks to acquire a taste aversion for the diet, manifesting no sign of discomfort except for the loss of appetite for that particular diet. When offered another flavored diet, the animal eats with gusto. Such losses of appetite may be conditioned taste aversions, and have been associated with exposure to low levels of ionizing radiation, improperly balanced diets, pregnancy, certain cancerous growths, and chemotherapeutic treatments. Whenever there is an unexplained loss of appetite for a familiar food or diet, a negative FB condition stemming from exogenous or endogenous sources should be suspected even if the subject offers no other signs of discomfort.

Not just any toxin will produce a conditioned taste aversion. For example, cyanide will not, because cyanosis works its deadly effect without nausea. However, rotary motion, a nontoxic agent producing nausea, will induce food aversions. The necessary and sufficient FB seems to be a nauseous malaise referred to the gastric region; discomfort and pain emanating from the upper or lower gut are not effective. However, the negative FB can operate without sensation of nausea and is effective in an unconscious subject.

The neurological mechanisms of the US-FB feeding adjustment are known only in broad outline. The taste receptors send afferents via the facial and glossopharyngeal nerves to the nucleus solitarius of the brain stem. The receptors in the viscera send vagal fibers converging to that same nucleus. The blood carries absorbed food products to the area postrema, where blood monitors report to the solitary nucleus. Vestibular influences also converge to this complex, and emesis is initiated here. The US and FB neural routes proceed rostrally to the parabrachial complex. Neurophysiological experiments indicate that a complex series of looping circuits bring influences from the hypothalamus, the limbic system, and the gustatory cortex to the palatability control mechanism. Accordingly, behavioral experiments indicate that taste aversions can be induced by motion sickness, endocrine products, emotional stress, cognitive associations, memories, and imagination.

If the CS-US-FB schema has generality, then the peculiarities of US-FB should be apparent in other systems of broad evolutionary significance. In the selective learning experiment, signal-shock learning and taste-nausea were not strictly comparable because the former is a CS-US cognitive processing of skin insult, while the latter is a motivational US-FB adjustment that can occur in unconscious animals. The signal-pain sequence requires a third FB term in order to be comparable with taste-nausea. Recently a different line of research has revealed the FB mechanisms that modulate the pain US in ways analogous to the feeding FB mechanisms (see Figure 1).

Endogenous FB analgesias are naturally induced by fear and/or pain. Experimentally, they can also be induced by direct stimulation of selected sites in the midbrain. These FBs raise the threshold for reflexive pain responses, and some of these mechanisms will do so in rats under deep anesthesia and will operate over long time periods. Such automatic modulation is advantageous because severe pain would hamper escape, but later, immobilizing pain promotes healing of wounds.

Comparable selective learning effects have been obtained with drug injections in both skin and gut defense. Drugs that interfere with motor responses (gallamine) or endogenous opioid analge-

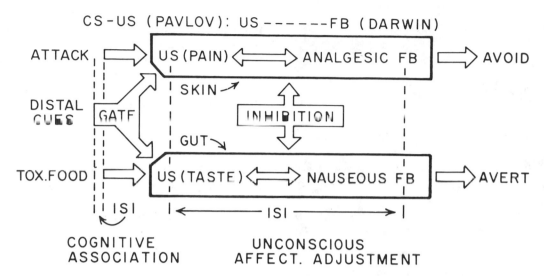

CS-US (PAVLOV): US------FB (DARWIN)

Figure 1. Skin-defense system against predatory attack and gut-defense system against toxic food. Distal cues (CS) impinging on the eyes, ears, and nose are cognitively associated with unconditioned stimulus (US) over brief interstimulus intervals (ISI), according to Pavlov. Subsequently, endogenous feedback (FB) unconsciously modulates the affective value of each US over a prolonged ISI commensurate with its adaptive value for the organism, concurring with Darwin. Activity in one function tends to inhibit the other function. *Reprinted with permission from S. B. Klein and R. R. Mower, eds. (1989). Contemporary learning theories, p. 187. Hillsdale, N.J.: Erlbaum.*

sia (naloxone) will produce strong avoidance of external place cues but weak taste aversions. By contrast, nauseous drugs have precisely the opposite effect. Furthermore, this skin-defense system against predatory attack is as widespread in phylogeny and ontogeny as is the gut-defense system against natural poisons in the foodstuffs of the world.

(See also FOOD AVERSION AND PREFERENCE LEARNING IN HUMANS.)

REFERENCES

Bernstein, I. L., and Borson, S. (1986). Learned food aversion: A component of anorexia syndromes. *Psychological Review 93* (4), 462–472.

Brower, L. P. (1981). Chemical defence in butterflies. *Symposium of the Royal Entomological Society of London 11,* 109–114.

Cabanac, M. (1979). Sensory pleasure. *Quarterly Review of Biology 54,* 1–29.

Garcia, J., Hankins, W. G., and Rusiniak, K. W. (1974). Behavioral regulations of the *milieu interne* in man and rat. *Science 185,* 824–831.

John Garcia

THORNDIKE, EDWARD

Edward Lee Thorndike was born on August 31, 1874, in Williamsburg, Massachusetts. He died on August 9, 1949, in Montrose, New York. Thorndike proceeded very rapidly through his graduate education. After receiving a B.A. at Wesleyan University in 1895, he transferred to Harvard University, where he received a second B.A. in 1896 and his M.A. the following year. In 1898, Thorndike completed his Ph.D. at Columbia University, where he spent virtually his entire academic career as a professor at Teachers College (1899–1940). While this article will not dwell on Thorndike's achievements in the applied area that came to be called *educational psychology,* it should be noted that he created that field and developed it during his entire career at Columbia.

Thorndike's experimental studies of learning in monkeys brought him his first position at Teachers College as an instructor in genetic psychology. The dean of Teachers College, James E. Russell, hired Thorndike because he thought those studies to be "a pretty good stepping stone to a study of the nature and behavior of children" (*Current Biography,* 1941, p. 857). The ingenuity of Thorn-

Figure 1. Edward Thorndike. *Courtesy Columbia University.*

dike's animal experiments had made a very favorable impression on William JAMES at Harvard, as well as on his major professors at Columbia, each of whom would have strongly endorsed him for the position in Teachers College. Thorndike's contributions to the fledgling science of psychology are of the highest importance and come down to us well into the end of the twentieth century.

To Thorndike goes the credit for putting what was to become the experimental psychology of animal learning (the study of animal intelligence) on a sound laboratory and theoretical footing. Thorndike's studies (1911), which began around 1896 at Harvard and continued at Columbia University, were much more controlled than those of any of his predecessors. He employed a variety of vertebrate species (fish, chicks, dogs, cats, monkeys) and typically placed them in a problem situation, such as a puzzle box or a maze, from which they had to escape in order to get food and/or join companions. He observed the number of errors or latency to escape across trials and generally

published quantitative information on the behavior of his experimental subjects. He attempted to control the life history or extra-experimental experiences of his animals and also kept the problem situation standard.

From his experimental observations, Thorndike proposed a general theory of learning that held that the animal learned the association between an act and a situation on the basis of the success of the act in bringing about a "satisfying" state of affairs. He proposed that it is through the Law of Effect that acts that bring about a satisfying state of affairs are gradually "stamped-in" the nervous system and those that lead to an annoying or discomforting state of affairs are gradually "stamped-out." Thorndike believed the animal had to behave actively to learn in the problem situation (Law of Exercise) and that the animal's particular movements in the particular situation are validated or made invalid depending on whether they lead to satisfying or annoying consequences. Learning was thus the gradual association of particular movements in particular situations leading to certain ends. Thorndike believed that the actual connections between nerve cells in the brain underlying situation-response (S-R) associations were strengthened by reward ("satisfaction") and weakened by punishment ("annoyance").

To better appreciate Thorndike's theoretical contribution, it is necessary to briefly recall the history of thought about learning. The dominant theme of the psychological process involved in learning has always been some sort of ASSOCIATIONISM, so that was not Thorndike's particular contribution. The change that Thorndike injected into the concept of associationism concerned the nature of the association: It was not ideas that animals associated, it was movements (R) in a given situation (S) that led to satisfying consequences. Thorndike spoke of neuronal connections in the brain and hypothesized that the synaptic links between them were gradually made more traversable by use and by satisfactory consequences, whereas disuse or annoying consequences made the neuronal connections underlying other S-R associations less traversable. This was Thorndike's neurological account of trial-and-error learning, later reintroduced and expanded in a significant way by Donald O. HEBB (1949).

The foregoing represents Thorndike's bequest to what became "general behavior (learning) theory" in the field of psychological science in the 1940s. Today, general behavior theory no longer holds such a central place in psychological science.

Thorndike also made three influential contributions to comparative (animal) psychology. First, by the introduction of the puzzle box and other standard testing situations, and the careful quantification of his observations, he set the comparative psychology of learning on an objective course from which it has rarely deviated. Thorndike also incidentally helped pave the way for the methodological and theoretical BEHAVIORISM of John B. WATSON a decade later, but it is clear that a number of other significant intellectual threads were tending in that same direction around (and even before) the turn of the century: Ivan Sechenov's "reflexes of the brain" (1863), Ivan PAVLOV's highly quantitative conditioning procedures (Yerkes and Morgulis, 1909), Jacques Loeb's (1912) physicochemical reductionism and his tropistic theory of psychology (movements are "forced" by external stimuli), and especially H. S. Jennings's (1906) objective experimental approach to behavioral adaptation in single-celled paramecia, among other protozoan and lower metazoan organisms. In fact, with the publication of Watson's *Behavior: An Introduction to Comparative Psychology* (1914) and *Psychology from the Standpoint of a Behaviorist* (1919), virtually all of the general psychology became objective in methodology. Psychology became the study of behavior (instead of the mind), with the conditioned response (reflex) as its primary unit of analysis and conditioning as its tool. (Not all would agree that psychology should be limited to the study of reflexes or conditioning, so cognitive psychology has become quite popular in the late 1900s.)

Second, Thorndike postulated that *all* learning involved the Law of Exercise (use and disuse) and the Law of Effect. Therefore, from the comparative-psychological viewpoint, according to Thorndike, animals differed merely in "the delicacy, number, complexity, and permanence of associations." On these measures, dogs were somewhat more intelligent than cats, dogs and cats exceeded fish, monkeys exceeded dogs and cats, and humankind exceeded monkeys. (However, a real "gauge" of intelligence or learning ability—or a genuine application of a gauge—was still lacking.) According to Thorndike, nonhuman animals did not have ideas: *Homo sapiens* had ideas but these were derived from learning via exercise and effect.

These issues (S-R association and the roles of behavioral activity and reinforcement) have remained prominent to this day in general learning (behavior) theory, which one might define somewhat mischievously as the noncomparative approach to animal intelligence—if we understand by "comparative" the search for species *differences* as well as similarities not only in behavioral adjustment per se but also in the psychological processes mediating these adjustments. General behavior theory holds that principles of conditioning are applicable across all vertebrate species, including humans, and that cognitive psychology will one day be explicable in terms of principles of conditioning. The power or influence of conditioning theory has waned considerably in the final decades of the 1900s, whereas cognitive psychology is in the ascendancy.

Third, one of Thorndike's least appreciated contributions to comparative psychology is embodied in his notion that as we "ascend" the vertebrate series of animals, we likely have the possibility for the learning of more associations more quickly and lastingly because the trend is for the brain to be larger and thus to have more connections (synapses) in it. Thorndike does not give us his authority for this generalization about the evolution of the brain, but likely he was following Herbert Spencer and the writings of more contemporaneous, neurologically well-versed writers such as the Herrick brothers (Clarence Luther, the originator of psychobiology, and his younger brother C. Judson). In any event, this grand generalization resurfaced, with new trappings, in Hebb's (1949) concept of the A/S ratio: the ratio of association area to sensory projection area of the brain. Although there are no exact figures available, the ratio of association to primary sensory areas increases rather remarkably from the "lower" vertebrates (fishes, amphibians, reptiles) to the "higher" ones (birds and mammals).

By inference, Hebb (1949) assumed this ratio to be relevant "to the greater speed with which the 'lower' species can learn to respond selectively to the environment, and to the comparative simplicity of the behavior when it is fully developed" (p. 126). He also predicted the relevance of the ratio to the slow initial or primary learning of higher vertebrates (especially primates), in which the sensory projections are small relative to the size of the association areas: "If the sensory projection is small, association cortex large, the [environmental] control will take longer; the period of 'primary learning,' that is, will be long" (p. 124). Finally, the larger association area of the higher vertebrates (birds and mammals) would account for their greater efficiency at maturity. For Hebb, the learning capacity of higher species at maturity is not merely the capacity for a greater number of associations (Thorndike); it also reflects an emancipation from direct control by the stimulus of the moment from the immediate environment (i.e., an evolutionary difference in central or psychological mediation).

In recent years, an important tome has appeared to put some meat on the bare bones of Thorndike's and Hebb's speculations on the increase in the size of the brain in the vertebrate lineage: Harry Jerison's *Evolution of the Brain and Intelligence* (1973). There has indeed been a progressive enlargement of the brain even when the general increase in body size in higher versus lower vertebrates is calculated in the equation. Birds and mammals stand out conspicuously in "encephalization quotient" when compared with lower vertebrates of the same body size: Birds and mammals have "extra neurons" when their brain size is compared to the size it ought to be, given a high correlation between brain and body size across species (not, however, across individuals *within* a species). The conventional explanation for the increase in brain size in birds and mammals is "that they had invaded new niches in which there was an adaptive advantage for enlarged brains" (Jerison, 1973, p. 16).

With Jerison's elegant statistical formulas we at last have a metric or gauge (however gross it may be) for the evolution of the brain. But what of the evolution of intelligence? Is it valid to continue to ask whether intelligence (learning ability) has evolved in the usual sense that transcends ecological niches and ecological considerations? If so, can it be meaningfully and validly measured in the laboratory? What is the psychological gauge? These issues bedevil us to the present day with supporters on both sides of the controversy. (See also EVOLUTION AND LEARNING.)

[*Some material for this entry was excerpted, with permission, from G. Gottlieb (1979), "Comparative Psychology and Ethology," in E. Hearst, ed.,* The First Century of Experimental Psychology. *Hillsdale, N.J.: Erlbaum.*]

REFERENCES

Bitterman, M. E. (1965). Phyletic differences in learning. *American Psychologist 20,* 396–410.

Gottlieb, G. (1984). Evolutionary trends and evolutionary origins: Relevance to theory in comparative psychology. *Psychological Review 91,* 448–456.

Hebb, D. O. (1949). *The organization of behavior.* New York: Wiley.

Hodos, W., and Campbell, C. B. G. (1969). Scala naturae: Why there is no theory in comparative psychology. *Psychological Review 76,* 337–350.

Jennings, H. S. (1906). *The behavior of lower organisms.* New York: Macmillan.

Jerison, H. (1973). *Evolution of the brain and intelligence.* New York: Academic Press.

Loeb, J. (1964). *The mechanistic conception of life.* Ed. D. Fleming. Cambridge, Mass.: Harvard University Press. (Originally published 1912.)

Sechenov, I. M. (1965). *Reflexes of the brain.* Trans. S. Belsky. Cambridge, Mass.: MIT Press. (Initially published serially in the Russian journal *Meditsinsky vestnik* in 1863 and in revised book form in 1866.)

Thorndike, E. L. (1965). *Animal intelligence.* New York: Hafner. (Originally published 1911.)

Watson, J. B. (1914). *Behavior: An introduction to comparative psychology.* New York: Henry Holt.

———— (1919). *Psychology from the standpoint of a behaviorist.* Philadelphia: Lippincott.

Yerkes, R. M., and Morgulis, S. (1909). The method of Pawlow in animal psychology. *Psychological Bulletin 6,* 257–273.

Gilbert Gottlieb

TIP-OF-THE-TONGUE PHENOMENON

We have all had the experience of being temporarily unable to recall a name or other word that we are confident of ultimately retrieving. Brown and McNeill called this experience the tip-of-the-tongue (TOT) phenomenon, and characterized it in graphic terms: "The signs of it were unmistakable; [the subject] would appear to be in mild torment, something like the brink of a sneeze, and if he found the word his relief was considerable" (Brown and McNeill, 1966, p. 326). The TOT state provides a window onto lexical activation processes that is valuable to students both of human memory and of language production. One of the most interesting aspects of the phenomenon is that the person in a TOT state is often able to volunteer partial information about the desired target word, information which is frequently confirmed when the target is eventually recalled in full. The mechanisms that control this sequence from partial to full retrieval are not completely understood.

The occurrence of a TOT state is generally a noteworthy, albeit minor, intrusion into a person's discourse. Thus it is not surprising that psychological discussion of the TOT phenomenon has a considerable history, although prior to Brown and McNeill's article the phenomenon was usually considered under a less specific title, such as "partial recall." For most of this time, the evidence under review was essentially anecdotal. An important representative of this tradition was William JAMES (1890), who described the occurrence of the TOT state within what he termed the stream of thought. Greater popular fame attaches to FREUD's approximately contemporaneous interpretation of memory problems and other mistakes as manifestations of the psychopathology of everyday life—as Freudian slips. However, it has been forcefully argued (Timpanaro, 1976) that such slips in general may be understood without recourse to Freud's interpretation of them as manifestations of repressed, unconscious urges.

Until the work of Brown and McNeill, systematic data on the TOT state had been gathered in a relatively uncontrolled way by assembling a corpus of descriptions of naturally occurring instances. Nevertheless, this work had succeeded in demonstrating that people in TOT states often produce incorrect words that are related in meaning or in sound to their target words (these may be termed semantic and phonological interlopers, respectively). For example, Woodworth (1929) collected misnamings such as "Underwood" for "Overstreet" and "Macdonald" for "McDougall." Table 1 shows examples from a modern diary study carried out by Lucas and reported by Reason and Mycielska (1982).

The production of an interloper that is related in meaning to the target word is not very surprising. Clearly, the meaning of a word is normally a major factor in its selection for utterance. Thus any imperfection in this selection process is liable to result in the production of a word whose meaning is partially related to that of the target. Indeed, it may be noted that the examples listed as phonological interlopers in Table 1 tend to be related to their targets not only in sound but also in meaning (e.g., both words may be female names). However, the mechanism by which relatedness in sound between target and interloper arises is less obvious, and will be returned to later.

The major contribution of Brown and McNeill was to bring the TOT phenomenon into the realm of quantitative laboratory investigation. They discovered that a TOT state could be reliably induced on roughly 10 percent of occasions by reading people definitions of moderately rare words such as *apse* or *ambergris*. Once in a TOT state, a participant was able to state both the target word's initial letter and its number of syllables at levels of accuracy of approximately 50 percent. This figure is particularly striking for initial letters, where a simple baseline for correct guessing of one letter of the alphabet at random would be only 1/26, approximately 4 percent. In the case of word length, Brown and McNeill used only words of one to four syllables, giving rise to a simple guessing baseline of 25 percent. When relatively long target

Table 1.   Sequences of Interloper Words in Naturally Occurring Tip-of-the-Tongue States

| Target | Interloper | | |
	First	Second	Third
Semantic Interlopers			
Guernica	Picasso	Correrra	
Ice screw	Ice pick	Ice ax	Ice bolt
Initiative	Alone	Unaided	
Phonological Interlopers			
Evelyn	Eva	Esther	
Alison	Andrea	Angela	Anthea
Pomander	Potpourri		

words are used, and sophisticated guessing strategies are considered, it has been found that the estimation of the number of syllables in TOT states may be little above chance. Nevertheless, the main point is that people in TOT states frequently do have available to them at least some phonological information about their targets. Indeed, given that people in such states frequently produce words similar in sound to targets, it would be surprising if this were not so. So how do such interlopers come to be produced? Jones (1989) distinguished two possibilities.

The first possibility, proposal of which can be traced at least as far back as Woodworth, is that the interloper is instrumental in causing the TOT state. Activation of target word phonology is derailed by the activation of a similar, more accessible word. The second possibility, advanced by Brown and McNeill (1966), is that phonological interlopers are facilitative rather than obstructive in action. As an example, one might attempt to recall the dish Barbary duck, but suffer a TOT state in which the phrase *Barnaby duck* repeatedly occurred. On the first account, activation beyond a skeleton such as the four-syllable Bar' a' y u has been derailed by a matching distractor, conjecturally the title of Dickens's book *Barnaby Rudge*. On the second account, the word's incomplete retrieval merely reflects weak initial encoding of, for example, all except its initial syllable; in this case, *Barnaby* may have served to assist progress from Bar' ' to Bar' a' y along the path to complete retrieval of *Barbary*. Experimental comparison of the obstructive and the facilitative accounts of phonological interlopers is not as yet conclusive.

Recent research has also investigated a number of other aspects of the TOT state (for a general review, see Brown, 1991). It has been shown that among collections of naturally occurring TOT states the target word is most often a proper noun (especially the name of a friend or acquaintance). A possible reason is that when a person fails to retrieve a word other than a name, an approximate synonym can be substituted and the matter given little attention. However, if the word is a name, there is frequently no synonym available for substitution and therefore a memory problem is more likely to be recorded. Another aspect of names is that the frequency of use of many of them varies greatly among different members of the population, meaning that normative word frequencies are not of assistance in analyzing their incidence. More generally, although it has sometimes been assumed

that TOT states are more likely to occur for rare than for common target words, there is in fact little evidence that this is true. Another common belief is that the incidence of TOT states increases with advancing age in adults. This proposition, in contrast, has received support from both naturalistic and experimental studies.

(See also RETRIEVAL PROCESSES).

REFERENCES

Brown, A. S. (1991). A review of the tip-of-the-tongue experience. *Psychological Bulletin, 109,* 204–223.

Brown, R., and McNeill, D. (1966). The "tip of the tongue" phenomenon. *Journal of Verbal Learning and Verbal Behavior 5,* 325–337.

James, W. (1890). *Principles of psychology,* vol. 1. New York: Holt; London: Macmillan.

Jones, G. V. (1989). Back to Woodworth: Role of interlopers in the tip-of-the-tongue phenomenon. *Memory and Cognition 17,* 69–76.

Reason, J., and Mycielska, K. (1982). *Absent-minded? The psychology of mental lapses and everyday errors.* Englewood Cliffs, N.J.: Prentice-Hall.

Timpanaro, S. (1976). *The Freudian slip,* trans. K. Soper. London: NLB. First published as *Il lapsus freudiano* (1974).

Woodworth, R. S. (1929). *Psychology,* 2nd rev. ed. New York: Holt.

Gregory V. Jones

TOLMAN, EDWARD C.

The American psychologist Edward Chace Tolman (1886–1959) was a forerunner of modern cognitive psychology who showed that animals in learning mazes acquire organized spatial and temporal information about the maze and about the consequences of various alternative behaviors. In developing this approach he was combating the dominant views of his time which emphasized the acquisition of conditioned reflexes rather than knowledge about environmental events. Although several short biographies of Tolman have been written (e.g., Crutchfield, 1961; Crutchfield et al., 1960; Hilgard, 1980; Ritchie, 1964; Tolman, 1952), it is especially appropriate that one be included in an encyclopedia of learning and memory because people in this field today are using ideas

Figure 1. Edward Tolman. *Courtesy University of California, Berkeley.*

that were initiated and often developed by Tolman, although they do not necessarily recognize the source. Tolman's concepts and findings have helped to shape the field of learning and memory, and that of modern cognition.

Tolman was born in Newton, Massachusetts, on April 14, 1886, into a prosperous family that valued hard work, high thinking, and social responsibility. Following high school he attended the Massachusetts Institute of Technology, where his father served on the board of trustees. In his autobiography (1952) Tolman comments, "I went to MIT not because I wanted to be an engineer but because I had been good at mathematics and physics in high school and because of family pressure. After graduating from Technology (in electrochemistry) I became more certain of my own wants and transferred to Harvard for graduate work in philosophy and psychology" (p. 323). Among the experiences at Harvard that Tolman mentions as having influenced his later life were Ralph Barton Perry's course in ethics, which "laid the basis for my later interest in motivation and indeed gave me the main concepts (reinforced by a reading of McDougall's *Social Psychology* as part of the requirement of the course) which I have retained ever since;

. . . Holt's seminar in epistemology in which I was introduced to and excited by the 'New Realism'; and Yerkes' course in comparative, using Watson's *Behavior—An Introduction to Comparative Psychology* which was just out, as a text" (p. 325; see WATSON, JOHN B.). Tolman also spent the summer of 1912 at the University of Giessen in Germany, where he studied with Kurt Koffka, one of the founders of Gestalt psychology. Tolman returned to Giessen for another period with Koffka in 1923.

In 1915, Tolman married Kathleen Drew and received the Ph.D. He then spent three years as an instructor at Northwestern University before accepting a position at the University of California at Berkeley in 1918. Except for brief periods, Tolman spent the rest of his life at Berkeley, where he had a distinguished scientific career and was an intellectual leader in the university community. In the course of this career, Tolman received many honors, including election to the Society of Experimental Psychologists, the National Academy of Sciences, the American Philosophical Society, and the American Academy of Arts and Sciences. He was an honorary fellow of the British Psychological Society and was awarded honorary degrees by a number of universities. Tolman was president of the American Psychological Association in 1937, president of the Society for the Psychological Study of Social Issues in 1940, and vice president of the American Association for the Advancement of Science in 1942. The Fourteenth International Congress of Psychology was scheduled to be held in the United States in 1954, and Tolman was to be its president. When it became apparent that the United States, because of its anticommunist policy, was likely to refuse admission to many participants from abroad, the venue was changed to Canada, and Tolman became copresident along with Canadian psychologist Edward A. Bott.

In 1949, Tolman took a leadership role in the Berkeley faculty's resistance to the imposition of a loyalty oath by the university. Prevented from teaching, he spent the academic year of 1949–1950 away from Berkeley. The nonsigners finally won their case in 1953, gaining recognition of tenure at the University, and Tolman's professorship was restored.

The line of research that occupied most of Tolman's life started when, on arrival in Berkeley, he "found it was up to me to suggest a new course. Remembering Yerkes' course and Watson's textbook I proposed 'Comparative Psychology' and it was this that finally launched me down the behaviorist slope" (Tolman, 1952, p. 329). This slope may have been behaviorist (see BEHAVIORISM), but it was of a new and unusual kind that reflected Tolman's education at Harvard.

Tolman's early experimental papers on animal behavior were on the rat's behavior in the maze rather than in other types of apparatus because it gave opportunities for observing the animal's solution to problems in space, in getting from here to there. He believed that when a rat ran from the start of a maze to the goal, its behavior reflected a purpose—getting to the goal *in order to* get something—and knowledge about the spatial layout. In referring to such knowledge, Tolman used terms such as "sign-gestalt-expectation"; this referred to his assumption that the rat was learning that if in the presence of a certain sign (that is, the events at the start box and on into the maze), it behaved in such and such a way, it would achieve certain goals. The term *gestalt* referred to Tolman's assumption that the rat was acquiring a "cognitive map" which would allow it to use its organized information in getting to the goal. In Tolman's early writings, including his major book, *Purposive Behavior in Animals and Men* (1932), he maintained the neorealist argument that knowledge and purpose could be directly observed in the behavior of the rat in the maze. But by 1932 he was also working with a different idea: that knowledge and purpose were inferences from behavior rather than characteristics of behavior. These inferences Tolman came to call "intervening variables," a term which carried the idea that knowledge and purpose intervened between the stimulus and behavior and guided the behavior (e.g., Tolman, 1938). In his autobiography Tolman (1952) takes the position that such intervening variables are not only summary statements which bring together data but also refer to real events that presumably are causal in nature.

In the course of developing these ideas, Tolman and his students conducted a vigorous, broad program of research on learning and problem solving in rats that served both to test his ideas and to change them in the light of new data. Two lines of research will be mentioned briefly here. The first, latent learning experiments, showed that rats learn about the layout of a complex maze even though, in the absence of reward, they show little or no evidence of such learning. When, after some trials, they are first rewarded in the goal box, they show virtually error-free behavior on the next trial. These latent learning experiments demonstrated several points. First, learning can be distinguished from performance and is occurring even when there is no clear evidence for it. Two reviews (Richardson-Klavehn and Bjork, 1988; Spear et al., 1990) show how research of this sort continues to grow and to prove fruitful, even though neither review cites Tolman. Second, the latent learning experiments showed that rats were gaining organized knowledge of the maze which could not be described in terms of stimulus-response connections. Third, Tolman argued that these experiments showed that the behavior of the animal was suited to its purposes.

A second line of research, closely related to the first, asked in a variety of cleverly constructed experiments whether the animal could make inferences from its knowledge of the maze about what to do in new situations. Thus a rat would be guided to the goal along a circuitous route for a number of trials and then would be deprived of that route but exposed to a variety of alternatives, one of which would lead more directly to the goal. The results showed that the animal was able to use its knowledge about the spatial arrangements in the room to make the appropriate inference and take the direct route. Other research by Tolman and his students was aimed at what might be called control processes, such as selective testing of alternative possible solutions ("hypotheses" and "vicarious trial and error").

At a time when learning theorists were still trying to establish *the* theory of learning, Tolman (1949) published an article entitled "There Is More Than One Kind of Learning." In it he proposed that some of the basic disputes about learning might be resolved if investigators agreed that there are a number of kinds of learning; "the theory and laws appropriate to one kind may well be different to those appropriate to other kinds" (p. 144). Not only does this proposal have a modern sound, but some of the types of learning that Tolman proposed are being investigated at present.

Although Tolman, like his contemporaries, thought mostly in terms of the plasticity of behavior, he did not ignore genetic influences. In fact, in 1924 he was the first to apply the technique of selective breeding to the study of genetics of behavior, obtaining "maze-bright" and "maze-dull" strains of rats. His student Robert Tryon then carried out a successful program of selective breeding for maze ability over several generations. This was replicated in other laboratories and extended to other kinds of behavior. As McClearn and Foch

(1988, pp. 685–686) have pointed out, this clear evidence for the influence of genes on behaviors was important in holding a place for behavior genetics during the period when environmentalism was dominant.

All of Tolman's research showed a remarkably coherent but nevertheless broad ranging character. Although during much of this time his position was one of dissent from the mainstream of animal learning during the 1930s through 1950s, there is no doubt that Tolman's position has become a dominant one in animal learning of the 1980s and 1990s.

(See also LEARNING THEORY.)

REFERENCES

Crutchfield, R. S. (1961). Edward Chace Tolman. *American Journal of Psychology 74,* 135–141.

Crutchfield, R. S., Krech, D., and Tryon, R. C. (1960). Edward Chace Tolman: A Life of Scientific and Social Purpose. *Science 131* (March 11), 714–716.

Hilgard, E. R. (1980). Edward Chace Tolman. *Dictionary of American Biography,* Supp. 6, pp. 639–641. New York: Scribner's.

McClearn, G. E. and Foch, T. T. (1988). Behavioral genetics. In R. C. Atkinson, R. J. Herrnstein, G. Lindzey, and R. D. Luce, eds., *Steven's handbook of experimental psychology,* 2nd ed., vol. 1, pp. 677–764. New York: Wiley.

Richardson-Klavehn, A., and Bjork, R. A. (1988). Measures of memory. *Annual Review of Psychology 39,* 475–543.

Ritchie, B. F. (1964). Edward Chace Tolman. *Biographical Memoirs. National Academy of Sciences,* vol. 37, pp. 293–324. New York: Columbia University Press. (This is mainly a reprint of Tolman [1952] with an introductory statement and two final notes by Ritchie and a full list of publications.)

Spear, N. E., Miller, J. S., and Jagiclo, J. A. (1990). Animal memory and learning. *Annual Review of Psychology 41,* 169–211.

Tolman, E. C. (1920). Instinct and purpose. *Psychological Review 27,* 217–233.

—— (1924). The inheritance of maze-learning ability in rats. *Journal of Comparative Psychology 4,* 1–18.

—— (1932). *Purposive behavior in animals and men.* New York: Century.

—— (1938). The determiners of behavior at a choice point. *Psychological Review 45,* 1–41.

—— (1949). There is more than one kind of learning. *Psychological Review 27,* 217–233.

—— (1952). Autobiography. In E. G. Boring et al., eds., *A history of psychology in autobiography,* vol. 4, pp. 323–339. Worcester, Mass.: Clark University Press.

Mark R. Rosenzweig
Donald A. Riley

UNICELLULAR ORGANISMS, LEARNING AND ADAPTIVE PLASTICITY IN

Like neurons (see GUIDE TO THE ANATOMY OF THE BRAIN), protozoa produce receptor potentials in response to sensory stimuli and action potentials when depolarized above threshold. The Ca^{++} and K^+ channels responsible for these potentials have properties analogous to those of neuron ion channels. Therefore, the mechanisms underlying learning in protozoa also may be analogous. The discovery of these mechanisms in protozoa is facilitated by the close correlation between action potential production and the behaviors of ciliary reversal and bodily contraction allowing electrophysiological changes produced by drugs, mutations, or learning to be inferred directly from behavioral observation. Biochemical analyses also are facilitated in protozoa because protozoa can be cloned to form masses of genetically uniform cells. Last, all of these experimental approaches can be applied to a single class of organism. Given these experimental advantages, protozoa may serve as model systems in the analysis of some types of learning.

Nonassociative Learning

The all-or-none bodily contractions elicited by mechanical stimulation in some protozoa habituate during stimulus repetition, and two species also have been reported to habituate to electrical stimuli. Seven of the nine parametric characteristics used to define habituation have been observed in *Stentor* and *Spirostomum*. Dishabituation has not been observed. In both species habituation to mechanical stimuli is specific to that stimulus modality and does not generalize to electrical or photic stimuli. In *Stentor* habituation is correlated with a decrease in mechanoreceptor potential amplitude resulting from modification of its mechanoreceptor channels (Wood, 1988).

Individual reports indicate that mechanical agitation sensitizes *Stylonychia* to avoid rough surfaces and that previous exposure to warmth sensitizes *Paramecia* to avoid lighted areas. Neither of these phenomena has been characterized, nor has the mechanism producing them been studied.

Associative Learning

Paramecia and *Stentor* placed into the top of a fluid-filled capillary tube eventually exit the bottom of the tube after numerous, seemingly random reorientations in their swimming direction. This "escape" behavior occurs more rapidly over trials, but such apparent instrumental learning occurs only with capillaries of specific sizes and in specific orientations, and hence does not represent a general learning capability.

Paramecia repetitively presented with a bacteria-baited wire collect near the wire and attach themselves to it more frequently than do naive animals. However, this conditioned approach behavior does not develop if the medium in the area of the wire insertion is stirred between trials, suggesting that this medium becomes enriched with bacteria rather than that the *Paramecia* become conditioned.

The classical conditioning of protozoa using

paired light and touch or shock stimulation has been reported but has not proven replicable. A well-controlled study reported the development of conditioned responses to vibrational stimuli after their pairing with shock (Hennessey, Rucker, and McDiarmid, 1979), but confirmatory data is needed before any conclusions can be drawn.

Protozoa also have been trained in conditioned avoidance paradigms by being placed in a chamber half of which is illuminated and warmed (or shocked) while the other half is dark and cool (or not shocked). Animals are tested for their avoidance of illuminated areas when the temperature throughout the chamber is uniform. All studies reporting successful conditioning either have not been replicated by other investigators or have been shown to be missing a crucial control group.

In sum, protozoa clearly habituate to some stimuli and may show sensitization to others, but no unequivocal examples of associative learning have been reported.

REFERENCES

Applewhite, P. B. (1979). Learning in protozoa. In M. Levandowsky and S. H. Hutner, eds., *Biochemistry and physiology of protozoa*, pp. 341–355. New York: Academic Press.

Corning, W. C., and Von Burg, R. (1973). Protozoa. In W. C. Corning, J. A. Dyal, and A. O. D. Willows, eds., *Invertebrate learning*, vol. 1, pp. 49–122. New York: Plenum.

Hennessey, T. M., Rucker, W. B., and McDiarmid, C. G. (1979). Classical conditioning in *Paramecia. Animal Learning and Behavior 7*, 417–423.

Wood, D. C. (1988). Habituation in *Stentor*: Produced by mechanoreceptor channel modification. *Journal of Neuroscience 8*, 2254–2258.

David C. Wood

VISUAL MEMORY

See Modality Effects; Primates, Visual Perception and Memory in Nonhuman; Visual Memory, Brightness and Flux in; Visual Object Agnosia

VISUAL MEMORY, BRIGHTNESS AND FLUX IN

The study of simple visual discriminations reveals fundamental properties of learning and memory in the nervous system. Physical measures of the light source include energy emitted (*flux*) or reflected (*reflectance*) from the stimulus per unit area. Heinrich Klüver (1942) called it *brightness* if the total amount of light was measured over the whole stimulus source (including contours and edges), and *density of luminous flux* if measured over a unit area of the stimulus. He concluded that visually decorticated monkeys could solve a luminous-flux problem but not a brightness problem.

Using this definition, a brightness discrimination includes both light intensity and light contrast on edges that contribute to pattern perception. A flux discrimination, on the other hand, pertains to differences in light intensity per unit area. This intensity can be for the whole stimulus (total flux) or for parts of the stimulus (local flux). For example, a horizontal-versus-vertical-stripes pattern problem can be equated for total flux and for total brightness (same number of contrasting contours) and yet the edges of the stimulus cards have differences in local flux. Discrimination tasks for intensity that are used for testing animals, whether black and white cards with edges or black and white alleys with an edge that creates a contrast (the wall separating the alleys), normally are not purely flux discriminations but are brightness discriminations that include elements of pattern discrimination. Discriminations more purely restricted to flux can be achieved by use of contact lenses that diffuse light and obscure edges, by successive discrimination problems in which both alleys being lit means to go one way or both alleys being dark means to go the other way, or by a shuttle box in which the subject sits in the middle of the apparatus, one alley is lit, and the alley 180 degrees away is not. The distinguishing feature between a flux and a brightness discrimination is that the latter has contours created by contrasting levels of flux within the same stimulus.

In the simplest visual discrimination a subject distinguishes between a black and a white stimulus card. With this task Karl LASHLEY (1935) studied the role of cerebral neocortex in his search for the physical manifestation of memory, for the *engram*. Rats without any neocortex cannot discriminate visual patterns (Lavond and Dewberry, 1980). However, rudimentary visual functions remain in that decorticated rats can see moving objects, can detect the deep side of a visual cliff, and can learn or relearn the brightness discrimination.

Importantly, the results of brightness discrimination training illustrate the property of behavioral *recovery of function* following brain injury. Lashley trained rats on a brightness discrimination and then systematically removed fractions of the cerebral neocortex. After removal of visual neocortex there was no evidence for retention of the brightness discrimination. With continued training, however, the rats reacquired the discrimination, taking as many trials as initially required to learn. One possible conclusion would be that the lesion destroyed the memory and, once it was removed, a new memory could be reestablished with the same effort. However, this is a somewhat fortuitous result in that it is an outcome of the training criterion used, because posteriorly decorticated subjects perform better when trained with less stringent criteria and worse when trained to successively more stringent criteria (Spear and Braun, 1969). This indicates that normal learning and learning by posteriorly decorticated subjects are by different mechanisms.

The recovery of brightness discriminations is consistent with Lashley's previous observations on maze learning (1929) where he found *equipotentiality* (all parts of the neocortex have the same capacity for supporting memory) and *mass action* (large areas of neocortex contribute to the memory). There is one caveat, however, in that he confined these properties to visual cortex for visual discriminations. Lashley did not think that the anterior neocortex participated in visual discriminations as it does for maze learning. However, more recent work supports the generalization of visual function to the entire neocortex (Cloud, Meyer, and Meyer, 1982).

Bauer and Cooper (1964) suggested that memory was not stored in the neocortex at all, but that visual cortex was necessary for seeing the stimulus as a pattern discrimination (a brightness discrimination). They suggested that learning after a visual cortical lesion was by using a different stimulus feature (i.e., a flux discrimination). However, there is evidence that both brightness and flux are learned simultaneously. Meyer and Meyer showed that a neural stimulant facilitates recovery of the flux discrimination but not a pattern discrimination (see Meyer and Meyer, 1977, for review). They suggest that the role of the neocortex is to add context in facilitating access to subcortically established engrams rather than to act as a store for memories. LeVere and Morlock supported this conclusion using a behavioral interference test, a simultaneous brightness discrimination (lit versus dark alleys, 1973), and a successive flux discrimination (both alleys lit means go one way, both dark means go the other way, 1974). Rats were initially trained to one habit, then had the visual neocortex removed. If the cortical lesion actually destroyed the memory, then it should not matter whether the subjects were trained to the same habit or to the opposite habit (go the other way). LeVere and Morlock found that training to the opposite habit took substantially longer to learn, indicating that the old memory still existed and interfered with learning the opposite habit.

As was true in Lashley's time, no one has yet localized the memory for a flux discrimination. Lesions of visual subcortical structures (superior colliculus, lateral geniculate, pretectal area, accessory optic nuclei) or of the limbic system (septum, hippocampus, amygdala), in combination with visual decortication, do not prevent relearning. The fault probably lies within Walter HUNTER's criticisms (1930) that there is not enough experimental control over the instrumental training task used in this research. The more general question is whether the neocortex is involved in any memory. Squire (1987, chap. 8) reviews the best evidence for cortical memory, which can also be interpreted as suggesting that the cortex is necessary for perception of the stimuli but not for memory itself. Clearly, these are issues that are not resolved and continue to be of interest.

REFERENCES

Bauer, J. H., and Cooper, R. M. (1964). Effects of posterior cortical lesions on performance of a brightness discrimination task. *Journal of Comparative and Physiological Psychology 58*, 84–93.

Cloud, M. D., Meyer, D. R., and Meyer, P. M. (1982). Induction of recoveries from injuries to the cortex: Dissociation of equipotential and regionally specific mechanisms. *Physiological Psychology 10*, 66–73.

Hunter, W. S. (1930). A consideration of Lashley's theory of the equipotentiality of cerebral action. *Journal of Genetic Psychology 3*, 455–468.

Klüver, H. (1942). Functional significance of the geniculo-striate system. In H. Klüver, ed., *Visual mechanisms*. Lancaster, Pa.: Jaques Cattell Press.

Lashley, K. S. (1929). *Brain mechanisms and intelligence: A quantitative study of injuries to the brain*. Chicago: University of Chicago Press, 1929.

——— (1935). The mechanism of vision: XII. Nervous structures concerned in the acquisition and retention of habits based on reactions to light. *Comparative Psychology Monographs 11*, 43–79.

Lavond, D. G., and Dewberry, R. G. (1980). Visual form perception is a function of the visual cortex: II. The rotated horizontal-vertical and oblique-stripes pattern problems. *Physiological Psychology 8*, 1–8.

LeVere, T. E., and Morlock, G. W. (1973). Nature of visual recovery following posterior neodecortication in the hooded rat. *Journal of Comparative and Physiological Psychology 83*, 62–67.

Meyer, D. R., and Meyer, P. M. (1977). Dynamics and bases of recoveries of functions after injuries to the cerebral cortex. *Physiological Psychology* 5, 133–165.

Spear, P. D., and Braun, J. J. (1969). Nonequivalence of normal and posteriorly neodecorticated rats on two brightness discrimination problems. *Journal of Comparative and Physiological Psychology* 67, 235–239.

Squire, L. R. (1987). *Memory and the brain.* New York: Oxford University Press.

David Lavond

VISUAL OBJECT AGNOSIA

Visual object agnosia refers to the impairment of object recognition in the presence of relatively intact elementary visual perception, memory, and general intellectual function. This article will review the different subtypes of agnosia, their major clinical features, and their implications for cognitive neuroscience theories of visual object recognition.

The study of agnosia has a long history of controversy, with some authors doubting that the condition even exists. For example, Bay (1953) suggested that the appearance of disproportionate difficulty with visual object recognition could invariably be explained by synergistic interactions between mild perceptual impairments on the one hand, and mild general intellectual impairments on the other. The rarity of visual object agnosia has contributed to the slowness with which this issue has been resolved, but several decades of careful case studies have convinced most neuropsychologists that visual object recognition can be selectively impaired. For example, it has been shown that agnosic patients may be no more impaired in their elementary visual capabilities and their general intellectual functioning than many patients who are not agnosic (Ettlinger, 1956). Therefore, most current research on agnosia focuses on a new set of questions: Are there different types of visual object agnosia, corresponding to different underlying impairments? At what level of visual and/or memory representation do these impairments occur? What theories of normal visual object recognition can be ruled out, or supported, by observations of agnosic patients? What brain regions are critically involved in visual object recognition?

The Apperceptive/Associative Distinction

Lissauer (1890) reasoned that visual object recognition could be disrupted in two different ways: by impairing higher levels of visual perception, in which case patients would be unable to recognize objects because they could not see them properly, and by impairing the process of associating a percept with its meaning, in which case patients would be unable to recognize objects because they could not use the percept to access their knowledge of the object. He termed the first kind of agnosia *apperceptive agnosia* and the second kind *associative agnosia,* terminology that is still used today.

One might wonder whether apperceptive agnosics should be considered agnosics at all, given that the definition of agnosia cited at the beginning of this article excludes patients whose problems are caused by elementary visual impairments. The difference between apperceptive agnosics and patients who fall outside of the exclusionary criteria for agnosia is that the former have relatively good acuity, brightness discrimination, color vision, and other so-called elementary visual capabilities. Despite these capabilities, their perception of objects is markedly abnormal, and this prevents them from recognizing objects. Figure 1 shows the attempts of one such patient to copy columns of simple shapes. The dissociability of elementary visual perception from higher-level visual perception suggests a complex, many-stage architecture for object vision. The different subtypes of apperceptive agnosia provide additional clues to the organization and subprocesses of object perception. Because the apperceptive agnosias are uncontroversially considered impairments of visual perception, as opposed to memory, they will not be discussed further in this article. (Interested readers may consult Farah, 1990, chs. 2 and 3).

Associative Agnosia

In associative agnosia, visual perception is much better than in apperceptive agnosia. Compare, for example, the copies made by two associative agno-

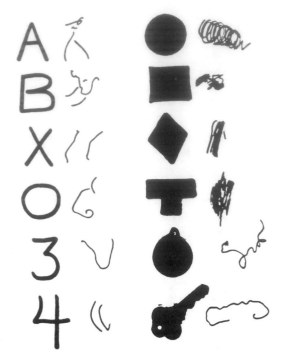

Figure 1. Attempts at copying by an apperceptive agnosic. *Reprinted with permission from Benson, D. F., and Greenberg, J. P., "Visual form agnosia."* Archives of Neurology 20, 82–89. Copyright 1969 American Medical Association.

sics in Figure 2 with the copies shown in Figure 1. Nevertheless, object recognition is impaired. Associative agnosic patients may be able to recognize an object by its feel in their hand, or from a spoken definition, demonstrating that they have intact general knowledge of the object in addition to being able to see it well enough to copy it, but they cannot recognize the same object by sight alone. The impairment is not simply a naming deficit for visual stimuli; associative agnosics cannot indicate their recognition of objects by nonverbal means, such as pantomiming the use of an object or grouping together dissimilar-looking objects from the same semantic category. The case of Rubens and Benson shows all of the cardinal signs of associative agnosia:

> The patient could not identify common objects presented visually, and did not know what was on his plate until he tasted it. He identified objects immediately on touching them. When shown a stethoscope, he described it as "a long cord with a round thing at the end," and asked if it could be a watch. He identified a can opener as "could be a key. . . ." He was never able to describe or demonstrate the use of an object if he could not name it. . . . He could match identical objects but not group objects by categories (clothing, food). He could draw the outlines of objects which he could not identify. . . . Remarkably, he could make excellent copies of line drawings and still fail to name the subject. (1971, pp. 308–309)

Explaining Associative Agnosia

Disconnection Accounts

Is associative agnosia a problem with perception, with memory, or with both? There are three different ways in which associative agnosia has been explained that suggest different answers to this question. The simplest way to explain agnosia is by a disconnection between visual representations and other brain centers responsible for language or memory. For example, Geschwind (1965) proposed that associative agnosia is a visual-verbal disconnection. This hypothesis accounts well for agnosics' impaired naming of visual stimuli, but it cannot account for their inability to convey recognition nonverbally.

The syndrome of *optic aphasia* may correspond to this type of hypothesized visual-verbal disconnection. Optic aphasics cannot name visually presented objects even though they can name the same objects if they touch them or hear them, and can use nonverbal means of demonstrating their recognition of the visually presented objects. Optic aphasia has often been considered a type of associative agnosia, but it differs from a true agnosia in a number of ways, most notably in the preservation of nonverbal recognition ability. Although it is a fascinating syndrome in its own right, it falls outside the scope of the present article. A classic case of optic aphasia was described by Lhermitte and Beauvois (1973). Farah (1990, chs. 4 and 5) reviews the published cases and their interpretations.

Associative agnosia has also been explained as a disconnection between visual representations and medial temporal memory centers (e.g., Albert et al., 1979). This would account for a modality-specific impairment in new learning, not the inability to access old knowledge through vision. Patients with visual learning impairments subsequent to visual-limbic disconnection have been described (Ross, 1980).

Figure 2. Copies by two associative agnosic patients, who were unable to recognize what they were copying. *Reprinted with permission from Farah, M. J., McMullen, P. A., and Meyer, M. M. 1991. "Can recognition of living things be selectively impaired?"* Neuropsychologia 29, 185 193.

Loss of Stored Visual Memories

The inadequacy of the disconnection accounts leads us to consider theories of associative agnosia in which some component of perception and/or memory has been damaged. Perhaps the most widely accepted account of associative agnosia is that stored visual memory representations have been damaged. According to this type of account, stimuli can be processed perceptually up to some end-state visual representation, which would normally be matched against stored visual representations. In associative agnosia the stored representations are no longer available and recognition therefore fails. An assumption of this account is that two identical tokens of the object representation normally exist, one that is derived from the stimulus and one that is stored in memory, and that these are compared in much the same way as a data base might be searched in a computer. This account is not directly disconfirmed by any of the available evidence. However, there are some reasons to question it, and to suspect that subtle impairments in perception may underlie associative agnosia.

Impaired High-Level Visual Perception

Although the good copies and successful matching performance of associative agnosics might seem to exonerate perception, a closer look at the manner in which these tasks are accomplished suggests that perception is not normal in associative agnosia, and suggests yet a third explanation of associative agnosia. Typically, these patients are described as copying drawings "slavishly" and "line by line." In matching tasks, they rely on slow, sequential, feature-by-feature checking. It is therefore premature to conclude that faulty perception is not the cause of associative agnosia. Recent studies of the visual capabilities of associative agnosic patients confirm that there are subtle visual perceptual impairments present in all cases studied (see Farah, 1990, chs. 4 and 5 for a review). If the possibility of impaired recognition with intact perception is consistent with the use of a computational architecture in which separate perceptual and memory representations are compared, then the absence of such a case suggests that a different type of computational architecture may underlie object recognition. Parallel distributed processing (PDP) systems exemplify an alternative architecture, in which the perceptual and memory representations cannot be dissociated (see Rumelhart and McClelland, 1986, for an introduction to PDP computation; see also Farah, 1990, ch. 5, for a discussion of PDP models and agnosia). In a PDP system, the memory of the stimulus would consist of a pattern of connection strengths among a number of neuronlike units. The "perceptual" representation resulting from the presentation of a stimulus will depend upon the pattern of connection strengths among the units directly or indirectly activated by the stimulus. Thus, if memory is altered by damaging the network, perception will be altered as well. On this account, associative agnosia is not a result of an impairment to perception *or* to memory; rather, the two are in principle inseparable, and the impairment is better described as a loss of high-level visual perceptual representations that are shaped by, and embody the memory of, visual experience. It will thus be of great interest to see whether future studies of associative agnosics will ever document a case of impaired recognition with intact perception. (See also PARALLEL DISTRIBUTED PROCESSING MODELS OF MEMORY).

Subtypes and Neuroanatomical Bases of Associative Agnosia

The scope of the agnosic deficit varies from case to case. Some cases encounter difficulty mainly with face recognition, while others demonstrate better face recognition than object recognition. Printed word recognition is similarly impaired in some cases but not others. The selectivity of these impairments suggests the existence of specialized subsystems necessary for recognizing stimuli from at least certain domains, such as faces or words. As these category-specific recognition impairments are the subject of another article in this volume (see MATERIAL-SPECIFIC MEMORY DEFICITS), they are mentioned here only insofar as they help to clarify the neuropathology of associative agnosia.

If one regards associative agnosia as a single undifferentiated category, it is impossible to make any generalizations about the brain regions responsible for visual object recognition. Although the intrahemispheric location of damage is generally occipitotemporal, involving both gray and white matter, cases of associative agnosia have been reported following unilateral right hemisphere lesions, unilateral left hemisphere lesions, and bilateral lesions. (Cambier et al., 1980, describe a case of associative agnosia following bilateral occipitotemporal gray matter damage with no interruption of white matter pathways, verified by autopsy. This fortuitous lesion suggests that white matter damage may not be critical for producing agnosia.) However, if one views associative agnosia as spanning a spectrum from impairments of face recognition on one end (perhaps requiring the most holistic visual representations; see Farah, 1990, ch. 5) to printed word recognition on the other end (requiring the representation of many separate parts), with most common objects in between, then a pattern emerges in the associated neuropathology. When face recognition alone is impaired, or when face and object recognition are impaired but reading is spared, the lesions are generally either on the right or bilateral. When reading alone is impaired, or when reading and object recognition are impaired but face recognition is spared, the lesions are generally on the left. When recognition of all three types of stimuli is impaired, the lesions are generally bilateral.

REFERENCES

Albert, M. L., Soffer, D., Silverberg, R., and Reches, A. (1979). The anatomic basis of visual agnosia. *Neurology 25,* 876–879.

Bay, E. (1953). Disturbances of visual perception and their examination. *Brain 76,* 515–530.

Cambier, J., Masson, M., Elghozi, D., Henin, D., and Viader, F. (1980). Visual agnosia without right hemianopia in a right-handed patient. *Revue Neurologique 136,* 727–740.

Ettlinger, G. (1956). Sensory deficits in visual agnosia. *Journal of Neurology, Neurosurgery and Psychiatry 19,* 297–301.

Farah, M. J. (1990). *Visual agnosia: Disorders of object recognition and what they tell us about normal vision.* Cambridge, Mass.: MIT Press.

Geschwind, N. (1965). Disconnexion syndromes in animal and man. Part II. *Brain 88,* 585–645.

Lhermitte, F., and Beauvois, M. F. (1973). A visual-speech disconnexion syndrome: Report of a case with optic aphasia, agnosic alexia, and color agnosia. *Brain 96,* 695–714.

Lissauer, H. (1890). Ein Fall von Seelenblindheit nebst einem Beitrage zur Theorie derselben. *Archiv für Psychiatrie und Nervenkrankheiten 21,* 222–270.

Ross, E. D. (1980). Sensory-specific and fractional disorders of recent memory in man: I. Isolated loss of recent visual memory. *Archives of Neurology 24,* 305–316.

Rubens, A. B., and Benson, D. F. (1971). Associative visual agnosia. *Archives of Neurology 24,* 305–316.

Rumelhart, D. E., and McClelland, J. L., eds. (1986). *Parallel distributed processing: Explorations in the microstructure of cognition.* Cambridge, Mass.: MIT Press.

Martha J. Farah

WATSON, JOHN B.

John Broadus Watson (1878–1958), the founder of behaviorism, was born January 9, 1878, near Greenville, South Carolina. He spent his preadolescent years in a farm community, where he acquired numerous manual skills and an affectionate familiarity with the behavior of many animals. At about the time his father deserted the family, the Watsons moved into the cotton-mill town of Greenville, which his mother thought would provide a better educational and religious atmosphere for the children. Watson later characterized himself as a mediocre student and a lazy, rebellious teenager (with a couple of arrests to brag about). Nevertheless, he managed to persuade officials at Furman University in Greenville to admit him. An average student at Furman from 1894 to 1899, Watson graduated with an A.M. degree; only philosophy and psychology had interested him at all. His mother's death in 1900 removed any remaining pressure to pursue a career in theology; by then, in any case, he had become antagonistic to established religion. Gordon Moore, his professor in philosophy and psychology, had attended and favorably described the University of Chicago, so Watson wrote to its president about his ambitions to attend a "real university" and "amount to" something professionally. Persuasive once again, he started graduate work there in 1900.

Watson had expected to concentrate on philosophy, with the eminent John Dewey as his mentor. However, he "never knew what Dewey was talking about" and, despite taking a variety of philosophy courses to fulfill a minor-area requirement, he later confessed that only some of the British empiricists (who emphasized past experience and principles of association as the crucial sources of human knowledge) aroused his interest. Typically for the turn of the century, psychology was part of the philosophy department, and Watson soon gravitated toward James R. Angell as his major professor. Angell was experimentally oriented and a leader of the burgeoning school of functionalism, which tolerated differing conceptions of the field of psychology but stressed the role of evolutionary factors, environmental adaptation, objectivity, and practical matters. This outlook contrasted with that

Figure 1. John B. Watson. *Reproduced with permission from Watson, 1936. Courtesy Clark University Press.*

of experimental introspectionists (e.g., the "structuralists"), who used human observers reporting on their private conscious experience, without regard for biological or practical implications.

Watson felt uncomfortable when asked to introspect in the standard ways, and he did not produce consistent reports under those conditions; but he said he felt at home with animals. Working under Angell and Henry Donaldson (who along with Jacques Loeb, an extremely mechanistic and materialistic biologist, handled Watson's other minor area, neurology), he studied possible correlations between problem-solving skills and the degree of medullation (myelination) in the brains of white rats at various ages. After 3 years of intense dedication to university duties and various odd jobs that he took to support himself—overwork that presumably caused the relatively brief breakdown he suffered during his final year—in 1903 Watson received the first Ph.D. in psychology to be awarded by Chicago. His dissertation, *Animal Education,* was published in the same year.

Watson remained at Chicago until 1908, first as Angell's assistant and then as an instructor. Even though he taught his students about orthodox introspective methods with human observers, his own research involved only animals. With Harvey Carr he carried out influential work on the sensory basis of maze learning in rats (neither vision nor audition nor smell was presumably crucial; rather, what was important was feedback stimulation from the animal's own movements: kinesthesis or the "muscle sense"); with Robert Yerkes he began studies of color vision that eventually involved several nonhuman species; and he failed to find good evidence for learning by imitation in monkeys. In addition, Watson spent the first of several summers on an island near Florida, observing the natural, instinctive behavior of birds (noddy terns and sooty terns), some of which he isolated at birth. His bird studies were thoughtful and creative; besides homing behavior, he investigated what today we would call IMPRINTING, instinctive drift, territoriality, and egg, mate, and nest recognition. This nonlaboratory work is particularly noteworthy because, somewhat ironically, B. F. Skinner later assessed it as Watson's best research, and the ethologist Konrad LORENZ falsely concluded that "if J. B. Watson had only once reared a young bird in isolation," he would never have stressed conditioning as much as he did.

As early as 1903–1904 Watson confided to some Chicago colleagues his growing belief that psychology could become an objective and practical science only if it rid itself of unverifiable, unreliable introspective methods and focused instead on the study of observable behavior—events that could be recorded by an outsider—rather than on inferred, private states of consciousness or experience. Associates like Angell argued that his suggestion might be appropriate for animal research but would hardly be satisfactory for human beings. Another 10 years passed before Watson publicly proposed such ideas as the main bases for the approach he called behaviorism.

In 1908 Watson became full professor of experimental and comparative psychology at Johns Hopkins University in Baltimore. He continued his animal research, and soon assumed the leadership of the Johns Hopkins psychology program and the editorship of several important journals in experimental psychology. With the encouragement and stimulation of Knight Dunlap and Karl Lashley, he began to concentrate on developing his behavioristic psychology, first presented to a large audience in a landmark *Psychological Review* article in 1913. In a radical redefinition of psychology, Watson claimed that his field, animal learning and behavior—which had generally been relegated to a minor position in psychology or had not been viewed as part of psychology at all—was the one truly objective, scientific area of psychology. Furthermore, he maintained that the techniques used in the animal laboratory could be profitably, objectively, and practically applied to human beings; the goal of psychology was to predict and control behavior, not to analyze consciousness into its elements or to study vague "functions" or processes like perception, imagery, and volition. According to Watson, psychology had not yet emancipated itself from philosophy and religion, which it must do to become a true science—the science of behavior, of stimulus (S) and response (R: movements and secretions).

Historians of psychology have had no difficulty tracing possible antecedents for virtually all of Watson's specific ideas and arguments. Among others, they have cited views of philosophers (empiricists-associationists, materialists, positivists, pragmatists), biologists (evolutionary theorists, naturalists, objectivists, reflexologists), and early psychologists (nonmentalistic students of animal and human sensation, learning, memory, and intelligence—as well as functionalists like Angell). However, the direct influence on Watson of most of these views is unclear. In any event, his approach was original because of how it combined a variety of emphases, dissatisfactions, and opinions in a unique, revolutionary way. He offered a straightforward, bold program that was easy to understand (and easy to attack).

Generally favorable opinions about Watson's approach (as well as his established reputation as a researcher, administrator, and editor) led to his election as president of the American Psychological Association (APA) 2 years after the publication of his behaviorist manifesto. Many psychologists correctly believed that institutional and societal support for independent departments of psychology and new research facilities would be increased by redefining psychology along practical and objective lines like those offered by Watson.

In his APA presidential address (1915) Watson described research with both animals and humans, but for the first time in his career he stressed the latter. The talk offered a specific positive alternative to the techniques for studying human psychology that he had condemned in print 2 years before. Such an extension of his approach would presumably help convert to behaviorism those psychologists who believed that animal studies could not be of great significance for human affairs. The new method was essentially the conditioned-reflex procedure of Ivan Pavlov and Vladimir Bekhterev, which Watson had only recently begun to examine and appreciate. (Previously he had stressed the associationist laws of frequency and recency; he frowned on Edward L. Thorndike's law of effect because the notion of strengthening or weakening S-R bonds by means of subsequent satisfaction or discomfort seemed subjective to him, although it is the forerunner of Skinner's law of operant REINFORCEMENT.) From his own studies with human beings Watson illustrated a variety of Pavlovian conditioning phenomena that seemed relevant for everyday human behavior. He boasted that "We give no more instruction to our human subjects than we give to our animal subjects."

Except for a minor study with rats, the rest of Watson's academic career (suddenly aborted within 5 years) involved work with humans, especially young infants in the Phipps Psychiatric Clinic directed by Adolf Meyer. There was one brief interruption, when Watson served in the army during World War I (1917–1918) as a psychologist concerned mainly with aviation skills. Despite his irritation with the military establishment, Watson's views on the technological potential of psychology were bolstered.

Immediately after the war, Watson worked with a graduate student, Rosalie Rayner, on his most famous single study. It originated from his claim that emotional behavior in human infants was based on three fundamental types of unlearned, well-defined stimulus-response (S-R) patterns: fear, rage, and love. More complex emotional reactions, to specific objects and situations, arose through associative learning and transfer—and supposedly could not be attributed to hereditary predispositions. Primarily by means of Pavlovian procedures adopted directly from animal research, 11-month-old Albert B. was conditioned to fear a white rat by associating presentations of the rat with a very loud noise. Soon the mere sight of the rat caused Albert to whimper, cry, and move as far away as he could. In addition, this fear reaction transferred to other furry objects, like a rabbit or a Santa Claus mask. Unfortunately, Albert left the nursery too soon for Watson to attempt to eliminate the child's newly acquired habits. A few years later, Mary Cover Jones, whose research at Columbia University was unofficially supervised by Watson, compared various methods for removing children's fears of animals. Some treatments were more successful than others. This research, supplemented by Watson's and Jones's comments about its practical implications, marks the beginning of the fields of behavior modification and behavior therapy.

Watson denied any significant initiating or mediating role for the brain, and he would not consider possible cognitive processes intervening between the external S and the subject's R. His approach was thus peripheralistic in its focus on movements and secretions, and not on changes in the central nervous system. He worried that serious consideration of the existence of such intervening, unobservable processes would be subjective and unscientific; and in any case it was unnecessary for behavioral prediction and control. However, Watson did include implicit or covert behavior and "verbal reports" within his behaviorism. For example, he viewed thinking as basically silent speech, talking to yourself, that was potentially measurable by means of sensitive recording instruments attached to appropriate muscles (of the lips, tongue, larynx, etc.)—a general idea, not really original with Watson, that stimulated much research. Furthermore, a person's regular, overt utterances could be objectively recorded as a form of behavior. Nevertheless, Watson was accused of making an alarming concession: of retaining introspection under another guise, the verbal report.

In 1920, while engrossed in his work with infants and other experiments involving adult human learning, Watson was faced with divorce proceedings initiated by his wife, who had discovered his love affair with Rayner. The participants were so well known (the Rayner family was politically and socially prominent in Maryland) that the case became a local and national sensation. Although Watson had probably believed that he was too important a figure at Johns Hopkins and in American psychology to lose his job over such a personal matter, he was forced to resign from the university in 1920. He never again held any official academic position. He and Rayner were married as soon as the divorce was final.

Resilient and self-reliant, Watson began an entirely new career at the J. Walter Thompson Agency, viewed by its president, Stanley Resor, as a "university of advertising." Watson started at the bottom, surveying the demand for different kinds of rubber boots along the Mississippi River and acting as a salesman in Macy's department store to observe consumer reactions. He eventually became a vice president of the agency and was directly involved in many campaigns for specific products. He favored emotional over rational appeals but did not contribute any strikingly novel methods to the field of advertising, as some writers have claimed. Financially successful compared with his academic years, he asserted that "It can be just as thrilling to watch the growth of a sales curve of a new product as to watch the learning curve of animals or men."

After his dismissal from Johns Hopkins, Watson continued to write and lecture about behaviorism, but the books, radio broadcasts, and magazine articles were directed mainly at a popular audience. Aside from FREUD, he was probably the psychologist best known to the American public in the first half of the twentieth century. Unfortunately, Watson's views became progressively more simplistic, dogmatic, brash, and extreme. Nevertheless, his book *Behaviorism* (1924), though hastily written, had a favorable popular reception; a *New York Times* reviewer said that it marked a new "epoch in the intellectual history of man," and the *New York Herald-Tribune* declared that "perhaps this is the most important book ever written." Even Bertrand Russell said it was "massively impressive."

In this and later writings Watson repudiated his earlier acceptance of the existence of certain human instincts and instead presented an extremely environmentalist, learning-based point of view. A widely cited passage, usually quoted without some qualifications that he did add, claimed that with the right kind of early experience and training, one could make any healthy infant into a "doctor, lawyer, artist . . . even beggar-man and thief, regardless of the talents . . . abilities, vocations, and race of his ancestors." Such a democratic view, combined with Watson's optimistic vision of psychology's general role in transforming society, was attractive to the American public, which was becoming increasingly urbanized and seemed to recognize the need for an effective technology of behavior (for example, in education and retraining). Interestingly, behaviorism never gained strong support in Europe, perhaps because traditional values there tended to be more intellectual, philosophical, and abstract; democratic, practical ideals were not so prevalent.

Watson's popular book *Psychological Care of Infant and Child* (1928), dedicated to "the first mother who brings up a happy child," had a definite influence on American child-rearing practices in the 1930s. Some writers have described Watson as the Dr. Spock of his day, but unlike Spock he maintained that the upbringing of children should be quite objective and routinized, with minimal affection and sentimentality. His own children said that he was "all business," believing that tenderness would have a harmful effect on their independence and emotional control. In Watson's autobiographical sketch (1936) he apologized for the infant-care book, admitting that he had insufficient knowledge to write it. He did not, however, retract any of its specific advice.

Different varieties of behaviorism had emerged almost as soon as Watson proposed his own brand, but in the 1930s to 1960s more sophisticated "neo-behaviorists" (e.g., Edwin Guthrie, Clark Hull, B. F. Skinner, and Edward Tolman) flourished during the so-called golden age of learning theory. These persons and their current impact are discussed elsewhere in this volume, along with views of contemporary cognitive psychologists, who generally reject many of behaviorism's assumptions and emphases—but not its objective methodology.

Rosalie Watson's death in 1936 left her husband depressed for a long time. Although he worked at an advertising firm for another decade, he preferred the isolation of his rural Connecticut home and farm, part of which he had built himself, to social and intellectual activities. The APA presented Watson with a special award in 1957, the year before his death on September 25, 1958, and almost 40 years after he left academia. He was honored as the initiator of a "revolution in psychological thought" and a person whose work was a vital determinant of "the form and substance of modern psychology."

(See also ASSOCIATIONISM; BEHAVIORISM; BEHAVIOR THERAPY; CONDITIONING, CLASSICAL AND INSTRUMENTAL; GUTHRIE, EDWIN; HULL, CLARK; LEARNING THEORY; PAVLOV, IVAN; SKINNER, B. F.; THORNDIKE, EDWARD; TOLMAN, EDWARD.)

REFERENCES

Boakes, R. A. (1984). *From Darwin to behaviourism: Psychology and the minds of animals.* Cambridge: Cambridge University Press. A well-written and accurate portrayal, on many levels, of the history of work on animal behavior.

Buckley, K. W. (1989). *Mechanical man: John Broadus Watson and the beginnings of behaviorism.* New York: Guilford Press. The best available biography of Watson, with extensive discussion of the social and intellectual context surrounding the development of behaviorism.

Cohen, D. (1979). *J. B. Watson: The founder of behaviourism.* London: Routledge and Kegan Paul. The only biography besides Buckley's; it is inaccurate and unscholarly but very readable.

Harrell, W., and Harrison, R. (1938). The rise and fall of behaviorism. *Journal of General Psychology 18,* 367–421. Contains an extensive reference list of more than 400 items.

O'Donnell, J. M. (1985). *The origins of behaviorism: American psychology, 1870–1920.* New York: New York University Press. The best social and institutional history of the early development of psychology and behaviorism in the United States.

Watson, J. B. (1913). Psychology as the behaviorist views it. *Psychological Review 20,* 158–177.

—— (1914). *Behavior: An introduction to comparative psychology.* New York: Henry Holt.

—— (1919). *Psychology from the standpoint of a behaviorist.* Philadelphia: Lippincott.

—— (1924). *Behaviorism.* New York: W. W. Norton.

—— (1928). *Psychological care of infant and child.* New York: W. W. Norton.

—— (1936). John Broadus Watson (autobiographical sketch). In C. Murchison, ed., *A history of psychology in autobiography,* vol. 3, pp. 271–281. Worcester, Mass.: Clark University Press.

Eliot Hearst

WORKING MEMORY

[This entry consists of two articles: Animals *by David S. Olton, Alicja L. Markowska, and Mary Lou Voytko, and* Humans *by Alan Baddeley.]*

Animals

Many events that we wish to remember are small variations of repeated themes. We regularly eat dinner, yet what we eat varies from evening to evening. We regularly drive our car to the shopping mall, yet where we park it varies from trip to trip. We often meet with our friends, yet what we discuss varies from meeting to meeting. Remembering the content of each episode, and distinguishing it from each other episode, requires *working memory.*

Similar problems face animals in their natural habitats. Birds and insects that retrieve nectar from flowers must remember the flowers they have visited recently in order to avoid returning to them before the flowers have produced an adequate supply of nectar. Birds that cache seeds must remember whether the food remains in the cache, in which case it should be revisited, or whether food has been moved, in which case it should be avoided. Responding correctly can substantially increase benefits (the amount of food obtained) and reduce costs (the amount of energy expended, the length of time exposed to predators), thereby conferring an adaptive advantage on individuals that solve these problems efficiently. Analyses of *optimal foraging* indicate the importance of mnemonic abilities in solving these problems, and have described numerous examples of species-specific specializations of memory to enhance performance (Harvey and Krebs, 1990; Sherry, 1987; see also FORAGING).

Impairments of working memory are characteristic of *amnesic syndromes* in humans, regardless of their origin: head trauma, neurodegenerative diseases such as ALZHEIMER'S DISEASE, stroke. Amnesic individuals often complain about having difficulties remembering recently presented familiar items. The possibility of an impairment in working memory is often assessed in a simple screening test, similar to the following. The individual is presented with three words, each the name of a common object (car, chair, ball), and asked to repeat these words immediately. This immediate repetition ensures that the individual has heard the words, understands the instructions, is motivated to perform the task, and can speak the words. A short interval of distraction, produced by performance of a different task, prevents explicit rehearsal of the correct words. After an appropriate delay, the individual is asked to recall the words presented earlier. Normal individuals almost always perform perfectly. Amnesic individuals make errors, with the number and type of errors depending on the severity of the amnesic syndrome (Ingram et al., 1988; Olton et al., 1985; Olton and Wenk, 1987; Squire, 1987).

Because experiments with animals are required in order to identify the neural mechanisms of memory, many procedures have been developed to assess working memory in animals. Variations of a *delayed conditional discrimination* are very similar to the clinical procedure described above, and assess working memory. At the beginning of each trial, some information is presented to the animal and then removed. A delay follows, after which two or more response alternatives are presented to the animal. The response that is correct at the end of the delay depends on (is conditional upon) the stimuli presented before the delay. Again, as in the clinical procedures, the interval between presentation of the stimuli and the opportunity to respond varies in duration. In normal animals accuracy of choice varies with the duration of the interval, being very good with short intervals and near chance with extremely long intervals. The amount of time required to go from high accuracy to chance performance is influenced by many parameters, and can range from a few seconds to many months. (See also DISCRIMINATION AND GENERALIZATION.)

For rats, spatially organized tasks are learned rapidly and performed accurately. Consequently, many of the delayed conditional discriminations use a procedure in a *spatial maze*. A spatial alternation procedure in a *radial arm maze* has been an effective way of assessing working memory. The maze has a central platform from which a set of arms radiate like spokes from the hub of a wheel. At the beginning of each test session, reinforcement, such as a small pellet of food, is placed at the end of each arm. This reinforcement is not replaced during the test session. Consequently, the optimal strategy for the rat is to choose each arm once and only once during each test session. The rats use recent memory to follow this strategy

and to develop a list of arms that have been chosen previously during that session. This list has many of the expected mnemonic characteristics.

Long delays, imposed by removing the rat from the maze and returning it later, decrease choice accuracy. Choices made at the beginning of the session are remembered better than those made in the middle, a *primacy effect*. Choices made near the end of the session are remembered better than those made in the middle of the session, a *recency effect*. Remembering choices made earlier in the test session interferes with remembering subsequent choices, *proactive interference*. Remembering choices made later in the session interferes with the memory of previously made choices, *retroactive interference*. *Aging* impairs recent memory as assessed by choice accuracy on this task. All of these results are consistent with what we know about working memory in humans, suggesting that these two species share similar cognitive mechanisms for recent memory (Olton, 1979).

Birds also have been tested for the characteristics of recent memory in laboratory settings. A small arboretum was constructed of tree branches. Each branch had many holes, each of which could be used by the bird to cache a seed. At the beginning of each experimental session, a bowl of seeds was placed in the room. The bird was allowed to cache seeds in some of the holes, and then removed from the room. A small cover was placed over each hole so that the bird could not determine if a seed was in the hole. The bird was returned to the arboretum and allowed to search freely among the holes. As might be expected from the previous description of optimal foraging, the birds were highly accurate in searching the holes. They avoided the holes in which they did not cache a seed, and visited each hole in which they did cache a seed only once (Sherry, 1987).

Monkeys have been tested in numerous variations of delayed conditional discriminations. *Delayed response* tests the memory for spatial locations, as the radial arm maze does for rats, but rewards the monkey for returning to a particular location rather than avoiding it. In delayed response, each trial begins with the monkey receiving information about a given location. After a delay, the monkey is given a choice between responding to this location and at least one other. A reward is provided for a response only to the previously presented location. Thus, the optimal strategy for the monkey is to remember the previously presented location during the delay, and to respond to it when given the opportunity at the end of the delay (Bartus et al., 1978).

Visual *recognition memory* in monkeys has been assessed by a delayed nonmatch-to-sample procedure with real objects or pictures of objects as stimuli. At the beginning of each trial, one or more sample stimuli are presented. Following a delay, the monkey is given a choice between each of these previously presented stimuli and a novel stimulus. The correct strategy is for the monkey to respond to the novel stimulus. The demand on memory can be increased by increasing the delay between the presentation of the sample stimuli and the opportunity to respond, or by increasing the number of sample stimuli prior to the delay; both of these manipulations reduce choice accuracy (Presty et al., 1987).

The hippocampus (see GUIDE TO THE ANATOMY OF THE BRAIN) is one of a number of brain areas required for spatial working memory. Damage to the hippocampus or its connections with the rest of the brain can produce substantial impairments in the performance of tasks that require spatial working memory. Species of birds that use recent memory to forage for food have a larger hippocampus than species of birds that use other strategies. Changes in hippocampal function that occur with normal aging in rats are strongly correlated with the ability to perform tasks that require working memory (Harvey and Krebs, 1990; Olton et al., 1991; Squire, 1987).

The neurotransmitter *acetylcholine* is importantly involved in working memory. Neurons in the basal forebrain send their axons to the hippocampus and cortex, and release acetylcholine there. Interfering with the ability of these cells to release acetylcholine produces mnemonic impairments. For example, inhibiting the release of acetylcholine from *medial septal* axons in the hippocampus produced memory deficits similar to those caused by destruction of the hippocampus. Consequently, the cholinergic input from the medial septal area is necessary for normal hippocampal functions (Givens and Olton, 1990; see also AGING ANIMALS, PHARMACOLOGICAL MANIPULATIONS OF MEMORY IN).

Five important challenges face investigators who are examining the neural bases of working memory:

1. What are the characteristics of working memory that distinguish it from other kinds of memory, and why do these characteristics require hippocampal function?

2. What is the appropriate description of mnemonic processes? An interesting exercise might be to think about how you would provide a comprehensive description of memory.

3. What are the molecular bases of working memory in the hippocampus? Detailed information is available about many neurobiological mechanisms, and these must be involved in the substrate of working memory.

4. How does the hippocampus integrate its function with those of other brain areas that are required for normal performance in delayed conditional discriminations (Voytko, 1986)?

5. How can working memory be improved? The search for cognitive enhancers is intense, and several promising leads suggest ways in which enhancement of cholinergic function can improve working memory.

REFERENCES

Bartus, R. T., Fleming, D., and Johnson, H. R. (1978). Aging in the rhesus monkey: Debilitating effects on short-term memory. *Journal of Gerontology 33,* 858–871.

Givens, G. L., and Olton, D. S. (1990). Cholinergic and GABAergic modulation of medial septal area: Effect on working memory." *Behavioral Neuroscience 104,* 849–855.

Harvey, P. H., and Krebs, J. R. (1990). Comparing brains. *Science 249,* 140–146.

Ingram, D. K., Bartus, R. T., Olton, D. S., and Khachaturian, Z. S. (1988). Special issue: Experimental models of age-related memory dysfunction and neurodegeneration. *Neurobiology of Aging 9,* 443–765,

Olton, D. S. (1979). Mazes, maps, and memory. *American Psychologist 34,* 583–596.

Olton, D. S., Gamzu, E., and Corkin, S. (1985). *Memory dysfunctions: An integration of animal and human research from preclinical and clinical perspectives.* New York: New York Academy of Sciences.

Olton, D. S., Markowska, A. L., Breckler, S. J., Wenk, G. L., Pang, K. C., Koliatsos, V., and Price, D. L. (1991). Individual differences in aging: Behavioral and neural analyses. *Biomedical and Environmental Science 4,* 166–172.

Olton, D. S., and Wenk, G. L. (1987). Dementia: Animal models of the cognitive impairments produced by degeneration of the basal forebrain cholinergic system. In H. Y. Meltzer, ed., *Psychopharmacology: The third generation of progress,* pp. 941–953. New York: Raven Press.

Presty, S. K., Bachevalier, J., Walker, L. C., Struble, R. G., Price, D. L., Mishkin, M., and Cork, L. C. (1987). Age differences in recognition memory of the rhesus monkey (*Macaca mulatta*). *Neurobiology of Aging* 8, 435–440.

Sherry, D. F. (1987). Learning and adaptation in food-storing birds. In R. C. Bolles and M. D. Beecher, eds., *Evolution and learning,* pp. 79–95. Hillsdale, N.J.: Erlbaum.

Squire, L. R. (1987). *Memory and Brain.* New York: Oxford University Press.

Voytko, M. L. (1986). Visual learning and retention examined with reversible cold lesions of the anterior temporal lobe. *Behavioral Brain Research 22,* 25–39.

David S. Olton
Alicja L. Markowska
Mary Lou Voytko

Humans

Working memory is a system that provides temporary storage of information that is being used in such complex cognitive activities as reasoning, comprehending, and learning.

Suppose you ordered three bottles of mineral water at $1.80 a bottle and gave the waiter $10. How much change would you expect? In order to work this out, you would almost certainly need to hold the results of your initial calculations while performing other operations, storing interim results for which you had no need once the answer was reached, and which you probably would be unable to recall if subsequently asked about them. The temporary storage of information that is required to perform this, and many other, tasks is often termed *working memory.*

The idea that there might be a temporary store, separate from the system involved in long-term storage and possibly associated with consciousness, has been current for many years. In the 1880s, Sir Francis Galton (1883) referred to "the empty chamber of consciousness," and William JAMES (1890) proposed the term "primary memory" to refer to a form of temporary storage that was at least in part responsible for the experience of what he termed "the specious present," experience that time is continuous, extending beyond the specific microsecond one is currently encountering.

In the 1890s, London schoolmaster John Jacobs devised a deceptively simple method for measuring the mental capacity of his pupils. This technique, known as the *digit span,* involves presenting a sequence of numbers and requiring the subject to repeat them back in the same order. The sequence length is gradually increased to a point at which perfect recall is no longer possible. This is the subject's digit span, and in the case of normal adults is typically about six digits. Although it does not correlate particularly highly with more general measures of intelligence, digit span has continued to be included in intelligence tests because it appears to reflect something important. (See also MEMORY SPAN.)

Despite the widespread use of digit span in testing, the twentieth century saw little interest in short-term or working memory, until the 1950s, when two factors produced a revival. The first was a growth of interest in the information-processing approach to the analysis of human cognition, with the newly developed digital computer being used as a basis for new theories as to how the mind might work. This, coupled with some of the practical problems that have arisen from the attempt to apply psychology to wartime issues, led to a resurgence of interest in both attention and short-term storage, an interest that was crystallized and popularized by Broadbent (1958).

The second source of revived interest was the demonstration by John Brown (1958) in England, and by Lloyd and Margaret Peterson in the United States, that even small amounts of information are rapidly forgotten if the subject is prevented from rehearsing it. In the initial study (Peterson and Peterson, 1959) subjects were presented with groups of three unrelated consonants, which they were required to recall after a delay ranging from 3 to 18 seconds, during which their attention was occupied by requiring them to count backward by threes from a starting number. Percentage of correct recall declined from 80 percent after 3 seconds to 10 percent after 18 seconds. Subsequent studies have shown that a similar effect can be obtained when subjects are trying to recall words or nonverbal material such as patterns or tactile stimuli. The Petersons interpreted their results as reflecting the gradual fading of a short-term memory trace.

A third experimental procedure that initially appeared to provide evidence for a rapidly fading memory trace came from the task known as *free recall,* in which subjects are presented with a string of unrelated words and then asked to recall as many as possible in any order they wish. Given a list of, say, sixteen words, subjects will typically remember about half, with the probability of remembering early words being relatively low but with the last few words having a very high probability of correct recall. This is termed the *recency effect*, since it is the most recent words that are best recalled. If recall is delayed for a few seconds, however, during which the subject is required to perform some distracting task such as counting, then the recency effect disappears, leaving a comparatively flat function with almost all items being equally likely to be recalled. This phenomenon has been extensively studied, principally by Murray Glanzer (1972), who has shown that although the recency effect is very sensitive to disruption by subsequent items, it is unaffected by factors such as the familiarity of the words, their frequency within the language, or the rate of presentation, all variables that influence the performance of items earlier in the test, and that in general affect long-term learning. Glanzer suggested that the recency effect is based on the operation of a short-term memory store.

By the late 1960s, despite considerable earlier controversy (e.g. Melton, 1963), the available evidence appeared to support the separation of memory into at least two systems, a short-term store of limited capacity that is able to hold information for a matter of seconds, and a long-term store of much greater capacity and longer durability, fed by the short-term store. The dominant model of this period was that proposed by Atkinson and Shiffrin (1968; see Figure 1). This proposes that information passes through a series of brief sensory registers, which perhaps can best be regarded as part of the processes of perception (see SENSORY MEMORY), then moves into a limited-capacity short-term store. The latter acts as a working memory, using a series of strategies or control processes to organize and maintain incoming material so as to optimize its learning and to facilitate its subsequent recall. This model appears to give a good account of the available data, and is still presented as the dominant view of memory in many introductory textbooks.

However, despite its attractive simplicity, the model soon began to encounter problems. One difficulty concerned its learning assumption: the longer an item is held in short-term storage (STS), the greater its probability of being transferred into long-term memory. A number of studies began to appear suggesting that time in the STS is much

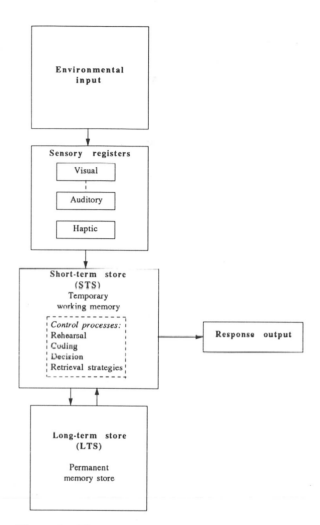

Figure 1. The structure of memory proposed by Atkinson and Shiffrin. The boxes labeled Sensory registers, Short-term store, and Long-term store represent proposed stages or subsystems of memory.

less important than the type of processing or encoding carried out by the subject. In particular, Craik and Lockhart (1972) pointed out that probability of learning appears to be a function of *depth of processing*, with words that have been processed only in terms of their superficial visual appearance being very poorly retained, words that have been categorized in terms of their sound being somewhat better recalled, and the best learning tending to be associated with deeper or richer semantic encoding (see CODING PROCESSES: LEVELS OF PROCESSING). Total time in STS did not seem to lead to good learning if the subject was merely maintaining the trace at a superficial level.

A second source of problems came from evidence that at first seemed to support the two-store model. Patients suffering from amnesia following brain damage appeared to show drastic impairment of long-term learning, preserved operation of the short-term store, normal performance on the Peterson task, and normal recency in free recall (Baddeley and Warrington, 1970). Conversely, Shallice and Warrington (1970) identified other patients showing exactly the opposite pattern: normal long-term learning, a digit span of only one or two items, and greatly impaired performance on the Peterson test and on the recency component in free recall. Such patients fitted the Atkinson and Shiffrin model quite nicely, except for one crucial point. If, as the model proposed, short-term storage acted as a crucial working memory, then how could patients with a gross disruption of the short-term store learn and recall normally? A defective short-term store should have led to massive problems in learning, memory, and general cognitive functioning if this system indeed served as a working memory.

Baddeley and Hitch (1974) tried to tackle this problem by attempting to simulate the deficit shown in short-term memory patients using normal subjects. They studied the role of the short-term store in learning, reasoning, and comprehension by attempting to disrupt its function through requiring the subject to perform a memory span task while attempting to learn, reason, or comprehend. The two-store model should predict that requiring the subject to maintain a string of, for example, six digits should virtually completely fill the limited-capacity short-term store; if the latter acts as a crucial working memory, then the subject's capacity to perform other tasks should be almost totally disrupted. The pattern of results obtained across a range of activities was quite consistent. While impairment was observed, even a concurrent load of six numbers produced a comparatively modest amount of disruption, even in the capacity to perform quite demanding reasoning tasks. Baddeley and Hitch concluded that these results were inconsistent with the Atkinson and Shiffrin model (1968). A particularly damning finding for the original model came from a study in which subjects were required to hear and repeat back sequences of six random digits at the same time they attempted to learn visually presented lists of words, which were subsequently tested by free recall. While the concurrent digit span task caused a clear though not catastrophic impairment in the long-term part of the curve, it did not influence the recency effect. This result was entirely at variance with the model's assumption that recency represented the output of the same limited-capacity store that was used for performing the digit span task.

Baddeley and Hitch (1974) proposed to replace the concept of a unitary short-term store with that of a multicomponent working memory system. They proposed three main components: an attentional control system they termed the *central executive*, and two subsidiary slave systems, the *phonological loop*, which maintains and manipulates speech-based information, and the *visuospatial sketchpad*, which provides a temporary storage system for visuospatial information.

The phonological loop is assumed to comprise two components, a store that will hold auditory-verbal memory traces for about 2 seconds, and a subvocal rehearsal process. This process can both maintain the items within the store by recycling them subvocally and register visually presented items in the store by means of subvocalization. The model is able to account for a relatively wide range of results, including the following:

1. *The phonological similarity effect.* The memory span for items that sound alike, such as the letters *GCTPV* is much poorer than that for dissimilar letters such as *XKWRY*. This is assumed to occur because the store is based on an acoustic or phonological code; acoustically similar letters are harder to discriminate during the process of recall (Conrad, 1962).

2. *The irrelevant speech effect.* Memory span for sequences of items presented visually or auditorily is impaired when the subject must try to ignore irrelevant spoken material, even when the latter is in an unfamiliar language (Colle and Welsh, 1976). This is assumed to occur because such spoken material inevitably gains access to the phonological store, corrupting the memory trace (Salamé and Baddeley, 1982).

3. *The word length effect.* Memory span decreases with the length of the words being remembered. This occurs because long words take more time to rehearse than short ones. Memory span is determined by two factors: the rate at which the memory trace fades and the speed with which the subject can revive it through rehearsal. Long words take longer to say, and consequently fewer can be maintained (Baddeley et al., 1975).

4. *Articulatory suppression.* When subjects are required continuously to utter some irrelevant sound, such as *blah,* their memory span is impaired. This is assumed to occur because suppression prevents the subject from using articulatory rehearsal and from recoding visually presented items into a speech-based code. Suppression also interferes with the operation of the phonological similarity, irrelevant speech, and word-length effects in systematic and predictable ways (Baddeley et al., 1984).

5. *Short-term memory patients.* These patients are assumed to have a deficit in the phonological store. This causes specific disruption to their capacity to learn new phonological material, such as the vocabulary of a foreign language, but does not interfere with visual learning or verbal learning based on meaning rather than sound (Baddeley et al., 1988).

The short-term phonological storage system appears to play an important role in children's acquisition of the vocabulary of their native language, and it has been suggested that a defect in this system may lead to a major disruption of normal language learning (Gathercole and Baddeley, 1989, 1990).

The visuospatial sketchpad appears to represent a quite separate system that is specialized for the maintenance of visuospatial images. There is evidence to suggest that it may comprise two subsystems, one principally concerned with spatial information and the relative location of objects, and the other concerned with pattern information. Patients with a disruption to the operation of the spatial system may have difficulty in finding their way around, but have no problem in recalling or using information concerning the visual characteristics of objects, such as the color of a banana or the shape of a dachshund's ears. Other patients show the opposite pattern of deficits (Farah, 1988; see also VISUAL OBJECT AGNOSIA). The system appears to play a role in long-term learning of verbal material when visual imagery mnemonics are used (Baddeley and Lieberman, 1980).

The central executive, the most complex and least understood component of working memory, has been suggested to operate along the lines of the model of attentional control proposed by Norman and Shallice (1980). This assumes that ongoing activity is controlled in two major ways: by the running off of existing programs or scripts, or by the intervention of the *supervisory attentional system* (SAS). The latter is capable of interrupting ongoing semiautomatic programs when they reach an impasse or when longer-term goals demand a departure from the ongoing activity. In this respect, the SAS resembles the function that we tend to refer to as "the will" in everyday conversation.

Norman and Shallice (1980) use their model to give an account of slips of action, such as setting out in the evening and finding oneself driving to work, rather than to the theater as intended. Here, a strongly overlearned response pattern is triggered at a time when the SAS is probably concerning itself with other activity, such as carrying on an interesting conversation. Shallice (1982) uses the model to account for the puzzling patterns of behavior sometimes shown by patients with bilateral damage to the frontal lobes of the brain. This is characterized by a combination of rigidity coupled on occasions with excessive distractability. Shallice suggests that such patients have a defect in the operation of the SAS, with the result that their attentional processes are at the mercy of surrounding stimuli, becoming locked onto a dominant program on some occasions and responding to the presence of many different response triggers on others.

Over the years, then, the concept of a working memory that provides the temporary storage necessary for a wide range of cognitive activity has proved a useful one. While our theoretical ideas have changed and become more complex, the relationship between memory and such diverse factors as perception, attention, comprehension, and reasoning is likely to remain an area of great significance.

REFERENCES

Atkinson, R. C., and Shiffrin, R. M. (1968). Human memory: A proposed system and its control processes. In K. W. Spence, ed., *The psychology of learning and motivation: Advances in research and theory,* vol. 2, pp. 89–195. New York: Academic Press.

Baddeley, A. D., and Hitch, G. (1974). Working memory. In G. H. Bower, ed., *Recent advances in learning and motivation,* vol. 8. New York: Academic Press.

Baddeley, A. D., Lewis, V. J., and Vallar, G. (1984). Exploring the articulatory loop. *Quarterly Journal of Experimental Psychology 36,* 233–252.

Baddeley, A. D., and Lieberman, K. (1980). Spatial working memory. In R. S. Nickerson, ed., *Attention and performance*, vol. 8, pp. 521–539. Hillsdale, N.J.: Erlbaum.

Baddeley, A. D., Papagno, C., and Vallar, G. (1988). When long-term learning depends on long-term storage. *Journal of Memory and Language 27*, 586–595.

Baddeley, A. D., Thomson, N., and Buchanan, M. (1975). Word length and the structure of short-term memory. *Journal of Verbal Learning and Verbal Behavior 14*, 575–589.

Baddeley, A. D., and Warrington, E. K. (1970). Amnesia and the distinction between long- and short-term memory. *Journal of Verbal Learning and Verbal Behavior 9*, 176–189.

Broadbent, D. E. (1958). *Perception and communication.* London: Pergamon Press.

Brown, J. (1958). Some tests of the decay theory of immediate memory. *Quarterly Journal of Experimental Psychology 10*, 12–21.

Colle, H. A., and Welsh, A. (1976). Acoustic masking in primary memory. *Journal of Verbal Learning and Verbal Behavior 15*, 17–32.

Conrad, R. (1962). An association between memory errors and errors due to acoustic masking of speech. *Nature 193*, 1314–1315.

Craik, F. I. M., and Lockhart, R. S. (1972). Levels of processing: A framework for memory research. *Journal of Verbal Learning and Verbal Behavior 11*, 671–684.

Farah, M. J. (1988). Is visual memory really visual? Overlooked evidence from neuropsychology. *Psychological Review 95*, 307–317.

Galton, F. (1883). *Inquiries into human faculty and its development.* London: Dent.

Gathercole, S., and Baddeley, A. D. (1989). Evaluation of the role of phonological STM in the development of vocabulary in children: A longitudinal study. *Journal of Memory and Language 28*, 200–213.

—— (1990). Phonological memory deficits in language-disordered children: Is there a causal connection. *Journal of Memory and Language 29*, 336–360.

Glanzer, M. (1972). Storage mechanisms in recall. In G. H. Bower, ed., *The psychology of learning and motivation: Advances in research and theory*, vol. 5. New York: Academic Press.

James, W. (1890). *The principles of psychology.* New York: Holt, Rinehart and Winston.

Melton, A. W. (1963). Implications of short-term memory for a general theory of memory. *Journal of Verbal Learning and Verbal Behavior 2*, 1–21.

Norman, D. A., and Shallice, T. (1980). *Attention to action: Willed and automatic control of behavior.* CHIP Report 99. San Diego: University of California, San Diego.

Peterson, L. R., and Peterson, M. J. (1959). Short-term retention of individual verbal items. *Journal of Experimental Psychology 58*, 193–198.

Salamé, P., and Baddeley, A. D. (1982). Disruption of short-term memory by unattended speech: Implications for the structure of working memory. *Journal of Verbal Learning and Verbal Behavior 21*, 150–164.

Shallice, T. (1982). Specific impairments of planning. *Philosophical Transactions of the Royal Society London B 298*, 199–209.

Shallice, T., and Warrington, E. K. (1970). Independent functioning of verbal memory stores: A neuropsychological study. *Quarterly Journal of Experimental Psychology 22*, 261–273.

Alan D. Baddeley

Index

Page numbers in boldface indicate a major discussion. Page numbers in italic indicate illustrations.